Joel Whitburn Presents

Billboard's

TOP 10 CHARTS

A WEEK BY WEEK HISTORY OF THE HOTTEST OF THE HOT 100 1958-1988

Compiled from *Billboard's* **Hot 100** charts, 1958-1988.

Record Research Inc.
P.O. Box 200
Menomonee Falls, Wisconsin 53051

ISBN 0-89820-066-0

Published by Record Research Inc.
P.O. Box 200, Menomonee Falls, Wisconsin 53051

CONTENTS

AUTHOR'S NOTE

August 4, 1958 – The debut of *Billboard's* **Hot 100** chart.

January 13, 1962 – "The Twist" by Chubby Checker returns to the #1 spot, 68 weeks after its last #1 appearance.

April 4, 1964 – The Beatles rule the upper half of the **Top 10**.

August 31, 1968 – "Harper Valley P.T.A." by Jeannie C. Riley jumps from 81 to 7 - the biggest **Hot 100** move ever.

March 21, 1970 – The highest **Hot 100** debut in history: The Beatles' "Let It Be" enters the chart at position 6.

December 17, 1977 – Debby Boone's "You Light Up My Life" is the first single to log 10 weeks at #1.

February 25, 1978 – Independent label RSO controls half of the **Top 10**.

July 2, 1988 – "Dirty Diana" jumps to the top of the charts, making Michael Jackson the first artist to have five #1 hits from one album.

This is the diary of America's musical fancies. The collector's checklist. The trivia enthusiast's wellspring. The nostalgia buff's freeway to the back alleys of memory. The historian's documentation of countless pop music trends.

It is the unedited life story of the upper tenth of the nation's premier and most-quoted popular music chart, *Billboard Magazine's* **Hot 100**. For the last 30 years, this survey, based on national sales and airplay, has been a parallel of American popular culture. The upper echelon of the **Hot 100** is the marrow of the chart, the ultimate goal of every single fortunate to break into the **Hot 100**.

To commemorate this minority, each week's **Top 10** is reproduced as it was first presented. Chart bullets, current and previous weeks' chart positions, weeks charted, titles, artists, and labels are noted as originally shown. The highest-debuting and fastest-moving singles of each week's entire **Hot 100** are also listed. Singles at the peak of their chart career are noted in **bold typeface.**

So, it is in homage to the **Top 10** that the data, from each **Hot 100** chart of the past three decades, is duplicated as it was originally published. Read on, you'll find that every page produces a weekly soundtrack to the diary of your life.

JOEL WHITBURN

THE TOP 10 CHARTS

Beginning with the very first **Hot 100** chart on August 4, 1958 and ending with the **Hot 100** on July 9, 1988, *Top 10 Charts* is a comprehensive, week-by-week, chart-by-chart history of the Top 10. In keeping with the original chart format, each week's current and previous chart positions are shown, along with the artist and original label and number.

BULLETS

The original chart bullets are also shown, highlighting those records making substantial gains for the week. *Billboard* changed its methodology for awarding bullets over the years, which explains the scarcity of bullets during the early years and the large influx of bullets later on.

PEAK POSITIONS

All records at their peak positions are shown in boldface type - making the charts even more useful than when originally published. At a glance you can see exactly when each record was at its peak of popularity.

HIGHEST DEBUTS

The week's highest debuting record is shown at the bottom of each chart, along with its debut position. If a record is a re-entry (a record off for several weeks before returning to the charts) it is not counted as a debut.

BIGGEST MOVERS

The biggest moving record of each week is also shown at the bottom of each chart, along with its previous and current weeks' chart positions. In the case of a tie for biggest mover, the record positioned at a higher ranking for that week is the one shown.

Just prior to the **Hot 100**, *Billboard* published the following Pop charts: **Best Sellers In Stores** (ended on 10/13/58), **Most Played By Jockeys**, and the **Top 100**. The following titles were in the Top 10 during the first few weeks of the **Hot 100** charts, however, they reached their peak on the Pop charts mentioned above:

Patricia...Perez Prado (#1 on *Top 100* and *Jockey* charts)
Hard Headed Woman...Elvis Presley (#1 on *Best Seller* and *Jockey* charts)

Yakety Yak...The Coasters (#1 on *Top 100*)
Bird Dog...The Everly Brothers (#1 on *Best Seller* chart –
after debut of *Hot 100*)

TIES

During the pre-**Hot 100** years *Billboard*, on occasion, showed records tying at the same position. You will note that this practice carried over into the first month of the **Hot 100,** and then ceased.

YEAR-END CHARTS 1976-PRESENT

Billboard made slight adjustments to their chart dates over the years, therefore, you will find a few dates that seem out of sequence. Also, due to holiday constraints, *Billboard* has not published a chart during the last week of each year since 1976. To account for the missing chart, one week is added to the total weeks charted for each entry on the next chart published.

EXPLANATION OF HEADINGS & DATA:

All titles at their peak positions are shown in **boldface type.**

Chart bullets are indicated by showing the current week's chart position in reverse type (ex.:**❺**).

TW – Current week's **Hot 100** chart position
LW – Last week's **Hot 100** chart position
WK – Total weeks charted on the **Hot 100***

HIGHEST DEBUT:

The record debuting at the highest position on the **Hot 100** for the week.

BIGGEST MOVER:

The record advancing the most positions on the **Hot 100** for the week.

*A record which re-enters the Top 10 after several years, has its original weeks charted included with its current weeks charted.

TW	LW	WK	Billboard	AUGUST 4, 1958	HOT 100.
①	-	1	**Poor Little Fool**..	*Ricky Nelson* ... Imperial 5528	
②	-	1	**Patricia**..	*Perez Prado* ... RCA 7245	
③	-	1	**Splish Splash**..	*Bobby Darin* ... Atco 6117	
④	-	1	**Hard Headed Woman**.....................................	*Elvis Presley* ... RCA 7280	
⑤	-	1	**When**..	*Kalin Twins* ... Decca 30642	
⑥	-	1	**Rebel-'Rouser**...	*Duane Eddy* ... Jamie 1104	
⑦	-	1	**Yakety Yak**..	*The Coasters* ... Atco 6116	
⑧	-	1	**My True Love**..	*Jack Scott* ... Carlton 462	
⑨	-	1	**Willie And The Hand Jive**	*The Johnny Otis Show* ... Capitol 3966	
⑩	-	1	**Fever**...	*Peggy Lee* ... Capitol 3998	

first Hot 100 — no Highest Debut or Biggest Mover

TW	LW	WK	Billboard	AUGUST 11, 1958	HOT 100.
①	1	2	**Poor Little Fool**..	*Ricky Nelson* ... Imperial 5528	
❷	54	2	**Nel Blu Dipinto Di Blu (Volare)**	*Domenico Modugno* ... Decca 30677	
③	2	2	**Patricia**	*Perez Prado* ... RCA 7245	
④	3	2	**Splish Splash**	*Bobby Darin* ... Atco 6117	
⑤	5	2	**When**	*Kalin Twins* ... Decca 30642	
⑥	8	2	**My True Love**	*Jack Scott* ... Carlton 462	
⑦	4	2	**Hard Headed Woman**	*Elvis Presley* ... RCA 7280	
⑧	6	2	**Rebel-'Rouser**..	*Duane Eddy* ... Jamie 1104	
⑨	9	2	**Willie And The Hand Jive**	*The Johnny Otis Show* ... Capitol 3966	
⑨	12	2	**Just A Dream**	*Jimmy Clanton* ... Ace 546	

★ *HIGHEST DEBUT* ★ POS 42	★ *BIGGEST MOVER* ★ 93 to 26
Susie Darlin'......................*Robin Luke*	Are You Really Mine ....*Jimmie Rodgers*

TW	LW	WK	Billboard	AUGUST 18, 1958	HOT 100.
①	2	3	**Nel Blu Dipinto Di Blu (Volare)** ....*Domenico Modugno* ... Decca 30677		
❷	14	3	**Little Star**...	*The Elegants* ... Apt 25005	
③	6	3	**My True Love**...	*Jack Scott* ... Carlton 462	
④	1	3	**Poor Little Fool**	*Ricky Nelson* ... Imperial 5528	
⑤	3	3	**Patricia**	*Perez Prado* ... RCA 7245	
⑤	9	3	**Just A Dream**	*Jimmy Clanton* ... Ace 546	
⑦	5	3	**When**	*Kalin Twins* ... Decca 30642	
⑧	8	3	**Rebel-'Rouser**..	*Duane Eddy* ... Jamie 1104	
⑨	13	3	**Fever**	*Peggy Lee* ... Capitol 3998	
⑩	4	3	**Splish Splash**...	*Bobby Darin* ... Atco 6117	

★ *HIGHEST DEBUT* ★ POS 52	★ *BIGGEST MOVER* ★ 92 to 47
How The Time Flies ....*Jerry Wallace*	La Paloma ....*Billy Vaughn*

Billboard — AUGUST 25, 1958 — HOT 100

TW	LW	WK	Title	Artist	Label
①	2	4	**Little Star**	The Elegants	Apt 25005
②	1	4	**Nel Blu Dipinto Di Blu (Volare)**	Domenico Modugno	Decca 30677
❸	17	4	**Bird Dog**	The Everly Brothers	Cadence 1350
④	5	4	**Just A Dream**	Jimmy Clanton	Ace 546
⑤	3	4	**My True Love**	Jack Scott	Carlton 462
⑥	4	4	**Poor Little Fool**	Ricky Nelson	Imperial 5528
⑦	5	4	**Patricia**	Perez Prado	RCA 7245
⑧	9	4	**Fever**	Peggy Lee	Capitol 3998
⑧	16	4	**Born Too Late**	Poni-Tails	ABC-Paramount 9934
⑩	7	4	**When**	Kalin Twins	Decca 30642

★ **HIGHEST DEBUT** ★ POS 40
It's All In The Game .... Tommy Edwards

★ **BIGGEST MOVER** ★ 63 to 26
Tears On My Pillow .... Little Anthony & The Imperials

Billboard — SEPTEMBER 1, 1958 — HOT 100

TW	LW	WK	Title	Artist	Label
①	2	5	**Nel Blu Dipinto Di Blu (Volare)**	Domenico Modugno	Decca 30677
②	1	5	**Little Star**	The Elegants	Apt 25005
③	3	5	**Bird Dog**	The Everly Brothers	Cadence 1350
④	4	5	**Just A Dream**	Jimmy Clanton	Ace 546
⑤	6	5	**Poor Little Fool**	Ricky Nelson	Imperial 5528
⑥	7	5	**Patricia**	Perez Prado	RCA 7245
⑦	5	5	**My True Love**	Jack Scott	Carlton 462
⑧	10	5	**When**	Kalin Twins	Decca 30642
⑨	17	5	**Ginger Bread**	Frankie Avalon	Chancellor 1021
⑩	20	5	**Are You Really Mine**	Jimmie Rodgers	Roulette 4090

★ **HIGHEST DEBUT** ★ POS 74
Tea For Two Cha Cha .... The Tommy Dorsey Orchestra

★ **BIGGEST MOVER** ★ 87 to 43
Down The Aisle Of Love .... The Quin-Tones

Billboard — SEPTEMBER 8, 1958 — HOT 100

TW	LW	WK	Title	Artist	Label
①	1	6	**Nel Blu Dipinto Di Blu (Volare)**	Domenico Modugno	Decca 30677
②	2	6	**Little Star**	The Elegants	Apt 25005
③	3	6	**Bird Dog**	The Everly Brothers	Cadence 1350
④	4	6	**Just A Dream**	Jimmy Clanton	Ace 546
⑤	6	6	**Patricia**	Perez Prado	RCA 7245
⑥	5	6	**Poor Little Fool**	Ricky Nelson	Imperial 5528
⑦	7	6	**My True Love**	Jack Scott	Carlton 462
❽	17	6	**Rock-in Robin**	Bobby Day	Class 229
⑨	9	6	**Ginger Bread**	Frankie Avalon	Chancellor 1021
⑩	14	6	**Western Movies**	The Olympics	Demon 1508

★ **HIGHEST DEBUT** ★ POS 72
Your Cheatin' Heart .... George Hamilton IV

★ **BIGGEST MOVER** ★ 84 to 43
No One Knows .... Dion & The Belmonts

TW	LW	WK	Billboard	SEPTEMBER 15, 1958	HOT 100
①	1	7	**Nel Blu Dipinto Di Blu (Volare)** ....Domenico Modugno ... Decca 30677		
②	3	7	Bird Dog ....The Everly Brothers ... Cadence 1350		
③	2	7	Little Star ....The Elegants ... Apt 25005		
④	11	4	It's All In The Game ....Tommy Edwards ... MGM 12688		
⑤	4	7	Just A Dream ....Jimmy Clanton ... Ace 546		
⑥	8	7	Rock-in Robin ....Bobby Day ... Class 229		
⑦	14	7	**Born Too Late** ....Poni-Tails ... ABC-Paramount 9934		
⑧	10	7	**Western Movies** ....The Olympics ... Demon 1508		
⑨	13	6	Tears On My Pillow ....Little Anthony & The Imperials ... End 1027		
⑩	28	6	Susie Darlin' ....Robin Luke ... Dot 15781		

★ HIGHEST DEBUT ★ POS 59	★ BIGGEST MOVER ★ 88 to 44
Ten Commandments Of Love........Harvey & The Moonglows	Firefly ....Tony Bennett

TW	LW	WK	Billboard	SEPTEMBER 22, 1958	HOT 100
①	1	8	**Nel Blu Dipinto Di Blu (Volare)** ....Domenico Modugno ... Decca 30677		
②	2	8	**Bird Dog** ....The Everly Brothers ... Cadence 1350		
③	4	5	③ It's All In The Game ....Tommy Edwards ... MGM 12688		
④	3	8	Little Star ....The Elegants ... Apt 25005		
⑤	6	8	Rock-in Robin ....Bobby Day ... Class 229		
⑥	5	8	Just A Dream ....Jimmy Clanton ... Ace 546		
⑦	9	7	Tears On My Pillow ....Little Anthony & The Imperials ... End 1027		
⑧	10	7	Susie Darlin' ....Robin Luke ... Dot 15781		
⑨	7	8	Born Too Late ....Poni-Tails ... ABC-Paramount 9934		
⑩	14	7	**Devoted To You** ....The Everly Brothers ... Cadence 1350		

★ HIGHEST DEBUT ★ POS 54	★ BIGGEST MOVER ★ 87 to 49
For My Good Fortune ....Pat Boone	The End ....Earl Grant

TW	LW	WK	Billboard	SEPTEMBER 29, 1958	HOT 100
①	3	6	**It's All In The Game** ....Tommy Edwards ... MGM 12688		
②	1	9	Nel Blu Dipinto Di Blu (Volare) ....Domenico Modugno ... Decca 30677		
③	2	9	Bird Dog ....The Everly Brothers ... Cadence 1350		
④	5	9	Rock-in Robin ....Bobby Day ... Class 229		
⑤	4	9	Little Star ....The Elegants ... Apt 25005		
⑥	7	8	Tears On My Pillow ....Little Anthony & The Imperials ... End 1027		
⑦	8	8	Susie Darlin' ....Robin Luke ... Dot 15781		
⑧	11	9	**Summertime Blues**.................................Eddie Cochran ... Liberty 55144		
⑨	6	9	Just A Dream ....Jimmy Clanton ... Ace 546		
⑩	12	7	**Near You** ....Roger Williams ... Kapp 233		

★ HIGHEST DEBUT ★ POS 59	★ BIGGEST MOVER ★ 49 to 15
No One But You (In My Heart) ....The Ames Brothers	The End ....Earl Grant

Billboard 🔴 OCTOBER 6, 1958 🔴 HOT 100

TW	LW	WK		
①	1	7	It's All In The Game	Tommy Edwards ... MGM 12688
②	3	10	Bird Dog	The Everly Brothers ... Cadence 1350
③	4	10	Rock-in Robin	Bobby Day ... Class 229
④	2	10	Nel Blu Dipinto Di Blu (Volare)	Domenico Modugno ... Decca 30677
⑤	5	10	Little Star	The Elegants ... Apt 25005
⑥	6	9	Tears On My Pillow	Little Anthony & The Imperials ... End 1027
⑦	7	9	Susie Darlin'	Robin Luke ... Dot 15781
⑧	14	6	Tea For Two Cha Cha	The Tommy Dorsey Orchestra ... Decca 30704
⑨	8	10	Summertime Blues	Eddie Cochran ... Liberty 55144
⑩	10	8	Near You	Roger Williams ... Kapp 233

★ **HIGHEST DEBUT** ★ POS 69
Hoopa Hoola ....Betty Johnson

★ **BIGGEST MOVER** ★ 83 to 37
Tom Dooley ....The Kingston Trio

Billboard 🔴 OCTOBER 13, 1958 🔴 HOT 100

TW	LW	WK		
①	1	8	It's All In The Game	Tommy Edwards ... MGM 12688
②	3	11	Rock-in Robin	Bobby Day ... Class 229
③	2	11	Bird Dog	The Everly Brothers ... Cadence 1350
④	6	10	Tears On My Pillow	Little Anthony & The Imperials ... End 1027
⑤	7	10	Susie Darlin'	Robin Luke ... Dot 15781
⑥	4	11	Nel Blu Dipinto Di Blu (Volare)	Domenico Modugno ... Decca 30677
⑦	13	5	The End	Earl Grant ... Decca 30719
⑧	5	11	Little Star	The Elegants ... Apt 25005
⑨	8	7	Tea For Two Cha Cha	The Tommy Dorsey Orchestra ... Decca 30704
⑩	10	9	Near You	Roger Williams ... Kapp 233

★ **HIGHEST DEBUT** ★ POS 70
I Got A Feeling ....Ricky Nelson

★ **BIGGEST MOVER** ★ 54 to 23
For My Good Fortune ....Pat Boone

Billboard 🔴 OCTOBER 20, 1958 🔴 HOT 100

TW	LW	WK		
①	1	9	It's All In The Game	Tommy Edwards ... MGM 12688
②	2	12	Rock-in Robin	Bobby Day ... Class 229
③	13	9	Topsy II	Cozy Cole ... Love 5004
④	3	12	Bird Dog	The Everly Brothers ... Cadence 1350
⑤	16	6	It's Only Make Believe	Conway Twitty ... MGM 12677
⑥	5	11	Susie Darlin'	Robin Luke ... Dot 15781
⑦	4	11	Tears On My Pillow	Little Anthony & The Imperials ... End 1027
⑧	17	4	Tom Dooley	The Kingston Trio ... Capitol 4049
⑨	9	8	Tea For Two Cha Cha	The Tommy Dorsey Orchestra ... Decca 30704
⑩	11	12	Chantilly Lace	Big Bopper ... Mercury 71343

★ **HIGHEST DEBUT** ★ POS 51
Poor Boy ....The Royaltones

★ **BIGGEST MOVER** ★ 70 to 21
I Got A Feeling ....Ricky Nelson

TW	LW	WK	Billboard.	OCTOBER 27, 1958	HOT 100.
①	1	10	It's All In The Game	Tommy Edwards . . . MGM 12688	
②	5	7	It's Only Make Believe	Conway Twitty . . . MGM 12677	
③	8	5	Tom Dooley	The Kingston Trio . . . Capitol 4049	
④	3	10	Topsy II	Cozy Cole . . . Love 5004	
⑤	2	13	Rock-in Robin	Bobby Day . . . Class 229	
⑥	7	12	Tears On My Pillow	Little Anthony & The Imperials . . . End 1027	
⑦	4	13	Bird Dog	The Everly Brothers . . . Cadence 1350	
⑧	9	9	Tea For Two Cha Cha	The Tommy Dorsey Orchestra . . . Decca 30704	
⑨	6	12	Susie Darlin'	Robin Luke . . . Dot 15781	
⑩	10	13	Chantilly Lace	Big Bopper . . . Mercury 71343	

★ HIGHEST DEBUT ★ POS 67	★ BIGGEST MOVER ★ 86 to 18
The Day The Rains Came . . . . Raymond LeFevre	Lonesome Town . . . . Ricky Nelson

TW	LW	WK	Billboard.	NOVEMBER 3, 1958	HOT 100.
①	1	11	It's All In The Game	Tommy Edwards . . . MGM 12688	
②	2	8	It's Only Make Believe	Conway Twitty . . . MGM 12677	
③	4	11	Topsy II	Cozy Cole . . . Love 5004	
④	3	6	Tom Dooley	The Kingston Trio . . . Capitol 4049	
⑤	5	14	Rock-in Robin	Bobby Day . . . Class 229	
⑥	10	14	Chantilly Lace	Big Bopper . . . Mercury 71343	
⑦	8	10	Tea For Two Cha Cha	The Tommy Dorsey Orchestra . . . Decca 30704	
⑧	11	8	The End	Earl Grant . . . Decca 30719	
⑨	6	13	Tears On My Pillow	Little Anthony & The Imperials . . . End 1027	
⑩	7	14	Bird Dog	The Everly Brothers . . . Cadence 1350	

★ HIGHEST DEBUT ★ POS 54	★ BIGGEST MOVER ★ 67 to 30
Beep Beep . . . . The Playmates	The Day The Rains Came . . . . Raymond LeFevre

TW	LW	WK	Billboard.	NOVEMBER 10, 1958	HOT 100.
①	2	9	It's Only Make Believe	Conway Twitty . . . MGM 12677	
②	4	7	Tom Dooley	The Kingston Trio . . . Capitol 4049	
③	1	12	It's All In The Game	Tommy Edwards . . . MGM 12688	
④	3	12	Topsy II	Cozy Cole . . . Love 5004	
⑤	11	8	To Know Him, Is To Love Him	The Teddy Bears . . . Dore 503	
⑥	6	15	Chantilly Lace	Big Bopper . . . Mercury 71343	
⑦	7	11	Tea For Two Cha Cha	The Tommy Dorsey Orchestra . . . Decca 30704	
⑧	8	9	The End	Earl Grant . . . Decca 30719	
⑨	5	15	Rock-in Robin	Bobby Day . . . Class 229	
⑩	13	5	I Got A Feeling	Ricky Nelson . . . Imperial 5545	

★ HIGHEST DEBUT ★ POS 30	★ BIGGEST MOVER ★ 65 to 18
One Night . . . . Elvis Presley	I Got Stung . . . . Elvis Presley

Billboard — NOVEMBER 17, 1958 — HOT 100

TW	LW	WK			
①	2	8	Tom Dooley	The Kingston Trio	Capitol 4049
②	1	10	It's Only Make Believe	Conway Twitty	MGM 12677
③	4	13	Topsy II	Cozy Cole	Love 5004
④	3	13	It's All In The Game	Tommy Edwards	MGM 12688
⑤	5	9	To Know Him, Is To Love Him	The Teddy Bears	Dore 503
⑥	19	3	Beep Beep	The Playmates	Roulette 4115
⑦	6	16	Chantilly Lace	Big Bopper	Mercury 71343
⑧	11	5	Lonesome Town	Ricky Nelson	Imperial 5545
⑨	13	7	Queen Of The Hop	Bobby Darin	Atco 6127
⑩	10	6	I Got A Feeling	Ricky Nelson	Imperial 5545

★ **HIGHEST DEBUT** ★ POS 71
Pledging My Love .... Roy Hamilton

★ **BIGGEST MOVER** ★ 71 to 25
Cannonball .... Duane Eddy

Billboard — NOVEMBER 24, 1958 — HOT 100

TW	LW	WK			
①	2	11	It's Only Make Believe	Conway Twitty	MGM 12677
②	1	9	Tom Dooley	The Kingston Trio	Capitol 4049
③	5	10	To Know Him, Is To Love Him	The Teddy Bears	Dore 503
④	3	14	Topsy II	Cozy Cole	Love 5004
⑤	4	14	It's All In The Game	Tommy Edwards	MGM 12688
⑥	6	4	Beep Beep	The Playmates	Roulette 4115
⑦	14	3	One Night	Elvis Presley	RCA 7410
⑧	11	4	I Got Stung	Elvis Presley	RCA 7410
⑨	8	6	Lonesome Town	Ricky Nelson	Imperial 5545
⑩	9	8	Queen Of The Hop	Bobby Darin	Atco 6127

★ **HIGHEST DEBUT** ★ POS 72
Need Your Love .... Bobby Freeman

★ **BIGGEST MOVER** ★ 86 to 50
Smoke Gets In Your Eyes .... The Platters

Billboard — DECEMBER 1, 1958 — HOT 100

TW	LW	WK			
①	3	11	To Know Him, Is To Love Him	The Teddy Bears	Dore 503
②	2	10	Tom Dooley	The Kingston Trio	Capitol 4049
③	1	12	It's Only Make Believe	Conway Twitty	MGM 12677
④	6	5	Beep Beep	The Playmates	Roulette 4115
⑤	7	4	One Night	Elvis Presley	RCA 7410
⑥	4	15	Topsy II	Cozy Cole	Love 5004
⑦	9	7	Lonesome Town	Ricky Nelson	Imperial 5545
⑧	17	4	Problems	The Everly Brothers	Cadence 1355
⑨	8	5	I Got Stung	Elvis Presley	RCA 7410
⑩	5	15	It's All In The Game	Tommy Edwards	MGM 12688

★ **HIGHEST DEBUT** ★ POS 62
The Chipmunk Song .... The Chipmunks

★ **BIGGEST MOVER** ★ 88 to 42
Lonely Teardrops .... Jackie Wilson

TW	LW	WK	Billboard.	DECEMBER 8, 1958	HOT 100.
①	1	12	**To Know Him, Is To Love Him**..............*The Teddy Bears* ... Dore 503		
②	2	11	Tom Dooley ....*The Kingston Trio* ... Capitol 4049		
③	3	13	It's Only Make Believe ....*Conway Twitty* ... MGM 12677		
④	4	6	**Beep Beep** ....*The Playmates* ... Roulette 4115		
⑤	5	5	One Night ....*Elvis Presley* ... RCA 7410		
⑥	8	5	Problems ....*The Everly Brothers* ... Cadence 1355		
⑦	7	8	**Lonesome Town**...*Ricky Nelson* ... Imperial 5545		
⑧	6	16	Topsy II ....*Cozy Cole* ... Love 5004		
⑨	9	6	I Got Stung ....*Elvis Presley* ... RCA 7410		
⑩	11	10	Queen Of The Hop ....*Bobby Darin* ... Atco 6127		

★ HIGHEST DEBUT ★ POS 57	★ BIGGEST MOVER ★ 87 to 42
My Happiness ....*Connie Francis*	The Teen Commandments ....*Paul Anka-George Hamilton IV-Johnny Nash*

TW	LW	WK	Billboard.	DECEMBER 15, 1958	HOT 100.
①	1	13	**To Know Him, Is To Love Him**..............*The Teddy Bears* ... Dore 503		
②	6	6	**Problems**...*The Everly Brothers* ... Cadence 1355		
③	2	12	Tom Dooley ....*The Kingston Trio* ... Capitol 4049		
④	5	6	**One Night** ....*Elvis Presley* ... RCA 7410		
⑤	4	7	Beep Beep ....*The Playmates* ... Roulette 4115		
⑥	11	5	Smoke Gets In Your Eyes ....*The Platters* ... Mercury 71383		
⑦	7	9	**Lonesome Town**...*Ricky Nelson* ... Imperial 5545		
⑧	3	14	It's Only Make Believe ....*Conway Twitty* ... MGM 12677		
⑨	9	7	I Got Stung ....*Elvis Presley* ... RCA 7410		
⑩	37	3	The Chipmunk Song...........................*The Chipmunks* ... Liberty 55168		

★ HIGHEST DEBUT ★ POS 66	★ BIGGEST MOVER ★ 73 to 40
Donde Esta Santa Claus? ....*Augie Rios*	Love Of My Life...................*The Everly Brothers*

TW	LW	WK	Billboard.	DECEMBER 22, 1958	HOT 100.
❶	10	4	**The Chipmunk Song** ....*The Chipmunks* ... Liberty 55168		
②	6	6	Smoke Gets In Your Eyes ....*The Platters* ... Mercury 71383		
③	1	14	To Know Him, Is To Love Him ....*The Teddy Bears* ... Dore 503		
④	2	7	Problems ....*The Everly Brothers* ... Cadence 1355		
⑤	3	13	Tom Dooley ....*The Kingston Trio* ... Capitol 4049		
⑥	4	7	One Night ....*Elvis Presley* ... RCA 7410		
⑦	5	8	Beep Beep ....*The Playmates* ... Roulette 4115		
⑧	7	10	Lonesome Town ....*Ricky Nelson* ... Imperial 5545		
⑨	8	15	It's Only Make Believe ....*Conway Twitty* ... MGM 12677		
⑩	13	11	A Lover's Question ....*Clyde McPhatter* ... Atlantic 1199		

★ HIGHEST DEBUT ★ POS 39	★ BIGGEST MOVER ★ 75 to 45
(All Of A Sudden) My Heart Sings.......*Paul Anka*	I Cried A Tear...............................*LaVern Baker*

TW	LW	WK	Billboard. 🔊 DECEMBER 29, 1958 🔊 HOT 100.
①	1	5	**The Chipmunk Song** ....*The Chipmunks* ... Liberty 55168
②	2	7	**Smoke Gets In Your Eyes** ....*The Platters* ... Mercury 71383
③	3	15	**To Know Him, Is To Love Him** ....*The Teddy Bears* ... Dore 503
④	6	8	**One Night** ....*Elvis Presley* ... RCA 7410
⑤	4	8	**Problems** ....*The Everly Brothers* ... Cadence 1355
⑥	5	14	**Tom Dooley** ....*The Kingston Trio* ... Capitol 4049
⑦	8	11	**Lonesome Town**.....................................*Ricky Nelson* ... Imperial 5545
⑧	7	9	**Beep Beep** ....*The Playmates* ... Roulette 4115
⑨	10	12	**A Lover's Question** ....*Clyde McPhatter* ... Atlantic 1199
⑩	12	7	**Whole Lotta Loving** ....*Fats Domino* ... Imperial 5553

★ *HIGHEST DEBUT* ★ POS 44	★ *BIGGEST MOVER* ★ 88 to 29
Green Chritma............................*Stan Freberg*	The Little Drummer Boy..........*The Harry Simeone Chorale*

Billboard — JANUARY 5, 1959 — HOT 100

TW	LW	WK	Title	Artist	Label
①	1	6	The Chipmunk Song	The Chipmunks	Liberty 55168
②	2	8	Smoke Gets In Your Eyes	The Platters	Mercury 71383
③	3	16	To Know Him, Is To Love Him	The Teddy Bears	Dore 503
④	5	9	Problems	The Everly Brothers	Cadence 1355
⑤	4	9	One Night	Elvis Presley	RCA 7410
⑥	13	5	My Happiness	Connie Francis	MGM 12738
⑦	6	15	Tom Dooley	The Kingston Trio	Capitol 4049
⑧	9	13	A Lover's Question	Clyde McPhatter	Atlantic 1199
⑨	11	7	Gotta Travel On	Billy Grammer	Monument 400
⑩	10	8	Whole Lotta Loving	Fats Domino	Imperial 5553

★ HIGHEST DEBUT ★ POS 73
You Are Beautiful......................Johnny Mathis

★ BIGGEST MOVER ★ 100 to 60
Red River Rose......................The Ames Brothers

Billboard — JANUARY 12, 1959 — HOT 100

TW	LW	WK	Title	Artist	Label
①	1	7	The Chipmunk Song	The Chipmunks	Liberty 55168
②	2	9	Smoke Gets In Your Eyes	The Platters	Mercury 71383
③	6	6	My Happiness	Connie Francis	MGM 12738
④	9	8	Gotta Travel On	Billy Grammer	Monument 400
⑤	3	17	To Know Him, Is To Love Him	The Teddy Bears	Dore 503
⑥	10	9	Whole Lotta Loving	Fats Domino	Imperial 5553
⑦	8	14	A Lover's Question	Clyde McPhatter	Atlantic 1199
⑧	5	10	One Night	Elvis Presley	RCA 7410
⑨	4	10	Problems	The Everly Brothers	Cadence 1355
⑩	11	13	Lonesome Town	Ricky Nelson	Imperial 5545

★ HIGHEST DEBUT ★ POS 69
The Children's Marching Song......Cyril Stapleton

★ BIGGEST MOVER ★ 84 to 46
May You Always ....The McGuire Sisters

Billboard — JANUARY 19, 1959 — HOT 100

TW	LW	WK	Title	Artist	Label
①	2	10	Smoke Gets In Your Eyes	The Platters	Mercury 71383
②	3	7	My Happiness	Connie Francis	MGM 12738
③	1	8	The Chipmunk Song	The Chipmunks	Liberty 55168
④	15	9	Donna	Ritchie Valens	Del-Fi 4110
⑤	12	9	16 Candles	The Crests	Coed 506
⑥	7	15	A Lover's Question	Clyde McPhatter	Atlantic 1199
⑦	4	9	Gotta Travel On	Billy Grammer	Monument 400
⑧	6	10	Whole Lotta Loving	Fats Domino	Imperial 5553
⑨	21	7	Stagger Lee	Lloyd Price	ABC-Paramount 9972
⑩	5	18	To Know Him, Is To Love Him	The Teddy Bears	Dore 503

★ HIGHEST DEBUT ★ POS 71
Don't Take Your Guns To Town ......Johnny Cash

★ BIGGEST MOVER ★ 97 to 50
With The Wind And The Rain In Your
Hair ....Pat Boone

TW	LW	WK	Billboard. 🔴 JANUARY 26, 1959 🔴 HOT 100.
①	1	11	**Smoke Gets In Your Eyes** ....*The Platters* . . . Mercury 71383
②	2	8	**My Happiness** ....*Connie Francis* . . . MGM 12738
③	4	10	**Donna** ....*Ritchie Valens* . . . Del-Fi 4110
④	5	10	**16 Candles** ....*The Crests* . . . Coed 506
⑤	9	8	**Stagger Lee** ....*Lloyd Price* . . . ABC-Paramount 9972
⑥	7	10	**Gotta Travel On** ....*Billy Grammer* . . . Monument 400
⑦	6	16	**A Lover's Question** ....*Clyde McPhatter* . . . Atlantic 1199
⑧	12	10	**Lonely Teardrops** ....*Jackie Wilson* . . . Brunswick 55105
⑨	15	7	**Goodbye Baby** ....*Jack Scott* . . . Carlton 493
⑩	8	11	**Whole Lotta Loving** ....*Fats Domino* . . . Imperial 5553

★ *HIGHEST DEBUT* ★ POS 64	★ *BIGGEST MOVER* ★ 89 to 62
Ambrose (Part Five) ....*Linda Laurie*	The Lonely One ....*Duane Eddy*

TW	LW	WK	Billboard. 🔴 FEBRUARY 2, 1959 🔴 HOT 100.
①	1	12	**Smoke Gets In Your Eyes** ....*The Platters* . . . Mercury 71383
❷	12	7	**The All American Boy** ....*Bill Parsons* . . . Fraternity 835
③	3	11	**Donna** ....*Ritchie Valens* . . . Del-Fi 4110
④	4	11	**16 Candles** ....*The Crests* . . . Coed 506
⑤	5	9	**Stagger Lee** ....*Lloyd Price* . . . ABC-Paramount 9972
⑥	2	9	**My Happiness** ....*Connie Francis* . . . MGM 12738
⑦	6	11	**Gotta Travel On** ....*Billy Grammer* . . . Monument 400
⑧	8	11	**Lonely Teardrops** ....*Jackie Wilson* . . . Brunswick 55105
⑨	7	17	**A Lover's Question** ....*Clyde McPhatter* . . . Atlantic 1199
⑩	9	8	**Goodbye Baby** ....*Jack Scott* . . . Carlton 493

★ *HIGHEST DEBUT* ★ POS 69	★ *BIGGEST MOVER* ★ 84 to 45
Charlie Brown ....*The Coasters*	I Got A Wife ....*The Mark IV*

TW	LW	WK	Billboard. 🔴 FEBRUARY 9, 1959 🔴 HOT 100.
①	5	10	**Stagger Lee** ....*Lloyd Price* . . . ABC-Paramount 9972
②	4	12	**16 Candles** ....*The Crests* . . . Coed 506
③	3	12	**Donna** ....*Ritchie Valens* . . . Del-Fi 4110
④	1	13	**Smoke Gets In Your Eyes** ....*The Platters* . . . Mercury 71383
⑤	2	8	**The All American Boy** ....*Bill Parsons* . . . Fraternity 835
⑥	6	10	**My Happiness** ....*Connie Francis* . . . MGM 12738
⑦	8	12	**Lonely Teardrops** ....*Jackie Wilson* . . . Brunswick 55105
⑧	7	12	**Gotta Travel On** ....*Billy Grammer* . . . Monument 400
⑨	10	9	**Goodbye Baby** ....*Jack Scott* . . . Carlton 493
⑩	11	10	**Manhattan Spiritual** ....*Reg Owen & His Orchestra* . . . Palette 5005

★ *HIGHEST DEBUT* ★ POS 88	★ *BIGGEST MOVER* ★ 69 to 29
Nola ....*The Morgan Brothers*	Charlie Brown ....*The Coasters*

Billboard — FEBRUARY 16, 1959 — HOT 100.

TW	LW	WK		
①	1	11	**Stagger Lee**	Lloyd Price . . . ABC-Paramount 9972
②	2	13	**16 Candles**	The Crests . . . Coed 506
③	3	13	**Donna**	Ritchie Valens . . . Del-Fi 4110
④	4	14	**Smoke Gets In Your Eyes**	The Platters . . . Mercury 71383
⑤	5	9	**The All American Boy**	Bill Parsons . . . Fraternity 835
⑥	6	11	**My Happiness**	Connie Francis . . . MGM 12738
⑦	7	13	**Lonely Teardrops**	Jackie Wilson . . . Brunswick 55105
⑧	9	10	**Goodbye Baby**	Jack Scott . . . Carlton 493
⑨	8	13	**Gotta Travel On**	Billy Grammer . . . Monument 400
⑩	10	11	**Manhattan Spiritual**	Reg Owen & His Orchestra . . . Palette 5005

★ **HIGHEST DEBUT** ★ POS 65
Anthony Boy .... Chuck Berry

★ **BIGGEST MOVER** ★ 99 to 53
Venus .... Frankie Avalon

Billboard — FEBRUARY 23, 1959 — HOT 100.

TW	LW	WK		
①	1	12	**Stagger Lee**	Lloyd Price . . . ABC-Paramount 9972
②	3	14	**Donna**	Ritchie Valens . . . Del-Fi 4110
③	2	14	**16 Candles**	The Crests . . . Coed 506
④	5	10	**The All American Boy**	Bill Parsons . . . Fraternity 835
❺	20	4	**Charlie Brown**	The Coasters . . . Atco 6132
⑥	14	12	**I Cried A Tear**	LaVern Baker . . . Atlantic 2007
⑦	12	8	**Tall Paul**	Annette & the Afterbeats . . . Disneyland 118
⑧	13	7	**Petite Fleur**	Chris Barber's Jazz Band . . . Laurie 3022
⑨	7	14	**Lonely Teardrops**	Jackie Wilson . . . Brunswick 55105
⑩	16	8	**Peter Gunn**	Ray Anthony & His Orchestra . . . Capitol 4041

★ **HIGHEST DEBUT** ★ POS 65
Never Be Anyone Else But You .... Ricky Nelson

★ **BIGGEST MOVER** ★ 70 to 30
Alvin's Harmonica .... David Seville & The Chipmunks

Billboard — MARCH 2, 1959 — HOT 100.

TW	LW	WK		
①	1	13	**Stagger Lee**	Lloyd Price . . . ABC-Paramount 9972
②	2	15	**Donna**	Ritchie Valens . . . Del-Fi 4110
③	5	5	**Charlie Brown**	The Coasters . . . Atco 6132
④	3	15	**16 Candles**	The Crests . . . Coed 506
⑤	8	8	**Petite Fleur**	Chris Barber's Jazz Band . . . Laurie 3022
⑥	6	13	**I Cried A Tear**	LaVern Baker . . . Atlantic 2007
❼	28	4	**Venus**	Frankie Avalon . . . Chancellor 1031
⑧	10	9	**Peter Gunn**	Ray Anthony & His Orchestra . . . Capitol 4041
⑨	4	11	**The All American Boy**	Bill Parsons . . . Fraternity 835
⑩	30	3	**Alvin's Harmonica**	David Seville & The Chipmunks . . . Liberty 55179

★ **HIGHEST DEBUT** ★ POS 70
No Other Arms, No Other Lips ..... The Chordettes

★ **BIGGEST MOVER** ★ 82 to 45
It Doesn't Matter Anymore .... Buddy Holly

Billboard — MARCH 9, 1959 — HOT 100

TW	LW	WK	Title	Artist	Label
1	7	5	Venus	Frankie Avalon	Chancellor 1031
2	3	6	Charlie Brown	The Coasters	Atco 6132
3	1	14	Stagger Lee	Lloyd Price	ABC-Paramount 9972
4	2	16	Donna	Ritchie Valens	Del-Fi 4110
5	10	4	Alvin's Harmonica	David Seville & The Chipmunks	Liberty 55179
6	13	7	I've Had It	The Bell Notes	Time 1004
7	15	7	It's Just A Matter Of Time	Brook Benton	Mercury 71394
8	5	9	Petite Fleur	Chris Barber's Jazz Band	Laurie 3022
9	6	14	I Cried A Tear	LaVern Baker	Atlantic 2007
10	4	16	16 Candles	The Crests	Coed 506

★ **HIGHEST DEBUT** ★ POS 55
Come Softly To Me .... The Fleetwoods

★ **BIGGEST MOVER** ★ 91 to 44
It's Late .... Ricky Nelson

Billboard — MARCH 16, 1959 — HOT 100

TW	LW	WK	Title	Artist	Label
1	1	6	Venus	Frankie Avalon	Chancellor 1031
2	2	7	Charlie Brown	The Coasters	Atco 6132
3	5	5	Alvin's Harmonica	David Seville & The Chipmunks	Liberty 55179
4	7	8	It's Just A Matter Of Time	Brook Benton	Mercury 71394
5	3	15	Stagger Lee	Lloyd Price	ABC-Paramount 9972
6	6	8	I've Had It	The Bell Notes	Time 1004
7	4	17	Donna	Ritchie Valens	Del-Fi 4110
8	15	8	Tragedy	Thomas Wayne	Fernwood 109
9	19	4	Never Be Anyone Else But You	Ricky Nelson	Imperial 5565
10	12	11	Peter Gunn	Ray Anthony & His Orchestra	Capitol 4041

★ **HIGHEST DEBUT** ★ POS 68
The Happy Organ .... Dave 'Baby' Cortez

★ **BIGGEST MOVER** ★ 55 to 16
Come Softly To Me .... The Fleetwoods

Billboard — MARCH 23, 1959 — HOT 100

TW	LW	WK	Title	Artist	Label
1	1	7	Venus	Frankie Avalon	Chancellor 1031
2	2	8	Charlie Brown	The Coasters	Atco 6132
3	3	6	Alvin's Harmonica	David Seville & The Chipmunks	Liberty 55179
4	4	9	It's Just A Matter Of Time	Brook Benton	Mercury 71394
5	8	9	Tragedy	Thomas Wayne	Fernwood 109
6	16	3	Come Softly To Me	The Fleetwoods	Dolphin 1
7	6	9	I've Had It	The Bell Notes	Time 1004
8	5	16	Stagger Lee	Lloyd Price	ABC-Paramount 9972
9	9	5	Never Be Anyone Else But You	Ricky Nelson	Imperial 5565
10	7	18	Donna	Ritchie Valens	Del-Fi 4110

★ **HIGHEST DEBUT** ★ POS 64
(Now And Then There's) A Fool Such As
I .... Elvis Presley

★ **BIGGEST MOVER** ★ 96 to 60
Heavenly Lover .... Teresa Brewer

Billboard — MARCH 30, 1959 — HOT 100

TW	LW	WK		
①	1	8	**Venus**	*Frankie Avalon* . . . Chancellor 1031
②	6	4	**Come Softly To Me**	*The Fleetwoods* . . . Dolphin 1
③	2	9	**Charlie Brown**	*The Coasters* . . . Atco 6132
④	4	10	**It's Just A Matter Of Time**	*Brook Benton* . . . Mercury 71394
⑤	5	10	**Tragedy**	*Thomas Wayne* . . . Fernwood 109
⑥	3	7	**Alvin's Harmonica**	*David Seville & The Chipmunks* . . . Liberty 55179
⑦	9	6	**Never Be Anyone Else But You**	*Ricky Nelson* . . . Imperial 5565
⑧	11	7	**Pink Shoe Laces**	*Dodie Stevens* . . . Crystalette 724
⑨	7	10	**I've Had It**	*The Bell Notes* . . . Time 1004
⑩	17	5	**It's Late**	*Ricky Nelson* . . . Imperial 5565

★ **HIGHEST DEBUT** ★ POS 33
I Need Your Love Tonight...............*Elvis Presley*

★ **BIGGEST MOVER** ★ 72 to 32
The Tijuana Jail ....*The Kingston Trio*

Billboard — APRIL 6, 1959 — HOT 100

TW	LW	WK		
①	1	9	**Venus**	*Frankie Avalon* . . . Chancellor 1031
②	2	5	**Come Softly To Me**	*The Fleetwoods* . . . Dolphin 1
③	4	11	**It's Just A Matter Of Time**	*Brook Benton* . . . Mercury 71394
④	8	8	**Pink Shoe Laces**	*Dodie Stevens* . . . Crystalette 724
⑤	5	11	**Tragedy**	*Thomas Wayne* . . . Fernwood 109
⑥	7	7	**Never Be Anyone Else But You**	*Ricky Nelson* . . . Imperial 5565
⑦	3	10	**Charlie Brown**	*The Coasters* . . . Atco 6132
⑧	6	8	**Alvin's Harmonica**	*David Seville & The Chipmunks* . . . Liberty 55179
⑨	10	6	**It's Late**	*Ricky Nelson* . . . Imperial 5565
⑩	14	5	**Guitar Boogie Shuffle**	*The Virtues* . . . Hunt 324

★ **HIGHEST DEBUT** ★ POS 77
So Fine ....*The Fiestas*

★ **BIGGEST MOVER** ★ 84 to 35
Enchanted ....*The Platters*

Billboard — APRIL 13, 1959 — HOT 100

TW	LW	WK		
①	2	6	**Come Softly To Me**	*The Fleetwoods* . . . Dolphin 1
②	1	10	**Venus**	*Frankie Avalon* . . . Chancellor 1031
③	4	9	**Pink Shoe Laces**	*Dodie Stevens* . . . Crystalette 724
④	3	12	**It's Just A Matter Of Time**	*Brook Benton* . . . Mercury 71394
⑤	5	12	**Tragedy**	*Thomas Wayne* . . . Fernwood 109
⑥	6	8	**Never Be Anyone Else But You**	*Ricky Nelson* . . . Imperial 5565
⑦	7	11	**Charlie Brown**	*The Coasters* . . . Atco 6132
⑧	13	4	**(Now And Then There's) A Fool Such As I**	*Elvis Presley* . . . RCA 7506
⑨	10	6	**Guitar Boogie Shuffle**	*The Virtues* . . . Hunt 324
⑩	12	3	**I Need Your Love Tonight**	*Elvis Presley* . . . RCA 7506

★ **HIGHEST DEBUT** ★ POS 70
Goodbye Jimmy, Goodbye ....*Kathy Linden*

★ **BIGGEST MOVER** ★ 73 to 30
That's Why (I Love You So) ....*Jackie Wilson*

Billboard — HOT 100 — APRIL 20, 1959

TW	LW	WK	Title	Artist	Label
①	1	7	Come Softly To Me	The Fleetwoods	Dolphin 1
②	2	11	Venus	Frankie Avalon	Chancellor 1031
③	3	10	Pink Shoe Laces	Dodie Stevens	Crystalette 724
④	10	4	I Need Your Love Tonight	Elvis Presley	RCA 7506
⑤	8	5	(Now And Then There's) A Fool Such As I	Elvis Presley	RCA 7506
⑥	6	9	Never Be Anyone Else But You	Ricky Nelson	Imperial 5565
⑦	9	7	Guitar Boogie Shuffle	The Virtues	Hunt 324
⑧	4	13	It's Just A Matter Of Time	Brook Benton	Mercury 71394
⑨	5	13	Tragedy	Thomas Wayne	Fernwood 109
⑩	11	8	It's Late	Ricky Nelson	Imperial 5565

★ **HIGHEST DEBUT** ★ POS 62
The Wang Dang Taffy-Apple Tango ....Pat Boone

★ **BIGGEST MOVER** ★ 79 to 43
Only You..............Franck Pourcel's French Fiddles

Billboard — HOT 100 — APRIL 27, 1959

TW	LW	WK	Title	Artist	Label
①	1	8	Come Softly To Me	The Fleetwoods	Dolphin 1
②	5	6	(Now And Then There's) A Fool Such As I	Elvis Presley	RCA 7506
③	2	12	Venus	Frankie Avalon	Chancellor 1031
④	3	11	Pink Shoe Laces	Dodie Stevens	Crystalette 724
⑤	7	8	Guitar Boogie Shuffle	The Virtues	Hunt 324
⑥	13	7	The Happy Organ	Dave 'Baby' Cortez	Clock 1009
⑦	4	5	I Need Your Love Tonight	Elvis Presley	RCA 7506
⑧	11	6	Tell Him No	Travis & Bob	Sandy 1017
⑨	20	7	Sorry (I Ran All The Way Home)	The Impalas	Cub 9022
⑩	17	5	Turn Me Loose	Fabian	Chancellor 1033

★ **HIGHEST DEBUT** ★ POS 65
Personality ....Lloyd Price

★ **BIGGEST MOVER** ★ 71 to 24
Kansas City ....Wilbert Harrison

Billboard — HOT 100 — MAY 4, 1959

TW	LW	WK	Title	Artist	Label
①	1	9	Come Softly To Me	The Fleetwoods	Dolphin 1
②	6	8	The Happy Organ	Dave 'Baby' Cortez	Clock 1009
③	9	8	Sorry (I Ran All The Way Home)	The Impalas	Cub 9022
④	4	12	Pink Shoe Laces	Dodie Stevens	Crystalette 724
⑤	5	9	Guitar Boogie Shuffle	The Virtues	Hunt 324
⑥	2	7	(Now And Then There's) A Fool Such As I	Elvis Presley	RCA 7506
⑦	7	6	I Need Your Love Tonight	Elvis Presley	RCA 7506
⑧	8	7	Tell Him No	Travis & Bob	Sandy 1017
⑨	3	13	Venus	Frankie Avalon	Chancellor 1031
⑩	10	6	Turn Me Loose	Fabian	Chancellor 1033

★ **HIGHEST DEBUT** ★ POS 73
Kansas City ....Hank Ballard & The Midnighters

★ **BIGGEST MOVER** ★ 93 to 36
The Battle Of New Orleans............Johnny Horton

Billboard · MAY 11, 1959 · HOT 100.

TW	LW	WK	Title	Artist · Label
①	2	9	The Happy Organ	*Dave 'Baby' Cortez* ... Clock 1009
②	3	9	Sorry (I Ran All The Way Home)	*The Impalas* ... Cub 9022
③	1	10	Come Softly To Me	*The Fleetwoods* ... Dolphin 1
❹	19	4	Kookie, Kookie (Lend Me Your Comb)	*Edward Byrnes & Connie Stevens* ... Warner 5047
⑤	6	8	(Now And Then There's) A Fool Such As I	*Elvis Presley* ... RCA 7506
❻	16	5	Kansas City	*Wilbert Harrison* ... Fury 1023
⑦	5	10	Guitar Boogie Shuffle	*The Virtues* ... Hunt 324
⑧	4	13	Pink Shoe Laces	*Dodie Stevens* ... Crystalette 724
⑨	10	7	Turn Me Loose	*Fabian* ... Chancellor 1033
⑩	7	7	I Need Your Love Tonight	*Elvis Presley* ... RCA 7506

★ HIGHEST DEBUT ★ POS 75
I'm Ready......*Fats Domino*

★ BIGGEST MOVER ★ 98 to 60
Kansas City......*Rocky Olson*

Billboard · MAY 18, 1959 · HOT 100.

TW	LW	WK	Title	Artist · Label
①	6	6	Kansas City	*Wilbert Harrison* ... Fury 1023
②	2	10	Sorry (I Ran All The Way Home)	*The Impalas* ... Cub 9022
③	1	10	The Happy Organ	*Dave 'Baby' Cortez* ... Clock 1009
④	4	5	Kookie, Kookie (Lend Me Your Comb)	*Edward Byrnes & Connie Stevens* ... Warner 5047
⑤	12	5	A Teenager In Love	*Dion & The Belmonts* ... Laurie 3027
❻	16	5	Dream Lover	*Bobby Darin* ... Atco 6140
❼	23	4	The Battle Of New Orleans	*Johnny Horton* ... Columbia 41339
❽	19	6	Quiet Village	*Martin Denny* ... Liberty 55162
⑨	9	8	Turn Me Loose	*Fabian* ... Chancellor 1033
⑩	8	14	Pink Shoe Laces	*Dodie Stevens* ... Crystalette 724

★ HIGHEST DEBUT ★ POS 57
Lipstick On Your Collar......*Connie Francis*

★ BIGGEST MOVER ★ 96 to 53
Tallahassee Lassie......*Freddy Cannon*

Billboard · MAY 25, 1959 · HOT 100.

TW	LW	WK	Title	Artist · Label
①	1	7	Kansas City	*Wilbert Harrison* ... Fury 1023
②	7	5	The Battle Of New Orleans	*Johnny Horton* ... Columbia 41339
③	6	6	Dream Lover	*Bobby Darin* ... Atco 6140
④	2	11	Sorry (I Ran All The Way Home)	*The Impalas* ... Cub 9022
⑤	4	6	Kookie, Kookie (Lend Me Your Comb)	*Edward Byrnes & Connie Stevens* ... Warner 5047
⑥	3	11	The Happy Organ	*Dave 'Baby' Cortez* ... Clock 1009
⑦	5	6	A Teenager In Love	*Dion & The Belmonts* ... Laurie 3027
⑧	8	7	Quiet Village	*Martin Denny* ... Liberty 55162
⑨	22	5	Personality	*Lloyd Price* ... ABC-Paramount 10018
⑩	14	8	Only You	*Franck Pourcel's French Fiddles* ... Capitol 4165

★ HIGHEST DEBUT ★ POS 60
Bobby Sox To Stockings......*Frankie Avalon*

★ BIGGEST MOVER ★ 80 to 48
Bongo Rock......*Preston Epps*

JUNE 1, 1959 — Billboard HOT 100

TW	LW	WK	Title — Artist — Label
①	2	6	**The Battle Of New Orleans**..............*Johnny Horton* . . . Columbia 41339
②	1	8	**Kansas City** ....*Wilbert Harrison* . . . Fury 1023
③	3	7	**Dream Lover** ....*Bobby Darin* . . . Atco 6140
④	8	8	**Quiet Village**..*Martin Denny* . . . Liberty 55162
⑤	9	6	**Personality**...*Lloyd Price* . . . ABC-Paramount 10018
⑥	7	7	**A Teenager In Love**.........................*Dion & The Belmonts* . . . Laurie 3027
⑦	5	7	**Kookie, Kookie (Lend Me Your Comb)**.......................... *Edward Byrnes & Connie Stevens* . . . Warner 5047
⑧	4	12	**Sorry (I Ran All The Way Home)**.......................*The Impalas* . . . Cub 9022
⑨	10	9	**Only You**...........................*Franck Pourcel's French Fiddles* . . . Capitol 4165
⑩	6	12	**The Happy Organ**.................................*Dave 'Baby' Cortez* . . . Clock 1009

★ HIGHEST DEBUT ★ POS 52
Lonely Boy ....*Paul Anka*

★ BIGGEST MOVER ★ 98 to 66
Waterloo ....*Stonewall Jackson*

JUNE 8, 1959 — Billboard HOT 100

TW	LW	WK	Title — Artist — Label
①	1	7	**The Battle Of New Orleans**..............*Johnny Horton* . . . Columbia 41339
②	3	8	**Dream Lover** ....*Bobby Darin* . . . Atco 6140
③	5	7	**Personality**...*Lloyd Price* . . . ABC-Paramount 10018
④	2	9	**Kansas City** ....*Wilbert Harrison* . . . Fury 1023
⑤	4	9	**Quiet Village**..*Martin Denny* . . . Liberty 55162
⑥	6	8	**A Teenager In Love**.........................*Dion & The Belmonts* . . . Laurie 3027
⑦	7	8	**Kookie, Kookie (Lend Me Your Comb)**.......................... *Edward Byrnes & Connie Stevens* . . . Warner 5047
⑧	8	13	**Sorry (I Ran All The Way Home)**.......................*The Impalas* . . . Cub 9022
⑨	9	10	**Only You**...........................*Franck Pourcel's French Fiddles* . . . Capitol 4165
⑩	10	13	**The Happy Organ**.................................*Dave 'Baby' Cortez* . . . Clock 1009

★ HIGHEST DEBUT ★ POS 67
I'm Gonna Change Him......................*Cathy Carr*

★ BIGGEST MOVER ★ 52 to 18
Lonely Boy ....*Paul Anka*

JUNE 15, 1959 — Billboard HOT 100

TW	LW	WK	Title — Artist — Label
①	1	8	**The Battle Of New Orleans**..............*Johnny Horton* . . . Columbia 41339
②	3	8	**Personality**...*Lloyd Price* . . . ABC-Paramount 10018
③	2	9	**Dream Lover** ....*Bobby Darin* . . . Atco 6140
④	5	10	**Quiet Village**..*Martin Denny* . . . Liberty 55162
⑤	4	10	**Kansas City** ....*Wilbert Harrison* . . . Fury 1023
⑥	6	9	**A Teenager In Love**.........................*Dion & The Belmonts* . . . Laurie 3027
⑦	11	6	**Tallahassee Lassie**...*Freddy Cannon* . . . Swan 4031
❽	18	3	**Lonely Boy** ....*Paul Anka* . . . ABC-Paramount 10022
⑨	7	9	**Kookie, Kookie (Lend Me Your Comb)**.......................... *Edward Byrnes & Connie Stevens* . . . Warner 5047
⑩	9	11	**Only You**...........................*Franck Pourcel's French Fiddles* . . . Capitol 4165

★ HIGHEST DEBUT ★ POS 55
Tiger..*Fabian*

★ BIGGEST MOVER ★ 69 to 28
A Boy Without A Girl ....*Frankie Avalon*

Billboard — JUNE 22, 1959 — HOT 100

TW	LW	WK	Title	Artist ... Label
①	1	9	**The Battle Of New Orleans**	Johnny Horton ... Columbia 41339
②	2	9	**Personality**	Lloyd Price ... ABC-Paramount 10018
③	3	10	Dream Lover	Bobby Darin ... Atco 6140
④	8	4	Lonely Boy	Paul Anka ... ABC-Paramount 10022
⑤	5	11	Kansas City	Wilbert Harrison ... Fury 1023
⑥	4	11	Quiet Village	Martin Denny ... Liberty 55162
⑦	7	7	Tallahassee Lassie	Freddy Cannon ... Swan 4031
⑧	6	10	A Teenager In Love	Dion & The Belmonts ... Laurie 3027
⑨	13	6	**Along Came Jones**	The Coasters ... Atco 6141
⑩	15	6	Lipstick On Your Collar	Connie Francis ... MGM 12793

★ **HIGHEST DEBUT** ★ POS 56
Back In The U.S.A. ....Chuck Berry

★ **BIGGEST MOVER** ★ 96 to 50
Forty Miles Of Bad Road ....Duane Eddy

Billboard — JUNE 29, 1959 — HOT 100

TW	LW	WK	Title	Artist ... Label
①	1	10	**The Battle Of New Orleans**	Johnny Horton ... Columbia 41339
②	2	10	**Personality**	Lloyd Price ... ABC-Paramount 10018
③	4	5	Lonely Boy	Paul Anka ... ABC-Paramount 10022
④	3	11	Dream Lover	Bobby Darin ... Atco 6140
⑤	10	7	**Lipstick On Your Collar**	Connie Francis ... MGM 12793
⑥	7	8	**Tallahassee Lassie**	Freddy Cannon ... Swan 4031
⑦	5	12	Kansas City	Wilbert Harrison ... Fury 1023
⑧	6	12	Quiet Village	Martin Denny ... Liberty 55162
⑨	9	7	**Along Came Jones**	The Coasters ... Atco 6141
⑩	8	11	A Teenager In Love	Dion & The Belmonts ... Laurie 3027

★ **HIGHEST DEBUT** ★ POS 63
Just A Little Too Much ....Ricky Nelson

★ **BIGGEST MOVER** ★ 83 to 55
Like Young ....Andre Previn & David Rose

Billboard — JULY 6, 1959 — HOT 100

TW	LW	WK	Title	Artist ... Label
①	1	11	**The Battle Of New Orleans**	Johnny Horton ... Columbia 41339
②	3	6	Lonely Boy	Paul Anka ... ABC-Paramount 10022
③	2	11	Personality	Lloyd Price ... ABC-Paramount 10018
④	4	12	Dream Lover	Bobby Darin ... Atco 6140
⑤	5	8	**Lipstick On Your Collar**	Connie Francis ... MGM 12793
⑥	12	7	Waterloo	Stonewall Jackson ... Columbia 41393
⑦	6	9	Tallahassee Lassie	Freddy Cannon ... Swan 4031
⑧	13	7	**Bobby Sox To Stockings**	Frankie Avalon ... Chancellor 1036
⑨	11	8	**Frankie**	Connie Francis ... MGM 12793
⑩	19	4	Tiger	Fabian ... Chancellor 1037

★ **HIGHEST DEBUT** ★ POS 43
A Big Hunk O' Love ....Elvis Presley

★ **BIGGEST MOVER** ★ 74 to 45
Cap And Gown ....Marty Robbins

Billboard — JULY 13, 1959 — HOT 100

TW	LW	WK	Title	Artist	Label
①	2	7	Lonely Boy	Paul Anka	ABC-Paramount 10022
②	1	12	The Battle Of New Orleans	Johnny Horton	Columbia 41339
③	3	12	Personality	Lloyd Price	ABC-Paramount 10018
④	6	8	Waterloo	Stonewall Jackson	Columbia 41393
⑤	5	9	Lipstick On Your Collar	Connie Francis	MGM 12793
⑥	10	5	Tiger	Fabian	Chancellor 1037
⑦	4	13	Dream Lover	Bobby Darin	Atco 6140
⑧	7	10	Tallahassee Lassie	Freddy Cannon	Swan 4031
⑨	13	13	My Heart Is An Open Book	Carl Dobkins, Jr.	Decca 30803
⑩	12	8	A Boy Without A Girl	Frankie Avalon	Chancellor 1036

★ **HIGHEST DEBUT** ★ POS 39
My Wish Came True .... Elvis Presley

★ **BIGGEST MOVER** ★ 82 to 43
What'd I Say (Part I) .... Ray Charles

Billboard — JULY 20, 1959 — HOT 100

TW	LW	WK	Title	Artist	Label
①	1	8	Lonely Boy	Paul Anka	ABC-Paramount 10022
②	2	13	The Battle Of New Orleans	Johnny Horton	Columbia 41339
③	6	6	Tiger	Fabian	Chancellor 1037
④	4	9	Waterloo	Stonewall Jackson	Columbia 41393
⑤	3	13	Personality	Lloyd Price	ABC-Paramount 10018
⑥	9	14	My Heart Is An Open Book	Carl Dobkins, Jr.	Decca 30803
⑦	8	11	Tallahassee Lassie	Freddy Cannon	Swan 4031
⑧	5	10	Lipstick On Your Collar	Connie Francis	MGM 12793
⑨	25	3	A Big Hunk O' Love	Elvis Presley	RCA 7600
⑩	7	14	Dream Lover	Bobby Darin	Atco 6140

★ **HIGHEST DEBUT** ★ POS 79
Sugaree .... Rusty York

★ **BIGGEST MOVER** ★ 84 to 57
Lonely Guitar .... Annette

Billboard — JULY 27, 1959 — HOT 100

TW	LW	WK	Title	Artist	Label
①	1	9	Lonely Boy	Paul Anka	ABC-Paramount 10022
②	2	14	The Battle Of New Orleans	Johnny Horton	Columbia 41339
③	3	7	Tiger	Fabian	Chancellor 1037
④	4	10	Waterloo	Stonewall Jackson	Columbia 41393
⑤	9	4	A Big Hunk O' Love	Elvis Presley	RCA 7600
⑥	6	15	My Heart Is An Open Book	Carl Dobkins, Jr.	Decca 30803
⑦	16	9	There Goes My Baby	The Drifters	Atlantic 2025
⑧	8	11	Lipstick On Your Collar	Connie Francis	MGM 12793
⑨	12	7	Forty Miles Of Bad Road	Duane Eddy	Jamie 1126
⑩	5	14	Personality	Lloyd Price	ABC-Paramount 10018

★ **HIGHEST DEBUT** ★ POS 63
The Three Bells .... The Browns

★ **BIGGEST MOVER** ★ 98 to 66
Makin' Love .... Floyd Robinson

Billboard — AUGUST 3, 1959 — HOT 100

TW	LW	WK	Title	Artist ... Label
1	1	10	**Lonely Boy**	*Paul Anka* ... ABC-Paramount 10022
2	5	5	**A Big Hunk O' Love**	*Elvis Presley* ... RCA 7600
3	6	16	**My Heart Is An Open Book**	*Carl Dobkins, Jr.* ... Decca 30803
4	2	15	**The Battle Of New Orleans**	*Johnny Horton* ... Columbia 41339
5	3	8	**Tiger**	*Fabian* ... Chancellor 1037
6	7	10	**There Goes My Baby**	*The Drifters* ... Atlantic 2025
7	4	11	**Waterloo**	*Stonewall Jackson* ... Columbia 41393
8	12	7	**Lavender-Blue**	*Sammy Turner* ... Big Top 3016
9	15	5	**Sweeter Than You**	*Ricky Nelson* ... Imperial 5595
10	9	8	**Forty Miles Of Bad Road**	*Duane Eddy* ... Jamie 1126

★ **HIGHEST DEBUT** ★ POS 65
Baby Talk .... *Jan & Dean*

★ **BIGGEST MOVER** ★ 63 to 32
The Three Bells .... *The Browns*

Billboard — AUGUST 10, 1959 — HOT 100

TW	LW	WK	Title	Artist ... Label
1	2	6	**A Big Hunk O' Love**	*Elvis Presley* ... RCA 7600
2	1	11	**Lonely Boy**	*Paul Anka* ... ABC-Paramount 10022
3	3	17	**My Heart Is An Open Book**	*Carl Dobkins, Jr.* ... Decca 30803
4	6	11	**There Goes My Baby**	*The Drifters* ... Atlantic 2025
5	8	8	**Lavender-Blue**	*Sammy Turner* ... Big Top 3016
6	5	9	**Tiger**	*Fabian* ... Chancellor 1037
7	4	16	**The Battle Of New Orleans**	*Johnny Horton* ... Columbia 41339
8	13	12	**What A Diff'rence A Day Makes**	*Dinah Washington* ... Mercury 71435
9	15	6	**What'd I Say (Part I)**	*Ray Charles* ... Atlantic 2031
10	7	12	**Waterloo**	*Stonewall Jackson* ... Columbia 41393

★ **HIGHEST DEBUT** ★ POS 46
I Want To Walk You Home .... *Fats Domino*

★ **BIGGEST MOVER** ★ 76 to 42
My Own True Love .... *Jimmy Clanton*

Billboard — AUGUST 17, 1959 — HOT 100

TW	LW	WK	Title	Artist ... Label
1	1	7	**A Big Hunk O' Love**	*Elvis Presley* ... RCA 7600
2	4	12	**There Goes My Baby**	*The Drifters* ... Atlantic 2025
3	3	18	**My Heart Is An Open Book**	*Carl Dobkins, Jr.* ... Decca 30803
4	5	9	**Lavender-Blue**	*Sammy Turner* ... Big Top 3016
5	2	12	**Lonely Boy**	*Paul Anka* ... ABC-Paramount 10022
6	9	7	**What'd I Say (Part I)**	*Ray Charles* ... Atlantic 2031
7	16	4	**The Three Bells**	*The Browns* ... RCA 7555
8	8	13	**What A Diff'rence A Day Makes**	*Dinah Washington* ... Mercury 71435
9	13	8	**Just A Little Too Much**	*Ricky Nelson* ... Imperial 5595
10	11	10	**Forty Miles Of Bad Road**	*Duane Eddy* ... Jamie 1126

★ **HIGHEST DEBUT** ★ POS 56
('Til) I Kissed You .... *The Everly Brothers*

★ **BIGGEST MOVER** ★ 65 to 35
I'm Gonna Get Married .... *Lloyd Price*

TW	LW	WK	Billboard AUGUST 24, 1959 HOT 100.
①	7	5	The Three Bells ....*The Browns* . . . RCA 7555
②	22	8	Sea Of Love...*Phil Phillips* . . . Mercury 71465
③	4	10	Lavender-Blue...*Sammy Turner* . . . Big Top 3016
④	1	8	A Big Hunk O' Love...................................*Elvis Presley* . . . RCA 7600
⑤	3	19	My Heart Is An Open Book ....*Carl Dobkins, Jr.* . . . Decca 30803
⑥	6	8	What'd I Say (Part I).................................*Ray Charles* . . . Atlantic 2031
⑦	2	13	There Goes My Baby ....*The Drifters* . . . Atlantic 2025
⑧	33	5	Sleep Walk...............................*Santo & Johnny* . . . Canadian American 103
⑨	8	14	What A Diff'rence A Day Makes ....*Dinah Washington* . . . Mercury 71435
⑩	24	3	I Want To Walk You Home ....*Fats Domino* . . . Imperial 5606

★ HIGHEST DEBUT ★ POS 59	★ BIGGEST MOVER ★ 86 to 51
Mack The Knife ....*Bobby Darin*	Primrose Lane ....*Jerry Wallace*

TW	LW	WK	Billboard AUGUST 31, 1959 HOT 100.
①	1	6	The Three Bells ....*The Browns* . . . RCA 7555
②	2	9	Sea Of Love...*Phil Phillips* . . . Mercury 71465
③	8	6	Sleep Walk...............................*Santo & Johnny* . . . Canadian American 103
④	3	11	Lavender-Blue ....*Sammy Turner* . . . Big Top 3016
⑤	11	4	I'm Gonna Get Married ....*Lloyd Price* . . . ABC-Paramount 10032
⑥	6	9	What'd I Say (Part I).................................*Ray Charles* . . . Atlantic 2031
⑦	4	9	A Big Hunk O' Love...................................*Elvis Presley* . . . RCA 7600
⑧	7	14	There Goes My Baby ....*The Drifters* . . . Atlantic 2025
⑨	20	5	Red River Rock ....*Johnny & The Hurricanes* . . . Warwick 509
⑩	10	4	I Want To Walk You Home ....*Fats Domino* . . . Imperial 5606

★ HIGHEST DEBUT ★ POS 65	★ BIGGEST MOVER ★ 81 to 51
Just Ask Your Heart....................*Frankie Avalon*	The Mummy.......................*Bob McFadden & Dor*

TW	LW	WK	Billboard SEPTEMBER 7, 1959 HOT 100.
①	1	7	The Three Bells ....*The Browns* . . . RCA 7555
②	3	7	Sleep Walk...............................*Santo & Johnny* . . . Canadian American 103
③	2	10	Sea Of Love ....*Phil Phillips* . . . Mercury 71465
④	5	5	I'm Gonna Get Married ....*Lloyd Price* . . . ABC-Paramount 10032
⑤	9	6	Red River Rock ....*Johnny & The Hurricanes* . . . Warwick 509
⑥	13	4	('Til) I Kissed You...........................*The Everly Brothers* . . . Cadence 1369
⑦	14	8	Broken-Hearted Melody....................*Sarah Vaughan* . . . Mercury 71477
⑧	4	12	Lavender-Blue ....*Sammy Turner* . . . Big Top 3016
⑨	6	10	What'd I Say (Part I).................................*Ray Charles* . . . Atlantic 2031
⑩	10	5	I Want To Walk You Home ....*Fats Domino* . . . Imperial 5606

★ HIGHEST DEBUT ★ POS 71	★ BIGGEST MOVER ★ 67 to 41
I'm A Hog For You....................*The Coasters*	Put Your Head On My Shoulder..........*Paul Anka*

Billboard. 🔴 SEPTEMBER 14, 1959 🔴 HOT 100.

TW	LW	WK		
①	1	8	**The Three Bells** ....*The Browns* ... RCA 7555	
②	2	8	**Sleep Walk**.............................*Santo & Johnny* ... Canadian American 103	
③	4	6	**I'm Gonna Get Married**...................*Lloyd Price* ... ABC-Paramount 10032	
④	3	11	**Sea Of Love** ....*Phil Phillips* ... Mercury 71465	
⑤	6	5	**('Til) I Kissed You**............................*The Everly Brothers* ... Cadence 1369	
⑥	5	7	**Red River Rock** ....*Johnny & The Hurricanes* ... Warwick 509	
⑦	7	9	**Broken-Hearted Melody**..................*Sarah Vaughan* ... Mercury 71477	
⑧	10	6	**I Want To Walk You Home** ....*Fats Domino* ... Imperial 5606	
⑨	24	4	**Mack The Knife**..*Bobby Darin* ... Atco 6147	
⑩	11	7	**Baby Talk**...*Jan & Dean* ... Dore 522	

★ HIGHEST DEBUT ★ POS 68	★ BIGGEST MOVER ★ 84 to 28
Fools Hall Of Fame ....*Pat Boone*	Teen Beat...*Sandy Nelson*

Billboard. 🔴 SEPTEMBER 21, 1959 🔴 HOT 100.

TW	LW	WK		
①	2	9	**Sleep Walk**.............................*Santo & Johnny* ... Canadian American 103	
②	1	9	**The Three Bells**...*The Browns* ... RCA 7555	
③	3	7	**I'm Gonna Get Married**...................*Lloyd Price* ... ABC-Paramount 10032	
④	5	6	**('Til) I Kissed You**............................*The Everly Brothers* ... Cadence 1369	
⑤	4	12	**Sea Of Love** ....*Phil Phillips* ... Mercury 71465	
⑥	6	8	**Red River Rock** ....*Johnny & The Hurricanes* ... Warwick 509	
⑦	9	5	**Mack The Knife**..*Bobby Darin* ... Atco 6147	
⑧	7	10	**Broken-Hearted Melody** ....*Sarah Vaughan* ... Mercury 71477	
⑨	8	7	**I Want To Walk You Home** ....*Fats Domino* ... Imperial 5606	
⑩	29	4	**Put Your Head On My Shoulder** ....*Paul Anka* ... ABC-Paramount 10040	

★ HIGHEST DEBUT ★ POS 62	★ BIGGEST MOVER ★ 90 to 40
Got The Feeling ....*Fabian*	A Worried Man ....*The Kingston Trio*

Billboard. 🔴 SEPTEMBER 28, 1959 🔴 HOT 100.

TW	LW	WK		
①	1	10	**Sleep Walk**.............................*Santo & Johnny* ... Canadian American 103	
②	7	6	**Mack The Knife**..*Bobby Darin* ... Atco 6147	
③	2	10	**The Three Bells**...*The Browns* ... RCA 7555	
④	4	7	**('Til) I Kissed You** ....*The Everly Brothers* ... Cadence 1369	
⑤	3	8	**I'm Gonna Get Married** ....*Lloyd Price* ... ABC-Paramount 10032	
⑥	5	13	**Sea Of Love** ....*Phil Phillips* ... Mercury 71465	
⑦	10	5	**Put Your Head On My Shoulder** ....*Paul Anka* ... ABC-Paramount 10040	
⑧	6	9	**Red River Rock** ....*Johnny & The Hurricanes* ... Warwick 509	
⑨	15	4	**Teen Beat**...*Sandy Nelson* ... Original Sound 5	
⑩	8	11	**Broken-Hearted Melody** ....*Sarah Vaughan* ... Mercury 71477	

★ HIGHEST DEBUT ★ POS 70	★ BIGGEST MOVER ★ 71 to 42
Darling, I Love You..........................*Al Martino*	Say Man...*Bo Diddley*

Billboard OCTOBER 5, 1959 HOT 100

TW	LW	WK		
①	2	7	Mack The Knife	Bobby Darin ... Atco 6147
②	7	6	Put Your Head On My Shoulder	Paul Anka ... ABC-Paramount 10040
③	1	11	Sleep Walk	Santo & Johnny ... Canadian American 103
④	4	8	('Til) I Kissed You	The Everly Brothers ... Cadence 1369
⑤	3	11	The Three Bells	The Browns ... RCA 7555
⑥	9	5	Teen Beat	Sandy Nelson ... Original Sound 5
⑦	5	9	I'm Gonna Get Married	Lloyd Price ... ABC-Paramount 10032
⑧	12	5	Mr. Blue	The Fleetwoods ... Dolton 5
⑨	8	10	Red River Rock	Johnny & The Hurricanes ... Warwick 509
⑩	11	7	Poison Ivy	The Coasters ... Atco 6146

★ **HIGHEST DEBUT** ★ POS 45
Woo-Hoo .... Rock-A-Teens

★ **BIGGEST MOVER** ★ 95 to 46
In The Mood .... Ernie Field's Orch.

Billboard OCTOBER 12, 1959 HOT 100

TW	LW	WK		
①	1	8	Mack The Knife	Bobby Darin ... Atco 6147
②	2	7	Put Your Head On My Shoulder	Paul Anka ... ABC-Paramount 10040
③	8	6	Mr. Blue	The Fleetwoods ... Dolton 5
④	3	12	Sleep Walk	Santo & Johnny ... Canadian American 103
⑤	4	9	('Til) I Kissed You	The Everly Brothers ... Cadence 1369
⑥	6	6	Teen Beat	Sandy Nelson ... Original Sound 5
⑦	10	8	Poison Ivy	The Coasters ... Atco 6146
⑧	5	12	The Three Bells	The Browns ... RCA 7555
⑨	12	7	Just Ask Your Heart	Frankie Avalon ... Chancellor 1040
⑩	14	6	Lonely Street	Andy Williams ... Cadence 1370

★ **HIGHEST DEBUT** ★ POS 67
We Got Love .... Bobby Rydell

★ **BIGGEST MOVER** ★ 81 to 45
The Enchanted Sea .... The Islanders

Billboard OCTOBER 19, 1959 HOT 100

TW	LW	WK		
①	1	9	Mack The Knife	Bobby Darin ... Atco 6147
②	2	8	Put Your Head On My Shoulder	Paul Anka ... ABC-Paramount 10040
③	3	7	Mr. Blue	The Fleetwoods ... Dolton 5
④	6	7	Teen Beat	Sandy Nelson ... Original Sound 5
⑤	5	10	('Til) I Kissed You	The Everly Brothers ... Cadence 1369
⑥	4	13	Sleep Walk	Santo & Johnny ... Canadian American 103
⑦	10	7	Lonely Street	Andy Williams ... Cadence 1370
⑧	7	9	Poison Ivy	The Coasters ... Atco 6146
⑨	9	8	Just Ask Your Heart	Frankie Avalon ... Chancellor 1040
⑩	8	13	The Three Bells	The Browns ... RCA 7555

★ **HIGHEST DEBUT** ★ POS 60
So Many Ways .... Brook Benton

★ **BIGGEST MOVER** ★ 73 to 41
Oh! Carol .... Neil Sedaka

Billboard 🔴 OCTOBER 26, 1959 🔴 HOT 100.

TW	LW	WK			
①	1	10	Mack The Knife	Bobby Darin	Atco 6147
②	3	8	Mr. Blue	The Fleetwoods	Dolton 5
③	2	9	Put Your Head On My Shoulder	Paul Anka	ABC-Paramount 10040
④	4	8	Teen Beat	Sandy Nelson	Original Sound 5
⑤	13	6	Don't You Know	Della Reese	RCA 7591
⑥	7	8	Lonely Street	Andy Williams	Cadence 1370
⑦	9	9	Just Ask Your Heart	Frankie Avalon	Chancellor 1040
⑧	11	11	Primrose Lane	Jerry Wallace	Challenge 59047
⑨	8	10	Poison Ivy	The Coasters	Atco 6146
⑩	15	7	Deck Of Cards	Wink Martindale	Dot 15968

★ **HIGHEST DEBUT** ★ POS 52
Believe Me ....Royal Teens

★ **BIGGEST MOVER** ★ 97 to 51
High School U.S.A....................Tommy Facenda

Billboard 🔴 NOVEMBER 2, 1959 🔴 HOT 100.

TW	LW	WK			
①	1	11	Mack The Knife	Bobby Darin	Atco 6147
②	2	9	Mr. Blue	The Fleetwoods	Dolton 5
③	3	10	Put Your Head On My Shoulder	Paul Anka	ABC-Paramount 10040
④	5	7	Don't You Know	Della Reese	RCA 7591
⑤	4	9	Teen Beat	Sandy Nelson	Original Sound 5
⑥	6	9	Lonely Street	Andy Williams	Cadence 1370
⑦	10	8	Deck Of Cards	Wink Martindale	Dot 15968
⑧	8	12	Primrose Lane	Jerry Wallace	Challenge 59047
⑨	7	10	Just Ask Your Heart	Frankie Avalon	Chancellor 1040
⑩	9	11	Poison Ivy	The Coasters	Atco 6146

★ **HIGHEST DEBUT** ★ POS 75
Always ....Sammy Turner

★ **BIGGEST MOVER** ★ 88 to 55
Come Into My Heart ....Lloyd Price

Billboard 🔴 NOVEMBER 9, 1959 🔴 HOT 100.

TW	LW	WK			
①	1	12	Mack The Knife	Bobby Darin	Atco 6147
②	2	10	Mr. Blue	The Fleetwoods	Dolton 5
③	3	11	Put Your Head On My Shoulder	Paul Anka	ABC-Paramount 10040
④	4	8	Don't You Know	Della Reese	RCA 7591
⑤	6	10	Lonely Street	Andy Williams	Cadence 1370
⑥	5	10	Teen Beat	Sandy Nelson	Original Sound 5
⑦	7	9	Deck Of Cards	Wink Martindale	Dot 15968
⑧	8	13	Primrose Lane	Jerry Wallace	Challenge 59047
⑨	15	9	Seven Little Girls Sitting In The Back Seat	Paul Evans	Guaranteed 200
⑩	12	6	Heartaches By The Number	Guy Mitchell	Columbia 41476

★ **HIGHEST DEBUT** ★ POS 80
Marina ....Rocco Granata

★ **BIGGEST MOVER** ★ 95 to 45
Reveille Rock ....Johnny & The Hurricanes

Billboard — NOVEMBER 16, 1959 — HOT 100

TW	LW	WK	Title	Artist	Label
①	2	11	**Mr. Blue**	The Fleetwoods	Dolton 5
②	1	13	**Mack The Knife**	Bobby Darin	Atco 6147
③	4	9	**Don't You Know**	Della Reese	RCA 7591
④	3	12	**Put Your Head On My Shoulder**	Paul Anka	ABC-Paramount 10040
❺	10	7	**Heartaches By The Number**	Guy Mitchell	Columbia 41476
⑥	5	11	**Lonely Street**	Andy Williams	Cadence 1370
⑦	6	11	**Teen Beat**	Sandy Nelson	Original Sound 5
⑧	7	10	**Deck Of Cards**	Wink Martindale	Dot 15968
⑨	12	5	**So Many Ways**	Brook Benton	Mercury 71512
⑩	8	14	**Primrose Lane**	Jerry Wallace	Challenge 59047

★ **HIGHEST DEBUT** ★ POS 55
The Big Hurt .... Miss Toni Fisher

★ **BIGGEST MOVER** ★ 100 to 43
Wont'cha Come Home .... Lloyd Price

Billboard — NOVEMBER 23, 1959 — HOT 100

TW	LW	WK	Title	Artist	Label
①	2	14	**Mack The Knife**	Bobby Darin	Atco 6147
②	1	12	**Mr. Blue**	The Fleetwoods	Dolton 5
③	3	10	**Don't You Know**	Della Reese	RCA 7591
④	5	8	**Heartaches By The Number**	Guy Mitchell	Columbia 41476
⑤	4	13	**Put Your Head On My Shoulder**	Paul Anka	ABC-Paramount 10040
⑥	9	6	**So Many Ways**	Brook Benton	Mercury 71512
⑦	8	11	**Deck Of Cards**	Wink Martindale	Dot 15968
⑧	11	10	**In The Mood**	Ernie Field's Orch.	Rendezvous 110
⑨	10	15	**Primrose Lane**	Jerry Wallace	Challenge 59047
⑩	12	7	**We Got Love**	Bobby Rydell	Cameo 169

★ **HIGHEST DEBUT** ★ POS 61
This Friendly World .... Fabian

★ **BIGGEST MOVER** ★ 81 to 42
Hound Dog Man .... Fabian

Billboard — NOVEMBER 30, 1959 — HOT 100

TW	LW	WK	Title	Artist	Label
①	1	15	**Mack The Knife**	Bobby Darin	Atco 6147
②	3	11	**Don't You Know**	Della Reese	RCA 7591
③	2	13	**Mr. Blue**	The Fleetwoods	Dolton 5
④	4	9	**Heartaches By The Number**	Guy Mitchell	Columbia 41476
⑤	8	11	**In The Mood**	Ernie Field's Orch.	Rendezvous 110
⑥	6	7	**So Many Ways**	Brook Benton	Mercury 71512
⑦	5	14	**Put Your Head On My Shoulder**	Paul Anka	ABC-Paramount 10040
⑧	10	8	**We Got Love**	Bobby Rydell	Cameo 169
❾	14	6	**Be My Guest**	Fats Domino	Imperial 5629
⑩	12	12	**Seven Little Girls Sitting In The Back Seat**	Paul Evans	Guaranteed 200

★ **HIGHEST DEBUT** ★ POS 50
I Wanna Be Loved .... Ricky Nelson

★ **BIGGEST MOVER** ★ 95 to 53
Why .... Frankie Avalon

Billboard — DECEMBER 7, 1959 — HOT 100

TW	LW	WK	Title	Artist ... Label
①	1	16	Mack The Knife	Bobby Darin ... Atco 6147
②	4	10	Heartaches By The Number	Guy Mitchell ... Columbia 41476
③	3	14	Mr. Blue	The Fleetwoods ... Dolton 5
④	2	12	Don't You Know	Della Reese ... RCA 7591
⑤	5	12	In The Mood	Ernie Field's Orch. ... Rendezvous 110
⑥	8	9	We Got Love	Bobby Rydell ... Cameo 169
⑦	6	8	So Many Ways	Brook Benton ... Mercury 71512
⑧	9	7	Be My Guest	Fats Domino ... Imperial 5629
⑨	13	9	Oh! Carol	Neil Sedaka ... RCA 7595
⑩	14	11	Danny Boy	Conway Twitty ... MGM 12826

★ HIGHEST DEBUT ★ POS 71
A Year Ago Tonight .... The Crests

★ BIGGEST MOVER ★ 98 to 65
Smokie - Part 2 .... Bill Black's Combo

Billboard — DECEMBER 14, 1959 — HOT 100

TW	LW	WK	Title	Artist ... Label
①	2	11	Heartaches By The Number	Guy Mitchell ... Columbia 41476
②	3	15	Mr. Blue	The Fleetwoods ... Dolton 5
③	1	17	Mack The Knife	Bobby Darin ... Atco 6147
④	5	13	In The Mood	Ernie Field's Orch. ... Rendezvous 110
⑤	24	4	Why	Frankie Avalon ... Chancellor 1045
⑥	6	10	We Got Love	Bobby Rydell ... Cameo 169
⑦	4	13	Don't You Know	Della Reese ... RCA 7591
⑧	7	9	So Many Ways	Brook Benton ... Mercury 71512
⑨	18	4	It's Time To Cry	Paul Anka ... ABC-Paramount 10064
⑩	17	5	The Big Hurt	Miss Toni Fisher ... Signet 275

★ HIGHEST DEBUT ★ POS 70
The Village Of St. Bernadette .... Andy Williams

★ BIGGEST MOVER ★ 100 to 54
Uh! Oh! Part 1 .... The Nutty Squirrels

Billboard — DECEMBER 21, 1959 — HOT 100

TW	LW	WK	Title	Artist ... Label
①	1	12	Heartaches By The Number	Guy Mitchell ... Columbia 41476
②	5	5	Why	Frankie Avalon ... Chancellor 1045
③	11	7	El Paso	Marty Robbins ... Columbia 41511
④	10	6	The Big Hurt	Miss Toni Fisher ... Signet 275
⑤	13	5	Way Down Yonder In New Orleans	Freddie Cannon ... Swan 4043
⑥	9	5	It's Time To Cry	Paul Anka ... ABC-Paramount 10064
⑦	3	18	Mack The Knife	Bobby Darin ... Atco 6147
⑧	6	11	We Got Love	Bobby Rydell ... Cameo 169
⑨	21	5	Among My Souvenirs	Connie Francis ... MGM 12841
⑩	16	6	Hound Dog Man	Fabian ... Chancellor 1044

★ HIGHEST DEBUT ★ POS 82
Climb Ev'ry Mountain .... Tony Bennett

★ BIGGEST MOVER ★ 99 to 47
The Little Drummer Boy .... The Harry Simeone Chorale

TW	LW	WK	**Billboard**® 🎯 DECEMBER 28, 1959 🎯	**HOT 100**®
①	2	6	**Why**	*Frankie Avalon* . . . Chancellor 1045
②	3	8	**El Paso**	*Marty Robbins* . . . Columbia 41511
③	4	7	**The Big Hurt**	*Miss Toni Fisher* . . . Signet 275
④	6	6	**It's Time To Cry**	*Paul Anka* . . . ABC-Paramount 10064
⑤	5	6	**Way Down Yonder In New Orleans**	*Freddie Cannon* . . . Swan 4043
⑥	1	13	**Heartaches By The Number**	*Guy Mitchell* . . . Columbia 41476
⑦	9	6	**Among My Souvenirs**	*Connie Francis* . . . MGM 12841
⑧	7	19	**Mack The Knife**	*Bobby Darin* . . . Atco 6147
⑨	10	7	**Hound Dog Man**	*Fabian* . . . Chancellor 1044
⑩	19	6	**Pretty Blue Eyes**	*Steve Lawrence* . . . ABC-Paramount 10058

★ *HIGHEST DEBUT* ★ POS 58	★ *BIGGEST MOVER* ★ 100 to 50
He'll Have To Go ....*Jim Reeves*	Teen Angel ....*Mark Dinning*

TW	LW	WK	Billboard ● JANUARY 4, 1960 ● HOT 100.
①	2	9	El Paso ....*Marty Robbins* ... Columbia 41511
②	1	7	Why...*Frankie Avalon* ... Chancellor 1045
③	3	8	The Big Hurt ....*Miss Toni Fisher* ... Signet 275
❹	11	12	Running Bear.................................*Johnny Preston* ... Mercury 71474
⑤	5	7	Way Down Yonder In New Orleans............*Freddie Cannon* ... Swan 4043
⑥	6	14	Heartaches By The Number ....*Guy Mitchell* ... Columbia 41476
⑦	4	7	It's Time To Cry ....*Paul Anka* ... ABC-Paramount 10064
⑧	7	7	Among My Souvenirs................................*Connie Francis* ... MGM 12841
⑨	10	7	Pretty Blue Eyes..................*Steve Lawrence* ... ABC-Paramount 10058
⑩	19	5	Go, Jimmy, Go ....*Jimmy Clanton* ... Ace 575

★ HIGHEST DEBUT ★ POS 68
Crazy Arms....................*Bob Beckham*

★ BIGGEST MOVER ★ 83 to 46
Bonnie Came Back.....................*Duane Eddy*

TW	LW	WK	Billboard ● JANUARY 11, 1960 ● HOT 100.
①	1	10	El Paso ....*Marty Robbins* ... Columbia 41511
②	2	8	Why...*Frankie Avalon* ... Chancellor 1045
③	5	8	Way Down Yonder In New Orleans.....*Freddie Cannon* ... Swan 4043
④	4	13	Running Bear.................................*Johnny Preston* ... Mercury 71474
⑤	3	9	The Big Hurt...*Miss Toni Fisher* ... Signet 275
⑥	7	8	It's Time To Cry ....*Paul Anka* ... ABC-Paramount 10064
⑦	10	6	Go, Jimmy, Go ....*Jimmy Clanton* ... Ace 575
⑧	8	8	Among My Souvenirs................................*Connie Francis* ... MGM 12841
⑨	9	8	Pretty Blue Eyes..................*Steve Lawrence* ... ABC-Paramount 10058
⑩	6	15	Heartaches By The Number ....*Guy Mitchell* ... Columbia 41476

★ HIGHEST DEBUT ★ POS 75
What In The World's Come Over You........*Jack Scott*

★ BIGGEST MOVER ★ 80 to 46
Run Red Run ....*The Coasters*

TW	LW	WK	Billboard ● JANUARY 18, 1960 ● HOT 100.
①	4	14	Running Bear.................................*Johnny Preston* ... Mercury 71474
②	2	9	Why...*Frankie Avalon* ... Chancellor 1045
③	1	11	El Paso ....*Marty Robbins* ... Columbia 41511
④	5	10	The Big Hurt...*Miss Toni Fisher* ... Signet 275
⑤	3	9	Way Down Yonder In New Orleans............*Freddie Cannon* ... Swan 4043
⑥	7	7	Go, Jimmy, Go ....*Jimmy Clanton* ... Ace 575
❼	14	5	Teen Angel ....*Mark Dinning* ... MGM 12845
⑧	12	6	The Village Of St. Bernadette...................*Andy Williams* ... Cadence 1374
⑨	9	9	Pretty Blue Eyes..................*Steve Lawrence* ... ABC-Paramount 10058
⑩	8	9	Among My Souvenirs................................*Connie Francis* ... MGM 12841

★ HIGHEST DEBUT ★ POS 74
Beyond The Sea....................*Bobby Darin*

★ BIGGEST MOVER ★ 96 to 43
The Theme From "A Summer Place" ....*Percy Faith*

Billboard — JANUARY 25, 1960 — HOT 100

TW	LW	WK	Title	Artist ... Label
①	1	15	**Running Bear**	*Johnny Preston* ... Mercury 71474
②	3	12	El Paso	*Marty Robbins* ... Columbia 41511
③	2	10	Why	*Frankie Avalon* ... Chancellor 1045
④	7	6	Teen Angel	*Mark Dinning* ... MGM 12845
⑤	5	10	Way Down Yonder In New Orleans	*Freddie Cannon* ... Swan 4043
⑥	4	11	The Big Hurt	*Miss Toni Fisher* ... Signet 275
⑦	8	7	**The Village Of St. Bernadette**	*Andy Williams* ... Cadence 1374
⑧	6	8	Go, Jimmy, Go	*Jimmy Clanton* ... Ace 575
⑨	9	10	**Pretty Blue Eyes**	*Steve Lawrence* ... ABC-Paramount 10058
⑩	13	5	Where Or When	*Dion & The Belmonts* ... Laurie 3044

★ **HIGHEST DEBUT** ★ POS 70
Midnite Special ....*Paul Evans*

★ **BIGGEST MOVER** ★ 74 to 34
Beyond The Sea ....*Bobby Darin*

Billboard — FEBRUARY 1, 1960 — HOT 100

TW	LW	WK	Title	Artist ... Label
①	1	16	**Running Bear**	*Johnny Preston* ... Mercury 71474
②	4	7	Teen Angel	*Mark Dinning* ... MGM 12845
③	2	13	El Paso	*Marty Robbins* ... Columbia 41511
❹	10	6	Where Or When	*Dion & The Belmonts* ... Laurie 3044
⑤	8	9	**Go, Jimmy, Go**	*Jimmy Clanton* ... Ace 575
⑥	3	11	Why	*Frankie Avalon* ... Chancellor 1045
❼	14	6	Handy Man	*Jimmy Jones* ... Cub 9049
⑧	6	12	The Big Hurt	*Miss Toni Fisher* ... Signet 275
⑨	5	11	Way Down Yonder In New Orleans	*Freddie Cannon* ... Swan 4043
⑩	9	11	Pretty Blue Eyes	*Steve Lawrence* ... ABC-Paramount 10058

★ **HIGHEST DEBUT** ★ POS 61
Country Boy ....*Fats Domino*

★ **BIGGEST MOVER** ★ 80 to 44
Am I That Easy To Forget..........*Debbie Reynolds*

Billboard — FEBRUARY 8, 1960 — HOT 100

TW	LW	WK	Title	Artist ... Label
①	2	8	**Teen Angel**	*Mark Dinning* ... MGM 12845
②	1	17	**Running Bear**	*Johnny Preston* ... Mercury 71474
③	4	7	**Where Or When**	*Dion & The Belmonts* ... Laurie 3044
④	3	14	El Paso	*Marty Robbins* ... Columbia 41511
⑤	7	7	Handy Man	*Jimmy Jones* ... Cub 9049
❻	14	7	**Lonely Blue Boy**	*Conway Twitty* ... MGM 12857
❼	12	5	What In The World's Come Over You	*Jack Scott* ... Top Rank 2028
❽	17	7	He'll Have To Go	*Jim Reeves* ... RCA 7643
⑨	6	12	Why	*Frankie Avalon* ... Chancellor 1045
⑩	13	15	**You Got What It Takes**	*Marv Johnson* ... United Artists 185

★ **HIGHEST DEBUT** ★ POS 61
Eternally ....*Sarah Vaughan*

★ **BIGGEST MOVER** ★ 72 to 29
Wild One ....*Bobby Rydell*

Billboard — FEBRUARY 15, 1960 — HOT 100

TW	LW	WK	Title	Artist / Label
①	1	9	**Teen Angel**	*Mark Dinning* . . . MGM 12845
②	2	18	**Running Bear**	*Johnny Preston* . . . Mercury 71474
③	5	8	**Handy Man**	*Jimmy Jones* . . . Cub 9049
④	8	8	**He'll Have To Go**	*Jim Reeves* . . . RCA 7643
⑤	3	8	**Where Or When**	*Dion & The Belmonts* . . . Laurie 3044
❻	12	6	**The Theme From "A Summer Place"**	*Percy Faith* . . . Columbia 41490
⑦	7	6	**What In The World's Come Over You**	*Jack Scott* . . . Top Rank 2028
⑧	6	8	**Lonely Blue Boy**	*Conway Twitty* . . . MGM 12857
⑨	13	6	**Let It Be Me**	*The Everly Brothers* . . . Cadence 1376
⑩	4	15	**El Paso**	*Marty Robbins* . . . Columbia 41511

★ HIGHEST DEBUT ★ POS 69	★ BIGGEST MOVER ★ 90 to 62
Beatnik Fly....................*Johnny & The Hurricanes*	Bad Boy..*Marty Wilde*

Billboard — FEBRUARY 22, 1960 — HOT 100

TW	LW	WK	Title	Artist / Label
❶	6	7	**The Theme From "A Summer Place"**	*Percy Faith* . . . Columbia 41490
②	1	10	**Teen Angel**	*Mark Dinning* . . . MGM 12845
③	3	9	**Handy Man**	*Jimmy Jones* . . . Cub 9049
④	4	9	**He'll Have To Go**	*Jim Reeves* . . . RCA 7643
⑤	7	7	**What In The World's Come Over You**	*Jack Scott* . . . Top Rank 2028
⑥	2	19	**Running Bear**	*Johnny Preston* . . . Mercury 71474
⑦	9	7	**Let It Be Me**	*The Everly Brothers* . . . Cadence 1376
⑧	11	6	**Beyond The Sea**	*Bobby Darin* . . . Atco 6158
⑨	8	9	**Lonely Blue Boy**	*Conway Twitty* . . . MGM 12857
⑩	5	9	**Where Or When**	*Dion & The Belmonts* . . . Laurie 3044

★ HIGHEST DEBUT ★ POS 60	★ BIGGEST MOVER ★ 69 to 36
(Welcome) New Lovers.....................*Pat Boone*	Beatnik Fly.....................*Johnny & The Hurricanes*

Billboard — FEBRUARY 29, 1960 — HOT 100

TW	LW	WK	Title	Artist / Label
①	1	8	**The Theme From "A Summer Place"**	*Percy Faith* . . . Columbia 41490
②	3	10	**Handy Man**	*Jimmy Jones* . . . Cub 9049
③	4	10	**He'll Have To Go**	*Jim Reeves* . . . RCA 7643
④	2	11	**Teen Angel**	*Mark Dinning* . . . MGM 12845
⑤	5	8	**What In The World's Come Over You**	*Jack Scott* . . . Top Rank 2028
⑥	8	7	**Beyond The Sea**	*Bobby Darin* . . . Atco 6158
⑦	6	20	**Running Bear**	*Johnny Preston* . . . Mercury 71474
⑧	7	8	**Let It Be Me**	*The Everly Brothers* . . . Cadence 1376
⑨	12	6	**Baby (You've Got What It Takes)**	*Dinah Washington & Brook Benton* . . . Mercury 71565
⑩	11	5	**Wild One**	*Bobby Rydell* . . . Cameo 171

★ HIGHEST DEBUT ★ POS 53	★ BIGGEST MOVER ★ 99 to 70
About This Thing Called Love ....*Fabian*	El Matador ....*The Kingston Trio*

Billboard — MARCH 7, 1960 — HOT 100

TW	LW	WK	Title / Artist
1	1	9	**The Theme From "A Summer Place"** .... *Percy Faith* ... Columbia 41490
2	3	11	**He'll Have To Go** .... *Jim Reeves* ... RCA 7643
3	2	11	**Handy Man** .... *Jimmy Jones* ... Cub 9049
4	10	6	**Wild One** .... *Bobby Rydell* ... Cameo 171
5	5	9	**What In The World's Come Over You** .... *Jack Scott* ... Top Rank 2028
6	4	12	**Teen Angel** .... *Mark Dinning* ... MGM 12845
7	6	8	**Beyond The Sea** .... *Bobby Darin* ... Atco 6158
8	9	7	**Baby (You've Got What It Takes)** ...... *Dinah Washington & Brook Benton* ... Mercury 71565
9	8	9	**Let It Be Me** .... *The Everly Brothers* ... Cadence 1376
10	7	21	**Running Bear** .... *Johnny Preston* ... Mercury 71474

★ **HIGHEST DEBUT** ★ POS 69
Sink The Bismarck .... *Johnny Horton*

★ **BIGGEST MOVER** ★ 71 to 33
Alvin's Orchestra ..... *David Seville & The Chipmunks*

Billboard — MARCH 14, 1960 — HOT 100

TW	LW	WK	Title / Artist
1	1	10	**The Theme From "A Summer Place"** .... *Percy Faith* ... Columbia 41490
2	2	12	**He'll Have To Go** .... *Jim Reeves* ... RCA 7643
3	4	7	**Wild One** .... *Bobby Rydell* ... Cameo 171
4	3	12	**Handy Man** .... *Jimmy Jones* ... Cub 9049
5	5	10	**What In The World's Come Over You** .... *Jack Scott* ... Top Rank 2028
6	8	8	**Baby (You've Got What It Takes)** ...... *Dinah Washington & Brook Benton* ... Mercury 71565
7	6	13	**Teen Angel** .... *Mark Dinning* ... MGM 12845
8	7	9	**Beyond The Sea** .... *Bobby Darin* ... Atco 6158
9	17	4	**Puppy Love** .... *Paul Anka* ... ABC-Paramount 10082
10	12	8	**Harbor Lights** .... *The Platters* ... Mercury 71563

★ **HIGHEST DEBUT** ★ POS 65
Don't Throw Away All Those
Teardrops .... *Frankie Avalon*

★ **BIGGEST MOVER** ★ 69 to 30
Sink The Bismarck .... *Johnny Horton*

Billboard — MARCH 21, 1960 — HOT 100

TW	LW	WK	Title / Artist
1	1	11	**The Theme From "A Summer Place"** .... *Percy Faith* ... Columbia 41490
2	2	13	**He'll Have To Go** .... *Jim Reeves* ... RCA 7643
3	3	8	**Wild One** .... *Bobby Rydell* ... Cameo 171
4	4	13	**Handy Man** .... *Jimmy Jones* ... Cub 9049
5	6	9	**Baby (You've Got What It Takes)** ...... *Dinah Washington & Brook Benton* ... Mercury 71565
6	5	11	**What In The World's Come Over You** .... *Jack Scott* ... Top Rank 2028
7	9	5	**Puppy Love** .... *Paul Anka* ... ABC-Paramount 10082
8	11	14	**Sweet Nothin's** .... *Brenda Lee* ... Decca 30967
9	7	14	**Teen Angel** .... *Mark Dinning* ... MGM 12845
10	10	9	**Harbor Lights** .... *The Platters* ... Mercury 71563

★ **HIGHEST DEBUT** ★ POS 82
Shazam! .... *Duane Eddy*

★ **BIGGEST MOVER** ★ 52 to 27
Money (That's What I Want) .... *Barrett Strong*

TW	LW	WK	Billboard		MARCH 28, 1960		HOT 100.
①	1	12	The Theme From "A Summer Place"			Percy Faith ... Columbia 41490	
②	3	9	Wild One			Bobby Rydell ... Cameo 171	
③	2	14	He'll Have To Go			Jim Reeves ... RCA 7643	
④	7	6	Puppy Love			Paul Anka ... ABC-Paramount 10082	
⑤	8	15	Sweet Nothin's			Brenda Lee ... Decca 30967	
⑥	5	10	Baby (You've Got What It Takes)			Dinah Washington & Brook Benton ... Mercury 71565	
⑦	4	14	Handy Man			Jimmy Jones ... Cub 9049	
⑧	10	10	Harbor Lights			The Platters ... Mercury 71563	
⑨	12	10	Forever			The Little Dippers ... University 210	
⑩	17	6	O Dio Mio			Annette ... Vista 354	

★ HIGHEST DEBUT ★ POS 76	★ BIGGEST MOVER ★ 81 to 35
Cradle Of Love .... Johnny Preston	The Old Lamplighter .... The Browns

TW	LW	WK	Billboard		APRIL 4, 1960		HOT 100.
①	1	13	The Theme From "A Summer Place"			Percy Faith ... Columbia 41490	
②	4	7	Puppy Love			Paul Anka ... ABC-Paramount 10082	
③	2	10	Wild One			Bobby Rydell ... Cameo 171	
④	3	15	He'll Have To Go			Jim Reeves ... RCA 7643	
⑤	5	16	Sweet Nothin's			Brenda Lee ... Decca 30967	
⑥	14	5	Sink The Bismarck			Johnny Horton ... Columbia 41568	
⑦	25	5	Footsteps			Steve Lawrence ... ABC-Paramount 10085	
⑧	8	11	Harbor Lights			The Platters ... Mercury 71563	
⑨	11	7	Mama			Connie Francis ... MGM 12878	
⑩	6	11	Baby (You've Got What It Takes)			... Mercury 71565	

★ HIGHEST DEBUT ★ POS 81	★ BIGGEST MOVER ★ 76 to 38
Doggin' Around .... Jackie Wilson	Cradle Of Love .... Johnny Preston

TW	LW	WK	Billboard		APRIL 11, 1960		HOT 100.
①	1	14	The Theme From "A Summer Place"			Percy Faith ... Columbia 41490	
②	2	8	Puppy Love			Paul Anka ... ABC-Paramount 10082	
③	4	16	He'll Have To Go			Jim Reeves ... RCA 7643	
④	3	11	Wild One			Bobby Rydell ... Cameo 171	
⑤	12	8	Greenfields			The Brothers Four ... Columbia 41571	
⑥	5	17	Sweet Nothin's			Brenda Lee ... Decca 30967	
⑦	6	6	Sink The Bismarck			Johnny Horton ... Columbia 41568	
⑧	9	8	Mama			Connie Francis ... MGM 12878	
⑨	14	6	I Love The Way You Love			Marv Johnson ... United Artists 208	
⑩	7	6	Footsteps			Steve Lawrence ... ABC-Paramount 10085	

★ HIGHEST DEBUT ★ POS 71	★ BIGGEST MOVER ★ 84 to 17
Fame And Fortune .... Elvis Presley	Stuck On You .... Elvis Presley

TW	LW	WK	Billboard	APRIL 18, 1960	HOT 100
①	1	15	The Theme From "A Summer Place"	Percy Faith	Columbia 41490
②	5	9	Greenfields	The Brothers Four	Columbia 41571
③	2	9	Puppy Love	Paul Anka	ABC-Paramount 10082
④	6	18	Sweet Nothin's	Brenda Lee	Decca 30967
⑤	7	7	Sink The Bismarck	Johnny Horton	Columbia 41568
❻	17	3	Stuck On You	Elvis Presley	RCA 7740
⑦	4	12	Wild One	Bobby Rydell	Cameo 171
⑧	3	17	He'll Have To Go	Jim Reeves	RCA 7643
⑨	11	12	Sixteen Reasons	Connie Stevens	Warner 5137
⑩	8	9	Mama	Connie Francis	MGM 12878

★ **HIGHEST DEBUT** ★ POS 67
Good Timin' .... Jimmy Jones

★ **BIGGEST MOVER** ★ 79 to 33
Mr. Lucky .... Henry Mancini

TW	LW	WK	Billboard	APRIL 25, 1960	HOT 100
❶	6	4	Stuck On You	Elvis Presley	RCA 7740
②	2	10	Greenfields	The Brothers Four	Columbia 41571
③	5	8	Sink The Bismarck	Johnny Horton	Columbia 41568
④	1	16	The Theme From "A Summer Place"	Percy Faith	Columbia 41490
⑤	8	18	He'll Have To Go	Jim Reeves	RCA 7643
⑥	9	13	Sixteen Reasons	Connie Stevens	Warner 5137
⑦	3	10	Puppy Love	Paul Anka	ABC-Paramount 10082
❽	16	7	The Old Lamplighter	The Browns	RCA 7700
⑨	12	8	White Silver Sands	Bill Black's Combo	Hi 2021
⑩	4	19	Sweet Nothin's	Brenda Lee	Decca 30967

★ **HIGHEST DEBUT** ★ POS 85
When You Wish Upon A Star .... Dion & The Belmonts

★ **BIGGEST MOVER** ★ 79 to 44
The Madison .... Al Brown's Tunetoppers

TW	LW	WK	Billboard	MAY 2, 1960	HOT 100
①	1	5	Stuck On You	Elvis Presley	RCA 7740
②	2	11	Greenfields	The Brothers Four	Columbia 41571
③	6	14	Sixteen Reasons	Connie Stevens	Warner 5137
④	3	9	Sink The Bismarck	Johnny Horton	Columbia 41568
⑤	8	8	The Old Lamplighter	The Browns	RCA 7700
❻	13	7	Night	Jackie Wilson	Brunswick 55166
❼	12	6	Cradle Of Love	Johnny Preston	Mercury 71598
❽	18	12	Let The Little Girl Dance	Billy Bland	Old Town 1076
⑨	4	17	The Theme From "A Summer Place"	Percy Faith	Columbia 41490
⑩	10	20	Sweet Nothin's	Brenda Lee	Decca 30967

★ **HIGHEST DEBUT** ★ POS 37
He'll Have To Stay .... Jeanne Black

★ **BIGGEST MOVER** ★ 74 to 15
Cathy's Clown .... The Everly Brothers

Billboard — MAY 9, 1960 — HOT 100

TW	LW	WK	Title	Artist
①	1	6	Stuck On You	Elvis Presley . . . RCA 7740
②	2	12	Greenfields	The Brothers Four . . . Columbia 41571
③	15	4	Cathy's Clown	The Everly Brothers . . . Warner 5151
④	6	8	Night	Jackie Wilson . . . Brunswick 55166
⑤	3	15	Sixteen Reasons	Connie Stevens . . . Warner 5137
⑥	4	10	Sink The Bismarck	Johnny Horton . . . Columbia 41568
⑦	5	9	The Old Lamplighter	The Browns . . . RCA 7700
⑧	7	7	Cradle Of Love	Johnny Preston . . . Mercury 71598
⑨	11	7	Stairway To Heaven	Neil Sedaka . . . RCA 7709
⑩	8	13	Let The Little Girl Dance	Billy Bland . . . Old Town 1076

★ **HIGHEST DEBUT** ★ POS 52
Everybody's Somebody's Fool......Connie Francis

★ **BIGGEST MOVER** ★ 96 to 59
Tell Me That You Love Me...............Fats Domino

Billboard — MAY 16, 1960 — HOT 100

TW	LW	WK	Title	Artist
①	1	7	Stuck On You	Elvis Presley . . . RCA 7740
②	3	5	Cathy's Clown	The Everly Brothers . . . Warner 5151
③	2	13	Greenfields	The Brothers Four . . . Columbia 41571
④	4	9	Night	Jackie Wilson . . . Brunswick 55166
⑤	13	5	Good Timin'	Jimmy Jones . . . Cub 9067
⑥	5	16	Sixteen Reasons	Connie Stevens . . . Warner 5137
⑦	10	14	Let The Little Girl Dance	Billy Bland . . . Old Town 1076
⑧	8	8	Cradle Of Love	Johnny Preston . . . Mercury 71598
⑨	6	11	Sink The Bismarck	Johnny Horton . . . Columbia 41568
⑩	21	3	He'll Have To Stay	Jeanne Black . . . Capitol 4368

★ **HIGHEST DEBUT** ★ POS 71
Always It's You ....The Everly Brothers

★ **BIGGEST MOVER** ★ 97 to 56
Wonderful World ....Sam Cooke

Billboard — MAY 23, 1960 — HOT 100

TW	LW	WK	Title	Artist
①	2	6	Cathy's Clown	The Everly Brothers . . . Warner 5151
②	1	8	Stuck On You	Elvis Presley . . . RCA 7740
③	5	6	Good Timin'	Jimmy Jones . . . Cub 9067
④	3	14	Greenfields	The Brothers Four . . . Columbia 41571
⑤	4	10	Night	Jackie Wilson . . . Brunswick 55166
⑥	6	17	Sixteen Reasons	Connie Stevens . . . Warner 5137
⑦	8	9	Cradle Of Love	Johnny Preston . . . Mercury 71598
⑧	10	4	He'll Have To Stay	Jeanne Black . . . Capitol 4368
⑨	7	15	Let The Little Girl Dance	Billy Bland . . . Old Town 1076
⑩	12	7	Paper Roses	Anita Bryant . . . Carlton 528

★ **HIGHEST DEBUT** ★ POS 61
A Rockin' Good Way ....Dinah Washington & Brook Benton

★ **BIGGEST MOVER** ★ 73 to 41
Happy-Go-Lucky-Me........................Paul Evans

TW	LW	WK	Billboard	MAY 30, 1960	HOT 100
①	1	7	Cathy's Clown	The Everly Brothers	Warner 5151
②	2	9	Stuck On You	Elvis Presley	RCA 7740
③	3	7	Good Timin'	Jimmy Jones	Cub 9067
④	8	5	He'll Have To Stay	Jeanne Black	Capitol 4368
⑤	4	15	Greenfields	The Brothers Four	Columbia 41571
⑥	5	11	Night	Jackie Wilson	Brunswick 55166
⑦	10	8	Paper Roses	Anita Bryant	Carlton 528
⑧	6	18	Sixteen Reasons	Connie Stevens	Warner 5137
⑨	11	7	Burning Bridges	Jack Scott	Top Rank 2041
⑩	7	10	Cradle Of Love	Johnny Preston	Mercury 71598

★ HIGHEST DEBUT ★ POS 76	★ BIGGEST MOVER ★ 85 to 42
I'm Sorry ....Brenda Lee	Because They're Young ....Duane Eddy

TW	LW	WK	Billboard	JUNE 6, 1960	HOT 100
①	1	8	Cathy's Clown	The Everly Brothers	Warner 5151
②	2	10	Stuck On You	Elvis Presley	RCA 7740
③	3	8	Good Timin'	Jimmy Jones	Cub 9067
④	4	6	He'll Have To Stay	Jeanne Black	Capitol 4368
⑤	9	8	Burning Bridges	Jack Scott	Top Rank 2041
⑥	7	9	Paper Roses	Anita Bryant	Carlton 528
⑦	6	12	Night	Jackie Wilson	Brunswick 55166
⑧	20	5	Everybody's Somebody's Fool	Connie Francis	MGM 12899
⑨	14	10	Love You So	Ron Holden with The Thunderbirds	Donna 1315
⑩	5	16	Greenfields	The Brothers Four	Columbia 41571

★ HIGHEST DEBUT ★ POS 78	★ BIGGEST MOVER ★ 76 to 38
That's All You Gotta Do ....Brenda Lee	I'm Sorry ....Brenda Lee

TW	LW	WK	Billboard	JUNE 13, 1960	HOT 100
①	1	9	Cathy's Clown	The Everly Brothers	Warner 5151
②	8	6	Everybody's Somebody's Fool	Connie Francis	MGM 12899
③	5	9	Burning Bridges	Jack Scott	Top Rank 2041
④	3	9	Good Timin'	Jimmy Jones	Cub 9067
⑤	6	10	Paper Roses	Anita Bryant	Carlton 528
⑥	4	7	He'll Have To Stay	Jeanne Black	Capitol 4368
⑦	9	11	Love You So	Ron Holden with The Thunderbirds	Donna 1315
⑧	2	11	Stuck On You	Elvis Presley	RCA 7740
⑨	13	6	Swingin' School	Bobby Rydell	Cameo 175
⑩	17	7	Happy-Go-Lucky-Me	Paul Evans	Guaranteed 208

★ HIGHEST DEBUT ★ POS 76	★ BIGGEST MOVER ★ 75 to 28
Mister Lonely ....The Videls	Alley-Oop ....Dante & The Evergreens

Billboard — JUNE 20, 1960 — HOT 100

TW	LW	WK	Title	Artist	Label
①	1	10	**Cathy's Clown**	*The Everly Brothers*	Warner 5151
②	2	7	Everybody's Somebody's Fool	*Connie Francis*	MGM 12899
③	3	10	**Burning Bridges**	*Jack Scott*	Top Rank 2041
④	4	10	Good Timin'	*Jimmy Jones*	Cub 9067
⑤	9	7	**Swingin' School**	*Bobby Rydell*	Cameo 175
❻	12	4	Alley-Oop	*Hollywood Argyles*	Lute 5905
⑦	5	11	Paper Roses	*Anita Bryant*	Carlton 528
⑧	7	12	Love You So	*Ron Holden with The Thunderbirds*	Donna 1315
⑨	6	8	He'll Have To Stay	*Jeanne Black*	Capitol 4368
⑩	8	12	Stuck On You	*Elvis Presley*	RCA 7740

★ **HIGHEST DEBUT** ★ POS 57
Walking To New Orleans .... *Fats Domino*

★ **BIGGEST MOVER** ★ 78 to 52
One Of Us (Will Weep Tonight) .... *Patti Page*

Billboard — JUNE 27, 1960 — HOT 100

TW	LW	WK	Title	Artist	Label
①	2	8	**Everybody's Somebody's Fool**	*Connie Francis*	MGM 12899
②	1	11	Cathy's Clown	*The Everly Brothers*	Warner 5151
③	6	5	Alley-Oop	*Hollywood Argyles*	Lute 5905
④	3	11	Burning Bridges	*Jack Scott*	Top Rank 2041
❺	11	6	Because They're Young	*Duane Eddy*	Jamie 1156
❻	14	5	I'm Sorry	*Brenda Lee*	Decca 31093
❼	13	6	**A Rockin' Good Way**	*Dinah Washington & Brook Benton*	Mercury 71629
⑧	7	12	Paper Roses	*Anita Bryant*	Carlton 528
⑨	4	11	Good Timin'	*Jimmy Jones*	Cub 9067
⑩	5	8	Swingin' School	*Bobby Rydell*	Cameo 175

★ **HIGHEST DEBUT** ★ POS 71
Josephine .... *Bill Black's Combo*

★ **BIGGEST MOVER** ★ 72 to 40
Tell Laura I Love Her .... *Ray Peterson*

Billboard — JULY 4, 1960 — HOT 100

TW	LW	WK	Title	Artist	Label
①	1	9	**Everybody's Somebody's Fool**	*Connie Francis*	MGM 12899
②	3	6	Alley-Oop	*Hollywood Argyles*	Lute 5905
③	6	6	I'm Sorry	*Brenda Lee*	Decca 31093
④	5	7	**Because They're Young**	*Duane Eddy*	Jamie 1156
⑤	2	12	Cathy's Clown	*The Everly Brothers*	Warner 5151
❻	17	5	**That's All You Gotta Do**	*Brenda Lee*	Decca 31093
⑦	4	12	Burning Bridges	*Jack Scott*	Top Rank 2041
⑧	11	7	**My Home Town**	*Paul Anka*	ABC-Paramount 10106
⑨	15	7	Mule Skinner Blues	*The Fendermen*	Soma 1137
⑩	7	7	A Rockin' Good Way	*Dinah Washington & Brook Benton*	Mercury 71629

★ **HIGHEST DEBUT** ★ POS 59
Itsy Bitsy Teenie Weenie Yellow Polkadot
Bikini .... *Brian Hyland*

★ **BIGGEST MOVER** ★ 71 to 33
Josephine .... *Bill Black's Combo*

Billboard — JULY 11, 1960 — HOT 100

TW	LW	WK	Title	Artist
①	2	7	Alley-Oop	Hollywood Argyles . . . Lute 5905
②	3	7	I'm Sorry	Brenda Lee . . . Decca 31093
③	1	10	Everybody's Somebody's Fool	Connie Francis . . . MGM 12899
④	4	8	Because They're Young	Duane Eddy . . . Jamie 1156
⑤	9	8	Mule Skinner Blues	The Fendermen . . . Soma 1137
❻	11	6	Only The Lonely	Roy Orbison . . . Monument 421
⑦	6	6	That's All You Gotta Do	Brenda Lee . . . Decca 31093
⑧	8	8	My Home Town	Paul Anka . . . ABC-Paramount 10106
⑨	10	8	A Rockin' Good Way	Dinah Washington & Brook Benton . . . Mercury 71629
❿	20	7	When Will I Be Loved	The Everly Brothers . . . Cadence 1380

★ HIGHEST DEBUT ★ POS 79	★ BIGGEST MOVER ★ 79 to 34
I'll Be There ....Bobby Darin	Mission Bell ....Donnie Brooks

Billboard — JULY 18, 1960 — HOT 100

TW	LW	WK	Title	Artist
①	2	8	I'm Sorry	Brenda Lee . . . Decca 31093
②	1	8	Alley-Oop	Hollywood Argyles . . . Lute 5905
③	3	11	Everybody's Somebody's Fool	Connie Francis . . . MGM 12899
④	6	7	Only The Lonely	Roy Orbison . . . Monument 421
⑤	4	9	Because They're Young	Duane Eddy . . . Jamie 1156
⑥	7	7	That's All You Gotta Do	Brenda Lee . . . Decca 31093
⑦	5	9	Mule Skinner Blues	The Fendermen . . . Soma 1137
⑧	10	8	When Will I Be Loved	The Everly Brothers . . . Cadence 1380
⑨	12	6	Tell Laura I Love Her	Ray Peterson . . . RCA 7745
❿	20	3	Itsy Bitsy Teenie Weenie Yellow Polkadot Bikini	Brian Hyland . . . Leader 805

★ HIGHEST DEBUT ★ POS 44	★ BIGGEST MOVER ★ 94 to 61
It's Now Or Never ....Elvis Presley	In My Little Corner Of The World .....Anita Bryant

Billboard — JULY 25, 1960 — HOT 100

TW	LW	WK	Title	Artist
①	1	9	I'm Sorry	Brenda Lee . . . Decca 31093
②	4	8	Only The Lonely	Roy Orbison . . . Monument 421
③	2	9	Alley-Oop	Hollywood Argyles . . . Lute 5905
④	3	12	Everybody's Somebody's Fool	Connie Francis . . . MGM 12899
❺	10	4	Itsy Bitsy Teenie Weenie Yellow Polkadot Bikini	Brian Hyland . . . Leader 805
⑥	7	10	Mule Skinner Blues	The Fendermen . . . Soma 1137
❼	14	8	Image Of A Girl	Safaris . . . Eldo 101
⑧	9	7	Tell Laura I Love Her	Ray Peterson . . . RCA 7745
⑨	15	10	Please Help Me, I'm Falling	Hank Locklin . . . RCA 7692
❿	6	8	That's All You Gotta Do	Brenda Lee . . . Decca 31093

★ HIGHEST DEBUT ★ POS 53	★ BIGGEST MOVER ★ 88 to 39
A Mess Of Blues ....Elvis Presley	Walk—Don't Run ....The Ventures

AUGUST 1, 1960 — Billboard HOT 100

TW	LW	WK		
①	1	10	I'm Sorry	Brenda Lee ... Decca 31093
②	5	5	Itsy Bitsy Teenie Weenie Yellow Polkadot Bikini	Brian Hyland ... Leader 805
❸	14	3	It's Now Or Never	Elvis Presley ... RCA 7777
④	2	9	Only The Lonely	Roy Orbison ... Monument 421
⑤	3	10	Alley-Oop	Hollywood Argyles ... Lute 5905
⑥	7	9	Image Of A Girl	Safaris ... Eldo 101
⑦	8	8	Tell Laura I Love Her	Ray Peterson ... RCA 7745
⑧	9	11	Please Help Me, I'm Falling	Hank Locklin ... RCA 7692
⑨	6	11	Mule Skinner Blues	The Fendermen ... Soma 1137
⑩	10	9	That's All You Gotta Do	Brenda Lee ... Decca 31093

★ HIGHEST DEBUT ★ POS 49 — The Twist ... Chubby Checker
★ BIGGEST MOVER ★ 80 to 34 — A Woman, A Lover, A Friend ... Jackie Wilson

AUGUST 8, 1960 — Billboard HOT 100

TW	LW	WK		
①	2	6	Itsy Bitsy Teenie Weenie Yellow Polkadot Bikini	Brian Hyland ... Leader 805
②	1	11	I'm Sorry	Brenda Lee ... Decca 31093
③	3	4	It's Now Or Never	Elvis Presley ... RCA 7777
④	4	10	Only The Lonely	Roy Orbison ... Monument 421
⑤	5	11	Alley-Oop	Hollywood Argyles ... Lute 5905
⑥	6	10	Image Of A Girl	Safaris ... Eldo 101
❼	18	4	Walk--Don't Run	The Ventures ... Dolton 25
⑧	7	9	Tell Laura I Love Her	Ray Peterson ... RCA 7745
⑨	8	12	Please Help Me, I'm Falling	Hank Locklin ... RCA 7692
⑩	13	8	Walking To New Orleans	Fats Domino ... Imperial 5675

★ HIGHEST DEBUT ★ POS 59 — Kiddio ... Brook Benton
★ BIGGEST MOVER ★ 85 to 36 — Theme From The Apartment ... Ferrante & Teicher

AUGUST 15, 1960 — Billboard HOT 100

TW	LW	WK		
①	3	5	It's Now Or Never	Elvis Presley ... RCA 7777
②	1	7	Itsy Bitsy Teenie Weenie Yellow Polkadot Bikini	Brian Hyland ... Leader 805
③	2	12	I'm Sorry	Brenda Lee ... Decca 31093
④	4	11	Only The Lonely	Roy Orbison ... Monument 421
⑤	7	5	Walk--Don't Run	The Ventures ... Dolton 25
⑥	10	9	Walking To New Orleans	Fats Domino ... Imperial 5675
❼	15	14	Finger Poppin' Time	Hank Ballard & The Midnighters ... King 5341
⑧	11	3	The Twist	Chubby Checker ... Parkway 811
⑨	8	10	Tell Laura I Love Her	Ray Peterson ... RCA 7745
⑩	6	11	Image Of A Girl	Safaris ... Eldo 101

★ HIGHEST DEBUT ★ POS 56 — My Heart Has A Mind Of Its Own ... Connie Francis
★ BIGGEST MOVER ★ 93 to 42 — Hot Rod Lincoln ... Johnny Bond

Billboard — AUGUST 22, 1960 — HOT 100.

TW	LW	WK		
①	1	6	**It's Now Or Never**	*Elvis Presley* . . . RCA 7777
②	2	8	Itsy Bitsy Teenie Weenie Yellow Polkadot Bikini	*Brian Hyland* . . . Kapp 342
③	5	6	Walk—Don't Run	*The Ventures* . . . Dolton 25
④	8	4	The Twist	*Chubby Checker* . . . Parkway 811
⑤	3	13	I'm Sorry	*Brenda Lee* . . . Decca 31093
⑥	4	12	Only The Lonely	*Roy Orbison* . . . Monument 421
⑦	11	6	Volare	*Bobby Rydell* . . . Cameo 179
⑧	7	15	Finger Poppin' Time	*Hank Ballard & The Midnighters* . . . King 5341
⑨	12	11	Mission Bell	*Donnie Brooks* . . . Era 3018
⑩	10	12	Image Of A Girl	*Safaris* . . . Eldo 101

★ HIGHEST DEBUT ★ POS 61	★ BIGGEST MOVER ★ 79 to 54
The Same One . . . *Brook Benton*	Chain Gang . . . *Sam Cooke*

Billboard — AUGUST 29, 1960 — HOT 100.

TW	LW	WK		
①	1	7	**It's Now Or Never**	*Elvis Presley* . . . RCA 7777
②	3	7	**Walk--Don't Run**	*The Ventures* . . . Dolton 25
③	4	5	The Twist	*Chubby Checker* . . . Parkway 811
④	5	14	I'm Sorry	*Brenda Lee* . . . Decca 31093
⑤	7	7	Volare	*Bobby Rydell* . . . Cameo 179
⑥	2	9	Itsy Bitsy Teenie Weenie Yellow Polkadot Bikini	*Brian Hyland* . . . Kapp 342
⑦	8	16	**Finger Poppin' Time**	*Hank Ballard & The Midnighters* . . . King 5341
⑧	9	12	Mission Bell	*Donnie Brooks* . . . Era 3018
⑨	6	13	Only The Lonely	*Roy Orbison* . . . Monument 421
⑩	14	8	**In My Little Corner Of The World**	*Anita Bryant* . . . Carlton 530

★ HIGHEST DEBUT ★ POS 65	★ BIGGEST MOVER ★ 95 to 52
Mr. Custer . . . *Larry Verne*	A Million To One . . . *Jimmy Charles*

Billboard — SEPTEMBER 5, 1960 — HOT 100.

TW	LW	WK		
①	1	8	**It's Now Or Never**	*Elvis Presley* . . . RCA 7777
②	3	6	The Twist	*Chubby Checker* . . . Parkway 811
③	2	8	Walk--Don't Run	*The Ventures* . . . Dolton 25
④	5	8	**Volare**	*Bobby Rydell* . . . Cameo 179
⑤	4	15	I'm Sorry	*Brenda Lee* . . . Decca 31093
⑥	6	10	Itsy Bitsy Teenie Weenie Yellow Polkadot Bikini	*Brian Hyland* . . . Kapp 342
⑦	8	13	**Mission Bell**	*Donnie Brooks* . . . Era 3018
⑧	7	17	Finger Poppin' Time	*Hank Ballard & The Midnighters* . . . King 5341
⑨	16	4	My Heart Has A Mind Of Its Own	*Connie Francis* . . . MGM 12923
⑩	12	7	**Theme From The Apartment**	*Ferrante & Teicher* . . . United Artists 231

★ HIGHEST DEBUT ★ POS 47	★ BIGGEST MOVER ★ 65 to 13
So Sad (To Watch Good Love Go Bad) . . . *The Everly Brothers*	Mr. Custer . . . *Larry Verne*

Billboard 🔴 SEPTEMBER 12, 1960 🔴 HOT 100.

TW	LW	WK			
①	1	9	It's Now Or Never	Elvis Presley	RCA 7777
②	2	7	The Twist	Chubby Checker	Parkway 811
③	9	5	My Heart Has A Mind Of Its Own	Connie Francis	MGM 12923
④	13	3	Mr. Custer	Larry Verne	Era 3024
⑤	3	9	Walk—Don't Run	The Ventures	Dolton 25
⑥	22	5	Chain Gang	Sam Cooke	RCA 7783
⑦	4	9	Volare	Bobby Rydell	Cameo 179
⑧	17	6	Kiddio	Brook Benton	Mercury 71652
⑨	14	6	Yogi	The Ivy Three	Shell 720
⑩	7	14	Mission Bell	Donnie Brooks	Era 3018

★ **HIGHEST DEBUT** ★ POS 67
I Want To Be Wanted................Brenda Lee

★ **BIGGEST MOVER** ★ 76 to 35
Three Nights A Week................Fats Domino

Billboard 🔴 SEPTEMBER 19, 1960 🔴 HOT 100.

TW	LW	WK			
①	2	8	The Twist	Chubby Checker	Parkway 811
②	3	6	My Heart Has A Mind Of Its Own	Connie Francis	MGM 12923
③	1	10	It's Now Or Never	Elvis Presley	RCA 7777
④	4	4	Mr. Custer	Larry Verne	Era 3024
⑤	6	6	Chain Gang	Sam Cooke	RCA 7783
⑥	5	10	Walk—Don't Run	The Ventures	Dolton 25
⑦	8	7	Kiddio	Brook Benton	Mercury 71652
⑧	9	7	Yogi	The Ivy Three	Shell 720
⑨	7	10	Volare	Bobby Rydell	Cameo 179
⑩	13	5	A Million To One	Jimmy Charles	Promo 1002

★ **HIGHEST DEBUT** ★ POS 87
Let's Go, Let's Go, Let's Go..........Hank Ballard &
The Midnighters

★ **BIGGEST MOVER** ★ 80 to 43
Yes Sir, That's My Baby................Ricky Nelson

Billboard 🔴 SEPTEMBER 26, 1960 🔴 HOT 100.

TW	LW	WK			
①	2	7	My Heart Has A Mind Of Its Own	Connie Francis	MGM 12923
②	1	9	The Twist	Chubby Checker	Parkway 811
③	5	7	Chain Gang	Sam Cooke	RCA 7783
④	4	5	Mr. Custer	Larry Verne	Era 3024
⑤	10	6	A Million To One	Jimmy Charles	Promo 1002
⑥	3	11	It's Now Or Never	Elvis Presley	RCA 7777
⑦	6	11	Walk—Don't Run	The Ventures	Dolton 25
⑧	7	8	Kiddio	Brook Benton	Mercury 71652
⑨	11	4	So Sad (To Watch Good Love Go Bad)	The Everly Brothers	Warner 5163
⑩	18	4	Save The Last Dance For Me	The Drifters	Atlantic 2071

★ **HIGHEST DEBUT** ★ POS 75
Somebody To Love..................Bobby Darin

★ **BIGGEST MOVER** ★ 91 to 56
You Talk Too Much ....Joe Jones

TW	LW	WK	Billboard.	OCTOBER 3, 1960	HOT 100.
①	1	8	**My Heart Has A Mind Of Its Own** ....*Connie Francis* ... MGM 12923		
②	3	8	**Chain Gang**...*Sam Cooke* ... RCA 7783		
③	4	6	Mr. Custer ....*Larry Verne* ... Era 3024		
④	2	10	The Twist...*Chubby Checker* ... Parkway 811		
⑤	5	7	**A Million To One** ....*Jimmy Charles* ... Promo 1002		
⑥	10	5	Save The Last Dance For Me.......................*The Drifters* ... Atlantic 2071		
⑦	6	12	It's Now Or Never...*Elvis Presley* ... RCA 7777		
⑧	7	12	Walk--Don't Run...*The Ventures* ... Dolton 25		
⑨	9	5	So Sad (To Watch Good Love Go Bad) .... *The Everly Brothers* ... Warner 5163		
⑩	12	11	**Theme From The Apartment**............................*Ferrante & Teicher* ... United Artists 231		

★ HIGHEST DEBUT ★ POS 78	★ BIGGEST MOVER ★ 90 to 55
Love Walked In ....*Dinah Washington*	Artificial Flowers ....*Bobby Darin*

TW	LW	WK	Billboard.	OCTOBER 10, 1960	HOT 100.
①	3	7	**Mr. Custer**...*Larry Verne* ... Era 3024		
②	2	9	**Chain Gang**...*Sam Cooke* ... RCA 7783		
③	1	9	My Heart Has A Mind Of Its Own ....*Connie Francis* ... MGM 12923		
④	6	6	**Save The Last Dance For Me**.......................*The Drifters* ... Atlantic 2071		
⑤	4	11	The Twist.....................................*Chubby Checker* ... Parkway 811		
⑥	5	8	A Million To One ....*Jimmy Charles* ... Promo 1002		
⑦	9	6	**So Sad (To Watch Good Love Go Bad)**............ *The Everly Brothers* ... Warner 5163		
⑧	12	11	**Devil Or Angel** ....*Bobby Vee* ... Liberty 55270		
❾	14	5	I Want To Be Wanted ....*Brenda Lee* ... Decca 31149		
⑩	11	10	Kiddio ....*Brook Benton* ... Mercury 71652		

★ HIGHEST DEBUT ★ POS 72	★ BIGGEST MOVER ★ 86 to 40
To Each His Own ....*The Platters*	Stay ....*Maurice Williams & The Zodiacs*

TW	LW	WK	Billboard.	OCTOBER 17, 1960	HOT 100.
①	4	7	**Save The Last Dance For Me**.................*The Drifters* ... Atlantic 2071		
②	3	10	My Heart Has A Mind Of Its Own ....*Connie Francis* ... MGM 12923		
③	2	10	Chain Gang.......................................*Sam Cooke* ... RCA 7783		
❹	9	6	I Want To Be Wanted ....*Brenda Lee* ... Decca 31149		
⑤	5	12	The Twist...*Chubby Checker* ... Parkway 811		
⑥	8	12	**Devil Or Angel** ....*Bobby Vee* ... Liberty 55270		
⑦	1	8	Mr. Custer ....*Larry Verne* ... Era 3024		
⑧	6	9	A Million To One ....*Jimmy Charles* ... Promo 1002		
⑨	7	7	So Sad (To Watch Good Love Go Bad) .... *The Everly Brothers* ... Warner 5163		
⑩	11	14	It's Now Or Never...*Elvis Presley* ... RCA 7777		

★ HIGHEST DEBUT ★ POS 71	★ BIGGEST MOVER ★ 99 to 63
New Orleans ...............................*U.S. Bonds*	Last Date ....*Floyd Cramer*

Billboard — OCTOBER 24, 1960 — HOT 100

TW	LW	WK	Title	Artist	Label
1	4	7	I Want To Be Wanted	Brenda Lee	Decca 31149
2	1	8	Save The Last Dance For Me	The Drifters	Atlantic 2071
3	5	13	The Twist	Chubby Checker	Parkway 811
4	2	11	My Heart Has A Mind Of Its Own	Connie Francis	MGM 12923
5	3	11	Chain Gang	Sam Cooke	RCA 7783
6	6	13	Devil Or Angel	Bobby Vee	Liberty 55270
7	11	8	Let's Think About Living	Bob Luman	Warner 5172
8	9	8	So Sad (To Watch Good Love Go Bad)	The Everly Brothers	Warner 5163
9	7	9	Mr. Custer	Larry Verne	Era 3024
10	14	14	Theme From The Apartment	Ferrante & Teicher	United Artists 231

★ **HIGHEST DEBUT** ★ POS 67
A Thousand Stars .... Kathy Young with The Innocents

★ **BIGGEST MOVER** ★ 67 to 41
Peter Gunn .... Duane Eddy

Billboard — OCTOBER 31, 1960 — HOT 100

TW	LW	WK	Title	Artist	Label
1	2	9	Save The Last Dance For Me	The Drifters	Atlantic 2071
2	1	8	I Want To Be Wanted	Brenda Lee	Decca 31149
3	4	12	My Heart Has A Mind Of Its Own	Connie Francis	MGM 12923
4	3	14	The Twist	Chubby Checker	Parkway 811
5	5	12	Chain Gang	Sam Cooke	RCA 7783
6	12	7	You Talk Too Much	Joe Jones	Roulette 4304
7	6	14	Devil Or Angel	Bobby Vee	Liberty 55270
8	7	9	Let's Think About Living	Bob Luman	Warner 5172
9	26	4	Poetry In Motion	Johnny Tillotson	Cadence 1384
10	11	6	Georgia On My Mind	Ray Charles	ABC-Paramount 10135

★ **HIGHEST DEBUT** ★ POS 63
He Will Break Your Heart .... Jerry Butler

★ **BIGGEST MOVER** ★ 90 to 59
I'll Save The Last Dance For You .... Damita Jo

Billboard — NOVEMBER 7, 1960 — HOT 100

TW	LW	WK	Title	Artist	Label
1	1	10	Save The Last Dance For Me	The Drifters	Atlantic 2071
2	2	9	I Want To Be Wanted	Brenda Lee	Decca 31149
3	9	5	Poetry In Motion	Johnny Tillotson	Cadence 1384
4	10	7	Georgia On My Mind	Ray Charles	ABC-Paramount 10135
5	6	8	You Talk Too Much	Joe Jones	Roulette 4304
6	3	13	My Heart Has A Mind Of Its Own	Connie Francis	MGM 12923
7	19	6	Stay	Maurice Williams & The Zodiacs	Herald 552
8	14	8	Let's Go, Let's Go, Let's Go	Hank Ballard & The Midnighters	King 5400
9	15	8	Blue Angel	Roy Orbison	Monument 425
10	7	15	Devil Or Angel	Bobby Vee	Liberty 55270

★ **HIGHEST DEBUT** ★ POS 54
Sway .... Bobby Rydell

★ **BIGGEST MOVER** ★ 78 to 44
Perfidia .... The Ventures

Billboard — NOVEMBER 14, 1960 — HOT 100

TW	LW	WK	Title	Artist	Label
①	4	8	Georgia On My Mind	Ray Charles	ABC-Paramount 10135
②	3	6	Poetry In Motion	Johnny Tillotson	Cadence 1384
③	5	9	You Talk Too Much	Joe Jones	Roulette 4304
④	2	10	I Want To Be Wanted	Brenda Lee	Decca 31149
⑤	1	11	Save The Last Dance For Me	The Drifters	Atlantic 2071
⑥	7	7	Stay	Maurice Williams & The Zodiacs	Herald 552
⑦	8	9	Let's Go, Let's Go, Let's Go	Hank Ballard & The Midnighters	King 5400
⑧	16	6	Last Date	Floyd Cramer	RCA 7775
⑨	22	4	A Thousand Stars	Kathy Young with The Innocents	Indigo 108
⑩	9	9	Blue Angel	Roy Orbison	Monument 425

★ **HIGHEST DEBUT** ★ POS 35
Are You Lonesome To-night?.........Elvis Presley

★ **BIGGEST MOVER** ★ 92 to 51
Ol' MacDonald ....Frank Sinatra

Billboard — NOVEMBER 21, 1960 — HOT 100

TW	LW	WK	Title	Artist	Label
❶	6	8	Stay	Maurice Williams & The Zodiacs	Herald 552
❷	35	2	Are You Lonesome To-night?	Elvis Presley	RCA 7810
③	2	7	Poetry In Motion	Johnny Tillotson	Cadence 1384
④	8	7	Last Date	Floyd Cramer	RCA 7775
⑤	1	9	Georgia On My Mind	Ray Charles	ABC-Paramount 10135
⑥	7	10	Let's Go, Let's Go, Let's Go	Hank Ballard & The Midnighters	King 5400
⑦	9	5	A Thousand Stars	Kathy Young with The Innocents	Indigo 108
⑧	11	6	New Orleans	U.S. Bonds	Legrand 1003
⑨	3	10	You Talk Too Much	Joe Jones	Roulette 4304
⑩	5	12	Save The Last Dance For Me	The Drifters	Atlantic 2071

★ **HIGHEST DEBUT** ★ POS 64
Ruby ....Ray Charles

★ **BIGGEST MOVER** ★ 35 to 2
Are You Lonesome To-night?.........Elvis Presley

Billboard — NOVEMBER 28, 1960 — HOT 100

TW	LW	WK	Title	Artist	Label
①	2	3	Are You Lonesome To-night?	Elvis Presley	RCA 7810
②	4	8	Last Date	Floyd Cramer	RCA 7775
③	1	9	Stay	Maurice Williams & The Zodiacs	Herald 552
④	3	8	Poetry In Motion	Johnny Tillotson	Cadence 1384
⑤	7	6	A Thousand Stars	Kathy Young with The Innocents	Indigo 108
⑥	8	7	New Orleans	U.S. Bonds	Legrand 1003
❼	12	11	North To Alaska	Johnny Horton	Columbia 41782
❽	13	8	Alone At Last	Jackie Wilson	Brunswick 55170
⑨	6	11	Let's Go, Let's Go, Let's Go	Hank Ballard & The Midnighters	King 5400
⑩	5	10	Georgia On My Mind	Ray Charles	ABC-Paramount 10135

★ **HIGHEST DEBUT** ★ POS 67
Rubber Ball ....Bobby Vee

★ **BIGGEST MOVER** ★ 50 to 22
Like Strangers.....................The Everly Brothers

Billboard — DECEMBER 5, 1960 — HOT 100

TW	LW	WK		
①	1	4	**Are You Lonesome To-night?**	*Elvis Presley* ... RCA 7810
②	2	9	**Last Date**	*Floyd Cramer* ... RCA 7775
③	4	9	Poetry In Motion	*Johnny Tillotson* ... Cadence 1384
④	3	10	Stay	*Maurice Williams & The Zodiacs* ... Herald 552
⑤	5	7	A Thousand Stars	*Kathy Young with The Innocents* ... Indigo 108
⑥	7	12	North To Alaska	*Johnny Horton* ... Columbia 41782
⑦	11	6	**He Will Break Your Heart**	*Jerry Butler* ... Vee-Jay 354
⑧	6	8	New Orleans	*U.S. Bonds* ... Legrand 1003
⑨	12	7	Sailor (Your Home Is The Sea)	*Lolita* ... Kapp 349
⑩	9	12	Let's Go, Let's Go, Let's Go	*Hank Ballard & The Midnighters* ... King 5400

★ HIGHEST DEBUT ★ POS 69	★ BIGGEST MOVER ★ 75 to 41
Sad Mood ...*Sam Cooke*	Blue Tango ...*Bill Black's Combo*

Billboard — DECEMBER 12, 1960 — HOT 100

TW	LW	WK		
①	1	5	**Are You Lonesome To-night?**	*Elvis Presley* ... RCA 7810
②	2	10	**Last Date**	*Floyd Cramer* ... RCA 7775
③	5	8	**A Thousand Stars**	*Kathy Young with The Innocents* ... Indigo 108
❹	13	5	Wonderland By Night	*Bert Kaempfert* ... Decca 31141
⑤	6	13	North To Alaska	*Johnny Horton* ... Columbia 41782
⑥	9	8	Sailor (Your Home Is The Sea)	*Lolita* ... Kapp 349
⑦	7	7	**He Will Break Your Heart**	*Jerry Butler* ... Vee-Jay 354
⑧	11	6	Many Tears Ago	*Connie Francis* ... MGM 12964
⑨	3	10	Poetry In Motion	*Johnny Tillotson* ... Cadence 1384
⑩	30	5	Exodus	*Ferrante & Teicher* ... United Artists 274

★ HIGHEST DEBUT ★ POS 40	★ BIGGEST MOVER ★ 74 to 36
Angel Baby ...*Rosie & The Originals*	Don't Go To Strangers ...*Etta Jones*

Billboard — DECEMBER 19, 1960 — HOT 100

TW	LW	WK		
①	1	6	**Are You Lonesome To-night?**	*Elvis Presley* ... RCA 7810
②	2	11	**Last Date**	*Floyd Cramer* ... RCA 7775
③	4	6	**Wonderland By Night**	*Bert Kaempfert* ... Decca 31141
④	5	14	**North To Alaska**	*Johnny Horton* ... Columbia 41782
⑤	6	9	**Sailor (Your Home Is The Sea)**	*Lolita* ... Kapp 349
⑥	10	6	Exodus	*Ferrante & Teicher* ... United Artists 274
⑦	3	9	A Thousand Stars	*Kathy Young with The Innocents* ... Indigo 108
⑧	8	7	Many Tears Ago	*Connie Francis* ... MGM 12964
⑨	12	8	You're Sixteen	*Johnny Burnette* ... Liberty 55285
⑩	7	8	He Will Break Your Heart	*Jerry Butler* ... Vee-Jay 354

★ HIGHEST DEBUT ★ POS 62	★ BIGGEST MOVER ★ 64 to 26
Rudolph The Red Nosed Reindeer ...*David Seville & The Chipmunks*	Rockin' Around The Christmas Tree ...*Brenda Lee*

TW	LW	WK	Billboard.	DECEMBER 26, 1960	HOT 100.
①	1	7	**Are You Lonesome To-night?** ....*Elvis Presley* . . . RCA 7810		
②	3	7	**Wonderland By Night** ....*Bert Kaempfert* . . . Decca 31141		
③	2	12	**Last Date**...*Floyd Cramer* . . . RCA 7775		
④	7	10	**A Thousand Stars**................*Kathy Young with The Innocents* . . . Indigo 108		
⑤	6	7	**Exodus** ....*Ferrante & Teicher* . . . United Artists 274		
⑥	4	15	**North To Alaska** ....*Johnny Horton* . . . Columbia 41782		
⑦	8	8	**Many Tears Ago** ....*Connie Francis* . . . MGM 12964		
⑧	9	9	**You're Sixteen**................................*Johnny Burnette* . . . Liberty 55285		
⑨	5	10	**Sailor (Your Home Is The Sea)**................................*Lolita* . . . Kapp 349		
⑩	27	6	**Corinna, Corinna** ....*Ray Peterson* . . . Dunes 2002		

★ **HIGHEST DEBUT** ★ POS 63	★ **BIGGEST MOVER** ★ 100 to 57
You Are The Only One..................*Ricky Nelson*	Calendar Girl ....*Neil Sedaka*

TW	LW	WK	Billboard.	DECEMBER 31, 1960	HOT 100.
①	1	8	**Are You Lonesome To-night?** ....*Elvis Presley* . . . RCA 7810		
②	2	8	**Wonderland By Night** ....*Bert Kaempfert* . . . Decca 31141		
③	3	13	**Last Date**...*Floyd Cramer* . . . RCA 7775		
④	5	8	**Exodus** ....*Ferrante & Teicher* . . . United Artists 274		
⑤	4	11	**A Thousand Stars**................*Kathy Young with The Innocents* . . . Indigo 108		
⑥	6	16	**North To Alaska** ....*Johnny Horton* . . . Columbia 41782		
⑦	7	9	**Many Tears Ago** ....*Connie Francis* . . . MGM 12964		
⑧	8	10	**You're Sixteen**................................*Johnny Burnette* . . . Liberty 55285		
⑨	13	4	**Angel Baby** ....*Rosie & The Originals* . . . Highland 1011		
⑩	10	7	**Corinna, Corinna** ....*Ray Peterson* . . . Dunes 2002		

★ **HIGHEST DEBUT** ★ POS 72	★ **BIGGEST MOVER** ★ 98 to 61
C'est Si Bon ....*Conway Twitty*	There She Goes ....*Jerry Wallace*

TW	LW	WK	Billboard	JANUARY 9, 1961	HOT 100.
①	2	9	Wonderland By Night	............................*Bert Kaempfert* ... Decca 31141
②	1	9	Are You Lonesome To-night?	.....................*Elvis Presley* ... RCA 7810
③	4	9	Exodus	....*Ferrante & Teicher* ... United Artists 274
④	3	14	Last Date	....*Floyd Cramer* ... RCA 7775
⑤	14	8	Will You Love Me Tomorrow	.....................*The Shirelles* ... Scepter 1211
⑥	11	7	Rubber Ball	....*Bobby Vee* ... Liberty 55287
⑦	9	5	Angel Baby	................................*Rosie & The Originals* ... Highland 1011
⑧	6	17	North To Alaska	................................*Johnny Horton* ... Columbia 41782
⑨	10	8	Corinna, Corinna	....*Ray Peterson* ... Dunes 2002
⑩	8	11	You're Sixteen	....*Johnny Burnette* ... Liberty 55285

★ HIGHEST DEBUT ★ POS 60	★ BIGGEST MOVER ★ 83 to 48
My Empty Arms ....*Jackie Wilson*	Emotions ....*Brenda Lee*

TW	LW	WK	Billboard	JANUARY 16, 1961	HOT 100.
①	1	10	Wonderland By Night	............................*Bert Kaempfert* ... Decca 31141
②	2	10	Are You Lonesome To-night?	.....................*Elvis Presley* ... RCA 7810
③	3	10	Exodus	....*Ferrante & Teicher* ... United Artists 274
④	5	9	Will You Love Me Tomorrow	.....................*The Shirelles* ... Scepter 1211
⑤	13	6	Calcutta	....*Lawrence Welk* ... Dot 16161
⑥	7	6	Angel Baby	..........................*Rosie & The Originals* ... Highland 1011
⑦	6	8	Rubber Ball	....*Bobby Vee* ... Liberty 55287
⑧	4	15	Last Date	....*Floyd Cramer* ... RCA 7775
⑨	9	9	Corinna, Corinna	.................................*Ray Peterson* ... Dunes 2002
⑩	8	18	North To Alaska	........................*Johnny Horton* ... Columbia 41782

★ HIGHEST DEBUT ★ POS 72	★ BIGGEST MOVER ★ 81 to 48
No One ....*Connie Francis*	Wheels ....*The String-A-Longs*

TW	LW	WK	Billboard	JANUARY 23, 1961	HOT 100.
①	1	11	Wonderland By Night	............................*Bert Kaempfert* ... Decca 31141
②	3	11	Exodus	....*Ferrante & Teicher* ... United Artists 274
③	5	7	Calcutta	....*Lawrence Welk* ... Dot 16161
④	4	10	Will You Love Me Tomorrow	.....................*The Shirelles* ... Scepter 1211
⑤	6	7	Angel Baby	...........................*Rosie & The Originals* ... Highland 1011
⑥	2	11	Are You Lonesome To-night?	.....................*Elvis Presley* ... RCA 7810
⑦	12	7	Shop Around	...........................*The Miracles* ... Tamla 54034
⑧	14	6	Calendar Girl	..............................*Neil Sedaka* ... RCA 7829
⑨	7	9	Rubber Ball	....*Bobby Vee* ... Liberty 55287
⑩	9	10	Corinna, Corinna	.........................*Ray Peterson* ... Dunes 2002

★ HIGHEST DEBUT ★ POS 49	★ BIGGEST MOVER ★ 90 to 42
Pony Time ....*Chubby Checker*	Where The Boys Are ....*Connie Francis*

TW	LW	WK	Billboard.	JANUARY 30, 1961	HOT 100.
①	4	11	**Will You Love Me Tomorrow** ....*The Shirelles* . . . Scepter 1211		
②	3	8	Calcutta ....*Lawrence Welk* . . . Dot 16161		
③	2	12	Exodus ....*Ferrante & Teicher* . . . United Artists 274		
④	1	12	Wonderland By Night ....*Bert Kaempfert* . . . Decca 31141		
⑤	7	8	Shop Around ....*The Miracles* . . . Tamla 54034		
⑥	5	8	Angel Baby...............................*Rosie & The Originals* . . . Highland 1011		
⑦	8	7	Calendar Girl ....*Neil Sedaka* . . . RCA 7829		
❽	13	5	Emotions ....*Brenda Lee* . . . Decca 31195		
⑨	9	10	Rubber Ball...*Bobby Vee* . . . Liberty 55287		
⑩	6	12	Are You Lonesome To-night?....................*Elvis Presley* . . . RCA 7810		

★ **HIGHEST DEBUT** ★ POS 43	★ **BIGGEST MOVER** ★ 78 to 52
I'm Learning About Love.................*Brenda Lee*	What A Price ....*Fats Domino*

TW	LW	WK	Billboard.	FEBRUARY 6, 1961	HOT 100.
①	1	12	**Will You Love Me Tomorrow** ....*The Shirelles* . . . Scepter 1211		
②	2	9	Calcutta ....*Lawrence Welk* . . . Dot 16161		
③	3	13	Exodus ....*Ferrante & Teicher* . . . United Artists 274		
④	5	9	Shop Around...*The Miracles* . . . Tamla 54034		
⑤	7	8	Calendar Girl ....*Neil Sedaka* . . . RCA 7829		
⑥	4	13	Wonderland By Night ....*Bert Kaempfert* . . . Decca 31141		
⑦	6	9	Angel Baby...............................*Rosie & The Originals* . . . Highland 1011		
⑧	8	6	Emotions ....*Brenda Lee* . . . Decca 31195		
❾	15	5	**My Empty Arms**...............................*Jackie Wilson* . . . Brunswick 55201		
⑩	9	11	Rubber Ball...*Bobby Vee* . . . Liberty 55287		

★ **HIGHEST DEBUT** ★ POS 66	★ **BIGGEST MOVER** ★ 71 to 40
Little Boy Sad ....*Johnny Burnette*	Jimmy's Girl.................................*Johnny Tillotson*

TW	LW	WK	Billboard.	FEBRUARY 13, 1961	HOT 100.
①	2	10	**Calcutta** ....*Lawrence Welk* . . . Dot 16161		
②	1	13	Will You Love Me Tomorrow ....*The Shirelles* . . . Scepter 1211		
③	4	10	Shop Around...*The Miracles* . . . Tamla 54034		
④	5	9	**Calendar Girl** ....*Neil Sedaka* . . . RCA 7829		
⑤	3	14	Exodus ....*Ferrante & Teicher* . . . United Artists 274		
⑥	7	10	Angel Baby...............................*Rosie & The Originals* . . . Highland 1011		
⑦	8	7	**Emotions** ....*Brenda Lee* . . . Decca 31195		
⑧	6	14	Wonderland By Night ....*Bert Kaempfert* . . . Decca 31141		
❾	15	4	Pony Time..*Chubby Checker* . . . Parkway 818		
⑩	16	7	There's A Moon Out Tonight ....*The Capris* . . . Old Town 1094		

★ **HIGHEST DEBUT** ★ POS 69	★ **BIGGEST MOVER** ★ 94 to 50
Stayin' In................................*Bobby Vee*	Lazy River ....*Bobby Darin*

Billboard — FEBRUARY 20, 1961 — HOT 100

TW	LW	WK			
①	1	11	**Calcutta**	*Lawrence Welk* ...	Dot 16161
②	3	11	**Shop Around**	*The Miracles* ...	Tamla 54034
③	2	14	Will You Love Me Tomorrow	*The Shirelles* ...	Scepter 1211
❹	9	5	Pony Time	*Chubby Checker* ...	Parkway 818
❺	10	8	There's A Moon Out Tonight	*The Capris* ...	Old Town 1094
⑥	4	10	Calendar Girl	*Neil Sedaka* ...	RCA 7829
⑦	7	8	**Emotions**	*Brenda Lee* ...	Decca 31195
⑧	5	15	**Exodus**	*Ferrante & Teicher* ...	United Artists 274
⑨	13	9	Dedicated To The One I Love	*The Shirelles* ...	Scepter 1203
⑩	15	7	Wheels	*The String-A-Longs* ...	Warwick 603

★ **HIGHEST DEBUT** ★ POS 24
Surrender ....*Elvis Presley*

★ **BIGGEST MOVER** ★ 97 to 57
Cherie ....*Bobby Rydell*

Billboard — FEBRUARY 27, 1961 — HOT 100

TW	LW	WK			
①	4	6	**Pony Time**	*Chubby Checker* ...	Parkway 818
②	1	12	Calcutta	*Lawrence Welk* ...	Dot 16161
③	5	9	**There's A Moon Out Tonight**	*The Capris* ...	Old Town 1094
❹	24	2	Surrender	*Elvis Presley* ...	RCA 7850
❺	15	5	Don't Worry	*Marty Robbins* ...	Columbia 41922
⑥	9	10	Dedicated To The One I Love	*The Shirelles* ...	Scepter 1203
⑦	11	7	Where The Boys Are	*Connie Francis* ...	MGM 12971
⑧	2	12	Shop Around	*The Miracles* ...	Tamla 54034
⑨	18	5	Ebony Eyes	*The Everly Brothers* ...	Warner 5199
⑩	10	8	Wheels	*The String-A-Longs* ...	Warwick 603

★ **HIGHEST DEBUT** ★ POS 71
Please Love Me Forever ....*Cathy Jean & The Roommates*

★ **BIGGEST MOVER** ★ 97 to 63
Pony Express ....*Danny & The Juniors*

Billboard — MARCH 6, 1961 — HOT 100

TW	LW	WK			
①	1	7	**Pony Time**	*Chubby Checker* ...	Parkway 818
②	4	3	Surrender	*Elvis Presley* ...	RCA 7850
❸	10	9	**Wheels**	*The String-A-Longs* ...	Warwick 603
④	5	6	Don't Worry	*Marty Robbins* ...	Columbia 41922
⑤	7	8	Where The Boys Are	*Connie Francis* ...	MGM 12971
⑥	2	13	Calcutta	*Lawrence Welk* ...	Dot 16161
❼	12	9	Baby Sittin' Boogie	*Buzz Clifford* ...	Columbia 41876
⑧	6	11	Dedicated To The One I Love	*The Shirelles* ...	Scepter 1203
⑨	3	10	There's A Moon Out Tonight	*The Capris* ...	Old Town 1094
⑩	9	6	Ebony Eyes	*The Everly Brothers* ...	Warner 5199

★ **HIGHEST DEBUT** ★ POS 51
On The Rebound ....*Floyd Cramer*

★ **BIGGEST MOVER** ★ 84 to 44
Lonely Man ....*Elvis Presley*

Billboard — MARCH 13, 1961 — HOT 100

TW	LW	WK	Title	Artist	Label
1	1	8	**Pony Time**	Chubby Checker	Parkway 818
2	2	4	**Surrender**	Elvis Presley	RCA 7850
3	3	10	**Wheels**	The String-A-Longs	Warwick 603
4	4	7	**Don't Worry**	Marty Robbins	Columbia 41922
5	5	9	**Where The Boys Are**	Connie Francis	MGM 12971
6	7	10	**Baby Sittin' Boogie**	Buzz Clifford	Columbia 41876
7	8	12	**Dedicated To The One I Love**	The Shirelles	Scepter 1203
8	6	14	**Calcutta**	Lawrence Welk	Dot 16161
9	10	7	**Ebony Eyes**	The Everly Brothers	Warner 5199
10	13	11	**Spanish Harlem**	Ben E. King	Atco 6185

★ **HIGHEST DEBUT** ★ POS 56
Tonight My Love, Tonight .... Paul Anka

★ **BIGGEST MOVER** ★ 87 to 59
Blue Moon .... The Marcels

Billboard — MARCH 20, 1961 — HOT 100

TW	LW	WK	Title	Artist	Label
1	2	5	**Surrender**	Elvis Presley	RCA 7850
2	1	9	**Pony Time**	Chubby Checker	Parkway 818
3	4	8	**Don't Worry**	Marty Robbins	Columbia 41922
4	5	10	**Where The Boys Are**	Connie Francis	MGM 12971
5	7	13	**Dedicated To The One I Love**	The Shirelles	Scepter 1203
6	11	9	**Apache**	Jorgen Ingmann	Atco 6184
7	3	11	**Wheels**	The String-A-Longs	Warwick 603
8	9	8	**Ebony Eyes**	The Everly Brothers	Warner 5199
9	13	7	**Walk Right Back**	The Everly Brothers	Warner 5199
10	6	11	**Baby Sittin' Boogie**	Buzz Clifford	Columbia 41876

★ **HIGHEST DEBUT** ★ POS 75
Love Theme From One Eyed Jacks .... Ferrante & Teicher

★ **BIGGEST MOVER** ★ 59 to 21
Blue Moon .... The Marcels

Billboard — MARCH 27, 1961 — HOT 100

TW	LW	WK	Title	Artist	Label
1	1	6	**Surrender**	Elvis Presley	RCA 7850
2	2	10	**Pony Time**	Chubby Checker	Parkway 818
3	5	14	**Dedicated To The One I Love**	The Shirelles	Scepter 1203
4	6	10	**Apache**	Jorgen Ingmann	Atco 6184
5	3	9	**Don't Worry**	Marty Robbins	Columbia 41922
6	21	4	**Blue Moon**	The Marcels	Colpix 186
7	9	8	**Walk Right Back**	The Everly Brothers	Warner 5199
8	7	12	**Wheels**	The String-A-Longs	Warwick 603
9	4	11	**Where The Boys Are**	Connie Francis	MGM 12971
10	12	9	**Gee Whiz (Look At His Eyes)**	Carla Thomas	Atlantic 2086

★ **HIGHEST DEBUT** ★ POS 55
Mother-In-Law .... Ernie K-Doe

★ **BIGGEST MOVER** ★ 84 to 41
Fell In Love On Monday .... Fats Domino

Billboard — APRIL 3, 1961 — HOT 100

TW	LW	WK		
①	6	5	**Blue Moon**	The Marcels . . . Colpix 186
②	4	11	**Apache**	Jorgen Ingmann . . . Atco 6184
③	1	7	**Surrender**	Elvis Presley . . . RCA 7850
④	2	11	**Pony Time**	Chubby Checker . . . Parkway 818
⑤	3	15	**Dedicated To The One I Love**	The Shirelles . . . Scepter 1203
⑥	5	10	**Don't Worry**	Marty Robbins . . . Columbia 41922
⑦	11	5	**On The Rebound**	Floyd Cramer . . . RCA 7840
⑧	7	9	**Walk Right Back**	The Everly Brothers . . . Warner 5199
⑨	21	5	**Runaway**	Del Shannon . . . Big Top 3067
⑩	17	7	**But I Do**	Clarence Henry . . . Argo 5378

★ **HIGHEST DEBUT** ★ POS 72
Welcome Home . . . . .Sammy Kaye & His Orchestra

★ **BIGGEST MOVER** ★ 71 to 26
A Hundred Pounds Of Clay . . . . .Gene McDaniels

Billboard — APRIL 10, 1961 — HOT 100

TW	LW	WK		
①	1	6	**Blue Moon**	The Marcels . . . Colpix 186
②	2	12	**Apache**	Jorgen Ingmann . . . Atco 6184
③	5	16	**Dedicated To The One I Love**	The Shirelles . . . Scepter 1203
④	9	6	**Runaway**	Del Shannon . . . Big Top 3067
⑤	7	6	**On The Rebound**	Floyd Cramer . . . RCA 7840
⑥	10	8	**But I Do**	Clarence Henry . . . Argo 5378
⑦	3	8	**Surrender**	Elvis Presley . . . RCA 7850
⑧	6	11	**Don't Worry**	Marty Robbins . . . Columbia 41922
⑨	23	3	**Mother-In-Law**	Ernie K-Doe . . . Minit 623
⑩	8	10	**Walk Right Back**	The Everly Brothers . . . Warner 5199

★ **HIGHEST DEBUT** ★ POS 62
Frogg .The Brothers Four

★ **BIGGEST MOVER** ★ 83 to 48
Like, Long Hair . . . . .Paul Revere & The Raiders

Billboard — APRIL 17, 1961 — HOT 100

TW	LW	WK		
①	1	7	**Blue Moon**	The Marcels . . . Colpix 186
②	4	7	**Runaway**	Del Shannon . . . Big Top 3067
③	9	4	**Mother-In-Law**	Ernie K-Doe . . . Minit 623
④	5	7	**On The Rebound**	Floyd Cramer . . . RCA 7840
⑤	6	9	**But I Do**	Clarence Henry . . . Argo 5378
⑥	2	13	**Apache**	Jorgen Ingmann . . . Atco 6184
⑦	3	17	**Dedicated To The One I Love**	The Shirelles . . . Scepter 1203
⑧	12	9	**Asia Minor**	Kokomo . . . Felsted 8612
⑨	20	5	**A Hundred Pounds Of Clay**	Gene McDaniels . . . Liberty 55308
⑩	7	9	**Surrender**	Elvis Presley . . . RCA 7850

★ **HIGHEST DEBUT** ★ POS 56
Breakin' In A Brand New Broken
Heart . . . . .Connie Francis

★ **BIGGEST MOVER** ★ 79 to 53
What'd I Say . . . . .Jerry Lee Lewis

TW	LW	WK	Billboard.	APRIL 24, 1961	HOT 100.
1	2	8	**Runaway**	*Del Shannon* . . .	Big Top 3067
2	1	8	**Blue Moon**	*The Marcels* . . .	Colpix 186
3	3	5	**Mother-In-Law**	*Ernie K-Doe* . . .	Minit 623
4	5	10	**But I Do**	*Clarence Henry* . . .	Argo 5378
5	4	8	On The Rebound	*Floyd Cramer* . . .	RCA 7840
6	9	6	A Hundred Pounds Of Clay	*Gene McDaniels* . . .	Liberty 55308
7	18	7	I've Told Every Little Star	*Linda Scott* . . .	Canadian American 123
8	16	5	You Can Depend On Me	*Brenda Lee* . . .	Decca 31231
9	11	7	Take Good Care Of Her	*Adam Wade* . . .	Coed 546
10	14	8	One Mint Julep	*Ray Charles* . . .	Impulse 200

★ **HIGHEST DEBUT** ★ POS 71
Travelin' Man ....*Ricky Nelson*

★ **BIGGEST MOVER** ★ 85 to 34
Flaming Star ....*Elvis Presley*

TW	LW	WK	Billboard.	MAY 1, 1961	HOT 100.
1	1	9	**Runaway**	*Del Shannon* . . .	Big Top 3067
2	3	6	**Mother-In-Law**	*Ernie K-Doe* . . .	Minit 623
3	7	8	**I've Told Every Little Star**	*Linda Scott* . . .	Canadian American 123
4	6	7	**A Hundred Pounds Of Clay**	*Gene McDaniels* . . .	Liberty 55308
5	2	9	Blue Moon	*The Marcels* . . .	Colpix 186
6	4	11	But I Do	*Clarence Henry* . . .	Argo 5378
7	9	8	**Take Good Care Of Her**	*Adam Wade* . . .	Coed 546
8	10	9	**One Mint Julep**	*Ray Charles* . . .	Impulse 200
9	8	6	You Can Depend On Me	*Brenda Lee* . . .	Decca 31231
10	5	9	On The Rebound	*Floyd Cramer* . . .	RCA 7840

★ **HIGHEST DEBUT** ★ POS 53
That Old Black Magic ....*Bobby Rydell*

★ **BIGGEST MOVER** ★ 79 to 28
Dance The Mess Around ....*Chubby Checker*

TW	LW	WK	Billboard.	MAY 8, 1961	HOT 100.
1	1	10	**Runaway**	*Del Shannon* . . .	Big Top 3067
2	2	7	Mother-In-Law	*Ernie K-Doe* . . .	Minit 623
3	4	8	**A Hundred Pounds Of Clay**	*Gene McDaniels* . . .	Liberty 55308
4	3	9	I've Told Every Little Star	*Linda Scott* . . .	Canadian American 123
5	5	10	Blue Moon	*The Marcels* . . .	Colpix 186
6	9	7	**You Can Depend On Me**	*Brenda Lee* . . .	Decca 31231
7	7	9	**Take Good Care Of Her**	*Adam Wade* . . .	Coed 546
8	8	10	**One Mint Julep**	*Ray Charles* . . .	Impulse 200
9	11	10	**Portrait Of My Love**	*Steve Lawrence* . . .	United Artists 291
10	10	10	On The Rebound	*Floyd Cramer* . . .	RCA 7840

★ **HIGHEST DEBUT** ★ POS 75
Stand By Me.....................*Ben E. King*

★ **BIGGEST MOVER** ★ 73 to 27
Hello Mary Lou ....*Ricky Nelson*

Billboard — MAY 15, 1961 — HOT 100

TW	LW	WK	Title	Artist / Label
①	1	11	**Runaway**	*Del Shannon* . . . Big Top 3067
②	2	8	Mother-In-Law	*Ernie K-Doe* . . . Minit 623
③	3	9	**A Hundred Pounds Of Clay**	*Gene McDaniels* . . . Liberty 55308
④	4	10	I've Told Every Little Star	*Linda Scott* . . . Canadian American 123
⑤	12	8	Daddy's Home	*Shep & The Limelites* . . . Hull 740
⑥	6	8	**You Can Depend On Me**	*Brenda Lee* . . . Decca 31231
⑦	5	11	Blue Moon	*The Marcels* . . . Colpix 186
⑧	18	4	Travelin' Man	*Ricky Nelson* . . . Imperial 5741
⑨	14	5	Mama Said	*The Shirelles* . . . Scepter 1217
⑩	7	10	Take Good Care Of Her	*Adam Wade* . . . Coed 546

★ **HIGHEST DEBUT** ★ POS 43
I Feel So Bad .... *Elvis Presley*

★ **BIGGEST MOVER** ★ 95 to 58
Rama Lama Ding Dong .... *The Edsels*

Billboard — MAY 22, 1961 — HOT 100

TW	LW	WK	Title	Artist / Label
①	2	9	**Mother-In-Law**	*Ernie K-Doe* . . . Minit 623
②	1	12	Runaway	*Del Shannon* . . . Big Top 3067
③	5	9	Daddy's Home	*Shep & The Limelites* . . . Hull 740
④	3	10	A Hundred Pounds Of Clay	*Gene McDaniels* . . . Liberty 55308
⑤	8	5	Travelin' Man	*Ricky Nelson* . . . Imperial 5741
⑥	9	6	Mama Said	*The Shirelles* . . . Scepter 1217
⑦	16	7	**Running Scared**	*Roy Orbison* . . . Monument 438
⑧	11	6	Breakin' In A Brand New Broken Heart	*Connie Francis* . . . MGM 12995
⑨	15	4	**Hello Mary Lou**	*Ricky Nelson* . . . Imperial 5741
⑩	4	11	I've Told Every Little Star	*Linda Scott* . . . Canadian American 123

★ **HIGHEST DEBUT** ★ POS 81
Tell Me Why .... *The Belmonts*

★ **BIGGEST MOVER** ★ 76 to 48
You Always Hurt The One You Love ..... *Clarence Henry*

Billboard — MAY 29, 1961 — HOT 100

TW	LW	WK	Title	Artist / Label
①	5	6	**Travelin' Man**	*Ricky Nelson* . . . Imperial 5741
②	3	10	**Daddy's Home**	*Shep & The Limelites* . . . Hull 740
③	7	8	Running Scared	*Roy Orbison* . . . Monument 438
④	6	7	**Mama Said**	*The Shirelles* . . . Scepter 1217
⑤	1	10	Mother-In-Law	*Ernie K-Doe* . . . Minit 623
⑥	2	13	Runaway	*Del Shannon* . . . Big Top 3067
⑦	8	7	**Breakin' In A Brand New Broken Heart**	*Connie Francis* . . . MGM 12995
⑧	4	11	A Hundred Pounds Of Clay	*Gene McDaniels* . . . Liberty 55308
⑨	17	3	I Feel So Bad	*Elvis Presley* . . . RCA 7880
⑩	16	7	**Tragedy**	*The Fleetwoods* . . . Dolton 40

★ **HIGHEST DEBUT** ★ POS 67
Dance On Little Girl .... *Paul Anka*

★ **BIGGEST MOVER** ★ 99 to 65
Quarter To Three .... *U.S. Bonds*

TW	LW	WK	Billboard		JUNE 5, 1961		HOT 100
①	3	9	**Running Scared**			*Roy Orbison* . . .	Monument 438
②	1	7	Travelin' Man			*Ricky Nelson* . . .	Imperial 5741
③	2	11	Daddy's Home			*Shep & The Limelites* . . .	Hull 740
④	4	8	**Mama Said**			*The Shirelles* . . .	Scepter 1217
⑤	9	4	**I Feel So Bad**			*Elvis Presley* . . .	RCA 7880
❻	13	5	Stand By Me			*Ben E. King* . . .	Atco 6194
❼	14	6	Moody River			*Pat Boone* . . .	Dot 16209
⑧	8	12	A Hundred Pounds Of Clay			*Gene McDaniels* . . .	Liberty 55308
⑨	15	6	Raindrops			*Dee Clark* . . .	Vee-Jay 383
⑩	7	8	Breakin' In A Brand New Broken Heart			*Connie Francis* . . .	MGM 12995

★ **HIGHEST DEBUT** ★ POS 73	★ **BIGGEST MOVER** ★ 94 to 59
Wild In The Country............*Elvis Presley*	Temptation............*The Everly Brothers*

TW	LW	WK	Billboard		JUNE 12, 1961		HOT 100
①	2	8	**Travelin' Man**			*Ricky Nelson* . . .	Imperial 5741
❷	7	7	Moody River			*Pat Boone* . . .	Dot 16209
③	1	10	**Running Scared**			*Roy Orbison* . . .	Monument 438
④	6	6	**Stand By Me**			*Ben E. King* . . .	Atco 6194
⑤	9	7	Raindrops			*Dee Clark* . . .	Vee-Jay 383
❻	18	5	The Writing On The Wall			*Adam Wade* . . .	Coed 550
⑦	5	5	I Feel So Bad			*Elvis Presley* . . .	RCA 7880
⑧	21	5	Every Beat Of My Heart			*Pips* . . .	Vee-Jay 386
⑨	33	4	Quarter To Three			*U.S. Bonds* . . .	Legrand 1008
⑩	26	5	The Boll Weevil Song			*Brook Benton* . . .	Mercury 71820

★ **HIGHEST DEBUT** ★ POS 72	★ **BIGGEST MOVER** ★ 97 to 50
I'm Comin' On Back To You............*Jackie Wilson*	Stick With Me Baby ....*The Everly Brothers*

TW	LW	WK	Billboard		JUNE 19, 1961		HOT 100
①	2	8	**Moody River**			*Pat Boone* . . .	Dot 16209
②	1	9	Travelin' Man			*Ricky Nelson* . . .	Imperial 5741
❸	9	5	Quarter To Three			*U.S. Bonds* . . .	Legrand 1008
④	4	7	**Stand By Me**			*Ben E. King* . . .	Atco 6194
⑤	5	8	**Raindrops**			*Dee Clark* . . .	Vee-Jay 383
⑥	6	6	**The Writing On The Wall**			*Adam Wade* . . .	Coed 550
❼	17	9	Tossin' And Turnin'			*Bobby Lewis* . . .	Beltone 1002
⑧	8	6	**Every Beat Of My Heart**			*Pips* . . .	Vee-Jay 386
⑨	10	6	**The Boll Weevil Song**			*Brook Benton* . . .	Mercury 71820
⑩	11	8	**Those Oldies But Goodies**			*Little Caesar & The Romans* . . .	Del-Fi 4158

★ **HIGHEST DEBUT** ★ POS 68	★ **BIGGEST MOVER** ★ 70 to 33
You Can't Sit Down, Part 2..........*Philip Upchurch* Combo	Hats Off To Larry ....*Del Shannon*

Billboard 🔴 JUNE 26, 1961 🔴 HOT 100

TW	LW	WK		
①	3	6	Quarter To Three	U.S. Bonds ... Legrand 1008
②	5	9	Raindrops	Dee Clark ... Vee-Jay 383
③	1	9	Moody River	Pat Boone ... Dot 16209
④	7	10	Tossin' And Turnin'	Bobby Lewis ... Beltone 1002
⑤	2	10	Travelin' Man	Ricky Nelson ... Imperial 5741
⑥	6	7	The Writing On The Wall	Adam Wade ... Coed 550
⑦	9	7	The Boll Weevil Song	Brook Benton ... Mercury 71820
⑧	8	7	Every Beat Of My Heart	Pips ... Vee-Jay 386
⑨	10	9	Those Oldies But Goodies	Little Caesar & The Romans ... Del-Fi 4158
⑩	4	8	Stand By Me	Ben E. King ... Atco 6194

★ HIGHEST DEBUT ★ POS 48	★ BIGGEST MOVER ★ 69 to 31
Together ....Connie Francis	Dum Dum ....Brenda Lee

Billboard 🔴 JULY 3, 1961 🔴 HOT 100

TW	LW	WK		
①	1	7	Quarter To Three	U.S. Bonds ... Legrand 1008
②	4	11	Tossin' And Turnin'	Bobby Lewis ... Beltone 1002
③	7	8	The Boll Weevil Song	Brook Benton ... Mercury 71820
④	2	10	Raindrops	Dee Clark ... Vee-Jay 383
⑤	6	8	The Writing On The Wall	Adam Wade ... Coed 550
⑥	3	10	Moody River	Pat Boone ... Dot 16209
⑦	5	11	Travelin' Man	Ricky Nelson ... Imperial 5741
⑧	8	8	Every Beat Of My Heart	Pips ... Vee-Jay 386
⑨	9	10	Those Oldies But Goodies	Little Caesar & The Romans ... Del-Fi 4158
⑩	11	6	Yellow Bird	Arthur Lyman Group ... Hi Fi 5024

★ HIGHEST DEBUT ★ POS 60	★ BIGGEST MOVER ★ 99 to 59
The Fish................Bobby Rydell	Rainin' In My Heart.................Slim Harpo

Billboard 🔴 JULY 10, 1961 🔴 HOT 100

TW	LW	WK		
①	2	12	Tossin' And Turnin'	Bobby Lewis ... Beltone 1002
②	3	9	The Boll Weevil Song	Brook Benton ... Mercury 71820
③	1	8	Quarter To Three	U.S. Bonds ... Legrand 1008
④	4	11	Raindrops	Dee Clark ... Vee-Jay 383
⑤	5	9	The Writing On The Wall	Adam Wade ... Coed 550
⑥	8	9	Every Beat Of My Heart	Pips ... Vee-Jay 386
⑦	6	11	Moody River	Pat Boone ... Dot 16209
⑧	10	7	Yellow Bird	Arthur Lyman Group ... Hi Fi 5024
⑨	13	6	Hats Off To Larry	Del Shannon ... Big Top 3075
⑩	12	7	Dance On Little Girl	Paul Anka ... ABC-Paramount 10220

★ HIGHEST DEBUT ★ POS 79	★ BIGGEST MOVER ★ 74 to 46
Ready For Your Love..........Shep & The Limelites	Pretty Little Angel Eyes ....Curtis Lee

Billboard ⊙ JULY 17, 1961 ⊙ HOT 100

TW	LW	WK	Title	Artist	Label
①	1	13	Tossin' And Turnin'	Bobby Lewis	Beltone 1002
②	2	10	The Boll Weevil Song	Brook Benton	Mercury 71820
③	3	9	Quarter To Three	U.S. Bonds	Legrand 1008
④	4	12	Raindrops	Dee Clark	Vee-Jay 383
⑤	8	8	Yellow Bird	Arthur Lyman Group	Hi Fi 5024
⑥	9	7	Hats Off To Larry	Del Shannon	Big Top 3075
⑦	6	10	Every Beat Of My Heart	Pips	Vee-Jay 386
⑧	11	7	San Antonio Rose	Floyd Cramer	RCA 7893
⑨	14	8	I Like It Like That	Chris Kenner	Instant 3229
⑩	13	5	Dum Dum	Brenda Lee	Decca 31272

★ **HIGHEST DEBUT** ★ POS 82
My Memories Of You........Donnie & The Dreamers

★ **BIGGEST MOVER** ★ 100 to 69
Michael.....................The Highwaymen

Billboard ⊙ JULY 24, 1961 ⊙ HOT 100

TW	LW	WK	Title	Artist	Label
①	1	14	Tossin' And Turnin'	Bobby Lewis	Beltone 1002
②	2	11	The Boll Weevil Song	Brook Benton	Mercury 71820
③	3	10	Quarter To Three	U.S. Bonds	Legrand 1008
④	5	9	Yellow Bird	Arthur Lyman Group	Hi Fi 5024
⑤	9	9	I Like It Like That	Chris Kenner	Instant 3229
⑥	6	8	Hats Off To Larry	Del Shannon	Big Top 3075
⑦	4	13	Raindrops	Dee Clark	Vee-Jay 383
⑧	10	6	Dum Dum	Brenda Lee	Decca 31272
⑨	14	5	Together	Connie Francis	MGM 13019
⑩	15	6	Let's Twist Again	Chubby Checker	Parkway 824

★ **HIGHEST DEBUT** ★ POS 52
School Is Out.........................Gary (U.S.) Bonds

★ **BIGGEST MOVER** ★ 79 to 47
Runaround.............................The Regents

Billboard ⊙ JULY 31, 1961 ⊙ HOT 100

TW	LW	WK	Title	Artist	Label
①	1	15	Tossin' And Turnin'	Bobby Lewis	Beltone 1002
②	5	10	I Like It Like That	Chris Kenner	Instant 3229
③	2	12	The Boll Weevil Song	Brook Benton	Mercury 71820
④	8	7	Dum Dum	Brenda Lee	Decca 31272
⑤	6	9	Hats Off To Larry	Del Shannon	Big Top 3075
⑥	3	11	Quarter To Three	U.S. Bonds	Legrand 1008
⑦	12	5	Last Night	Mar-Keys	Satellite 107
⑧	9	6	Together	Connie Francis	MGM 13019
⑨	10	7	Let's Twist Again	Chubby Checker	Parkway 824
⑩	4	10	Yellow Bird	Arthur Lyman Group	Hi Fi 5024

★ **HIGHEST DEBUT** ★ POS 72
Amor.............................Ben E. King

★ **BIGGEST MOVER** ★ 66 to 35
Hurt.............................Timi Yuro

Billboard — AUGUST 7, 1961 — HOT 100

TW	LW	WK	Title	Artist	Label
1	1	16	Tossin' And Turnin'	Bobby Lewis	Beltone 1002
2	2	11	I Like It Like That	Chris Kenner	Instant 3229
3	7	6	Last Night	Mar-Keys	Satellite 107
4	4	8	Dum Dum	Brenda Lee	Decca 31272
5	5	10	Hats Off To Larry	Del Shannon	Big Top 3075
6	8	7	Together	Connie Francis	MGM 13019
7	16	6	Pretty Little Angel Eyes	Curtis Lee	Dunes 2007
8	9	8	Let's Twist Again	Chubby Checker	Parkway 824
9	13	7	Wooden Heart	Joe Dowell	Smash 1708
10	23	5	Michael	The Highwaymen	United Artists 258

★ HIGHEST DEBUT ★ POS 66
Who Put The Bomp (In The Bomp, Bomp, Bomp) ....Barry Mann

★ BIGGEST MOVER ★ 59 to 32
As If I Didn't Know ....Adam Wade

Billboard — AUGUST 14, 1961 — HOT 100

TW	LW	WK	Title	Artist	Label
1	1	17	Tossin' And Turnin'	Bobby Lewis	Beltone 1002
2	2	12	I Like It Like That	Chris Kenner	Instant 3229
3	3	7	Last Night	Mar-Keys	Satellite 107
4	4	9	Dum Dum	Brenda Lee	Decca 31272
5	9	8	Wooden Heart	Joe Dowell	Smash 1708
6	10	6	Michael	The Highwaymen	United Artists 258
7	7	7	Pretty Little Angel Eyes	Curtis Lee	Dunes 2007
8	8	9	Let's Twist Again	Chubby Checker	Parkway 824
9	6	8	Together	Connie Francis	MGM 13019
10	16	4	School Is Out	Gary (U.S.) Bonds	Legrand 1009

★ HIGHEST DEBUT ★ POS 71
Crying..................................Roy Orbison

★ BIGGEST MOVER ★ 87 to 41
Take Good Care Of My Baby ....Bobby Vee

Billboard — AUGUST 21, 1961 — HOT 100

TW	LW	WK	Title	Artist	Label
1	1	18	Tossin' And Turnin'	Bobby Lewis	Beltone 1002
2	5	9	Wooden Heart	Joe Dowell	Smash 1708
3	6	7	Michael	The Highwaymen	United Artists 258
4	3	8	Last Night	Mar-Keys	Satellite 107
5	2	13	I Like It Like That	Chris Kenner	Instant 3229
6	11	7	You Don't Know What You've Got (Until You Lose It)	Ral Donner	Gone 5108
7	7	8	Pretty Little Angel Eyes	Curtis Lee	Dunes 2007
8	4	10	Dum Dum	Brenda Lee	Decca 31272
9	8	10	Let's Twist Again	Chubby Checker	Parkway 824
10	10	5	School Is Out	Gary (U.S.) Bonds	Legrand 1009

★ HIGHEST DEBUT ★ POS 61
Little Sister..................................Elvis Presley

★ BIGGEST MOVER ★ 76 to 46
When We Get Married ....The Dreamlovers

Billboard HOT 100 — AUGUST 28, 1961

TW	LW	WK	Title	Artist	Label
①	2	10	Wooden Heart	Joe Dowell	Smash 1708
②	1	19	Tossin' And Turnin'	Bobby Lewis	Beltone 1002
③	3	8	Michael	The Highwaymen	United Artists 258
④	4	9	Last Night	Mar-Keys	Satellite 107
⑤	6	8	You Don't Know What You've Got (Until You Lose It)	Ral Donner	Gone 5108
⑥	5	14	I Like It Like That	Chris Kenner	Instant 3229
⑦	10	6	School Is Out	Gary (U.S.) Bonds	Legrand 1009
⑧	7	9	Pretty Little Angel Eyes	Curtis Lee	Dunes 2007
⑨	11	9	Don't Bet Money Honey	Linda Scott	Canadian American 127
⑩	12	6	Hurt	Timi Yuro	Liberty 55343

★ HIGHEST DEBUT ★ POS 60
Kissin' On The Phone...........Paul Anka

★ BIGGEST MOVER ★ 61 to 26
Little Sister...........Elvis Presley

Billboard HOT 100 — SEPTEMBER 4, 1961

TW	LW	WK	Title	Artist	Label
①	3	9	Michael	The Highwaymen	United Artists 258
②	1	11	Wooden Heart	Joe Dowell	Smash 1708
③	2	20	Tossin' And Turnin'	Bobby Lewis	Beltone 1002
④	5	9	You Don't Know What You've Got (Until You Lose It)	Ral Donner	Gone 5108
⑤	7	7	School Is Out	Gary (U.S.) Bonds	Legrand 1009
⑥	23	5	Take Good Care Of My Baby	Bobby Vee	Liberty 55354
⑦	13	10	My True Story	The Jive Five	Beltone 1006
⑧	10	7	Hurt	Timi Yuro	Liberty 55343
⑨	9	10	Don't Bet Money Honey	Linda Scott	Canadian American 127
⑩	11	7	As If I Didn't Know	Adam Wade	Coed 553

★ HIGHEST DEBUT ★ POS 67
You Must Have Been A Beautiful Baby ....Bobby Darin

★ BIGGEST MOVER ★ 66 to 32
(Marie's the Name) His Latest Flame.........Elvis Presley

Billboard HOT 100 — SEPTEMBER 11, 1961

TW	LW	WK	Title	Artist	Label
①	1	10	Michael	The Highwaymen	United Artists 258
②	6	6	Take Good Care Of My Baby	Bobby Vee	Liberty 55354
③	7	11	My True Story	The Jive Five	Beltone 1006
④	8	8	Hurt	Timi Yuro	Liberty 55343
⑤	4	10	You Don't Know What You've Got (Until You Lose It)	Ral Donner	Gone 5108
⑥	2	12	Wooden Heart	Joe Dowell	Smash 1708
⑦	11	6	Does Your Chewing Gum Lose It's Flavor (On The Bedpost Over Night)	Lonnie Donegan	Dot 15911
⑧	14	6	Who Put The Bomp (In The Bomp, Bomp, Bomp)	Barry Mann	ABC-Paramount 10237
⑨	15	4	Little Sister	Elvis Presley	RCA 7908
⑩	10	8	As If I Didn't Know	Adam Wade	Coed 553

★ HIGHEST DEBUT ★ POS 55
Hit The Road Jack ....Ray Charles

★ BIGGEST MOVER ★ 67 to 34
You Must Have Been A Beautiful Baby ....Bobby Darin

Billboard — SEPTEMBER 18, 1961 — HOT 100.

TW	LW	WK		
①	2	7	Take Good Care Of My Baby	Bobby Vee ... Liberty 55354
②	1	11	Michael	The Highwaymen ... United Artists 258
③	3	12	My True Story	The Jive Five ... Beltone 1006
④	22	4	(Marie's the Name) His Latest Flame	Elvis Presley ... RCA 7908
⑤	11	6	Crying	Roy Orbison ... Monument 447
⑥	7	7	Does Your Chewing Gum Lose It's Flavor (On The Bedpost Over Night)	Lonnie Donegan ... Dot 15911
➐	14	7	Without You	Johnny Tillotson ... Cadence 1404
⑧	6	13	Wooden Heart	Joe Dowell ... Smash 1708
⑨	29	4	One Track Mind	Bobby Lewis ... Beltone 1012
⑩	13	8	When We Get Married	The Dreamlovers ... Heritage 102

★ **HIGHEST DEBUT** ★ POS 75
This Time ... Troy Shondell

★ **BIGGEST MOVER** ★ 74 to 39
Bristol Stomp ... The Dovells

Billboard — SEPTEMBER 25, 1961 — HOT 100.

TW	LW	WK		
①	1	8	Take Good Care Of My Baby	Bobby Vee ... Liberty 55354
❷	15	9	The Mountain's High	Dick & DeeDee ... Liberty 55350
③	2	12	Michael	The Highwaymen ... United Artists 258
④	5	7	Crying	Roy Orbison ... Monument 447
⑤	6	8	Does Your Chewing Gum Lose It's Flavor (On The Bedpost Over Night)	Lonnie Donegan ... Dot 15911
⑥	13	6	Little Sister	Elvis Presley ... RCA 7908
➐	17	8	Who Put The Bomp (In The Bomp, Bomp, Bomp)	Barry Mann ... ABC-Paramount 10237
⑧	3	13	My True Story	The Jive Five ... Beltone 1006
⑨	7	8	Without You	Johnny Tillotson ... Cadence 1404
⑩	4	5	(Marie's the Name) His Latest Flame	Elvis Presley ... RCA 7908

★ **HIGHEST DEBUT** ★ POS 42
Runaround Sue ... Dion

★ **BIGGEST MOVER** ★ 75 to 24
This Time ... Troy Shondell

Billboard — OCTOBER 2, 1961 — HOT 100.

TW	LW	WK		
①	1	9	Take Good Care Of My Baby	Bobby Vee ... Liberty 55354
②	2	10	The Mountain's High	Dick & DeeDee ... Liberty 55350
③	4	8	Crying	Roy Orbison ... Monument 447
④	13	4	Hit The Road Jack	Ray Charles ... ABC-Paramount 10244
⑤	6	7	Little Sister	Elvis Presley ... RCA 7908
⑥	3	13	Michael	The Highwaymen ... United Artists 258
➐	12	8	Mexico	Bob Moore ... Monument 446
❽	16	5	You Must Have Been A Beautiful Baby	Bobby Darin ... Atco 6206
⑨	5	9	Does Your Chewing Gum Lose It's Flavor (On The Bedpost Over Night)	Lonnie Donegan ... Dot 15911
⑩	14	4	Bristol Stomp	The Dovells ... Parkway 827

★ **HIGHEST DEBUT** ★ POS 53
Big Bad John ... Jimmy Dean

★ **BIGGEST MOVER** ★ 87 to 46
Don't Blame Me ... The Everly Brothers

Billboard — OCTOBER 9, 1961 — HOT 100

TW	LW	WK	Title	Artist ... Label
1	4	5	**Hit The Road Jack**	*Ray Charles* ... ABC-Paramount 10244
2	3	9	**Crying**	*Roy Orbison* ... Monument 447
3	1	10	**Take Good Care Of My Baby**	*Bobby Vee* ... Liberty 55354
4	21	3	**Runaround Sue**	*Dion* ... Laurie 3110
5	10	5	**Bristol Stomp**	*The Dovells* ... Parkway 827
6	8	6	**You Must Have Been A Beautiful Baby**	*Bobby Darin* ... Atco 6206
7	2	11	**The Mountain's High**	*Dick & DeeDee* ... Liberty 55350
8	5	8	**Little Sister**	*Elvis Presley* ... RCA 7908
9	15	6	**Let's Get Together**	*Hayley Mills* ... Vista 385
10	7	9	**Mexico**	*Bob Moore* ... Monument 446

★ **HIGHEST DEBUT** ★ POS 67
Moon River .... *Jerry Butler*

★ **BIGGEST MOVER** ★ 84 to 45
Tower Of Strength .... *Gene McDaniels*

Billboard — OCTOBER 16, 1961 — HOT 100

TW	LW	WK	Title	Artist ... Label
1	1	6	**Hit The Road Jack**	*Ray Charles* ... ABC-Paramount 10244
2	4	4	**Runaround Sue**	*Dion* ... Laurie 3110
3	5	6	**Bristol Stomp**	*The Dovells* ... Parkway 827
4	2	10	**Crying**	*Roy Orbison* ... Monument 447
5	6	7	**You Must Have Been A Beautiful Baby**	*Bobby Darin* ... Atco 6206
6	3	11	**Take Good Care Of My Baby**	*Bobby Vee* ... Liberty 55354
7	18	7	**Sad Movies (Make Me Cry)**	*Sue Thompson* ... Hickory 1153
8	17	3	**Big Bad John**	*Jimmy Dean* ... Columbia 42175
9	10	10	**Mexico**	*Bob Moore* ... Monument 446
10	14	6	**Ya Ya**	*Lee Dorsey* ... Fury 1053

★ **HIGHEST DEBUT** ★ POS 75
Young Boy Blues .... *Ben E. King*

★ **BIGGEST MOVER** ★ 71 to 48
Hollywood .... *Connie Francis*

Billboard — OCTOBER 23, 1961 — HOT 100

TW	LW	WK	Title	Artist ... Label
1	2	5	**Runaround Sue**	*Dion* ... Laurie 3110
2	3	7	**Bristol Stomp**	*The Dovells* ... Parkway 827
3	8	4	**Big Bad John**	*Jimmy Dean* ... Columbia 42175
4	1	7	**Hit The Road Jack**	*Ray Charles* ... ABC-Paramount 10244
5	7	8	**Sad Movies (Make Me Cry)**	*Sue Thompson* ... Hickory 1153
6	11	6	**This Time**	*Troy Shondell* ... Liberty 55353
7	12	8	**I Love How You Love Me**	*The Paris Sisters* ... Gregmark 6
8	13	8	**Let's Get Together**	*Hayley Mills* ... Vista 385
9	10	7	**Ya Ya**	*Lee Dorsey* ... Fury 1053
10	14	5	**The Fly**	*Chubby Checker* ... Parkway 830

★ **HIGHEST DEBUT** ★ POS 59
School Is In .... *Gary (U.S.) Bonds*

★ **BIGGEST MOVER** ★ 77 to 49
September In The Rain .... *Dinah Washington*

Billboard — OCTOBER 30, 1961 — HOT 100

TW	LW	WK	Title	Artist	Label
1	1	6	Runaround Sue	Dion	Laurie 3110
2	2	8	Bristol Stomp	The Dovells	Parkway 827
3	3	5	Big Bad John	Jimmy Dean	Columbia 42175
4	4	8	Hit The Road Jack	Ray Charles	ABC-Paramount 10244
5	7	9	I Love How You Love Me	The Paris Sisters	Gregmark 6
6	5	9	Sad Movies (Make Me Cry)	Sue Thompson	Hickory 1153
7	9	8	Ya Ya	Lee Dorsey	Fury 1053
8	8	9	Let's Get Together	Hayley Mills	Vista 385
9	10	6	The Fly	Chubby Checker	Parkway 830
10	6	7	This Time	Troy Shondell	Liberty 55353

★ HIGHEST DEBUT ★ POS 86	★ BIGGEST MOVER ★ 100 to 77
Danny Boy ....Andy Williams	Blue Moon ....The Ventures

Billboard — NOVEMBER 6, 1961 — HOT 100

TW	LW	WK	Title	Artist	Label
1	3	6	Big Bad John	Jimmy Dean	Columbia 42175
2	1	7	Runaround Sue	Dion	Laurie 3110
3	2	9	Bristol Stomp	The Dovells	Parkway 827
4	4	9	Hit The Road Jack	Ray Charles	ABC-Paramount 10244
5	17	6	Fool #1	Brenda Lee	Decca 31309
6	6	10	Sad Movies (Make Me Cry)	Sue Thompson	Hickory 1153
7	10	8	This Time	Troy Shondell	Liberty 55353
8	9	7	The Fly	Chubby Checker	Parkway 830
9	5	10	I Love How You Love Me	The Paris Sisters	Gregmark 6
10	11	6	Tower Of Strength	Gene McDaniels	Liberty 55371

★ HIGHEST DEBUT ★ POS 77	★ BIGGEST MOVER ★ 82 to 54
Your Ma Said You Cried In Your Sleep Last Night ....Kenny Dino	In The Middle Of A Heartache .....Wanda Jackson

Billboard — NOVEMBER 13, 1961 — HOT 100

TW	LW	WK	Title	Artist	Label
1	1	7	Big Bad John	Jimmy Dean	Columbia 42175
2	2	8	Runaround Sue	Dion	Laurie 3110
3	5	7	Fool #1	Brenda Lee	Decca 31309
4	3	10	Bristol Stomp	The Dovells	Parkway 827
5	10	7	Tower Of Strength	Gene McDaniels	Liberty 55371
6	4	10	Hit The Road Jack	Ray Charles	ABC-Paramount 10244
7	8	8	The Fly	Chubby Checker	Parkway 830
8	7	9	This Time	Troy Shondell	Liberty 55353
9	17	11	Please Mr. Postman	The Marvelettes	Tamla 54046
10	6	11	Sad Movies (Make Me Cry)	Sue Thompson	Hickory 1153

★ HIGHEST DEBUT ★ POS 55	★ BIGGEST MOVER ★ 89 to 46
The Twist ....Chubby Checker	Walk On By ....Leroy Van Dyke

TW	LW	WK	Billboard. 🎵 NOVEMBER 20, 1961 🎵 HOT 100.
①	1	8	**Big Bad John** ....*Jimmy Dean* ... Columbia 42175
②	2	9	**Runaround Sue** ....*Dion* ... Laurie 3110
③	3	8	**Fool #1**..*Brenda Lee* ... Decca 31309
❹	12	6	**Goodbye Cruel World**...............................*James Darren* ... Colpix 609
⑤	4	11	**Bristol Stomp**...*The Dovells* ... Parkway 827
⑥	5	8	**Tower Of Strength**................................*Gene McDaniels* ... Liberty 55371
⑦	6	11	**Hit The Road Jack**........................*Ray Charles* ... ABC-Paramount 10244
⑧	9	12	**Please Mr. Postman** ....*The Marvelettes* ... Tamla 54046
⑨	8	10	**This Time**...*Troy Shondell* ... Liberty 55353
⑩	7	9	**The Fly** ....*Chubby Checker* ... Parkway 830

★ **HIGHEST DEBUT** ★ POS 68	★ **BIGGEST MOVER** ★ 84 to 51
Peppermint Twist...........*Joey Dee & The Starliters*	Up A Lazy River ....*Si Zenter & His Orchestra*

TW	LW	WK	Billboard. 🎵 NOVEMBER 27, 1961 🎵 HOT 100.
①	1	9	**Big Bad John** ....*Jimmy Dean* ... Columbia 42175
②	2	10	**Runaround Sue** ....*Dion* ... Laurie 3110
❸	8	13	**Please Mr. Postman** ....*The Marvelettes* ... Tamla 54046
④	4	7	**Goodbye Cruel World**...............................*James Darren* ... Colpix 609
⑤	3	9	**Fool #1**..*Brenda Lee* ... Decca 31309
⑥	5	12	**Bristol Stomp**...*The Dovells* ... Parkway 827
❼	19	8	**Heartaches** ....*The Marcels* ... Colpix 612
⑧	6	9	**Tower Of Strength**................................*Gene McDaniels* ... Liberty 55371
❾	15	6	**Crazy** ....*Patsy Cline* ... Decca 31317
⑩	9	11	**This Time**...*Troy Shondell* ... Liberty 55353

★ **HIGHEST DEBUT** ★ POS 62	★ **BIGGEST MOVER** ★ 89 to 55
Unchain My Heart ....*Ray Charles*	When I Fall In Love ....*The Lettermen*

TW	LW	WK	Billboard. 🎵 DECEMBER 4, 1961 🎵 HOT 100.
①	1	10	**Big Bad John**...*Jimmy Dean* ... Columbia 42175
②	3	14	**Please Mr. Postman** ....*The Marvelettes* ... Tamla 54046
③	4	8	**Goodbye Cruel World** ....*James Darren* ... Colpix 609
④	2	11	**Runaround Sue**..*Dion* ... Laurie 3110
⑤	5	10	**Fool #1** ....*Brenda Lee* ... Decca 31309
❻	16	22	**The Twist**...*Chubby Checker* ... Parkway 811
❼	12	6	**Walk On By**...*Leroy Van Dyke* ... Mercury 71834
⑧	8	10	**Tower Of Strength**................................*Gene McDaniels* ... Liberty 55371
❾	14	12	**I Understand (Just How You Feel)** ....*The G-Clefs* ... Terrace 7500
⑩	9	7	**Crazy** ....*Patsy Cline* ... Decca 31317

★ **HIGHEST DEBUT** ★ POS 57	★ **BIGGEST MOVER** ★ 88 to 60
Can't Help Falling In Love ....*Elvis Presley*	Soothe Me...*Sims Twins*

Billboard — DECEMBER 11, 1961 — HOT 100

TW	LW	WK	Title	Artist	Label
1	2	15	**Please Mr. Postman**	The Marvelettes	Tamla 54046
2	1	11	Big Bad John	Jimmy Dean	Columbia 42175
3	3	9	**Goodbye Cruel World**	James Darren	Colpix 609
4	6	23	The Twist	Chubby Checker	Parkway 811
5	7	7	**Walk On By**	Leroy Van Dyke	Mercury 71834
6	17	5	The Lion Sleeps Tonight	The Tokens	RCA 7954
7	11	5	Run To Him	Bobby Vee	Liberty 55388
8	12	9	**Tonight**	Ferrante & Teicher	United Artists 373
9	16	7	Let There Be Drums	Sandy Nelson	Imperial 5775
10	21	5	Happy Birthday, Sweet Sixteen	Neil Sedaka	RCA 7957

★ **HIGHEST DEBUT** ★ POS 63
Jambalaya (On The Bayou)............*Fats Domino*

★ **BIGGEST MOVER** ★ 86 to 60
Small Sad Sam..............................*Phil McLean*

Billboard — DECEMBER 18, 1961 — HOT 100

TW	LW	WK	Title	Artist	Label
1	6	6	**The Lion Sleeps Tonight**	The Tokens	RCA 7954
2	1	16	Please Mr. Postman	The Marvelettes	Tamla 54046
3	7	6	Run To Him	Bobby Vee	Liberty 55388
4	4	24	The Twist	Chubby Checker	Parkway 811
5	5	8	**Walk On By**	Leroy Van Dyke	Mercury 71834
6	3	10	Goodbye Cruel World	James Darren	Colpix 609
7	9	8	**Let There Be Drums**	Sandy Nelson	Imperial 5775
8	10	6	Happy Birthday, Sweet Sixteen	Neil Sedaka	RCA 7957
9	2	12	Big Bad John	Jimmy Dean	Columbia 42175
10	15	5	Peppermint Twist	Joey Dee & The Starliters	Roulette 4401

★ **HIGHEST DEBUT** ★ POS 52
Rudolph The Red Nosed Reindeer ....*David Seville & The Chipmunks*

★ **BIGGEST MOVER** ★ 66 to 33
White Christmas ....*Bing Crosby*

Billboard — DECEMBER 25, 1961 — HOT 100

TW	LW	WK	Title	Artist	Label
1	1	7	**The Lion Sleeps Tonight**	The Tokens	RCA 7954
2	3	7	**Run To Him**	Bobby Vee	Liberty 55388
3	4	25	The Twist	Chubby Checker	Parkway 811
4	6	11	Goodbye Cruel World	James Darren	Colpix 609
5	5	9	**Walk On By**	Leroy Van Dyke	Mercury 71834
6	10	6	Peppermint Twist	Joey Dee & The Starliters	Roulette 4401
7	2	17	Please Mr. Postman	The Marvelettes	Tamla 54046
8	8	7	Happy Birthday, Sweet Sixteen	Neil Sedaka	RCA 7957
9	7	9	Let There Be Drums	Sandy Nelson	Imperial 5775
10	18	4	Can't Help Falling In Love	Elvis Presley	RCA 7968

★ **HIGHEST DEBUT** ★ POS 76
She's Everything (I Wanted You To Be) ....*Ral Donner*

★ **BIGGEST MOVER** ★ 69 to 34
The Little Drummer Boy..........*The Harry Simeone Chorale*

TW	LW	WK	Billboard		JANUARY 6, 1962		HOT 100.
①	1	8	The Lion Sleeps Tonight ....The Tokens ... RCA 7954
②	3	26	The Twist...Chubby Checker ... Parkway 811
③	2	8	Run To Him...Bobby Vee ... Liberty 55388
④	6	7	Peppermint Twist.................Joey Dee & The Starliters ... Roulette 4401
⑤	10	5	Can't Help Falling In Love ....Elvis Presley ... RCA 7968
⑥	8	8	Happy Birthday, Sweet Sixteen.................Neil Sedaka ... RCA 7957
⑦	4	12	Goodbye Cruel World...........................James Darren ... Colpix 609
⑧	5	10	Walk On By ....Leroy Van Dyke ... Mercury 71834
⑨	13	7	When I Fall In Love..............................The Lettermen ... Capitol 4658
⑩	14	6	Unchain My Heart.......................Ray Charles ... ABC-Paramount 10266

★ HIGHEST DEBUT ★ POS 55	★ BIGGEST MOVER ★ 52 to 28
Dear Ivan...Jimmy Dean	A Little Bitty Tear.......................................Burl Ives

TW	LW	WK	Billboard		JANUARY 13, 1962		HOT 100.
①	2	27	The Twist ....Chubby Checker ... Parkway 811
②	1	9	The Lion Sleeps Tonight ....The Tokens ... RCA 7954
③	4	8	Peppermint Twist......................Joey Dee & The Starliters ... Roulette 4401
④	5	6	Can't Help Falling In Love ....Elvis Presley ... RCA 7968
⑤	15	9	I Know (You Don't Love Me No More)........Barbara George ... A.F.O. 302
⑥	6	9	Happy Birthday, Sweet Sixteen ....Neil Sedaka ... RCA 7957
⑦	8	11	Walk On By ....Leroy Van Dyke ... Mercury 71834
⑧	3	9	Run To Him ....Bobby Vee ... Liberty 55388
⑨	10	7	Unchain My Heart.........................Ray Charles ... ABC-Paramount 10266
⑩	11	8	When The Boy In Your Arms (Is The Boy In Your Heart)........ Connie Francis ... MGM 13051

★ HIGHEST DEBUT ★ POS 56	★ BIGGEST MOVER ★ 46 to 17
Break It To Me Gently ....Brenda Lee	Norman.......................................Sue Thompson

TW	LW	WK	Billboard		JANUARY 20, 1962		HOT 100.
①	1	28	The Twist ....Chubby Checker ... Parkway 811
②	3	9	Peppermint Twist......................Joey Dee & The Starliters ... Roulette 4401
③	2	10	The Lion Sleeps Tonight ....The Tokens ... RCA 7954
④	4	7	Can't Help Falling In Love ....Elvis Presley ... RCA 7968
⑤	5	10	I Know (You Don't Love Me No More)........Barbara George ... A.F.O. 302
⑥	6	10	Happy Birthday, Sweet Sixteen ....Neil Sedaka ... RCA 7957
⑦	7	12	Walk On By ....Leroy Van Dyke ... Mercury 71834
⑧	8	10	Run To Him ....Bobby Vee ... Liberty 55388
⑨	12	9	When I Fall In Love..............................The Lettermen ... Capitol 4658
⑩	17	7	Norman...Sue Thompson ... Hickory 1159

★ HIGHEST DEBUT ★ POS 80	★ BIGGEST MOVER ★ 93 to 49
To A Sleeping Beauty.....................Jimmy Dean	Duke Of Earl ....Gene Chandler

TW	LW	WK	Billboard	JANUARY 27, 1962	HOT 100
①	2	10	**Peppermint Twist**...................*Joey Dee & The Starliters* . . . Roulette 4401
②	1	29	The Twist..*Chubby Checker* . . . Parkway 811
③	5	11	**I Know (You Don't Love Me No More)** .... *Barbara George* . . . A.F.O. 302
④	4	8	Can't Help Falling In Love ....*Elvis Presley* . . . RCA 7968
⑤	10	8	Norman...*Sue Thompson* . . . Hickory 1159
⑥	3	11	The Lion Sleeps Tonight ....*The Tokens* . . . RCA 7954
⑦	9	10	**When I Fall In Love** ....*The Lettermen* . . . Capitol 4658
⑧	18	8	The Wanderer..*Dion* . . . Laurie 3115
⑨	15	6	Baby It's You ....*The Shirelles* . . . Scepter 1227
⑩	7	13	Walk On By ....*Leroy Van Dyke* . . . Mercury 71834

★ HIGHEST DEBUT ★ POS 69	★ BIGGEST MOVER ★ 96 to 63
The Cajun Queen...........................*Jimmy Dean*	Chip Chip....................................*Gene McDaniels*

TW	LW	WK	Billboard	FEBRUARY 3, 1962	HOT 100
①	1	11	**Peppermint Twist**...................*Joey Dee & The Starliters* . . . Roulette 4401
②	4	9	**Can't Help Falling In Love** ....*Elvis Presley* . . . RCA 7968
③	2	30	The Twist..*Chubby Checker* . . . Parkway 811
④	5	9	Norman...*Sue Thompson* . . . Hickory 1159
⑤	3	12	I Know (You Don't Love Me No More)........*Barbara George* . . . A.F.O. 302
⑥	8	9	The Wanderer..*Dion* . . . Laurie 3115
❼	20	4	Duke Of Earl...............................*Gene Chandler* . . . Vee-Jay 416
⑧	9	7	**Baby It's You**....................................*The Shirelles* . . . Scepter 1227
⑨	17	4	Break It To Me Gently ....*Brenda Lee* . . . Decca 31348
⑩	6	12	The Lion Sleeps Tonight ....*The Tokens* . . . RCA 7954

★ HIGHEST DEBUT ★ POS 66	★ BIGGEST MOVER ★ 69 to 41
Her Royal Majesty...........................*James Darren*	The Cajun Queen...........................*Jimmy Dean*

TW	LW	WK	Billboard	FEBRUARY 10, 1962	HOT 100
①	1	12	**Peppermint Twist**...................*Joey Dee & The Starliters* . . . Roulette 4401
❷	7	5	Duke Of Earl...............................*Gene Chandler* . . . Vee-Jay 416
③	3	31	The Twist..*Chubby Checker* . . . Parkway 811
④	2	10	Can't Help Falling In Love ....*Elvis Presley* . . . RCA 7968
⑤	5	13	I Know (You Don't Love Me No More)........*Barbara George* . . . A.F.O. 302
⑥	4	10	Norman...*Sue Thompson* . . . Hickory 1159
⑦	6	10	The Wanderer..*Dion* . . . Laurie 3115
⑧	9	5	Break It To Me Gently ....*Brenda Lee* . . . Decca 31348
⑨	12	8	**A Little Bitty Tear** ....*Burl Ives* . . . Decca 31330
⑩	11	9	Dear Lady Twist ....*Gary (U.S.) Bonds* . . . Legrand 1015

★ HIGHEST DEBUT ★ POS 66	★ BIGGEST MOVER ★ 79 to 47
Don't Break The Heart That Loves You ....*Connie Francis*	Midnight In Moscow ......*Kenny Ball & His Jazzmen*

TW	LW	WK	Billboard	FEBRUARY 17, 1962	HOT 100
①	2	6	**Duke Of Earl**	*Gene Chandler*	Vee-Jay 416
②	1	13	**Peppermint Twist**	*Joey Dee & The Starliters*	Roulette 4401
③	3	32	**The Twist**	*Chubby Checker*	Parkway 811
④	6	11	**Norman**	*Sue Thompson*	Hickory 1159
⑤	7	11	**The Wanderer**	*Dion*	Laurie 3115
⑥	8	6	**Break It To Me Gently**	*Brenda Lee*	Decca 31348
⑦	5	14	**I Know (You Don't Love Me No More)**	*Barbara George*	A.F.O. 302
⑧	4	11	**Can't Help Falling In Love**	*Elvis Presley*	RCA 7968
⑨	14	6	**Crying In The Rain**	*The Everly Brothers*	Warner 5250
⑩	10	10	**Dear Lady Twist**	*Gary (U.S.) Bonds*	Legrand 1015

★ **HIGHEST DEBUT** ★ POS 64
Hey, Let's Twist.............*Joey Dee & The Starliters*

★ **BIGGEST MOVER** ★ 72 to 47
What's Your Name.........................*Don & Juan*

TW	LW	WK	Billboard	FEBRUARY 24, 1962	HOT 100
①	1	7	**Duke Of Earl**	*Gene Chandler*	Vee-Jay 416
②	5	12	**The Wanderer**	*Dion*	Laurie 3115
③	4	12	**Norman**	*Sue Thompson*	Hickory 1159
④	3	33	**The Twist**	*Chubby Checker*	Parkway 811
❺	13	5	**Hey! Baby**	*Bruce Channel*	Smash 1731
⑥	6	7	**Break It To Me Gently**	*Brenda Lee*	Decca 31348
⑦	2	14	**Peppermint Twist**	*Joey Dee & The Starliters*	Roulette 4401
⑧	9	7	**Crying In The Rain**	*The Everly Brothers*	Warner 5250
⑨	10	11	**Dear Lady Twist**	*Gary (U.S.) Bonds*	Legrand 1015
⑩	11	10	**A Little Bitty Tear**	*Burl Ives*	Decca 31330

★ **HIGHEST DEBUT** ★ POS 64
You Win Again.........................*Fats Domino*

★ **BIGGEST MOVER** ★ 77 to 53
Dream Baby.................................*Roy Orbison*

TW	LW	WK	Billboard	MARCH 3, 1962	HOT 100
①	1	8	**Duke Of Earl**	*Gene Chandler*	Vee-Jay 416
②	5	6	**Hey! Baby**	*Bruce Channel*	Smash 1731
③	2	13	**The Wanderer**	*Dion*	Laurie 3115
④	6	8	**Break It To Me Gently**	*Brenda Lee*	Decca 31348
⑤	4	34	**The Twist**	*Chubby Checker*	Parkway 811
⑥	8	8	**Crying In The Rain**	*The Everly Brothers*	Warner 5250
⑦	3	13	**Norman**	*Sue Thompson*	Hickory 1159
❽	16	5	**Midnight In Moscow**	*Kenny Ball & His Jazzmen*	Kapp 442
⑨	7	15	**Peppermint Twist**	*Joey Dee & The Starliters*	Roulette 4401
⑩	11	7	**Chip Chip**	*Gene McDaniels*	Liberty 55405

★ **HIGHEST DEBUT** ★ POS 60
Slow Twistin'.............*Chubby Checker*

★ **BIGGEST MOVER** ★ 81 to 57
Please Don't Ask About Barbara.......*Bobby Vee*

TW	LW	WK	Billboard®	MARCH 10, 1962	HOT 100®
①	2	7	**Hey! Baby** ....*Bruce Channel* . . . Smash 1731
②	1	9	Duke Of Earl..*Gene Chandler* . . . Vee-Jay 416
❸	8	6	Midnight In Moscow.....................*Kenny Ball & His Jazzmen* . . . Kapp 442
❹	13	5	Don't Break The Heart That Loves You .....*Connie Francis* . . . MGM 13059
❺	12	10	Let Me In..*The Sensations* . . . Argo 5405
⑥	6	9	**Crying In The Rain** ....*The Everly Brothers* . . . Warner 5250
⑦	4	9	Break It To Me Gently ....*Brenda Lee* . . . Decca 31348
❽	16	6	Her Royal Majesty...............................*James Darren* . . . Colpix 622
⑨	3	14	The Wanderer...*Dion* . . . Laurie 3115
⑩	20	5	What's Your Name.............................*Don & Juan* . . . Big Top 3079

★ **HIGHEST DEBUT** ★ POS 75	★ **BIGGEST MOVER** ★ 81 to 50
If A Woman Answers ....*Leroy Van Dyke*	Johnny Angel.............................*Shelley Fabares*

TW	LW	WK	Billboard®	MARCH 17, 1962	HOT 100®
①	1	8	**Hey! Baby** ....*Bruce Channel* . . . Smash 1731
②	3	7	**Midnight In Moscow**..................*Kenny Ball & His Jazzmen* . . . Kapp 442
③	4	6	Don't Break The Heart That Loves You .....*Connie Francis* . . . MGM 13059
④	5	11	**Let Me In**..*The Sensations* . . . Argo 5405
⑤	2	10	Duke Of Earl..*Gene Chandler* . . . Vee-Jay 416
⑥	8	7	**Her Royal Majesty**...............................*James Darren* . . . Colpix 622
⑦	10	6	**What's Your Name**.............................*Don & Juan* . . . Big Top 3079
⑧	6	10	Crying In The Rain ....*The Everly Brothers* . . . Warner 5250
⑨	7	10	Break It To Me Gently ....*Brenda Lee* . . . Decca 31348
⑩	12	10	**Percolator (Twist)** ....*Billy Joe & The Checkmates* . . . Dore 620

★ **HIGHEST DEBUT** ★ POS 51	★ **BIGGEST MOVER** ★ 85 to 61
Good Luck Charm ....*Elvis Presley*	She Can't Find Her Keys...............*Paul Petersen*

TW	LW	WK	Billboard®	MARCH 24, 1962	HOT 100®
①	1	9	**Hey! Baby** ....*Bruce Channel* . . . Smash 1731
②	3	7	Don't Break The Heart That Loves You .....*Connie Francis* . . . MGM 13059
③	2	8	Midnight In Moscow.......................*Kenny Ball & His Jazzmen* . . . Kapp 442
④	4	12	**Let Me In**..*The Sensations* . . . Argo 5405
⑤	5	11	Duke Of Earl..*Gene Chandler* . . . Vee-Jay 416
❻	18	6	Dream Baby...............................*Roy Orbison* . . . Monument 456
❼	14	4	Slow Twistin' ....*Chubby Checker* . . . Parkway 835
⑧	7	7	What's Your Name.............................*Don & Juan* . . . Big Top 3079
⑨	13	8	**Twistin' The Night Away**.......................*Sam Cooke* . . . RCA 7983
⑩	6	8	Her Royal Majesty...............................*James Darren* . . . Colpix 622

★ **HIGHEST DEBUT** ★ POS 63	★ **BIGGEST MOVER** ★ 51 to 14
Soldier Boy ....*The Shirelles*	Good Luck Charm ....*Elvis Presley*

Billboard — MARCH 31, 1962 — HOT 100

TW	LW	WK	Title	Artist / Label
①	2	8	**Don't Break The Heart That Loves You**	*Connie Francis* ... MGM 13059
②	1	10	Hey! Baby	*Bruce Channel* ... Smash 1731
❸	11	5	Johnny Angel	*Shelley Fabares* ... Colpix 621
④	6	7	**Dream Baby**	*Roy Orbison* ... Monument 456
⑤	3	9	Midnight In Moscow	*Kenny Ball & His Jazzmen* ... Kapp 442
⑥	7	5	Slow Twistin'	*Chubby Checker* ... Parkway 835
⑦	8	8	**What's Your Name**	*Don & Juan* ... Big Top 3079
⑧	4	13	Let Me In	*The Sensations* ... Argo 5405
⑨	14	3	Good Luck Charm	*Elvis Presley* ... RCA 7992
⑩	9	9	Twistin' The Night Away	*Sam Cooke* ... RCA 7983

★ **HIGHEST DEBUT** ★ POS 64
At The Club .... *Ray Charles*

★ **BIGGEST MOVER** ★ 68 to 36
Shout .... *Joey Dee & The Starliters*

Billboard — APRIL 7, 1962 — HOT 100

TW	LW	WK	Title	Artist / Label
①	3	6	**Johnny Angel**	*Shelley Fabares* ... Colpix 621
②	1	9	Don't Break The Heart That Loves You	*Connie Francis* ... MGM 13059
❸	9	4	Good Luck Charm	*Elvis Presley* ... RCA 7992
④	6	6	Slow Twistin'	*Chubby Checker* ... Parkway 835
⑤	4	8	Dream Baby	*Roy Orbison* ... Monument 456
⑥	2	11	Hey! Baby	*Bruce Channel* ... Smash 1731
⑦	5	10	Midnight In Moscow	*Kenny Ball & His Jazzmen* ... Kapp 442
⑧	12	6	Young World	*Rick Nelson* ... Imperial 5805
⑨	11	7	Love Letters	*Ketty Lester* ... Era 3068
⑩	15	6	Mashed Potato Time	*Dee Dee Sharp* ... Cameo 212

★ **HIGHEST DEBUT** ★ POS 65
Funny Way Of Laughin' .... *Burl Ives*

★ **BIGGEST MOVER** ★ 68 to 32
Twist, Twist Senora .... *Gary "U.S." Bonds*

Billboard — APRIL 14, 1962 — HOT 100

TW	LW	WK	Title	Artist / Label
①	1	7	**Johnny Angel**	*Shelley Fabares* ... Colpix 621
②	3	5	Good Luck Charm	*Elvis Presley* ... RCA 7992
③	4	7	**Slow Twistin'**	*Chubby Checker* ... Parkway 835
❹	10	7	Mashed Potato Time	*Dee Dee Sharp* ... Cameo 212
⑤	9	8	**Love Letters**	*Ketty Lester* ... Era 3068
⑥	8	7	Young World	*Rick Nelson* ... Imperial 5805
⑦	2	10	**Don't Break The Heart That Loves You**	*Connie Francis* ... MGM 13059
❽	16	7	Lover Please	*Clyde McPhatter* ... Mercury 71941
⑨	7	11	Midnight In Moscow	*Kenny Ball & His Jazzmen* ... Kapp 442
⑩	6	12	Hey! Baby	*Bruce Channel* ... Smash 1731

★ **HIGHEST DEBUT** ★ POS 66
Everybody Loves Me But You .... *Brenda Lee*

★ **BIGGEST MOVER** ★ 97 to 61
Old Rivers .... *Walter Brennan*

Billboard — APRIL 21, 1962 — HOT 100

TW	LW	WK	Title	Artist
①	2	6	**Good Luck Charm**	*Elvis Presley* ... RCA 7992
②	1	8	Johnny Angel	*Shelley Fabares* ... Colpix 621
③	4	8	Mashed Potato Time	*Dee Dee Sharp* ... Cameo 212
④	3	8	Slow Twistin'	*Chubby Checker* ... Parkway 835
⑤	6	8	**Young World**	*Rick Nelson* ... Imperial 5805
⑥	11	5	Soldier Boy	*The Shirelles* ... Scepter 1228
⑦	8	8	**Lover Please**	*Clyde McPhatter* ... Mercury 71941
⑧	5	9	Love Letters	*Ketty Lester* ... Era 3068
⑨	14	5	Shout	*Joey Dee & The Starliters* ... Roulette 4416
⑩	19	6	Stranger On The Shore	*Mr. Acker Bilk* ... Atco 6217

★ **HIGHEST DEBUT** ★ POS 80
I Sold My Heart To The Junkman ....*The Blue-Belles*

★ **BIGGEST MOVER** ★ 61 to 39
Old Rivers ....*Walter Brennan*

Billboard — APRIL 28, 1962 — HOT 100

TW	LW	WK	Title	Artist
①	1	7	**Good Luck Charm**	*Elvis Presley* ... RCA 7992
②	2	9	Johnny Angel	*Shelley Fabares* ... Colpix 621
③	3	9	Mashed Potato Time	*Dee Dee Sharp* ... Cameo 212
④	6	6	Soldier Boy	*The Shirelles* ... Scepter 1228
⑤	4	9	Slow Twistin'	*Chubby Checker* ... Parkway 835
⑥	5	9	Young World	*Rick Nelson* ... Imperial 5805
⑦	10	7	Stranger On The Shore	*Mr. Acker Bilk* ... Atco 6217
⑧	7	9	Lover Please	*Clyde McPhatter* ... Mercury 71941
⑨	9	6	Shout	*Joey Dee & The Starliters* ... Roulette 4416
⑩	12	5	Twist, Twist Senora	*Gary "U.S." Bonds* ... Legrand 1018

★ **HIGHEST DEBUT** ★ POS 78
Hearts ....*Jackie Wilson*

★ **BIGGEST MOVER** ★ 86 to 64
Lovers Who Wander ....*Dion*

Billboard — MAY 5, 1962 — HOT 100

TW	LW	WK	Title	Artist
①	4	7	**Soldier Boy**	*The Shirelles* ... Scepter 1228
②	3	10	**Mashed Potato Time**	*Dee Dee Sharp* ... Cameo 212
③	2	10	Johnny Angel	*Shelley Fabares* ... Colpix 621
④	7	8	Stranger On The Shore	*Mr. Acker Bilk* ... Atco 6217
⑤	1	8	Good Luck Charm	*Elvis Presley* ... RCA 7992
⑥	9	7	**Shout**	*Joey Dee & The Starliters* ... Roulette 4416
⑦	8	10	**Lover Please**	*Clyde McPhatter* ... Mercury 71941
⑧	5	10	Slow Twistin'	*Chubby Checker* ... Parkway 835
⑨	12	6	P.T. 109	*Jimmy Dean* ... Columbia 42338
⑩	10	6	Twist, Twist Senora	*Gary "U.S." Bonds* ... Legrand 1018

★ **HIGHEST DEBUT** ★ POS 80
Lemon Tree ....*Peter, Paul & Mary*

★ **BIGGEST MOVER** ★ 64 to 33
Lovers Who Wander ....*Dion*

Billboard — MAY 12, 1962 — HOT 100

TW	LW	WK	Title	Artist	Label
①	1	8	**Soldier Boy**	*The Shirelles*	Scepter 1228
②	2	11	**Mashed Potato Time**	*Dee Dee Sharp*	Cameo 212
③	4	9	**Stranger On The Shore**	*Mr. Acker Bilk*	Atco 6217
④	3	11	**Johnny Angel**	*Shelley Fabares*	Colpix 621
⑤	5	9	**Good Luck Charm**	*Elvis Presley*	RCA 7992
⑥	13	9	**She Cried**	*Jay & The Americans*	United Artists 415
⑦	15	6	**Old Rivers**	*Walter Brennan*	Liberty 55436
⑧	16	7	**Shout! Shout! (Knock Yourself Out)**	*Ernie Maresca*	Seville 117
⑨	10	7	**Twist, Twist Senora**	*Gary "U.S." Bonds*	Legrand 1018
⑩	6	8	**Shout**	*Joey Dee & The Starliters*	Roulette 4416

★ **HIGHEST DEBUT** ★ POS 58
Follow That Dream ....*Elvis Presley*

★ **BIGGEST MOVER** ★ 86 to 53
I Can't Stop Loving You ....*Ray Charles*

Billboard — MAY 19, 1962 — HOT 100

TW	LW	WK	Title	Artist	Label
①	1	9	**Soldier Boy**	*The Shirelles*	Scepter 1228
②	3	10	**Stranger On The Shore**	*Mr. Acker Bilk*	Atco 6217
③	2	12	**Mashed Potato Time**	*Dee Dee Sharp*	Cameo 212
④	4	12	**Johnny Angel**	*Shelley Fabares*	Colpix 621
⑤	6	10	**She Cried**	*Jay & The Americans*	United Artists 415
⑥	8	8	**Shout! Shout! (Knock Yourself Out)**	*Ernie Maresca*	Seville 117
⑦	7	7	**Old Rivers**	*Walter Brennan*	Liberty 55436
⑧	12	6	**Everybody Loves Me But You**	*Brenda Lee*	Decca 31379
⑨	11	8	**P.T. 109**	*Jimmy Dean*	Columbia 42338
⑩	14	7	**Funny Way Of Laughin'**	*Burl Ives*	Decca 31371

★ **HIGHEST DEBUT** ★ POS 72
Where Are You ....*Dinah Washington*

★ **BIGGEST MOVER** ★ 75 to 40
Second Hand Love ....*Connie Francis*

Billboard — MAY 26, 1962 — HOT 100

TW	LW	WK	Title	Artist	Label
①	2	11	**Stranger On The Shore**	*Mr. Acker Bilk*	Atco 6217
②	1	10	**Soldier Boy**	*The Shirelles*	Scepter 1228
③	3	13	**Mashed Potato Time**	*Dee Dee Sharp*	Cameo 212
④	21	4	**I Can't Stop Loving You**	*Ray Charles*	ABC-Paramount 10330
⑤	7	8	**Old Rivers**	*Walter Brennan*	Liberty 55436
⑥	8	7	**Everybody Loves Me But You**	*Brenda Lee*	Decca 31379
⑦	5	11	**She Cried**	*Jay & The Americans*	United Artists 415
⑧	9	9	**P.T. 109**	*Jimmy Dean*	Columbia 42338
⑨	4	13	**Johnny Angel**	*Shelley Fabares*	Colpix 621
⑩	13	6	**Lovers Who Wander**	*Dion*	Laurie 3123

★ **HIGHEST DEBUT** ★ POS 80
Wolverton Mountain......................*Claude King*

★ **BIGGEST MOVER** ★ 69 to 44
Walk On The Wild Side ....*Jimmy Smith*

Billboard 🔵 JUNE 2, 1962 🔵 HOT 100.

TW	LW	WK			
①	4	5	**I Can't Stop Loving You** ....*Ray Charles* ... ABC-Paramount 10330		
②	1	12	**Stranger On The Shore** ....*Mr. Acker Bilk* ... Atco 6217		
③	2	11	**Soldier Boy**..*The Shirelles* ... Scepter 1228		
❹	10	7	**Lovers Who Wander** ....*Dion* ... Laurie 3123		
⑤	3	14	**Mashed Potato Time** ....*Dee Dee Sharp* ... Cameo 212		
⑥	6	8	**Everybody Loves Me But You** ....*Brenda Lee* ... Decca 31379		
⑦	11	10	**Shout! Shout! (Knock Yourself Out)**.............*Ernie Maresca* ... Seville 117		
⑧	5	9	**Old Rivers**..*Walter Brennan* ... Liberty 55436		
⑨	12	11	**The One Who Really Loves You**.....................*Mary Wells* ... Motown 1024		
⑩	21	6	**(The Man Who Shot) Liberty Valance** ....*Gene Pitney* ... Musicor 1020		

★ HIGHEST DEBUT ★ POS 72	★ BIGGEST MOVER ★ 62 to 28
Theme From Dr. Kildare........*Richard Chamberlain*	The Stripper....................................*David Rose*

Billboard 🔵 JUNE 9, 1962 🔵 HOT 100.

TW	LW	WK			
①	1	6	**I Can't Stop Loving You** ....*Ray Charles* ... ABC-Paramount 10330		
②	2	13	**Stranger On The Shore** ....*Mr. Acker Bilk* ... Atco 6217		
③	4	8	**Lovers Who Wander** ....*Dion* ... Laurie 3123		
④	3	12	**Soldier Boy**..*The Shirelles* ... Scepter 1228		
⑤	10	7	**(The Man Who Shot) Liberty Valance** ....*Gene Pitney* ... Musicor 1020		
⑥	12	5	**It Keeps Right On A-Hurtin'**..................*Johnny Tillotson* ... Cadence 1418		
⑦	16	5	**Second Hand Love** ....*Connie Francis* ... MGM 13074		
⑧	9	12	**The One Who Really Loves You**.............*Mary Wells* ... Motown 1024		
⑨	17	5	**Palisades Park**.......................................*Freddy Cannon* ... Swan 4106		
⑩	19	6	**Playboy**....................................*The Marvelettes* ... Tamla 54060		

★ HIGHEST DEBUT ★ POS 68	★ BIGGEST MOVER ★ 62 to 30
Roses Are Red.............................*Bobby Vinton*	Al Di La' ....*Emilio Pericoli*

Billboard 🔵 JUNE 16, 1962 🔵 HOT 100.

TW	LW	WK			
①	1	7	**I Can't Stop Loving You** ....*Ray Charles* ... ABC-Paramount 10330		
②	2	14	**Stranger On The Shore** ....*Mr. Acker Bilk* ... Atco 6217		
③	6	6	**It Keeps Right On A-Hurtin'**..............*Johnny Tillotson* ... Cadence 1418		
④	5	8	**(The Man Who Shot) Liberty Valance**........................*Gene Pitney* ... Musicor 1020		
⑤	9	6	**Palisades Park**.......................................*Freddy Cannon* ... Swan 4106		
⑥	3	9	**Lovers Who Wander** ....*Dion* ... Laurie 3123		
⑦	7	6	**Second Hand Love** ....*Connie Francis* ... MGM 13074		
❽	15	6	**The Stripper** ....*David Rose* ... MGM 13064		
⑨	10	7	**Playboy**....................................*The Marvelettes* ... Tamla 54060		
⑩	8	13	**The One Who Really Loves You**....................*Mary Wells* ... Motown 1024		

★ HIGHEST DEBUT ★ POS 61	★ BIGGEST MOVER ★ 68 to 31
Gravy (For My Mashed Potatoes) ....*Dee Dee Sharp*	Roses Are Red.............................*Bobby Vinton*

Billboard — JUNE 23, 1962 — HOT 100

TW	LW	WK	Title	Artist ... Label
①	1	8	I Can't Stop Loving You	Ray Charles ... ABC-Paramount 10330
❷	8	7	The Stripper	David Rose ... MGM 13064
③	5	7	Palisades Park	Freddy Cannon ... Swan 4106
④	3	7	It Keeps Right On A-Hurtin'	Johnny Tillotson ... Cadence 1418
⑤	2	15	Stranger On The Shore	Mr. Acker Bilk ... Atco 6217
⑥	4	9	(The Man Who Shot) Liberty Valance	Gene Pitney ... Musicor 1020
⑦	9	8	Playboy	The Marvelettes ... Tamla 54060
⑧	12	7	Cindy's Birthday	Johnny Crawford ... Del-Fi 4178
⑨	13	7	That's Old Fashioned	The Everly Brothers ... Warner 5273
⑩	7	7	Second Hand Love	Connie Francis ... MGM 13074

★ HIGHEST DEBUT ★ POS 68
Seven Day Weekend .... Gary (U.S.) Bonds

★ BIGGEST MOVER ★ 60 to 30
The Wah Watusi............................ The Orlons

Billboard — JUNE 30, 1962 — HOT 100

TW	LW	WK	Title	Artist ... Label
①	1	9	I Can't Stop Loving You	Ray Charles ... ABC-Paramount 10330
②	2	8	The Stripper	David Rose ... MGM 13064
③	3	8	Palisades Park	Freddy Cannon ... Swan 4106
④	4	8	It Keeps Right On A-Hurtin'	Johnny Tillotson ... Cadence 1418
❺	16	4	Roses Are Red	Bobby Vinton ... Epic 9509
⑥	6	10	(The Man Who Shot) Liberty Valance	Gene Pitney ... Musicor 1020
⑦	7	9	Playboy	The Marvelettes ... Tamla 54060
⑧	8	8	Cindy's Birthday	Johnny Crawford ... Del-Fi 4178
⑨	5	16	Stranger On The Shore	Mr. Acker Bilk ... Atco 6217
⑩	12	7	Al Di La'	Emilio Pericoli ... Warner 5259

★ HIGHEST DEBUT ★ POS 57
It Started All Over Again.................. Brenda Lee

★ BIGGEST MOVER ★ 88 to 50
Welcome Home Baby .... The Shirelles

Billboard — JULY 7, 1962 — HOT 100

TW	LW	WK	Title	Artist ... Label
①	2	9	The Stripper	David Rose ... MGM 13064
②	5	5	Roses Are Red	Bobby Vinton ... Epic 9509
③	1	10	I Can't Stop Loving You	Ray Charles ... ABC-Paramount 10330
④	3	9	Palisades Park	Freddy Cannon ... Swan 4106
⑤	4	9	It Keeps Right On A-Hurtin'	Johnny Tillotson ... Cadence 1418
⑥	10	8	Al Di La'	Emilio Pericoli ... Warner 5259
❼	13	7	Wolverton Mountain	Claude King ... Columbia 42352
⑧	11	8	Snap Your Fingers	Joe Henderson ... Todd 1072
❾	14	7	Johnny Get Angry	Joanie Sommers ... Warner 5275
⑩	7	10	Playboy	The Marvelettes ... Tamla 54060

★ HIGHEST DEBUT ★ POS 65
Heart In Hand................................ Brenda Lee

★ BIGGEST MOVER ★ 66 to 26
Breaking Up Is Hard To Do.............. Neil Sedaka

JULY 14, 1962 — Billboard HOT 100

TW	LW	WK	Title	Artist	Label
1	2	6	**Roses Are Red**	*Bobby Vinton*	Epic 9509
2	1	10	**The Stripper**	*David Rose*	MGM 13064
3	3	11	**I Can't Stop Loving You**	*Ray Charles*	ABC-Paramount 10330
4	14	6	**The Wah Watusi**	*The Orlons*	Cameo 218
5	12	6	**Sealed With A Kiss**	*Brian Hyland*	ABC-Paramount 10336
6	4	10	**Palisades Park**	*Freddy Cannon*	Swan 4106
7	7	8	**Wolverton Mountain**	*Claude King*	Columbia 42352
8	5	10	**It Keeps Right On A-Hurtin'**	*Johnny Tillotson*	Cadence 1418
9	16	5	**Gravy (For My Mashed Potatoes)**	*Dee Dee Sharp*	Cameo 219
10	6	9	**Al Di La'**	*Emilio Pericoli*	Warner 5259

★ **HIGHEST DEBUT** ★ POS 80
Ben Crazy .... *Dickie Goodman*

★ **BIGGEST MOVER** ★ 47 to 18
Ahab, The Arab .... *Ray Stevens*

JULY 21, 1962 — Billboard HOT 100

TW	LW	WK	Title	Artist	Label
1	1	7	**Roses Are Red**	*Bobby Vinton*	Epic 9509
2	4	7	**The Wah Watusi**	*The Orlons*	Cameo 218
3	3	12	**I Can't Stop Loving You**	*Ray Charles*	ABC-Paramount 10330
4	2	11	**The Stripper**	*David Rose*	MGM 13064
5	5	7	**Sealed With A Kiss**	*Brian Hyland*	ABC-Paramount 10336
6	7	9	**Wolverton Mountain**	*Claude King*	Columbia 42352
7	11	9	**Johnny Get Angry**	*Joanie Sommers*	Warner 5275
8	13	6	**Speedy Gonzales**	*Pat Boone*	Dot 16368
9	9	6	**Gravy (For My Mashed Potatoes)**	*Dee Dee Sharp*	Cameo 219
10	6	11	**Palisades Park**	*Freddy Cannon*	Swan 4106

★ **HIGHEST DEBUT** ★ POS 70
A Swingin' Safari .... *Billy Vaughn*

★ **BIGGEST MOVER** ★ 85 to 49
Bring It On Home To Me .... *Sam Cooke*

JULY 28, 1962 — Billboard HOT 100

TW	LW	WK	Title	Artist	Label
1	1	8	**Roses Are Red**	*Bobby Vinton*	Epic 9509
2	2	8	**The Wah Watusi**	*The Orlons*	Cameo 218
3	5	8	**Sealed With A Kiss**	*Brian Hyland*	ABC-Paramount 10336
4	3	13	**I Can't Stop Loving You**	*Ray Charles*	ABC-Paramount 10330
5	4	12	**The Stripper**	*David Rose*	MGM 13064
6	8	7	**Speedy Gonzales**	*Pat Boone*	Dot 16368
7	6	10	**Wolverton Mountain**	*Claude King*	Columbia 42352
8	13	5	**Breaking Up Is Hard To Do**	*Neil Sedaka*	RCA 8046
9	9	7	**Gravy (For My Mashed Potatoes)**	*Dee Dee Sharp*	Cameo 219
10	12	5	**Ahab, The Arab**	*Ray Stevens*	Mercury 71966

★ **HIGHEST DEBUT** ★ POS 56
You Don't Know Me .... *Ray Charles*

★ **BIGGEST MOVER** ★ 93 to 76
Call Me Mr. In-Between .... *Burl Ives*

AUGUST 4, 1962 — Billboard HOT 100

TW	LW	WK	Title	Artist	Label
1	1	9	**Roses Are Red**	*Bobby Vinton*	Epic 9509
2	8	6	**Breaking Up Is Hard To Do**	*Neil Sedaka*	RCA 8046
3	3	9	**Sealed With A Kiss**	*Brian Hyland*	ABC-Paramount 10336
4	2	9	The Wah Watusi	*The Orlons*	Cameo 218
5	10	6	**Ahab, The Arab**	*Ray Stevens*	Mercury 71966
6	6	8	**Speedy Gonzales**	*Pat Boone*	Dot 16368
7	4	14	I Can't Stop Loving You	*Ray Charles*	ABC-Paramount 10330
8	14	6	The Loco-Motion	*Little Eva*	Dimension 1000
9	5	13	The Stripper	*David Rose*	MGM 13064
10	13	10	**Theme From Dr. Kildare**	*Richard Chamberlain*	MGM 13075

★ **HIGHEST DEBUT** ★ POS 57
She's Not You .... *Elvis Presley*

★ **BIGGEST MOVER** ★ 76 to 42
Call Me Mr. In-Between .... *Burl Ives*

AUGUST 11, 1962 — Billboard HOT 100

TW	LW	WK	Title	Artist	Label
1	2	7	**Breaking Up Is Hard To Do**	*Neil Sedaka*	RCA 8046
2	1	10	Roses Are Red	*Bobby Vinton*	Epic 9509
3	4	10	The Wah Watusi	*The Orlons*	Cameo 218
4	8	7	The Loco-Motion	*Little Eva*	Dimension 1000
5	5	7	**Ahab, The Arab**	*Ray Stevens*	Mercury 71966
6	6	9	**Speedy Gonzales**	*Pat Boone*	Dot 16368
7	3	10	Sealed With A Kiss	*Brian Hyland*	ABC-Paramount 10336
8	13	9	**You'll Lose A Good Thing**	*Barbara Lynn*	Jamie 1220
9	16	6	Things	*Bobby Darin*	Atco 6229
10	9	14	The Stripper	*David Rose*	MGM 13064

★ **HIGHEST DEBUT** ★ POS 69
Your Nose Is Gonna Grow .... *Johnny Crawford*

★ **BIGGEST MOVER** ★ 99 to 65
Love Me As I Love You .... *George Maharis*

AUGUST 18, 1962 — Billboard HOT 100

TW	LW	WK	Title	Artist	Label
1	1	8	**Breaking Up Is Hard To Do**	*Neil Sedaka*	RCA 8046
2	4	8	The Loco-Motion	*Little Eva*	Dimension 1000
3	2	11	Roses Are Red	*Bobby Vinton*	Epic 9509
4	3	11	The Wah Watusi	*The Orlons*	Cameo 218
5	11	4	You Don't Know Me	*Ray Charles*	ABC-Paramount 10345
6	9	7	Things	*Bobby Darin*	Atco 6229
7	5	8	Ahab, The Arab	*Ray Stevens*	Mercury 71966
8	13	7	**Little Diane**	*Dion*	Laurie 3134
9	6	10	Speedy Gonzales	*Pat Boone*	Dot 16368
10	7	11	Sealed With A Kiss	*Brian Hyland*	ABC-Paramount 10336

★ **HIGHEST DEBUT** ★ POS 74
Venus In Blue Jeans .... *Jimmy Clanton*

★ **BIGGEST MOVER** ★ 63 to 34
Ramblin' Rose .... *Nat King Cole*

Billboard 🔴 AUGUST 25, 1962 🔴 HOT 100

TW	LW	WK			
①	2	9	**The Loco-Motion**	Little Eva	Dimension 1000
②	1	9	**Breaking Up Is Hard To Do**	Neil Sedaka	RCA 8046
③	6	8	**Things**	Bobby Darin	Atco 6229
④	5	5	**You Don't Know Me**	Ray Charles	ABC-Paramount 10345
❺	12	5	**Sheila**	Tommy Roe	ABC-Paramount 10329
⑥	3	12	**Roses Are Red**	Bobby Vinton	Epic 9509
⑦	11	9	**Party Lights**	Claudine Clark	Chancellor 1113
❽	13	4	**She's Not You**	Elvis Presley	RCA 8041
⑨	7	9	**Ahab, The Arab**	Ray Stevens	Mercury 71966
⑩	8	8	**Little Diane**	Dion	Laurie 3134

★ HIGHEST DEBUT ★ POS 61	★ BIGGEST MOVER ★ 90 to 59
Patches .... Dickey Lee	If I Had A Hammer .... Peter, Paul & Mary

Billboard 🔴 SEPTEMBER 1, 1962 🔴 HOT 100

TW	LW	WK			
①	5	6	**Sheila**	Tommy Roe	ABC-Paramount 10329
②	1	10	**The Loco-Motion**	Little Eva	Dimension 1000
③	2	10	**Breaking Up Is Hard To Do**	Neil Sedaka	RCA 8046
④	4	6	**You Don't Know Me**	Ray Charles	ABC-Paramount 10345
⑤	7	10	**Party Lights**	Claudine Clark	Chancellor 1113
⑥	8	5	**She's Not You**	Elvis Presley	RCA 8041
⑦	3	9	**Things**	Bobby Darin	Atco 6229
⑧	6	13	**Roses Are Red**	Bobby Vinton	Epic 9509
⑨	12	6	**Vacation**	Connie Francis	MGM 13087
⑩	10	9	**Little Diane**	Dion	Laurie 3134

★ HIGHEST DEBUT ★ POS 78	★ BIGGEST MOVER ★ 65 to 22
Punish Her .... Bobby Vee	Sherry .... The 4 Seasons

Billboard 🔴 SEPTEMBER 8, 1962 🔴 HOT 100

TW	LW	WK			
①	1	7	**Sheila**	Tommy Roe	ABC-Paramount 10329
②	4	7	**You Don't Know Me**	Ray Charles	ABC-Paramount 10345
③	2	11	**The Loco-Motion**	Little Eva	Dimension 1000
❹	11	6	**Ramblin' Rose**	Nat King Cole	Capitol 4804
⑤	6	6	**She's Not You**	Elvis Presley	RCA 8041
⑥	3	11	**Breaking Up Is Hard To Do**	Neil Sedaka	RCA 8046
⑦	5	11	**Party Lights**	Claudine Clark	Chancellor 1113
⑧	7	10	**Things**	Bobby Darin	Atco 6229
❾	17	5	**Teen Age Idol**	Rick Nelson	Imperial 5864
⑩	9	7	**Vacation**	Connie Francis	MGM 13087

★ HIGHEST DEBUT ★ POS 72	★ BIGGEST MOVER ★ 45 to 20
Monster Mash .... Bobby "Boris" Pickett	Patches .... Dickey Lee

TW	LW	WK	Billboard	SEPTEMBER 15, 1962	HOT 100
❶	11	4	**Sherry**	*The 4 Seasons* . . . Vee-Jay 456	
②	1	8	**Sheila**	*Tommy Roe* . . . ABC-Paramount 10329	
③	4	7	**Ramblin' Rose**	*Nat King Cole* . . . Capitol 4804	
④	3	12	**The Loco-Motion**	*Little Eva* . . . Dimension 1000	
❺	22	6	**Green Onions**	*Booker T. & The MG's* . . . Stax 127	
⑥	5	7	**She's Not You**	*Elvis Presley* . . . RCA 8041	
⑦	9	6	**Teen Age Idol**	*Rick Nelson* . . . Imperial 5864	
⑧	2	8	**You Don't Know Me**	*Ray Charles* . . . ABC-Paramount 10345	
❾	20	4	**Patches**	*Dickey Lee* . . . Smash 1758	
⑩	12	10	**Rinky Dink**	*Baby Cortez* . . . Chess 1829	

★ HIGHEST DEBUT ★ POS 68	★ BIGGEST MOVER ★ 72 to 37
Only Love Can Break A Heart . . . . *Gene Pitney*	Monster Mash . . . . *Bobby "Boris" Pickett*

TW	LW	WK	Billboard	SEPTEMBER 22, 1962	HOT 100
①	1	5	**Sherry**	*The 4 Seasons* . . . Vee-Jay 456	
②	3	8	**Ramblin' Rose**	*Nat King Cole* . . . Capitol 4804	
③	2	9	**Sheila**	*Tommy Roe* . . . ABC-Paramount 10329	
④	5	7	**Green Onions**	*Booker T. & The MG's* . . . Stax 127	
⑤	7	7	**Teen Age Idol**	*Rick Nelson* . . . Imperial 5864	
❻	15	7	**Let's Dance**	*Chris Montez* . . . Monogram 505	
❼	13	8	**You Belong To Me**	*The Duprees* . . . Coed 569	
⑧	9	5	**Patches**	*Dickey Lee* . . . Smash 1758	
⑨	12	7	**You Beat Me To The Punch**	*Mary Wells* . . . Motown 1032	
⑩	6	8	**She's Not You**	*Elvis Presley* . . . RCA 8041	

★ HIGHEST DEBUT ★ POS 58	★ BIGGEST MOVER ★ 53 to 27
Save All Your Lovin' For Me . . . . *Brenda Lee*	I Remember You . . . . *Frank Ifield*

TW	LW	WK	Billboard	SEPTEMBER 29, 1962	HOT 100
①	1	6	**Sherry**	*The 4 Seasons* . . . Vee-Jay 456	
②	2	9	**Ramblin' Rose**	*Nat King Cole* . . . Capitol 4804	
③	4	8	**Green Onions**	*Booker T. & The MG's* . . . Stax 127	
❹	13	4	**Monster Mash**	*Bobby "Boris" Pickett* . . . Garpax 44167	
⑤	3	10	**Sheila**	*Tommy Roe* . . . ABC-Paramount 10329	
⑥	6	8	**Let's Dance**	*Chris Montez* . . . Monogram 505	
❼	12	10	**Alley Cat**	*Bent Fabric* . . . Atco 6226	
⑧	8	6	**Patches**	*Dickey Lee* . . . Smash 1758	
⑨	7	9	**You Belong To Me**	*The Duprees* . . . Coed 569	
⑩	5	8	**Teen Age Idol**	*Rick Nelson* . . . Imperial 5864	

★ HIGHEST DEBUT ★ POS 50	★ BIGGEST MOVER ★ 66 to 44
All Alone Am I . . . . *Brenda Lee*	He's A Rebel . . . . *The Crystals*

TW	LW	WK	Billboard	OCTOBER 6, 1962	HOT 100
①	1	7	**Sherry**	The 4 Seasons	Vee-Jay 456
②	4	5	Monster Mash	Bobby "Boris" Pickett	Garpax 44167
③	2	10	Ramblin' Rose	Nat King Cole	Capitol 4804
④	6	9	**Let's Dance**	Chris Montez	Monogram 505
⑤	3	9	Green Onions	Booker T. & The MG's	Stax 127
⑥	8	7	**Patches**	Dickey Lee	Smash 1758
❼	13	8	**Venus In Blue Jeans**	Jimmy Clanton	Ace 8001
❽	17	5	I Remember You	Frank Ifield	Vee-Jay 457
⑨	7	11	Alley Cat	Bent Fabric	Atco 6226
⑩	11	9	You Beat Me To The Punch	Mary Wells	Motown 1032

★ **HIGHEST DEBUT** ★ POS 77
Next Door To An Angel ....Neil Sedaka

★ **BIGGEST MOVER** ★ 76 to 49
Warmed Over Kisses ....Brian Hyland

TW	LW	WK	Billboard	OCTOBER 13, 1962	HOT 100
①	1	8	**Sherry**	The 4 Seasons	Vee-Jay 456
②	2	6	Monster Mash	Bobby "Boris" Pickett	Garpax 44167
③	3	11	Ramblin' Rose	Nat King Cole	Capitol 4804
④	4	10	**Let's Dance**	Chris Montez	Monogram 505
⑤	8	6	**I Remember You**	Frank Ifield	Vee-Jay 457
⑥	5	10	Green Onions	Booker T. & The MG's	Stax 127
❼	15	10	Do You Love Me	The Contours	Gordy 7005
⑧	6	8	Patches	Dickey Lee	Smash 1758
⑨	9	12	Alley Cat	Bent Fabric	Atco 6226
⑩	14	9	**If I Had A Hammer**	Peter, Paul & Mary	Warner 5296

★ **HIGHEST DEBUT** ★ POS 69
The Cha-Cha-Cha ....Bobby Rydell

★ **BIGGEST MOVER** ★ 77 to 44
Next Door To An Angel ....Neil Sedaka

TW	LW	WK	Billboard	OCTOBER 20, 1962	HOT 100
①	2	7	**Monster Mash**	Bobby "Boris" Pickett	Garpax 44167
②	1	9	Sherry	The 4 Seasons	Vee-Jay 456
③	7	11	**Do You Love Me**	The Contours	Gordy 7005
❹	11	7	He's A Rebel	The Crystals	Philles 106
⑤	5	7	**I Remember You**	Frank Ifield	Vee-Jay 457
⑥	8	9	**Patches**	Dickey Lee	Smash 1758
⑦	3	12	Ramblin' Rose	Nat King Cole	Capitol 4804
❽	13	6	Only Love Can Break A Heart	Gene Pitney	Musicor 1022
⑨	6	11	Green Onions	Booker T. & The MG's	Stax 127
⑩	4	11	Let's Dance	Chris Montez	Monogram 505

★ **HIGHEST DEBUT** ★ POS 66
Big Girls Don't Cry ....The 4 Seasons

★ **BIGGEST MOVER** ★ 88 to 57
I Was Such A Fool........................Connie Francis

Billboard — OCTOBER 27, 1962 — HOT 100

TW	LW	WK	Title	Artist	Label
①	1	8	Monster Mash	Bobby "Boris" Pickett	Garpax 44167
②	4	8	He's A Rebel	The Crystals	Philles 106
③	3	12	Do You Love Me	The Contours	Gordy 7005
④	8	7	Only Love Can Break A Heart	Gene Pitney	Musicor 1022
⑤	2	10	Sherry	The 4 Seasons	Vee-Jay 456
❻	15	5	All Alone Am I	Brenda Lee	Decca 31424
⑦	6	10	Patches	Dickey Lee	Smash 1758
⑧	7	13	Ramblin' Rose	Nat King Cole	Capitol 4804
❾	20	6	Gina	Johnny Mathis	Columbia 42582
⑩	5	8	I Remember You	Frank Ifield	Vee-Jay 457

★ HIGHEST DEBUT ★ POS 77
Somebody Have Mercy......................Sam Cooke

★ BIGGEST MOVER ★ 66 to 17
Big Girls Don't Cry.......................The 4 Seasons

Billboard — NOVEMBER 3, 1962 — HOT 100

TW	LW	WK	Title	Artist	Label
①	2	9	He's A Rebel	The Crystals	Philles 106
②	4	8	Only Love Can Break A Heart	Gene Pitney	Musicor 1022
③	3	13	Do You Love Me	The Contours	Gordy 7005
④	1	9	Monster Mash	Bobby "Boris" Pickett	Garpax 44167
⑤	6	6	All Alone Am I	Brenda Lee	Decca 31424
❻	17	3	Big Girls Don't Cry	The 4 Seasons	Vee-Jay 465
⑦	9	7	Gina	Johnny Mathis	Columbia 42582
❽	18	9	Limbo Rock	Chubby Checker	Parkway 849
❾	15	5	Next Door To An Angel	Neil Sedaka	RCA 8086
⑩	20	3	Return To Sender	Elvis Presley	RCA 8100

★ HIGHEST DEBUT ★ POS 80
Let's Go................................The Routers

★ BIGGEST MOVER ★ 95 to 64
The Lonely Bull......................The Tijuana Brass

Billboard — NOVEMBER 10, 1962 — HOT 100

TW	LW	WK	Title	Artist	Label
①	1	10	He's A Rebel	The Crystals	Philles 106
②	6	4	Big Girls Don't Cry	The 4 Seasons	Vee-Jay 465
③	5	7	All Alone Am I	Brenda Lee	Decca 31424
❹	10	4	Return To Sender	Elvis Presley	RCA 8100
⑤	2	9	Only Love Can Break A Heart	Gene Pitney	Musicor 1022
⑥	9	6	Next Door To An Angel	Neil Sedaka	RCA 8086
⑦	7	8	Gina	Johnny Mathis	Columbia 42582
⑧	4	10	Monster Mash	Bobby "Boris" Pickett	Garpax 44167
⑨	3	14	Do You Love Me	The Contours	Gordy 7005
⑩	14	9	Popeye The Hitchhiker	Chubby Checker	Parkway 849

★ HIGHEST DEBUT ★ POS 74
Love Came To Me......................Dion

★ BIGGEST MOVER ★ 95 to 66
Rumors................................Johnny Crawford

Billboard — NOVEMBER 17, 1962 — HOT 100

TW	LW	WK	Title	Artist	Label
①	2	5	Big Girls Don't Cry	The 4 Seasons	Vee-Jay 465
②	4	5	Return To Sender	Elvis Presley	RCA 8100
③	1	11	He's A Rebel	The Crystals	Philles 106
④	3	8	All Alone Am I	Brenda Lee	Decca 31424
⑤	6	7	Next Door To An Angel	Neil Sedaka	RCA 8086
⑥	7	9	Gina	Johnny Mathis	Columbia 42582
❼	19	5	Bobby's Girl	Marcie Blane	Seville 120
❽	16	6	Don't Hang Up	The Orlons	Cameo 231
⑨	11	11	Limbo Rock	Chubby Checker	Parkway 849
⑩	14	6	The Cha-Cha-Cha	Bobby Rydell	Cameo 228

★ HIGHEST DEBUT ★ POS 75
Zip-A-Dee Doo-Dah .... Bob B. Soxx & The Blue Jeans

★ BIGGEST MOVER ★ 89 to 52
Dear Lonely Hearts .... Nat King Cole

Billboard — NOVEMBER 24, 1962 — HOT 100

TW	LW	WK	Title	Artist	Label
①	1	6	Big Girls Don't Cry	The 4 Seasons	Vee-Jay 465
②	2	6	Return To Sender	Elvis Presley	RCA 8100
③	4	9	All Alone Am I	Brenda Lee	Decca 31424
④	7	6	Bobby's Girl	Marcie Blane	Seville 120
⑤	5	8	Next Door To An Angel	Neil Sedaka	RCA 8086
⑥	9	12	Limbo Rock	Chubby Checker	Parkway 849
⑦	8	7	Don't Hang Up	The Orlons	Cameo 231
⑧	3	12	He's A Rebel	The Crystals	Philles 106
⑨	6	10	Gina	Johnny Mathis	Columbia 42582
⑩	13	6	Ride!	Dee Dee Sharp	Cameo 230

★ HIGHEST DEBUT ★ POS 65
Hotel Happiness .... Brook Benton

★ BIGGEST MOVER ★ 85 to 54
Go Away Little Girl .... Steve Lawrence

Billboard — DECEMBER 1, 1962 — HOT 100

TW	LW	WK	Title	Artist	Label
①	1	7	Big Girls Don't Cry	The 4 Seasons	Vee-Jay 465
②	2	7	Return To Sender	Elvis Presley	RCA 8100
③	4	7	Bobby's Girl	Marcie Blane	Seville 120
④	6	13	Limbo Rock	Chubby Checker	Parkway 849
⑤	3	10	All Alone Am I	Brenda Lee	Decca 31424
⑥	7	8	Don't Hang Up	The Orlons	Cameo 231
⑦	11	6	The Lonely Bull	The Tijuana Brass	A&M 703
⑧	10	7	Ride!	Dee Dee Sharp	Cameo 230
⑨	8	13	He's A Rebel	The Crystals	Philles 106
⑩	5	9	Next Door To An Angel	Neil Sedaka	RCA 8086

★ HIGHEST DEBUT ★ POS 64
Two Lovers .... Mary Wells

★ BIGGEST MOVER ★ 65 to 42
Hotel Happiness .... Brook Benton

Billboard — DECEMBER 8, 1962 — HOT 100

TW	LW	WK	Title	Artist	Label
①	1	8	Big Girls Don't Cry	The 4 Seasons	Vee-Jay 465
②	2	8	Return To Sender	Elvis Presley	RCA 8100
③	3	8	Bobby's Girl	Marcie Blane	Seville 120
④	6	9	Don't Hang Up	The Orlons	Cameo 231
⑤	8	8	Ride!	Dee Dee Sharp	Cameo 230
⑥	7	7	The Lonely Bull	The Tijuana Brass	A&M 703
❼	13	6	Telstar	The Tornadoes	London 9561
⑧	4	14	Limbo Rock	Chubby Checker	Parkway 849
⑨	5	11	All Alone Am I	Brenda Lee	Decca 31424
⑩	16	7	Release Me	"Little Esther" Phillips	Lenox 5555

★ HIGHEST DEBUT ★ POS 66	★ BIGGEST MOVER ★ 94 to 53
The Little Drummer Boy..........The Harry Simeone Chorale	Everybody Loves A Lover..............The Shirelles

Billboard — DECEMBER 15, 1962 — HOT 100

TW	LW	WK	Title	Artist	Label
①	1	9	Big Girls Don't Cry	The 4 Seasons	Vee-Jay 465
②	2	9	Return To Sender	Elvis Presley	RCA 8100
③	3	9	Bobby's Girl	Marcie Blane	Seville 120
④	8	15	Limbo Rock	Chubby Checker	Parkway 849
⑤	7	7	Telstar	The Tornadoes	London 9561
⑥	4	10	Don't Hang Up	The Orlons	Cameo 231
⑦	6	8	The Lonely Bull	The Tijuana Brass	A&M 703
⑧	5	9	Ride!	Dee Dee Sharp	Cameo 230
⑨	10	8	Release Me	"Little Esther" Phillips	Lenox 5555
⑩	20	6	Go Away Little Girl	Steve Lawrence	Columbia 42601

★ HIGHEST DEBUT ★ POS 56	★ BIGGEST MOVER ★ 72 to 37
Santa Claus Is Coming To Town..............The 4 Seasons	Pepino The Italian Mouse..................Lou Monte

Billboard — DECEMBER 22, 1962 — HOT 100

TW	LW	WK	Title	Artist	Label
①	5	8	Telstar	The Tornadoes	London 9561
②	4	16	Limbo Rock	Chubby Checker	Parkway 849
③	2	10	Return To Sender	Elvis Presley	RCA 8100
④	3	10	Bobby's Girl	Marcie Blane	Seville 120
⑤	1	10	Big Girls Don't Cry	The 4 Seasons	Vee-Jay 465
⑥	6	11	Don't Hang Up	The Orlons	Cameo 231
⑦	10	7	Go Away Little Girl	Steve Lawrence	Columbia 42601
⑧	9	9	Release Me	"Little Esther" Phillips	Lenox 5555
⑨	11	6	You Are My Sunshine	Ray Charles	ABC-Paramount 10375
⑩	14	7	Love Came To Me	Dion	Laurie 3145

★ HIGHEST DEBUT ★ POS 80	★ BIGGEST MOVER ★ 84 to 57
Loop De Loop..............Johnny Thunder	Half Heaven - Half Heartache..........Gene Pitney

TW	LW	WK	Billboard.	🎄 DECEMBER 29, 1962 🎄	HOT 100.
①	1	9	**Telstar**	*The Tornadoes*	London 9561
②	2	17	**Limbo Rock**	*Chubby Checker*	Parkway 849
③	4	11	**Bobby's Girl**	*Marcie Blane*	Seville 120
④	7	8	**Go Away Little Girl**	*Steve Lawrence*	Columbia 42601
⑤	5	11	**Big Girls Don't Cry**	*The 4 Seasons*	Vee-Jay 465
⑥	3	11	**Return To Sender**	*Elvis Presley*	RCA 8100
⑦	9	7	**You Are My Sunshine**	*Ray Charles*	ABC-Paramount 10375
⑧	8	10	**Release Me**	*"Little Esther" Phillips*	Lenox 5555
⑨	16	7	**Zip-A-Dee Doo-Dah**	*Bob B. Soxx & The Blue Jeans*	Philles 107
⑩	14	6	**Hotel Happiness**	*Brook Benton*	Mercury 72055

★ *HIGHEST DEBUT* ★ POS 79	★ *BIGGEST MOVER* ★ 89 to 67
The Cinnamon Cinder ....*The Pastel Six*	My Coloring Book ....*Kitty Kallen*

JANUARY 5, 1963 — Billboard HOT 100

TW	LW	WK	Title	Artist	Label
①	1	10	Telstar	The Tornadoes	London 9561
②	4	9	Go Away Little Girl	Steve Lawrence	Columbia 42601
③	2	18	Limbo Rock	Chubby Checker	Parkway 849
④	3	12	Bobby's Girl	Marcie Blane	Seville 120
⑤	5	12	Big Girls Don't Cry	The 4 Seasons	Vee-Jay 465
❻	10	7	Hotel Happiness	Brook Benton	Mercury 72055
❼	11	5	Pepino The Italian Mouse	Lou Monte	Reprise 20106
⑧	6	12	Return To Sender	Elvis Presley	RCA 8100
⑨	9	8	Zip-A-Dee Doo-Dah	Bob B. Soxx & The Blue Jeans	Philles 107
⑩	14	6	Tell Him	The Exciters	United Artists 544

★ HIGHEST DEBUT ★ POS 71
Walk Right In .... The Rooftop Singers

★ BIGGEST MOVER ★ 96 to 53
Hey Paula .... Paul & Paula

JANUARY 12, 1963 — Billboard HOT 100

TW	LW	WK	Title	Artist	Label
①	2	10	Go Away Little Girl	Steve Lawrence	Columbia 42601
②	1	11	Telstar	The Tornadoes	London 9561
③	3	19	Limbo Rock	Chubby Checker	Parkway 849
④	6	8	Hotel Happiness	Brook Benton	Mercury 72055
⑤	7	6	Pepino The Italian Mouse	Lou Monte	Reprise 20106
❻	10	7	Tell Him	The Exciters	United Artists 544
❼	14	6	The Night Has A Thousand Eyes	Bobby Vee	Liberty 55521
⑧	9	9	Zip-A-Dee Doo-Dah	Bob B. Soxx & The Blue Jeans	Philles 107
⑨	15	7	Two Lovers	Mary Wells	Motown 1035
⑩	11	9	My Dad	Paul Petersen	Colpix 663

★ HIGHEST DEBUT ★ POS 77
Chicken Feed .... Bent Fabric

★ BIGGEST MOVER ★ 71 to 35
Walk Right In .... The Rooftop Singers

JANUARY 19, 1963 — Billboard HOT 100

TW	LW	WK	Title	Artist	Label
①	1	11	Go Away Little Girl	Steve Lawrence	Columbia 42601
②	2	12	Telstar	The Tornadoes	London 9561
③	4	9	Hotel Happiness	Brook Benton	Mercury 72055
④	6	8	Tell Him	The Exciters	United Artists 544
⑤	7	7	The Night Has A Thousand Eyes	Bobby Vee	Liberty 55521
⑥	3	20	Limbo Rock	Chubby Checker	Parkway 849
⑦	9	8	Two Lovers	Mary Wells	Motown 1035
⑧	10	10	My Dad	Paul Petersen	Colpix 663
⑨	5	7	Pepino The Italian Mouse	Lou Monte	Reprise 20106
⑩	30	4	Hey Paula	Paul & Paula	Philips 40084

★ HIGHEST DEBUT ★ POS 66
Love (Makes The World Go 'Round) .... Paul Anka

★ BIGGEST MOVER ★ 35 to 11
Walk Right In .... The Rooftop Singers

Billboard 🔴 JANUARY 26, 1963 🔴 HOT 100®

TW	LW	WK		
①	11	4	**Walk Right In** .... *The Rooftop Singers* ... Vanguard 35017
②	10	5	Hey Paula .... *Paul & Paula* ... Philips 40084
③	1	12	Go Away Little Girl .... *Steve Lawrence* ... Columbia 42601
④	4	9	**Tell Him** .... *The Exciters* ... United Artists 544
⑤	5	8	The Night Has A Thousand Eyes .... *Bobby Vee* ... Liberty 55521
⑥	8	11	**My Dad** .... *Paul Petersen* ... Colpix 663
⑦	7	9	**Two Lovers** .... *Mary Wells* ... Motown 1035
⑧	2	13	Telstar .... *The Tornadoes* ... London 9561
⑨	12	7	It's Up To You .... *Rick Nelson* ... Imperial 5901
⑩	6	21	Limbo Rock .... *Chubby Checker* ... Parkway 849

★ HIGHEST DEBUT ★ POS 40	★ BIGGEST MOVER ★ 69 to 31
Walk Like A Man ....*The 4 Seasons*	Ruby Baby ....*Dion*

Billboard 🔴 FEBRUARY 2, 1963 🔴 HOT 100®

TW	LW	WK		
①	1	5	**Walk Right In** .... *The Rooftop Singers* ... Vanguard 35017
②	2	6	Hey Paula... *Paul & Paula* ... Philips 40084
③	5	9	**The Night Has A Thousand Eyes** .... *Bobby Vee* ... Liberty 55521
④	3	13	Go Away Little Girl .... *Steve Lawrence* ... Columbia 42601
⑤	13	7	**Loop De Loop**................................... *Johnny Thunder* ... Diamond 129
⑥	9	8	**It's Up To You** .... *Rick Nelson* ... Imperial 5901
⑦	11	14	Up On The Roof .... *The Drifters* ... Atlantic 2162
⑧	4	10	Tell Him... *The Exciters* ... United Artists 544
⑨	7	10	Two Lovers.. *Mary Wells* ... Motown 1035
⑩	6	12	My Dad... *Paul Petersen* ... Colpix 663

★ HIGHEST DEBUT ★ POS 80	★ BIGGEST MOVER ★ 56 to 30
Only You (And You Alone) ....*Mr. Acker Bilk*	You're The Reason I'm Living..........*Bobby Darin*

Billboard 🔴 FEBRUARY 9, 1963 🔴 HOT 100®

TW	LW	WK		
①	2	7	**Hey Paula**...*Paul & Paula* ... Philips 40084
②	1	6	Walk Right In................................... *The Rooftop Singers* ... Vanguard 35017
③	3	10	**The Night Has A Thousand Eyes** .... *Bobby Vee* ... Liberty 55521
④	5	8	**Loop De Loop**.. *Johnny Thunder* ... Diamond 129
⑤	7	15	**Up On The Roof** .... *The Drifters* ... Atlantic 2162
⑥	15	3	Walk Like A Man .... *The 4 Seasons* ... Vee-Jay 485
⑦	12	4	Ruby Baby .... *Dion* ... Columbia 42662
⑧	11	10	**You've Really Got A Hold On Me**........... *The Miracles* ... Tamla 54073
⑨	19	5	**Rhythm Of The Rain** .... *The Cascades* ... Valiant 6026
⑩	4	14	Go Away Little Girl .... *Steve Lawrence* ... Columbia 42601

★ HIGHEST DEBUT ★ POS 72	★ BIGGEST MOVER ★ 66 to 33
I Really Don't Want To Know.........*"Little Esther"* Phillips	What Will Mary Say ....*Johnny Mathis*

Billboard — FEBRUARY 16, 1963 — HOT 100

TW	LW	WK	Title	Artist	Label
1	1	8	Hey Paula	Paul & Paula	Philips 40084
2	2	7	Walk Right In	The Rooftop Singers	Vanguard 35017
3	6	4	Walk Like A Man	The 4 Seasons	Vee-Jay 485
4	7	5	Ruby Baby	Dion	Columbia 42662
5	9	6	Rhythm Of The Rain	The Cascades	Valiant 6026
6	11	8	From A Jack To A King	Ned Miller	Fabor 114
7	3	11	The Night Has A Thousand Eyes	Bobby Vee	Liberty 55521
8	8	11	You've Really Got A Hold On Me	The Miracles	Tamla 54073
9	4	9	Loop De Loop	Johnny Thunder	Diamond 129
10	5	16	Up On The Roof	The Drifters	Atlantic 2162

★ **HIGHEST DEBUT** ★ POS 59
One Broken Heart For Sale............Elvis Presley

★ **BIGGEST MOVER** ★ 86 to 51
Boss Guitar.................................Duane Eddy

Billboard — FEBRUARY 23, 1963 — HOT 100

TW	LW	WK	Title	Artist	Label
1	1	9	Hey Paula	Paul & Paula	Philips 40084
2	4	6	Ruby Baby	Dion	Columbia 42662
3	3	5	Walk Like A Man	The 4 Seasons	Vee-Jay 485
4	2	8	Walk Right In	The Rooftop Singers	Vanguard 35017
5	5	7	Rhythm Of The Rain	The Cascades	Valiant 6026
6	6	9	From A Jack To A King	Ned Miller	Fabor 114
7	12	6	You're The Reason I'm Living	Bobby Darin	Capitol 4897
8	18	6	Blame It On The Bossa Nova	Eydie Gorme	Columbia 42661
9	8	12	You've Really Got A Hold On Me	The Miracles	Tamla 54073
10	15	9	Wild Weekend	The Rebels	Swan 4125

★ **HIGHEST DEBUT** ★ POS 74
They Remind Me Too Much Of You............Elvis Presley

★ **BIGGEST MOVER** ★ 59 to 25
One Broken Heart For Sale.............Elvis Presley

Billboard — MARCH 2, 1963 — HOT 100

TW	LW	WK	Title	Artist	Label
1	3	6	Walk Like A Man	The 4 Seasons	Vee-Jay 485
2	2	7	Ruby Baby	Dion	Columbia 42662
3	1	10	Hey Paula	Paul & Paula	Philips 40084
4	5	8	Rhythm Of The Rain	The Cascades	Valiant 6026
5	4	9	Walk Right In	The Rooftop Singers	Vanguard 35017
6	7	7	You're The Reason I'm Living	Bobby Darin	Capitol 4897
7	8	7	Blame It On The Bossa Nova	Eydie Gorme	Columbia 42661
8	6	10	From A Jack To A King	Ned Miller	Fabor 114
9	10	10	Wild Weekend	The Rebels	Swan 4125
10	17	6	What Will Mary Say	Johnny Mathis	Columbia 42666

★ **HIGHEST DEBUT** ★ POS 65
Do The Bird............Dee Dee Sharp

★ **BIGGEST MOVER** ★ 87 to 41
He's So Fine............The Chiffons

TW	LW	WK	Billboard. MARCH 9, 1963 HOT 100.
①	1	7	**Walk Like A Man**......................................*The 4 Seasons* . . . Vee-Jay 485
②	2	8	**Ruby Baby**...*Dion* . . . Columbia 42662
③	4	9	**Rhythm Of The Rain**............................*The Cascades* . . . Valiant 6026
④	3	11	Hey Paula...*Paul & Paula* . . . Philips 40084
⑤	6	8	You're The Reason I'm Living......................*Bobby Darin* . . . Capitol 4897
❻	11	5	Our Day Will Come ....*Ruby & The Romantics* . . . Kapp 501
❼	12	7	The End Of The World................................*Skeeter Davis* . . . RCA 8098
⑧	9	11	**Wild Weekend**...*The Rebels* . . . Swan 4125
⑨	10	7	**What Will Mary Say** ....*Johnny Mathis* . . . Columbia 42666
⑩	5	10	Walk Right In.............................*The Rooftop Singers* . . . Vanguard 35017

★ **HIGHEST DEBUT** ★ POS 77
You Don't Love Me Anymore ....*Rick Nelson*

★ **BIGGEST MOVER** ★ 89 to 59
Sandy...*Dion*

TW	LW	WK	Billboard. MARCH 16, 1963 HOT 100.
①	1	8	**Walk Like A Man**...............................*The 4 Seasons* . . . Vee-Jay 485
❷	6	6	**Our Day Will Come** ....*Ruby & The Romantics* . . . Kapp 501
③	5	9	**You're The Reason I'm Living** ....*Bobby Darin* . . . Capitol 4897
❹	7	8	The End Of The World................................*Skeeter Davis* . . . RCA 8098
⑤	3	10	Rhythm Of The Rain ....*The Cascades* . . . Valiant 6026
⑥	2	9	Ruby Baby..*Dion* . . . Columbia 42662
⑦	4	12	Hey Paula..*Paul & Paula* . . . Philips 40084
❽	11	9	Blame It On The Bossa Nova...................*Eydie Gorme* . . . Columbia 42661
⑨	9	8	**What Will Mary Say** ....*Johnny Mathis* . . . Columbia 42666
⑩	19	4	He's So Fine..*The Chiffons* . . . Laurie 3152

★ **HIGHEST DEBUT** ★ POS 58
Young Lovers ....*Paul & Paula*

★ **BIGGEST MOVER** ★ 81 to 50
Baby Workout................................*Jackie Wilson*

TW	LW	WK	Billboard. MARCH 23, 1963 HOT 100.
①	2	7	**Our Day Will Come**.....................*Ruby & The Romantics* . . . Kapp 501
②	4	9	**The End Of The World**............................*Skeeter Davis* . . . RCA 8098
③	3	10	**You're The Reason I'm Living** ....*Bobby Darin* . . . Capitol 4897
❹	10	5	He's So Fine..*The Chiffons* . . . Laurie 3152
⑤	1	9	Walk Like A Man.................................*The 4 Seasons* . . . Vee-Jay 485
⑥	5	11	Rhythm Of The Rain ....*The Cascades* . . . Valiant 6026
❼	16	6	South Street...*The Orlons* . . . Cameo 243
⑧	8	10	Blame It On The Bossa Nova...................*Eydie Gorme* . . . Columbia 42661
⑨	9	9	**What Will Mary Say** ....*Johnny Mathis* . . . Columbia 42666
⑩	13	7	In Dreams ....*Roy Orbison* . . . Monument 806

★ **HIGHEST DEBUT** ★ POS 74
Surfin' U.S.A.............................*The Beach Boys*

★ **BIGGEST MOVER** ★ 50 to 25
Baby Workout................................*Jackie Wilson*

Billboard — MARCH 30, 1963 — HOT 100

TW	LW	WK	Title	Artist / Label
1	4	6	He's So Fine	The Chiffons . . . Laurie 3152
2	1	8	Our Day Will Come	Ruby & The Romantics . . . Kapp 501
3	2	10	The End Of The World	Skeeter Davis . . . RCA 8098
4	7	7	South Street	The Orlons . . . Cameo 243
5	3	11	You're The Reason I'm Living	Bobby Darin . . . Capitol 4897
6	6	12	Rhythm Of The Rain	The Cascades . . . Valiant 6026
7	10	8	In Dreams	Roy Orbison . . . Monument 806
8	25	4	Baby Workout	Jackie Wilson . . . Brunswick 55239
9	13	9	Our Winter Love	Bill Pursell . . . Columbia 42619
10	8	11	Blame It On The Bossa Nova	Eydie Gorme . . . Columbia 42661

★ HIGHEST DEBUT ★ POS 75
Charms ....Bobby Vee

★ BIGGEST MOVER ★ 90 to 62
I Will Follow Him ....Little Peggy March

Billboard — APRIL 6, 1963 — HOT 100

TW	LW	WK	Title	Artist / Label
1	1	7	He's So Fine	The Chiffons . . . Laurie 3152
2	2	9	Our Day Will Come	Ruby & The Romantics . . . Kapp 501
3	3	11	The End Of The World	Skeeter Davis . . . RCA 8098
4	4	8	South Street	The Orlons . . . Cameo 243
5	18	6	Can't Get Used To Losing You	Andy Williams . . . Columbia 42674
6	8	5	Baby Workout	Jackie Wilson . . . Brunswick 55239
7	7	9	In Dreams	Roy Orbison . . . Monument 806
8	5	12	You're The Reason I'm Living	Bobby Darin . . . Capitol 4897
9	6	13	Rhythm Of The Rain	The Cascades . . . Valiant 6026
10	26	4	Young Lovers	Paul & Paula . . . Philips 40096

★ HIGHEST DEBUT ★ POS 82
Losing You ....Brenda Lee

★ BIGGEST MOVER ★ 62 to 30
I Will Follow Him ....Little Peggy March

Billboard — APRIL 13, 1963 — HOT 100

TW	LW	WK	Title	Artist / Label
1	1	8	He's So Fine	The Chiffons . . . Laurie 3152
2	5	7	Can't Get Used To Losing You	Andy Williams . . . Columbia 42674
3	4	9	South Street	The Orlons . . . Cameo 243
4	3	12	The End Of The World	Skeeter Davis . . . RCA 8098
5	6	6	Baby Workout	Jackie Wilson . . . Brunswick 55239
6	2	10	Our Day Will Come	Ruby & The Romantics . . . Kapp 501
7	30	4	I Will Follow Him	Little Peggy March . . . RCA 8139
8	11	5	Puff The Magic Dragon	Peter, Paul & Mary . . . Warner 5348
9	10	5	Young Lovers	Paul & Paula . . . Philips 40096
10	12	7	Do The Bird	Dee Dee Sharp . . . Cameo 244

★ HIGHEST DEBUT ★ POS 70
Take These Chains From My Heart ....Ray Charles

★ BIGGEST MOVER ★ 78 to 50
If You Wanna Be Happy ....Jimmy Soul

TW	LW	WK	Billboard	APRIL 20, 1963	HOT 100
①	1	9	He's So Fine	The Chiffons	Laurie 3152
②	2	8	Can't Get Used To Losing You	Andy Williams	Columbia 42674
③	7	5	I Will Follow Him	Little Peggy March	RCA 8139
④	8	6	Puff The Magic Dragon	Peter, Paul & Mary	Warner 5348
⑤	5	7	Baby Workout	Jackie Wilson	Brunswick 55239
⑥	9	6	Young Lovers	Paul & Paula	Philips 40096
⑦	3	10	South Street	The Orlons	Cameo 243
⑧	13	8	Don't Say Nothin' Bad (About My Baby)	The Cookies	Dimension 1008
⑨	12	8	Pipeline	Chantay's	Dot 16440
⑩	10	8	Do The Bird	Dee Dee Sharp	Cameo 244

★ **HIGHEST DEBUT** ★ POS 66
Another Saturday Night .... Sam Cooke

★ **BIGGEST MOVER** ★ 62 to 31
Reverend Mr. Black .... The Kingston Trio

TW	LW	WK	Billboard	APRIL 27, 1963	HOT 100
①	3	6	I Will Follow Him	Little Peggy March	RCA 8139
②	2	9	Can't Get Used To Losing You	Andy Williams	Columbia 42674
③	1	10	He's So Fine	The Chiffons	Laurie 3152
④	4	7	Puff The Magic Dragon	Peter, Paul & Mary	Warner 5348
⑤	5	8	Baby Workout	Jackie Wilson	Brunswick 55239
⑥	9	9	Pipeline	Chantay's	Dot 16440
⑦	8	9	Don't Say Nothin' Bad (About My Baby)	The Cookies	Dimension 1008
⑧	6	7	Young Lovers	Paul & Paula	Philips 40096
⑨	12	6	On Broadway	The Drifters	Atlantic 2182
⑩	14	7	Watermelon Man	Mongo Santamaria	Battle 45909

★ **HIGHEST DEBUT** ★ POS 67
You Can't Sit Down .... The Dovells

★ **BIGGEST MOVER** ★ 86 to 51
Ain't That A Shame! .... The 4 Seasons

TW	LW	WK	Billboard	MAY 4, 1963	HOT 100
①	1	7	I Will Follow Him	Little Peggy March	RCA 8139
②	2	10	Can't Get Used To Losing You	Andy Williams	Columbia 42674
③	4	8	Puff The Magic Dragon	Peter, Paul & Mary	Warner 5348
④	6	10	Pipeline	Chantay's	Dot 16440
⑤	3	11	He's So Fine	The Chiffons	Laurie 3152
⑥	15	6	If You Wanna Be Happy	Jimmy Soul	S.P.Q.R. 3305
⑦	7	10	Don't Say Nothin' Bad (About My Baby)	The Cookies	Dimension 1008
⑧	11	7	Surfin' U.S.A.	The Beach Boys	Capitol 4932
⑨	9	7	On Broadway	The Drifters	Atlantic 2182
⑩	10	8	Watermelon Man	Mongo Santamaria	Battle 45909

★ **HIGHEST DEBUT** ★ POS 80
Hello Stranger .... Barbara Lewis

★ **BIGGEST MOVER** ★ 80 to 54
Da Doo Ron Ron .... The Crystals

Billboard — MAY 11, 1963 — HOT 100

TW	LW	WK		
①	1	8	**I Will Follow Him**	*Little Peggy March* . . . RCA 8139
②	3	9	**Puff The Magic Dragon**	*Peter, Paul & Mary* . . . Warner 5348
❸	6	7	**If You Wanna Be Happy**	*Jimmy Soul* . . . S.P.Q.R. 3305
④	4	11	**Pipeline**	*Chantay's* . . . Dot 16440
⑤	2	11	Can't Get Used To Losing You	*Andy Williams* . . . Columbia 42674
❻	13	8	Foolish Little Girl	*The Shirelles* . . . Scepter 1248
⑦	8	8	Surfin' U.S.A.	*The Beach Boys* . . . Capitol 4932
⑧	5	12	He's So Fine	*The Chiffons* . . . Laurie 3152
❾	14	6	Reverend Mr. Black	*The Kingston Trio* . . . Capitol 4951
⑩	18	6	Losing You	*Brenda Lee* . . . Decca 31478

★ **HIGHEST DEBUT** ★ POS 60
It's My Party ....*Lesley Gore*

★ **BIGGEST MOVER** ★ 71 to 40
El Watusi ....*Ray Barretto*

Billboard — MAY 18, 1963 — HOT 100

TW	LW	WK		
①	3	8	**If You Wanna Be Happy**	*Jimmy Soul* . . . S.P.Q.R. 3305
②	1	9	I Will Follow Him	*Little Peggy March* . . . RCA 8139
③	2	10	Puff The Magic Dragon	*Peter, Paul & Mary* . . . Warner 5348
❹	7	9	**Surfin' U.S.A.**	*The Beach Boys* . . . Capitol 4932
⑤	6	9	Foolish Little Girl	*The Shirelles* . . . Scepter 1248
⑥	4	12	Pipeline	*Chantay's* . . . Dot 16440
❼	10	7	Losing You	*Brenda Lee* . . . Decca 31478
⑧	9	7	**Reverend Mr. Black**	*The Kingston Trio* . . . Capitol 4951
⑨	5	12	Can't Get Used To Losing You	*Andy Williams* . . . Columbia 42674
⑩	23	7	I Love You Because	*Al Martino* . . . Capitol 4930

★ **HIGHEST DEBUT** ★ POS 72
My Summer Love ....*Ruby & The Romantics*

★ **BIGGEST MOVER** ★ 93 to 55
18 Yellow Roses ....*Bobby Darin*

Billboard — MAY 25, 1963 — HOT 100

TW	LW	WK		
①	1	9	**If You Wanna Be Happy**	*Jimmy Soul* . . . S.P.Q.R. 3305
②	2	10	I Will Follow Him	*Little Peggy March* . . . RCA 8139
③	4	10	**Surfin' U.S.A.**	*The Beach Boys* . . . Capitol 4932
④	5	10	**Foolish Little Girl**	*The Shirelles* . . . Scepter 1248
❺	10	8	**I Love You Because**	*Al Martino* . . . Capitol 4930
⑥	7	8	**Losing You**	*Brenda Lee* . . . Decca 31478
❼	11	9	Two Faces Have I	*Lou Christie* . . . Roulette 4481
❽	12	7	**Take These Chains From My Heart**	*Ray Charles* . . . ABC-Paramount 10435
❾	26	3	It's My Party	*Lesley Gore* . . . Mercury 72119
❿	14	6	**Another Saturday Night**	*Sam Cooke* . . . RCA 8164

★ **HIGHEST DEBUT** ★ POS 72
String Along ....*Rick Nelson*

★ **BIGGEST MOVER** ★ 99 to 73
Pride And Joy ....*Marvin Gaye*

TW	LW	WK	Billboard.	JUNE 1, 1963	HOT 100.
①	9	4	It's My Party	Lesley Gore	Mercury 72119
②	1	10	If You Wanna Be Happy	Jimmy Soul	S.P.Q.R. 3305
③	5	9	I Love You Because	Al Martino	Capitol 4930
④	3	11	Surfin' U.S.A.	The Beach Boys	Capitol 4932
⑤	13	6	Da Doo Ron Ron	The Crystals	Philles 112
⑥	7	10	Two Faces Have I	Lou Christie	Roulette 4481
⑦	15	6	You Can't Sit Down	The Dovells	Parkway 867
⑧	2	11	I Will Follow Him	Little Peggy March	RCA 8139
⑨	6	9	Losing You	Brenda Lee	Decca 31478
⑩	20	4	Sukiyaki	Kyu Sakamoto	Capitol 4945

★ HIGHEST DEBUT ★ POS 66	★ BIGGEST MOVER ★ 79 to 45
One Fine Day ....The Chiffons	If My Pillow Could Talk................Connie Francis

TW	LW	WK	Billboard.	JUNE 8, 1963	HOT 100.
①	1	5	It's My Party	Lesley Gore	Mercury 72119
②	10	5	Sukiyaki	Kyu Sakamoto	Capitol 4945
③	5	7	Da Doo Ron Ron	The Crystals	Philles 112
④	3	10	I Love You Because	Al Martino	Capitol 4930
⑤	7	7	You Can't Sit Down	The Dovells	Parkway 867
⑥	6	11	Two Faces Have I	Lou Christie	Roulette 4481
⑦	2	11	If You Wanna Be Happy	Jimmy Soul	S.P.Q.R. 3305
⑧	11	9	Still	Bill Anderson	Decca 31458
⑨	16	5	Those Lazy-Hazy-Crazy Days Of Summer	Nat King Cole	... Capitol 4965
⑩	4	12	Surfin' U.S.A.	The Beach Boys	Capitol 4932

★ HIGHEST DEBUT ★ POS 76	★ BIGGEST MOVER ★ 90 to 55
Falling...Roy Orbison	First Quarrel ....Paul & Paula

TW	LW	WK	Billboard.	JUNE 15, 1963	HOT 100.
①	2	6	Sukiyaki	Kyu Sakamoto	Capitol 4945
②	1	6	It's My Party	Lesley Gore	Mercury 72119
③	5	8	You Can't Sit Down	The Dovells	Parkway 867
④	3	8	Da Doo Ron Ron	The Crystals	Philles 112
⑤	4	11	I Love You Because	Al Martino	Capitol 4930
⑥	14	5	Blue On Blue	Bobby Vinton	Epic 9593
⑦	9	6	Those Lazy-Hazy-Crazy Days Of Summer	Nat King Cole	... Capitol 4965
⑧	8	10	Still	Bill Anderson	Decca 31458
⑨	13	7	Hello Stranger	Barbara Lewis	Atlantic 2184
⑩	11	6	18 Yellow Roses	Bobby Darin	Capitol 4970

★ HIGHEST DEBUT ★ POS 68	★ BIGGEST MOVER ★ 90 to 57
Surf City...Jan & Dean	Memphis...Lonnie Mack

Billboard — JUNE 22, 1963 — HOT 100

TW	LW	WK	Title	Artist ... Label
①	1	7	**Sukiyaki**	*Kyu Sakamoto* ... Capitol 4945
②	2	7	**It's My Party**	*Lesley Gore* ... Mercury 72119
❸	9	8	**Hello Stranger**	*Barbara Lewis* ... Atlantic 2184
④	3	9	**You Can't Sit Down**	*The Dovells* ... Parkway 867
⑤	6	6	**Blue On Blue**	*Bobby Vinton* ... Epic 9593
⑥	4	9	**Da Doo Ron Ron**	*The Crystals* ... Philles 112
⑦	7	7	**Those Lazy-Hazy-Crazy Days Of Summer**	*Nat King Cole* ... Capitol 4965
⑧	8	11	**Still**	*Bill Anderson* ... Decca 31458
⑨	5	12	**I Love You Because**	*Al Martino* ... Capitol 4930
❿	17	4	**One Fine Day**	*The Chiffons* ... Laurie 3179

★ **HIGHEST DEBUT** ★ POS 62
Without Love (There Is Nothing).......*Ray Charles*

★ **BIGGEST MOVER** ★ 68 to 20
Surf City....................*Jan & Dean*

Billboard — JUNE 29, 1963 — HOT 100

TW	LW	WK	Title	Artist ... Label
①	1	8	**Sukiyaki**	*Kyu Sakamoto* ... Capitol 4945
②	2	8	**It's My Party**	*Lesley Gore* ... Mercury 72119
③	3	9	**Hello Stranger**	*Barbara Lewis* ... Atlantic 2184
④	5	7	**Blue On Blue**	*Bobby Vinton* ... Epic 9593
❺	15	4	**Easier Said Than Done**	*The Essex* ... Roulette 4494
⑥	7	8	**Those Lazy-Hazy-Crazy Days Of Summer**	*Nat King Cole* ... Capitol 4965
❼	10	5	**One Fine Day**	*The Chiffons* ... Laurie 3179
⑧	4	10	**You Can't Sit Down**	*The Dovells* ... Parkway 867
⑨	25	4	**Memphis**	*Lonnie Mack* ... Fraternity 906
❿	20	3	**Surf City**	*Jan & Dean* ... Liberty 55580

★ **HIGHEST DEBUT** ★ POS 77
Tips Of My Fingers ....*Roy Clark*

★ **BIGGEST MOVER** ★ 86 to 51
Wipe Out ....*The Surfaris*

Billboard — JULY 6, 1963 — HOT 100

TW	LW	WK	Title	Artist ... Label
❶	5	5	**Easier Said Than Done**	*The Essex* ... Roulette 4494
②	1	9	**Sukiyaki**	*Kyu Sakamoto* ... Capitol 4945
③	4	8	**Blue On Blue**	*Bobby Vinton* ... Epic 9593
④	3	10	**Hello Stranger**	*Barbara Lewis* ... Atlantic 2184
⑤	2	9	**It's My Party**	*Lesley Gore* ... Mercury 72119
⑥	7	6	**One Fine Day**	*The Chiffons* ... Laurie 3179
❼	10	4	**Surf City**	*Jan & Dean* ... Liberty 55580
⑧	9	5	**Memphis**	*Lonnie Mack* ... Fraternity 906
⑨	13	6	**So Much In Love**	*The Tymes* ... Parkway 871
❿	14	5	**Tie Me Kangaroo Down, Sport**	*Rolf Harris* ... Epic 9596

★ **HIGHEST DEBUT** ★ POS 75
Be Careful Of Stones That You Throw........*Dion*

★ **BIGGEST MOVER** ★ 58 to 18
Fingertips - Pt 2 ....*Little Stevie Wonder*

Billboard 🔵 JULY 13, 1963 🔵 HOT 100

TW	LW	WK	Title	Artist ... Label
①	1	6	**Easier Said Than Done**	*The Essex* ... Roulette 4494
②	7	5	Surf City	*Jan & Dean* ... Liberty 55580
③	10	6	**Tie Me Kangaroo Down, Sport**	*Rolf Harris* ... Epic 9596
④	9	7	So Much In Love	*The Tymes* ... Parkway 871
⑤	6	7	**One Fine Day**	*The Chiffons* ... Laurie 3179
⑥	2	10	Sukiyaki	*Kyu Sakamoto* ... Capitol 4945
⑦	8	6	Memphis	*Lonnie Mack* ... Fraternity 906
⑧	3	9	Blue On Blue	*Bobby Vinton* ... Epic 9593
⑨	4	11	Hello Stranger	*Barbara Lewis* ... Atlantic 2184
⑩	17	4	Wipe Out	*The Surfaris* ... Dot 16479

★ **HIGHEST DEBUT** ★ POS 70
I Wonder ......*Brenda Lee*

★ **BIGGEST MOVER** ★ 49 to 16
(You're the) Devil In Disguise......*Elvis Presley*

Billboard 🔵 JULY 20, 1963 🔵 HOT 100

TW	LW	WK	Title	Artist ... Label
①	2	6	**Surf City**	*Jan & Dean* ... Liberty 55580
②	1	7	**Easier Said Than Done**	*The Essex* ... Roulette 4494
③	4	8	So Much In Love	*The Tymes* ... Parkway 871
④	3	7	Tie Me Kangaroo Down, Sport	*Rolf Harris* ... Epic 9596
⑤	7	7	**Memphis**	*Lonnie Mack* ... Fraternity 906
⑥	11	5	Fingertips – Pt 2	*Little Stevie Wonder* ... Tamla 54080
⑦	10	5	Wipe Out	*The Surfaris* ... Dot 16479
⑧	6	11	Sukiyaki	*Kyu Sakamoto* ... Capitol 4945
⑨	16	4	(You're the) Devil In Disguise	*Elvis Presley* ... RCA 8188
⑩	13	10	**Pride And Joy**	*Marvin Gaye* ... Tamla 54079

★ **HIGHEST DEBUT** ★ POS 67
Sometimes You Gotta Cry A Little ......*Bobby Bland*

★ **BIGGEST MOVER** ★ 52 to 23
Judy's Turn To Cry......*Lesley Gore*

Billboard 🔵 JULY 27, 1963 🔵 HOT 100

TW	LW	WK	Title	Artist ... Label
①	1	7	**Surf City**	*Jan & Dean* ... Liberty 55580
②	3	9	So Much In Love	*The Tymes* ... Parkway 871
③	6	6	Fingertips – Pt 2	*Little Stevie Wonder* ... Tamla 54080
④	2	8	Easier Said Than Done	*The Essex* ... Roulette 4494
⑤	7	6	Wipe Out	*The Surfaris* ... Dot 16479
⑥	4	8	Tie Me Kangaroo Down, Sport	*Rolf Harris* ... Epic 9596
⑦	9	5	(You're the) Devil In Disguise	*Elvis Presley* ... RCA 8188
⑧	14	5	Blowin' In The Wind	*Peter, Paul & Mary* ... Warner 5368
⑨	5	8	Memphis	*Lonnie Mack* ... Fraternity 906
⑩	15	8	**Just One Look**	*Doris Troy* ... Atlantic 2188

★ **HIGHEST DEBUT** ★ POS 68
Hey, Girl......*Freddie Scott*

★ **BIGGEST MOVER** ★ 50 to 28
More ......*Kai Winding*

Billboard — AUGUST 3, 1963 — HOT 100

TW	LW	WK	Title	Artist	Label
1	2	10	So Much In Love	The Tymes	Parkway 871
2	3	7	Fingertips - Pt 2	Little Stevie Wonder	Tamla 54080
3	1	8	Surf City	Jan & Dean	Liberty 55580
4	7	6	(You're the) Devil In Disguise	Elvis Presley	RCA 8188
5	5	7	Wipe Out	The Surfaris	Dot 16479
6	8	6	Blowin' In The Wind	Peter, Paul & Mary	Warner 5368
7	4	9	Easier Said Than Done	The Essex	Roulette 4494
8	11	5	Judy's Turn To Cry	Lesley Gore	Mercury 72143
9	6	9	Tie Me Kangaroo Down, Sport	Rolf Harris	Epic 9596
10	10	9	Just One Look	Doris Troy	Atlantic 2188

★ HIGHEST DEBUT ★ POS 45
Hello Mudduh, Hello Fadduh! ....Allan Sherman

★ BIGGEST MOVER ★ 89 to 60
Frankie And Johnny ....Sam Cooke

Billboard — AUGUST 10, 1963 — HOT 100

TW	LW	WK	Title	Artist	Label
1	2	8	Fingertips - Pt 2	Little Stevie Wonder	Tamla 54080
2	5	8	Wipe Out	The Surfaris	Dot 16479
3	4	7	(You're the) Devil In Disguise	Elvis Presley	RCA 8188
4	6	7	Blowin' In The Wind	Peter, Paul & Mary	Warner 5368
5	1	11	So Much In Love	The Tymes	Parkway 871
6	8	6	Judy's Turn To Cry	Lesley Gore	Mercury 72143
7	3	9	Surf City	Jan & Dean	Liberty 55580
8	11	6	Candy Girl	Four Seasons	Vee-Jay 539
9	7	10	Easier Said Than Done	The Essex	Roulette 4494
10	19	6	More	Kai Winding	Verve 10295

★ HIGHEST DEBUT ★ POS 75
You Can Never Stop Me Loving You ....Johnny Tillotson

★ BIGGEST MOVER ★ 75 to 31
My Boyfriend's Back ....The Angels

Billboard — AUGUST 17, 1963 — HOT 100

TW	LW	WK	Title	Artist	Label
1	1	9	Fingertips - Pt 2	Little Stevie Wonder	Tamla 54080
2	4	8	Blowin' In The Wind	Peter, Paul & Mary	Warner 5368
3	3	8	(You're the) Devil In Disguise	Elvis Presley	RCA 8188
4	2	9	Wipe Out	The Surfaris	Dot 16479
5	6	7	Judy's Turn To Cry	Lesley Gore	Mercury 72143
6	8	7	Candy Girl	Four Seasons	Vee-Jay 539
7	17	3	Hello Mudduh, Hello Fadduh!	Allan Sherman	Warner 5378
8	5	12	So Much In Love	The Tymes	Parkway 871
9	10	7	More	Kai Winding	Verve 10295
10	31	3	My Boyfriend's Back	The Angels	Smash 1834

★ HIGHEST DEBUT ★ POS 71
Then He Kissed Me ....The Crystals

★ BIGGEST MOVER ★ 78 to 53
Blue Velvet ....Bobby Vinton

TW	LW	WK	Billboard	AUGUST 24, 1963	HOT 100
①	1	10	**Fingertips – Pt 2** ....*Little Stevie Wonder* ... Tamla 54080
②	7	4	**Hello Mudduh, Hello Fadduh!** ....*Allan Sherman* ... Warner 5378
③	6	8	**Candy Girl**..*Four Seasons* ... Vee-Jay 539
④	10	4	**My Boyfriend's Back** ....*The Angels* ... Smash 1834
⑤	5	8	**Judy's Turn To Cry** ....*Lesley Gore* ... Mercury 72143
⑥	2	9	**Blowin' In The Wind**.............................*Peter, Paul & Mary* ... Warner 5368
⑦	4	10	**Wipe Out**..*The Surfaris* ... Dot 16479
⑧	9	8	**More** ....*Kai Winding* ... Verve 10295
⑨	3	9	**(You're the) Devil In Disguise**.......................*Elvis Presley* ... RCA 8188
⑩	15	11	**Denise** ....*Randy & The Rainbows* ... Rust 5059

★ *HIGHEST DEBUT* ★ POS 70
Why Don't You Believe Me ....*The Duprees*

★ *BIGGEST MOVER* ★ 89 to 51
Wonderful! Wonderful! ....*The Tymes*

TW	LW	WK	Billboard	AUGUST 31, 1963	HOT 100
❶	4	5	**My Boyfriend's Back** ....*The Angels* ... Smash 1834
②	2	5	**Hello Mudduh, Hello Fadduh!** ....*Allan Sherman* ... Warner 5378
③	1	11	**Fingertips – Pt 2** ....*Little Stevie Wonder* ... Tamla 54080
④	3	9	**Candy Girl**..*Four Seasons* ... Vee-Jay 539
⑤	6	10	**Blowin' In The Wind**.............................*Peter, Paul & Mary* ... Warner 5368
❻	11	6	**If I Had A Hammer** ....*Trini Lopez* ... Reprise 20198
⑦	5	9	**Judy's Turn To Cry** ....*Lesley Gore* ... Mercury 72143
❽	12	11	**Mockingbird**....................................*Inez & Charlie Foxx* ... Symbol 919
⑨	8	9	**More** ....*Kai Winding* ... Verve 10295
⑩	10	12	**Denise** ....*Randy & The Rainbows* ... Rust 5059

★ *HIGHEST DEBUT* ★ POS 63
Sally, Go 'Round The Roses ....*The Jaynetts*

★ *BIGGEST MOVER* ★ 90 to 66
A Walkin' Miracle.................................*The Essex*

TW	LW	WK	Billboard	SEPTEMBER 7, 1963	HOT 100
①	1	6	**My Boyfriend's Back** ....*The Angels* ... Smash 1834
②	2	6	**Hello Mudduh, Hello Fadduh!** ....*Allan Sherman* ... Warner 5378
❸	6	7	**If I Had A Hammer** ....*Trini Lopez* ... Reprise 20198
❹	11	5	**Blue Velvet**..*Bobby Vinton* ... Epic 9614
⑤	4	10	**Candy Girl**..*Four Seasons* ... Vee-Jay 539
❻	14	6	**Heat Wave** ....*Martha & The Vandellas* ... Gordy 7022
⑦	8	12	**Mockingbird**....................................*Inez & Charlie Foxx* ... Symbol 919
❽	12	9	**The Monkey Time** ....*Major Lance* ... Okeh 7175
⑨	5	11	**Blowin' In The Wind**.............................*Peter, Paul & Mary* ... Warner 5368
⑩	15	7	**Hey, Girl** ....*Freddie Scott* ... Colpix 692

★ *HIGHEST DEBUT* ★ POS 66
Busted ....*Ray Charles*

★ *BIGGEST MOVER* ★ 69 to 31
Cry Baby ....*Garnet Mimms & The Enchanters*

TW	LW	WK	Billboard	SEPTEMBER 14, 1963	HOT 100.
①	1	7	My Boyfriend's Back	*The Angels* . . . Smash 1834	
②	4	6	Blue Velvet	*Bobby Vinton* . . . Epic 9614	
③	3	8	If I Had A Hammer	*Trini Lopez* . . . Reprise 20198	
④	2	7	Hello Mudduh, Hello Fadduh!	*Allan Sherman* . . . Warner 5378	
⑤	6	7	Heat Wave	*Martha & The Vandellas* . . . Gordy 7022	
⑥	15	5	Then He Kissed Me	*The Crystals* . . . Philles 115	
⑦	12	7	Surfer Girl	*The Beach Boys* . . . Capitol 5009	
⑧	8	10	The Monkey Time	*Major Lance* . . . Okeh 7175	
⑨	29	3	Sally, Go 'Round The Roses	*The Jaynetts* . . . Tuff 369	
⑩	7	13	Mockingbird	*Inez & Charlie Foxx* . . . Symbol 919	

★ **HIGHEST DEBUT** ★ POS 67
Don't Think Twice, It's All Right . . . . . . *Peter, Paul & Mary*

★ **BIGGEST MOVER** ★ 55 to 20
Be My Baby . . . . *The Ronettes*

TW	LW	WK	Billboard	SEPTEMBER 21, 1963	HOT 100.
①	2	7	Blue Velvet	*Bobby Vinton* . . . Epic 9614	
②	1	8	My Boyfriend's Back	*The Angels* . . . Smash 1834	
③	3	9	If I Had A Hammer	*Trini Lopez* . . . Reprise 20198	
④	5	8	Heat Wave	*Martha & The Vandellas* . . . Gordy 7022	
⑤	9	4	Sally, Go 'Round The Roses	*The Jaynetts* . . . Tuff 369	
⑥	6	6	Then He Kissed Me	*The Crystals* . . . Philles 115	
⑦	7	8	Surfer Girl	*The Beach Boys* . . . Capitol 5009	
⑧	15	6	Mickey's Monkey	*The Miracles* . . . Tamla 54083	
⑨	4	8	Hello Mudduh, Hello Fadduh!	*Allan Sherman* . . . Warner 5378	
⑩	13	6	Cry Baby	*Garnet Mimms & The Enchanters* . . . United Artists 629	

★ **HIGHEST DEBUT** ★ POS 65
Sugar Shack . . . . *Jimmy Gilmer & The Fireballs*

★ **BIGGEST MOVER** ★ 58 to 27
Honolulu Lulu . . . . *Jan & Dean*

TW	LW	WK	Billboard	SEPTEMBER 28, 1963	HOT 100.
①	1	8	Blue Velvet	*Bobby Vinton* . . . Epic 9614	
②	5	5	Sally, Go 'Round The Roses	*The Jaynetts* . . . Tuff 369	
③	12	5	Be My Baby	*The Ronettes* . . . Philles 116	
④	4	9	Heat Wave	*Martha & The Vandellas* . . . Gordy 7022	
⑤	2	9	My Boyfriend's Back	*The Angels* . . . Smash 1834	
⑥	6	7	Then He Kissed Me	*The Crystals* . . . Philles 115	
⑦	11	7	Wonderful! Wonderful!	*The Tymes* . . . Parkway 884	
⑧	8	7	Mickey's Monkey	*The Miracles* . . . Tamla 54083	
⑨	10	7	Cry Baby	*Garnet Mimms & The Enchanters* . . . United Artists 629	
⑩	3	10	If I Had A Hammer	*Trini Lopez* . . . Reprise 20198	

★ **HIGHEST DEBUT** ★ POS 70
You Lost The Sweetest Boy . . . . *Mary Wells*

★ **BIGGEST MOVER** ★ 65 to 19
Sugar Shack . . . . *Jimmy Gilmer & The Fireballs*

TW	LW	WK	Billboard.	OCTOBER 5, 1963	HOT 100.
①	1	9	**Blue Velvet**..*Bobby Vinton* . . . Epic 9614
②	2	6	**Sally, Go 'Round The Roses** ....*The Jaynetts* . . . Tuff 369
③	3	6	Be My Baby ....*The Ronettes* . . . Philles 116
④	19	3	Sugar Shack..............................*Jimmy Gilmer & The Fireballs* . . . Dot 16487
⑤	9	8	Cry Baby ....*Garnet Mimms & The Enchanters* . . . United Artists 629
⑥	5	10	My Boyfriend's Back ....*The Angels* . . . Smash 1834
⑦	7	8	**Wonderful! Wonderful!**..................................*The Tymes* . . . Parkway 884
⑧	4	10	Heat Wave ....*Martha & The Vandellas* . . . Gordy 7022
⑨	13	5	Busted..*Ray Charles* . . . ABC-Paramount 10481
⑩	6	8	Then He Kissed Me ....*The Crystals* . . . Philles 115

★ *HIGHEST DEBUT* ★ POS 63	★ *BIGGEST MOVER* ★ 69 to 38
Workout Stevie, Workout ....*Little Stevie Wonder*	Washington Square ....*The Village Stompers*

TW	LW	WK	Billboard.	OCTOBER 12, 1963	HOT 100.
❶	4	4	**Sugar Shack**..............................*Jimmy Gilmer & The Fireballs* . . . Dot 16487
②	3	7	**Be My Baby** ....*The Ronettes* . . . Philles 116
③	1	10	Blue Velvet ....*Bobby Vinton* . . . Epic 9614
④	5	9	**Cry Baby**..................*Garnet Mimms & The Enchanters* . . . United Artists 629
⑤	2	7	Sally, Go 'Round The Roses...............................*The Jaynetts* . . . Tuff 369
❻	9	6	Busted.....................................*Ray Charles* . . . ABC-Paramount 10481
⑦	6	11	My Boyfriend's Back ....*The Angels* . . . Smash 1834
❽	16	6	Mean Woman Blues...................................*Roy Orbison* . . . Monument 824
⑨	8	11	Heat Wave ....*Martha & The Vandellas* . . . Gordy 7022
⑩	17	5	Donna The Prima Donna ....*Dion DiMucci* . . . Columbia 42852

★ *HIGHEST DEBUT* ★ POS 68	★ *BIGGEST MOVER* ★ 96 to 71
Everybody.......................................*Tommy Roe*	500 Miles Away From Home............*Bobby Bare*

TW	LW	WK	Billboard.	OCTOBER 19, 1963	HOT 100.
①	1	5	**Sugar Shack**............................*Jimmy Gilmer & The Fireballs* . . . Dot 16487
②	2	8	**Be My Baby** ....*The Ronettes* . . . Philles 116
③	3	11	Blue Velvet ....*Bobby Vinton* . . . Epic 9614
④	6	7	**Busted** ....*Ray Charles* . . . ABC-Paramount 10481
⑤	4	10	Cry Baby ....*Garnet Mimms & The Enchanters* . . . United Artists 629
⑥	5	8	Sally, Go 'Round The Roses...............................*The Jaynetts* . . . Tuff 369
⑦	8	7	Mean Woman Blues....................................*Roy Orbison* . . . Monument 824
⑧	10	6	Donna The Prima Donna ....*Dion DiMucci* . . . Columbia 42852
❾	20	6	Deep Purple.....................*Nino Tempo & April Stevens* . . . Atco 6273
⑩	14	6	Don't Think Twice, It's All Right ....*Peter, Paul & Mary* . . . Warner 5385

★ *HIGHEST DEBUT* ★ POS 72	★ *BIGGEST MOVER* ★ 79 to 50
Witchcraft ....*Elvis Presley*	New Mexican Rose.................*The Four Seasons*

TW	LW	WK	Billboard	OCTOBER 26, 1963	HOT 100
①	1	6	**Sugar Shack**......................*Jimmy Gilmer & The Fireballs* ... Dot 16487
②	2	9	**Be My Baby** ....*The Ronettes* ... Philles 116
❸	9	7	**Deep Purple**.........................*Nino Tempo & April Stevens* ... Atco 6273
④	4	8	**Busted** ....*Ray Charles* ... ABC-Paramount 10481
⑤	3	12	**Blue Velvet** ....*Bobby Vinton* ... Epic 9614
⑥	8	7	**Donna The Prima Donna** ....*Dion DiMucci* ... Columbia 42852
⑦	7	8	**Mean Woman Blues**............................*Roy Orbison* ... Monument 824
❽	17	6	**Washington Square** ....*The Village Stompers* ... Epic 9617
⑨	10	7	**Don't Think Twice, It's All Right** ....*Peter, Paul & Mary* ... Warner 5385
⑩	5	11	**Cry Baby** ....*Garnet Mimms & The Enchanters* ... United Artists 629

★ HIGHEST DEBUT ★ POS 71	★ BIGGEST MOVER ★ 77 to 41
I Adore Him............................*The Angels*	Bossa Nova Baby............................*Elvis Presley*

TW	LW	WK	Billboard	NOVEMBER 2, 1963	HOT 100
①	1	7	**Sugar Shack**......................*Jimmy Gilmer & The Fireballs* ... Dot 16487
②	3	8	**Deep Purple**.........................*Nino Tempo & April Stevens* ... Atco 6273
❸	8	7	**Washington Square** ....*The Village Stompers* ... Epic 9617
④	4	9	**Busted** ....*Ray Charles* ... ABC-Paramount 10481
⑤	7	9	**Mean Woman Blues**............................*Roy Orbison* ... Monument 824
⑥	6	8	**Donna The Prima Donna** ....*Dion DiMucci* ... Columbia 42852
❼	12	9	**I Can't Stay Mad At You** ....*Skeeter Davis* ... RCA 8219
⑧	2	10	**Be My Baby** ....*The Ronettes* ... Philles 116
⑨	15	6	**It's All Right** ....*The Impressions* ... ABC-Paramount 10487
⑩	18	7	**Maria Elena**............................*Los Indios Tabajaras* ... RCA 8216

★ HIGHEST DEBUT ★ POS 66	★ BIGGEST MOVER ★ 73 to 44
Wonderful Summer........................*Robin Ward*	Little Red Rooster ....*Sam Cooke*

TW	LW	WK	Billboard	NOVEMBER 9, 1963	HOT 100
①	1	8	**Sugar Shack**......................*Jimmy Gilmer & The Fireballs* ... Dot 16487
②	2	9	**Deep Purple**.........................*Nino Tempo & April Stevens* ... Atco 6273
③	3	8	**Washington Square** ....*The Village Stompers* ... Epic 9617
④	9	7	**It's All Right**...............................*The Impressions* ... ABC-Paramount 10487
⑤	5	10	**Mean Woman Blues**............................*Roy Orbison* ... Monument 824
❻	11	6	**I'm Leaving It Up To You**......................*Dale & Grace* ... Montel 921
❼	10	8	**Maria Elena**............................*Los Indios Tabajaras* ... RCA 8216
⑧	4	10	**Busted**.................................*Ray Charles* ... ABC-Paramount 10481
❾	25	4	**Bossa Nova Baby**.....................................*Elvis Presley* ... RCA 8243
⑩	7	10	**I Can't Stay Mad At You** ....*Skeeter Davis* ... RCA 8219

★ HIGHEST DEBUT ★ POS 64	★ BIGGEST MOVER ★ 84 to 56
Dominique ....*The Singing Nun*	You Don't Have To Be A Baby To Cry ....*The Caravelles*

TW	LW	WK	Billboard.	NOVEMBER 16, 1963	HOT 100.
①	2	10	**Deep Purple**	*Nino Tempo & April Stevens* . . . Atco 6273	
②	1	9	**Sugar Shack**	*Jimmy Gilmer & The Fireballs* . . . Dot 16487	
③	3	9	**Washington Square**	*The Village Stompers* . . . Epic 9617	
④	6	7	**I'm Leaving It Up To You**	*Dale & Grace* . . . Montel 921	
⑤	4	8	**It's All Right**	*The Impressions* . . . ABC-Paramount 10487	
⑥	7	9	**Maria Elena**	*Los Indios Tabajaras* . . . RCA 8216	
❼	11	8	**She's A Fool**	*Lesley Gore* . . . Mercury 72180	
⑧	9	5	**Bossa Nova Baby**	*Elvis Presley* . . . RCA 8243	
❾	14	6	**Everybody**	*Tommy Roe* . . . ABC-Paramount 10478	
⑩	15	7	**500 Miles Away From Home**	*Bobby Bare* . . . RCA 8238	

★ **HIGHEST DEBUT** ★ POS 73
Drip Drop ....*Dion DiMucci*

★ **BIGGEST MOVER** ★ 64 to 19
Dominique ....*The Singing Nun*

TW	LW	WK	Billboard.	NOVEMBER 23, 1963	HOT 100.
❶	4	8	**I'm Leaving It Up To You**	*Dale & Grace* . . . Montel 921	
②	3	10	**Washington Square**	*The Village Stompers* . . . Epic 9617	
③	1	11	Deep Purple	*Nino Tempo & April Stevens* . . . Atco 6273	
④	2	10	Sugar Shack	*Jimmy Gilmer & The Fireballs* . . . Dot 16487	
⑤	5	9	It's All Right	*The Impressions* . . . ABC-Paramount 10487	
⑥	7	9	She's A Fool	*Lesley Gore* . . . Mercury 72180	
⑦	9	7	Everybody	*Tommy Roe* . . . ABC-Paramount 10478	
⑧	8	6	**Bossa Nova Baby**	*Elvis Presley* . . . RCA 8243	
❾	19	3	Dominique	*The Singing Nun* . . . Philips 40152	
⑩	6	10	Maria Elena	*Los Indios Tabajaras* . . . RCA 8216	

★ **HIGHEST DEBUT** ★ POS 75
Quicksand ....*Martha & The Vandellas*

★ **BIGGEST MOVER** ★ 73 to 38
Drip Drop ....*Dion DiMucci*

TW	LW	WK	Billboard.	NOVEMBER 30, 1963	HOT 100.
①	1	9	**I'm Leaving It Up To You**	*Dale & Grace* . . . Montel 921	
❷	9	4	**Dominique**	*The Singing Nun* . . . Philips 40152	
③	2	11	**Washington Square**	*The Village Stompers* . . . Epic 9617	
④	4	11	Sugar Shack	*Jimmy Gilmer & The Fireballs* . . . Dot 16487	
⑤	5	10	It's All Right	*The Impressions* . . . ABC-Paramount 10487	
⑥	6	10	She's A Fool	*Lesley Gore* . . . Mercury 72180	
⑦	7	8	Everybody	*Tommy Roe* . . . ABC-Paramount 10478	
⑧	3	12	Deep Purple	*Nino Tempo & April Stevens* . . . Atco 6273	
❾	11	10	**(Down At) Papa Joe's**	*The Dixiebelles* . . . Sound Stage 7 2507	
⑩	8	7	Bossa Nova Baby	*Elvis Presley* . . . RCA 8243	

★ **HIGHEST DEBUT** ★ POS 50
There! I've Said It Again ....*Bobby Vinton*

★ **BIGGEST MOVER** ★ 75 to 45
Quicksand ....*Martha & The Vandellas*

TW	LW	WK	Billboard	DECEMBER 7, 1963	HOT 100.
①	2	5	**Dominique** ....*The Singing Nun* ... Philips 40152
②	1	10	**I'm Leaving It Up To You**..........................*Dale & Grace* ... Montel 921
③	7	9	**Everybody** ....*Tommy Roe* ... ABC-Paramount 10478
④	23	5	**Louie Louie** ....*The Kingsmen* ... Wand 143
⑤	6	11	**She's A Fool** ....*Lesley Gore* ... Mercury 72180
⑥	4	12	**Sugar Shack**..........................*Jimmy Gilmer & The Fireballs* ... Dot 16487
⑦	19	6	**You Don't Have To Be A Baby To Cry** ....*The Caravelles* ... Smash 1852
⑧	14	6	**Be True To Your School**..........................*The Beach Boys* ... Capitol 5069
⑨	3	12	**Washington Square** ....*The Village Stompers* ... Epic 9617
⑩	11	10	**Walking The Dog** ....*Rufus Thomas* ... Stax 140

★ HIGHEST DEBUT ★ POS 70	★ BIGGEST MOVER ★ 63 to 32
Drag City.............................*Jan & Dean*	Popsicles And Icicles.................*The Murmaids*

TW	LW	WK	Billboard	DECEMBER 14, 1963	HOT 100.
①	1	6	**Dominique** ....*The Singing Nun* ... Philips 40152
②	4	6	**Louie Louie**...*The Kingsmen* ... Wand 143
③	3	10	**Everybody** ....*Tommy Roe* ... ABC-Paramount 10478
④	2	11	**I'm Leaving It Up To You**..........................*Dale & Grace* ... Montel 921
⑤	7	7	**You Don't Have To Be A Baby To Cry** ....*The Caravelles* ... Smash 1852
⑥	14	8	**Since I Fell For You** ....*Lenny Welch* ... Cadence 1439
⑦	8	7	**Be True To Your School**..........................*The Beach Boys* ... Capitol 5069
⑧	15	5	**Drip Drop**..*Dion DiMucci* ... Columbia 42917
⑨	22	3	**There! I've Said It Again** ....*Bobby Vinton* ... Epic 9638
⑩	10	11	**Walking The Dog** ....*Rufus Thomas* ... Stax 140

★ HIGHEST DEBUT ★ POS 60	★ BIGGEST MOVER ★ 97 to 70
Pretty Paper ....*Roy Orbison*	Surfin' Bird ....*The Trashmen*

TW	LW	WK	Billboard	DECEMBER 21, 1963	HOT 100.
①	1	7	**Dominique** ....*The Singing Nun* ... Philips 40152
②	2	7	**Louie Louie**...*The Kingsmen* ... Wand 143
③	5	8	**You Don't Have To Be A Baby To Cry** ....*The Caravelles* ... Smash 1852
④	9	4	**There! I've Said It Again**...............................*Bobby Vinton* ... Epic 9638
⑤	6	9	**Since I Fell For You** ....*Lenny Welch* ... Cadence 1439
⑥	7	8	**Be True To Your School**......................*The Beach Boys* ... Capitol 5069
⑦	8	6	**Drip Drop**..*Dion DiMucci* ... Columbia 42917
⑧	4	12	**I'm Leaving It Up To You**..........................*Dale & Grace* ... Montel 921
⑨	3	11	**Everybody** ....*Tommy Roe* ... ABC-Paramount 10478
⑩	16	5	**Popsicles And Icicles** ....*The Murmaids* ... Chattahoochee 628

★ HIGHEST DEBUT ★ POS 80	★ BIGGEST MOVER ★ 60 to 33
Whispering ....*Nino Tempo & April Stevens*	Pretty Paper ....*Roy Orbison*

TW	LW	WK	Billboard.	DECEMBER 28, 1963	HOT 100.
①	1	8	**Dominique**	*The Singing Nun* ... Philips 40152	
②	4	5	**There! I've Said It Again**	*Bobby Vinton* ... Epic 9638	
③	2	8	**Louie Louie**	*The Kingsmen* ... Wand 143	
④	5	10	**Since I Fell For You**	*Lenny Welch* ... Cadence 1439	
⑤	3	9	You Don't Have To Be A Baby To Cry	*The Caravelles* ... Smash 1852	
⑥	7	7	**Drip Drop**	*Dion DiMucci* ... Columbia 42917	
❼	13	8	Forget Him	*Bobby Rydell* ... Cameo 280	
⑧	10	6	Popsicles And Icicles	*The Murmaids* ... Chattahoochee 628	
⑨	11	8	Talk Back Trembling Lips	*Johnny Tillotson* ... MGM 13181	
⑩	6	9	Be True To Your School	*The Beach Boys* ... Capitol 5069	

★ HIGHEST DEBUT ★ POS 61	★ BIGGEST MOVER ★ 80 to 37
For You ....*Rick Nelson*	Whispering ....*Nino Tempo & April Stevens*

Billboard 🔴 JANUARY 4, 1964 🔴 HOT 100.

TW	LW	WK		
①	2	6	**There! I've Said It Again**	*Bobby Vinton* . . . Epic 9638
②	3	9	**Louie Louie**	*The Kingsmen* . . . Wand 143
③	1	9	**Dominique**	*The Singing Nun* . . . Philips 40152
④	4	11	**Since I Fell For You**	*Lenny Welch* . . . Cadence 1439
⑤	7	9	**Forget Him**	*Bobby Rydell* . . . Cameo 280
⑥	8	7	**Popsicles And Icicles**	*The Murmaids* . . . Chattahoochee 628
⑦	9	9	**Talk Back Trembling Lips**	*Johnny Tillotson* . . . MGM 13181
❽	12	7	**Quicksand**	*Martha & The Vandellas* . . . Gordy 7025
❾	13	8	**The Nitty Gritty**	*Shirley Ellis* . . . Congress 202
⑩	11	9	**Midnight Mary**	*Joey Powers* . . . Amy 892

★ HIGHEST DEBUT ★ POS 58	★ BIGGEST MOVER ★ 64 to 32
Um, Um, Um, Um, Um, Um ....*Major Lance*	Anyone Who Had A Heart..........*Dionne Warwick*

Billboard 🔴 JANUARY 11, 1964 🔴 HOT 100.

TW	LW	WK		
①	1	7	**There! I've Said It Again**	*Bobby Vinton* . . . Epic 9638
②	2	10	**Louie Louie**	*The Kingsmen* . . . Wand 143
❸	6	8	**Popsicles And Icicles**	*The Murmaids* . . . Chattahoochee 628
④	3	10	**Dominique**	*The Singing Nun* . . . Philips 40152
⑤	5	10	**Forget Him**	*Bobby Rydell* . . . Cameo 280
⑥	4	12	Since I Fell For You	*Lenny Welch* . . . Cadence 1439
❼	13	6	**Surfin' Bird**	*The Trashmen* . . . Garrett 4002
⑧	9	9	**The Nitty Gritty**	*Shirley Ellis* . . . Congress 202
⑨	7	10	Talk Back Trembling Lips	*Johnny Tillotson* . . . MGM 13181
⑩	10	10	**Midnight Mary**	*Joey Powers* . . . Amy 892

★ HIGHEST DEBUT ★ POS 65	★ BIGGEST MOVER ★ 58 to 31
A Fool Never Learns ....*Andy Williams*	Um, Um, Um, Um, Um, Um ....*Major Lance*

Billboard 🔴 JANUARY 18, 1964 🔴 HOT 100.

TW	LW	WK		
①	1	8	**There! I've Said It Again**	*Bobby Vinton* . . . Epic 9638
②	2	11	**Louie Louie**	*The Kingsmen* . . . Wand 143
③	3	9	**Popsicles And Icicles**	*The Murmaids* . . . Chattahoochee 628
④	5	11	**Forget Him**	*Bobby Rydell* . . . Cameo 280
⑤	7	7	**Surfin' Bird**	*The Trashmen* . . . Garrett 4002
⑥	4	11	**Dominique**	*The Singing Nun* . . . Philips 40152
❼	19	6	**Hey Little Cobra**	*The Rip Chords* . . . Columbia 42921
⑧	8	10	**The Nitty Gritty**	*Shirley Ellis* . . . Congress 202
⑨	20	7	**Out Of Limits**	*The Marketts* . . . Warner 5391
⑩	13	7	**Drag City**	*Jan & Dean* . . . Liberty 55641

★ HIGHEST DEBUT ★ POS 45	★ BIGGEST MOVER ★ 78 to 53
I Want To Hold Your Hand ....*The Beatles*	Java...*Al Hirt*

Billboard — JANUARY 25, 1964 — HOT 100

TW	LW	WK	Title	Artist	Label
①	1	9	There! I've Said It Again	Bobby Vinton	Epic 9638
②	2	12	Louie Louie	The Kingsmen	Wand 143
❸	45	2	I Want To Hold Your Hand	The Beatles	Capitol 5112
④	5	8	Surfin' Bird	The Trashmen	Garrett 4002
⑤	3	10	Popsicles And Icicles	The Murmaids	Chattahoochee 628
❻	9	8	Out Of Limits	The Marketts	Warner 5391
⑦	7	7	Hey Little Cobra	The Rip Chords	Columbia 42921
⑧	4	12	Forget Him	Bobby Rydell	Cameo 280
❾	14	4	Um, Um, Um, Um, Um, Um	Major Lance	Okeh 7187
⑩	10	8	Drag City	Jan & Dean	Liberty 55641

★ **HIGHEST DEBUT** ★ POS 66
Stop And Think It Over ....Dale & Grace

★ **BIGGEST MOVER** ★ 45 to 3
I Want To Hold Your Hand ....The Beatles

Billboard — FEBRUARY 1, 1964 — HOT 100

TW	LW	WK	Title	Artist	Label
①	3	3	I Want To Hold Your Hand	The Beatles	Capitol 5112
❷	13	6	You Don't Own Me	Lesley Gore	Mercury 72206
❸	6	9	Out Of Limits	The Marketts	Warner 5391
④	4	9	Surfin' Bird	The Trashmen	Garrett 4002
⑤	7	8	Hey Little Cobra	The Rip Chords	Columbia 42921
⑥	2	13	Louie Louie	The Kingsmen	Wand 143
⑦	1	10	There! I've Said It Again	Bobby Vinton	Epic 9638
⑧	9	5	Um, Um, Um, Um, Um, Um	Major Lance	Okeh 7187
❾	16	9	Anyone Who Had A Heart	Dionne Warwick	Scepter 1262
⑩	14	6	For You	Rick Nelson	Decca 31574

★ **HIGHEST DEBUT** ★ POS 64
Vaya Con Dios ....The Drifters

★ **BIGGEST MOVER** ★ 69 to 21
She Loves You ....The Beatles

Billboard — FEBRUARY 8, 1964 — HOT 100

TW	LW	WK	Title	Artist	Label
①	1	4	I Want To Hold Your Hand	The Beatles	Capitol 5112
②	2	7	You Don't Own Me	Lesley Gore	Mercury 72206
③	3	10	Out Of Limits	The Marketts	Warner 5391
④	5	9	Hey Little Cobra	The Rip Chords	Columbia 42921
❺	8	6	Um, Um, Um, Um, Um, Um	Major Lance	Okeh 7187
⑥	4	10	Surfin' Bird	The Trashmen	Garrett 4002
❼	21	3	She Loves You	The Beatles	Swan 4152
⑧	10	7	For You	Rick Nelson	Decca 31574
⑨	9	10	Anyone Who Had A Heart	Dionne Warwick	Scepter 1262
⑩	7	11	There! I've Said It Again	Bobby Vinton	Epic 9638

★ **HIGHEST DEBUT** ★ POS 68
I Saw Her Standing There ....The Beatles

★ **BIGGEST MOVER** ★ 75 to 24
Dawn (Go Away) ....The Four Seasons

Billboard — FEBRUARY 15, 1964 — HOT 100

TW	LW	WK	Title	Artist
①	1	5	I Want To Hold Your Hand	The Beatles ... Capitol 5112
②	2	8	You Don't Own Me	Lesley Gore ... Mercury 72206
❸	7	4	She Loves You	The Beatles ... Swan 4152
④	4	10	Hey Little Cobra	The Rip Chords ... Columbia 42921
⑤	5	7	Um, Um, Um, Um, Um, Um	Major Lance ... Okeh 7187
⑥	8	8	For You	Rick Nelson ... Decca 31574
⑦	3	11	Out Of Limits	The Marketts ... Warner 5391
⑧	9	11	Anyone Who Had A Heart	Dionne Warwick ... Scepter 1262
⑨	13	7	Java	Al Hirt ... RCA 8280
⑩	11	10	What Kind Of Fool (Do You Think I Am)	The Tams ... ABC-Paramount 10502

★ **HIGHEST DEBUT** ★ POS 67
My Bonnie .... The Beatles with Tony Sheridan

★ **BIGGEST MOVER** ★ 95 to 61
Bird Dance Beat .... The Trashmen

Billboard — FEBRUARY 22, 1964 — HOT 100

TW	LW	WK	Title	Artist
①	1	6	I Want To Hold Your Hand	The Beatles ... Capitol 5112
②	3	5	She Loves You	The Beatles ... Swan 4152
❸	11	4	Dawn (Go Away)	The Four Seasons ... Philips 40166
④	2	9	You Don't Own Me	Lesley Gore ... Mercury 72206
❺	9	8	Java	Al Hirt ... RCA 8280
⑥	5	8	Um, Um, Um, Um, Um, Um	Major Lance ... Okeh 7187
⑦	4	11	Hey Little Cobra	The Rip Chords ... Columbia 42921
⑧	14	5	California Sun	The Rivieras ... Riviera 1401
⑨	10	11	What Kind Of Fool (Do You Think I Am)	The Tams ... ABC-Paramount 10502
⑩	21	5	Navy Blue	Diane Renay ... 20th Century 456

★ **HIGHEST DEBUT** ★ POS 63
Kissin' Cousins .... Elvis Presley

★ **BIGGEST MOVER** ★ 69 to 27
Fun, Fun, Fun .... The Beach Boys

Billboard — FEBRUARY 29, 1964 — HOT 100

TW	LW	WK	Title	Artist
①	1	7	I Want To Hold Your Hand	The Beatles ... Capitol 5112
②	2	6	She Loves You	The Beatles ... Swan 4152
③	3	5	Dawn (Go Away)	The Four Seasons ... Philips 40166
④	5	9	Java	Al Hirt ... RCA 8280
❺	8	6	California Sun	The Rivieras ... Riviera 1401
⑥	29	5	Please Please Me	The Beatles ... Vee-Jay 581
⑦	4	10	You Don't Own Me	Lesley Gore ... Mercury 72206
⑧	10	6	Navy Blue	Diane Renay ... 20th Century 456
⑨	12	6	Stop And Think It Over	Dale & Grace ... Montel 922
⑩	6	9	Um, Um, Um, Um, Um, Um	Major Lance ... Okeh 7187

★ **HIGHEST DEBUT** ★ POS 65
My Heart Belongs To Only You .... Bobby Vinton

★ **BIGGEST MOVER** ★ 29 to 6
Please Please Me .... The Beatles

TW	LW	WK	Billboard	MARCH 7, 1964	HOT 100
①	1	8	**I Want To Hold Your Hand**	.......................The Beatles ...	Capitol 5112
②	2	7	She Loves You	.......................The Beatles ...	Swan 4152
③	3	6	**Dawn (Go Away)**	.......................The Four Seasons ...	Philips 40166
④	6	6	Please Please Me	.......................The Beatles ...	Vee-Jay 581
⑤	4	10	Java	.......................Al Hirt ...	RCA 8280
⑥	5	7	California Sun	.......................The Rivieras ...	Riviera 1401
⑦	8	7	Navy Blue	.......................Diane Renay ...	20th Century 456
⑧	9	7	**Stop And Think It Over**	.......................Dale & Grace ...	Montel 922
❾	17	4	Fun, Fun, Fun	.......................The Beach Boys ...	Capitol 5118
⑩	12	9	See The Funny Little Clown	...........Bobby Goldsboro ...	United Artists 672

★ **HIGHEST DEBUT** ★ POS 72
(You Can't Let The Boy Overpower) The Man In You ....The Miracles

★ **BIGGEST MOVER** ★ 78 to 44
It Hurts Me ....Elvis Presley

TW	LW	WK	Billboard	MARCH 14, 1964	HOT 100
①	1	9	**I Want To Hold Your Hand**	.......................The Beatles ...	Capitol 5112
②	2	8	She Loves You	.......................The Beatles ...	Swan 4152
③	4	7	**Please Please Me**	.......................The Beatles ...	Vee-Jay 581
④	3	7	Dawn (Go Away)	.......................The Four Seasons ...	Philips 40166
⑤	5	11	Java	.......................Al Hirt ...	RCA 8280
⑥	7	8	**Navy Blue**	.......................Diane Renay ...	20th Century 456
⑦	9	5	Fun, Fun, Fun	.......................The Beach Boys ...	Capitol 5118
⑧	6	8	California Sun	.......................The Rivieras ...	Riviera 1401
⑨	10	10	**See The Funny Little Clown**	......Bobby Goldsboro ...	United Artists 672
⑩	11	7	I Love You More And More Every Day	.............Al Martino ...	Capitol 5108

★ **HIGHEST DEBUT** ★ POS 55
Twist And Shout........................The Beatles

★ **BIGGEST MOVER** ★ 75 to 46
Needles And Pins ....The Searchers

TW	LW	WK	Billboard	MARCH 21, 1964	HOT 100
①	2	9	**She Loves You**	.......................The Beatles ...	Swan 4152
②	1	10	I Want To Hold Your Hand	.......................The Beatles ...	Capitol 5112
③	3	8	**Please Please Me**	.......................The Beatles ...	Vee-Jay 581
④	4	8	Dawn (Go Away)	.......................The Four Seasons ...	Philips 40166
⑤	7	6	**Fun, Fun, Fun**	.......................The Beach Boys ...	Capitol 5118
⑥	6	9	**Navy Blue**	.......................Diane Renay ...	20th Century 456
❼	55	2	Twist And Shout	.......................The Beatles ...	Tollie 9001
⑧	5	12	Java	.......................Al Hirt ...	RCA 8280
⑨	10	8	I Love You More And More Every Day	.....Al Martino ...	Capitol 5108
❿	13	6	Hello, Dolly!	.......................Louis Armstrong ...	Kapp 573

★ **HIGHEST DEBUT** ★ POS 73
We Love You Beatles........................The Carefrees

★ **BIGGEST MOVER** ★ 55 to 7
Twist And Shout........................The Beatles

TW	LW	WK	Billboard.	MARCH 28, 1964	HOT 100.
①	1	10	**She Loves You**..*The Beatles* . . . Swan 4152
②	2	11	**I Want To Hold Your Hand**..............................*The Beatles* . . . Capitol 5112
❸	7	3	**Twist And Shout**...*The Beatles* . . . Tollie 9001
④	3	9	**Please Please Me**...*The Beatles* . . . Vee-Jay 581
⑤	4	9	**Dawn (Go Away)**......................................*The Four Seasons* . . . Philips 40166
⑥	5	7	**Fun, Fun, Fun**..*The Beach Boys* . . . Capitol 5118
❼	19	6	**Suspicion**..*Terry Stafford* . . . Crusader 101
⑧	10	7	**Hello, Dolly!**...*Louis Armstrong* . . . Kapp 573
⑨	13	5	**My Heart Belongs To Only You**.................*Bobby Vinton* . . . Epic 9662
⑩	15	7	**Glad All Over**.......................................*The Dave Clark Five* . . . Epic 9656

★ *HIGHEST DEBUT* ★ POS 27	★ *BIGGEST MOVER* ★ 54 to 23
Can't Buy Me Love ....*The Beatles*	You're A Wonderful One.................*Marvin Gaye*

TW	LW	WK	Billboard.	APRIL 4, 1964	HOT 100.
❶	27	2	**Can't Buy Me Love** ....*The Beatles* . . . Capitol 5150
②	3	4	**Twist And Shout** ....*The Beatles* . . . Tollie 9001
③	1	11	**She Loves You** ....*The Beatles* . . . Swan 4152
④	2	12	**I Want To Hold Your Hand**..........................*The Beatles* . . . Capitol 5112
⑤	4	10	**Please Please Me**.......................................*The Beatles* . . . Vee-Jay 581
⑥	7	7	**Suspicion**..*Terry Stafford* . . . Crusader 101
⑦	8	8	**Hello, Dolly!**...*Louis Armstrong* . . . Kapp 573
❽	16	6	**The Shoop Shoop Song (It's In His Kiss)**.........................*Betty Everett* . . . Vee-Jay 585
⑨	9	6	**My Heart Belongs To Only You** ....*Bobby Vinton* . . . Epic 9662
⑩	10	8	**Glad All Over**...*The Dave Clark Five* . . . Epic 9656

★ *HIGHEST DEBUT* ★ POS 48	★ *BIGGEST MOVER* ★ 72 to 39
Bits And Pieces ....*The Dave Clark Five*	That's The Way Boys Are...............*Lesley Gore*

TW	LW	WK	Billboard.	APRIL 11, 1964	HOT 100.
①	1	3	**Can't Buy Me Love** ....*The Beatles* . . . Capitol 5150
②	2	5	**Twist And Shout** ....*The Beatles* . . . Tollie 9001
❸	6	8	**Suspicion** ....*Terry Stafford* . . . Crusader 101
④	3	12	**She Loves You** ....*The Beatles* . . . Swan 4152
⑤	7	9	**Hello, Dolly!** ....*Louis Armstrong* . . . Kapp 573
⑥	8	7	**The Shoop Shoop Song (It's In His Kiss)**..................*Betty Everett* . . . Vee-Jay 585
⑦	4	13	**I Want To Hold Your Hand**..........................*The Beatles* . . . Capitol 5112
⑧	10	9	**Glad All Over**...*The Dave Clark Five* . . . Epic 9656
⑨	5	11	**Please Please Me**.......................................*The Beatles* . . . Vee-Jay 581
⑩	14	7	**Don't Let The Rain Come Down (Crooked Little Man)** ....*The Serendipity Singers* . . . Philips 40175

★ *HIGHEST DEBUT* ★ POS 59	★ *BIGGEST MOVER* ★ 46 to 14
Ronnie ....*The 4 Seasons*	Do You Want To Know A Secret.......*The Beatles*

Billboard — APRIL 18, 1964 — HOT 100

TW	LW	WK	Title	Artist ... Label
①	1	4	**Can't Buy Me Love**	*The Beatles* ... Capitol 5150
②	2	6	**Twist And Shout**	*The Beatles* ... Tollie 9001
③	3	9	**Suspicion**	*Terry Stafford* ... Crusader 101
④	5	10	Hello, Dolly!	*Louis Armstrong* ... Kapp 573
❺	14	4	Do You Want To Know A Secret	*The Beatles* ... Vee-Jay 587
⑥	6	8	**The Shoop Shoop Song (It's In His Kiss)**	*Betty Everett* ... Vee-Jay 585
⑦	8	10	Glad All Over	*The Dave Clark Five* ... Epic 9656
⑧	4	13	She Loves You	*The Beatles* ... Swan 4152
⑨	10	8	Don't Let The Rain Come Down (Crooked Little Man)	*The Serendipity Singers* ... Philips 40175
⑩	15	7	Dead Man's Curve	*Jan & Dean* ... Liberty 55672

★ **HIGHEST DEBUT** ★ POS 66
Slip-In Mules ... *Sugar Pie DeSanto*

★ **BIGGEST MOVER** ★ 77 to 44
Kiss Me Sailor ... *Diane Renay*

Billboard — APRIL 25, 1964 — HOT 100

TW	LW	WK	Title	Artist ... Label
①	1	5	**Can't Buy Me Love**	*The Beatles* ... Capitol 5150
②	2	7	**Twist And Shout**	*The Beatles* ... Tollie 9001
③	5	5	**Do You Want To Know A Secret**	*The Beatles* ... Vee-Jay 587
④	4	11	Hello, Dolly!	*Louis Armstrong* ... Kapp 573
⑤	3	10	Suspicion	*Terry Stafford* ... Crusader 101
⑥	7	11	**Glad All Over**	*The Dave Clark Five* ... Epic 9656
❼	11	4	**Bits And Pieces**	*The Dave Clark Five* ... Epic 9671
⑧	9	9	Don't Let The Rain Come Down (Crooked Little Man)	*The Serendipity Singers* ... Philips 40175
❾	14	4	My Guy	*Mary Wells* ... Motown 1056
⑩	10	8	Dead Man's Curve	*Jan & Dean* ... Liberty 55672

★ **HIGHEST DEBUT** ★ POS 77
The Wonder Of You ... *Ray Peterson*

★ **BIGGEST MOVER** ★ 60 to 28
It's Over ... *Roy Orbison*

Billboard — MAY 2, 1964 — HOT 100

TW	LW	WK	Title	Artist ... Label
①	1	6	**Can't Buy Me Love**	*The Beatles* ... Capitol 5150
②	4	12	Hello, Dolly!	*Louis Armstrong* ... Kapp 573
③	3	6	Do You Want To Know A Secret	*The Beatles* ... Vee-Jay 587
❹	7	5	**Bits And Pieces**	*The Dave Clark Five* ... Epic 9671
❺	9	5	My Guy	*Mary Wells* ... Motown 1056
⑥	8	10	**Don't Let The Rain Come Down (Crooked Little Man)**	*The Serendipity Singers* ... Philips 40175
⑦	2	8	Twist And Shout	*The Beatles* ... Tollie 9001
⑧	5	11	Suspicion	*Terry Stafford* ... Crusader 101
⑨	10	9	Dead Man's Curve	*Jan & Dean* ... Liberty 55672
⑩	17	4	Ronnie	*The 4 Seasons* ... Philips 40185

★ **HIGHEST DEBUT** ★ POS 53
Do You Love Me ... *The Dave Clark Five*

★ **BIGGEST MOVER** ★ 67 to 32
Love Me Do ... *The Beatles*

Billboard — MAY 9, 1964 — HOT 100

TW	LW	WK	Title	Artist	Label
1	2	13	Hello, Dolly!	Louis Armstrong	Kapp 573
2	3	7	Do You Want To Know A Secret	The Beatles	Vee-Jay 587
3	5	6	My Guy	Mary Wells	Motown 1056
4	4	6	Bits And Pieces	The Dave Clark Five	Epic 9671
5	1	7	Can't Buy Me Love	The Beatles	Capitol 5150
6	6	11	Don't Let The Rain Come Down (Crooked Little Man)	The Serendipity Singers	Philips 40175
7	10	5	Ronnie	The 4 Seasons	Philips 40185
8	9	10	Dead Man's Curve	Jan & Dean	Liberty 55672
9	8	12	Suspicion	Terry Stafford	Crusader 101
10	11	10	White On White	Danny Williams	United Artists 685

★ HIGHEST DEBUT ★ POS 64
P.S. I Love You ....The Beatles

★ BIGGEST MOVER ★ 72 to 42
Chapel Of Love.............................The Dixie Cups

Billboard — MAY 16, 1964 — HOT 100

TW	LW	WK	Title	Artist	Label
1	3	7	My Guy	Mary Wells	Motown 1056
2	1	14	Hello, Dolly!	Louis Armstrong	Kapp 573
3	12	6	Love Me Do	The Beatles	Tollie 9008
4	4	7	Bits And Pieces	The Dave Clark Five	Epic 9671
5	2	8	Do You Want To Know A Secret	The Beatles	Vee-Jay 587
6	7	6	Ronnie	The 4 Seasons	Philips 40185
7	6	12	Don't Let The Rain Come Down (Crooked Little Man)	The Serendipity Singers	Philips 40175
8	8	11	Dead Man's Curve	Jan & Dean	Liberty 55672
9	10	11	White On White	Danny Williams	United Artists 685
10	13	6	It's Over	Roy Orbison	Monument 837

★ HIGHEST DEBUT ★ POS 76
Tears And Roses ....Al Martino

★ BIGGEST MOVER ★ 76 to 30
A World Without Love.................Peter & Gordon

Billboard — MAY 23, 1964 — HOT 100

TW	LW	WK	Title	Artist	Label
1	1	8	My Guy	Mary Wells	Motown 1056
2	3	7	Love Me Do	The Beatles	Tollie 9008
3	2	15	Hello, Dolly!	Louis Armstrong	Kapp 573
4	14	4	Chapel Of Love	The Dixie Cups	Red Bird 001
5	12	7	Love Me With All Your Heart	The Ray Charles Singers	Command 4046
6	4	8	Bits And Pieces	The Dave Clark Five	Epic 9671
7	13	7	(Just Like) Romeo & Juliet	The Reflections	Golden World 9
8	6	7	Ronnie	The 4 Seasons	Philips 40185
9	10	7	It's Over	Roy Orbison	Monument 837
10	30	3	A World Without Love	Peter & Gordon	Capitol 5175

★ HIGHEST DEBUT ★ POS 50
What'd I Say.................................Elvis Presley

★ BIGGEST MOVER ★ 76 to 52
Tears And Roses ....Al Martino

TW	LW	WK	Billboard.		MAY 30, 1964		HOT 100.
①	2	8	**Love Me Do** ....*The Beatles* . . . Tollie 9008
②	4	5	Chapel Of Love ....*The Dixie Cups* . . . Red Bird 001
③	1	9	My Guy ....*Mary Wells* . . . Motown 1056
④	5	8	Love Me With All Your Heart................. *The Ray Charles Singers* . . . Command 4046
⑤	3	16	Hello, Dolly! ....*Louis Armstrong* . . . Kapp 573
⑥	7	8	**(Just Like) Romeo & Juliet** ....*The Reflections* . . . Golden World 9
❼	10	4	A World Without Love ....*Peter & Gordon* . . . Capitol 5175
❽	11	7	Little Children., ...*Billy J. Kramer* . . . Imperial 66027
⑨	9	8	**It's Over** ....*Roy Orbison* . . . Monument 837
❿	16	6	Walk On By ....*Dionne Warwick* . . . Scepter 1274

★ **HIGHEST DEBUT** ★ POS 69
Don't Throw Your Love Away........*The Searchers*

★ **BIGGEST MOVER** ★ 90 to 48
My Boy Lollipop................................*Millie Small*

TW	LW	WK	Billboard.		JUNE 6, 1964		HOT 100.
①	2	6	**Chapel Of Love** ....*The Dixie Cups* . . . Red Bird 001
②	1	9	Love Me Do ....*The Beatles* . . . Tollie 9008
③	3	10	My Guy ....*Mary Wells* . . . Motown 1056
④	4	9	Love Me With All Your Heart............................. *The Ray Charles Singers* . . . Command 4046
⑤	5	17	Hello, Dolly! ....*Louis Armstrong* . . . Kapp 573
⑥	7	5	A World Without Love ....*Peter & Gordon* . . . Capitol 5175
❼	10	7	Walk On By...*Dionne Warwick* . . . Scepter 1274
⑧	8	8	Little Children...........................*Billy J. Kramer* . . . Imperial 66027
⑨	6	9	(Just Like) Romeo & Juliet ....*The Reflections* . . . Golden World 9
❿	11	5	**P.S. I Love You**................................*The Beatles* . . . Tollie 9008

★ **HIGHEST DEBUT** ★ POS 77
Good Times.....................................*Sam Cooke*

★ **BIGGEST MOVER** ★ 78 to 43
No Particular Place To Go...............*Chuck Berry*

TW	LW	WK	Billboard.		JUNE 13, 1964		HOT 100.
①	1	7	**Chapel Of Love** ....*The Dixie Cups* . . . Red Bird 001
❷	6	6	A World Without Love ....*Peter & Gordon* . . . Capitol 5175
③	4	10	**Love Me With All Your Heart**...................... *The Ray Charles Singers* . . . Command 4046
④	2	10	Love Me Do ....*The Beatles* . . . Tollie 9008
⑤	3	11	My Guy ....*Mary Wells* . . . Motown 1056
⑥	7	8	**Walk On By**...*Dionne Warwick* . . . Scepter 1274
⑦	8	9	**Little Children** ....*Billy J. Kramer* . . . Imperial 66027
⑧	5	18	Hello, Dolly! ....*Louis Armstrong* . . . Kapp 573
❾	12	11	People ....*Barbra Streisand* . . . Columbia 42965
❿	17	4	I Get Around ....*The Beach Boys* . . . Capitol 5174

★ **HIGHEST DEBUT** ★ POS 68
Can't You See That She's Mine............*The Dave Clark Five*

★ **BIGGEST MOVER** ★ 61 to 26
Bad To Me ....*Billy J. Kramer*

Billboard — JUNE 20, 1964 — HOT 100

TW	LW	WK			
①	1	8	**Chapel Of Love**	The Dixie Cups	Red Bird 001
②	2	7	A World Without Love	Peter & Gordon	Capitol 5175
❸	10	5	I Get Around	The Beach Boys	Capitol 5174
④	3	11	Love Me With All Your Heart	The Ray Charles Singers	Command 4046
❺	16	5	My Boy Lollipop	Millie Small	Smash 1893
⑥	6	9	**Walk On By**	Dionne Warwick	Scepter 1274
⑦	4	11	Love Me Do	The Beatles	Tollie 9008
⑧	9	12	People	Barbra Streisand	Columbia 42965
❾	20	5	Don't Let The Sun Catch You Crying	Gerry & The Pacemakers	Laurie 3251
⑩	11	10	**Diane**	The Bachelors	London 9639

★ **HIGHEST DEBUT** ★ POS 53
Rag Doll ....The 4 Seasons

★ **BIGGEST MOVER** ★ 68 to 31
Can't You See That She's Mine..........The Dave Clark Five

Billboard — JUNE 27, 1964 — HOT 100

TW	LW	WK			
①	2	8	**A World Without Love**	Peter & Gordon	Capitol 5175
②	3	6	I Get Around	The Beach Boys	Capitol 5174
③	1	9	Chapel Of Love	The Dixie Cups	Red Bird 001
④	5	6	My Boy Lollipop	Millie Small	Smash 1893
❺	8	13	**People**	Barbra Streisand	Columbia 42965
❻	15	5	Memphis	Johnny Rivers	Imperial 66032
⑦	9	6	Don't Let The Sun Catch You Crying	Gerry & The Pacemakers	Laurie 3251
⑧	4	12	Love Me With All Your Heart	The Ray Charles Singers	Command 4046
❾	16	5	**Bad To Me**	Billy J. Kramer	Imperial 66027
⑩	6	10	Walk On By	Dionne Warwick	Scepter 1274

★ **HIGHEST DEBUT** ★ POS 60
The Little Old Lady (From Pasadena) ....Jan & Dean

★ **BIGGEST MOVER** ★ 53 to 18
Rag Doll ....The 4 Seasons

Billboard — JULY 4, 1964 — HOT 100

TW	LW	WK			
①	2	7	**I Get Around**	The Beach Boys	Capitol 5174
②	4	7	**My Boy Lollipop**	Millie Small	Smash 1893
❸	6	6	**Memphis**	Johnny Rivers	Imperial 66032
❹	7	7	**Don't Let The Sun Catch You Crying**	Gerry & The Pacemakers	Laurie 3251
⑤	5	14	**People**	Barbra Streisand	Columbia 42965
⑥	1	9	A World Without Love	Peter & Gordon	Capitol 5175
⑦	3	10	Chapel Of Love	The Dixie Cups	Red Bird 001
❽	18	3	Rag Doll	The 4 Seasons	Philips 40211
❾	9	6	**Bad To Me**	Billy J. Kramer	Imperial 66027
⑩	16	4	Can't You See That She's Mine	The Dave Clark Five	Epic 9692

★ **HIGHEST DEBUT** ★ POS 74
I Want To Hold Your Hand..............Boston Pops Orchestra

★ **BIGGEST MOVER** ★ 60 to 22
The Little Old Lady (From Pasadena) ....Jan & Dean

Billboard HOT 100 — JULY 11, 1964

TW	LW	WK	Title	Artist	Label
①	1	8	I Get Around	The Beach Boys	Capitol 5174
②	3	7	Memphis	Johnny Rivers	Imperial 66032
❸	8	4	Rag Doll	The 4 Seasons	Philips 40211
④	4	8	Don't Let The Sun Catch You Crying	Gerry & The Pacemakers	Laurie 3251
❺	10	5	Can't You See That She's Mine	The Dave Clark Five	Epic 9692
⑥	2	8	My Boy Lollipop	Millie Small	Smash 1893
⑦	5	15	People	Barbra Streisand	Columbia 42965
⑧	6	10	A World Without Love	Peter & Gordon	Capitol 5175
⑨	12	6	The Girl From Ipanema	Stan Getz/Astrud Gilberto	Verve 10323
⑩	11	8	No Particular Place To Go	Chuck Berry	Chess 1898

★ **HIGHEST DEBUT** ★ POS 75
Sugar Lips .... Al Hirt

★ **BIGGEST MOVER** ★ 62 to 31
Under The Boardwalk .... The Drifters

Billboard HOT 100 — JULY 18, 1964

TW	LW	WK	Title	Artist	Label
①	3	5	Rag Doll	The 4 Seasons	Philips 40211
②	2	8	Memphis	Johnny Rivers	Imperial 66032
③	1	9	I Get Around	The Beach Boys	Capitol 5174
④	5	6	Can't You See That She's Mine	The Dave Clark Five	Epic 9692
❺	9	7	The Girl From Ipanema	Stan Getz/Astrud Gilberto	Verve 10323
❻	12	4	The Little Old Lady (From Pasadena)	Jan & Dean	Liberty 55704
⑦	4	9	Don't Let The Sun Catch You Crying	Gerry & The Pacemakers	Laurie 3251
❽	13	6	Dang Me	Roger Miller	Smash 1881
⑨	6	9	My Boy Lollipop	Millie Small	Smash 1893
⑩	18	7	Keep On Pushing	The Impressions	ABC-Paramount 10554

★ **HIGHEST DEBUT** ★ POS 21
A Hard Day's Night .... The Beatles

★ **BIGGEST MOVER** ★ 100 to 58
C'mon And Swim .... Bobby Freeman

Billboard HOT 100 — JULY 25, 1964

TW	LW	WK	Title	Artist	Label
①	1	6	Rag Doll	The 4 Seasons	Philips 40211
❷	21	2	A Hard Day's Night	The Beatles	Capitol 5222
③	3	10	I Get Around	The Beach Boys	Capitol 5174
④	2	9	Memphis	Johnny Rivers	Imperial 66032
⑤	5	8	The Girl From Ipanema	Stan Getz/Astrud Gilberto	Verve 10323
⑥	6	5	The Little Old Lady (From Pasadena)	Jan & Dean	Liberty 55704
⑦	4	7	Can't You See That She's Mine	The Dave Clark Five	Epic 9692
⑧	8	7	Dang Me	Roger Miller	Smash 1881
⑨	12	6	Wishin' And Hopin'	Dusty Springfield	Philips 40207
⑩	10	8	Keep On Pushing	The Impressions	ABC-Paramount 10554

★ **HIGHEST DEBUT** ★ POS 75
I Should Have Known Better .... The Beatles

★ **BIGGEST MOVER** ★ 72 to 47
People Say .... The Dixie Cups

TW	LW	WK	Billboard		AUGUST 1, 1964		HOT 100.
①	2	3	**A Hard Day's Night**		*The Beatles* ...		Capitol 5222
②	1	7	Rag Doll		*The 4 Seasons* ...		Philips 40211
❸	6	6	**The Little Old Lady (From Pasadena)**		*Jan & Dean*		... Liberty 55704
❹	11	6	Everybody Loves Somebody		*Dean Martin* ...		Reprise 0281
❺	18	4	Where Did Our Love Go		*The Supremes* ...		Motown 1060
❻	9	7	**Wishin' And Hopin'**		*Dusty Springfield* ...		Philips 40207
⑦	8	8	**Dang Me**		*Roger Miller* ...		Smash 1881
⑧	3	11	I Get Around		*The Beach Boys* ...		Capitol 5174
⑨	4	10	Memphis		*Johnny Rivers* ...		Imperial 66032
⑩	5	9	The Girl From Ipanema		*Stan Getz/Astrud Gilberto* ...		Verve 10323

★ HIGHEST DEBUT ★ POS 60	★ BIGGEST MOVER ★ 85 to 54
Because ....*The Dave Clark Five*	I'll Keep You Satisfied ....*Billy J. Kramer*

TW	LW	WK	Billboard		AUGUST 8, 1964		HOT 100.
①	1	4	**A Hard Day's Night**		*The Beatles* ...		Capitol 5222
②	4	7	**Everybody Loves Somebody**		*Dean Martin* ...		Reprise 0281
③	5	5	**Where Did Our Love Go**		*The Supremes* ...		Motown 1060
④	3	7	**The Little Old Lady (From Pasadena)**		*Jan & Dean* ...		Liberty 55704
⑤	2	8	Rag Doll		*The 4 Seasons* ...		Philips 40211
⑥	6	8	**Wishin' And Hopin'**		*Dusty Springfield* ...		Philips 40207
❼	11	7	Under The Boardwalk		*The Drifters* ...		Atlantic 2237
⑧	7	9	Dang Me		*Roger Miller* ...		Smash 1881
❾	15	8	**I Wanna Love Him So Bad**		*The Jelly Beans* ...		Red Bird 10003
⑩	8	12	I Get Around		*The Beach Boys* ...		Capitol 5174

★ HIGHEST DEBUT ★ POS 60	★ BIGGEST MOVER ★ 60 to 22
The House Of The Rising Sun ....*The Animals*	Because ....*The Dave Clark Five*

TW	LW	WK	Billboard		AUGUST 15, 1964		HOT 100.
①	2	8	**Everybody Loves Somebody**		*Dean Martin* ...		Reprise 0281
②	3	6	**Where Did Our Love Go**		*The Supremes* ...		Motown 1060
③	1	5	A Hard Day's Night		*The Beatles* ...		Capitol 5222
④	5	9	Rag Doll		*The 4 Seasons* ...		Philips 40211
⑤	7	8	Under The Boardwalk		*The Drifters* ...		Atlantic 2237
⑥	6	9	**Wishin' And Hopin'**		*Dusty Springfield* ...		Philips 40207
⑦	4	8	**The Little Old Lady (From Pasadena)**		*Jan & Dean* ...		Liberty 55704
❽	13	6	C'mon And Swim		*Bobby Freeman* ...		Autumn 2
⑨	9	9	**I Wanna Love Him So Bad**		*The Jelly Beans* ...		Red Bird 10003
⑩	60	2	The House Of The Rising Sun		*The Animals* ...		MGM 13264

★ HIGHEST DEBUT ★ POS 56	★ BIGGEST MOVER ★ 60 to 10
Bread And Butter ....*The Newbeats*	The House Of The Rising Sun ....*The Animals*

Billboard 🎵 AUGUST 22, 1964 🎵 HOT 100.

TW	LW	WK	Title	Artist	Label
①	2	7	**Where Did Our Love Go**	*The Supremes*	Motown 1060
②	1	9	Everybody Loves Somebody	*Dean Martin*	Reprise 0281
③	3	6	A Hard Day's Night	*The Beatles*	Capitol 5222
④	5	9	**Under The Boardwalk**	*The Drifters*	Atlantic 2237
⑤	10	3	The House Of The Rising Sun	*The Animals*	MGM 13264
⑥	8	7	C'mon And Swim	*Bobby Freeman*	Autumn 2
⑦	14	4	Because	*The Dave Clark Five*	Epic 9704
⑧	13	7	**Walk-Don't Run '64**	*The Ventures*	Dolton 96
⑨	6	10	Wishin' And Hopin'	*Dusty Springfield*	Philips 40207
⑩	16	7	How Do You Do It?	*Gerry & The Pacemakers*	Laurie 3261

★ **HIGHEST DEBUT** ★ POS 66
I'm On The Outside (Looking In).....*Little Anthony & The Imperials*

★ **BIGGEST MOVER** ★ 90 to 54
Baby I Need Your Loving ....*Four Tops*

Billboard 🎵 AUGUST 29, 1964 🎵 HOT 100.

TW	LW	WK	Title	Artist	Label
①	1	8	**Where Did Our Love Go**	*The Supremes*	Motown 1060
②	5	4	The House Of The Rising Sun	*The Animals*	MGM 13264
③	2	10	Everybody Loves Somebody	*Dean Martin*	Reprise 0281
④	3	7	A Hard Day's Night	*The Beatles*	Capitol 5222
⑤	6	8	**C'mon And Swim**	*Bobby Freeman*	Autumn 2
⑥	4	10	Under The Boardwalk	*The Drifters*	Atlantic 2237
⑦	7	5	Because	*The Dave Clark Five*	Epic 9704
⑧	8	8	**Walk-Don't Run '64**	*The Ventures*	Dolton 96
⑨	23	3	Bread And Butter	*The Newbeats*	Hickory 1269
⑩	10	8	How Do You Do It?	*Gerry & The Pacemakers*	Laurie 3261

★ **HIGHEST DEBUT** ★ POS 51
Oh, Pretty Woman ....*Roy Orbison*

★ **BIGGEST MOVER** ★ 78 to 47
Remember (Walkin' In The Sand)...............*The Shangri-Las*

Billboard 🎵 SEPTEMBER 5, 1964 🎵 HOT 100.

TW	LW	WK	Title	Artist	Label
①	2	5	**The House Of The Rising Sun**	*The Animals*	MGM 13264
②	1	9	Where Did Our Love Go	*The Supremes*	Motown 1060
③	3	11	Everybody Loves Somebody	*Dean Martin*	Reprise 0281
④	7	6	Because	*The Dave Clark Five*	Epic 9704
⑤	5	9	**C'mon And Swim**	*Bobby Freeman*	Autumn 2
⑥	9	4	Bread And Butter	*The Newbeats*	Hickory 1269
⑦	6	11	Under The Boardwalk	*The Drifters*	Atlantic 2237
⑧	4	8	A Hard Day's Night	*The Beatles*	Capitol 5222
⑨	10	9	**How Do You Do It?**	*Gerry & The Pacemakers*	Laurie 3261
⑩	15	6	G.T.O.	*Ronny & The Daytonas*	Mala 481

★ **HIGHEST DEBUT** ★ POS 58
Do Wah Diddy Diddy ....*Manfred Mann*

★ **BIGGEST MOVER** ★ 47 to 13
Remember (Walkin' In The Sand)...............*The Shangri-Las*

Billboard — SEPTEMBER 12, 1964 — HOT 100

TW	LW	WK	Title	Artist	Label
①	1	6	The House Of The Rising Sun	The Animals	MGM 13264
②	2	10	Where Did Our Love Go	The Supremes	Motown 1060
③	4	7	Because	The Dave Clark Five	Epic 9704
④	3	12	Everybody Loves Somebody	Dean Martin	Reprise 0281
⑤	6	5	Bread And Butter	The Newbeats	Hickory 1269
⑥	5	10	C'mon And Swim	Bobby Freeman	Autumn 2
❼	10	7	G.T.O.	Ronny & The Daytonas	Mala 481
⑧	8	9	A Hard Day's Night	The Beatles	Capitol 5222
⑨	13	4	Remember (Walkin' In The Sand)	The Shangri-Las	Red Bird 008
⑩	27	3	Oh, Pretty Woman	Roy Orbison	Monument 851

★ HIGHEST DEBUT ★ POS 65
Girl (Why You Wanna Make Me Blue) .... The Temptations

★ BIGGEST MOVER ★ 81 to 42
Matchbox .... The Beatles

Billboard — SEPTEMBER 19, 1964 — HOT 100

TW	LW	WK	Title	Artist	Label
①	1	7	The House Of The Rising Sun	The Animals	MGM 13264
❷	5	6	Bread And Butter	The Newbeats	Hickory 1269
③	2	11	Where Did Our Love Go	The Supremes	Motown 1060
❹	10	4	Oh, Pretty Woman	Roy Orbison	Monument 851
⑤	7	8	G.T.O.	Ronny & The Daytonas	Mala 481
⑥	4	13	Everybody Loves Somebody	Dean Martin	Reprise 0281
⑦	9	5	Remember (Walkin' In The Sand)	The Shangri-Las	Red Bird 008
⑧	3	8	Because	The Dave Clark Five	Epic 9704
⑨	31	3	Do Wah Diddy Diddy	Manfred Mann	Ascot 2157
⑩	25	5	Dancing In The Street	Martha & The Vandellas	Gordy 7033

★ HIGHEST DEBUT ★ POS 78
That's What Love Is Made Of .... The Miracles

★ BIGGEST MOVER ★ 96 to 71
Funny Girl .... Barbra Streisand

Billboard — SEPTEMBER 26, 1964 — HOT 100

TW	LW	WK	Title	Artist	Label
❶	4	5	Oh, Pretty Woman	Roy Orbison	Monument 851
②	2	7	Bread And Butter	The Newbeats	Hickory 1269
③	1	8	The House Of The Rising Sun	The Animals	MGM 13264
④	5	9	G.T.O.	Ronny & The Daytonas	Mala 481
⑤	7	6	Remember (Walkin' In The Sand)	The Shangri-Las	Red Bird 008
❻	9	4	Do Wah Diddy Diddy	Manfred Mann	Ascot 2157
⑦	3	12	Where Did Our Love Go	The Supremes	Motown 1060
⑧	10	6	Dancing In The Street	Martha & The Vandellas	Gordy 7033
⑨	16	11	It Hurts To Be In Love	Gene Pitney	Musicor 1040
⑩	18	5	Save It For Me	The 4 Seasons	Philips 40225

★ HIGHEST DEBUT ★ POS 66
I Like It .... Gerry & The Pacemakers

★ BIGGEST MOVER ★ 81 to 52
Baby Don't You Do It .... Marvin Gaye

Billboard — OCTOBER 3, 1964 — HOT 100

TW	LW	WK		
1	1	6	**Oh, Pretty Woman**	Roy Orbison . . . Monument 851
2	6	5	Do Wah Diddy Diddy	Manfred Mann . . . Ascot 2157
3	2	8	Bread And Butter	The Newbeats . . . Hickory 1269
4	8	7	Dancing In The Street	Martha & The Vandellas . . . Gordy 7033
5	5	7	**Remember (Walkin' In The Sand)**	The Shangri-Las . . . Red Bird 008
6	4	10	G.T.O.	Ronny & The Daytonas . . . Mala 481
7	9	12	**It Hurts To Be In Love**	Gene Pitney . . . Musicor 1040
8	3	9	The House Of The Rising Sun	The Animals . . . MGM 13264
9	14	9	We'll Sing In The Sunshine	Gale Garnett . . . RCA 8388
10	10	6	**Save It For Me**	The 4 Seasons . . . Philips 40225

★ **HIGHEST DEBUT** ★ POS 51
Baby Love . . . The Supremes

★ **BIGGEST MOVER** ★ 81 to 55
I Don't Want To See Tomorrow . . . Nat King Cole

Billboard — OCTOBER 10, 1964 — HOT 100

TW	LW	WK		
1	1	7	**Oh, Pretty Woman**	Roy Orbison . . . Monument 851
2	2	6	Do Wah Diddy Diddy	Manfred Mann . . . Ascot 2157
3	4	8	Dancing In The Street	Martha & The Vandellas . . . Gordy 7033
4	3	9	Bread And Butter	The Newbeats . . . Hickory 1269
5	5	8	**Remember (Walkin' In The Sand)**	The Shangri-Las . . . Red Bird 008
6	9	10	We'll Sing In The Sunshine	Gale Garnett . . . RCA 8388
7	7	13	It Hurts To Be In Love	Gene Pitney . . . Musicor 1040
8	6	11	G.T.O.	Ronny & The Daytonas . . . Mala 481
9	14	6	Last Kiss	J. Frank Wilson & The Cavaliers . . . Josie 923
10	12	9	A Summer Song	Chad Stuart & Jeremy Clyde . . . World Artists 1027

★ **HIGHEST DEBUT** ★ POS 76
Ain't That Loving You Baby . . . Elvis Presley

★ **BIGGEST MOVER** ★ 94 to 68
So Long Dearie . . . Louis Armstrong

Billboard — OCTOBER 17, 1964 — HOT 100

TW	LW	WK		
1	2	7	**Do Wah Diddy Diddy**	Manfred Mann . . . Ascot 2157
2	3	9	**Dancing In The Street**	Martha & The Vandellas . . . Gordy 7033
3	1	8	Oh, Pretty Woman	Roy Orbison . . . Monument 851
4	6	11	**We'll Sing In The Sunshine**	Gale Garnett . . . RCA 8388
5	9	7	**Last Kiss**	J. Frank Wilson & The Cavaliers . . . Josie 923
6	5	9	Remember (Walkin' In The Sand)	The Shangri-Las . . . Red Bird 008
7	10	10	**A Summer Song**	Chad Stuart & Jeremy Clyde . . . World Artists 1027
8	7	14	It Hurts To Be In Love	Gene Pitney . . . Musicor 1040
9	11	7	**When I Grow Up (To Be A Man)**	The Beach Boys . . . Capitol 5245
10	14	7	Let It Be Me	Betty Everett & Jerry Butler . . . Vee-Jay 613

★ **HIGHEST DEBUT** ★ POS 68
Is It True . . . Brenda Lee

★ **BIGGEST MOVER** ★ 76 to 47
Ain't That Loving You Baby . . . Elvis Presley

Billboard ● OCTOBER 24, 1964 ● HOT 100

TW	LW	WK	Title	Artist	Label
①	1	8	**Do Wah Diddy Diddy**	Manfred Mann	Ascot 2157
②	2	10	**Dancing In The Street**	Martha & The Vandellas	Gordy 7033
③	5	8	**Last Kiss**	J. Frank Wilson & The Cavaliers	Josie 923
④	4	12	**We'll Sing In The Sunshine**	Gale Garnett	RCA 8388
⑤	3	9	**Oh, Pretty Woman**	Roy Orbison	Monument 851
⑥	12	4	**Baby Love**	The Supremes	Motown 1066
⑦	7	11	**A Summer Song**	Chad Stuart & Jeremy Clyde	World Artists 1027
⑧	10	8	**Let It Be Me**	Betty Everett & Jerry Butler	Vee-Jay 613
⑨	9	8	**When I Grow Up (To Be A Man)**	The Beach Boys	Capitol 5245
⑩	20	6	**Have I The Right?**	The Honeycombs	Interphon 7707

★ **HIGHEST DEBUT** ★ POS 74
I'm Gonna Be Strong ....Gene Pitney

★ **BIGGEST MOVER** ★ 59 to 20
Leader Of The Pack ....The Shangri-Las

Billboard ● OCTOBER 31, 1964 ● HOT 100

TW	LW	WK	Title	Artist	Label
❶	6	5	**Baby Love**	The Supremes	Motown 1066
②	1	9	**Do Wah Diddy Diddy**	Manfred Mann	Ascot 2157
③	3	9	**Last Kiss**	J. Frank Wilson & The Cavaliers	Josie 923
④	4	13	**We'll Sing In The Sunshine**	Gale Garnett	RCA 8388
⑤	2	11	**Dancing In The Street**	Martha & The Vandellas	Gordy 7033
⑥	8	9	**Let It Be Me**	Betty Everett & Jerry Butler	Vee-Jay 613
❼	10	7	**Have I The Right?**	The Honeycombs	Interphon 7707
⑧	5	10	**Oh, Pretty Woman**	Roy Orbison	Monument 851
⑨	11	8	**Little Honda**	The Hondells	Mercury 72324
⑩	12	9	**Chug-A-Lug**	Roger Miller	Smash 1926

★ **HIGHEST DEBUT** ★ POS 62
Ringo ....Lorne Greene

★ **BIGGEST MOVER** ★ 89 to 64
You Should Have Seen The Way He Looked At Me.................................The Dixie Cups

Billboard ● NOVEMBER 7, 1964 ● HOT 100

TW	LW	WK	Title	Artist	Label
①	1	6	**Baby Love**	The Supremes	Motown 1066
②	3	10	**Last Kiss**	J. Frank Wilson & The Cavaliers	Josie 923
③	2	10	**Do Wah Diddy Diddy**	Manfred Mann	Ascot 2157
④	14	5	**Leader Of The Pack**	The Shangri-Las	Red Bird 014
⑤	6	10	**Let It Be Me**	Betty Everett & Jerry Butler	Vee-Jay 613
⑥	7	8	**Have I The Right?**	The Honeycombs	Interphon 7707
❼	11	9	**Come A Little Bit Closer**	Jay & The Americans	United Artists 759
❽	12	7	**The Door Is Still Open To My Heart**	Dean Martin	Reprise 0307
⑨	10	10	**Chug-A-Lug**	Roger Miller	Smash 1926
⑩	4	14	**We'll Sing In The Sunshine**	Gale Garnett	RCA 8388

★ **HIGHEST DEBUT** ★ POS 75
Goin' Out Of My Head..........Little Anthony & The Imperials

★ **BIGGEST MOVER** ★ 78 to 40
Everything's Alright ....The Newbeats

Billboard NOVEMBER 14, 1964 HOT 100

TW	LW	WK	Title	Artist	Label
1	1	7	Baby Love	The Supremes	Motown 1066
2	4	6	Leader Of The Pack	The Shangri-Las	Red Bird 014
3	2	11	Last Kiss	J. Frank Wilson & The Cavaliers	Josie 923
4	7	10	Come A Little Bit Closer	Jay & The Americans	United Artists 759
5	6	9	Have I The Right?	The Honeycombs	Interphon 7707
6	8	8	The Door Is Still Open To My Heart	Dean Martin	Reprise 0307
7	3	11	Do Wah Diddy Diddy	Manfred Mann	Ascot 2157
8	5	11	Let It Be Me	Betty Everett & Jerry Butler	Vee-Jay 613
9	22	5	She's Not There	The Zombies	Parrot 9695
10	28	3	Ringo	Lorne Greene	RCA 8444

★ HIGHEST DEBUT ★ POS 66
Come See About Me .... The Supremes

★ BIGGEST MOVER ★ 61 to 33
Mountain Of Love .... Johnny Rivers

Billboard NOVEMBER 21, 1964 HOT 100

TW	LW	WK	Title	Artist	Label
1	1	8	Baby Love	The Supremes	Motown 1066
2	2	7	Leader Of The Pack	The Shangri-Las	Red Bird 014
3	4	11	Come A Little Bit Closer	Jay & The Americans	United Artists 759
4	3	12	Last Kiss	J. Frank Wilson & The Cavaliers	Josie 923
5	9	6	She's Not There	The Zombies	Parrot 9695
6	10	4	Ringo	Lorne Greene	RCA 8444
7	5	10	Have I The Right?	The Honeycombs	Interphon 7707
8	13	9	You Really Got Me	The Kinks	Reprise 0306
9	6	9	The Door Is Still Open To My Heart	Dean Martin	Reprise 0307
10	18	6	Time Is On My Side	The Rolling Stones	London 9708

★ HIGHEST DEBUT ★ POS 81
The Wedding .... Julie Rogers

★ BIGGEST MOVER ★ 66 to 31
Come See About Me .... The Supremes

Billboard NOVEMBER 28, 1964 HOT 100

TW	LW	WK	Title	Artist	Label
1	2	8	Leader Of The Pack	The Shangri-Las	Red Bird 014
2	1	9	Baby Love	The Supremes	Motown 1066
3	3	12	Come A Little Bit Closer	Jay & The Americans	United Artists 759
4	5	7	She's Not There	The Zombies	Parrot 9695
5	6	5	Ringo	Lorne Greene	RCA 8444
6	11	5	Mr. Lonely	Bobby Vinton	Epic 9730
7	8	10	You Really Got Me	The Kinks	Reprise 0306
8	10	7	Time Is On My Side	The Rolling Stones	London 9708
9	4	13	Last Kiss	J. Frank Wilson & The Cavaliers	Josie 923
10	19	5	Mountain Of Love	Johnny Rivers	Imperial 66075

★ HIGHEST DEBUT ★ POS 68
Without The One You Love .... Four Tops

★ BIGGEST MOVER ★ 96 to 59
Amen .... The Impressions

Billboard • DECEMBER 5, 1964 • HOT 100

TW	LW	WK	Title	Artist	Label
❶	5	6	Ringo	Lorne Greene	RCA 8444
❷	6	6	Mr. Lonely	Bobby Vinton	Epic 9730
③	1	9	Leader Of The Pack	The Shangri-Las	Red Bird 014
④	4	8	She's Not There	The Zombies	Parrot 9695
⑤	2	10	Baby Love	The Supremes	Motown 1066
⑥	8	8	Time Is On My Side	The Rolling Stones	London 9708
⑦	7	11	You Really Got Me	The Kinks	Reprise 0306
❽	13	4	Come See About Me	The Supremes	Motown 1068
⑨	10	6	Mountain Of Love	Johnny Rivers	Imperial 66075
⑩	11	7	I'm Gonna Be Strong	Gene Pitney	Musicor 1045

★ HIGHEST DEBUT ★ POS 22	★ BIGGEST MOVER ★ 81 to 50
I Feel Fine................The Beatles	As Tears Go By ....Marianne Faithfull

Billboard • DECEMBER 12, 1964 • HOT 100

TW	LW	WK	Title	Artist	Label
①	2	7	Mr. Lonely	Bobby Vinton	Epic 9730
②	4	9	She's Not There	The Zombies	Parrot 9695
③	1	7	Ringo	Lorne Greene	RCA 8444
❹	8	5	Come See About Me	The Supremes	Motown 1068
❺	22	2	I Feel Fine	The Beatles	Capitol 5327
⑥	6	9	Time Is On My Side	The Rolling Stones	London 9708
⑦	7	12	You Really Got Me	The Kinks	Reprise 0306
⑧	5	11	Baby Love	The Supremes	Motown 1066
⑨	10	8	I'm Gonna Be Strong	Gene Pitney	Musicor 1045
⑩	13	6	Dance, Dance, Dance	The Beach Boys	Capitol 5306

★ HIGHEST DEBUT ★ POS 70	★ BIGGEST MOVER ★ 80 to 58
You're Nobody Till Somebody Loves You ....Dean Martin	Leader Of The Laundromat..........The Detergents

Billboard • DECEMBER 19, 1964 • HOT 100

TW	LW	WK	Title	Artist	Label
❶	4	6	Come See About Me	The Supremes	Motown 1068
❷	5	3	I Feel Fine	The Beatles	Capitol 5327
③	1	8	Mr. Lonely	Bobby Vinton	Epic 9730
④	2	10	She's Not There	The Zombies	Parrot 9695
⑤	3	8	Ringo	Lorne Greene	RCA 8444
⑥	6	10	Time Is On My Side	The Rolling Stones	London 9708
❼	14	7	Goin' Out Of My Head	Little Anthony & The Imperials	DCP 1119
⑧	10	7	Dance, Dance, Dance	The Beach Boys	Capitol 5306
⑨	9	9	I'm Gonna Be Strong	Gene Pitney	Musicor 1045
⑩	7	13	You Really Got Me	The Kinks	Reprise 0306

★ HIGHEST DEBUT ★ POS 75	★ BIGGEST MOVER ★ 58 to 33
Hold What You've Got ....Joe Tex	Leader Of The Laundromat..........The Detergents

TW	LW	WK	Billboard.	DECEMBER 26, 1964	HOT 100.
①	2	4	**I Feel Fine**	*The Beatles* . . .	Capitol 5327
②	1	7	**Come See About Me**	*The Supremes* . . .	Motown 1068
③	3	9	**Mr. Lonely**	*Bobby Vinton* . . .	Epic 9730
❹	14	4	**She's A Woman**	*The Beatles* . . .	Capitol 5327
⑤	4	11	**She's Not There**	*The Zombies* . . .	Parrot 9695
⑥	7	8	**Goin' Out Of My Head**	*Little Anthony & The Imperials* . . .	DCP 1119
⑦	5	9	**Ringo**	*Lorne Greene* . . .	RCA 8444
⑧	8	8	**Dance, Dance, Dance**	*The Beach Boys* . . .	Capitol 5306
❾	12	7	**The Jerk**	*The Larks* . . .	Money 106
⑩	6	11	**Time Is On My Side**	*The Rolling Stones* . . .	London 9708

★ *HIGHEST DEBUT* ★ POS 69	★ *BIGGEST MOVER* ★ 87 to 41
All Day And All Of The Night *The Kinks*	**Downtown** *Petula Clark*

Billboard — JANUARY 2, 1965 — HOT 100

TW	LW	WK	Title	Artist ... Label
①	1	5	I Feel Fine	The Beatles ... Capitol 5327
②	2	8	Come See About Me	The Supremes ... Motown 1068
③	3	10	Mr. Lonely	Bobby Vinton ... Epic 9730
④	4	5	She's A Woman	The Beatles ... Capitol 5327
❺	11	6	Love Potion Number Nine	The Searchers ... Kapp 27
⑥	6	9	Goin' Out Of My Head	Little Anthony & The Imperials ... DCP 1119
⑦	5	12	She's Not There	The Zombies ... Parrot 9695
❽	12	7	Amen	The Impressions ... ABC-Paramount 10602
⑨	9	8	The Jerk	The Larks ... Money 106
❿	14	7	The Wedding	Julie Rogers ... Mercury 72332

★ **HIGHEST DEBUT** ★ POS 78
Paper Tiger ......Sue Thompson

★ **BIGGEST MOVER** ★ 41 to 12
Downtown ......Petula Clark

Billboard — JANUARY 9, 1965 — HOT 100

TW	LW	WK	Title	Artist ... Label
①	1	6	I Feel Fine	The Beatles ... Capitol 5327
②	2	9	Come See About Me	The Supremes ... Motown 1068
③	3	11	Mr. Lonely	Bobby Vinton ... Epic 9730
④	5	7	Love Potion Number Nine	The Searchers ... Kapp 27
❺	12	4	Downtown	Petula Clark ... Warner 5494
⑥	6	10	Goin' Out Of My Head	Little Anthony & The Imperials ... DCP 1119
⑦	8	8	Amen	The Impressions ... ABC-Paramount 10602
⑧	9	9	The Jerk	The Larks ... Money 106
⑨	14	5	You've Lost That Lovin' Feelin'	The Righteous Brothers ... Philles 124
❿	10	8	The Wedding	Julie Rogers ... Mercury 72332

★ **HIGHEST DEBUT** ★ POS 73
Shake ......Sam Cooke

★ **BIGGEST MOVER** ★ 90 to 71
Use Your Head ......Mary Wells

Billboard — JANUARY 16, 1965 — HOT 100

TW	LW	WK	Title	Artist ... Label
①	2	10	Come See About Me	The Supremes ... Motown 1068
②	1	7	I Feel Fine	The Beatles ... Capitol 5327
③	4	8	Love Potion Number Nine	The Searchers ... Kapp 27
④	5	5	Downtown	Petula Clark ... Warner 5494
❺	9	6	You've Lost That Lovin' Feelin'	The Righteous Brothers ... Philles 124
⑥	3	12	Mr. Lonely	Bobby Vinton ... Epic 9730
⑦	8	10	The Jerk	The Larks ... Money 106
⑧	6	11	Goin' Out Of My Head	Little Anthony & The Imperials ... DCP 1119
⑨	15	9	How Sweet It Is To Be Loved By You	Marvin Gaye ... Tamla 54107
❿	13	9	Keep Searchin'	Del Shannon ... Amy 915

★ **HIGHEST DEBUT** ★ POS 65
This Diamond Ring ......Gary Lewis & The Playboys

★ **BIGGEST MOVER** ★ 73 to 36
Shake ......Sam Cooke

Billboard — JANUARY 23, 1965 — HOT 100

TW	LW	WK			
1	4	6	Downtown	Petula Clark	Warner 5494
2	5	7	You've Lost That Lovin' Feelin'	The Righteous Brothers	Philles 124
3	3	9	Love Potion Number Nine	The Searchers	Kapp 27
4	2	8	I Feel Fine	The Beatles	Capitol 5327
5	1	11	Come See About Me	The Supremes	Motown 1068
6	20	7	The Name Game	Shirley Ellis	Congress 230
7	6	13	Mr. Lonely	Bobby Vinton	Epic 9730
8	7	11	The Jerk	The Larks	Money 106
9	9	10	How Sweet It Is To Be Loved By You	Marvin Gaye	Tamla 54107
10	10	10	Keep Searchin'	Del Shannon	Amy 915

★ HIGHEST DEBUT ★ POS 75
Lemon Tree.....................................Trini Lopez

★ BIGGEST MOVER ★ 65 to 34
This Diamond Ring ......Gary Lewis & The Playboys

Billboard — JANUARY 30, 1965 — HOT 100

TW	LW	WK			
1	1	7	Downtown	Petula Clark	Warner 5494
2	2	8	You've Lost That Lovin' Feelin'	The Righteous Brothers	Philles 124
3	6	8	The Name Game	Shirley Ellis	Congress 230
4	3	10	Love Potion Number Nine	The Searchers	Kapp 27
5	11	7	Hold What You've Got	Joe Tex	Dial 4001
6	9	11	How Sweet It Is To Be Loved By You	Marvin Gaye	Tamla 54107
7	34	3	This Diamond Ring	Gary Lewis & The Playboys	Liberty 55756
8	5	12	Come See About Me	The Supremes	Motown 1068
9	10	11	Keep Searchin'	Del Shannon	Amy 915
10	19	6	All Day And All Of The Night	The Kinks	Reprise 0334

★ HIGHEST DEBUT ★ POS 63
King Of The Road ....Roger Miller

★ BIGGEST MOVER ★ 61 to 29
Bye, Bye, Baby (Baby Goodbye)..............The 4 Seasons

Billboard — FEBRUARY 6, 1965 — HOT 100

TW	LW	WK			
1	2	9	You've Lost That Lovin' Feelin'	The Righteous Brothers	Philles 124
2	1	8	Downtown	Petula Clark	Warner 5494
3	3	9	The Name Game	Shirley Ellis	Congress 230
4	7	4	This Diamond Ring	Gary Lewis & The Playboys	Liberty 55756
5	5	8	Hold What You've Got	Joe Tex	Dial 4001
6	4	11	Love Potion Number Nine	The Searchers	Kapp 27
7	10	7	All Day And All Of The Night	The Kinks	Reprise 0334
8	12	4	My Girl	The Temptations	Gordy 7038
9	6	12	How Sweet It Is To Be Loved By You	Marvin Gaye	Tamla 54107
10	15	5	Shake	Sam Cooke	RCA 8486

★ HIGHEST DEBUT ★ POS 61
Ferry Across The Mersey.................Gerry & The Pacemakers

★ BIGGEST MOVER ★ 68 to 40
The Birds And The Bees ....Jewel Akens

Billboard — FEBRUARY 13, 1965 — HOT 100

TW	LW	WK		
①	1	10	**You've Lost That Lovin' Feelin'**..................	*The Righteous Brothers* ... Philles 124
②	2	9	**Downtown**	*Petula Clark* ... Warner 5494
③	4	5	**This Diamond Ring**	*Gary Lewis & The Playboys* ... Liberty 55756
④	3	10	**The Name Game**	*Shirley Ellis* ... Congress 230
❺	8	5	**My Girl**	*The Temptations* ... Gordy 7038
⑥	5	9	**Hold What You've Got**	*Joe Tex* ... Dial 4001
⑦	7	8	**All Day And All Of The Night**	*The Kinks* ... Reprise 0334
⑧	10	6	**Shake**	*Sam Cooke* ... RCA 8486
⑨	14	6	**The Jolly Green Giant**	*The Kingsmen* ... Wand 172
❿	16	6	**I Go To Pieces**	*Peter & Gordon* ... Capitol 5335

★ **HIGHEST DEBUT** ★ POS 61
Goodnight .... *Roy Orbison*

★ **BIGGEST MOVER** ★ 63 to 38
Hurt So Bad .... *Little Anthony & The Imperials*

Billboard — FEBRUARY 20, 1965 — HOT 100

TW	LW	WK		
①	3	6	**This Diamond Ring**	*Gary Lewis & The Playboys* ... Liberty 55756
②	1	11	**You've Lost That Lovin' Feelin'**.......	*The Righteous Brothers* ... Philles 124
③	2	10	**Downtown**	*Petula Clark* ... Warner 5494
④	5	6	**My Girl**	*The Temptations* ... Gordy 7038
⑤	4	11	**The Name Game**	*Shirley Ellis* ... Congress 230
❻	9	7	**The Jolly Green Giant**	*The Kingsmen* ... Wand 172
⑦	7	9	**All Day And All Of The Night**	*The Kinks* ... Reprise 0334
⑧	8	7	**Shake**	*Sam Cooke* ... RCA 8486
⑨	10	7	**I Go To Pieces**.....................................	*Peter & Gordon* ... Capitol 5335
❿	15	6	**The Boy From New York City**	*The Ad Libs* ... Blue Cat 102

★ **HIGHEST DEBUT** ★ POS 53
Eight Days A Week .... *The Beatles*

★ **BIGGEST MOVER** ★ 61 to 34
Goodnight .... *Roy Orbison*

Billboard — FEBRUARY 27, 1965 — HOT 100

TW	LW	WK		
①	1	7	**This Diamond Ring**	*Gary Lewis & The Playboys* ... Liberty 55756
②	2	12	**You've Lost That Lovin' Feelin'**.......	*The Righteous Brothers* ... Philles 124
③	4	7	**My Girl**	*The Temptations* ... Gordy 7038
④	3	11	**Downtown**	*Petula Clark* ... Warner 5494
⑤	6	8	**The Jolly Green Giant**	*The Kingsmen* ... Wand 172
❻	11	8	**Tell Her No**	*The Zombies* ... Parrot 9723
⑦	8	8	**Shake**	*Sam Cooke* ... RCA 8486
⑧	10	7	**The Boy From New York City**	*The Ad Libs* ... Blue Cat 102
⑨	9	8	**I Go To Pieces**.....................................	*Peter & Gordon* ... Capitol 5335
❿	17	5	**King Of The Road**...................................	*Roger Miller* ... Smash 1965

★ **HIGHEST DEBUT** ★ POS 68
Do The Clam .... *Elvis Presley*

★ **BIGGEST MOVER** ★ 80 to 41
Stop! In The Name Of Love .... *The Supremes*

Billboard — MARCH 6, 1965 — HOT 100

TW	LW	WK	Title	Artist	Label
①	3	8	My Girl	The Temptations	Gordy 7038
②	1	8	This Diamond Ring	Gary Lewis & The Playboys	Liberty 55756
③	2	13	You've Lost That Lovin' Feelin'	The Righteous Brothers	Philles 124
④	5	9	The Jolly Green Giant	The Kingsmen	Wand 172
❺	19	3	Eight Days A Week	The Beatles	Capitol 5371
⑥	6	9	Tell Her No	The Zombies	Parrot 9723
❼	10	6	King Of The Road	Roger Miller	Smash 1965
❽	13	7	The Birds And The Bees	Jewel Akens	Era 3141
⑨	12	5	Ferry Across The Mersey	Gerry & The Pacemakers	Laurie 3284
⑩	4	12	Downtown	Petula Clark	Warner 5494

★ **HIGHEST DEBUT** ★ POS 74
When I'm Gone ....Brenda Holloway

★ **BIGGEST MOVER** ★ 89 to 58
The Race Is On ....Jack Jones

Billboard — MARCH 13, 1965 — HOT 100

TW	LW	WK	Title	Artist	Label
❶	5	4	Eight Days A Week	The Beatles	Capitol 5371
②	1	9	My Girl	The Temptations	Gordy 7038
❸	13	4	Stop! In The Name Of Love	The Supremes	Motown 1074
④	2	9	This Diamond Ring	Gary Lewis & The Playboys	Liberty 55756
❺	8	8	The Birds And The Bees	Jewel Akens	Era 3141
⑥	7	7	King Of The Road	Roger Miller	Smash 1965
⑦	9	6	Ferry Across The Mersey	Gerry & The Pacemakers	Laurie 3284
❽	19	7	Can't You Hear My Heartbeat	Herman's Hermits	MGM 13310
⑨	4	10	The Jolly Green Giant	The Kingsmen	Wand 172
⑩	12	6	Hurt So Bad	Little Anthony & The Imperials	DCP 1128

★ **HIGHEST DEBUT** ★ POS 62
Tired Of Waiting For You ....The Kinks

★ **BIGGEST MOVER** ★ 80 to 48
Long Lonely Nights........................Bobby Vinton

Billboard — MARCH 20, 1965 — HOT 100

TW	LW	WK	Title	Artist	Label
①	1	5	Eight Days A Week	The Beatles	Capitol 5371
②	3	5	Stop! In The Name Of Love	The Supremes	Motown 1074
③	5	9	The Birds And The Bees	Jewel Akens	Era 3141
④	6	8	King Of The Road	Roger Miller	Smash 1965
❺	8	8	Can't You Hear My Heartbeat	Herman's Hermits	MGM 13310
⑥	7	7	Ferry Across The Mersey	Gerry & The Pacemakers	Laurie 3284
⑦	2	10	My Girl	The Temptations	Gordy 7038
⑧	4	10	This Diamond Ring	Gary Lewis & The Playboys	Liberty 55756
⑨	11	8	Goldfinger	Shirley Bassey	United Artists 790
⑩	14	6	Shotgun	Jr. Walker & The All Stars	Soul 35008

★ **HIGHEST DEBUT** ★ POS 63
Game Of Love ....Wayne Fontana & The Mindbenders

★ **BIGGEST MOVER** ★ 71 to 42
I'm Telling You Now.........Freddie & The Dreamers

TW	LW	WK	Billboard ⦿ MARCH 27, 1965 ⦿ HOT 100®
①	2	6	**Stop! In The Name Of Love**.................*The Supremes* . . . Motown 1074
❷	5	9	**Can't You Hear My Heartbeat**.........*Herman's Hermits* . . . MGM 13310
③	3	10	**The Birds And The Bees**............................*Jewel Akens* . . . Era 3141
④	1	6	**Eight Days A Week** ....*The Beatles* . . . Capitol 5371
⑤	4	9	**King Of The Road**..*Roger Miller* . . . Smash 1965
⑥	6	8	**Ferry Across The Mersey** ....*Gerry & The Pacemakers* . . . Laurie 3284
❼	10	7	**Shotgun** ....*Jr. Walker & The All Stars* . . . Soul 35008
⑧	9	9	**Goldfinger**...*Shirley Bassey* . . . United Artists 790
⑨	7	11	**My Girl** ....*The Temptations* . . . Gordy 7038
⑩	8	11	**This Diamond Ring** ....*Gary Lewis & The Playboys* . . . Liberty 55756

★ **HIGHEST DEBUT** ★ POS 79
The Last Time.......................*The Rolling Stones*

★ **BIGGEST MOVER** ★ 94 to 50
I Know A Place................................*Petula Clark*

TW	LW	WK	Billboard ⦿ APRIL 3, 1965 ⦿ HOT 100®
①	1	7	**Stop! In The Name Of Love**.................*The Supremes* . . . Motown 1074
②	2	10	**Can't You Hear My Heartbeat**.........*Herman's Hermits* . . . MGM 13310
❸	20	4	**I'm Telling You Now** ....*Freddie & The Dreamers* . . . Tower 125
❹	7	8	**Shotgun** ....*Jr. Walker & The All Stars* . . . Soul 35008
⑤	3	11	**The Birds And The Bees**....................................*Jewel Akens* . . . Era 3141
⑥	5	10	**King Of The Road**..*Roger Miller* . . . Smash 1965
⑦	4	7	**Eight Days A Week** ....*The Beatles* . . . Capitol 5371
⑧	8	10	**Goldfinger**...*Shirley Bassey* . . . United Artists 790
❾	12	6	**Nowhere To Run** ....*Martha & The Vandellas* . . . Gordy 7039
❿	15	9	**Red Roses For A Blue Lady** ....*Vic Dana* . . . Dolton 304

★ **HIGHEST DEBUT** ★ POS 69
She's About A Mover.............*Sir Douglas Quintet*

★ **BIGGEST MOVER** ★ 79 to 46
The Last Time ....*The Rolling Stones*

TW	LW	WK	Billboard ⦿ APRIL 10, 1965 ⦿ HOT 100®
①	3	5	**I'm Telling You Now**.....................*Freddie & The Dreamers* . . . Tower 125
②	1	8	**Stop! In The Name Of Love** ....*The Supremes* . . . Motown 1074
③	2	11	**Can't You Hear My Heartbeat**.................*Herman's Hermits* . . . MGM 13310
④	4	9	**Shotgun** ....*Jr. Walker & The All Stars* . . . Soul 35008
⑤	5	12	**The Birds And The Bees**....................................*Jewel Akens* . . . Era 3141
⑥	6	11	**King Of The Road**..*Roger Miller* . . . Smash 1965
❼	17	4	**Game Of Love**.............*Wayne Fontana & The Mindbenders* . . . Fontana 1509
⑧	9	7	**Nowhere To Run**....................*Martha & The Vandellas* . . . Gordy 7039
❾	28	4	**I Know A Place** ....*Petula Clark* . . . Warner 5612
⑩	10	10	**Red Roses For A Blue Lady** ....*Vic Dana* . . . Dolton 304

★ **HIGHEST DEBUT** ★ POS 56
Just Once In My Life ....*The Righteous Brothers*

★ **BIGGEST MOVER** ★ 76 to 44
Silhouettes................................*Herman's Hermits*

Billboard — APRIL 17, 1965 — HOT 100

TW	LW	WK			
1	1	6	I'm Telling You Now	Freddie & The Dreamers	Tower 125
2	2	9	Stop! In The Name Of Love	The Supremes	Motown 1074
3	7	5	Game Of Love	Wayne Fontana & The Mindbenders	Fontana 1509
4	9	5	I Know A Place	Petula Clark	Warner 5612
5	4	10	Shotgun	Jr. Walker & The All Stars	Soul 35008
6	3	12	Can't You Hear My Heartbeat	Herman's Hermits	MGM 13310
7	13	6	Tired Of Waiting For You	The Kinks	Reprise 0347
8	8	8	Nowhere To Run	Martha & The Vandellas	Gordy 7039
9	19	5	The Clapping Song	Shirley Ellis	Congress 234
10	15	9	Go Now!	The Moody Blues	London 9726

★ **HIGHEST DEBUT** ★ POS 12
Mrs. Brown You've Got A Lovely Daughter .... Herman's Hermits

★ **BIGGEST MOVER** ★ 62 to 29
Count Me In .... Gary Lewis & The Playboys

Billboard — APRIL 24, 1965 — HOT 100

TW	LW	WK			
1	3	6	Game Of Love	Wayne Fontana & The Mindbenders	Fontana 1509
2	12	2	Mrs. Brown You've Got A Lovely Daughter	Herman's Hermits	MGM 13341
3	1	7	I'm Telling You Now	Freddie & The Dreamers	Tower 125
4	4	6	I Know A Place	Petula Clark	Warner 5612
5	2	10	Stop! In The Name Of Love	The Supremes	Motown 1074
6	7	7	Tired Of Waiting For You	The Kinks	Reprise 0347
7	14	5	I'll Never Find Another You	The Seekers	Capitol 5383
8	9	6	The Clapping Song	Shirley Ellis	Congress 234
9	5	11	Shotgun	Jr. Walker & The All Stars	Soul 35008
10	19	4	Silhouettes	Herman's Hermits	MGM 13332

★ **HIGHEST DEBUT** ★ POS 59
Ticket To Ride .... The Beatles

★ **BIGGEST MOVER** ★ 75 to 48
It's Not Unusual .... Tom Jones

Billboard — MAY 1, 1965 — HOT 100

TW	LW	WK			
1	2	3	Mrs. Brown You've Got A Lovely Daughter	Herman's Hermits	MGM 13341
2	1	7	Game Of Love	Wayne Fontana & The Mindbenders	Fontana 1509
3	4	7	I Know A Place	Petula Clark	Warner 5612
4	3	8	I'm Telling You Now	Freddie & The Dreamers	Tower 125
5	7	6	I'll Never Find Another You	The Seekers	Capitol 5383
6	6	8	Tired Of Waiting For You	The Kinks	Reprise 0347
7	11	5	Count Me In	Gary Lewis & The Playboys	Liberty 55778
8	10	5	Silhouettes	Herman's Hermits	MGM 13332
9	12	6	The Last Time	The Rolling Stones	London 9741
10	5	11	Stop! In The Name Of Love	The Supremes	Motown 1074

★ **HIGHEST DEBUT** ★ POS 66
You Were Made For Me .... Freddie & The Dreamers

★ **BIGGEST MOVER** ★ 59 to 18
Ticket To Ride .... The Beatles

Billboard — MAY 8, 1965 — HOT 100

TW	LW	WK		
①	1	4	**Mrs. Brown You've Got A Lovely Daughter** ....*Herman's Hermits* ... MGM 13341	
❷	7	6	**Count Me In** ....*Gary Lewis & The Playboys* ... Liberty 55778	
❸	18	3	Ticket To Ride..*The Beatles* ... Capitol 5407	
④	2	8	**Game Of Love**.............*Wayne Fontana & The Mindbenders* ... Fontana 1509	
⑤	5	7	**I'll Never Find Another You** ....*The Seekers* ... Capitol 5383	
⑥	3	8	**I Know A Place** ....*Petula Clark* ... Warner 5612	
⑦	8	6	Silhouettes ....*Herman's Hermits* ... MGM 13332	
⑧	4	9	**I'm Telling You Now** ....*Freddie & The Dreamers* ... Tower 125	
⑨	9	7	**The Last Time**................................*The Rolling Stones* ... London 9741	
⑩	12	8	**Cast Your Fate To The Wind**.........*Sounds Orchestral* ... Parkway 942	

★ **HIGHEST DEBUT** ★ POS 73
Last Chance To Turn Around............*Gene Pitney*

★ **BIGGEST MOVER** ★ 68 to 38
Back In My Arms Again ....*The Supremes*

Billboard — MAY 15, 1965 — HOT 100

TW	LW	WK		
①	1	5	**Mrs. Brown You've Got A Lovely Daughter** ....*Herman's Hermits* ... MGM 13341	
②	2	7	**Count Me In** ....*Gary Lewis & The Playboys* ... Liberty 55778	
③	3	4	Ticket To Ride..*The Beatles* ... Capitol 5407	
④	5	8	**I'll Never Find Another You** ....*The Seekers* ... Capitol 5383	
⑤	7	7	**Silhouettes** ....*Herman's Hermits* ... MGM 13332	
❻	21	5	Help Me, Rhonda ....*The Beach Boys* ... Capitol 5395	
⑦	6	9	**I Know A Place** ....*Petula Clark* ... Warner 5612	
❽	11	9	**I'll Be Doggone**...*Marvin Gaye* ... Tamla 54112	
❾	12	6	**Just Once In My Life** ....*The Righteous Brothers* ... Philles 127	
⑩	14	7	Wooly Bully.........................*Sam The Sham & The Pharoahs* ... MGM 13322	

★ **HIGHEST DEBUT** ★ POS 65
Before And After..........................*Chad & Jeremy*

★ **BIGGEST MOVER** ★ 78 to 47
Engine Engine #9 ....*Roger Miller*

Billboard — MAY 22, 1965 — HOT 100

TW	LW	WK		
①	3	5	**Ticket To Ride**...*The Beatles* ... Capitol 5407	
②	1	6	Mrs. Brown You've Got A Lovely Daughter................*Herman's Hermits* ... MGM 13341	
③	2	8	Count Me In..................*Gary Lewis & The Playboys* ... Liberty 55778	
④	6	6	Help Me, Rhonda ....*The Beach Boys* ... Capitol 5395	
⑤	4	9	**I'll Never Find Another You** ....*The Seekers* ... Capitol 5383	
❻	15	4	Back In My Arms Again............................*The Supremes* ... Motown 1075	
⑦	5	8	Silhouettes ....*Herman's Hermits* ... MGM 13332	
⑧	10	8	Wooly Bully.........................*Sam The Sham & The Pharoahs* ... MGM 13322	
⑨	9	7	**Just Once In My Life** ....*The Righteous Brothers* ... Philles 127	
⑩	20	5	**Crying In The Chapel** ....*Elvis Presley* ... RCA 0643	

★ **HIGHEST DEBUT** ★ POS 77
(Remember Me) I'm The One Who Loves
You ....*Dean Martin*

★ **BIGGEST MOVER** ★ 67 to 32
I Can't Help Myself.........................*Four Tops*

Billboard HOT 100 — MAY 29, 1965

TW	LW	WK	Title	Artist	Label
1	4	7	Help Me, Rhonda	The Beach Boys	Capitol 5395
2	1	6	Ticket To Ride	The Beatles	Capitol 5407
3	6	5	Back In My Arms Again	The Supremes	Motown 1075
4	2	7	Mrs. Brown You've Got A Lovely Daughter	Herman's Hermits	MGM 13341
5	8	9	Wooly Bully	Sam The Sham & The Pharoahs	MGM 13322
6	10	6	Crying In The Chapel	Elvis Presley	RCA 0643
7	3	9	Count Me In	Gary Lewis & The Playboys	Liberty 55778
8	5	10	I'll Never Find Another You	The Seekers	Capitol 5383
9	19	7	Just A Little	The Beau Brummels	Autumn 10
10	15	8	It's Not Unusual	Tom Jones	Parrot 9737

★ HIGHEST DEBUT ★ POS 50
Wonderful World .... Herman's Hermits

★ BIGGEST MOVER ★ 77 to 54
(Remember Me) I'm The One Who Loves You .... Dean Martin

Billboard HOT 100 — JUNE 5, 1965

TW	LW	WK	Title	Artist	Label
1	1	8	Help Me, Rhonda	The Beach Boys	Capitol 5395
2	5	10	Wooly Bully	Sam The Sham & The Pharoahs	MGM 13322
3	3	6	Back In My Arms Again	The Supremes	Motown 1075
4	6	7	Crying In The Chapel	Elvis Presley	RCA 0643
5	2	7	Ticket To Ride	The Beatles	Capitol 5407
6	4	8	Mrs. Brown You've Got A Lovely Daughter	Herman's Hermits	MGM 13341
7	17	4	I Can't Help Myself	Four Tops	Motown 1076
8	9	8	Just A Little	The Beau Brummels	Autumn 10
9	19	5	Engine Engine #9	Roger Miller	Smash 1983
10	10	9	It's Not Unusual	Tom Jones	Parrot 9737

★ HIGHEST DEBUT ★ POS 63
Seventh Son .... Johnny Rivers

★ BIGGEST MOVER ★ 55 to 17
Mr. Tambourine Man .... The Byrds

Billboard HOT 100 — JUNE 12, 1965

TW	LW	WK	Title	Artist	Label
1	3	7	Back In My Arms Again	The Supremes	Motown 1075
2	2	11	Wooly Bully	Sam The Sham & The Pharoahs	MGM 13322
3	4	8	Crying In The Chapel	Elvis Presley	RCA 0643
4	7	5	I Can't Help Myself	Four Tops	Motown 1076
5	1	9	Help Me, Rhonda	The Beach Boys	Capitol 5395
6	17	5	Mr. Tambourine Man	The Byrds	Columbia 43271
7	9	6	Engine Engine #9	Roger Miller	Smash 1983
8	25	3	Wonderful World	Herman's Hermits	MGM 13354
9	5	8	Ticket To Ride	The Beatles	Capitol 5407
10	8	9	Just A Little	The Beau Brummels	Autumn 10

★ HIGHEST DEBUT ★ POS 67
(I Can't Get No) Satisfaction .... The Rolling Stones

★ BIGGEST MOVER ★ 77 to 54
Cara, Mia .... Jay & The Americans

Billboard — JUNE 19, 1965 — HOT 100

TW	LW	WK	Title	Artist	Label
❶	4	6	I Can't Help Myself	Four Tops	Motown 1076
❷	6	6	Mr. Tambourine Man	The Byrds	Columbia 43271
③	2	12	Wooly Bully	Sam The Sham & The Pharoahs	MGM 13322
④	3	9	Crying In The Chapel	Elvis Presley	RCA 0643
⑤	1	8	Back In My Arms Again	The Supremes	Motown 1075
⑥	8	4	Wonderful World	Herman's Hermits	MGM 13354
⑦	5	10	Help Me, Rhonda	The Beach Boys	Capitol 5395
⑧	7	7	Engine Engine #9	Roger Miller	Smash 1983
⑨	13	6	For Your Love	The Yardbirds	Epic 9790
⑩	14	9	Hush, Hush, Sweet Charlotte	Patti Page	Columbia 43251

★ **HIGHEST DEBUT** ★ POS 70
(Such An) Easy Question.................Elvis Presley

★ **BIGGEST MOVER** ★ 67 to 26
(I Can't Get No) Satisfaction.............The Rolling Stones

Billboard — JUNE 26, 1965 — HOT 100

TW	LW	WK	Title	Artist	Label
①	2	7	Mr. Tambourine Man	The Byrds	Columbia 43271
②	1	7	I Can't Help Myself	Four Tops	Motown 1076
③	3	13	Wooly Bully	Sam The Sham & The Pharoahs	MGM 13322
❹	26	3	(I Can't Get No) Satisfaction	The Rolling Stones	London 9766
⑤	6	5	Wonderful World	Herman's Hermits	MGM 13354
⑥	4	10	Crying In The Chapel	Elvis Presley	RCA 0643
⑦	9	7	For Your Love	The Yardbirds	Epic 9790
⑧	10	10	Hush, Hush, Sweet Charlotte	Patti Page	Columbia 43251
⑨	7	11	Help Me, Rhonda	The Beach Boys	Capitol 5395
⑩	15	4	Seventh Son	Johnny Rivers	Imperial 66112

★ **HIGHEST DEBUT** ★ POS 67
Theme From "A Summer Place" ....The Lettermen

★ **BIGGEST MOVER** ★ 79 to 41
What's New Pussycat? ....Tom Jones

Billboard — JULY 3, 1965 — HOT 100

TW	LW	WK	Title	Artist	Label
①	2	8	I Can't Help Myself	Four Tops	Motown 1076
②	4	4	(I Can't Get No) Satisfaction	The Rolling Stones	London 9766
③	1	8	Mr. Tambourine Man	The Byrds	Columbia 43271
④	3	14	Wooly Bully	Sam The Sham & The Pharoahs	MGM 13322
⑤	5	6	Wonderful World	Herman's Hermits	MGM 13354
⑥	7	8	For Your Love	The Yardbirds	Epic 9790
⑦	10	5	Seventh Son	Johnny Rivers	Imperial 66112
⑧	6	11	Crying In The Chapel	Elvis Presley	RCA 0643
⑨	12	8	Yes, I'm Ready	Barbara Mason	Arctic 105
⑩	15	7	What The World Needs Now Is Love	Jackie DeShannon	Imperial 66110

★ **HIGHEST DEBUT** ★ POS 42
I'm Henry VIII, I Am ....Herman's Hermits

★ **BIGGEST MOVER** ★ 73 to 49
Sitting In The Park ....Billy Stewart

Billboard — JULY 10, 1965 — HOT 100

TW	LW	WK		
①	2	5	**(I Can't Get No) Satisfaction**..........*The Rolling Stones* ... London 9766
②	1	9	I Can't Help Myself.............................*Four Tops* ... Motown 1076
③	3	9	Mr. Tambourine Man ....*The Byrds* ... Columbia 43271
④	5	7	**Wonderful World** ....*Herman's Hermits* ... MGM 13354
⑤	4	15	Wooly Bully.....................*Sam The Sham & The Pharoahs* ... MGM 13322
❻	9	9	Yes, I'm Ready ....*Barbara Mason* ... Arctic 105
⑦	7	6	**Seventh Son** ....*Johnny Rivers* ... Imperial 66112
❽	11	6	Cara, Mia ....*Jay & The Americans* ... United Artists 881
❾	12	8	You Turn Me On ....*Ian Whitcomb* ... Tower 134
⑩	10	8	What The World Needs Now Is Love ....*Jackie DeShannon* ... Imperial 66110

★ **HIGHEST DEBUT** ★ POS 66
Pretty Little Baby...........................*Marvin Gaye*

★ **BIGGEST MOVER** ★ 42 to 13
I'm Henry VIII, I Am ....*Herman's Hermits*

Billboard — JULY 17, 1965 — HOT 100

TW	LW	WK		
①	1	6	**(I Can't Get No) Satisfaction**..........*The Rolling Stones* ... London 9766
②	2	10	I Can't Help Myself.............................*Four Tops* ... Motown 1076
❸	13	3	I'm Henry VIII, I Am ....*Herman's Hermits* ... MGM 13367
④	3	10	Mr. Tambourine Man ....*The Byrds* ... Columbia 43271
❺	8	7	Cara, Mia ....*Jay & The Americans* ... United Artists 881
⑥	6	10	Yes, I'm Ready ....*Barbara Mason* ... Arctic 105
⑦	7	7	**Seventh Son** ....*Johnny Rivers* ... Imperial 66112
⑧	9	9	**You Turn Me On**...........................*Ian Whitcomb* ... Tower 134
❾	10	9	What The World Needs Now Is Love ....*Jackie DeShannon* ... Imperial 66110
⑩	17	5	**What's New Pussycat?**......................*Tom Jones* ... Parrot 9765

★ **HIGHEST DEBUT** ★ POS 72
Unchained Melody ....*The Righteous Brothers*

★ **BIGGEST MOVER** ★ 99 to 70
One Dyin' And A Buryin' ....*Roger Miller*

Billboard — JULY 24, 1965 — HOT 100

TW	LW	WK		
①	1	7	**(I Can't Get No) Satisfaction**..........*The Rolling Stones* ... London 9766
②	3	4	I'm Henry VIII, I Am ....*Herman's Hermits* ... MGM 13367
③	2	11	I Can't Help Myself.............................*Four Tops* ... Motown 1076
❹	10	6	What's New Pussycat?......................*Tom Jones* ... Parrot 9765
⑤	5	8	Cara, Mia ....*Jay & The Americans* ... United Artists 881
⑥	6	11	Yes, I'm Ready ....*Barbara Mason* ... Arctic 105
⑦	9	10	**What The World Needs Now Is Love** ....*Jackie DeShannon* ... Imperial 66110
⑧	7	8	**Seventh Son** ....*Johnny Rivers* ... Imperial 66112
⑨	4	11	Mr. Tambourine Man ....*The Byrds* ... Columbia 43271
⑩	8	10	You Turn Me On ....*Ian Whitcomb* ... Tower 134

★ **HIGHEST DEBUT** ★ POS 68
Since I Lost My Baby.................*The Temptations*

★ **BIGGEST MOVER** ★ 40 to 13
Save Your Heart For Me...........*Gary Lewis & The Playboys*

Billboard 🔴 JULY 31, 1965 🔴 HOT 100

TW	LW	WK			
①	1	8	(I Can't Get No) Satisfaction	The Rolling Stones	London 9766
②	2	5	I'm Henry VIII, I Am	Herman's Hermits	MGM 13367
③	4	7	What's New Pussycat?	Tom Jones	Parrot 9765
④	5	9	Cara, Mia	Jay & The Americans	United Artists 881
⑤	6	12	Yes, I'm Ready	Barbara Mason	Arctic 105
⑥	3	12	I Can't Help Myself	Four Tops	Motown 1076
⑦	7	11	What The World Needs Now Is Love	Jackie DeShannon	Imperial 66110
⑧	13	5	Save Your Heart For Me	Gary Lewis & The Playboys	Liberty 55809
⑨	12	7	I Like It Like That	The Dave Clark Five	Epic 9811
⑩	8	9	Seventh Son	Johnny Rivers	Imperial 66112

★ **HIGHEST DEBUT** ★ POS 54
It's The Same Old Song ... Four Tops

★ **BIGGEST MOVER** ★ 57 to 22
I Got You Babe ... Sonny & Cher

Billboard 🔴 AUGUST 7, 1965 🔴 HOT 100

TW	LW	WK			
①	2	6	I'm Henry VIII, I Am	Herman's Hermits	MGM 13367
②	1	9	(I Can't Get No) Satisfaction	The Rolling Stones	London 9766
③	3	8	What's New Pussycat?	Tom Jones	Parrot 9765
④	8	6	Save Your Heart For Me	Gary Lewis & The Playboys	Liberty 55809
⑤	22	5	I Got You Babe	Sonny & Cher	Atco 6359
⑥	5	13	Yes, I'm Ready	Barbara Mason	Arctic 105
⑦	9	8	I Like It Like That	The Dave Clark Five	Epic 9811
⑧	4	10	Cara, Mia	Jay & The Americans	United Artists 881
⑨	6	13	I Can't Help Myself	Four Tops	Motown 1076
⑩	14	7	Don't Just Stand There	Patty Duke	United Artists 875

★ **HIGHEST DEBUT** ★ POS 41
Help! ... The Beatles

★ **BIGGEST MOVER** ★ 88 to 47
Nothing But Heartaches ... The Supremes

Billboard 🔴 AUGUST 14, 1965 🔴 HOT 100

TW	LW	WK			
①	5	6	I Got You Babe	Sonny & Cher	Atco 6359
②	2	10	(I Can't Get No) Satisfaction	The Rolling Stones	London 9766
③	4	7	Save Your Heart For Me	Gary Lewis & The Playboys	Liberty 55809
④	1	7	I'm Henry VIII, I Am	Herman's Hermits	MGM 13367
⑤	3	9	What's New Pussycat?	Tom Jones	Parrot 9765
⑥	15	5	Unchained Melody	The Righteous Brothers	Philles 129
⑦	17	3	It's The Same Old Song	Four Tops	Motown 1081
⑧	10	8	Don't Just Stand There	Patty Duke	United Artists 875
⑨	28	4	California Girls	The Beach Boys	Capitol 5464
⑩	14	7	Down In The Boondocks	Billy Joe Royal	Columbia 43305

★ **HIGHEST DEBUT** ★ POS 71
Action ... Freddy Cannon

★ **BIGGEST MOVER** ★ 41 to 14
Help! ... The Beatles

Billboard — AUGUST 21, 1965 — HOT 100

TW	LW	WK	Title	Artist	Label
1	1	7	**I Got You Babe**	Sonny & Cher	Atco 6359
2	3	8	**Save Your Heart For Me**	Gary Lewis & The Playboys	Liberty 55809
3	14	3	**Help!**	The Beatles	Capitol 5476
4	9	5	**California Girls**	The Beach Boys	Capitol 5464
5	6	6	**Unchained Melody**	The Righteous Brothers	Philles 129
6	2	11	**(I Can't Get No) Satisfaction**	The Rolling Stones	London 9766
7	7	4	**It's The Same Old Song**	Four Tops	Motown 1081
8	8	9	**Don't Just Stand There**	Patty Duke	United Artists 875
9	4	8	**I'm Henry VIII, I Am**	Herman's Hermits	MGM 13367
10	10	8	**Down In The Boondocks**	Billy Joe Royal	Columbia 43305

★ **HIGHEST DEBUT** ★ POS 58
Eve Of Destruction .... Barry McGuire

★ **BIGGEST MOVER** ★ 99 to 67
Hang On Sloopy .... The McCoys

Billboard — AUGUST 28, 1965 — HOT 100

TW	LW	WK	Title	Artist	Label
1	1	8	**I Got You Babe**	Sonny & Cher	Atco 6359
2	3	4	**Help!**	The Beatles	Capitol 5476
3	4	6	**California Girls**	The Beach Boys	Capitol 5464
4	5	7	**Unchained Melody**	The Righteous Brothers	Philles 129
5	7	5	**It's The Same Old Song**	Four Tops	Motown 1081
6	16	6	**Like A Rolling Stone**	Bob Dylan	Columbia 43346
7	2	9	**Save Your Heart For Me**	Gary Lewis & The Playboys	Liberty 55809
8	13	10	**Hold Me, Thrill Me, Kiss Me**	Mel Carter	Imperial 66113
9	10	9	**Down In The Boondocks**	Billy Joe Royal	Columbia 43305
10	14	7	**Papa's Got A Brand New Bag**	James Brown	King 5999

★ **HIGHEST DEBUT** ★ POS 70
I'll Make All Your Dreams Come True ..... Ronnie Dove

★ **BIGGEST MOVER** ★ 58 to 27
Eve Of Destruction .... Barry McGuire

Billboard — SEPTEMBER 4, 1965 — HOT 100

TW	LW	WK	Title	Artist	Label
1	2	5	**Help!**	The Beatles	Capitol 5476
2	6	7	**Like A Rolling Stone**	Bob Dylan	Columbia 43346
3	3	7	**California Girls**	The Beach Boys	Capitol 5464
4	4	8	**Unchained Melody**	The Righteous Brothers	Philles 129
5	5	6	**It's The Same Old Song**	Four Tops	Motown 1081
6	1	9	**I Got You Babe**	Sonny & Cher	Atco 6359
7	12	7	**You Were On My Mind**	We Five	A&M 770
8	10	8	**Papa's Got A Brand New Bag**	James Brown	King 5999
9	27	3	**Eve Of Destruction**	Barry McGuire	Dunhill 4009
10	8	11	**Hold Me, Thrill Me, Kiss Me**	Mel Carter	Imperial 66113

★ **HIGHEST DEBUT** ★ POS 80
Some Enchanted Evening ..... Jay & The Americans

★ **BIGGEST MOVER** ★ 49 to 22
Hang On Sloopy .... The McCoys

'65

Billboard — SEPTEMBER 11, 1965 — HOT 100

TW	LW	WK	Title	Artist ... Label
1	1	6	**Help!**	The Beatles ... Capitol 5476
2	2	8	**Like A Rolling Stone**	Bob Dylan ... Columbia 43346
3	9	4	Eve Of Destruction	Barry McGuire ... Dunhill 4009
4	7	8	You Were On My Mind	We Five ... A&M 770
5	3	8	California Girls	The Beach Boys ... Capitol 5464
6	4	9	Unchained Melody	The Righteous Brothers ... Philles 129
7	6	10	I Got You Babe	Sonny & Cher ... Atco 6359
8	8	9	**Papa's Got A Brand New Bag**	James Brown ... King 5999
9	12	6	It Ain't Me Babe	The Turtles ... White Whale 222
10	15	7	The "In" Crowd	Ramsey Lewis Trio ... Argo 5506

★ HIGHEST DEBUT ★ POS 72 — Kansas City Star ... Roger Miller
★ BIGGEST MOVER ★ 83 to 56 — Treat Her Right ... Roy Head

Billboard — SEPTEMBER 18, 1965 — HOT 100

TW	LW	WK	Title	Artist ... Label
1	1	7	**Help!**	The Beatles ... Capitol 5476
2	3	5	Eve Of Destruction	Barry McGuire ... Dunhill 4009
3	2	9	Like A Rolling Stone	Bob Dylan ... Columbia 43346
4	4	9	You Were On My Mind	We Five ... A&M 770
5	13	5	Catch Us If You Can	The Dave Clark Five ... Epic 9833
6	10	8	The "In" Crowd	Ramsey Lewis Trio ... Argo 5506
7	11	6	Hang On Sloopy	The McCoys ... Bang 506
8	9	7	**It Ain't Me Babe**	The Turtles ... White Whale 222
9	7	11	I Got You Babe	Sonny & Cher ... Atco 6359
10	14	8	Heart Full Of Soul	The Yardbirds ... Epic 9823

★ HIGHEST DEBUT ★ POS 64 — Just A Little Bit Better ... Herman's Hermits
★ BIGGEST MOVER ★ 56 to 26 — Treat Her Right ... Roy Head

Billboard — SEPTEMBER 25, 1965 — HOT 100

TW	LW	WK	Title	Artist ... Label
1	2	6	**Eve Of Destruction**	Barry McGuire ... Dunhill 4009
2	7	7	**Hang On Sloopy**	The McCoys ... Bang 506
3	4	10	**You Were On My Mind**	We Five ... A&M 770
4	5	6	**Catch Us If You Can**	The Dave Clark Five ... Epic 9833
5	1	8	Help!	The Beatles ... Capitol 5476
6	6	9	The "In" Crowd	Ramsey Lewis Trio ... Argo 5506
7	3	10	Like A Rolling Stone	Bob Dylan ... Columbia 43346
8	8	8	**It Ain't Me Babe**	The Turtles ... White Whale 222
9	10	9	**Heart Full Of Soul**	The Yardbirds ... Epic 9823
10	14	6	**Laugh At Me**	Sonny ... Atco 6369

★ HIGHEST DEBUT ★ POS 45 — Yesterday ... The Beatles
★ BIGGEST MOVER ★ 88 to 60 — Make Me Your Baby ... Barbara Lewis

TW	LW	WK	Billboard		OCTOBER 2, 1965		HOT 100
①	2	8	**Hang On Sloopy**			*The McCoys* ... Bang 506	
②	1	7	**Eve Of Destruction**			*Barry McGuire* ... Dunhill 4009	
❸	45	2	**Yesterday**			*The Beatles* ... Capitol 5498	
④	4	7	**Catch Us If You Can**			*The Dave Clark Five* ... Epic 9833	
⑤	3	11	**You Were On My Mind**			*We Five* ... A&M 770	
⑥	6	10	**The "In" Crowd**			*Ramsey Lewis Trio* ... Argo 5506	
❼	12	5	**Treat Her Right**			*Roy Head* ... Back Beat 546	
❽	11	7	**You've Got Your Troubles**			*The Fortunes* ... Press 9773	
❾	14	7	**Baby Don't Go**			*Sonny & Cher* ... Reprise 0309	
⑩	10	7	**Laugh At Me**			*Sonny* ... Atco 6369	

★ **HIGHEST DEBUT** ★ POS 66
Positively 4th Street ....*Bob Dylan*

★ **BIGGEST MOVER** ★ 85 to 42
Everybody Loves A Clown........*Gary Lewis & The Playboys*

TW	LW	WK	Billboard		OCTOBER 9, 1965		HOT 100
①	3	3	**Yesterday**..			*The Beatles* ... Capitol 5498	
②	1	9	**Hang On Sloopy**			*The McCoys* ... Bang 506	
❸	7	6	**Treat Her Right**			*Roy Head* ... Back Beat 546	
④	2	8	**Eve Of Destruction**			*Barry McGuire* ... Dunhill 4009	
⑤	6	11	**The "In" Crowd**			*Ramsey Lewis Trio* ... Argo 5506	
⑥	4	8	**Catch Us If You Can**			*The Dave Clark Five* ... Epic 9833	
⑦	8	8	**You've Got Your Troubles**			*The Fortunes* ... Press 9773	
⑧	9	8	**Baby Don't Go**...			*Sonny & Cher* ... Reprise 0309	
⑨	5	12	**You Were On My Mind**			*We Five* ... A&M 770	
⑩	12	8	**Do You Believe In Magic** ....*The Lovin' Spoonful* ... Kama Sutra 201				

★ **HIGHEST DEBUT** ★ POS 64
Get Off Of My Cloud ....*The Rolling Stones*

★ **BIGGEST MOVER** ★ 66 to 34
Positively 4th Street ....*Bob Dylan*

TW	LW	WK	Billboard		OCTOBER 16, 1965		HOT 100
①	1	4	**Yesterday**..			*The Beatles* ... Capitol 5498	
②	3	7	**Treat Her Right**			*Roy Head* ... Back Beat 546	
③	2	10	**Hang On Sloopy**			*The McCoys* ... Bang 506	
❹	19	6	**A Lover's Concerto**			*The Toys* ... DynoVoice 209	
❺	14	6	**Keep On Dancing**			*The Gentrys* ... MGM 13379	
⑥	5	12	**The "In" Crowd**			*Ramsey Lewis Trio* ... Argo 5506	
❼	12	5	**Just A Little Bit Better**.....................*Herman's Hermits* ... MGM 13398				
⑧	8	9	**Baby Don't Go**...			*Sonny & Cher* ... Reprise 0309	
⑨	10	9	**Do You Believe In Magic** ....*The Lovin' Spoonful* ... Kama Sutra 201				
⑩	4	9	**Eve Of Destruction**			*Barry McGuire* ... Dunhill 4009	

★ **HIGHEST DEBUT** ★ POS 80
I Found A Girl ....*Jan & Dean*

★ **BIGGEST MOVER** ★ 64 to 14
Get Off Of My Cloud ....*The Rolling Stones*

Billboard — OCTOBER 23, 1965 — HOT 100

TW	LW	WK		
①	1	5	**Yesterday**..	*The Beatles* ... Capitol 5498
②	2	8	**Treat Her Right**	*Roy Head* ... Back Beat 546
③	4	7	A Lover's Concerto	*The Toys* ... DynoVoice 209
❹	14	3	Get Off Of My Cloud	*The Rolling Stones* ... London 9792
⑤	5	7	Keep On Dancing	*The Gentrys* ... MGM 13379
⑥	3	11	Hang On Sloopy	*The McCoys* ... Bang 506
⑦	7	6	**Just A Little Bit Better**......................	*Herman's Hermits* ... MGM 13398
❽	12	5	Everybody Loves A Clown......	*Gary Lewis & The Playboys* ... Liberty 55818
❾	18	4	Positively 4th Street	*Bob Dylan* ... Columbia 43389
❿	16	6	You're The One	*The Vogues* ... Co & Ce 229

★ **HIGHEST DEBUT** ★ POS 74	★ **BIGGEST MOVER** ★ 48 to 19
My Baby.............................*The Temptations*	1-2-3...*Len Barry*

Billboard — OCTOBER 30, 1965 — HOT 100

TW	LW	WK		
①	1	6	**Yesterday**..	*The Beatles* ... Capitol 5498
②	3	8	**A Lover's Concerto**	*The Toys* ... DynoVoice 209
③	4	4	Get Off Of My Cloud	*The Rolling Stones* ... London 9792
④	5	8	**Keep On Dancing**.......................................	*The Gentrys* ... MGM 13379
❺	8	6	Everybody Loves A Clown......	*Gary Lewis & The Playboys* ... Liberty 55818
⑥	2	9	Treat Her Right	*Roy Head* ... Back Beat 546
❼	10	7	You're The One	*The Vogues* ... Co & Ce 229
⑧	9	5	Positively 4th Street	*Bob Dylan* ... Columbia 43389
⑨	6	12	Hang On Sloopy	*The McCoys* ... Bang 506
❿	19	6	1-2-3	*Len Barry* ... Decca 31827

★ **HIGHEST DEBUT** ★ POS 39	★ **BIGGEST MOVER** ★ 68 to 44
I Hear A Symphony ....*The Supremes*	Where Do You Go...*Cher*

Billboard — NOVEMBER 6, 1965 — HOT 100

TW	LW	WK		
①	3	5	**Get Off Of My Cloud**....................	*The Rolling Stones* ... London 9792
②	2	9	**A Lover's Concerto**	*The Toys* ... DynoVoice 209
③	1	7	Yesterday	*The Beatles* ... Capitol 5498
④	5	7	**Everybody Loves A Clown**	*Gary Lewis & The Playboys* ... Liberty 55818
⑤	4	9	Keep On Dancing	*The Gentrys* ... MGM 13379
⑥	7	8	You're The One...	*The Vogues* ... Co & Ce 229
⑦	8	6	**Positively 4th Street**..................................	*Bob Dylan* ... Columbia 43389
⑧	10	7	1-2-3	*Len Barry* ... Decca 31827
❾	14	6	Rescue Me	*Fontella Bass* ... Checker 1120
❿	15	7	Taste Of Honey......................	*Herb Alpert & The Tijuana Brass* ... A&M 775

★ **HIGHEST DEBUT** ★ POS 74	★ **BIGGEST MOVER** ★ 61 to 31
Kiss Away...*Ronnie Dove*	Turn! Turn! Turn! ....*The Byrds*

'65

TW	LW	WK	Billboard	NOVEMBER 13, 1965	HOT 100
①	1	6	Get Off Of My Cloud	The Rolling Stones	London 9792
②	2	10	A Lover's Concerto	The Toys	DynoVoice 209
③	8	8	1-2-3	Len Barry	Decca 31827
④	6	9	You're The One	The Vogues	Co & Ce 229
⑤	12	3	I Hear A Symphony	The Supremes	Motown 1083
⑥	9	7	Rescue Me	Fontella Bass	Checker 1120
⑦	4	8	Everybody Loves A Clown	Gary Lewis & The Playboys	Liberty 55818
⑧	13	6	Let's Hang On!	The 4 Seasons	Philips 40317
⑨	10	8	Taste Of Honey	Herb Alpert & The Tijuana Brass	A&M 775
⑩	15	6	Ain't That Peculiar	Marvin Gaye	Tamla 54122

★ HIGHEST DEBUT ★ POS 58 — Something About You ... Four Tops
★ BIGGEST MOVER ★ 88 to 51 — I Can Never Go Home Anymore ... The Shangri-Las

TW	LW	WK	Billboard	NOVEMBER 20, 1965	HOT 100
❶	5	4	I Hear A Symphony	The Supremes	Motown 1083
②	3	9	1-2-3	Len Barry	Decca 31827
③	1	7	Get Off Of My Cloud	The Rolling Stones	London 9792
④	6	8	Rescue Me	Fontella Bass	Checker 1120
❺	8	7	Let's Hang On!	The 4 Seasons	Philips 40317
❻	12	5	Turn! Turn! Turn!	The Byrds	Columbia 43424
⑦	2	11	A Lover's Concerto	The Toys	DynoVoice 209
⑧	10	7	Ain't That Peculiar	Marvin Gaye	Tamla 54122
⑨	9	9	Taste Of Honey	Herb Alpert & The Tijuana Brass	A&M 775
⑩	4	10	You're The One	The Vogues	Co & Ce 229

★ HIGHEST DEBUT ★ POS 61 — Hang On Sloopy ... Ramsey Lewis Trio
★ BIGGEST MOVER ★ 68 to 14 — I Got You (I Feel Good) ... James Brown

TW	LW	WK	Billboard	NOVEMBER 27, 1965	HOT 100
①	1	5	I Hear A Symphony	The Supremes	Motown 1083
❷	6	6	Turn! Turn! Turn!	The Byrds	Columbia 43424
③	2	10	1-2-3	Len Barry	Decca 31827
④	5	8	Let's Hang On!	The 4 Seasons	Philips 40317
⑤	3	8	Get Off Of My Cloud	The Rolling Stones	London 9792
⑥	4	9	Rescue Me	Fontella Bass	Checker 1120
⑦	9	10	Taste Of Honey	Herb Alpert & The Tijuana Brass	A&M 775
⑧	8	8	Ain't That Peculiar	Marvin Gaye	Tamla 54122
❾	14	3	I Got You (I Feel Good)	James Brown	King 6015
⑩	12	7	You've Got To Hide Your Love Away	The Silkie	Fontana 1525

★ HIGHEST DEBUT ★ POS 69 — The Little Girl I Once Knew ... The Beach Boys
★ BIGGEST MOVER ★ 61 to 28 — Hang On Sloopy ... Ramsey Lewis Trio

Billboard — DECEMBER 4, 1965 — HOT 100

TW	LW	WK			
①	2	7	**Turn! Turn! Turn!**	*The Byrds*	Columbia 43424
②	1	6	I Hear A Symphony	*The Supremes*	Motown 1083
③	3	11	1-2-3	*Len Barry*	Decca 31827
④	4	9	Let's Hang On!	*The 4 Seasons*	Philips 40317
⑤	9	4	I Got You (I Feel Good)	*James Brown*	King 6015
⑥	6	10	Rescue Me	*Fontella Bass*	Checker 1120
⑦	7	11	Taste Of Honey	*Herb Alpert & The Tijuana Brass*	A&M 775
⑧	8	9	**Ain't That Peculiar**	*Marvin Gaye*	Tamla 54122
⑨	12	5	I Can Never Go Home Anymore	*The Shangri-Las*	Red Bird 043
⑩	16	4	Over And Over	*The Dave Clark Five*	Epic 9863

★ **HIGHEST DEBUT** ★ POS 41
Ebb Tide.........................*The Righteous Brothers*

★ **BIGGEST MOVER** ★ 65 to 34
The Sounds Of Silence ....*Simon & Garfunkel*

Billboard — DECEMBER 11, 1965 — HOT 100

TW	LW	WK			
①	1	8	**Turn! Turn! Turn!**	*The Byrds*	Columbia 43424
②	2	7	I Hear A Symphony	*The Supremes*	Motown 1083
③	4	10	**Let's Hang On!**	*The 4 Seasons*	Philips 40317
④	5	5	I Got You (I Feel Good)	*James Brown*	King 6015
⑤	10	5	**Over And Over**	*The Dave Clark Five*	Epic 9863
⑥	9	6	**I Can Never Go Home Anymore**	*The Shangri-Las* ... Red Bird 043	
⑦	3	12	1-2-3	*Len Barry*	Decca 31827
⑧	7	12	Taste Of Honey	*Herb Alpert & The Tijuana Brass*	A&M 775
⑨	6	11	Rescue Me	*Fontella Bass*	Checker 1120
⑩	13	7	**I Will**	*Dean Martin*	Reprise 0415

★ **HIGHEST DEBUT** ★ POS 57
She's Just My Style .....*Gary Lewis & The Playboys*

★ **BIGGEST MOVER** ★ 67 to 40
Five O'Clock World.........................*The Vogues*

Billboard — DECEMBER 18, 1965 — HOT 100

TW	LW	WK			
①	1	9	**Turn! Turn! Turn!**	*The Byrds*	Columbia 43424
②	5	6	**Over And Over**	*The Dave Clark Five*	Epic 9863
③	4	6	I Got You (I Feel Good)	*James Brown*	King 6015
④	3	11	Let's Hang On!	*The 4 Seasons*	Philips 40317
⑤	2	8	I Hear A Symphony	*The Supremes*	Motown 1083
⑥	6	7	**I Can Never Go Home Anymore**	*The Shangri-Las* ... Red Bird 043	
⑦	14	10	**Make The World Go Away**	*Eddy Arnold*	RCA 8679
⑧	12	7	**England Swings**	*Roger Miller*	Smash 2010
⑨	13	6	**Fever**	*The McCoys*	Bang 511
⑩	10	8	I Will	*Dean Martin*	Reprise 0415

★ **HIGHEST DEBUT** ★ POS 36
We Can Work It Out.........................*The Beatles*

★ **BIGGEST MOVER** ★ 78 to 52
No Matter What Shape (Your Stomach's In) ....*The T-Bones*

TW	LW	WK	Billboard.	DECEMBER 25, 1965	HOT 100.
①	2	7	**Over And Over**............................	*The Dave Clark Five* . . .	Epic 9863
②	1	10	**Turn! Turn! Turn!**..........................	*The Byrds* . . .	Columbia 43424
③	3	7	**I Got You (I Feel Good)**..................	*James Brown* . . .	King 6015
④	4	12	**Let's Hang On!**	*The 4 Seasons* . . .	Philips 40317
⑤	16	6	**The Sounds Of Silence**...................	*Simon & Garfunkel* . . .	Columbia 43396
⑥	7	11	**Make The World Go Away**	*Eddy Arnold* . . .	RCA 8679
⑦	9	7	**Fever**....................................	*The McCoys* . . .	Bang 511
⑧	8	8	**England Swings**	*Roger Miller* . . .	Smash 2010
⑨	12	4	**Ebb Tide**	*The Righteous Brothers* . . .	Philles 130
⑩	6	8	**I Can Never Go Home Anymore**	*The Shangri-Las* . . .	Red Bird 043

★ HIGHEST DEBUT ★ POS 48	★ BIGGEST MOVER ★ 56 to 28
A Must To Avoid ....*Herman's Hermits*	Day Tripper ....*The Beatles*

Billboard — JANUARY 1, 1966 — HOT 100

TW	LW	WK			
❶	5	7	The Sounds Of Silence	Simon & Garfunkel	Columbia 43396
❷	11	3	We Can Work It Out	The Beatles	Capitol 5555
③	3	8	I Got You (I Feel Good)	James Brown	King 6015
④	2	11	Turn! Turn! Turn!	The Byrds	Columbia 43424
⑤	1	8	Over And Over	The Dave Clark Five	Epic 9863
⑥	4	13	Let's Hang On!	The 4 Seasons	Philips 40317
⑦	7	8	Fever	The McCoys	Bang 511
⑧	9	5	Ebb Tide	The Righteous Brothers	Philles 130
⑨	8	9	England Swings	Roger Miller	Smash 2010
⑩	6	12	Make The World Go Away	Eddy Arnold	RCA 8679

★ HIGHEST DEBUT ★ POS 75
Tell Me Why .... Elvis Presley

★ BIGGEST MOVER ★ 79 to 48
As Tears Go By .... The Rolling Stones

Billboard — JANUARY 8, 1966 — HOT 100

TW	LW	WK			
①	2	4	We Can Work It Out	The Beatles	Capitol 5555
②	1	8	The Sounds Of Silence	Simon & Garfunkel	Columbia 43396
❸	16	5	She's Just My Style	Gary Lewis & The Playboys	Liberty 55846
❹	12	9	Flowers On The Wall	The Statler Brothers	Columbia 43315
❺	8	6	Ebb Tide	The Righteous Brothers	Philles 130
⑥	5	9	Over And Over	The Dave Clark Five	Epic 9863
⑦	3	9	I Got You (I Feel Good)	James Brown	King 6015
❽	11	7	Five O'Clock World	The Vogues	Co & Ce 232
⑨	4	12	Turn! Turn! Turn!	The Byrds	Columbia 43424
⑩	18	4	Day Tripper	The Beatles	Capitol 5555

★ HIGHEST DEBUT ★ POS 81
Call Me .... Chris Montez

★ BIGGEST MOVER ★ 48 to 14
As Tears Go By .... The Rolling Stones

Billboard — JANUARY 15, 1966 — HOT 100

TW	LW	WK			
①	1	5	We Can Work It Out	The Beatles	Capitol 5555
②	2	9	The Sounds Of Silence	Simon & Garfunkel	Columbia 43396
③	3	6	She's Just My Style	Gary Lewis & The Playboys	Liberty 55846
❹	8	8	Five O'Clock World	The Vogues	Co & Ce 232
⑤	5	7	Ebb Tide	The Righteous Brothers	Philles 130
❻	10	5	Day Tripper	The Beatles	Capitol 5555
⑦	4	10	Flowers On The Wall	The Statler Brothers	Columbia 43315
❽	24	4	The Men In My Little Girl's Life	Mike Douglas	Epic 9876
⑨	14	4	As Tears Go By	The Rolling Stones	London 9808
⑩	13	6	No Matter What Shape (Your Stomach's In)	The T-Bones	Liberty 55836

★ HIGHEST DEBUT ★ POS 75
Cleo's Mood .... Jr. Walker & The All Stars

★ BIGGEST MOVER ★ 98 to 69
Michelle .... David & Jonathan

TW	LW	WK	Billboard.	JANUARY 22, 1966	HOT 100.
①	2	10	**The Sounds Of Silence**	*Simon & Garfunkel* . . . Columbia 43396	
②	1	6	We Can Work It Out	*The Beatles* . . . Capitol 5555	
③	3	7	**She's Just My Style**	*Gary Lewis & The Playboys* . . . Liberty 55846	
④	4	9	**Five O'Clock World**	*The Vogues* . . . Co & Ce 232	
⑤	6	6	**Day Tripper**	*The Beatles* . . . Capitol 5555	
⑥	10	7	No Matter What Shape (Your Stomach's In)	*The T-Bones* . . . Liberty 55836	
⑦	8	5	The Men In My Little Girl's Life	*Mike Douglas* . . . Epic 9876	
⑧	11	5	**A Must To Avoid**	*Herman's Hermits* . . . MGM 13437	
⑨	9	5	As Tears Go By	*The Rolling Stones* . . . London 9808	
⑩	12	9	**You Didn't Have To Be So Nice**	*The Lovin' Spoonful* . . . Kama Sutra 205	

★ HIGHEST DEBUT ★ POS 58	★ BIGGEST MOVER ★ 78 to 46
A Hard Day's Night ....*Ramsey Lewis Trio*	My World Is Empty Without You.................*The Supremes*

TW	LW	WK	Billboard.	JANUARY 29, 1966	HOT 100.
①	2	7	**We Can Work It Out**	*The Beatles* . . . Capitol 5555	
②	15	5	**Barbara Ann**	*The Beach Boys* . . . Capitol 5561	
③	3	8	**She's Just My Style**	*Gary Lewis & The Playboys* . . . Liberty 55846	
④	6	8	**No Matter What Shape (Your Stomach's In)**	*The T-Bones* . . . Liberty 55836	
⑤	4	10	Five O'Clock World	*The Vogues* . . . Co & Ce 232	
⑥	9	6	**As Tears Go By**	*The Rolling Stones* . . . London 9808	
⑦	7	6	The Men In My Little Girl's Life	*Mike Douglas* . . . Epic 9876	
⑧	8	6	**A Must To Avoid**	*Herman's Hermits* . . . MGM 13437	
⑨	17	6	My Love	*Petula Clark* . . . Warner 5684	
⑩	16	8	**Jenny Take A Ride!**	*Mitch Ryder & The Detroit Wheels* . . . New Voice 806	

★ HIGHEST DEBUT ★ POS 63	★ BIGGEST MOVER ★ 74 to 50
Working My Way Back To You .....*The 4 Seasons*	These Boots Are Made For Walkin' ....*Nancy Sinatra*

TW	LW	WK	Billboard.	FEBRUARY 5, 1966	HOT 100.
①	9	7	**My Love**	*Petula Clark* . . . Warner 5684	
②	2	6	**Barbara Ann**	*The Beach Boys* . . . Capitol 5561	
③	4	9	**No Matter What Shape (Your Stomach's In)**	*The T-Bones* . . . Liberty 55836	
④	1	8	We Can Work It Out	*The Beatles* . . . Capitol 5555	
⑤	20	7	Lightnin' Strikes	*Lou Christie* . . . MGM 13412	
⑥	7	7	**The Men In My Little Girl's Life**	*Mike Douglas* . . . Epic 9876	
⑦	3	9	She's Just My Style	*Gary Lewis & The Playboys* . . . Liberty 55846	
⑧	5	11	Five O'Clock World	*The Vogues* . . . Co & Ce 232	
⑨	8	7	A Must To Avoid	*Herman's Hermits* . . . MGM 13437	
⑩	16	9	**Crying Time**	*Ray Charles* . . . ABC-Paramount 10739	

★ HIGHEST DEBUT ★ POS 71	★ BIGGEST MOVER ★ 57 to 34
You Baby.............................*The Turtles*	When Liking Turns To Loving.........*Ronnie Dove*

FEBRUARY 12, 1966 — Billboard HOT 100

TW	LW	WK	Title	Artist	Label
①	1	8	**My Love**	Petula Clark	Warner 5684
②	5	8	**Lightnin' Strikes**	Lou Christie	MGM 13412
③	16	9	**Uptight (Everything's Alright)**	Stevie Wonder	Tamla 54124
④	2	7	**Barbara Ann**	The Beach Boys	Capitol 5561
⑤	4	9	**We Can Work It Out**	The Beatles	Capitol 5555
⑥	3	10	**No Matter What Shape (Your Stomach's In)**	The T-Bones	Liberty 55836
❼	10	10	**Crying Time**	Ray Charles	ABC-Paramount 10739
❽	13	5	**My World Is Empty Without You**	The Supremes	Motown 1089
⑨	8	12	**Five O'Clock World**	The Vogues	Co & Ce 232
⑩	19	7	**Don't Mess With Bill**	The Marvelettes	Tamla 54126

★ **HIGHEST DEBUT** ★ POS 81
634-5789 ....Wilson Pickett

★ **BIGGEST MOVER** ★ 87 to 51
The Ballad Of The Green Berets.........SSgt Barry Sadler

FEBRUARY 19, 1966 — Billboard HOT 100

TW	LW	WK	Title	Artist	Label
①	2	9	**Lightnin' Strikes**	Lou Christie	MGM 13412
❷	15	5	**These Boots Are Made For Walkin'**	Nancy Sinatra	Reprise 0432
③	3	10	**Uptight (Everything's Alright)**	Stevie Wonder	Tamla 54124
④	1	9	**My Love**	Petula Clark	Warner 5684
❺	8	6	**My World Is Empty Without You**	The Supremes	Motown 1089
⑥	7	11	**Crying Time**	Ray Charles	ABC-Paramount 10739
⑦	4	8	**Barbara Ann**	The Beach Boys	Capitol 5561
⑧	10	8	**Don't Mess With Bill**	The Marvelettes	Tamla 54126
⑨	6	11	**No Matter What Shape (Your Stomach's In)**	The T-Bones	Liberty 55836
⑩	51	3	**The Ballad Of The Green Berets**	SSgt Barry Sadler	RCA 8739

★ **HIGHEST DEBUT** ★ POS 41
Listen People ....Herman's Hermits

★ **BIGGEST MOVER** ★ 51 to 10
The Ballad Of The Green Berets.........SSgt Barry Sadler

FEBRUARY 26, 1966 — Billboard HOT 100

TW	LW	WK	Title	Artist	Label
①	2	6	**These Boots Are Made For Walkin'**	Nancy Sinatra	Reprise 0432
②	1	10	**Lightnin' Strikes**	Lou Christie	MGM 13412
③	10	4	**The Ballad Of The Green Berets**	SSgt Barry Sadler	RCA 8739
④	3	11	**Uptight (Everything's Alright)**	Stevie Wonder	Tamla 54124
⑤	5	7	**My World Is Empty Without You**	The Supremes	Motown 1089
⑥	4	10	**My Love**	Petula Clark	Warner 5684
⑦	8	9	**Don't Mess With Bill**	The Marvelettes	Tamla 54126
❽	16	8	**California Dreamin'**	The Mamas & The Papas	Dunhill 4020
⑨	20	6	**Elusive Butterfly**	Bob Lind	World Pacific 77808
⑩	15	5	**Working My Way Back To You**	The 4 Seasons	Philips 40350

★ **HIGHEST DEBUT** ★ POS 46
19th Nervous Breakdown ....The Rolling Stones

★ **BIGGEST MOVER** ★ 41 to 13
Listen People ....Herman's Hermits

Billboard — MARCH 5, 1966 — HOT 100

TW	LW	WK	Title	Artist	Label
①	3	5	The Ballad Of The Green Berets	SSgt Barry Sadler	RCA 8739
②	1	7	These Boots Are Made For Walkin'	Nancy Sinatra	Reprise 0432
③	2	11	Lightnin' Strikes	Lou Christie	MGM 13412
❹	13	3	Listen People	Herman's Hermits	MGM 13462
❺	8	9	California Dreamin'	The Mamas & The Papas	Dunhill 4020
❻	9	7	Elusive Butterfly	Bob Lind	World Pacific 77808
⑦	6	11	My Love	Petula Clark	Warner 5684
⑧	4	12	Uptight (Everything's Alright)	Stevie Wonder	Tamla 54124
⑨	10	6	Working My Way Back To You	The 4 Seasons	Philips 40350
⑩	5	8	My World Is Empty Without You	The Supremes	Motown 1089

★ HIGHEST DEBUT ★ POS 25
Nowhere Man ......The Beatles

★ BIGGEST MOVER ★ 46 to 12
19th Nervous Breakdown ......The Rolling Stones

Billboard — MARCH 12, 1966 — HOT 100

TW	LW	WK	Title	Artist	Label
①	1	6	The Ballad Of The Green Berets	SSgt Barry Sadler	RCA 8739
②	2	8	These Boots Are Made For Walkin'	Nancy Sinatra	Reprise 0432
③	4	4	Listen People	Herman's Hermits	MGM 13462
④	5	10	California Dreamin'	The Mamas & The Papas	Dunhill 4020
⑤	6	8	Elusive Butterfly	Bob Lind	World Pacific 77808
❻	12	3	19th Nervous Breakdown	The Rolling Stones	London 9823
❼	25	2	Nowhere Man	The Beatles	Capitol 5587
⑧	3	12	Lightnin' Strikes	Lou Christie	MGM 13412
⑨	11	7	I Fought The Law	Bobby Fuller Four	Mustang 3014
⑩	16	5	Homeward Bound	Simon & Garfunkel	Columbia 43511

★ HIGHEST DEBUT ★ POS 75
Bang Bang (My Baby Shot Me Down) ......Cher

★ BIGGEST MOVER ★ 90 to 45
(You're My) Soul And Inspiration ......The Righteous Brothers

Billboard — MARCH 19, 1966 — HOT 100

TW	LW	WK	Title	Artist	Label
①	1	7	The Ballad Of The Green Berets	SSgt Barry Sadler	RCA 8739
❷	6	4	19th Nervous Breakdown	The Rolling Stones	London 9823
③	2	9	These Boots Are Made For Walkin'	Nancy Sinatra	Reprise 0432
❹	7	3	Nowhere Man	The Beatles	Capitol 5587
⑤	5	9	Elusive Butterfly	Bob Lind	World Pacific 77808
⑥	3	5	Listen People	Herman's Hermits	MGM 13462
⑦	4	11	California Dreamin'	The Mamas & The Papas	Dunhill 4020
⑧	10	6	Homeward Bound	Simon & Garfunkel	Columbia 43511
⑨	9	8	I Fought The Law	Bobby Fuller Four	Mustang 3014
⑩	25	4	Daydream	The Lovin' Spoonful	Kama Sutra 208

★ HIGHEST DEBUT ★ POS 60
Secret Agent Man ......Johnny Rivers

★ BIGGEST MOVER ★ 75 to 41
Bang Bang (My Baby Shot Me Down) ......Cher

Billboard 🔊 MARCH 26, 1966 🔊 HOT 100.

TW	LW	WK		
①	1	8	**The Ballad Of The Green Berets** ....*SSgt Barry Sadler* . . . RCA 8739
②	2	5	**19th Nervous Breakdown** ....*The Rolling Stones* . . . London 9823
③	4	4	**Nowhere Man** ....*The Beatles* . . . Capitol 5587
④	3	10	**These Boots Are Made For Walkin'** ....*Nancy Sinatra* . . . Reprise 0432
⑤	8	7	**Homeward Bound** ....*Simon & Garfunkel* . . . Columbia 43511
⑥	10	5	**Daydream** ....*The Lovin' Spoonful* . . . Kama Sutra 208
⑦	7	12	**California Dreamin'**.................*The Mamas & The Papas* . . . Dunhill 4020
⑧	14	4	**(You're My) Soul And Inspiration** ....*The Righteous Brothers* . . . Verve 10383
⑨	5	10	**Elusive Butterfly** ....*Bob Lind* . . . World Pacific 77808
⑩	6	6	**Listen People** ....*Herman's Hermits* . . . MGM 13462

★ HIGHEST DEBUT ★ POS 70	★ BIGGEST MOVER ★ 60 to 22
A Sign Of The Times ....*Petula Clark*	Secret Agent Man.......................*Johnny Rivers*

Billboard 🔊 APRIL 2, 1966 🔊 HOT 100.

TW	LW	WK		
①	1	9	**The Ballad Of The Green Berets** ....*SSgt Barry Sadler* . . . RCA 8739
②	2	6	**19th Nervous Breakdown** ....*The Rolling Stones* . . . London 9823
③	8	5	**(You're My) Soul And Inspiration** ....*The Righteous Brothers* . . . Verve 10383
④	6	6	**Daydream** ....*The Lovin' Spoonful* . . . Kama Sutra 208
⑤	5	8	**Homeward Bound** ....*Simon & Garfunkel* . . . Columbia 43511
⑥	3	5	**Nowhere Man** ....*The Beatles* . . . Capitol 5587
⑦	7	13	**California Dreamin'**.......................*The Mamas & The Papas* . . . Dunhill 4020
⑧	4	11	**These Boots Are Made For Walkin'** ....*Nancy Sinatra* . . . Reprise 0432
⑨	17	4	**Bang Bang (My Baby Shot Me Down)**...................*Cher* . . . Imperial 66160
⑩	14	5	**Sure Gonna Miss Her** ....*Gary Lewis & The Playboys* . . . Liberty 55865

★ HIGHEST DEBUT ★ POS 68	★ BIGGEST MOVER ★ 70 to 36
Sloop John B ....*The Beach Boys*	A Sign Of The Times ....*Petula Clark*

Billboard 🔊 APRIL 9, 1966 🔊 HOT 100.

TW	LW	WK		
①	3	6	**(You're My) Soul And Inspiration** ....*The Righteous Brothers* . . . Verve 10383
②	4	7	**Daydream** ....*The Lovin' Spoonful* . . . Kama Sutra 208
③	2	7	**19th Nervous Breakdown**...................*The Rolling Stones* . . . London 9823
④	9	5	**Bang Bang (My Baby Shot Me Down)**...................*Cher* . . . Imperial 66160
⑤	1	10	**The Ballad Of The Green Berets**.............*SSgt Barry Sadler* . . . RCA 8739
⑥	6	6	**Nowhere Man** ....*The Beatles* . . . Capitol 5587
⑦	15	4	**Secret Agent Man**...............................*Johnny Rivers* . . . Imperial 66159
⑧	11	8	**I'm So Lonesome I Could Cry** ..............*B.J. Thomas* . . . Scepter 12129
⑨	10	6	**Sure Gonna Miss Her** ....*Gary Lewis & The Playboys* . . . Liberty 55865
⑩	7	14	**California Dreamin'**.......................*The Mamas & The Papas* . . . Dunhill 4020

★ HIGHEST DEBUT ★ POS 65	★ BIGGEST MOVER ★ 68 to 35
Leaning On The Lamp Post ......*Herman's Hermits*	Sloop John B ....*The Beach Boys*

TW	LW	WK	**Billboard**	APRIL 16, 1966	**HOT 100**
①	1	7	(You're My) Soul And Inspiration	.... The Righteous Brothers ... Verve 10383	
②	2	8	**Daydream**	..................................The Lovin' Spoonful ... Kama Sutra 208	
③	4	6	Bang Bang (My Baby Shot Me Down)	...................Cher ... Imperial 66160	
④	7	5	Secret Agent Man	..................................Johnny Rivers ... Imperial 66159	
⑤	11	9	Time Won't Let Me	...........................The Outsiders ... Capitol 5573	
⑥	3	8	19th Nervous Breakdown	................The Rolling Stones ... London 9823	
⑦	5	11	The Ballad Of The Green Berets	........SSgt Barry Sadler ... RCA 8739	
⑧	8	9	I'm So Lonesome I Could Cry	..............B.J. Thomas ... Scepter 12129	
⑨	16	6	Good Lovin'	....The Young Rascals ... Atlantic 2321	
⑩	18	5	Kicks	..................................Paul Revere & The Raiders ... Columbia 43556	

★ HIGHEST DEBUT ★ POS 71	★ BIGGEST MOVER ★ 79 to 34
Rainy Day Women #12 & 35..............Bob Dylan	Monday, Monday............The Mamas & The Papas

TW	LW	WK	**Billboard**	APRIL 23, 1966	**HOT 100**
①	1	8	(You're My) Soul And Inspiration	.... The Righteous Brothers ... Verve 10383	
②	3	7	**Bang Bang (My Baby Shot Me Down)**	............Cher ... Imperial 66160	
③	4	6	**Secret Agent Man**	..................................Johnny Rivers ... Imperial 66159	
④	2	9	Daydream	.....................................The Lovin' Spoonful ... Kama Sutra 208	
⑤	5	10	**Time Won't Let Me**	...............................The Outsiders ... Capitol 5573	
⑥	9	7	Good Lovin'	.....................................The Young Rascals ... Atlantic 2321	
⑦	10	6	Kicks	..................................Paul Revere & The Raiders ... Columbia 43556	
⑧	13	4	Sloop John B	....The Beach Boys ... Capitol 5602	
⑨	8	10	I'm So Lonesome I Could Cry	....................B.J. Thomas ... Scepter 12129	
⑩	34	3	Monday, Monday	.........................The Mamas & The Papas ... Dunhill 4026	

★ HIGHEST DEBUT ★ POS 49	★ BIGGEST MOVER ★ 71 to 38
How Does That Grab You, Darlin'?...........Nancy Sinatra	Rainy Day Women #12 & 35..............Bob Dylan

TW	LW	WK	**Billboard**	APRIL 30, 1966	**HOT 100**
①	6	8	**Good Lovin'**	....The Young Rascals ... Atlantic 2321	
②	1	9	(You're My) Soul And Inspiration	......................The Righteous Brothers ... Verve 10383	
③	10	4	**Monday, Monday**	........................The Mamas & The Papas ... Dunhill 4026	
④	8	5	**Sloop John B**	....The Beach Boys ... Capitol 5602	
⑤	3	7	Secret Agent Man	..................................Johnny Rivers ... Imperial 66159	
⑥	7	7	Kicks	..................................Paul Revere & The Raiders ... Columbia 43556	
⑦	5	11	Time Won't Let Me	...........................The Outsiders ... Capitol 5573	
⑧	2	8	Bang Bang (My Baby Shot Me Down)	...................Cher ... Imperial 66160	
⑨	4	10	Daydream	.....................................The Lovin' Spoonful ... Kama Sutra 208	
⑩	15	4	Leaning On The Lamp Post	...................Herman's Hermits ... MGM 13500	

★ HIGHEST DEBUT ★ POS 62	★ BIGGEST MOVER ★ 99 to 64
Love Is Like An Itching In My Heart............The Supremes	Come On Let's Go ....The McCoys

Billboard — MAY 7, 1966 — HOT 100

TW	LW	WK		
1	3	5	Monday, Monday ....The Mamas & The Papas	Dunhill 4026
2	1	9	Good Lovin' ....The Young Rascals	Atlantic 2321
3	4	6	Sloop John B...The Beach Boys	Capitol 5602
4	2	10	(You're My) Soul And Inspiration ....The Righteous Brothers	Verve 10383
5	6	8	Kicks................................Paul Revere & The Raiders	Columbia 43556
6	5	8	Secret Agent Man...Johnny Rivers	Imperial 66159
7	14	4	Rainy Day Women #12 & 35.....................Bob Dylan	Columbia 43592
8	8	9	Bang Bang (My Baby Shot Me Down)....................Cher	Imperial 66160
9	10	5	Leaning On The Lamp Post ....Herman's Hermits	MGM 13500
10	11	8	Gloria ....The Shadows Of Knight	Dunwich 116

★ HIGHEST DEBUT ★ POS 62
I Am A Rock.........................Simon & Garfunkel

★ BIGGEST MOVER ★ 70 to 31
It's A Man's Man's Man's World.....James Brown

Billboard — MAY 14, 1966 — HOT 100

TW	LW	WK		
1	1	6	Monday, Monday ....The Mamas & The Papas	Dunhill 4026
2	2	10	Good Lovin' ....The Young Rascals	Atlantic 2321
3	7	5	Rainy Day Women #12 & 35.....................Bob Dylan	Columbia 43592
4	5	9	Kicks ....Paul Revere & The Raiders	Columbia 43556
5	3	7	Sloop John B...The Beach Boys	Capitol 5602
6	4	11	(You're My) Soul And Inspiration ....The Righteous Brothers	Verve 10383
7	15	4	How Does That Grab You, Darlin'?.....Nancy Sinatra	Reprise 0461
8	13	7	Message To Michael.........................Dionne Warwick	Scepter 12133
9	16	6	When A Man Loves A Woman......................Percy Sledge	Atlantic 2326
10	10	9	Gloria ....The Shadows Of Knight	Dunwich 116

★ HIGHEST DEBUT ★ POS 48
Paint It, Black.........................The Rolling Stones

★ BIGGEST MOVER ★ 65 to 25
Did You Ever Have To Make Up Your
Mind? ....The Lovin' Spoonful

Billboard — MAY 21, 1966 — HOT 100

TW	LW	WK		
1	1	7	Monday, Monday ....The Mamas & The Papas	Dunhill 4026
2	3	6	Rainy Day Women #12 & 35.................Bob Dylan	Columbia 43592
3	2	11	Good Lovin' ....The Young Rascals	Atlantic 2321
4	9	7	When A Man Loves A Woman......................Percy Sledge	Atlantic 2326
5	13	6	A Groovy Kind Of Love.........................The Mindbenders	Fontana 1541
6	4	10	Kicks................................Paul Revere & The Raiders	Columbia 43556
7	7	5	How Does That Grab You, Darlin'?.....Nancy Sinatra	Reprise 0461
8	8	8	Message To Michael.........................Dionne Warwick	Scepter 12133
9	5	8	Sloop John B...The Beach Boys	Capitol 5602
10	15	4	Love Is Like An Itching In My Heart.........The Supremes	Motown 1094

★ HIGHEST DEBUT ★ POS 63
Opus 17 (Don't You Worry 'Bout Me) ....The 4
Seasons

★ BIGGEST MOVER ★ 48 to 19
Paint It, Black.........................The Rolling Stones

Billboard — MAY 28, 1966 — HOT 100

TW	LW	WK	Title	Artist	Label
1	4	8	When A Man Loves A Woman	Percy Sledge	Atlantic 2326
2	5	7	A Groovy Kind Of Love	The Mindbenders	Fontana 1541
3	1	8	Monday, Monday	The Mamas & The Papas	Dunhill 4026
4	19	3	Paint It, Black	The Rolling Stones	London 901
5	2	7	Rainy Day Women #12 & 35	Bob Dylan	Columbia 43592
6	17	4	I Am A Rock	Simon & Garfunkel	Columbia 43617
7	16	4	Did You Ever Have To Make Up Your Mind?	The Lovin' Spoonful	Kama Sutra 209
8	3	12	Good Lovin'	The Young Rascals	Atlantic 2321
9	10	5	Love Is Like An Itching In My Heart	The Supremes	Motown 1094
10	18	5	It's A Man's Man's Man's World	James Brown	King 6035

★ **HIGHEST DEBUT** ★ POS 66
Crying ....Jay & The Americans

★ **BIGGEST MOVER** ★ 63 to 31
Opus 17 (Don't You Worry 'Bout Me)........The 4 Seasons

Billboard — JUNE 4, 1966 — HOT 100

TW	LW	WK	Title	Artist	Label
1	1	9	When A Man Loves A Woman	Percy Sledge	Atlantic 2326
2	2	8	A Groovy Kind Of Love	The Mindbenders	Fontana 1541
3	4	4	Paint It, Black	The Rolling Stones	London 901
4	7	5	Did You Ever Have To Make Up Your Mind?	The Lovin' Spoonful	Kama Sutra 209
5	6	5	I Am A Rock	Simon & Garfunkel	Columbia 43617
6	3	9	Monday, Monday	The Mamas & The Papas	Dunhill 4026
7	5	8	Rainy Day Women #12 & 35	Bob Dylan	Columbia 43592
8	10	6	It's A Man's Man's Man's World	James Brown	King 6035
9	12	4	Green Grass	Gary Lewis & The Playboys	Liberty 55880
10	27	5	Strangers In The Night	Frank Sinatra	Reprise 0470

★ **HIGHEST DEBUT** ★ POS 66
Popsicle ....Jan & Dean

★ **BIGGEST MOVER** ★ 65 to 35
Red Rubber Ball ....The Cyrkle

Billboard — JUNE 11, 1966 — HOT 100

TW	LW	WK	Title	Artist	Label
1	3	5	Paint It, Black	The Rolling Stones	London 901
2	4	6	Did You Ever Have To Make Up Your Mind?	The Lovin' Spoonful	Kama Sutra 209
3	5	6	I Am A Rock	Simon & Garfunkel	Columbia 43617
4	1	10	When A Man Loves A Woman	Percy Sledge	Atlantic 2326
5	2	9	A Groovy Kind Of Love	The Mindbenders	Fontana 1541
6	10	6	Strangers In The Night	Frank Sinatra	Reprise 0470
7	6	10	Monday, Monday	The Mamas & The Papas	Dunhill 4026
8	8	7	It's A Man's Man's Man's World	James Brown	King 6035
9	9	5	Green Grass	Gary Lewis & The Playboys	Liberty 55880
10	12	8	Barefootin'	Robert Parker	Nola 721

★ **HIGHEST DEBUT** ★ POS 28
Paperback Writer ....The Beatles

★ **BIGGEST MOVER** ★ 89 to 52
He ....The Righteous Brothers

Billboard — JUNE 18, 1966 — HOT 100

TW	LW	WK	Title	Artist	Label
①	1	6	**Paint It, Black**	*The Rolling Stones* . . . London 901	
②	2	7	**Did You Ever Have To Make Up Your Mind?**	*The Lovin' Spoonful* . . . Kama Sutra 209	
③	3	7	**I Am A Rock**	*Simon & Garfunkel* . . . Columbia 43617	
④	4	11	**When A Man Loves A Woman**	*Percy Sledge* . . . Atlantic 2326	
⑤	6	7	**Strangers In The Night**	*Frank Sinatra* . . . Reprise 0470	
⑥	5	10	**A Groovy Kind Of Love**	*The Mindbenders* . . . Fontana 1541	
7	10	9	**Barefootin'**	*Robert Parker* . . . Nola 721	
⑧	9	6	**Green Grass**	*Gary Lewis & The Playboys* . . . Liberty 55880	
⑨	12	8	**Cool Jerk**	*The Capitols* . . . Karen 1524	
⑩	19	5	**Red Rubber Ball**	*The Cyrkle* . . . Columbia 43589	

★ **HIGHEST DEBUT** ★ POS 72
You Better Run ....*The Young Rascals*

★ **BIGGEST MOVER** ★ 72 to 42
Rain ....*The Beatles*

Billboard — JUNE 25, 1966 — HOT 100

TW	LW	WK	Title	Artist	Label
❶	15	3	**Paperback Writer**	*The Beatles* . . . Capitol 5651	
❷	5	8	**Strangers In The Night**	*Frank Sinatra* . . . Reprise 0470	
③	1	7	**Paint It, Black**	*The Rolling Stones* . . . London 901	
④	2	8	**Did You Ever Have To Make Up Your Mind?**	*The Lovin' Spoonful* . . . Kama Sutra 209	
⑤	3	8	**I Am A Rock**	*Simon & Garfunkel* . . . Columbia 43617	
❻	10	6	**Red Rubber Ball**	*The Cyrkle* . . . Columbia 43589	
⑦	7	10	**Barefootin'**	*Robert Parker* . . . Nola 721	
⑧	9	9	**Cool Jerk**	*The Capitols* . . . Karen 1524	
❾	12	6	**You Don't Have To Say You Love Me**	*Dusty Springfield* . . . Philips 40371	
⑩	11	8	**Sweet Talkin' Guy**	*The Chiffons* . . . Laurie 3340	

★ **HIGHEST DEBUT** ★ POS 75
Wild Thing ....*The Troggs*

★ **BIGGEST MOVER** ★ 93 to 55
Lil' Red Riding Hood............*Sam The Sham & The Pharoahs*

Billboard — JULY 2, 1966 — HOT 100

TW	LW	WK	Title	Artist	Label
①	2	9	**Strangers In The Night**	*Frank Sinatra* . . . Reprise 0470	
②	1	4	**Paperback Writer**	*The Beatles* . . . Capitol 5651	
❸	6	7	**Red Rubber Ball**	*The Cyrkle* . . . Columbia 43589	
④	3	8	**Paint It, Black**	*The Rolling Stones* . . . London 901	
❺	9	7	**You Don't Have To Say You Love Me**	*Dusty Springfield* . . . Philips 40371	
❻	15	5	**Hanky Panky**	*Tommy James & The Shondells* . . . Roulette 4686	
⑦	8	10	**Cool Jerk**	*The Capitols* . . . Karen 1524	
⑧	5	9	**I Am A Rock**	*Simon & Garfunkel* . . . Columbia 43617	
⑨	4	9	**Did You Ever Have To Make Up Your Mind?**	*The Lovin' Spoonful* . . . Kama Sutra 209	
⑩	7	11	**Barefootin'**	*Robert Parker* . . . Nola 721	

★ **HIGHEST DEBUT** ★ POS 53
I Saw Her Again ....*The Mamas & The Papas*

★ **BIGGEST MOVER** ★ 75 to 47
Wild Thing ....*The Troggs*

JULY 9, 1966 — Billboard HOT 100

TW	LW	WK	Title	Artist	Label
①	2	5	**Paperback Writer**	The Beatles	Capitol 5651
②	3	8	**Red Rubber Ball**	The Cyrkle	Columbia 43589
③	1	10	**Strangers In The Night**	Frank Sinatra	Reprise 0470
④	6	6	**Hanky Panky**	Tommy James & The Shondells	Roulette 4686
⑤	5	8	**You Don't Have To Say You Love Me**	Dusty Springfield	Philips 40371
❻	47	3	**Wild Thing**	The Troggs	Atco 6415/Fontana 1548
⑦	7	11	**Cool Jerk**	The Capitols	Karen 1524
❽	11	6	**Little Girl**	Syndicate Of Sound	Bell 640
⑨	4	9	**Paint It, Black**	The Rolling Stones	London 901
❿	19	6	**Along Comes Mary**	The Association	Valiant 741

★ **HIGHEST DEBUT** ★ POS 70
Mothers Little Helper .... The Rolling Stones

★ **BIGGEST MOVER** ★ 47 to 6
Wild Thing .... The Troggs

JULY 16, 1966 — Billboard HOT 100

TW	LW	WK	Title	Artist	Label
❶	4	7	**Hanky Panky**	Tommy James & The Shondells	Roulette 4686
❷	6	4	**Wild Thing**	The Troggs	Atco 6415/Fontana 1548
③	2	9	**Red Rubber Ball**	The Cyrkle	Columbia 43589
④	5	9	**You Don't Have To Say You Love Me**	Dusty Springfield	Philips 40371
⑤	1	6	**Paperback Writer**	The Beatles	Capitol 5651
⑥	3	11	**Strangers In The Night**	Frank Sinatra	Reprise 0470
❼	10	7	**Along Comes Mary**	The Association	Valiant 741
⑧	8	7	**Little Girl**	Syndicate Of Sound	Bell 640
❾	12	6	**Lil' Red Riding Hood**	Sam The Sham & The Pharoahs	MGM 13506
❿	15	5	**Hungry**	Paul Revere & The Raiders	Columbia 43678

★ **HIGHEST DEBUT** ★ POS 53
Summer In The City .... The Lovin' Spoonful

★ **BIGGEST MOVER** ★ 70 to 38
Mothers Little Helper .... The Rolling Stones

JULY 23, 1966 — Billboard HOT 100

TW	LW	WK	Title	Artist	Label
①	1	8	**Hanky Panky**	Tommy James & The Shondells	Roulette 4686
❷	2	5	**Wild Thing**	The Troggs	Atco 6415/Fontana 1548
❸	9	7	**Lil' Red Riding Hood**	Sam The Sham & The Pharoahs	MGM 13506
❹	12	7	**The Pied Piper**	Crispian St. Peters	Jamie 1320
⑤	4	10	**You Don't Have To Say You Love Me**	Dusty Springfield	Philips 40371
⑥	5	7	**Paperback Writer**	The Beatles	Capitol 5651
❼	10	6	**Hungry**	Paul Revere & The Raiders	Columbia 43678
⑧	3	10	**Red Rubber Ball**	The Cyrkle	Columbia 43589
❾	14	4	**I Saw Her Again**	The Mamas & The Papas	Dunhill 4031
❿	15	7	**Sweet Pea**	Tommy Roe	ABC-Paramount 10762

★ **HIGHEST DEBUT** ★ POS 50
They're Coming To Take Me Away, Ha-Haaa! .... Napoleon XIV

★ **BIGGEST MOVER** ★ 53 to 21
Summer In The City .... The Lovin' Spoonful

Billboard HOT 100 — JULY 30, 1966

TW	LW	WK	Title / Artist / Label
①	2	6	**Wild Thing** ....*The Troggs* . . . Atco 6415/Fontana 1548
②	1	9	**Hanky Panky** ....*Tommy James & The Shondells* . . . Roulette 4686
③	3	8	**Lil' Red Riding Hood**..........*Sam The Sham & The Pharoahs* . . . MGM 13506
④	4	8	**The Pied Piper** ....*Crispian St. Peters* . . . Jamie 1320
⑤	9	5	**I Saw Her Again**.......................*The Mamas & The Papas* . . . Dunhill 4031
⑥	7	7	**Hungry**..................................*Paul Revere & The Raiders* . . . Columbia 43678
⑦	21	3	**Summer In The City** ....*The Lovin' Spoonful* . . . Kama Sutra 211
⑧	10	8	**Sweet Pea**...*Tommy Roe* . . . ABC-Paramount 10762
⑨	17	4	**Mothers Little Helper**............................*The Rolling Stones* . . . London 902
⑩	14	7	**Somewhere, My Love** ....*Ray Conniff & The Singers* . . . Columbia 43626

★ HIGHEST DEBUT ★ POS 61	★ BIGGEST MOVER ★ 50 to 11
Guantanamera...........................*The Sandpipers*	They're Coming To Take Me Away, Ha-Haaa! ....*Napoleon XIV*

Billboard HOT 100 — AUGUST 6, 1966

TW	LW	WK	Title / Artist / Label
①	1	7	**Wild Thing**...............................*The Troggs* . . . Atco 6415/Fontana 1548
②	3	9	**Lil' Red Riding Hood**......*Sam The Sham & The Pharoahs* . . . MGM 13506
③	7	4	**Summer In The City** ....*The Lovin' Spoonful* . . . Kama Sutra 211
④	4	9	**The Pied Piper** ....*Crispian St. Peters* . . . Jamie 1320
⑤	11	3	**They're Coming To Take Me Away, Ha-Haaa!** ....*Napoleon XIV* . . . Warner 5831
⑥	5	6	**I Saw Her Again** ....*The Mamas & The Papas* . . . Dunhill 4031
⑦	2	10	**Hanky Panky** ....*Tommy James & The Shondells* . . . Roulette 4686
⑧	8	9	**Sweet Pea**..*Tommy Roe* . . . ABC-Paramount 10762
⑨	9	5	**Mothers Little Helper**............................*The Rolling Stones* . . . London 902
⑩	10	8	**Somewhere, My Love** ....*Ray Conniff & The Singers* . . . Columbia 43626

★ HIGHEST DEBUT ★ POS 70	★ BIGGEST MOVER ★ 76 to 43
Respectable....................................*The Outsiders*	Land Of 1000 Dances...................*Wilson Pickett*

Billboard HOT 100 — AUGUST 13, 1966

TW	LW	WK	Title / Artist / Label
①	3	5	**Summer In The City** ....*The Lovin' Spoonful* . . . Kama Sutra 211
②	2	10	**Lil' Red Riding Hood**......*Sam The Sham & The Pharoahs* . . . MGM 13506
③	5	4	**They're Coming To Take Me Away, Ha-Haaa!** ....*Napoleon XIV* . . . Warner 5831
④	1	8	**Wild Thing** ....*The Troggs* . . . Atco 6415/Fontana 1548
⑤	4	10	**The Pied Piper**.................................*Crispian St. Peters* . . . Jamie 1320
⑥	6	7	**I Saw Her Again** ....*The Mamas & The Papas* . . . Dunhill 4031
⑦	11	8	**Sunny**...*Bobby Hebb* . . . Philips 40365
⑧	9	6	**Mothers Little Helper**.......................*The Rolling Stones* . . . London 902
⑨	10	9	**Somewhere, My Love**.......*Ray Conniff & The Singers* . . . Columbia 43626
⑩	8	10	**Sweet Pea** ....*Tommy Roe* . . . ABC-Paramount 10762

★ HIGHEST DEBUT ★ POS 66	★ BIGGEST MOVER ★ 61 to 20
You Can't Hurry Love....................*The Supremes*	Sunshine Superman ....*Donovan*

Billboard — AUGUST 20, 1966 — HOT 100

TW	LW	WK		
①	1	6	**Summer In The City** ....*The Lovin' Spoonful* . . . Kama Sutra 211	
②	7	9	**Sunny** ....*Bobby Hebb* . . . Philips 40365	
③	2	11	**Lil' Red Riding Hood**..........*Sam The Sham & The Pharoahs* . . . MGM 13506	
④	4	9	**Wild Thing** ....*The Troggs* . . . Atco 6415/Fontana 1548	
⑤	3	5	**They're Coming To Take Me Away, Ha-Haaa!** ....*Napoleon XIV* . . . Warner 5831	
⑥	14	7	**See You In September**.........................*The Happenings* . . . B.T. Puppy 520	
⑦	5	11	**The Pied Piper**......................................*Crispian St. Peters* . . . Jamie 1320	
⑧	8	7	**Mothers Little Helper**......................*The Rolling Stones* . . . London 902	
⑨	11	6	**I Couldn't Live Without Your Love** ....*Petula Clark* . . . Warner 5835	
⑩	20	4	**Sunshine Superman**..*Donovan* . . . Epic 10045	

★ **HIGHEST DEBUT** ★ POS 52
Yellow Submarine....................*The Beatles*

★ **BIGGEST MOVER** ★ 66 to 28
You Can't Hurry Love..................*The Supremes*

Billboard — AUGUST 27, 1966 — HOT 100

TW	LW	WK		
①	1	7	**Summer In The City** ....*The Lovin' Spoonful* . . . Kama Sutra 211	
②	2	10	**Sunny** ....*Bobby Hebb* . . . Philips 40365	
③	6	8	**See You In September**......................*The Happenings* . . . B.T. Puppy 520	
④	3	12	**Lil' Red Riding Hood**..........*Sam The Sham & The Pharoahs* . . . MGM 13506	
⑤	10	5	**Sunshine Superman**..*Donovan* . . . Epic 10045	
⑥	4	10	**Wild Thing** ....*The Troggs* . . . Atco 6415/Fontana 1548	
⑦	28	3	**You Can't Hurry Love** ....*The Supremes* . . . Motown 1097	
⑧	52	2	**Yellow Submarine**...............................*The Beatles* . . . Capitol 5715	
⑨	9	7	**I Couldn't Live Without Your Love** ....*Petula Clark* . . . Warner 5835	
⑩	16	7	**Summertime** ....*Billy Stewart* . . . Chess 1966	

★ **HIGHEST DEBUT** ★ POS 65
Eleanor Rigby ....*The Beatles*

★ **BIGGEST MOVER** ★ 52 to 8
Yellow Submarine..........................*The Beatles*

Billboard — SEPTEMBER 3, 1966 — HOT 100

TW	LW	WK		
❶	5	6	**Sunshine Superman** ....*Donovan* . . . Epic 10045	
❷	1	8	**Summer In The City** ....*The Lovin' Spoonful* . . . Kama Sutra 211	
❸	3	9	**See You In September**......................*The Happenings* . . . B.T. Puppy 520	
❹	7	4	**You Can't Hurry Love** ....*The Supremes* . . . Motown 1097	
❺	8	3	**Yellow Submarine** ....*The Beatles* . . . Capitol 5715	
❻	2	11	**Sunny**..*Bobby Hebb* . . . Philips 40365	
❼	15	6	**Land Of 1000 Dances** ....*Wilson Pickett* . . . Atlantic 2348	
❽	12	7	**Working In The Coal Mine** ....*Lee Dorsey* . . . Amy 958	
❾	11	7	**Blowin In The Wind** ....*Stevie Wonder* . . . Tamla 54136	
❿	10	8	**Summertime** ....*Billy Stewart* . . . Chess 1966	

★ **HIGHEST DEBUT** ★ POS 71
I Chose To Sing The Blues..............*Ray Charles*

★ **BIGGEST MOVER** ★ 66 to 27
Cherish ....*The Association*

Billboard — SEPTEMBER 10, 1966 — HOT 100

TW	LW	WK		
1	4	5	You Can't Hurry Love...........................The Supremes	Motown 1097
2	1	7	Sunshine Superman..Donovan	Epic 10045
3	5	4	Yellow Submarine ....The Beatles	Capitol 5715
4	3	10	See You In September....................The Happenings	B.T. Puppy 520
5	2	9	Summer In The City ....The Lovin' Spoonful	Kama Sutra 211
6	7	7	Land Of 1000 Dances ....Wilson Pickett	Atlantic 2348
7	6	12	Sunny...Bobby Hebb	Philips 40365
8	8	8	Working In The Coal Mine ....Lee Dorsey	Amy 958
9	18	8	Bus Stop ....The Hollies	Imperial 66186
10	16	7	Guantanamera ....The Sandpipers	A&M 806

★ HIGHEST DEBUT ★ POS 67	★ BIGGEST MOVER ★ 83 to 41
Last Train To Clarksville................The Monkees	I've Got You Under My Skin ....The 4 Seasons

Billboard — SEPTEMBER 17, 1966 — HOT 100

TW	LW	WK		
1	1	6	You Can't Hurry Love...........................The Supremes	Motown 1097
2	3	5	Yellow Submarine ....The Beatles	Capitol 5715
3	2	8	Sunshine Superman..Donovan	Epic 10045
4	14	4	Cherish ....The Association	Valiant 747
5	9	9	Bus Stop ....The Hollies	Imperial 66186
6	4	11	See You In September....................The Happenings	B.T. Puppy 520
7	6	8	Land Of 1000 Dances ....Wilson Pickett	Atlantic 2348
8	11	8	Wouldn't It Be Nice ....The Beach Boys	Capitol 5706
9	10	8	Guantanamera ....The Sandpipers	A&M 806
10	7	13	Sunny...Bobby Hebb	Philips 40365

★ HIGHEST DEBUT ★ POS 75	★ BIGGEST MOVER ★ 79 to 42
Hooray For Hazel ....Tommy Roe	Psychotic Reaction ....Count Five

Billboard — SEPTEMBER 24, 1966 — HOT 100

TW	LW	WK		
1	4	5	Cherish ....The Association	Valiant 747
2	1	7	You Can't Hurry Love ....The Supremes	Motown 1097
3	3	9	Sunshine Superman..Donovan	Epic 10045
4	2	6	Yellow Submarine ....The Beatles	Capitol 5715
5	5	10	Bus Stop ....The Hollies	Imperial 66186
6	11	6	Beauty Is Only Skin Deep ....The Temptations	Gordy 7055
7	18	7	Black Is Black ....Los Bravos	Press 60002
8	25	4	96 Tears ....?(Question Mark) & The Mysterians	Cameo 428
9	8	9	Wouldn't It Be Nice ....The Beach Boys	Capitol 5706
10	26	4	Reach Out I'll Be There ....Four Tops	Motown 1098

★ HIGHEST DEBUT ★ POS 81	★ BIGGEST MOVER ★ 85 to 53
If I Were A Carpenter ....Bobby Darin	See See Rider ....Eric Burdon & The Animals

OCTOBER 1, 1966 — HOT 100

TW	LW	WK	Title	Artist	Label
1	1	6	**Cherish**	The Association	Valiant 747
2	2	8	**You Can't Hurry Love**	The Supremes	Motown 1097
3	6	7	**Beauty Is Only Skin Deep**	The Temptations	Gordy 7055
4	7	8	**Black Is Black**	Los Bravos	Press 60002
5	5	11	**Bus Stop**	The Hollies	Imperial 66186
6	8	5	**96 Tears**	?(Question Mark) & The Mysterians	Cameo 428
7	10	5	**Reach Out I'll Be There**	Four Tops	Motown 1098
8	4	7	**Yellow Submarine**	The Beatles	Capitol 5715
9	3	10	**Sunshine Superman**	Donovan	Epic 10045
10	14	7	**Cherry, Cherry**	Neil Diamond	Bang 528

★ **HIGHEST DEBUT** ★ POS 72
Little Man ....Sonny & Cher

★ **BIGGEST MOVER** ★ 72 to 42
Poor Side Of Town ....Johnny Rivers

OCTOBER 8, 1966 — HOT 100

TW	LW	WK	Title	Artist	Label
1	1	7	**Cherish**	The Association	Valiant 747
2	7	6	**Reach Out I'll Be There**	Four Tops	Motown 1098
3	6	6	**96 Tears**	?(Question Mark) & The Mysterians	Cameo 428
4	4	9	**Black Is Black**	Los Bravos	Press 60002
5	3	8	**Beauty Is Only Skin Deep**	The Temptations	Gordy 7055
6	18	5	**Last Train To Clarksville**	The Monkees	Colgems 1001
7	10	8	**Cherry, Cherry**	Neil Diamond	Bang 528
8	2	9	**You Can't Hurry Love**	The Supremes	Motown 1097
9	15	5	**Psychotic Reaction**	Count Five	Double Shot 104
10	12	6	**I've Got You Under My Skin**	The 4 Seasons	Philips 40393

★ **HIGHEST DEBUT** ★ POS 40
Have You Seen Your Mother, Baby, Standing In The Shadow? ....The Rolling Stones

★ **BIGGEST MOVER** ★ 89 to 48
Dandy ....Herman's Hermits

OCTOBER 15, 1966 — HOT 100

TW	LW	WK	Title	Artist	Label
1	2	7	**Reach Out I'll Be There**	Four Tops	Motown 1098
2	1	8	**Cherish**	The Association	Valiant 747
3	3	7	**96 Tears**	?(Question Mark) & The Mysterians	Cameo 428
4	6	6	**Last Train To Clarksville**	The Monkees	Colgems 1001
5	9	6	**Psychotic Reaction**	Count Five	Double Shot 104
6	7	9	**Cherry, Cherry**	Neil Diamond	Bang 528
7	14	6	**Walk Away Renee**	The Left Banke	Smash 2041
8	11	9	**What Becomes Of The Brokenhearted**	Jimmy Ruffin	Soul 35022
9	10	7	**I've Got You Under My Skin**	The 4 Seasons	Philips 40393
10	8	10	**You Can't Hurry Love**	The Supremes	Motown 1097

★ **HIGHEST DEBUT** ★ POS 73
Secret Love ....Billy Stewart

★ **BIGGEST MOVER** ★ 48 to 15
Dandy ....Herman's Hermits

Billboard 🎵 OCTOBER 22, 1966 🎵 HOT 100.

TW	LW	WK	Title	Artist	Label
①	1	8	**Reach Out I'll Be There**	*Four Tops*	Motown 1098
②	3	8	**96 Tears**	*?(Question Mark) & The Mysterians*	Cameo 428
③	4	7	**Last Train To Clarksville**	*The Monkees*	Colgems 1001
④	2	9	**Cherish**	*The Association*	Valiant 747
⑤	5	7	**Psychotic Reaction**	*Count Five*	Double Shot 104
⑥	7	7	**Walk Away Renee**	*The Left Banke*	Smash 2041
❼	11	6	**Poor Side Of Town**	*Johnny Rivers*	Imperial 66205
⑧	8	10	**What Becomes Of The Brokenhearted**	*Jimmy Ruffin*	Soul 35022
⑨	15	4	**Dandy**	*Herman's Hermits*	MGM 13603
⑩	14	6	**See See Rider**	*Eric Burdon & The Animals*	MGM 13582

★ **HIGHEST DEBUT** ★ POS 65
Look Through My Window ....*The Mamas & The Papas*

★ **BIGGEST MOVER** ★ 76 to 40
Rain On The Roof ....*The Lovin' Spoonful*

Billboard 🎵 OCTOBER 29, 1966 🎵 HOT 100.

TW	LW	WK	Title	Artist	Label
①	2	9	**96 Tears**	*?(Question Mark) & The Mysterians*	Cameo 428
②	3	8	**Last Train To Clarksville**	*The Monkees*	Colgems 1001
③	1	9	**Reach Out I'll Be There**	*Four Tops*	Motown 1098
❹	7	7	**Poor Side Of Town**	*Johnny Rivers*	Imperial 66205
⑤	6	8	**Walk Away Renee**	*The Left Banke*	Smash 2041
❻	9	5	**Dandy**	*Herman's Hermits*	MGM 13603
⑦	8	11	**What Becomes Of The Brokenhearted**	*Jimmy Ruffin*	Soul 35022
❽	11	7	**Hooray For Hazel**	*Tommy Roe*	ABC 10852
❾	13	4	**Have You Seen Your Mother, Baby, Standing In The Shadow?**	*The Rolling Stones*	London 903
⑩	10	7	**See See Rider**	*Eric Burdon & The Animals*	MGM 13582

★ **HIGHEST DEBUT** ★ POS 66
Winchester Cathedral .....*The New Vaudeville Band*

★ **BIGGEST MOVER** ★ 81 to 38
Good Vibrations........................*The Beach Boys*

Billboard 🎵 NOVEMBER 5, 1966 🎵 HOT 100.

TW	LW	WK	Title	Artist	Label
①	2	9	**Last Train To Clarksville**	*The Monkees*	Colgems 1001
②	1	10	**96 Tears**	*?(Question Mark) & The Mysterians*	Cameo 428
③	4	8	**Poor Side Of Town**	*Johnny Rivers*	Imperial 66205
④	3	10	**Reach Out I'll Be There**	*Four Tops*	Motown 1098
⑤	6	6	**Dandy**	*Herman's Hermits*	MGM 13603
⑥	8	8	**Hooray For Hazel**	*Tommy Roe*	ABC 10852
⑦	7	12	**What Becomes Of The Brokenhearted**	*Jimmy Ruffin*	Soul 35022
❽	11	7	**If I Were A Carpenter**	*Bobby Darin*	Atlantic 2350
⑨	9	5	**Have You Seen Your Mother, Baby, Standing In The Shadow?**	*The Rolling Stones*	London 903
⑩	5	9	**Walk Away Renee**	*The Left Banke*	Smash 2041

★ **HIGHEST DEBUT** ★ POS 81
A Hazy Shade Of Winter ....*Simon & Garfunkel*

★ **BIGGEST MOVER** ★ 66 to 24
Winchester Cathedral .....*The New Vaudeville Band*

TW	LW	WK	Billboard	NOVEMBER 12, 1966	HOT 100
①	3	9	**Poor Side Of Town**.................................Johnny Rivers ... Imperial 66205
②	1	10	Last Train To Clarksville ....The Monkees ... Colgems 1001
③	2	11	**96 Tears** ....?(Question Mark) & The Mysterians ... Cameo 428
④	17	4	Good Vibrations ....The Beach Boys ... Capitol 5676
⑤	5	7	**Dandy**...Herman's Hermits ... MGM 13603
⑥	24	3	Winchester Cathedral...............The New Vaudeville Band ... Fontana 1562
⑦	27	3	You Keep Me Hangin' On ....The Supremes ... Motown 1101
⑧	8	8	**If I Were A Carpenter**...............................Bobby Darin ... Atlantic 2350
⑨	18	6	Devil With A Blue Dress On & Good Golly Miss Molly .... Mitch Ryder & The Detroit Wheels ... New Voice 817
⑩	11	8	I'm Your Puppet.................................James & Bobby Purify ... Bell 648

★ HIGHEST DEBUT ★ POS 65	★ BIGGEST MOVER ★ 81 to 47
Mellow Yellow ....Donovan	A Hazy Shade Of Winter ....Simon & Garfunkel

TW	LW	WK	Billboard	NOVEMBER 19, 1966	HOT 100
①	7	4	**You Keep Me Hangin' On** ....The Supremes ... Motown 1101
②	4	5	Good Vibrations ....The Beach Boys ... Capitol 5676
③	6	4	Winchester Cathedral................The New Vaudeville Band ... Fontana 1562
④	2	11	Last Train To Clarksville ....The Monkees ... Colgems 1001
⑤	1	10	Poor Side Of Town ....Johnny Rivers ... Imperial 66205
⑥	9	7	Devil With A Blue Dress On & Good Golly Miss Molly .... Mitch Ryder & The Detroit Wheels ... New Voice 817
⑦	10	9	I'm Your Puppet.................................James & Bobby Purify ... Bell 648
⑧	3	12	96 Tears ....?(Question Mark) & The Mysterians ... Cameo 428
⑨	8	9	If I Were A Carpenter ....Bobby Darin ... Atlantic 2350
⑩	15	6	**Rain On The Roof**........................The Lovin' Spoonful ... Kama Sutra 216

★ HIGHEST DEBUT ★ POS 75	★ BIGGEST MOVER ★ 65 to 24
That's Life ....Frank Sinatra	Mellow Yellow ....Donovan

TW	LW	WK	Billboard	NOVEMBER 26, 1966	HOT 100
①	1	5	**You Keep Me Hangin' On** ....The Supremes ... Motown 1101
②	2	6	Good Vibrations ....The Beach Boys ... Capitol 5676
③	3	5	Winchester Cathedral................The New Vaudeville Band ... Fontana 1562
④	6	8	**Devil With A Blue Dress On & Good Golly Miss Molly** .... Mitch Ryder & The Detroit Wheels ... New Voice 817
⑤	5	11	Poor Side Of Town ....Johnny Rivers ... Imperial 66205
⑥	7	10	**I'm Your Puppet**.................................James & Bobby Purify ... Bell 648
⑦	4	12	Last Train To Clarksville ....The Monkees ... Colgems 1001
⑧	11	8	Lady Godiva ....Peter & Gordon ... Capitol 5740
⑨	24	3	Mellow Yellow...Donovan ... Epic 10098
⑩	12	14	Born Free...Roger Williams ... Kapp 767

★ HIGHEST DEBUT ★ POS 66	★ BIGGEST MOVER ★ 82 to 45
Mustang Sally ....Wilson Pickett	Mame ....Herb Alpert & The Tijuana Brass

Billboard ⊙ DECEMBER 3, 1966 ⊙ HOT 100

TW	LW	WK	Title	Artist	Label
❶	3	6	**Winchester Cathedral**...........*The New Vaudeville Band* . . . Fontana 1562		
②	2	7	Good Vibrations ....*The Beach Boys* . . . Capitol 5676		
③	1	6	You Keep Me Hangin' On ....*The Supremes* . . . Motown 1101		
④	4	9	**Devil With A Blue Dress On & Good Golly Miss Molly**		
			Mitch Ryder & The Detroit Wheels . . . New Voice 817		
❺	9	4	Mellow Yellow..*Donovan* . . . Epic 10098		
⑥	6	11	**I'm Your Puppet** ....*James & Bobby Purify* . . . Bell 648		
⑦	8	9	Lady Godiva ....*Peter & Gordon* . . . Capitol 5740		
⑧	10	15	Born Free ....*Roger Williams* . . . Kapp 767		
⑨	5	12	Poor Side Of Town ....*Johnny Rivers* . . . Imperial 66205		
⑩	7	13	Last Train To Clarksville ....*The Monkees* . . . Colgems 1001		

★ HIGHEST DEBUT ★ POS 78	★ BIGGEST MOVER ★ 100 to 57
Tell It Like It Is.............................*Aaron Neville*	Cry...*Ronnie Dove*

Billboard ⊙ DECEMBER 10, 1966 ⊙ HOT 100

TW	LW	WK	Title	Artist	Label
①	2	8	**Good Vibrations**..................................*The Beach Boys* . . . Capitol 5676		
❷	5	5	**Mellow Yellow**..*Donovan* . . . Epic 10098		
③	1	7	Winchester Cathedral...........*The New Vaudeville Band* . . . Fontana 1562		
④	4	10	**Devil With A Blue Dress On & Good Golly Miss Molly**		
			Mitch Ryder & The Detroit Wheels . . . New Voice 817		
⑤	3	7	You Keep Me Hangin' On ....*The Supremes* . . . Motown 1101		
⑥	7	10	**Lady Godiva**...*Peter & Gordon* . . . Capitol 5740		
❼	13	7	**Stop Stop Stop** ....*The Hollies* . . . Imperial 66214		
⑧	8	16	Born Free ....*Roger Williams* . . . Kapp 767		
❾	12	7	**I'm Ready For Love**...................*Martha & The Vandellas* . . . Gordy 7056		
⑩	15	4	That's Life ....*Frank Sinatra* . . . Reprise 0531		

★ HIGHEST DEBUT ★ POS 44	★ BIGGEST MOVER ★ 81 to 46
I'm A Believer...............................*The Monkees*	Words Of Love..............*The Mamas & The Papas*

Billboard ⊙ DECEMBER 17, 1966 ⊙ HOT 100

TW	LW	WK	Title	Artist	Label
❶	3	8	**Winchester Cathedral**...........*The New Vaudeville Band* . . . Fontana 1562		
②	2	6	**Mellow Yellow** ....*Donovan* . . . Epic 10098		
③	1	9	Good Vibrations ....*The Beach Boys* . . . Capitol 5676		
④	4	11	**Devil With A Blue Dress On & Good Golly Miss Molly**		
			Mitch Ryder & The Detroit Wheels . . . New Voice 817		
⑤	5	8	You Keep Me Hangin' On ....*The Supremes* . . . Motown 1101		
⑥	10	5	That's Life ....*Frank Sinatra* . . . Reprise 0531		
⑦	8	17	**Born Free**...*Roger Williams* . . . Kapp 767		
⑧	44	2	I'm A Believer ....*The Monkees* . . . Colgems 1002		
⑨	16	5	Sugar Town..*Nancy Sinatra* . . . Reprise 0527		
⑩	14	6	A Place In The Sun....................................*Stevie Wonder* . . . Tamla 54139		

★ HIGHEST DEBUT ★ POS 30	★ BIGGEST MOVER ★ 44 to 8
Snoopy Vs. The Red Baron.................*The Royal Guardsmen*	I'm A Believer...................................*The Monkees*

TW	LW	WK	Billboard.	🔵 DECEMBER 24, 1966 🔵	HOT 100.
①	1	9	Winchester Cathedral...........*The New Vaudeville Band* . . . Fontana 1562		
②	2	7	Mellow Yellow.....................................*Donovan* . . . Epic 10098		
③	8	3	I'm A Believer ....*The Monkees* . . . Colgems 1002		
④	6	6	That's Life................................*Frank Sinatra* . . . Reprise 0531		
⑤	4	12	Devil With A Blue Dress On & Good Golly Miss Molly .... *Mitch Ryder & The Detroit Wheels* . . . New Voice 817		
⑥	9	6	Sugar Town.....................................*Nancy Sinatra* . . . Reprise 0527		
⑦	30	2	Snoopy Vs. The Red Baron..............*The Royal Guardsmen* . . . Laurie 3366		
⑧	3	10	Good Vibrations ....*The Beach Boys* . . . Capitol 5676		
⑨	10	7	A Place In The Sun................................*Stevie Wonder* . . . Tamla 54139		
⑩	12	6	(I Know) I'm Losing You............................*The Temptations* . . . Gordy 7057		

★ HIGHEST DEBUT ★ POS 65	★ BIGGEST MOVER ★ 86 to 45
Gallant Men ....*Senator Everett McKinley Dirksen*	Nashville Cats......................*The Lovin' Spoonful*

TW	LW	WK	Billboard.	🔵 DECEMBER 31, 1966 🔵	HOT 100.
❶	3	4	I'm A Believer ....*The Monkees* . . . Colgems 1002		
❷	7	3	Snoopy Vs. The Red Baron ....*The Royal Guardsmen* . . . Laurie 3366		
❸	1	10	Winchester Cathedral.................*The New Vaudeville Band* . . . Fontana 1562		
❹	4	7	That's Life................................*Frank Sinatra* . . . Reprise 0531		
❺	6	7	Sugar Town...................................*Nancy Sinatra* . . . Reprise 0527		
❻	2	8	Mellow Yellow.......................................*Donovan* . . . Epic 10098		
❼	14	5	Tell It Like It Is.................................*Aaron Neville* . . . Par-Lo 101		
❽	10	7	(I Know) I'm Losing You ....*The Temptations* . . . Gordy 7057		
❾	9	8	A Place In The Sun................................*Stevie Wonder* . . . Tamla 54139		
❿	27	5	Good Thing ....*Paul Revere & The Raiders* . . . Columbia 43907		

★ HIGHEST DEBUT ★ POS 86	★ BIGGEST MOVER ★ 69 to 38
Music To Watch Girls By ....*The Bob Crewe Generation*	Color My World...............................*Petula Clark*

TW	LW	WK	**Billboard**	JANUARY 7, 1967	HOT 100
①	1	5	**I'm A Believer**	*The Monkees*	Colgems 1002
②	2	4	**Snoopy Vs. The Red Baron**	*The Royal Guardsmen*	Laurie 3366
❸	7	6	**Tell It Like It Is**	*Aaron Neville*	Par-Lo 101
④	3	11	**Winchester Cathedral**	*The New Vaudeville Band*	Fontana 1562
⑤	5	8	**Sugar Town**	*Nancy Sinatra*	Reprise 0527
⑥	4	8	**That's Life**	*Frank Sinatra*	Reprise 0531
❼	10	6	**Good Thing**	*Paul Revere & The Raiders*	Columbia 43907
❽	19	6	**Words Of Love**	*The Mamas & The Papas*	Dunhill 4057
⑨	15	4	**Standing In The Shadows Of Love**	*Four Tops*	Motown 1102
⑩	6	9	**Mellow Yellow**	*Donovan*	Epic 10098

★ **HIGHEST DEBUT** ★ POS 77
Wild Thing ....*Senator Bobby*

★ **BIGGEST MOVER** ★ 71 to 41
Knight In Rusty Armour.............*Peter & Gordon*

TW	LW	WK	**Billboard**	JANUARY 14, 1967	HOT 100
①	1	6	**I'm A Believer**	*The Monkees*	Colgems 1002
②	2	5	**Snoopy Vs. The Red Baron**	*The Royal Guardsmen*	Laurie 3366
③	3	7	**Tell It Like It Is**	*Aaron Neville*	Par-Lo 101
❹	7	7	**Good Thing**	*Paul Revere & The Raiders*	Columbia 43907
⑤	5	9	**Sugar Town**	*Nancy Sinatra*	Reprise 0527
⑥	8	7	**Words Of Love**	*The Mamas & The Papas*	Dunhill 4057
⑦	9	5	**Standing In The Shadows Of Love**	*Four Tops*	Motown 1102
⑧	4	12	**Winchester Cathedral**	*The New Vaudeville Band*	Fontana 1562
⑨	6	9	**That's Life**	*Frank Sinatra*	Reprise 0531
⑩	20	7	**Georgy Girl**	*The Seekers*	Capitol 5756

★ **HIGHEST DEBUT** ★ POS 72
The Beat Goes On ....*Sonny & Cher*

★ **BIGGEST MOVER** ★ 77 to 52
Wild Thing ....*Senator Bobby*

TW	LW	WK	**Billboard**	JANUARY 21, 1967	HOT 100
①	1	7	**I'm A Believer**	*The Monkees*	Colgems 1002
②	2	6	**Snoopy Vs. The Red Baron**	*The Royal Guardsmen*	Laurie 3366
③	3	8	**Tell It Like It Is**	*Aaron Neville*	Par-Lo 101
④	4	8	**Good Thing**	*Paul Revere & The Raiders*	Columbia 43907
⑤	6	8	**Words Of Love**	*The Mamas & The Papas*	Dunhill 4057
⑥	7	6	**Standing In The Shadows Of Love**	*Four Tops*	Motown 1102
❼	10	8	**Georgy Girl**	*The Seekers*	Capitol 5756
⑧	5	10	**Sugar Town**	*Nancy Sinatra*	Reprise 0527
⑨	16	6	**Nashville Cats**	*The Lovin' Spoonful*	Kama Sutra 219
⑩	12	7	**Tell It To The Rain**	*The 4 Seasons*	Philips 40412

★ **HIGHEST DEBUT** ★ POS 78
Ruby Tuesday ....*The Rolling Stones*

★ **BIGGEST MOVER** ★ 42 to 15
Kind Of A Drag ....*The Buckinghams*

Billboard — JANUARY 28, 1967 — HOT 100

TW	LW	WK	Title	Artist	Label
①	1	8	**I'm A Believer**	*The Monkees*	Colgems 1002
②	3	9	**Tell It Like It Is**	*Aaron Neville*	Par-Lo 101
③	2	7	Snoopy Vs. The Red Baron	*The Royal Guardsmen*	Laurie 3366
❹	7	9	Georgy Girl	*The Seekers*	Capitol 5756
⑤	5	9	**Words Of Love**	*The Mamas & The Papas*	Dunhill 4057
⑥	6	7	**Standing In The Shadows Of Love**	*Four Tops*	Motown 1102
⑦	4	9	Good Thing	*Paul Revere & The Raiders*	Columbia 43907
⑧	9	7	**Nashville Cats**	*The Lovin' Spoonful*	Kama Sutra 219
❾	15	5	Kind Of A Drag	*The Buckinghams*	U.S.A. 860
❿	13	8	(We Ain't Got) Nothin' Yet	*Blues Magoos*	Mercury 72622

★ **HIGHEST DEBUT** ★ POS 47
Love Is Here And Now You're Gone ....*The Supremes*

★ **BIGGEST MOVER** ★ 78 to 43
Ruby Tuesday ....*The Rolling Stones*

Billboard — FEBRUARY 4, 1967 — HOT 100

TW	LW	WK	Title	Artist	Label
①	1	9	**I'm A Believer**	*The Monkees*	Colgems 1002
②	4	10	**Georgy Girl**	*The Seekers*	Capitol 5756
③	3	8	Snoopy Vs. The Red Baron	*The Royal Guardsmen*	Laurie 3366
④	2	10	Tell It Like It Is	*Aaron Neville*	Par-Lo 101
❺	9	6	**Kind Of A Drag**	*The Buckinghams*	U.S.A. 860
⑥	5	10	Words Of Love	*The Mamas & The Papas*	Dunhill 4057
❼	10	9	(We Ain't Got) Nothin' Yet	*Blues Magoos*	Mercury 72622
❽	11	9	98.6	*Keith*	Mercury 72639
⑨	7	10	Good Thing	*Paul Revere & The Raiders*	Columbia 43907
❿	6	8	Standing In The Shadows Of Love	*Four Tops*	Motown 1102

★ **HIGHEST DEBUT** ★ POS 77
Everybody Needs Somebody To Love .....*Wilson Pickett*

★ **BIGGEST MOVER** ★ 43 to 11
Ruby Tuesday ....*The Rolling Stones*

Billboard — FEBRUARY 11, 1967 — HOT 100

TW	LW	WK	Title	Artist	Label
①	1	10	**I'm A Believer**	*The Monkees*	Colgems 1002
②	2	11	**Georgy Girl**	*The Seekers*	Capitol 5756
③	5	7	Kind Of A Drag	*The Buckinghams*	U.S.A. 860
❹	11	4	**Ruby Tuesday**	*The Rolling Stones*	London 904
⑤	7	10	**(We Ain't Got) Nothin' Yet**	*Blues Magoos*	Mercury 72622
⑥	4	11	Tell It Like It Is	*Aaron Neville*	Par-Lo 101
⑦	8	10	**98.6**	*Keith*	Mercury 72639
⑧	3	9	Snoopy Vs. The Red Baron	*The Royal Guardsmen*	Laurie 3366
❾	27	3	Love Is Here And Now You're Gone	*The Supremes*	Motown 1103
❿	16	5	The Beat Goes On	*Sonny & Cher*	Atco 6461

★ **HIGHEST DEBUT** ★ POS 69
Epistle To Dippy ....*Donovan*

★ **BIGGEST MOVER** ★ 81 to 49
Baby I Need Your Lovin' ....*Johnny Rivers*

Billboard — FEBRUARY 18, 1967 — HOT 100

TW	LW	WK			
1	3	8	Kind Of A Drag	The Buckinghams	U.S.A. 860
2	1	11	I'm A Believer	The Monkees	Colgems 1002
3	4	5	Ruby Tuesday	The Rolling Stones	London 904
4	2	12	Georgy Girl	The Seekers	Capitol 5756
5	5	11	(We Ain't Got) Nothin' Yet	Blues Magoos	Mercury 72622
6	9	4	Love Is Here And Now You're Gone	The Supremes	Motown 1103
7	7	11	98.6	Keith	Mercury 72639
8	6	12	Tell It Like It Is	Aaron Neville	Par-Lo 101
9	10	6	The Beat Goes On	Sonny & Cher	Atco 6461
10	17	8	Gimme Some Lovin'	The Spencer Davis Group	United Artists 50108

★ **HIGHEST DEBUT** ★ POS 77
Ups And Downs .... *Paul Revere & The Raiders*

★ **BIGGEST MOVER** ★ 90 to 54
There's A Kind Of Hush .... *Herman's Hermits*

Billboard — FEBRUARY 25, 1967 — HOT 100

TW	LW	WK			
1	1	9	Kind Of A Drag	The Buckinghams	U.S.A. 860
2	6	5	Love Is Here And Now You're Gone	The Supremes	Motown 1103
3	3	6	Ruby Tuesday	The Rolling Stones	London 904
4	2	12	I'm A Believer	The Monkees	Colgems 1002
5	4	13	Georgy Girl	The Seekers	Capitol 5756
6	9	7	The Beat Goes On	Sonny & Cher	Atco 6461
7	10	9	Gimme Some Lovin'	The Spencer Davis Group	United Artists 50108
8	13	7	Then You Can Tell Me Goodbye	The Casinos	Fraternity 977
9	5	12	(We Ain't Got) Nothin' Yet	Blues Magoos	Mercury 72622
10	19	4	Baby I Need Your Lovin'	Johnny Rivers	Imperial 66227

★ **HIGHEST DEBUT** ★ POS 57
Dedicated To The One I Love .... *The Mamas & The Papas*

★ **BIGGEST MOVER** ★ 95 to 62
The Love I Saw In You Was Just A Mirage .... *Smokey Robinson & The Miracles*

Billboard — MARCH 4, 1967 — HOT 100

TW	LW	WK			
1	3	7	Ruby Tuesday	The Rolling Stones	London 904
2	2	6	Love Is Here And Now You're Gone	The Supremes	Motown 1103
3	1	10	Kind Of A Drag	The Buckinghams	U.S.A. 860
4	10	5	Baby I Need Your Lovin'	Johnny Rivers	Imperial 66227
5	5	14	Georgy Girl	The Seekers	Capitol 5756
6	6	8	The Beat Goes On	Sonny & Cher	Atco 6461
7	7	10	Gimme Some Lovin'	The Spencer Davis Group	United Artists 50108
8	8	8	Then You Can Tell Me Goodbye	The Casinos	Fraternity 977
9	14	5	Sock It To Me-Baby!	Mitch Ryder & The Detroit Wheels	New Voice 820
10	4	13	I'm A Believer	The Monkees	Colgems 1002

★ **HIGHEST DEBUT** ★ POS 80
I Never Loved A Man (The Way I Love You) .... *Aretha Franklin*

★ **BIGGEST MOVER** ★ 85 to 36
Penny Lane .... *The Beatles*

Billboard — MARCH 11, 1967 — HOT 100

TW	LW	WK	Title	Artist	Label
①	2	7	**Love Is Here And Now You're Gone**	The Supremes	Motown 1103
②	1	8	**Ruby Tuesday**	The Rolling Stones	London 904
③	4	6	**Baby I Need Your Lovin'**	Johnny Rivers	Imperial 66227
④	3	11	**Kind Of A Drag**	The Buckinghams	U.S.A. 860
⑤	36	3	**Penny Lane**	The Beatles	Capitol 5810
⑥	8	9	**Then You Can Tell Me Goodbye**	The Casinos	Fraternity 977
⑦	9	6	**Sock It To Me-Baby!**	Mitch Ryder & The Detroit Wheels	New Voice 820
⑧	21	5	**Happy Together**	The Turtles	White Whale 244
⑨	13	8	**My Cup Runneth Over**	Ed Ames	RCA 9002
⑩	26	3	**Dedicated To The One I Love**	The Mamas & The Papas	Dunhill 4077

★ **HIGHEST DEBUT** ★ POS 65
Bernadette ....Four Tops

★ **BIGGEST MOVER** ★ 90 to 57
This Is My Song ....Petula Clark

Billboard — MARCH 18, 1967 — HOT 100

TW	LW	WK	Title	Artist	Label
❶	5	4	**Penny Lane**	The Beatles	Capitol 5810
❷	8	6	**Happy Together**	The Turtles	White Whale 244
❸	3	7	**Baby I Need Your Lovin'**	Johnny Rivers	Imperial 66227
❹	1	8	**Love Is Here And Now You're Gone**	The Supremes	Motown 1103
❺	2	9	**Ruby Tuesday**	The Rolling Stones	London 904
❻	10	4	**Dedicated To The One I Love**	The Mamas & The Papas	Dunhill 4077
❼	7	7	**Sock It To Me-Baby!**	Mitch Ryder & The Detroit Wheels	New Voice 820
❽	12	6	**There's A Kind Of Hush**	Herman's Hermits	MGM 13681
❾	9	9	**My Cup Runneth Over**	Ed Ames	RCA 9002
❿	6	10	**Then You Can Tell Me Goodbye**	The Casinos	Fraternity 977

★ **HIGHEST DEBUT** ★ POS 50
Somethin' Stupid ......Nancy Sinatra & Frank Sinatra

★ **BIGGEST MOVER** ★ 65 to 23
Bernadette ....Four Tops

Billboard — MARCH 25, 1967 — HOT 100

TW	LW	WK	Title	Artist	Label
①	2	7	**Happy Together**	The Turtles	White Whale 244
❷	6	5	**Dedicated To The One I Love**	The Mamas & The Papas	Dunhill 4077
③	1	5	**Penny Lane**	The Beatles	Capitol 5810
❹	8	7	**There's A Kind Of Hush**	Herman's Hermits	MGM 13681
⑤	3	8	**Baby I Need Your Lovin'**	Johnny Rivers	Imperial 66227
⑥	7	8	**Sock It To Me-Baby!**	Mitch Ryder & The Detroit Wheels	New Voice 820
❼	12	9	**For What It's Worth**	The Buffalo Springfield	Atco 6459
⑧	9	10	**My Cup Runneth Over**	Ed Ames	RCA 9002
⑨	4	9	**Love Is Here And Now You're Gone**	The Supremes	Motown 1103
⑩	5	10	**Ruby Tuesday**	The Rolling Stones	London 904

★ **HIGHEST DEBUT** ★ POS 32
A Little Bit Me, A Little Bit You ......The Monkees

★ **BIGGEST MOVER** ★ 99 to 64
On A Carousel ....The Hollies

Billboard HOT 100 — APRIL 1, 1967

TW	LW	WK		
①	1	8	**Happy Together**....................................*The Turtles* . . . White Whale 244	
②	2	6	**Dedicated To The One I Love** .... *The Mamas & The Papas* . . . Dunhill 4077	
③	3	6	**Penny Lane** ....*The Beatles* . . . Capitol 5810	
④	4	8	**There's A Kind Of Hush**....................*Herman's Hermits* . . . MGM 13681	
⑤	18	4	**Bernadette**...*Four Tops* . . . Motown 1104	
⑥	19	5	**This Is My Song**.................................*Petula Clark* . . . Warner 7002	
⑦	7	10	**For What It's Worth** ....*The Buffalo Springfield* . . . Atco 6459	
⑧	11	6	**Strawberry Fields Forever** ....*The Beatles* . . . Capitol 5810	
⑨	29	3	**Somethin' Stupid**.................*Nancy Sinatra & Frank Sinatra* . . . Reprise 0561	
⑩	28	5	**Western Union** ....*The Five Americans* . . . Abnak 118	

★ **HIGHEST DEBUT** ★ POS 65
Get Me To The World On Time.........*The Electric Prunes*

★ **BIGGEST MOVER** ★ 58 to 34
At The Zoo..............................*Simon & Garfunkel*

Billboard HOT 100 — APRIL 8, 1967

TW	LW	WK		
①	1	9	**Happy Together**....................................*The Turtles* . . . White Whale 244	
②	2	7	**Dedicated To The One I Love** .... *The Mamas & The Papas* . . . Dunhill 4077	
③	9	4	**Somethin' Stupid**.................*Nancy Sinatra & Frank Sinatra* . . . Reprise 0561	
④	5	5	**Bernadette**...*Four Tops* . . . Motown 1104	
⑤	6	6	**This Is My Song**.................................*Petula Clark* . . . Warner 7002	
⑥	3	7	**Penny Lane** ....*The Beatles* . . . Capitol 5810	
⑦	10	6	**Western Union** ....*The Five Americans* . . . Abnak 118	
⑧	12	9	**I Think We're Alone Now** ....*Tommy James & The Shondells* . . . Roulette 4720	
⑨	19	3	**A Little Bit Me, A Little Bit You** ....*The Monkees* . . . Colgems 1004	
⑩	4	9	**There's A Kind Of Hush**....................*Herman's Hermits* . . . MGM 13681	

★ **HIGHEST DEBUT** ★ POS 57
The Happening ....*The Supremes*

★ **BIGGEST MOVER** ★ 83 to 48
You Got What It Takes..........*The Dave Clark Five*

Billboard HOT 100 — APRIL 15, 1967

TW	LW	WK		
①	3	5	**Somethin' Stupid**..............*Nancy Sinatra & Frank Sinatra* . . . Reprise 0561	
②	1	10	**Happy Together** ....*The Turtles* . . . White Whale 244	
③	5	7	**This Is My Song**.................................*Petula Clark* . . . Warner 7002	
④	4	6	**Bernadette**...*Four Tops* . . . Motown 1104	
⑤	9	4	**A Little Bit Me, A Little Bit You** ....*The Monkees* . . . Colgems 1004	
⑥	7	7	**Western Union** ....*The Five Americans* . . . Abnak 118	
⑦	8	10	**I Think We're Alone Now** ....*Tommy James & The Shondells* . . . Roulette 4720	
⑧	2	8	**Dedicated To The One I Love** .....*The Mamas & The Papas* . . . Dunhill 4077	
⑨	12	7	**I Never Loved A Man (The Way I Love You)**..........*Aretha Franklin* . . . Atlantic 2386	
⑩	11	8	**Jimmy Mack**.................................*Martha & The Vandellas* . . . Gordy 7058	

★ **HIGHEST DEBUT** ★ POS 82
Shake A Tail Feather..........*James & Bobby Purify*

★ **BIGGEST MOVER** ★ 57 to 19
The Happening ....*The Supremes*

Billboard — APRIL 22, 1967 — HOT 100

TW	LW	WK	Title	Artist	Label
①	1	6	**Somethin' Stupid**	*Nancy Sinatra & Frank Sinatra*	Reprise 0561
②	2	11	Happy Together	*The Turtles*	White Whale 244
③	5	5	A Little Bit Me, A Little Bit You	*The Monkees*	Colgems 1004
❹	7	11	I Think We're Alone Now	*Tommy James & The Shondells*	Roulette 4720
⑤	6	8	**Western Union**	*The Five Americans*	Abnak 118
⑥	3	8	This Is My Song	*Petula Clark*	Warner 7002
❼	11	7	Sweet Soul Music	*Arthur Conley*	Atco 6463
⑧	4	7	Bernadette	*Four Tops*	Motown 1104
⑨	9	8	I Never Loved A Man (The Way I Love You)	*Aretha Franklin*	Atlantic 2386
⑩	10	9	**Jimmy Mack**	*Martha & The Vandellas*	Gordy 7058

★ HIGHEST DEBUT ★ POS 76
Melancholy Music Man .....*The Righteous Brothers*

★ BIGGEST MOVER ★ 61 to 38
When I Was Young.......*Eric Burdon & The Animals*

Billboard — APRIL 29, 1967 — HOT 100

TW	LW	WK	Title	Artist	Label
①	1	7	**Somethin' Stupid**	*Nancy Sinatra & Frank Sinatra*	Reprise 0561
②	3	6	**A Little Bit Me, A Little Bit You**	*The Monkees*	Colgems 1004
③	2	12	Happy Together	*The Turtles*	White Whale 244
❹	7	8	Sweet Soul Music	*Arthur Conley*	Atco 6463
⑤	4	12	I Think We're Alone Now	*Tommy James & The Shondells*	Roulette 4720
⑥	5	9	Western Union	*The Five Americans*	Abnak 118
⑦	6	9	This Is My Song	*Petula Clark*	Warner 7002
❽	11	4	The Happening	*The Supremes*	Motown 1107
⑨	8	8	Bernadette	*Four Tops*	Motown 1104
⑩	10	10	**Jimmy Mack**	*Martha & The Vandellas*	Gordy 7058

★ HIGHEST DEBUT ★ POS 50
Respect ......*Aretha Franklin*

★ BIGGEST MOVER ★ 79 to 49
Groovin' ......*The Young Rascals*

Billboard — MAY 6, 1967 — HOT 100

TW	LW	WK	Title	Artist	Label
①	1	8	**Somethin' Stupid**	*Nancy Sinatra & Frank Sinatra*	Reprise 0561
❷	8	5	The Happening	*The Supremes*	Motown 1107
③	4	9	Sweet Soul Music	*Arthur Conley*	Atco 6463
④	2	7	A Little Bit Me, A Little Bit You	*The Monkees*	Colgems 1004
⑤	3	13	Happy Together	*The Turtles*	White Whale 244
⑥	5	13	I Think We're Alone Now	*Tommy James & The Shondells*	Roulette 4720
❼	11	9	Don't You Care	*The Buckinghams*	Columbia 44053
❽	18	7	Close Your Eyes	*Peaches & Herb*	Date 1549
❾	12	6	You Got What It Takes	*The Dave Clark Five*	Epic 10144
❿	13	7	I'm A Man	*The Spencer Davis Group*	United Artists 50144

★ HIGHEST DEBUT ★ POS 79
Tramp ......*Otis & Carla*

★ BIGGEST MOVER ★ 81 to 42
All I Need......*The Temptations*

Billboard — MAY 13, 1967 — HOT 100

TW	LW	WK		
①	2	6	The Happening ....The Supremes . . .	Motown 1107
②	3	10	Sweet Soul Music ....Arthur Conley . . .	Atco 6463
③	1	9	Somethin' Stupid ....Nancy Sinatra & Frank Sinatra . . .	Reprise 0561
❹	19	4	Groovin' ....The Young Rascals . . .	Atlantic 2401
⑤	4	8	A Little Bit Me, A Little Bit You ....The Monkees . . .	Colgems 1004
⑥	7	10	Don't You Care ....The Buckinghams . . .	Columbia 44053
⑦	9	7	You Got What It Takes....................The Dave Clark Five . . .	Epic 10144
⑧	8	8	Close Your Eyes ....Peaches & Herb . . .	Date 1549
⑨	17	6	I Got Rhythm...............................The Happenings . . .	B.T. Puppy 527
⑩	6	14	I Think We're Alone Now ....Tommy James & The Shondells . . .	Roulette 4720

★ HIGHEST DEBUT ★ POS 78
Jump Back..............................King Curtis

★ BIGGEST MOVER ★ 44 to 22
Creeque Alley................The Mamas & The Papas

Billboard — MAY 20, 1967 — HOT 100

TW	LW	WK		
❶	4	5	Groovin' ....The Young Rascals . . .	Atlantic 2401
②	1	7	The Happening ....The Supremes . . .	Motown 1107
③	2	11	Sweet Soul Music ....Arthur Conley . . .	Atco 6463
④	3	10	Somethin' Stupid ....Nancy Sinatra & Frank Sinatra . . .	Reprise 0561
❺	14	4	Respect ....Aretha Franklin . . .	Atlantic 2403
❻	9	7	I Got Rhythm...............................The Happenings . . .	B.T. Puppy 527
❼	13	7	Release Me (And Let Me Love Again)............. Engelbert Humperdinck . . .	Parrot 40011
⑧	8	9	Close Your Eyes ....Peaches & Herb . . .	Date 1549
⑨	6	11	Don't You Care ....The Buckinghams . . .	Columbia 44053
⑩	7	8	You Got What It Takes ....The Dave Clark Five . . .	Epic 10144

★ HIGHEST DEBUT ★ POS 74
Can't Take My Eyes Off You ....Frankie Valli

★ BIGGEST MOVER ★ 88 to 58
She'd Rather Be With Me................The Turtles

Billboard — MAY 27, 1967 — HOT 100

TW	LW	WK		
①	1	6	Groovin' ....The Young Rascals . . .	Atlantic 2401
❷	5	5	Respect ....Aretha Franklin . . .	Atlantic 2403
❸	6	8	I Got Rhythm...............................The Happenings . . .	B.T. Puppy 527
❹	7	8	Release Me (And Let Me Love Again) .... Engelbert Humperdinck . . .	Parrot 40011
⑤	2	8	The Happening ....The Supremes . . .	Motown 1107
⑥	3	12	Sweet Soul Music ....Arthur Conley . . .	Atco 6463
❼	14	5	Him Or Me – What's It Gonna Be? ....Paul Revere & The Raiders . . .	Columbia 44094
❽	13	5	Creeque Alley ....The Mamas & The Papas . . .	Dunhill 4083
⑨	4	11	Somethin' Stupid................Nancy Sinatra & Frank Sinatra . . .	Reprise 0561
⑩	11	8	Girl, You'll Be A Woman Soon................Neil Diamond . . .	Bang 542

★ HIGHEST DEBUT ★ POS 52
Windy ....The Association

★ BIGGEST MOVER ★ 98 to 49
Sunday Will Never Be The Same.........Spanky & Our Gang

Billboard — JUNE 3, 1967 — HOT 100

TW	LW	WK		
①	2	6	**Respect** ....*Aretha Franklin* ... Atlantic 2403	
②	1	7	Groovin' ....*The Young Rascals* ... Atlantic 2401	
③	3	9	I Got Rhythm..*The Happenings* ... B.T. Puppy 527	
④	4	9	**Release Me (And Let Me Love Again)** .... *Engelbert Humperdinck* ... Parrot 40011	
⑤	8	6	**Creeque Alley** ....*The Mamas & The Papas* ... Dunhill 4083	
⑥	7	6	Him Or Me - What's It Gonna Be? ....*Paul Revere & The Raiders* ... Columbia 44094	
⑦	5	9	The Happening ....*The Supremes* ... Motown 1107	
⑧	6	13	Sweet Soul Music ....*Arthur Conley* ... Atco 6463	
⑨	17	10	Somebody To Love.....................................*Jefferson Airplane* ... RCA 9140	
⑩	15	6	All I Need..*The Temptations* ... Gordy 7061	

★ **HIGHEST DEBUT** ★ POS 70
The Tracks Of My Tears................*Johnny Rivers*

★ **BIGGEST MOVER** ★ 98 to 55
San Francisco (Be Sure To Wear Flowers In Your Hair)..............................*Scott McKenzie*

Billboard — JUNE 10, 1967 — HOT 100

TW	LW	WK		
①	1	7	**Respect** ....*Aretha Franklin* ... Atlantic 2403	
②	2	8	Groovin' ....*The Young Rascals* ... Atlantic 2401	
③	3	10	I Got Rhythm..*The Happenings* ... B.T. Puppy 527	
④	4	10	**Release Me (And Let Me Love Again)** .... *Engelbert Humperdinck* ... Parrot 40011	
⑤	6	7	**Him Or Me - What's It Gonna Be?** ....*Paul Revere & The Raiders* ... Columbia 44094	
⑥	9	11	Somebody To Love....................................*Jefferson Airplane* ... RCA 9140	
⑦	14	5	She'd Rather Be With Me.............................*The Turtles* ... White Whale 249	
⑧	17	5	Little Bit O' Soul.....................................*The Music Explosion* ... Laurie 3380	
⑨	10	7	All I Need..*The Temptations* ... Gordy 7061	
⑩	5	7	Creeque Alley ....*The Mamas & The Papas* ... Dunhill 4083	

★ **HIGHEST DEBUT** ★ POS 66
C'mon Marianne ....*The 4 Seasons*

★ **BIGGEST MOVER** ★ 83 to 44
Up-Up And Away ....*The 5th Dimension*

Billboard — JUNE 17, 1967 — HOT 100

TW	LW	WK		
①	2	9	**Groovin'** ....*The Young Rascals* ... Atlantic 2401	
②	1	8	Respect ....*Aretha Franklin* ... Atlantic 2403	
③	7	6	**She'd Rather Be With Me**.....................*The Turtles* ... White Whale 249	
④	4	11	**Release Me (And Let Me Love Again)** .... *Engelbert Humperdinck* ... Parrot 40011	
⑤	6	12	**Somebody To Love**..................................*Jefferson Airplane* ... RCA 9140	
⑥	8	6	Little Bit O' Soul.....................................*The Music Explosion* ... Laurie 3380	
⑦	12	4	Windy ....*The Association* ... Warner 7041	
⑧	9	8	All I Need ....*The Temptations* ... Gordy 7061	
⑨	3	11	I Got Rhythm..*The Happenings* ... B.T. Puppy 527	
⑩	11	8	Mirage.............................*Tommy James & The Shondells* ... Roulette 4736	

★ **HIGHEST DEBUT** ★ POS 73
Carrie-Anne................................*The Hollies*

★ **BIGGEST MOVER** ★ 66 to 33
C'mon Marianne ....*The 4 Seasons*

Billboard — JUNE 24, 1967 — HOT 100

TW	LW	WK	Title	Artist	Label
①	1	10	**Groovin'**	*The Young Rascals*	Atlantic 2401
②	2	9	Respect	*Aretha Franklin*	Atlantic 2403
③	3	7	**She'd Rather Be With Me**	*The Turtles*	White Whale 249
④	7	5	Windy	*The Association*	Warner 7041
⑤	6	7	Little Bit O' Soul	*The Music Explosion*	Laurie 3380
⑥	20	5	San Francisco (Be Sure To Wear Flowers In Your Hair)	*Scott McKenzie*	Ode 103
⑦	5	13	Somebody To Love	*Jefferson Airplane*	RCA 9140
⑧	11	6	Can't Take My Eyes Off You	*Frankie Valli*	Philips 40446
⑨	12	6	**Sunday Will Never Be The Same**	*Spanky & Our Gang*	Mercury 72679
⑩	15	7	Let's Live For Today	*The Grass Roots*	Dunhill 4084

★ **HIGHEST DEBUT** ★ POS 50
White Rabbit ....*Jefferson Airplane*

★ **BIGGEST MOVER** ★ 81 to 49
Mercy, Mercy, Mercy ....*The Buckinghams*

Billboard — JULY 1, 1967 — HOT 100

TW	LW	WK	Title	Artist	Label
❶	4	6	**Windy**	*The Association*	Warner 7041
②	1	11	Groovin'	*The Young Rascals*	Atlantic 2401
③	5	8	Little Bit O' Soul	*The Music Explosion*	Laurie 3380
④	6	6	**San Francisco (Be Sure To Wear Flowers In Your Hair)**	*Scott McKenzie*	Ode 103
⑤	3	8	**She'd Rather Be With Me**	*The Turtles*	White Whale 249
⑥	2	10	Respect	*Aretha Franklin*	Atlantic 2403
⑦	8	7	Can't Take My Eyes Off You	*Frankie Valli*	Philips 40446
⑧	10	8	**Let's Live For Today**	*The Grass Roots*	Dunhill 4084
⑨	11	9	Come On Down To My Boat	*Every Mothers' Son*	MGM 13733
⑩	20	5	Don't Sleep In The Subway	*Petula Clark*	Warner 7049

★ **HIGHEST DEBUT** ★ POS 77
I Like The Way ....*Tommy James & The Shondells*

★ **BIGGEST MOVER** ★ 80 to 28
A Whiter Shade Of Pale ....*Procol Harum*

Billboard — JULY 8, 1967 — HOT 100

TW	LW	WK	Title	Artist	Label
①	1	7	**Windy**	*The Association*	Warner 7041
②	3	9	**Little Bit O' Soul**	*The Music Explosion*	Laurie 3380
❸	7	8	**Can't Take My Eyes Off You**	*Frankie Valli*	Philips 40446
④	4	7	**San Francisco (Be Sure To Wear Flowers In Your Hair)**	*Scott McKenzie*	Ode 103
❺	10	6	**Don't Sleep In The Subway**	*Petula Clark*	Warner 7049
❻	9	10	**Come On Down To My Boat**	*Every Mothers' Son*	MGM 13733
❼	12	6	**Up-Up And Away**	*The 5th Dimension*	Soul City 756
⑧	8	9	**Let's Live For Today**	*The Grass Roots*	Dunhill 4084
⑨	2	12	**Groovin'**	*The Young Rascals*	Atlantic 2401
⑩	13	6	**The Tracks Of My Tears**	*Johnny Rivers*	Imperial 66244

★ **HIGHEST DEBUT** ★ POS 60
In The Chapel In The Moonlight ....*Dean Martin*

★ **BIGGEST MOVER** ★ 96 to 62
Your Unchanging Love ....*Marvin Gaye*

TW	LW	WK	Billboard®	JULY 15, 1967	HOT 100®
①	1	8	**Windy** ....*The Association* . . . Warner 7041		
②	2	10	**Little Bit O' Soul** ....*The Music Explosion* . . . Laurie 3380		
③	3	9	**Can't Take My Eyes Off You**....................*Frankie Valli* . . . Philips 40446		
④	4	8	**San Francisco (Be Sure To Wear Flowers In Your Hair)** .... *Scott McKenzie* . . . Ode 103		
⑤	5	7	**Don't Sleep In The Subway**.....................*Petula Clark* . . . Warner 7049		
⑥	6	11	**Come On Down To My Boat** ....*Every Mothers' Son* . . . MGM 13733		
⑦	7	7	**Up-Up And Away** ....*The 5th Dimension* . . . Soul City 756		
❽	12	7	**Light My Fire**...*The Doors* . . . Elektra 45615		
⑨	16	6	**C'mon Marianne** ....*The 4 Seasons* . . . Philips 40460		
➓	13	4	**A Whiter Shade Of Pale** ....*Procol Harum* . . . Deram 7507		

★ HIGHEST DEBUT ★ POS 52	★ BIGGEST MOVER ★ 88 to 64
My Mammy ....*The Happenings*	**The River Is Wide**............................*The Forum*

TW	LW	WK	Billboard®	JULY 22, 1967	HOT 100®
①	1	9	**Windy** ....*The Association* . . . Warner 7041		
②	3	10	**Can't Take My Eyes Off You** ....*Frankie Valli* . . . Philips 40446		
❸	8	8	**Light My Fire** ....*The Doors* . . . Elektra 45615		
④	4	9	**San Francisco (Be Sure To Wear Flowers In Your Hair)** .... *Scott McKenzie* . . . Ode 103		
⑤	2	11	**Little Bit O' Soul**............................*The Music Explosion* . . . Laurie 3380		
❻	11	7	**I Was Made To Love Her**..........................*Stevie Wonder* . . . Tamla 54151		
⑦	7	8	**Up-Up And Away** ....*The 5th Dimension* . . . Soul City 756		
⑧	10	5	**A Whiter Shade Of Pale** ....*Procol Harum* . . . Deram 7507		
⑨	9	7	**C'mon Marianne** ....*The 4 Seasons* . . . Philips 40460		
➓	6	12	**Come On Down To My Boat**...............*Every Mothers' Son* . . . MGM 13733		

★ HIGHEST DEBUT ★ POS 51	★ BIGGEST MOVER ★ 79 to 42
Pleasant Valley Sunday..................*The Monkees*	**To Love Somebody**.......................*The Bee Gees*

TW	LW	WK	Billboard®	JULY 29, 1967	HOT 100®
❶	3	9	**Light My Fire** ....*The Doors* . . . Elektra 45615		
❷	6	8	**I Was Made To Love Her** ....*Stevie Wonder* . . . Tamla 54151		
③	1	10	**Windy** ....*The Association* . . . Warner 7041		
④	2	11	**Can't Take My Eyes Off You**....................*Frankie Valli* . . . Philips 40446		
❺	8	6	**A Whiter Shade Of Pale** ....*Procol Harum* . . . Deram 7507		
⑥	5	12	**Little Bit O' Soul**............................*The Music Explosion* . . . Laurie 3380		
❼	11	7	**Mercy, Mercy, Mercy** ....*The Buckinghams* . . . Columbia 44182		
❽	12	6	**White Rabbit** ....*Jefferson Airplane* . . . RCA 9248		
⑨	7	9	**Up-Up And Away** ....*The 5th Dimension* . . . Soul City 756		
➓	9	8	**C'mon Marianne** ....*The 4 Seasons* . . . Philips 40460		

★ HIGHEST DEBUT ★ POS 64	★ BIGGEST MOVER ★ 71 to 29
Baby You're A Rich Man ....*The Beatles*	**All You Need Is Love** ....*The Beatles*

TW	LW	WK	Billboard	AUGUST 5, 1967		HOT 100.
①	1	10	**Light My Fire** ....*The Doors* . . . Elektra 45615			
②	2	9	**I Was Made To Love Her** ....*Stevie Wonder* . . . Tamla 54151			
❸	29	3	All You Need Is Love.....................................*The Beatles* . . . Capitol 5964			
④	3	11	Windy ....*The Association* . . . Warner 7041			
⑤	5	7	**A Whiter Shade Of Pale**........................*Procol Harum* . . . Deram 7507			
⑥	4	12	Can't Take My Eyes Off You.......................*Frankie Valli* . . . Philips 40446			
⑦	7	8	Mercy, Mercy, Mercy ....*The Buckinghams* . . . Columbia 44182			
⑧	8	7	**White Rabbit** ....*Jefferson Airplane* . . . RCA 9248			
❾	24	3	Pleasant Valley Sunday ....*The Monkees* . . . Colgems 1007			
⑩	6	13	Little Bit O' Soul...............................*The Music Explosion* . . . Laurie 3380			

★ **HIGHEST DEBUT** ★ POS 61	★ **BIGGEST MOVER** ★ 81 to 53
Heroes And Villains...................*The Beach Boys*	Fakin' It...................................*Simon & Garfunkel*

TW	LW	WK	Billboard	AUGUST 12, 1967		HOT 100.
①	1	11	**Light My Fire** ....*The Doors* . . . Elektra 45615			
②	3	4	All You Need Is Love....................................*The Beatles* . . . Capitol 5964			
③	2	10	I Was Made To Love Her............................*Stevie Wonder* . . . Tamla 54151			
❹	9	4	Pleasant Valley Sunday ....*The Monkees* . . . Colgems 1007			
⑤	7	9	**Mercy, Mercy, Mercy** ....*The Buckinghams* . . . Columbia 44182			
⑥	6	13	Can't Take My Eyes Off You.......................*Frankie Valli* . . . Philips 40446			
⑦	5	8	A Whiter Shade Of Pale ....*Procol Harum* . . . Deram 7507			
⑧	4	12	Windy ....*The Association* . . . Warner 7041			
⑨	16	9	**Carrie-Anne** ....*The Hollies* . . . Epic 10180			
⑩	11	5	**A Girl Like You** ....*The Young Rascals* . . . Atlantic 2424			

★ **HIGHEST DEBUT** ★ POS 61	★ **BIGGEST MOVER** ★ 71 to 21
Reflections ....*Diana Ross & The Supremes*	Ode To Billie Joe..........................*Bobbie Gentry*

TW	LW	WK	Billboard	AUGUST 19, 1967		HOT 100.
①	2	5	**All You Need Is Love**..................................*The Beatles* . . . Capitol 5964			
②	1	12	Light My Fire...*The Doors* . . . Elektra 45615			
③	4	5	**Pleasant Valley Sunday** ....*The Monkees* . . . Colgems 1007			
④	3	11	I Was Made To Love Her............................*Stevie Wonder* . . . Tamla 54151			
❺	11	5	Baby I Love You.....................................*Aretha Franklin* . . . Atlantic 2427			
⑥	5	10	Mercy, Mercy, Mercy ....*The Buckinghams* . . . Columbia 44182			
❼	21	3	Ode To Billie Joe ....*Bobbie Gentry* . . . Capitol 5950			
❽	20	6	Cold Sweat...*James Brown* . . . King 6110			
⑨	7	9	A Whiter Shade Of Pale ....*Procol Harum* . . . Deram 7507			
⑩	10	6	**A Girl Like You** ....*The Young Rascals* . . . Atlantic 2424			

★ **HIGHEST DEBUT** ★ POS 76	★ **BIGGEST MOVER** ★ 61 to 20
I Dig Rock And Roll Music.......*Peter, Paul & Mary*	Reflections ....*Diana Ross & The Supremes*

TW	LW	WK	Billboard	AUGUST 26, 1967	HOT 100
①	7	4	**Ode To Billie Joe**	*Bobbie Gentry*	Capitol 5950
②	1	6	All You Need Is Love	*The Beatles*	Capitol 5964
③	3	6	**Pleasant Valley Sunday**	*The Monkees*	Colgems 1007
④	2	13	Light My Fire	*The Doors*	Elektra 45615
⑤	5	6	Baby I Love You	*Aretha Franklin*	Atlantic 2427
⑥	4	12	I Was Made To Love Her	*Stevie Wonder*	Tamla 54151
⑦	8	7	**Cold Sweat**	*James Brown*	King 6110
⑧	20	3	Reflections	*Diana Ross & The Supremes*	Motown 1111
⑨	21	5	You're My Everything	*The Temptations*	Gordy 7063
⑩	9	10	A Whiter Shade Of Pale	*Procol Harum*	Deram 7507

★ HIGHEST DEBUT ★ POS 72	★ BIGGEST MOVER ★ 58 to 25
Twelve Thirty...............*The Mamas & The Papas*	The Letter...............*The Box Tops*

TW	LW	WK	Billboard	SEPTEMBER 2, 1967	HOT 100
①	1	5	**Ode To Billie Joe**	*Bobbie Gentry*	Capitol 5950
②	2	7	All You Need Is Love	*The Beatles*	Capitol 5964
③	8	4	**Reflections**	*Diana Ross & The Supremes*	Motown 1111
④	4	14	Light My Fire	*The Doors*	Elektra 45615
⑤	5	7	Baby I Love You	*Aretha Franklin*	Atlantic 2427
⑥	14	7	Come Back When You Grow Up	*Bobby Vee*	Liberty 55964
⑦	7	8	**Cold Sweat**	*James Brown*	King 6110
⑧	3	7	Pleasant Valley Sunday	*The Monkees*	Colgems 1007
⑨	9	6	You're My Everything	*The Temptations*	Gordy 7063
⑩	6	13	I Was Made To Love Her	*Stevie Wonder*	Tamla 54151

★ HIGHEST DEBUT ★ POS 71	★ BIGGEST MOVER ★ 72 to 36
Little Ole Man (Uptight-Everything's Alright) ....*Bill Cosby*	Twelve Thirty...............*The Mamas & The Papas*

TW	LW	WK	Billboard	SEPTEMBER 9, 1967	HOT 100
①	1	6	**Ode To Billie Joe**	*Bobbie Gentry*	Capitol 5950
②	3	5	**Reflections**	*Diana Ross & The Supremes*	Motown 1111
③	6	8	**Come Back When You Grow Up**	*Bobby Vee*	Liberty 55964
④	5	8	**Baby I Love You**	*Aretha Franklin*	Atlantic 2427
⑤	15	5	**The Letter**	*The Box Tops*	Mala 565
⑥	2	8	All You Need Is Love	*The Beatles*	Capitol 5964
⑦	9	7	You're My Everything	*The Temptations*	Gordy 7063
⑧	4	15	Light My Fire	*The Doors*	Elektra 45615
⑨	14	9	Apples, Peaches, Pumpkin Pie	*Jay & The Techniques*	Smash 2086
⑩	25	6	San Franciscan Nights	*Eric Burdon & The Animals*	MGM 13769

★ HIGHEST DEBUT ★ POS 73	★ BIGGEST MOVER ★ 59 to 25
Your Precious Love ....*Marvin Gaye & Tammi Terrell*	Never My Love...............*The Association*

Billboard — SEPTEMBER 16, 1967 — HOT 100

TW	LW	WK		
①	1	7	Ode To Billie Joe	Bobbie Gentry . . . Capitol 5950
②	2	6	Reflections	Diana Ross & The Supremes . . . Motown 1111
③	3	9	Come Back When You Grow Up	Bobby Vee . . . Liberty 55964
④	5	6	The Letter	The Box Tops . . . Mala 565
⑤	4	9	Baby I Love You	Aretha Franklin . . . Atlantic 2427
⑥	7	8	You're My Everything	The Temptations . . . Gordy 7063
⑦	9	10	Apples, Peaches, Pumpkin Pie	Jay & The Techniques . . . Smash 2086
⑧	6	9	All You Need Is Love	The Beatles . . . Capitol 5964
⑨	10	7	San Franciscan Nights	Eric Burdon & The Animals . . . MGM 13769
⑩	18	7	Funky Broadway	Wilson Pickett . . . Atlantic 2430

★ HIGHEST DEBUT ★ POS 75	★ BIGGEST MOVER ★ 80 to 43
You Keep Running Away . . . Four Tops	How Can I Be Sure . . . The Young Rascals

Billboard — SEPTEMBER 23, 1967 — HOT 100

TW	LW	WK		
❶	4	7	The Letter	The Box Tops . . . Mala 565
②	1	8	Ode To Billie Joe	Bobbie Gentry . . . Capitol 5950
③	3	10	Come Back When You Grow Up	Bobby Vee . . . Liberty 55964
④	2	7	Reflections	Diana Ross & The Supremes . . . Motown 1111
❺	15	5	Never My Love	The Association . . . Warner 7074
⑥	7	11	Apples, Peaches, Pumpkin Pie	Jay & The Techniques . . . Smash 2086
❼	12	7	(Your Love Keeps Lifting Me) Higher And Higher	Jackie Wilson . . . Brunswick 55336
⑧	6	9	You're My Everything	The Temptations . . . Gordy 7063
⑨	16	6	I Dig Rock And Roll Music	Peter, Paul & Mary . . . Warner 7067
⑩	10	8	Funky Broadway	Wilson Pickett . . . Atlantic 2430

★ HIGHEST DEBUT ★ POS 65	★ BIGGEST MOVER ★ 75 to 45
People Are Strange . . . The Doors	You Keep Running Away . . . Four Tops

Billboard — SEPTEMBER 30, 1967 — HOT 100

TW	LW	WK		
①	1	8	The Letter	The Box Tops . . . Mala 565
②	2	9	Ode To Billie Joe	Bobbie Gentry . . . Capitol 5950
③	5	6	Never My Love	The Association . . . Warner 7074
④	3	11	Come Back When You Grow Up	Bobby Vee . . . Liberty 55964
⑤	4	8	Reflections	Diana Ross & The Supremes . . . Motown 1111
⑥	6	12	Apples, Peaches, Pumpkin Pie	Jay & The Techniques . . . Smash 2086
⑦	7	8	(Your Love Keeps Lifting Me) Higher And Higher	Jackie Wilson . . . Brunswick 55336
⑧	10	9	Funky Broadway	Wilson Pickett . . . Atlantic 2430
⑨	9	7	I Dig Rock And Roll Music	Peter, Paul & Mary . . . Warner 7067
⑩	14	12	Brown Eyed Girl	Van Morrison . . . Bang 545

★ HIGHEST DEBUT ★ POS 69	★ BIGGEST MOVER ★ 90 to 63
Love Is Strange . . . Peaches & Herb	Let It Out (Let It All Hang Out) . . . The Hombres

TW	LW	WK	Billboard	OCTOBER 7, 1967	HOT 100
①	1	9	**The Letter**	*The Box Tops* . . . Mala 565	
②	3	7	**Never My Love**	*The Association* . . . Warner 7074	
③	2	10	**Ode To Billie Joe**	*Bobbie Gentry* . . . Capitol 5950	
④	4	12	**Come Back When You Grow Up**	*Bobby Vee* . . . Liberty 55964	
⑤	13	6	**Little Ole Man (Uptight-Everything's Alright)**	*Bill Cosby* . . . Warner 7072	
⑥	7	9	**(Your Love Keeps Lifting Me) Higher And Higher**	*Jackie Wilson* . . . Brunswick 55336	
⑦	5	9	**Reflections**	*Diana Ross & The Supremes* . . . Motown 1111	
⑧	6	13	**Apples, Peaches, Pumpkin Pie**	*Jay & The Techniques* . . . Smash 2086	
⑨	14	5	**How Can I Be Sure**	*The Young Rascals* . . . Atlantic 2438	
⑩	11	9	**Gimme Little Sign**	*Brenton Wood* . . . Double Shot 116	

★ **HIGHEST DEBUT** ★ POS 61
I'm Wondering ....*Stevie Wonder*

★ **BIGGEST MOVER** ★ 70 to 38
A Natural Woman ....*Aretha Franklin*

TW	LW	WK	Billboard	OCTOBER 14, 1967	HOT 100
①	1	10	**The Letter**	*The Box Tops* . . . Mala 565	
②	2	8	**Never My Love**	*The Association* . . . Warner 7074	
③	11	6	**To Sir With Love**	*Lulu* . . . Epic 10187	
④	5	7	**Little Ole Man (Uptight-Everything's Alright)**	*Bill Cosby* . . . Warner 7072	
⑤	3	11	**Ode To Billie Joe**	*Bobbie Gentry* . . . Capitol 5950	
⑥	6	10	**(Your Love Keeps Lifting Me) Higher And Higher**	*Jackie Wilson* . . . Brunswick 55336	
⑦	4	13	**Come Back When You Grow Up**	*Bobby Vee* . . . Liberty 55964	
⑧	9	6	**How Can I Be Sure**	*The Young Rascals* . . . Atlantic 2438	
⑨	10	10	**Gimme Little Sign**	*Brenton Wood* . . . Double Shot 116	
⑩	20	6	**Soul Man**	*Sam & Dave* . . . Stax 231	

★ **HIGHEST DEBUT** ★ POS 61
(Loneliness Made Me Realize) It's You That I Need ....*The Temptations*

★ **BIGGEST MOVER** ★ 59 to 34
Incense And Peppermints ....*Strawberry Alarm Clock*

TW	LW	WK	Billboard	OCTOBER 21, 1967	HOT 100
❶	3	7	**To Sir With Love**	*Lulu* . . . Epic 10187	
②	1	11	**The Letter**	*The Box Tops* . . . Mala 565	
③	2	9	**Never My Love**	*The Association* . . . Warner 7074	
❹	8	7	**How Can I Be Sure**	*The Young Rascals* . . . Atlantic 2438	
❺	15	8	**Expressway To Your Heart**	*Soul Survivors* . . . Crimson 1010	
❻	24	8	**It Must Be Him**	*Vikki Carr* . . . Liberty 55986	
❼	10	7	**Soul Man**	*Sam & Dave* . . . Stax 231	
⑧	4	8	**Little Ole Man (Uptight-Everything's Alright)**	*Bill Cosby* . . . Warner 7072	
⑨	9	11	**Gimme Little Sign**	*Brenton Wood* . . . Double Shot 116	
⑩	13	7	**Your Precious Love**	*Marvin Gaye & Tammi Terrell* . . . Tamla 54156	

★ **HIGHEST DEBUT** ★ POS 74
I Heard It Through The Grapevine ....*Gladys Knight & The Pips*

★ **BIGGEST MOVER** ★ 88 to 50
Lazy Day ....*Spanky & Our Gang*

Billboard — OCTOBER 28, 1967 — HOT 100

TW	LW	WK	Title	Artist	Label
1	1	8	To Sir With Love	Lulu	Epic 10187
2	2	12	The Letter	The Box Tops	Mala 565
3	3	10	Never My Love	The Association	Warner 7074
4	4	8	How Can I Be Sure	The Young Rascals	Atlantic 2438
5	5	9	Expressway To Your Heart	Soul Survivors	Crimson 1010
6	6	9	It Must Be Him	Vikki Carr	Liberty 55986
7	7	8	Soul Man	Sam & Dave	Stax 231
8	10	8	Your Precious Love	Marvin Gaye & Tammi Terrell	Tamla 54156
9	13	5	A Natural Woman	Aretha Franklin	Atlantic 2441
10	19	5	Incense And Peppermints	Strawberry Alarm Clock	Uni 55018

★ HIGHEST DEBUT ★ POS 62
Glad To Be Unhappy ......The Mamas & The Papas

★ BIGGEST MOVER ★ 100 to 64
Back On The Street Again ....The Sunshine Company

Billboard — NOVEMBER 4, 1967 — HOT 100

TW	LW	WK	Title	Artist	Label
1	1	9	To Sir With Love	Lulu	Epic 10187
2	7	9	Soul Man	Sam & Dave	Stax 231
3	6	10	It Must Be Him	Vikki Carr	Liberty 55986
4	5	10	Expressway To Your Heart	Soul Survivors	Crimson 1010
5	8	9	Your Precious Love	Marvin Gaye & Tammi Terrell	Tamla 54156
6	3	11	Never My Love	The Association	Warner 7074
7	10	6	Incense And Peppermints	Strawberry Alarm Clock	Uni 55018
8	9	6	A Natural Woman	Aretha Franklin	Atlantic 2441
9	19	6	The Rain, The Park & Other Things	The Cowsills	MGM 13810
10	15	6	Please Love Me Forever	Bobby Vinton	Epic 10228

★ HIGHEST DEBUT ★ POS 57
Stag-O-Lee ....Wilson Pickett

★ BIGGEST MOVER ★ 62 to 37
Glad To Be Unhappy ......The Mamas & The Papas

Billboard — NOVEMBER 11, 1967 — HOT 100

TW	LW	WK	Title	Artist	Label
1	1	10	To Sir With Love	Lulu	Epic 10187
2	2	10	Soul Man	Sam & Dave	Stax 231
3	3	11	It Must Be Him	Vikki Carr	Liberty 55986
4	7	7	Incense And Peppermints	Strawberry Alarm Clock	Uni 55018
5	5	10	Your Precious Love	Marvin Gaye & Tammi Terrell	Tamla 54156
6	9	7	The Rain, The Park & Other Things	The Cowsills	MGM 13810
7	10	7	Please Love Me Forever	Bobby Vinton	Epic 10228
8	8	7	A Natural Woman	Aretha Franklin	Atlantic 2441
9	4	11	Expressway To Your Heart	Soul Survivors	Crimson 1010
10	6	12	Never My Love	The Association	Warner 7074

★ HIGHEST DEBUT ★ POS 62
Yesterday ....Ray Charles

★ BIGGEST MOVER ★ 85 to 57
I Second That Emotion ....Smokey Robinson & The Miracles

Billboard — NOVEMBER 18, 1967 — HOT 100

TW	LW	WK	Title	Artist	Label
1	1	11	**To Sir With Love**	*Lulu*	Epic 10187
2	2	11	**Soul Man**	*Sam & Dave*	Stax 231
3	4	8	**Incense And Peppermints**	*Strawberry Alarm Clock*	Uni 55018
4	6	8	**The Rain, The Park & Other Things**	*The Cowsills*	MGM 13810
5	3	12	**It Must Be Him**	*Vikki Carr*	Liberty 55986
6	7	8	**Please Love Me Forever**	*Bobby Vinton*	Epic 10228
7	5	11	**Your Precious Love**	*Marvin Gaye & Tammi Terrell*	Tamla 54156
8	22	5	**I Say A Little Prayer**	*Dionne Warwick*	Scepter 12203
9	9	12	**Expressway To Your Heart**	*Soul Survivors*	Crimson 1010
10	11	6	**I Can See For Miles**	*The Who*	Decca 32206

★ **HIGHEST DEBUT** ★ POS 33
Daydream Believer ....*The Monkees*

★ **BIGGEST MOVER** ★ 84 to 58
An Open Letter To My Teenage Son ....*Victor Lundberg*

Billboard — NOVEMBER 25, 1967 — HOT 100

TW	LW	WK	Title	Artist	Label
1	3	9	**Incense And Peppermints**	*Strawberry Alarm Clock*	Uni 55018
2	1	12	**To Sir With Love**	*Lulu*	Epic 10187
3	4	9	**The Rain, The Park & Other Things**	*The Cowsills*	MGM 13810
4	2	12	**Soul Man**	*Sam & Dave*	Stax 231
5	33	2	**Daydream Believer**	*The Monkees*	Colgems 1012
6	6	9	**Please Love Me Forever**	*Bobby Vinton*	Epic 10228
7	8	6	**I Say A Little Prayer**	*Dionne Warwick*	Scepter 12203
8	5	13	**It Must Be Him**	*Vikki Carr*	Liberty 55986
9	10	7	**I Can See For Miles**	*The Who*	Decca 32206
10	9	13	**Expressway To Your Heart**	*Soul Survivors*	Crimson 1010

★ **HIGHEST DEBUT** ★ POS 71
And Get Away ....*The Esquires*

★ **BIGGEST MOVER** ★ 58 to 18
An Open Letter To My Teenage Son ....*Victor Lundberg*

Billboard — DECEMBER 2, 1967 — HOT 100

TW	LW	WK	Title	Artist	Label
1	5	3	**Daydream Believer**	*The Monkees*	Colgems 1012
2	3	10	**The Rain, The Park & Other Things**	*The Cowsills*	MGM 13810
3	1	10	**Incense And Peppermints**	*Strawberry Alarm Clock*	Uni 55018
4	2	13	**To Sir With Love**	*Lulu*	Epic 10187
5	7	7	**I Say A Little Prayer**	*Dionne Warwick*	Scepter 12203
6	6	10	**Please Love Me Forever**	*Bobby Vinton*	Epic 10228
7	4	13	**Soul Man**	*Sam & Dave*	Stax 231
8	16	7	**I Heard It Through The Grapevine**	*Gladys Knight & The Pips*	Soul 35039
9	9	8	**I Can See For Miles**	*The Who*	Decca 32206
10	18	4	**An Open Letter To My Teenage Son**	*Victor Lundberg*	Liberty 55996

★ **HIGHEST DEBUT** ★ POS 45
Hello Goodbye ....*The Beatles*

★ **BIGGEST MOVER** ★ 74 to 46
Wear Your Love Like Heaven ....*Donovan*

TW	LW	WK	Billboard	DECEMBER 9, 1967	HOT 100.

TW	LW	WK		
①	1	4	**Daydream Believer** ....*The Monkees* ... Colgems 1012
②	2	11	**The Rain, The Park & Other Things** ......*The Cowsills* ... MGM 13810
③	3	11	**Incense And Peppermints**.................*Strawberry Alarm Clock* ... Uni 55018
④	5	8	**I Say A Little Prayer**............................*Dionne Warwick* ... Scepter 12203
❺	8	8	**I Heard It Through The Grapevine** ....*Gladys Knight & The Pips* ... Soul 35039
⑥	4	14	**To Sir With Love** ....*Lulu* ... Epic 10187
❼	11	6	**I Second That Emotion** ....*Smokey Robinson & The Miracles* ... Tamla 54159
❽	45	2	**Hello Goodbye**...*The Beatles* ... Capitol 2056
⑨	13	5	**In And Out Of Love** ....*Diana Ross & The Supremes* ... Motown 1116
⑩	10	5	**An Open Letter To My Teenage Son** ....*Victor Lundberg* ... Liberty 55996

★ HIGHEST DEBUT ★ POS 64	★ BIGGEST MOVER ★ 45 to 8
I Am The Walrus ....*The Beatles*	Hello Goodbye ....*The Beatles*

TW	LW	WK	Billboard	DECEMBER 16, 1967	HOT 100.

TW	LW	WK		
①	1	5	**Daydream Believer** ....*The Monkees* ... Colgems 1012
❷	5	9	**I Heard It Through The Grapevine** ....*Gladys Knight & The Pips* ... Soul 35039
❸	8	3	**Hello Goodbye**.......................................*The Beatles* ... Capitol 2056
❹	7	7	**I Second That Emotion** ....*Smokey Robinson & The Miracles* ... Tamla 54159
⑤	2	12	**The Rain, The Park & Other Things** ....*The Cowsills* ... MGM 13810
⑥	3	12	**Incense And Peppermints**.................*Strawberry Alarm Clock* ... Uni 55018
⑦	4	9	**I Say A Little Prayer** ....*Dionne Warwick* ... Scepter 12203
❽	13	11	**Boogaloo Down Broadway** ....*The Fantastic Johnny C* ... Phil-L.A. of Soul 305
⑨	9	6	**In And Out Of Love** ....*Diana Ross & The Supremes* ... Motown 1116
⑩	12	8	**You Better Sit Down Kids** ....*Cher* ... Imperial 66261

★ HIGHEST DEBUT ★ POS 68	★ BIGGEST MOVER ★ 66 to 29
Green Tambourine ....*The Lemon Pipers*	Chain Of Fools ....*Aretha Franklin*

TW	LW	WK	Billboard	DECEMBER 23, 1967	HOT 100.

TW	LW	WK		
①	1	6	**Daydream Believer** ....*The Monkees* ... Colgems 1012
②	2	10	**I Heard It Through The Grapevine** ....*Gladys Knight & The Pips* ... Soul 35039
③	3	4	**Hello Goodbye**.......................................*The Beatles* ... Capitol 2056
④	4	8	**I Second That Emotion** ....*Smokey Robinson & The Miracles* ... Tamla 54159
❺	12	6	**Woman, Woman**.................................*The Union Gap* ... Columbia 44297
⑥	5	13	**The Rain, The Park & Other Things** ....*The Cowsills* ... MGM 13810
⑦	8	12	**Boogaloo Down Broadway** ....*The Fantastic Johnny C* ... Phil-L.A. of Soul 305
⑧	6	13	**Incense And Peppermints**.................*Strawberry Alarm Clock* ... Uni 55018
⑨	10	9	**You Better Sit Down Kids**...............................*Cher* ... Imperial 66261
⑩	7	10	**I Say A Little Prayer** ....*Dionne Warwick* ... Scepter 12203

★ HIGHEST DEBUT ★ POS 79	★ BIGGEST MOVER ★ 68 to 33
Explosion In Your Soul.................*Soul Survivors*	Green Tambourine ....*The Lemon Pipers*

TW	LW	WK	Billboard.	🔵 DECEMBER 30, 1967 🔵	HOT 100.
❶	3	5	**Hello Goodbye** .... *The Beatles* . . . Capitol 2056		
②	2	11	**I Heard It Through The Grapevine** .... *Gladys Knight & The Pips* . . . Soul 35039		
③	1	7	**Daydream Believer**................................... *The Monkees* . . . Colgems 1012		
④	4	9	**I Second That Emotion** .... *Smokey Robinson & The Miracles* . . . Tamla 54159		
⑤	5	7	**Woman, Woman**...................................... *The Union Gap* . . . Columbia 44297		
❻	11	6	**Judy In Disguise (With Glasses)**............. *John Fred & His Playboy Band* . . . Paula 282		
❼	17	4	**Chain Of Fools**.. *Aretha Franklin* . . . Atlantic 2464		
❽	13	5	**Bend Me, Shape Me**................................ *The American Breed* . . . Acta 811		
⑨	7	13	**Boogaloo Down Broadway** .... *The Fantastic Johnny C* . . . Phil-L.A. of Soul 305		
❿	15	10	**Skinny Legs And All** .... *Joe Tex* . . . Dial 4063		

★ *HIGHEST DEBUT* ★ POS 77	★ *BIGGEST MOVER* ★ 64 to 32
She's A Rainbow ....*The Rolling Stones*	Monterey ....*Eric Burdon & The Animals*

178

Billboard — JANUARY 6, 1968 — HOT 100

TW	LW	WK	Title	Artist
①	1	6	**Hello Goodbye**	*The Beatles* . . . Capitol 2056
②	3	8	**Daydream Believer**	*The Monkees* . . . Colgems 1012
❸	6	7	**Judy In Disguise (With Glasses)**	*John Fred & His Playboy Band* . . . Paula 282
④	2	12	**I Heard It Through The Grapevine**	*Gladys Knight & The Pips* . . . Soul 35039
⑤	5	8	**Woman, Woman**	*The Union Gap* . . . Columbia 44297
⑥	4	10	**I Second That Emotion**	*Smokey Robinson & The Miracles* . . . Tamla 54159
⑦	7	5	**Chain Of Fools**	*Aretha Franklin* . . . Atlantic 2464
⑧	8	6	**Bend Me, Shape Me**	*The American Breed* . . . Acta 811
⑨	9	14	**Boogaloo Down Broadway**	*The Fantastic Johnny C* . . . Phil-L.A. of Soul 305
⑩	10	11	**Skinny Legs And All**	*Joe Tex* . . . Dial 4063

★ **HIGHEST DEBUT** ★ POS 72
Some Velvet Morning . . . . *Nancy Sinatra & Lee Hazlewood*

★ **BIGGEST MOVER** ★ 77 to 48
She's A Rainbow . . . . *The Rolling Stones*

Billboard — JANUARY 13, 1968 — HOT 100

TW	LW	WK	Title	Artist
①	1	7	**Hello Goodbye**	*The Beatles* . . . Capitol 2056
②	3	8	**Judy In Disguise (With Glasses)**	*John Fred & His Playboy Band* . . . Paula 282
③	2	9	**Daydream Believer**	*The Monkees* . . . Colgems 1012
④	5	9	**Woman, Woman**	*The Union Gap* . . . Columbia 44297
⑤	4	13	**I Heard It Through The Grapevine**	*Gladys Knight & The Pips* . . . Soul 35039
⑥	7	6	**Chain Of Fools**	*Aretha Franklin* . . . Atlantic 2464
⑦	8	7	**Bend Me, Shape Me**	*The American Breed* . . . Acta 811
⑧	6	11	**I Second That Emotion**	*Smokey Robinson & The Miracles* . . . Tamla 54159
❾	12	5	**Green Tambourine**	*The Lemon Pipers* . . . Buddah 23
⑩	10	12	**Skinny Legs And All**	*Joe Tex* . . . Dial 4063

★ **HIGHEST DEBUT** ★ POS 56
I Wish It Would Rain . . . . *The Temptations*

★ **BIGGEST MOVER** ★ 47 to 23
Spooky . . . . *Classics IV*

Billboard — JANUARY 20, 1968 — HOT 100

TW	LW	WK	Title	Artist
①	2	9	**Judy In Disguise (With Glasses)**	*John Fred & His Playboy Band* . . . Paula 282
❷	6	7	**Chain Of Fools**	*Aretha Franklin* . . . Atlantic 2464
③	1	8	**Hello Goodbye**	*The Beatles* . . . Capitol 2056
④	4	10	**Woman, Woman**	*The Union Gap* . . . Columbia 44297
❺	9	6	**Green Tambourine**	*The Lemon Pipers* . . . Buddah 23
⑥	3	10	**Daydream Believer**	*The Monkees* . . . Colgems 1012
⑦	7	8	**Bend Me, Shape Me**	*The American Breed* . . . Acta 811
⑧	8	12	**I Second That Emotion**	*Smokey Robinson & The Miracles* . . . Tamla 54159
⑨	5	14	**I Heard It Through The Grapevine**	*Gladys Knight & The Pips* . . . Soul 35039
⑩	13	8	**If I Could Build My Whole World Around You**	*Marvin Gaye & Tammi Terrell* . . . Tamla 54161

★ **HIGHEST DEBUT** ★ POS 77
(Theme From) Valley Of The Dolls . . . . *Dionne Warwick*

★ **BIGGEST MOVER** ★ 84 to 47
Love Is Blue . . . . *Paul Mauriat*

TW	LW	WK	Billboard.	JANUARY 27, 1968	HOT 100.
①	1	10	**Judy In Disguise (With Glasses)**........John Fred & His Playboy Band ... Paula 282
②	2	8	**Chain Of Fools**.............................Aretha Franklin ... Atlantic 2464
❸	5	7	**Green Tambourine** ....The Lemon Pipers ... Buddah 23
④	4	11	**Woman, Woman** ....The Union Gap ... Columbia 44297
⑤	7	9	**Bend Me, Shape Me** ....The American Breed ... Acta 811
⑥	3	9	Hello Goodbye...............................The Beatles ... Capitol 2056
❼	16	6	Spooky ....Classics IV ... Imperial 66259
⑧	6	11	Daydream Believer..........................The Monkees ... Colgems 1012
⑨	9	15	I Heard It Through The Grapevine ....Gladys Knight & The Pips ... Soul 35039
⑩	10	9	**If I Could Build My Whole World Around You**............ Marvin Gaye & Tammi Terrell ... Tamla 54161

★ **HIGHEST DEBUT** ★ POS 67	★ **BIGGEST MOVER** ★ 45 to 15
(Sittin' On) The Dock Of The Bay ....Otis Redding	I Wish It Would Rain ....The Temptations

TW	LW	WK	Billboard.	FEBRUARY 3, 1968	HOT 100.
❶	3	8	**Green Tambourine**...........................The Lemon Pipers ... Buddah 23
②	1	11	Judy In Disguise (With Glasses)..............John Fred & His Playboy Band ... Paula 282
③	2	9	**Chain Of Fools**................................Aretha Franklin ... Atlantic 2464
❹	7	7	**Spooky** ....Classics IV ... Imperial 66259
⑤	5	10	**Bend Me, Shape Me** ....The American Breed ... Acta 811
⑥	4	12	Woman, Woman...............................The Union Gap ... Columbia 44297
❼	18	5	**Love Is Blue** ....Paul Mauriat ... Philips 40495
❽	12	9	**Nobody But Me**............................The Human Beinz ... Capitol 5990
⑨	17	9	Goin' Out Of My Head/Can't Take My Eyes Off You .... The Lettermen ... Capitol 2054
⑩	15	4	I Wish It Would Rain ....The Temptations ... Gordy 7068

★ **HIGHEST DEBUT** ★ POS 62	★ **BIGGEST MOVER** ★ 61 to 33
Everything That Touches You......The Association	(Theme From) Valley Of The Dolls..........Dionne Warwick

TW	LW	WK	Billboard.	FEBRUARY 10, 1968	HOT 100.
❶	7	6	**Love Is Blue** ....Paul Mauriat ... Philips 40495
②	1	9	Green Tambourine ....The Lemon Pipers ... Buddah 23
❸	4	8	**Spooky** ....Classics IV ... Imperial 66259
④	2	12	Judy In Disguise (With Glasses)..............John Fred & His Playboy Band ... Paula 282
⑤	3	10	Chain Of Fools................................Aretha Franklin ... Atlantic 2464
❻	10	5	I Wish It Would Rain ....The Temptations ... Gordy 7068
❼	9	10	**Goin' Out Of My Head/Can't Take My Eyes Off You** .... The Lettermen ... Capitol 2054
⑧	8	10	**Nobody But Me**............................The Human Beinz ... Capitol 5990
⑨	6	13	Woman, Woman...............................The Union Gap ... Columbia 44297
⑩	5	11	Bend Me, Shape Me ....The American Breed ... Acta 811

★ **HIGHEST DEBUT** ★ POS 63	★ **BIGGEST MOVER** ★ 97 to 56
Just Dropped In (To See What Condition My Condition Was In).................The First Edition	Carpet Man ....The 5th Dimension

TW	LW	WK	Billboard.	FEBRUARY 17, 1968	HOT 100.
①	1	7	Love Is Blue	Paul Mauriat . . . Philips 40495	
②	2	10	Green Tambourine	The Lemon Pipers . . . Buddah 23	
③	3	9	Spooky	Classics IV . . . Imperial 66259	
④	6	6	I Wish It Would Rain	The Temptations . . . Gordy 7068	
⑤	15	5	(Theme From) Valley Of The Dolls	Dionne Warwick . . . Scepter 12203	
⑥	28	4	(Sittin' On) The Dock Of The Bay	Otis Redding . . . Volt 157	
⑦	7	11	Goin' Out Of My Head/Can't Take My Eyes Off You	The Lettermen . . . Capitol 2054	
⑧	8	11	Nobody But Me	The Human Beinz . . . Capitol 5990	
⑨	4	13	Judy In Disguise (With Glasses)	John Fred & His Playboy Band . . . Paula 282	
⑩	13	9	I Wonder What She's Doing Tonite	Tommy Boyce & Bobby Hart . . . A&M 893	

★ **HIGHEST DEBUT** ★ POS 62
Country Girl - City Man . . . . Billy Vera & Judy Clay

★ **BIGGEST MOVER** ★ 98 to 53
Men Are Gettin' Scarce . . . . Joe Tex

TW	LW	WK	Billboard.	FEBRUARY 24, 1968	HOT 100.
①	1	8	Love Is Blue	Paul Mauriat . . . Philips 40495	
②	5	6	(Theme From) Valley Of The Dolls	Dionne Warwick . . . Scepter 12203	
③	3	10	Spooky	Classics IV . . . Imperial 66259	
④	4	7	I Wish It Would Rain	The Temptations . . . Gordy 7068	
⑤	6	5	(Sittin' On) The Dock Of The Bay	Otis Redding . . . Volt 157	
⑥	17	5	Simon Says	1910 Fruitgum Co. . . . Buddah 24	
⑦	2	11	Green Tambourine	The Lemon Pipers . . . Buddah 23	
⑧	10	10	I Wonder What She's Doing Tonite	Tommy Boyce & Bobby Hart . . . A&M 893	
⑨	7	12	Goin' Out Of My Head/Can't Take My Eyes Off You	The Lettermen . . . Capitol 2054	
⑩	8	12	Nobody But Me	The Human Beinz . . . Capitol 5990	

★ **HIGHEST DEBUT** ★ POS 66
A Question Of Temperature . . . . . . The Balloon Farm

★ **BIGGEST MOVER** ★ 82 to 52
Kiss Me Goodbye . . . . Petula Clark

TW	LW	WK	Billboard.	MARCH 2, 1968	HOT 100.
①	1	9	Love Is Blue	Paul Mauriat . . . Philips 40495	
②	2	7	(Theme From) Valley Of The Dolls	Dionne Warwick . . . Scepter 12203	
③	5	6	(Sittin' On) The Dock Of The Bay	Otis Redding . . . Volt 157	
④	4	8	I Wish It Would Rain	The Temptations . . . Gordy 7068	
⑤	6	6	Simon Says	1910 Fruitgum Co. . . . Buddah 24	
⑥	3	11	Spooky	Classics IV . . . Imperial 66259	
⑦	21	4	Just Dropped In (To See What Condition My Condition Was In)	The First Edition . . . Reprise 0655	
⑧	8	11	I Wonder What She's Doing Tonite	Tommy Boyce & Bobby Hart . . . A&M 893	
⑨	12	10	Bottle Of Wine	The Fireballs . . . Atco 6491	
⑩	15	5	Everything That Touches You	The Association . . . Warner 7163	

★ **HIGHEST DEBUT** ★ POS 31
(Sweet Sweet Baby) Since You've Been Gone . . . . Aretha Franklin

★ **BIGGEST MOVER** ★ 85 to 47
If You Can Want . . . . Smokey Robinson & The Miracles

TW	LW	WK	Billboard	MARCH 9, 1968	HOT 100
①	1	10	**Love Is Blue** ....*Paul Mauriat* . . . Philips 40495		
②	2	8	**(Theme From) Valley Of The Dolls**........................ *Dionne Warwick* ... Scepter 12203		
❸	3	7	**(Sittin' On) The Dock Of The Bay** ....*Otis Redding* . . . Volt 157		
④	5	7	**Simon Says**...*1910 Fruitgum Co.* . . . Buddah 24		
⑤	4	9	**I Wish It Would Rain** ....*The Temptations* . . . Gordy 7068		
❻	7	5	**Just Dropped In (To See What Condition My Condition Was In)** .... *The First Edition* . . . Reprise 0655		
⑦	6	12	**Spooky**..*Classics IV* . . . Imperial 66259		
⑧	8	12	**I Wonder What She's Doing Tonite**...... *Tommy Boyce & Bobby Hart* ... A&M 893		
❾	19	6	**La - La - Means I Love You**.................*The Delfonics* . . . Philly Groove 150		
⑩	10	6	**Everything That Touches You**...........*The Association* . . . Warner 7163		

★ HIGHEST DEBUT ★ POS 24	★ BIGGEST MOVER ★ 87 to 52
Valleri....................................*The Monkees*	Young Girl ....*The Union Gap*

TW	LW	WK	Billboard	MARCH 16, 1968	HOT 100
❶	3	8	**(Sittin' On) The Dock Of The Bay** ....*Otis Redding* . . . Volt 157		
②	2	9	**(Theme From) Valley Of The Dolls**........................ *Dionne Warwick* ... Scepter 12203		
③	1	11	**Love Is Blue** ....*Paul Mauriat* . . . Philips 40495		
❹	4	8	**Simon Says**...*1910 Fruitgum Co.* . . . Buddah 24		
⑤	6	6	**Just Dropped In (To See What Condition My Condition Was In)** .... *The First Edition* . . . Reprise 0655		
⑥	5	10	**I Wish It Would Rain** ....*The Temptations* . . . Gordy 7068		
❼	9	7	**La - La - Means I Love You**.................*The Delfonics* . . . Philly Groove 150		
❽	24	2	**Valleri**..*The Monkees* . . . Colgems 1019		
❾	17	3	**(Sweet Sweet Baby) Since You've Been Gone** ....*Aretha Franklin* . . . Atlantic 2486		
⑩	11	8	**I Thank You**..*Sam & Dave* . . . Stax 242		

★ HIGHEST DEBUT ★ POS 63	★ BIGGEST MOVER ★ 52 to 24
I Got The Feelin' ....*James Brown*	Young Girl ....*The Union Gap*

TW	LW	WK	Billboard	MARCH 23, 1968	HOT 100
①	1	9	**(Sittin' On) The Dock Of The Bay** ....*Otis Redding* . . . Volt 157		
②	3	12	**Love Is Blue** ....*Paul Mauriat* . . . Philips 40495		
③	2	10	**(Theme From) Valley Of The Dolls** ....*Dionne Warwick* . . . Scepter 12203		
④	4	9	**Simon Says**...*1910 Fruitgum Co.* . . . Buddah 24		
⑤	5	7	**Just Dropped In (To See What Condition My Condition Was In)** .... *The First Edition* . . . Reprise 0655		
❻	7	8	**La - La - Means I Love You** ....*The Delfonics* . . . Philly Groove 150		
❼	8	3	**Valleri**..*The Monkees* . . . Colgems 1019		
❽	9	4	**(Sweet Sweet Baby) Since You've Been Gone** ....*Aretha Franklin* . . . Atlantic 2486		
❾	10	9	**I Thank You** ....*Sam & Dave* . . . Stax 242		
⑩	17	6	**The Ballad Of Bonnie And Clyde**...................*Georgie Fame* . . . Epic 10283		

★ HIGHEST DEBUT ★ POS 23	★ BIGGEST MOVER ★ 63 to 33
Lady Madonna ....*The Beatles*	I Got The Feelin' ....*James Brown*

Billboard — MARCH 30, 1968 — HOT 100

TW	LW	WK	Title	Artist	Label
①	1	10	(Sittin' On) The Dock Of The Bay	Otis Redding	Volt 157
②	2	13	Love Is Blue	Paul Mauriat	Philips 40495
③	7	4	Valleri	The Monkees	Colgems 1019
④	4	10	Simon Says	1910 Fruitgum Co.	Buddah 24
⑤	8	5	(Sweet Sweet Baby) Since You've Been Gone	Aretha Franklin	Atlantic 2486
⑥	6	9	La - La - Means I Love You	The Delfonics	Philly Groove 150
⑦	12	5	Young Girl	The Union Gap	Columbia 44450
⑧	10	7	The Ballad Of Bonnie And Clyde	Georgie Fame	Epic 10283
⑨	23	2	Lady Madonna	The Beatles	Capitol 2138
⑩	3	11	(Theme From) Valley Of The Dolls	Dionne Warwick	Scepter 12203

★ **HIGHEST DEBUT** ★ POS 79
The Unknown Soldier ....The Doors

★ **BIGGEST MOVER** ★ 87 to 42
Cowboys To Girls ....The Intruders

Billboard — APRIL 6, 1968 — HOT 100

TW	LW	WK	Title	Artist	Label
①	1	11	(Sittin' On) The Dock Of The Bay	Otis Redding	Volt 157
②	7	6	Young Girl	The Union Gap	Columbia 44450
③	3	5	Valleri	The Monkees	Colgems 1019
④	6	10	La - La - Means I Love You	The Delfonics	Philly Groove 150
⑤	5	6	(Sweet Sweet Baby) Since You've Been Gone	Aretha Franklin	Atlantic 2486
⑥	15	6	Cry Like A Baby	The Box Tops	Mala 593
⑦	9	3	Lady Madonna	The Beatles	Capitol 2138
⑧	8	8	The Ballad Of Bonnie And Clyde	Georgie Fame	Epic 10283
⑨	2	14	Love Is Blue	Paul Mauriat	Philips 40495
⑩	23	3	Honey	Bobby Goldsboro	United Artists 50283

★ **HIGHEST DEBUT** ★ POS 70
Goodbye Baby (I Don't Want To See You Cry) ....Tommy Boyce & Bobby Hart

★ **BIGGEST MOVER** ★ 95 to 48
I Will Always Think About You ....The New Colony Six

Billboard — APRIL 13, 1968 — HOT 100

TW	LW	WK	Title	Artist	Label
❶	10	4	Honey	Bobby Goldsboro	United Artists 50283
❷	2	7	Young Girl	The Union Gap	Columbia 44450
③	1	12	(Sittin' On) The Dock Of The Bay	Otis Redding	Volt 157
❹	6	7	Cry Like A Baby	The Box Tops	Mala 593
⑤	5	7	(Sweet Sweet Baby) Since You've Been Gone	Aretha Franklin	Atlantic 2486
⑥	7	4	Lady Madonna	The Beatles	Capitol 2138
⑦	8	9	The Ballad Of Bonnie And Clyde	Georgie Fame	Epic 10283
⑧	4	11	La - La - Means I Love You	The Delfonics	Philly Groove 150
⑨	3	6	Valleri	The Monkees	Colgems 1019
⑩	11	7	Mighty Quinn (Quinn The Eskimo)	Manfred Mann	Mercury 72770

★ **HIGHEST DEBUT** ★ POS 56
A Beautiful Morning ....The Rascals

★ **BIGGEST MOVER** ★ 78 to 21
Ain't No Way ....Aretha Franklin

Billboard 🎵 APRIL 20, 1968 🎵 HOT 100

TW	LW	WK	Title	Artist
①	1	5	Honey	Bobby Goldsboro ... United Artists 50283
②	2	8	Young Girl	The Union Gap ... Columbia 44450
③	4	8	Cry Like A Baby	The Box Tops ... Mala 593
④	6	5	Lady Madonna	The Beatles ... Capitol 2138
⑤	5	8	(Sweet Sweet Baby) Since You've Been Gone	Aretha Franklin ... Atlantic 2486
⑥	3	13	(Sittin' On) The Dock Of The Bay	Otis Redding ... Volt 157
⑦	7	10	The Ballad Of Bonnie And Clyde	Georgie Fame ... Epic 10283
⑧	14	11	Dance To The Music	Sly & The Family Stone ... Epic 10256
⑨	11	6	I Got The Feelin'	James Brown ... King 6155
⑩	10	8	Mighty Quinn (Quinn The Eskimo)	Manfred Mann ... Mercury 72770

★ HIGHEST DEBUT ★ POS 71	★ BIGGEST MOVER ★ 56 to 31
Like To Get To Know You ......Spanky & Our Gang	A Beautiful Morning ....The Rascals

Billboard 🎵 APRIL 27, 1968 🎵 HOT 100

TW	LW	WK	Title	Artist
①	1	6	Honey	Bobby Goldsboro ... United Artists 50283
②	3	9	Cry Like A Baby	The Box Tops ... Mala 593
③	2	9	Young Girl	The Union Gap ... Columbia 44450
④	4	6	Lady Madonna	The Beatles ... Capitol 2138
⑤	5	9	(Sweet Sweet Baby) Since You've Been Gone	Aretha Franklin ... Atlantic 2486
⑥	9	7	I Got The Feelin'	James Brown ... King 6155
⑦	6	14	(Sittin' On) The Dock Of The Bay	Otis Redding ... Volt 157
⑧	8	12	Dance To The Music	Sly & The Family Stone ... Epic 10256
⑨	25	5	Tighten Up	Archie Bell & The Drells ... Atlantic 2478
⑩	7	11	The Ballad Of Bonnie And Clyde	Georgie Fame ... Epic 10283

★ HIGHEST DEBUT ★ POS 58	★ BIGGEST MOVER ★ 61 to 27
Mrs. Robinson ....Simon & Garfunkel	Do You Know The Way To San Jose ....Dionne Warwick

Billboard 🎵 MAY 4, 1968 🎵 HOT 100

TW	LW	WK	Title	Artist
①	1	7	Honey	Bobby Goldsboro ... United Artists 50283
②	2	10	Cry Like A Baby	The Box Tops ... Mala 593
③	3	10	Young Girl	The Union Gap ... Columbia 44450
④	4	7	Lady Madonna	The Beatles ... Capitol 2138
⑤	9	6	Tighten Up	Archie Bell & The Drells ... Atlantic 2478
⑥	6	8	I Got The Feelin'	James Brown ... King 6155
⑦	13	7	Cowboys To Girls	The Intruders ... Gamble 214
⑧	14	12	The Good, The Bad And The Ugly	Hugo Montenegro ... RCA 9423
⑨	19	4	A Beautiful Morning	The Rascals ... Atlantic 2493
⑩	12	7	The Unicorn	The Irish Rovers ... Decca 32254

★ HIGHEST DEBUT ★ POS 87	★ BIGGEST MOVER ★ 87 to 47
I Could Never Love Another (After Loving You) ....The Temptations	The Happy Song (Dum-Dum) ....Otis Redding

Billboard HOT 100 — MAY 11, 1968

TW	LW	WK	Title	Artist	Label
1	1	8	Honey	Bobby Goldsboro	United Artists 50283
2	5	7	Tighten Up	Archie Bell & The Drells	Atlantic 2478
3	3	11	Young Girl	The Union Gap	Columbia 44450
4	8	13	The Good, The Bad And The Ugly	Hugo Montenegro	RCA 9423
5	2	11	Cry Like A Baby	The Box Tops	Mala 593
6	9	5	A Beautiful Morning	The Rascals	Atlantic 2493
7	7	8	Cowboys To Girls	The Intruders	Gamble 214
8	10	8	The Unicorn	The Irish Rovers	Decca 32254
9	32	3	Mrs. Robinson	Simon & Garfunkel	Columbia 44511
10	4	8	Lady Madonna	The Beatles	Capitol 2138

★ **HIGHEST DEBUT** ★ POS 77
The Look Of Love ....Sergio Mendes & Brasil '66

★ **BIGGEST MOVER** ★ 69 to 36
If I Were A Carpenter ....Four Tops

Billboard HOT 100 — MAY 18, 1968

TW	LW	WK	Title	Artist	Label
1	2	8	Tighten Up	Archie Bell & The Drells	Atlantic 2478
2	9	4	Mrs. Robinson	Simon & Garfunkel	Columbia 44511
3	1	9	Honey	Bobby Goldsboro	United Artists 50283
4	4	14	The Good, The Bad And The Ugly	Hugo Montenegro	RCA 9423
5	6	6	A Beautiful Morning	The Rascals	Atlantic 2493
6	7	9	Cowboys To Girls	The Intruders	Gamble 214
7	11	13	Love Is All Around	The Troggs	Fontana 1607
8	8	9	The Unicorn	The Irish Rovers	Decca 32254
9	3	12	Young Girl	The Union Gap	Columbia 44450
10	19	6	Do You Know The Way To San Jose	Dionne Warwick	Scepter 12216

★ **HIGHEST DEBUT** ★ POS 67
Think ....Aretha Franklin

★ **BIGGEST MOVER** ★ 100 to 65
She's A Heartbreaker ....Gene Pitney

Billboard HOT 100 — MAY 25, 1968

TW	LW	WK	Title	Artist	Label
1	1	9	Tighten Up	Archie Bell & The Drells	Atlantic 2478
2	2	5	Mrs. Robinson	Simon & Garfunkel	Columbia 44511
3	5	7	A Beautiful Morning	The Rascals	Atlantic 2493
4	4	15	The Good, The Bad And The Ugly	Hugo Montenegro	RCA 9423
5	3	10	Honey	Bobby Goldsboro	United Artists 50283
6	6	10	Cowboys To Girls	The Intruders	Gamble 214
7	8	10	The Unicorn	The Irish Rovers	Decca 32254
8	14	7	Ain't Nothing Like The Real Thing	Marvin Gaye & Tammi Terrell	Tamla 54163
9	11	8	Shoo-Be-Doo-Be-Doo-Da-Day	Stevie Wonder	Tamla 54165
10	10	7	Do You Know The Way To San Jose	Dionne Warwick	Scepter 12216

★ **HIGHEST DEBUT** ★ POS 71
The Horse ....Cliff Nobles & Co.

★ **BIGGEST MOVER** ★ 67 to 16
Think ....Aretha Franklin

Billboard Hot 100 — JUNE 1, 1968

TW	LW	WK		
1	2	6	**Mrs. Robinson** ....*Simon & Garfunkel* ... Columbia 44511	
2	4	16	**The Good, The Bad And The Ugly** .....*Hugo Montenegro* ... RCA 9423	
3	3	8	**A Beautiful Morning** ....*The Rascals* ... Atlantic 2493	
4	1	10	**Tighten Up**..................................*Archie Bell & The Drells* ... Atlantic 2478	
5	5	11	**Honey**...*Bobby Goldsboro* ... United Artists 50283	
6	24	5	**Yummy Yummy Yummy**..............................*Ohio Express* ... Buddah 38	
7	12	9	**Mony Mony**......................*Tommy James & The Shondells* ... Roulette 7008	
8	8	8	**Ain't Nothing Like The Real Thing** ...... *Marvin Gaye & Tammi Terrell* ... Tamla 54163	
9	6	11	**Cowboys To Girls**...*The Intruders* ... Gamble 214	
10	10	8	**Do You Know The Way To San Jose** .... *Dionne Warwick* ... Scepter 12216	

★ **HIGHEST DEBUT** ★ POS 62
Choo Choo Train ....*The Box Tops*

★ **BIGGEST MOVER** ★ 75 to 32
Licking Stick - Licking Stick ....*James Brown*

Billboard Hot 100 — JUNE 8, 1968

TW	LW	WK		
1	1	7	**Mrs. Robinson** ....*Simon & Garfunkel* ... Columbia 44511	
2	4	11	**Tighten Up**....................................*Archie Bell & The Drells* ... Atlantic 2478	
3	11	4	**This Guy's In Love With You**...............................*Herb Alpert* ... A&M 929	
4	2	17	**The Good, The Bad And The Ugly** ....*Hugo Montenegro* ... RCA 9423	
5	7	10	**Mony Mony**......................*Tommy James & The Shondells* ... Roulette 7008	
6	6	6	**Yummy Yummy Yummy**..............................*Ohio Express* ... Buddah 38	
7	12	5	**MacArthur Park** ....*Richard Harris* ... Dunhill 4134	
8	3	9	**A Beautiful Morning**................................*The Rascals* ... Atlantic 2493	
9	13	4	**Think** ....*Aretha Franklin* ... Atlantic 2518	
10	5	12	**Honey**...*Bobby Goldsboro* ... United Artists 50283	

★ **HIGHEST DEBUT** ★ POS 62
Jumpin' Jack Flash ....*The Rolling Stones*

★ **BIGGEST MOVER** ★ 95 to 53
Stoned Soul Picnic ....*The 5th Dimension*

Billboard Hot 100 — JUNE 15, 1968

TW	LW	WK		
1	1	8	**Mrs. Robinson** ....*Simon & Garfunkel* ... Columbia 44511	
2	3	5	**This Guy's In Love With You**...............................*Herb Alpert* ... A&M 929	
3	5	11	**Mony Mony**......................*Tommy James & The Shondells* ... Roulette 7008	
4	6	7	**Yummy Yummy Yummy** ....*Ohio Express* ... Buddah 38	
5	7	6	**MacArthur Park** ....*Richard Harris* ... Dunhill 4134	
6	2	12	**Tighten Up**.................................*Archie Bell & The Drells* ... Atlantic 2478	
7	9	5	**Think** ....*Aretha Franklin* ... Atlantic 2518	
8	8	10	**A Beautiful Morning**................................*The Rascals* ... Atlantic 2493	
9	4	18	**The Good, The Bad And The Ugly** ....*Hugo Montenegro* ... RCA 9423	
10	13	6	**The Look Of Love** ....*Sergio Mendes & Brasil '66* ... A&M 924	

★ **HIGHEST DEBUT** ★ POS 61
D. W. Washburn ....*The Monkees*

★ **BIGGEST MOVER** ★ 77 to 40
Face It Girl, It's Over ....*Nancy Wilson*

JUNE 22, 1968 — Billboard HOT 100

TW	LW	WK		
1	2	6	**This Guy's In Love With You**	Herb Alpert ... A&M 929
2	5	7	**MacArthur Park**	Richard Harris ... Dunhill 4134
3	1	9	Mrs. Robinson	Simon & Garfunkel ... Columbia 44511
4	4	8	**Yummy Yummy Yummy**	Ohio Express ... Buddah 38
5	10	7	The Look Of Love	Sergio Mendes & Brasil '66 ... A&M 924
6	3	12	Mony Mony	Tommy James & The Shondells ... Roulette 7008
7	7	6	**Think**	Aretha Franklin ... Atlantic 2518
8	14	8	**Angel Of The Morning**	Merrilee Rush & The Turnabouts ... Bell 705
9	6	13	Tighten Up	Archie Bell & The Drells ... Atlantic 2478
10	22	6	**Reach Out Of The Darkness**	Friend And Lover ... Verve Forecast 5069

★ **HIGHEST DEBUT** ★ POS 71
People Sure Act Funny ... Arthur Conley

★ **BIGGEST MOVER** ★ 95 to 56
Turn Around, Look At Me ... The Vogues

JUNE 29, 1968 — Billboard HOT 100

TW	LW	WK		
1	1	7	**This Guy's In Love With You**	Herb Alpert ... A&M 929
2	15	6	**The Horse**	Cliff Nobles & Co. ... Phil-L.A. of Soul 313
3	2	8	MacArthur Park	Richard Harris ... Dunhill 4134
4	4	9	**Yummy Yummy Yummy**	Ohio Express ... Buddah 38
5	5	8	The Look Of Love	Sergio Mendes & Brasil '66 ... A&M 924
6	6	13	Mony Mony	Tommy James & The Shondells ... Roulette 7008
7	8	9	**Angel Of The Morning**	Merrilee Rush & The Turnabouts ... Bell 705
8	7	7	**Think**	Aretha Franklin ... Atlantic 2518
9	11	5	Here Comes The Judge	Shorty Long ... Soul 35044
10	10	7	**Reach Out Of The Darkness**	Friend And Lover ... Verve Forecast 5069

★ **HIGHEST DEBUT** ★ POS 73
Hitch It To The Horse ... The Fantastic Johnny C

★ **BIGGEST MOVER** ★ 95 to 46
I'm A Midnight Mover ... Wilson Pickett

JULY 6, 1968 — Billboard HOT 100

TW	LW	WK		
1	1	8	**This Guy's In Love With You**	Herb Alpert ... A&M 929
2	2	7	**The Horse**	Cliff Nobles & Co. ... Phil-L.A. of Soul 313
3	11	5	**Jumpin' Jack Flash**	The Rolling Stones ... London 908
4	5	9	The Look Of Love	Sergio Mendes & Brasil '66 ... A&M 924
5	13	5	**Grazing In The Grass**	Hugh Masekela ... Uni 55066
6	15	5	**Lady Willpower**	Gary Puckett & The Union Gap ... Columbia 44547
7	7	10	**Angel Of The Morning**	Merrilee Rush & The Turnabouts ... Bell 705
8	9	6	**Here Comes The Judge**	Shorty Long ... Soul 35044
9	3	9	MacArthur Park	Richard Harris ... Dunhill 4134
10	10	8	**Reach Out Of The Darkness**	Friend And Lover ... Verve Forecast 5069

★ **HIGHEST DEBUT** ★ POS 73
Dreams Of The Everyday Housewife ... Glen Campbell

★ **BIGGEST MOVER** ★ 90 to 44
Autumn Of My Life ... Bobby Goldsboro

Billboard — JULY 13, 1968 — HOT 100

TW	LW	WK	Title	Artist	Label
1	1	9	This Guy's In Love With You	Herb Alpert	A&M 929
2	2	8	The Horse	Cliff Nobles & Co.	Phil-L.A. of Soul 313
3	3	6	Jumpin' Jack Flash	The Rolling Stones	London 908
4	6	6	Lady Willpower	Gary Puckett & The Union Gap	Columbia 44547
5	5	6	Grazing In The Grass	Hugh Masekela	Uni 55066
6	4	10	The Look Of Love	Sergio Mendes & Brasil '66	A&M 924
7	7	11	Angel Of The Morning	Merrilee Rush & The Turnabouts	Bell 705
8	17	7	Stoned Soul Picnic	The 5th Dimension	Soul City 766
9	8	7	Here Comes The Judge	Shorty Long	Soul 35044
10	15	7	Indian Lake	The Cowsills	MGM 13944

★ HIGHEST DEBUT ★ POS 70
Born To Be Wild .... Steppenwolf

★ BIGGEST MOVER ★ 77 to 22
Hello, I Love You .... The Doors

Billboard — JULY 20, 1968 — HOT 100

TW	LW	WK	Title	Artist	Label
1	5	7	Grazing In The Grass	Hugh Masekela	Uni 55066
2	4	7	Lady Willpower	Gary Puckett & The Union Gap	Columbia 44547
3	3	7	Jumpin' Jack Flash	The Rolling Stones	London 908
4	1	10	This Guy's In Love With You	Herb Alpert	A&M 929
5	2	9	The Horse	Cliff Nobles & Co.	Phil-L.A. of Soul 313
6	8	8	Stoned Soul Picnic	The 5th Dimension	Soul City 766
7	12	5	Hurdy Gurdy Man	Donovan	Epic 10345
8	29	5	Classical Gas	Mason Williams	Warner 7190
9	22	3	Hello, I Love You	The Doors	Elektra 45635
10	10	8	Indian Lake	The Cowsills	MGM 13944

★ HIGHEST DEBUT ★ POS 64
People Got To Be Free .... The Rascals

★ BIGGEST MOVER ★ 84 to 52
Soul-Limbo .... Booker T. & The MG's

Billboard — JULY 27, 1968 — HOT 100

TW	LW	WK	Title	Artist	Label
1	1	8	Grazing In The Grass	Hugh Masekela	Uni 55066
2	2	8	Lady Willpower	Gary Puckett & The Union Gap	Columbia 44547
3	6	9	Stoned Soul Picnic	The 5th Dimension	Soul City 766
4	3	8	Jumpin' Jack Flash	The Rolling Stones	London 908
5	5	10	The Horse	Cliff Nobles & Co.	Phil-L.A. of Soul 313
6	7	6	Hurdy Gurdy Man	Donovan	Epic 10345
7	4	11	This Guy's In Love With You	Herb Alpert	A&M 929
8	8	6	Classical Gas	Mason Williams	Warner 7190
9	9	4	Hello, I Love You	The Doors	Elektra 45635
10	10	9	Indian Lake	The Cowsills	MGM 13944

★ HIGHEST DEBUT ★ POS 62
Light My Fire .... Jose Feliciano

★ BIGGEST MOVER ★ 96 to 54
Yesterday's Dreams .... Four Tops

Billboard HOT 100 — AUGUST 3, 1968

TW	LW	WK	Title	Artist	Label
1	9	5	Hello, I Love You	The Doors	Elektra 45635
2	8	7	Classical Gas	Mason Williams	Warner 7190
3	3	10	Stoned Soul Picnic	The 5th Dimension	Soul City 766
4	1	9	Grazing In The Grass	Hugh Masekela	Uni 55066
5	6	7	Hurdy Gurdy Man	Donovan	Epic 10345
6	4	9	Jumpin' Jack Flash	The Rolling Stones	London 908
7	2	9	Lady Willpower	Gary Puckett & The Union Gap	Columbia 44547
8	5	11	The Horse	Cliff Nobles & Co.	Phil-L.A. of Soul 313
9	11	8	Turn Around, Look At Me	The Vogues	Reprise 0686
10	18	19	Sunshine Of Your Love	Cream	Atco 6544

★ **HIGHEST DEBUT** ★ POS 80
Brown Eyed Woman ....Bill Medley

★ **BIGGEST MOVER** ★ 47 to 16
You Keep Me Hangin' On..............Vanilla Fudge

Billboard HOT 100 — AUGUST 10, 1968

TW	LW	WK	Title	Artist	Label
1	1	6	Hello, I Love You	The Doors	Elektra 45635
2	2	8	Classical Gas	Mason Williams	Warner 7190
3	3	11	Stoned Soul Picnic	The 5th Dimension	Soul City 766
4	4	10	Grazing In The Grass	Hugh Masekela	Uni 55066
5	13	4	People Got To Be Free	The Rascals	Atlantic 2537
6	5	8	Hurdy Gurdy Man	Donovan	Epic 10345
7	7	10	Lady Willpower	Gary Puckett & The Union Gap	Columbia 44547
8	9	9	Turn Around, Look At Me	The Vogues	Reprise 0686
9	10	20	Sunshine Of Your Love	Cream	Atco 6544
10	6	10	Jumpin' Jack Flash	The Rolling Stones	London 908

★ **HIGHEST DEBUT** ★ POS 61
The Fool On The Hill ....Sergio Mendes & Brasil '66

★ **BIGGEST MOVER** ★ 83 to 44
Please Return Your Love To Me..................The Temptations

Billboard HOT 100 — AUGUST 17, 1968

TW	LW	WK	Title	Artist	Label
1	5	5	People Got To Be Free	The Rascals	Atlantic 2537
2	1	7	Hello, I Love You	The Doors	Elektra 45635
3	2	9	Classical Gas	Mason Williams	Warner 7190
4	11	6	Born To Be Wild	Steppenwolf	Dunhill 4138
5	20	4	Light My Fire	Jose Feliciano	RCA 9550
6	3	12	Stoned Soul Picnic	The 5th Dimension	Soul City 766
7	8	10	Turn Around, Look At Me	The Vogues	Reprise 0686
8	9	21	Sunshine Of Your Love	Cream	Atco 6544
9	4	11	Grazing In The Grass	Hugh Masekela	Uni 55066
10	6	9	Hurdy Gurdy Man	Donovan	Epic 10345

★ **HIGHEST DEBUT** ★ POS 59
The House That Jack Built..........Aretha Franklin

★ **BIGGEST MOVER** ★ 51 to 29
Slip Away ....Clarence Carter

TW	LW	WK	Billboard	AUGUST 24, 1968	HOT 100.
①	1	6	**People Got To Be Free**	*The Rascals* . . . Atlantic 2537	
②	4	7	**Born To Be Wild**	*Steppenwolf* . . . Dunhill 4138	
③	2	8	Hello, I Love You	*The Doors* . . . Elektra 45635	
④	5	5	Light My Fire	*Jose Feliciano* . . . RCA 9550	
⑤	3	10	Classical Gas	*Mason Williams* . . . Warner 7190	
⑥	8	22	Sunshine Of Your Love	*Cream* . . . Atco 6544	
⑦	7	11	**Turn Around, Look At Me**	*The Vogues* . . . Reprise 0686	
⑧	6	13	Stoned Soul Picnic	*The 5th Dimension* . . . Soul City 766	
⑨	16	6	**I Can't Stop Dancing**	*Archie Bell & The Drells* . . . Atlantic 2534	
⑩	13	9	**Stay In My Corner**	*The Dells* . . . Cadet 5612	

★ HIGHEST DEBUT ★ POS 81	★ BIGGEST MOVER ★ 83 to 38
Harper Valley P.T.A. ....*Jeannie C. Riley*	Hush................................*Deep Purple*

TW	LW	WK	Billboard	AUGUST 31, 1968	HOT 100.
①	1	7	**People Got To Be Free**	*The Rascals* . . . Atlantic 2537	
②	2	8	**Born To Be Wild**	*Steppenwolf* . . . Dunhill 4138	
③	4	6	**Light My Fire**	*Jose Feliciano* . . . RCA 9550	
④	3	9	Hello, I Love You	*The Doors* . . . Elektra 45635	
⑤	6	23	**Sunshine Of Your Love**	*Cream* . . . Atco 6544	
⑥	11	13	**You Keep Me Hangin' On**	*Vanilla Fudge* . . . Atco 6590	
⑦	81	2	Harper Valley P.T.A.	*Jeannie C. Riley* . . . Plantation 3	
⑧	15	6	You're All I Need To Get By	*Marvin Gaye & Tammi Terrell* . . . Tamla 54169	
⑨	9	7	**I Can't Stop Dancing**	*Archie Bell & The Drells* . . . Atlantic 2534	
⑩	10	10	**Stay In My Corner**	*The Dells* . . . Cadet 5612	

★ HIGHEST DEBUT ★ POS 63	★ BIGGEST MOVER ★ 81 to 7
To Wait For Love ....*Herb Alpert*	Harper Valley P.T.A. ....*Jeannie C. Riley*

TW	LW	WK	Billboard	SEPTEMBER 7, 1968	HOT 100.
①	1	8	**People Got To Be Free**	*The Rascals* . . . Atlantic 2537	
②	2	9	**Born To Be Wild**	*Steppenwolf* . . . Dunhill 4138	
③	3	7	**Light My Fire**	*Jose Feliciano* . . . RCA 9550	
④	7	3	**Harper Valley P.T.A.**	*Jeannie C. Riley* . . . Plantation 3	
⑤	4	10	Hello, I Love You	*The Doors* . . . Elektra 45635	
⑥	20	4	**The House That Jack Built**	*Aretha Franklin* . . . Atlantic 2546	
⑦	12	7	**1, 2, 3, Red Light**	*1910 Fruitgum Co.* . . . Buddah 54	
⑧	8	7	You're All I Need To Get By	*Marvin Gaye & Tammi Terrell* . . . Tamla 54169	
⑨	9	8	**I Can't Stop Dancing**	*Archie Bell & The Drells* . . . Atlantic 2534	
⑩	10	11	**Stay In My Corner**	*The Dells* . . . Cadet 5612	

★ HIGHEST DEBUT ★ POS 60	★ BIGGEST MOVER ★ 69 to 45
Say It Loud - I'm Black And I'm Proud.....*James Brown*	Little Green Apples..............*O.C. Smith*

Billboard — SEPTEMBER 14, 1968 — HOT 100

TW	LW	WK	Title	Artist	Label
①	1	9	People Got To Be Free	The Rascals	Atlantic 2537
②	4	4	Harper Valley P.T.A.	Jeannie C. Riley	Plantation 3
③	3	8	Light My Fire	Jose Feliciano	RCA 9550
④	2	10	Born To Be Wild	Steppenwolf	Dunhill 4138
⑤	7	8	1, 2, 3, Red Light	1910 Fruitgum Co.	Buddah 54
⑥	6	5	The House That Jack Built	Aretha Franklin	Atlantic 2546
⑦	8	8	You're All I Need To Get By	Marvin Gaye & Tammi Terrell	Tamla 54169
⑧	13	5	Hush	Deep Purple	Tetragrammaton 1503
⑨	5	11	Hello, I Love You	The Doors	Elektra 45635
⑩	-	1	Hey Jude	The Beatles	Apple 2276

★ HIGHEST DEBUT ★ POS 10
Hey Jude ....The Beatles

★ BIGGEST MOVER ★ 60 to 31
Say It Loud - I'm Black And I'm Proud.....James Brown

Billboard — SEPTEMBER 21, 1968 — HOT 100

TW	LW	WK	Title	Artist	Label
❶	2	5	Harper Valley P.T.A.	Jeannie C. Riley	Plantation 3
②	1	10	People Got To Be Free	The Rascals	Atlantic 2537
❸	10	2	Hey Jude	The Beatles	Apple 2276
❹	8	6	Hush	Deep Purple	Tetragrammaton 1503
⑤	5	9	1, 2, 3, Red Light	1910 Fruitgum Co.	Buddah 54
⑥	3	9	Light My Fire	Jose Feliciano	RCA 9550
⑦	4	11	Born To Be Wild	Steppenwolf	Dunhill 4138
❽	11	7	The Fool On The Hill	Sergio Mendes & Brasil '66	A&M 961
❾	23	6	I've Gotta Get A Message To You	The Bee Gees	Atco 6603
⑩	6	6	The House That Jack Built	Aretha Franklin	Atlantic 2546

★ HIGHEST DEBUT ★ POS 54
Over You ....Gary Puckett & The Union Gap

★ BIGGEST MOVER ★ 60 to 15
Fire.....................The Crazy World Of Arthur Brown

Billboard — SEPTEMBER 28, 1968 — HOT 100

TW	LW	WK	Title	Artist	Label
❶	3	3	Hey Jude	The Beatles	Apple 2276
②	1	6	Harper Valley P.T.A.	Jeannie C. Riley	Plantation 3
③	2	11	People Got To Be Free	The Rascals	Atlantic 2537
④	4	7	Hush	Deep Purple	Tetragrammaton 1503
❺	15	4	Fire	The Crazy World Of Arthur Brown	Atlantic 2556
⑥	8	8	The Fool On The Hill	Sergio Mendes & Brasil '66	A&M 961
⑦	5	10	1, 2, 3, Red Light	1910 Fruitgum Co.	Buddah 54
❽	9	7	I've Gotta Get A Message To You	The Bee Gees	Atco 6603
⑨	16	7	Girl Watcher	The O'Kaysions	ABC 11094
⑩	13	12	Slip Away	Clarence Carter	Atlantic 2508

★ HIGHEST DEBUT ★ POS 69
I've Got Dreams To Remember ....Otis Redding

★ BIGGEST MOVER ★ 97 to 54
Elenore.....................................The Turtles

Billboard — OCTOBER 5, 1968 — HOT 100

TW	LW	WK			
1	1	4	Hey Jude	The Beatles	Apple 2276
2	2	7	Harper Valley P.T.A.	Jeannie C. Riley	Plantation 3
3	5	5	Fire	The Crazy World Of Arthur Brown	Atlantic 2556
4	20	8	Little Green Apples	O.C. Smith	Columbia 44616
5	9	8	Girl Watcher	The O'Kaysions	ABC 11094
6	10	13	Slip Away	Clarence Carter	Atlantic 2508
7	3	12	People Got To Be Free	The Rascals	Atlantic 2537
8	8	8	I've Gotta Get A Message To You	The Bee Gees	Atco 6603
9	7	11	1, 2, 3, Red Light	1910 Fruitgum Co.	Buddah 54
10	14	8	I Say A Little Prayer	Aretha Franklin	Atlantic 2546

★ **HIGHEST DEBUT** ★ POS 58
White Room................Cream

★ **BIGGEST MOVER** ★ 100 to 69
Peace Of Mind................Nancy Wilson

Billboard — OCTOBER 12, 1968 — HOT 100

TW	LW	WK			
1	1	5	Hey Jude	The Beatles	Apple 2276
2	2	8	Harper Valley P.T.A.	Jeannie C. Riley	Plantation 3
3	3	6	Fire	The Crazy World Of Arthur Brown	Atlantic 2556
4	4	9	Little Green Apples	O.C. Smith	Columbia 44616
5	5	9	Girl Watcher	The O'Kaysions	ABC 11094
6	17	7	Midnight Confessions	The Grass Roots	Dunhill 4144
7	18	6	My Special Angel	The Vogues	Reprise 0766
8	8	9	I've Gotta Get A Message To You	The Bee Gees	Atco 6603
9	25	4	Over You	Gary Puckett & The Union Gap	Columbia 44644
10	6	14	Slip Away	Clarence Carter	Atlantic 2508

★ **HIGHEST DEBUT** ★ POS 69
Keep On Lovin' Me Honey............Marvin Gaye & Tammi Terrell

★ **BIGGEST MOVER** ★ 54 to 18
Those Were The Days ....Mary Hopkin

Billboard — OCTOBER 19, 1968 — HOT 100

TW	LW	WK			
1	1	6	Hey Jude	The Beatles	Apple 2276
2	3	7	Fire	The Crazy World Of Arthur Brown	Atlantic 2556
3	4	10	Little Green Apples	O.C. Smith	Columbia 44616
4	2	9	Harper Valley P.T.A.	Jeannie C. Riley	Plantation 3
5	5	10	Girl Watcher	The O'Kaysions	ABC 11094
6	6	8	Midnight Confessions	The Grass Roots	Dunhill 4144
7	7	7	My Special Angel	The Vogues	Reprise 0766
8	8	10	I've Gotta Get A Message To You	The Bee Gees	Atco 6603
9	9	5	Over You	Gary Puckett & The Union Gap	Columbia 44644
10	14	7	Say It Loud – I'm Black And I'm Proud	James Brown	King 6187

★ **HIGHEST DEBUT** ★ POS 43
Love Child ....Diana Ross & The Supremes

★ **BIGGEST MOVER** ★ 69 to 38
Keep On Lovin' Me Honey............Marvin Gaye & Tammi Terrell

TW	LW	WK	Billboard.	OCTOBER 26, 1968	HOT 100.
①	1	7	**Hey Jude**..*The Beatles* . . . Apple 2276		
②	3	11	**Little Green Apples** ........................*O.C. Smith* . . . Columbia 44616		
③	2	8	**Fire**.......................*The Crazy World Of Arthur Brown* . . . Atlantic 2556		
❹	13	5	**Those Were The Days** ....*Mary Hopkin* . . . Apple 1801		
⑤	5	11	**Girl Watcher**...*The O'Kaysions* . . . ABC 11094		
⑥	6	9	**Midnight Confessions** ....*The Grass Roots* . . . Dunhill 4144		
⑦	9	6	**Over You**.....................*Gary Puckett & The Union Gap* . . . Columbia 44644		
⑧	4	10	**Harper Valley P.T.A.** ....*Jeannie C. Riley* . . . Plantation 3		
❾	14	6	**Elenore**...*The Turtles* . . . White Whale 276		
⑩	8	11	**I've Gotta Get A Message To You** ....*The Bee Gees* . . . Atco 6603		

★ HIGHEST DEBUT ★ POS 45	★ BIGGEST MOVER ★ 94 to 53
Who's Making Love....................*Johnnie Taylor*	Battle Hymn Of The Republic.........*Andy Williams*

TW	LW	WK	Billboard.	NOVEMBER 2, 1968	HOT 100.
①	1	8	**Hey Jude**..*The Beatles* . . . Apple 2276		
❷	4	6	**Those Were The Days** ....*Mary Hopkin* . . . Apple 1801		
③	2	12	**Little Green Apples** ........................*O.C. Smith* . . . Columbia 44616		
④	3	9	**Fire**.......................*The Crazy World Of Arthur Brown* . . . Atlantic 2556		
⑤	6	10	**Midnight Confessions** ....*The Grass Roots* . . . Dunhill 4144		
⑥	9	7	**Elenore**...*The Turtles* . . . White Whale 276		
⑦	7	7	**Over You**.....................*Gary Puckett & The Union Gap* . . . Columbia 44644		
❽	11	8	**Hold Me Tight** ....*Johnny Nash* . . . JAD 207		
❾	19	3	**Love Child** ....*Diana Ross & The Supremes* . . . Motown 1135		
⑩	15	5	**White Room** ....*Cream* . . . Atco 6617		

★ HIGHEST DEBUT ★ POS 64	★ BIGGEST MOVER ★ 66 to 35
I Love How You Love Me................*Bobby Vinton*	Abraham, Martin And John ....*Dion*

TW	LW	WK	Billboard.	NOVEMBER 9, 1968	HOT 100.
①	1	9	**Hey Jude**..*The Beatles* . . . Apple 2276		
②	2	7	**Those Were The Days** ....*Mary Hopkin* . . . Apple 1801		
❸	9	4	**Love Child** ....*Diana Ross & The Supremes* . . . Motown 1135		
④	3	13	**Little Green Apples** ........................*O.C. Smith* . . . Columbia 44616		
⑤	8	9	**Hold Me Tight** ....*Johnny Nash* . . . JAD 207		
❻	10	6	**White Room**...*Cream* . . . Atco 6617		
❼	12	6	**Magic Carpet Ride** ....*Steppenwolf* . . . Dunhill 4161		
⑧	6	8	**Elenore**...*The Turtles* . . . White Whale 276		
⑨	4	10	**Fire**.......................*The Crazy World Of Arthur Brown* . . . Atlantic 2556		
⑩	5	11	**Midnight Confessions** ....*The Grass Roots* . . . Dunhill 4144		

★ HIGHEST DEBUT ★ POS 73	★ BIGGEST MOVER ★ 79 to 35
Too Weak To Fight ....*Clarence Carter*	For Once In My Life....................*Stevie Wonder*

Billboard. NOVEMBER 16, 1968 — HOT 100.

TW	LW	WK		
①	1	10	**Hey Jude**	*The Beatles* . . . Apple 2276
②	2	8	**Those Were The Days**	*Mary Hopkin* . . . Apple 1801
❸	3	5	**Love Child**	*Diana Ross & The Supremes* . . . Motown 1135
④	7	7	**Magic Carpet Ride**	*Steppenwolf* . . . Dunhill 4161
⑤	5	10	**Hold Me Tight**	*Johnny Nash* . . . JAD 207
⑥	6	7	**White Room**	*Cream* . . . Atco 6617
⑦	4	14	**Little Green Apples**	*O.C. Smith* . . . Columbia 44616
❽	21	4	**Who's Making Love**	*Johnnie Taylor* . . . Stax 0009
❾	18	4	**Abraham, Martin And John**	*Dion* . . . Laurie 3464
⑩	8	9	**Elenore**.......................................	*The Turtles* . . . White Whale 276

★ **HIGHEST DEBUT** ★ POS 45	★ **BIGGEST MOVER** ★ 67 to 23
Cloud Nine ....*The Temptations*	**Wichita Lineman** ....*Glen Campbell*

Billboard. NOVEMBER 23, 1968 — HOT 100.

TW	LW	WK		
①	1	11	**Hey Jude**..	*The Beatles* . . . Apple 2276
②	3	6	**Love Child**	*Diana Ross & The Supremes* . . . Motown 1135
③	2	9	**Those Were The Days**	*Mary Hopkin* . . . Apple 1801
④	4	8	**Magic Carpet Ride**	*Steppenwolf* . . . Dunhill 4161
❺	9	5	**Abraham, Martin And John**	*Dion* . . . Laurie 3464
⑥	6	8	**White Room**	*Cream* . . . Atco 6617
⑦	5	11	**Hold Me Tight**	*Johnny Nash* . . . JAD 207
⑧	8	5	**Who's Making Love**	*Johnnie Taylor* . . . Stax 0009
⑨	7	15	**Little Green Apples**	*O.C. Smith* . . . Columbia 44616
❿	23	4	**Wichita Lineman**	*Glen Campbell* . . . Capitol 2302

★ **HIGHEST DEBUT** ★ POS 34	★ **BIGGEST MOVER** ★ 97 to 69
I Heard It Through The Grapevine...........*Marvin Gaye*	**Hooked On A Feeling**......................*B.J. Thomas*

Billboard. NOVEMBER 30, 1968 — HOT 100.

TW	LW	WK		
①	2	7	**Love Child** ....*Diana Ross & The Supremes* . . . Motown 1135	
②	1	12	**Hey Jude**..	*The Beatles* . . . Apple 2276
③	4	9	**Magic Carpet Ride**	*Steppenwolf* . . . Dunhill 4161
④	3	10	**Those Were The Days**	*Mary Hopkin* . . . Apple 1801
⑤	5	6	**Abraham, Martin And John**	*Dion* . . . Laurie 3464
❻	8	6	**Who's Making Love**	*Johnnie Taylor* . . . Stax 0009
❼	14	5	**For Once In My Life**..........................	*Stevie Wonder* . . . Tamla 54174
⑧	10	5	**Wichita Lineman**	*Glen Campbell* . . . Capitol 2302
⑨	7	12	**Hold Me Tight**	*Johnny Nash* . . . JAD 207
⑩	6	9	**White Room**	*Cream* . . . Atco 6617

★ **HIGHEST DEBUT** ★ POS 57	★ **BIGGEST MOVER** ★ 100 to 61
Papa's Got A Brand New Bag.........*Otis Redding*	**Lo Mucho Que Te Quiero**...............*Rene & Rene*

Billboard — DECEMBER 7, 1968 — HOT 100

TW	LW	WK	Title	Artist	Label
①	1	8	**Love Child**	*Diana Ross & The Supremes*	Motown 1135
②	2	13	Hey Jude	*The Beatles*	Apple 2276
❸	7	6	For Once In My Life	*Stevie Wonder*	Tamla 54174
❹	16	3	I Heard It Through The Grapevine	*Marvin Gaye*	Tamla 54176
⑤	6	7	Who's Making Love	*Johnnie Taylor*	Stax 0009
⑥	3	10	Magic Carpet Ride	*Steppenwolf*	Dunhill 4161
⑦	5	7	Abraham, Martin And John	*Dion*	Laurie 3464
⑧	8	6	Wichita Lineman	*Glen Campbell*	Capitol 2302
⑨	11	7	Stormy	*Classics IV featuring Dennis Yost*	Imperial 66328
⑩	4	11	Those Were The Days	*Mary Hopkin*	Apple 1801

★ **HIGHEST DEBUT** ★ POS 57
I'm Gonna Make You Love Me ....*Diana Ross & The Supremes & The Temptations*

★ **BIGGEST MOVER** ★ 100 to 63
If I Can Dream ....*Elvis Presley*

Billboard — DECEMBER 14, 1968 — HOT 100

TW	LW	WK	Title	Artist	Label
❶	4	4	**I Heard It Through The Grapevine**	*Marvin Gaye*	Tamla 54176
②	1	9	Love Child	*Diana Ross & The Supremes*	Motown 1135
③	3	7	For Once In My Life	*Stevie Wonder*	Tamla 54174
④	7	8	**Abraham, Martin And John**	*Dion*	Laurie 3464
⑤	5	8	**Who's Making Love**	*Johnnie Taylor*	Stax 0009
⑥	2	14	Hey Jude	*The Beatles*	Apple 2276
⑦	8	7	Wichita Lineman	*Glen Campbell*	Capitol 2302
⑧	9	8	Stormy	*Classics IV featuring Dennis Yost*	Imperial 66328
⑨	11	7	**I Love How You Love Me**	*Bobby Vinton*	Epic 10397
⑩	6	11	Magic Carpet Ride	*Steppenwolf*	Dunhill 4161

★ **HIGHEST DEBUT** ★ POS 74
Bluebirds Over The Mountain .....*The Beach Boys*

★ **BIGGEST MOVER** ★ 57 to 20
I'm Gonna Make You Love Me ....*Diana Ross & The Supremes & The Temptations*

Billboard — DECEMBER 21, 1968 — HOT 100

TW	LW	WK	Title	Artist	Label
①	1	5	**I Heard It Through The Grapevine**	*Marvin Gaye*	Tamla 54176
②	2	10	Love Child	*Diana Ross & The Supremes*	Motown 1135
③	3	8	For Once In My Life	*Stevie Wonder*	Tamla 54174
④	4	9	**Abraham, Martin And John**	*Dion*	Laurie 3464
❺	7	8	Wichita Lineman	*Glen Campbell*	Capitol 2302
❻	8	9	Stormy	*Classics IV featuring Dennis Yost*	Imperial 66328
⑦	5	9	Who's Making Love	*Johnnie Taylor*	Stax 0009
❽	11	7	**Both Sides Now**	*Judy Collins*	Elektra 45639
⑨	9	8	**I Love How You Love Me**	*Bobby Vinton*	Epic 10397
⑩	10	12	Magic Carpet Ride	*Steppenwolf*	Dunhill 4161

★ **HIGHEST DEBUT** ★ POS 61
I Started A Joke...........................*The Bee Gees*

★ **BIGGEST MOVER** ★ 85 to 39
Crimson And Clover ....*Tommy James & The Shondells*

TW	LW	WK	Billboard ⊙ DECEMBER 28, 1968 ⊙	HOT 100.
①	1	6	**I Heard It Through The Grapevine** ....*Marvin Gaye* . . . Tamla 54176	
②	3	9	**For Once In My Life**...............................*Stevie Wonder* . . . Tamla 54174	
③	2	11	Love Child ....*Diana Ross & The Supremes* . . . Motown 1135	
④	5	9	Wichita Lineman ....*Glen Campbell* . . . Capitol 2302	
⑤	6	10	**Stormy** ....*Classics IV featuring Dennis Yost* . . . Imperial 66328	
⑥	4	10	Abraham, Martin And John.......................................*Dion* . . . Laurie 3464	
❼	17	4	I'm Gonna Make You Love Me.. *Diana Ross & The Supremes & The Temptations* . . . Motown 1137	
⑧	7	10	Who's Making Love ....*Johnnie Taylor* . . . Stax 0009	
⑨	9	9	**I Love How You Love Me** ....*Bobby Vinton* . . . Epic 10397	
⑩	12	7	Cloud Nine...*The Temptations* . . . Gordy 7081	

★ *HIGHEST DEBUT* ★ POS 64	★ *BIGGEST MOVER* ★ 90 to 43
Daddy Sang Bass ....*Johnny Cash*	**Hey Jude**..................................*Wilson Pickett*

Billboard ★ JANUARY 4, 1969 ★ HOT 100

TW	LW	WK		
①	1	7	**I Heard It Through The Grapevine** ....*Marvin Gaye* . . . Tamla 54176	
②	2	10	**For Once In My Life**..........................*Stevie Wonder* . . . Tamla 54174	
❸	7	5	**I'm Gonna Make You Love Me**..	
			Diana Ross & The Supremes & The Temptations . . . Motown 1137	
❹	16	6	**Soulful Strut** ....*Young-Holt Unlimited* . . . Brunswick 55391	
⑤	4	10	**Wichita Lineman** ....*Glen Campbell* . . . Capitol 2302	
⑥	10	8	**Cloud Nine**.......................................*The Temptations* . . . Gordy 7081	
⑦	3	12	**Love Child** ....*Diana Ross & The Supremes* . . . Motown 1135	
⑧	5	11	**Stormy**........................*Classics IV featuring Dennis Yost* . . . Imperial 66328	
⑨	8	11	**Who's Making Love** ....*Johnnie Taylor* . . . Stax 0009	
⑩	13	8	**Hooked On A Feeling**..........................*B.J. Thomas* . . . Scepter 12230	

★ **HIGHEST DEBUT** ★ POS 53
Baby, Baby Don't Cry ......*Smokey Robinson & The Miracles*

★ **BIGGEST MOVER** ★ 66 to 29
Can I Change My Mind ....*Tyrone Davis*

Billboard ★ JANUARY 11, 1969 ★ HOT 100

TW	LW	WK		
①	1	8	**I Heard It Through The Grapevine** ....*Marvin Gaye* . . . Tamla 54176	
②	3	6	**I'm Gonna Make You Love Me**..	
			Diana Ross & The Supremes & The Temptations . . . Motown 1137	
③	5	11	**Wichita Lineman** ....*Glen Campbell* . . . Capitol 2302	
④	4	7	**Soulful Strut** ....*Young-Holt Unlimited* . . . Brunswick 55391	
⑤	10	9	**Hooked On A Feeling**..........................*B.J. Thomas* . . . Scepter 12230	
⑥	6	9	**Cloud Nine**.......................................*The Temptations* . . . Gordy 7081	
⑦	2	11	**For Once In My Life**..........................*Stevie Wonder* . . . Tamla 54174	
❽	17	5	**Crimson And Clover** ....*Tommy James & The Shondells* . . . Roulette 7028	
⑨	7	13	**Love Child** ....*Diana Ross & The Supremes* . . . Motown 1135	
⑩	11	11	**I Love How You Love Me** ....*Bobby Vinton* . . . Epic 10397	

★ **HIGHEST DEBUT** ★ POS 91
Games People Play ....*Joe South*

★ **BIGGEST MOVER** ★ 84 to 48
Build Me Up Buttercup ....*The Foundations*

Billboard ★ JANUARY 18, 1969 ★ HOT 100

TW	LW	WK		
①	1	9	**I Heard It Through The Grapevine** ....*Marvin Gaye* . . . Tamla 54176	
②	2	7	**I'm Gonna Make You Love Me**	
			Diana Ross & The Supremes & The Temptations . . . Motown 1137	
❸	4	8	**Soulful Strut**...........................*Young-Holt Unlimited* . . . Brunswick 55391	
❹	8	6	**Crimson And Clover** ....*Tommy James & The Shondells* . . . Roulette 7028	
⑤	5	10	**Hooked On A Feeling**..........................*B.J. Thomas* . . . Scepter 12230	
⑥	3	12	**Wichita Lineman** ....*Glen Campbell* . . . Capitol 2302	
⑦	7	12	**For Once In My Life**..........................*Stevie Wonder* . . . Tamla 54174	
❽	18	4	**Touch Me** ....*The Doors* . . . Elektra 45646	
⑨	23	5	**Worst That Could Happen** ....*Brooklyn Bridge* . . . Buddah 75	
⑩	13	8	**Son-Of-A Preacher Man**...................*Dusty Springfield* . . . Atlantic 2580	

★ **HIGHEST DEBUT** ★ POS 67
Take Care Of Your Homework ......*Johnnie Taylor*

★ **BIGGEST MOVER** ★ 83 to 47
Goodnight My Love ....*Paul Anka*

TW	LW	WK	Billboard	JANUARY 25, 1969	HOT 100
①	1	10	**I Heard It Through The Grapevine** ....*Marvin Gaye* ... Tamla 54176
❷	4	7	Crimson And Clover ....*Tommy James & The Shondells* ... Roulette 7028
③	2	8	I'm Gonna Make You Love Me..
			Diana Ross & The Supremes & The Temptations ... Motown 1137
④	3	9	Soulful Strut ....*Young-Holt Unlimited* ... Brunswick 55391
❺	15	9	Everyday People ....*Sly & The Family Stone* ... Epic 10407
⑥	5	11	Hooked On A Feeling...............................*B.J. Thomas* ... Scepter 12230
⑦	8	5	Touch Me...*The Doors* ... Elektra 45646
⑧	9	6	Worst That Could Happen ....*Brooklyn Bridge* ... Buddah 75
❾	16	6	I Started A Joke...*The Bee Gees* ... Atco 6639
⑩	10	9	**Son-Of-A Preacher Man**....................*Dusty Springfield* ... Atlantic 2580

★ HIGHEST DEBUT ★ POS 47	★ BIGGEST MOVER ★ 97 to 67
I'm Livin' In Shame ....*Diana Ross & The Supremes*	This Old Heart Of Mine ....*Tammi Terrell*

TW	LW	WK	Billboard	FEBRUARY 1, 1969	HOT 100
①	2	8	**Crimson And Clover** .....*Tommy James & The Shondells* ... Roulette 7028
❷	5	10	Everyday People ....*Sly & The Family Stone* ... Epic 10407
❸	8	7	**Worst That Could Happen** ....*Brooklyn Bridge* ... Buddah 75
❹	7	6	Touch Me..*The Doors* ... Elektra 45646
⑤	1	11	I Heard It Through The Grapevine.................*Marvin Gaye* ... Tamla 54176
⑥	3	9	I'm Gonna Make You Love Me..
			Diana Ross & The Supremes & The Temptations ... Motown 1137
⑦	9	7	I Started A Joke...*The Bee Gees* ... Atco 6639
⑧	6	12	Hooked On A Feeling...............................*B.J. Thomas* ... Scepter 12230
⑨	4	10	Soulful Strut ....*Young-Holt Unlimited* ... Brunswick 55391
⑩	28	5	Build Me Up Buttercup................................*The Foundations* ... Uni 55101

★ HIGHEST DEBUT ★ POS 46	★ BIGGEST MOVER ★ 99 to 65
Soul Shake ....*Peggy Scott & Jo Jo Benson*	Crossroads..*Cream*

TW	LW	WK	Billboard	FEBRUARY 8, 1969	HOT 100
①	1	9	**Crimson And Clover** .....*Tommy James & The Shondells* ... Roulette 7028
②	2	11	Everyday People ....*Sly & The Family Stone* ... Epic 10407
③	3	8	**Worst That Could Happen** ....*Brooklyn Bridge* ... Buddah 75
❹	4	7	Touch Me..*The Doors* ... Elektra 45646
❺	10	6	Build Me Up Buttercup................................*The Foundations* ... Uni 55101
⑥	7	8	**I Started A Joke** ....*The Bee Gees* ... Atco 6639
⑦	5	12	I Heard It Through The Grapevine.................*Marvin Gaye* ... Tamla 54176
⑧	6	10	I'm Gonna Make You Love Me..
			Diana Ross & The Supremes & The Temptations ... Motown 1137
❾	13	14	**Hang 'Em High**...............................*Booker T. & The MG's* ... Stax 0013
⑩	11	8	Can I Change My Mind ....*Tyrone Davis* ... Dakar 602

★ HIGHEST DEBUT ★ POS 60	★ BIGGEST MOVER ★ 92 to 40
Time Of The Season ....*The Zombies*	This Girl's In Love With You........*Dionne Warwick*

Billboard ⊙ FEBRUARY 15, 1969 ⊙ HOT 100.

TW	LW	WK			
①	2	12	**Everyday People**............................*Sly & The Family Stone* . . . Epic 10407		
②	1	10	**Crimson And Clover** ....*Tommy James & The Shondells* . . . Roulette 7028		
③	4	8	**Touch Me**..*The Doors* . . . Elektra 45646		
④	5	7	Build Me Up Buttercup..............................*The Foundations* . . . Uni 55101		
⑤	3	9	Worst That Could Happen ....*Brooklyn Bridge* . . . Buddah 75		
⑥	10	9	Can I Change My Mind..................................*Tyrone Davis* . . . Dakar 602		
❼	14	7	You Showed Me...*The Turtles* . . . White Whale 292		
⑧	7	13	I Heard It Through The Grapevine................*Marvin Gaye* . . . Tamla 54176		
⑨	9	15	Hang 'Em High....................................*Booker T. & The MG's* . . . Stax 0013		
⑩	8	11	I'm Gonna Make You Love Me.. *Diana Ross & The Supremes & The Temptations* . . . Motown 1137		

★ HIGHEST DEBUT ★ POS 50	★ BIGGEST MOVER ★ 90 to 59
My Whole World Ended (The Moment You Left Me) ....*David Ruffin*	Heaven..*The Rascals*

Billboard ⊙ FEBRUARY 22, 1969 ⊙ HOT 100.

TW	LW	WK			
①	1	13	**Everyday People**............................*Sly & The Family Stone* . . . Epic 10407		
②	2	11	**Crimson And Clover** ....*Tommy James & The Shondells* . . . Roulette 7028		
③	4	8	**Build Me Up Buttercup**.........................*The Foundations* . . . Uni 55101		
④	3	9	**Touch Me**..*The Doors* . . . Elektra 45646		
⑤	6	10	**Can I Change My Mind**..............................*Tyrone Davis* . . . Dakar 602		
⑥	5	10	Worst That Could Happen ....*Brooklyn Bridge* . . . Buddah 75		
⑦	7	8	You Showed Me...*The Turtles* . . . White Whale 292		
❽	12	9	This Magic Moment ....*Jay & The Americans* . . . United Artists 50475		
⑨	21	5	Proud Mary ....*Creedence Clearwater Revival* . . . Fantasy 619		
⑩	11	5	I'm Livin' In Shame ....*Diana Ross & The Supremes* . . . Motown 1139		

★ HIGHEST DEBUT ★ POS 52	★ BIGGEST MOVER ★ 70 to 38
The Weight................................*Aretha Franklin*	Run Away Child, Running Wild...................*The Temptations*

Billboard ⊙ MARCH 1, 1969 ⊙ HOT 100.

TW	LW	WK			
①	1	14	**Everyday People**............................*Sly & The Family Stone* . . . Epic 10407		
②	2	12	**Crimson And Clover** ....*Tommy James & The Shondells* . . . Roulette 7028		
③	3	9	**Build Me Up Buttercup**.........................*The Foundations* . . . Uni 55101		
④	4	10	**Touch Me**..*The Doors* . . . Elektra 45646		
❺	9	6	Proud Mary ....*Creedence Clearwater Revival* . . . Fantasy 619		
⑥	7	9	**You Showed Me** ....*The Turtles* . . . White Whale 292		
⑦	8	10	This Magic Moment ....*Jay & The Americans* . . . United Artists 50475		
❽	11	9	**Baby, Baby Don't Cry** .... *Smokey Robinson & The Miracles* . . . Tamla 54178		
⑨	6	11	Worst That Could Happen ....*Brooklyn Bridge* . . . Buddah 75		
⑩	25	5	Dizzy...*Tommy Roe* . . . ABC 11164		

★ HIGHEST DEBUT ★ POS 63	★ BIGGEST MOVER ★ 94 to 66
Rock Me................................*Steppenwolf*	Twenty-Five Miles ....*Edwin Starr*

TW	LW	WK	Billboard	MARCH 8, 1969	HOT 100.
①	1	15	**Everyday People**...........................Sly & The Family Stone ... Epic 10407
②	5	7	**Proud Mary**........................Creedence Clearwater Revival ... Fantasy 619
③	3	10	**Build Me Up Buttercup**........................The Foundations ... Uni 55101
❹	10	6	**Dizzy**...Tommy Roe ... ABC 11164
⑤	2	13	**Crimson And Clover** ....Tommy James & The Shondells ... Roulette 7028
⑥	7	11	**This Magic Moment** ....Jay & The Americans ... United Artists 50475
⑦	11	6	**This Girl's In Love With You** ....Dionne Warwick ... Scepter 12241
⑧	8	10	**Baby, Baby Don't Cry** .... Smokey Robinson & The Miracles ... Tamla 54178
⑨	4	11	**Touch Me**...The Doors ... Elektra 45646
⑩	16	7	**Indian Giver**.................................1910 Fruitgum Co. ... Buddah 91

★ **HIGHEST DEBUT** ★ POS 67
Blessed Is The Rain ....Brooklyn Bridge

★ **BIGGEST MOVER** ★ 87 to 47
Galveston ....Glen Campbell

TW	LW	WK	Billboard	MARCH 15, 1969	HOT 100.
❶	4	7	**Dizzy**...Tommy Roe ... ABC 11164
②	2	8	**Proud Mary**........................Creedence Clearwater Revival ... Fantasy 619
③	1	16	**Everyday People** ....Sly & The Family Stone ... Epic 10407
④	3	11	**Build Me Up Buttercup**........................The Foundations ... Uni 55101
❺	17	6	**Traces**...........................Classics IV featuring Dennis Yost ... Imperial 66352
⑥	5	14	**Crimson And Clover** ....Tommy James & The Shondells ... Roulette 7028
⑦	7	7	**This Girl's In Love With You** ....Dionne Warwick ... Scepter 12241
⑧	10	8	**Indian Giver**.................................1910 Fruitgum Co. ... Buddah 91
❾	20	6	**Time Of The Season**................................The Zombies ... Date 1628
⑩	6	12	**This Magic Moment** ....Jay & The Americans ... United Artists 50475

★ **HIGHEST DEBUT** ★ POS 54
I'll Try Something New ....Diana Ross & The
Supremes & The Temptations

★ **BIGGEST MOVER** ★ 89 to 37
Aquarius/Let The Sunshine In ....The 5th
Dimension

TW	LW	WK	Billboard	MARCH 22, 1969	HOT 100.
①	1	8	**Dizzy**...Tommy Roe ... ABC 11164
②	2	9	**Proud Mary**........................Creedence Clearwater Revival ... Fantasy 619
③	5	7	**Traces**...........................Classics IV featuring Dennis Yost ... Imperial 66352
④	4	12	**Build Me Up Buttercup**........................The Foundations ... Uni 55101
⑤	8	9	**Indian Giver** ....1910 Fruitgum Co. ... Buddah 91
⑥	9	7	**Time Of The Season**................................The Zombies ... Date 1628
⑦	7	8	**This Girl's In Love With You** ....Dionne Warwick ... Scepter 12241
⑧	3	17	**Everyday People** ....Sly & The Family Stone ... Epic 10407
⑨	6	15	**Crimson And Clover** ....Tommy James & The Shondells ... Roulette 7028
⑩	11	6	**Run Away Child, Running Wild** ....The Temptations ... Gordy 7084

★ **HIGHEST DEBUT** ★ POS 67
Memories...................................Elvis Presley

★ **BIGGEST MOVER** ★ 93 to 42
It's Your Thing ....The Isley Brothers

Billboard 🔴 MARCH 29, 1969 🔴 HOT 100

TW	LW	WK		
①	1	9	**Dizzy**	*Tommy Roe* . . . ABC 11164
②	3	8	**Traces**	*Classics IV featuring Dennis Yost* . . . Imperial 66352
③	6	8	**Time Of The Season**	*The Zombies* . . . Date 1628
④	14	4	**Aquarius/Let The Sunshine In**	*The 5th Dimension* . . . Soul City 772
⑤	2	10	**Proud Mary**	*Creedence Clearwater Revival* . . . Fantasy 619
⑥	10	7	**Run Away Child, Running Wild**	*The Temptations* . . . Gordy 7084
⑦	5	10	**Indian Giver**	*1910 Fruitgum Co.* . . . Buddah 91
⑧	11	5	**Galveston**	*Glen Campbell* . . . Capitol 2428
⑨	13	7	**My Whole World Ended (The Moment You Left Me)**	*David Ruffin* . . . Motown 1140
⑩	24	5	**Only The Strong Survive**	*Jerry Butler* . . . Mercury 72898

★ **HIGHEST DEBUT** ★ POS 69
My Way ....*Frank Sinatra*

★ **BIGGEST MOVER** ★ 70 to 35
Hair ....*The Cowsills*

Billboard 🔴 APRIL 5, 1969 🔴 HOT 100

TW	LW	WK		
①	1	10	**Dizzy**	*Tommy Roe* . . . ABC 11164
②	4	5	**Aquarius/Let The Sunshine In**	*The 5th Dimension* . . . Soul City 772
③	3	9	**Time Of The Season**	*The Zombies* . . . Date 1628
④	12	6	**You've Made Me So Very Happy**	*Blood, Sweat & Tears* . . . Columbia 44776
⑤	8	6	**Galveston**	*Glen Campbell* . . . Capitol 2428
⑥	6	8	**Run Away Child, Running Wild**	*The Temptations* . . . Gordy 7084
⑦	10	6	**Only The Strong Survive**	*Jerry Butler* . . . Mercury 72898
⑧	2	9	**Traces**	*Classics IV featuring Dennis Yost* . . . Imperial 66352
⑨	9	8	**My Whole World Ended (The Moment You Left Me)**	*David Ruffin* . . . Motown 1140
⑩	5	11	**Proud Mary**	*Creedence Clearwater Revival* . . . Fantasy 619

★ **HIGHEST DEBUT** ★ POS 61
I Don't Want Nobody To Give Me Nothing
(Open Up The Door, I'll Get It
Myself) ....*James Brown*

★ **BIGGEST MOVER** ★ 69 to 41
My Way ....*Frank Sinatra*

Billboard 🔴 APRIL 12, 1969 🔴 HOT 100

TW	LW	WK		
①	2	6	**Aquarius/Let The Sunshine In**	*The 5th Dimension* . . . Soul City 772
②	4	7	**You've Made Me So Very Happy**	*Blood, Sweat & Tears* . . . Columbia 44776
③	1	11	**Dizzy**	*Tommy Roe* . . . ABC 11164
④	5	7	**Galveston**	*Glen Campbell* . . . Capitol 2428
⑤	3	10	**Time Of The Season**	*The Zombies* . . . Date 1628
⑥	7	7	**Only The Strong Survive**	*Jerry Butler* . . . Mercury 72898
⑦	14	5	**It's Your Thing**	*The Isley Brothers* . . . T-Neck 901
⑧	18	5	**Hair**	*The Cowsills* . . . MGM 14026
⑨	6	9	**Run Away Child, Running Wild**	*The Temptations* . . . Gordy 7084
⑩	13	9	**Twenty-Five Miles**	*Edwin Starr* . . . Gordy 7083

★ **HIGHEST DEBUT** ★ POS 51
The Boxer ....*Simon & Garfunkel*

★ **BIGGEST MOVER** ★ 94 to 68
Gitarzan ....*Ray Stevens*

TW	LW	WK	Billboard ⊚ APRIL 19, 1969 ⊚ HOT 100.
①	1	7	**Aquarius/Let The Sunshine In** ....*The 5th Dimension* . . . Soul City 772
②	2	8	**You've Made Me So Very Happy** ....*Blood, Sweat & Tears* . . . Columbia 44776
❸	7	6	**It's Your Thing** ....*The Isley Brothers* . . . T-Neck 901
❹	6	8	**Only The Strong Survive** ....*Jerry Butler* . . . Mercury 72898
⑤	3	12	**Dizzy** ....*Tommy Roe* . . . ABC 11164
⑥	4	8	**Galveston** ....*Glen Campbell* . . . Capitol 2428
⑦	8	6	**Hair** ....*The Cowsills* . . . MGM 14026
⑧	10	10	**Twenty-Five Miles** ....*Edwin Starr* . . . Gordy 7083
⑨	5	11	**Time Of The Season** ....*The Zombies* . . . Date 1628
⑩	11	8	**Rock Me** ....*Steppenwolf* . . . Dunhill 4182

★ HIGHEST DEBUT ★ POS 53	★ BIGGEST MOVER ★ 51 to 20
The Composer...........*Diana Ross & The Supremes*	The Boxer ....*Simon & Garfunkel*

TW	LW	WK	Billboard ⊚ APRIL 26, 1969 ⊚ HOT 100.
①	1	8	**Aquarius/Let The Sunshine In** ....*The 5th Dimension* . . . Soul City 772
②	2	9	**You've Made Me So Very Happy** ....*Blood, Sweat & Tears* . . . Columbia 44776
③	3	7	**It's Your Thing** ....*The Isley Brothers* . . . T-Neck 901
❹	7	7	**Hair** ....*The Cowsills* . . . MGM 14026
⑤	4	9	**Only The Strong Survive** ....*Jerry Butler* . . . Mercury 72898
⑥	8	11	**Twenty-Five Miles** ....*Edwin Starr* . . . Gordy 7083
⑦	6	9	**Galveston** ....*Glen Campbell* . . . Capitol 2428
❽	24	7	**Time Is Tight**...............................*Booker T. & The MG's* . . . Stax 0028
⑨	5	13	**Dizzy** ....*Tommy Roe* . . . ABC 11164
⑩	12	6	**Sweet Cherry Wine**...........*Tommy James & The Shondells* . . . Roulette 7039

★ HIGHEST DEBUT ★ POS 67	★ BIGGEST MOVER ★ 74 to 34
Too Busy Thinking About My Baby ....*Marvin Gaye*	I Can't See Myself Leaving You ....*Aretha Franklin*

TW	LW	WK	Billboard ⊚ MAY 3, 1969 ⊚ HOT 100.
①	1	9	**Aquarius/Let The Sunshine In** ....*The 5th Dimension* . . . Soul City 772
②	3	8	**It's Your Thing**..................................*The Isley Brothers* . . . T-Neck 901
③	4	8	**Hair** ....*The Cowsills* . . . MGM 14026
④	2	10	**You've Made Me So Very Happy** ....*Blood, Sweat & Tears* . . . Columbia 44776
⑤	5	10	**Only The Strong Survive** ....*Jerry Butler* . . . Mercury 72898
❻	8	8	**Time Is Tight**...............................*Booker T. & The MG's* . . . Stax 0028
❼	10	7	**Sweet Cherry Wine** ......*Tommy James & The Shondells* . . . Roulette 7039
❽	13	9	**Hawaii Five-O** ....*The Ventures* . . . Liberty 56068
⑨	16	4	**The Boxer** ....*Simon & Garfunkel* . . . Columbia 44785
⑩	7	10	**Galveston**...*Glen Campbell* . . . Capitol 2428

★ HIGHEST DEBUT ★ POS 59	★ BIGGEST MOVER ★ 52 to 15
Where's The Playground Susie .....*Glen Campbell*	Love (Can Make You Happy) ....*Mercy*

Billboard — MAY 10, 1969 — HOT 100

TW	LW	WK		
①	1	10	**Aquarius/Let The Sunshine In**	*The 5th Dimension* . . . Soul City 772
②	3	9	**Hair**	*The Cowsills* . . . MGM 14026
③	2	9	**It's Your Thing**	*The Isley Brothers* . . . T-Neck 901
④	8	10	**Hawaii Five-O**	*The Ventures* . . . Liberty 56068
⑤	4	11	You've Made Me So Very Happy	*Blood, Sweat & Tears* . . . Columbia 44776
⑥	6	9	**Time Is Tight**	*Booker T. & The MG's* . . . Stax 0028
⑦	7	8	**Sweet Cherry Wine**	*Tommy James & The Shondells* . . . Roulette 7039
⑧	9	5	The Boxer	*Simon & Garfunkel* . . . Columbia 44785
⑨	19	6	Atlantis	*Donovan* . . . Epic 10434
⑩	-	1	Get Back	*The Beatles* . . . Apple 2490

★ HIGHEST DEBUT ★ POS 10	★ BIGGEST MOVER ★ 79 to 41
Get Back.............................*The Beatles*	In The Ghetto ....*Elvis Presley*

Billboard — MAY 17, 1969 — HOT 100

TW	LW	WK		
①	1	11	**Aquarius/Let The Sunshine In**	*The 5th Dimension* . . . Soul City 772
②	2	10	**Hair**	*The Cowsills* . . . MGM 14026
❸	10	2	**Get Back**	*The Beatles* . . . Apple 2490
④	3	10	**It's Your Thing**	*The Isley Brothers* . . . T-Neck 901
❺	11	6	**Love (Can Make You Happy)**	*Mercy* . . . Sundi 6811
⑥	4	11	Hawaii Five-O	*The Ventures* . . . Liberty 56068
⑦	8	6	**The Boxer**	*Simon & Garfunkel* . . . Columbia 44785
⑧	9	7	**Atlantis**	*Donovan* . . . Epic 10434
⑨	17	7	**Gitarzan**	*Ray Stevens* . . . Monument 1131
⑩	13	7	**These Eyes**	*The Guess Who* . . . RCA 0102

★ HIGHEST DEBUT ★ POS 77	★ BIGGEST MOVER ★ 100 to 66
The April Fools ....*Dionne Warwick*	Born To Be Wild ....*Wilson Pickett*

Billboard — MAY 24, 1969 — HOT 100

TW	LW	WK		
❶	3	3	**Get Back**	*The Beatles* . . . Apple 2490
②	1	12	Aquarius/Let The Sunshine In	*The 5th Dimension* . . . Soul City 772
③	5	7	Love (Can Make You Happy)	*Mercy* . . . Sundi 6811
④	2	11	Hair	*The Cowsills* . . . MGM 14026
❺	12	5	Oh Happy Day	*The Edwin Hawkins' Singers* . . . Pavilion 20001
⑥	4	11	It's Your Thing	*The Isley Brothers* . . . T-Neck 901
⑦	8	8	**Atlantis**	*Donovan* . . . Epic 10434
⑧	7	7	The Boxer	*Simon & Garfunkel* . . . Columbia 44785
⑨	9	8	Gitarzan	*Ray Stevens* . . . Monument 1131
⑩	10	8	These Eyes	*The Guess Who* . . . RCA 0102

★ HIGHEST DEBUT ★ POS 43	★ BIGGEST MOVER ★ 83 to 53
Don't Let The Joneses Get You Down........*The Temptations*	Let Me.........................*Paul Revere & The Raiders*

TW	LW	WK	Billboard		MAY 31, 1969		HOT 100.
①	1	4	**Get Back** ....*The Beatles* . . . Apple 2490
②	3	8	**Love (Can Make You Happy)**.........................*Mercy* . . . Sundi 6811
③	2	13	**Aquarius/Let The Sunshine In** ....*The 5th Dimension* . . . Soul City 772
④	5	6	**Oh Happy Day** ....*The Edwin Hawkins' Singers* . . . Pavilion 20001
⑤	4	12	**Hair**...*The Cowsills* . . . MGM 14026
⑥	10	9	**These Eyes** ....*The Guess Who* . . . RCA 0102
⑦	7	9	**Atlantis**...*Donovan* . . . Epic 10434
⑧	9	9	**Gitarzan**.....................................*Ray Stevens* . . . Monument 1131
⑨	17	5	**In The Ghetto** ....*Elvis Presley* . . . RCA 9741
⑩	12	9	**Grazing In The Grass**..............*The Friends Of Distinction* . . . RCA 0107

★ **HIGHEST DEBUT** ★ POS 60
Tomorrow Tomorrow ....*The Bee Gees*

★ **BIGGEST MOVER** ★ 79 to 45
Love Me Tonight ....*Tom Jones*

TW	LW	WK	Billboard		JUNE 7, 1969		HOT 100.
①	1	5	**Get Back** ....*The Beatles* . . . Apple 2490
②	2	9	**Love (Can Make You Happy)**.........................*Mercy* . . . Sundi 6811
③	10	10	**Grazing In The Grass**................*The Friends Of Distinction* . . . RCA 0107
④	4	7	**Oh Happy Day** ....*The Edwin Hawkins' Singers* . . . Pavilion 20001
⑤	14	6	**Bad Moon Rising**..................*Creedence Clearwater Revival* . . . Fantasy 622
⑥	9	6	**In The Ghetto** ....*Elvis Presley* . . . RCA 9741
⑦	3	14	**Aquarius/Let The Sunshine In** ....*The 5th Dimension* . . . Soul City 772
⑧	11	5	**Love Theme From Romeo & Juliet**................*Henry Mancini* . . . RCA 0131
⑨	6	10	**These Eyes**......................................*The Guess Who* . . . RCA 0102
⑩	15	7	**Too Busy Thinking About My Baby** ....*Marvin Gaye* . . . Tamla 54181

★ **HIGHEST DEBUT** ★ POS 83
Didn't We......................................*Richard Harris*

★ **BIGGEST MOVER** ★ 78 to 33
Spinning Wheel.................*Blood, Sweat & Tears*

TW	LW	WK	Billboard		JUNE 14, 1969		HOT 100.
①	1	6	**Get Back** ....*The Beatles* . . . Apple 2490
②	8	6	**Love Theme From Romeo & Juliet**................*Henry Mancini* . . . RCA 0131
③	6	7	**In The Ghetto** ....*Elvis Presley* . . . RCA 9741
④	5	7	**Bad Moon Rising**..................*Creedence Clearwater Revival* . . . Fantasy 622
⑤	2	10	**Love (Can Make You Happy)** ....*Mercy* . . . Sundi 6811
⑥	3	11	**Grazing In The Grass**..............*The Friends Of Distinction* . . . RCA 0107
⑦	4	8	**Oh Happy Day** ....*The Edwin Hawkins' Singers* . . . Pavilion 20001
⑧	10	8	**Too Busy Thinking About My Baby** ....*Marvin Gaye* . . . Tamla 54181
⑨	9	11	**These Eyes**......................................*The Guess Who* . . . RCA 0102
⑩	14	7	**One**...*Three Dog Night* . . . Dunhill 4191

★ **HIGHEST DEBUT** ★ POS 71
The Ballad Of John And Yoko ....*The Beatles*

★ **BIGGEST MOVER** ★ 89 to 57
Crystal Blue Persuasion ....*Tommy James & The Shondells*

Billboard — JUNE 21, 1969 — HOT 100

TW	LW	WK	Title	Artist	Label
①	1	7	Get Back	The Beatles	Apple 2490
②	2	7	Love Theme From Romeo & Juliet	Henry Mancini	RCA 0131
③	4	8	Bad Moon Rising	Creedence Clearwater Revival	Fantasy 622
④	3	8	In The Ghetto	Elvis Presley	RCA 9741
⑤	8	9	Too Busy Thinking About My Baby	Marvin Gaye	Tamla 54181
⑥	10	8	One	Three Dog Night	Dunhill 4191
⑦	5	11	Love (Can Make You Happy)	Mercy	Sundi 6811
⑧	6	12	Grazing In The Grass	The Friends Of Distinction	RCA 0107
⑨	15	5	Good Morning Starshine	Oliver	Jubilee 5659
⑩	18	4	Spinning Wheel	Blood, Sweat & Tears	Columbia 44871

★ **HIGHEST DEBUT** ★ POS 72
In The Year 2525 .... Zager & Evans

★ **BIGGEST MOVER** ★ 80 to 31
Mother Popcorn (You Got To Have A Mother For Me) .... James Brown

Billboard — JUNE 28, 1969 — HOT 100

TW	LW	WK	Title	Artist	Label
①	2	8	Love Theme From Romeo & Juliet	Henry Mancini	RCA 0131
②	3	9	Bad Moon Rising	Creedence Clearwater Revival	Fantasy 622
③	1	8	Get Back	The Beatles	Apple 2490
④	5	10	Too Busy Thinking About My Baby	Marvin Gaye	Tamla 54181
⑤	6	9	One	Three Dog Night	Dunhill 4191
⑥	10	5	Spinning Wheel	Blood, Sweat & Tears	Columbia 44871
⑦	4	9	In The Ghetto	Elvis Presley	RCA 9741
⑧	9	6	Good Morning Starshine	Oliver	Jubilee 5659
⑨	12	7	Israelites	Desmond Dekker & The Aces	Uni 55129
⑩	8	13	Grazing In The Grass	The Friends Of Distinction	RCA 0107

★ **HIGHEST DEBUT** ★ POS 59
Sweet Caroline .... Neil Diamond

★ **BIGGEST MOVER** ★ 72 to 35
In The Year 2525 .... Zager & Evans

Billboard — JULY 5, 1969 — HOT 100

TW	LW	WK	Title	Artist	Label
①	1	9	Love Theme From Romeo & Juliet	Henry Mancini	RCA 0131
②	6	6	Spinning Wheel	Blood, Sweat & Tears	Columbia 44871
③	2	10	Bad Moon Rising	Creedence Clearwater Revival	Fantasy 622
④	8	7	Good Morning Starshine	Oliver	Jubilee 5659
⑤	5	10	One	Three Dog Night	Dunhill 4191
⑥	3	9	Get Back	The Beatles	Apple 2490
⑦	18	5	Crystal Blue Persuasion	Tommy James & The Shondells	Roulette 7050
⑧	35	3	In The Year 2525	Zager & Evans	RCA 0174
⑨	13	7	Color Him Father	The Winstons	Metromedia 117
⑩	4	11	Too Busy Thinking About My Baby	Marvin Gaye	Tamla 54181

★ **HIGHEST DEBUT** ★ POS 73
Abraham, Martin And John .... Smokey Robinson & The Miracles

★ **BIGGEST MOVER** ★ 89 to 57
Abraham, Martin And John .... Moms Mabley

Billboard — JULY 12, 1969 — HOT 100

TW	LW	WK	Title / Artist / Label
1	8	4	**In The Year 2525** ....*Zager & Evans* ... RCA 0174
2	2	7	**Spinning Wheel** ....*Blood, Sweat & Tears* ... Columbia 44871
3	4	8	**Good Morning Starshine** ....*Oliver* ... Jubilee 5659
4	1	10	Love Theme From Romeo & Juliet.................*Henry Mancini* ... RCA 0131
5	5	11	**One**...*Three Dog Night* ... Dunhill 4191
6	7	6	Crystal Blue Persuasion.........................*Tommy James & The Shondells* ... Roulette 7050
7	3	11	**Bad Moon Rising**..................*Creedence Clearwater Revival* ... Fantasy 622
8	11	5	**The Ballad Of John And Yoko**...................*The Beatles* ... Apple 2531
9	9	8	**Color Him Father** ....*The Winstons* ... Metromedia 117
10	14	9	What Does It Take (To Win Your Love) ....*Jr. Walker & The All Stars* ... Soul 35062

★ HIGHEST DEBUT ★ POS 81
Hey Joe ....*Wilson Pickett*

★ BIGGEST MOVER ★ 86 to 57
Polk Salad Annie ....*Tony Joe White*

Billboard — JULY 19, 1969 — HOT 100

TW	LW	WK	Title / Artist / Label
1	1	5	**In The Year 2525** ....*Zager & Evans* ... RCA 0174
2	2	8	**Spinning Wheel** ....*Blood, Sweat & Tears* ... Columbia 44871
3	3	9	**Good Morning Starshine** ....*Oliver* ... Jubilee 5659
4	6	7	**Crystal Blue Persuasion**.........................*Tommy James & The Shondells* ... Roulette 7050
5	10	10	What Does It Take (To Win Your Love) ....*Jr. Walker & The All Stars* ... Soul 35062
6	5	12	**One**...*Three Dog Night* ... Dunhill 4191
7	9	9	**Color Him Father** ....*The Winstons* ... Metromedia 117
8	8	6	**The Ballad Of John And Yoko**...................*The Beatles* ... Apple 2531
9	11	8	**My Cherie Amour**.......................................*Stevie Wonder* ... Tamla 54180
10	4	11	Love Theme From Romeo & Juliet.................*Henry Mancini* ... RCA 0131

★ HIGHEST DEBUT ★ POS 70
Workin' On A Groovy Thing .....*The 5th Dimension*

★ BIGGEST MOVER ★ 83 to 62
Laughing................................*The Guess Who*

Billboard — JULY 26, 1969 — HOT 100

TW	LW	WK	Title / Artist / Label
1	1	6	**In The Year 2525** ....*Zager & Evans* ... RCA 0174
2	4	8	**Crystal Blue Persuasion** ....*Tommy James & The Shondells* ... Roulette 7050
3	2	9	**Spinning Wheel** ....*Blood, Sweat & Tears* ... Columbia 44871
4	9	9	**My Cherie Amour**.......................................*Stevie Wonder* ... Tamla 54180
5	5	11	What Does It Take (To Win Your Love) ....*Jr. Walker & The All Stars* ... Soul 35062
6	3	10	Good Morning Starshine ....*Oliver* ... Jubilee 5659
7	6	13	One...*Three Dog Night* ... Dunhill 4191
8	8	7	**The Ballad Of John And Yoko**...................*The Beatles* ... Apple 2531
9	14	10	**Baby, I Love You**.....................................*Andy Kim* ... Steed 716
10	10	12	Love Theme From Romeo & Juliet.................*Henry Mancini* ... RCA 0131

★ HIGHEST DEBUT ★ POS 42
A Boy Named Sue.......................*Johnny Cash*

★ BIGGEST MOVER ★ 79 to 28
Honky Tonk Women ....*The Rolling Stones*

Billboard HOT 100 — AUGUST 2, 1969

TW	LW	WK	Title / Artist
①	1	7	**In The Year 2525** ....*Zager & Evans* . . . RCA 0174
②	2	9	**Crystal Blue Persuasion** ....*Tommy James & The Shondells* . . . Roulette 7050
③	3	10	Spinning Wheel ....*Blood, Sweat & Tears* . . . Columbia 44871
④	4	10	**My Cherie Amour** ....*Stevie Wonder* . . . Tamla 54180
⑤	5	12	What Does It Take (To Win Your Love) ....*Jr. Walker & The All Stars* . . . Soul 35062
❻	15	9	**Ruby, Don't Take Your Love To Town**.. *Kenny Rogers & The First Edition* . . . Reprise 0829
⑦	13	6	Sweet Caroline ....*Neil Diamond* . . . Uni 55136
⑧	28	3	Honky Tonk Women ....*The Rolling Stones* . . . London 910
⑨	9	11	**Baby, I Love You**...*Andy Kim* . . . Steed 716
⑩	8	8	The Ballad Of John And Yoko.......................*The Beatles* . . . Apple 2531

★ **HIGHEST DEBUT** ★ POS 55
Share Your Love With Me ....*Aretha Franklin*

★ **BIGGEST MOVER** ★ 86 to 52
I'll Never Fall In Love Again.............*Tom Jones*

Billboard HOT 100 — AUGUST 9, 1969

TW	LW	WK	Title / Artist
①	1	8	**In The Year 2525**....................................*Zager & Evans* . . . RCA 0174
②	2	10	**Crystal Blue Persuasion** ....*Tommy James & The Shondells* . . . Roulette 7050
❸	8	4	Honky Tonk Women ....*The Rolling Stones* . . . London 910
④	5	13	**What Does It Take (To Win Your Love)**................................ *Jr. Walker & The All Stars* . . . Soul 35062
⑤	7	7	Sweet Caroline ....*Neil Diamond* . . . Uni 55136
⑥	6	10	**Ruby, Don't Take Your Love To Town**.. *Kenny Rogers & The First Edition* . . . Reprise 0829
❼	20	3	A Boy Named Sue ....*Johnny Cash* . . . Columbia 44944
⑧	4	11	My Cherie Amour.......................................*Stevie Wonder* . . . Tamla 54180
⑨	25	7	Put A Little Love In Your Heart..........*Jackie DeShannon* . . . Imperial 66385
⑩	9	12	Baby, I Love You ....*Andy Kim* . . . Steed 716

★ **HIGHEST DEBUT** ★ POS 77
Easy To Be Hard ....*Three Dog Night*

★ **BIGGEST MOVER** ★ 71 to 34
Commotion ....*Creedence Clearwater Revival*

Billboard HOT 100 — AUGUST 16, 1969

TW	LW	WK	Title / Artist
①	1	9	**In The Year 2525**.....................................*Zager & Evans* . . . RCA 0174
❷	3	5	Honky Tonk Women ....*The Rolling Stones* . . . London 910
③	2	11	Crystal Blue Persuasion...........................*Tommy James & The Shondells* . . . Roulette 7050
④	5	8	**Sweet Caroline**..*Neil Diamond* . . . Uni 55136
❺	7	4	A Boy Named Sue ....*Johnny Cash* . . . Columbia 44944
❻	9	8	Put A Little Love In Your Heart..........*Jackie DeShannon* . . . Imperial 66385
⑦	6	11	Ruby, Don't Take Your Love To Town .... *Kenny Rogers & The First Edition* . . . Reprise 0829
⑧	8	12	My Cherie Amour.......................................*Stevie Wonder* . . . Tamla 54180
⑨	4	14	What Does It Take (To Win Your Love) ....*Jr. Walker & The All Stars* . . . Soul 35062
⑩	10	13	Baby, I Love You ....*Andy Kim* . . . Steed 716

★ **HIGHEST DEBUT** ★ POS 65
Oh, What A Night ....*The Dells*

★ **BIGGEST MOVER** ★ 77 to 40
Easy To Be Hard ....*Three Dog Night*

TW	LW	WK	Billboard	AUGUST 23, 1969	HOT 100
①	2	6	**Honky Tonk Women**	*The Rolling Stones* . . . London 910	
②	5	5	**A Boy Named Sue**	*Johnny Cash* . . . Columbia 44944	
③	3	12	Crystal Blue Persuasion	*Tommy James & The Shondells* . . . Roulette 7050	
④	4	9	**Sweet Caroline**	*Neil Diamond* . . . Uni 55136	
⑤	1	10	In The Year 2525	*Zager & Evans* . . . RCA 0174	
⑥	6	9	Put A Little Love In Your Heart	*Jackie DeShannon* . . . Imperial 66385	
⑦	15	4	Green River	*Creedence Clearwater Revival* . . . Fantasy 625	
⑧	13	8	**Polk Salad Annie**	*Tony Joe White* . . . Monument 1104	
⑨	14	17	Get Together	*The Youngbloods* . . . RCA 9752	
⑩	12	7	**Laughing**	*The Guess Who* . . . RCA 0195	

★ **HIGHEST DEBUT** ★ POS 60
I'm A Better Man ....*Engelbert Humperdinck*

★ **BIGGEST MOVER** ★ 84 to 48
I Can't Get Next To You ....*The Temptations*

TW	LW	WK	Billboard	AUGUST 30, 1969	HOT 100
①	1	7	**Honky Tonk Women**	*The Rolling Stones* . . . London 910	
②	2	6	**A Boy Named Sue**	*Johnny Cash* . . . Columbia 44944	
③	14	6	Sugar, Sugar	*The Archies* . . . Calendar 1008	
④	6	10	**Put A Little Love In Your Heart**	*Jackie DeShannon* . . . Imperial 66385	
⑤	4	10	Sweet Caroline	*Neil Diamond* . . . Uni 55136	
⑥	9	18	Get Together	*The Youngbloods* . . . RCA 9752	
⑦	7	5	Green River	*Creedence Clearwater Revival* . . . Fantasy 625	
⑧	5	11	In The Year 2525	*Zager & Evans* . . . RCA 0174	
⑨	12	8	Lay Lady Lay	*Bob Dylan* . . . Columbia 44926	
⑩	3	13	Crystal Blue Persuasion	*Tommy James & The Shondells* . . . Roulette 7050	

★ **HIGHEST DEBUT** ★ POS 64
What's The Use Of Breaking Up ....*Jerry Butler*

★ **BIGGEST MOVER** ★ 75 to 49
That's The Way Love Is ....*Marvin Gaye*

TW	LW	WK	Billboard	SEPTEMBER 6, 1969	HOT 100
①	1	8	**Honky Tonk Women**	*The Rolling Stones* . . . London 910	
②	2	7	**A Boy Named Sue**	*Johnny Cash* . . . Columbia 44944	
③	3	7	Sugar, Sugar	*The Archies* . . . Calendar 1008	
④	7	6	Green River	*Creedence Clearwater Revival* . . . Fantasy 625	
⑤	6	19	**Get Together**	*The Youngbloods* . . . RCA 9752	
⑥	4	11	Put A Little Love In Your Heart	*Jackie DeShannon* . . . Imperial 66385	
⑦	9	9	**Lay Lady Lay**	*Bob Dylan* . . . Columbia 44926	
⑧	13	5	Easy To Be Hard	*Three Dog Night* . . . Dunhill 4203	
⑨	5	11	Sweet Caroline	*Neil Diamond* . . . Uni 55136	
⑩	14	14	I'll Never Fall In Love Again	*Tom Jones* . . . Parrot 40018	

★ **HIGHEST DEBUT** ★ POS 70
Carry Me Back ....*The Rascals*

★ **BIGGEST MOVER** ★ 66 to 34
Little Woman ....*Bobby Sherman*

Billboard — SEPTEMBER 13, 1969 — HOT 100

TW	LW	WK			
①	1	9	**Honky Tonk Women**	*The Rolling Stones*	London 910
②	3	8	Sugar, Sugar	*The Archies*	Calendar 1008
③	2	8	A Boy Named Sue	*Johnny Cash*	Columbia 44944
④	4	7	Green River	*Creedence Clearwater Revival*	Fantasy 625
⑤	5	20	**Get Together**	*The Youngbloods*	RCA 9752
⑥	10	15	**I'll Never Fall In Love Again**	*Tom Jones*	Parrot 40018
⑦	7	10	**Lay Lady Lay**	*Bob Dylan*	Columbia 44926
⑧	8	6	Easy To Be Hard	*Three Dog Night*	Dunhill 4203
⑨	6	12	Put A Little Love In Your Heart	*Jackie DeShannon*	Imperial 66385
⑩	11	5	**I Can't Get Next To You**	*The Temptations*	Gordy 7093

★ **HIGHEST DEBUT** ★ POS 69
The Weight ......*Diana Ross & The Supremes & The Temptations*

★ **BIGGEST MOVER** ★ 69 to 43
By The Time I Get To Phoenix ....*Isaac Hayes*

Billboard — SEPTEMBER 20, 1969 — HOT 100

TW	LW	WK			
❶	2	9	**Sugar, Sugar**	*The Archies*	Calendar 1008
②	1	10	**Honky Tonk Women**	*The Rolling Stones*	London 910
③	4	8	**Green River**	*Creedence Clearwater Revival*	Fantasy 625
④	3	9	A Boy Named Sue	*Johnny Cash*	Columbia 44944
❺	8	7	**Easy To Be Hard**	*Three Dog Night*	Dunhill 4203
⑥	6	16	**I'll Never Fall In Love Again**	*Tom Jones*	Parrot 40018
⑦	5	21	Get Together	*The Youngbloods*	RCA 9752
❽	18	6	**Jean**	*Oliver*	Crewe 334
❾	16	5	**Little Woman**	*Bobby Sherman*	Metromedia 121
⑩	10	6	I Can't Get Next To You	*The Temptations*	Gordy 7093

★ **HIGHEST DEBUT** ★ POS 61
Love Of The Common People ....*The Winstons*

★ **BIGGEST MOVER** ★ 77 to 36
Suspicious Minds ....*Elvis Presley*

Billboard — SEPTEMBER 27, 1969 — HOT 100

TW	LW	WK			
①	1	10	**Sugar, Sugar**	*The Archies*	Calendar 1008
②	3	9	**Green River**	*Creedence Clearwater Revival*	Fantasy 625
③	2	11	Honky Tonk Women	*The Rolling Stones*	London 910
④	5	8	**Easy To Be Hard**	*Three Dog Night*	Dunhill 4203
❺	9	6	**Little Woman**	*Bobby Sherman*	Metromedia 121
❻	10	7	**I Can't Get Next To You**	*The Temptations*	Gordy 7093
⑦	8	7	**Jean**	*Oliver*	Crewe 334
⑧	6	17	I'll Never Fall In Love Again	*Tom Jones*	Parrot 40018
❾	21	8	**Hot Fun In The Summertime**	*Sly & The Family Stone*	Epic 10497
⑩	11	7	**Oh, What A Night**	*The Dells*	Cadet 5649

★ **HIGHEST DEBUT** ★ POS 67
Wedding Bell Blues ....*The 5th Dimension*

★ **BIGGEST MOVER** ★ 90 to 57
You've Lost That Lovin' Feeling ....*Dionne Warwick*

Billboard — OCTOBER 4, 1969 — HOT 100

TW	LW	WK	Title	Artist / Label
1	1	11	**Sugar, Sugar**	*The Archies* . . . Calendar 1008
2	7	8	**Jean**	*Oliver* . . . Crewe 334
3	5	7	**Little Woman**	*Bobby Sherman* . . . Metromedia 121
4	4	9	**Easy To Be Hard**	*Three Dog Night* . . . Dunhill 4203
5	6	8	**I Can't Get Next To You**	*The Temptations* . . . Gordy 7093
6	3	12	**Honky Tonk Women**	*The Rolling Stones* . . . London 910
7	2	10	**Green River**	*Creedence Clearwater Revival* . . . Fantasy 625
8	17	8	**Everybody's Talkin'**	*Nilsson* . . . RCA 0161
9	9	9	**Hot Fun In The Summertime**	*Sly & The Family Stone* . . . Epic 10497
10	10	8	**Oh, What A Night**	*The Dells* . . . Cadet 5649

★ **HIGHEST DEBUT** ★ POS 66
Smile A Little Smile For Me ....*The Flying Machine*

★ **BIGGEST MOVER** ★ 67 to 35
Wedding Bell Blues ....*The 5th Dimension*

Billboard — OCTOBER 11, 1969 — HOT 100

TW	LW	WK	Title	Artist / Label
1	1	12	**Sugar, Sugar**	*The Archies* . . . Calendar 1008
2	2	9	**Jean**	*Oliver* . . . Crewe 334
3	3	8	**Little Woman**	*Bobby Sherman* . . . Metromedia 121
4	5	9	**I Can't Get Next To You**	*The Temptations* . . . Gordy 7093
5	9	10	**Hot Fun In The Summertime**	*Sly & The Family Stone* . . . Epic 10497
6	8	9	**Everybody's Talkin'**	*Nilsson* . . . RCA 0161
7	4	10	**Easy To Be Hard**	*Three Dog Night* . . . Dunhill 4203
8	6	13	**Honky Tonk Women**	*The Rolling Stones* . . . London 910
9	11	8	**This Girl Is A Woman Now**	*Gary Puckett & The Union Gap* . . . Columbia 44967
10	7	11	**Green River**	*Creedence Clearwater Revival* . . . Fantasy 625

★ **HIGHEST DEBUT** ★ POS 77
Groovy Grubworm.......*Harlow Wilcox & The Oakies*

★ **BIGGEST MOVER** ★ 82 to 52
Ball Of Fire ....*Tommy James & The Shondells*

Billboard — OCTOBER 18, 1969 — HOT 100

TW	LW	WK	Title	Artist / Label
1	4	10	**I Can't Get Next To You**	*The Temptations* . . . Gordy 7093
2	5	11	**Hot Fun In The Summertime**	*Sly & The Family Stone* . . . Epic 10497
3	1	13	**Sugar, Sugar**	*The Archies* . . . Calendar 1008
4	2	10	**Jean**	*Oliver* . . . Crewe 334
5	3	9	**Little Woman**	*Bobby Sherman* . . . Metromedia 121
6	11	6	**Suspicious Minds**	*Elvis Presley* . . . RCA 9764
7	12	9	**That's The Way Love Is**	*Marvin Gaye* . . . Tamla 54185
8	25	4	**Wedding Bell Blues**	*The 5th Dimension* . . . Soul City 779
9	7	11	**Easy To Be Hard**	*Three Dog Night* . . . Dunhill 4203
10	19	6	**Tracy**	*The Cuff Links* . . . Decca 32533

★ **HIGHEST DEBUT** ★ POS 20
Something........................*The Beatles*

★ **BIGGEST MOVER** ★ 67 to 33
Baby, I'm For Real ....*The Originals*

Billboard — OCTOBER 25, 1969 — HOT 100

TW	LW	WK	Title	Artist	Label
①	1	11	I Can't Get Next To You	The Temptations	Gordy 7093
②	2	12	Hot Fun In The Summertime	Sly & The Family Stone	Epic 10497
③	3	14	Sugar, Sugar	The Archies	Calendar 1008
④	4	11	Jean	Oliver	Crewe 334
❺	6	7	Suspicious Minds	Elvis Presley	RCA 9764
⑥	5	10	Little Woman	Bobby Sherman	Metromedia 121
❼	8	5	Wedding Bell Blues	The 5th Dimension	Soul City 779
⑧	13	8	Baby It's You	Smith	Dunhill 4206
❾	10	7	Tracy	The Cuff Links	Decca 32533
⑩	11	10	I'm Gonna Make You Mine	Lou Christie	Buddah 116

★ **HIGHEST DEBUT** ★ POS 61
Eli's Coming..........................Three Dog Night

★ **BIGGEST MOVER** ★ 94 to 59
Yester-Me, Yester-You, Yesterday............Stevie Wonder

Billboard — NOVEMBER 1, 1969 — HOT 100

TW	LW	WK	Title	Artist	Label
❶	5	8	Suspicious Minds	Elvis Presley	RCA 9764
❷	7	6	Wedding Bell Blues	The 5th Dimension	Soul City 779
③	3	15	Sugar, Sugar	The Archies	Calendar 1008
④	1	12	I Can't Get Next To You	The Temptations	Gordy 7093
⑤	8	9	Baby It's You	Smith	Dunhill 4206
⑥	2	13	Hot Fun In The Summertime	Sly & The Family Stone	Epic 10497
⑦	6	11	Little Woman	Bobby Sherman	Metromedia 121
⑧	4	12	Jean	Oliver	Crewe 334
⑨	9	8	Tracy	The Cuff Links	Decca 32533
❿	13	3	Come Together	The Beatles	Apple 2654

★ **HIGHEST DEBUT** ★ POS 58
Fortunate Son ....Creedence Clearwater Revival

★ **BIGGEST MOVER** ★ 58 to 30
Let A Man Come In And Do The Popcorn (Part One) ....James Brown

Billboard — NOVEMBER 8, 1969 — HOT 100

TW	LW	WK	Title	Artist	Label
❶	2	7	Wedding Bell Blues	The 5th Dimension	Soul City 779
②	1	9	Suspicious Minds	Elvis Presley	RCA 9764
❸	10	4	Come Together	The Beatles	Apple 2654
④	4	13	I Can't Get Next To You	The Temptations	Gordy 7093
⑤	5	10	Baby It's You	Smith	Dunhill 4206
⑥	3	16	Sugar, Sugar	The Archies	Calendar 1008
⑦	6	14	Hot Fun In The Summertime	Sly & The Family Stone	Epic 10497
❽	17	4	And When I Die	Blood, Sweat & Tears	Columbia 45008
⑨	11	4	Something	The Beatles	Apple 2654
⑩	12	6	Smile A Little Smile For Me	The Flying Machine	Congress 6000

★ **HIGHEST DEBUT** ★ POS 50
Someday We'll Be Together .....Diana Ross & The Supremes

★ **BIGGEST MOVER** ★ 93 to 54
We Love You, Call Collect ....Art Linkletter

Billboard — NOVEMBER 15, 1969 — HOT 100

TW	LW	WK	Title	Artist	Label
①	1	8	**Wedding Bell Blues**	*The 5th Dimension*	Soul City 779
②	3	5	Come Together	*The Beatles*	Apple 2654
❸	9	5	**Something**	*The Beatles*	Apple 2654
④	8	5	And When I Die	*Blood, Sweat & Tears*	Columbia 45008
⑤	5	11	**Baby It's You**	*Smith*	Dunhill 4206
⑥	4	14	I Can't Get Next To You	*The Temptations*	Gordy 7093
⑦	2	10	Suspicious Minds	*Elvis Presley*	RCA 9764
⑧	10	7	Smile A Little Smile For Me	*The Flying Machine*	Congress 6000
⑨	6	17	Sugar, Sugar	*The Archies*	Calendar 1008
⑩	18	5	Take A Letter Maria	*R.B. Greaves*	Atco 6714

★ HIGHEST DEBUT ★ POS 73	★ BIGGEST MOVER ★ 96 to 40
Midnight ....*Dennis Yost & The Classics IV*	Eleanor Rigby ....*Aretha Franklin*

Billboard — NOVEMBER 22, 1969 — HOT 100

TW	LW	WK	Title	Artist	Label
①	1	9	**Wedding Bell Blues**	*The 5th Dimension*	Soul City 779
❷	10	6	**Take A Letter Maria**	*R.B. Greaves*	Atco 6714
③	3	6	Something	*The Beatles*	Apple 2654
④	4	6	And When I Die	*Blood, Sweat & Tears*	Columbia 45008
❺	8	8	**Smile A Little Smile For Me**	*The Flying Machine*	Congress 6000
❻	11	6	**Na Na Hey Hey Kiss Him Goodbye**	*Steam*	Fontana 1667
⑦	2	6	Come Together	*The Beatles*	Apple 2654
❽	22	6	**Yester-Me, Yester-You, Yesterday**	*Stevie Wonder*	Tamla 54188
⑨	7	11	Suspicious Minds	*Elvis Presley*	RCA 9764
⑩	6	15	I Can't Get Next To You	*The Temptations*	Gordy 7093

★ HIGHEST DEBUT ★ POS 71	★ BIGGEST MOVER ★ 62 to 37
Ain't It Funky Now........................*James Brown*	Raindrops Keep Fallin' On My Head ...........*B.J. Thomas*

Billboard — NOVEMBER 29, 1969 — HOT 100

TW	LW	WK	Title	Artist	Label
❶	7	7	**Come Together/Something**	*The Beatles*	Apple 2654
❷	4	7	**And When I Die**	*Blood, Sweat & Tears*	Columbia 45008
③	1	10	Wedding Bell Blues	*The 5th Dimension*	Soul City 779
④	2	7	Take A Letter Maria	*R.B. Greaves*	Atco 6714
⑤	6	7	Na Na Hey Hey Kiss Him Goodbye	*Steam*	Fontana 1667
⑥	5	9	Smile A Little Smile For Me	*The Flying Machine*	Congress 6000
❼	12	6	**Leaving On A Jet Plane**	*Peter, Paul & Mary*	Warner 7340
⑧	8	7	Yester-Me, Yester-You, Yesterday	*Stevie Wonder*	Tamla 54188
❾	21	6	**Down On The Corner/Fortunate Son**	*Creedence Clearwater Revival*	Fantasy 634
⑩	18	6	**Eli's Coming**	*Three Dog Night*	Dunhill 4215

★ HIGHEST DEBUT ★ POS 73	★ BIGGEST MOVER ★ 91 to 45
Don't Cry Daddy/Rubberneckin' ......*Elvis Presley*	Whole Lotta Love..........................*Led Zeppelin*

Billboard — DECEMBER 6, 1969 — HOT 100

TW	LW	WK	Title / Artist / Label
①	5	8	**Na Na Hey Hey Kiss Him Goodbye**.................*Steam* . . . Fontana 1667
②	7	7	**Leaving On A Jet Plane**.......................*Peter, Paul & Mary* . . . Warner 7340
③	1	8	**Come Together/Something** ....*The Beatles* . . . Apple 2654
④	4	8	**Take A Letter Maria**..*R.B. Greaves* . . . Atco 6714
⑤	9	7	**Down On The Corner/Fortunate Son**.. *Creedence Clearwater Revival* . . . Fantasy 634
⑥	2	8	**And When I Die** ....*Blood, Sweat & Tears* . . . Columbia 45008
⑦	3	11	**Wedding Bell Blues**....................*The 5th Dimension* . . . Soul City 779
⑧	8	8	**Yester-Me, Yester-You, Yesterday** ....*Stevie Wonder* . . . Tamla 54188
⑨	11	5	**Someday We'll Be Together** ....*Diana Ross & The Supremes* . . . Motown 1156
⑩	10	7	**Eli's Coming**...*Three Dog Night* . . . Dunhill 4215

★ **HIGHEST DEBUT** ★ POS 71
Don't Let Him Take Your Love From Me.....*Four Tops*

★ **BIGGEST MOVER** ★ 90 to 53
Jingle Jangle ....*The Archies*

Billboard — DECEMBER 13, 1969 — HOT 100

TW	LW	WK	Title / Artist / Label
①	1	9	**Na Na Hey Hey Kiss Him Goodbye**.................*Steam* . . . Fontana 1667
②	2	8	**Leaving On A Jet Plane**.......................*Peter, Paul & Mary* . . . Warner 7340
③	9	6	**Someday We'll Be Together** ....*Diana Ross & The Supremes* . . . Motown 1156
④	3	9	**Come Together/Something** ....*The Beatles* . . . Apple 2654
⑤	5	8	**Down On The Corner/Fortunate Son**.. *Creedence Clearwater Revival* . . . Fantasy 634
⑥	4	9	**Take A Letter Maria**..*R.B. Greaves* . . . Atco 6714
⑦	8	9	**Yester-Me, Yester-You, Yesterday** ....*Stevie Wonder* . . . Tamla 54188
⑧	6	9	**And When I Die** ....*Blood, Sweat & Tears* . . . Columbia 45008
⑨	13	7	**Raindrops Keep Fallin' On My Head** ..........*B.J. Thomas* . . . Scepter 12265
⑩	11	9	**Backfield In Motion** ....*Mel & Tim* . . . Bamboo 107

★ **HIGHEST DEBUT** ★ POS 65
She......................*Tommy James & The Shondells*

★ **BIGGEST MOVER** ★ 81 to 60
Wonderful World, Beautiful People ....*Jimmy Cliff*

Billboard — DECEMBER 20, 1969 — HOT 100

TW	LW	WK	Title / Artist / Label
①	2	9	**Leaving On A Jet Plane** ....*Peter, Paul & Mary* . . . Warner 7340
②	3	7	**Someday We'll Be Together** ....*Diana Ross & The Supremes* . . . Motown 1156
③	5	9	**Down On The Corner/Fortunate Son** .... *Creedence Clearwater Revival* . . . Fantasy 634
④	1	10	**Na Na Hey Hey Kiss Him Goodbye** ....*Steam* . . . Fontana 1667
⑤	9	8	**Raindrops Keep Fallin' On My Head** ..........*B.J. Thomas* . . . Scepter 12265
⑥	4	10	**Come Together/Something** ....*The Beatles* . . . Apple 2654
⑦	7	10	**Yester-Me, Yester-You, Yesterday** ....*Stevie Wonder* . . . Tamla 54188
⑧	6	10	**Take A Letter Maria**..*R.B. Greaves* . . . Atco 6714
⑨	13	8	**Holly Holy** ....*Neil Diamond* . . . Uni 55175
⑩	8	10	**And When I Die**...........................*Blood, Sweat & Tears* . . . Columbia 45008

★ **HIGHEST DEBUT** ★ POS 72
Let A Man Come In And Do The Popcorn (Part Two) ....*James Brown*

★ **BIGGEST MOVER** ★ 77 to 31
Venus ....*The Shocking Blue*

TW	LW	WK	Billboard.	DECEMBER 27, 1969	HOT 100.
1	2	8	**Someday We'll Be Together**	*Diana Ross & The Supremes*	... Motown 1156
②	1	10	**Leaving On A Jet Plane**.........................	*Peter, Paul & Mary* ...	Warner 7340
3	5	9	**Raindrops Keep Fallin' On My Head**	*B.J. Thomas* ...	Scepter 12265
④	3	10	**Down On The Corner/Fortunate Son**..	*Creedence Clearwater Revival* ...	Fantasy 634
⑤	4	11	**Na Na Hey Hey Kiss Him Goodbye**.....................	*Steam* ...	Fontana 1667
⑥	9	9	**Holly Holy**..	*Neil Diamond* : .	Uni 55175
⑦	6	11	**Come Together/Something**	*The Beatles* ...	Apple 2654
8	17	7	**I Want You Back**	*The Jackson 5* ...	Motown 1157
9	12	6	**Whole Lotta Love**	*Led Zeppelin* ...	Atlantic 2690
⑩	8	11	**Take A Letter Maria**...................................	*R.B. Greaves* ...	Atco 6714

★ *HIGHEST DEBUT* ★ POS 50	★ *BIGGEST MOVER* ★ 64 to 40
Without Love (There Is Nothing)........*Tom Jones*	Point It Out..........*Smokey Robinson & The Miracles*

Billboard JANUARY 3, 1970 — HOT 100

TW	LW	WK	Title / Artist / Label
①	3	10	**Raindrops Keep Fallin' On My Head**..........................*B.J. Thomas* ...Scepter 12265
②	2	11	**Leaving On A Jet Plane**.......................*Peter, Paul & Mary* ...Warner 7340
③	1	9	**Someday We'll Be Together** .... *Diana Ross & The Supremes* ...Motown 1156
④	4	11	**Down On The Corner/Fortunate Son**.................................. *Creedence Clearwater Revival* ...Fantasy 634
⑤	5	12	**Na Na Hey Hey Kiss Him Goodbye**......................*Steam* ...Fontana 1667
❻	9	7	**Whole Lotta Love** ....*Led Zeppelin* ...Atlantic 2690
⑦	8	8	**I Want You Back** ....*The Jackson 5* ...Motown 1157
❽	19	4	**Venus** ....*The Shocking Blue* ...Colossus 108
⑨	6	10	**Holly Holy** ....*Neil Diamond* ...Uni 55175
⑩	14	7	**La La La (If I Had You)**.......................*Bobby Sherman* ...Metromedia 150

★ HIGHEST DEBUT ★ POS 54	★ BIGGEST MOVER ★ 50 to 29
Walk A Mile In My Shoes ....*Joe South*	Without Love (There Is Nothing).........*Tom Jones*

Billboard JANUARY 10, 1970 — HOT 100

TW	LW	WK	Title / Artist / Label
①	1	11	**Raindrops Keep Fallin' On My Head**..........................*B.J. Thomas* ...Scepter 12265
②	3	10	**Someday We'll Be Together** .... *Diana Ross & The Supremes* ...Motown 1156
③	2	12	**Leaving On A Jet Plane**.......................*Peter, Paul & Mary* ...Warner 7340
❹	7	9	**I Want You Back** ....*The Jackson 5* ...Motown 1157
❺	6	8	**Whole Lotta Love** ....*Led Zeppelin* ...Atlantic 2690
❻	8	5	**Venus** ....*The Shocking Blue* ...Colossus 108
⑦	4	12	**Down On The Corner/Fortunate Son**.................................. *Creedence Clearwater Revival* ...Fantasy 634
⑧	5	13	**Na Na Hey Hey Kiss Him Goodbye** ....*Steam* ...Fontana 1667
⑨	10	8	**La La La (If I Had You)** ....*Bobby Sherman* ...Metromedia 150
⑩	13	9	**Jam Up Jelly Tight**...*Tommy Roe* ...ABC 11247

★ HIGHEST DEBUT ★ POS 58	★ BIGGEST MOVER ★ 92 to 67
How Can I Forget ....*Marvin Gaye*	The Thrill Is Gone .............................*B.B. King*

Billboard JANUARY 17, 1970 — HOT 100

TW	LW	WK	Title / Artist / Label
①	1	12	**Raindrops Keep Fallin' On My Head**..........................*B.J. Thomas* ...Scepter 12265
❷	6	6	**Venus** ....*The Shocking Blue* ...Colossus 108
❸	4	10	**I Want You Back** ....*The Jackson 5* ...Motown 1157
④	2	11	**Someday We'll Be Together** .... *Diana Ross & The Supremes* ...Motown 1156
⑤	5	9	**Whole Lotta Love** ....*Led Zeppelin* ...Atlantic 2690
⑥	3	13	**Leaving On A Jet Plane**.......................*Peter, Paul & Mary* ...Warner 7340
❼	11	8	**Don't Cry Daddy/Rubberneckin'**......................*Elvis Presley* ...RCA 9768
⑧	10	10	**Jam Up Jelly Tight**...*Tommy Roe* ...ABC 11247
⑨	7	13	**Down On The Corner/Fortunate Son**.................................. *Creedence Clearwater Revival* ...Fantasy 634
⑩	12	12	**Midnight Cowboy** ....*Ferrante & Teicher* ...United Artists 50554

★ HIGHEST DEBUT ★ POS 78	★ BIGGEST MOVER ★ 100 to 70
Honey Come Back.......................*Glen Campbell*	Rainy Night In Georgia.................*Brook Benton*

Billboard — JANUARY 24, 1970 — HOT 100

TW	LW	WK		
①	1	13	**Raindrops Keep Fallin' On My Head**......................	*B.J. Thomas* ... Scepter 12265
②	2	7	**Venus**	*The Shocking Blue* ... Colossus 108
③	3	11	**I Want You Back**	*The Jackson 5* ... Motown 1157
④	4	12	**Someday We'll Be Together**	*Diana Ross & The Supremes* ... Motown 1156
⑤	5	10	**Whole Lotta Love**	*Led Zeppelin* ... Atlantic 2690
⑥	6	14	**Leaving On A Jet Plane**......................	*Peter, Paul & Mary* ... Warner 7340
⑦	7	9	**Don't Cry Daddy/Rubberneckin'**......................	*Elvis Presley* ... RCA 9768
⑧	14	5	**Without Love (There Is Nothing)**	*Tom Jones* ... Parrot 40045
⑨	8	11	**Jam Up Jelly Tight**.................................	*Tommy Roe* ... ABC 11247
⑩	16	5	**I'll Never Fall In Love Again**	*Dionne Warwick* ... Scepter 12273

★ HIGHEST DEBUT ★ POS 71	★ BIGGEST MOVER ★ 95 to 38
Evil Ways ....*Santana*	**Psychedelic Shack** ....*The Temptations*

Billboard — JANUARY 31, 1970 — HOT 100

TW	LW	WK		
①	3	12	**I Want You Back**.................................	*The Jackson 5* ... Motown 1157
②	2	8	**Venus**	*The Shocking Blue* ... Colossus 108
③	1	14	**Raindrops Keep Fallin' On My Head**	*B.J. Thomas* ... Scepter 12265
④	5	11	**Whole Lotta Love**	*Led Zeppelin* ... Atlantic 2690
⑤	8	6	**Without Love (There Is Nothing)**	*Tom Jones* ... Parrot 40045
⑥	7	10	**Don't Cry Daddy/Rubberneckin'**	*Elvis Presley* ... RCA 9768
⑦	10	6	**I'll Never Fall In Love Again**	*Dionne Warwick* ... Scepter 12273
⑧	15	5	**Thank You (Falettinme Be Mice Elf Agin)/Everybody Is A Star**	*Sly & The Family Stone* ... Epic 10555
⑨	4	13	**Someday We'll Be Together**	*Diana Ross & The Supremes* ... Motown 1156
⑩	6	15	**Leaving On A Jet Plane**......................	*Peter, Paul & Mary* ... Warner 7340

★ HIGHEST DEBUT ★ POS 50	★ BIGGEST MOVER ★ 63 to 34
Travelin' Band/Who'll Stop The Rain ....*Creedence Clearwater Revival*	**Rainy Night In Georgia**..................*Brook Benton*

Billboard — FEBRUARY 7, 1970 — HOT 100

TW	LW	WK		
①	2	9	**Venus**...................................	*The Shocking Blue* ... Colossus 108
②	1	13	**I Want You Back**	*The Jackson 5* ... Motown 1157
③	3	15	**Raindrops Keep Fallin' On My Head**	*B.J. Thomas* ... Scepter 12265
④	8	6	**Thank You (Falettinme Be Mice Elf Agin)/Everybody Is A Star**	*Sly & The Family Stone* ... Epic 10555
⑤	5	7	**Without Love (There Is Nothing)**	*Tom Jones* ... Parrot 40045
⑥	7	7	**I'll Never Fall In Love Again**	*Dionne Warwick* ... Scepter 12273
⑦	13	7	**Hey There Lonely Girl**	*Eddie Holman* ... ABC 11240
⑧	4	12	**Whole Lotta Love**	*Led Zeppelin* ... Atlantic 2690
⑨	17	8	**No Time**	*The Guess Who* ... RCA 0300
⑩	11	11	**Jingle Jangle**	*The Archies* ... Kirshner 5002

★ HIGHEST DEBUT ★ POS 49	★ BIGGEST MOVER ★ 71 to 33
Bridge Over Troubled Water ....*Simon & Garfunkel*	**Ma Belle Amie**...............................*The Tee Set*

TW	LW	WK	Billboard.	⊙ FEBRUARY 14, 1970 ⊙	HOT 100.
❶	4	7	Thank You (Falettinme Be Mice Elf Agin)/Everybody Is A Star .... *Sly & The Family Stone* ... Epic 10555		
②	2	14	I Want You Back ....*The Jackson 5* ... Motown 1157		
③	3	16	Raindrops Keep Fallin' On My Head ..........*B.J. Thomas* ... Scepter 12265		
④	1	10	Venus ....*The Shocking Blue* ... Colossus 108		
⑤	7	8	Hey There Lonely Girl ....*Eddie Holman* ... ABC 11240		
⑥	9	9	No Time ....*The Guess Who* ... RCA 0300		
⑦	6	8	I'll Never Fall In Love Again ....*Dionne Warwick* ... Scepter 12273		
⑧	11	5	Psychedelic Shack...................................*The Temptations* ... Gordy 7096		
⑨	18	3	Travelin' Band/Who'll Stop The Rain .... *Creedence Clearwater Revival* ... Fantasy 637		
⑩	13	11	**Arizona** ....*Mark Lindsay* ... Columbia 45037		

★ *HIGHEST DEBUT* ★ POS 83	★ *BIGGEST MOVER* ★ 49 to 13
It's A New Day..............................*James Brown*	Bridge Over Troubled Water ....*Simon & Garfunkel*

TW	LW	WK	Billboard.	⊙ FEBRUARY 21, 1970 ⊙	HOT 100.
①	1	8	Thank You (Falettinme Be Mice Elf Agin)/Everybody Is A Star .... *Sly & The Family Stone* ... Epic 10555		
②	5	9	**Hey There Lonely Girl**...................................*Eddie Holman* ... ABC 11240		
❸	13	3	**Bridge Over Troubled Water** ....*Simon & Garfunkel* ... Columbia 45079		
④	2	15	I Want You Back ....*The Jackson 5* ... Motown 1157		
⑤	9	4	Travelin' Band/Who'll Stop The Rain .... *Creedence Clearwater Revival* ... Fantasy 637		
⑥	6	10	No Time ....*The Guess Who* ... RCA 0300		
⑦	3	17	Raindrops Keep Fallin' On My Head ..........*B.J. Thomas* ... Scepter 12265		
⑧	8	6	Psychedelic Shack...................................*The Temptations* ... Gordy 7096		
⑨	4	11	Venus ....*The Shocking Blue* ... Colossus 108		
⑩	14	7	Rainy Night In Georgia...................................*Brook Benton* ... Cotillion 44057		

★ *HIGHEST DEBUT* ★ POS 64	★ *BIGGEST MOVER* ★ 96 to 40
Gotta Hold On To This Feeling..........*Jr. Walker & The All Stars*	Kentucky Rain ....*Elvis Presley*

TW	LW	WK	Billboard.	⊙ FEBRUARY 28, 1970 ⊙	HOT 100.
❶	3	4	**Bridge Over Troubled Water** ......*Simon & Garfunkel* ... Columbia 45079		
②	1	9	Thank You (Falettinme Be Mice Elf Agin)/Everybody Is A Star .... *Sly & The Family Stone* ... Epic 10555		
❸	5	5	Travelin' Band/Who'll Stop The Rain .... *Creedence Clearwater Revival* ... Fantasy 637		
④	2	10	Hey There Lonely Girl ....*Eddie Holman* ... ABC 11240		
⑤	6	11	**No Time** ....*The Guess Who* ... RCA 0300		
⑥	14	6	Ma Belle Amie ....*The Tee Set* ... Colossus 107		
⑦	8	7	**Psychedelic Shack** ....*The Temptations* ... Gordy 7096		
⑧	7	18	Raindrops Keep Fallin' On My Head ..........*B.J. Thomas* ... Scepter 12265		
⑨	10	8	Rainy Night In Georgia...................................*Brook Benton* ... Cotillion 44057		
⑩	9	12	Venus ....*The Shocking Blue* ... Colossus 108		

★ *HIGHEST DEBUT* ★ POS 48	★ *BIGGEST MOVER* ★ 68 to 28
Celebrate..............................*Three Dog Night*	Love Grows (Where My Rosemary Goes) ....*Edison Lighthouse*

MARCH 7, 1970 — Billboard HOT 100

TW	LW	WK		
①	1	5	**Bridge Over Troubled Water** ......*Simon & Garfunkel* . . . Columbia 45079	
②	3	6	**Travelin' Band/Who'll Stop The Rain**	
			Creedence Clearwater Revival . . . Fantasy 637	
③	2	10	**Thank You (Falettinme Be Mice Elf Agin)/Everybody Is A Star**	
			Sly & The Family Stone . . . Epic 10555	
❹	9	9	**Rainy Night In Georgia** ....*Brook Benton* . . . Cotillion 44057	
⑤	4	11	**Hey There Lonely Girl** ....*Eddie Holman* . . . ABC 11240	
⑥	6	7	**Ma Belle Amie** ....*The Tee Set* . . . Colossus 107	
❼	11	6	**The Rapper** ....*The Jaggerz* . . . Kama Sutra 502	
❽	16	8	**Give Me Just A Little More Time** .... *Chairmen Of The Board*	
			. . . Invictus 9074	
⑨	8	19	**Raindrops Keep Fallin' On My Head** .........*B.J. Thomas* . . . Scepter 12265	
⑩	17	12	**He Ain't Heavy, He's My Brother** ....*Hollies* . . . Epic 10532	

★ **HIGHEST DEBUT** ★ POS 57
Up The Ladder To The Roof ....*The Supremes*

★ **BIGGEST MOVER** ★ 65 to 33
Instant Karma (We All Shine On).........*John Ono Lennon*

MARCH 14, 1970 — Billboard HOT 100

TW	LW	WK		
①	1	6	**Bridge Over Troubled Water** ......*Simon & Garfunkel* . . . Columbia 45079	
②	2	7	**Travelin' Band/Who'll Stop The Rain**	
			Creedence Clearwater Revival . . . Fantasy 637	
❸	7	7	**The Rapper** ....*The Jaggerz* . . . Kama Sutra 502	
④	4	10	**Rainy Night In Georgia** ....*Brook Benton* . . . Cotillion 44057	
⑤	6	8	**Ma Belle Amie** ....*The Tee Set* . . . Colossus 107	
⑥	8	9	**Give Me Just A Little More Time** .... *Chairmen Of The Board*	
			. . . Invictus 9074	
⑦	3	11	**Thank You (Falettinme Be Mice Elf Agin)/Everybody Is A Star**	
			Sly & The Family Stone . . . Epic 10555	
⑧	5	12	**Hey There Lonely Girl** ....*Eddie Holman* . . . ABC 11240	
⑨	10	13	**He Ain't Heavy, He's My Brother** ....*Hollies* . . . Epic 10532	
⑩	15	8	**Evil Ways** ....*Santana* . . . Columbia 45069	

★ **HIGHEST DEBUT** ★ POS 41
ABC ....*The Jackson 5*

★ **BIGGEST MOVER** ★ 82 to 61
Love Or Let Me Be Lonely ....*The Friends Of Distinction*

MARCH 21, 1970 — Billboard HOT 100

TW	LW	WK		
①	1	7	**Bridge Over Troubled Water** ......*Simon & Garfunkel* . . . Columbia 45079	
②	3	8	**The Rapper** ....*The Jaggerz* . . . Kama Sutra 502	
③	6	10	**Give Me Just A Little More Time** .... *Chairmen Of The Board*	
			. . . Invictus 9074	
❹	15	4	**Instant Karma (We All Shine On)** ....*John Ono Lennon* . . . Apple 1818	
⑤	4	11	**Rainy Night In Georgia** ....*Brook Benton* . . . Cotillion 44057	
⑥	-	1	**Let It Be** ....*The Beatles* . . . Apple 2764	
⑦	9	14	**He Ain't Heavy, He's My Brother** ....*Hollies* . . . Epic 10532	
❽	13	5	**Love Grows (Where My Rosemary Goes)** ....*Edison Lighthouse*	
			. . . Bell 858	
⑨	10	9	**Evil Ways** ....*Santana* . . . Columbia 45069	
⑩	11	11	**Didn't I (Blow Your Mind This Time)** ....*The Delfonics*	
			. . . Philly Groove 161	

★ **HIGHEST DEBUT** ★ POS 6
Let It Be ....*The Beatles*

★ **BIGGEST MOVER** ★ 84 to 47
Tennessee Bird Walk........*Jack Blanchard & Misty Morgan*

Billboard 🔴 MARCH 28, 1970 🔴 HOT 100.

TW	LW	WK			
①	1	8	**Bridge Over Troubled Water**......*Simon & Garfunkel* . . . Columbia 45079		
②	6	2	**Let It Be** ....*The Beatles* . . . Apple 2764		
③	4	5	**Instant Karma (We All Shine On)** .....*John Ono Lennon* . . . Apple 1818		
④	2	9	**The Rapper** ....*The Jaggerz* . . . Kama Sutra 502		
⑤	8	6	**Love Grows (Where My Rosemary Goes)** .... *Edison Lighthouse* . . . Bell 858		
⑥	14	3	**ABC**...*The Jackson 5* . . . Motown 1163		
⑦	7	15	**He Ain't Heavy, He's My Brother** ....*Hollies* . . Epic 10532		
⑧	13	5	**Spirit In The Sky** ....*Norman Greenbaum* . . . Reprise 0885		
⑨	3	11	**Give Me Just A Little More Time** .... *Chairmen Of The Board* . . . Invictus 9074		
⑩	23	8	**Come And Get It** ....*Badfinger* . . . Apple 1815		

★ **HIGHEST DEBUT** ★ POS 68	★ **BIGGEST MOVER** ★ 87 to 41
Woodstock.................*Crosby, Stills, Nash & Young*	You Need Love Like I Do (Don't You).......*Gladys Knight & The Pips*

Billboard 🔴 APRIL 4, 1970 🔴 HOT 100.

TW	LW	WK			
①	1	9	**Bridge Over Troubled Water**......*Simon & Garfunkel* . . . Columbia 45079		
②	2	3	**Let It Be** ....*The Beatles* . . . Apple 2764		
③	3	6	**Instant Karma (We All Shine On)** .....*John Ono Lennon* . . . Apple 1818		
④	6	4	**ABC**...*The Jackson 5* . . . Motown 1163		
⑤	5	7	**Love Grows (Where My Rosemary Goes)** .... *Edison Lighthouse* . . . Bell 858		
⑥	8	6	**Spirit In The Sky** ....*Norman Greenbaum* . . . Reprise 0885		
⑦	11	9	**House Of The Rising Sun** ....*Frijid Pink* . . . Parrot 341		
⑧	4	10	**The Rapper** ....*The Jaggerz* . . . Kama Sutra 502		
⑨	10	9	**Come And Get It** ....*Badfinger* . . . Apple 1815		
⑩	12	9	**Easy Come, Easy Go** ....*Bobby Sherman* . . . Metromedia 177		

★ **HIGHEST DEBUT** ★ POS 69	★ **BIGGEST MOVER** ★ 68 to 35
The Girls' Song.......................*The 5th Dimension*	Woodstock.................*Crosby, Stills, Nash & Young*

Billboard 🔴 APRIL 11, 1970 🔴 HOT 100.

TW	LW	WK			
❶	2	4	**Let It Be** ....*The Beatles* . . . Apple 2764		
❷	4	5	**ABC**...*The Jackson 5* . . . Motown 1163		
③	3	7	**Instant Karma (We All Shine On)** .....*John Ono Lennon* . . . Apple 1818		
❹	6	7	**Spirit In The Sky** ....*Norman Greenbaum* . . . Reprise 0885		
⑤	1	10	**Bridge Over Troubled Water**...........*Simon & Garfunkel* . . . Columbia 45079		
⑥	5	8	**Love Grows (Where My Rosemary Goes)** ....*Edison Lighthouse* . . . Bell 858		
⑦	7	10	**House Of The Rising Sun** ....*Frijid Pink* . . . Parrot 341		
⑧	9	10	**Come And Get It** ....*Badfinger* . . . Apple 1815		
⑨	10	10	**Easy Come, Easy Go**.......................*Bobby Sherman* . . . Metromedia 177		
⑩	8	11	**The Rapper** ....*The Jaggerz* . . . Kama Sutra 502		

★ **HIGHEST DEBUT** ★ POS 56	★ **BIGGEST MOVER** ★ 75 to 38
Love On A Two-Way Street ....*The Moments*	Vehicle ....*The Ides Of March*

Billboard — APRIL 18, 1970 — HOT 100

TW	LW	WK	Title	Artist
①	1	5	**Let It Be**	*The Beatles* . . . Apple 2764
②	2	6	**ABC**	*The Jackson 5* . . . Motown 1163
③	4	8	**Spirit In The Sky**	*Norman Greenbaum* . . . Reprise 0885
④	3	8	**Instant Karma (We All Shine On)**	*John Ono Lennon* . . . Apple 1818
⑤	6	9	**Love Grows (Where My Rosemary Goes)**	*Edison Lighthouse* . . . Bell 858
⑥	5	11	**Bridge Over Troubled Water**	*Simon & Garfunkel* . . . Columbia 45079
⑦	8	11	**Come And Get It**	*Badfinger* . . . Apple 1815
⑧	14	7	Love Or Let Me Be Lonely	*The Friends Of Distinction* . . . RCA 0319
⑨	15	5	American Woman/No Sugar Tonight	*The Guess Who* . . . RCA 0325
⑩	11	7	**Up The Ladder To The Roof**	*The Supremes* . . . Motown 1162

★ **HIGHEST DEBUT** ★ POS 72
The Letter...................*Joe Cocker*

★ **BIGGEST MOVER** ★ 90 to 44
Airport Love Theme ....*Vincent Bell*

Billboard — APRIL 25, 1970 — HOT 100

TW	LW	WK	Title	Artist
①	2	7	**ABC**	*The Jackson 5* . . . Motown 1163
②	1	6	**Let It Be**	*The Beatles* . . . Apple 2764
③	3	9	**Spirit In The Sky**	*Norman Greenbaum* . . . Reprise 0885
④	4	9	**Instant Karma (We All Shine On)**	*John Ono Lennon* . . . Apple 1818
⑤	9	6	American Woman/No Sugar Tonight	*The Guess Who* . . . RCA 0325
⑥	5	10	Love Grows (Where My Rosemary Goes)	*Edison Lighthouse* . . . Bell 858
⑦	7	12	**Come And Get It**	*Badfinger* . . . Apple 1815
⑧	8	8	**Love Or Let Me Be Lonely**	*The Friends Of Distinction* . . . RCA 0319
⑨	6	12	**Bridge Over Troubled Water**	*Simon & Garfunkel* . . . Columbia 45079
⑩	16	6	**Turn Back The Hands Of Time**	*Tyrone Davis* . . . Dakar 616

★ **HIGHEST DEBUT** ★ POS 48
Up Around The Bend/Run Through The Jungle ....*Creedence Clearwater Revival*

★ **BIGGEST MOVER** ★ 86 to 56
Puppet Man.............................*The 5th Dimension*

Billboard — MAY 2, 1970 — HOT 100

TW	LW	WK	Title	Artist
①	1	8	**ABC**	*The Jackson 5* . . . Motown 1163
②	2	7	**Let It Be**	*The Beatles* . . . Apple 2764
③	3	10	**Spirit In The Sky**	*Norman Greenbaum* . . . Reprise 0885
④	5	7	**American Woman/No Sugar Tonight**	*The Guess Who* . . . RCA 0325
⑤	4	10	Instant Karma (We All Shine On)	*John Ono Lennon* . . . Apple 1818
⑥	8	9	**Love Or Let Me Be Lonely**	*The Friends Of Distinction* . . . RCA 0319
⑦	6	11	Love Grows (Where My Rosemary Goes)	*Edison Lighthouse* . . . Bell 858
⑧	7	13	Come And Get It	*Badfinger* . . . Apple 1815
⑨	19	6	**Vehicle**	*The Ides Of March* . . . Warner 7378
⑩	10	7	**Turn Back The Hands Of Time**	*Tyrone Davis* . . . Dakar 616

★ **HIGHEST DEBUT** ★ POS 49
Daughter Of Darkness ....*Tom Jones*

★ **BIGGEST MOVER** ★ 87 to 62
My Baby Loves Lovin' ....*White Plains*

Billboard — MAY 9, 1970 — HOT 100

TW	LW	WK	Title	Artist	Label
1	4	8	American Woman/No Sugar Tonight	The Guess Who	RCA 0325
2	1	9	ABC	The Jackson 5	Motown 1163
3	2	8	Let It Be	The Beatles	Apple 2764
4	9	7	Vehicle	The Ides Of March	Warner 7378
5	3	11	Spirit In The Sky	Norman Greenbaum	Reprise 0885
6	6	10	Love Or Let Me Be Lonely	The Friends Of Distinction	RCA 0319
7	16	6	Everything Is Beautiful	Ray Stevens	Barnaby 2011
8	5	11	Instant Karma (We All Shine On)	John Ono Lennon	Apple 1818
9	10	8	Turn Back The Hands Of Time	Tyrone Davis	Dakar 616
10	13	9	Reflections Of My Life	The Marmalade	London 20058

★ HIGHEST DEBUT ★ POS 79
Baby Hold On .... The Grass Roots

★ BIGGEST MOVER ★ 88 to 65
Mississippi Queen .... Mountain

Billboard — MAY 16, 1970 — HOT 100

TW	LW	WK	Title	Artist	Label
1	1	9	American Woman/No Sugar Tonight	The Guess Who	RCA 0325
2	2	10	ABC	The Jackson 5	Motown 1163
3	4	8	Vehicle	The Ides Of March	Warner 7378
4	3	9	Let It Be	The Beatles	Apple 2764
5	14	6	Cecilia	Simon & Garfunkel	Columbia 45133
6	5	12	Spirit In The Sky	Norman Greenbaum	Reprise 0885
7	7	7	Everything Is Beautiful	Ray Stevens	Barnaby 2011
8	9	9	Turn Back The Hands Of Time	Tyrone Davis	Dakar 616
9	13	4	Up Around The Bend/Run Through The Jungle	Creedence Clearwater Revival	Fantasy 641
10	10	10	Reflections Of My Life	The Marmalade	London 20058

★ HIGHEST DEBUT ★ POS 66
The Wonder Of You/Mama Liked The
Roses .... Elvis Presley

★ BIGGEST MOVER ★ 76 to 47
It's All In The Game .... Four Tops

Billboard — MAY 23, 1970 — HOT 100

TW	LW	WK	Title	Artist	Label
1	1	10	American Woman/No Sugar Tonight	The Guess Who	RCA 0325
2	3	9	Vehicle	The Ides Of March	Warner 7378
3	8	10	Turn Back The Hands Of Time	Tyrone Davis	Dakar 616
4	7	8	Everything Is Beautiful	Ray Stevens	Barnaby 2011
5	5	7	Cecilia	Simon & Garfunkel	Columbia 45133
6	4	10	Let It Be	The Beatles	Apple 2764
7	12	7	Love On A Two-Way Street	The Moments	Stang 5012
8	9	5	Up Around The Bend/Run Through The Jungle	Creedence Clearwater Revival	Fantasy 641
9	2	11	ABC	The Jackson 5	Motown 1163
10	10	11	Reflections Of My Life	The Marmalade	London 20058

★ HIGHEST DEBUT ★ POS 35
The Long And Winding Road/For You
Blue .... The Beatles

★ BIGGEST MOVER ★ 66 to 36
The Wonder Of You/Mama Liked The
Roses .... Elvis Presley

TW	LW	WK	Billboard	MAY 30, 1970	HOT 100.
①	4	9	**Everything Is Beautiful**..........................*Ray Stevens* ... Barnaby 2011		
②	1	11	American Woman/No Sugar Tonight....................... *The Guess Who* ... RCA 0325		
③	7	8	**Love On A Two-Way Street** ....*The Moments* ... Stang 5012		
④	5	8	**Cecilia**...................................*Simon & Garfunkel* ... Columbia 45133		
⑤	8	6	Up Around The Bend/Run Through The Jungle .... *Creedence Clearwater Revival* ... Fántasy 641		
❻	14	10	Which Way You Goin' Billy?...................*The Poppy Family* ... London 129		
❼	18	7	**The Letter**....................................*Joe Cocker* ... A&M 1174		
⑧	3	11	Turn Back The Hands Of Time ....*Tyrone Davis* ... Dakar 616		
⑨	2	10	Vehicle...................................*The Ides Of March* ... Warner 7378		
⑩	6	11	Let It Be ....*The Beatles* ... Apple 2764		

★ HIGHEST DEBUT ★ POS 45	★ BIGGEST MOVER ★ 80 to 41
The Love You Save ....*The Jackson 5*	Ball Of Confusion ....*The Temptations*

TW	LW	WK	Billboard	JUNE 6, 1970	HOT 100.
①	1	10	**Everything Is Beautiful**..........................*Ray Stevens* ... Barnaby 2011		
❷	6	11	**Which Way You Goin' Billy?** ....*The Poppy Family* ... London 129		
③	3	9	**Love On A Two-Way Street** ....*The Moments* ... Stang 5012		
④	5	7	**Up Around The Bend/Run Through The Jungle**......................... *Creedence Clearwater Revival* ... Fantasy 641		
⑤	4	9	**Cecilia** ....*Simon & Garfunkel* ... Columbia 45133		
❻	11	13	**Get Ready** ....*Rare Earth* ... Rare Earth 5012		
⑦	7	8	**The Letter**...............................*Joe Cocker* ... A&M 1174		
⑧	2	12	American Woman/No Sugar Tonight........................... *The Guess Who* ... RCA 0325		
❾	17	10	**Make Me Smile** ....*Chicago* ... Columbia 45127		
❿	12	3	The Long And Winding Road/For You Blue ....*The Beatles* ... Apple 2832		

★ HIGHEST DEBUT ★ POS 73	★ BIGGEST MOVER ★ 45 to 15
Tighter, Tighter...........................*Alive & Kicking*	The Love You Save ....*The Jackson 5*

TW	LW	WK	Billboard	JUNE 13, 1970	HOT 100.
①	10	4	**The Long And Winding Road/For You Blue** .... *The Beatles* ... Apple 2832		
②	2	12	**Which Way You Goin' Billy?** ....*The Poppy Family* ... London 129		
③	1	11	**Everything Is Beautiful**...............................*Ray Stevens* ... Barnaby 2011		
④	6	14	**Get Ready** ....*Rare Earth* ... Rare Earth 5012		
⑤	3	10	Love On A Two-Way Street.........................*The Moments* ... Stang 5012		
⑥	5	10	Cecilia ....*Simon & Garfunkel* ... Columbia 45133		
⑦	7	9	**The Letter**...............................*Joe Cocker* ... A&M 1174		
⑧	4	8	Up Around The Bend/Run Through The Jungle .... *Creedence Clearwater Revival* ... Fantasy 641		
❾	9	11	**Make Me Smile** ....*Chicago* ... Columbia 45127		
❿	15	3	The Love You Save ....*The Jackson 5* ... Motown 1166		

★ HIGHEST DEBUT ★ POS 49	★ BIGGEST MOVER ★ 85 to 56
A Song Of Joy ....*Miguel Rios*	Teach Your Children ....*Crosby, Stills, Nash & Young*

Billboard — JUNE 20, 1970 — HOT 100

TW	LW	WK	Title / Artist / Label
①	1	5	**The Long And Winding Road/For You Blue** .... *The Beatles* ... Apple 2832
❷	10	4	The Love You Save .... *The Jackson 5* ... Motown 1166
③	2	13	Which Way You Goin' Billy? .... *The Poppy Family* ... London 129
④	4	15	**Get Ready** .... *Rare Earth* ... Rare Earth 5012
❺	19	5	Mama Told Me (Not To Come) .... *Three Dog Night* ... Dunhill 4239
❻	20	5	Ball Of Confusion .... *The Temptations* ... Gordy 7099
⑦	5	11	Love On A Two-Way Street .... *The Moments* ... Stang 5012
⑧	7	10	The Letter .... *Joe Cocker* ... A&M 1174
⑨	16	14	Hitchin' A Ride .... *Vanity Fare* ... Page One 21029
⑩	11	9	Lay Down (Candles In The Rain) .... *Melanie with The Edwin Hawkins' Singers* ... Buddah 167

★ HIGHEST DEBUT ★ POS 56	★ BIGGEST MOVER ★ 90 to 42
(They Long To Be) Close To You .... *Carpenters*	Save The Country .... *The 5th Dimension*

Billboard — JUNE 27, 1970 — HOT 100

TW	LW	WK	Title / Artist / Label
❶	2	5	**The Love You Save** .... *The Jackson 5* ... Motown 1166
❷	5	6	Mama Told Me (Not To Come) .... *Three Dog Night* ... Dunhill 4239
❸	6	6	**Ball Of Confusion** .... *The Temptations* ... Gordy 7099
④	1	6	The Long And Winding Road/For You Blue .... *The Beatles* ... Apple 2832
❺	9	15	**Hitchin' A Ride** .... *Vanity Fare* ... Page One 21029
❻	11	8	Ride Captain Ride .... *Blues Image* ... Atco 6746
⑦	4	16	Get Ready .... *Rare Earth* ... Rare Earth 5012
❽	10	10	Lay Down (Candles In The Rain) .... *Melanie with The Edwin Hawkins' Singers* ... Buddah 167
❾	15	7	**The Wonder Of You/Mama Liked The Roses** *Elvis Presley* ... RCA 9835
⑩	3	14	Which Way You Goin' Billy? .... *The Poppy Family* ... London 129

★ HIGHEST DEBUT ★ POS 49	★ BIGGEST MOVER ★ 83 to 55
Signed, Sealed, Delivered I'm Yours .... *Stevie Wonder*	Silver Bird .... *Mark Lindsay*

Billboard — JULY 4, 1970 — HOT 100

TW	LW	WK	Title / Artist / Label
①	1	6	**The Love You Save** .... *The Jackson 5* ... Motown 1166
②	2	7	Mama Told Me (Not To Come) .... *Three Dog Night* ... Dunhill 4239
③	3	7	**Ball Of Confusion** .... *The Temptations* ... Gordy 7099
④	4	7	The Long And Winding Road/For You Blue .... *The Beatles* ... Apple 2832
⑤	5	16	**Hitchin' A Ride** .... *Vanity Fare* ... Page One 21029
⑥	6	9	Ride Captain Ride .... *Blues Image* ... Atco 6746
❼	11	11	Band Of Gold .... *Freda Payne* ... Invictus 9075
⑧	8	11	Lay Down (Candles In The Rain) .... *Melanie with The Edwin Hawkins' Singers* ... Buddah 167
⑨	9	8	**The Wonder Of You/Mama Liked The Roses** *Elvis Presley* ... RCA 9835
⑩	7	17	Get Ready .... *Rare Earth* ... Rare Earth 5012

★ HIGHEST DEBUT ★ POS 80	★ BIGGEST MOVER ★ 90 to 63
Everything A Man Could Ever Need .... *Glen Campbell*	My Marie .... *Engelbert Humperdinck*

TW	LW	WK	Billboard.	JULY 11, 1970	HOT 100.
❶	2	8	**Mama Told Me (Not To Come)** .... *Three Dog Night* . . . Dunhill 4239		
②	1	7	**The Love You Save** .... *The Jackson 5* . . . Motown 1166		
③	3	8	**Ball Of Confusion** .... *The Temptations* . . . Gordy 7099		
④	6	10	**Ride Captain Ride** .... *Blues Image* . . . Atco 6746		
⑤	7	12	**Band Of Gold** .... *Freda Payne* . . . Invictus 9075		
⑥	8	12	**Lay Down (Candles In The Rain)** .... *Melanie with The Edwin Hawkins' Singers* . . . Buddah 167		
❼	14	4	**(They Long To Be) Close To You** .... *Carpenters* . . . A&M 1183		
⑧	4	8	**The Long And Winding Road/For You Blue** .... *The Beatles* . . . Apple 2832		
⑨	9	9	**The Wonder Of You/Mama Liked The Roses** .... *Elvis Presley* . . . RCA 9835		
⑩	5	17	**Hitchin' A Ride** .... *Vanity Fare* . . . Page One 21029		

★ **HIGHEST DEBUT** ★ POS 72	★ **BIGGEST MOVER** ★ 44 to 20
War .... *Edwin Starr*	Make It With You .... *Bread*

TW	LW	WK	Billboard.	JULY 18, 1970	HOT 100.
①	1	9	**Mama Told Me (Not To Come)** .... *Three Dog Night* . . . Dunhill 4239		
②	2	8	**The Love You Save** .... *The Jackson 5* . . . Motown 1166		
❸	7	5	**(They Long To Be) Close To You** .... *Carpenters* . . . A&M 1183		
❹	5	13	**Band Of Gold** .... *Freda Payne* . . . Invictus 9075		
⑤	3	9	**Ball Of Confusion** .... *The Temptations* . . . Gordy 7099		
⑥	4	11	**Ride Captain Ride** .... *Blues Image* . . . Atco 6746		
⑦	6	13	**Lay Down (Candles In The Rain)** .... *Melanie with The Edwin Hawkins' Singers* . . . Buddah 167		
❽	12	10	**O-o-h Child** .... *The Five Stairsteps* . . . Buddah 165		
⑨	11	9	**Gimme Dat Ding** .... *The Pipkins* . . . Capitol 2819		
⑩	20	6	**Make It With You** .... *Bread* . . . Elektra 45686		

★ **HIGHEST DEBUT** ★ POS 72	★ **BIGGEST MOVER** ★ 72 to 44
Get Up (I Feel Like Being A) Sex Machine .... *James Brown*	War .... *Edwin Starr*

TW	LW	WK	Billboard.	JULY 25, 1970	HOT 100.
❶	3	6	**(They Long To Be) Close To You** .... *Carpenters* . . . A&M 1183		
②	1	10	**Mama Told Me (Not To Come)** .... *Three Dog Night* . . . Dunhill 4239		
③	4	14	**Band Of Gold** .... *Freda Payne* . . . Invictus 9075		
④	2	9	**The Love You Save** .... *The Jackson 5* . . . Motown 1166		
❺	10	7	**Make It With You** .... *Bread* . . . Elektra 45686		
⑥	5	10	**Ball Of Confusion** .... *The Temptations* . . . Gordy 7099		
⑦	6	12	**Ride Captain Ride** .... *Blues Image* . . . Atco 6746		
⑧	8	11	**O-o-h Child** .... *The Five Stairsteps* . . . Buddah 165		
⑨	18	5	**Signed, Sealed, Delivered I'm Yours** .... *Stevie Wonder* . . . Tamla 54196		
⑩	7	14	**Lay Down (Candles In The Rain)** .... *Melanie with The Edwin Hawkins' Singers* . . . Buddah 167		

★ **HIGHEST DEBUT** ★ POS 50	★ **BIGGEST MOVER** ★ 68 to 32
25 Or 6 To 4 .... *Chicago*	In The Summertime .... *Mungo Jerry*

Billboard — AUGUST 1, 1970 — HOT 100

TW	LW	WK	Title	Artist	Label
1	1	7	(They Long To Be) Close To You	Carpenters	A&M 1183
2	5	8	Make It With You	Bread	Elektra 45686
3	2	11	Mama Told Me (Not To Come)	Three Dog Night	Dunhill 4239
4	3	15	Band Of Gold	Freda Payne	Invictus 9075
5	9	6	Signed, Sealed, Delivered I'm Yours	Stevie Wonder	Tamla 54196
6	4	10	The Love You Save/I Found That Girl	The Jackson 5	Motown 1166
7	14	11	Spill The Wine	Eric Burdon & War	MGM 14118
8	6	11	Ball Of Confusion	The Temptations	Gordy 7099
9	11	9	Tighter, Tighter	Alive & Kicking	Roulette 7078
10	8	12	O-o-h Child	The Five Stairsteps	Buddah 165

★ HIGHEST DEBUT ★ POS 61
(I Know) I'm Losing You .... Rare Earth

★ BIGGEST MOVER ★ 60 to 29
Patches .... Clarence Carter

Billboard — AUGUST 8, 1970 — HOT 100

TW	LW	WK	Title	Artist	Label
1	1	8	(They Long To Be) Close To You	Carpenters	A&M 1183
2	2	9	Make It With You	Bread	Elektra 45686
3	5	7	Signed, Sealed, Delivered I'm Yours	Stevie Wonder	Tamla 54196
4	7	12	Spill The Wine	Eric Burdon & War	MGM 14118
5	4	16	Band Of Gold	Freda Payne	Invictus 9075
6	3	12	Mama Told Me (Not To Come)	Three Dog Night	Dunhill 4239
7	9	10	Tighter, Tighter	Alive & Kicking	Roulette 7078
8	6	11	The Love You Save/I Found That Girl	The Jackson 5	Motown 1166
9	8	12	Ball Of Confusion	The Temptations	Gordy 7099
10	10	13	O-o-h Child	The Five Stairsteps	Buddah 165

★ HIGHEST DEBUT ★ POS 46
Ain't No Mountain High Enough .... Diana Ross

★ BIGGEST MOVER ★ 85 to 47
I've Lost You/The Next Step Is Love .... Elvis Presley

Billboard — AUGUST 15, 1970 — HOT 100

TW	LW	WK	Title	Artist	Label
1	1	9	(They Long To Be) Close To You	Carpenters	A&M 1183
2	2	10	Make It With You	Bread	Elektra 45686
3	3	8	Signed, Sealed, Delivered I'm Yours	Stevie Wonder	Tamla 54196
4	4	13	Spill The Wine	Eric Burdon & War	MGM 14118
5	12	6	In The Summertime	Mungo Jerry	Janus 125
6	11	6	War	Edwin Starr	Gordy 7101
7	5	17	Band Of Gold	Freda Payne	Invictus 9075
8	6	13	Mama Told Me (Not To Come)	Three Dog Night	Dunhill 4239
9	7	11	Tighter, Tighter	Alive & Kicking	Roulette 7078
10	9	13	Ball Of Confusion	The Temptations	Gordy 7099

★ HIGHEST DEBUT ★ POS 59
Rubber Duckie .... Ernie

★ BIGGEST MOVER ★ 56 to 23
Lookin' Out My Back Door/Long As I Can See The Light .... Creedence Clearwater Revival

TW	LW	WK	Billboard.	AUGUST 22, 1970	HOT 100.
①	2	11	**Make It With You**	*Bread* . . . Elektra 45686
②	1	10	**(They Long To Be) Close To You**	*Carpenters* . . . A&M 1183
③	4	14	**Spill The Wine**	*Eric Burdon & War* . . . MGM 14118
❹	6	7	War	*Edwin Starr* . . . Gordy 7101
⑤	5	7	In The Summertime	*Mungo Jerry* . . . Janus 125
⑥	3	9	Signed, Sealed, Delivered I'm Yours	*Stevie Wonder* . . . Tamla 54196
❼	16	6	Patches	*Clarence Carter* . . . Atlantic 2748
⑧	7	18	Band Of Gold	*Freda Payne* . . . Invictus 9075
⑨	12	10	**I Just Can't Help Believing**	*B.J. Thomas* . . . Scepter 12283
⑩	9	12	Tighter, Tighter	*Alive & Kicking* . . . Roulette 7078

★ **HIGHEST DEBUT** ★ POS 46
I (Who Have Nothing) ....*Tom Jones*

★ **BIGGEST MOVER** ★ 92 to 65
Green-Eyed Lady ....*Sugarloaf*

TW	LW	WK	Billboard.	AUGUST 29, 1970	HOT 100.
①	4	8	**War**	*Edwin Starr* . . . Gordy 7101
②	1	12	**Make It With You**	*Bread* . . . Elektra 45686
③	2	11	**(They Long To Be) Close To You**	*Carpenters* . . . A&M 1183
④	5	8	**In The Summertime**	*Mungo Jerry* . . . Janus 125
⑤	3	15	Spill The Wine	*Eric Burdon & War* . . . MGM 14118
⑥	6	10	Signed, Sealed, Delivered I'm Yours	*Stevie Wonder* . . . Tamla 54196
⑦	7	7	Patches	*Clarence Carter* . . . Atlantic 2748
❽	12	11	**(If You Let Me Make Love To You Then) Why Can't I Touch You?**	*Ronnie Dyson* . . . Columbia 45110
⑨	17	4	Ain't No Mountain High Enough	*Diana Ross* . . . Motown 1169
⑩	13	6	25 Or 6 To 4	*Chicago* . . . Columbia 45194

★ **HIGHEST DEBUT** ★ POS 62
Sunday Morning Coming Down ....*Johnny Cash*

★ **BIGGEST MOVER** ★ 81 to 43
Neanderthal Man ....*Hotlegs*

TW	LW	WK	Billboard.	SEPTEMBER 5, 1970	HOT 100.
①	1	9	**War**	*Edwin Starr* . . . Gordy 7101
❷	9	5	Ain't No Mountain High Enough	*Diana Ross* . . . Motown 1169
③	2	13	**Make It With You**	*Bread* . . . Elektra 45686
④	4	9	In The Summertime	*Mungo Jerry* . . . Janus 125
⑤	3	12	(They Long To Be) Close To You	*Carpenters* . . . A&M 1183
❻	10	7	25 Or 6 To 4	*Chicago* . . . Columbia 45194
⑦	7	8	Patches	*Clarence Carter* . . . Atlantic 2748
⑧	8	12	**(If You Let Me Make Love To You Then) Why Can't I Touch You?**	*Ronnie Dyson* . . . Columbia 45110
⑨	5	16	Spill The Wine	*Eric Burdon & War* . . . MGM 14118
⑩	12	5	Lookin' Out My Back Door/Long As I Can See The Light	*Creedence Clearwater Revival* . . . Fantasy 645

★ **HIGHEST DEBUT** ★ POS 70
Look What They've Done To My Song
Ma ....*The New Seekers*

★ **BIGGEST MOVER** ★ 90 to 68
Out In The Country....................*Three Dog Night*

Billboard 🔵 SEPTEMBER 12, 1970 🔵 HOT 100.

TW	LW	WK		
①	1	10	**War** ....*Edwin Starr* . . . Gordy 7101	
②	2	6	**Ain't No Mountain High Enough**...................*Diana Ross* . . . Motown 1169	
③	4	10	**In The Summertime** ....*Mungo Jerry* . . . Janus 125	
④	6	8	**25 Or 6 To 4**...................................*Chicago* . . . Columbia 45194	
❺	10	6	**Lookin' Out My Back Door/Long As I Can See The Light**............... *Creedence Clearwater Revival* . . . Fantasy 645	
⑥	7	9	**Patches**...............................*Clarence Carter* . . . Atlantic 2748	
❼	13	7	**Julie, Do Ya Love Me** ....*Bobby Sherman* . . . Metromedia 194	
⑧	5	13	**(They Long To Be) Close To You** ....*Carpenters* . . . A&M 1183	
⑨	3	14	**Make It With You**.............................*Bread* . . . Elektra 45686	
⑩	9	17	**Spill The Wine** ....*Eric Burdon & War* . . . MGM 14118	

★ HIGHEST DEBUT ★ POS 54	★ BIGGEST MOVER ★ 86 to 45
El Condor Pasa....................*Simon & Garfunkel*	Indiana Wants Me......................*R. Dean Taylor*

Billboard 🔵 SEPTEMBER 19, 1970 🔵 HOT 100.

TW	LW	WK		
①	2	7	**Ain't No Mountain High Enough** ....*Diana Ross* . . . Motown 1169	
②	1	11	**War**..*Edwin Starr* . . . Gordy 7101	
③	5	7	**Lookin' Out My Back Door/Long As I Can See The Light**.................. *Creedence Clearwater Revival* . . . Fantasy 645	
❹	6	10	**Patches**...............................*Clarence Carter* . . . Atlantic 2748	
⑤	7	8	**Julie, Do Ya Love Me**......................*Bobby Sherman* . . . Metromedia 194	
⑥	4	9	**25 Or 6 To 4** ....*Chicago* . . . Columbia 45194	
⑦	3	11	**In The Summertime**.............................*Mungo Jerry* . . . Janus 125	
⑧	8	14	**(They Long To Be) Close To You** ....*Carpenters* . . . A&M 1183	
⑨	11	9	**Candida** ....*Dawn* . . . Bell 903	
⑩	9	15	**Make It With You**............................*Bread* . . . Elektra 45686	

★ HIGHEST DEBUT ★ POS 40	★ BIGGEST MOVER ★ 83 to 50
I'll Be There ....*The Jackson 5*	Fire And Rain.........................*James Taylor*

Billboard 🔵 SEPTEMBER 26, 1970 🔵 HOT 100.

TW	LW	WK		
①	1	8	**Ain't No Mountain High Enough** ....*Diana Ross* . . . Motown 1169	
②	2	12	**War**..*Edwin Starr* . . . Gordy 7101	
③	3	8	**Lookin' Out My Back Door/Long As I Can See The Light**............... *Creedence Clearwater Revival* . . . Fantasy 645	
④	4	11	**Patches**...............................*Clarence Carter* . . . Atlantic 2748	
⑤	5	9	**Julie, Do Ya Love Me**......................*Bobby Sherman* . . . Metromedia 194	
❻	12	6	**Cracklin' Rosie** ....*Neil Diamond* . . . Uni 55250	
❼	9	10	**Candida** ....*Dawn* . . . Bell 903	
❽	13	11	**Snowbird**................................*Anne Murray* . . . Capitol 2738	
❾	14	9	**(I Know) I'm Losing You** ....*Rare Earth* . . . Rare Earth 5017	
⑩	6	10	**25 Or 6 To 4** ....*Chicago* . . . Columbia 45194	

★ HIGHEST DEBUT ★ POS 75	★ BIGGEST MOVER ★ 84 to 59
See Me, Feel Me ....*The Who*	Our House ....*Crosby, Stills, Nash & Young*

Billboard — OCTOBER 3, 1970 — HOT 100

TW	LW	WK		
1	1	9	Ain't No Mountain High Enough	Diana Ross ... Motown 1169
2	3	9	Lookin' Out My Back Door/Long As I Can See The Light .... Creedence Clearwater Revival ... Fantasy 645	
3	7	11	Candida	Dawn ... Bell 903
4	6	7	Cracklin' Rosie	Neil Diamond ... Uni 55250
5	5	10	Julie, Do Ya Love Me	Bobby Sherman ... Metromedia 194
6	19	3	I'll Be There	The Jackson 5 ... Motown 1171
7	9	10	(I Know) I'm Losing You	Rare Earth ... Rare Earth 5017
8	8	12	Snowbird	Anne Murray ... Capitol 2738
9	2	13	War	Edwin Starr ... Gordy 7101
10	13	8	All Right Now	Free ... A&M 1206

★ HIGHEST DEBUT ★ POS 62
Lucretia Mac Evil .... Blood, Sweat & Tears

★ BIGGEST MOVER ★ 99 to 71
Sweetheart .... Engelbert Humperdinck

Billboard — OCTOBER 10, 1970 — HOT 100

TW	LW	WK		
1	4	8	Cracklin' Rosie	Neil Diamond ... Uni 55250
2	6	4	I'll Be There	The Jackson 5 ... Motown 1171
3	3	12	Candida	Dawn ... Bell 903
4	1	10	Ain't No Mountain High Enough	Diana Ross ... Motown 1169
5	10	9	All Right Now	Free ... A&M 1206
6	5	11	Julie, Do Ya Love Me	Bobby Sherman ... Metromedia 194
7	2	10	Lookin' Out My Back Door/Long As I Can See The Light .... Creedence Clearwater Revival ... Fantasy 645	
8	16	9	Green-Eyed Lady	Sugarloaf ... Liberty 56183
9	18	5	We've Only Just Begun	Carpenters ... A&M 1217
10	7	11	(I Know) I'm Losing You	Rare Earth ... Rare Earth 5017

★ HIGHEST DEBUT ★ POS 62
Cry Me A River .... Joe Cocker

★ BIGGEST MOVER ★ 70 to 43
Ungena Za Ulimwengu (Unite The World) .... The Temptations

Billboard — OCTOBER 17, 1970 — HOT 100

TW	LW	WK		
1	2	5	I'll Be There	The Jackson 5 ... Motown 1171
2	1	9	Cracklin' Rosie	Neil Diamond ... Uni 55250
3	8	10	Green-Eyed Lady	Sugarloaf ... Liberty 56183
4	5	10	All Right Now	Free ... A&M 1206
5	9	6	We've Only Just Begun	Carpenters ... A&M 1217
6	3	13	Candida	Dawn ... Bell 903
7	4	11	Ain't No Mountain High Enough	Diana Ross ... Motown 1169
8	7	11	Lookin' Out My Back Door/Long As I Can See The Light .... Creedence Clearwater Revival ... Fantasy 645	
9	6	12	Julie, Do Ya Love Me	Bobby Sherman ... Metromedia 194
10	17	6	Fire And Rain	James Taylor ... Warner 7423

★ HIGHEST DEBUT ★ POS 67
Heed The Call ...... Kenny Rogers & The First Edition

★ BIGGEST MOVER ★ 80 to 59
Fresh Air .... Quicksilver Messenger Service

Billboard — OCTOBER 24, 1970 — HOT 100

TW	LW	WK	Title	Artist ... Label
1	1	6	I'll Be There	The Jackson 5 ... Motown 1171
2	2	10	Cracklin' Rosie	Neil Diamond ... Uni 55250
3	3	11	Green-Eyed Lady	Sugarloaf ... Liberty 56183
4	5	7	We've Only Just Begun	Carpenters ... A&M 1217
5	4	11	All Right Now	Free ... A&M 1206
6	10	7	Fire And Rain	James Taylor ... Warner 7423
7	6	14	Candida	Dawn ... Bell 903
8	11	8	Indiana Wants Me	R. Dean Taylor ... Rare Earth 5013
9	12	9	Lola	The Kinks ... Reprise 0930
10	7	12	Ain't No Mountain High Enough	Diana Ross ... Motown 1169

★ **HIGHEST DEBUT** ★ POS 73
Share The Land ....The Guess Who

★ **BIGGEST MOVER** ★ 78 to 49
Heaven Help Us All ....Stevie Wonder

Billboard — OCTOBER 31, 1970 — HOT 100

TW	LW	WK	Title	Artist ... Label
1	1	7	I'll Be There	The Jackson 5 ... Motown 1171
2	4	8	We've Only Just Begun	Carpenters ... A&M 1217
3	6	8	Fire And Rain	James Taylor ... Warner 7423
4	2	11	Cracklin' Rosie	Neil Diamond ... Uni 55250
5	3	12	Green-Eyed Lady	Sugarloaf ... Liberty 56183
6	5	12	All Right Now	Free ... A&M 1206
7	8	9	Indiana Wants Me	R. Dean Taylor ... Rare Earth 5013
8	7	15	Candida	Dawn ... Bell 903
9	9	10	Lola	The Kinks ... Reprise 0930
10	17	9	It's Only Make Believe	Glen Campbell ... Capitol 2905

★ **HIGHEST DEBUT** ★ POS 79
No Matter What ....Badfinger

★ **BIGGEST MOVER** ★ 74 to 49
You Don't Have To Say You Love Me/Patch It Up ....Elvis Presley

Billboard — NOVEMBER 7, 1970 — HOT 100

TW	LW	WK	Title	Artist ... Label
1	1	8	I'll Be There	The Jackson 5 ... Motown 1171
2	2	9	We've Only Just Begun	Carpenters ... A&M 1217
3	3	9	Fire And Rain	James Taylor ... Warner 7423
4	5	13	Green-Eyed Lady	Sugarloaf ... Liberty 56183
5	7	10	Indiana Wants Me	R. Dean Taylor ... Rare Earth 5013
6	6	13	All Right Now	Free ... A&M 1206
7	17	5	I Think I Love You	The Partridge Family ... Bell 910
8	4	12	Cracklin' Rosie	Neil Diamond ... Uni 55250
9	8	16	Candida	Dawn ... Bell 903
10	9	11	Lola	The Kinks ... Reprise 0930

★ **HIGHEST DEBUT** ★ POS 61
Stoned Love ....The Supremes

★ **BIGGEST MOVER** ★ 98 to 66
Chains And Things ...............B.B. King

Billboard — NOVEMBER 14, 1970 — HOT 100

TW	LW	WK	Title	Artist	Label
①	1	9	I'll Be There	The Jackson 5	Motown 1171
②	2	10	We've Only Just Begun	Carpenters	A&M 1217
③	3	10	Fire And Rain	James Taylor	Warner 7423
❹	7	6	I Think I Love You	The Partridge Family	Bell 910
⑤	5	11	Indiana Wants Me	R. Dean Taylor	Rare Earth 5013
⑥	4	14	Green-Eyed Lady	Sugarloaf	Liberty 56183
❼	13	5	The Tears Of A Clown	Smokey Robinson & The Miracles	Tamla 54199
❽	12	11	Somebody's Been Sleeping	100 Proof Aged In Soul	Hot Wax 7004
❾	18	11	Gypsy Woman	Brian Hyland	Uni 55240
⑩	11	8	It Don't Matter To Me	Bread	Elektra 45701

★ HIGHEST DEBUT ★ POS 55
Black Magic Woman ....Santana

★ BIGGEST MOVER ★ 72 to 50
Does Anybody Really Know What Time It Is? ....Chicago

Billboard — NOVEMBER 21, 1970 — HOT 100

TW	LW	WK	Title	Artist	Label
❶	4	7	I Think I Love You	The Partridge Family	Bell 910
②	2	11	We've Only Just Begun	Carpenters	A&M 1217
③	1	10	I'll Be There	The Jackson 5	Motown 1171
❹	7	6	The Tears Of A Clown	Smokey Robinson & The Miracles	Tamla 54199
⑤	3	11	Fire And Rain	James Taylor	Warner 7423
⑥	5	12	Indiana Wants Me	R. Dean Taylor	Rare Earth 5013
⑦	6	15	Green-Eyed Lady	Sugarloaf	Liberty 56183
⑧	8	12	Somebody's Been Sleeping	100 Proof Aged In Soul	Hot Wax 7004
⑨	9	12	Gypsy Woman	Brian Hyland	Uni 55240
⑩	13	11	Montego Bay	Bobby Bloom	L&R/MGM 157

★ HIGHEST DEBUT ★ POS 55
One Man Band ....Three Dog Night

★ BIGGEST MOVER ★ 48 to 22
Stoned Love................................The Supremes

Billboard — NOVEMBER 28, 1970 — HOT 100

TW	LW	WK	Title	Artist	Label
①	1	8	I Think I Love You	The Partridge Family	Bell 910
❷	4	7	The Tears Of A Clown	Smokey Robinson & The Miracles	Tamla 54199
③	3	11	I'll Be There	The Jackson 5	Motown 1171
④	2	12	We've Only Just Begun	Carpenters	A&M 1217
⑤	5	12	Fire And Rain	James Taylor	Warner 7423
❻	9	13	Gypsy Woman	Brian Hyland	Uni 55240
⑦	6	13	Indiana Wants Me	R. Dean Taylor	Rare Earth 5013
⑧	10	12	Montego Bay	Bobby Bloom	L&R/MGM 157
⑨	16	7	Heaven Help Us All	Stevie Wonder	Tamla 54200
⑩	7	16	Green-Eyed Lady	Sugarloaf	Liberty 56183

★ HIGHEST DEBUT ★ POS 51
River Deep - Mountain High ....The Supremes & Four Tops

★ BIGGEST MOVER ★ 90 to 65
Knock Three Times................................Dawn

Billboard HOT 100 — DECEMBER 5, 1970

TW	LW	WK	Title / Artist / Label
1	1	9	**I Think I Love You**...............................*The Partridge Family* ... Bell 910
2	2	8	**The Tears Of A Clown** ....*Smokey Robinson & The Miracles* ... Tamla 54199
3	6	14	**Gypsy Woman** ....*Brian Hyland* ... Uni 55240
4	3	12	**I'll Be There**...*The Jackson 5* ... Motown 1171
5	4	13	**We've Only Just Begun** ....*Carpenters* ... A&M 1217
6	5	13	**Fire And Rain**..*James Taylor* ... Warner 7423
7	25	7	**One Less Bell To Answer**..........................*The 5th Dimension* ... Bell 940
8	24	6	**No Matter What**...*Badfinger* ... Apple 1822
9	9	8	**Heaven Help Us All**.............................*Stevie Wonder* ... Tamla 54200
10	16	7	**Share The Land**..*The Guess Who* ... RCA 0388

★ **HIGHEST DEBUT** ★ POS 79
The Green Grass Starts To Grow............*Dionne Warwick*

★ **BIGGEST MOVER** ★ 72 to 13
My Sweet Lord/Isn't It A Pity......*George Harrison*

Billboard HOT 100 — DECEMBER 12, 1970

TW	LW	WK	Title / Artist / Label
1	2	9	**The Tears Of A Clown** .... *Smokey Robinson & The Miracles* ... Tamla 54199
2	1	10	**I Think I Love You**...............................*The Partridge Family* ... Bell 910
3	3	15	**Gypsy Woman** ....*Brian Hyland* ... Uni 55240
4	7	8	**One Less Bell To Answer**.......................*The 5th Dimension* ... Bell 940
5	4	13	**I'll Be There**...*The Jackson 5* ... Motown 1171
6	13	3	**My Sweet Lord/Isn't It A Pity** ....*George Harrison* ... Apple 2995
7	17	5	**Black Magic Woman**...............................*Santana* ... Columbia 45270
8	8	7	**No Matter What**...*Badfinger* ... Apple 1822
9	16	6	**Does Anybody Really Know What Time It Is?**.....................*Chicago* ... Columbia 45264
10	10	8	**Share The Land**..*The Guess Who* ... RCA 0388

★ **HIGHEST DEBUT** ★ POS 67
Love The One You're With............*Stephen Stills*

★ **BIGGEST MOVER** ★ 81 to 56
Lonely Days......................................*Bee Gees*

Billboard HOT 100 — DECEMBER 19, 1970

TW	LW	WK	Title / Artist / Label
1	1	10	**The Tears Of A Clown** .... *Smokey Robinson & The Miracles* ... Tamla 54199
2	6	4	**My Sweet Lord/Isn't It A Pity** ....*George Harrison* ... Apple 2995
3	4	9	**One Less Bell To Answer**.......................*The 5th Dimension* ... Bell 940
4	2	11	**I Think I Love You**...............................*The Partridge Family* ... Bell 910
5	7	6	**Black Magic Woman**...............................*Santana* ... Columbia 45270
6	20	5	**Knock Three Times**...*Dawn* ... Bell 938
7	12	7	**Stoned Love**...*The Supremes* ... Motown 1172
8	9	7	**Does Anybody Really Know What Time It Is?**...................... *Chicago* ... Columbia 45264
9	3	16	**Gypsy Woman**...*Brian Hyland* ... Uni 55240
10	8	8	**No Matter What**...*Badfinger* ... Apple 1822

★ **HIGHEST DEBUT** ★ POS 62
Stop The War Now..........................*Edwin Starr*

★ **BIGGEST MOVER** ★ 67 to 39
Love The One You're With............*Stephen Stills*

TW	LW	WK	Billboard.	DECEMBER 26, 1970	HOT 100.
①	2	5	**My Sweet Lord/Isn't It A Pity**.................................*George Harrison* ... Apple 2995		
②	3	10	**One Less Bell To Answer**.....................*The 5th Dimension* ... Bell 940		
③	1	11	**The Tears Of A Clown** ....*Smokey Robinson & The Miracles* ... Tamla 54199		
④	6	6	**Knock Three Times**...*Dawn* ... Bell 938		
⑤	5	7	**Black Magic Woman**......................................*Santana* ... Columbia 45270		
⑥	4	12	**I Think I Love You**.................................*The Partridge Family* ... Bell 910		
⑦	7	8	**Stoned Love**...*The Supremes* ... Motown 1172		
⑧	8	8	**Does Anybody Really Know What Time It Is?**.........................*Chicago* ... Columbia 45264		
⑨	9	17	**Gypsy Woman**....................................*Brian Hyland* ... Uni 55240		
⑩	10	9	**No Matter What**..................................*Badfinger* ... Apple 1822		

★ *HIGHEST DEBUT* ★ POS 56	★ *BIGGEST MOVER* ★ 88 to 69
I Really Don't Want To Know/There Goes My Everything ....*Elvis Presley*	They Can't Take Away Our Music.....*Eric Burdon & War*

Billboard — JANUARY 2, 1971 — HOT 100

TW	LW	WK	Title / Artist
①	1	6	**My Sweet Lord/Isn't It A Pity**...............*George Harrison* . . . Apple 2995
②	2	11	**One Less Bell To Answer**.............*The 5th Dimension* . . . Bell 940
❸	4	7	**Knock Three Times**.............................*Dawn* . . . Bell 938
④	3	12	**The Tears Of A Clown** ....*Smokey Robinson & The Miracles* . . . Tamla 54199
⑤	5	8	**Black Magic Woman**.........................*Santana* . . . Columbia 45270
⑥	6	13	**I Think I Love You**...................*The Partridge Family* . . . Bell 910
⑦	8	9	**Does Anybody Really Know What Time It Is?** .... *Chicago* . . . Columbia 45264
⑧	7	9	**Stoned Love** ....*The Supremes* . . . Motown 1172
⑨	12	8	**Domino** ....*Van Morrison* . . . Warner 7434
⑩	9	18	**Gypsy Woman** ....*Brian Hyland* . . . Uni 55240

★ HIGHEST DEBUT ★ POS 53	★ BIGGEST MOVER ★ 90 to 62
Get Up, Get Into It, Get Involved ....*James Brown*	I Hear You Knocking ....*Dave Edmunds*

Billboard — JANUARY 9, 1971 — HOT 100

TW	LW	WK	Title / Artist
①	1	7	**My Sweet Lord/Isn't It A Pity**.......................*George Harrison* . . . Apple 2995
❷	3	8	**Knock Three Times**.............................*Dawn* . . . Bell 938
③	2	12	**One Less Bell To Answer**.............*The 5th Dimension* . . . Bell 940
④	5	9	**Black Magic Woman** ....*Santana* . . . Columbia 45270
⑤	6	14	**I Think I Love You**...................*The Partridge Family* . . . Bell 910
⑥	4	13	**The Tears Of A Clown** ....*Smokey Robinson & The Miracles* . . . Tamla 54199
⑦	7	10	**Does Anybody Really Know What Time It Is?** .... *Chicago* . . . Columbia 45264
⑧	8	10	**Stoned Love** ....*The Supremes* . . . Motown 1172
⑨	21	6	**Lonely Days**...........................*Bee Gees* . . . Atco 6795
⑩	12	11	**Stoney End**......................*Barbra Streisand* . . . Columbia 45236

★ HIGHEST DEBUT ★ POS 85	★ BIGGEST MOVER ★ 76 to 49
When I'm Dead And Gone.........*McGuinness Flint*	(Do The) Push And Pull................*Rufus Thomas*

Billboard — JANUARY 16, 1971 — HOT 100

TW	LW	WK	Title / Artist
①	1	8	**My Sweet Lord/Isn't It A Pity**...................*George Harrison* . . . Apple 2995
②	2	9	**Knock Three Times**.............................*Dawn* . . . Bell 938
③	3	13	**One Less Bell To Answer**.............*The 5th Dimension* . . . Bell 940
④	4	10	**Black Magic Woman** ....*Santana* . . . Columbia 45270
⑤	5	15	**I Think I Love You**...................*The Partridge Family* . . . Bell 910
❻	9	7	**Lonely Days**...........................*Bee Gees* . . . Atco 6795
❼	11	13	**Groove Me** ....*King Floyd* . . . Chimneyville 435
⑧	8	11	**Stoned Love** ....*The Supremes* . . . Motown 1172
⑨	10	12	**Stoney End**......................*Barbra Streisand* . . . Columbia 45236
⑩	6	14	**The Tears Of A Clown** ....*Smokey Robinson & The Miracles* . . . Tamla 54199

★ HIGHEST DEBUT ★ POS 81	★ BIGGEST MOVER ★ 87 to 60
Theme From Love Story ....*Henry Mancini*	Mother...................*John Lennon/Plastic Ono Band*

TW	LW	WK	Billboard. ⊙ JANUARY 23, 1971 ⊙ HOT 100.
①	2	10	**Knock Three Times** ....*Dawn* . . . Bell 938
②	1	9	My Sweet Lord/Isn't It A Pity ....*George Harrison* . . . Apple 2995
③	3	14	One Less Bell To Answer...........................*The 5th Dimension* . . . Bell 940
④	6	8	Lonely Days...*Bee Gees* . . . Atco 6795
⑤	4	11	Black Magic Woman..*Santana* . . . Columbia 45270
⑥	9	13	**Stoney End** ....*Barbra Streisand* . . . Columbia 45236
⑦	7	14	Groove Me ....*King Floyd* . . . Chimneyville 435
⑧	11	9	**Your Song** ....*Elton John* . . . Uni 55265
⑨	15	9	Rose Garden ....*Lynn Anderson* . . . Columbia 45252
⑩	12	11	**It's Impossible** ....*Perry Como* . . . RCA 0387

★ *HIGHEST DEBUT* ★ POS 79	★ *BIGGEST MOVER* ★ 81 to 53
Just Seven Numbers (Can Straighten Out My Life).............................*Four Tops*	Theme From Love Story ....*Henry Mancini*

TW	LW	WK	Billboard. ⊙ JANUARY 30, 1971 ⊙ HOT 100.
①	1	11	**Knock Three Times** ....*Dawn* . . . Bell 938
②	2	10	My Sweet Lord/Isn't It A Pity ....*George Harrison* . . . Apple 2995
③	4	9	**Lonely Days** ....*Bee Gees* . . . Atco 6795
④	3	15	One Less Bell To Answer...........................*The 5th Dimension* . . . Bell 940
⑤	9	10	**Rose Garden** ....*Lynn Anderson* . . . Columbia 45252
⑥	7	15	**Groove Me** ....*King Floyd* . . . Chimneyville 435
⑦	16	6	I Hear You Knocking ....*Dave Edmunds* . . . MAM 3601
⑧	8	10	**Your Song** ....*Elton John* . . . Uni 55265
⑨	34	5	One Bad Apple ....*The Osmonds* . . . MGM 14193
⑩	6	14	Stoney End...*Barbra Streisand* . . . Columbia 45236

★ *HIGHEST DEBUT* ★ POS 47	★ *BIGGEST MOVER* ★ 34 to 9
Mama's Pearl ....*The Jackson 5*	One Bad Apple............................*The Osmonds*

TW	LW	WK	Billboard. ⊙ FEBRUARY 6, 1971 ⊙ HOT 100.
①	1	12	**Knock Three Times** ....*Dawn* . . . Bell 938
②	9	6	One Bad Apple ....*The Osmonds* . . . MGM 14193
③	2	11	My Sweet Lord/Isn't It A Pity ....*George Harrison* . . . Apple 2995
④	3	10	Lonely Days...*Bee Gees* . . . Atco 6795
⑤	5	11	Rose Garden ....*Lynn Anderson* . . . Columbia 45252
⑥	7	7	I Hear You Knocking ....*Dave Edmunds* . . . MAM 3601
⑦	6	16	Groove Me ....*King Floyd* . . . Chimneyville 435
⑧	8	11	**Your Song** ....*Elton John* . . . Uni 55265
⑨	4	16	One Less Bell To Answer...........................*The 5th Dimension* . . . Bell 940
⑩	11	11	If I Were Your Woman................*Gladys Knight & The Pips* . . . Soul 35078

★ *HIGHEST DEBUT* ★ POS 60	★ *BIGGEST MOVER* ★ 99 to 63
She's A Lady.................................*Tom Jones*	Proud Mary ....*Ike & Tina Turner*

TW	LW	WK	Billboard	FEBRUARY 13, 1971	HOT 100
①	2	7	One Bad Apple	...............................*The Osmonds* ... MGM 14193	
②	1	13	Knock Three Times	....*Dawn* ... Bell 938	
③	5	12	Rose Garden	...............................*Lynn Anderson* ... Columbia 45252	
④	6	8	I Hear You Knocking	...............................*Dave Edmunds* ... MAM 3601	
⑤	4	11	Lonely Days	....*Bee Gees* ... Atco 6795	
⑥	3	12	My Sweet Lord/Isn't It A Pity	...................*George Harrison* ... Apple 2995	
⑦	7	17	Groove Me	....*King Floyd* ... Chimneyville 435	
⑧	8	12	Your Song	....*Elton John* ... Uni 55265	
⑨	10	12	If I Were Your Woman	..............*Gladys Knight & The Pips* ... Soul 35078	
⑩	25	3	Mama's Pearl	...............................*The Jackson 5* ... Motown 1177	

★ **HIGHEST DEBUT** ★ POS 57
Doesn't Somebody Want To Be Wanted......*The Partridge Family*

★ **BIGGEST MOVER** ★ 87 to 39
For All We Know ....*Carpenters*

TW	LW	WK	Billboard	FEBRUARY 20, 1971	HOT 100
①	1	8	One Bad Apple	....*The Osmonds* ... MGM 14193	
②	2	14	Knock Three Times	....*Dawn* ... Bell 938	
③	3	13	Rose Garden	...............................*Lynn Anderson* ... Columbia 45252	
④	4	9	I Hear You Knocking	...............................*Dave Edmunds* ... MAM 3601	
⑤	11	9	If You Could Read My Mind	.............*Gordon Lightfoot* ... Reprise 0974	
⑥	10	4	Mama's Pearl	...............................*The Jackson 5* ... Motown 1177	
⑦	7	18	Groove Me	...............................*King Floyd* ... Chimneyville 435	
⑧	15	9	Sweet Mary	...............................*Wadsworth Mansion* ... Sussex 209	
⑨	14	14	Mr. Bojangles	...............................*Nitty Gritty Dirt Band* ... Liberty 56197	
⑩	5	12	Lonely Days	....*Bee Gees* ... Atco 6795	

★ **HIGHEST DEBUT** ★ POS 81
What's Going On ....*Marvin Gaye*

★ **BIGGEST MOVER** ★ 51 to 29
Just My Imagination (Running Away With Me)...........................*The Temptations*

TW	LW	WK	Billboard	FEBRUARY 27, 1971	HOT 100
①	1	9	One Bad Apple	...............................*The Osmonds* ... MGM 14193	
②	6	5	Mama's Pearl	...............................*The Jackson 5* ... Motown 1177	
③	2	15	Knock Three Times	....*Dawn* ... Bell 938	
④	3	14	Rose Garden	...............................*Lynn Anderson* ... Columbia 45252	
⑤	5	10	If You Could Read My Mind	.............*Gordon Lightfoot* ... Reprise 0974	
⑥	4	10	I Hear You Knocking	...............................*Dave Edmunds* ... MAM 3601	
⑦	8	10	Sweet Mary	...............................*Wadsworth Mansion* ... Sussex 209	
⑧	12	18	Amos Moses	...............................*Jerry Reed* ... RCA 9904	
⑨	9	15	Mr. Bojangles	...............................*Nitty Gritty Dirt Band* ... Liberty 56197	
⑩	25	5	Me And Bobby McGee	...............................*Janis Joplin* ... Columbia 45314	

★ **HIGHEST DEBUT** ★ POS 66
What Is Life ....*George Harrison*

★ **BIGGEST MOVER** ★ 91 to 46
You're All I Need To Get By.........*Aretha Franklin*

Billboard — MARCH 6, 1971 — HOT 100

TW	LW	WK		
①	1	10	**One Bad Apple**	The Osmonds ... MGM 14193
②	2	6	**Mama's Pearl**	The Jackson 5 ... Motown 1177
③	10	6	**Me And Bobby McGee**	Janis Joplin ... Columbia 45314
④	16	5	**Just My Imagination (Running Away With Me)**	The Temptations ... Gordy 7105
⑤	5	11	**If You Could Read My Mind**	Gordon Lightfoot ... Reprise 0974
⑥	17	5	**She's A Lady**	Tom Jones ... Parrot 40058
⑦	12	5	**For All We Know**	Carpenters ... A&M 1243
⑧	8	19	**Amos Moses**	Jerry Reed ... RCA 9904
⑨	9	16	**Mr. Bojangles**	Nitty Gritty Dirt Band ... Liberty 56197
⑩	7	11	**Sweet Mary**	Wadsworth Mansion ... Sussex 209

★ **HIGHEST DEBUT** ★ POS 55
Another Day ... Paul McCartney

★ **BIGGEST MOVER** ★ 66 to 27
What Is Life ... George Harrison

Billboard — MARCH 13, 1971 — HOT 100

TW	LW	WK		
①	1	11	**One Bad Apple**	The Osmonds ... MGM 14193
②	3	7	**Me And Bobby McGee**	Janis Joplin ... Columbia 45314
③	7	6	**For All We Know**	Carpenters ... A&M 1243
④	4	6	**Just My Imagination (Running Away With Me)**	The Temptations ... Gordy 7105
⑤	6	6	**She's A Lady**	Tom Jones ... Parrot 40058
⑥	2	7	**Mama's Pearl**	The Jackson 5 ... Motown 1177
⑦	12	7	**Proud Mary**	Ike & Tina Turner ... Liberty 56216
⑧	11	7	**Have You Ever Seen The Rain**	Creedence Clearwater Revival ... Fantasy 655
⑨	15	5	**Doesn't Somebody Want To Be Wanted**	The Partridge Family ... Bell 963
⑩	5	12	**If You Could Read My Mind**	Gordon Lightfoot ... Reprise 0974

★ **HIGHEST DEBUT** ★ POS 53
Dream Baby (How Long Must I Dream) ... Glen Campbell

★ **BIGGEST MOVER** ★ 99 to 76
Stay Awhile ... The Bells

Billboard — MARCH 20, 1971 — HOT 100

TW	LW	WK		
①	2	8	**Me And Bobby McGee**	Janis Joplin ... Columbia 45314
②	5	7	**She's A Lady**	Tom Jones ... Parrot 40058
③	4	7	**Just My Imagination (Running Away With Me)**	The Temptations ... Gordy 7105
④	1	12	**One Bad Apple**	The Osmonds ... MGM 14193
⑤	3	7	**For All We Know**	Carpenters ... A&M 1243
⑥	7	8	**Proud Mary**	Ike & Tina Turner ... Liberty 56216
⑦	9	6	**Doesn't Somebody Want To Be Wanted**	The Partridge Family ... Bell 963
⑧	18	5	**What's Going On**	Marvin Gaye ... Tamla 54201
⑨	15	10	**Help Me Make It Through The Night**	Sammi Smith ... Mega 0015
⑩	10	13	**If You Could Read My Mind**	Gordon Lightfoot ... Reprise 0974

★ **HIGHEST DEBUT** ★ POS 72
I Won't Mention It Again ... Ray Price

★ **BIGGEST MOVER** ★ 76 to 56
Stay Awhile ... The Bells

Billboard HOT 100 — MARCH 27, 1971

TW	LW	WK	Title	Artist	Label
①	1	9	Me And Bobby McGee	Janis Joplin	Columbia 45314
❷	3	8	Just My Imagination (Running Away With Me)	The Temptations	Gordy 7105
③	2	8	She's A Lady	Tom Jones	Parrot 40058
④	6	9	Proud Mary	Ike & Tina Turner	Liberty 56216
⑤	5	8	For All We Know	Carpenters	A&M 1243
⑥	7	7	Doesn't Somebody Want To Be Wanted	The Partridge Family	Bell 963
❼	8	6	What's Going On	Marvin Gaye	Tamla 54201
⑧	9	11	Help Me Make It Through The Night	Sammi Smith	Mega 0015
⑨	4	13	One Bad Apple	The Osmonds	MGM 14193
❿	15	5	What Is Life	George Harrison	Apple 1828

★ **HIGHEST DEBUT** ★ POS 45
I Am...I Said ....Neil Diamond

★ **BIGGEST MOVER** ★ 71 to 37
Put Your Hand In The Hand ....Ocean

Billboard HOT 100 — APRIL 3, 1971

TW	LW	WK	Title	Artist	Label
①	2	9	Just My Imagination (Running Away With Me)	The Temptations	Gordy 7105
②	1	10	Me And Bobby McGee	Janis Joplin	Columbia 45314
③	5	9	For All We Know	Carpenters	A&M 1243
④	3	9	She's A Lady	Tom Jones	Parrot 40058
❺	7	7	What's Going On	Marvin Gaye	Tamla 54201
⑥	4	10	Proud Mary	Ike & Tina Turner	Liberty 56216
⑦	6	8	Doesn't Somebody Want To Be Wanted	The Partridge Family	Bell 963
⑧	8	12	Help Me Make It Through The Night	Sammi Smith	Mega 0015
❾	11	9	(Where Do I Begin) Love Story	Andy Williams	Columbia 45317
❿	14	5	Another Day/Oh Woman Oh Why	Paul McCartney	Apple 1829

★ **HIGHEST DEBUT** ★ POS 57
Never Can Say Goodbye ....The Jackson 5

★ **BIGGEST MOVER** ★ 72 to 39
If ....Bread

Billboard HOT 100 — APRIL 10, 1971

TW	LW	WK	Title	Artist	Label
①	1	10	Just My Imagination (Running Away With Me)	The Temptations	Gordy 7105
❷	5	8	What's Going On	Marvin Gaye	Tamla 54201
❸	11	5	Joy To The World	Three Dog Night	Dunhill 4272
④	4	10	She's A Lady	Tom Jones	Parrot 40058
⑤	3	10	For All We Know	Carpenters	A&M 1243
⑥	2	11	Me And Bobby McGee	Janis Joplin	Columbia 45314
⑦	7	9	Doesn't Somebody Want To Be Wanted	The Partridge Family	Bell 963
⑧	10	6	Another Day/Oh Woman Oh Why	Paul McCartney	Apple 1829
⑨	6	11	Proud Mary	Ike & Tina Turner	Liberty 56216
❿	16	9	One Toke Over The Line	Brewer & Shipley	Kama Sutra 516

★ **HIGHEST DEBUT** ★ POS 74
Love Her Madly ....The Doors

★ **BIGGEST MOVER** ★ 57 to 15
Never Can Say Goodbye ....The Jackson 5

Billboard HOT 100 — APRIL 17, 1971

TW	LW	WK	Title	Artist	Label
1	3	6	Joy To The World	Three Dog Night	Dunhill 4272
2	2	9	What's Going On	Marvin Gaye	Tamla 54201
3	1	11	Just My Imagination (Running Away With Me)	The Temptations	Gordy 7105
4	4	11	She's A Lady	Tom Jones	Parrot 40058
5	8	7	Another Day/Oh Woman Oh Why	Paul McCartney	Apple 1829
6	16	6	Put Your Hand In The Hand	Ocean	Kama Sutra 519
7	6	12	Me And Bobby McGee	Janis Joplin	Columbia 45314
8	7	10	Doesn't Somebody Want To Be Wanted	The Partridge Family	Bell 963
9	5	11	For All We Know	Carpenters	A&M 1243
10	10	10	One Toke Over The Line	Brewer & Shipley	Kama Sutra 516

★ **HIGHEST DEBUT** ★ POS 57
Bridge Over Troubled Water.........Aretha Franklin

★ **BIGGEST MOVER** ★ 74 to 45
Love Her Madly ....The Doors

Billboard HOT 100 — APRIL 24, 1971

TW	LW	WK	Title	Artist	Label
1	1	7	Joy To The World	Three Dog Night	Dunhill 4272
2	2	10	What's Going On	Marvin Gaye	Tamla 54201
3	6	7	Put Your Hand In The Hand	Ocean	Kama Sutra 519
4	13	4	Never Can Say Goodbye	The Jackson 5	Motown 1179
5	5	8	Another Day/Oh Woman Oh Why	Paul McCartney	Apple 1829
6	12	5	I Am...I Said	Neil Diamond	Uni 55278
7	3	12	Just My Imagination (Running Away With Me)	The Temptations	Gordy 7105
8	20	5	If	Bread	Elektra 45720
9	4	12	She's A Lady	Tom Jones	Parrot 40058
10	21	8	Stay Awhile	The Bells	Polydor 15023

★ **HIGHEST DEBUT** ★ POS 41
Battle Hymn Of Lt. Calley ....C Company Featuring Terry Nelson

★ **BIGGEST MOVER** ★ 57 to 24
Bridge Over Troubled Water.........Aretha Franklin

Billboard HOT 100 — MAY 1, 1971

TW	LW	WK	Title	Artist	Label
1	1	8	Joy To The World	Three Dog Night	Dunhill 4272
2	3	8	Put Your Hand In The Hand	Ocean	Kama Sutra 519
3	4	5	Never Can Say Goodbye	The Jackson 5	Motown 1179
4	2	11	What's Going On	Marvin Gaye	Tamla 54201
5	6	6	I Am...I Said	Neil Diamond	Uni 55278
6	8	6	If	Bread	Elektra 45720
7	10	9	Stay Awhile	The Bells	Polydor 15023
8	5	9	Another Day/Oh Woman Oh Why	Paul McCartney	Apple 1829
9	7	13	Just My Imagination (Running Away With Me)	The Temptations	Gordy 7105
10	17	9	Chick-A-Boom	Daddy Dewdrop	Sunflower 105

★ **HIGHEST DEBUT** ★ POS 40
Brown Sugar ....The Rolling Stones

★ **BIGGEST MOVER** ★ 96 to 61
Don't Knock My Love ....Wilson Pickett

Billboard — MAY 8, 1971 — HOT 100

TW	LW	WK	Title	Artist	Label
1	1	9	Joy To The World	Three Dog Night	Dunhill 4272
2	3	6	Never Can Say Goodbye	The Jackson 5	Motown 1179
3	2	9	Put Your Hand In The Hand	Ocean	Kama Sutra 519
4	5	7	I Am...I Said	Neil Diamond	Uni 55278
5	6	7	If	Bread	Elektra 45720
6	4	12	What's Going On	Marvin Gaye	Tamla 54201
7	7	10	Stay Awhile	The Bells	Polydor 15023
8	12	4	Bridge Over Troubled Water	Aretha Franklin	Atlantic 2796
9	10	10	Chick-A-Boom	Daddy Dewdrop	Sunflower 105
10	16	6	Me And You And A Dog Named Boo	Lobo	Big Tree 112

★ **HIGHEST DEBUT** ★ POS 61
When You're Hot, You're Hot............Jerry Reed

★ **BIGGEST MOVER** ★ 90 to 50
The Drum ....Bobby Sherman

Billboard — MAY 15, 1971 — HOT 100

TW	LW	WK	Title	Artist	Label
1	1	10	Joy To The World	Three Dog Night	Dunhill 4272
2	2	7	Never Can Say Goodbye	The Jackson 5	Motown 1179
3	3	10	Put Your Hand In The Hand	Ocean	Kama Sutra 519
4	5	8	If	Bread	Elektra 45720
5	10	7	Me And You And A Dog Named Boo	Lobo	Big Tree 112
6	13	3	Brown Sugar	The Rolling Stones	Rolling Stones 19100
7	8	5	Bridge Over Troubled Water	Aretha Franklin	Atlantic 2796
8	7	11	Stay Awhile	The Bells	Polydor 15023
9	4	8	I Am...I Said	Neil Diamond	Uni 55278
10	9	11	Chick-A-Boom	Daddy Dewdrop	Sunflower 105

★ **HIGHEST DEBUT** ★ POS 46
Rainy Days And Mondays.................Carpenters

★ **BIGGEST MOVER** ★ 84 to 47
It's Too Late ....Carole King

Billboard — MAY 22, 1971 — HOT 100

TW	LW	WK	Title	Artist	Label
1	1	11	Joy To The World	Three Dog Night	Dunhill 4272
2	2	8	Never Can Say Goodbye	The Jackson 5	Motown 1179
3	6	4	Brown Sugar	The Rolling Stones	Rolling Stones 19100
4	3	11	Put Your Hand In The Hand	Ocean	Kama Sutra 519
5	5	8	Me And You And A Dog Named Boo	Lobo	Big Tree 112
6	12	7	Want Ads	The Honey Cone	Hot Wax 7011
7	7	6	Bridge Over Troubled Water	Aretha Franklin	Atlantic 2796
8	13	4	It Don't Come Easy	Ringo Starr	Apple 1831
9	4	9	If	Bread	Elektra 45720
10	10	12	Chick-A-Boom	Daddy Dewdrop	Sunflower 105

★ **HIGHEST DEBUT** ★ POS 79
High Time We Went ....Joe Cocker

★ **BIGGEST MOVER** ★ 90 to 53
Double Lovin' ....The Osmonds

Billboard — HOT 100 — MAY 29, 1971

TW	LW	WK	Title	Artist	Label
❶	3	5	Brown Sugar	The Rolling Stones	Rolling Stones 19100
②	1	12	Joy To The World	Three Dog Night	Dunhill 4272
③	2	9	Never Can Say Goodbye	The Jackson 5	Motown 1179
④	6	8	Want Ads	The Honey Cone	Hot Wax 7011
⑤	8	5	It Don't Come Easy	Ringo Starr	Apple 1831
⑥	4	12	Put Your Hand In The Hand	Ocean	Kama Sutra 519
⑦	7	7	Bridge Over Troubled Water	Aretha Franklin	Atlantic 2796
⑧	13	10	Sweet And Innocent	Donny Osmond	MGM 14227
⑨	5	9	Me And You And A Dog Named Boo	Lobo	Big Tree 112
⑩	10	13	Chick-A-Boom	Daddy Dewdrop	Sunflower 105

★ HIGHEST DEBUT ★ POS 89	★ BIGGEST MOVER ★ 88 to 57
Walk Away ......The James Gang	Puppet Man......Tom Jones

Billboard — HOT 100 — JUNE 5, 1971

TW	LW	WK	Title	Artist	Label
①	1	6	Brown Sugar	The Rolling Stones	Rolling Stones 19100
②	2	13	Joy To The World	Three Dog Night	Dunhill 4272
③	4	9	Want Ads	The Honey Cone	Hot Wax 7011
④	5	6	It Don't Come Easy	Ringo Starr	Apple 1831
⑤	11	4	Rainy Days And Mondays	Carpenters	A&M 1260
⑥	7	8	Bridge Over Troubled Water	Aretha Franklin	Atlantic 2796
⑦	8	11	Sweet And Innocent	Donny Osmond	MGM 14227
⑧	3	10	Never Can Say Goodbye	The Jackson 5	Motown 1179
⑨	21	5	It's Too Late	Carole King	Ode 66015
⑩	9	10	Me And You And A Dog Named Boo	Lobo	Big Tree 112

★ HIGHEST DEBUT ★ POS 66	★ BIGGEST MOVER ★ 92 to 64
Bring The Boys Home ......Freda Payne	Mr. Big Stuff ......Jean Knight

Billboard — HOT 100 — JUNE 12, 1971

TW	LW	WK	Title	Artist	Label
①	3	10	Want Ads	The Honey Cone	Hot Wax 7011
②	1	7	Brown Sugar	The Rolling Stones	Rolling Stones 19100
③	5	5	Rainy Days And Mondays	Carpenters	A&M 1260
④	4	7	It Don't Come Easy	Ringo Starr	Apple 1831
⑤	2	14	Joy To The World	Three Dog Night	Dunhill 4272
⑥	9	6	It's Too Late/I Feel The Earth Move	Carole King	Ode 66015
⑦	7	12	Sweet And Innocent	Donny Osmond	MGM 14227
⑧	15	10	Treat Her Like A Lady	Cornelius Brothers & Sister Rose	United Artists 50721
⑨	11	6	I'll Meet You Halfway	The Partridge Family	Bell 996
⑩	6	9	Bridge Over Troubled Water/Brand New Me	Aretha Franklin	Atlantic 2796

★ HIGHEST DEBUT ★ POS 75	★ BIGGEST MOVER ★ 91 to 47
Escape-ism ......James Brown	I Don't Want To Do Wrong.....Gladys Knight & The Pips

Billboard — JUNE 19, 1971 — HOT 100

TW	LW	WK	Title	Artist / Label
1	6	7	**It's Too Late/I Feel The Earth Move**............................ *Carole King* ... Ode 66015
2	3	6	**Rainy Days And Mondays** ....*Carpenters* ... A&M 1260
③	1	11	**Want Ads**...*The Honey Cone* ... Hot Wax 7011
④	2	8	**Brown Sugar** ....*The Rolling Stones* ... Rolling Stones 19100
⑤	4	8	**It Don't Come Easy**...*Ringo Starr* ... Apple 1831
6	8	11	**Treat Her Like A Lady**.......................... *Cornelius Brothers & Sister Rose* ... United Artists 50721
7	11	11	**Indian Reservation** ....*Raiders* ... Columbia 45332
⑧	5	15	**Joy To The World**.....................................*Three Dog Night* ... Dunhill 4272
⑨	9	7	**I'll Meet You Halfway** ....*The Partridge Family* ... Bell 996
⑩	7	13	**Sweet And Innocent** ....*Donny Osmond* ... MGM 14227

★ **HIGHEST DEBUT** ★ POS 72
Love The One You're With ....*The Isley Brothers*

★ **BIGGEST MOVER** ★ 87 to 59
Stop, Look, Listen (To Your Heart) ....*The Stylistics*

Billboard — JUNE 26, 1971 — HOT 100

TW	LW	WK	Title	Artist / Label
①	1	8	**It's Too Late/I Feel The Earth Move**............................ *Carole King* ... Ode 66015
②	2	7	**Rainy Days And Mondays** ....*Carpenters* ... A&M 1260
③	3	12	**Want Ads**...*The Honey Cone* ... Hot Wax 7011
4	7	12	**Indian Reservation** ....*Raiders* ... Columbia 45332
⑤	6	12	**Treat Her Like A Lady**.......................... *Cornelius Brothers & Sister Rose* ... United Artists 50721
⑥	4	9	**Brown Sugar** ....*The Rolling Stones* ... Rolling Stones 19100
⑦	5	9	**It Don't Come Easy**...*Ringo Starr* ... Apple 1831
8	19	6	**Don't Pull Your Love**..........*Hamilton, Joe Frank & Reynolds* ... Dunhill 4276
9	12	8	**When You're Hot, You're Hot** ....*Jerry Reed* ... RCA 9976
⑩	10	14	**Sweet And Innocent** ....*Donny Osmond* ... MGM 14227

★ **HIGHEST DEBUT** ★ POS 70
Moon Shadow..................................*Cat Stevens*

★ **BIGGEST MOVER** ★ 85 to 47
Wild Horses ....*The Rolling Stones*

Billboard — JULY 3, 1971 — HOT 100

TW	LW	WK	Title	Artist / Label
①	1	9	**It's Too Late/I Feel The Earth Move**............................ *Carole King* ... Ode 66015
2	4	13	**Indian Reservation** ....*Raiders* ... Columbia 45332
③	5	13	**Treat Her Like A Lady** .... *Cornelius Brothers & Sister Rose* ... United Artists 50721
④	2	8	**Rainy Days And Mondays** ....*Carpenters* ... A&M 1260
5	8	7	**Don't Pull Your Love**..........*Hamilton, Joe Frank & Reynolds* ... Dunhill 4276
⑥	3	13	**Want Ads**...*The Honey Cone* ... Hot Wax 7011
⑦	6	10	**Brown Sugar** ....*The Rolling Stones* ... Rolling Stones 19100
8	14	5	**You've Got A Friend**.................................*James Taylor* ... Warner 7498
⑨	9	9	**When You're Hot, You're Hot** ....*Jerry Reed* ... RCA 9976
⑩	7	10	**It Don't Come Easy**...*Ringo Starr* ... Apple 1831

★ **HIGHEST DEBUT** ★ POS 70
Mercy Mercy Me (The Ecology) ....*Marvin Gaye*

★ **BIGGEST MOVER** ★ 73 to 39
How Can You Mend A Broken Heart......*The Bee Gees*

Billboard — JULY 10, 1971 — HOT 100

TW	LW	WK		
①	1	10	**It's Too Late/I Feel The Earth Move**	*Carole King* ... Ode 66015
②	2	14	**Indian Reservation**	*Raiders* ... Columbia 45332
③	3	14	**Treat Her Like A Lady**	*Cornelius Brothers & Sister Rose* ... United Artists 50721
④	4	9	**Rainy Days And Mondays**	*Carpenters* ... A&M 1260
⑤	5	8	**Don't Pull Your Love**	*Hamilton, Joe Frank & Reynolds* ... Dunhill 4276
⑥	8	6	**You've Got A Friend**	*James Taylor* ... Warner 7498
❼	12	7	**Mr. Big Stuff**	*Jean Knight* ... Stax 0088
⑧	6	14	**Want Ads**	*The Honey Cone* ... Hot Wax 7011
⑨	9	10	**When You're Hot, You're Hot**	*Jerry Reed* ... RCA 9976
⑩	16	13	**That's The Way I've Always Heard It Should Be**	*Carly Simon* ... Elektra 45724

★ **HIGHEST DEBUT** ★ POS 72
Liar...*Three Dog Night*

★ **BIGGEST MOVER** ★ 88 to 49
Hot Pants (She Got To Use What She Got, To Get What She Wants)................*James Brown*

Billboard — JULY 17, 1971 — HOT 100

TW	LW	WK		
①	1	11	**It's Too Late/I Feel The Earth Move**	*Carole King* ... Ode 66015
②	2	15	**Indian Reservation**	*Raiders* ... Columbia 45332
❸	6	7	**You've Got A Friend**	*James Taylor* ... Warner 7498
④	5	9	**Don't Pull Your Love**	*Hamilton, Joe Frank & Reynolds* ... Dunhill 4276
⑤	3	15	**Treat Her Like A Lady**	*Cornelius Brothers & Sister Rose* ... United Artists 50721
❻	7	8	**Mr. Big Stuff**	*Jean Knight* ... Stax 0088
⑦	4	10	**Rainy Days And Mondays**	*Carpenters* ... A&M 1260
❽	14	6	**Draggin' The Line**	*Tommy James* ... Roulette 7103
❾	16	4	**How Can You Mend A Broken Heart**	*The Bee Gees* ... Atco 6824
⑩	10	14	**That's The Way I've Always Heard It Should Be**	*Carly Simon* ... Elektra 45724

★ **HIGHEST DEBUT** ★ POS 68
Sweet Hitch-Hiker .....*Creedence Clearwater Revival*

★ **BIGGEST MOVER** ★ 84 to 49
What The World Needs Now Is Love/Abraham, Martin And John ....*Tom Clay*

Billboard — JULY 24, 1971 — HOT 100

TW	LW	WK		
①	2	16	**Indian Reservation**	*Raiders* ... Columbia 45332
②	1	12	**It's Too Late/I Feel The Earth Move**	*Carole King* ... Ode 66015
③	3	8	**You've Got A Friend**	*James Taylor* ... Warner 7498
④	4	10	**Don't Pull Your Love**	*Hamilton, Joe Frank & Reynolds* ... Dunhill 4276
⑤	6	9	**Mr. Big Stuff**	*Jean Knight* ... Stax 0088
⑥	5	16	**Treat Her Like A Lady**	*Cornelius Brothers & Sister Rose* ... United Artists 50721
❼	8	7	**Draggin' The Line**	*Tommy James* ... Roulette 7103
❽	9	5	**How Can You Mend A Broken Heart**	*The Bee Gees* ... Atco 6824
❾	12	14	**Take Me Home, Country Roads**	*John Denver* ... RCA 0445
⑩	13	8	**Sooner Or Later**	*The Grass Roots* ... Dunhill 4279

★ **HIGHEST DEBUT** ★ POS 68
It's Summer..........................*The Temptations*

★ **BIGGEST MOVER** ★ 68 to 37
Sweet Hitch-Hiker .....*Creedence Clearwater Revival*

Billboard — JULY 31, 1971 — HOT 100

TW	LW	WK	Title	Artist ... Label
①	3	9	**You've Got A Friend**	*James Taylor* ... Warner 7498
②	1	17	**Indian Reservation**	*Raiders* ... Columbia 45332
③	2	13	**It's Too Late/I Feel The Earth Move**	*Carole King* ... Ode 66015
④	5	10	**Mr. Big Stuff**	*Jean Knight* ... Stax 0088
⑤	7	8	**Draggin' The Line**	*Tommy James* ... Roulette 7103
⑥	8	6	**How Can You Mend A Broken Heart**	*The Bee Gees* ... Atco 6824
⑦	4	11	**Don't Pull Your Love**	*Hamilton, Joe Frank & Reynolds* ... Dunhill 4276
⑧	9	15	**Take Me Home, Country Roads**	*John Denver* ... RCA 0445
⑨	10	9	**Sooner Or Later**	*The Grass Roots* ... Dunhill 4279
⑩	26	4	**What The World Needs Now Is Love/Abraham, Martin And John**	*Tom Clay* ... Mowest 5002

★ **HIGHEST DEBUT** ★ POS 69
Spanish Harlem .... *Aretha Franklin*

★ **BIGGEST MOVER** ★ 90 to 68
Where You Lead .... *Barbra Streisand*

Billboard — AUGUST 7, 1971 — HOT 100

TW	LW	WK	Title	Artist ... Label
①	6	7	**How Can You Mend A Broken Heart**	*The Bee Gees* ... Atco 6824
②	2	18	**Indian Reservation**	*Raiders* ... Columbia 45332
③	1	10	**You've Got A Friend**	*James Taylor* ... Warner 7498
④	4	11	**Mr. Big Stuff**	*Jean Knight* ... Stax 0088
⑤	5	9	**Draggin' The Line**	*Tommy James* ... Roulette 7103
⑥	8	16	**Take Me Home, Country Roads**	*John Denver* ... RCA 0445
⑦	3	14	**It's Too Late/I Feel The Earth Move**	*Carole King* ... Ode 66015
⑧	16	7	**Beginnings/Colour My World**	*Chicago* ... Columbia 45417
⑨	10	5	**What The World Needs Now Is Love/Abraham, Martin And John**	*Tom Clay* ... Mowest 5002
⑩	11	6	**Mercy Mercy Me (The Ecology)**	*Marvin Gaye* ... Tamla 54207

★ **HIGHEST DEBUT** ★ POS 68
Stick-Up .... *The Honey Cone*

★ **BIGGEST MOVER** ★ 69 to 29
Spanish Harlem .... *Aretha Franklin*

Billboard — AUGUST 14, 1971 — HOT 100

TW	LW	WK	Title	Artist ... Label
①	1	8	**How Can You Mend A Broken Heart**	*The Bee Gees* ... Atco 6824
②	4	12	**Mr. Big Stuff**	*Jean Knight* ... Stax 0088
③	6	17	**Take Me Home, Country Roads**	*John Denver* ... RCA 0445
④	5	10	**Draggin' The Line**	*Tommy James* ... Roulette 7103
⑤	3	11	**You've Got A Friend**	*James Taylor* ... Warner 7498
⑥	2	19	**Indian Reservation**	*Raiders* ... Columbia 45332
⑦	8	8	**Beginnings/Colour My World**	*Chicago* ... Columbia 45417
⑧	9	6	**What The World Needs Now Is Love/Abraham, Martin And John**	*Tom Clay* ... Mowest 5002
⑨	10	7	**Mercy Mercy Me (The Ecology)**	*Marvin Gaye* ... Tamla 54207
⑩	15	12	**Signs**	*Five Man Electrical Band* ... Lionel 3213

★ **HIGHEST DEBUT** ★ POS 63
I Woke Up In Love This Morning ..... *The Partridge Family*

★ **BIGGEST MOVER** ★ 89 to 44
Go Away Little Girl .... *Donny Osmond*

Billboard AUGUST 21, 1971 — HOT 100

TW	LW	WK	Title	Artist	Label
①	1	9	How Can You Mend A Broken Heart	The Bee Gees	Atco 6824
②	2	13	Mr. Big Stuff	Jean Knight	Stax 0088
③	3	18	Take Me Home, Country Roads	John Denver	RCA 0445
④	9	8	Mercy Mercy Me (The Ecology)	Marvin Gaye	Tamla 54207
⑤	5	12	You've Got A Friend	James Taylor	Warner 7498
⑥	15	6	Sweet Hitch-Hiker	Creedence Clearwater Revival	Fantasy 665
⑦	7	9	Beginnings/Colour My World	Chicago	Columbia 45417
⑧	10	13	Signs	Five Man Electrical Band	Lionel 3213
⑨	4	11	Draggin' The Line	Tommy James	Roulette 7103
⑩	14	7	Liar	Three Dog Night	Dunhill 4282

★ **HIGHEST DEBUT** ★ POS 64
Marianne ...... Stephen Stills

★ **BIGGEST MOVER** ★ 65 to 21
Uncle Albert/Admiral Halsey ...... Paul & Linda McCartney

Billboard AUGUST 28, 1971 — HOT 100

TW	LW	WK	Title	Artist	Label
①	1	10	How Can You Mend A Broken Heart	The Bee Gees	Atco 6824
②	3	19	Take Me Home, Country Roads	John Denver	RCA 0445
③	8	14	Signs	Five Man Electrical Band	Lionel 3213
④	4	9	Mercy Mercy Me (The Ecology)	Marvin Gaye	Tamla 54207
⑤	2	14	Mr. Big Stuff	Jean Knight	Stax 0088
⑥	6	7	Sweet Hitch-Hiker	Creedence Clearwater Revival	Fantasy 665
⑦	10	8	Liar	Three Dog Night	Dunhill 4282
⑧	12	10	Smiling Faces Sometimes	The Undisputed Truth	Gordy 7108
⑨	14	5	Spanish Harlem	Aretha Franklin	Atlantic 2817
⑩	24	4	Go Away Little Girl	Donny Osmond	MGM 14285

★ **HIGHEST DEBUT** ★ POS 65
Make It Funky ...... James Brown

★ **BIGGEST MOVER** ★ 99 to 77
Trapped By A Thing Called Love ...... Denise LaSalle

Billboard SEPTEMBER 4, 1971 — HOT 100

TW	LW	WK	Title	Artist	Label
❶	12	4	Uncle Albert/Admiral Halsey	Paul & Linda McCartney	Apple 1837
②	1	11	How Can You Mend A Broken Heart	The Bee Gees	Atco 6824
❸	8	11	Smiling Faces Sometimes	The Undisputed Truth	Gordy 7108
④	9	6	Spanish Harlem	Aretha Franklin	Atlantic 2817
⑤	10	5	Go Away Little Girl	Donny Osmond	MGM 14285
⑥	13	8	Ain't No Sunshine	Bill Withers	Sussex 219
⑦	2	20	Take Me Home, Country Roads	John Denver	RCA 0445
⑧	3	15	Signs	Five Man Electrical Band	Lionel 3213
⑨	7	9	Liar	Three Dog Night	Dunhill 4282
⑩	18	8	I Just Want To Celebrate	Rare Earth	Rare Earth 5031

★ **HIGHEST DEBUT** ★ POS 49
Superstar ...... Carpenters

★ **BIGGEST MOVER** ★ 71 to 39
So Far Away/Smackwater Jack ...... Carole King

TW	LW	WK	Billboard®	SEPTEMBER 11, 1971	HOT 100®
①	5	6	Go Away Little Girl	Donny Osmond	MGM 14285
②	4	7	Spanish Harlem	Aretha Franklin	Atlantic 2817
③	3	12	Smiling Faces Sometimes	The Undisputed Truth	Gordy 7108
④	6	9	Ain't No Sunshine	Bill Withers	Sussex 219
⑤	1	5	Uncle Albert/Admiral Halsey	Paul & Linda McCartney	Apple 1837
⑥	2	12	How Can You Mend A Broken Heart	The Bee Gees	Atco 6824
⑦	10	9	I Just Want To Celebrate	Rare Earth	Rare Earth 5031
⑧	7	21	Take Me Home, Country Roads	John Denver	RCA 0445
⑨	8	16	Signs	Five Man Electrical Band	Lionel 3213
⑩	19	9	Maggie May/Reason To Believe	Rod Stewart	Mercury 73224

★ HIGHEST DEBUT ★ POS 75
One Fine Morning.................Lighthouse

★ BIGGEST MOVER ★ 49 to 17
Superstar.................................Carpenters

TW	LW	WK	Billboard®	SEPTEMBER 18, 1971	HOT 100®
①	1	7	Go Away Little Girl	Donny Osmond	MGM 14285
②	2	8	Spanish Harlem	Aretha Franklin	Atlantic 2817
③	4	10	Ain't No Sunshine	Bill Withers	Sussex 219
④	10	10	Maggie May/Reason To Believe	Rod Stewart	Mercury 73224
⑤	5	6	Uncle Albert/Admiral Halsey	Paul & Linda McCartney	Apple 1837
⑥	3	13	Smiling Faces Sometimes	The Undisputed Truth	Gordy 7108
⑦	7	10	I Just Want To Celebrate	Rare Earth	Rare Earth 5031
⑧	12	6	The Night They Drove Old Dixie Down	Joan Baez	Vanguard 35138
⑨	6	13	How Can You Mend A Broken Heart	The Bee Gees	Atco 6824
⑩	11	12	Whatcha See Is Whatcha Get	Dramatics	Volt 4058

★ HIGHEST DEBUT ★ POS 81
Charity Ball ....Fanny

★ BIGGEST MOVER ★ 85 to 40
Yo-Yo.................................The Osmonds

TW	LW	WK	Billboard®	SEPTEMBER 25, 1971	HOT 100®
①	1	8	Go Away Little Girl	Donny Osmond	MGM 14285
②	4	11	Maggie May/Reason To Believe	Rod Stewart	Mercury 73224
③	3	11	Ain't No Sunshine	Bill Withers	Sussex 219
④	8	7	The Night They Drove Old Dixie Down	Joan Baez	Vanguard 35138
⑤	2	9	Spanish Harlem	Aretha Franklin	Atlantic 2817
⑥	5	7	Uncle Albert/Admiral Halsey	Paul & Linda McCartney	Apple 1837
⑦	6	14	Smiling Faces Sometimes	The Undisputed Truth	Gordy 7108
⑧	12	4	Superstar	Carpenters	A&M 1289
⑨	10	13	Whatcha See Is Whatcha Get	Dramatics	Volt 4058
⑩	7	11	I Just Want To Celebrate	Rare Earth	Rare Earth 5031

★ HIGHEST DEBUT ★ POS 71
Only You Know And I Know ......Delaney & Bonnie

★ BIGGEST MOVER ★ 89 to 61
Never My Love ....The 5th Dimension

Billboard 🔴 OCTOBER 2, 1971 🔴 HOT 100

TW	LW	WK		
❶	2	12	Maggie May/Reason To Believe	Rod Stewart ... Mercury 73224
②	1	9	Go Away Little Girl	Donny Osmond ... MGM 14285
③	4	8	The Night They Drove Old Dixie Down	Joan Baez ... Vanguard 35138
❹	8	5	Superstar	Carpenters ... A&M 1289
⑤	3	12	Ain't No Sunshine	Bill Withers ... Sussex 219
⑥	6	8	Uncle Albert/Admiral Halsey	Paul & Linda McCartney ... Apple 1837
⑦	5	10	Spanish Harlem	Aretha Franklin ... Atlantic 2817
⑧	7	15	Smiling Faces Sometimes	The Undisputed Truth ... Gordy 7108
❾	19	4	Yo-Yo	The Osmonds ... MGM 14295
❿	12	10	Do You Know What I Mean	Lee Michaels ... A&M 1262

★ HIGHEST DEBUT ★ POS 79	★ BIGGEST MOVER ★ 88 to 50
Spill The Wine .... The Isley Brothers	Peace Train .... Cat Stevens

Billboard 🔴 OCTOBER 9, 1971 🔴 HOT 100

TW	LW	WK		
①	1	13	Maggie May/Reason To Believe	Rod Stewart ... Mercury 73224
②	2	10	Go Away Little Girl	Donny Osmond ... MGM 14285
③	4	6	Superstar	Carpenters ... A&M 1289
④	3	9	The Night They Drove Old Dixie Down	Joan Baez ... Vanguard 35138
❺	9	5	Yo-Yo	The Osmonds ... MGM 14295
❻	10	11	Do You Know What I Mean	Lee Michaels ... A&M 1262
⑦	6	9	Uncle Albert/Admiral Halsey	Paul & Linda McCartney ... Apple 1837
⑧	5	13	Ain't No Sunshine	Bill Withers ... Sussex 219
❾	12	9	If You Really Love Me	Stevie Wonder ... Tamla 54208
❿	14	9	Sweet City Woman	Stampeders ... Bell 45120

★ HIGHEST DEBUT ★ POS 62	★ BIGGEST MOVER ★ 89 to 51
Inner City Blues (Make Me Wanna Holler) .... Marvin Gaye	What Are You Doing Sunday .... Dawn featuring Tony Orlando

Billboard 🔴 OCTOBER 16, 1971 🔴 HOT 100

TW	LW	WK		
①	1	14	Maggie May/Reason To Believe	Rod Stewart ... Mercury 73224
②	3	7	Superstar	Carpenters ... A&M 1289
❸	5	6	Yo-Yo	The Osmonds ... MGM 14295
④	4	10	The Night They Drove Old Dixie Down	Joan Baez ... Vanguard 35138
⑤	2	11	Go Away Little Girl	Donny Osmond ... MGM 14285
⑥	6	12	Do You Know What I Mean	Lee Michaels ... A&M 1262
⑦	7	10	Uncle Albert/Admiral Halsey	Paul & Linda McCartney ... Apple 1837
⑧	9	10	If You Really Love Me	Stevie Wonder ... Tamla 54208
⑨	10	10	Sweet City Woman	Stampeders ... Bell 45120
❿	28	5	Gypsys, Tramps & Thieves	Cher ... Kapp 2146

★ HIGHEST DEBUT ★ POS 50	★ BIGGEST MOVER ★ 87 to 54
Theme From Shaft .... Isaac Hayes	Desiderata .... Les Crane

TW	LW	WK	Billboard	OCTOBER 23, 1971	HOT 100.
①	1	15	**Maggie May/Reason To Believe** .... *Rod Stewart* ... Mercury 73224		
②	2	8	**Superstar** ....*Carpenters* ... A&M 1289		
③	3	7	**Yo-Yo** ....*The Osmonds* ... MGM 14295		
④	10	6	Gypsys, Tramps & Thieves..................................*Cher* ... Kapp 2146		
⑤	4	11	The Night They Drove Old Dixie Down ....*Joan Baez* ... Vanguard 35138		
⑥	6	13	**Do You Know What I Mean** ....*Lee Michaels* ... A&M 1262		
⑦	5	12	Go Away Little Girl....................*Donny Osmond* ... MGM 14285		
⑧	9	11	**Sweet City Woman** ....*Stampeders* ... Bell 45120		
⑨	50	2	**Theme From Shaft** ....*Isaac Hayes* ... Enterprise 9038		
⑩	8	11	If You Really Love Me ....*Stevie Wonder* ... Tamla 54208		

★ HIGHEST DEBUT ★ POS 20	★ BIGGEST MOVER ★ 50 to 9
Imagine..................*John Lennon Plastic Ono Band*	Theme From Shaft ....*Isaac Hayes*

TW	LW	WK	Billboard	OCTOBER 30, 1971	HOT 100.
①	1	16	**Maggie May/Reason To Believe** .... *Rod Stewart* ... Mercury 73224		
❷	4	7	**Gypsys, Tramps & Thieves**..................................*Cher* ... Kapp 2146		
③	3	8	**Yo-Yo** ....*The Osmonds* ... MGM 14295		
④	2	9	Superstar..*Carpenters* ... A&M 1289		
❺	9	3	**Theme From Shaft** ....*Isaac Hayes* ... Enterprise 9038		
❻	20	2	**Imagine** ....*John Lennon Plastic Ono Band* ... Apple 1840		
⑦	6	14	Do You Know What I Mean ....*Lee Michaels* ... A&M 1262		
⑧	5	12	The Night They Drove Old Dixie Down ....*Joan Baez* ... Vanguard 35138		
❾	15	6	Peace Train.................................*Cat Stevens* ... A&M 1291		
⑩	11	22	I've Found Someone Of My Own ....*The Free Movement* ... Decca 32818		

★ HIGHEST DEBUT ★ POS 69	★ BIGGEST MOVER ★ 60 to 21
Rock Steady ....*Aretha Franklin*	Have You Seen Her ....*Chi-Lites*

TW	LW	WK	Billboard	NOVEMBER 6, 1971	HOT 100.
❶	2	8	**Gypsys, Tramps & Thieves** ....*Cher* ... Kapp 2146		
❷	5	4	**Theme From Shaft** ....*Isaac Hayes* ... Enterprise 9038		
③	1	17	Maggie May/Reason To Believe ....*Rod Stewart* ... Mercury 73224		
④	6	3	**Imagine** ....*John Lennon Plastic Ono Band* ... Apple 1840		
⑤	3	9	Yo-Yo ....*The Osmonds* ... MGM 14295		
⑥	4	10	Superstar..*Carpenters* ... A&M 1289		
⑦	9	7	**Peace Train**.................................*Cat Stevens* ... A&M 1291		
⑧	10	23	I've Found Someone Of My Own ....*The Free Movement* ... Decca 32818		
❾	19	5	**Inner City Blues (Make Me Wanna Holler)**.................*Marvin Gaye* ... Tamla 54209		
⑩	8	13	The Night They Drove Old Dixie Down ....*Joan Baez* ... Vanguard 35138		

★ HIGHEST DEBUT ★ POS 50	★ BIGGEST MOVER ★ 89 to 39
Family Affair ....*Sly & The Family Stone*	Got To Be There........................*Michael Jackson*

TW	LW	WK	Billboard	NOVEMBER 13, 1971	HOT 100
①	1	9	**Gypsys, Tramps & Thieves** ....*Cher* ... Kapp 2146
②	2	5	**Theme From Shaft** ....*Isaac Hayes* ... Enterprise 9038
③	4	4	**Imagine**...........................*John Lennon Plastic Ono Band* ... Apple 1840
④	3	18	**Maggie May/Reason To Believe** ....*Rod Stewart* ... Mercury 73224
⑤	8	24	**I've Found Someone Of My Own** ....*The Free Movement* ... Decca 32818
⑥	5	10	**Yo-Yo** ....*The Osmonds* ... MGM 14295
⑦	7	8	**Peace Train**...........................*Cat Stevens* ... A&M 1291
⑧	14	4	**Have You Seen Her** ....*Chi-Lites* ... Brunswick 55462
⑨	9	6	**Inner City Blues (Make Me Wanna Holler)**...............*Marvin Gaye* ... Tamla 54209
⑩	6	11	**Superstar**...........................*Carpenters* ... A&M 1289

★ **HIGHEST DEBUT** ★ POS 61
I'm A Greedy Man...........................*James Brown*

★ **BIGGEST MOVER** ★ 87 to 40
Cherish ....*David Cassidy*

TW	LW	WK	Billboard	NOVEMBER 20, 1971	HOT 100
❶	2	6	**Theme From Shaft** ....*Isaac Hayes* ... Enterprise 9038
❷	1	10	**Gypsys, Tramps & Thieves**...........................*Cher* ... Kapp 2146
❸	3	5	**Imagine**...........................*John Lennon Plastic Ono Band* ... Apple 1840
❹	11	5	**Baby I'm-A Want You** ....*Bread* ... Elektra 45751
❺	8	5	**Have You Seen Her**...........................*Chi-Lites* ... Brunswick 55462
❻	4	19	**Maggie May/Reason To Believe** ....*Rod Stewart* ... Mercury 73224
❼	7	9	**Peace Train**...........................*Cat Stevens* ... A&M 1291
❽	21	3	**Family Affair**...........................*Sly & The Family Stone* ... Epic 10805
❾	13	4	**Got To Be There** ....*Michael Jackson* ... Motown 1191
❿	6	11	**Yo-Yo**...........................*The Osmonds* ... MGM 14295

★ **HIGHEST DEBUT** ★ POS 74
One Monkey Don't Stop No Show ......*The Honey Cone*

★ **BIGGEST MOVER** ★ 77 to 39
An Old Fashioned Love Song .....*Three Dog Night*

TW	LW	WK	Billboard	NOVEMBER 27, 1971	HOT 100
①	1	7	**Theme From Shaft**...........................*Isaac Hayes* ... Enterprise 9038
②	2	11	**Gypsys, Tramps & Thieves**...........................*Cher* ... Kapp 2146
③	4	6	**Baby I'm-A Want You**...........................*Bread* ... Elektra 45751
④	5	6	**Have You Seen Her**...........................*Chi-Lites* ... Brunswick 55462
⑤	8	4	**Family Affair**...........................*Sly & The Family Stone* ... Epic 10805
⑥	3	6	**Imagine** ....*John Lennon Plastic Ono Band* ... Apple 1840
⑦	9	5	**Got To Be There** ....*Michael Jackson* ... Motown 1191
⑧	7	10	**Peace Train**...........................*Cat Stevens* ... A&M 1291
⑨	15	5	**Rock Steady** ....*Aretha Franklin* ... Atlantic 2838
⑩	13	8	**Desiderata** ....*Les Crane* ... Warner 7520

★ **HIGHEST DEBUT** ★ POS 69
American Pie ....*Don McLean*

★ **BIGGEST MOVER** ★ 79 to 38
(I Know) I'm Losing You...........*Rod Stewart with Faces*

TW	LW	WK	Billboard	DECEMBER 4, 1971	HOT 100
①	5	5	**Family Affair**....................................*Sly & The Family Stone* . . . Epic 10805
②	1	8	**Theme From Shaft** ....*Isaac Hayes* . . . Enterprise 9038
③	3	7	**Baby I'm-A Want You**...............................*Bread* . . . Elektra 45751
④	4	7	**Have You Seen Her**..........................*Chi-Lites* . . . Brunswick 55462
⑤	2	12	**Gypsys, Tramps & Thieves**.........................*Cher* . . . Kapp 2146
⑥	7	6	**Got To Be There** ....*Michael Jackson* . . . Motown 1191
⑦	14	4	**An Old Fashioned Love Song**..................*Three Dog Night* . . . Dunhill 4294
⑧	10	9	**Desiderata** ....*Les Crane* . . . Warner 7520
⑨	9	6	**Rock Steady** ....*Aretha Franklin* . . . Atlantic 2838
⑩	6	7	**Imagine** ....*John Lennon Plastic Ono Band* . . . Apple 1840

★ HIGHEST DEBUT ★ POS 61	★ BIGGEST MOVER ★ 70 to 32
I'd Like To Teach The World To Sing...........*The New Seekers*	Hey Girl/I Knew You When ....*Donny Osmond*

TW	LW	WK	Billboard	DECEMBER 11, 1971	HOT 100
①	1	6	**Family Affair**....................................*Sly & The Family Stone* . . . Epic 10805
②	2	9	**Theme From Shaft** ....*Isaac Hayes* . . . Enterprise 9038
③	4	8	**Have You Seen Her**..........................*Chi-Lites* . . . Brunswick 55462
④	6	7	**Got To Be There**..........................*Michael Jackson* . . . Motown 1191
⑤	7	5	**An Old Fashioned Love Song**..................*Three Dog Night* . . . Dunhill 4294
⑥	3	8	**Baby I'm-A Want You**...............................*Bread* . . . Elektra 45751
⑦	5	13	**Gypsys, Tramps & Thieves**.........................*Cher* . . . Kapp 2146
⑧	11	9	**All I Ever Need Is You** ....*Sonny & Cher* . . . Kapp 2151
⑨	15	7	**Brand New Key**...............................*Melanie* . . . Neighborhood 4201
⑩	8	10	**Desiderata**...................................*Les Crane* . . . Warner 7520

★ HIGHEST DEBUT ★ POS 61	★ BIGGEST MOVER ★ 93 to 56
Anticipation...........................*Carly Simon*	George Jackson ....*Bob Dylan*

TW	LW	WK	Billboard	DECEMBER 18, 1971	HOT 100
①	1	7	**Family Affair**....................................*Sly & The Family Stone* . . . Epic 10805
②	9	8	**Brand New Key**...............................*Melanie* . . . Neighborhood 4201
③	3	9	**Have You Seen Her**..........................*Chi-Lites* . . . Brunswick 55462
④	5	6	**An Old Fashioned Love Song** ....*Three Dog Night* . . . Dunhill 4294
⑤	4	8	**Got To Be There** ....*Michael Jackson* . . . Motown 1191
⑥	2	10	**Theme From Shaft** ....*Isaac Hayes* . . . Enterprise 9038
⑦	6	9	**Baby I'm-A Want You**...............................*Bread* . . . Elektra 45751
⑧	8	10	**All I Ever Need Is You** ....*Sonny & Cher* . . . Kapp 2151
⑨	25	4	**American Pie** ....*Don McLean* . . . United Artists 50856
⑩	11	7	**Cherish** ....*David Cassidy* . . . Bell 45150

★ HIGHEST DEBUT ★ POS 57	★ BIGGEST MOVER ★ 72 to 45
It's One Of Those Nights (Yes Love)...........*The Partridge Family*	Sugar Daddy ....*The Jackson 5*

TW	LW	WK	Billboard. 🔆 DECEMBER 25, 1971 🔆	HOT 100.
1	2	9	**Brand New Key** ....*Melanie* ... Neighborhood 4201	
②	1	8	Family Affair.................................*Sly & The Family Stone* ... Epic 10805	
3	9	5	American Pie ....*Don McLean* ... United Artists 50856	
④	4	7	**An Old Fashioned Love Song** ....*Three Dog Night* ... Dunhill 4294	
⑤	5	9	Got To Be There...................................*Michael Jackson* ... Motown 1191	
⑥	3	10	Have You Seen Her.................................*Chi-Lites* ... Brunswick 55462	
7	8	11	**All I Ever Need Is You** ....*Sonny & Cher* ... Kapp 2151	
8	11	9	Scorpio ....*Dennis Coffey & The Detroit Guitar Band* ... Sussex 226	
9	10	8	**Cherish**..*David Cassidy* ... Bell 45150	
⑩	12	5	Hey Girl/I Knew You When ....*Donny Osmond* ... MGM 14322	

★ *HIGHEST DEBUT* ★ POS 67	★ *BIGGEST MOVER* ★ 83 to 48
Black Dog...............................*Led Zeppelin*	Make Me The Woman That You Go Home To ....*Gladys Knight & The Pips*

Billboard HOT 100 — JANUARY 1, 1972

TW	LW	WK	Title / Artist / Label
1	1	10	**Brand New Key** ....*Melanie* . . . Neighborhood 4201
2	3	6	American Pie ....*Don McLean* . . . United Artists 50856
3	2	9	Family Affair...............................*Sly & The Family Stone* . . . Epic 10805
4	4	8	**An Old Fashioned Love Song** ....*Three Dog Night* . . . Dunhill 4294
5	5	10	Got To Be There.................................*Michael Jackson* . . . Motown 1191
6	6	11	Have You Seen Her.................................*Chi-Lites* . . . Brunswick 55462
7	8	10	Scorpio ....*Dennis Coffey & The Detroit Guitar Band* . . . Sussex 226
8	13	8	Sunshine..................................*Jonathan Edwards* . . . Capricorn 8021
9	9	9	**Cherish**...*David Cassidy* . . . Bell 45150
10	10	6	Hey Girl/I Knew You When ....*Donny Osmond* . . . MGM 14322

★ HIGHEST DEBUT ★ POS 56	★ BIGGEST MOVER ★ 81 to 43
Stay With Me ....*Faces*	Never Been To Spain ....*Three Dog Night*

Billboard HOT 100 — JANUARY 8, 1972

TW	LW	WK	Title / Artist / Label
1	1	11	**Brand New Key** ....*Melanie* . . . Neighborhood 4201
2	2	7	American Pie ....*Don McLean* . . . United Artists 50856
3	3	10	Family Affair...............................*Sly & The Family Stone* . . . Epic 10805
4	14	6	Let's Stay Together ....*Al Green* . . . Hi 2202
5	5	11	Got To Be There.................................*Michael Jackson* . . . Motown 1191
6	7	11	Scorpio ....*Dennis Coffey & The Detroit Guitar Band* . . . Sussex 226
7	8	9	Sunshine..................................*Jonathan Edwards* . . . Capricorn 8021
8	12	6	I'd Like To Teach The World To Sing .... *The New Seekers* . . . Elektra 45762
9	9	10	**Cherish**...*David Cassidy* . . . Bell 45150
10	10	7	Hey Girl/I Knew You When ....*Donny Osmond* . . . MGM 14322

★ HIGHEST DEBUT ★ POS 83	★ BIGGEST MOVER ★ 43 to 24
Another Puff ....*Jerry Reed*	Never Been To Spain ....*Three Dog Night*

Billboard HOT 100 — JANUARY 15, 1972

TW	LW	WK	Title / Artist / Label
1	2	8	**American Pie** ....*Don McLean* . . . United Artists 50856
2	1	12	Brand New Key.....................................*Melanie* . . . Neighborhood 4201
3	4	7	**Let's Stay Together** ....*Al Green* . . . Hi 2202
4	7	10	**Sunshine**..................................*Jonathan Edwards* . . . Capricorn 8021
5	3	11	Family Affair...............................*Sly & The Family Stone* . . . Epic 10805
6	6	12	**Scorpio** ....*Dennis Coffey & The Detroit Guitar Band* . . . Sussex 226
7	8	7	**I'd Like To Teach The World To Sing** .... *The New Seekers* . . . Elektra 45762
8	5	12	Got To Be There.................................*Michael Jackson* . . . Motown 1191
9	10	8	**Hey Girl/I Knew You When**..................*Donny Osmond* . . . MGM 14322
10	13	8	Clean Up Woman..............................*Betty Wright* . . . Alston 4601

★ HIGHEST DEBUT ★ POS 74	★ BIGGEST MOVER ★ 90 to 49
Baby Won't You Let Me Rock 'N Roll You ....*Ten Years After*	Joy ....*Apollo 100*

Billboard JANUARY 22, 1972 HOT 100

TW	LW	WK		
①	1	9	**American Pie**	*Don McLean* . . . United Artists 50856
②	2	13	Brand New Key	*Melanie* . . . Neighborhood 4201
❸	3	8	Let's Stay Together	*Al Green* . . . Hi 2202
④	4	11	**Sunshine**	*Jonathan Edwards* . . . Capricorn 8021
⑤	14	8	Day After Day	*Badfinger* . . . Apple 1841
⑥	6	13	Scorpio	*Dennis Coffey & The Detroit Guitar Band* . . . Sussex 226
⑦	7	8	**I'd Like To Teach The World To Sing**	*The New Seekers* . . . Elektra 45762
❽	10	9	Clean Up Woman	*Betty Wright* . . . Alston 4601
❾	11	12	**You Are Everything**	*The Stylistics* . . . Avco 4581
❿	12	7	**Sugar Daddy**	*The Jackson 5* . . . Motown 1194

★ **HIGHEST DEBUT** ★ POS 68
Down By The Lazy River . . . . *The Osmonds*

★ **BIGGEST MOVER** ★ 76 to 38
Hurting Each Other . . . . *Carpenters*

Billboard JANUARY 29, 1972 HOT 100

TW	LW	WK		
①	1	10	**American Pie**	*Don McLean* . . . United Artists 50856
②	2	14	**Brand New Key**	*Melanie* . . . Neighborhood 4201
③	3	9	Let's Stay Together	*Al Green* . . . Hi 2202
④	4	12	**Sunshine**	*Jonathan Edwards* . . . Capricorn 8021
⑤	5	9	Day After Day	*Badfinger* . . . Apple 1841
⑥	8	10	**Clean Up Woman**	*Betty Wright* . . . Alston 4601
⑦	6	14	Scorpio	*Dennis Coffey & The Detroit Guitar Band* . . . Sussex 226
❽	11	6	Never Been To Spain	*Three Dog Night* . . . Dunhill 4299
⑨	9	13	**You Are Everything**	*The Stylistics* . . . Avco 4581
❿	10	8	**Sugar Daddy**	*The Jackson 5* . . . Motown 1194

★ **HIGHEST DEBUT** ★ POS 60
Everything I Own . . . . *Bread*

★ **BIGGEST MOVER** ★ 68 to 32
Down By The Lazy River . . . . *The Osmonds*

Billboard FEBRUARY 5, 1972 HOT 100

TW	LW	WK		
①	1	11	**American Pie**	*Don McLean* . . . United Artists 50856
②	3	10	Let's Stay Together	*Al Green* . . . Hi 2202
③	2	15	Brand New Key	*Melanie* . . . Neighborhood 4201
④	5	10	**Day After Day**	*Badfinger* . . . Apple 1841
⑤	14	8	Without You	*Nilsson* . . . RCA 0604
⑥	8	7	Never Been To Spain	*Three Dog Night* . . . Dunhill 4299
⑦	4	13	Sunshine	*Jonathan Edwards* . . . Capricorn 8021
❽	16	6	Precious And Few	*Climax* . . . Rocky Road 30055
⑨	13	4	Hurting Each Other	*Carpenters* . . . A&M 1322
❿	15	6	Joy	*Apollo 100* . . . Mega 0050

★ **HIGHEST DEBUT** ★ POS 62
Heart Of Gold . . . . *Neil Young*

★ **BIGGEST MOVER** ★ 77 to 35
Sweet Seasons . . . . *Carole King*

Billboard — FEBRUARY 12, 1972 — HOT 100

TW	LW	WK	Title	Artist	Label
①	2	11	Let's Stay Together	Al Green	Hi 2202
②	1	12	American Pie	Don McLean	United Artists 50856
❸	5	9	Without You	Nilsson	RCA 0604
❹	8	7	Precious And Few	Climax	Rocky Road 30055
❺	6	8	Never Been To Spain	Three Dog Night	Dunhill 4299
❻	9	5	Hurting Each Other	Carpenters	A&M 1322
❼	12	4	Down By The Lazy River	The Osmonds	MGM 14324
❽	10	7	Joy	Apollo 100	Mega 0050
⑨	3	16	Brand New Key	Melanie	Neighborhood 4201
⑩	4	11	Day After Day	Badfinger	Apple 1841

★ HIGHEST DEBUT ★ POS 61
Talking Loud And Saying Nothing ....James Brown

★ BIGGEST MOVER ★ 87 to 52
Runnin' Away ....Sly & The Family Stone

Billboard — FEBRUARY 19, 1972 — HOT 100

TW	LW	WK	Title	Artist	Label
❶	3	10	Without You	Nilsson	RCA 0604
②	1	12	Let's Stay Together	Al Green	Hi 2202
❸	6	6	Hurting Each Other	Carpenters	A&M 1322
④	4	8	Precious And Few	Climax	Rocky Road 30055
⑤	5	9	Never Been To Spain	Three Dog Night	Dunhill 4299
❻	7	5	Down By The Lazy River	The Osmonds	MGM 14324
⑦	2	13	American Pie	Don McLean	United Artists 50856
⑧	8	8	Joy	Apollo 100	Mega 0050
⑨	14	8	The Lion Sleeps Tonight	Robert John	Atlantic 2846
⑩	28	4	Everything I Own	Bread	Elektra 45765

★ HIGHEST DEBUT ★ POS 66
Could It Be Forever......................David Cassidy

★ BIGGEST MOVER ★ 88 to 62
Roundabout ....Yes

Billboard — FEBRUARY 26, 1972 — HOT 100

TW	LW	WK	Title	Artist	Label
①	1	11	Without You	Nilsson	RCA 0604
②	3	7	Hurting Each Other	Carpenters	A&M 1322
③	4	9	Precious And Few	Climax	Rocky Road 30055
④	2	13	Let's Stay Together	Al Green	Hi 2202
⑤	6	6	Down By The Lazy River	The Osmonds	MGM 14324
⑥	8	9	Joy	Apollo 100	Mega 0050
❼	9	9	The Lion Sleeps Tonight	Robert John	Atlantic 2846
❽	10	5	Everything I Own	Bread	Elektra 45765
⑨	7	14	American Pie	Don McLean	United Artists 50856
⑩	11	5	Sweet Seasons	Carole King	Ode 66022

★ HIGHEST DEBUT ★ POS 60
Puppy Love......................Donny Osmond

★ BIGGEST MOVER ★ 84 to 47
A Horse With No Name........................America

TW	LW	WK	Billboard.	MARCH 4, 1972	HOT 100.
①	1	12	**Without You**	Nilsson	RCA 0604
②	2	8	**Hurting Each Other**	Carpenters	A&M 1322
③	3	10	**Precious And Few**	Climax	Rocky Road 30055
④	5	7	**Down By The Lazy River**	The Osmonds	MGM 14324
❺	8	6	**Everything I Own**	Bread	Elektra 45765
⑥	7	10	The Lion Sleeps Tonight	Robert John	Atlantic 2846
❼	13	5	Heart Of Gold	Neil Young	Reprise 1065
⑧	4	14	Let's Stay Together	Al Green	Hi 2202
⑨	10	6	**Sweet Seasons**	Carole King	Ode 66022
⑩	14	10	**Bang A Gong (Get It On)**	T. Rex	Reprise 1032

★ **HIGHEST DEBUT** ★ POS 62
Take A Look Around .... The Temptations

★ **BIGGEST MOVER** ★ 47 to 20
A Horse With No Name .... America

TW	LW	WK	Billboard.	MARCH 11, 1972	HOT 100.
①	1	13	**Without You**	Nilsson	RCA 0604
❷	7	6	Heart Of Gold	Neil Young	Reprise 1065
❸	6	11	**The Lion Sleeps Tonight**	Robert John	Atlantic 2846
④	4	8	**Down By The Lazy River**	The Osmonds	MGM 14324
⑤	5	7	**Everything I Own**	Bread	Elektra 45765
⑥	3	11	**Precious And Few**	Climax	Rocky Road 30055
❼	20	4	A Horse With No Name	America	Warner 7555
⑧	2	9	Hurting Each Other	Carpenters	A&M 1322
⑨	11	7	The Way Of Love	Cher	Kapp 2158
⑩	10	11	**Bang A Gong (Get It On)**	T. Rex	Reprise 1032

★ **HIGHEST DEBUT** ★ POS 68
Rockin' Robin .... Michael Jackson

★ **BIGGEST MOVER** ★ 38 to 11
Puppy Love .... Donny Osmond

TW	LW	WK	Billboard.	MARCH 18, 1972	HOT 100.
①	2	7	**Heart Of Gold**	Neil Young	Reprise 1065
❷	7	5	A Horse With No Name	America	Warner 7555
③	3	12	**The Lion Sleeps Tonight**	Robert John	Atlantic 2846
④	1	14	**Without You**	Nilsson	RCA 0604
⑤	5	8	**Everything I Own**	Bread	Elektra 45765
❻	12	7	Mother And Child Reunion	Paul Simon	Columbia 45547
⑦	6	12	**Precious And Few**	Climax	Rocky Road 30055
⑧	9	8	The Way Of Love	Cher	Kapp 2158
⑨	11	4	Puppy Love	Donny Osmond	MGM 14367
⑩	4	9	**Down By The Lazy River**	The Osmonds	MGM 14324

★ **HIGHEST DEBUT** ★ POS 58
Day Dreaming .... Aretha Franklin

★ **BIGGEST MOVER** ★ 68 to 33
Rockin' Robin .... Michael Jackson

Billboard — MARCH 25, 1972 — HOT 100

TW	LW	WK	Title	Artist	Label
❶	2	6	**A Horse With No Name**	*America*	Warner 7555
②	1	8	Heart Of Gold	*Neil Young*	Reprise 1065
③	3	13	**The Lion Sleeps Tonight**	*Robert John*	Atlantic 2846
❹	9	5	Puppy Love	*Donny Osmond*	MGM 14367
⑤	6	8	Mother And Child Reunion	*Paul Simon*	Columbia 45547
⑥	4	15	Without You	*Nilsson*	RCA 0604
⑦	8	9	**The Way Of Love**	*Cher*	Kapp 2158
❽	11	11	**Jungle Fever**	*The Chakachas*	Polydor 15030
⑨	5	9	Everything I Own	*Bread*	Elektra 45765
⑩	14	10	I Gotcha	*Joe Tex*	Dial 1010

★ HIGHEST DEBUT ★ POS 74	★ BIGGEST MOVER ★ 58 to 32
Help Me Make It Through The Night........*Gladys Knight & The Pips*	Day Dreaming ....*Aretha Franklin*

Billboard — APRIL 1, 1972 — HOT 100

TW	LW	WK	Title	Artist	Label
①	1	7	**A Horse With No Name**	*America*	Warner 7555
②	2	9	**Heart Of Gold**	*Neil Young*	Reprise 1065
③	4	6	**Puppy Love**	*Donny Osmond*	MGM 14367
④	5	9	**Mother And Child Reunion**	*Paul Simon*	Columbia 45547
⑤	3	14	The Lion Sleeps Tonight	*Robert John*	Atlantic 2846
❻	10	11	I Gotcha	*Joe Tex*	Dial 1010
⑦	6	16	Without You	*Nilsson*	RCA 0604
⑧	8	12	**Jungle Fever**	*The Chakachas*	Polydor 15030
⑨	14	4	Rockin' Robin	*Michael Jackson*	Motown 1197
⑩	17	5	The First Time Ever I Saw Your Face	*Roberta Flack*	Atlantic 2864

★ HIGHEST DEBUT ★ POS 44	★ BIGGEST MOVER ★ 79 to 36
Look What You Done For Me ....*Al Green*	The Family Of Man....................*Three Dog Night*

Billboard — APRIL 8, 1972 — HOT 100

TW	LW	WK	Title	Artist	Label
①	1	8	**A Horse With No Name**	*America*	Warner 7555
②	2	10	Heart Of Gold	*Neil Young*	Reprise 1065
❸	10	6	The First Time Ever I Saw Your Face	*Roberta Flack*	Atlantic 2864
❹	6	12	I Gotcha	*Joe Tex*	Dial 1010
❺	9	5	Rockin' Robin	*Michael Jackson*	Motown 1197
⑥	3	7	Puppy Love	*Donny Osmond*	MGM 14367
⑦	4	10	Mother And Child Reunion	*Paul Simon*	Columbia 45547
⑧	8	13	**Jungle Fever**	*The Chakachas*	Polydor 15030
❾	11	7	In The Rain	*Dramatics*	Volt 4075
⑩	5	15	The Lion Sleeps Tonight	*Robert John*	Atlantic 2846

★ HIGHEST DEBUT ★ POS 63	★ BIGGEST MOVER ★ 88 to 42
I'll Take You There.................*The Staple Singers*	Back Off Boogaloo..........................*Ringo Starr*

Billboard — APRIL 15, 1972 — HOT 100

TW	LW	WK	Title	Artist ... Label
1	3	7	**The First Time Ever I Saw Your Face**	*Roberta Flack* ... Atlantic 2864
2	1	9	**A Horse With No Name**	*America* ... Warner 7555
3	4	13	**I Gotcha**	*Joe Tex* ... Dial 1010
4	5	6	**Rockin' Robin**	*Michael Jackson* ... Motown 1197
5	2	11	**Heart Of Gold**	*Neil Young* ... Reprise 1065
6	9	8	**In The Rain**	*Dramatics* ... Volt 4075
7	6	8	**Puppy Love**	*Donny Osmond* ... MGM 14367
8	11	8	**Betcha By Golly, Wow**	*The Stylistics* ... Avco 4591
9	12	5	**Day Dreaming**	*Aretha Franklin* ... Atlantic 2866
10	13	8	**A Cowboys Work Is Never Done**	*Sonny & Cher* ... Kapp 2163

★ **HIGHEST DEBUT** ★ POS 86
Iko Iko .... *Dr. John*

★ **BIGGEST MOVER** ★ 80 to 35
Oh Girl .... *Chi-Lites*

Billboard — APRIL 22, 1972 — HOT 100

TW	LW	WK	Title	Artist ... Label
1	1	8	**The First Time Ever I Saw Your Face**	*Roberta Flack* ... Atlantic 2864
2	4	7	**Rockin' Robin**	*Michael Jackson* ... Motown 1197
3	3	14	**I Gotcha**	*Joe Tex* ... Dial 1010
4	2	10	**A Horse With No Name**	*America* ... Warner 7555
5	6	9	**In The Rain**	*Dramatics* ... Volt 4075
6	8	9	**Betcha By Golly, Wow**	*The Stylistics* ... Avco 4591
7	9	6	**Day Dreaming**	*Aretha Franklin* ... Atlantic 2866
8	5	12	**Heart Of Gold**	*Neil Young* ... Reprise 1065
9	10	9	**A Cowboys Work Is Never Done**	*Sonny & Cher* ... Kapp 2163
10	16	6	**Doctor My Eyes**	*Jackson Browne* ... Asylum 11004

★ **HIGHEST DEBUT** ★ POS 62
Little Bitty Pretty One .... *The Jackson 5*

★ **BIGGEST MOVER** ★ 78 to 53
Sylvia's Mother .... *Dr. Hook & The Medicine Show*

Billboard — APRIL 29, 1972 — HOT 100

TW	LW	WK	Title	Artist ... Label
1	1	9	**The First Time Ever I Saw Your Face**	*Roberta Flack* ... Atlantic 2864
2	2	8	**Rockin' Robin**	*Michael Jackson* ... Motown 1197
3	3	15	**I Gotcha**	*Joe Tex* ... Dial 1010
4	6	10	**Betcha By Golly, Wow**	*The Stylistics* ... Avco 4591
5	4	11	**A Horse With No Name**	*America* ... Warner 7555
6	7	7	**Day Dreaming**	*Aretha Franklin* ... Atlantic 2866
7	5	10	**In The Rain**	*Dramatics* ... Volt 4075
8	9	10	**A Cowboys Work Is Never Done**	*Sonny & Cher* ... Kapp 2163
9	10	7	**Doctor My Eyes**	*Jackson Browne* ... Asylum 11004
10	12	5	**Look What You Done For Me**	*Al Green* ... Hi 2211

★ **HIGHEST DEBUT** ★ POS 50
Tumbling Dice .... *The Rolling Stones*

★ **BIGGEST MOVER** ★ 62 to 32
Little Bitty Pretty One .... *The Jackson 5*

TW	LW	WK	Billboard.	MAY 6, 1972	HOT 100.
①	1	10	The First Time Ever I Saw Your Face		Roberta Flack ... Atlantic 2864
②	3	16	I Gotcha		Joe Tex ... Dial 1010
③	4	11	Betcha By Golly, Wow		The Stylistics ... Avco 4591
④	2	9	Rockin' Robin		Michael Jackson ... Motown 1197
⑤	6	8	Day Dreaming		Aretha Franklin ... Atlantic 2866
⑥	5	12	A Horse With No Name		America ... Warner 7555
⑦	18	5	I'll Take You There		The Staple Singers ... Stax 0125
⑧	9	8	Doctor My Eyes		Jackson Browne ... Asylum 11004
⑨	10	6	Look What You Done For Me		Al Green ... Hi 2211
⑩	11	6	Back Off Boogaloo		Ringo Starr ... Apple 1849

★ HIGHEST DEBUT ★ POS 67	★ BIGGEST MOVER ★ 79 to 43
Song Sung Blue ... Neil Diamond	It's Going To Take Some Time ... Carpenters

TW	LW	WK	Billboard.	MAY 13, 1972	HOT 100.
①	1	11	The First Time Ever I Saw Your Face		Roberta Flack ... Atlantic 2864
②	2	17	I Gotcha		Joe Tex ... Dial 1010
③	11	6	Oh Girl		Chi-Lites ... Brunswick 55471
④	7	6	I'll Take You There		The Staple Singers ... Stax 0125
⑤	4	10	Rockin' Robin		Michael Jackson ... Motown 1197
⑥	3	12	Betcha By Golly, Wow		The Stylistics ... Avco 4591
⑦	9	7	Look What You Done For Me		Al Green ... Hi 2211
⑧	5	9	Day Dreaming		Aretha Franklin ... Atlantic 2866
⑨	10	7	Back Off Boogaloo		Ringo Starr ... Apple 1849
⑩	6	13	A Horse With No Name		America ... Warner 7555

★ HIGHEST DEBUT ★ POS 71	★ BIGGEST MOVER ★ 100 to 62
Troglodyte (Cave Man) ... The Jimmy Castor Bunch	There It Is ... James Brown

TW	LW	WK	Billboard.	MAY 20, 1972	HOT 100.
①	1	12	The First Time Ever I Saw Your Face		Roberta Flack ... Atlantic 2864
②	3	7	Oh Girl		Chi-Lites ... Brunswick 55471
③	4	7	I'll Take You There		The Staple Singers ... Stax 0125
④	2	18	I Gotcha		Joe Tex ... Dial 1010
⑤	7	8	Look What You Done For Me		Al Green ... Hi 2211
⑥	5	11	Rockin' Robin		Michael Jackson ... Motown 1197
⑦	6	13	Betcha By Golly, Wow		The Stylistics ... Avco 4591
⑧	11	4	Tumbling Dice		The Rolling Stones ... Rolling Stones 19103
⑨	9	8	Back Off Boogaloo		Ringo Starr ... Apple 1849
⑩	15	8	Morning Has Broken		Cat Stevens ... A&M 1335

★ HIGHEST DEBUT ★ POS 59	★ BIGGEST MOVER ★ 71 to 46
Amazing Grace ... The Royal Scots Dragoon Guards	Troglodyte (Cave Man) ... The Jimmy Castor Bunch

TW	LW	WK	Billboard	MAY 27, 1972	HOT 100
①	2	8	**Oh Girl** ....*Chi-Lites* . . . Brunswick 55471		
②	3	8	**I'll Take You There** ....*The Staple Singers* . . . Stax 0125		
③	1	13	**The First Time Ever I Saw Your Face** ....*Roberta Flack* . . . Atlantic 2864		
④	5	9	**Look What You Done For Me** ....*Al Green* . . . Hi 2211		
⑤	13	12	**The Candy Man**......................................*Sammy Davis, Jr.* . . . MGM 14320		
⑥	10	9	**Morning Has Broken**.......................................*Cat Stevens* . . . A&M 1335		
⑦	8	5	**Tumbling Dice**........................*The Rolling Stones* . . . Rolling Stones 19103		
⑧	4	19	**I Gotcha**..*Joe Tex* . . . Dial 1010		
⑨	14	9	**Sylvia's Mother** ....*Dr. Hook & The Medicine Show* . . . Columbia 45562		
⑩	12	10	**Hot Rod Lincoln** ....*Commander Cody & His Lost Planet Airmen* . . . Paramount 0146		

★ HIGHEST DEBUT ★ POS 59	★ BIGGEST MOVER ★ 59 to 31
I Wanna Be Where You Are ....*Michael Jackson*	Amazing Grace ....*The Royal Scots Dragoon Guards*

TW	LW	WK	Billboard	JUNE 3, 1972	HOT 100
❶	2	9	**I'll Take You There**............................*The Staple Singers* . . . Stax 0125		
②	1	9	**Oh Girl**..*Chi-Lites* . . . Brunswick 55471		
③	3	14	**The First Time Ever I Saw Your Face** ....*Roberta Flack* . . . Atlantic 2864		
❹	5	13	**The Candy Man**......................................*Sammy Davis, Jr.* . . . MGM 14320		
❺	9	10	**Sylvia's Mother**..........*Dr. Hook & The Medicine Show* . . . Columbia 45562		
⑥	6	10	**Morning Has Broken**.......................................*Cat Stevens* . . . A&M 1335		
⑦	7	6	**Tumbling Dice**........................*The Rolling Stones* . . . Rolling Stones 19103		
❽	11	15	**Nice To Be With You** ....*Gallery* . . . Sussex 232		
⑨	10	11	**Hot Rod Lincoln**.................*Commander Cody & His Lost Planet Airmen* . . . Paramount 0146		
⑩	4	10	**Look What You Done For Me**..............................*Al Green* . . . Hi 2211		

★ HIGHEST DEBUT ★ POS 64	★ BIGGEST MOVER ★ 84 to 63
(If Loving You Is Wrong) I Don't Want To Be Right ....*Luther Ingram*	Conquistador.................................*Procol Harum*

TW	LW	WK	Billboard	JUNE 10, 1972	HOT 100
❶	4	14	**The Candy Man**......................................*Sammy Davis, Jr.* . . . MGM 14320		
②	1	10	**I'll Take You There** ....*The Staple Singers* . . . Stax 0125		
③	2	10	**Oh Girl**..*Chi-Lites* . . . Brunswick 55471		
④	12	6	**Song Sung Blue**...*Neil Diamond* . . . Uni 55326		
⑤	5	11	**Sylvia's Mother**..........*Dr. Hook & The Medicine Show* . . . Columbia 45562		
⑥	8	16	**Nice To Be With You** ....*Gallery* . . . Sussex 232		
⑦	3	15	**The First Time Ever I Saw Your Face** ....*Roberta Flack* . . . Atlantic 2864		
⑧	6	11	**Morning Has Broken** ....*Cat Stevens* . . . A&M 1335		
⑨	17	8	**Outa-Space** ....*Billy Preston* . . . A&M 1320		
⑩	11	11	**(Last Night) I Didn't Get To Sleep At All**...................*The 5th Dimension* . . . Bell 45195		

★ HIGHEST DEBUT ★ POS 68	★ BIGGEST MOVER ★ 75 to 49
Where Is The Love...........*Roberta Flack & Donny Hathaway*	All The King's Horses ....*Aretha Franklin*

Billboard — JUNE 17, 1972 — HOT 100

TW	LW	WK	Title	Artist	Label
1	1	15	**The Candy Man**	Sammy Davis, Jr.	MGM 14320
2	2	11	I'll Take You There	The Staple Singers	Stax 0125
3	4	7	Song Sung Blue	Neil Diamond	Uni 55326
4	3	11	Oh Girl	Chi-Lites	Brunswick 55471
5	6	17	Nice To Be With You	Gallery	Sussex 232
6	9	9	Outa-Space	Billy Preston	A&M 1320
7	13	6	Troglodyte (Cave Man)	The Jimmy Castor Bunch	RCA 1029
8	10	12	(Last Night) I Didn't Get To Sleep At All	The 5th Dimension	Bell 45195
9	5	12	Sylvia's Mother	Dr. Hook & The Medicine Show	Columbia 45562
10	20	9	Lean On Me	Bill Withers	Sussex 235

★ HIGHEST DEBUT ★ POS 68
Brandy (You're A Fine Girl) .... Looking Glass

★ BIGGEST MOVER ★ 72 to 35
Too Young .... Donny Osmond

Billboard — JUNE 24, 1972 — HOT 100

TW	LW	WK	Title	Artist	Label
1	1	16	**The Candy Man**	Sammy Davis, Jr.	MGM 14320
2	3	8	Song Sung Blue	Neil Diamond	Uni 55326
3	6	10	Outa-Space	Billy Preston	A&M 1320
4	5	18	Nice To Be With You	Gallery	Sussex 232
5	2	12	I'll Take You There	The Staple Singers	Stax 0125
6	7	7	Troglodyte (Cave Man)	The Jimmy Castor Bunch	RCA 1029
7	10	10	Lean On Me	Bill Withers	Sussex 235
8	8	13	(Last Night) I Didn't Get To Sleep At All	The 5th Dimension	Bell 45195
9	4	12	Oh Girl	Chi-Lites	Brunswick 55471
10	23	5	Too Late To Turn Back Now	Cornelius Brothers & Sister Rose	United Artists 50910

★ HIGHEST DEBUT ★ POS 74
Honky Tonk .... James Brown

★ BIGGEST MOVER ★ 88 to 59
Alone Again (Naturally) .... Gilbert O'Sullivan

Billboard — JULY 1, 1972 — HOT 100

TW	LW	WK	Title	Artist	Label
1	2	9	**Song Sung Blue**	Neil Diamond	Uni 55326
2	1	17	The Candy Man	Sammy Davis, Jr.	MGM 14320
3	3	11	Outa-Space	Billy Preston	A&M 1320
4	7	11	Lean On Me	Bill Withers	Sussex 235
5	10	6	Too Late To Turn Back Now	Cornelius Brothers & Sister Rose	United Artists 50910
6	6	8	Troglodyte (Cave Man)	The Jimmy Castor Bunch	RCA 1029
7	4	19	Nice To Be With You	Gallery	Sussex 232
8	14	9	Rocket Man	Elton John	Uni 55328
9	13	7	I Need You	America	Warner 7580
10	15	11	Daddy Don't You Walk So Fast	Wayne Newton	Chelsea 0100

★ HIGHEST DEBUT ★ POS 60
You Don't Mess Around With Jim .... Jim Croce

★ BIGGEST MOVER ★ 59 to 34
Alone Again (Naturally) .... Gilbert O'Sullivan

'72

TW	LW	WK	Billboard	JULY 8, 1972	HOT 100
①	4	12	**Lean On Me**..*Bill Withers* . . . Sussex 235
②	3	12	**Outa-Space** ....*Billy Preston* . . . A&M 1320
③	1	10	**Song Sung Blue**................................*Neil Diamond* . . . Uni 55326
④	5	7	**Too Late To Turn Back Now** .... *Cornelius Brothers & Sister Rose* . . . United Artists 50910
⑤	2	18	**The Candy Man**...............................*Sammy Davis, Jr.* . . . MGM 14320
⑥	6	9	**Troglodyte (Cave Man)**.............*The Jimmy Castor Bunch* . . . RCA 1029
⑦	8	10	**Rocket Man**......................................*Elton John* . . . Uni 55328
⑧	10	12	**Daddy Don't You Walk So Fast**................*Wayne Newton* . . . Chelsea 0100
⑨	9	8	**I Need You** ....*America* . . . Warner 7580
⑩	14	6	**(If Loving You Is Wrong) I Don't Want To Be Right** .... *Luther Ingram* . . . KoKo 2111

★ HIGHEST DEBUT ★ POS 57	★ BIGGEST MOVER ★ 76 to 39
I'm Still In Love With You ....*Al Green*	Hold Her Tight ....*The Osmonds*

TW	LW	WK	Billboard	JULY 15, 1972	HOT 100
①	1	13	**Lean On Me**..*Bill Withers* . . . Sussex 235
②	4	8	**Too Late To Turn Back Now** .... *Cornelius Brothers & Sister Rose* . . . United Artists 50910
③	2	13	**Outa-Space** ....*Billy Preston* . . . A&M 1320
④	3	11	**Song Sung Blue**................................*Neil Diamond* . . . Uni 55326
⑤	12	5	**Brandy (You're A Fine Girl)**........................*Looking Glass* . . . Epic 10874
⑥	7	11	**Rocket Man** ....*Elton John* . . . Uni 55328
⑦	8	13	**Daddy Don't You Walk So Fast**................*Wayne Newton* . . . Chelsea 0100
⑧	20	5	**Alone Again (Naturally)** ....*Gilbert O'Sullivan* . . . MAM 3619
⑨	10	7	**(If Loving You Is Wrong) I Don't Want To Be Right** .... *Luther Ingram* . . . KoKo 2111
⑩	19	6	**Where Is The Love** ....*Roberta Flack & Donny Hathaway* . . . Atlantic 2879

★ HIGHEST DEBUT ★ POS 68	★ BIGGEST MOVER ★ 99 to 70
Goodbye To Love ....*Carpenters*	When You Say Love ....*Sonny & Cher*

TW	LW	WK	Billboard	JULY 22, 1972	HOT 100
①	1	14	**Lean On Me**..*Bill Withers* . . . Sussex 235
②	2	9	**Too Late To Turn Back Now** .... *Cornelius Brothers & Sister Rose* . . . United Artists 50910
③	8	6	**Alone Again (Naturally)** ....*Gilbert O'Sullivan* . . . MAM 3619
④	5	6	**Brandy (You're A Fine Girl)**........................*Looking Glass* . . . Epic 10874
⑤	9	8	**(If Loving You Is Wrong) I Don't Want To Be Right** .... *Luther Ingram* . . . KoKo 2111
⑥	7	14	**Daddy Don't You Walk So Fast**................*Wayne Newton* . . . Chelsea 0100
⑦	10	7	**Where Is The Love** ....*Roberta Flack & Donny Hathaway* . . . Atlantic 2879
⑧	11	13	**How Do You Do?**...............................*Mouth & MacNeal* . . . Philips 40715
⑨	6	12	**Rocket Man**......................................*Elton John* . . . Uni 55328
⑩	12	8	**School's Out** ....*Alice Cooper* . . . Warner 7596

★ HIGHEST DEBUT ★ POS 70	★ BIGGEST MOVER ★ 68 to 38
Join Together.............................*The Who*	Goodbye To Love.............................*Carpenters*

Billboard 🔴 JULY 29, 1972 🔴 HOT 100®

TW	LW	WK			
❶	3	7	**Alone Again (Naturally)** ....*Gilbert O'Sullivan* . . . MAM 3619		
❷	4	7	**Brandy (You're A Fine Girl)**........................*Looking Glass* . . Epic 10874		
③	2	10	**Too Late To Turn Back Now** .... *Cornelius Brothers & Sister Rose* . . . United Artists 50910		
④	5	9	**(If Loving You Is Wrong) I Don't Want To Be Right** .... *Luther Ingram* . . . KoKo 2111		
❺	6	15	**Daddy Don't You Walk So Fast**................*Wayne Newton* . . . Chelsea 0100		
❻	7	8	**Where Is The Love** ....*Roberta Flack & Donny Hathaway* . . . Atlantic 2879		
❼	10	9	**School's Out**..*Alice Cooper* . . . Warner 7596		
⑧	8	14	**How Do You Do?**................................*Mouth & MacNeal* . . . Philips 40715		
⑨	1	15	**Lean On Me**..*Bill Withers* . . . Sussex 235		
❿	18	6	**Long Cool Woman (In A Black Dress)**.............*The Hollies* . . . Epic 10871		

★ HIGHEST DEBUT ★ POS 62	★ BIGGEST MOVER ★ 84 to 50
The Guitar Man.................................*Bread*	Rock And Roll Part 2.......................*Gary Glitter*

Billboard 🔴 AUGUST 5, 1972 🔴 HOT 100®

TW	LW	WK			
①	1	8	**Alone Again (Naturally)** ....*Gilbert O'Sullivan* . . . MAM 3619		
②	2	8	**Brandy (You're A Fine Girl)**........................*Looking Glass* . . . Epic 10874		
③	4	10	**(If Loving You Is Wrong) I Don't Want To Be Right**................... *Luther Ingram* . . . KoKo 2111		
④	5	16	**Daddy Don't You Walk So Fast**..........*Wayne Newton* . . . Chelsea 0100		
⑤	3	11	**Too Late To Turn Back Now** .... *Cornelius Brothers & Sister Rose* . . . United Artists 50910		
⑥	6	9	**Where Is The Love** ....*Roberta Flack & Donny Hathaway* . . . Atlantic 2879		
⑦	7	10	**School's Out**..*Alice Cooper* . . . Warner 7596		
⑧	8	15	**How Do You Do?**................................*Mouth & MacNeal* . . . Philips 40715		
⑨	10	7	**Long Cool Woman (In A Black Dress)**.............*The Hollies* . . . Epic 10871		
⑩	11	23	**Layla** ....*Derek & The Dominos* . . . Atco 6809		

★ HIGHEST DEBUT ★ POS 60	★ BIGGEST MOVER ★ 62 to 39
Saturday In The Park ....*Chicago*	The Guitar Man ....*Bread*

Billboard 🔴 AUGUST 12, 1972 🔴 HOT 100®

TW	LW	WK			
①	1	9	**Alone Again (Naturally)** ....*Gilbert O'Sullivan* . . . MAM 3619		
②	2	9	**Brandy (You're A Fine Girl)**........................*Looking Glass* . . . Epic 10874		
③	3	11	**(If Loving You Is Wrong) I Don't Want To Be Right**................... *Luther Ingram* . . . KoKo 2111		
④	4	17	**Daddy Don't You Walk So Fast**..........*Wayne Newton* . . . Chelsea 0100		
⑤	6	10	**Where Is The Love**......*Roberta Flack & Donny Hathaway* . . . Atlantic 2879		
⑥	9	8	**Long Cool Woman (In A Black Dress)**.............*The Hollies* . . . Epic 10871		
❼	15	6	**I'm Still In Love With You** ....*Al Green* . . . Hi 2216		
⑧	5	12	**Too Late To Turn Back Now** .... *Cornelius Brothers & Sister Rose* . . . United Artists 50910		
⑨	8	16	**How Do You Do?** ....*Mouth & MacNeal* . . . Philips 40715		
⑩	7	11	**School's Out** ....*Alice Cooper* . . . Warner 7596		

★ HIGHEST DEBUT ★ POS 61	★ BIGGEST MOVER ★ 89 to 62
Black & White ....*Three Dog Night*	Speak To The Sky ....*Rick Springfield*

Billboard HOT 100 — AUGUST 19, 1972

TW	LW	WK	Title	Artist	Label
①	1	10	Alone Again (Naturally)	Gilbert O'Sullivan	MAM 3619
②	2	10	Brandy (You're A Fine Girl)	Looking Glass	Epic 10874
❸	6	9	Long Cool Woman (In A Black Dress)	The Hollies	Epic 10871
④	3	12	(If Loving You Is Wrong) I Don't Want To Be Right	Luther Ingram	KoKo 2111
⑤	7	7	I'm Still In Love With You	Al Green	Hi 2216
⑥	5	11	Where Is The Love	Roberta Flack & Donny Hathaway	Atlantic 2879
⑦	4	18	Daddy Don't You Walk So Fast	Wayne Newton	Chelsea 0100
❽	18	10	Hold Your Head Up	Argent	Epic 10852
⑨	11	11	Coconut	Nilsson	RCA 0718
❿	12	6	Goodbye To Love	Carpenters	A&M 1367

★ HIGHEST DEBUT ★ POS 83
If You Leave Me Tonight I'll Cry .....Jerry Wallace

★ BIGGEST MOVER ★ 87 to 55
Play Me...Neil Diamond

Billboard HOT 100 — AUGUST 26, 1972

TW	LW	WK	Title	Artist	Label
①	2	11	Brandy (You're A Fine Girl)	Looking Glass	Epic 10874
②	1	11	Alone Again (Naturally)	Gilbert O'Sullivan	MAM 3619
③	3	10	Long Cool Woman (In A Black Dress)	The Hollies	Epic 10871
❹	5	8	I'm Still In Love With You	Al Green	Hi 2216
❺	8	11	Hold Your Head Up	Argent	Epic 10852
⑥	4	13	(If Loving You Is Wrong) I Don't Want To Be Right	Luther Ingram	KoKo 2111
❼	10	7	Goodbye To Love	Carpenters	A&M 1367
⑧	9	12	Coconut	Nilsson	RCA 0718
⑨	12	9	You Don't Mess Around With Jim	Jim Croce	ABC 11328
❿	18	9	Baby Don't Get Hooked On Me	Mac Davis	Columbia 45618

★ HIGHEST DEBUT ★ POS 80
Use Me...Bill Withers

★ BIGGEST MOVER ★ 47 to 23
Black & White ....Three Dog Night

Billboard HOT 100 — SEPTEMBER 2, 1972

TW	LW	WK	Title	Artist	Label
①	2	12	Alone Again (Naturally)	Gilbert O'Sullivan	MAM 3619
❷	3	11	Long Cool Woman (In A Black Dress)	The Hollies	Epic 10871
❸	4	9	I'm Still In Love With You	Al Green	Hi 2216
④	1	12	Brandy (You're A Fine Girl)	Looking Glass	Epic 10874
⑤	5	12	Hold Your Head Up	Argent	Epic 10852
⑥	10	10	Baby Don't Get Hooked On Me	Mac Davis	Columbia 45618
⑦	7	8	Goodbye To Love	Carpenters	A&M 1367
⑧	9	10	You Don't Mess Around With Jim	Jim Croce	ABC 11328
⑨	17	7	Rock And Roll Part 2	Gary Glitter	Bell 45237
❿	14	7	Back Stabbers	O'Jays	Philadelphia International 3517

★ HIGHEST DEBUT ★ POS 78
For Emily, Whenever I May Find Her .....Simon & Garfunkel

★ BIGGEST MOVER ★ 80 to 53
Use Me...................................Bill Withers

TW	LW	WK	Billboard. SEPTEMBER 9, 1972 HOT 100.
①	1	13	**Alone Again (Naturally)** ....*Gilbert O'Sullivan* ... MAM 3619
②	2	12	**Long Cool Woman (In A Black Dress)** ....*The Hollies* ... Epic 10871
③	3	10	**I'm Still In Love With You** ....*Al Green* ... Hi 2216
❹	6	11	**Baby Don't Get Hooked On Me** ....*Mac Davis* ... Columbia 45618
⑤	4	13	**Brandy (You're A Fine Girl)** ....*Looking Glass* ... Epic 10874
❻	10	8	**Back Stabbers** ....*O'Jays* ... Philadelphia International 3517
⑦	9	8	**Rock And Roll Part 2** ....*Gary Glitter* ... Bell 45237
⑧	8	11	**You Don't Mess Around With Jim** ....*Jim Croce* ... ABC 11328
⑨	14	5	**Black & White** ....*Three Dog Night* ... Dunhill 4317
⑩	15	6	**Saturday In The Park** ....*Chicago* ... Columbia 45657

★ HIGHEST DEBUT ★ POS 71	★ BIGGEST MOVER ★ 89 to 62
If I Could Reach You ....*The 5th Dimension*	Listen To The Music ....*The Doobie Brothers*

TW	LW	WK	Billboard. SEPTEMBER 16, 1972 HOT 100.
❶	9	6	**Black & White** ....*Three Dog Night* ... Dunhill 4317
❷	4	12	**Baby Don't Get Hooked On Me** ....*Mac Davis* ... Columbia 45618
③	1	14	**Alone Again (Naturally)** ....*Gilbert O'Sullivan* ... MAM 3619
❹	10	7	**Saturday In The Park** ....*Chicago* ... Columbia 45657
⑤	6	9	**Back Stabbers** ....*O'Jays* ... Philadelphia International 3517
⑥	2	13	**Long Cool Woman (In A Black Dress)** ....*The Hollies* ... Epic 10871
⑦	7	9	**Rock And Roll Part 2** ....*Gary Glitter* ... Bell 45237
⑧	5	14	**Brandy (You're A Fine Girl)** ....*Looking Glass* ... Epic 10874
❾	13	6	**Honky Cat** ....*Elton John* ... Uni 55343
⑩	3	11	**I'm Still In Love With You** ....*Al Green* ... Hi 2216

★ HIGHEST DEBUT ★ POS 70	★ BIGGEST MOVER ★ 94 to 68
Midnight Rider...............................*Joe Cocker*	Don't Hide Your Love ....*Cher*

TW	LW	WK	Billboard. SEPTEMBER 23, 1972 HOT 100.
❶	2	13	**Baby Don't Get Hooked On Me** ....*Mac Davis* ... Columbia 45618
②	1	7	**Black & White**...............................*Three Dog Night* ... Dunhill 4317
❸	4	8	**Saturday In The Park**..................................*Chicago* ... Columbia 45657
❹	5	10	**Back Stabbers** ....*O'Jays* ... Philadelphia International 3517
⑤	3	15	**Alone Again (Naturally)** ....*Gilbert O'Sullivan* ... MAM 3619
❻	13	8	**Ben** ....*Michael Jackson* ... Motown 1207
❼	16	11	**Everybody Plays The Fool**...............*The Main Ingredient* ... RCA 0731
⑧	9	7	**Honky Cat**...*Elton John* ... Uni 55343
⑨	12	13	**Go All The Way** ....*Raspberries* ... Capitol 3348
⑩	7	10	**Rock And Roll Part 2** ....*Gary Glitter* ... Bell 45237

★ HIGHEST DEBUT ★ POS 80	★ BIGGEST MOVER ★ 87 to 65
Let It Rain................................*Eric Clapton*	I Am Woman................................*Helen Reddy*

Billboard — SEPTEMBER 30, 1972 — HOT 100

TW	LW	WK			
①	1	14	**Baby Don't Get Hooked On Me** ....*Mac Davis* ... Columbia 45618		
②	2	8	**Black & White**..............................*Three Dog Night* ... Dunhill 4317		
③	3	9	**Saturday In The Park**......................*Chicago* ... Columbia 45657		
④	4	11	**Back Stabbers**................................*O'Jays* ... Philadelphia International 3517		
⑤	6	9	**Ben**...*Michael Jackson* ... Motown 1207		
⑥	7	12	**Everybody Plays The Fool**....................*The Main Ingredient* ... RCA 0731		
⑦	9	14	**Go All The Way** ....*Raspberries* ... Capitol 3348		
⑧	13	6	**Use Me** ....*Bill Withers* ... Sussex 241		
⑨	18	7	**Burning Love** ....*Elvis Presley* ... RCA 0769		
⑩	14	13	**Popcorn** ....*Hot Butter* ... Musicor 1458		

★ **HIGHEST DEBUT** ★ POS 81
A Lonely Man/The Man & The Woman........*The Chi-Lites*

★ **BIGGEST MOVER** ★ 90 to 63
American City Suite ....*Cashman & West*

Billboard — OCTOBER 7, 1972 — HOT 100

TW	LW	WK			
①	1	15	**Baby Don't Get Hooked On Me** ....*Mac Davis* ... Columbia 45618		
②	5	10	**Ben** ....*Michael Jackson* ... Motown 1207		
③	4	12	**Back Stabbers**..............................*O'Jays* ... Philadelphia International 3517		
④	6	13	**Everybody Plays The Fool**....................*The Main Ingredient* ... RCA 0731		
⑤	7	15	**Go All The Way**..............................*Raspberries* ... Capitol 3348		
⑥	8	7	**Use Me** ....*Bill Withers* ... Sussex 241		
⑦	9	8	**Burning Love** ....*Elvis Presley* ... RCA 0769		
⑧	2	9	**Black & White**..............................*Three Dog Night* ... Dunhill 4317		
⑨	13	10	**My Ding-A-Ling**.............................*Chuck Berry* ... Chess 2131		
⑩	10	14	**Popcorn** ....*Hot Butter* ... Musicor 1458		

★ **HIGHEST DEBUT** ★ POS 67
Elected............................*Alice Cooper*

★ **BIGGEST MOVER** ★ 86 to 61
If You Don't Know Me By Now.....*Harold Melvin & The Bluenotes*

Billboard — OCTOBER 14, 1972 — HOT 100

TW	LW	WK			
①	2	11	**Ben** ....*Michael Jackson* ... Motown 1207		
②	6	8	**Use Me**......................................*Bill Withers* ... Sussex 241		
③	4	14	**Everybody Plays The Fool** ....*The Main Ingredient* ... RCA 0731		
④	7	9	**Burning Love** ....*Elvis Presley* ... RCA 0769		
⑤	5	16	**Go All The Way**..............................*Raspberries* ... Capitol 3348		
⑥	1	16	**Baby Don't Get Hooked On Me**..................*Mac Davis* ... Columbia 45618		
⑦	9	11	**My Ding-A-Ling**.............................*Chuck Berry* ... Chess 2131		
⑧	12	11	**Nights In White Satin**......................*The Moody Blues* ... Deram 85023		
⑨	3	13	**Back Stabbers**..............................*O'Jays* ... Philadelphia International 3517		
⑩	10	15	**Popcorn** ....*Hot Butter* ... Musicor 1458		

★ **HIGHEST DEBUT** ★ POS 78
Operator (That's Not The Way It Feels)........*Jim Croce*

★ **BIGGEST MOVER** ★ 67 to 48
Elected................................*Alice Cooper*

Billboard — OCTOBER 21, 1972 — HOT 100

TW	LW	WK		
1	7	12	My Ding-A-Ling...*Chuck Berry* . . . Chess 2131	
2	2	9	Use Me..*Bill Withers* . . . Sussex 241	
3	4	10	Burning Love ....*Elvis Presley* . . . RCA 0769	
4	3	15	Everybody Plays The Fool....................*The Main Ingredient* . . . RCA 0731	
5	8	12	Nights In White Satin...............................*The Moody Blues* . . . Deram 85023	
6	1	12	Ben...*Michael Jackson* . . . Motown 1207	
7	6	17	Baby Don't Get Hooked On Me ....*Mac Davis* . . . Columbia 45618	
8	12	13	Garden Party...........*Rick Nelson & The Stone Canyon Band* . . . Decca 32980	
9	10	16	Popcorn ....*Hot Butter* . . . Musicor 1458	
10	5	17	Go All The Way ....*Raspberries* . . . Capitol 3348	

★ **HIGHEST DEBUT** ★ POS 63
Ventura Highway ....*America*

★ **BIGGEST MOVER** ★ 83 to 54
Papa Was A Rollin' Stone ....*The Temptations*

Billboard — OCTOBER 28, 1972 — HOT 100

TW	LW	WK		
1	1	13	My Ding-A-Ling...*Chuck Berry* . . . Chess 2131	
2	3	11	Burning Love ....*Elvis Presley* . . . RCA 0769	
3	5	13	Nights In White Satin...............................*The Moody Blues* . . . Deram 85023	
4	2	10	Use Me..*Bill Withers* . . . Sussex 241	
5	20	8	I Can See Clearly Now................................*Johnny Nash* . . . Epic 10902	
6	12	11	Freddie's Dead (Theme From "Superfly") ....*Curtis Mayfield* . . . Curtom 1975	
7	8	14	Garden Party...........*Rick Nelson & The Stone Canyon Band* . . . Decca 32980	
8	6	13	Ben...*Michael Jackson* . . . Motown 1207	
9	4	16	Everybody Plays The Fool....................*The Main Ingredient* . . . RCA 0731	
10	14	9	Good Time Charlie's Got The Blues ......*Danny O'Keefe* . . . Signpost 70006	

★ **HIGHEST DEBUT** ★ POS 72
Dialogue (Part I & II) ....*Chicago*

★ **BIGGEST MOVER** ★ 91 to 59
You Ought To Be With Me..................*Al Green*

Billboard — NOVEMBER 4, 1972 — HOT 100

TW	LW	WK		
1	5	9	I Can See Clearly Now ....*Johnny Nash* . . . Epic 10902	
2	3	14	Nights In White Satin ....*The Moody Blues* . . . Deram 85023	
3	1	14	My Ding-A-Ling...*Chuck Berry* . . . Chess 2131	
4	6	12	Freddie's Dead (Theme From "Superfly") ....*Curtis Mayfield* . . . Curtom 1975	
5	2	12	Burning Love ....*Elvis Presley* . . . RCA 0769	
6	7	15	Garden Party........*Rick Nelson & The Stone Canyon Band* . . . Decca 32980	
7	14	12	I'll Be Around..*Spinners* . . . Atlantic 2904	
8	15	7	I'd Love You To Want Me......................................*Lobo* . . . Big Tree 147	
9	10	10	Good Time Charlie's Got The Blues ....*Danny O'Keefe* . . . Signpost 70006	
10	8	14	Ben...*Michael Jackson* . . . Motown 1207	

★ **HIGHEST DEBUT** ★ POS 71
I Didn't Know I Loved You (Till I Saw You Rock And Roll)....................*Gary Glitter*

★ **BIGGEST MOVER** ★ 86 to 53
Clair...*Gilbert O'Sullivan*

Billboard — NOVEMBER 11, 1972 — HOT 100

TW	LW	WK		
①	1	10	**I Can See Clearly Now** ....*Johnny Nash* . . . Epic 10902
②	2	15	**Nights In White Satin** ....*The Moody Blues* . . . Deram 85023
❸	8	8	**I'd Love You To Want Me**..*Lobo* . . . Big Tree 147
④	4	13	**Freddie's Dead (Theme From "Superfly")** ....*Curtis Mayfield* . . . Curtom 1975
❺	7	13	**I'll Be Around** ....*Spinners* . . . Atlantic 2904
⑥	6	16	**Garden Party**........*Rick Nelson & The Stone Canyon Band* . . . Decca 32980
⑦	3	15	**My Ding-A-Ling**...*Chuck Berry* . . . Chess 2131
❽	12	12	**I Am Woman**...*Helen Reddy* . . . Capitol 3350
❾	26	4	**Convention '72** ....*The Delegates* . . . Mainstream 5525
❿	15	10	**Witchy Woman**..*Eagles* . . . Asylum 11008

★ **HIGHEST DEBUT** ★ POS 55
Sweet Surrender ....*Bread*

★ **BIGGEST MOVER** ★ 74 to 48
Me And Mrs. Jones...........................*Billy Paul*

Billboard — NOVEMBER 18, 1972 — HOT 100

TW	LW	WK		
①	1	11	**I Can See Clearly Now** ....*Johnny Nash* . . . Epic 10902
②	3	9	**I'd Love You To Want Me** ....*Lobo* . . . Big Tree 147
❸	5	14	**I'll Be Around**...*Spinners* . . . Atlantic 2904
❹	8	13	**I Am Woman**...*Helen Reddy* . . . Capitol 3350
⑤	2	16	**Nights In White Satin**.........................*The Moody Blues* . . . Deram 85023
❻	13	6	**Papa Was A Rollin' Stone**.......................*The Temptations* . . . Gordy 7121
⑦	4	14	**Freddie's Dead (Theme From "Superfly")** ....*Curtis Mayfield* . . . Curtom 1975
⑧	9	5	**Convention '72**...................................*The Delegates* . . . Mainstream 5525
⑨	10	11	**Witchy Woman**..*Eagles* . . . Asylum 11008
❿	16	11	**Summer Breeze** ....*Seals & Crofts* . . . Warner 7606

★ **HIGHEST DEBUT** ★ POS 63
Alive...............................*The Bee Gees*

★ **BIGGEST MOVER** ★ 85 to 51
Walk On Water...............................*Neil Diamond*

Billboard — NOVEMBER 25, 1972 — HOT 100

TW	LW	WK		
①	1	12	**I Can See Clearly Now** ....*Johnny Nash* . . . Epic 10902
②	2	10	**I'd Love You To Want Me** ....*Lobo* . . . Big Tree 147
③	3	15	**I'll Be Around**...*Spinners* . . . Atlantic 2904
④	4	14	**I Am Woman**...*Helen Reddy* . . . Capitol 3350
❺	6	7	**Papa Was A Rollin' Stone**.......................*The Temptations* . . . Gordy 7121
❻	10	12	**Summer Breeze** ....*Seals & Crofts* . . . Warner 7606
❼	13	9	**If You Don't Know Me By Now**.................*Harold Melvin & The Bluenotes* . . . Philadelphia International 3520
❽	15	6	**You Ought To Be With Me** ....*Al Green* . . . Hi 2227
⑨	5	17	**Nights In White Satin**.........................*The Moody Blues* . . . Deram 85023
❿	11	12	**If I Could Reach You** ....*The 5th Dimension* . . . Bell 45261

★ **HIGHEST DEBUT** ★ POS 77
I Wanna Be With You.......................*Raspberries*

★ **BIGGEST MOVER** ★ 83 to 40
Superfly.......................*Curtis Mayfield*

266

Billboard — HOT 100 — DECEMBER 2, 1972

TW	LW	WK		
①	5	8	**Papa Was A Rollin' Stone**	*The Temptations* . . . Gordy 7121
②	4	15	I Am Woman	*Helen Reddy* . . . Capitol 3350
③	1	13	I Can See Clearly Now	*Johnny Nash* . . . Epic 10902
④	2	11	I'd Love You To Want Me	*Lobo* . . . Big Tree 147
⑤	7	10	If You Don't Know Me By Now	*Harold Melvin & The Bluenotes* . . . Philadelphia International 3520
⑥	6	13	**Summer Breeze**	*Seals & Crofts* . . . Warner 7606
❼	8	7	You Ought To Be With Me	*Al Green* . . . Hi 2227
❽	14	7	It Never Rains In Southern California	*Albert Hammond* . . . Mums 6011
⑨	3	16	I'll Be Around	*Spinners* . . . Atlantic 2904
⑩	13	7	Ventura Highway	*America* . . . Warner 7641

★ **HIGHEST DEBUT** ★ POS 60
Don't Let Me Be Lonely Tonight .....*James Taylor*

★ **BIGGEST MOVER** ★ 88 to 50
Been To Canaan ....*Carole King*

Billboard — HOT 100 — DECEMBER 9, 1972

TW	LW	WK		
①	2	16	**I Am Woman**	*Helen Reddy* . . . Capitol 3350
②	1	9	Papa Was A Rollin' Stone	*The Temptations* . . . Gordy 7121
❸	5	11	**If You Don't Know Me By Now**	*Harold Melvin & The Bluenotes* . . . Philadelphia International 3520
④	3	14	I Can See Clearly Now	*Johnny Nash* . . . Epic 10902
❺	7	8	You Ought To Be With Me	*Al Green* . . . Hi 2227
⑥	13	6	Me And Mrs. Jones	*Billy Paul* . . . Philadelphia International 3521
❼	8	8	It Never Rains In Southern California	*Albert Hammond* . . . Mums 6011
❽	10	8	**Ventura Highway**	*America* . . . Warner 7641
⑨	12	7	Clair	*Gilbert O'Sullivan* . . . MAM 3626
⑩	11	9	**I'm Stone In Love With You**	*The Stylistics* . . . Avco 4603

★ **HIGHEST DEBUT** ★ POS 73
Crocodile Rock................................*Elton John*

★ **BIGGEST MOVER** ★ 99 to 60
You're So Vain ....*Carly Simon*

Billboard — HOT 100 — DECEMBER 16, 1972

TW	LW	WK		
①	6	7	**Me And Mrs. Jones**	*Billy Paul* . . . Philadelphia International 3521
②	1	17	I Am Woman	*Helen Reddy* . . . Capitol 3350
③	3	12	**If You Don't Know Me By Now**	*Harold Melvin & The Bluenotes* . . . Philadelphia International 3520
❹	5	9	You Ought To Be With Me	*Al Green* . . . Hi 2227
❺	7	9	**It Never Rains In Southern California**	*Albert Hammond* . . . Mums 6011
⑥	2	10	Papa Was A Rollin' Stone	*The Temptations* . . . Gordy 7121
❼	9	8	Clair	*Gilbert O'Sullivan* . . . MAM 3626
⑧	8	9	**Ventura Highway**	*America* . . . Warner 7641
⑨	4	15	I Can See Clearly Now	*Johnny Nash* . . . Epic 10902
⑩	10	10	**I'm Stone In Love With You**	*The Stylistics* . . . Avco 4603

★ **HIGHEST DEBUT** ★ POS 81
Trouble Man ....*Marvin Gaye*

★ **BIGGEST MOVER** ★ 73 to 46
Crocodile Rock................................*Elton John*

TW	LW	WK	Billboard.	DECEMBER 23, 1972	HOT 100.
①	1	8	**Me And Mrs. Jones** ....*Billy Paul* ... Philadelphia International 3521		
②	2	18	I Am Woman..*Helen Reddy* ... Capitol 3350		
❸	4	10	**You Ought To Be With Me** ....*Al Green* ... Hi 2227		
❹	7	9	Clair...*Gilbert O'Sullivan* ... MAM 3626		
⑤	5	10	**It Never Rains In Southern California** .... Albert Hammond ... Mums 6011		
⑥	3	13	If You Don't Know Me By Now............... *Harold Melvin & The Bluenotes* ... Philadelphia International 3520		
❼	12	13	**Funny Face**...*Donna Fargo* ... Dot 17429		
⑧	6	11	Papa Was A Rollin' Stone.......................*The Temptations* ... Gordy 7121		
❾	37	4	You're So Vain..*Carly Simon* ... Elektra 45824		
⑩	11	12	**Rockin' Pneumonia - Boogie Woogie Flu**.......................*Johnny Rivers* ... United Artists 50960		

★ HIGHEST DEBUT ★ POS 74	★ BIGGEST MOVER ★ 100 to 42
I'm Never Gonna Be Alone Anymore ....*Cornelius Brothers & Sister Rose*	Hi, Hi, Hi ....*Wings*

TW	LW	WK	Billboard.	DECEMBER 30, 1972	HOT 100.
①	1	9	**Me And Mrs. Jones** ....*Billy Paul* ... Philadelphia International 3521		
❷	4	10	**Clair** ....*Gilbert O'Sullivan* ... MAM 3626		
❸	3	11	**You Ought To Be With Me** ....*Al Green* ... Hi 2227		
❹	9	5	You're So Vain..*Carly Simon* ... Elektra 45824		
⑤	5	11	**It Never Rains In Southern California** .... Albert Hammond ... Mums 6011		
⑥	7	14	**Funny Face**...*Donna Fargo* ... Dot 17429		
⑦	2	19	I Am Woman..*Helen Reddy* ... Capitol 3350		
❽	10	13	**Rockin' Pneumonia - Boogie Woogie Flu**.......................*Johnny Rivers* ... United Artists 50960		
❾	12	7	**Superfly** ....*Curtis Mayfield* ... Curtom 1978		
⑩	14	8	**Your Mama Don't Dance** ....*Kenny Loggins & Jim Messina* .:. Columbia 45719		

★ HIGHEST DEBUT ★ POS 73	★ BIGGEST MOVER ★ 98 to 78
Peaceful Easy Feeling............................*Eagles*	What My Baby Needs Now Is A Little More Lovin' ....*James Brown-Lyn Collins*

Billboard — JANUARY 6, 1973 — HOT 100

TW	LW	WK	Title	Artist ... Label
1	4	6	**You're So Vain**	*Carly Simon* . . . Elektra 45824
2	2	11	**Clair**	*Gilbert O'Sullivan* . . . MAM 3626
3	1	10	Me And Mrs. Jones	*Billy Paul* . . . Philadelphia International 3521
4	16	8	Superstition	*Stevie Wonder* . . . Tamla 54226
5	6	15	**Funny Face**	*Donna Fargo* . . . Dot 17429
6	5	12	It Never Rains In Southern California	*Albert Hammond* . . . Mums 6011
7	8	14	Rockin' Pneumonia - Boogie Woogie Flu	*Johnny Rivers* . . . United Artists 50960
8	10	9	Your Mama Don't Dance	*Kenny Loggins & Jim Messina* . . . Columbia 45719
9	9	8	Superfly	*Curtis Mayfield* . . . Curtom 1978
10	3	12	You Ought To Be With Me	*Al Green* . . . Hi 2227

★· **HIGHEST DEBUT** ★ POS 76
Living Together, Growing Together ....*The 5th Dimension*

★ **BIGGEST MOVER** ★ 81 to 54
Don't Expect Me To Be Your Friend ....*Lobo*

Billboard — JANUARY 13, 1973 — HOT 100

TW	LW	WK	Title	Artist ... Label
1	1	7	**You're So Vain**	*Carly Simon* . . . Elektra 45824
2	4	9	Superstition	*Stevie Wonder* . . . Tamla 54226
3	3	11	Me And Mrs. Jones	*Billy Paul* . . . Philadelphia International 3521
4	2	12	Clair...	*Gilbert O'Sullivan* . . . MAM 3626
5	5	16	**Funny Face**	*Donna Fargo* . . . Dot 17429
6	8	10	Your Mama Don't Dance	*Kenny Loggins & Jim Messina* . . . Columbia 45719
7	7	15	Rockin' Pneumonia - Boogie Woogie Flu	*Johnny Rivers* . . . United Artists 50960
8	9	9	**Superfly**	*Curtis Mayfield* . . . Curtom 1978
9	13	6	Crocodile Rock..	*Elton John* . . . MCA 40000
10	11	10	**Keeper Of The Castle**	*The Four Tops* . . . Dunhill 4330

★ **HIGHEST DEBUT** ★ POS 80
Dueling Banjos.......*Eric Weissberg & Steve Mandell*

★ **BIGGEST MOVER** ★ 54 to 33
Don't Expect Me To Be Your Friend ....*Lobo*

Billboard — JANUARY 20, 1973 — HOT 100

TW	LW	WK	Title	Artist ... Label
1	1	8	**You're So Vain**	*Carly Simon* . . . Elektra 45824
2	2	10	Superstition	*Stevie Wonder* . . . Tamla 54226
3	3	12	Me And Mrs. Jones	*Billy Paul* . . . Philadelphia International 3521
4	9	7	Crocodile Rock..	*Elton John* . . . MCA 40000
5	6	11	Your Mama Don't Dance	*Kenny Loggins & Jim Messina* . . . Columbia 45719
6	7	16	**Rockin' Pneumonia - Boogie Woogie Flu**	*Johnny Rivers* . . . United Artists 50960
7	4	13	Clair...	*Gilbert O'Sullivan* . . . MAM 3626
8	8	10	**Superfly**	*Curtis Mayfield* . . . Curtom 1978
9	13	9	Why Can't We Live Together	*Timmy Thomas* . . . Glades 1703
10	15	8	**Oh, Babe, What Would You Say?**	*Hurricane Smith* . . . Capitol 3383

★ **HIGHEST DEBUT** ★ POS 61
Love Train...*O'Jays*

★ **BIGGEST MOVER** ★ 98 to 71
Good Morning Heartache ....*Diana Ross*

Billboard — JANUARY 27, 1973 — HOT 100

TW	LW	WK	Title	Artist ... Label
1	2	11	**Superstition**	Stevie Wonder ... Tamla 54226
2	1	9	You're So Vain	Carly Simon ... Elektra 45824
3	4	8	Crocodile Rock	Elton John ... MCA 40000
4	5	12	**Your Mama Don't Dance**	Kenny Loggins & Jim Messina ... Columbia 45719
5	9	10	Why Can't We Live Together	Timmy Thomas ... Glades 1703
6	3	13	Me And Mrs. Jones	Billy Paul ... Philadelphia International 3521
7	10	9	Oh, Babe, What Would You Say?	Hurricane Smith ... Capitol 3383
8	13	7	Trouble Man	Marvin Gaye ... Tamla 54228
9	6	17	Rockin' Pneumonia - Boogie Woogie Flu	Johnny Rivers ... United Artists 50960
10	15	11	**The World Is A Ghetto**	War ... United Artists 50975

★ **HIGHEST DEBUT** ★ POS 54
Killing Me Softly With His Song......Roberta Flack

★ **BIGGEST MOVER** ★ 79 to 51
I Got Ants In My Pants (and i want to dance) ....James Brown

Billboard — FEBRUARY 3, 1973 — HOT 100

TW	LW	WK	Title	Artist ... Label
1	3	9	**Crocodile Rock**	Elton John ... MCA 40000
2	2	10	You're So Vain	Carly Simon ... Elektra 45824
3	1	12	Superstition	Stevie Wonder ... Tamla 54226
4	5	11	Why Can't We Live Together	Timmy Thomas ... Glades 1703
5	4	13	Your Mama Don't Dance	Kenny Loggins & Jim Messina ... Columbia 45719
6	7	10	Oh, Babe, What Would You Say?	Hurricane Smith ... Capitol 3383
7	8	8	**Trouble Man**	Marvin Gaye ... Tamla 54228
8	10	12	The World Is A Ghetto	War ... United Artists 50975
9	13	12	Do It Again	Steely Dan ... ABC 11338
10	11	8	**Hi, Hi, Hi**	Wings ... Apple 1857

★ **HIGHEST DEBUT** ★ POS 58
I'm Just A Singer (In A Rock And Roll Band) ....The Moody Blues

★ **BIGGEST MOVER** ★ 86 to 62
Neither One Of Us (Wants To Be The First To Say Goodbye) ....Gladys Knight & The Pips

Billboard — FEBRUARY 10, 1973 — HOT 100

TW	LW	WK	Title	Artist ... Label
1	1	10	**Crocodile Rock**	Elton John ... MCA 40000
2	2	11	You're So Vain	Carly Simon ... Elektra 45824
3	4	12	**Why Can't We Live Together**	Timmy Thomas ... Glades 1703
4	6	11	Oh, Babe, What Would You Say?	Hurricane Smith ... Capitol 3383
5	3	13	Superstition	Stevie Wonder ... Tamla 54226
6	9	13	**Do It Again**	Steely Dan ... ABC 11338
7	8	13	**The World Is A Ghetto**	War ... United Artists 50975
8	7	9	Trouble Man	Marvin Gaye ... Tamla 54228
9	12	7	Don't Expect Me To Be Your Friend	Lobo ... Big Tree 158
10	13	7	Could It Be I'm Falling In Love	Spinners ... Atlantic 2927

★ **HIGHEST DEBUT** ★ POS 77
Master Of Eyes..........................Aretha Franklin

★ **BIGGEST MOVER** ★ 74 to 50
Also Sprach Zarathustra (2001) ....Deodato

Billboard — FEBRUARY 17, 1973 — HOT 100

TW	LW	WK	Title / Artist / Label
1	1	11	**Crocodile Rock** ....*Elton John* . . . MCA 40000
2	2	12	You're So Vain ....*Carly Simon* . . . Elektra 45824
3	4	12	**Oh, Babe, What Would You Say?** ......*Hurricane Smith* . . . Capitol 3383
4	11	6	Dueling Banjos ....*Eric Weissberg & Steve Mandell* . . . Warner 7659
5	15	4	Killing Me Softly With His Song..................*Roberta Flack* . . . Atlantic 2940
6	6	14	**Do It Again** ....*Steely Dan* . . . ABC 11338
7	10	8	Could It Be I'm Falling In Love.........................*Spinners* . . . Atlantic 2927
8	9	8	**Don't Expect Me To Be Your Friend**................*Lobo* . . . Big Tree 158
9	3	13	Why Can't We Live Together ....*Timmy Thomas* . . . Glades 1703
10	12	13	Rocky Mountain High ....*John Denver* . . . RCA 0829

★ **HIGHEST DEBUT** ★ POS 73
Call Me (Come Back Home)..................*Al Green*

★ **BIGGEST MOVER** ★ 88 to 53
Break Up To Make Up..................*The Stylistics*

Billboard — FEBRUARY 24, 1973 — HOT 100

TW	LW	WK	Title / Artist / Label
1	5	5	**Killing Me Softly With His Song**...........*Roberta Flack* . . . Atlantic 2940
2	4	7	**Dueling Banjos** ....*Eric Weissberg & Steve Mandell* . . . Warner 7659
3	1	12	Crocodile Rock...*Elton John* . . . MCA 40000
4	2	13	You're So Vain ....*Carly Simon* . . . Elektra 45824
5	7	9	Could It Be I'm Falling In Love.........................*Spinners* . . . Atlantic 2927
6	6	15	Do It Again ....*Steely Dan* . . . ABC 11338
7	13	11	Last Song...*Edward Bear* . . . Capitol 3452
8	8	9	**Don't Expect Me To Be Your Friend**................*Lobo* . . . Big Tree 158
9	15	6	Love Train ....*O'Jays* . . . Philadelphia International 3524
10	10	14	Rocky Mountain High ....*John Denver* . . . RCA 0829

★ **HIGHEST DEBUT** ★ POS 61
Sing ....*Carpenters*

★ **BIGGEST MOVER** ★ 73 to 48
Call Me (Come Back Home).................*Al Green*

Billboard — MARCH 3, 1973 — HOT 100

TW	LW	WK	Title / Artist / Label
1	1	6	**Killing Me Softly With His Song**...........*Roberta Flack* . . . Atlantic 2940
2	2	8	**Dueling Banjos** ....*Eric Weissberg & Steve Mandell* . . . Warner 7659
3	7	12	**Last Song**...*Edward Bear* . . . Capitol 3452
4	5	10	**Could It Be I'm Falling In Love**.....................*Spinners* . . . Atlantic 2927
5	3	13	Crocodile Rock...*Elton John* . . . MCA 40000
6	4	14	You're So Vain ....*Carly Simon* . . . Elektra 45824
7	9	7	Love Train ....*O'Jays* . . . Philadelphia International 3524
8	18	5	Also Sprach Zarathustra (2001)...............................*Deodato* . . . CTI 12
9	10	15	**Rocky Mountain High**.................................*John Denver* . . . RCA 0829
10	8	10	Don't Expect Me To Be Your Friend.....................*Lobo* . . . Big Tree 158

★ **HIGHEST DEBUT** ★ POS 75
One Man Parade ....*James Taylor*

★ **BIGGEST MOVER** ★ 80 to 59
The Night The Lights Went Out In Georgia ....*Vicki Lawrence*

Billboard — MARCH 10, 1973 — HOT 100

TW	LW	WK	Title / Artist / Label
1	1	7	**Killing Me Softly With His Song** ....*Roberta Flack* ... Atlantic 2940
2	2	9	**Dueling Banjos** ....*Eric Weissberg & Steve Mandell* ... Warner 7659
3	3	13	**Last Song**..*Edward Bear* ... Capitol 3452
4	4	11	**Could It Be I'm Falling In Love**...................*Spinners* ... Atlantic 2927
5	7	8	Love Train ....*O'Jays* ... Philadelphia International 3524
6	8	6	Also Sprach Zarathustra (2001)............................*Deodato* ... CTI 12
7	5	14	Crocodile Rock...*Elton John* ... MCA 40000
8	11	15	The Cover Of "Rolling Stone" ....*Dr. Hook & The Medicine Show* ... Columbia 45732
9	9	16	**Rocky Mountain High**................................*John Denver* ... RCA 0829
10	12	14	Daddy's Home ....*Jermaine Jackson* ... Motown 1216

★ HIGHEST DEBUT ★ POS 80	★ BIGGEST MOVER ★ 49 to 31
Oh La De Da ....*The Staple Singers*	Sing ....*Carpenters*

Billboard — MARCH 17, 1973 — HOT 100

TW	LW	WK	Title / Artist / Label
1	1	8	**Killing Me Softly With His Song** ....*Roberta Flack* ... Atlantic 2940
2	2	10	**Dueling Banjos** ....*Eric Weissberg & Steve Mandell* ... Warner 7659
3	5	9	**Love Train** ....*O'Jays* ... Philadelphia International 3524
4	6	7	**Also Sprach Zarathustra (2001)**............................*Deodato* ... CTI 12
5	3	14	Last Song..*Edward Bear* ... Capitol 3452
6	8	16	**The Cover Of "Rolling Stone"** ....*Dr. Hook & The Medicine Show* ... Columbia 45732
7	4	12	Could It Be I'm Falling In Love ....*Spinners* ... Atlantic 2927
8	16	8	Neither One Of Us (Wants To Be The First To Say Goodbye)............ *Gladys Knight & The Pips* ... Soul 35098
9	10	15	**Daddy's Home** ....*Jermaine Jackson* ... Motown 1216
10	15	11	Danny's Song......................................*Anne Murray* ... Capitol 3481

★ HIGHEST DEBUT ★ POS 76	★ BIGGEST MOVER ★ 69 to 45
You Are The Sunshine Of My Life............*Stevie Wonder*	The Cisco Kid ....*War*

Billboard — MARCH 24, 1973 — HOT 100

TW	LW	WK	Title / Artist / Label
1	3	10	**Love Train**...................................*O'Jays* ... Philadelphia International 3524
2	1	9	**Killing Me Softly With His Song**..................*Roberta Flack* ... Atlantic 2940
3	4	8	**Also Sprach Zarathustra (2001)**............................*Deodato* ... CTI 12
4	8	9	**Neither One Of Us (Wants To Be The First To Say Goodbye)**............ *Gladys Knight & The Pips* ... Soul 35098
5	5	15	Last Song..*Edward Bear* ... Capitol 3452
6	6	17	**The Cover Of "Rolling Stone"** ....*Dr. Hook & The Medicine Show* ... Columbia 45732
7	2	11	Dueling Banjos ....*Eric Weissberg & Steve Mandell* ... Warner 7659
8	10	12	Danny's Song.................................*Anne Murray* ... Capitol 3481
9	11	7	Break Up To Make Up................................*The Stylistics* ... Avco 4611
10	14	8	Ain't No Woman (Like The One I've Got)........*Four Tops* ... Dunhill 4339

★ HIGHEST DEBUT ★ POS 83	★ BIGGEST MOVER ★ 55 to 29
Playground In My Mind ....*Clint Holmes*	The Twelfth Of Never ....*Donny Osmond*

Billboard · MARCH 31, 1973 · HOT 100.

TW	LW	WK	Title / Artist / Label
①	2	10	**Killing Me Softly With His Song** ....*Roberta Flack* ... Atlantic 2940
②	3	9	**Also Sprach Zarathustra (2001)** ....*Deodato* ... CTI 12
③	4	10	**Neither One Of Us (Wants To Be The First To Say Goodbye)** .... *Gladys Knight & The Pips* ... Soul 35098
④	1	11	**Love Train** ....*O'Jays* ... Philadelphia International 3524
⑤	10	9	**Ain't No Woman (Like The One I've Got)** ....*Four Tops* ... Dunhill 4339
⑥	9	8	**Break Up To Make Up** ....*The Stylistics* ... Avco 4611
⑦	5	16	**Last Song** ....*Edward Bear* ... Capitol 3452
⑧	8	13	**Danny's Song** ....*Anne Murray* ... Capitol 3481
⑨	11	6	**Sing** ....*Carpenters* ... A&M 1413
⑩	16	8	**The Night The Lights Went Out In Georgia** ....*Vicki Lawrence* ... Bell 45303

★ **HIGHEST DEBUT** ★ POS 70
The Right Thing To Do.....................*Carly Simon*

★ **BIGGEST MOVER** ★ 56 to 29
You Are The Sunshine Of My Life.............*Stevie Wonder*

Billboard · APRIL 7, 1973 · HOT 100.

TW	LW	WK	Title / Artist / Label
❶	10	9	**The Night The Lights Went Out In Georgia** ....*Vicki Lawrence* ... Bell 45303
②	3	11	**Neither One Of Us (Wants To Be The First To Say Goodbye)**. *Gladys Knight & The Pips* ... Soul 35098
③	1	11	**Killing Me Softly With His Song**.................*Roberta Flack* ... Atlantic 2940
④	5	10	**Ain't No Woman (Like The One I've Got)** .... *Four Tops* ... Dunhill 4339
⑤	6	9	**Break Up To Make Up** ....*The Stylistics* ... Avco 4611
❻	13	8	**Tie A Yellow Ribbon Round The Ole Oak Tree** .... *Dawn featuring Tony Orlando* ... Bell 45318
❼	9	7	**Sing**..*Carpenters* ... A&M 1413
⑧	8	14	**Danny's Song**.............................*Anne Murray* ... Capitol 3481
⑨	2	10	**Also Sprach Zarathustra (2001)**.........................*Deodato* ... CTI 12
⑩	21	6	**The Cisco Kid** ....*War* ... United Artists 163

★ **HIGHEST DEBUT** ★ POS 77
Daniel ....*Elton John*

★ **BIGGEST MOVER** ★ 78 to 59
Frankenstein....................*The Edgar Winter Group*

Billboard · APRIL 14, 1973 · HOT 100.

TW	LW	WK	Title / Artist / Label
①	1	10	**The Night The Lights Went Out In Georgia** ....*Vicki Lawrence* ... Bell 45303
②	2	12	**Neither One Of Us (Wants To Be The First To Say Goodbye)**. *Gladys Knight & The Pips* ... Soul 35098
❸	6	9	**Tie A Yellow Ribbon Round The Ole Oak Tree** .... *Dawn featuring Tony Orlando* ... Bell 45318
④	4	11	**Ain't No Woman (Like The One I've Got)** .... *Four Tops* ... Dunhill 4339
❺	7	8	**Sing** ....*Carpenters* ... A&M 1413
❻	10	7	**The Cisco Kid** ....*War* ... United Artists 163
⑦	8	15	**Danny's Song**.................................*Anne Murray* ... Capitol 3481
⑧	5	10	**Break Up To Make Up**................................*The Stylistics* ... Avco 4611
⑨	3	12	**Killing Me Softly With His Song**.................*Roberta Flack* ... Atlantic 2940
⑩	11	9	**Call Me (Come Back Home)** ....*Al Green* ... Hi 2235

★ **HIGHEST DEBUT** ★ POS 73
My Love ....*Paul McCartney & Wings*

★ **BIGGEST MOVER** ★ 77 to 46
Daniel ....*Elton John*

TW	LW	WK	Billboard	APRIL 21, 1973	HOT 100
❶	3	10	Tie A Yellow Ribbon Round The Ole Oak Tree.......... *Dawn featuring Tony Orlando* . . . Bell 45318		
②	1	11	The Night The Lights Went Out In Georgia...................*Vicki Lawrence* . . . Bell 45303		
❸	5	9	Sing...*Carpenters* . . . A&M 1413		
❹	6	8	The Cisco Kid...*War* . . . United Artists 163		
⑤	4	12	Ain't No Woman (Like The One I've Got).........*Four Tops* . . . Dunhill 4339		
⑥	2	13	Neither One Of Us (Wants To Be The First To Say Goodbye)............ *Gladys Knight & The Pips* . . . Soul 35098		
❼	12	14	Little Willy...*The Sweet* . . . Bell 45251		
❽	11	9	Masterpiece...*The Temptations* . . . Gordy 7126		
⑨	7	16	Danny's Song...*Anne Murray* . . . Capitol 3481		
❿	15	8	The Twelfth Of Never................................*Donny Osmond* . . . MGM 14503		

★ HIGHEST DEBUT ★ POS 84	★ BIGGEST MOVER ★ 54 to 30
Long Train Runnin'..............*The Doobie Brothers*	Pillow Talk...*Sylvia*

TW	LW	WK	Billboard	APRIL 28, 1973	HOT 100
①	1	11	Tie A Yellow Ribbon Round The Ole Oak Tree........................ *Dawn featuring Tony Orlando* . . . Bell 45318		
❷	4	9	The Cisco Kid...................................*War* . . . United Artists 163		
③	3	10	Sing...*Carpenters* . . . A&M 1413		
④	2	12	The Night The Lights Went Out In Georgia...................*Vicki Lawrence* . . . Bell 45303		
❺	7	15	Little Willy...*The Sweet* . . . Bell 45251		
❻	11	7	You Are The Sunshine Of My Life.............*Stevie Wonder* . . . Tamla 54232		
⑦	8	10	Masterpiece ....*The Temptations* . . . Gordy 7126		
❽	10	9	The Twelfth Of Never................................*Donny Osmond* . . . MGM 14503		
❾	13	9	Stuck In The Middle With You ....*Stealers Wheel* . . . A&M 1416		
❿	5	13	Ain't No Woman (Like The One I've Got).........*Four Tops* . . . Dunhill 4339		

★ HIGHEST DEBUT ★ POS 71	★ BIGGEST MOVER ★ 62 to 36
One Of A Kind (Love Affair)..................*Spinners*	My Love ....*Paul McCartney & Wings*

TW	LW	WK	Billboard	MAY 5, 1973	HOT 100
①	1	12	Tie A Yellow Ribbon Round The Ole Oak Tree........................ *Dawn featuring Tony Orlando* . . . Bell 45318		
②	2	10	The Cisco Kid...................................*War* . . . United Artists 163		
❸	5	16	Little Willy...*The Sweet* . . . Bell 45251		
❹	6	8	You Are The Sunshine Of My Life.............*Stevie Wonder* . . . Tamla 54232		
⑤	4	13	The Night The Lights Went Out In Georgia...................*Vicki Lawrence* . . . Bell 45303		
❻	11	11	Drift Away...*Dobie Gray* . . . Decca 33057		
❼	9	10	Stuck In The Middle With You ....*Stealers Wheel* . . . A&M 1416		
❽	8	10	The Twelfth Of Never................................*Donny Osmond* . . . MGM 14503		
⑨	3	11	Sing...*Carpenters* . . . A&M 1413		
❿	15	9	Frankenstein.......................................*The Edgar Winter Group* . . . Epic 10967		

★ HIGHEST DEBUT ★ POS 84	★ BIGGEST MOVER ★ 57 to 37
With A Child's Heart..................*Michael Jackson*	I'm Gonna Love You Just A Little More Baby ....*Barry White*

Billboard · MAY 12, 1973 · HOT 100.

TW	LW	WK	
①	1	13	**Tie A Yellow Ribbon Round The Ole Oak Tree** .... *Dawn featuring Tony Orlando* ... Bell 45318
❷	4	9	You Are The Sunshine Of My Life ....*Stevie Wonder* ... Tamla 54232
③	3	17	**Little Willy** ....*The Sweet* ... Bell 45251
④	2	11	The Cisco Kid ....*War* ... United Artists 163
⑤	6	12	Drift Away ....*Dobie Gray* ... Decca 33057
⑥	7	11	**Stuck In The Middle With You** ....*Stealers Wheel* ... A&M 1416
❼	10	10	Frankenstein ....*The Edgar Winter Group* ... Epic 10967
⑧	5	14	The Night The Lights Went Out In Georgia ....*Vicki Lawrence* ... Bell 45303
❾	14	6	Daniel ....*Elton John* ... MCA 40046
⑩	8	11	The Twelfth Of Never ....*Donny Osmond* ... MGM 14503

★ HIGHEST DEBUT ★ POS 81	★ BIGGEST MOVER ★ 97 to 82
Diamond Girl ....*Seals & Crofts*	So Very Hard To Go ....*Tower Of Power*

Billboard · MAY 19, 1973 · HOT 100.

TW	LW	WK	
❶	2	10	**You Are The Sunshine Of My Life** ......*Stevie Wonder* ... Tamla 54232
②	1	14	Tie A Yellow Ribbon Round The Ole Oak Tree .... *Dawn featuring Tony Orlando* ... Bell 45318
③	3	18	**Little Willy** ....*The Sweet* ... Bell 45251
❹	7	11	Frankenstein ....*The Edgar Winter Group* ... Epic 10967
❺	9	7	Daniel ....*Elton John* ... MCA 40046
❻	13	6	My Love ....*Paul McCartney & Wings* ... Apple 1861
⑦	5	13	Drift Away ....*Dobie Gray* ... Decca 33057
⑧	6	12	Stuck In The Middle With You ....*Stealers Wheel* ... A&M 1416
❾	14	9	Pillow Talk ....*Sylvia* .. Vibration 521
⑩	12	14	Wildflower ....*Skylark* ... Capitol 3511

★ HIGHEST DEBUT ★ POS 59	★ BIGGEST MOVER ★ 85 to 63
Give Me Love (Give Me Peace On Earth) ....*George Harrison*	Boogie Woogie Bugle Boy ....*Bette Midler*

Billboard · MAY 26, 1973 · HOT 100.

TW	LW	WK	
❶	4	12	**Frankenstein** ....*The Edgar Winter Group* ... Epic 10967
❷	6	7	My Love ....*Paul McCartney & Wings* ... Apple 1861
❸	5	8	Daniel ....*Elton John* ... MCA 40046
④	2	15	Tie A Yellow Ribbon Round The Ole Oak Tree .... *Dawn featuring Tony Orlando* ... Bell 45318
⑤	1	11	You Are The Sunshine Of My Life ....*Stevie Wonder* ... Tamla 54232
❻	9	10	Pillow Talk ....*Sylvia* ... Vibration 521
⑦	3	19	Little Willy ....*The Sweet* ... Bell 45251
⑧	7	14	Drift Away ....*Dobie Gray* ... Decca 33057
❾	10	15	Wildflower ....*Skylark* ... Capitol 3511
⑩	13	13	Hocus Pocus ....*Focus* ... Sire 704

★ HIGHEST DEBUT ★ POS 83	★ BIGGEST MOVER ★ 59 to 34
What About Me..................*Anne Murray*	Give Me Love (Give Me Peace On Earth) ....*George Harrison*

TW	LW	WK	Billboard	JUNE 2, 1973	HOT 100
❶	2	8	My Love	Paul McCartney & Wings	Apple 1861
②	3	9	Daniel	Elton John	MCA 40046
③	1	13	Frankenstein	The Edgar Winter Group	Epic 10967
❹	6	11	Pillow Talk	Sylvia	Vibration 521
⑤	4	16	Tie A Yellow Ribbon Round The Ole Oak Tree	Dawn featuring Tony Orlando	Bell 45318
⑥	5	12	You Are The Sunshine Of My Life	Stevie Wonder	Tamla 54232
❼	12	8	I'm Gonna Love You Just A Little More Baby	Barry White	20th Century 2018
⑧	7	20	Little Willy	The Sweet	Bell 45251
⑨	10	14	Hocus Pocus	Focus	Sire 704
❿	14	11	Playground In My Mind	Clint Holmes	Epic 10891

★ HIGHEST DEBUT ★ POS 79
Yesterday Once More ....Carpenters

★ BIGGEST MOVER ★ 57 to 28
Kodachrome ....Paul Simon

TW	LW	WK	Billboard	JUNE 9, 1973	HOT 100
①	1	9	My Love	Paul McCartney & Wings	Apple 1861
②	3	14	Frankenstein	The Edgar Winter Group	Epic 10967
③	4	12	Pillow Talk	Sylvia	Vibration 521
④	2	10	Daniel	Elton John	MCA 40046
⑤	10	12	Playground In My Mind	Clint Holmes	Epic 10891
⑥	7	9	I'm Gonna Love You Just A Little More Baby	Barry White	20th Century 2018
⑦	5	17	Tie A Yellow Ribbon Round The Ole Oak Tree	Dawn featuring Tony Orlando	Bell 45318
⑧	6	13	You Are The Sunshine Of My Life	Stevie Wonder	Tamla 54232
⑨	9	15	Hocus Pocus	Focus	Sire 704
❿	22	8	Long Train Runnin'	The Doobie Brothers	Warner 7698

★ HIGHEST DEBUT ★ POS 73
There's No Me Without You ....Manhattans

★ BIGGEST MOVER ★ 96 to 63
Misdemeanor ....Foster Sylvers

TW	LW	WK	Billboard	JUNE 16, 1973	HOT 100
①	1	10	My Love	Paul McCartney & Wings	Apple 1861
❷	5	13	Playground In My Mind	Clint Holmes	Epic 10891
③	3	13	Pillow Talk	Sylvia	Vibration 521
④	6	10	I'm Gonna Love You Just A Little More Baby	Barry White	20th Century 2018
⑤	4	11	Daniel	Elton John	MCA 40046
⑥	2	15	Frankenstein	The Edgar Winter Group	Epic 10967
❼	14	12	Will It Go Round In Circles	Billy Preston	A&M 1411
❽	13	5	Give Me Love (Give Me Peace On Earth)	George Harrison	Apple 1862
❾	17	5	Kodachrome	Paul Simon	Columbia 45859
❿	7	18	Tie A Yellow Ribbon Round The Ole Oak Tree	Dawn featuring Tony Orlando	Bell 45318

★ HIGHEST DEBUT ★ POS 71
Goin' Home ....The Osmonds

★ BIGGEST MOVER ★ 69 to 38
Yesterday Once More ....Carpenters

Billboard 🔵 JUNE 23, 1973 🔵 HOT 100®

TW	LW	WK		
①	1	11	**My Love**...*Paul McCartney & Wings* ... Apple 1861	
②	2	14	**Playground In My Mind**..............................*Clint Holmes* ... Epic 10891	
③	4	11	**I'm Gonna Love You Just A Little More Baby**.......... *Barry White* ... 20th Century 2018	
④	7	13	**Will It Go Round In Circles**..............................*Billy Preston* ... A&M 1411	
⑤	8	6	**Give Me Love (Give Me Peace On Earth)** ....*George Harrison* ... Apple 1862	
⑥	3	14	**Pillow Talk**...*Sylvia* ... Vibration 521	
⑦	9	6	**Kodachrome**...*Paul Simon* ... Columbia 45859	
⑧	5	12	**Daniel** ....*Elton John* ... MCA 40046	
⑨	12	10	**Long Train Runnin'**...........................*The Doobie Brothers* ... Warner 7698	
⑩	11	11	**Right Place Wrong Time** ....*Dr. John* ... Atco 6914	

★ **HIGHEST DEBUT** ★ POS 75
Feelin' Stronger Every Day..................*Chicago*

★ **BIGGEST MOVER** ★ 77 to 51
The Plastic Man ....*The Temptations*

Billboard 🔵 JUNE 30, 1973 🔵 HOT 100®

TW	LW	WK		
❶	5	7	**Give Me Love (Give Me Peace On Earth)**.............*George Harrison* ... Apple 1862	
②	1	12	**My Love** ....*Paul McCartney & Wings* ... Apple 1861	
③	4	14	**Will It Go Round In Circles**..............................*Billy Preston* ... A&M 1411	
④	3	12	**I'm Gonna Love You Just A Little More Baby** .... *Barry White* ... 20th Century 2018	
❺	7	7	**Kodachrome**...*Paul Simon* ... Columbia 45859	
⑥	6	15	**Pillow Talk**...*Sylvia* ... Vibration 521	
⑦	2	15	**Playground In My Mind** ....*Clint Holmes* ... Epic 10891	
⑧	9	11	**Long Train Runnin'** ....*The Doobie Brothers* ... Warner 7698	
⑨	10	12	**Right Place Wrong Time** ....*Dr. John* ... Atco 6914	
⑩	11	7	**Shambala** ....*Three Dog Night* ... Dunhill 4352	

★ **HIGHEST DEBUT** ★ POS 78
If You Want Me To Stay ....*Sly & The Family Stone*

★ **BIGGEST MOVER** ★ 57 to 39
I'll Always Love My Mama ....*The Intruders*

Billboard 🔵 JULY 7, 1973 🔵 HOT 100®

TW	LW	WK		
①	3	15	**Will It Go Round In Circles**........................*Billy Preston* ... A&M 1411	
❷	5	8	**Kodachrome** ....*Paul Simon* ... Columbia 45859	
③	2	13	**My Love** ....*Paul McCartney & Wings* ... Apple 1861	
④	1	8	**Give Me Love (Give Me Peace On Earth)** ....*George Harrison* ... Apple 1862	
❺	12	12	**Bad, Bad Leroy Brown** ....*Jim Croce* ... ABC 11359	
⑥	7	16	**Playground In My Mind** ....*Clint Holmes* ... Epic 10891	
❼	10	8	**Shambala** ....*Three Dog Night* ... Dunhill 4352	
❽	13	6	**Yesterday Once More**..........................*Carpenters* ... A&M 1446	
⑨	9	13	**Right Place Wrong Time** ....*Dr. John* ... Atco 6914	
⑩	4	13	**I'm Gonna Love You Just A Little More Baby** .... *Barry White* ... 20th Century 2018	

★ **HIGHEST DEBUT** ★ POS 69
Live And Let Die ....*Wings*

★ **BIGGEST MOVER** ★ 86 to 42
The Morning After ....*Maureen McGovern*

Billboard — JULY 14, 1973 — HOT 100

TW	LW	WK	Title	Artist ... Label
①	1	16	**Will It Go Round In Circles**	*Billy Preston* ... A&M 1411
②	2	9	**Kodachrome**	*Paul Simon* ... Columbia 45859
③	5	13	**Bad, Bad Leroy Brown**	*Jim Croce* ... ABC 11359
❹	7	9	**Shambala**	*Three Dog Night* ... Dunhill 4352
⑤	4	9	**Give Me Love (Give Me Peace On Earth)**	*George Harrison* ... Apple 1862
⑥	8	7	**Yesterday Once More**	*Carpenters* ... A&M 1446
⑦	6	17	**Playground In My Mind**	*Clint Holmes* ... Epic 10891
❽	11	8	**Smoke On The Water**	*Deep Purple* ... Warner 7710
⑨	3	14	**My Love**	*Paul McCartney & Wings* ... Apple 1861
⑩	9	14	**Right Place Wrong Time**	*Dr. John* ... Atco 6914

★ **HIGHEST DEBUT** ★ POS 68
Say, Has Anybody Seen My Sweet Gypsy Rose ... *Tony Orlando & Dawn*

★ **BIGGEST MOVER** ★ 73 to 46
Here I Am (Come And Take Me) ... *Al Green*

Billboard — JULY 21, 1973 — HOT 100

TW	LW	WK	Title	Artist ... Label
①	3	14	**Bad, Bad Leroy Brown**	*Jim Croce* ... ABC 11359
②	1	17	**Will It Go Round In Circles**	*Billy Preston* ... A&M 1411
❸	6	8	**Yesterday Once More**	*Carpenters* ... A&M 1446
④	4	10	**Shambala**	*Three Dog Night* ... Dunhill 4352
⑤	2	10	**Kodachrome**	*Paul Simon* ... Columbia 45859
⑥	5	10	**Give Me Love (Give Me Peace On Earth)**	*George Harrison* ... Apple 1862
⑦	8	9	**Smoke On The Water**	*Deep Purple* ... Warner 7710
❽	14	11	**Boogie Woogie Bugle Boy**	*Bette Midler* ... Atlantic 2964
⑨	7	18	**Playground In My Mind**	*Clint Holmes* ... Epic 10891
⑩	12	14	**Natural High**	*Bloodstone* ... London 1046

★ **HIGHEST DEBUT** ★ POS 66
Gypsy Man ... *War*

★ **BIGGEST MOVER** ★ 74 to 50
Let's Get It On ... *Marvin Gaye*

Billboard — JULY 28, 1973 — HOT 100

TW	LW	WK	Title	Artist ... Label
①	1	15	**Bad, Bad Leroy Brown**	*Jim Croce* ... ABC 11359
②	3	9	**Yesterday Once More**	*Carpenters* ... A&M 1446
③	4	11	**Shambala**	*Three Dog Night* ... Dunhill 4352
❹	7	10	**Smoke On The Water**	*Deep Purple* ... Warner 7710
⑤	2	18	**Will It Go Round In Circles**	*Billy Preston* ... A&M 1411
⑥	11	12	**Diamond Girl**	*Seals & Crofts* ... Warner 7708
⑦	5	11	**Kodachrome**	*Paul Simon* ... Columbia 45859
⑧	8	12	**Boogie Woogie Bugle Boy**	*Bette Midler* ... Atlantic 2964
⑨	20	6	**The Morning After**	*Maureen McGovern* ... 20th Century 2010
⑩	6	11	**Give Me Love (Give Me Peace On Earth)**	*George Harrison* ... Apple 1862

★ **HIGHEST DEBUT** ★ POS 81
My Maria ... *B.W. Stevenson*

★ **BIGGEST MOVER** ★ 87 to 58
Everyone's Agreed That Everything Will Turn Out Fine ... *Stealers Wheel*

TW	LW	WK	Billboard	AUGUST 4, 1973	HOT 100
①	9	7	The Morning After	Maureen McGovern ...	20th Century 2010
②	1	16	Bad, Bad Leroy Brown	Jim Croce ...	ABC 11359
③	21	5	Live And Let Die	Wings ...	Apple 1863
④	4	11	Smoke On The Water	Deep Purple ...	Warner 7710
⑤	2	10	Yesterday Once More	Carpenters ...	A&M 1446
⑥	6	13	Diamond Girl	Seals & Crofts ...	Warner 7708
⑦	11	10	Touch Me In The Morning	Diana Ross ...	Motown 1239
⑧	20	7	Brother Louie	Stories ...	Kama Sutra 577
⑨	5	19	Will It Go Round In Circles	Billy Preston ...	A&M 1411
⑩	3	12	Shambala	Three Dog Night ...	Dunhill 4352

★ HIGHEST DEBUT ★ POS 60
Loves Me Like A Rock....................Paul Simon

★ BIGGEST MOVER ★ 74 to 49
Future Shock ....Curtis Mayfield

TW	LW	WK	Billboard	AUGUST 11, 1973	HOT 100
①	1	8	The Morning After	Maureen McGovern ...	20th Century 2010
②	3	6	Live And Let Die	Wings ...	Apple 1863
③	8	8	Brother Louie	Stories ...	Kama Sutra 577
④	7	11	Touch Me In The Morning	Diana Ross ...	Motown 1239
⑤	2	17	Bad, Bad Leroy Brown	Jim Croce ...	ABC 11359
⑥	4	12	Smoke On The Water	Deep Purple ...	Warner 7710
⑦	17	5	Let's Get It On	Marvin Gaye ...	Tamla 54234
⑧	5	11	Yesterday Once More	Carpenters ...	A&M 1446
⑨	15	7	Uneasy Rider	Charlie Daniels ...	Kama Sutra 576
⑩	12	32	Monster Mash	Bobby "Boris" Pickett ...	Parrot 348

★ HIGHEST DEBUT ★ POS 77
You've Never Been This Far Before.......Conway Twitty

★ BIGGEST MOVER ★ 74 to 34
Saturday Night's Alright For Fighting.........Elton John

TW	LW	WK	Billboard	AUGUST 18, 1973	HOT 100
①	4	12	Touch Me In The Morning	Diana Ross ...	Motown 1239
②	2	7	Live And Let Die	Wings ...	Apple 1863
③	3	9	Brother Louie	Stories ...	Kama Sutra 577
④	1	9	The Morning After	Maureen McGovern ...	20th Century 2010
⑤	7	6	Let's Get It On	Marvin Gaye ...	Tamla 54234
⑥	5	18	Bad, Bad Leroy Brown	Jim Croce ...	ABC 11359
⑦	13	9	Get Down	Gilbert O'Sullivan ...	MAM 3629
⑧	15	9	Delta Dawn	Helen Reddy ...	Capitol 3645
⑨	9	8	Uneasy Rider	Charlie Daniels ...	Kama Sutra 576
⑩	11	9	Feelin' Stronger Every Day	Chicago ...	Columbia 45880

★ HIGHEST DEBUT ★ POS 64
Ghetto Child................................Spinners

★ BIGGEST MOVER ★ 57 to 29
We're An American Band ....Grand Funk

Billboard 🔘 AUGUST 25, 1973 🔘 HOT 100.

TW	LW	WK	Title	Artist ... Label
①	3	10	**Brother Louie**	*Stories* . . . Kama Sutra 577
②	2	8	**Live And Let Die**	*Wings* . . . Apple 1863
③	1	13	**Touch Me In The Morning**	*Diana Ross* . . . Motown 1239
④	5	7	**Let's Get It On**	*Marvin Gaye* . . . Tamla 54234
⑤	4	10	**The Morning After**	*Maureen McGovern* . . . 20th Century 2010
⑥	8	10	**Delta Dawn**	*Helen Reddy* . . . Capitol 3645
⑦	7	10	**Get Down**	*Gilbert O'Sullivan* . . . MAM 3629
⑧	14	7	**Say, Has Anybody Seen My Sweet Gypsy Rose**	*Tony Orlando & Dawn* . . . Bell 45374
⑨	9	9	**Uneasy Rider**	*Charlie Daniels* . . . Kama Sutra 576
⑩	6	19	**Bad, Bad Leroy Brown**	*Jim Croce* . . . ABC 11359

★ HIGHEST DEBUT ★ POS 79	★ BIGGEST MOVER ★ 73 to 51
Keep On Truckin' . . . . *Eddie Kendricks*	**Higher Ground** . . . . *Stevie Wonder*

Billboard 🔘 SEPTEMBER 1, 1973 🔘 HOT 100.

TW	LW	WK	Title	Artist ... Label
①	1	11	**Brother Louie**	*Stories* . . . Kama Sutra 577
②	4	8	**Let's Get It On**	*Marvin Gaye* . . . Tamla 54234
③	6	11	**Delta Dawn**	*Helen Reddy* . . . Capitol 3645
④	3	14	**Touch Me In The Morning**	*Diana Ross* . . . Motown 1239
⑤	2	9	**Live And Let Die**	*Wings* . . . Apple 1863
⑥	8	8	**Say, Has Anybody Seen My Sweet Gypsy Rose**	*Tony Orlando & Dawn* . . . Bell 45374
⑦	5	11	**The Morning After**	*Maureen McGovern* . . . 20th Century 2010
⑧	7	11	**Get Down**	*Gilbert O'Sullivan* . . . MAM 3629
⑨	16	5	**Loves Me Like A Rock**	*Paul Simon* . . . Columbia 45907
⑩	11	11	**Feelin' Stronger Every Day**	*Chicago* . . . Columbia 45880

★ HIGHEST DEBUT ★ POS 71	★ BIGGEST MOVER ★ 85 to 58
Midnight Train To Georgia . . . . . *Gladys Knight & The Pips*	**Ramblin Man** . . . . *The Allman Brothers Band*

Billboard 🔘 SEPTEMBER 8, 1973 🔘 HOT 100.

TW	LW	WK	Title	Artist ... Label
①	2	9	**Let's Get It On**	*Marvin Gaye* . . . Tamla 54234
②	1	12	**Brother Louie**	*Stories* . . . Kama Sutra 577
③	3	12	**Delta Dawn**	*Helen Reddy* . . . Capitol 3645
④	6	9	**Say, Has Anybody Seen My Sweet Gypsy Rose**	*Tony Orlando & Dawn* . . . Bell 45374
⑤	4	15	**Touch Me In The Morning**	*Diana Ross* . . . Motown 1239
⑥	9	6	**Loves Me Like A Rock**	*Paul Simon* . . . Columbia 45907
⑦	5	10	**Live And Let Die**	*Wings* . . . Apple 1863
⑧	11	7	**We're An American Band**	*Grand Funk* . . . Capitol 3660
⑨	15	8	**Gypsy Man**	*War* . . . United Artists 281
⑩	14	10	**Here I Am (Come And Take Me)**	*Al Green* . . . Hi 2247

★ HIGHEST DEBUT ★ POS 75	★ BIGGEST MOVER ★ 58 to 35
Angie . . . . *The Rolling Stones*	**Ramblin Man** . . . . *The Allman Brothers Band*

Billboard ⊙ SEPTEMBER 15, 1973 ⊙ HOT 100

TW	LW	WK			
①	3	13	**Delta Dawn**	*Helen Reddy* ...	Capitol 3645
②	1	10	**Let's Get It On**	*Marvin Gaye* ...	Tamla 54234
③	4	10	**Say, Has Anybody Seen My Sweet Gypsy Rose**		
				Tony Orlando & Dawn ...	Bell 45374
④	6	7	**Loves Me Like A Rock**	*Paul Simon* ...	Columbia 45907
❺	8	8	**We're An American Band**	*Grand Funk* ...	Capitol 3660
⑥	2	13	**Brother Louie**	*Stories* ...	Kama Sutra 577
⑦	5	16	**Touch Me In The Morning**	*Diana Ross* ...	Motown 1239
⑧	9	9	**Gypsy Man**	*War* ...	United Artists 281
⑨	7	11	**Live And Let Die**	*Wings* ...	Apple 1863
⑩	10	11	**Here I Am (Come And Take Me)**	*Al Green* ...	Hi 2247

★ **HIGHEST DEBUT** ★ POS 79
All I Know .... *Garfunkel*

★ **BIGGEST MOVER** ★ 73 to 48
Rhapsody In Blue .... *Deodato*

Billboard ⊙ SEPTEMBER 22, 1973 ⊙ HOT 100

TW	LW	WK			
①	2	11	**Let's Get It On**	*Marvin Gaye* ...	Tamla 54234
❷	5	9	**We're An American Band**	*Grand Funk* ...	Capitol 3660
③	1	14	**Delta Dawn**	*Helen Reddy* ...	Capitol 3645
④	4	8	**Loves Me Like A Rock**	*Paul Simon* ...	Columbia 45907
⑤	3	11	**Say, Has Anybody Seen My Sweet Gypsy Rose**		
				Tony Orlando & Dawn ...	Bell 45374
⑥	6	14	**Brother Louie**	*Stories* ...	Kama Sutra 577
❼	11	8	**Half-Breed**	*Cher* ...	MCA 40102
❽	13	6	**Higher Ground**	*Stevie Wonder* ...	Tamla 54235
⑨	7	17	**Touch Me In The Morning**	*Diana Ross* ...	Motown 1239
⑩	15	11	**That Lady**	*Isley Brothers* ...	T-Neck 2251

★ **HIGHEST DEBUT** ★ POS 75
Space Race .... *Billy Preston*

★ **BIGGEST MOVER** ★ 55 to 22
Angie .... *The Rolling Stones*

Billboard ⊙ SEPTEMBER 29, 1973 ⊙ HOT 100

TW	LW	WK			
①	2	10	**We're An American Band**	*Grand Funk* ...	Capitol 3660
②	1	12	**Let's Get It On**	*Marvin Gaye* ...	Tamla 54234
❸	7	9	**Half-Breed**	*Cher* ...	MCA 40102
④	4	9	**Loves Me Like A Rock**	*Paul Simon* ...	Columbia 45907
⑤	3	15	**Delta Dawn**	*Helen Reddy* ...	Capitol 3645
⑥	8	7	**Higher Ground**	*Stevie Wonder* ...	Tamla 54235
⑦	5	12	**Say, Has Anybody Seen My Sweet Gypsy Rose**		
				Tony Orlando & Dawn ...	Bell 45374
⑧	10	12	**That Lady**	*Isley Brothers* ...	T-Neck 2251
⑨	11	10	**My Maria**	*B.W. Stevenson* ...	RCA 0030
⑩	15	6	**Ramblin Man**	*The Allman Brothers Band* ...	Capricorn 0027

★ **HIGHEST DEBUT** ★ POS 71
Just You 'N' Me .... *Chicago*

★ **BIGGEST MOVER** ★ 72 to 43
Paper Roses .... *Marie Osmond*

TW	LW	WK	Billboard.	OCTOBER 6, 1973	HOT 100.
①	3	10	Half-Breed	....*Cher* . . . MCA 40102	
②	4	10	Loves Me Like A Rock	........................*Paul Simon* . . . Columbia 45907	
③	2	13	Let's Get It On	...........................*Marvin Gaye* . . . Tamla 54234	
④	1	11	We're An American Band	..........................*Grand Funk* . . . Capitol 3660	
⑤	6	8	Higher Ground	..............................*Stevie Wonder* . . . Tamla 54235	
⑥	8	13	That Lady	..............................*Isley Brothers* . . . T-Neck 2251	
❼	10	7	Ramblin Man	........................*The Allman Brothers Band* . . . Capricorn 0027	
❽	13	5	Angie	........................*The Rolling Stones* . . . Rolling Stones 19105	
⑨	5	16	Delta Dawn	................................*Helen Reddy* . . . Capitol 3645	
⑩	12	7	Keep On Truckin'	........................*Eddie Kendricks* . . . Tamla 54238	

★ HIGHEST DEBUT ★ POS 66	★ BIGGEST MOVER ★ 94 to 68
You're A Special Part Of Me ....*Diana Ross &* *Marvin Gaye*	The Love I Lost.......*Harold Melvin & The Bluenotes*

TW	LW	WK	Billboard.	OCTOBER 13, 1973	HOT 100.
①	1	11	Half-Breed	....*Cher* . . . MCA 40102	
❷	7	8	Ramblin Man	........................*The Allman Brothers Band* . . . Capricorn 0027	
③	3	14	Let's Get It On	...........................*Marvin Gaye* . . . Tamla 54234	
④	5	9	Higher Ground	..............................*Stevie Wonder* . . . Tamla 54235	
❺	8	6	Angie	........................*The Rolling Stones* . . . Rolling Stones 19105	
⑥	6	14	That Lady	..............................*Isley Brothers* . . . T-Neck 2251	
⑦	2	11	Loves Me Like A Rock	........................*Paul Simon* . . . Columbia 45907	
❽	11	7	Midnight Train To Georgia	..........*Gladys Knight & The Pips* . . . Buddah 383	
⑨	10	8	Keep On Truckin'	........................*Eddie Kendricks* . . . Tamla 54238	
⑩	4	12	We're An American Band	..........................*Grand Funk* . . . Capitol 3660	

★ HIGHEST DEBUT ★ POS 77	★ BIGGEST MOVER ★ 76 to 40
Cheaper To Keep Her...................*Johnnie Taylor*	I Got A Name......................................*Jim Croce*

TW	LW	WK	Billboard.	OCTOBER 20, 1973	HOT 100.
❶	5	7	Angie	........................*The Rolling Stones* . . . Rolling Stones 19105	
②	1	12	Half-Breed	....*Cher* . . . MCA 40102	
③	2	9	Ramblin Man	........................*The Allman Brothers Band* . . . Capricorn 0027	
④	3	15	Let's Get It On	...........................*Marvin Gaye* . . . Tamla 54234	
❺	8	8	Midnight Train To Georgia	..........*Gladys Knight & The Pips* . . . Buddah 383	
⑥	6	15	That Lady	..............................*Isley Brothers* . . . T-Neck 2251	
❼	9	9	Keep On Truckin'	........................*Eddie Kendricks* . . . Tamla 54238	
⑧	4	10	Higher Ground	..............................*Stevie Wonder* . . . Tamla 54235	
❾	12	7	Heartbeat - It's A Lovebeat	................................*The DeFranco Family* . . . 20th Century 2030	
⑩	13	6	Paper Roses	........................*Marie Osmond* . . . MGM 14609	

★ HIGHEST DEBUT ★ POS 77	★ BIGGEST MOVER ★ 60 to 29
Sail Around The World...................*David Gates*	Photograph ....*Ringo Starr*

Billboard — OCTOBER 27, 1973 — HOT 100.

TW	LW	WK	Title	Artist	Label
1	5	9	**Midnight Train To Georgia**.....*Gladys Knight & The Pips* ... Buddah 383		
2	1	8	Angie ....*The Rolling Stones* ... Rolling Stones 19105		
3	2	13	Half-Breed ....*Cher* ... MCA 40102		
4	3	10	Ramblin Man ....*The Allman Brothers Band* ... Capricorn 0027		
5	7	10	Keep On Truckin' ....*Eddie Kendricks* ... Tamla 54238		
6	4	16	Let's Get It On ....*Marvin Gaye* ... Tamla 54234		
7	10	7	Paper Roses ....*Marie Osmond* ... MGM 14609		
8	9	8	Heartbeat - It's A Lovebeat .... *The DeFranco Family* ... 20th Century 2030		
9	6	16	That Lady ....*Isley Brothers* ... T-Neck 2251		
10	8	11	Higher Ground ....*Stevie Wonder* ... Tamla 54235		

★ **HIGHEST DEBUT** ★ POS 62
Goodbye Yellow Brick Road..............*Elton John*

★ **BIGGEST MOVER** ★ 57 to 38
Cheaper To Keep Her..................*Johnnie Taylor*

Billboard — NOVEMBER 3, 1973 — HOT 100.

TW	LW	WK	Title	Artist	Label
1	1	10	**Midnight Train To Georgia**.....*Gladys Knight & The Pips* ... Buddah 383		
2	2	9	Angie ....*The Rolling Stones* ... Rolling Stones 19105		
3	5	11	Keep On Truckin' ....*Eddie Kendricks* ... Tamla 54238		
4	3	14	Half-Breed ....*Cher* ... MCA 40102		
5	7	8	**Paper Roses** ....*Marie Osmond* ... MGM 14609		
6	8	9	Heartbeat - It's A Lovebeat .... *The DeFranco Family* ... 20th Century 2030		
7	4	11	Ramblin Man ....*The Allman Brothers Band* ... Capricorn 0027		
8	6	17	Let's Get It On ....*Marvin Gaye* ... Tamla 54234		
9	15	7	Space Race......................................*Billy Preston* ... A&M 1463		
10	11	8	All I Know......................................*Garfunkel* ... Columbia 45926		

★ **HIGHEST DEBUT** ★ POS 82
Come Get To This ....*Marvin Gaye*

★ **BIGGEST MOVER** ★ 99 to 65
Never, Never Gonna Give Ya Up.......*Barry White*

Billboard — NOVEMBER 10, 1973 — HOT 100.

TW	LW	WK	Title	Artist	Label
1	3	12	**Keep On Truckin'** ....*Eddie Kendricks* ... Tamla 54238		
2	1	11	Midnight Train To Georgia ....*Gladys Knight & The Pips* ... Buddah 383		
3	2	10	Angie ....*The Rolling Stones* ... Rolling Stones 19105		
4	6	10	Heartbeat - It's A Lovebeat .... *The DeFranco Family* ... 20th Century 2030		
5	5	9	**Paper Roses**......................................*Marie Osmond* ... MGM 14609		
6	11	6	Photograph ....*Ringo Starr* ... Apple 1865		
7	9	8	Space Race......................................*Billy Preston* ... A&M 1463		
8	4	15	Half-Breed ....*Cher* ... MCA 40102		
9	10	9	**All I Know**......................................*Garfunkel* ... Columbia 45926		
10	13	6	Top Of The World......................................*Carpenters* ... A&M 1468		

★ **HIGHEST DEBUT** ★ POS 76
Mind Games..................*John Lennon*

★ **BIGGEST MOVER** ★ 90 to 59
Leave Me Alone (Ruby Red Dress)..........*Helen Reddy*

Billboard 🔴 NOVEMBER 17, 1973 🔴 HOT 100

TW	LW	WK	Title	Artist
①	1	13	**Keep On Truckin'**	*Eddie Kendricks* ... Tamla 54238
②	2	12	**Midnight Train To Georgia**	*Gladys Knight & The Pips* ... Buddah 383
③	4	11	**Heartbeat – It's A Lovebeat**	*The DeFranco Family* ... 20th Century 2030
❹	6	7	Photograph	*Ringo Starr* ... Apple 1865
❺	7	9	Space Race	*Billy Preston* ... A&M 1463
⑥	5	10	Paper Roses	*Marie Osmond* ... MGM 14609
❼	10	7	Top Of The World	*Carpenters* ... A&M 1468
⑧	3	11	Angie	*The Rolling Stones* ... Rolling Stones 19105
⑨	12	8	Just You 'N' Me	*Chicago* ... Columbia 45933
⑩	11	7	**I Got A Name**	*Jim Croce* ... ABC 11389

★ HIGHEST DEBUT ★ POS 79	★ BIGGEST MOVER ★ 59 to 29
Time In A Bottle ....*Jim Croce*	Leave Me Alone (Ruby Red Dress).........*Helen Reddy*

Billboard 🔴 NOVEMBER 24, 1973 🔴 HOT 100

TW	LW	WK	Title	Artist
❶	4	8	**Photograph**	*Ringo Starr* ... Apple 1865
②	1	14	**Keep On Truckin'**	*Eddie Kendricks* ... Tamla 54238
❸	7	8	**Top Of The World**	*Carpenters* ... A&M 1468
④	5	10	**Space Race**	*Billy Preston* ... A&M 1463
⑤	3	12	Heartbeat – It's A Lovebeat	*The DeFranco Family* ... 20th Century 2030
⑥	2	13	**Midnight Train To Georgia**	*Gladys Knight & The Pips* ... Buddah 383
❼	9	9	**Just You 'N' Me**	*Chicago* ... Columbia 45933
⑧	6	11	Paper Roses	*Marie Osmond* ... MGM 14609
⑨	15	5	Goodbye Yellow Brick Road	*Elton John* ... MCA 40148
⑩	13	9	The Love I Lost	*Harold Melvin & The Bluenotes* ... Philadelphia International 3533

★ HIGHEST DEBUT ★ POS 66	★ BIGGEST MOVER ★ 79 to 48
Helen Wheels ....*Paul McCartney & Wings*	Time In A Bottle ....*Jim Croce*

Billboard 🔴 DECEMBER 1, 1973 🔴 HOT 100

TW	LW	WK	Title	Artist
❶	3	9	**Top Of The World**	*Carpenters* ... A&M 1468
②	1	9	Photograph	*Ringo Starr* ... Apple 1865
❸	9	6	Goodbye Yellow Brick Road	*Elton John* ... MCA 40148
④	4	11	**Space Race**	*Billy Preston* ... A&M 1463
⑤	2	15	Keep On Truckin'	*Eddie Kendricks* ... Tamla 54238
⑥	7	10	Just You 'N' Me	*Chicago* ... Columbia 45933
⑦	6	14	Midnight Train To Georgia	*Gladys Knight & The Pips* ... Buddah 383
❽	10	10	The Love I Lost	*Harold Melvin & The Bluenotes* ... Philadelphia International 3533
⑨	5	13	Heartbeat – It's A Lovebeat	*The DeFranco Family* ... 20th Century 2030
⑩	12	10	The Most Beautiful Girl	*Charlie Rich* ... Epic 11040

★ HIGHEST DEBUT ★ POS 82	★ BIGGEST MOVER ★ 48 to 18
American Tune ....*Paul Simon*	Time In A Bottle ....*Jim Croce*

Billboard — DECEMBER 8, 1973 — HOT 100

TW	LW	WK	Title	Artist	Label
①	1	10	**Top Of The World**	*Carpenters*	A&M 1468
②	3	7	**Goodbye Yellow Brick Road**	*Elton John*	MCA 40148
③	10	11	**The Most Beautiful Girl**	*Charlie Rich*	Epic 11040
④	6	11	**Just You 'N' Me**	*Chicago*	Columbia 45933
⑤	2	10	**Photograph**	*Ringo Starr*	Apple 1865
⑥	4	12	**Space Race**	*Billy Preston*	A&M 1463
⑦	8	11	**The Love I Lost**	*Harold Melvin & The Bluenotes*	Philadelphia International 3533
⑧	11	10	**Hello It's Me**	*Todd Rundgren*	Bearsville 0009
⑨	5	16	**Keep On Truckin'**	*Eddie Kendricks*	Tamla 54238
⑩	13	6	**Leave Me Alone (Ruby Red Dress)**	*Helen Reddy*	Capitol 3768

★ **HIGHEST DEBUT** ★ POS 85
Livin' For You ....*Al Green*

★ **BIGGEST MOVER** ★ 69 to 45
Until You Come Back To Me (That's What I'm Gonna Do) ....*Aretha Franklin*

Billboard — DECEMBER 15, 1973 — HOT 100

TW	LW	WK	Title	Artist	Label
①	3	12	**The Most Beautiful Girl**	*Charlie Rich*	Epic 11040
②	2	8	**Goodbye Yellow Brick Road**	*Elton John*	MCA 40148
③	1	11	**Top Of The World**	*Carpenters*	A&M 1468
④	4	12	**Just You 'N' Me**	*Chicago*	Columbia 45933
⑤	13	5	**Time In A Bottle**	*Jim Croce*	ABC 11405
⑥	8	11	**Hello It's Me**	*Todd Rundgren*	Bearsville 0009
⑦	10	7	**Leave Me Alone (Ruby Red Dress)**	*Helen Reddy*	Capitol 3768
⑧	5	11	**Photograph**	*Ringo Starr*	Apple 1865
⑨	15	9	**The Joker**	*Steve Miller Band*	Capitol 3732
⑩	12	8	**If You're Ready (Come Go With Me)**	*The Staple Singers*	Stax 0179

★ **HIGHEST DEBUT** ★ POS 75
You're Sixteen..................................*Ringo Starr*

★ **BIGGEST MOVER** ★ 79 to 50
Love's Theme ....*Love Unlimited Orchestra*

Billboard — DECEMBER 22, 1973 — HOT 100

TW	LW	WK	Title	Artist	Label
①	1	13	**The Most Beautiful Girl**	*Charlie Rich*	Epic 11040
②	2	9	**Goodbye Yellow Brick Road**	*Elton John*	MCA 40148
③	5	6	**Time In A Bottle**	*Jim Croce*	ABC 11405
④	7	8	**Leave Me Alone (Ruby Red Dress)**	*Helen Reddy*	Capitol 3768
⑤	6	12	**Hello It's Me**	*Todd Rundgren*	Bearsville 0009
⑥	9	10	**The Joker**	*Steve Miller Band*	Capitol 3732
⑦	3	12	**Top Of The World**	*Carpenters*	A&M 1468
⑧	4	13	**Just You 'N' Me**	*Chicago*	Columbia 45933
⑨	10	9	**If You're Ready (Come Go With Me)**	*The Staple Singers*	Stax 0179
⑩	14	9	**Never, Never Gonna Give Ya Up**	*Barry White*	20th Century 2058

★ **HIGHEST DEBUT** ★ POS 71
Put Your Hands Together ....*The O'Jays*

★ **BIGGEST MOVER** ★ 97 to 66
Jungle Boogie ....*Kool & The Gang*

TW	LW	WK	Billboard.	DECEMBER 29, 1973	HOT 100.
❶	3	7	**Time In A Bottle**..*Jim Croce* . . . ABC 11405
②	1	14	**The Most Beautiful Girl** ....*Charlie Rich* . . . Epic 11040
③	4	9	**Leave Me Alone (Ruby Red Dress)**........*Helen Reddy* . . . Capitol 3768
❹	6	11	**The Joker** ....*Steve Miller Band* . . . Capitol 3732
⑤	2	10	**Goodbye Yellow Brick Road**............................*Elton John* . . . MCA 40148
⑥	5	13	**Hello It's Me**..*Todd Rundgren* . . . Bearsville 0009
⑦	7	13	**Top Of The World**...*Carpenters* . . . A&M 1468
❽	11	11	**Show And Tell**...*Al Wilson* . . . Rocky Road 30073
❾	12	10	**Smokin' In The Boy's Room**............*Brownsville Station* . . . Big Tree 16011
⑩	10	10	**Never, Never Gonna Give Ya Up** ....*Barry White* . . . 20th Century 2058

★ *HIGHEST DEBUT* ★ POS 77	★ *BIGGEST MOVER* ★ 50 to 27
It Doesn't Have To Be That Way.........*Jim Croce*	You're Sixteen................................*Ringo Starr*

TW	LW	WK	Billboard		JANUARY 5, 1974		HOT 100.
①	1	8	**Time In A Bottle**..*Jim Croce* . . . ABC 11405
②	4	12	The Joker ....*Steve Miller Band* . . . Capitol 3732
③	3	10	**Leave Me Alone (Ruby Red Dress)**........*Helen Reddy* . . . Capitol 3768
④	2	15	The Most Beautiful Girl ....*Charlie Rich* . . . Epic 11040
⑤	8	12	Show And Tell................................*Al Wilson* . . . Rocky Road 30073
⑥	9	11	Smokin' In The Boy's Room............*Brownsville Station* . . . Big Tree 16011
⑦	5	11	Goodbye Yellow Brick Road.........................*Elton John* . . . MCA 40148
⑧	10	11	Never, Never Gonna Give Ya Up ....*Barry White* . . . 20th Century 2058
⑨	11	9	Living For The City ....*Stevie Wonder* . . . Tamla 54242
⑩	14	7	I've Got To Use My Imagination.....................*Gladys Knight & The Pips* . . . Buddah 393

★ HIGHEST DEBUT ★ POS 65	★ BIGGEST MOVER ★ 65 to 46
Americans....................*Byron MacGregor*	Let Your Hair Down..................*The Temptations*

TW	LW	WK	Billboard		JANUARY 12, 1974		HOT 100.
①	2	13	**The Joker**................................*Steve Miller Band* . . . Capitol 3732
②	1	9	Time In A Bottle ....*Jim Croce* . . . ABC 11405
③	5	13	Show And Tell................................*Al Wilson* . . . Rocky Road 30073
④	6	12	Smokin' In The Boy's Room............*Brownsville Station* . . . Big Tree 16011
⑤	10	8	I've Got To Use My Imagination.....................*Gladys Knight & The Pips* . . . Buddah 393
⑥	16	5	You're Sixteen ....*Ringo Starr* . . . Apple 1870
⑦	8	12	**Never, Never Gonna Give Ya Up** ......*Barry White* . . . 20th Century 2058
⑧	9	10	**Living For The City** ....*Stevie Wonder* . . . Tamla 54242
⑨	13	9	Let Me Be There ....*Olivia Newton-John* . . . MCA 40101
⑩	12	8	**Helen Wheels** ....*Paul McCartney & Wings* . . . Apple 1869

★ HIGHEST DEBUT ★ POS 83	★ BIGGEST MOVER ★ 65 to 33
Doo Doo Doo Doo Doo (Heartbreaker) ....*The Rolling Stones*	Americans..............................*Byron MacGregor*

TW	LW	WK	Billboard		JANUARY 19, 1974		HOT 100.
①	3	14	**Show And Tell**................................*Al Wilson* . . . Rocky Road 30073
②	1	14	The Joker ....*Steve Miller Band* . . . Capitol 3732
③	4	13	**Smokin' In The Boy's Room** ....*Brownsville Station* . . . Big Tree 16011
④	5	9	**I've Got To Use My Imagination** ....*Gladys Knight & The Pips* . . . Buddah 393
⑤	6	6	You're Sixteen ....*Ringo Starr* . . . Apple 1870
⑥	2	10	Time In A Bottle ....*Jim Croce* . . . ABC 11405
⑦	11	9	The Way We Were ....*Barbra Streisand* . . . Columbia 45944
⑧	8	11	**Living For The City** ....*Stevie Wonder* . . . Tamla 54242
⑨	9	10	Let Me Be There ....*Olivia Newton-John* . . . MCA 40101
⑩	13	8	Love's Theme ....*Love Unlimited Orchestra* . . . 20th Century 2069

★ HIGHEST DEBUT ★ POS 82	★ BIGGEST MOVER ★ 98 to 62
Dark Lady....................*Cher*	The Americans (A Canadian's Opinion) ....*Gordon Sinclair*

'74

| TW | LW | WK | Billboard. | 🔵 JANUARY 26, 1974 🔵 | HOT 100. |

TW	LW	WK			
①	5	7	**You're Sixteen**	*Ringo Starr*	Apple 1870
②	1	15	Show And Tell	*Al Wilson*	Rocky Road 30073
❸	7	10	The Way We Were	*Barbra Streisand*	Columbia 45944
④	4	10	**I've Got To Use My Imagination**	*Gladys Knight & The Pips*	Buddah 393
⑤	2	15	The Joker	*Steve Miller Band*	Capitol 3732
❻	10	9	Love's Theme	*Love Unlimited Orchestra*	20th Century 2069
⑦	3	14	Smokin' In The Boy's Room	*Brownsville Station*	Big Tree 16011
⑧	9	11	Let Me Be There	*Olivia Newton-John*	MCA 40101
⑨	6	11	Time In A Bottle	*Jim Croce*	ABC 11405
❿	17	4	Americans	*Byron MacGregor*	Westbound 222

★ *HIGHEST DEBUT* ★ POS 80	★ *BIGGEST MOVER* ★ 62 to 28
You Sure Love To Ball ....*Marvin Gaye*	The Americans (A Canadian's Opinion) ....*Gordon Sinclair*

| TW | LW | WK | Billboard. | 🔵 FEBRUARY 2, 1974 🔵 | HOT 100. |

TW	LW	WK			
①	3	11	**The Way We Were**	*Barbra Streisand*	Columbia 45944
②	1	8	You're Sixteen	*Ringo Starr*	Apple 1870
❸	6	10	Love's Theme	*Love Unlimited Orchestra*	20th Century 2069
④	2	16	Show And Tell	*Al Wilson*	Rocky Road 30073
❺	10	5	Americans	*Byron MacGregor*	Westbound 222
⑥	4	11	I've Got To Use My Imagination	*Gladys Knight & The Pips*	Buddah 393
⑦	8	12	Let Me Be There	*Olivia Newton-John*	MCA 40101
❽	11	11	Until You Come Back To Me (That's What I'm Gonna Do)	*Aretha Franklin*	Atlantic 2995
⑨	5	16	The Joker	*Steve Miller Band*	Capitol 3732
❿	14	13	Spiders & Snakes	*Jim Stafford*	MGM 14648

★ *HIGHEST DEBUT* ★ POS 80	★ *BIGGEST MOVER* ★ 72 to 49
Mockingbird..............*Carly Simon & James Taylor*	Seasons In The Sun........................*Terry Jacks*

| TW | LW | WK | Billboard. | 🔵 FEBRUARY 9, 1974 🔵 | HOT 100. |

TW	LW	WK			
①	3	11	**Love's Theme**	*Love Unlimited Orchestra*	20th Century 2069
②	1	12	The Way We Were	*Barbra Streisand*	Columbia 45944
③	2	9	You're Sixteen	*Ringo Starr*	Apple 1870
④	5	6	**Americans**	*Byron MacGregor*	Westbound 222
❺	8	12	Until You Come Back To Me (That's What I'm Gonna Do)	*Aretha Franklin*	Atlantic 2995
⑥	7	13	**Let Me Be There**	*Olivia Newton-John*	MCA 40101
❼	10	14	Spiders & Snakes	*Jim Stafford*	MGM 14648
⑧	4	17	Show And Tell	*Al Wilson*	Rocky Road 30073
⑨	6	12	I've Got To Use My Imagination	*Gladys Knight & The Pips*	Buddah 393
❿	14	10	Jungle Boogie	*Kool & The Gang*	De-Lite 559

★ *HIGHEST DEBUT* ★ POS 69	★ *BIGGEST MOVER* ★ 77 to 51
Jet.........................*Paul McCartney & Wings*	Sunshine On My Shoulders.............*John Denver*

TW	LW	WK	Billboard	FEBRUARY 16, 1974	HOT 100
①	2	13	**The Way We Were**................................*Barbra Streisand* . . . Columbia 45944
②	1	12	**Love's Theme**......................*Love Unlimited Orchestra* . . . 20th Century 2069
③	3	10	**You're Sixteen**...*Ringo Starr* . . . Apple 1870
④	5	13	**Until You Come Back To Me (That's What I'm Gonna Do)**................ *Aretha Franklin* . . . Atlantic 2995
❺	7	15	**Spiders & Snakes**......................................*Jim Stafford* . . . MGM 14648
⑥	4	7	**Americans** ....*Byron MacGregor* . . . Westbound 222
⑦	6	14	**Let Me Be There** ....*Olivia Newton-John* . . . MCA 40101
⑧	10	11	**Jungle Boogie** ....*Kool & The Gang* . . . De-Lite 559
⑨	14	7	**Boogie Down**.................................*Eddie Kendricks* . . . Tamla 54243
⑩	13	15	**Rock On** ....*David Essex* . . . Columbia 45940

★ *HIGHEST DEBUT* ★ POS 69	★ *BIGGEST MOVER* ★ 66 to 30
Bennie And The Jets......................*Elton John*	**Mockingbird**.............*Carly Simon & James Taylor*

TW	LW	WK	Billboard	FEBRUARY 23, 1974	HOT 100
①	1	14	**The Way We Were**................................*Barbra Streisand* . . . Columbia 45944
❷	12	7	**Seasons In The Sun**...*Terry Jacks* . . . Bell 45432
③	4	14	**Until You Come Back To Me (That's What I'm Gonna Do)** ...... *Aretha Franklin* . . . Atlantic 2995
④	5	16	**Spiders & Snakes**......................................*Jim Stafford* . . . MGM 14648
⑤	2	13	**Love's Theme**......................*Love Unlimited Orchestra* . . . 20th Century 2069
❻	8	12	**Jungle Boogie** ....*Kool & The Gang* . . . De-Lite 559
❼	9	8	**Boogie Down**.................................*Eddie Kendricks* . . . Tamla 54243
❽	10	16	**Rock On** ....*David Essex* . . . Columbia 45940
⑨	3	11	**You're Sixteen** ....*Ringo Starr* . . . Apple 1870
⑩	7	15	**Let Me Be There** ....*Olivia Newton-John* . . . MCA 40101

★ *HIGHEST DEBUT* ★ POS 63	★ *BIGGEST MOVER* ★ 87 to 59
A Very Special Love Song.............*Charlie Rich*	**Hooked On A Feeling**......................*Blue Swede*

TW	LW	WK	Billboard	MARCH 2, 1974	HOT 100
①	2	8	**Seasons In The Sun**...*Terry Jacks* . . . Bell 45432
②	1	15	**The Way We Were** ....*Barbra Streisand* . . . Columbia 45944
③	4	17	**Spiders & Snakes**......................................*Jim Stafford* . . . MGM 14648
❹	7	9	**Boogie Down**.................................*Eddie Kendricks* . . . Tamla 54243
⑤	6	13	**Jungle Boogie** ....*Kool & The Gang* . . . De-Lite 559
❻	8	17	**Rock On** ....*David Essex* . . . Columbia 45940
⑦	3	15	**Until You Come Back To Me (That's What I'm Gonna Do)**................... *Aretha Franklin* . . . Atlantic 2995
⑧	5	14	**Love's Theme** ....*Love Unlimited Orchestra* . . . 20th Century 2069
⑨	16	7	**Dark Lady**...*Cher* . . . MCA 40161
⑩	11	11	**Put Your Hands Together**...*The O'Jays* . . . Philadelphia International 3535

★ *HIGHEST DEBUT* ★ POS 65	★ *BIGGEST MOVER* ★ 100 to 77
TSOP (The Sound Of Philadelphia) ....*MFSB* *featuring The Three Degrees*	**Honey Please, Can't Ya See** ....*Barry White*

TW	LW	WK	**Billboard**	MARCH 9, 1974	HOT 100.
①	1	9	Seasons In The Sun .... *Terry Jacks* . . . Bell 45432
❷	4	10	Boogie Down .... *Eddie Kendricks* . . . Tamla 54243
③	2	16	The Way We Were .... *Barbra Streisand* . . . Columbia 45944
④	5	14	Jungle Boogie .... *Kool & The Gang* . . . De-Lite 559
⑤	6	18	Rock On .... *David Essex* . . . Columbia 45940
❻	9	8	Dark Lady .... *Cher* . . . MCA 40161
⑦	3	18	Spiders & Snakes .... *Jim Stafford* . . . MGM 14648
❽	13	6	Mockingbird .... *Carly Simon & James Taylor* . . . Elektra 45880
⑨	7	16	Until You Come Back To Me (That's What I'm Gonna Do)................... *Aretha Franklin* . . . Atlantic 2995
⑩	17	7	Sunshine On My Shoulders .... *John Denver* . . . RCA 0213

★ *HIGHEST DEBUT* ★ POS 65	★ *BIGGEST MOVER* ★ 65 to 42
Oh My My .... *Ringo Starr*	TSOP (The Sound Of Philadelphia) .... *MFSB* featuring The Three Degrees

TW	LW	WK	**Billboard**	MARCH 16, 1974	HOT 100.
①	1	10	Seasons In The Sun.. *Terry Jacks* . . . Bell 45432
②	2	11	Boogie Down .... *Eddie Kendricks* . . . Tamla 54243
❸	6	9	Dark Lady .... *Cher* . . . MCA 40161
❹	10	8	Sunshine On My Shoulders .... *John Denver* . . . RCA 0213
⑤	3	17	The Way We Were .... *Barbra Streisand* . . . Columbia 45944
❻	8	7	Mockingbird .... *Carly Simon & James Taylor* . . . Elektra 45880
⑦	4	15	Jungle Boogie .... *Kool & The Gang* . . . De-Lite 559
⑧	5	19	Rock On .... *David Essex* . . . Columbia 45940
⑨	7	19	Spiders & Snakes .... *Jim Stafford* . . . MGM 14648
⑩	14	6	Jet.. *Paul McCartney & Wings* . . . Apple 1871

★ *HIGHEST DEBUT* ★ POS 79	★ *BIGGEST MOVER* ★ 86 to 58
Dancing Machine .... *The Jackson 5*	Keep On Singing .... *Helen Reddy*

TW	LW	WK	**Billboard**	MARCH 23, 1974	HOT 100.
①	3	10	Dark Lady.. *Cher* . . . MCA 40161
②	1	11	Seasons In The Sun .... *Terry Jacks* . . . Bell 45432
③	4	9	Sunshine On My Shoulders .... *John Denver* . . . RCA 0213
④	2	12	Boogie Down .... *Eddie Kendricks* . . . Tamla 54243
⑤	6	8	Mockingbird........................ *Carly Simon & James Taylor* . . . Elektra 45880
❻	12	6	Bennie And The Jets... *Elton John* . . . MCA 40198
❼	14	6	Hooked On A Feeling .... *Blue Swede* . . . EMI 3627
❽	10	7	Jet.. *Paul McCartney & Wings* . . . Apple 1871
⑨	11	11	Eres Tu (Touch The Wind).......................... *Mocedades* . . . Tara 100
⑩	7	16	Jungle Boogie .... *Kool & The Gang* . . . De-Lite 559

★ *HIGHEST DEBUT* ★ POS 81	★ *BIGGEST MOVER* ★ 79 to 58
The Payback .... *James Brown*	Dancing Machine .... *The Jackson 5*

TW	LW	WK	Billboard®	MARCH 30, 1974	HOT 100®
①	3	10	**Sunshine On My Shoulders**.........................*John Denver* . . . RCA 0213		
❷	7	7	**Hooked On A Feeling**...............................*Blue Swede* . . . EMI 3627		
③	2	12	**Seasons In The Sun**..................................*Terry Jacks* . . . Bell 45432		
④	6	7	**Bennie And The Jets**................................*Elton John* . . . MCA 40198		
⑤	1	11	**Dark Lady**..*Cher* . . . MCA 40161		
⑥	5	9	**Mockingbird** ....*Carly Simon & James Taylor* . . . Elektra 45880		
⑦	8	8	**Jet**..*Paul McCartney & Wings* . . . Apple 1871		
❽	11	12	**Come And Get Your Love**........................*Redbone* . . . Epic 11035		
⑨	9	12	**Eres Tu (Touch The Wind)**.....................*Mocedades* . . . Tara 100		
⑩	14	6	**The Lord's Prayer**...........................*Sister Janet Mead* . . . A&M 1491		

★ **HIGHEST DEBUT** ★ POS 81	★ **BIGGEST MOVER** ★ 58 to 40
All In Love Is Fair......................*Barbra Streisand*	Dancing Machine ....*The Jackson 5*

TW	LW	WK	Billboard®	APRIL 6, 1974	HOT 100®
①	2	8	**Hooked On A Feeling**...............................*Blue Swede* . . . EMI 3627		
❷	4	8	**Bennie And The Jets**................................*Elton John* . . . MCA 40198		
③	1	11	**Sunshine On My Shoulders** ....*John Denver* . . . RCA 0213		
④	3	13	**Seasons In The Sun**..................................*Terry Jacks* . . . Bell 45432		
❺	10	7	**The Lord's Prayer**...........................*Sister Janet Mead* . . . A&M 1491		
❻	8	13	**Come And Get Your Love**........................*Redbone* . . . Epic 11035		
⑦	5	12	**Dark Lady**..*Cher* . . . MCA 40161		
❽	12	6	**TSOP (The Sound Of Philadelphia)** .... *MFSB featuring The Three Degrees* . . . Philadelphia International 3540		
⑨	6	10	**Mockingbird** ....*Carly Simon & James Taylor* . . . Elektra 45880		
⑩	14	8	**Best Thing That Ever Happened To Me**.......... *Gladys Knight & The Pips* . . . Buddah 403		

★ **HIGHEST DEBUT** ★ POS 73	★ **BIGGEST MOVER** ★ 70 to 48
Don't You Worry 'Bout A Thing......*Stevie Wonder*	You Make Me Feel Brand New ....*The Stylistics*

TW	LW	WK	Billboard®	APRIL 13, 1974	HOT 100®
①	2	9	**Bennie And The Jets** ....*Elton John* . . . MCA 40198		
②	1	9	**Hooked On A Feeling**................................*Blue Swede* . . . EMI 3627		
❸	8	7	**TSOP (The Sound Of Philadelphia)** .... *MFSB featuring The Three Degrees* . . . Philadelphia International 3540		
④	5	8	**The Lord's Prayer**...............................*Sister Janet Mead* . . . A&M 1491		
⑤	6	14	**Come And Get Your Love**...........................*Redbone* . . . Epic 11035		
⑥	3	12	**Sunshine On My Shoulders** ....*John Denver* . . . RCA 0213		
❼	10	9	**Best Thing That Ever Happened To Me**.......... *Gladys Knight & The Pips* . . . Buddah 403		
⑧	4	14	**Seasons In The Sun**.................................*Terry Jacks* . . . Bell 45432		
⑨	12	6	**Oh My My** ....*Ringo Starr* . . . Apple 1872		
⑩	9	11	**Mockingbird** ....*Carly Simon & James Taylor* . . . Elektra 45880		

★ **HIGHEST DEBUT** ★ POS 70	★ **BIGGEST MOVER** ★ 80 to 61
I Won't Last A Day Without You ....*Carpenters*	Let's Get Married.............................*Al Green*

Billboard — APRIL 20, 1974 — HOT 100

TW	LW	WK		
❶	3	8	**TSOP (The Sound Of Philadelphia)**	
			MFSB featuring The Three Degrees . . . Philadelphia International 3540	
②	1	10	**Bennie And The Jets**..*Elton John* . . . MCA 40198	
③	2	10	**Hooked On A Feeling** ....*Blue Swede* . . . EMI 3627	
❹	7	10	**Best Thing That Ever Happened To Me**..........*Gladys Knight & The Pips* . . . Buddah 403	
⑤	5	15	**Come And Get Your Love**................................*Redbone* . . . Epic 11035	
❻	9	7	**Oh My My** ....*Ringo Starr* . . . Apple 1872	
⑦	6	13	**Sunshine On My Shoulders** ....*John Denver* . . . RCA 0213	
❽	17	7	**The Loco-Motion** ....*Grand Funk* . . . Capitol 3840	
⑨	4	9	**The Lord's Prayer**..*Sister Janet Mead* . . . A&M 1491	
⑩	13	8	**I'll Have To Say I Love You In A Song** ....*Jim Croce* . . . ABC 11424	

★ HIGHEST DEBUT ★ POS 68	★ BIGGEST MOVER ★ 84 to 54
Band On The Run ....*Paul McCartney & Wings*	The Streak ....*Ray Stevens*

Billboard — APRIL 27, 1974 — HOT 100

TW	LW	WK		
①	1	9	**TSOP (The Sound Of Philadelphia)**	
			MFSB featuring The Three Degrees . . . Philadelphia International 3540	
②	2	11	**Bennie And The Jets**..*Elton John* . . . MCA 40198	
③	4	11	**Best Thing That Ever Happened To Me**	
			Gladys Knight & The Pips . . . Buddah 403	
❹	8	8	**The Loco-Motion**...*Grand Funk* . . . Capitol 3840	
⑤	6	8	**Oh My My**...*Ringo Starr* . . . Apple 1872	
⑥	3	11	**Hooked On A Feeling** ....*Blue Swede* . . . EMI 3627	
⑦	5	16	**Come And Get Your Love**....................................*Redbone* . . . Epic 11035	
❽	13	7	**Dancing Machine**...*The Jackson 5* . . . Motown 1286	
⑨	10	9	**I'll Have To Say I Love You In A Song**.......*Jim Croce* . . . ABC 11424	
⑩	11	13	**Lookin' For A Love** ....*Bobby Womack* . . . United Artists 375	

★ HIGHEST DEBUT ★ POS 89	★ BIGGEST MOVER ★ 54 to 19
(I'm A) YoYo Man ....*Rick Cunha*	The Streak ....*Ray Stevens*

Billboard — MAY 4, 1974 — HOT 100

TW	LW	WK		
❶	4	9	**The Loco-Motion** ....*Grand Funk* . . . Capitol 3840	
②	1	10	TSOP (The Sound Of Philadelphia)	
			MFSB featuring The Three Degrees . . . Philadelphia International 3540	
③	2	12	**Bennie And The Jets**..*Elton John* . . . MCA 40198	
④	3	12	**Best Thing That Ever Happened To Me**..........*Gladys Knight & The Pips* . . . Buddah 403	
❺	8	8	**Dancing Machine**...................................*The Jackson 5* . . . Motown 1286	
⑥	19	4	**The Streak**...*Ray Stevens* . . . Barnaby 600	
⑦	6	12	**Hooked On A Feeling** ....*Blue Swede* . . . EMI 3627	
❽	12	11	**Tubular Bells**...*Mike Oldfield* . . . Virgin 55100	
⑨	13	8	**The Show Must Go On** ....*Three Dog Night* . . . Dunhill 4382	
⑩	11	14	**Just Don't Want To Be Lonely** ....*The Main Ingredient* . . . RCA 0205	

★ HIGHEST DEBUT ★ POS 80	★ BIGGEST MOVER ★ 78 to 57
I Don't See Me In Your Eyes Anymore ....*Charlie Rich*	Billy, Don't Be A Hero...........*Bo Donaldson & The Heywoods*

TW	LW	WK	Billboard.	MAY 11, 1974	HOT 100.
①	1	10	**The Loco-Motion**	*Grand Funk* . . . Capitol 3840	
②	6	5	**The Streak**	*Ray Stevens* . . . Barnaby 600	
③	5	9	Dancing Machine	*The Jackson 5* . . . Motown 1286	
④	11	8	The Entertainer	*Marvin Hamlisch* . . . MCA 40174	
⑤	3	13	Bennie And The Jets	*Elton John* . . . MCA 40198	
⑥	9	9	The Show Must Go On	*Three Dog Night* . . . Dunhill 4382	
⑦	8	12	**Tubular Bells**	*Mike Oldfield* . . . Virgin 55100	
⑧	2	11	TSOP (The Sound Of Philadelphia)		
			MFSB featuring The Three Degrees . . . Philadelphia International 3540		
⑨	12	9	**(I've Been) Searchin' So Long**	*Chicago* . . . Columbia 46020	
⑩	15	12	Midnight At The Oasis	*Maria Muldaur* . . . Reprise 1183	

★ *HIGHEST DEBUT* ★ POS 74	★ *BIGGEST MOVER* ★ 89 to 54
Son Of Sagittarius ....*Eddie Kendricks*	Be Thankful For What You Got..............*William DeVaughn*

TW	LW	WK	Billboard.	MAY 18, 1974	HOT 100.
①	2	6	**The Streak**	*Ray Stevens* . . . Barnaby 600	
②	3	10	**Dancing Machine**	*The Jackson 5* . . . Motown 1286	
③	4	9	**The Entertainer**	*Marvin Hamlisch* . . . MCA 40174	
④	1	11	The Loco-Motion	*Grand Funk* . . . Capitol 3840	
⑤	6	10	The Show Must Go On	*Three Dog Night* . . . Dunhill 4382	
⑥	5	14	Bennie And The Jets	*Elton John* . . . MCA 40198	
⑦	14	5	**Band On The Run**	*Paul McCartney & Wings* . . . Apple 1873	
⑧	10	13	Midnight At The Oasis	*Maria Muldaur* . . . Reprise 1183	
⑨	9	10	**(I've Been) Searchin' So Long**	*Chicago* . . . Columbia 46020	
⑩	13	9	You Make Me Feel Brand New	*The Stylistics* . . . Avco 4634	

★ *HIGHEST DEBUT* ★ POS 84	★ *BIGGEST MOVER* ★ 54 to 30
I'm Coming Home ....*Spinners*	Be Thankful For What You Got..............*William DeVaughn*

TW	LW	WK	Billboard.	MAY 25, 1974	HOT 100.
①	1	7	**The Streak**	*Ray Stevens* . . . Barnaby 600	
②	2	11	**Dancing Machine**	*The Jackson 5* . . . Motown 1286	
③	3	10	**The Entertainer**	*Marvin Hamlisch* . . . MCA 40174	
④	5	11	**The Show Must Go On**	*Three Dog Night* . . . Dunhill 4382	
⑤	7	6	**Band On The Run**	*Paul McCartney & Wings* . . . Apple 1873	
⑥	10	10	You Make Me Feel Brand New	*The Stylistics* . . . Avco 4634	
⑦	8	14	Midnight At The Oasis	*Maria Muldaur* . . . Reprise 1183	
⑧	4	12	The Loco-Motion	*Grand Funk* . . . Capitol 3840	
⑨	9	11	**(I've Been) Searchin' So Long**	*Chicago* . . . Columbia 46020	
⑩	14	11	Help Me	*Joni Mitchell* . . . Asylum 11034	

★ *HIGHEST DEBUT* ★ POS 70	★ *BIGGEST MOVER* ★ 84 to 60
On And On....................*Gladys Knight & The Pips*	I'm Coming Home ....*Spinners*

TW	LW	WK	Billboard.	JUNE 1, 1974	HOT 100.
①	1	8	**The Streak**	....*Ray Stevens* . . . Barnaby 600
②	5	7	**Band On The Run**	............................*Paul McCartney & Wings* . . . Apple 1873
③	2	12	**Dancing Machine**	...............................*The Jackson 5* . . . Motown 1286
④	6	11	**You Make Me Feel Brand New**	......................*The Stylistics* . . . Avco 4634
⑤	3	11	**The Entertainer**	..................................*Marvin Hamlisch* . . . MCA 40174
⑥	7	15	**Midnight At The Oasis**	.......................*Maria Muldaur* . . . Reprise 1183
⑦	12	8	**Sundown**	....*Gordon Lightfoot* . . . Reprise 1194
⑧	10	12	**Help Me**	....*Joni Mitchell* . . . Asylum 11034
⑨	13	7	**Billy, Don't Be A Hero**	.........*Bo Donaldson & The Heywoods* . . . ABC 11435
⑩	14	12	**Oh Very Young**	....*Cat Stevens* . . . A&M 1503

★ HIGHEST DEBUT ★ POS 76	★ BIGGEST MOVER ★ 70 to 40
Waterloo ....*Abba*	On And On ....*Gladys Knight & The Pips*

TW	LW	WK	Billboard.	JUNE 8, 1974	HOT 100.
①	2	8	**Band On The Run**	......................*Paul McCartney & Wings* . . . Apple 1873
②	1	9	**The Streak**	....*Ray Stevens* . . . Barnaby 600
③	4	12	**You Make Me Feel Brand New**	......................*The Stylistics* . . . Avco 4634
④	3	13	**Dancing Machine**	...............................*The Jackson 5* . . . Motown 1286
⑤	7	9	**Sundown**	....*Gordon Lightfoot* . . . Reprise 1194
⑥	9	8	**Billy, Don't Be A Hero**	.........*Bo Donaldson & The Heywoods* . . . ABC 11435
⑦	8	13	**Help Me**	....*Joni Mitchell* . . . Asylum 11034
⑧	5	12	**The Entertainer**	..................................*Marvin Hamlisch* . . . MCA 40174
⑨	6	16	**Midnight At The Oasis**	.......................*Maria Muldaur* . . . Reprise 1183
⑩	11	9	**For The Love Of Money**	.................*O'Jays* . . . Philadelphia International 3544

★ HIGHEST DEBUT ★ POS 77	★ BIGGEST MOVER ★ 93 to 62
If You Talk In Your Sleep ....*Elvis Presley*	Rock Your Baby ....*George McCrae*

TW	LW	WK	Billboard.	JUNE 15, 1974	HOT 100.
❶	6	9	**Billy, Don't Be A Hero**	.....*Bo Donaldson & The Heywoods* . . . ABC 11435
②	3	13	**You Make Me Feel Brand New**	................*The Stylistics* . . . Avco 4634
❸	5	10	**Sundown**	....*Gordon Lightfoot* . . . Reprise 1194
④	2	10	**The Streak**	....*Ray Stevens* . . . Barnaby 600
⑤	1	9	**Band On The Run**	............................*Paul McCartney & Wings* . . . Apple 1873
⑥	4	14	**Dancing Machine**	...............................*The Jackson 5* . . . Motown 1286
❼	11	7	**Be Thankful For What You Got**	...........*William DeVaughn* . . . Roxbury 0236
⑧	8	13	**The Entertainer**	..................................*Marvin Hamlisch* . . . MCA 40174
⑨	10	10	**For The Love Of Money**	.............*O'Jays* . . . Philadelphia International 3544
⑩	9	17	**Midnight At The Oasis**	.............................*Maria Muldaur* . . . Reprise 1183

★ HIGHEST DEBUT ★ POS 75	★ BIGGEST MOVER ★ 62 to 34
Jive Turkey ....*Ohio Players*	Rock Your Baby ....*George McCrae*

TW	LW	WK	Billboard.	JUNE 22, 1974	HOT 100.
①	1	10	**Billy, Don't Be A Hero** .....*Bo Donaldson & The Heywoods* . . . ABC 11435
②	2	14	**You Make Me Feel Brand New**.................*The Stylistics* . . . Avco 4634
③	3	11	**Sundown**..................................*Gordon Lightfoot* . . . Reprise 1194
④	4	11	**The Streak** ....*Ray Stevens* . . . Barnaby 600
⑤	7	8	**Be Thankful For What You Got** ....*William DeVaughn* . . . Roxbury 0236
⑥	5	10	**Band On The Run**.....................*Paul McCartney & Wings* . . . Apple 1873
⑦	11	11	**If You Love Me (Let Me Know)** ....*Olivia Newton-John* . . . MCA 40209
⑧	6	15	**Dancing Machine**................................*The Jackson 5* . . . Motown 1286
⑨	13	10	**Hollywood Swinging** ....*Kool & The Gang* . . . De-Lite 561
⑩	8	14	**The Entertainer** ....*Marvin Hamlisch* . . . MCA 40174

★ HIGHEST DEBUT ★ POS 70	★ BIGGEST MOVER ★ 91 to 62
Don't Let The Sun Go Down On Me...........*Elton John*	Fish Ain't Bitin' ....*Lamont Dozier*

TW	LW	WK	Billboard.	JUNE 29, 1974	HOT 100.
①	3	12	**Sundown**..................................*Gordon Lightfoot* . . . Reprise 1194
②	1	11	**Billy, Don't Be A Hero** ....*Bo Donaldson & The Heywoods* . . . ABC 11435
③	2	15	**You Make Me Feel Brand New** ....*The Stylistics* . . . Avco 4634
④	5	9	**Be Thankful For What You Got** .....*William DeVaughn* . . . Roxbury 0236
⑤	7	12	**If You Love Me (Let Me Know)** ....*Olivia Newton-John* . . . MCA 40209
⑥	12	6	**Rock The Boat** ....*The Hues Corporation* . . . RCA 0232
⑦	9	11	**Hollywood Swinging** ....*Kool & The Gang* . . . De-Lite 561
⑧	6	11	**Band On The Run**.....................*Paul McCartney & Wings* . . . Apple 1873
⑨	15	5	**Rock Your Baby**................................*George McCrae* . . . T.K. 1004
⑩	27	5	**Annie's Song**..............................*John Denver* . . . RCA 0295	←

★ HIGHEST DEBUT ★ POS 79	★ BIGGEST MOVER ★ 78 to 53
Hang On In There Baby ....*Johnny Bristol*	Feel Like Makin' Love ....*Roberta Flack*

TW	LW	WK	Billboard.	JULY 6, 1974	HOT 100.
❶	6	7	**Rock The Boat** ....*The Hues Corporation* . . . RCA 0232
②	1	13	**Sundown**..................................*Gordon Lightfoot* . . . Reprise 1194
③	2	12	**Billy, Don't Be A Hero** ....*Bo Donaldson & The Heywoods* . . . ABC 11435
❹	9	6	**Rock Your Baby**................................*George McCrae* . . . T.K. 1004
⑤	5	13	**If You Love Me (Let Me Know)** ....*Olivia Newton-John* . . . MCA 40209
⑥	7	12	**Hollywood Swinging**............................*Kool & The Gang* . . . De-Lite 561
⑦	3	16	**You Make Me Feel Brand New** ....*The Stylistics* . . . Avco 4634
❽	10	6	**Annie's Song** ....*John Denver* . . . RCA 0295	←
⑨	12	12	**You Won't See Me** ....*Anne Murray* . . . Capitol 3867
⑩	13	7	**On And On** ....*Gladys Knight & The Pips* . . . Buddah 423

★ HIGHEST DEBUT ★ POS 82	★ BIGGEST MOVER ★ 50 to 25
(You're) Having My Baby ....*Paul Anka*	Don't Let The Sun Go Down On Me...........*Elton John*

Billboard — JULY 13, 1974 — HOT 100

TW	LW	WK	Title	Artist	Label
1	4	7	Rock Your Baby	George McCrae	T.K. 1004
2	8	7	Annie's Song	John Denver	RCA 0295
3	1	8	Rock The Boat	The Hues Corporation	RCA 0232
4	2	14	Sundown	Gordon Lightfoot	Reprise 1194
5	10	8	On And On	Gladys Knight & The Pips	Buddah 423
6	25	4	Don't Let The Sun Go Down On Me	Elton John	MCA 40259
7	3	13	Billy, Don't Be A Hero	Bo Donaldson & The Heywoods	ABC 11435
8	9	13	You Won't See Me	Anne Murray	Capitol 3867
9	11	13	The Air That I Breathe	The Hollies	Epic 11100
10	15	8	Rock And Roll Heaven	The Righteous Brothers	Haven 7002

★ HIGHEST DEBUT ★ POS 63
Shinin' On ....Grand Funk

★ BIGGEST MOVER ★ 71 to 38
Sure As I'm Sittin' Here ....Three Dog Night

Billboard — JULY 20, 1974 — HOT 100

TW	LW	WK	Title	Artist	Label
1	1	8	Rock Your Baby	George McCrae	T.K. 1004
2	2	8	Annie's Song	John Denver	RCA 0295
3	10	9	Rock And Roll Heaven	The Righteous Brothers	Haven 7002
4	6	5	Don't Let The Sun Go Down On Me	Elton John	MCA 40259
5	5	9	On And On	Gladys Knight & The Pips	Buddah 423
6	3	9	Rock The Boat	The Hues Corporation	RCA 0232
7	13	11	Rikki Don't Lose That Number	Steely Dan	ABC 11439
8	8	14	You Won't See Me	Anne Murray	Capitol 3867
9	9	14	The Air That I Breathe	The Hollies	Epic 11100
10	12	15	If You Love Me (Let Me Know)	Olivia Newton-John	MCA 40209

★ HIGHEST DEBUT ★ POS 71
Clap For The Wolfman ....The Guess Who

★ BIGGEST MOVER ★ 63 to 34
Shinin' On ....Grand Funk

Billboard — JULY 27, 1974 — HOT 100

TW	LW	WK	Title	Artist	Label
1	2	9	Annie's Song	John Denver	RCA 0295
2	4	6	Don't Let The Sun Go Down On Me	Elton John	MCA 40259
3	3	10	Rock And Roll Heaven	The Righteous Brothers	Haven 7002
4	1	9	Rock Your Baby	George McCrae	T.K. 1004
5	7	12	Rikki Don't Lose That Number	Steely Dan	ABC 11439
6	16	6	Feel Like Makin' Love	Roberta Flack	Atlantic 3025
7	9	15	The Air That I Breathe	The Hollies	Epic 11100
8	6	10	Rock The Boat	The Hues Corporation	RCA 0232
9	19	9	Please Come To Boston	Dave Loggins	Epic 11115
10	23	6	Call On Me	Chicago	Columbia 46062

★ HIGHEST DEBUT ★ POS 51
Then Came You ....Dionne Warwicke & Spinners

★ BIGGEST MOVER ★ 62 to 42
I Shot The Sheriff ....Eric Clapton

Billboard — AUGUST 3, 1974 — HOT 100

TW	LW	WK	Title	Artist ... Label
1	1	10	**Annie's Song**	*John Denver* ... RCA 0295
2	2	7	**Don't Let The Sun Go Down On Me**	*Elton John* ... MCA 40259
3	6	7	**Feel Like Makin' Love**	*Roberta Flack* ... Atlantic 3025
4	5	13	**Rikki Don't Lose That Number**	*Steely Dan* ... ABC 11439
5	14	8	**The Night Chicago Died**	*Paper Lace* ... Mercury 73492
6	7	16	**The Air That I Breathe**	*The Hollies* ... Epic 11100
7	3	11	**Rock And Roll Heaven**	*The Righteous Brothers* ... Haven 7002
8	9	10	**Please Come To Boston**	*Dave Loggins* ... Epic 11115
9	10	7	**Call On Me**	*Chicago* ... Columbia 46062
10	11	12	**Sideshow**	*Blue Magic* ... Atco 6961

★ **HIGHEST DEBUT** ★ POS 51
Can't Get Enough Of Your Love, Babe ......*Barry White*

★ **BIGGEST MOVER** ★ 93 to 72
Sweet Home Alabama ....*Lynyrd Skynyrd*

Billboard — AUGUST 10, 1974 — HOT 100

TW	LW	WK	Title	Artist ... Label
1	3	8	**Feel Like Makin' Love**	*Roberta Flack* ... Atlantic 3025
2	5	9	**The Night Chicago Died**	*Paper Lace* ... Mercury 73492
3	1	11	**Annie's Song**	*John Denver* ... RCA 0295
4	2	8	**Don't Let The Sun Go Down On Me**	*Elton John* ... MCA 40259
5	8	11	**Please Come To Boston**	*Dave Loggins* ... Epic 11115
6	9	8	**Call On Me**	*Chicago* ... Columbia 46062
7	11	11	**Waterloo**	*Abba* ... Atlantic 3035
8	10	13	**Sideshow**	*Blue Magic* ... Atco 6961
9	14	6	**Wildwood Weed**	*Jim Stafford* ... MGM 14737
10	19	9	**Tell Me Something Good**	*Rufus* ... ABC 11427

★ **HIGHEST DEBUT** ★ POS 84
Tell Her Love Has Felt The Need ....*Eddie Kendricks*

★ **BIGGEST MOVER** ★ 93 to 51
You Haven't Done Nothin ....*Stevie Wonder*

Billboard — AUGUST 17, 1974 — HOT 100

TW	LW	WK	Title	Artist ... Label
1	2	10	**The Night Chicago Died**	*Paper Lace* ... Mercury 73492
2	1	9	**Feel Like Makin' Love**	*Roberta Flack* ... Atlantic 3025
3	13	7	**(You're) Having My Baby**	*Paul Anka* ... United Artists 454
4	10	10	**Tell Me Something Good**	*Rufus* ... ABC 11427
5	5	12	**Please Come To Boston**	*Dave Loggins* ... Epic 11115
6	6	9	**Call On Me**	*Chicago* ... Columbia 46062
7	7	12	**Waterloo**	*Abba* ... Atlantic 3035
8	9	7	**Wildwood Weed**	*Jim Stafford* ... MGM 14737
9	19	7	**I'm Leaving It (All) Up To You** ....*Donny & Marie Osmond* ... MGM 14735
10	8	14	**Sideshow**	*Blue Magic* ... Atco 6961

★ **HIGHEST DEBUT** ★ POS 63
I Honestly Love You ....*Olivia Newton-John*

★ **BIGGEST MOVER** ★ 79 to 34
It's Only Rock 'N Roll (But I Like It) ....*The Rolling Stones*

Billboard — AUGUST 24, 1974 — HOT 100

TW	LW	WK		
①	3	8	(You're) Having My Baby	Paul Anka . . . United Artists 454
②	1	11	The Night Chicago Died	Paper Lace . . . Mercury 73492
③	4	11	Tell Me Something Good	Rufus . . . ABC 11427
④	2	10	Feel Like Makin' Love	Roberta Flack . . . Atlantic 3025
⑤	13	7	I Shot The Sheriff	Eric Clapton . . . RSO 409
⑥	7	13	Waterloo	Abba . . . Atlantic 3035
⑦	8	8	Wildwood Weed	Jim Stafford . . . MGM 14737
⑧	9	8	I'm Leaving It (All) Up To You	Donny & Marie Osmond . . . MGM 14735
⑨	15	10	Rock Me Gently	Andy Kim . . . Capitol 3895
⑩	11	14	Keep On Smilin'	Wet Willie . . . Capricorn 0043

★ **HIGHEST DEBUT** ★ POS 75
Do It Baby . . . . The Miracles

★ **BIGGEST MOVER** ★ 72 to 47
Earache My Eye Featuring Alice Bowie . . . . Cheech & Chong

Billboard — AUGUST 31, 1974 — HOT 100

TW	LW	WK		
①	1	9	(You're) Having My Baby	Paul Anka . . . United Artists 454
②	5	8	I Shot The Sheriff	Eric Clapton . . . RSO 409
③	3	12	Tell Me Something Good	Rufus . . . ABC 11427
④	2	12	The Night Chicago Died	Paper Lace . . . Mercury 73492
⑤	4	11	Feel Like Makin' Love	Roberta Flack . . . Atlantic 3025
⑥	8	9	I'm Leaving It (All) Up To You	Donny & Marie Osmond . . . MGM 14735
⑦	7	9	Wildwood Weed	Jim Stafford . . . MGM 14737
⑧	9	11	Rock Me Gently	Andy Kim . . . Capitol 3895
⑨	15	5	Can't Get Enough Of Your Love, Babe	Barry White . . . 20th Century 2120
⑩	12	12	You And Me Against The World	Helen Reddy . . . Capitol 3897

★ **HIGHEST DEBUT** ★ POS 83
Love Me For A Reason . . . . The Osmonds

★ **BIGGEST MOVER** ★ 77 to 50
Never My Love . . . . Blue Swede

Billboard — SEPTEMBER 7, 1974 — HOT 100

TW	LW	WK		
①	1	10	(You're) Having My Baby	Paul Anka . . . United Artists 454
②	2	9	I Shot The Sheriff	Eric Clapton . . . RSO 409
③	3	13	Tell Me Something Good	Rufus . . . ABC 11427
④	8	12	Rock Me Gently	Andy Kim . . . Capitol 3895
⑤	6	10	I'm Leaving It (All) Up To You	Donny & Marie Osmond . . . MGM 14735
⑥	9	6	Can't Get Enough Of Your Love, Babe	Barry White . . . 20th Century 2120
⑦	12	9	Nothing From Nothing	Billy Preston . . . A&M 1544
⑧	4	13	The Night Chicago Died	Paper Lace . . . Mercury 73492
⑨	10	13	You And Me Against The World	Helen Reddy . . . Capitol 3897
⑩	11	7	Then Came You	Dionne Warwicke & Spinners . . . Atlantic 3202

★ **HIGHEST DEBUT** ★ POS 45
Skin Tight . . . . Ohio Players

★ **BIGGEST MOVER** ★ 70 to 39
Steppin' Out (Gonna Boogie Tonight) . . . . Tony Orlando & Dawn

Billboard — SEPTEMBER 14, 1974 — HOT 100

TW	LW	WK	Title / Artist / Label
1	2	10	**I Shot The Sheriff**......................................*Eric Clapton* ... RSO 409
2	1	11	(You're) Having My Baby.........................*Paul Anka* ... United Artists 454
3	4	13	Rock Me Gently ....*Andy Kim* ... Capitol 3895
4	5	11	**I'm Leaving It (All) Up To You**...................*Donny & Marie Osmond* ... MGM 14735
5	6	7	Can't Get Enough Of Your Love, Babe ....*Barry White* ... 20th Century 2120
6	7	10	Nothing From Nothing ....*Billy Preston* ... A&M 1544
7	3	14	Tell Me Something Good...........................*Rufus* ... ABC 11427
8	10	8	Then Came You.....................*Dionne Warwicke & Spinners* ... Atlantic 3202
9	9	14	**You And Me Against The World**..............*Helen Reddy* ... Capitol 3897
10	13	9	Clap For The Wolfman...............................*The Guess Who* ... RCA 0324

★ **HIGHEST DEBUT** ★ POS 84
The Need To Be ....*Jim Weatherly*

★ **BIGGEST MOVER** ★ 90 to 68
Life Is A Rock (But The Radio Rolled Me) ....*Reunion*

Billboard — SEPTEMBER 21, 1974 — HOT 100

TW	LW	WK	Title / Artist / Label
1	5	8	**Can't Get Enough Of Your Love, Babe**......................*Barry White* ... 20th Century 2120
2	3	14	Rock Me Gently ....*Andy Kim* ... Capitol 3895
3	12	6	I Honestly Love You.............................*Olivia Newton-John* ... MCA 40280
4	6	11	Nothing From Nothing ....*Billy Preston* ... A&M 1544
5	1	11	I Shot The Sheriff.....................................*Eric Clapton* ... RSO 409
6	8	9	Then Came You.....................*Dionne Warwicke & Spinners* ... Atlantic 3202
7	2	12	(You're) Having My Baby.........................*Paul Anka* ... United Artists 454
8	10	10	Clap For The Wolfman...............................*The Guess Who* ... RCA 0324
9	11	8	You Haven't Done Nothin ....*Stevie Wonder* ... Tamla 54252
10	13	13	Hang On In There Baby ....*Johnny Bristol* ... MGM 14715

★ **HIGHEST DEBUT** ★ POS 65
You Ain't Seen Nothing Yet........*Bachman-Turner Overdrive*

★ **BIGGEST MOVER** ★ 60 to 37
Love Me For A Reason.................*The Osmonds*

Billboard — SEPTEMBER 28, 1974 — HOT 100

TW	LW	WK	Title / Artist / Label
1	2	15	**Rock Me Gently**...*Andy Kim* ... Capitol 3895
2	3	7	I Honestly Love You.............................*Olivia Newton-John* ... MCA 40280
3	4	12	Nothing From Nothing ....*Billy Preston* ... A&M 1544
4	6	10	Then Came You.....................*Dionne Warwicke & Spinners* ... Atlantic 3202
5	12	11	Beach Baby ....*First Class* ... UK 49022
6	9	9	You Haven't Done Nothin ....*Stevie Wonder* ... Tamla 54252
7	8	11	Clap For The Wolfman...............................*The Guess Who* ... RCA 0324
8	11	9	Another Saturday Night ....*Cat Stevens* ... A&M 1602
9	10	14	Hang On In There Baby ....*Johnny Bristol* ... MGM 14715
10	14	10	Sweet Home Alabama ....*Lynyrd Skynyrd* ... MCA 40258

★ **HIGHEST DEBUT** ★ POS 53
Whatever Gets You Thru The Night ....*John Lennon with The Plastic Ono Nuclear Band*

★ **BIGGEST MOVER** ★ 87 to 63
Everlasting Love ....*Carl Carlton*

Billboard — OCTOBER 5, 1974 — HOT 100

TW	LW	WK	Title	Artist	Label
1	2	8	I Honestly Love You	Olivia Newton-John	MCA 40280
2	3	13	Nothing From Nothing	Billy Preston	A&M 1544
3	4	11	Then Came You	Dionne Warwicke & Spinners	Atlantic 3202
4	5	12	Beach Baby	First Class	UK 49022
5	6	10	You Haven't Done Nothin	Stevie Wonder	Tamla 54252
6	7	12	Clap For The Wolfman	The Guess Who	RCA 0324
7	8	10	Another Saturday Night	Cat Stevens	A&M 1602
8	9	15	Hang On In There Baby	Johnny Bristol	MGM 14715
9	10	11	Sweet Home Alabama	Lynyrd Skynyrd	MCA 40258
10	11	9	Earache My Eye Featuring Alice Bowie	Cheech & Chong	Ode 66102

★ HIGHEST DEBUT ★ POS 59
Longfellow Serenade .... Neil Diamond

★ BIGGEST MOVER ★ 60 to 38
Do It ('Til You're Satisfied) .... B.T. Express

Billboard — OCTOBER 12, 1974 — HOT 100

TW	LW	WK	Title	Artist	Label
1	1	9	I Honestly Love You	Olivia Newton-John	MCA 40280
2	2	14	Nothing From Nothing	Billy Preston	A&M 1544
3	3	12	Then Came You	Dionne Warwicke & Spinners	Atlantic 3202
4	4	13	Beach Baby	First Class	UK 49022
5	5	11	You Haven't Done Nothin	Stevie Wonder	Tamla 54252
6	7	11	Another Saturday Night	Cat Stevens	A&M 1602
7	18	6	The Bitch Is Back	Elton John	MCA 40297
8	13	8	Never My Love	Blue Swede	EMI 3938
9	10	10	Earache My Eye Featuring Alice Bowie	Cheech & Chong	Ode 66102
10	11	9	Can't Get Enough	Bad Company	Swan Song 70015

★ HIGHEST DEBUT ★ POS 63
Rockin' Soul .... The Hues Corporation

★ BIGGEST MOVER ★ 65 to 33
My Melody Of Love .... Bobby Vinton

Billboard — OCTOBER 19, 1974 — HOT 100

TW	LW	WK	Title	Artist	Label
1	2	15	Nothing From Nothing	Billy Preston	A&M 1544
2	3	13	Then Came You	Dionne Warwicke & Spinners	Atlantic 3202
3	5	12	You Haven't Done Nothin	Stevie Wonder	Tamla 54252
4	1	10	I Honestly Love You	Olivia Newton-John	MCA 40280
5	15	8	Jazzman	Carole King	Ode 66101
6	7	7	The Bitch Is Back	Elton John	MCA 40297
7	8	9	Never My Love	Blue Swede	EMI 3938
8	10	10	Can't Get Enough	Bad Company	Swan Song 70015
9	11	9	Steppin' Out (Gonna Boogie Tonight)	Tony Orlando & Dawn	Bell 45601
10	17	8	Love Me For A Reason	The Osmonds	MGM 14746

★ HIGHEST DEBUT ★ POS 56
Wishing You Were Here .... Chicago

★ BIGGEST MOVER ★ 72 to 40
When Will I See You Again ..... The Three Degrees

Billboard — OCTOBER 26, 1974 — HOT 100

TW	LW	WK	Title	Artist	Label
1	2	14	**Then Came You**	*Dionne Warwicke & Spinners*	Atlantic 3202
2	3	13	**You Haven't Done Nothin**	*Stevie Wonder*	Tamla 54252
3	17	6	**You Ain't Seen Nothing Yet/Free Wheelin'**	*Bachman-Turner Overdrive*	Mercury 73622
4	5	9	**Jazzman**	*Carole King*	Ode 66101
5	6	8	**The Bitch Is Back**	*Elton John*	MCA 40297
6	8	11	**Can't Get Enough**	*Bad Company*	Swan Song 70015
7	9	10	**Steppin' Out (Gonna Boogie Tonight)**	*Tony Orlando & Dawn*	Bell 45601
8	15	14	**Sweet Home Alabama**	*Lynyrd Skynyrd*	MCA 40258
9	11	10	**Stop And Smell The Roses**	*Mac Davis*	Columbia 10018
10	10	9	**Love Me For A Reason**	*The Osmonds*	MGM 14746

★ **HIGHEST DEBUT** ★ POS 82
Let's Straighten It Out ....*Latimore*

★ **BIGGEST MOVER** ★ 79 to 51
You Got The Love ......*Rufus Featuring Chaka Khan*

Billboard — NOVEMBER 2, 1974 — HOT 100

TW	LW	WK	Title	Artist	Label
1	2	14	**You Haven't Done Nothin**	*Stevie Wonder*	Tamla 54252
2	3	7	**You Ain't Seen Nothing Yet/Free Wheelin'**	*Bachman-Turner Overdrive*	Mercury 73622
3	4	10	**Jazzman**	*Carole King*	Ode 66101
4	5	9	**The Bitch Is Back**	*Elton John*	MCA 40297
5	6	12	**Can't Get Enough**	*Bad Company*	Swan Song 70015
6	12	6	**Whatever Gets You Thru The Night**	*John Lennon with The Plastic Ono Nuclear Band*	Apple 1874
7	7	11	**Steppin' Out (Gonna Boogie Tonight)**	*Tony Orlando & Dawn*	Bell 45601
8	8	15	**Sweet Home Alabama**	*Lynyrd Skynyrd*	MCA 40258
9	9	11	**Stop And Smell The Roses**	*Mac Davis*	Columbia 10018
10	11	11	**Tin Man**	*America*	Warner 7839

★ **HIGHEST DEBUT** ★ POS 60
You're The First, The Last, My Everything ....*Barry White*

★ **BIGGEST MOVER** ★ 86 to 48
Promised Land............*Elvis Presley*

Billboard — NOVEMBER 9, 1974 — HOT 100

TW	LW	WK	Title	Artist	Label
1	2	8	**You Ain't Seen Nothing Yet/Free Wheelin'**	*Bachman-Turner Overdrive*	Mercury 73622
2	3	11	**Jazzman**	*Carole King*	Ode 66101
3	6	7	**Whatever Gets You Thru The Night**	*John Lennon with The Plastic Ono Nuclear Band*	Apple 1874
4	10	12	**Tin Man**	*America*	Warner 7839
5	11	8	**Back Home Again**	*John Denver*	RCA 10065
6	17	8	**My Melody Of Love**	*Bobby Vinton*	ABC 12022
7	14	7	**Do It ('Til You're Satisfied)**	*B.T. Express*	Scepter 12395
8	4	10	**The Bitch Is Back**	*Elton John*	MCA 40297
9	12	10	**Life Is A Rock (But The Radio Rolled Me)**	*Reunion*	RCA 10056
10	13	11	**Carefree Highway**	*Gordon Lightfoot*	Reprise 1309

★ **HIGHEST DEBUT** ★ POS 59
Junior's Farm/Sally G ......*Paul McCartney & Wings*

★ **BIGGEST MOVER** ★ 55 to 33
Kung Fu Fighting ....*Carl Douglas*

Billboard — NOVEMBER 16, 1974 — HOT 100

TW	LW	WK	Title / Artist / Label
1	3	8	**Whatever Gets You Thru The Night** .... *John Lennon with The Plastic Ono Nuclear Band* ... Apple 1874
2	7	8	**Do It ('Til You're Satisfied)** ..................*B.T. Express* ... Scepter 12395
3	6	9	**My Melody Of Love** ....*Bobby Vinton* ... ABC 12022
4	4	13	**Tin Man** ....*America* ... Warner 7839
5	5	9	**Back Home Again** ....*John Denver* ... RCA 10065
6	15	8	**I Can Help** ....*Billy Swan* ... Monument 8621
7	13	7	**Longfellow Serenade** ....*Neil Diamond* ... Columbia 10043
8	9	11	**Life Is A Rock (But The Radio Rolled Me)** .... *Reunion* ... RCA 10056
9	11	9	**Everlasting Love** ....*Carl Carlton* ... Back Beat 27001
10	10	12	**Carefree Highway** ....*Gordon Lightfoot* ... Reprise 1309

★ **HIGHEST DEBUT** ★ POS 62
Boogie On Reggae Woman ....*Stevie Wonder*

★ **BIGGEST MOVER** ★ 64 to 40
Ain't Too Proud To Beg ....*The Rolling Stones*

Billboard — NOVEMBER 23, 1974 — HOT 100

TW	LW	WK	Title / Artist / Label
1	6	9	**I Can Help** ....*Billy Swan* ... Monument 8621
2	2	9	**Do It ('Til You're Satisfied)** ..................*B.T. Express* ... Scepter 12395
3	3	10	**My Melody Of Love** ....*Bobby Vinton* ... ABC 12022
4	4	14	**Tin Man** ....*America* ... Warner 7839
5	7	8	**Longfellow Serenade** ....*Neil Diamond* ... Columbia 10043
6	9	10	**Everlasting Love** ....*Carl Carlton* ... Back Beat 27001
7	27	7	**Kung Fu Fighting** ....*Carl Douglas* ... 20th Century 2140
8	16	9	**When Will I See You Again** ....*The Three Degrees* ... Philadelphia International 3550
9	5	10	**Back Home Again** ....*John Denver* ... RCA 10065
10	22	8	**Cat's In The Cradle** ....*Harry Chapin* ... Elektra 45203

★ **HIGHEST DEBUT** ★ POS 69
Dark Horse ....*George Harrison*

★ **BIGGEST MOVER** ★ 27 to 7
Kung Fu Fighting ....*Carl Douglas*

Billboard — NOVEMBER 30, 1974 — HOT 100

TW	LW	WK	Title / Artist / Label
1	1	10	**I Can Help** ....*Billy Swan* ... Monument 8621
2	7	8	**Kung Fu Fighting** ....*Carl Douglas* ... 20th Century 2140
3	8	10	**When Will I See You Again** .... *The Three Degrees* ... Philadelphia International 3550
4	2	10	**Do It ('Til You're Satisfied)** ..................*B.T. Express* ... Scepter 12395
5	5	9	**Longfellow Serenade** ....*Neil Diamond* ... Columbia 10043
6	6	11	**Everlasting Love** ....*Carl Carlton* ... Back Beat 27001
7	3	11	**My Melody Of Love** ....*Bobby Vinton* ... ABC 12022
8	34	11	**You Ain't Seen Nothing Yet** ....*Bachman-Turner Overdrive* ... Mercury 73622
9	10	9	**Cat's In The Cradle** ....*Harry Chapin* ... Elektra 45203
10	14	7	**Angie Baby** ....*Helen Reddy* ... Capitol 3972

★ **HIGHEST DEBUT** ★ POS 48
Lucy In The Sky With Diamonds ....*Elton John*

★ **BIGGEST MOVER** ★ 34 to 8
You Ain't Seen Nothing Yet ....*Bachman-Turner Overdrive*

Billboard DECEMBER 7, 1974 HOT 100.

TW	LW	WK	Title	Artist / Label
❶	2	9	**Kung Fu Fighting**	*Carl Douglas* . . . 20th Century 2140
②	1	11	I Can Help	*Billy Swan* . . . Monument 8621
③	3	11	When Will I See You Again	*The Three Degrees* . . . Philadelphia International 3550
④	4	11	Do It ('Til You're Satisfied)	*B.T. Express* . . . Scepter 12395
⑤	9	10	Cat's In The Cradle	*Harry Chapin* . . . Elektra 45203
⑥	10	8	Angie Baby	*Helen Reddy* . . . Capitol 3972
⑦	7	12	My Melody Of Love	*Bobby Vinton* . . . ABC 12022
⑧	8	12	You Ain't Seen Nothing Yet/Free Wheelin'	*Bachman-Turner Overdrive* . . . Mercury 73622
⑨	13	11	Sha-La-La (Make Me Happy)	*Al Green* . . . Hi 2274
⑩	17	6	You're The First, The Last, My Everything	*Barry White* . . . 20th Century 2133

★ HIGHEST DEBUT ★ POS 81	★ BIGGEST MOVER ★ 56 to 39
Pick Up The Pieces ....*AWB*	Please Mr. Postman.........................*Carpenters*

Billboard DECEMBER 14, 1974 HOT 100.

TW	LW	WK	Title	Artist / Label
❶	1	10	**Kung Fu Fighting**	*Carl Douglas* . . . 20th Century 2140
②	3	12	**When Will I See You Again**	*The Three Degrees* . . . Philadelphia International 3550
③	2	12	I Can Help	*Billy Swan* . . . Monument 8621
④	5	11	Cat's In The Cradle	*Harry Chapin* . . . Elektra 45203
⑤	6	9	Angie Baby	*Helen Reddy* . . . Capitol 3972
⑥	4	12	Do It ('Til You're Satisfied)	*B.T. Express* . . . Scepter 12395
❼	10	7	You're The First, The Last, My Everything	*Barry White* . . . 20th Century 2133
⑧	9	12	Sha-La-La (Make Me Happy)	*Al Green* . . . Hi 2274
⑨	36	3	Lucy In The Sky With Diamonds	*Elton John* . . . MCA 40344
⑩	12	6	Junior's Farm/Sally G	*Paul McCartney & Wings* . . . Apple 1875

★ HIGHEST DEBUT ★ POS 67	★ BIGGEST MOVER ★ 87 to 50
Some Kind Of Wonderful ....*Grand Funk*	Rock N' Roll (I Gave You The Best Years Of My Life) ....*Mac Davis*

Billboard DECEMBER 21, 1974 HOT 100.

TW	LW	WK	Title	Artist / Label
❶	4	12	**Cat's In The Cradle**	*Harry Chapin* . . . Elektra 45203
②	1	11	Kung Fu Fighting	*Carl Douglas* . . . 20th Century 2140
❸	5	10	Angie Baby	*Helen Reddy* . . . Capitol 3972
④	2	13	When Will I See You Again	*The Three Degrees* . . . Philadelphia International 3550
❺	7	8	You're The First, The Last, My Everything	*Barry White* . . . 20th Century 2133
⑥	9	4	Lucy In The Sky With Diamonds	*Elton John* . . . MCA 40344
⑦	8	13	**Sha-La-La (Make Me Happy)**	*Al Green* . . . Hi 2274
⑧	10	7	Junior's Farm/Sally G	*Paul McCartney & Wings* . . . Apple 1875
⑨	3	13	I Can Help	*Billy Swan* . . . Monument 8621
⑩	6	13	Do It ('Til You're Satisfied)	*B.T. Express* . . . Scepter 12395

★ HIGHEST DEBUT ★ POS 68	★ BIGGEST MOVER ★ 67 to 38
#9 Dream.............................*John Lennon*	Some Kind Of Wonderful ....*Grand Funk*

TW	LW	WK	Billboard.	DECEMBER 28, 1974	HOT 100.
❶	3	11	**Angie Baby**...*Helen Reddy* . . . Capitol 3972
❷	6	5	**Lucy In The Sky With Diamonds** ....*Elton John* . . . MCA 40344
❸	5	9	**You're The First, The Last, My Everything**..........................*Barry White* . . . 20th Century 2133
④	2	12	**Kung Fu Fighting**.................................*Carl Douglas* . . . 20th Century 2140
⑤	1	13	**Cat's In The Cradle** ....*Harry Chapin* . . . Elektra 45203
⑥	8	8	**Junior's Farm/Sally G** ....*Paul McCartney & Wings* . . . Apple 1875
⑦	4	14	**When Will I See You Again**.................................*The Three Degrees* . . . Philadelphia International 3550
⑧	12	11	**Laughter In The Rain** ....*Neil Sedaka* . . . Rocket 40313
⑨	14	7	**Only You**...*Ringo Starr* . . . Apple 1876
⑩	13	7	**Boogie On Reggae Woman** ....*Stevie Wonder* . . . Tamla 54254

★ *HIGHEST DEBUT* ★ POS 77	★ *BIGGEST MOVER* ★ 59 to 24
Lonely People ....*America*	Fire ....*Ohio Players*

Billboard — JANUARY 4, 1975 — HOT 100

TW	LW	WK	Title	Artist	Label
1	2	6	Lucy In The Sky With Diamonds	Elton John	MCA 40344
2	3	10	You're The First, The Last, My Everything	Barry White	20th Century 2133
3	4	13	Kung Fu Fighting	Carl Douglas	20th Century 2140
4	6	9	Junior's Farm/Sally G	Paul McCartney & Wings	Apple 1875
5	8	12	Laughter In The Rain	Neil Sedaka	Rocket 40313
6	1	12	Angie Baby	Helen Reddy	Capitol 3972
7	9	8	Only You	Ringo Starr	Apple 1876
8	10	8	Boogie On Reggae Woman	Stevie Wonder	Tamla 54254
9	11	7	Please Mr. Postman	Carpenters	A&M 1646
10	12	8	Mandy	Barry Manilow	Bell 45613

★ **HIGHEST DEBUT** ★ POS 67
Nightingale .... Carole King

★ **BIGGEST MOVER** ★ 63 to 41
Look In My Eyes Pretty Woman ...... Tony Orlando & Dawn

Billboard — JANUARY 11, 1975 — HOT 100

TW	LW	WK	Title	Artist	Label
1	1	7	Lucy In The Sky With Diamonds	Elton John	MCA 40344
2	2	11	You're The First, The Last, My Everything	Barry White	20th Century 2133
3	4	10	Junior's Farm/Sally G	Paul McCartney & Wings	Apple 1875
4	5	13	Laughter In The Rain	Neil Sedaka	Rocket 40313
5	10	9	Mandy	Barry Manilow	Bell 45613
6	7	9	Only You	Ringo Starr	Apple 1876
7	8	9	Boogie On Reggae Woman	Stevie Wonder	Tamla 54254
8	9	8	Please Mr. Postman	Carpenters	A&M 1646
9	3	14	Kung Fu Fighting	Carl Douglas	20th Century 2140
10	13	10	One Man Woman/One Woman Man	Paul Anka with Odia Coates	United Artists 569

★ **HIGHEST DEBUT** ★ POS 81
Ding Dong; Ding Dong .... George Harrison

★ **BIGGEST MOVER** ★ 64 to 37
Sweet Surrender .... John Denver ⟵

Billboard — JANUARY 18, 1975 — HOT 100

TW	LW	WK	Title	Artist	Label
1	5	10	Mandy	Barry Manilow	Bell 45613
2	8	9	Please Mr. Postman	Carpenters	A&M 1646
3	4	14	Laughter In The Rain	Neil Sedaka	Rocket 40313
4	2	12	You're The First, The Last, My Everything	Barry White	20th Century 2133
5	1	8	Lucy In The Sky With Diamonds	Elton John	MCA 40344
6	7	10	Boogie On Reggae Woman	Stevie Wonder	Tamla 54254
7	3	11	Junior's Farm/Sally G	Paul McCartney & Wings	Apple 1875
8	10	11	One Man Woman/One Woman Man	Paul Anka with Odia Coates	United Artists 569
9	11	10	Morning Side Of The Mountain	Donny & Marie Osmond	MGM 14765
10	14	12	Never Can Say Goodbye	Gloria Gaynor	MGM 14748

★ **HIGHEST DEBUT** ★ POS 67
Roll On Down The Highway .... Bachman-Turner Overdrive

★ **BIGGEST MOVER** ★ 81 to 59
Ding Dong; Ding Dong .... George Harrison

Billboard — JANUARY 25, 1975 — HOT 100

TW	LW	WK	Title	Artist	Label
1	2	10	**Please Mr. Postman**	*Carpenters*	A&M 1646
2	3	15	**Laughter In The Rain**	*Neil Sedaka*	Rocket 40313
3	1	11	**Mandy**	*Barry Manilow*	Bell 45613
4	11	7	**Fire**	*Ohio Players*	Mercury 73643
5	6	11	**Boogie On Reggae Woman**	*Stevie Wonder*	Tamla 54254
6	21	8	**You're No Good**	*Linda Ronstadt*	Capitol 3990
7	8	12	**One Man Woman/One Woman Man**	*Paul Anka with Odia Coates*	United Artists 569
8	9	11	**Morning Side Of The Mountain**	*Donny & Marie Osmond*	MGM 14765
9	10	13	**Never Can Say Goodbye**	*Gloria Gaynor*	MGM 14748
10	14	8	**Pick Up The Pieces**	*AWB*	Atlantic 3229

★ **HIGHEST DEBUT** ★ POS 63
Have You Never Been Mellow..................*Olivia Newton-John*

★ **BIGGEST MOVER** ★ 86 to 62
Up In A Puff Of Smoke ....*Polly Brown*

Billboard — FEBRUARY 1, 1975 — HOT 100

TW	LW	WK	Title	Artist	Label
1	2	16	**Laughter In The Rain**	*Neil Sedaka*	Rocket 40313
2	4	8	**Fire**	*Ohio Players*	Mercury 73643
3	5	12	**Boogie On Reggae Woman**	*Stevie Wonder*	Tamla 54254
4	6	9	**You're No Good**	*Linda Ronstadt*	Capitol 3990
5	10	9	**Pick Up The Pieces**	*AWB*	Atlantic 3229
6	1	11	**Please Mr. Postman**	*Carpenters*	A&M 1646
7	3	12	**Mandy**	*Barry Manilow*	Bell 45613
8	8	12	**Morning Side Of The Mountain**	*Donny & Marie Osmond*	MGM 14765
9	15	10	**Best Of My Love**	*The Eagles*	Asylum 45218
10	12	8	**Some Kind Of Wonderful**	*Grand Funk*	Capitol 4002

★ **HIGHEST DEBUT** ★ POS 73
I've Been This Way Before.............*Neil Diamond*

★ **BIGGEST MOVER** ★ 85 to 42
Express.....................................*B.T. Express*

Billboard — FEBRUARY 8, 1975 — HOT 100

TW	LW	WK	Title	Artist	Label
1	2	9	**Fire**	*Ohio Players*	Mercury 73643
2	4	10	**You're No Good**	*Linda Ronstadt*	Capitol 3990
3	3	13	**Boogie On Reggae Woman**	*Stevie Wonder*	Tamla 54254
4	5	10	**Pick Up The Pieces**	*AWB*	Atlantic 3229
5	9	11	**Best Of My Love**	*The Eagles*	Asylum 45218
6	10	9	**Some Kind Of Wonderful**	*Grand Funk*	Capitol 4002
7	16	8	**Black Water**	*The Doobie Brothers*	Warner 8062
8	1	17	**Laughter In The Rain**	*Neil Sedaka*	Rocket 40313
9	24	7	**Lonely People**	*America*	Warner 8048
10	11	12	**Get Dancin'**	*Disco Tex & The Sex-O-Lettes*	Chelsea 3004

★ **HIGHEST DEBUT** ★ POS 72
Emotion ....*Helen Reddy*

★ **BIGGEST MOVER** ★ 69 to 42
My Boy.....................................*Elvis Presley*

Billboard — FEBRUARY 15, 1975 — HOT 100

TW	LW	WK	Title	Artist	Label
1	2	11	You're No Good	Linda Ronstadt	Capitol 3990
2	4	11	Pick Up The Pieces	AWB	Atlantic 3229
3	5	12	Best Of My Love	The Eagles	Asylum 45218
4	6	10	Some Kind Of Wonderful	Grand Funk	Capitol 4002
5	7	9	Black Water	The Doobie Brothers	Warner 8062
6	1	10	Fire	Ohio Players	Mercury 73643
7	9	8	Lonely People	America	Warner 8048
8	3	14	Boogie On Reggae Woman	Stevie Wonder	Tamla 54254
9	12	13	My Eyes Adored You	Frankie Valli	Private Stock 45003
10	13	9	#9 Dream	John Lennon	Apple 1878

★ **HIGHEST DEBUT** ★ POS 79
Once You Get Started........Rufus Featuring Chaka Khan

★ **BIGGEST MOVER** ★ 78 to 58
No No Song/Snookeroo ....Ringo Starr

Billboard — FEBRUARY 22, 1975 — HOT 100

TW	LW	WK	Title	Artist	Label
1	2	12	Pick Up The Pieces	AWB	Atlantic 3229
2	3	13	Best Of My Love	The Eagles	Asylum 45218
3	4	11	Some Kind Of Wonderful	Grand Funk	Capitol 4002
4	5	10	Black Water	The Doobie Brothers	Warner 8062
5	18	5	Have You Never Been Mellow	Olivia Newton-John	MCA 40349
6	7	9	Lonely People	America	Warner 8048
7	9	14	My Eyes Adored You	Frankie Valli	Private Stock 45003
8	1	12	You're No Good	Linda Ronstadt	Capitol 3990
9	10	10	#9 Dream	John Lennon	Apple 1878
10	15	8	Nightingale	Carole King	Ode 66106

★ **HIGHEST DEBUT** ★ POS 55
Harry Truman ....Chicago

★ **BIGGEST MOVER** ★ 81 to 44
(Hey Won't You Play) Another Somebody Done Somebody Wrong Song ............B.J. Thomas

Billboard — MARCH 1, 1975 — HOT 100

TW	LW	WK	Title	Artist	Label
1	2	14	Best Of My Love	The Eagles	Asylum 45218
2	5	6	Have You Never Been Mellow	Olivia Newton-John	MCA 40349
3	4	11	Black Water	The Doobie Brothers	Warner 8062
4	7	15	My Eyes Adored You	Frankie Valli	Private Stock 45003
5	3	12	Some Kind Of Wonderful	Grand Funk	Capitol 4002
6	6	10	Lonely People	America	Warner 8048
7	1	13	Pick Up The Pieces	AWB	Atlantic 3229
8	17	9	Lady Marmalade	LaBelle	Epic 50048
9	10	9	Nightingale	Carole King	Ode 66106
10	14	12	Lady	Styx	Wooden Nickel 10102

★ **HIGHEST DEBUT** ★ POS 69
L-O-V-E (Love) ....Al Green

★ **BIGGEST MOVER** ★ 92 to 65
The Bertha Butt Boogie ....The Jimmy Castor Bunch

TW	LW	WK	Billboard.	MARCH 8, 1975	HOT 100.
①	2	7	**Have You Never Been Mellow**	*Olivia Newton-John*	... MCA 40349
❷	3	12	**Black Water**	*The Doobie Brothers* ... Warner 8062	
❸	4	16	**My Eyes Adored You**	*Frankie Valli* ... Private Stock 45003	
④	8	10	**Lady Marmalade**	*LaBelle* ... Epic 50048	
⑤	6	11	**Lonely People**	*America* ... Warner 8048	
⑥	10	13	**Lady**	*Styx* ... Wooden Nickel 10102	
⑦	1	15	**Best Of My Love**	*The Eagles* ... Asylum 45218	
⑧	22	8	**Lovin' You**	*Minnie Riperton* ... Epic 50057	
⑨	7	14	**Pick Up The Pieces**	*AWB* ... Atlantic 3229	
⑩	11	12	**Can't Get It Out Of My Head**	*Electric Light Orchestra* ... United Artists 573	

★ HIGHEST DEBUT ★ POS 53	★ BIGGEST MOVER ★ 45 to 28
Philadelphia Freedom ....*The Elton John Band*	Once You Get Started........*Rufus Featuring Chaka Khan*

TW	LW	WK	Billboard.	MARCH 15, 1975	HOT 100.
①	2	13	**Black Water**	*The Doobie Brothers* ... Warner 8062	
❷	3	17	**My Eyes Adored You**	*Frankie Valli* ... Private Stock 45003	
❸	4	11	**Lady Marmalade**	*LaBelle* ... Epic 50048	
④	1	8	**Have You Never Been Mellow**	*Olivia Newton-John* ... MCA 40349	
⑤	8	9	**Lovin' You**	*Minnie Riperton* ... Epic 50057	
⑥	6	14	**Lady**	*Styx* ... Wooden Nickel 10102	
⑦	5	12	**Lonely People**	*America* ... Warner 8048	
⑧	13	8	**Express**	*B.T. Express* ... Roadshow 7001	
⑨	10	13	**Can't Get It Out Of My Head**	*Electric Light Orchestra* ... United Artists 573	
⑩	11	15	**Don't Call Us, We'll Call You**	*Sugarloaf/Jerry Corbetta* ... Claridge 402	

★ HIGHEST DEBUT ★ POS 55	★ BIGGEST MOVER ★ 76 to 50
He Don't Love You (Like I Love You)..........*Tony Orlando & Dawn*	What Am I Gonna Do With You.........*Barry White*

TW	LW	WK	Billboard.	MARCH 22, 1975	HOT 100.
①	2	18	**My Eyes Adored You**	*Frankie Valli* ... Private Stock 45003	
❷	3	12	**Lady Marmalade**	*LaBelle* ... Epic 50048	
❸	5	10	**Lovin' You**	*Minnie Riperton* ... Epic 50057	
④	1	14	**Black Water**	*The Doobie Brothers* ... Warner 8062	
⑤	4	9	**Have You Never Been Mellow**	*Olivia Newton-John* ... MCA 40349	
⑥	8	9	**Express**	*B.T. Express* ... Roadshow 7001	
⑦	12	11	**You Are So Beautiful**	*Joe Cocker* ... A&M 1641	
⑧	11	12	**Poetry Man**	*Phoebe Snow* ... Shelter 40353	
⑨	14	7	**No No Song/Snookeroo**	*Ringo Starr* ... Apple 1880	
⑩	10	16	**Don't Call Us, We'll Call You**	*Sugarloaf/Jerry Corbetta* ... Claridge 402	

★ HIGHEST DEBUT ★ POS 81	★ BIGGEST MOVER ★ 35 to 11
Shakey Ground ....*The Temptations*	Philadelphia Freedom ....*The Elton John Band*

Billboard — MARCH 29, 1975 — HOT 100

TW	LW	WK	Title	Artist
1	2	13	**Lady Marmalade**	LaBelle ... Epic 50048
2	3	11	Lovin' You	*Minnie Riperton* ... Epic 50057
3	11	4	Philadelphia Freedom	*The Elton John Band* ... MCA 40364
4	6	10	**Express**	*B.T. Express* ... Roadshow 7001
5	7	12	**You Are So Beautiful**	*Joe Cocker* ... A&M 1641
6	9	8	No No Song/Snookeroo	*Ringo Starr* ... Apple 1880
7	8	13	Poetry Man	*Phoebe Snow* ... Shelter 40353
8	1	19	My Eyes Adored You	*Frankie Valli* ... Private Stock 45003
9	10	17	**Don't Call Us, We'll Call You**	*Sugarloaf/Jerry Corbetta* ... Claridge 402
10	5	10	Have You Never Been Mellow	*Olivia Newton-John* ... MCA 40349

★ **HIGHEST DEBUT** ★ POS 74
Only Yesterday ....*Carpenters*

★ **BIGGEST MOVER** ★ 82 to 60
Thank God I'm A Country Boy ....*John Denver*

Billboard — APRIL 5, 1975 — HOT 100

TW	LW	WK	Title	Artist
1	2	12	**Lovin' You**	*Minnie Riperton* ... Epic 50057
2	3	5	**Philadelphia Freedom**	*The Elton John Band* ... MCA 40364
3	6	9	**No No Song/Snookeroo**	*Ringo Starr* ... Apple 1880
4	4	11	**Express**	*B.T. Express* ... Roadshow 7001
5	5	13	**You Are So Beautiful**	*Joe Cocker* ... A&M 1641
6	7	14	Poetry Man	*Phoebe Snow* ... Shelter 40353
7	1	14	Lady Marmalade	*LaBelle* ... Epic 50048
8	11	10	(Hey Won't You Play) Another Somebody Done Somebody Wrong Song	*B.J. Thomas* ... ABC 12054
9	10	11	Have You Never Been Mellow	*Olivia Newton-John* ... MCA 40349
10	8	20	My Eyes Adored You	*Frankie Valli* ... Private Stock 45003

★ **HIGHEST DEBUT** ★ POS 69
Bad Time ....*Grand Funk*

★ **BIGGEST MOVER** ★ 74 to 47
Only Yesterday ....*Carpenters*

Billboard — APRIL 12, 1975 — HOT 100

TW	LW	WK	Title	Artist
1	2	6	**Philadelphia Freedom**	*The Elton John Band* ... MCA 40364
2	1	13	Lovin' You	*Minnie Riperton* ... Epic 50057
3	3	10	**No No Song/Snookeroo**	*Ringo Starr* ... Apple 1880
4	4	12	**Express**	*B.T. Express* ... Roadshow 7001
5	6	15	**Poetry Man**	*Phoebe Snow* ... Shelter 40353
6	8	11	(Hey Won't You Play) Another Somebody Done Somebody Wrong Song	*B.J. Thomas* ... ABC 12054
7	7	15	Lady Marmalade	*LaBelle* ... Epic 50048
8	12	11	Chevy Van	*Sammy Johns* ... GRC 2046
9	14	6	What Am I Gonna Do With You	*Barry White* ... 20th Century 2177
10	11	9	**Once You Get Started**	*Rufus Featuring Chaka Khan* ... ABC 12066

★ **HIGHEST DEBUT** ★ POS 76
Cut The Cake.................................*AWB*

★ **BIGGEST MOVER** ★ 88 to 66
I'm Not Lisa.................................*Jessi Colter*

TW	LW	WK	Billboard.	APRIL 19, 1975	HOT 100.
①	1	7	**Philadelphia Freedom** ....*The Elton John Band* . . . MCA 40364		
②	6	12	**(Hey Won't You Play) Another Somebody Done Somebody Wrong Song**..*B.J. Thomas* . . . ABC 12054		
③	2	14	**Lovin' You**...*Minnie Riperton* . . . Epic 50057		
④	3	11	**No No Song/Snookeroo**..............................*Ringo Starr* . . . Apple 1880		
⑤	23	6	**He Don't Love You (Like I Love You)**...................*Tony Orlando & Dawn* . . . Elektra 45240		
⑥	12	11	**Supernatural Thing**..*Ben E. King* . . . Atlantic 3241		
⑦	8	12	**Chevy Van**..*Sammy Johns* . . . GRC 2046		
⑧	9	7	**What Am I Gonna Do With You** ....*Barry White* . . . 20th Century 2177		
⑨	11	11	**Emma**...*Hot Chocolate* . . . Big Tree 16031		
⑩	14	12	**Before The Next Teardrop Falls**............*Freddy Fender* . . . ABC/Dot 17540		

★ **HIGHEST DEBUT** ★ POS 77
Trampled Under Foot.....................*Led Zeppelin*

★ **BIGGEST MOVER** ★ 81 to 52
When Will I Be Loved..................*Linda Ronstadt*

TW	LW	WK	Billboard.	APRIL 26, 1975	HOT 100.
①	2	13	**(Hey Won't You Play) Another Somebody Done Somebody Wrong Song**..*B.J. Thomas* . . . ABC 12054		
②	1	8	**Philadelphia Freedom** ....*The Elton John Band* . . . MCA 40364		
③	5	7	**He Don't Love You (Like I Love You)**...................*Tony Orlando & Dawn* . . . Elektra 45240		
④	3	15	**Lovin' You**...*Minnie Riperton* . . . Epic 50057		
⑤	6	12	**Supernatural Thing** ....*Ben E. King* . . . Atlantic 3241		
⑥	7	13	**Chevy Van**..*Sammy Johns* . . . GRC 2046		
⑦	10	13	**Before The Next Teardrop Falls**............*Freddy Fender* . . . ABC/Dot 17540		
⑧	9	12	**Emma** ....*Hot Chocolate* . . . Big Tree 16031		
⑨	8	8	**What Am I Gonna Do With You** ....*Barry White* . . . 20th Century 2177		
⑩	12	12	**Walking In Rhythm**....................................*The Blackbyrds* . . . Fantasy 736		

★ **HIGHEST DEBUT** ★ POS 68
Old Days ....*Chicago*

★ **BIGGEST MOVER** ★ 58 to 36
Cut The Cake...*AWB*

TW	LW	WK	Billboard.	MAY 3, 1975	HOT 100.
①	3	8	**He Don't Love You (Like I Love You)** ....*Tony Orlando & Dawn* . . . Elektra 45240		
②	1	14	**(Hey Won't You Play) Another Somebody Done Somebody Wrong Song**..*B.J. Thomas* . . . ABC 12054		
③	7	14	**Before The Next Teardrop Falls**............*Freddy Fender* . . . ABC/Dot 17540		
④	2	9	**Philadelphia Freedom** ....*The Elton John Band* . . . MCA 40364		
⑤	6	14	**Chevy Van** ....*Sammy Johns* . . . GRC 2046		
⑥	14	13	**Jackie Blue**.................*Ozark Mountain Daredevils* . . . A&M 1654		
⑦	11	12	**Shining Star**.................................*Earth, Wind & Fire* . . . Columbia 10090		
⑧	10	13	**Walking In Rhythm**....................................*The Blackbyrds* . . . Fantasy 736		
⑨	12	11	**Long Tall Glasses (I Can Dance)**.............*Leo Sayer* . . . Warner 8043		
⑩	21	6	**Only Yesterday**...*Carpenters* . . . A&M 1677		

★ **HIGHEST DEBUT** ★ POS 77
Take Me In Your Arms (Rock Me) .....*The Doobie Brothers*

★ **BIGGEST MOVER** ★ 68 to 43
Old Days ....*Chicago*

Billboard — MAY 10, 1975 — HOT 100

TW	LW	WK	Title	Artist
①	1	9	**He Don't Love You (Like I Love You)**	Tony Orlando & Dawn ... Elektra 45240
②	3	15	Before The Next Teardrop Falls	Freddy Fender ... ABC/Dot 17540
③	2	15	(Hey Won't You Play) Another Somebody Done Somebody Wrong Song	B.J. Thomas ... ABC 12054
④	6	14	Jackie Blue	Ozark Mountain Daredevils ... A&M 1654
⑤	7	13	Shining Star	Earth, Wind & Fire ... Columbia 10090
⑥	8	14	**Walking In Rhythm**	The Blackbyrds ... Fantasy 736
⑦	4	10	Philadelphia Freedom	The Elton John Band .. MCA 40364
⑧	10	7	Only Yesterday	Carpenters ... A&M 1677
⑨	9	12	**Long Tall Glasses (I Can Dance)**	Leo Sayer ... Warner 8043
⑩	11	9	I Don't Like To Sleep Alone	Paul Anka ... United Artists 615

★ **HIGHEST DEBUT** ★ POS 71
Attitude Dancing .... Carly Simon

★ **BIGGEST MOVER** ★ 43 to 17
Old Days .... Chicago

Billboard — MAY 17, 1975 — HOT 100

TW	LW	WK	Title	Artist
①	1	10	**He Don't Love You (Like I Love You)**	Tony Orlando & Dawn ... Elektra 45240
②	2	16	Before The Next Teardrop Falls	Freddy Fender ... ABC/Dot 17540
③	4	15	**Jackie Blue**	Ozark Mountain Daredevils ... A&M 1654
④	5	14	Shining Star	Earth, Wind & Fire ... Columbia 10090
⑤	8	8	Only Yesterday	Carpenters ... A&M 1677
⑥	6	15	**Walking In Rhythm**	The Blackbyrds ... Fantasy 736
⑦	14	9	Thank God I'm A Country Boy	John Denver ... RCA 10239
⑧	11	11	How Long	Ace ... Anchor 21000
⑨	10	10	I Don't Like To Sleep Alone	Paul Anka ... United Artists 615
⑩	3	16	(Hey Won't You Play) Another Somebody Done Somebody Wrong Song	B.J. Thomas ... ABC 12054

★ **HIGHEST DEBUT** ★ POS 82
Swearin' To God .... Frankie Valli

★ **BIGGEST MOVER** ★ 82 to 58
Judy Mae .... Boomer Castleman

Billboard — MAY 24, 1975 — HOT 100

TW	LW	WK	Title	Artist
①	4	15	**Shining Star**	Earth, Wind & Fire ... Columbia 10090
②	2	17	Before The Next Teardrop Falls	Freddy Fender ... ABC/Dot 17540
③	3	16	**Jackie Blue**	Ozark Mountain Daredevils ... A&M 1654
④	5	9	**Only Yesterday**	Carpenters ... A&M 1677
⑤	7	10	**Thank God I'm A Country Boy**	John Denver ... RCA 10239
⑥	8	12	How Long	Ace ... Anchor 21000
⑦	1	11	He Don't Love You (Like I Love You)	Tony Orlando & Dawn ... Elektra 45240
⑧	9	11	**I Don't Like To Sleep Alone**	Paul Anka ... United Artists 615
⑨	15	8	Bad Time	Grand Funk ... Capitol 4046
⑩	14	5	Old Days	Chicago ... Columbia 10131

★ **HIGHEST DEBUT** ★ POS 76
Black Friday .... Steely Dan

★ **BIGGEST MOVER** ★ 71 to 48
T-R-O-U-B-L-E .... Elvis Presley

Billboard Hot 100 — MAY 31, 1975

TW	LW	WK	Title	Artist	Label
1	2	18	Before The Next Teardrop Falls	Freddy Fender	ABC/Dot 17540
2	5	11	Thank God I'm A Country Boy	John Denver	RCA 10239
3	6	13	How Long	Ace	Anchor 21000
4	4	10	Only Yesterday	Carpenters	A&M 1677
5	11	9	Sister Golden Hair	America	Warner 8086
6	9	9	Bad Time	Grand Funk	Capitol 4046
7	10	6	Old Days	Chicago	Columbia 10131
8	1	16	Shining Star	Earth, Wind & Fire	Columbia 10090
9	8	12	I Don't Like To Sleep Alone	Paul Anka	United Artists 615
10	14	8	When Will I Be Loved	Linda Ronstadt	Capitol 4050

★ HIGHEST DEBUT ★ POS 65
Listen To What The Man Said.................Wings

★ BIGGEST MOVER ★ 76 to 63
Black Friday.......................................Steely Dan

Billboard Hot 100 — JUNE 7, 1975

TW	LW	WK	Title	Artist	Label
1	2	12	Thank God I'm A Country Boy	John Denver	RCA 10239
2	5	10	Sister Golden Hair	America	Warner 8086
3	3	14	How Long	Ace	Anchor 21000
4	6	10	Bad Time	Grand Funk	Capitol 4046
5	7	7	Old Days	Chicago	Columbia 10131
6	10	9	When Will I Be Loved	Linda Ronstadt	Capitol 4050
7	1	19	Before The Next Teardrop Falls	Freddy Fender	ABC/Dot 17540
8	15	10	I'm Not Lisa	Jessi Colter	Capitol 4009
9	11	11	Love Won't Let Me Wait	Major Harris	Atlantic 3248
10	12	14	Philadelphia Freedom	The Elton John Band	MCA 40364

★ HIGHEST DEBUT ★ POS 65
Please Mr. Please ....Olivia Newton-John

★ BIGGEST MOVER ★ 65 to 35
Listen To What The Man Said.................Wings

Billboard Hot 100 — JUNE 14, 1975

TW	LW	WK	Title	Artist	Label
1	2	11	Sister Golden Hair	America	Warner 8086
2	12	9	Love Will Keep Us Together	The Captain & Tennille	A&M 1672
3	6	10	When Will I Be Loved	Linda Ronstadt	Capitol 4050
4	4	11	Bad Time	Grand Funk	Capitol 4046
5	5	8	Old Days	Chicago	Columbia 10131
6	8	11	I'm Not Lisa	Jessi Colter	Capitol 4009
7	9	12	Love Won't Let Me Wait	Major Harris	Atlantic 3248
8	1	13	Thank God I'm A Country Boy	John Denver	RCA 10239
9	10	15	Philadelphia Freedom	The Elton John Band	MCA 40364
10	14	11	Get Down, Get Down (Get On The Floor)	Joe Simon	Spring 156

★ HIGHEST DEBUT ★ POS 81
Got To Get You Into My Life........Blood, Sweat & Tears

★ BIGGEST MOVER ★ 65 to 46
Please Mr. Please ....Olivia Newton-John

Billboard JUNE 21, 1975 HOT 100

TW	LW	WK		
①	2	10	**Love Will Keep Us Together**........*The Captain & Tennille* ... A&M 1672	
②	3	11	**When Will I Be Loved**............................*Linda Ronstadt* ... Capitol 4050	←
③	12	13	**Wildfire**..*Michael Murphey* ... Epic 50084	
④	6	12	**I'm Not Lisa**...*Jessi Colter* ... Capitol 4009	
⑤	7	13	**Love Won't Let Me Wait** ....*Major Harris* ... Atlantic 3248	
⑥	1	12	**Sister Golden Hair** ....*America* ... Warner 8086	
⑦	29	10	**The Hustle**..................*Van McCoy & The Soul City Symphony* ... Avco 4653	
⑧	10	12	**Get Down, Get Down (Get On The Floor)** ....*Joe Simon* ... Spring 156	
⑨	22	4	**Listen To What The Man Said** ....*Wings* ... Capitol 4091	
⑩	11	11	**Cut The Cake**..*AWB* ... Atlantic 3261	

★ HIGHEST DEBUT ★ POS 79	★ BIGGEST MOVER ★ 65 to 41
Fight The Power......................*The Isley Brothers*	**Jive Talkin'** ....*Bee Gees*

Billboard JUNE 28, 1975 HOT 100

TW	LW	WK		
①	1	11	**Love Will Keep Us Together**........*The Captain & Tennille* ... A&M 1672	
②	2	12	**When Will I Be Loved**............................*Linda Ronstadt* ... Capitol 4050	←
③	3	14	**Wildfire**..*Michael Murphey* ... Epic 50084	
④	4	13	**I'm Not Lisa**...*Jessi Colter* ... Capitol 4009	
⑤	5	14	**Love Won't Let Me Wait** ....*Major Harris* ... Atlantic 3248	
⑥	7	11	**The Hustle**..................*Van McCoy & The Soul City Symphony* ... Avco 4653	
⑦	9	5	**Listen To What The Man Said** ....*Wings* ... Capitol 4091	
⑧	8	13	**Get Down, Get Down (Get On The Floor)** ....*Joe Simon* ... Spring 156	
⑨	13	13	**Magic**..*Pilot* ... EMI 3992	
⑩	10	12	**Cut The Cake**..*AWB* ... Atlantic 3261	

★ HIGHEST DEBUT ★ POS 81	★ BIGGEST MOVER ★ 79 to 55
Could It Be Magic ....*Barry Manilow*	**Fight The Power**......................*The Isley Brothers*

Billboard JULY 5, 1975 HOT 100

TW	LW	WK		
①	1	12	**Love Will Keep Us Together**........*The Captain & Tennille* ... A&M 1672	
②	6	12	**The Hustle**..................*Van McCoy & The Soul City Symphony* ... Avco 4653	
③	7	6	**Listen To What The Man Said** ....*Wings* ... Capitol 4091	
④	3	15	**Wildfire**..*Michael Murphey* ... Epic 50084	
⑤	5	15	**Love Won't Let Me Wait** ....*Major Harris* ... Atlantic 3248	
⑥	9	14	**Magic**..*Pilot* ... EMI 3992	
⑦	4	14	**I'm Not Lisa** ....*Jessi Colter* ... Capitol 4009	
⑧	2	13	**When Will I Be Loved** ....*Linda Ronstadt* ... Capitol 4050	←
⑨	16	6	**One Of These Nights** ....*Eagles* ... Asylum 45257	
⑩	15	5	**Please Mr. Please** ....*Olivia Newton-John* ... MCA 40418	

★ HIGHEST DEBUT ★ POS 51	★ BIGGEST MOVER ★ 72 to 48
Someone Saved My Life Tonight........*Elton John*	**Mornin' Beautiful**.................*Tony Orlando & Dawn*

TW	LW	WK	Billboard.	JULY 12, 1975	HOT 100.
①	1	13	**Love Will Keep Us Together**........*The Captain & Tennille* . . . A&M 1672		
②	2	13	The Hustle..................*Van McCoy & The Soul City Symphony* . . . Avco 4653		
③	3	7	Listen To What The Man Said ....*Wings* . . . Capitol 4091		
④	4	16	Wildfire...*Michael Murphey* . . . Epic 50084		
⑤	6	15	**Magic** ....*Pilot* . . . EMI 3992		
⑥	10	6	Please Mr. Please ....*Olivia Newton-John* . . . MCA 40418		
⑦	9	7	One Of These Nights ....*Eagles* . . . Asylum 45257		
⑧	12	9	Swearin' To God ....*Frankie Valli* . . . Private Stock 45021		
⑨	8	14	When Will I Be Loved ....*Linda Ronstadt* . . . Capitol 4050		
⑩	11	9	I'm Not In Love...*10cc* . . . Mercury 73678		

★ **HIGHEST DEBUT** ★ POS 77	★ *BIGGEST MOVER* ★ 51 to 25
Glasshouse ....*The Temptations*	Someone Saved My Life Tonight........*Elton John*

TW	LW	WK	Billboard.	JULY 19, 1975	HOT 100.
①	3	8	**Listen To What The Man Said** ....*Wings* . . . Capitol 4091		
②	2	14	The Hustle..................*Van McCoy & The Soul City Symphony* . . . Avco 4653		
③	10	10	I'm Not In Love...*10cc* . . . Mercury 73678		
④	7	8	One Of These Nights ....*Eagles* . . . Asylum 45257		
⑤	6	7	Please Mr. Please ....*Olivia Newton-John* . . . MCA 40418		
⑥	5	16	Magic..*Pilot* . . . EMI 3992		
⑦	8	10	Swearin' To God ....*Frankie Valli* . . . Private Stock 45021		
⑧	1	14	Love Will Keep Us Together ....*The Captain & Tennille* . . . A&M 1672		
⑨	22	8	Jive Talkin' ....*Bee Gees* . . . RSO 510		
⑩	11	10	Rockin' Chair ....*Gwen McCrae* . . . Cat 1996		

★ **HIGHEST DEBUT** ★ POS 76	★ *BIGGEST MOVER* ★ 57 to 33
Two Fine People ....*Cat Stevens*	Fallin' In Love........*Hamilton, Joe Frank & Reynolds*

TW	LW	WK	Billboard.	JULY 26, 1975	HOT 100.
①	2	15	**The Hustle** ....*Van McCoy & The Soul City Symphony* . . . Avco 4653		
②	3	11	I'm Not In Love...*10cc* . . . Mercury 73678		
③	4	9	One Of These Nights ....*Eagles* . . . Asylum 45257		
④	5	8	Please Mr. Please ....*Olivia Newton-John* . . . MCA 40418		
⑤	1	9	Listen To What The Man Said ....*Wings* . . . Capitol 4091		
⑥	7	11	**Swearin' To God**...........................*Frankie Valli* . . . Private Stock 45021		
⑦	9	9	Jive Talkin' ....*Bee Gees* . . . RSO 510		
⑧	15	4	Someone Saved My Life Tonight ....*Elton John* . . . MCA 40421		
⑨	11	12	Midnight Blue ....*Melissa Manchester* . . . Arista 0116		
⑩	10	11	Rockin' Chair ....*Gwen McCrae* . . . Cat 1996		

★ **HIGHEST DEBUT** ★ POS 68	★ *BIGGEST MOVER* ★ 80 to 51
(I Believe) There's Nothing Stronger Than Our Love ....*Paul Anka with Odia Coates*	Get Down Tonight.........*K.C. & The Sunshine Band*

Billboard — AUGUST 2, 1975 — HOT 100

TW	LW	WK	Title	Artist ... Label
1	3	10	**One Of These Nights**	*Eagles* ... Asylum 45257
2	2	12	**I'm Not In Love**	*10cc* ... Mercury 73678
3	7	10	**Jive Talkin'**	*Bee Gees* ... RSO 510
4	4	9	**Please Mr. Please**	*Olivia Newton-John* ... MCA 40418
5	1	16	**The Hustle**	*Van McCoy & The Soul City Symphony* ... Avco 4653
6	8	5	**Someone Saved My Life Tonight**	*Elton John* ... MCA 40421
7	9	13	**Midnight Blue**	*Melissa Manchester* ... Arista 0116
8	5	10	**Listen To What The Man Said**	*Wings* ... Capitol 4091
9	10	12	**Rockin' Chair**	*Gwen McCrae* ... Cat 1996
10	11	17	**Dynomite**	*Bazuka* ... A&M 1666

★ HIGHEST DEBUT ★ POS 76
Solitaire ......*Carpenters*

★ BIGGEST MOVER ★ 51 to 32
Get Down Tonight......*K.C. & The Sunshine Band*

Billboard — AUGUST 9, 1975 — HOT 100

TW	LW	WK	Title	Artist ... Label
1	3	11	**Jive Talkin'**	*Bee Gees* ... RSO 510
2	2	13	**I'm Not In Love**	*10cc* ... Mercury 73678
3	4	10	**Please Mr. Please**	*Olivia Newton-John* ... MCA 40418
4	1	11	**One Of These Nights**	*Eagles* ... Asylum 45257
5	6	6	**Someone Saved My Life Tonight**	*Elton John* ... MCA 40421
6	7	14	**Midnight Blue**	*Melissa Manchester* ... Arista 0116
7	14	11	**Rhinestone Cowboy**	*Glen Campbell* ... Capitol 4095
8	12	15	**Why Can't We Be Friends?**	*War* ... United Artists 629
9	15	8	**How Sweet It Is (To Be Loved By You)**	*James Taylor* ... Warner 8109
10	13	13	**The Rockford Files**	*Mike Post* ... MGM 14772

★ HIGHEST DEBUT ★ POS 82
They Just Can't Stop It the (Games People Play) ......*Spinners*

★ BIGGEST MOVER ★ 58 to 44
(I Believe) There's Nothing Stronger Than Our Love ......*Paul Anka with Odia Coates*

Billboard — AUGUST 16, 1975 — HOT 100

TW	LW	WK	Title	Artist ... Label
1	1	12	**Jive Talkin'**	*Bee Gees* ... RSO 510
2	4	12	**One Of These Nights**	*Eagles* ... Asylum 45257
3	3	11	**Please Mr. Please**	*Olivia Newton-John* ... MCA 40418
4	5	7	**Someone Saved My Life Tonight**	*Elton John* ... MCA 40421
5	15	9	**Fallin' In Love**	*Hamilton, Joe Frank & Reynolds* ... Playboy 6024
6	7	12	**Rhinestone Cowboy**	*Glen Campbell* ... Capitol 4095
7	8	16	**Why Can't We Be Friends?**	*War* ... United Artists 629
8	9	9	**How Sweet It Is (To Be Loved By You)**	*James Taylor* ... Warner 8109
9	6	15	**Midnight Blue**	*Melissa Manchester* ... Arista 0116
10	10	14	**The Rockford Files**	*Mike Post* ... MGM 14772

★ HIGHEST DEBUT ★ POS 64
Calypso/I'm Sorry......*John Denver*

★ BIGGEST MOVER ★ 65 to 40
Solitaire ......*Carpenters*

Billboard — AUGUST 23, 1975 — HOT 100

TW	LW	WK	Title	Artist	Label
1	5	10	**Fallin' In Love**	*Hamilton, Joe Frank & Reynolds*	Playboy 6024
2	2	13	One Of These Nights	*Eagles*	Asylum 45257
3	12	7	Get Down Tonight	*K.C. & The Sunshine Band*	T.K. 1009
4	1	13	Jive Talkin'	*Bee Gees*	RSO 510
5	6	13	Rhinestone Cowboy	*Glen Campbell*	Capitol 4095
6	7	17	**Why Can't We Be Friends?**	*War*	United Artists 629
7	8	10	How Sweet It Is (To Be Loved By You)	*James Taylor*	Warner 8109
8	4	8	Someone Saved My Life Tonight	*Elton John*	MCA 40421
9	16	11	At Seventeen	*Janis Ian*	Columbia 10154
10	3	12	Please Mr. Please	*Olivia Newton-John*	MCA 40418

★ HIGHEST DEBUT ★ POS 64
Do It Any Way You Wanna ....*People's Choice*

★ BIGGEST MOVER ★ 70 to 48
They Just Can't Stop It the (Games People Play) ....*Spinners*

Billboard — AUGUST 30, 1975 — HOT 100

TW	LW	WK	Title	Artist	Label
1	3	8	**Get Down Tonight**	*K.C. & The Sunshine Band*	T.K. 1009
2	1	11	Fallin' In Love	*Hamilton, Joe Frank & Reynolds*	Playboy 6024
3	5	14	Rhinestone Cowboy	*Glen Campbell*	Capitol 4095
4	2	14	One Of These Nights	*Eagles*	Asylum 45257
5	7	11	**How Sweet It Is (To Be Loved By You)**	*James Taylor*	Warner 8109
6	4	14	Jive Talkin'	*Bee Gees*	RSO 510
7	9	12	At Seventeen	*Janis Ian*	Columbia 10154
8	8	9	Someone Saved My Life Tonight	*Elton John*	MCA 40421
9	6	18	Why Can't We Be Friends?	*War*	United Artists 629
10	11	11	Fight The Power	*The Isley Brothers*	T-Neck 2256

★ HIGHEST DEBUT ★ POS 70
You're All I Need To Get By ....*Tony Orlando & Dawn*

★ BIGGEST MOVER ★ 49 to 20
I'm Sorry ....*John Denver*

Billboard — SEPTEMBER 6, 1975 — HOT 100

TW	LW	WK	Title	Artist	Label
1	3	15	**Rhinestone Cowboy**	*Glen Campbell*	Capitol 4095
2	2	12	Fallin' In Love	*Hamilton, Joe Frank & Reynolds*	Playboy 6024
3	1	9	Get Down Tonight	*K.C. & The Sunshine Band*	T.K. 1009
4	7	13	At Seventeen	*Janis Ian*	Columbia 10154
5	5	12	**How Sweet It Is (To Be Loved By You)**	*James Taylor*	Warner 8109
6	6	15	Jive Talkin'	*Bee Gees*	RSO 510
7	11	11	Fame	*David Bowie*	RCA 10320
8	10	12	Fight The Power	*The Isley Brothers*	T-Neck 2256
9	12	11	Could It Be Magic	*Barry Manilow*	Arista 0126
10	4	15	One Of These Nights	*Eagles*	Asylum 45257

★ HIGHEST DEBUT ★ POS 49
Mr. Jaws.................................*Dickie Goodman*

★ BIGGEST MOVER ★ 65 to 44
Theme From "Jaws".......................*John Williams*

Billboard SEPTEMBER 13, 1975 HOT 100

TW	LW	WK			
①	1	16	**Rhinestone Cowboy**.....................................*Glen Campbell* . . . Capitol 4095
②	2	13	Fallin' In Love....................*Hamilton, Joe Frank & Reynolds* . . . Playboy 6024
❸	4	14	**At Seventeen** ....*Janis Ian* . . . Columbia 10154
④	3	10	Get Down Tonight.....................*K.C. & The Sunshine Band* . . . T.K. 1009
⑤	7	12	Fame...*David Bowie* . . . RCA 10320
⑥	8	13	Fight The Power.....................................*The Isley Brothers* . . . T-Neck 2256
❼	9	12	Could It Be Magic...*Barry Manilow* . . . Arista 0126
⑧	15	5	I'm Sorry ....*John Denver* . . . RCA 10353
⑨	19	7	Run Joey Run...*David Geddes* . . . Big Tree 16044
⑩	11	13	**Wasted Days And Wasted Nights**..........*Freddy Fender* . . . ABC/Dot 17558

★ **HIGHEST DEBUT** ★ POS 66
Bad Blood...............................*Neil Sedaka*

★ **BIGGEST MOVER** ★ 49 to 31
Mr. Jaws...................................*Dickie Goodman*

Billboard SEPTEMBER 20, 1975 HOT 100

TW	LW	WK			
①	5	13	**Fame**..*David Bowie* . . . RCA 10320
②	1	17	Rhinestone Cowboy ....*Glen Campbell* . . . Capitol 4095
③	3	15	**At Seventeen** ....*Janis Ian* . . . Columbia 10154
❹	8	6	**I'm Sorry** ....*John Denver* . . . RCA 10353
⑤	6	14	**Fight The Power** ....*The Isley Brothers* . . . T-Neck 2256
⑥	7	13	**Could It Be Magic** ....*Barry Manilow* . . . Arista 0126
❼	9	8	Run Joey Run...*David Geddes* . . . Big Tree 16044
⑧	2	14	Fallin' In Love....................*Hamilton, Joe Frank & Reynolds* . . . Playboy 6024
⑨	10	14	**Wasted Days And Wasted Nights**..........*Freddy Fender* . . . ABC/Dot 17558
⑩	11	12	**Feel Like Makin' Love**....................*Bad Company* . . . Swan Song 70106

★ **HIGHEST DEBUT** ★ POS 64
Sweet Sticky Thing....................*Ohio Players*

★ **BIGGEST MOVER** ★ 66 to 32
Bad Blood...................................*Neil Sedaka*

Billboard SEPTEMBER 27, 1975 HOT 100

TW	LW	WK			
①	4	7	**I'm Sorry** ....*John Denver* . . . RCA 10353
②	1	14	Fame..*David Bowie* . . . RCA 10320
③	2	18	Rhinestone Cowboy ....*Glen Campbell* . . . Capitol 4095
④	5	15	**Fight The Power** ....*The Isley Brothers* . . . T-Neck 2256
⑤	7	9	Run Joey Run...*David Geddes* . . . Big Tree 16044
⑥	6	14	**Could It Be Magic** ....*Barry Manilow* . . . Arista 0126
⑦	3	16	At Seventeen...*Janis Ian* . . . Columbia 10154
⑧	9	15	**Wasted Days And Wasted Nights**...........................*Freddy Fender* . . . ABC/Dot 17558
⑨	11	16	Ballroom Blitz ....*Sweet* . . . Capitol 4055
⑩	10	13	**Feel Like Makin' Love**....................*Bad Company* . . . Swan Song 70106

★ **HIGHEST DEBUT** ★ POS 80
The Way I Want To Touch You...........*Captain & Tennille*

★ **BIGGEST MOVER** ★ 75 to 49
You....................................*George Harrison*

TW	LW	WK	Billboard		OCTOBER 4, 1975		HOT 100
①	2	15	**Fame**			*David Bowie*	RCA 10320
②	1	8	I'm Sorry			*John Denver*	RCA 10353
③	3	19	Rhinestone Cowboy			*Glen Campbell*	Capitol 4095
④	5	10	**Run Joey Run**			*David Geddes*	Big Tree 16044
❺	14	5	Mr. Jaws			*Dickie Goodman*	Cash 451
❻	25	4	Bad Blood			*Neil Sedaka*	Rocket 40460
❼	9	17	Ballroom Blitz			*Sweet*	Capitol 4055
⑧	12	12	Dance With Me			*Orleans*	Asylum 45261
⑨	11	9	Ain't No Way To Treat A Lady			*Helen Reddy*	Capitol 4128
⑩	24	12	Rocky			*Austin Roberts*	Private Stock 45020

★ HIGHEST DEBUT ★ POS 74	★ BIGGEST MOVER ★ 80 to 33
Letting Go......................*Wings*	The Way I Want To Touch You ....*Captain & Tennille*

TW	LW	WK	Billboard		OCTOBER 11, 1975		HOT 100
①	6	5	**Bad Blood**			*Neil Sedaka*	Rocket 40460
②	2	9	Calypso/I'm Sorry			*John Denver*	RCA 10353
③	1	16	Fame			*David Bowie*	RCA 10320
④	5	6	**Mr. Jaws**			*Dickie Goodman*	Cash 451
❺	22	8	Miracles			*Jefferson Starship*	Grunt 10367
⑥	7	18	Ballroom Blitz			*Sweet*	Capitol 4055
⑦	8	13	Dance With Me			*Orleans*	Asylum 45261
⑧	9	10	**Ain't No Way To Treat A Lady**			*Helen Reddy*	Capitol 4128
⑨	10	13	**Rocky**			*Austin Roberts*	Private Stock 45020
⑩	18	5	Lyin' Eyes			*The Eagles*	Asylum 45279

★ HIGHEST DEBUT ★ POS 49	★ BIGGEST MOVER ★ 52 to 19
Island Girl......................*Elton John*	Something Better To Do ....*Olivia Newton-John*

TW	LW	WK	Billboard		OCTOBER 18, 1975		HOT 100
①	1	6	**Bad Blood**			*Neil Sedaka*	Rocket 40460
②	2	10	Calypso/I'm Sorry			*John Denver*	RCA 10353
❸	5	9	**Miracles**			*Jefferson Starship*	Grunt 10367
❹	10	6	**Lyin' Eyes**			*The Eagles*	Asylum 45279
⑤	6	19	Ballroom Blitz			*Sweet*	Capitol 4055
⑥	7	14	**Dance With Me**			*Orleans*	Asylum 45261
❼	11	18	Feelings			*Morris Albert*	RCA 10279
⑧	8	11	**Ain't No Way To Treat A Lady**			*Helen Reddy*	Capitol 4128
⑨	13	11	They Just Can't Stop It the (Games People Play)			*Spinners*	... Atlantic 3284
⑩	14	9	Who Loves You			*Four Seasons*	Warner 8122

★ HIGHEST DEBUT ★ POS 81	★ BIGGEST MOVER ★ 87 to 48
My Little Town......................*Simon & Garfunkel*	Fly, Robin, Fly ....*Silver Convention*

Billboard — OCTOBER 25, 1975 — HOT 100

TW	LW	WK	Title	Artist	Label
1	1	7	Bad Blood	Neil Sedaka	Rocket 40460
2	2	11	Calypso/I'm Sorry	John Denver	RCA 10353
3	3	10	Miracles	Jefferson Starship	Grunt 10367
4	4	7	Lyin' Eyes	The Eagles	Asylum 45279
5	9	12	They Just Can't Stop It the (Games People Play)	Spinners	Atlantic 3284
6	7	19	Feelings	Morris Albert	RCA 10279
7	10	10	Who Loves You	Four Seasons	Warner 8122
8	36	3	Island Girl	Elton John	MCA 40461
9	5	20	Ballroom Blitz	Sweet	Capitol 4055
10	11	14	It Only Takes A Minute	Tavares	Capitol 4111

★ HIGHEST DEBUT ★ POS 50 — That's The Way (I Like It)....KC & The Sunshine Band
★ BIGGEST MOVER ★ 81 to 47 — My Little Town....Simon & Garfunkel

Billboard — NOVEMBER 1, 1975 — HOT 100

TW	LW	WK	Title	Artist	Label
1	8	4	Island Girl	Elton John	MCA 40461
2	2	12	Calypso/I'm Sorry	John Denver	RCA 10353
3	3	11	Miracles	Jefferson Starship	Grunt 10367
4	4	8	Lyin' Eyes	The Eagles	Asylum 45279
5	5	13	They Just Can't Stop It the (Games People Play)	Spinners	Atlantic 3284
6	7	11	Who Loves You	Four Seasons	Warner 8122
7	6	20	Feelings	Morris Albert	RCA 10279
8	1	8	Bad Blood	Neil Sedaka	Rocket 40460
9	12	9	Heat Wave/Love Is A Rose	Linda Ronstadt	Asylum 45282
10	16	10	This Will Be	Natalie Cole	Capitol 4109

★ HIGHEST DEBUT ★ POS 70 — I Love Music (Part 1)....O'Jays
★ BIGGEST MOVER ★ 68 to 37 — Let's Do It Again....The Staple Singers

Billboard — NOVEMBER 8, 1975 — HOT 100

TW	LW	WK	Title	Artist	Label
1	1	5	Island Girl	Elton John	MCA 40461
2	4	9	Lyin' Eyes	The Eagles	Asylum 45279
3	2	13	Calypso/I'm Sorry	John Denver	RCA 10353
4	6	12	Who Loves You	Four Seasons	Warner 8122
5	3	12	Miracles	Jefferson Starship	Grunt 10367
6	9	10	Heat Wave/Love Is A Rose	Linda Ronstadt	Asylum 45282
7	5	14	They Just Can't Stop It the (Games People Play)	Spinners	Atlantic 3284
8	10	11	This Will Be	Natalie Cole	Capitol 4109
9	7	21	Feelings	Morris Albert	RCA 10279
10	14	7	The Way I Want To Touch You	Captain & Tennille	A&M 1725

★ HIGHEST DEBUT ★ POS 74 — Part Time Love....Gladys Knight & The Pips
★ BIGGEST MOVER ★ 82 to 60 — Venus And Mars Rock Show....Wings

TW	LW	WK	Billboard.	NOVEMBER 15, 1975	HOT 100.
❶	1	6	**Island Girl** ....*Elton John* . . . MCA 40461
②	2	10	**Lyin' Eyes** ....*The Eagles* . . . Asylum 45279
❸	4	13	**Who Loves You** ....*Four Seasons* . . . Warner 8122
④	5	13	**Miracles** ....*Jefferson Starship* . . . Grunt 10367
⑤	6	11	**Heat Wave/Love Is A Rose** ....*Linda Ronstadt* . . . Asylum 45282
⑥	19	4	**That's The Way (I Like It)** ....*KC & The Sunshine Band* . . . T.K. 1015
⑦	8	12	**This Will Be** ....*Natalie Cole* . . . Capitol 4109
⑧	9	22	**Feelings** ....*Morris Albert* . . . RCA 10279
❾	10	8	**The Way I Want To Touch You** ....*Captain & Tennille* . . . A&M 1725
❿	12	9	**Low Rider** ....*War* . . . United Artists 706

★ *HIGHEST DEBUT* ★ POS 44	★ *BIGGEST MOVER* ★ 79 to 53
The Last Game Of The Season (A Blind Man In The Bleachers) ....*David Geddes*	Theme From Mahogany (Do You Know Where You're Going To)........................*Diana Ross*

TW	LW	WK	Billboard.	NOVEMBER 22, 1975	HOT 100.
❶	6	5	**That's The Way (I Like It)** ....*KC & The Sunshine Band* . . . T.K. 1015
❷	16	7	**Fly, Robin, Fly** ....*Silver Convention* . . . Midland International 10339
❸	3	14	**Who Loves You** ....*Four Seasons* . . . Warner 8122
④	1	7	**Island Girl**...*Elton John* . . . MCA 40461
❺	9	9	**The Way I Want To Touch You**...............*Captain & Tennille* . . . A&M 1725
⑥	7	13	**This Will Be**...*Natalie Cole* . . . Capitol 4109
⑦	8	23	**Feelings**...*Morris Albert* . . . RCA 10279
⑧	10	10	**Low Rider** ....*War* . . . United Artists 706
❾	13	13	**Sky High**...*Jigsaw* . . . Chelsea 3022
❿	21	5	**Let's Do It Again** ....*The Staple Singers* . . . Curtom 0109

★ *HIGHEST DEBUT* ★ POS 73	★ *BIGGEST MOVER* ★ 63 to 40
Sing A Song............................*Earth, Wind & Fire*	Country Boy (You Got Your Feet In L.A.) ....*Glen Campbell*

TW	LW	WK	Billboard.	NOVEMBER 29, 1975	HOT 100.
❶	2	8	**Fly, Robin, Fly** ....*Silver Convention* . . . Midland International 10339
②	1	6	**That's The Way (I Like It)** ....*KC & The Sunshine Band* . . . T.K. 1015
❸	4	8	**Island Girl**...*Elton John* . . . MCA 40461
④	5	10	**The Way I Want To Touch You**..........*Captain & Tennille* . . . A&M 1725
❺	10	6	**Let's Do It Again** ....*The Staple Singers* . . . Curtom 0109
⑥	9	14	**Sky High**...*Jigsaw* . . . Chelsea 3022
⑦	8	11	**Low Rider** ....*War* . . . United Artists 706
⑧	6	14	**This Will Be**...*Natalie Cole* . . . Capitol 4109
❾	11	9	**Nights On Broadway** ....*Bee Gees* . . . RSO 515
❿	3	15	**Who Loves You** ....*Four Seasons* . . . Warner 8122

★ *HIGHEST DEBUT* ★ POS 81	★ *BIGGEST MOVER* ★ 60 to 37
School Boy Crush................................*AWB*	Walk Away From Love...................*David Ruffin*

Billboard — DECEMBER 6, 1975 — HOT 100

TW	LW	WK	Title	Artist
1	1	9	**Fly, Robin, Fly**	*Silver Convention* . . . Midland International 10339
2	2	7	That's The Way (I Like It)	*KC & The Sunshine Band* . . . T.K. 1015
3	6	15	**Sky High**	*Jigsaw* . . . Chelsea 3022
4	5	7	Let's Do It Again	*The Staple Singers* . . . Curtom 0109
5	4	11	The Way I Want To Touch You	*Captain & Tennille* . . . A&M 1725
6	3	9	Island Girl	*Elton John* . . . MCA 40461
7	7	12	**Low Rider**	*War* . . . United Artists 706
8	9	10	Nights On Broadway	*Bee Gees* . . . RSO 515
9	11	9	Saturday Night	*Bay City Rollers* . . . Arista 0149
10	12	8	**My Little Town**	*Simon & Garfunkel* . . . Columbia 10230

★ **HIGHEST DEBUT** ★ POS 55
Love To Love You Baby ....*Donna Summer*

★ **BIGGEST MOVER** ★ 81 to 51
School Boy Crush.....................................*AWB*

Billboard — DECEMBER 13, 1975 — HOT 100

TW	LW	WK	Title	Artist
1	1	10	**Fly, Robin, Fly**	*Silver Convention* . . . Midland International 10339
2	4	8	Let's Do It Again	*The Staple Singers* . . . Curtom 0109
3	3	16	**Sky High**	*Jigsaw* . . . Chelsea 3022
4	2	8	That's The Way (I Like It)	*KC & The Sunshine Band* . . . T.K. 1015
5	9	10	Saturday Night	*Bay City Rollers* . . . Arista 0149
6	12	5	Love Rollercoaster	*Ohio Players* . . . Mercury 73734
7	8	11	**Nights On Broadway**	*Bee Gees* . . . RSO 515
8	19	7	Theme From Mahogany (Do You Know Where You're Going To)	*Diana Ross* . . . Motown 1377
9	10	9	**My Little Town**	*Simon & Garfunkel* . . . Columbia 10230
10	11	5	Fox On The Run	*Sweet* . . . Capitol 4157

★ **HIGHEST DEBUT** ★ POS 75
Play On Love ....*Jefferson Starship*

★ **BIGGEST MOVER** ★ 82 to 29
Convoy..*C.W. McCall*

Billboard — DECEMBER 20, 1975 — HOT 100

TW	LW	WK	Title	Artist
1	4	9	**That's The Way (I Like It)**	*KC & The Sunshine Band* . . . T.K. 1015
2	2	9	Let's Do It Again	*The Staple Singers* . . . Curtom 0109
3	1	11	Fly, Robin, Fly	*Silver Convention* . . . Midland International 10339
4	5	11	Saturday Night	*Bay City Rollers* . . . Arista 0149
5	6	6	Love Rollercoaster	*Ohio Players* . . . Mercury 73734
6	8	8	Theme From Mahogany (Do You Know Where You're Going To)	*Diana Ross* . . . Motown 1377
7	3	17	Sky High	*Jigsaw* . . . Chelsea 3022
8	11	6	I Write The Songs	*Barry Manilow* . . . Arista 0157
9	10	6	Fox On The Run	*Sweet* . . . Capitol 4157
10	7	12	Nights On Broadway	*Bee Gees* . . . RSO 515

★ **HIGHEST DEBUT** ★ POS 74
50 Ways To Leave Your Lover ....*Paul Simon*

★ **BIGGEST MOVER** ★ 79 to 59
Breaking Up Is Hard To Do..............*Neil Sedaka*

TW	LW	WK	Billboard® ⓭ DECEMBER 27, 1975 ⓭	HOT 100®
❶	2	10	**Let's Do It Again**............................*The Staple Singers* . . . Curtom 0109	
❷	4	12	**Saturday Night** ....*Bay City Rollers* . . . Arista 0149	
③	1	10	**That's The Way (I Like It)** ....*KC & The Sunshine Band* . . . T.K. 1015	
❹	5	7	**Love Rollercoaster** ....*Ohio Players* . . . Mercury 73734	
❺	6	9	**Theme From Mahogany (Do You Know Where You're Going To)** .... *Diana Ross* . . . Motown 1377	
❻	8	7	**I Write The Songs**........................*Barry Manilow* . . . Arista 0157	
❼	14	4	**Convoy** ....*C.W. McCall* . . . MGM 14839	
❽	9	7	**Fox On The Run** ....*Sweet* . . . Capitol 4157	
⑨	3	12	**Fly, Robin, Fly** ....*Silver Convention* . . . Midland International 10339	
❿	12	9	**I Love Music (Part 1)**.....................*O'Jays* . . . Philadelphia International 3577	

★ *HIGHEST DEBUT* ★ POS 70	★ *BIGGEST MOVER* ★ 59 to 34
Let The Music Play........................*Barry White*	**Breaking Up Is Hard To Do**..............*Neil Sedaka*

Billboard — JANUARY 3, 1976 — HOT 100

TW	LW	WK		
❶	2	13	**Saturday Night**...*Bay City Rollers* ... Arista 0149	
❷	6	8	**I Write The Songs**..*Barry Manilow* ... Arista 0157	
❸	5	10	**Theme From Mahogany (Do You Know Where You're Going To)** .... *Diana Ross* ... Motown 1377	
❹	4	8	**Love Rollercoaster** ....*Ohio Players* ... Mercury 73734	
⑤	1	11	**Let's Do It Again** ....*The Staple Singers* ... Curtom 0109	
❻	7	5	**Convoy**...*C.W. McCall* ... MGM 14839	
❼	8	8	**Fox On The Run** ....*Sweet* ... Capitol 4157	
⑧	3	11	**That's The Way (I Like It)** ....*KC & The Sunshine Band* ... T.K. 1015	
⑨	10	10	**I Love Music (Part 1)**.......................*O'Jays* ... Philadelphia International 3577	
⑩	9	13	**Fly, Robin, Fly** ....*Silver Convention* ... Midland International 10339	

★ HIGHEST DEBUT ★ POS 73	★ BIGGEST MOVER ★ 41 to 25
Back To The Island ....*Leon Russell*	Love Hurts...*Nazareth*

Billboard — JANUARY 10, 1976 — HOT 100

TW	LW	WK		
❶	6	6	**Convoy**..*C.W. McCall* ... MGM 14839	
❷	2	9	**I Write The Songs**..*Barry Manilow* ... Arista 0157	
❸	3	11	**Theme From Mahogany (Do You Know Where You're Going To)** .... *Diana Ross* ... Motown 1377	
❹	4	9	**Love Rollercoaster** ....*Ohio Players* ... Mercury 73734	
⑤	1	14	**Saturday Night** ....*Bay City Rollers* ... Arista 0149	
⑥	7	9	**Fox On The Run** ....*Sweet* ... Capitol 4157	
❼	9	11	**I Love Music (Part 1)**.......................*O'Jays* ... Philadelphia International 3577	
⑧	8	12	**That's The Way (I Like It)** ....*KC & The Sunshine Band* ... T.K. 1015	
⑨	11	6	**Love To Love You Baby** ....*Donna Summer* ... Oasis 401	
⑩	12	9	**Times Of Your Life** ....*Paul Anka* ... United Artists 737	

★ HIGHEST DEBUT ★ POS 68	★ BIGGEST MOVER ★ 77 to 57
Junk Food Junkie...........................*Larry Groce*	The White Knight ....*Cledus Maggard & The Citizen's Band*

Billboard — JANUARY 17, 1976 — HOT 100

TW	LW	WK		
❶	2	10	**I Write The Songs** ....*Barry Manilow* ... Arista 0157	
❷	3	12	**Theme From Mahogany (Do You Know Where You're Going To)** .... *Diana Ross* ... Motown 1377	
③	1	7	**Convoy** ....*C.W. McCall* ... MGM 14839	
④	4	10	**Love Rollercoaster** ....*Ohio Players* ... Mercury 73734	
⑤	6	10	**Fox On The Run** ....*Sweet* ... Capitol 4157	
⑥	7	12	**I Love Music (Part 1)**.......................*O'Jays* ... Philadelphia International 3577	
❼	9	7	**Love To Love You Baby** ....*Donna Summer* ... Oasis 401	
⑧	14	12	**You Sexy Thing**.......................................*Hot Chocolate* ... Big Tree 16047	
⑨	10	10	**Times Of Your Life** ....*Paul Anka* ... United Artists 737	
⑩	11	11	**Walk Away From Love**.....................................*David Ruffin* ... Motown 1376	

★ HIGHEST DEBUT ★ POS 86	★ BIGGEST MOVER ★ 52 to 40
Quiet Storm ....*Smokey Robinson*	Fanny (Be Tender With My Love)........*Bee Gees*

TW	LW	WK	Billboard.	JANUARY 24, 1976	HOT 100.
❶	2	13	**Theme From Mahogany (Do You Know Where You're Going To)**... *Diana Ross* ... Motown 1377		
②	1	11	I Write The Songs.......................................*Barry Manilow* ... Arista 0157		
❸	4	11	Love Rollercoaster ....*Ohio Players* ... Mercury 73734		
❹	7	8	Love To Love You Baby ....*Donna Summer* ... Oasis 401		
❺	6	13	**I Love Music (Part 1)**.................*O'Jays* ... Philadelphia International 3577		
❻	8	13	You Sexy Thing................................*Hot Chocolate* ... Big Tree 16047		
❼	3	8	Convoy ....*C.W. McCall* ... MGM 14839		
❽	9	11	Times Of Your Life ....*Paul Anka* ... United Artists 737		
❾	10	12	**Walk Away From Love** ....*David Ruffin* ... Motown 1376		
❿	12	10	Sing A Song ....*Earth, Wind & Fire* ... Columbia 10251		

★ HIGHEST DEBUT ★ POS 55	★ BIGGEST MOVER ★ 78 to 60
Grow Some Funk Of Your Own/I Feel Like A Bullet (In The Gun Of Robert Ford).......*Elton John*	Dream Weaver................................*Gary Wright*

TW	LW	WK	Billboard.	JANUARY 31, 1976	HOT 100.
❶	3	12	**Love Rollercoaster**................................*Ohio Players* ... Mercury 73734		
②	2	12	I Write The Songs...*Barry Manilow* ... Arista 0157		
❸	4	9	Love To Love You Baby ....*Donna Summer* ... Oasis 401		
❹	6	14	You Sexy Thing................................*Hot Chocolate* ... Big Tree 16047		
❺	5	14	**I Love Music (Part 1)**.................*O'Jays* ... Philadelphia International 3577		
❻	7	9	Convoy ....*C.W. McCall* ... MGM 14839		
❼	10	11	Sing A Song ....*Earth, Wind & Fire* ... Columbia 10251		
❽	8	12	Times Of Your Life ....*Paul Anka* ... United Artists 737		
❾	9	13	**Walk Away From Love** ....*David Ruffin* ... Motown 1376		
❿	14	7	50 Ways To Leave Your Lover...................*Paul Simon* ... Columbia 10270		

★ HIGHEST DEBUT ★ POS 88	★ BIGGEST MOVER ★ 55 to 31
Let Your Love Flow ....*Bellamy Brothers*	Grow Some Funk Of Your Own/I Feel Like A Bullet (In The Gun Of Robert Ford).......*Elton John*

TW	LW	WK	Billboard.	FEBRUARY 7, 1976	HOT 100.
❶	10	8	**50 Ways To Leave Your Lover**.............*Paul Simon* ... Columbia 10270		
❷	3	10	**Love To Love You Baby**.........................*Donna Summer* ... Oasis 401		
❸	4	15	**You Sexy Thing** ....*Hot Chocolate* ... Big Tree 16047		
④	2	13	I Write The Songs...*Barry Manilow* ... Arista 0157		
❺	7	12	Sing A Song.......................................*Earth, Wind & Fire* ... Columbia 10251		
❻	1	13	Love Rollercoaster ....*Ohio Players* ... Mercury 73734		
❼	8	13	**Times Of Your Life** ....*Paul Anka* ... United Artists 737		
❽	17	13	Theme From S.W.A.T. ....*Rhythm Heritage* ... ABC 12135		
❾	6	10	Convoy ....*C.W. McCall* ... MGM 14839		
❿	16	9	Breaking Up Is Hard To Do ....*Neil Sedaka* ... Rocket 40500		

★ HIGHEST DEBUT ★ POS 51	★ BIGGEST MOVER ★ 50 to 25
Money Honey..........................*Bay City Rollers*	Lonely Night (Angel Face)........*Captain & Tennille*

Billboard ● FEBRUARY 14, 1976 ● HOT 100.

TW	LW	WK		
❶	1	9	**50 Ways To Leave Your Lover**.............*Paul Simon* . . . Columbia 10270	
②	2	11	**Love To Love You Baby**.........................*Donna Summer* . . . Oasis 401	
③	3	16	**You Sexy Thing** ....*Hot Chocolate* . . . Big Tree 16047	
❹	8	14	Theme From S.W.A.T. ....*Rhythm Heritage* . . . ABC 12135	
⑤	5	13	**Sing A Song**..*Earth, Wind & Fire* . . . Columbia 10251	
⑥	4	14	I Write The Songs.................................*Barry Manilow* . . . Arista 0157	
⑦	6	14	Love Rollercoaster ....*Ohio Players* . . . Mercury 73734	
❽	11	17	Love Machine (Part 1).........................*The Miracles* . . . Tamla 54262	
⑨	10	10	Breaking Up Is Hard To Do ....*Neil Sedaka* . . . Rocket 40500	
❿	13	14	**Evil Woman** ....*Electric Light Orchestra* . . . United Artists 729	

★ *HIGHEST DEBUT* ★ POS 77	★ *BIGGEST MOVER* ★ 87 to 65
Only Love Is Real ....*Carole King*	Disco Lady..............................*Johnnie Taylor*

Billboard ● FEBRUARY 21, 1976 ● HOT 100.

TW	LW	WK		
❶	1	10	**50 Ways To Leave Your Lover**.............*Paul Simon* . . . Columbia 10270	
②	4	15	Theme From S.W.A.T. ....*Rhythm Heritage* . . . ABC 12135	
③	3	17	**You Sexy Thing** ....*Hot Chocolate* . . . Big Tree 16047	
④	2	12	Love To Love You Baby ....*Donna Summer* . . . Oasis 401	
❺	8	18	Love Machine (Part 1).........................*The Miracles* . . . Tamla 54262	
⑥	6	15	I Write The Songs.................................*Barry Manilow* . . . Arista 0157	
❼	14	10	All By Myself ....*Eric Carmen* . . . Arista 0165	
⑧	9	11	**Breaking Up Is Hard To Do**....................*Neil Sedaka* . . . Rocket 40500	
⑨	12	10	Take It To The Limit ....*Eagles* . . . Asylum 45293	
❿	10	15	**Evil Woman** ....*Electric Light Orchestra* . . . United Artists 729	

★ *HIGHEST DEBUT* ★ POS 83	★ *BIGGEST MOVER* ★ 53 to 38
The Jam..........................*Graham Central Station*	Cupid ....*Tony Orlando & Dawn*

Billboard ● FEBRUARY 28, 1976 ● HOT 100.

TW	LW	WK		
❶	2	16	**Theme From S.W.A.T.**...........................*Rhythm Heritage* . . . ABC 12135	
②	1	11	50 Ways To Leave Your Lover....................*Paul Simon* . . . Columbia 10270	
③	5	19	Love Machine (Part 1).........................*The Miracles* . . . Tamla 54262	
④	7	11	All By Myself ....*Eric Carmen* . . . Arista 0165	
⑤	12	10	**December, 1963 (Oh, What a Night)**.....*The Four Seasons* . . . Warner 8168	
⑥	3	18	You Sexy Thing...................................*Hot Chocolate* . . . Big Tree 16047	
❼	9	11	Take It To The Limit ....*Eagles* . . . Asylum 45293	
⑧	18	9	Dream Weaver ....*Gary Wright* . . . Warner 8167	
⑨	13	6	Lonely Night (Angel Face).......................*Captain & Tennille* . . . A&M 1782	
❿	11	15	Love Hurts...*Nazareth* . . . A&M 1671	

★ *HIGHEST DEBUT* ★ POS 75	★ *BIGGEST MOVER* ★ 85 to 62
There's A Kind Of Hush (All Over The World) ....*Carpenters*	Right Back Where We Started From ....*Maxine Nightingale*

Billboard — MARCH 6, 1976 — HOT 100

TW	LW	WK			
1	3	20	Love Machine (Part 1)	The Miracles	Tamla 54262
2	4	12	All By Myself	Eric Carmen	Arista 0165
3	5	11	December, 1963 (Oh, What a Night)	The Four Seasons	Warner 8168
4	1	17	Theme From S.W.A.T.	Rhythm Heritage	ABC 12135
5	7	12	Take It To The Limit	Eagles	Asylum 45293
6	8	10	Dream Weaver	Gary Wright	Warner 8167
7	9	7	Lonely Night (Angel Face)	Captain & Tennille	A&M 1782
8	2	12	50 Ways To Leave Your Lover	Paul Simon	Columbia 10270
9	10	16	Love Hurts	Nazareth	A&M 1671
10	6	19	You Sexy Thing	Hot Chocolate	Big Tree 16047

★ **HIGHEST DEBUT** ★ POS 61
Looking For Space .... John Denver

★ **BIGGEST MOVER** ★ 46 to 26
Disco Lady .... Johnnie Taylor

Billboard — MARCH 13, 1976 — HOT 100

TW	LW	WK			
1	3	12	December, 1963 (Oh, What a Night)	The Four Seasons	Warner 8168
2	2	13	All By Myself	Eric Carmen	Arista 0165
3	1	21	Love Machine (Part 1)	The Miracles	Tamla 54262
4	5	13	Take It To The Limit	Eagles	Asylum 45293
5	6	11	Dream Weaver	Gary Wright	Warner 8167
6	7	8	Lonely Night (Angel Face)	Captain & Tennille	A&M 1782
7	4	18	Theme From S.W.A.T.	Rhythm Heritage	ABC 12135
8	9	17	Love Hurts	Nazareth	A&M 1671
9	11	11	Sweet Thing	Rufus Featuring Chaka Khan	ABC 12149
10	13	10	Junk Food Junkie	Larry Groce	Warner 8165

★ **HIGHEST DEBUT** ★ POS 71
Strange Magic .... Electric Light Orchestra

★ **BIGGEST MOVER** ★ 79 to 51
Livin' For The Weekend .... The O'Jays

Billboard — MARCH 20, 1976 — HOT 100

TW	LW	WK			
1	1	13	December, 1963 (Oh, What a Night)	The Four Seasons	Warner 8168
2	2	14	All By Myself	Eric Carmen	Arista 0165
3	5	12	Dream Weaver	Gary Wright	Warner 8167
4	4	14	Take It To The Limit	Eagles	Asylum 45293
5	6	9	Lonely Night (Angel Face)	Captain & Tennille	A&M 1782
6	3	22	Love Machine (Part 1)	The Miracles	Tamla 54262
7	9	12	Sweet Thing	Rufus Featuring Chaka Khan	ABC 12149
8	16	20	Dream On	Aerosmith	Columbia 10278
9	10	11	Junk Food Junkie	Larry Groce	Warner 8165
10	12	7	Disco Lady	Johnnie Taylor	Columbia 10281

★ **HIGHEST DEBUT** ★ POS 59
I Thought It Took A Little Time (But Today I Fell In Love) .... Diana Ross

★ **BIGGEST MOVER** ★ 75 to 57
Fooled Around And Fell In Love ...... Elvin Bishop

Billboard — MARCH 27, 1976 — HOT 100

TW	LW	WK	Title	Artist / Label
1	1	14	**December, 1963 (Oh, What a Night)**	*The Four Seasons* ... Warner 8168
2	3	13	**Dream Weaver**	*Gary Wright* ... Warner 8167
3	5	10	**Lonely Night (Angel Face)**	*Captain & Tennille* ... A&M 1782
4	2	15	**All By Myself**	*Eric Carmen* ... Arista 0165
5	10	8	**Disco Lady**	*Johnnie Taylor* ... Columbia 10281
6	7	13	**Sweet Thing**	*Rufus Featuring Chaka Khan* ... ABC 12149
7	8	21	**Dream On**	*Aerosmith* ... Columbia 10278
8	17	9	**Let Your Love Flow**	*Bellamy Brothers* ... Warner 8169
9	14	7	**Right Back Where We Started From**	*Maxine Nightingale* ... United Artists 752
10	11	8	**Money Honey**	*Bay City Rollers* ... Arista 0170

★ **HIGHEST DEBUT** ★ POS 84
Welcome Back ... *John Sebastian*

★ **BIGGEST MOVER** ★ 57 to 41
Fooled Around And Fell In Love ... *Elvin Bishop*

Billboard — APRIL 3, 1976 — HOT 100

TW	LW	WK	Title	Artist / Label
1	5	9	**Disco Lady**	*Johnnie Taylor* ... Columbia 10281
2	2	14	**Dream Weaver**	*Gary Wright* ... Warner 8167
3	3	11	**Lonely Night (Angel Face)**	*Captain & Tennille* ... A&M 1782
4	8	10	**Let Your Love Flow**	*Bellamy Brothers* ... Warner 8169
5	6	14	**Sweet Thing**	*Rufus Featuring Chaka Khan* ... ABC 12149
6	9	8	**Right Back Where We Started From**	*Maxine Nightingale* ... United Artists 752
7	7	22	**Dream On**	*Aerosmith* ... Columbia 10278
8	1	15	**December, 1963 (Oh, What a Night)**	*The Four Seasons* ... Warner 8168
9	10	9	**Money Honey**	*Bay City Rollers* ... Arista 0170
10	11	17	**Golden Years**	*David Bowie* ... RCA 10441

★ **HIGHEST DEBUT** ★ POS 77
Anytime (I'll Be There) ... *Paul Anka*

★ **BIGGEST MOVER** ★ 84 to 59
Welcome Back ... *John Sebastian*

Billboard — APRIL 10, 1976 — HOT 100

TW	LW	WK	Title	Artist / Label
1	1	10	**Disco Lady**	*Johnnie Taylor* ... Columbia 10281
2	2	15	**Dream Weaver**	*Gary Wright* ... Warner 8167
3	3	12	**Lonely Night (Angel Face)**	*Captain & Tennille* ... A&M 1782
4	4	11	**Let Your Love Flow**	*Bellamy Brothers* ... Warner 8169
5	6	9	**Right Back Where We Started From**	*Maxine Nightingale* ... United Artists 752
6	7	23	**Dream On**	*Aerosmith* ... Columbia 10278
7	16	9	**Boogie Fever**	*Sylvers* ... Capitol 4179
8	11	15	**Only Sixteen**	*Dr. Hook* ... Capitol 4171
9	12	16	**Sweet Love**	*Commodores* ... Motown 1381
10	10	18	**Golden Years**	*David Bowie* ... RCA 10441

★ **HIGHEST DEBUT** ★ POS 58
Silly Love Songs ... *Wings*

★ **BIGGEST MOVER** ★ 59 to 20
Welcome Back ... *John Sebastian*

Billboard — APRIL 17, 1976 — HOT 100

TW	LW	WK	Title	Artist ... Label & Number
1	1	11	**Disco Lady**	*Johnnie Taylor* ... Columbia 10281
2	4	12	Let Your Love Flow	*Bellamy Brothers* ... Warner 8169
3	5	10	Right Back Where We Started From	*Maxine Nightingale* ... United Artists 752
4	3	13	Lonely Night (Angel Face)	*Captain & Tennille* ... A&M 1782
5	7	10	Boogie Fever	*Sylvers* ... Capitol 4179
6	8	16	**Only Sixteen**	*Dr. Hook* ... Capitol 4171
7	9	17	Sweet Love	*Commodores* ... Motown 1381
8	2	16	Dream Weaver	*Gary Wright* ... Warner 8167
9	11	9	Show Me The Way	*Peter Frampton* ... A&M 1795
10	12	16	Bohemian Rhapsody	*Queen* ... Elektra 45297

★ **HIGHEST DEBUT** ★ POS 71
One Piece At A Time .... *Johnny Cash*

★ **BIGGEST MOVER** ★ 58 to 35
Silly Love Songs .... *Wings*

Billboard — APRIL 24, 1976 — HOT 100

TW	LW	WK	Title	Artist ... Label & Number
1	1	12	**Disco Lady**	*Johnnie Taylor* ... Columbia 10281
2	2	13	Let Your Love Flow	*Bellamy Brothers* ... Warner 8169
3	3	11	Right Back Where We Started From	*Maxine Nightingale* ... United Artists 752
4	5	11	Boogie Fever	*Sylvers* ... Capitol 4179
5	7	18	**Sweet Love**	*Commodores* ... Motown 1381
6	6	17	**Only Sixteen**	*Dr. Hook* ... Capitol 4171
7	11	5	Welcome Back	*John Sebastian* ... Reprise 1349
8	9	10	Show Me The Way	*Peter Frampton* ... A&M 1795
9	10	17	**Bohemian Rhapsody**	*Queen* ... Elektra 45297
10	12	8	Fooled Around And Fell In Love	*Elvin Bishop* ... Capricorn 0252

★ **HIGHEST DEBUT** ★ POS 63
Fool To Cry .... *The Rolling Stones*

★ **BIGGEST MOVER** ★ 66 to 44
Love In The Shadows .... *Neil Sedaka*

Billboard — MAY 1, 1976 — HOT 100

TW	LW	WK	Title	Artist ... Label & Number
1	2	14	**Let Your Love Flow**	*Bellamy Brothers* ... Warner 8169
2	3	12	**Right Back Where We Started From**	*Maxine Nightingale* ... United Artists 752
3	4	12	Boogie Fever	*Sylvers* ... Capitol 4179
4	7	6	Welcome Back	*John Sebastian* ... Reprise 1349
5	5	19	**Sweet Love**	*Commodores* ... Motown 1381
6	1	13	Disco Lady	*Johnnie Taylor* ... Columbia 10281
7	8	11	Show Me The Way	*Peter Frampton* ... A&M 1795
8	10	9	Fooled Around And Fell In Love	*Elvin Bishop* ... Capricorn 0252
9	9	18	**Bohemian Rhapsody**	*Queen* ... Elektra 45297
10	29	5	Love Hangover	*Diana Ross* ... Motown 1392

★ **HIGHEST DEBUT** ★ POS 62
Shop Around .... *Captain & Tennille*

★ **BIGGEST MOVER** ★ 29 to 10
Love Hangover .... *Diana Ross*

Billboard — MAY 8, 1976 — HOT 100

TW	LW	WK	Title	Artist / Label
1	4	7	**Welcome Back**	John Sebastian . . . Reprise 1349
2	2	13	**Right Back Where We Started From**	Maxine Nightingale . . . United Artists 752
3	3	13	**Boogie Fever**	Sylvers . . . Capitol 4179
4	8	10	**Fooled Around And Fell In Love**	Elvin Bishop . . . Capricorn 0252
5	12	5	**Silly Love Songs**	Wings . . . Capitol 4256
6	7	12	**Show Me The Way**	Peter Frampton . . . A&M 1795
7	10	6	**Love Hangover**	Diana Ross . . . Motown 1392
8	13	9	**Get Up And Boogie (That's Right)**	Silver Convention . . . Midland International 10571
9	1	15	**Let Your Love Flow**	Bellamy Brothers . . . Warner 8169
10	6	14	**Disco Lady**	Johnnie Taylor . . . Columbia 10281

★ **HIGHEST DEBUT** ★ POS 80
It Makes Me Giggle ....John Denver

★ **BIGGEST MOVER** ★ 46 to 20
Fool To Cry..............................The Rolling Stones

Billboard — MAY 15, 1976 — HOT 100

TW	LW	WK	Title	Artist / Label
1	3	14	**Boogie Fever**	Sylvers . . . Capitol 4179
2	1	8	**Welcome Back**	John Sebastian . . . Reprise 1349
3	5	6	**Silly Love Songs**	Wings . . . Capitol 4256
4	4	11	**Fooled Around And Fell In Love**	Elvin Bishop . . . Capricorn 0252
5	7	7	**Love Hangover**	Diana Ross . . . Motown 1392
6	6	13	**Show Me The Way**	Peter Frampton . . . A&M 1795
7	8	10	**Get Up And Boogie (That's Right)**	Silver Convention . . . Midland International 10571
8	2	14	**Right Back Where We Started From**	Maxine Nightingale . . . United Artists 752
9	19	7	**Happy Days**	Pratt & McClain . . . Reprise 1351
10	12	12	**Shannon**	Henry Gross . . . Lifesong 45002

★ **HIGHEST DEBUT** ★ POS 81
Today's The Day ....America

★ **BIGGEST MOVER** ★ 72 to 47
I'll Be Good To You............The Brothers Johnson

Billboard — MAY 22, 1976 — HOT 100

TW	LW	WK	Title	Artist / Label
1	3	7	**Silly Love Songs**	Wings . . . Capitol 4256
2	5	8	**Love Hangover**	Diana Ross . . . Motown 1392
3	4	12	**Fooled Around And Fell In Love**	Elvin Bishop . . . Capricorn 0252
4	1	15	**Boogie Fever**	Sylvers . . . Capitol 4179
5	7	11	**Get Up And Boogie (That's Right)**	Silver Convention . . . Midland International 10571
6	2	9	**Welcome Back**	John Sebastian . . . Reprise 1349
7	9	8	**Happy Days**	Pratt & McClain . . . Reprise 1351
8	14	10	**Misty Blue**	Dorthy Moore . . . Malaco 1029
9	10	13	**Shannon**	Henry Gross . . . Lifesong 45002
10	11	10	**Tryin' To Get The Feeling Again**	Barry Manilow . . . Arista 0172

★ **HIGHEST DEBUT** ★ POS 77
Let It Shine ....Santana

★ **BIGGEST MOVER** ★ 83 to 35
I.O.U. ....Jimmy Dean

Billboard HOT 100 — MAY 29, 1976

TW	LW	WK	Title	Artist	Label
1	2	9	**Love Hangover**	Diana Ross	Motown 1392
2	1	8	Silly Love Songs	Wings	Capitol 4256
3	3	13	**Fooled Around And Fell In Love**	Elvin Bishop	Capricorn 0252
4	5	12	**Get Up And Boogie (That's Right)**	Silver Convention	Midland International 10571
5	8	11	Misty Blue	Dorthy Moore	Malaco 1029
6	7	9	Happy Days	Pratt & McClain	Reprise 1351
7	6	10	Welcome Back	John Sebastian	Reprise 1349
8	9	14	Shannon	Henry Gross	Lifesong 45002
9	11	18	Sara Smile	Daryl Hall & John Oates	RCA 10530
10	10	11	**Tryin' To Get The Feeling Again**	Barry Manilow	Arista 0172

★ **HIGHEST DEBUT** ★ POS 73
Young Hearts Run Free .... Candi Staton

★ **BIGGEST MOVER** ★ 66 to 44
Afternoon Delight .... Starland Vocal Band

Billboard HOT 100 — JUNE 5, 1976

TW	LW	WK	Title	Artist	Label
1	1	10	**Love Hangover**	Diana Ross	Motown 1392
2	2	9	**Silly Love Songs**	Wings	Capitol 4256
3	4	13	**Get Up And Boogie (That's Right)**	Silver Convention	Midland International 10571
4	5	12	Misty Blue	Dorthy Moore	Malaco 1029
5	6	10	**Happy Days**	Pratt & McClain	Reprise 1351
6	8	15	**Shannon**	Henry Gross	Lifesong 45002
7	7	11	Welcome Back	John Sebastian	Reprise 1349
8	9	19	Sara Smile	Daryl Hall & John Oates	RCA 10530
9	14	6	Shop Around	Captain & Tennille	A&M 1817
10	11	7	**Fool To Cry**	The Rolling Stones	Rolling Stones 19304

★ **HIGHEST DEBUT** ★ POS 61
Somebody's Gettin' It .... Johnnie Taylor

★ **BIGGEST MOVER** ★ 89 to 63
Sophisticated Lady (She's A Different Lady) .... Natalie Cole

Billboard HOT 100 — JUNE 12, 1976

TW	LW	WK	Title	Artist	Label
1	2	10	**Silly Love Songs**	Wings	Capitol 4256
2	3	14	**Get Up And Boogie (That's Right)**	Silver Convention	Midland International 10571
3	4	13	**Misty Blue**	Dorthy Moore	Malaco 1029
4	1	11	Love Hangover	Diana Ross	Motown 1392
5	5	11	**Happy Days**	Pratt & McClain	Reprise 1351
6	6	16	**Shannon**	Henry Gross	Lifesong 45002
7	8	20	Sara Smile	Daryl Hall & John Oates	RCA 10530
8	9	7	Shop Around	Captain & Tennille	A&M 1817
9	13	14	More, More, More (Pt. 1)	Andrea True Connection	Buddah 515
10	10	8	**Fool To Cry**	The Rolling Stones	Rolling Stones 19304

★ **HIGHEST DEBUT** ★ POS 52
Last Child .... Aerosmith

★ **BIGGEST MOVER** ★ 75 to 58
Rock And Roll Music .... The Beach Boys

TW	LW	WK	Billboard	JUNE 19, 1976	HOT 100
①	1	11	**Silly Love Songs** ....*Wings* ... Capitol 4256
②	2	15	**Get Up And Boogie (That's Right)** ....*Silver Convention* ... Midland International 10571
③	3	14	**Misty Blue** ....*Dorthy Moore* ... Malaco 1029
④	4	12	**Love Hangover**...*Diana Ross* ... Motown 1392
⑤	7	21	**Sara Smile**.....................................*Daryl Hall & John Oates* ... RCA 10530
⑥	6	17	**Shannon**..*Henry Gross* ... Lifesong 45002
⑦	8	8	**Shop Around** ....*Captain & Tennille* ... A&M 1817
⑧	9	15	**More, More, More (Pt. 1)**.............*Andrea True Connection* ... Buddah 515
⑨	25	7	**Afternoon Delight**...............................*Starland Vocal Band* ... Windsong 10588
⑩	13	8	**I'll Be Good To You** ....*The Brothers Johnson* ... A&M 1806

★ HIGHEST DEBUT ★ POS 55	★ BIGGEST MOVER ★ 54 to 29
If You Know What I Mean ....*Neil Diamond*	Got To Get You Into My Life ....*The Beatles*

TW	LW	WK	Billboard	JUNE 26, 1976	HOT 100
①	1	12	**Silly Love Songs** ....*Wings* ... Capitol 4256
②	2	16	**Get Up And Boogie (That's Right)** ....*Silver Convention* ... Midland International 10571
③	3	15	**Misty Blue** ....*Dorthy Moore* ... Malaco 1029
④	5	22	**Sara Smile**.....................................*Daryl Hall & John Oates* ... RCA 10530
⑤	7	9	**Shop Around** ....*Captain & Tennille* ... A&M 1817
⑥	8	16	**More, More, More (Pt. 1)**.............*Andrea True Connection* ... Buddah 515
⑦	9	8	**Afternoon Delight**...........................*Starland Vocal Band* ... Windsong 10588
⑧	4	13	**Love Hangover**...*Diana Ross* ... Motown 1392
⑨	10	9	**I'll Be Good To You** ....*The Brothers Johnson* ... A&M 1806
⑩	12	11	**Kiss And Say Goodbye**.........................*Manhattans* ... Columbia 10310

★ HIGHEST DEBUT ★ POS 63	★ BIGGEST MOVER ★ 55 to 24
Hot Stuff/Fool To Cry ....*The Rolling Stones*	If You Know What I Mean ....*Neil Diamond*

TW	LW	WK	Billboard	JULY 4, 1976	HOT 100
①	1	13	**Silly Love Songs** ....*Wings* ... Capitol 4256
②	7	9	**Afternoon Delight**...........................*Starland Vocal Band* ... Windsong 10588
③	3	16	**Misty Blue** ....*Dorthy Moore* ... Malaco 1029
④	4	23	**Sara Smile**.....................................*Daryl Hall & John Oates* ... RCA 10530
⑤	5	10	**Shop Around** ....*Captain & Tennille* ... A&M 1817
⑥	6	17	**More, More, More (Pt. 1)**.............*Andrea True Connection* ... Buddah 515
⑦	2	17	**Get Up And Boogie (That's Right)** ....*Silver Convention* ... Midland International 10571
⑧	9	10	**I'll Be Good To You** ....*The Brothers Johnson* ... A&M 1806
⑨	10	12	**Kiss And Say Goodbye**.........................*Manhattans* ... Columbia 10310
⑩	11	12	**Love Is Alive** ....*Gary Wright* ... Warner 8143

★ HIGHEST DEBUT ★ POS 59	★ BIGGEST MOVER ★ 77 to 56
Let 'Em In ....*Wings*	Baby, I Love Your Way ....*Peter Frampton*

JULY 10, 1976 — Billboard HOT 100

TW	LW	WK	Title	Artist	Label
1	2	10	Afternoon Delight	Starland Vocal Band	Windsong 10588
2	9	13	Kiss And Say Goodbye	Manhattans	Columbia 10310
3	8	11	I'll Be Good To You	The Brothers Johnson	A&M 1806
4	5	11	Shop Around	Captain & Tennille	A&M 1817
5	6	18	More, More, More (Pt. 1)	Andrea True Connection	Buddah 515
6	1	14	Silly Love Songs	Wings	Capitol 4256
7	3	17	Misty Blue	Dorthy Moore	Malaco 1029
8	10	13	Love Is Alive	Gary Wright	Warner 8143
9	4	24	Sara Smile	Daryl Hall & John Oates	RCA 10530
10	12	5	Got To Get You Into My Life	The Beatles	Capitol 4274

★ HIGHEST DEBUT ★ POS 79
(Shake, Shake, Shake) Shake Your Booty ....KC & The Sunshine Band

★ BIGGEST MOVER ★ 66 to 46
Don't Go Breaking My Heart ......Elton John & Kiki Dee

JULY 17, 1976 — Billboard HOT 100

TW	LW	WK	Title	Artist	Label
1	1	11	Afternoon Delight	Starland Vocal Band	Windsong 10588
2	2	14	Kiss And Say Goodbye	Manhattans	Columbia 10310
3	3	12	I'll Be Good To You	The Brothers Johnson	A&M 1806
4	5	19	More, More, More (Pt. 1)	Andrea True Connection	Buddah 515
5	13	14	Moonlight Feels Right	Starbuck	Private Stock 45039
6	8	14	Love Is Alive	Gary Wright	Warner 8143
7	4	12	Shop Around	Captain & Tennille	A&M 1817
8	10	6	Got To Get You Into My Life	The Beatles	Capitol 4274
9	6	15	Silly Love Songs	Wings	Capitol 4256
10	15	7	Rock And Roll Music	The Beach Boys	Brother 1354

★ HIGHEST DEBUT ★ POS 78
Gotta Be The One ......Maxine Nightingale

★ BIGGEST MOVER ★ 51 to 25
You Should Be Dancing ......Bee Gees

JULY 24, 1976 — Billboard HOT 100

TW	LW	WK	Title	Artist	Label
1	2	15	Kiss And Say Goodbye	Manhattans	Columbia 10310
2	1	12	Afternoon Delight	Starland Vocal Band	Windsong 10588
3	3	13	I'll Be Good To You	The Brothers Johnson	A&M 1806
4	5	15	Moonlight Feels Right	Starbuck	Private Stock 45039
5	6	15	Love Is Alive	Gary Wright	Warner 8143
6	16	15	Get Closer	Seals & Crofts	Warner 8190
7	8	7	Got To Get You Into My Life	The Beatles	Capitol 4274
8	23	4	Don't Go Breaking My Heart	Elton John & Kiki Dee	Rocket 40585
9	10	8	Rock And Roll Music	The Beach Boys	Brother 1354
10	11	13	Let Her In	John Travolta	Midland International 10623

★ HIGHEST DEBUT ★ POS 67
Teddy Bear ......Red Sovine

★ BIGGEST MOVER ★ 79 to 55
Getaway ......Earth, Wind & Fire

TW	LW	WK	Billboard	JULY 31, 1976	HOT 100.
❶	1	16	**Kiss And Say Goodbye** ....*Manhattans* . . . Columbia 10310
❷	5	16	**Love Is Alive**...*Gary Wright* . . . Warner 8143
❸	4	16	**Moonlight Feels Right**...........................*Starbuck* . . . Private Stock 45039
④	2	13	Afternoon Delight.......................*Starland Vocal Band* . . . Windsong 10588
❺	8	5	Don't Go Breaking My Heart ....*Elton John & Kiki Dee* . . . Rocket 40585
⑥	6	16	**Get Closer** ....*Seals & Crofts* . . . Warner 8190
❼	7	8	**Got To Get You Into My Life** ....*The Beatles* . . . Capitol 4274
❽	9	9	Rock And Roll Music...............................*The Beach Boys* . . . Brother 1354
⑨	3	14	I'll Be Good To You ....*The Brothers Johnson* . . . A&M 1806
❿	19	5	Let 'Em In...*Wings* . . . Capitol 4293

★ HIGHEST DEBUT ★ POS 69	★ BIGGEST MOVER ★ 67 to 52
Still The One ....*Orleans*	Teddy Bear.......................................*Red Sovine*

TW	LW	WK	Billboard	AUGUST 7, 1976	HOT 100.
❶	5	6	**Don't Go Breaking My Heart** ....*Elton John & Kiki Dee* . . . Rocket 40585
②	2	17	**Love Is Alive**...*Gary Wright* . . . Warner 8143
③	3	17	**Moonlight Feels Right**...........................*Starbuck* . . . Private Stock 45039
❹	10	6	**Let 'Em In**...*Wings* . . . Capitol 4293
❺	11	6	You Should Be Dancing................................*Bee Gees* . . . RSO 853
⑥	8	10	Rock And Roll Music ....*The Beach Boys* . . . Brother 1354
⑦	7	9	**Got To Get You Into My Life** ....*The Beatles* . . . Capitol 4274
⑧	1	17	**Kiss And Say Goodbye**.............................*Manhattans* . . . Columbia 10310
⑨	13	10	You'll Never Find Another Love Like Mine..............................*Lou Rawls* . . . Philadelphia International 3592
❿	4	14	Afternoon Delight.......................*Starland Vocal Band* . . . Windsong 10588

★ HIGHEST DEBUT ★ POS 58	★ BIGGEST MOVER ★ 69 to 51
One Love In My Lifetime.................*Diana Ross*	Still The One ....*Orleans*

TW	LW	WK	Billboard	AUGUST 14, 1976	HOT 100.
❶	1	7	**Don't Go Breaking My Heart** ....*Elton John & Kiki Dee* . . . Rocket 40585
❷	5	7	You Should Be Dancing................................*Bee Gees* . . . RSO 853
❸	4	7	Let 'Em In...*Wings* . . . Capitol 4293
❹	9	11	You'll Never Find Another Love Like Mine..........................*Lou Rawls* . . . Philadelphia International 3592
⑤	6	11	**Rock And Roll Music** ....*The Beach Boys* . . . Brother 1354
⑥	2	18	Love Is Alive ....*Gary Wright* . . . Warner 8143
❼	19	10	I'd Really Love To See You Tonight ......*England Dan & John Ford Coley* . . . Big Tree 16069
❽	26	6	(Shake, Shake, Shake) Shake Your Booty ......*KC & The Sunshine Band* . . . T.K. 1019
⑨	8	18	Kiss And Say Goodbye.............................*Manhattans* . . . Columbia 10310
❿	12	19	**Turn The Beat Around** ....*Vicki Sue Robinson* . . . RCA 10562

★ HIGHEST DEBUT ★ POS 60	★ BIGGEST MOVER ★ 78 to 59
If You Leave Me Now ....*Chicago*	I Can't Hear You No More...............*Helen Reddy*

Billboard — AUGUST 21, 1976 — HOT 100

TW	LW	WK	Title	Artist	Label
1	1	8	Don't Go Breaking My Heart	Elton John & Kiki Dee	Rocket 40585
2	2	8	You Should Be Dancing	Bee Gees	RSO 853
3	3	8	Let 'Em In	Wings	Capitol 4293
4	4	12	You'll Never Find Another Love Like Mine	Lou Rawls	Philadelphia International 3592
5	7	11	I'd Really Love To See You Tonight	England Dan & John Ford Coley	Big Tree 16069
6	8	7	(Shake, Shake, Shake) Shake Your Booty	KC & The Sunshine Band	T.K. 1019
7	5	12	Rock And Roll Music	The Beach Boys	Brother 1354
8	9	19	Kiss And Say Goodbye	Manhattans	Columbia 10310
9	11	19	Get Closer	Seals & Crofts	Warner 8190
10	10	20	Turn The Beat Around	Vicki Sue Robinson	RCA 10562

★ HIGHEST DEBUT ★ POS 71
That'll Be The Day ....Linda Ronstadt

★ BIGGEST MOVER ★ 60 to 28
If You Leave Me Now ....Chicago

Billboard — AUGUST 28, 1976 — HOT 100

TW	LW	WK	Title	Artist	Label
1	1	9	Don't Go Breaking My Heart	Elton John & Kiki Dee	Rocket 40585
2	2	9	You Should Be Dancing	Bee Gees	RSO 853
3	3	9	Let 'Em In	Wings	Capitol 4293
4	4	13	You'll Never Find Another Love Like Mine	Lou Rawls	Philadelphia International 3592
5	5	12	I'd Really Love To See You Tonight	England Dan & John Ford Coley	Big Tree 16069
6	6	8	(Shake, Shake, Shake) Shake Your Booty	KC & The Sunshine Band	T.K. 1019
7	12	11	Play That Funky Music	Wild Cherry	Epic 50225
8	13	14	A Fifth Of Beethoven	Walter Murphy & The Big Apple Band	Private Stock 45073
9	9	20	Get Closer	Seals & Crofts	Warner 8190
10	11	12	This Masquerade	George Benson	Warner 8209

★ HIGHEST DEBUT ★ POS 70
The Wreck Of The Edmund Fitzgerald ....Gordon Lightfoot

★ BIGGEST MOVER ★ 79 to 63
Disco Duck (Part 1) ....Rick Dees & His Cast Of Idiots

Billboard — SEPTEMBER 4, 1976 — HOT 100

TW	LW	WK	Title	Artist	Label
1	2	10	You Should Be Dancing	Bee Gees	RSO 853
2	4	14	You'll Never Find Another Love Like Mine	Lou Rawls	Philadelphia International 3592
3	3	10	Let 'Em In	Wings	Capitol 4293
4	5	13	I'd Really Love To See You Tonight	England Dan & John Ford Coley	Big Tree 16069
5	6	9	(Shake, Shake, Shake) Shake Your Booty	KC & The Sunshine Band	T.K. 1019
6	7	12	Play That Funky Music	Wild Cherry	Epic 50225
7	8	15	A Fifth Of Beethoven	Walter Murphy & The Big Apple Band	Private Stock 45073
8	1	10	Don't Go Breaking My Heart	Elton John & Kiki Dee	Rocket 40585
9	16	10	Lowdown	Boz Scaggs	Columbia 10367
10	10	13	This Masquerade	George Benson	Warner 8209

★ HIGHEST DEBUT ★ POS 77
Fernando ....Abba

★ BIGGEST MOVER ★ 63 to 34
Disco Duck (Part 1) ....Rick Dees & His Cast Of Idiots

TW	LW	WK	Billboard.	🔴 SEPTEMBER 11, 1976 🔴	HOT 100.
❶	5	10	**(Shake, Shake, Shake) Shake Your Booty** .... *KC & The Sunshine Band* ... T.K. 1019		
②	2	15	**You'll Never Find Another Love Like Mine** ....*Lou Rawls* ... Philadelphia International 3592		
❸	6	13	**Play That Funky Music** ....*Wild Cherry* ... Epic 50225		
❹	4	14	**I'd Really Love To See You Tonight** ......*England Dan & John Ford Coley* ... Big Tree 16069		
❺	7	16	**A Fifth Of Beethoven** .... *Walter Murphy & The Big Apple Band* ... Private Stock 45073		
⑥	1	11	**You Should Be Dancing** ....*Bee Gees* ... RSO 853		
❼	9	11	**Lowdown**...*Boz Scaggs* ... Columbia 10367		
⑧	3	11	**Let 'Em In** ....*Wings* ... Capitol 4293		
⑨	8	11	**Don't Go Breaking My Heart** ....*Elton John & Kiki Dee* ... Rocket 40585		
⑩	11	10	**Summer** ....*War* ... United Artists 834		

★ *HIGHEST DEBUT* ★ POS 74	★ *BIGGEST MOVER* ★ 83 to 54
Like A Sad Song ....*John Denver*	I Only Want To Be With You ....*Bay City Rollers*

TW	LW	WK	Billboard.	🔴 SEPTEMBER 18, 1976 🔴	HOT 100.
❶	3	14	**Play That Funky Music** ....*Wild Cherry* ... Epic 50225		
②	1	11	**(Shake, Shake, Shake) Shake Your Booty** ......*KC & The Sunshine Band* ... T.K. 1019		
❸	4	15	**I'd Really Love To See You Tonight** ......*England Dan & John Ford Coley* ... Big Tree 16069		
❹	5	17	**A Fifth Of Beethoven** .... *Walter Murphy & The Big Apple Band* ... Private Stock 45073		
⑤	2	16	**You'll Never Find Another Love Like Mine**...........................*Lou Rawls* ... Philadelphia International 3592		
❻	7	12	**Lowdown**...*Boz Scaggs* ... Columbia 10367		
❼	13	12	**Devil Woman** ....*Cliff Richard* ... Rocket 40574		
❽	10	11	**Summer** ....*War* ... United Artists 834		
⑨	11	6	**If You Leave Me Now** ....*Chicago* ... Columbia 10390		
⑩	6	12	**You Should Be Dancing** ....*Bee Gees* ... RSO 853		

★ *HIGHEST DEBUT* ★ POS 70	★ *BIGGEST MOVER* ★ 84 to 62
Love So Right ....*Bee Gees*	The Rubberband Man ....*Spinners*

TW	LW	WK	Billboard.	🔴 SEPTEMBER 25, 1976 🔴	HOT 100.
❶	1	15	**Play That Funky Music** ....*Wild Cherry* ... Epic 50225		
❷	3	16	**I'd Really Love To See You Tonight** .... *England Dan & John Ford Coley* ... Big Tree 16069		
❸	4	18	**A Fifth Of Beethoven** .... *Walter Murphy & The Big Apple Band* ... Private Stock 45073		
④	2	12	**(Shake, Shake, Shake) Shake Your Booty** ......*KC & The Sunshine Band* ... T.K. 1019		
❺	6	13	**Lowdown**...*Boz Scaggs* ... Columbia 10367		
❻	7	13	**Devil Woman**...*Cliff Richard* ... Rocket 40574		
❼	8	12	**Summer** ....*War* ... United Artists 834		
❽	9	7	**If You Leave Me Now** ....*Chicago* ... Columbia 10390		
⑨	13	7	**Disco Duck (Part 1)** ....*Rick Dees & His Cast Of Idiots* ... RSO 857		
⑩	5	17	**You'll Never Find Another Love Like Mine**...........................*Lou Rawls* ... Philadelphia International 3592		

★ *HIGHEST DEBUT* ★ POS 68	★ *BIGGEST MOVER* ★ 85 to 57
Muskrat Love ....*Captain & Tennille*	Just To Be Close To You ....*Commodores*

TW	LW	WK	**Billboard** OCTOBER 2, 1976	HOT 100
❶	1	16	**Play That Funky Music** ....*Wild Cherry* ... Epic 50225	
②	2	17	**I'd Really Love To See You Tonight** .... *England Dan & John Ford Coley* ... Big Tree 16069	
❸	3	19	**A Fifth Of Beethoven** .... *Walter Murphy & The Big Apple Band* ... Private Stock 45073	
④	9	8	**Disco Duck (Part 1)** ....*Rick Dees & His Cast Of Idiots* ... RSO 857	
⑤	5	14	**Lowdown**...*Boz Scaggs* ... Columbia 10367	
⑥	6	14	**Devil Woman**...*Cliff Richard* ... Rocket 40574	
⑦	7	13	**Summer** ....*War* ... United Artists 834	
⑧	8	8	**If You Leave Me Now** ....*Chicago* ... Columbia 10390	
⑨	4	13	**(Shake, Shake, Shake) Shake Your Booty** ...... *KC & The Sunshine Band* ... T.K. 1019	
❿	13	10	**Still The One**...*Orleans* ... Asylum 45336	

★ HIGHEST DEBUT ★ POS 58	★ BIGGEST MOVER ★ 76 to 55
A Dose Of Rock 'N' Roll ....*Ringo Starr*	More Than A Feeling ....*Boston*

TW	LW	WK	**Billboard** OCTOBER 9, 1976	HOT 100
❶	3	20	**A Fifth Of Beethoven** .... *Walter Murphy & The Big Apple Band* ... Private Stock 45073	
②	1	17	**Play That Funky Music** ....*Wild Cherry* ... Epic 50225	
❸	5	15	**Lowdown** ....*Boz Scaggs* ... Columbia 10367	
④	4	9	**Disco Duck (Part 1)** ....*Rick Dees & His Cast Of Idiots* ... RSO 857	
⑤	8	9	**If You Leave Me Now** ....*Chicago* ... Columbia 10390	
⑥	6	15	**Devil Woman**...*Cliff Richard* ... Rocket 40574	
❼	10	11	**Still The One**...*Orleans* ... Asylum 45336	
⑧	2	18	**I'd Really Love To See You Tonight** ...... *England Dan & John Ford Coley* ... Big Tree 16069	
⑨	9	14	**(Shake, Shake, Shake) Shake Your Booty** ...... *KC & The Sunshine Band* ... T.K. 1019	
❿	14	20	**She's Gone**.................................*Daryl Hall & John Oates* ... Atlantic 3332	

★ HIGHEST DEBUT ★ POS 74	★ BIGGEST MOVER ★ 48 to 32
Stand Tall ....*Burton Cummings*	Muskrat Love ....*Captain & Tennille*

TW	LW	WK	**Billboard** OCTOBER 16, 1976	HOT 100
❶	4	10	**Disco Duck (Part 1)** ....*Rick Dees & His Cast Of Idiots* ... RSO 857	
②	1	21	**A Fifth Of Beethoven** .... *Walter Murphy & The Big Apple Band* ... Private Stock 45073	
③	3	16	**Lowdown** ....*Boz Scaggs* ... Columbia 10367	
④	5	10	**If You Leave Me Now** ....*Chicago* ... Columbia 10390	
⑤	2	18	**Play That Funky Music** ....*Wild Cherry* ... Epic 50225	
⑥	7	12	**Still The One**...*Orleans* ... Asylum 45336	
⑦	6	16	**Devil Woman** ....*Cliff Richard* ... Rocket 40574	
⑧	9	15	**(Shake, Shake, Shake) Shake Your Booty** ...... *KC & The Sunshine Band* ... T.K. 1019	
⑨	10	21	**She's Gone**.................................*Daryl Hall & John Oates* ... Atlantic 3332	
❿	8	19	**I'd Really Love To See You Tonight** ...... *England Dan & John Ford Coley* ... Big Tree 16069	

★ HIGHEST DEBUT ★ POS 70	★ BIGGEST MOVER ★ 71 to 42
Hello Old Friend...........................*Eric Clapton*	Tonight's The Night (Gonna Be Alright).......*Rod Stewart*

Billboard — OCTOBER 23, 1976 — HOT 100

TW	LW	WK	Title	Artist ... Label
1	4	11	If You Leave Me Now	Chicago ... Columbia 10390
2	1	11	Disco Duck (Part 1)	Rick Dees & His Cast Of Idiots ... RSO 857
3	2	22	A Fifth Of Beethoven	Walter Murphy & The Big Apple Band ... Private Stock 45073
4	3	17	Lowdown	Boz Scaggs ... Columbia 10367
5	6	13	Still The One	Orleans ... Asylum 45336
6	5	19	Play That Funky Music	Wild Cherry ... Epic 50225
7	8	16	(Shake, Shake, Shake) Shake Your Booty	KC & The Sunshine Band ... T.K. 1019
8	9	22	She's Gone	Daryl Hall & John Oates ... Atlantic 3332
9	16	6	Love So Right	Bee Gees ... RSO 859
10	11	11	Rock'n Me	Steve Miller ... Capitol 4323

★ HIGHEST DEBUT ★ POS 68
You Make Me Feel Like Dancing .... Leo Sayer

★ BIGGEST MOVER ★ 90 to 77
Breezin' .... George Benson

Billboard — OCTOBER 30, 1976 — HOT 100

TW	LW	WK	Title	Artist ... Label
1	1	12	If You Leave Me Now	Chicago ... Columbia 10390
2	2	12	Disco Duck (Part 1)	Rick Dees & His Cast Of Idiots ... RSO 857
3	10	12	Rock'n Me	Steve Miller ... Capitol 4323
4	15	10	The Wreck Of The Edmund Fitzgerald	Gordon Lightfoot ... Reprise 1369
5	3	23	A Fifth Of Beethoven	Walter Murphy & The Big Apple Band ... Private Stock 45073
6	9	7	Love So Right	Bee Gees ... RSO 859
7	8	23	She's Gone	Daryl Hall & John Oates ... Atlantic 3332
8	6	20	Play That Funky Music	Wild Cherry ... Epic 50225
9	18	6	Muskrat Love	Captain & Tennille ... A&M 1870
10	13	16	Magic Man	Heart ... Mushroom 7011

★ HIGHEST DEBUT ★ POS 70
Whenever I'm Away From You .... John Travolta

★ BIGGEST MOVER ★ 88 to 60
Livin' Thing .... Electric Light Orchestra

Billboard — NOVEMBER 6, 1976 — HOT 100

TW	LW	WK	Title	Artist ... Label
1	3	13	Rock'n Me	Steve Miller ... Capitol 4323
2	2	13	Disco Duck (Part 1)	Rick Dees & His Cast Of Idiots ... RSO 857
3	4	11	The Wreck Of The Edmund Fitzgerald	Gordon Lightfoot ... Reprise 1369
4	1	13	If You Leave Me Now	Chicago ... Columbia 10390
5	6	8	Love So Right	Bee Gees ... RSO 859
6	9	7	Muskrat Love	Captain & Tennille ... A&M 1870
7	7	24	She's Gone	Daryl Hall & John Oates ... Atlantic 3332
8	22	6	Tonight's The Night (Gonna Be Alright)	Rod Stewart ... Warner 8262
9	10	17	Magic Man	Heart ... Mushroom 7011
10	17	8	Just To Be Close To You	Commodores ... Motown 1402

★ HIGHEST DEBUT ★ POS 76
Every Face Tells A Story .... Olivia Newton-John

★ BIGGEST MOVER ★ 22 to 8
Tonight's The Night (Gonna Be Alright) .... Rod Stewart

Billboard — NOVEMBER 13, 1976 — HOT 100

TW	LW	WK		
1	8	7	Tonight's The Night (Gonna Be Alright)	Rod Stewart ... Warner 8262
2	2	14	Disco Duck (Part 1)	Rick Dees & His Cast Of Idiots ... RSO 857
3	3	12	The Wreck Of The Edmund Fitzgerald	Gordon Lightfoot ... Reprise 1369
4	5	9	Love So Right	Bee Gees ... RSO 859
5	6	8	Muskrat Love	Captain & Tennille ... A&M 1870
6	1	14	Rock'n Me	Steve Miller ... Capitol 4323
7	4	14	If You Leave Me Now	Chicago ... Columbia 10390
8	10	9	Just To Be Close To You	Commodores ... Motown 1402
9	15	10	The Rubberband Man	Spinners ... Atlantic 3355
10	11	9	Do You Feel Like We Do	Peter Frampton ... A&M 1867

★ HIGHEST DEBUT ★ POS 54
Sorry Seems To Be The Hardest Word ......Elton John

★ BIGGEST MOVER ★ 68 to 53
Dazz......Brick

Billboard — NOVEMBER 20, 1976 — HOT 100

TW	LW	WK		
1	1	8	Tonight's The Night (Gonna Be Alright)	Rod Stewart ... Warner 8262
2	3	13	The Wreck Of The Edmund Fitzgerald	Gordon Lightfoot ... Reprise 1369
3	4	10	Love So Right	Bee Gees ... RSO 859
4	5	9	Muskrat Love	Captain & Tennille ... A&M 1870
5	2	15	Disco Duck (Part 1)	Rick Dees & His Cast Of Idiots ... RSO 857
6	9	11	The Rubberband Man	Spinners ... Atlantic 3355
7	6	15	Rock'n Me	Steve Miller ... Capitol 4323
8	8	10	Just To Be Close To You	Commodores ... Motown 1402
9	11	12	Beth	Kiss ... Casablanca 863
10	10	10	Do You Feel Like We Do	Peter Frampton ... A&M 1867

★ HIGHEST DEBUT ★ POS 78
Saturday Nite ......Earth, Wind & Fire

★ BIGGEST MOVER ★ 54 to 28
Sorry Seems To Be The Hardest Word ......Elton John

Billboard — NOVEMBER 27, 1976 — HOT 100

TW	LW	WK		
1	1	9	Tonight's The Night (Gonna Be Alright)	Rod Stewart ... Warner 8262
2	2	14	The Wreck Of The Edmund Fitzgerald	Gordon Lightfoot ... Reprise 1369
3	3	11	Love So Right	Bee Gees ... RSO 859
4	4	10	Muskrat Love	Captain & Tennille ... A&M 1870
5	6	12	The Rubberband Man	Spinners ... Atlantic 3355
6	5	16	Disco Duck (Part 1)	Rick Dees & His Cast Of Idiots ... RSO 857
7	8	11	Just To Be Close To You	Commodores ... Motown 1402
8	9	13	Beth	Kiss ... Casablanca 863
9	12	11	More Than A Feeling	Boston ... Epic 50266
10	11	14	Nadia's Theme (The Young And The Restless)	Barry DeVorzon & Perry Botkin, Jr. ... A&M 1856

★ HIGHEST DEBUT ★ POS 45
Somebody To Love ......Queen

★ BIGGEST MOVER ★ 78 to 48
Saturday Nite ......Earth, Wind & Fire

TW	LW	WK	Billboard® ⊙ DECEMBER 4, 1976 ⊙ HOT 100®
❶	1	10	**Tonight's The Night (Gonna Be Alright)** .... *Rod Stewart* ... Warner 8262
❷	5	13	**The Rubberband Man** ....*Spinners* ... Atlantic 3355
❸	3	12	**Love So Right** ....*Bee Gees* ... RSO 859
❹	4	11	**Muskrat Love**...............................*Captain & Tennille* ... A&M 1870
⑤	2	15	**The Wreck Of The Edmund Fitzgerald**........................*Gordon Lightfoot* ... Reprise 1369
❻	14	13	**You Don't Have To Be A Star (To Be In My Show)** .... *Marilyn McCoo & Billy Davis, Jr.* ... ABC 12208
⑦	8	14	**Beth** ....*Kiss* ... Casablanca 863
⑧	9	12	**More Than A Feeling** ....*Boston* ... Epic 50266
❾	10	15	**Nadia's Theme (The Young And The Restless)** .... *Barry DeVorzon & Perry Botkin, Jr.* ... A&M 1856
⑩	12	16	**You Are The Woman** ....*Firefall* ... Atlantic 3335

★ HIGHEST DEBUT ★ POS 40	★ BIGGEST MOVER ★ 72 to 60
I Wish...............................*Stevie Wonder*	What Can I Say...............................*Boz Scaggs*

TW	LW	WK	Billboard® ⊙ DECEMBER 11, 1976 ⊙ HOT 100®
❶	1	11	**Tonight's The Night (Gonna Be Alright)** .... *Rod Stewart* ... Warner 8262
❷	2	14	**The Rubberband Man** ....*Spinners* ... Atlantic 3355
③	3	13	**Love So Right** ....*Bee Gees* ... RSO 859
❹	4	12	**Muskrat Love**...............................*Captain & Tennille* ... A&M 1870
❺	6	14	**You Don't Have To Be A Star (To Be In My Show)** .... *Marilyn McCoo & Billy Davis, Jr.* ... ABC 12208
❻	12	8	**You Make Me Feel Like Dancing**....................*Leo Sayer* ... Warner 8283
❼	8	13	**More Than A Feeling** ....*Boston* ... Epic 50266
❽	9	16	**Nadia's Theme (The Young And The Restless)** .... *Barry DeVorzon & Perry Botkin, Jr.* ... A&M 1856
❾	10	17	**You Are The Woman** ....*Firefall* ... Atlantic 3335
⑩	11	10	**Nights Are Forever Without You** ..... *England Dan & John Ford Coley* ... Big Tree 16079

★ HIGHEST DEBUT ★ POS 72	★ BIGGEST MOVER ★ 42 to 22
Love Theme From "A Star Is Born" (Evergreen) ....*Barbra Streisand*	Car Wash......................................*Rose Royce*

Billboard · DECEMBER 18, 1976 · HOT 100

TW	LW	WK		
①	1	12	**Tonight's The Night (Gonna Be Alright)** .... *Rod Stewart*	... Warner 8262
②	2	15	**The Rubberband Man** .... *Spinners* ... Atlantic 3355	
③	5	15	**You Don't Have To Be A Star (To Be In My Show)** .... *Marilyn McCoo & Billy Davis, Jr.* .... ABC 12208	
④	4	13	**Muskrat Love** .... *Captain & Tennille* ... A&M 1870	
⑤	6	9	**You Make Me Feel Like Dancing** .... *Leo Sayer* ... Warner 8283	
⑥	7	14	**More Than A Feeling** .... *Boston* ... Epic 50266	
⑦	11	6	**Sorry Seems To Be The Hardest Word** .... *Elton John* ... MCA/Rocket 40645	
⑧	8	17	**Nadia's Theme (The Young And The Restless)** .... *Barry DeVorzon & Perry Botkin, Jr.* .... A&M 1856	
⑨	9	18	**You Are The Woman** .... *Firefall* ... Atlantic 3335	
⑩	10	11	**Nights Are Forever Without You** ..... *England Dan & John Ford Coley* ... Big Tree 16079	

★ HIGHEST DEBUT ★ POS 48	★ BIGGEST MOVER ★ 59 to 40
New Kid In Town .... *Eagles*	Blinded By The Light .... *Manfred Mann's Earth Band*

Billboard · DECEMBER 25, 1976 · HOT 100

TW	LW	WK		
①	1	13	**Tonight's The Night (Gonna Be Alright)** .... *Rod Stewart* ... Warner 8262	
②	3	16	**You Don't Have To Be A Star (To Be In My Show)** .... *Marilyn McCoo & Billy Davis, Jr.* .... ABC 12208	
③	2	16	**The Rubberband Man** .... *Spinners* ... Atlantic 3355	
④	5	10	**You Make Me Feel Like Dancing** .... *Leo Sayer* ... Warner 8283	
⑤	6	15	**More Than A Feeling** .... *Boston* ... Epic 50266	
⑥	7	7	**Sorry Seems To Be The Hardest Word** .... *Elton John* ... MCA/Rocket 40645	
⑦	18	4	**I Wish** .... *Stevie Wonder* ... Tamla 54274	
⑧	12	10	**Dazz** .... *Brick* ... Bang 727	
⑨	17	10	**Car Wash** .... *Rose Royce* ... MCA 40615	
⑩	11	10	**After The Lovin'** .... *Engelbert Humperdinck* ... Epic 50270	

★ HIGHEST DEBUT ★ POS 79	★ BIGGEST MOVER ★ 48 to 20
Baby, You Look Good To Me Tonight .... *John Denver*	New Kid In Town .... *Eagles*

Billboard HOT 100 — JANUARY 8, 1977

TW	LW	WK	Title / Artist / Label
1	2	18	**You Don't Have To Be A Star (To Be In My Show)** .... *Marilyn McCoo & Billy Davis, Jr.* . . . . ABC 12208
2	4	12	**You Make Me Feel Like Dancing** .... *Leo Sayer* . . . Warner 8283
3	1	15	**Tonight's The Night (Gonna Be Alright)** .... *Rod Stewart* . . . Warner 8262
4	7	6	**I Wish** .... *Stevie Wonder* . . . Tamla 54274
5	9	12	**Car Wash** .... *Rose Royce* . . . MCA 40615
6	6	9	**Sorry Seems To Be The Hardest Word** .... *Elton John* . . . MCA/Rocket 40645
7	8	12	**Dazz** .... *Brick* . . . Bang 727
8	3	18	**The Rubberband Man** .... *Spinners* . . . Atlantic 3355
9	10	12	**After The Lovin'** .... *Engelbert Humperdinck* . . . Epic 50270
10	11	14	**Stand Tall** .... *Burton Cummings* . . . Portrait 70001

★ **HIGHEST DEBUT** ★ POS 71
Go Your Own Way .... *Fleetwood Mac*

★ **BIGGEST MOVER** ★ 82 to 59
Moody Blue/She Thinks I Still Care .... *Elvis Presley*

Billboard HOT 100 — JANUARY 15, 1977

TW	LW	WK	Title / Artist / Label
1	2	13	**You Make Me Feel Like Dancing** .... *Leo Sayer* . . . Warner 8283
2	4	7	**I Wish** .... *Stevie Wonder* . . . Tamla 54274
3	5	13	**Car Wash** .... *Rose Royce* . . . MCA 40615
4	1	19	**You Don't Have To Be A Star (To Be In My Show)** .... *Marilyn McCoo & Billy Davis, Jr.* . . . . ABC 12208
5	7	13	**Dazz** .... *Brick* . . . Bang 727
6	3	16	**Tonight's The Night (Gonna Be Alright)** .... *Rod Stewart* . . . Warner 8262
7	6	10	**Sorry Seems To Be The Hardest Word** .... *Elton John* . . . MCA/Rocket 40645
8	11	15	**Hot Line** .... *The Sylvers* . . . Capitol 4336
9	9	13	**After The Lovin'** .... *Engelbert Humperdinck* . . . Epic 50270
10	10	15	**Stand Tall** .... *Burton Cummings* . . . Portrait 70001

★ **HIGHEST DEBUT** ★ POS 72
Baby Don't You Know .... *Wild Cherry*

★ **BIGGEST MOVER** ★ 86 to 63
The Things We Do For Love *10cc*

Billboard HOT 100 — JANUARY 22, 1977

TW	LW	WK	Title / Artist / Label
1	2	8	**I Wish** .... *Stevie Wonder* . . . Tamla 54274
2	3	14	**Car Wash** .... *Rose Royce* . . . MCA 40615
3	1	14	**You Make Me Feel Like Dancing** .... *Leo Sayer* . . . Warner 8283
4	5	14	**Dazz** .... *Brick* . . . Bang 727
5	4	20	**You Don't Have To Be A Star (To Be In My Show)** .... *Marilyn McCoo & Billy Davis, Jr.* . . . . ABC 12208
6	8	16	**Hot Line** .... *The Sylvers* . . . Capitol 4336
7	12	6	**New Kid In Town** .... *Eagles* . . . Asylum 45373
8	9	14	**After The Lovin'** .... *Engelbert Humperdinck* . . . Epic 50270
9	19	10	**Blinded By The Light** .... *Manfred Mann's Earth Band* . . . Warner 8252
10	20	10	**Torn Between Two Lovers** .... *Mary MacGregor* . . . Ariola America 7638

★ **HIGHEST DEBUT** ★ POS 80
Darlin' Darlin' Baby (Sweet, Tender, Love) .... *O'Jays*

★ **BIGGEST MOVER** ★ 84 to 57
Boogie Child .... *Bee Gees*

Billboard — JANUARY 29, 1977 — HOT 100

TW	LW	WK			
①	2	15	**Car Wash**	Rose Royce	MCA 40615
②	1	9	I Wish	Stevie Wonder	Tamla 54274
③	4	15	**Dazz**	Brick	Bang 727
④	3	15	You Make Me Feel Like Dancing	Leo Sayer	Warner 8283
⑤	6	17	**Hot Line**	The Sylvers	Capitol 4336
⑥	7	7	New Kid In Town	Eagles	Asylum 45373
⑦	10	11	Torn Between Two Lovers	Mary MacGregor	Ariola America 7638
⑧	9	11	Blinded By The Light	Manfred Mann's Earth Band	Warner 8252
⑨	20	8	Love Theme From "A Star Is Born" (Evergreen)	Barbra Streisand	Columbia 10450
⑩	12	11	**Walk This Way**	Aerosmith	Columbia 10449

★ **HIGHEST DEBUT** ★ POS 62
Long Time .... Boston

★ **BIGGEST MOVER** ★ 57 to 38
Boogie Child .... Bee Gees

Billboard — FEBRUARY 5, 1977 — HOT 100

TW	LW	WK			
①	7	12	**Torn Between Two Lovers**	Mary MacGregor	Ariola America 7638
②	1	16	Car Wash	Rose Royce	MCA 40615
③	3	16	**Dazz**	Brick	Bang 727
④	6	8	New Kid In Town	Eagles	Asylum 45373
⑤	5	18	**Hot Line**	The Sylvers	Capitol 4336
⑥	8	12	Blinded By The Light	Manfred Mann's Earth Band	Warner 8252
⑦	9	9	Love Theme From "A Star Is Born" (Evergreen)	Barbra Streisand	Columbia 10450
⑧	2	10	I Wish	Stevie Wonder	Tamla 54274
⑨	11	13	Enjoy Yourself	The Jacksons	Epic 50289
⑩	10	12	**Walk This Way**	Aerosmith	Columbia 10449

★ **HIGHEST DEBUT** ★ POS 64
Here Come Those Tears Again .... Jackson Browne

★ **BIGGEST MOVER** ★ 71 to 38
Rich Girl .... Daryl Hall & John Oates

Billboard — FEBRUARY 12, 1977 — HOT 100

TW	LW	WK			
①	1	13	**Torn Between Two Lovers**	Mary MacGregor	Ariola America 7638
②	4	9	New Kid In Town	Eagles	Asylum 45373
③	6	13	Blinded By The Light	Manfred Mann's Earth Band	Warner 8252
④	2	17	Car Wash	Rose Royce	MCA 40615
⑤	7	10	Love Theme From "A Star Is Born" (Evergreen)	Barbra Streisand	Columbia 10450
⑥	3	17	Dazz	Brick	Bang 727
⑦	9	14	Enjoy Yourself	The Jacksons	Epic 50289
⑧	8	11	I Wish	Stevie Wonder	Tamla 54274
⑨	12	15	I Like Dreamin'	Kenny Nolan	20th Century 2287
⑩	11	12	**Lost Without Your Love**	Bread	Elektra 45365

★ **HIGHEST DEBUT** ★ POS 56
Bite Your Lip (Get up and dance!) ...... Elton John

★ **BIGGEST MOVER** ★ 77 to 60
So In To You .... Atlanta Rhythm Section

Billboard ⊙ FEBRUARY 19, 1977 ⊙ HOT 100.

TW	LW	WK		
❶	3	14	**Blinded By The Light** ....*Manfred Mann's Earth Band* ... Warner 8252
❷	2	10	**New Kid In Town**..*Eagles* ... Asylum 45373
③	1	14	**Torn Between Two Lovers** ....*Mary MacGregor* ... Ariola America 7638
❹	5	11	**Love Theme From "A Star Is Born" (Evergreen)**......... *Barbra Streisand* ... Columbia 10450
⑤	9	16	**I Like Dreamin'**................................*Kenny Nolan* ... 20th Century 2287
⑥	7	15	**Enjoy Yourself**...*The Jacksons* ... Epic 50289
⑦	4	18	**Car Wash** ....*Rose Royce* ... MCA 40615
⑧	11	10	**Fly Like An Eagle** ....*Steve Miller* ... Capitol 4372
⑨	10	13	**Lost Without Your Love**...............................*Bread* ... Elektra 45365
⑩	14	11	**Night Moves** ....*Bob Seger* ... Capitol 4369

★ HIGHEST DEBUT ★ POS 72	★ BIGGEST MOVER ★ 77 to 46
All Strung Out On You....................*John Travolta*	The First Cut Is The Deepest ....*Rod Stewart*

Billboard ⊙ FEBRUARY 26, 1977 ⊙ HOT 100.

TW	LW	WK		
❶	2	11	**New Kid In Town**..*Eagles* ... Asylum 45373
❷	4	12	**Love Theme From "A Star Is Born" (Evergreen)**......... *Barbra Streisand* ... Columbia 10450
③	1	15	**Blinded By The Light** ....*Manfred Mann's Earth Band* ... Warner 8252
❹	8	11	**Fly Like An Eagle** ....*Steve Miller* ... Capitol 4372
⑤	5	17	**I Like Dreamin'**................................*Kenny Nolan* ... 20th Century 2287
⑥	6	16	**Enjoy Yourself**...*The Jacksons* ... Epic 50289
⑦	3	15	**Torn Between Two Lovers** ....*Mary MacGregor* ... Ariola America 7638
⑧	10	12	**Night Moves** ....*Bob Seger* ... Capitol 4369
⑨	14	12	**Dancing Queen** ....*Abba* ... Atlantic 3372
⑩	11	14	**Weekend In New England** ....*Barry Manilow* ... Arista 0212

★ HIGHEST DEBUT ★ POS 72	★ BIGGEST MOVER ★ 86 to 65
Hotel California ....*Eagles*	Southern Nights ....*Glen Campbell*

Billboard ⊙ MARCH 5, 1977 ⊙ HOT 100.

TW	LW	WK		
❶	2	13	**Love Theme From "A Star Is Born" (Evergreen)** ....*Barbra Streisand* ... Columbia 10450
②	1	12	**New Kid In Town**..*Eagles* ... Asylum 45373
❸	4	12	**Fly Like An Eagle** ....*Steve Miller* ... Capitol 4372
④	5	18	**I Like Dreamin'**................................*Kenny Nolan* ... 20th Century 2287
⑤	3	16	**Blinded By The Light** ....*Manfred Mann's Earth Band* ... Warner 8252
⑥	8	13	**Night Moves** ....*Bob Seger* ... Capitol 4369
❼	9	13	**Dancing Queen**...*Abba* ... Atlantic 3372
⑧	11	13	**Year Of The Cat**..*Al Stewart* ... Janus 266
⑨	7	16	**Torn Between Two Lovers** ....*Mary MacGregor* ... Ariola America 7638
⑩	10	15	**Weekend In New England** ....*Barry Manilow* ... Arista 0212

★ HIGHEST DEBUT ★ POS 81	★ BIGGEST MOVER ★ 65 to 39
Phantom Writer ....*Gary Wright*	Southern Nights ....*Glen Campbell*

TW	LW	WK	Billboard	MARCH 12, 1977	HOT 100
❶	1	14	Love Theme From "A Star Is Born" (Evergreen)		
				Barbra Streisand ... Columbia 10450	
❷	3	13	Fly Like An Eagle	*Steve Miller* ... Capitol 4372	
③	4	19	I Like Dreamin'	*Kenny Nolan* ... 20th Century 2287	
④	6	14	Night Moves..	*Bob Seger* ... Capitol 4369	
⑤	5	17	Blinded By The Light	*Manfred Mann's Earth Band* ... Warner 8252	
⑥	7	14	Dancing Queen..	*Abba* ... Atlantic 3372	
❼	9	17	Torn Between Two Lovers	*Mary MacGregor* ... Ariola America 7638	
⑧	8	14	Year Of The Cat...	*Al Stewart* ... Janus 266	
⑨	12	8	Rich Girl	*Daryl Hall & John Oates* ... RCA 10860	
⑩	11	10	Go Your Own Way....................................	*Fleetwood Mac* ... Warner 8304	

★ HIGHEST DEBUT ★ POS 72	★ BIGGEST MOVER ★ 79 to 50
Lido Shuffle ....*Boz Scaggs*	I Wanna Get Next To You ....*Rose Royce*

TW	LW	WK	Billboard	MARCH 19, 1977	HOT 100
❶	1	15	Love Theme From "A Star Is Born" (Evergreen)		
				Barbra Streisand ... Columbia 10450	
②	2	14	Fly Like An Eagle	*Steve Miller* ... Capitol 4372	
❸	9	9	Rich Girl ....*Daryl Hall & John Oates* ... RCA 10860		
④	4	15	Night Moves..	*Bob Seger* ... Capitol 4369	
⑤	6	15	Dancing Queen..	*Abba* ... Atlantic 3372	
⑥	3	20	I Like Dreamin'..	*Kenny Nolan* ... 20th Century 2287	
⑦	7	18	Torn Between Two Lovers ....*Mary MacGregor* ... Ariola America 7638		
⑧	17	8	Don't Give Up On Us.................................*David Soul* ... Private Stock 45129		
⑨	11	14	Don't Leave Me This Way......................*Thelma Houston* ... Tamla 54278		
⑩	10	11	Go Your Own Way..	*Fleetwood Mac* ... Warner 8304	

★ HIGHEST DEBUT ★ POS 71	★ BIGGEST MOVER ★ 72 to 37
Calling Dr. Love ....*Kiss*	Lido Shuffle ....*Boz Scaggs*

TW	LW	WK	Billboard	MARCH 26, 1977	HOT 100
❶	3	10	Rich Girl ....*Daryl Hall & John Oates* ... RCA 10860		
②	1	16	Love Theme From "A Star Is Born" (Evergreen).........	*Barbra Streisand*	
				... Columbia 10450	
❸	5	16	Dancing Queen..	*Abba* ... Atlantic 3372	
④	8	9	Don't Give Up On Us...............................*David Soul* ... Private Stock 45129		
⑤	9	15	Don't Leave Me This Way......................*Thelma Houston* ... Tamla 54278		
⑥	2	15	Fly Like An Eagle	*Steve Miller* ... Capitol 4372	
⑦	4	16	Night Moves	*Bob Seger* ... Capitol 4369	
⑧	11	12	The Things We Do For Love...............................*10cc* ... Mercury 73875		
⑨	6	21	I Like Dreamin'..	*Kenny Nolan* ... 20th Century 2287	
⑩	7	19	Torn Between Two Lovers ....*Mary MacGregor* ... Ariola America 7638		

★ HIGHEST DEBUT ★ POS 71	★ BIGGEST MOVER ★ 75 to 45
Whodunit ....*Tavares*	Can't Stop Dancin' ....*Captain & Tennille*

TW	LW	WK	Billboard		APRIL 2, 1977		HOT 100.
❶	1	11	**Rich Girl** ....*Daryl Hall & John Oates* ... RCA 10860
②	3	17	Dancing Queen...*Abba* ... Atlantic 3372
③	4	10	Don't Give Up On Us...............................*David Soul* ... Private Stock 45129
❹	5	16	Don't Leave Me This Way ....*Thelma Houston* ... Tamla 54278
⑤	2	17	Love Theme From "A Star Is Born" (Evergreen)......... *Barbra Streisand* ... Columbia 10450
❻	16	8	Southern Nights ....*Glen Campbell* ... Capitol 4376
❼	8	13	The Things We Do For Love.............................*10cc* ... Mercury 73875
❽	17	6	Hotel California ....*Eagles* ... Asylum 45386
❾	12	10	I've Got Love On My Mind..........................*Natalie Cole* ... Capitol 4360
⑩	11	8	**Maybe I'm Amazed**.................................*Wings* ... Capitol 4385

★ HIGHEST DEBUT ★ POS 74	★ BIGGEST MOVER ★ 89 to 70
Sir Duke ....*Stevie Wonder*	Feels Like The First Time................*Foreigner*

TW	LW	WK	Billboard		APRIL 9, 1977		HOT 100.
❶	2	18	**Dancing Queen**...*Abba* ... Atlantic 3372
❷	3	11	Don't Give Up On Us...............................*David Soul* ... Private Stock 45129
❸	4	17	Don't Leave Me This Way ....*Thelma Houston* ... Tamla 54278
④	1	12	Rich Girl ....*Daryl Hall & John Oates* ... RCA 10860
❺	6	9	Southern Nights ....*Glen Campbell* ... Capitol 4376
❻	7	14	The Things We Do For Love.............................*10cc* ... Mercury 73875
❼	8	7	Hotel California ....*Eagles* ... Asylum 45386
❽	9	11	I've Got Love On My Mind..........................*Natalie Cole* ... Capitol 4360
⑨	5	18	Love Theme From "A Star Is Born" (Evergreen)......... *Barbra Streisand* ... Columbia 10450
⑩	12	11	So In To You ....*Atlanta Rhythm Section* ... Polydor 14373

★ HIGHEST DEBUT ★ POS 82	★ BIGGEST MOVER ★ 74 to 48
Slow Dancin' Don't Turn Me On.......*Addrisi Bros.*	Sir Duke ....*Stevie Wonder*

TW	LW	WK	Billboard		APRIL 16, 1977		HOT 100.
❶	2	12	**Don't Give Up On Us** ....*David Soul* ... Private Stock 45129
❷	3	18	Don't Leave Me This Way ....*Thelma Houston* ... Tamla 54278
❸	5	10	Southern Nights ....*Glen Campbell* ... Capitol 4376
④	7	8	Hotel California ....*Eagles* ... Asylum 45386
⑤	6	15	**The Things We Do For Love**............................*10cc* ... Mercury 73875
⑥	1	19	Dancing Queen...*Abba* ... Atlantic 3372
❼	8	12	I've Got Love On My Mind..........................*Natalie Cole* ... Capitol 4360
⑧	9	19	Love Theme From "A Star Is Born" (Evergreen)......... *Barbra Streisand* ... Columbia 10450
❾	10	12	So In To You ....*Atlanta Rhythm Section* ... Polydor 14373
⑩	4	13	Rich Girl ....*Daryl Hall & John Oates* ... RCA 10860

★ HIGHEST DEBUT ★ POS 50	★ BIGGEST MOVER ★ 90 to 63
Got To Give It Up (Pt. I)................*Marvin Gaye*	Show You The Way To Go ....*The Jacksons*

Billboard — APRIL 23, 1977 — HOT 100

TW	LW	WK	Title	Artist ... Label
1	2	19	**Don't Leave Me This Way**	Thelma Houston ... Tamla 54278
2	3	11	Southern Nights	Glen Campbell ... Capitol 4376
3	4	9	Hotel California	Eagles ... Asylum 45386
4	1	13	Don't Give Up On Us	David Soul ... Private Stock 45129
5	5	16	**The Things We Do For Love**	10cc ... Mercury 73875
6	7	13	I've Got Love On My Mind	Natalie Cole ... Capitol 4360
7	8	20	Love Theme From "A Star Is Born" (Evergreen)	Barbra Streisand ... Columbia 10450
8	9	13	So In To You	Atlanta Rhythm Section ... Polydor 14373
9	13	9	When I Need You	Leo Sayer ... Warner 8332
10	11	13	Right Time Of The Night	Jennifer Warnes ... Arista 0223

★ **HIGHEST DEBUT** ★ POS 73
High School Dance .... The Sylvers

★ **BIGGEST MOVER** ★ 77 to 56
Dreams .... Fleetwood Mac

Billboard — APRIL 30, 1977 — HOT 100

TW	LW	WK	Title	Artist ... Label
1	2	12	**Southern Nights**	Glen Campbell ... Capitol 4376
2	3	10	Hotel California	Eagles ... Asylum 45386
3	1	20	Don't Leave Me This Way	Thelma Houston ... Tamla 54278
4	9	10	When I Need You	Leo Sayer ... Warner 8332
5	6	14	**I've Got Love On My Mind**	Natalie Cole ... Capitol 4360
6	4	14	Don't Give Up On Us	David Soul ... Private Stock 45129
7	8	14	**So In To You**	Atlanta Rhythm Section ... Polydor 14373
8	10	14	Right Time Of The Night	Jennifer Warnes ... Arista 0223
9	19	5	Sir Duke	Stevie Wonder ... Tamla 54281
10	11	11	**Tryin' To Love Two**	William Bell ... Mercury 73839

★ **HIGHEST DEBUT** ★ POS 71
Jet Airliner .... The Steve Miller Band

★ **BIGGEST MOVER** ★ 84 to 58
Gonna Fly Now (Theme From "Rocky") .... Bill Conti

Billboard — MAY 7, 1977 — HOT 100

TW	LW	WK	Title	Artist ... Label
1	2	11	**Hotel California**	Eagles ... Asylum 45386
2	4	11	When I Need You	Leo Sayer ... Warner 8332
3	1	13	Southern Nights	Glen Campbell ... Capitol 4376
4	9	6	Sir Duke	Stevie Wonder ... Tamla 54281
5	3	21	Don't Leave Me This Way	Thelma Houston ... Tamla 54278
6	8	15	**Right Time Of The Night**	Jennifer Warnes ... Arista 0223
7	7	15	**So In To You**	Atlanta Rhythm Section ... Polydor 14373
8	5	15	I've Got Love On My Mind	Natalie Cole ... Capitol 4360
9	12	12	Couldn't Get It Right	Climax Blues Band ... Sire 736
10	11	11	**I Wanna Get Next To You**	Rose Royce ... MCA 40662

★ **HIGHEST DEBUT** ★ POS 73
Back Together Again .... Daryl Hall & John Oates

★ **BIGGEST MOVER** ★ 58 to 29
Gonna Fly Now (Theme From "Rocky") .... Bill Conti

TW	LW	WK	Billboard.		MAY 14, 1977		HOT 100.
❶	2	12	When I Need You		Leo Sayer . . . Warner 8332		
❷	4	7	Sir Duke		Stevie Wonder . . . Tamla 54281		
③	1	12	Hotel California		Eagles . . . Asylum 45386		
④	3	14	Southern Nights		Glen Campbell . . . Capitol 4376		
❺	9	13	Couldn't Get It Right		Climax Blues Band . . . Sire 736		
⑥	6	16	Right Time Of The Night		Jennifer Warnes . . . Arista 0223		
⑦	7	16	So In To You		Atlanta Rhythm Section . . . Polydor 14373		
❽	11	12	I'm Your Boogie Man		KC & The Sunshine Band . . . T.K. 1022		
❾	14	5	Got To Give It Up (Pt. I)		Marvin Gaye . . . Tamla 54280		
⑩	10	12	I Wanna Get Next To You		Rose Royce . . . MCA 40662		

★ **HIGHEST DEBUT** ★ POS 73
Life In The Fast Lane............................*Eagles*

★ **BIGGEST MOVER** ★ 88 to 66
Looks Like We Made It................*Barry Manilow*

TW	LW	WK	Billboard.		MAY 21, 1977		HOT 100.
❶	2	8	Sir Duke		Stevie Wonder . . . Tamla 54281		
②	1	13	When I Need You		Leo Sayer . . . Warner 8332		
❸	5	14	Couldn't Get It Right		Climax Blues Band . . . Sire 736		
❹	8	13	I'm Your Boogie Man		KC & The Sunshine Band . . . T.K. 1022		
❺	9	6	Got To Give It Up (Pt. I)		Marvin Gaye . . . Tamla 54280		
❻	14	6	Dreams		Fleetwood Mac . . . Warner 8371		
❼	21	5	Gonna Fly Now (Theme From "Rocky")		Bill Conti . . . United Artists 940		
⑧	3	13	Hotel California		Eagles . . . Asylum 45386		
⑨	4	15	Southern Nights		Glen Campbell . . . Capitol 4376		
⑩	12	9	Lucille		Kenny Rogers . . . United Artists 929		

★ **HIGHEST DEBUT** ★ POS 52
My Heart Belongs To Me............*Barbra Streisand*

★ **BIGGEST MOVER** ★ 73 to 53
Life In The Fast Lane...............................*Eagles*

TW	LW	WK	Billboard.		MAY 28, 1977		HOT 100.
❶	1	9	Sir Duke		Stevie Wonder . . . Tamla 54281		
②	2	14	When I Need You		Leo Sayer . . . Warner 8332		
③	4	14	I'm Your Boogie Man		KC & The Sunshine Band . . . T.K. 1022		
❹	6	7	Dreams		Fleetwood Mac . . . Warner 8371		
❺	5	7	Got To Give It Up (Pt. I)		Marvin Gaye . . . Tamla 54280		
❻	7	6	Gonna Fly Now (Theme From "Rocky")		Bill Conti . . . United Artists 940		
⑦	3	15	Couldn't Get It Right		Climax Blues Band . . . Sire 736		
❽	10	10	Lucille		Kenny Rogers . . . United Artists 929		
❾	12	11	Lonely Boy		Andrew Gold . . . Asylum 45384		
⑩	14	10	Feels Like The First Time		Foreigner . . . Atlantic 3394		

★ **HIGHEST DEBUT** ★ POS 68
I'm In You...................................*Peter Frampton*

★ **BIGGEST MOVER** ★ 53 to 28
Life In The Fast Lane...............................*Eagles*

Billboard — JUNE 4, 1977 — HOT 100

TW	LW	WK	Title	Artist	Label
❶	1	10	**Sir Duke**	Stevie Wonder	Tamla 54281
❷	3	15	I'm Your Boogie Man	KC & The Sunshine Band	T.K. 1022
❸	4	8	Dreams	Fleetwood Mac	Warner 8371
❹	5	8	Got To Give It Up (Pt. I)	Marvin Gaye	Tamla 54280
❺	6	7	Gonna Fly Now (Theme From "Rocky")	Bill Conti	United Artists 940
❻	7	16	Couldn't Get It Right	Climax Blues Band	Sire 736
❼	8	11	Lucille	Kenny Rogers	United Artists 929
❽	9	12	Lonely Boy	Andrew Gold	Asylum 45384
❾	10	11	Feels Like The First Time	Foreigner	Atlantic 3394
❿	2	15	When I Need You	Leo Sayer	Warner 8332

★ **HIGHEST DEBUT** ★ POS 69
You Made Me Believe In Magic ....Bay City Rollers

★ **BIGGEST MOVER** ★ 68 to 49
I'm In You ....Peter Frampton

Billboard — JUNE 11, 1977 — HOT 100

TW	LW	WK	Title	Artist	Label
❶	2	16	**I'm Your Boogie Man**	KC & The Sunshine Band	T.K. 1022
❷	3	9	Dreams	Fleetwood Mac	Warner 8371
❸	4	9	Got To Give It Up (Pt. I)	Marvin Gaye	Tamla 54280
❹	5	8	Gonna Fly Now (Theme From "Rocky")	Bill Conti	United Artists 940
❺	9	12	Feels Like The First Time	Foreigner	Atlantic 3394
❻	7	12	Lucille	Kenny Rogers	United Artists 929
❼	8	13	**Lonely Boy**	Andrew Gold	Asylum 45384
❽	11	11	Undercover Angel	Alan O'Day	Pacific 001
❾	1	11	Sir Duke	Stevie Wonder	Tamla 54281
❿	6	17	Couldn't Get It Right	Climax Blues Band	Sire 736

★ **HIGHEST DEBUT** ★ POS 80
Come In From The Rain ....Captain & Tennille

★ **BIGGEST MOVER** ★ 49 to 31
I'm In You ....Peter Frampton

Billboard — JUNE 18, 1977 — HOT 100

TW	LW	WK	Title	Artist	Label
❶	2	10	**Dreams**	Fleetwood Mac	Warner 8371
❷	3	10	Got To Give It Up (Pt. I)	Marvin Gaye	Tamla 54280
❸	4	9	Gonna Fly Now (Theme From "Rocky")	Bill Conti	United Artists 940
❹	5	13	**Feels Like The First Time**	Foreigner	Atlantic 3394
❺	6	13	**Lucille**	Kenny Rogers	United Artists 929
❻	8	12	Undercover Angel	Alan O'Day	Pacific 001
❼	7	14	**Lonely Boy**	Andrew Gold	Asylum 45384
❽	1	17	I'm Your Boogie Man	KC & The Sunshine Band	T.K. 1022
❾	9	12	Sir Duke	Stevie Wonder	Tamla 54281
❿	11	18	Angel In Your Arms	Hot	Big Tree 16085

★ **HIGHEST DEBUT** ★ POS 80
Handy Man ....James Taylor

★ **BIGGEST MOVER** ★ 64 to 47
Easy ....Commodores

TW	LW	WK	Billboard.	JUNE 25, 1977	HOT 100.
①	2	11	**Got To Give It Up (Pt. I)** ....*Marvin Gaye* . . . Tamla 54280
②	3	10	**Gonna Fly Now (Theme From "Rocky")**......*Bill Conti* . . . United Artists 940
③	6	13	**Undercover Angel**..*Alan O'Day* . . . Pacific 001
④	4	14	**Feels Like The First Time** ....*Foreigner* . . . Atlantic 3394
⑤	5	14	**Lucille** ....*Kenny Rogers* . . . United Artists 929
⑥	1	11	**Dreams** ....*Fleetwood Mac* . . . Warner 8371
⑦	7	15	**Lonely Boy** ....*Andrew Gold* . . . Asylum 45384
⑧	16	7	**Da Doo Ron Ron** ....*Shaun Cassidy* . . . Warner 8365
⑨	10	19	**Angel In Your Arms** ....*Hot* . . . Big Tree 16085
⑩	11	9	**Jet Airliner**.............................*The Steve Miller Band* . . . Capitol 4424

★ *HIGHEST DEBUT* ★ POS 70	★ *BIGGEST MOVER* ★ 70 to 50
Way Down.........................*Elvis Presley*	Best Of My Love ....*Emotions*

TW	LW	WK	Billboard.	JULY 2, 1977	HOT 100.
①	2	11	**Gonna Fly Now (Theme From "Rocky")**.........................*Bill Conti* . . . United Artists 940
②	3	14	**Undercover Angel**..*Alan O'Day* . . . Pacific 001
③	1	12	**Got To Give It Up (Pt. I)** ....*Marvin Gaye* . . . Tamla 54280
④	8	8	**Da Doo Ron Ron** ....*Shaun Cassidy* . . . Warner 8365
⑤	13	9	**Looks Like We Made It** ....*Barry Manilow* . . . Arista 0244
⑥	6	12	**Dreams** ....*Fleetwood Mac* . . . Warner 8371
⑦	15	11	**I Just Want To Be Your Everything**......................*Andy Gibb* . . . RSO 872
⑧	9	20	**Angel In Your Arms** ....*Hot* . . . Big Tree 16085
⑨	10	10	**Jet Airliner**.............................*The Steve Miller Band* . . . Capitol 4424
⑩	12	14	**Margaritaville**...............................*Jimmy Buffett* . . . ABC 12254

★ *HIGHEST DEBUT* ★ POS 71	★ *BIGGEST MOVER* ★ 70 to 49
Strawberry Letter 23...........*The Brothers Johnson*	Way Down.......................................*Elvis Presley*

TW	LW	WK	Billboard.	JULY 9, 1977	HOT 100.
①	2	15	**Undercover Angel**..*Alan O'Day* . . . Pacific 001
②	4	9	**Da Doo Ron Ron** ....*Shaun Cassidy* . . . Warner 8365
③	5	10	**Looks Like We Made It** ....*Barry Manilow* . . . Arista 0244
④	1	12	**Gonna Fly Now (Theme From "Rocky")**......*Bill Conti* . . . United Artists 940
⑤	7	12	**I Just Want To Be Your Everything**......................*Andy Gibb* . . . RSO 872
⑥	3	13	**Got To Give It Up (Pt. I)** ....*Marvin Gaye* . . . Tamla 54280
⑦	8	21	**Angel In Your Arms** ....*Hot* . . . Big Tree 16085
⑧	9	11	**Jet Airliner**.............................*The Steve Miller Band* . . . Capitol 4424
⑨	10	15	**Margaritaville**...............................*Jimmy Buffett* . . . ABC 12254
⑩	12	8	**My Heart Belongs To Me**....................*Barbra Streisand* . . . Columbia 10555

★ *HIGHEST DEBUT* ★ POS 72	★ *BIGGEST MOVER* ★ 30 to 14
Don't Stop.........................*Fleetwood Mac*	Best Of My Love ....*Emotions*

TW	LW	WK	Billboard	JULY 16, 1977	HOT 100
❶	2	10	**Da Doo Ron Ron** ....*Shaun Cassidy* . . . Warner 8365
❷	3	11	**Looks Like We Made It** ....*Barry Manilow* . . . Arista 0244
③	1	16	Undercover Angel...*Alan O'Day* . . . Pacific 001
❹	5	13	I Just Want To Be Your Everything......................*Andy Gibb* . . . RSO 872
❺	11	8	I'm In You...*Peter Frampton* . . . A&M 1941
❻	7	22	**Angel In Your Arms** ....*Hot* . . . Big Tree 16085
❼	10	9	My Heart Belongs To Me....................*Barbra Streisand* . . . Columbia 10555
⑧	8	12	**Jet Airliner**....................................*The Steve Miller Band* . . . Capitol 4424
⑨	9	16	Margaritaville...*Jimmy Buffett* . . . ABC 12254
⑩	12	13	Do You Wanna Make Love...............*Peter McCann* . . . 20th Century 2335

★ HIGHEST DEBUT ★ POS 77	★ BIGGEST MOVER ★ 77 to 55
Christine Sixteen.......................................*Kiss*	How Much Love ....*Leo Sayer*

TW	LW	WK	Billboard	JULY 23, 1977	HOT 100
❶	2	12	**Looks Like We Made It** ....*Barry Manilow* . . . Arista 0244
❷	4	14	**I Just Want To Be Your Everything**......................*Andy Gibb* . . . RSO 872
③	1	11	Da Doo Ron Ron ....*Shaun Cassidy* . . . Warner 8365
❹	5	9	I'm In You...*Peter Frampton* . . . A&M 1941
❺	7	10	My Heart Belongs To Me....................*Barbra Streisand* . . . Columbia 10555
⑥	6	23	**Angel In Your Arms** ....*Hot* . . . Big Tree 16085
⑦	3	17	Undercover Angel...*Alan O'Day* . . . Pacific 001
❽	9	17	**Margaritaville** ....*Jimmy Buffett* . . . ABC 12254
❾	10	14	Do You Wanna Make Love...............*Peter McCann* . . . 20th Century 2335
⑩	12	7	Best Of My Love..*Emotions* . . . Columbia 10544

★ HIGHEST DEBUT ★ POS 76	★ BIGGEST MOVER ★ 60 to 31
Edge Of The Universe ....*Bee Gees*	Don't Stop..................................*Fleetwood Mac*

TW	LW	WK	Billboard	JULY 30, 1977	HOT 100
❶	2	15	**I Just Want To Be Your Everything** ....*Andy Gibb* . . . RSO 872
❷	4	10	**I'm In You** ....*Peter Frampton* . . . A&M 1941
③	1	13	Looks Like We Made It ....*Barry Manilow* . . . Arista 0244
❹	5	11	**My Heart Belongs To Me**................*Barbra Streisand* . . . Columbia 10555
❺	3	12	Da Doo Ron Ron ....*Shaun Cassidy* . . . Warner 8365
❻	10	8	Best Of My Love..*Emotions* . . . Columbia 10544
❼	9	15	Do You Wanna Make Love...............*Peter McCann* . . . 20th Century 2335
⑧	8	18	**Margaritaville** ....*Jimmy Buffett* . . . ABC 12254
❾	11	13	(Your Love Has Lifted Me) Higher And Higher.................*Rita Coolidge* . . . A&M 1922
⑩	12	16	Whatcha Gonna Do? ....*Pablo Cruise* . . . A&M 1920

★ HIGHEST DEBUT ★ POS 77	★ BIGGEST MOVER ★ 81 to 60
Little Darling (I Need You) ....*The Doobie Brothers*	Cold As Ice ....*Foreigner*

Billboard · AUGUST 6, 1977 · HOT 100

TW	LW	WK		
1	1	16	**I Just Want To Be Your Everything**	*Andy Gibb* . . . RSO 872
2	2	11	**I'm In You**	*Peter Frampton* . . . A&M 1941
3	6	9	**Best Of My Love**	*Emotions* . . . Columbia 10544
4	4	12	**My Heart Belongs To Me**	*Barbra Streisand* . . . Columbia 10555
5	7	16	**Do You Wanna Make Love**	*Peter McCann* . . . 20th Century 2335
6	5	13	**Da Doo Ron Ron**	*Shaun Cassidy* . . . Warner 8365
7	9	14	**(Your Love Has Lifted Me) Higher And Higher**	*Rita Coolidge* . . . A&M 1922
8	13	10	**Easy**	*Commodores* . . . Motown 1418
9	10	17	**Whatcha Gonna Do?**	*Pablo Cruise* . . . A&M 1920
10	11	15	**You And Me**	*Alice Cooper* . . . Warner 8349

★ HIGHEST DEBUT ★ POS 71	★ BIGGEST MOVER ★ 66 to 52
Star Wars Theme/Cantina Band ....*Meco*	Hard Rock Cafe..........................*Carole King*

Billboard · AUGUST 13, 1977 · HOT 100

TW	LW	WK		
1	1	17	**I Just Want To Be Your Everything**	*Andy Gibb* . . . RSO 872
2	2	12	**I'm In You**	*Peter Frampton* . . . A&M 1941
3	3	10	**Best Of My Love**	*Emotions* . . . Columbia 10544
4	7	15	**(Your Love Has Lifted Me) Higher And Higher**	*Rita Coolidge* . . . A&M 1922
5	5	17	**Do You Wanna Make Love**	*Peter McCann* . . . 20th Century 2335
6	4	13	**My Heart Belongs To Me**	*Barbra Streisand* . . . Columbia 10555
7	8	11	**Easy**	*Commodores* . . . Motown 1418
8	9	18	**Whatcha Gonna Do?**	*Pablo Cruise* . . . A&M 1920
9	10	16	**You And Me**	*Alice Cooper* . . . Warner 8349
10	11	11	**You Made Me Believe In Magic**	*Bay City Rollers* . . . Arista 0256

★ HIGHEST DEBUT ★ POS 70	★ BIGGEST MOVER ★ 89 to 54
Cat Scratch Fever...........................*Ted Nugent*	The Greatest Love Of All ....*George Benson*

Billboard · AUGUST 20, 1977 · HOT 100

TW	LW	WK		
1	3	11	**Best Of My Love**	*Emotions* . . . Columbia 10544
2	1	18	**I Just Want To Be Your Everything**	*Andy Gibb* . . . RSO 872
3	4	16	**(Your Love Has Lifted Me) Higher And Higher**	*Rita Coolidge* . . . A&M 1922
4	2	13	**I'm In You**	*Peter Frampton* . . . A&M 1941
5	7	12	**Easy**	*Commodores* . . . Motown 1418
6	8	19	**Whatcha Gonna Do?**	*Pablo Cruise* . . . A&M 1920
7	5	18	**Do You Wanna Make Love**	*Peter McCann* . . . 20th Century 2335
8	11	13	**Just A Song Before I Go** ....*Crosby, Stills & Nash* . . . Atlantic 3401	
9	9	17	**You And Me**	*Alice Cooper* . . . Warner 8349
10	10	12	**You Made Me Believe In Magic**	*Bay City Rollers* . . . Arista 0256

★ HIGHEST DEBUT ★ POS 78	★ BIGGEST MOVER ★ 62 to 49
I Wouldn't Want To Be Like You .....*Alan Parsons*	Jungle Love ....*The Steve Miller Band*

Billboard ⊙ AUGUST 27, 1977 ⊙ HOT 100.

TW	LW	WK		
①	1	12	**Best Of My Love**..*Emotions* . . . Columbia 10544	
②	2	19	I Just Want To Be Your Everything.....................*Andy Gibb* . . . RSO 872	
③	3	17	(Your Love Has Lifted Me) Higher And Higher.................*Rita Coolidge* . . . A&M 1922	
④	5	13	**Easy**...*Commodores* . . . Motown 1418	
⑤	12	11	Handy Man.....................................*James Taylor* . . . Columbia 10557	
⑥	6	20	**Whatcha Gonna Do?**....................................*Pablo Cruise* . . . A&M 1920	
⑦	8	14	**Just A Song Before I Go** ....*Crosby, Stills & Nash* . . . Atlantic 3401	
⑧	13	8	Float On ....*The Floaters* . . . ABC 12284	
⑨	11	8	Don't Stop...*Fleetwood Mac* . . . Warner 8413	
⑩	23	9	Strawberry Letter 23...........................*The Brothers Johnson* . . . A&M 1949	

★ HIGHEST DEBUT ★ POS 72	★ BIGGEST MOVER ★ 23 to 10
Brick House..............................*Commodores*	Strawberry Letter 23...........*The Brothers Johnson*

Billboard ⊙ SEPTEMBER 3, 1977 ⊙ HOT 100.

TW	LW	WK		
①	1	13	**Best Of My Love**..*Emotions* . . . Columbia 10544	
②	2	20	I Just Want To Be Your Everything.....................*Andy Gibb* . . . RSO 872	
③	3	18	(Your Love Has Lifted Me) Higher And Higher.................*Rita Coolidge* . . . A&M 1922	
④	4	14	**Easy**...*Commodores* . . . Motown 1418	
⑤	5	12	Handy Man.....................................*James Taylor* . . . Columbia 10557	
⑥	8	9	Float On ....*The Floaters* . . . ABC 12284	
⑦	7	15	**Just A Song Before I Go** ....*Crosby, Stills & Nash* . . . Atlantic 3401	
⑧	9	9	Don't Stop...*Fleetwood Mac* . . . Warner 8413	
⑨	10	10	Strawberry Letter 23...........................*The Brothers Johnson* . . . A&M 1949	
⑩	13	13	Telephone Line.....................*Electric Light Orchestra* . . . United Artists 1000	

★ HIGHEST DEBUT ★ POS 71	★ BIGGEST MOVER ★ 75 to 49
You Light Up My Life ....*Debby Boone*	Signed, Sealed, Delivered (I'm Yours) ....*Peter Frampton*

Billboard ⊙ SEPTEMBER 10, 1977 ⊙ HOT 100.

TW	LW	WK		
①	1	14	**Best Of My Love**..*Emotions* . . . Columbia 10544	
②	3	19	**(Your Love Has Lifted Me) Higher And Higher** ....*Rita Coolidge* . . . A&M 1922	
③	2	21	I Just Want To Be Your Everything.....................*Andy Gibb* . . . RSO 872	
④	5	13	**Handy Man**.....................................*James Taylor* . . . Columbia 10557	
⑤	6	10	**Float On** ....*The Floaters* . . . ABC 12284	
⑥	8	10	**Don't Stop**...*Fleetwood Mac* . . . Warner 8413	
⑦	4	15	Easy...*Commodores* . . . Motown 1418	
⑧	9	11	Strawberry Letter 23...........................*The Brothers Johnson* . . . A&M 1949	
⑨	10	14	Telephone Line.....................*Electric Light Orchestra* . . . United Artists 1000	
⑩	12	13	Smoke From A Distant Fire.......................*The Sanford/Townsend Band* . . . Warner 8370	

★ HIGHEST DEBUT ★ POS 78	★ BIGGEST MOVER ★ 73 to 54
I Just Want To Make Love To You..........*Foghat*	She Did It ....*Eric Carmen*

Billboard — SEPTEMBER 17, 1977 — HOT 100

TW	LW	WK	Title / Artist / Label
1	3	22	I Just Want To Be Your Everything ....*Andy Gibb* ... RSO 872
2	5	11	Float On ....*The Floaters* ... ABC 12284
③	1	15	Best Of My Love..*Emotions* ... Columbia 10544
④	4	14	Handy Man...*James Taylor* ... Columbia 10557
⑤	6	11	Don't Stop...*Fleetwood Mac* ... Warner 8413
⑥	15	8	Keep It Comin' Love.....................*KC & The Sunshine Band* ... T.K. 1023
⑦	8	12	Strawberry Letter 23..........................*The Brothers Johnson* ... A&M 1949
⑧	9	15	Telephone Line....................*Electric Light Orchestra* ... United Artists 1000
⑨	10	14	Smoke From A Distant Fire..................*The Sanford/Townsend Band* ... Warner 8370
⑩	11	11	Star Wars (Main Title) ....*The London Symphony Orchestra* ... 20th Century 2345

★ HIGHEST DEBUT ★ POS 76	★ BIGGEST MOVER ★ 89 to 40
Do Ya Wanna Get Funky With Me ....*Peter Brown*	The King Is Gone....................*Ronnie McDowell*

Billboard — SEPTEMBER 24, 1977 — HOT 100

TW	LW	WK	Title / Artist / Label
1	3	16	Best Of My Love..*Emotions* ... Columbia 10544
②	2	12	Float On ....*The Floaters* ... ABC 12284
③	5	12	Don't Stop...*Fleetwood Mac* ... Warner 8413
④	6	9	Keep It Comin' Love.....................*KC & The Sunshine Band* ... T.K. 1023
⑤	7	13	Strawberry Letter 23..........................*The Brothers Johnson* ... A&M 1949
⑥	1	23	I Just Want To Be Your Everything......................*Andy Gibb* ... RSO 872
⑦	8	16	Telephone Line ....*Electric Light Orchestra* ... United Artists 1000
⑧	13	8	Star Wars Theme/Cantina Band..........................*Meco* ... Millennium 604
⑨	14	10	That's Rock 'N' Roll ....*Shaun Cassidy* ... Warner 8423
⑩	12	10	Cold As Ice ....*Foreigner* ... Atlantic 3410

★ HIGHEST DEBUT ★ POS 70	★ BIGGEST MOVER ★ 76 to 53
Baby, What A Big Surprise....................*Chicago*	Do Ya Wanna Get Funky With Me ....*Peter Brown*

Billboard — OCTOBER 1, 1977 — HOT 100

TW	LW	WK	Title / Artist / Label
1	8	9	Star Wars Theme/Cantina Band...................*Meco* ... Millennium 604
②	4	10	Keep It Comin' Love ....*KC & The Sunshine Band* ... T.K. 1023
③	3	13	Don't Stop...*Fleetwood Mac* ... Warner 8413
④	1	17	Best Of My Love..*Emotions* ... Columbia 10544
⑤	5	14	Strawberry Letter 23......................*The Brothers Johnson* ... A&M 1949
⑥	12	11	Nobody Does It Better ....*Carly Simon* ... Elektra 45413
⑦	7	17	Telephone Line ....*Electric Light Orchestra* ... United Artists 1000
⑧	9	11	That's Rock 'N' Roll ....*Shaun Cassidy* ... Warner 8423
⑨	10	11	Cold As Ice ....*Foreigner* ... Atlantic 3410
⑩	6	24	I Just Want To Be Your Everything......................*Andy Gibb* ... RSO 872

★ HIGHEST DEBUT ★ POS 80	★ BIGGEST MOVER ★ 83 to 49
Could Heaven Ever Be Like This ....*Idris Muhammad*	How Deep Is Your Love ....*Bee Gees*

Billboard — OCTOBER 8, 1977 — HOT 100.

TW	LW	WK			
1	1	10	**Star Wars Theme/Cantina Band**	*Meco*	Millennium 604
2	2	11	**Keep It Comin' Love**	*KC & The Sunshine Band*	T.K. 1023
3	15	6	**You Light Up My Life**	*Debby Boone*	Warner 8455
4	6	12	**Nobody Does It Better**	*Carly Simon*	Elektra 45413
5	8	12	**That's Rock 'N' Roll**	*Shaun Cassidy*	Warner 8423
6	4	18	**Best Of My Love**	*Emotions*	Columbia 10544
7	11	12	**Boogie Nights**	*Heatwave*	Epic 50370
8	9	12	**Cold As Ice**	*Foreigner*	Atlantic 3410
9	16	7	**Brick House**	*Commodores*	Motown 1425
10	10	25	**I Just Want To Be Your Everything**	*Andy Gibb*	RSO 872

★ HIGHEST DEBUT ★ POS 71	★ BIGGEST MOVER ★ 82 to 66
Calling Occupants Of Interplanetary Craft ....*Carpenters*	Daybreak ....*Barry Manilow*

Billboard — OCTOBER 15, 1977 — HOT 100.

TW	LW	WK			
1	3	7	**You Light Up My Life**	*Debby Boone*	Warner 8455
2	2	12	**Keep It Comin' Love**	*KC & The Sunshine Band*	T.K. 1023
3	4	13	**Nobody Does It Better**	*Carly Simon*	Elektra 45413
4	5	13	**That's Rock 'N' Roll**	*Shaun Cassidy*	Warner 8423
5	1	11	**Star Wars Theme/Cantina Band**	*Meco*	Millennium 604
6	7	13	**Boogie Nights**	*Heatwave*	Epic 50370
7	8	13	**Cold As Ice**	*Foreigner*	Atlantic 3410
8	9	8	**Brick House**	*Commodores*	Motown 1425
9	13	11	**I Feel Love**	*Donna Summer*	Casablanca 884
10	10	26	**I Just Want To Be Your Everything**	*Andy Gibb*	RSO 872

★ HIGHEST DEBUT ★ POS 73	★ BIGGEST MOVER ★ 66 to 45
You Make Loving Fun ....*Fleetwood Mac*	Daybreak ....*Barry Manilow*

Billboard — OCTOBER 22, 1977 — HOT 100.

TW	LW	WK			
1	1	8	**You Light Up My Life**	*Debby Boone*	Warner 8455
2	3	14	**Nobody Does It Better**	*Carly Simon*	Elektra 45413
3	4	14	**That's Rock 'N' Roll**	*Shaun Cassidy*	Warner 8423
4	2	13	**Keep It Comin' Love**	*KC & The Sunshine Band*	T.K. 1023
5	6	14	**Boogie Nights**	*Heatwave*	Epic 50370
6	7	14	**Cold As Ice**	*Foreigner*	Atlantic 3410
7	8	9	**Brick House**	*Commodores*	Motown 1425
8	9	12	**I Feel Love**	*Donna Summer*	Casablanca 884
9	5	12	**Star Wars Theme/Cantina Band**	*Meco*	Millennium 604
10	11	18	**Swayin' To The Music (Slow Dancin')**	*Johnny Rivers*	Big Tree 16094

★ HIGHEST DEBUT ★ POS 79	★ BIGGEST MOVER ★ 88 to 64
Draw The Line ....*Aerosmith*	(Every Time I Turn Around) Back In Love Again ....*L.T.D.*

Billboard — OCTOBER 29, 1977 — HOT 100

TW	LW	WK		
1	1	9	You Light Up My Life	Debby Boone ... Warner 8455
2	2	15	Nobody Does It Better	Carly Simon ... Elektra 45413
3	3	15	That's Rock 'N' Roll	Shaun Cassidy ... Warner 8423
4	5	15	Boogie Nights	Heatwave ... Epic 50370
5	4	14	Keep It Comin' Love	KC & The Sunshine Band ... T.K. 1023
6	7	10	Brick House	Commodores ... Motown 1425
7	8	13	I Feel Love	Donna Summer ... Casablanca 884
8	11	11	It's Ecstasy When You Lay Down Next To Me	Barry White ... 20th Century 2350
9	9	13	Star Wars Theme/Cantina Band	Meco ... Millennium 604
10	12	12	Don't It Make My Brown Eyes Blue	Crystal Gayle ... United Artists 1016

★ **HIGHEST DEBUT** ★ POS 80
You're In My Heart (The Final Acclaim).......Rod Stewart

★ **BIGGEST MOVER** ★ 58 to 32
Isn't It Time ....The Babys

Billboard — NOVEMBER 5, 1977 — HOT 100

TW	LW	WK		
1	1	10	You Light Up My Life	Debby Boone ... Warner 8455
2	2	16	Nobody Does It Better	Carly Simon ... Elektra 45413
3	4	16	Boogie Nights	Heatwave ... Epic 50370
4	3	16	That's Rock 'N' Roll	Shaun Cassidy ... Warner 8423
5	6	11	Brick House	Commodores ... Motown 1425
6	8	12	It's Ecstasy When You Lay Down Next To Me	Barry White ... 20th Century 2350
7	7	14	I Feel Love	Donna Summer ... Casablanca 884
8	10	13	Don't It Make My Brown Eyes Blue	Crystal Gayle ... United Artists 1016
9	11	7	Baby, What A Big Surprise	Chicago ... Columbia 10620
10	12	12	Heaven On The 7th Floor	Paul Nicholas ... RSO 878

★ **HIGHEST DEBUT** ★ POS 81
As................................Stevie Wonder

★ **BIGGEST MOVER** ★ 75 to 62
We Are The Champions.........................Queen

Billboard — NOVEMBER 12, 1977 — HOT 100

TW	LW	WK		
1	1	11	You Light Up My Life	Debby Boone ... Warner 8455
2	3	17	Boogie Nights	Heatwave ... Epic 50370
3	2	17	Nobody Does It Better	Carly Simon ... Elektra 45413
4	6	13	It's Ecstasy When You Lay Down Next To Me	Barry White ... 20th Century 2350
5	8	14	Don't It Make My Brown Eyes Blue	Crystal Gayle ... United Artists 1016
6	7	15	I Feel Love	Donna Summer ... Casablanca 884
7	9	8	Baby, What A Big Surprise	Chicago ... Columbia 10620
8	10	13	Heaven On The 7th Floor	Paul Nicholas ... RSO 878
9	11	8	How Deep Is Your Love	Bee Gees ... RSO 882
10	13	9	We're All Alone	Rita Coolidge ... A&M 1965

★ **HIGHEST DEBUT** ★ POS 75
My Way ....Elvis Presley

★ **BIGGEST MOVER** ★ 82 to 53
Gettin' Ready For Love...................Diana Ross

'77

TW	LW	WK	Billboard	NOVEMBER 19, 1977	HOT 100
①	1	12	You Light Up My Life	Debby Boone	Warner 8455
②	2	18	Boogie Nights	Heatwave	Epic 50370
③	5	15	Don't It Make My Brown Eyes Blue	Crystal Gayle	United Artists 1016
④	4	14	It's Ecstasy When You Lay Down Next To Me	Barry White	20th Century 2350
⑤	7	9	Baby, What A Big Surprise	Chicago	Columbia 10620
⑥	9	9	How Deep Is Your Love	Bee Gees	RSO 882
⑦	8	14	Heaven On The 7th Floor	Paul Nicholas	RSO 878
⑧	10	10	We're All Alone	Rita Coolidge	A&M 1965
⑨	11	11	Blue Bayou	Linda Ronstadt	Asylum 45431
⑩	3	18	Nobody Does It Better	Carly Simon	Elektra 45413

★ **HIGHEST DEBUT** ★ POS 81
Turn To Stone...................Electric Light Orchestra

★ **BIGGEST MOVER** ★ 85 to 61
Point Of Know Return..........................Kansas

TW	LW	WK	Billboard	NOVEMBER 26, 1977	HOT 100
①	1	13	You Light Up My Life	Debby Boone	Warner 8455
②	3	16	Don't It Make My Brown Eyes Blue	Crystal Gayle	United Artists 1016
③	6	10	How Deep Is Your Love	Bee Gees	RSO 882
④	2	19	Boogie Nights	Heatwave	Epic 50370
⑤	5	10	Baby, What A Big Surprise	Chicago	Columbia 10620
⑥	7	15	Heaven On The 7th Floor	Paul Nicholas	RSO 878
⑦	8	11	We're All Alone	Rita Coolidge	A&M 1965
⑧	9	12	Blue Bayou	Linda Ronstadt	Asylum 45431
⑨	4	15	It's Ecstasy When You Lay Down Next To Me	Barry White	20th Century 2350
⑩	16	8	It's So Easy	Linda Ronstadt	Asylum 45438

★ **HIGHEST DEBUT** ★ POS 84
Kick It Out...................Heart

★ **BIGGEST MOVER** ★ 64 to 40
Hey Deanie.........................Shaun Cassidy

TW	LW	WK	Billboard	DECEMBER 3, 1977	HOT 100
①	1	14	You Light Up My Life	Debby Boone	Warner 8455
②	2	17	Don't It Make My Brown Eyes Blue	Crystal Gayle	United Artists 1016
③	3	11	How Deep Is Your Love	Bee Gees	RSO 882
④	5	11	Baby, What A Big Surprise	Chicago	Columbia 10620
⑤	8	13	Blue Bayou	Linda Ronstadt	Asylum 45431
⑥	6	16	Heaven On The 7th Floor	Paul Nicholas	RSO 878
⑦	7	12	We're All Alone	Rita Coolidge	A&M 1965
⑧	4	20	Boogie Nights	Heatwave	Epic 50370
⑨	10	9	It's So Easy	Linda Ronstadt	Asylum 45438
⑩	11	8	(Every Time I Turn Around) Back In Love Again	L.T.D.	A&M 1974

★ **HIGHEST DEBUT** ★ POS 70
Desiree...................Neil Diamond

★ **BIGGEST MOVER** ★ 67 to 49
Native New Yorker.........................Odyssey

Billboard 🔵 DECEMBER 10, 1977 🔵 HOT 100.

TW	LW	WK	Title	Artist ... Label
①	1	15	**You Light Up My Life** ....*Debby Boone* ... Warner 8455
②	2	18	**Don't It Make My Brown Eyes Blue** ....*Crystal Gayle* ... United Artists 1016
③	3	12	**How Deep Is Your Love** ....*Bee Gees* ... RSO 882
④	5	14	**Blue Bayou**..*Linda Ronstadt* ... Asylum 45431
⑤	9	10	**It's So Easy** ....*Linda Ronstadt* ... Asylum 45438
⑥	6	17	**Heaven On The 7th Floor** ....*Paul Nicholas* ... RSO 878
⑦	7	13	**We're All Alone** ....*Rita Coolidge* ... A&M 1965
⑧	10	9	**(Every Time I Turn Around) Back In Love Again** ......*L.T.D.* ... A&M 1974
⑨	4	12	**Baby, What A Big Surprise**............................*Chicago* ... Columbia 10620
⑩	11	9	**You Make Loving Fun** ....*Fleetwood Mac* ... Warner 8483

★ **HIGHEST DEBUT** ★ POS 65
Stayin' Alive.........................*Bee Gees*

★ **BIGGEST MOVER** ★ 70 to 47
Desiree ....*Neil Diamond*

Billboard 🔵 DECEMBER 17, 1977 🔵 HOT 100.

TW	LW	WK	Title	Artist ... Label
①	1	16	**You Light Up My Life** ....*Debby Boone* ... Warner 8455
②	3	13	**How Deep Is Your Love** ....*Bee Gees* ... RSO 882
③	4	15	**Blue Bayou** ....*Linda Ronstadt* ... Asylum 45431
④	2	19	**Don't It Make My Brown Eyes Blue** .....*Crystal Gayle* ... United Artists 1016
⑤	5	11	**It's So Easy** ....*Linda Ronstadt* ... Asylum 45438
⑥	8	10	**(Every Time I Turn Around) Back In Love Again** ......*L.T.D.* ... A&M 1974
⑦	7	14	**We're All Alone**...................................*Rita Coolidge* ... A&M 1965
⑧	11	12	**Baby Come Back** ....*Player* ... RSO 879
⑨	10	10	**You Make Loving Fun** ....*Fleetwood Mac* ... Warner 8483
⑩	12	10	**Here You Come Again** ....*Dolly Parton* ... RCA 11123

★ **HIGHEST DEBUT** ★ POS 77
Too Hot Ta Trot.........................*Commodores*

★ **BIGGEST MOVER** ★ 64 to 50
Sometimes When We Touch ....*Dan Hill*

Billboard 🔵 DECEMBER 24, 1977 🔵 HOT 100.

TW	LW	WK	Title	Artist ... Label
①	2	14	**How Deep Is Your Love** ....*Bee Gees* ... RSO 882
②	1	17	**You Light Up My Life** ....*Debby Boone* ... Warner 8455
③	3	16	**Blue Bayou** ....*Linda Ronstadt* ... Asylum 45431
④	6	11	**(Every Time I Turn Around) Back In Love Again** .............*L.T.D.* ... A&M 1974
⑤	5	12	**It's So Easy** ....*Linda Ronstadt* ... Asylum 45438
⑥	8	13	**Baby Come Back** ....*Player* ... RSO 879
⑦	4	20	**Don't It Make My Brown Eyes Blue** .....*Crystal Gayle* ... United Artists 1016
⑧	10	11	**Here You Come Again** ....*Dolly Parton* ... RCA 11123
⑨	11	11	**Sentimental Lady** ....*Bob Welch* ... Capitol 4479
⑩	13	11	**Slip Slidin' Away** ....*Paul Simon* ... Columbia 10630

★ **HIGHEST DEBUT** ★ POS 81
Theme From "Close Encounters Of The Third Kind" ....*John Williams*

★ **BIGGEST MOVER** ★ 77 to 56
Too Hot Ta Trot...........................*Commodores*

Billboard ® JANUARY 7, 1978 HOT 100 ®

TW	LW	WK		
❶	1	16	**How Deep Is Your Love**	*Bee Gees* . . . RSO 882
❷	6	15	Baby Come Back	*Player* . . . RSO 879
③	3	18	**Blue Bayou**	*Linda Ronstadt* . . . Asylum 45431 ←
④	4	13	**(Every Time I Turn Around) Back In Love Again**	*L.T.D.* . . . A&M 1974
⑤	8	13	Here You Come Again	*Dolly Parton* . . . RCA 11123
⑥	2	19	You Light Up My Life	*Debby Boone* . . . Warner 8455
❼	10	13	Slip Slidin' Away	*Paul Simon* . . . Columbia 10630
⑧	9	13	**Sentimental Lady**	*Bob Welch* . . . Capitol 4479
❾	11	11	You're In My Heart (The Final Acclaim)	*Rod Stewart* . . . Warner 8475
❿	15	9	Hey Deanie	*Shaun Cassidy* . . . Warner 8488

★ HIGHEST DEBUT ★ POS 61	★ BIGGEST MOVER ★ 75 to 50
Theme From Close Encounters . . . . *Meco*	Ffun . . . . *Con Funk Shun*

Billboard ® JANUARY 14, 1978 HOT 100 ®

TW	LW	WK		
❶	2	16	**Baby Come Back**	*Player* . . . RSO 879
②	1	17	How Deep Is Your Love	*Bee Gees* . . . RSO 882
❸	5	14	**Here You Come Again**	*Dolly Parton* . . . RCA 11123
④	9	12	**You're In My Heart (The Final Acclaim)**	*Rod Stewart* . . . Warner 8475
⑤	4	14	(Every Time I Turn Around) Back In Love Again	*L.T.D.* . . . A&M 1974
⑥	7	14	Slip Slidin' Away	*Paul Simon* . . . Columbia 10630
❼	10	10	**Hey Deanie**	*Shaun Cassidy* . . . Warner 8488
⑧	8	14	**Sentimental Lady**	*Bob Welch* . . . Capitol 4479
⑨	11	17	Come Sail Away	*Styx* . . . A&M 1977
❿	13	13	We Are The Champions	*Queen* . . . Elektra 45441

★ HIGHEST DEBUT ★ POS 73	★ BIGGEST MOVER ★ 71 to 48
Jack And Jill . . . . *Raydio*	Theme From "Close Encounters Of The Third Kind" . . . . *John Williams*

Billboard ® JANUARY 21, 1978 HOT 100 ®

TW	LW	WK		
❶	1	17	**Baby Come Back**	*Player* . . . RSO 879
②	2	18	How Deep Is Your Love	*Bee Gees* . . . RSO 882
③	3	15	**Here You Come Again**	*Dolly Parton* . . . RCA 11123
④	4	13	**You're In My Heart (The Final Acclaim)**	*Rod Stewart* . . . Warner 8475
❺	15	11	**Short People**	*Randy Newman* . . . Warner 8492
⑥	6	15	Slip Slidin' Away	*Paul Simon* . . . Columbia 10630
⑦	7	11	**Hey Deanie**	*Shaun Cassidy* . . . Warner 8488
❽	10	14	**We Are The Champions**	*Queen* . . . Elektra 45441
⑨	9	18	Come Sail Away	*Styx* . . . A&M 1977
❿	17	7	Stayin' Alive	*Bee Gees* . . . RSO 885

★ HIGHEST DEBUT ★ POS 81	★ BIGGEST MOVER ★ 53 to 37
(What A) Wonderful World . . . . *Art Garfunkel with James Taylor & Paul Simon*	Happy Anniversary . . . . *Little River Band*

TW	LW	WK	Billboard.	JANUARY 28, 1978	HOT 100.
❶	1	18	**Baby Come Back**..*Player* . . . RSO 879
❷	5	12	**Short People** ....*Randy Newman* . . . Warner 8492
❸	10	8	Stayin' Alive...*Bee Gees* . . . RSO 885
④	4	14	**You're In My Heart (The Final Acclaim)**.................... *Rod Stewart* . . . Warner 8475
⑤	6	16	**Slip Slidin' Away** ....*Paul Simon* . . . Columbia 10630
⑥	8	15	We Are The Champions..*Queen* . . . Elektra 45441
⑦	2	19	How Deep Is Your Love ....*Bee Gees* . . . RSO 882
⑧	9	19	**Come Sail Away**..*Styx* . . . A&M 1977
⑨	11	12	**Just The Way You Are** ....*Billy Joel* . . . Columbia 10646
❿	14	13	**(Love Is) Thicker Than Water** ....*Andy Gibb* . . . RSO 883

★ *HIGHEST DEBUT* ★ POS 78
Poor Poor Pitiful Me....................*Linda Ronstadt*

★ *BIGGEST MOVER* ★ 85 to 69
Shout It Out Loud...*Kiss*

TW	LW	WK	Billboard.	FEBRUARY 4, 1978	HOT 100.
❶	3	9	**Stayin' Alive**...*Bee Gees* . . . RSO 885
❷	2	13	**Short People** ....*Randy Newman* . . . Warner 8492
❸	1	19	Baby Come Back ....*Player* . . . RSO 879
④	6	16	**We Are The Champions** ....*Queen* . . . Elektra 45441
⑤	10	14	**(Love Is) Thicker Than Water** ....*Andy Gibb* . . . RSO 883
⑥	9	13	**Just The Way You Are** ....*Billy Joel* . . . Columbia 10646
⑦	7	20	How Deep Is Your Love ....*Bee Gees* . . . RSO 882
⑧	11	11	Sometimes When We Touch........................*Dan Hill* . . . 20th Century 2355
⑨	4	15	**You're In My Heart (The Final Acclaim)**........*Rod Stewart* . . . Warner 8475
❿	17	12	Emotion...............................*Samantha Sang* . . . Private Stock 45178

★ *HIGHEST DEBUT* ★ POS 63
Can't Smile Without You...............*Barry Manilow*

★ *BIGGEST MOVER* ★ 58 to 38
The Way You Do The Things You Do..........*Rita Coolidge*

TW	LW	WK	Billboard.	FEBRUARY 11, 1978	HOT 100.
❶	1	10	**Stayin' Alive**..*Bee Gees* . . . RSO 885
②	2	14	**Short People** ....*Randy Newman* . . . Warner 8492
③	5	15	**(Love Is) Thicker Than Water** ....*Andy Gibb* . . . RSO 883
④	4	17	**We Are The Champions** ....*Queen* . . . Elektra 45441
⑤	6	14	Just The Way You Are ....*Billy Joel* . . . Columbia 10646
⑥	8	12	Sometimes When We Touch........................*Dan Hill* . . . 20th Century 2355
⑦	3	20	Baby Come Back ....*Player* . . . RSO 879
⑧	10	13	Emotion...............................*Samantha Sang* . . . Private Stock 45178
⑨	11	16	Dance, Dance, Dance (Yowsah, Yowsah, Yowsah)...................... *Chic* . . . Atlantic 3435
❿	7	21	How Deep Is Your Love ....*Bee Gees* . . . RSO 882

★ *HIGHEST DEBUT* ★ POS 72
Running On Empty.....................*Jackson Browne*

★ *BIGGEST MOVER* ★ 76 to 32
Night Fever..*Bee Gees*

Billboard. ⊚ FEBRUARY 18, 1978 ⊚ HOT 100.

TW	LW	WK		
❶	1	11	**Stayin' Alive**..*Bee Gees* ... RSO 885	
❷	3	16	**(Love Is) Thicker Than Water** ....*Andy Gibb* ... RSO 883	
❸	5	15	**Just The Way You Are**...........................*Billy Joel* ... Columbia 10646	
④	4	18	**We Are The Champions**............................*Queen* ... Elektra 45441	
❺	6	13	**Sometimes When We Touch** ....*Dan Hill* ... 20th Century 2355	
❻	8	14	**Emotion**............................*Samantha Sang* ... Private Stock 45178	
❼	9	17	**Dance, Dance, Dance (Yowsah, Yowsah, Yowsah)**.....................*Chic* ... Atlantic 3435	
(8)	2	15	**Short People** ....*Randy Newman* ... Warner 8492	
(9)	7	21	**Baby Come Back** ....*Player* ... RSO 879	
(10)	10	22	**How Deep Is Your Love** ....*Bee Gees* ... RSO 882	

★ *HIGHEST DEBUT* ★ POS 78	★ *BIGGEST MOVER* ★ 32 to 17
Sweet Talkin' Woman........*Electric Light Orchestra*	Night Fever..................................*Bee Gees*

Billboard. ⊚ FEBRUARY 25, 1978 ⊚ HOT 100.

TW	LW	WK		
❶	1	12	**Stayin' Alive**..*Bee Gees* ... RSO 885	
❷	2	17	**(Love Is) Thicker Than Water** ....*Andy Gibb* ... RSO 883	
③	3	16	**Just The Way You Are**...........................*Billy Joel* ... Columbia 10646	
④	5	14	**Sometimes When We Touch** ....*Dan Hill* ... 20th Century 2355	
❺	6	15	**Emotion**............................*Samantha Sang* ... Private Stock 45178	
❻	7	18	**Dance, Dance, Dance (Yowsah, Yowsah, Yowsah)**...........*Chic* ... Atlantic 3435	
⑦	4	19	**We Are The Champions**.................................*Queen* ... Elektra 45441	
⑧	17	4	**Night Fever** ....*Bee Gees* ... RSO 889	
⑨	11	8	**Lay Down Sally**................................*Eric Clapton* ... RSO 886	
(10)	10	23	**How Deep Is Your Love** ....*Bee Gees* ... RSO 882	

★ *HIGHEST DEBUT* ★ POS 70	★ *BIGGEST MOVER* ★ 79 to 38
We'll Never Have To Say Goodbye Again ....*England Dan & John Ford Coley*	Flash Light..*Parliament*

Billboard. ⊚ MARCH 4, 1978 ⊚ HOT 100.

TW	LW	WK		
❶	2	18	**(Love Is) Thicker Than Water** ....*Andy Gibb* ... RSO 883	
②	1	13	**Stayin' Alive**.....................................*Bee Gees* ... RSO 885	
❸	4	15	**Sometimes When We Touch** ....*Dan Hill* ... 20th Century 2355	
④	5	16	**Emotion**............................*Samantha Sang* ... Private Stock 45178	
❺	8	5	**Night Fever** ....*Bee Gees* ... RSO 889	
❻	6	19	**Dance, Dance, Dance (Yowsah, Yowsah, Yowsah)**...........*Chic* ... Atlantic 3435	
❼	9	9	**Lay Down Sally**................................*Eric Clapton* ... RSO 886	
⑧	3	17	**Just The Way You Are** ....*Billy Joel* ... Columbia 10646	
❾	11	28	**I Go Crazy**...*Paul Davis* ... Bang 733	
(10)	10	24	**How Deep Is Your Love** ....*Bee Gees* ... RSO 882	

★ *HIGHEST DEBUT* ★ POS 70	★ *BIGGEST MOVER* ★ 70 to 50
Imaginary Lover ....*Atlanta Rhythm Section*	We'll Never Have To Say Goodbye Again ....*England Dan & John Ford Coley*

Billboard — MARCH 11, 1978 — HOT 100

TW	LW	WK		
①	1	19	**(Love Is) Thicker Than Water**	*Andy Gibb* ... RSO 883
②	5	6	**Night Fever**	*Bee Gees* ... RSO 889
③	3	16	**Sometimes When We Touch**	*Dan Hill* ... 20th Century 2355
④	4	17	**Emotion**	*Samantha Sang* ... Private Stock 45178
⑤	7	10	**Lay Down Sally**	*Eric Clapton* ... RSO 886
⑥	2	14	**Stayin' Alive**	*Bee Gees* ... RSO 885
⑦	6	20	**Dance, Dance, Dance (Yowsah, Yowsah, Yowsah)**	*Chic* ... Atlantic 3435
⑧	9	29	**I Go Crazy**	*Paul Davis* ... Bang 733
⑨	8	18	**Just The Way You Are**	*Billy Joel* ... Columbia 10646
⑩	17	6	**Can't Smile Without You**	*Barry Manilow* ... Arista 0305

★ **HIGHEST DEBUT** ★ POS 70
Count On Me................*Jefferson Starship*

★ **BIGGEST MOVER** ★ 63 to 48
The Closer I Get To You ....*Roberta Flack with Donny Hathaway*

Billboard — MARCH 18, 1978 — HOT 100

TW	LW	WK		
①	2	7	**Night Fever**	*Bee Gees* ... RSO 889
②	6	15	**Stayin' Alive**	*Bee Gees* ... RSO 885
③	4	18	**Emotion**	*Samantha Sang* ... Private Stock 45178
④	5	11	**Lay Down Sally**	*Eric Clapton* ... RSO 886
⑤	1	20	**(Love Is) Thicker Than Water**	*Andy Gibb* ... RSO 883
⑥	10	7	**Can't Smile Without You**	*Barry Manilow* ... Arista 0305
⑦	8	30	**I Go Crazy**	*Paul Davis* ... Bang 733
⑧	3	17	**Sometimes When We Touch**	*Dan Hill* ... 20th Century 2355
⑨	7	21	**Dance, Dance, Dance (Yowsah, Yowsah, Yowsah)**	*Chic* ... Atlantic 3435
⑩	9	19	**Just The Way You Are**	*Billy Joel* ... Columbia 10646

★ **HIGHEST DEBUT** ★ POS 69
Two Doors Down ....*Dolly Parton*

★ **BIGGEST MOVER** ★ 75 to 60
More Than A Woman................*Tavares*

Billboard — MARCH 25, 1978 — HOT 100

TW	LW	WK		
①	1	8	**Night Fever**	*Bee Gees* ... RSO 889
②	2	16	**Stayin' Alive**	*Bee Gees* ... RSO 885
③	3	19	**Emotion**	*Samantha Sang* ... Private Stock 45178
④	4	12	**Lay Down Sally**	*Eric Clapton* ... RSO 886
⑤	6	8	**Can't Smile Without You**	*Barry Manilow* ... Arista 0305
⑥	5	21	**(Love Is) Thicker Than Water**	*Andy Gibb* ... RSO 883
⑦	7	31	**I Go Crazy**	*Paul Davis* ... Bang 733
⑧	8	18	**Sometimes When We Touch**	*Dan Hill* ... 20th Century 2355
⑨	14	9	**If I Can't Have You**	*Yvonne Elliman* ... RSO 884
⑩	11	15	**Thunder Island**	*Jay Ferguson* ... Asylum 45444

★ **HIGHEST DEBUT** ★ POS 70
With A Little Luck ....*Wings*

★ **BIGGEST MOVER** ★ 58 to 35
Count On Me................*Jefferson Starship*

April 1, 1978 — Billboard Hot 100

TW	LW	WK	Title	Artist	Label
1	1	9	Night Fever	Bee Gees	RSO 889
2	2	17	Stayin' Alive	Bee Gees	RSO 885
3	4	13	Lay Down Sally	Eric Clapton	RSO 886
4	5	9	Can't Smile Without You	Barry Manilow	Arista 0305
5	3	20	Emotion	Samantha Sang	Private Stock 45178
6	9	10	If I Can't Have You	Yvonne Elliman	RSO 884
7	7	32	I Go Crazy	Paul Davis	Bang 733
8	6	22	(Love Is) Thicker Than Water	Andy Gibb	RSO 883
9	10	16	Thunder Island	Jay Ferguson	Asylum 45444
10	12	10	Dust In The Wind	Kansas	Kirshner 4274

★ HIGHEST DEBUT ★ POS 65
You're The One That I Want......John Travolta & Olivia Newton-John

★ BIGGEST MOVER ★ 69 to 54
Movin' Out (Anthony's Song)......Billy Joel

April 8, 1978 — Billboard Hot 100

TW	LW	WK	Title	Artist	Label
1	1	10	Night Fever	Bee Gees	RSO 889
2	2	18	Stayin' Alive	Bee Gees	RSO 885
3	3	14	Lay Down Sally	Eric Clapton	RSO 886
4	4	10	Can't Smile Without You	Barry Manilow	Arista 0305
5	6	11	If I Can't Have You	Yvonne Elliman	RSO 884
6	5	21	Emotion	Samantha Sang	Private Stock 45178
7	10	11	Dust In The Wind	Kansas	Kirshner 4274
8	8	23	(Love Is) Thicker Than Water	Andy Gibb	RSO 883
9	9	17	Thunder Island	Jay Ferguson	Asylum 45444
10	11	13	Jack And Jill	Raydio	Arista 0283

★ HIGHEST DEBUT ★ POS 78
Make You Feel Love Again......Wet Willie

★ BIGGEST MOVER ★ 57 to 17
With A Little Luck......Wings

April 15, 1978 — Billboard Hot 100

TW	LW	WK	Title	Artist	Label
1	1	11	Night Fever	Bee Gees	RSO 889
2	2	19	Stayin' Alive	Bee Gees	RSO 885
3	3	15	Lay Down Sally	Eric Clapton	RSO 886
4	4	11	Can't Smile Without You	Barry Manilow	Arista 0305
5	5	12	If I Can't Have You	Yvonne Elliman	RSO 884
6	7	12	Dust In The Wind	Kansas	Kirshner 4274
7	13	9	The Closer I Get To You	Roberta Flack with Donny Hathaway	Atlantic 3463
8	10	14	Jack And Jill	Raydio	Arista 0283
9	12	8	We'll Never Have To Say Goodbye Again	England Dan & John Ford Coley	Big Tree 16110
10	11	14	Our Love	Natalie Cole	Capitol 4509

★ HIGHEST DEBUT ★ POS 65
Ego......Elton John

★ BIGGEST MOVER ★ 95 to 82
Stay......Rufus/Chaka Khan

Billboard — APRIL 22, 1978 — HOT 100

TW	LW	WK		
1	1	12	**Night Fever** ....*Bee Gees* . . . RSO 889	
2	5	13	**If I Can't Have You**.................................*Yvonne Elliman* . . . RSO 884	
3	4	12	**Can't Smile Without You** ....*Barry Manilow* . . . Arista 0305	
4	3	16	**Lay Down Sally**..*Eric Clapton* . . . RSO 886	
5	7	10	**The Closer I Get To You** ....*Roberta Flack with Donny Hathaway* . . . Atlantic 3463	
6	6	13	**Dust In The Wind**...*Kansas* . . . Kirshner 4274	
7	12	5	**With A Little Luck**..*Wings* . . . Capitol 4559	
8	8	15	**Jack And Jill**...*Raydio* . . . Arista 0283	
9	9	9	**We'll Never Have To Say Goodbye Again** ....*England Dan & John Ford Coley* . . . Big Tree 16110	
10	10	15	**Our Love**...*Natalie Cole* . . . Capitol 4509	

★ HIGHEST DEBUT ★ POS 69	★ BIGGEST MOVER ★ 69 to 30
Take A Chance On Me.....................*Abba*	Shadow Dancing ....*Andy Gibb*

Billboard — APRIL 29, 1978 — HOT 100

TW	LW	WK		
1	1	13	**Night Fever** ....*Bee Gees* . . . RSO 889	
2	2	14	**If I Can't Have You**.................................*Yvonne Elliman* . . . RSO 884	
3	3	13	**Can't Smile Without You** ....*Barry Manilow* . . . Arista 0305	
4	5	11	**The Closer I Get To You** ....*Roberta Flack with Donny Hathaway* . . . Atlantic 3463	
5	7	6	**With A Little Luck**..*Wings* . . . Capitol 4559	
6	4	17	**Lay Down Sally**..*Eric Clapton* . . . RSO 886	
7	6	14	**Dust In The Wind** ....*Kansas* . . . Kirshner 4274	
8	8	16	**Jack And Jill** ....*Raydio* . . . Arista 0283	
9	11	5	**You're The One That I Want** ....*John Travolta & Olivia Newton-John* . . . RSO 891	
10	20	5	**Too Much, Too Little, Too Late**..............*Johnny Mathis/Deniece Williams* . . . Columbia 10693	

★ HIGHEST DEBUT ★ POS 70	★ BIGGEST MOVER ★ 79 to 58
I Was Only Joking ....*Rod Stewart*	You Belong To Me ....*Carly Simon*

Billboard — MAY 6, 1978 — HOT 100

TW	LW	WK		
1	1	14	**Night Fever** ....*Bee Gees* . . . RSO 889	
2	2	15	**If I Can't Have You**.................................*Yvonne Elliman* . . . RSO 884	
3	3	14	**Can't Smile Without You** ....*Barry Manilow* . . . Arista 0305	
4	4	12	**The Closer I Get To You** ....*Roberta Flack with Donny Hathaway* . . . Atlantic 3463	
5	5	7	**With A Little Luck**...*Wings* . . . Capitol 4559	
6	10	6	**Too Much, Too Little, Too Late**..............*Johnny Mathis/Deniece Williams* . . . Columbia 10693	
7	9	6	**You're The One That I Want** ....*John Travolta & Olivia Newton-John* . . . RSO 891	
8	6	18	**Lay Down Sally**..*Eric Clapton* . . . RSO 886	
9	7	15	**Dust In The Wind** ....*Kansas* . . . Kirshner 4274	
10	12	9	**Count On Me**................................*Jefferson Starship* . . . Grunt 11196	

★ HIGHEST DEBUT ★ POS 70	★ BIGGEST MOVER ★ 58 to 31
The Groove Line.....................*Heatwave*	You Belong To Me ....*Carly Simon*

Billboard HOT 100 — MAY 13, 1978

TW	LW	WK	Title — Artist — Label
❶	2	16	**If I Can't Have You**.....................Yvonne Elliman ... RSO 884
❷	4	13	**The Closer I Get To You** ....Roberta Flack with Donny Hathaway ... Atlantic 3463
❸	5	8	**With A Little Luck**................................Wings ... Capitol 4559
❹	6	7	**Too Much, Too Little, Too Late**..............Johnny Mathis/Deniece Williams ... Columbia 10693
⑤	1	15	Night Fever...Bee Gees ... RSO 889
⑥	7	7	You're The One That I Want ....John Travolta & Olivia Newton-John ... RSO 891
⑦	3	15	Can't Smile Without You..........................Barry Manilow ... Arista 0305
⑧	10	10	**Count On Me** ....Jefferson Starship ... Grunt 11196
⑨	9	16	Dust In The Wind ....Kansas ... Kirshner 4274
⑩	12	11	Imaginary Lover ....Atlanta Rhythm Section ... Polydor 14459

★ HIGHEST DEBUT ★ POS 73	★ BIGGEST MOVER ★ 75 to 59
Still The Same..........Bob Seger & The Silver Bullet Band	Oh What A Night For Dancing ....Barry White

Billboard HOT 100 — MAY 20, 1978

TW	LW	WK	Title — Artist — Label
❶	3	9	**With A Little Luck** ....Wings ... Capitol 4559
②	2	14	**The Closer I Get To You** ....Roberta Flack with Donny Hathaway ... Atlantic 3463
❸	4	8	**Too Much, Too Little, Too Late**.............. Johnny Mathis/Deniece Williams ... Columbia 10693
❹	6	8	**You're The One That I Want** ....John Travolta & Olivia Newton-John ... RSO 891
⑤	1	17	If I Can't Have You.....................................Yvonne Elliman ... RSO 884
⑥	11	6	Shadow Dancing.....................................Andy Gibb ... RSO 893
⑦	12	15	Feels So Good ....Chuck Mangione ... A&M 2001
⑧	8	11	**Count On Me** ....Jefferson Starship ... Grunt 11196
⑨	10	12	Imaginary Lover ....Atlanta Rhythm Section ... Polydor 14459
⑩	5	16	Night Fever...Bee Gees ... RSO 889

★ HIGHEST DEBUT ★ POS 82	★ BIGGEST MOVER ★ 67 to 41
Darlin' ....Paul Davis featuring Susan Collins	Bluer Than Blue ....Michael Johnson

Billboard HOT 100 — MAY 27, 1978

TW	LW	WK	Title — Artist — Label
❶	1	10	**With A Little Luck** ....Wings ... Capitol 4559
❷	3	9	Too Much, Too Little, Too Late..............Johnny Mathis/Deniece Williams ... Columbia 10693
❸	4	9	You're The One That I Want ....John Travolta & Olivia Newton-John ... RSO 891
❹	6	7	Shadow Dancing.....................................Andy Gibb ... RSO 893
⑤	2	15	The Closer I Get To You ....Roberta Flack with Donny Hathaway ... Atlantic 3463
⑥	7	16	Feels So Good ....Chuck Mangione ... A&M 2001
⑦	5	18	If I Can't Have You.....................................Yvonne Elliman ... RSO 884
⑧	9	13	Imaginary Lover ....Atlanta Rhythm Section ... Polydor 14459
⑨	8	12	Count On Me.....................................Jefferson Starship ... Grunt 11196
⑩	11	12	On Broadway ....George Benson ... Warner 8542

★ HIGHEST DEBUT ★ POS 69	★ BIGGEST MOVER ★ 58 to 47
Grease ....Frankie Valli	Still The Same..........Bob Seger & The Silver Bullet Band

Billboard — JUNE 3, 1978 — HOT 100

TW	LW	WK		
1	2	10	**Too Much, Too Little, Too Late** .... *Johnny Mathis/Deniece Williams* ... Columbia 10693	
2	3	10	You're The One That I Want .... *John Travolta & Olivia Newton-John* ... RSO 891	
3	4	8	Shadow Dancing .... *Andy Gibb* ... RSO 893	
4	1	11	With A Little Luck .... *Wings* ... Capitol 4559	
5	6	17	Feels So Good .... *Chuck Mangione* ... A&M 2001	
6	5	16	The Closer I Get To You .... *Roberta Flack with Donny Hathaway* ... Atlantic 3463	
7	8	14	*Imaginary Lover* .... *Atlanta Rhythm Section* ... Polydor 14459	
8	10	13	On Broadway .... *George Benson* ... Warner 8542	
9	13	7	Take A Chance On Me .... *Abba* ... Atlantic 3457	
10	12	13	**This Time I'm In It For Love** .... *Player* ... RSO 890	

★ **HIGHEST DEBUT** ★ POS 67
FM (No Static At All) .... *Steely Dan*

★ **BIGGEST MOVER** ★ 67 to 38
Last Dance .... *Donna Summer*

Billboard — JUNE 10, 1978 — HOT 100

TW	LW	WK		
1	2	11	**You're The One That I Want** .... *John Travolta & Olivia Newton-John* ... RSO 891	
2	3	9	Shadow Dancing .... *Andy Gibb* ... RSO 893	
3	1	11	Too Much, Too Little, Too Late .... *Johnny Mathis/Deniece Williams* ... Columbia 10693	
4	5	18	**Feels So Good** .... *Chuck Mangione* ... A&M 2001	
5	14	8	Baker Street .... *Gerry Rafferty* ... United Artists 1192	
6	15	12	It's A Heartache .... *Bonnie Tyler* ... RCA 11249	
7	8	14	**On Broadway** .... *George Benson* ... Warner 8542	
8	9	8	Take A Chance On Me .... *Abba* ... Atlantic 3457	
9	4	12	With A Little Luck .... *Wings* ... Capitol 4559	
10	10	14	**This Time I'm In It For Love** .... *Player* ... RSO 890	

★ **HIGHEST DEBUT** ★ POS 68
Copacabana (At The Copa) .... *Barry Manilow*

★ **BIGGEST MOVER** ★ 53 to 37
Miss You .... *The Rolling Stones*

Billboard — JUNE 17, 1978 — HOT 100

TW	LW	WK		
1	2	10	**Shadow Dancing** .... *Andy Gibb* ... RSO 893	
2	1	12	You're The One That I Want .... *John Travolta & Olivia Newton-John* ... RSO 891	
3	5	9	Baker Street .... *Gerry Rafferty* ... United Artists 1192	
4	6	13	It's A Heartache .... *Bonnie Tyler* ... RCA 11249	
5	3	12	Too Much, Too Little, Too Late .... *Johnny Mathis/Deniece Williams* ... Columbia 10693	
6	8	9	Take A Chance On Me .... *Abba* ... Atlantic 3457	
7	4	19	Feels So Good .... *Chuck Mangione* ... A&M 2001	
8	7	15	On Broadway .... *George Benson* ... Warner 8542	
9	16	10	You Belong To Me .... *Carly Simon* ... Elektra 45477	
10	12	18	Love Is Like Oxygen .... *Sweet* ... Capitol 4549	

★ **HIGHEST DEBUT** ★ POS 67
Songbird .... *Barbra Streisand*

★ **BIGGEST MOVER** ★ 83 to 59
I'm Not Gonna Let It Bother Me Tonight .... *Atlanta Rhythm Section*

Billboard — JUNE 24, 1978 — HOT 100

TW	LW	WK	Title	Artist ... Label
①	1	11	**Shadow Dancing**	*Andy Gibb* ... RSO 893
②	3	10	**Baker Street**	*Gerry Rafferty* ... United Artists 1192
③	4	14	**It's A Heartache**	*Bonnie Tyler* ... RCA 11249
④	2	13	You're The One That I Want	*John Travolta & Olivia Newton-John* ... RSO 891
⑤	6	10	Take A Chance On Me	*Abba* ... Atlantic 3457
⑥	9	11	**You Belong To Me**	*Carly Simon* ... Elektra 45477
⑦	12	9	Use Ta Be My Girl	*The O'Jays* ... Philadelphia International 3642
⑧	10	19	**Love Is Like Oxygen**	*Sweet* ... Capitol 4549
⑨	16	7	Still The Same	*Bob Seger & The Silver Bullet Band* ... Capitol 4581
⑩	11	17	Dance With Me	*Peter Brown* ... Drive 6269

★ HIGHEST DEBUT ★ POS 79	★ BIGGEST MOVER ★ 67 to 51
Mr. Blue Sky ....*Electric Light Orchestra*	Songbird ....*Barbra Streisand*

Billboard — JULY 1, 1978 — HOT 100

TW	LW	WK	Title	Artist ... Label
①	1	12	**Shadow Dancing**	*Andy Gibb* ... RSO 893
②	2	11	**Baker Street**	*Gerry Rafferty* ... United Artists 1192
③	3	15	It's A Heartache	*Bonnie Tyler* ... RCA 11249
④	5	11	Take A Chance On Me	*Abba* ... Atlantic 3457
⑤	7	10	Use Ta Be My Girl	*The O'Jays* ... Philadelphia International 3642
⑥	6	12	You Belong To Me	*Carly Simon* ... Elektra 45477
⑦	9	8	Still The Same	*Bob Seger & The Silver Bullet Band* ... Capitol 4581
⑧	8	20	**Love Is Like Oxygen**	*Sweet* ... Capitol 4549
⑨	10	18	Dance With Me	*Peter Brown* ... Drive 6269
⑩	11	9	The Groove Line	*Heatwave* ... Epic 50524

★ HIGHEST DEBUT ★ POS 52	★ BIGGEST MOVER ★ 50 to 31
Hot Blooded ....*Foreigner*	Life's Been Good ....*Joe Walsh*

Billboard — JULY 8, 1978 — HOT 100

TW	LW	WK	Title	Artist ... Label
①	1	13	**Shadow Dancing**	*Andy Gibb* ... RSO 893
②	2	12	**Baker Street**	*Gerry Rafferty* ... United Artists 1192
③	4	12	**Take A Chance On Me**	*Abba* ... Atlantic 3457
④	5	11	**Use Ta Be My Girl**	*The O'Jays* ... Philadelphia International 3642
⑤	7	9	**Still The Same**	*Bob Seger & The Silver Bullet Band* ... Capitol 4581
⑥	3	16	It's A Heartache	*Bonnie Tyler* ... RCA 11249
⑦	14	7	Miss You	*The Rolling Stones* ... Rolling Stones 19307
⑧	9	19	**Dance With Me**	*Peter Brown* ... Drive 6269
⑨	10	10	The Groove Line	*Heatwave* ... Epic 50524
⑩	6	13	You Belong To Me	*Carly Simon* ... Elektra 45477

★ HIGHEST DEBUT ★ POS 68	★ BIGGEST MOVER ★ 49 to 26
Hopelessly Devoted To You ....*Olivia Newton-John*	Three Times A Lady ....*Commodores*

Billboard — JULY 15, 1978 — HOT 100

TW	LW	WK	Title	Artist	Label
1	1	14	Shadow Dancing	Andy Gibb	RSO 893
2	2	13	Baker Street	Gerry Rafferty	United Artists 1192
3	3	13	Take A Chance On Me	Abba	Atlantic 3457
4	4	12	Use Ta Be My Girl	The O'Jays	Philadelphia International 3642
5	5	10	Still The Same	Bob Seger & The Silver Bullet Band	Capitol 4581
6	7	8	Miss You	The Rolling Stones	Rolling Stones 19307
7	9	11	The Groove Line	Heatwave	Epic 50524
8	8	20	Dance With Me	Peter Brown	Drive 6269
9	6	17	It's A Heartache	Bonnie Tyler	RCA 11249
10	13	10	Last Dance	Donna Summer	Casablanca 926

★ **HIGHEST DEBUT** ★ POS 73
An Everlasting Love .... Andy Gibb

★ **BIGGEST MOVER** ★ 85 to 72
Kiss You All Over .... Exile

Billboard — JULY 22, 1978 — HOT 100

TW	LW	WK	Title	Artist	Label
1	1	15	Shadow Dancing	Andy Gibb	RSO 893
2	2	14	Baker Street	Gerry Rafferty	United Artists 1192
3	6	9	Miss You	The Rolling Stones	Rolling Stones 19307
4	5	11	Still The Same	Bob Seger & The Silver Bullet Band	Capitol 4581
5	10	11	Last Dance	Donna Summer	Casablanca 926
6	11	9	Grease	Frankie Valli	RSO 897
7	7	12	The Groove Line	Heatwave	Epic 50524
8	4	13	Use Ta Be My Girl	The O'Jays	Philadelphia International 3642
9	3	14	Take A Chance On Me	Abba	Atlantic 3457
10	21	6	Three Times A Lady	Commodores	Motown 1443

★ **HIGHEST DEBUT** ★ POS 80
Got To Get You Into My Life .... Earth, Wind & Fire

★ **BIGGEST MOVER** ★ 73 to 40
An Everlasting Love .... Andy Gibb

Billboard — JULY 29, 1978 — HOT 100

TW	LW	WK	Title	Artist	Label
1	1	16	Shadow Dancing	Andy Gibb	RSO 893
2	2	15	Baker Street	Gerry Rafferty	United Artists 1192
3	3	10	Miss You	The Rolling Stones	Rolling Stones 19307
4	5	12	Last Dance	Donna Summer	Casablanca 926
5	6	10	Grease	Frankie Valli	RSO 897
6	10	7	Three Times A Lady	Commodores	Motown 1443
7	4	12	Still The Same	Bob Seger & The Silver Bullet Band	Capitol 4581
8	8	14	Use Ta Be My Girl	The O'Jays	Philadelphia International 3642
9	7	13	The Groove Line	Heatwave	Epic 50524
10	11	9	Love Will Find A Way	Pablo Cruise	A&M 2048

★ **HIGHEST DEBUT** ★ POS 79
Love Theme From "Eyes Of Laura Mars"
(Prisoner) .... Barbra Streisand

★ **BIGGEST MOVER** ★ 92 to 75
A Rock 'N' Roll Fantasy .... The Kinks

Billboard • AUGUST 5, 1978 • HOT 100.

TW	LW	WK	Title	Artist	Label
1	3	11	Miss You	The Rolling Stones	Rolling Stones 19307
2	6	8	Three Times A Lady	Commodores	Motown 1443
3	5	11	Grease	Frankie Valli	RSO 897
4	4	13	Last Dance	Donna Summer	Casablanca 926
5	1	17	Shadow Dancing	Andy Gibb	RSO 893
6	2	16	Baker Street	Gerry Rafferty	United Artists 1192
7	8	15	Use Ta Be My Girl	The O'Jays	Philadelphia International 3642
8	11	6	Hot Blooded	Foreigner	Atlantic 3488
9	10	10	Love Will Find A Way	Pablo Cruise	A&M 2048
10	7	13	Still The Same	Bob Seger & The Silver Bullet Band	Capitol 4581

★ **HIGHEST DEBUT** ★ POS 66
Summer Nights ....John Travolta & Olivia Newton-John & Cast

★ **BIGGEST MOVER** ★ 69 to 39
Got To Get You Into My Life ....Earth, Wind & Fire

Billboard • AUGUST 12, 1978 • HOT 100.

TW	LW	WK	Title	Artist	Label
1	2	9	Three Times A Lady	Commodores	Motown 1443
2	3	12	Grease	Frankie Valli	RSO 897
3	4	14	Last Dance	Donna Summer	Casablanca 926
4	1	12	Miss You	The Rolling Stones	Rolling Stones 19307
5	8	7	Hot Blooded	Foreigner	Atlantic 3488
6	17	8	Boogie Oogie Oogie	A Taste Of Honey	Capitol 4565
7	9	11	Love Will Find A Way	Pablo Cruise	A&M 2048
8	12	10	Copacabana (At The Copa)	Barry Manilow	Arista 0339
9	11	12	Magnet And Steel	Walter Egan	Columbia 10719
10	16	5	An Everlasting Love	Andy Gibb	RSO 904

★ **HIGHEST DEBUT** ★ POS 68
Oh! Darling ....Robin Gibb

★ **BIGGEST MOVER** ★ 56 to 34
Reminiscing ....Little River Band

Billboard • AUGUST 19, 1978 • HOT 100.

TW	LW	WK	Title	Artist	Label
1	1	10	Three Times A Lady	Commodores	Motown 1443
2	2	13	Grease	Frankie Valli	RSO 897
3	3	15	Last Dance	Donna Summer	Casablanca 926
4	4	13	Miss You	The Rolling Stones	Rolling Stones 19307
5	5	8	Hot Blooded	Foreigner	Atlantic 3488
6	6	9	Boogie Oogie Oogie	A Taste Of Honey	Capitol 4565
7	7	12	Love Will Find A Way	Pablo Cruise	A&M 2048
8	8	11	Copacabana (At The Copa)	Barry Manilow	Arista 0339
9	9	13	Magnet And Steel	Walter Egan	Columbia 10719
10	10	6	An Everlasting Love	Andy Gibb	RSO 904

★ **HIGHEST DEBUT** ★ POS 62
Don't Look Back ....Boston

★ **BIGGEST MOVER** ★ 78 to 38
Hollywood Nights ......Bob Seger & The Silver Bullet Band

TW	LW	WK	Billboard	AUGUST 26, 1978	HOT 100.
❶	2	14	**Grease**	*Frankie Valli* . . . RSO 897	
❷	1	11	Three Times A Lady	*Commodores* . . . Motown 1443	
③	4	14	Miss You	*The Rolling Stones* . . . Rolling Stones 19307	
④	6	10	Boogie Oogie Oogie	*A Taste Of Honey* . . . Capitol 4565	
⑤	5	9	Hot Blooded	*Foreigner* . . . Atlantic 3488	
⑥	7	13	**Love Will Find A Way**	*Pablo Cruise* . . . A&M 2048	
❼	11	8	Hopelessly Devoted To You	*Olivia Newton-John* . . . RSO 903	
⑧	9	14	**Magnet And Steel**	*Walter Egan* . . . Columbia 10719	
⑨	10	7	An Everlasting Love	*Andy Gibb* . . . RSO 904	
⑩	3	16	Last Dance	*Donna Summer* . . . Casablanca 926	

★ *HIGHEST DEBUT* ★ POS 70	★ *BIGGEST MOVER* ★ 62 to 36
Who Are You ....*The Who*	Don't Look Back ....*Boston*

TW	LW	WK	Billboard	SEPTEMBER 2, 1978	HOT 100.
❶	1	15	**Grease**	*Frankie Valli* . . . RSO 897	
②	2	12	Three Times A Lady	*Commodores* . . . Motown 1443	
③	4	11	Boogie Oogie Oogie	*A Taste Of Honey* . . . Capitol 4565	
④	5	10	Hot Blooded	*Foreigner* . . . Atlantic 3488	
⑤	7	9	Hopelessly Devoted To You	*Olivia Newton-John* . . . RSO 903	
⑥	3	15	Miss You	*The Rolling Stones* . . . Rolling Stones 19307	
❼	11	9	Kiss You All Over	*Exile* . . . Warner 8589	
⑧	9	8	An Everlasting Love	*Andy Gibb* . . . RSO 904	
⑨	8	15	Magnet And Steel	*Walter Egan* . . . Columbia 10719	
⑩	12	12	Shame	*Evelyn "Champagne" King* . . . RCA 11122	

★ *HIGHEST DEBUT* ★ POS 81	★ *BIGGEST MOVER* ★ 36 to 19
Takin' It Easy ....*Seals & Crofts*	Don't Look Back ....*Boston*

TW	LW	WK	Billboard	SEPTEMBER 9, 1978	HOT 100.
❶	3	12	**Boogie Oogie Oogie**	*A Taste Of Honey* . . . Capitol 4565	
❷	2	13	Three Times A Lady	*Commodores* . . . Motown 1443	
❸	4	11	**Hot Blooded**	*Foreigner* . . . Atlantic 3488	
④	5	10	Hopelessly Devoted To You	*Olivia Newton-John* . . . RSO 903	
⑤	7	10	Kiss You All Over	*Exile* . . . Warner 8589	
⑥	1	16	Grease	*Frankie Valli* . . . RSO 897	
❼	8	9	An Everlasting Love	*Andy Gibb* . . . RSO 904	
⑧	15	6	Summer Nights	*John Travolta & Olivia Newton-John & Cast* . . . RSO 906	
⑨	10	13	**Shame**	*Evelyn "Champagne" King* . . . RCA 11122	
⑩	11	8	Got To Get You Into My Life	*Earth, Wind & Fire* . . . Columbia 10796	

★ *HIGHEST DEBUT* ★ POS 70	★ *BIGGEST MOVER* ★ 60 to 41
Beast Of Burden ....*The Rolling Stones*	Who Are You ....*The Who*

TW	LW	WK	Billboard	SEPTEMBER 16, 1978	HOT 100.
❶	1	13	**Boogie Oogie Oogie** ....*A Taste Of Honey* ... Capitol 4565
②	2	14	Three Times A Lady.................................*Commodores* ... Motown 1443
③	3	12	**Hot Blooded**..*Foreigner* ... Atlantic 3488
④	4	11	Hopelessly Devoted To You ....*Olivia Newton-John* ... RSO 903
⑤	5	11	Kiss You All Over...*Exile* ... Warner 8589
⑥	7	10	An Everlasting Love................................*Andy Gibb* ... RSO 904
❼	8	7	Summer Nights .... *John Travolta & Olivia Newton-John & Cast* ... RSO 906
❽	12	5	Don't Look Back ....*Boston* ... Epic 50590
⑨	10	9	**Got To Get You Into My Life**......*Earth, Wind & Fire* ... Columbia 10796
⑩	9	14	Shame ....*Evelyn "Champagne" King* ... RCA 11122

★ *HIGHEST DEBUT* ★ POS 70	★ *BIGGEST MOVER* ★ 70 to 52
Ready To Take A Chance Again ....*Barry Manilow*	Beast Of Burden.....................*The Rolling Stones*

TW	LW	WK	Billboard	SEPTEMBER 23, 1978	HOT 100.
❶	1	14	**Boogie Oogie Oogie** ....*A Taste Of Honey* ... Capitol 4565
❷	5	12	**Kiss You All Over**.......................................*Exile* ... Warner 8589
❸	4	12	**Hopelessly Devoted To You** ....*Olivia Newton-John* ... RSO 903
④	2	15	Three Times A Lady.................................*Commodores* ... Motown 1443
⑤	6	11	**An Everlasting Love** ....*Andy Gibb* ... RSO 904
⑥	7	8	Summer Nights .... *John Travolta & Olivia Newton-John & Cast* ... RSO 906
❼	8	6	Don't Look Back ....*Boston* ... Epic 50590
⑧	3	13	Hot Blooded ....*Foreigner* ... Atlantic 3488
❾	11	16	Hot Child In The City................................*Nick Gilder* ... Chrysalis 2226
⑩	15	9	Reminiscing ....*Little River Band* ... Harvest 4605

★ *HIGHEST DEBUT* ★ POS 67	★ *BIGGEST MOVER* ★ 75 to 50
Double Vision ....*Foreigner*	MacArthur Park ....*Donna Summer*

TW	LW	WK	Billboard	SEPTEMBER 30, 1978	HOT 100.
❶	2	13	**Kiss You All Over** ....*Exile* ... Warner 8589
②	1	15	Boogie Oogie Oogie ....*A Taste Of Honey* ... Capitol 4565
③	3	13	**Hopelessly Devoted To You** ....*Olivia Newton-John* ... RSO 903
④	4	16	Three Times A Lady.................................*Commodores* ... Motown 1443
⑤	6	9	**Summer Nights**.................... *John Travolta & Olivia Newton-John & Cast* ... RSO 906
⑥	7	7	Don't Look Back ....*Boston* ... Epic 50590
❼	9	17	Hot Child In The City................................*Nick Gilder* ... Chrysalis 2226
⑧	10	10	Reminiscing ....*Little River Band* ... Harvest 4605
⑨	11	12	Love Is In The Air ....*John Paul Young* ... Scotti Brothers 402
⑩	5	12	An Everlasting Love...*Andy Gibb* ... RSO 904

★ *HIGHEST DEBUT* ★ POS 73	★ *BIGGEST MOVER* ★ 67 to 38
Greased Lightnin'..........................*John Travolta*	Double Vision ....*Foreigner*

Billboard OCTOBER 7, 1978 HOT 100.

TW	LW	WK		
❶	1	14	**Kiss You All Over** ....*Exile* ... Warner 8589	
②	2	16	Boogie Oogie Oogie ....*A Taste Of Honey* ... Capitol 4565	
❸	7	18	Hot Child In The City...................................*Nick Gilder* ... Chrysalis 2226	
④	6	8	**Don't Look Back**..*Boston* ... Epic 50590	
⑤	5	10	**Summer Nights**................... *John Travolta & Olivia Newton-John & Cast* ... RSO 906	
⑥	8	11	Reminiscing ....*Little River Band* ... Harvest 4605	
⑦	3	14	Hopelessly Devoted To You ....*Olivia Newton-John* ... RSO 903	
⑧	9	13	Love Is In The Air ....*John Paul Young* ... Scotti Brothers 402	
⑨	11	13	You Needed Me ....*Anne Murray* ... Capitol 4574	
⑩	12	11	Whenever I Call You "Friend" ....*Kenny Loggins* ... Columbia 10794	

★ *HIGHEST DEBUT* ★ POS 81
Martha (Your Lovers Come And Go) ....*Gabriel*

★ *BIGGEST MOVER* ★ 92 to 77
Dreadlock Holiday.................................*10cc*

Billboard OCTOBER 14, 1978 HOT 100.

TW	LW	WK		
❶	1	15	**Kiss You All Over** ....*Exile* ... Warner 8589	
②	3	19	Hot Child In The City...................................*Nick Gilder* ... Chrysalis 2226	
③	2	17	Boogie Oogie Oogie ....*A Taste Of Honey* ... Capitol 4565	
④	4	9	**Don't Look Back**..*Boston* ... Epic 50590	
⑤	6	12	Reminiscing ....*Little River Band* ... Harvest 4605	
⑥	9	14	You Needed Me ....*Anne Murray* ... Capitol 4574	
⑦	8	14	**Love Is In The Air**.......................*John Paul Young* ... Scotti Brothers 402	
⑧	10	12	Whenever I Call You "Friend" ....*Kenny Loggins* ... Columbia 10794	
⑨	5	11	Summer Nights .... *John Travolta & Olivia Newton-John & Cast* ... RSO 906	
⑩	7	15	Hopelessly Devoted To You ....*Olivia Newton-John* ... RSO 903	

★ *HIGHEST DEBUT* ★ POS 70
(Our Love) Don't Throw It All Away.....*Andy Gibb*

★ *BIGGEST MOVER* ★ 75 to 50
Time Passages ....*Al Stewart*

Billboard OCTOBER 21, 1978 HOT 100.

TW	LW	WK		
❶	1	16	**Kiss You All Over** ....*Exile* ... Warner 8589	
②	2	20	Hot Child In The City...................................*Nick Gilder* ... Chrysalis 2226	
③	3	18	Boogie Oogie Oogie ....*A Taste Of Honey* ... Capitol 4565	
④	5	13	Reminiscing ....*Little River Band* ... Harvest 4605	
⑤	6	15	You Needed Me ....*Anne Murray* ... Capitol 4574	
⑥	8	13	Whenever I Call You "Friend" ....*Kenny Loggins* ... Columbia 10794	
⑦	7	15	**Love Is In The Air**.......................*John Paul Young* ... Scotti Brothers 402	
⑧	11	7	MacArthur Park ....*Donna Summer* ... Casablanca 939	
⑨	4	10	Don't Look Back ....*Boston* ... Epic 50590	
⑩	9	12	Summer Nights .... *John Travolta & Olivia Newton-John & Cast* ... RSO 906	

★ *HIGHEST DEBUT* ★ POS 63
Alive Again ....*Chicago*

★ *BIGGEST MOVER* ★ 62 to 45
Strange Way ....*Firefall*

TW	LW	WK	Billboard.	OCTOBER 28, 1978	HOT 100.
❶	2	21	**Hot Child In The City** ....*Nick Gilder* . . . Chrysalis 2226
❷	5	16	You Needed Me ....*Anne Murray* . . . Capitol 4574
❸	4	14	**Reminiscing**..................................*Little River Band* . . . Harvest 4605
❹	8	8	MacArthur Park ....*Donna Summer* . . . Casablanca 939
❺	6	14	**Whenever I Call You "Friend"** ....*Kenny Loggins* . . . Columbia 10794
❻	1	17	Kiss You All Over...*Exile* . . . Warner 8589
❼	13	6	**Double Vision** ....*Foreigner* . . . Atlantic 3514
❽	7	16	Love Is In The Air ....*John Paul Young* . . . Scotti Brothers 402
❾	11	9	How Much I Feel................................*Ambrosia* . . . Warner 8640
❿	3	19	Boogie Oogie Oogie ....*A Taste Of Honey* . . . Capitol 4565

★ HIGHEST DEBUT ★ POS 48	★ BIGGEST MOVER ★ 63 to 40
You Don't Bring Me Flowers ....*Barbra Streisand & Neil Diamond*	Alive Again ....*Chicago*

TW	LW	WK	Billboard.	NOVEMBER 4, 1978	HOT 100.
❶	2	17	**You Needed Me** ....*Anne Murray* . . . Capitol 4574
❷	4	9	MacArthur Park ....*Donna Summer* . . . Casablanca 939
❸	3	15	**Reminiscing**.................................*Little River Band* . . . Harvest 4605
❹	7	7	Double Vision ....*Foreigner* . . . Atlantic 3514
❺	5	15	**Whenever I Call You "Friend"** ....*Kenny Loggins* . . . Columbia 10794
❻	1	22	Hot Child In The City..............................*Nick Gilder* . . . Chrysalis 2226
❼	6	18	Kiss You All Over...*Exile* . . . Warner 8589
❽	9	10	How Much I Feel................................*Ambrosia* . . . Warner 8640
❾	11	9	Beast Of Burden ....*The Rolling Stones* . . . Rolling Stones 19309
❿	13	16	Get Off...*Foxy* . . . Dash 5046

★ HIGHEST DEBUT ★ POS 69	★ BIGGEST MOVER ★ 46 to 26
My Life................................*Billy Joel*	(Our Love) Don't Throw It All Away.....*Andy Gibb*

TW	LW	WK	Billboard.	NOVEMBER 11, 1978	HOT 100.
❶	2	10	**MacArthur Park**..................................*Donna Summer* . . . Casablanca 939
②	1	18	You Needed Me ....*Anne Murray* . . . Capitol 4574
❸	4	8	Double Vision ....*Foreigner* . . . Atlantic 3514
❹	8	11	How Much I Feel................................*Ambrosia* . . . Warner 8640
⑤	6	23	Hot Child In The City..............................*Nick Gilder* . . . Chrysalis 2226
⑥	7	19	Kiss You All Over...*Exile* . . . Warner 8589
⑦	5	16	Whenever I Call You "Friend" ....*Kenny Loggins* . . . Columbia 10794
⑧	9	10	**Beast Of Burden** ....*The Rolling Stones* . . . Rolling Stones 19309
⑨	10	17	**Get Off** ....*Foxy* . . . Dash 5046
❿	16	10	I Just Wanna Stop...............................*Gino Vannelli* . . . A&M 2072

★ HIGHEST DEBUT ★ POS 59	★ BIGGEST MOVER ★ 68 to 31
Ooh Baby Baby................................*Linda Ronstadt*	Y.M.C.A. ....*Village People*

Billboard · NOVEMBER 18, 1978 · HOT 100

TW	LW	WK		
❶	1	11	**MacArthur Park**..................................*Donna Summer* . . . Casablanca 939	
❷	3	9	**Double Vision** ....*Foreigner* . . . Atlantic 3514	
❸	4	12	**How Much I Feel** ....*Ambrosia* . . . Warner 8640	
④	2	19	**You Needed Me** ....*Anne Murray* . . . Capitol 4574	
❺	16	4	**You Don't Bring Me Flowers** ....*Barbra Streisand & Neil Diamond* . . . Columbia 10840	
⑥	5	24	**Hot Child In The City**....................................*Nick Gilder* . . . Chrysalis 2226	
⑦	6	20	**Kiss You All Over**...*Exile* . . . Warner 8589	
⑧	10	11	**I Just Wanna Stop**......................................*Gino Vannelli* . . . A&M 2072	
⑨	7	17	**Whenever I Call You "Friend"** ....*Kenny Loggins* . . . Columbia 10794	
⑩	11	16	**You Never Done It Like That**.............*Captain & Tennille* . . . A&M 2063	

★ HIGHEST DEBUT ★ POS 35	★ BIGGEST MOVER ★ 63 to 34
Too Much Heaven..............................*Bee Gees*	Part-Time Love.................................*Elton John*

Billboard · NOVEMBER 25, 1978 · HOT 100

TW	LW	WK		
❶	1	12	**MacArthur Park**..................................*Donna Summer* . . . Casablanca 939	
②	2	10	**Double Vision** ....*Foreigner* . . . Atlantic 3514	
③	3	13	**How Much I Feel** ....*Ambrosia* . . . Warner 8640	
❹	5	5	**You Don't Bring Me Flowers** ....*Barbra Streisand & Neil Diamond* . . . Columbia 10840	
⑤	4	20	**You Needed Me** ....*Anne Murray* . . . Capitol 4574	
❻	37	5	**Le Freak** ....*Chic* . . . Atlantic 3519	
❼	8	12	**I Just Wanna Stop**......................................*Gino Vannelli* . . . A&M 2072	
⑧	12	21	**I Love The Nightlife (Disco 'Round)**..........*Alicia Bridges* . . . Polydor 14483	
⑨	15	9	**Time Passages**..*Al Stewart* . . . Arista 0362	
⑩	10	17	**You Never Done It Like That** ....*Captain & Tennille* . . . A&M 2063	

★ HIGHEST DEBUT ★ POS 68	★ BIGGEST MOVER ★ 37 to 6
A Little More Love.................*Olivia Newton-John*	Le Freak ....*Chic*

Billboard · DECEMBER 2, 1978 · HOT 100

TW	LW	WK		
❶	4	6	**You Don't Bring Me Flowers** ....*Barbra Streisand & Neil Diamond* . . . Columbia 10840	
❷	1	13	**MacArthur Park** ....*Donna Summer* . . . Casablanca 939	
③	3	14	**How Much I Feel** ....*Ambrosia* . . . Warner 8640	
❹	6	6	**Le Freak** ....*Chic* . . . Atlantic 3519	
❺	7	13	**I Just Wanna Stop**......................................*Gino Vannelli* . . . A&M 2072	
⑥	2	11	**Double Vision** ....*Foreigner* . . . Atlantic 3514	
❼	8	22	**I Love The Nightlife (Disco 'Round)**..........*Alicia Bridges* . . . Polydor 14483	
⑧	9	10	**Time Passages**..*Al Stewart* . . . Arista 0362	
⑨	16	5	**My Life** ....*Billy Joel* . . . Columbia 10853	
⑩	12	12	**Sharing The Night Together** ....*Dr. Hook* . . . Capitol 4621	

★ HIGHEST DEBUT ★ POS 78	★ BIGGEST MOVER ★ 68 to 52
Got To Be Real...............................*Cheryl Lynn*	A Little More Love.................*Olivia Newton-John*

Billboard — DECEMBER 9, 1978 — HOT 100

TW	LW	WK	Title	Artist ... Label
1	4	7	**Le Freak**	*Chic* ... Atlantic 3519
2	2	14	MacArthur Park	*Donna Summer* ... Casablanca 939
3	1	7	You Don't Bring Me Flowers	*Barbra Streisand & Neil Diamond* ... Columbia 10840
4	5	14	**I Just Wanna Stop**	*Gino Vannelli* ... A&M 2072
5	3	15	How Much I Feel	*Ambrosia* ... Warner 8640
6	7	23	I Love The Nightlife (Disco 'Round)	*Alicia Bridges* ... Polydor 14483
7	8	11	**Time Passages**	*Al Stewart* ... Arista 0362
8	9	6	My Life	*Billy Joel* ... Columbia 10853
9	10	13	Sharing The Night Together	*Dr. Hook* ... Capitol 4621
10	11	9	(Our Love) Don't Throw It All Away	*Andy Gibb* ... RSO 911

★ **HIGHEST DEBUT** ★ POS 78
Please Come Home For Christmas .... *Eagles*

★ **BIGGEST MOVER** ★ 76 to 51
Lotta Love .... *Nicolette Larson*

Billboard — DECEMBER 16, 1978 — HOT 100

TW	LW	WK	Title	Artist ... Label
1	3	8	**You Don't Bring Me Flowers**	*Barbra Streisand & Neil Diamond* ... Columbia 10840
2	1	8	Le Freak	*Chic* ... Atlantic 3519
3	12	5	Too Much Heaven	*Bee Gees* ... RSO 913
4	4	15	**I Just Wanna Stop**	*Gino Vannelli* ... A&M 2072
5	8	7	My Life	*Billy Joel* ... Columbia 10853
6	6	24	I Love The Nightlife (Disco 'Round)	*Alicia Bridges* ... Polydor 14483
7	7	12	**Time Passages**	*Al Stewart* ... Arista 0362
8	9	14	Sharing The Night Together	*Dr. Hook* ... Capitol 4621
9	10	10	(Our Love) Don't Throw It All Away	*Andy Gibb* ... RSO 911
10	2	15	MacArthur Park	*Donna Summer* ... Casablanca 939

★ **HIGHEST DEBUT** ★ POS 75
Somewhere In The Night .... *Barry Manilow*

★ **BIGGEST MOVER** ★ 78 to 45
Please Come Home For Christmas .... *Eagles*

Billboard — DECEMBER 23, 1978 — HOT 100

TW	LW	WK	Title	Artist ... Label
1	2	9	**Le Freak**	*Chic* ... Atlantic 3519
2	3	6	Too Much Heaven	*Bee Gees* ... RSO 913
3	1	9	You Don't Bring Me Flowers	*Barbra Streisand & Neil Diamond* ... Columbia 10840
4	5	8	My Life	*Billy Joel* ... Columbia 10853
5	6	25	**I Love The Nightlife (Disco 'Round)**	*Alicia Bridges* ... Polydor 14483
6	4	16	I Just Wanna Stop	*Gino Vannelli* ... A&M 2072
7	8	15	Sharing The Night Together	*Dr. Hook* ... Capitol 4621
8	12	10	Y.M.C.A.	*Village People* ... Casablanca 945
9	9	11	(Our Love) Don't Throw It All Away	*Andy Gibb* ... RSO 911
10	13	12	Hold The Line	*Toto* ... Columbia 10830

★ **HIGHEST DEBUT** ★ POS 40
Da Ya Think I'm Sexy? .... *Rod Stewart*

★ **BIGGEST MOVER** ★ 45 to 20
Please Come Home For Christmas .... *Eagles*

Billboard HOT 100 — JANUARY 6, 1979

TW	LW	WK	Title	Artist	Label
1	2	8	Too Much Heaven	Bee Gees	RSO 913
2	1	11	Le Freak	Chic	Atlantic 3519
3	4	10	My Life	Billy Joel	Columbia 10853
4	3	11	You Don't Bring Me Flowers	Barbra Streisand & Neil Diamond	Columbia 10840
5	5	27	I Love The Nightlife (Disco 'Round)	Alicia Bridges	Polydor 14483
6	7	17	Sharing The Night Together	Dr. Hook	Capitol 4621
7	8	12	Y.M.C.A.	Village People	Casablanca 945
8	10	14	Hold The Line	Toto	Columbia 10830
9	9	13	(Our Love) Don't Throw It All Away	Andy Gibb	RSO 911
10	11	9	Ooh Baby Baby	Linda Ronstadt	Asylum 45546

★ HIGHEST DEBUT ★ POS 70
The Football Card .... Glenn Sutton

★ BIGGEST MOVER ★ 57 to 31
Somewhere In The Night .... Barry Manilow

Billboard HOT 100 — JANUARY 13, 1979

TW	LW	WK	Title	Artist	Label
1	1	9	Too Much Heaven	Bee Gees	RSO 913
2	2	12	Le Freak	Chic	Atlantic 3519
3	3	11	My Life	Billy Joel	Columbia 10853
4	4	12	You Don't Bring Me Flowers	Barbra Streisand & Neil Diamond	Columbia 10840
5	8	15	Hold The Line	Toto	Columbia 10830
6	6	18	Sharing The Night Together	Dr. Hook	Capitol 4621
7	7	13	Y.M.C.A.	Village People	Casablanca 945
8	10	10	Ooh Baby Baby	Linda Ronstadt	Asylum 45546
9	9	14	(Our Love) Don't Throw It All Away	Andy Gibb	RSO 911
10	11	14	Promises	Eric Clapton & His Band	RSO 910

★ HIGHEST DEBUT ★ POS 77
Heaven Knows .... Donna Summer with Brooklyn Dreams

★ BIGGEST MOVER ★ 70 to 52
The Football Card .... Glenn Sutton

Billboard HOT 100 — JANUARY 20, 1979

TW	LW	WK	Title	Artist	Label
1	2	13	Le Freak	Chic	Atlantic 3519
2	1	10	Too Much Heaven	Bee Gees	RSO 913
3	3	12	My Life	Billy Joel	Columbia 10853
4	7	14	Y.M.C.A.	Village People	Casablanca 945
5	5	16	Hold The Line	Toto	Columbia 10830
6	4	13	You Don't Bring Me Flowers	Barbra Streisand & Neil Diamond	Columbia 10840
7	8	11	Ooh Baby Baby	Linda Ronstadt	Asylum 45546
8	11	9	A Little More Love	Olivia Newton-John	MCA 40975
9	10	15	Promises	Eric Clapton & His Band	RSO 910
10	22	5	Da Ya Think I'm Sexy?	Rod Stewart	Warner 8724

★ HIGHEST DEBUT ★ POS 72
Crazy Love .... Poco

★ BIGGEST MOVER ★ 77 to 40
Heaven Knows .... Donna Summer with Brooklyn Dreams

Billboard HOT 100 — JANUARY 27, 1979

TW	LW	WK	Title	Artist	Label
1	1	14	Le Freak	Chic	Atlantic 3519
2	2	11	Too Much Heaven	Bee Gees	RSO 913
3	4	15	Y.M.C.A.	Village People	Casablanca 945
4	10	6	Da Ya Think I'm Sexy?	Rod Stewart	Warner 8724
5	3	13	My Life	Billy Joel	Columbia 10853
6	8	10	A Little More Love	Olivia Newton-John	MCA 40975
7	7	12	Ooh Baby Baby	Linda Ronstadt	Asylum 45546
8	5	17	Hold The Line	Toto	Columbia 10830
9	11	12	Every 1's A Winner	Hot Chocolate	Infinity 50002
10	12	11	September	Earth, Wind & Fire	ARC 10854

★ **HIGHEST DEBUT** ★ POS 57
I Just Fall In Love Again .... Anne Murray

★ **BIGGEST MOVER** ★ 35 to 20
I Will Survive .... Gloria Gaynor

Billboard HOT 100 — FEBRUARY 3, 1979

TW	LW	WK	Title	Artist	Label
1	1	15	Le Freak	Chic	Atlantic 3519
2	3	16	Y.M.C.A.	Village People	Casablanca 945
3	4	7	Da Ya Think I'm Sexy?	Rod Stewart	Warner 8724
4	6	11	A Little More Love	Olivia Newton-John	MCA 40975
5	2	12	Too Much Heaven	Bee Gees	RSO 913
6	5	14	My Life	Billy Joel	Columbia 10853
7	9	13	Every 1's A Winner	Hot Chocolate	Infinity 50002
8	11	13	Fire	Pointer Sisters	Planet 45901
9	10	12	September	Earth, Wind & Fire	ARC 10854
10	20	8	I Will Survive	Gloria Gaynor	Polydor 14508

★ **HIGHEST DEBUT** ★ POS 82
Dog & Butterfly .... Heart

★ **BIGGEST MOVER** ★ 62 to 41
What A Fool Believes .... The Doobie Brothers

Billboard HOT 100 — FEBRUARY 10, 1979

TW	LW	WK	Title	Artist	Label
1	3	8	Da Ya Think I'm Sexy?	Rod Stewart	Warner 8724
2	2	17	Y.M.C.A.	Village People	Casablanca 945
3	1	16	Le Freak	Chic	Atlantic 3519
4	4	12	A Little More Love	Olivia Newton-John	MCA 40975
5	8	14	Fire	Pointer Sisters	Planet 45901
6	7	14	Every 1's A Winner	Hot Chocolate	Infinity 50002
7	10	9	I Will Survive	Gloria Gaynor	Polydor 14508
8	9	13	September	Earth, Wind & Fire	ARC 10854
9	5	13	Too Much Heaven	Bee Gees	RSO 913
10	11	12	Lotta Love	Nicolette Larson	Warner 8664

★ **HIGHEST DEBUT** ★ POS 29
Tragedy .... Bee Gees

★ **BIGGEST MOVER** ★ 78 to 49
Stumblin' In .... Suzi Quatro & Chris Norman

Billboard — FEBRUARY 17, 1979 — HOT 100

TW	LW	WK	Title	Artist	Label
1	1	9	**Da Ya Think I'm Sexy?**	Rod Stewart	Warner 8724
2	2	18	**Y.M.C.A.**	Village People	Casablanca 945
3	4	13	**A Little More Love**	Olivia Newton-John	MCA 40975
4	5	15	**Fire**	Pointer Sisters	Planet 45901
5	7	10	**I Will Survive**	Gloria Gaynor	Polydor 14508
6	6	15	**Every 1's A Winner**	Hot Chocolate	Infinity 50002
7	3	17	**Le Freak**	Chic	Atlantic 3519
8	10	13	**Lotta Love**	Nicolette Larson	Warner 8664
9	11	10	**Somewhere In The Night**	Barry Manilow	Arista 0382
10	12	15	**I Was Made For Dancin'**	Leif Garrett	Scotti Brothers 403

★ HIGHEST DEBUT ★ POS 81 — Sinner Man .... Sarah Dash
★ BIGGEST MOVER ★ 47 to 33 — Sultans Of Swing .... Dire Straits

Billboard — FEBRUARY 24, 1979 — HOT 100

TW	LW	WK	Title	Artist	Label
1	1	10	**Da Ya Think I'm Sexy?**	Rod Stewart	Warner 8724
2	4	16	**Fire**	Pointer Sisters	Planet 45901
3	3	14	**A Little More Love**	Olivia Newton-John	MCA 40975
4	5	11	**I Will Survive**	Gloria Gaynor	Polydor 14508
5	2	19	**Y.M.C.A.**	Village People	Casablanca 945
6	19	3	**Tragedy**	Bee Gees	RSO 918
7	7	18	**Le Freak**	Chic	Atlantic 3519
8	8	14	**Lotta Love**	Nicolette Larson	Warner 8664
9	9	11	**Somewhere In The Night**	Barry Manilow	Arista 0382
10	10	16	**I Was Made For Dancin'**	Leif Garrett	Scotti Brothers 403

★ HIGHEST DEBUT ★ POS 77 — Watch Out For Lucy .... Eric Clapton & His Band
★ BIGGEST MOVER ★ 19 to 6 — Tragedy .... Bee Gees

Billboard — MARCH 3, 1979 — HOT 100

TW	LW	WK	Title	Artist	Label
1	1	11	**Da Ya Think I'm Sexy?**	Rod Stewart	Warner 8724
2	2	17	**Fire**	Pointer Sisters	Planet 45901
3	4	12	**I Will Survive**	Gloria Gaynor	Polydor 14508
4	6	4	**Tragedy**	Bee Gees	RSO 918
5	3	15	**A Little More Love**	Olivia Newton-John	MCA 40975
6	11	8	**Heaven Knows**	Donna Summer with Brooklyn Dreams	Casablanca 959
7	7	19	**Le Freak**	Chic	Atlantic 3519
8	5	20	**Y.M.C.A.**	Village People	Casablanca 945
9	8	15	**Lotta Love**	Nicolette Larson	Warner 8664
10	23	7	**What A Fool Believes**	The Doobie Brothers	Warner 8725

★ HIGHEST DEBUT ★ POS 66 — Rubber Biscuit .... Blues Brothers
★ BIGGEST MOVER ★ 51 to 23 — Big Shot .... Billy Joel

Billboard — MARCH 10, 1979 — HOT 100

TW	LW	WK	Title	Artist	Label
1	3	13	I Will Survive	Gloria Gaynor	Polydor 14508
2	1	12	Da Ya Think I'm Sexy?	Rod Stewart	Warner 8724
3	4	5	Tragedy	Bee Gees	RSO 918
4	2	18	Fire	Pointer Sisters	Planet 45901
5	6	9	Heaven Knows	Donna Summer with Brooklyn Dreams	Casablanca 959
6	5	16	A Little More Love	Olivia Newton-John	MCA 40975
7	11	13	Shake Your Groove Thing	Peaches & Herb	Polydor 14514
8	10	8	What A Fool Believes	The Doobie Brothers	Warner 8725
9	8	21	Y.M.C.A.	Village People	Casablanca 945
10	13	5	Sultans Of Swing	Dire Straits	Warner 8736

★ **HIGHEST DEBUT** ★ POS 81
Love Is The Answer.......England Dan & John Ford Coley

★ **BIGGEST MOVER** ★ 65 to 51
I Got My Mind Made Up (You Can Get It Girl)..............................Instant Funk

Billboard — MARCH 17, 1979 — HOT 100

TW	LW	WK	Title	Artist	Label
1	1	14	I Will Survive	Gloria Gaynor	Polydor 14508
2	3	6	Tragedy	Bee Gees	RSO 918
3	2	13	Da Ya Think I'm Sexy?	Rod Stewart	Warner 8724
4	5	10	Heaven Knows	Donna Summer with Brooklyn Dreams	Casablanca 959
5	7	14	Shake Your Groove Thing	Peaches & Herb	Polydor 14514
6	8	9	What A Fool Believes	The Doobie Brothers	Warner 8725
7	4	19	Fire	Pointer Sisters	Planet 45901
8	10	6	Sultans Of Swing	Dire Straits	Warner 8736
9	6	17	A Little More Love	Olivia Newton-John	MCA 40975
10	15	13	What You Won't Do For Love	Bobby Caldwell	Clouds 11

★ **HIGHEST DEBUT** ★ POS 67
In The Navy ....Village People

★ **BIGGEST MOVER** ★ 47 to 26
Heart Of Glass ....Blondie

Billboard — MARCH 24, 1979 — HOT 100

TW	LW	WK	Title	Artist	Label
1	2	7	Tragedy	Bee Gees	RSO 918
2	1	15	I Will Survive	Gloria Gaynor	Polydor 14508
3	6	10	What A Fool Believes	The Doobie Brothers	Warner 8725
4	4	11	Heaven Knows	Donna Summer with Brooklyn Dreams	Casablanca 959
5	5	15	Shake Your Groove Thing	Peaches & Herb	Polydor 14514
6	3	14	Da Ya Think I'm Sexy?	Rod Stewart	Warner 8724
7	8	7	Sultans Of Swing	Dire Straits	Warner 8736
8	7	20	Fire	Pointer Sisters	Planet 45901
9	10	14	What You Won't Do For Love	Bobby Caldwell	Clouds 11
10	9	18	A Little More Love	Olivia Newton-John	MCA 40975

★ **HIGHEST DEBUT** ★ POS 77
Bridge Over Troubled Water...........Linda Clifford

★ **BIGGEST MOVER** ★ 67 to 49
In The Navy ....Village People

Billboard — MARCH 31, 1979 — HOT 100

TW	LW	WK	Title	Artist	Label
①	1	8	**Tragedy**	*Bee Gees*	RSO 918
②	2	16	I Will Survive	*Gloria Gaynor*	Polydor 14508
③	3	11	What A Fool Believes	*The Doobie Brothers*	Warner 8725
④	4	12	**Heaven Knows**	*Donna Summer with Brooklyn Dreams*	Casablanca 959
⑤	5	16	**Shake Your Groove Thing**	*Peaches & Herb*	Polydor 14514
⑥	7	8	Sultans Of Swing	*Dire Straits*	Warner 8736
⑦	6	15	Da Ya Think I'm Sexy?	*Rod Stewart*	Warner 8724
⑧	15	10	Knock On Wood	*Amii Stewart*	Ariola 7736
⑨	9	15	**What You Won't Do For Love**	*Bobby Caldwell*	Clouds 11
⑩	11	20	**Don't Cry Out Loud**	*Melissa Manchester*	Arista 0373

★ **HIGHEST DEBUT** ★ POS 38
Goodnight Tonight......................*Wings*

★ **BIGGEST MOVER** ★ 66 to 26
Reunited................................*Peaches & Herb*

Billboard — APRIL 7, 1979 — HOT 100

TW	LW	WK	Title	Artist	Label
①	2	17	**I Will Survive**	*Gloria Gaynor*	Polydor 14508
②	3	12	**What A Fool Believes**	*The Doobie Brothers*	Warner 8725
③	1	9	Tragedy	*Bee Gees*	RSO 918
④	6	9	**Sultans Of Swing**	*Dire Straits*	Warner 8736
⑤	5	17	**Shake Your Groove Thing**	*Peaches & Herb*	Polydor 14514
⑥	18	11	Music Box Dancer	*Frank Mills*	Polydor 14517
⑦	8	11	Knock On Wood	*Amii Stewart*	Ariola 7736
⑧	7	16	Da Ya Think I'm Sexy?	*Rod Stewart*	Warner 8724
⑨	15	8	Heart Of Glass	*Blondie*	Chrysalis 2295
⑩	11	14	Lady	*Little River Band*	Harvest 4667

★ **HIGHEST DEBUT** ★ POS 72
Old Time Rock & Roll........*Bob Seger & The Silver Bullet Band*

★ **BIGGEST MOVER** ★ 69 to 35
Love Takes Time ....*Orleans*

Billboard — APRIL 14, 1979 — HOT 100

TW	LW	WK	Title	Artist	Label
①	2	13	**What A Fool Believes**	*The Doobie Brothers*	Warner 8725
②	1	18	I Will Survive	*Gloria Gaynor*	Polydor 14508
③	7	12	Knock On Wood	*Amii Stewart*	Ariola 7736
④	4	10	**Sultans Of Swing**	*Dire Straits*	Warner 8736
⑤	6	12	Music Box Dancer	*Frank Mills*	Polydor 14517
⑥	3	10	Tragedy	*Bee Gees*	RSO 918
⑦	15	5	Reunited	*Peaches & Herb*	Polydor 14547
⑧	9	9	Heart Of Glass	*Blondie*	Chrysalis 2295
⑨	11	12	Stumblin' In	*Suzi Quatro & Chris Norman*	RSO 917
⑩	10	15	Lady	*Little River Band*	Harvest 4667

★ **HIGHEST DEBUT** ★ POS 73
Little Bit Of Soap..................*Nigel Olsson*

★ **BIGGEST MOVER** ★ 87 to 65
I (Who Have Nothing) ....*Sylvester*

Billboard HOT 100 — APRIL 21, 1979

TW	LW	WK	Title	Artist	Label
1	3	13	**Knock On Wood**	Amii Stewart	Ariola 7736
2	2	19	I Will Survive	Gloria Gaynor	Polydor 14508
3	8	10	Heart Of Glass	Blondie	Chrysalis 2295
4	5	13	Music Box Dancer	Frank Mills	Polydor 14517
5	1	14	What A Fool Believes	The Doobie Brothers	Warner 8725
6	7	6	Reunited	Peaches & Herb	Polydor 14547
7	9	13	Stumblin' In	Suzi Quatro & Chris Norman	RSO 917
8	6	11	Tragedy	Bee Gees	RSO 918
9	11	11	I Want Your Love	Chic	Atlantic 3557
10	4	11	Sultans Of Swing	Dire Straits	Warner 8736

★ **HIGHEST DEBUT** ★ POS 37
Love You Inside Out..........Bee Gees

★ **BIGGEST MOVER** ★ 78 to 54
Dancer..........Gino Soccio

Billboard HOT 100 — APRIL 28, 1979

TW	LW	WK	Title	Artist	Label
1	3	11	**Heart Of Glass**	Blondie	Chrysalis 2295
2	6	7	Reunited	Peaches & Herb	Polydor 14547
3	1	14	Knock On Wood	Amii Stewart	Ariola 7736
4	4	14	Music Box Dancer	Frank Mills	Polydor 14517
5	2	20	I Will Survive	Gloria Gaynor	Polydor 14508
6	7	14	Stumblin' In	Suzi Quatro & Chris Norman	RSO 917
7	5	15	What A Fool Believes	The Doobie Brothers	Warner 8725
8	9	12	I Want Your Love	Chic	Atlantic 3557
9	11	5	Goodnight Tonight	Wings	Columbia 10939
10	12	7	In The Navy	Village People	Casablanca 973

★ **HIGHEST DEBUT** ★ POS 61
She Believes In Me..........Kenny Rogers

★ **BIGGEST MOVER** ★ 79 to 29
Hot Stuff..........Donna Summer

Billboard HOT 100 — MAY 5, 1979

TW	LW	WK	Title	Artist	Label
1	2	8	**Reunited**	Peaches & Herb	Polydor 14547
2	1	12	Heart Of Glass	Blondie	Chrysalis 2295
3	4	15	**Music Box Dancer**	Frank Mills	Polydor 14517
4	3	15	Knock On Wood	Amii Stewart	Ariola 7736
5	6	15	Stumblin' In	Suzi Quatro & Chris Norman	RSO 917
6	10	8	In The Navy	Village People	Casablanca 973
7	8	13	**I Want Your Love**	Chic	Atlantic 3557
8	9	6	Goodnight Tonight	Wings	Columbia 10939
9	12	13	Take Me Home	Cher	Casablanca 965
10	11	13	He's The Greatest Dancer	Sister Sledge	Cotillion 44245

★ **HIGHEST DEBUT** ★ POS 67
Minute By Minute..........The Doobie Brothers

★ **BIGGEST MOVER** ★ 77 to 59
You Take My Breath Away..........Rex Smith

Billboard — MAY 12, 1979 — HOT 100

TW	LW	WK	Title	Artist	Label
❶	1	9	Reunited	Peaches & Herb	Polydor 14547
②	2	13	Heart Of Glass	Blondie	Chrysalis 2295
❸	20	4	Hot Stuff	Donna Summer	Casablanca 978
④	5	16	Stumblin' In	Suzi Quatro & Chris Norman	RSO 917
❺	6	9	In The Navy	Village People	Casablanca 973
❻	8	7	Goodnight Tonight	Wings	Columbia 10939
⑦	7	14	I Want Your Love	Chic	Atlantic 3557
❽	9	14	Take Me Home	Cher	Casablanca 965
❾	10	14	He's The Greatest Dancer	Sister Sledge	Cotillion 44245
❿	12	13	Shake Your Body (Down To The Ground)	The Jacksons	Epic 50656

★ **HIGHEST DEBUT** ★ POS 69
Boogie Wonderland .....Earth, Wind & Fire with The Emotions

★ **BIGGEST MOVER** ★ 59 to 30
You Take My Breath Away ....Rex Smith

Billboard — MAY 19, 1979 — HOT 100

TW	LW	WK	Title	Artist	Label
❶	1	10	Reunited	Peaches & Herb	Polydor 14547
❷	3	5	Hot Stuff	Donna Summer	Casablanca 978
❸	5	10	In The Navy	Village People	Casablanca 973
④	4	17	Stumblin' In	Suzi Quatro & Chris Norman	RSO 917
❺	6	8	Goodnight Tonight	Wings	Columbia 10939
❻	11	5	Love You Inside Out	Bee Gees	RSO 925
❼	10	14	Shake Your Body (Down To The Ground)	The Jacksons	Epic 50656
⑧	8	15	Take Me Home	Cher	Casablanca 965
⑨	9	15	He's The Greatest Dancer	Sister Sledge	Cotillion 44245
❿	2	14	Heart Of Glass	Blondie	Chrysalis 2295

★ **HIGHEST DEBUT** ★ POS 57
Shine A Little Love ....Electric Light Orchestra

★ **BIGGEST MOVER** ★ 69 to 42
Boogie Wonderland .....Earth, Wind & Fire with The Emotions

Billboard — MAY 26, 1979 — HOT 100

TW	LW	WK	Title	Artist	Label
❶	1	11	Reunited	Peaches & Herb	Polydor 14547
❷	2	6	Hot Stuff	Donna Summer	Casablanca 978
③	3	11	In The Navy	Village People	Casablanca 973
❹	6	6	Love You Inside Out	Bee Gees	RSO 925
❺	5	9	Goodnight Tonight	Wings	Columbia 10939
❻	13	5	We Are Family	Sister Sledge	Cotillion 44251
⑦	7	15	Shake Your Body (Down To The Ground)	The Jacksons	Epic 50656
❽	15	10	Just When I Needed You Most	Randy Vanwarmer	Bearsville 0334
⑨	4	18	Stumblin' In	Suzi Quatro & Chris Norman	RSO 917
❿	11	12	Love Is The Answer	England Dan & John Ford Coley	Big Tree 16131

★ **HIGHEST DEBUT** ★ POS 55
Bad Girls ....Donna Summer

★ **BIGGEST MOVER** ★ 73 to 39
Ring My Bell ....Anita Ward

Billboard — JUNE 2, 1979 — HOT 100

TW	LW	WK	Title	Artist	Label
1	2	7	**Hot Stuff**	*Donna Summer*	Casablanca 978
2	1	12	Reunited	*Peaches & Herb*	Polydor 14547
3	4	7	Love You Inside Out	*Bee Gees*	RSO 925
4	6	6	We Are Family	*Sister Sledge*	Cotillion 44251
5	5	10	**Goodnight Tonight**	*Wings*	Columbia 10939
6	8	11	Just When I Needed You Most	*Randy Vanwarmer*	Bearsville 0334
7	7	16	**Shake Your Body (Down To The Ground)**	*The Jacksons*	Epic 50656
8	3	12	In The Navy	*Village People*	Casablanca 973
9	12	11	The Logical Song	*Supertramp*	A&M 2128
10	10	13	**Love Is The Answer**	*England Dan & John Ford Coley*	Big Tree 16131

★ **HIGHEST DEBUT** ★ POS 68
Days Gone Down (Still Got The Light In Your Eyes)............*Gerry Rafferty*

★ **BIGGEST MOVER** ★ 39 to 19
Ring My Bell............*Anita Ward*

Billboard — JUNE 9, 1979 — HOT 100

TW	LW	WK	Title	Artist	Label
1	3	8	**Love You Inside Out**	*Bee Gees*	RSO 925
2	1	8	Hot Stuff	*Donna Summer*	Casablanca 978
3	4	7	We Are Family	*Sister Sledge*	Cotillion 44251
4	2	13	Reunited	*Peaches & Herb*	Polydor 14547
5	6	12	Just When I Needed You Most	*Randy Vanwarmer*	Bearsville 0334
6	19	5	Ring My Bell	*Anita Ward*	Juana 3422
7	9	12	The Logical Song	*Supertramp*	A&M 2128
8	11	7	Chuck E.'s In Love	*Rickie Lee Jones*	Warner 8825
9	7	17	Shake Your Body (Down To The Ground)	*The Jacksons*	Epic 50656
10	14	7	She Believes In Me	*Kenny Rogers*	United Artists 1273

★ **HIGHEST DEBUT** ★ POS 69
Mama Can't Buy You Love............*Elton John*

★ **BIGGEST MOVER** ★ 68 to 47
Days Gone Down (Still Got The Light In Your Eyes)............*Gerry Rafferty*

Billboard — JUNE 16, 1979 — HOT 100

TW	LW	WK	Title	Artist	Label
1	2	9	**Hot Stuff**	*Donna Summer*	Casablanca 978
2	3	8	**We Are Family**	*Sister Sledge*	Cotillion 44251
3	6	6	Ring My Bell	*Anita Ward*	Juana 3422
4	5	13	**Just When I Needed You Most**	*Randy Vanwarmer*	Bearsville 0334
5	1	9	Love You Inside Out	*Bee Gees*	RSO 925
6	7	13	**The Logical Song**	*Supertramp*	A&M 2128
7	8	8	Chuck E.'s In Love	*Rickie Lee Jones*	Warner 8825
8	10	8	She Believes In Me	*Kenny Rogers*	United Artists 1273
9	4	14	Reunited	*Peaches & Herb*	Polydor 14547
10	19	6	Boogie Wonderland	*Earth, Wind & Fire with The Emotions*	ARC 10956

★ **HIGHEST DEBUT** ★ POS 64
Getting Closer............*Wings*

★ **BIGGEST MOVER** ★ 68 to 50
Up On The Roof............*James Taylor*

Billboard HOT 100 — JUNE 23, 1979

TW	LW	WK	Title	Artist	Label
1	1	10	**Hot Stuff**	*Donna Summer*	Casablanca 978
2	2	9	**We Are Family**	*Sister Sledge*	Cotillion 44251
3	3	7	Ring My Bell	*Anita Ward*	Juana 3422
4	4	14	**Just When I Needed You Most**	*Randy Vanwarmer*	Bearsville 0334
5	11	5	Bad Girls	*Donna Summer*	Casablanca 988
6	6	14	**The Logical Song**	*Supertramp*	A&M 2128
7	7	9	Chuck E.'s In Love	*Rickie Lee Jones*	Warner 8825
8	8	9	She Believes In Me	*Kenny Rogers*	United Artists 1273
9	10	7	Boogie Wonderland	*Earth, Wind & Fire with The Emotions*	ARC 10956
10	12	10	**You Take My Breath Away**	*Rex Smith*	Columbia 10908

★ **HIGHEST DEBUT** ★ POS 81
The Devil Went Down To Georgia......*The Charlie Daniels Band*

★ **BIGGEST MOVER** ★ 58 to 40
Mama Can't Buy You Love...............*Elton John*

Billboard HOT 100 — JUNE 30, 1979

TW	LW	WK	Title	Artist	Label
1	3	8	**Ring My Bell**	*Anita Ward*	Juana 3422
2	1	11	Hot Stuff	*Donna Summer*	Casablanca 978
3	5	6	Bad Girls	*Donna Summer*	Casablanca 988
4	2	10	We Are Family	*Sister Sledge*	Cotillion 44251
5	7	10	Chuck E.'s In Love	*Rickie Lee Jones*	Warner 8825
6	6	15	**The Logical Song**	*Supertramp*	A&M 2128
7	8	10	She Believes In Me	*Kenny Rogers*	United Artists 1273
8	9	8	Boogie Wonderland	*Earth, Wind & Fire with The Emotions*	ARC 10956
9	4	15	Just When I Needed You Most	*Randy Vanwarmer*	Bearsville 0334
10	10	11	**You Take My Breath Away**	*Rex Smith*	Columbia 10908

★ **HIGHEST DEBUT** ★ POS 80
Let's Go..............................*The Cars*

★ **BIGGEST MOVER** ★ 51 to 37
Getting Closer ....*Wings*

Billboard HOT 100 — JULY 7, 1979

TW	LW	WK	Title	Artist	Label
1	1	9	**Ring My Bell**	*Anita Ward*	Juana 3422
2	3	7	**Bad Girls**	*Donna Summer*	Casablanca 988
3	2	12	**Hot Stuff**	*Donna Summer*	Casablanca 978
4	5	11	**Chuck E.'s In Love**	*Rickie Lee Jones*	Warner 8825
5	7	11	**She Believes In Me**	*Kenny Rogers*	United Artists 1273
6	6	16	**The Logical Song**	*Supertramp*	A&M 2128
7	8	9	Boogie Wonderland	*Earth, Wind & Fire with The Emotions*	ARC 10956
8	4	11	We Are Family	*Sister Sledge*	Cotillion 44251
9	13	15	Makin' It	*David Naughton*	RSO 916
10	12	11	I Want You To Want Me	*Cheap Trick*	Epic 50680

★ **HIGHEST DEBUT** ★ POS 77
After The Love Has Gone ....*Earth, Wind & Fire*

★ **BIGGEST MOVER** ★ 50 to 25
Good Times...*Chic*

TW	LW	WK	Billboard		JULY 14, 1979		HOT 100.
1	2	8	**Bad Girls**..*Donna Summer* . . . Casablanca 988
②	1	10	**Ring My Bell**...*Anita Ward* . . . Juana 3422
③	3	13	**Hot Stuff**...*Donna Summer* . . . Casablanca 978
④	4	12	**Chuck E.'s In Love**............................*Rickie Lee Jones* . . . Warner 8825
⑤	5	12	**She Believes In Me** ....*Kenny Rogers* . . . United Artists 1273
6	7	10	**Boogie Wonderland** ....*Earth, Wind & Fire with The Emotions* . . . ARC 10956
7	9	16	**Makin' It**...*David Naughton* . . . RSO 916
8	10	12	**I Want You To Want Me**....................*Cheap Trick* . . . Epic 50680
9	13	9	**Shine A Little Love**...........................*Electric Light Orchestra* . . . Jet 5057
10	11	9	**Gold**...*John Stewart* . . . RSO 931

★ HIGHEST DEBUT ★ POS 80	★ BIGGEST MOVER ★ 69 to 51
The Boss............................*Diana Ross*	**Let's Go**............................*The Cars*

TW	LW	WK	Billboard		JULY 21, 1979		HOT 100.
1	1	9	**Bad Girls**..*Donna Summer* . . . Casablanca 988
②	2	11	**Ring My Bell**...*Anita Ward* . . . Juana 3422
③	3	14	**Hot Stuff**...*Donna Summer* . . . Casablanca 978
4	13	6	**Good Times**...*Chic* . . . Atlantic 3584
5	7	17	**Makin' It**...*David Naughton* . . . RSO 916
⑥	6	11	**Boogie Wonderland** ....*Earth, Wind & Fire with The Emotions* . . . ARC 10956
7	8	13	**I Want You To Want Me** ....*Cheap Trick* . . . Epic 50680
8	9	10	**Shine A Little Love**...........................*Electric Light Orchestra* . . . Jet 5057
9	10	10	**Gold**...*John Stewart* . . . RSO 931
⑩	5	13	**She Believes In Me** ....*Kenny Rogers* . . . United Artists 1273

★ HIGHEST DEBUT ★ POS 63	★ BIGGEST MOVER ★ 68 to 46
Lonesome Loser.......................*Little River Band*	**After The Love Has Gone** ....*Earth, Wind & Fire*

TW	LW	WK	Billboard		JULY 28, 1979		HOT 100.
1	1	10	**Bad Girls**..*Donna Summer* . . . Casablanca 988
②	2	12	**Ring My Bell**...*Anita Ward* . . . Juana 3422
3	4	7	**Good Times**...*Chic* . . . Atlantic 3584
④	3	15	**Hot Stuff**...*Donna Summer* . . . Casablanca 978
⑤	5	18	**Makin' It**...*David Naughton* . . . RSO 916
6	9	11	**Gold**...*John Stewart* . . . RSO 931
⑦	7	14	**I Want You To Want Me** ....*Cheap Trick* . . . Epic 50680
8	8	11	**Shine A Little Love**...........................*Electric Light Orchestra* . . . Jet 5057
9	11	16	**When You're In Love With A Beautiful Woman**......................*Dr. Hook* . . . Capitol 4705
10	16	7	**The Main Event/Fight**.......................*Barbra Streisand* . . . Columbia 11008

★ HIGHEST DEBUT ★ POS 74	★ BIGGEST MOVER ★ 63 to 44
Young Blood ....*Rickie Lee Jones*	**Lonesome Loser**......................*Little River Band*

Billboard — AUGUST 4, 1979 — HOT 100

TW	LW	WK			
1	1	11	**Bad Girls**...	*Donna Summer* . . .	Casablanca 988
2	3	8	**Good Times**...	*Chic* . . .	Atlantic 3584
3	2	13	**Ring My Bell**...	*Anita Ward* . . .	Juana 3422
4	10	8	**The Main Event/Fight**..........................	*Barbra Streisand* . . .	Columbia 11008
5	6	12	**Gold**...	*John Stewart* . . .	RSO 931
6	18	7	**My Sharona**...	*The Knack* . . .	Capitol 4731
7	5	19	**Makin' It**...	*David Naughton* . . .	RSO 916
8	9	17	**When You're In Love With A Beautiful Woman**......................	*Dr. Hook*	. . . Capitol 4705
9	4	16	**Hot Stuff**...	*Donna Summer* . . .	Casablanca 978
10	7	15	**I Want You To Want Me**................................	*Cheap Trick* . . .	Epic 50680

★ HIGHEST DEBUT ★ POS 41	★ BIGGEST MOVER ★ 84 to 59
Don't Bring Me Down ....*Electric Light Orchestra*	Why Leave Us Alone ....*Five Special*

Billboard — AUGUST 11, 1979 — HOT 100

TW	LW	WK			
1	1	12	**Bad Girls**...	*Donna Summer* . . .	Casablanca 988
2	2	9	**Good Times**...	*Chic* . . .	Atlantic 3584
3	4	9	**The Main Event/Fight**	*Barbra Streisand* . . .	Columbia 11008
4	6	8	**My Sharona**	*The Knack* . . .	Capitol 4731
5	5	13	**Gold**	*John Stewart* . . .	RSO 931
6	8	18	**When You're In Love With A Beautiful Woman**	*Dr. Hook*	. . . Capitol 4705
7	3	14	**Ring My Bell**...	*Anita Ward* . . .	Juana 3422
8	7	20	**Makin' It**...	*David Naughton* . . .	RSO 916
9	9	17	**Hot Stuff**...	*Donna Summer* . . .	Casablanca 978
10	11	16	**You Can't Change That**................................	*Raydio* . . .	Arista 0399

★ HIGHEST DEBUT ★ POS 61	★ BIGGEST MOVER ★ 41 to 18
Pop Muzik..*M*	Don't Bring Me Down ....*Electric Light Orchestra*

Billboard — AUGUST 18, 1979 — HOT 100

TW	LW	WK			
1	2	10	**Good Times**...	*Chic* . . .	Atlantic 3584
2	4	9	**My Sharona**	*The Knack* . . .	Capitol 4731
3	3	10	**The Main Event/Fight**	*Barbra Streisand* . . .	Columbia 11008
4	1	13	**Bad Girls**	*Donna Summer* . . .	Casablanca 988
5	19	7	**After The Love Has Gone**	*Earth, Wind & Fire* . . .	ARC 11033
6	6	19	**When You're In Love With A Beautiful Woman**	*Dr. Hook*	. . . Capitol 4705
7	7	15	**Ring My Bell**...	*Anita Ward* . . .	Juana 3422
8	21	9	**The Devil Went Down To Georgia**	*The Charlie Daniels Band*	. . . Epic 50700
9	10	17	**You Can't Change That**................................	*Raydio* . . .	Arista 0399
10	12	11	**Mama Can't Buy You Love**................................	*Elton John* . . .	MCA 41042

★ HIGHEST DEBUT ★ POS 81	★ BIGGEST MOVER ★ 68 to 37
Rolene..*Moon Martin*	Sail On..*Commodores*

'79

Billboard — AUGUST 25, 1979 — HOT 100

TW	LW	WK	Title	Artist
1	2	10	My Sharona	The Knack ... Capitol 4731
2	1	11	Good Times	Chic ... Atlantic 3584
3	3	11	The Main Event/Fight	Barbra Streisand ... Columbia 11008
4	5	8	After The Love Has Gone	Earth, Wind & Fire ... ARC 11033
5	4	14	Bad Girls	Donna Summer ... Casablanca 988
6	14	4	Don't Bring Me Down	Electric Light Orchestra ... Jet 5060
7	8	10	The Devil Went Down To Georgia	The Charlie Daniels Band ... Epic 50700
8	13	14	Lead Me On	Maxine Nightingale ... Windsong 11530
9	10	12	Mama Can't Buy You Love	Elton John ... MCA 41042
10	12	15	Sad Eyes	Robert John ... EMI America 8015

★ **HIGHEST DEBUT** ★ POS 70
Dim All The Lights .... Donna Summer

★ **BIGGEST MOVER** ★ 68 to 51
Get It Right Next Time .... Gerry Rafferty

Billboard — SEPTEMBER 1, 1979 — HOT 100

TW	LW	WK	Title	Artist
1	1	11	My Sharona	The Knack ... Capitol 4731
2	2	12	Good Times	Chic ... Atlantic 3584
3	3	12	The Main Event/Fight	Barbra Streisand ... Columbia 11008
4	4	9	After The Love Has Gone	Earth, Wind & Fire ... ARC 11033
5	6	5	Don't Bring Me Down	Electric Light Orchestra ... Jet 5060
6	7	11	The Devil Went Down To Georgia	The Charlie Daniels Band ... Epic 50700
7	8	15	Lead Me On	Maxine Nightingale ... Windsong 11530
8	10	16	Sad Eyes	Robert John ... EMI America 8015
9	9	13	Mama Can't Buy You Love	Elton John ... MCA 41042
10	14	11	I'll Never Love This Way Again	Dionne Warwick ... Arista 0419

★ **HIGHEST DEBUT** ★ POS 80
Voulez-Vous .... Abba

★ **BIGGEST MOVER** ★ 54 to 35
Don't Stop 'Til You Get Enough .... Michael Jackson

Billboard — SEPTEMBER 8, 1979 — HOT 100

TW	LW	WK	Title	Artist
1	1	12	My Sharona	The Knack ... Capitol 4731
2	2	13	Good Times	Chic ... Atlantic 3584
3	4	10	After The Love Has Gone	Earth, Wind & Fire ... ARC 11033
4	5	6	Don't Bring Me Down	Electric Light Orchestra ... Jet 5060
5	6	12	The Devil Went Down To Georgia	The Charlie Daniels Band ... Epic 50700
6	7	16	Lead Me On	Maxine Nightingale ... Windsong 11530
7	8	17	Sad Eyes	Robert John ... EMI America 8015
8	3	13	The Main Event/Fight	Barbra Streisand ... Columbia 11008
9	10	12	I'll Never Love This Way Again	Dionne Warwick ... Arista 0419
10	12	8	Lonesome Loser	Little River Band ... Capitol 4748

★ **HIGHEST DEBUT** ★ POS 65
Dirty White Boy .... Foreigner

★ **BIGGEST MOVER** ★ 82 to 61
Good Girls Don't .... The Knack

Billboard — SEPTEMBER 15, 1979 — HOT 100

TW	LW	WK	Title	Artist ... Label
1	1	13	**My Sharona**	The Knack ... Capitol 4731
2	3	11	**After The Love Has Gone**	Earth, Wind & Fire ... ARC 11033
3	5	13	**The Devil Went Down To Georgia**	The Charlie Daniels Band ... Epic 50700
4	4	7	**Don't Bring Me Down**	Electric Light Orchestra ... Jet 5060
5	6	17	**Lead Me On**	Maxine Nightingale ... Windsong 11530
6	7	18	**Sad Eyes**	Robert John ... EMI America 8015
7	10	9	**Lonesome Loser**	Little River Band ... Capitol 4748
8	9	13	**I'll Never Love This Way Again**	Dionne Warwick ... Arista 0419
9	2	14	**Good Times**	Chic ... Atlantic 3584
10	12	6	**Sail On**	Commodores ... Motown 1466

★ **HIGHEST DEBUT** ★ POS 81 — Hell On Wheels ...Cher
★ **BIGGEST MOVER** ★ 65 to 50 — Dirty White Boy ...Foreigner

Billboard — SEPTEMBER 22, 1979 — HOT 100

TW	LW	WK	Title	Artist ... Label
1	1	14	**My Sharona**	The Knack ... Capitol 4731
2	2	12	**After The Love Has Gone**	Earth, Wind & Fire ... ARC 11033
3	3	14	**The Devil Went Down To Georgia**	The Charlie Daniels Band ... Epic 50700
4	12	9	**Rise**	Herb Alpert ... A&M 2151
5	5	18	**Lead Me On**	Maxine Nightingale ... Windsong 11530
6	6	19	**Sad Eyes**	Robert John ... EMI America 8015
7	7	10	**Lonesome Loser**	Little River Band ... Capitol 4748
8	8	14	**I'll Never Love This Way Again**	Dionne Warwick ... Arista 0419
9	10	7	**Sail On**	Commodores ... Motown 1466
10	4	8	**Don't Bring Me Down**	Electric Light Orchestra ... Jet 5060

★ **HIGHEST DEBUT** ★ POS 76 — Broken Hearted Me ...Anne Murray
★ **BIGGEST MOVER** ★ 60 to 37 — You Decorated My Life ...Kenny Rogers

Billboard — SEPTEMBER 29, 1979 — HOT 100

TW	LW	WK	Title	Artist ... Label
1	1	15	**My Sharona**	The Knack ... Capitol 4731
2	6	20	**Sad Eyes**	Robert John ... EMI America 8015
3	4	10	**Rise**	Herb Alpert ... A&M 2151
4	12	10	**Don't Stop 'Til You Get Enough**	Michael Jackson ... Epic 50742
5	2	13	**After The Love Has Gone**	Earth, Wind & Fire ... ARC 11033
6	7	11	**Lonesome Loser**	Little River Baad ... Capitol 4748
7	8	15	**I'll Never Love This Way Again**	Dionne Warwick ... Arista 0419
8	9	8	**Sail On**	Commodores ... Motown 1466
9	3	15	**The Devil Went Down To Georgia**	The Charlie Daniels Band ... Epic 50700
10	10	9	**Don't Bring Me Down**	Electric Light Orchestra ... Jet 5060

★ **HIGHEST DEBUT** ★ POS 68 — Still ...Commodores
★ **BIGGEST MOVER** ★ 63 to 40 — Come To Me ...France Joli

Billboard · OCTOBER 6, 1979 · HOT 100

TW	LW	WK	Title	Artist	Label
1	2	21	**Sad Eyes**	Robert John	EMI America 8015
2	4	11	**Don't Stop 'Til You Get Enough**	Michael Jackson	Epic 50742
3	3	11	**Rise**	Herb Alpert	A&M 2151
4	1	16	**My Sharona**	The Knack	Capitol 4731
5	8	9	**Sail On**	Commodores	Motown 1466
6	6	12	**Lonesome Loser**	Little River Band	Capitol 4748
7	7	16	**I'll Never Love This Way Again**	Dionne Warwick	Arista 0419
8	11	9	**Pop Muzik**	M	Sire 49033
9	5	14	**After The Love Has Gone**	Earth, Wind & Fire	ARC 11033
10	19	7	**Dim All The Lights**	Donna Summer	Casablanca 2201

★ **HIGHEST DEBUT** ★ POS 52
Heartache Tonight ....*Eagles*

★ **BIGGEST MOVER** ★ 68 to 47
Still..*Commodores*

Billboard · OCTOBER 13, 1979 · HOT 100

TW	LW	WK	Title	Artist	Label
1	2	12	**Don't Stop 'Til You Get Enough**	Michael Jackson	Epic 50742
2	3	12	**Rise**	Herb Alpert	A&M 2151
3	1	22	**Sad Eyes**	Robert John	EMI America 8015
4	5	10	**Sail On**	Commodores	Motown 1466
5	4	17	**My Sharona**	The Knack	Capitol 4731
6	7	17	**I'll Never Love This Way Again**	Dionne Warwick	Arista 0419
7	8	10	**Pop Muzik**	M	Sire 49033
8	10	8	**Dim All The Lights**	Donna Summer	Casablanca 2201
9	6	13	**Lonesome Loser**	Little River Band	Capitol 4748
10	9	15	**After The Love Has Gone**	Earth, Wind & Fire	ARC 11033

★ **HIGHEST DEBUT** ★ POS 57
Ships..*Barry Manilow*

★ **BIGGEST MOVER** ★ 52 to 15
Heartache Tonight ....*Eagles*

Billboard · OCTOBER 20, 1979 · HOT 100

TW	LW	WK	Title	Artist	Label
1	2	13	**Rise**	Herb Alpert	A&M 2151
2	1	13	**Don't Stop 'Til You Get Enough**	Michael Jackson	Epic 50742
3	7	11	**Pop Muzik**	M	Sire 49033
4	4	11	**Sail On**	Commodores	Motown 1466
5	6	18	**I'll Never Love This Way Again**	Dionne Warwick	Arista 0419
6	8	9	**Dim All The Lights**	Donna Summer	Casablanca 2201
7	3	23	**Sad Eyes**	Robert John	EMI America 8015
8	5	18	**My Sharona**	The Knack	Capitol 4731
9	15	3	**Heartache Tonight**	Eagles	Asylum 46545
10	38	4	**Still**	Commodores	Motown 1474

★ **HIGHEST DEBUT** ★ POS 59
No More Tears (Enough Is Enough) ....*Barbra Streisand/Donna Summer*

★ **BIGGEST MOVER** ★ 38 to 10
Still..*Commodores*

Billboard — OCTOBER 27, 1979 — HOT 100

TW	LW	WK	Title	Artist
①	1	14	**Rise** ....*Herb Alpert* ... A&M 2151
②	3	12	**Pop Muzik**...*M* ... Sire 49033
③	2	14	**Don't Stop 'Til You Get Enough** ....*Michael Jackson* ... Epic 50742
④	6	10	**Dim All The Lights** ....*Donna Summer* ... Casablanca 2201
⑤	5	19	**I'll Never Love This Way Again** ....*Dionne Warwick* ... Arista 0419
⑥	4	12	**Sail On** ....*Commodores* ... Motown 1466
⑦	9	4	**Heartache Tonight** ....*Eagles* ... Asylum 46545
⑧	10	5	**Still**.....................................*Commodores* ... Motown 1474
⑨	15	4	**Tusk** ....*Fleetwood Mac* ... Warner 49077
⑩	12	8	**You Decorated My Life** ....*Kenny Rogers* ... United Artists 1315

★ **HIGHEST DEBUT** ★ POS 78
What Can I Do With This Broken Heart ....*England Dan & John Ford Coley*

★ **BIGGEST MOVER** ★ 59 to 33
No More Tears (Enough Is Enough) ....*Barbra Streisand/Donna Summer*

Billboard — NOVEMBER 3, 1979 — HOT 100

TW	LW	WK	Title	Artist
①	2	13	**Pop Muzik**...*M* ... Sire 49033
②	7	5	**Heartache Tonight** ....*Eagles* ... Asylum 46545
③	4	11	**Dim All The Lights** ....*Donna Summer* ... Casablanca 2201
④	1	15	**Rise** ....*Herb Alpert* ... A&M 2151
⑤	8	6	**Still**.....................................*Commodores* ... Motown 1474
⑥	3	15	**Don't Stop 'Til You Get Enough** ....*Michael Jackson* ... Epic 50742
⑦	14	5	**Babe**.....................................*Styx* ... A&M 2188
⑧	9	5	**Tusk**.....................................*Fleetwood Mac* ... Warner 49077
⑨	10	9	**You Decorated My Life** ....*Kenny Rogers* ... United Artists 1315
⑩	33	3	**No More Tears (Enough Is Enough)**.....................*Barbra Streisand/Donna Summer* ... Columbia 11125

★ **HIGHEST DEBUT** ★ POS 51
Send One Your Love ....*Stevie Wonder*

★ **BIGGEST MOVER** ★ 33 to 10
No More Tears (Enough Is Enough) ....*Barbra Streisand/Donna Summer*

Billboard — NOVEMBER 10, 1979 — HOT 100

TW	LW	WK	Title	Artist
①	2	6	**Heartache Tonight**.................................*Eagles* ... Asylum 46545
②	3	12	**Dim All The Lights** ....*Donna Summer* ... Casablanca 2201
③	5	7	**Still**.....................................*Commodores* ... Motown 1474
④	4	16	**Rise** ....*Herb Alpert* ... A&M 2151
⑤	1	14	**Pop Muzik**...*M* ... Sire 49033
⑥	7	6	**Babe**.....................................*Styx* ... A&M 2188
⑦	10	4	**No More Tears (Enough Is Enough)**.....................*Barbra Streisand/Donna Summer* ... Columbia 11125
⑧	8	6	**Tusk**.....................................*Fleetwood Mac* ... Warner 49077
⑨	9	10	**You Decorated My Life** ....*Kenny Rogers* ... United Artists 1315
⑩	11	12	**Please Don't Go** ...........................*K.C. & The Sunshine Band* ... T.K. 1035

★ **HIGHEST DEBUT** ★ POS 63
Head Games ....*Foreigner*

★ **BIGGEST MOVER** ★ 56 to 25
Ladies Night.....................*Kool & The Gang*

TW	LW	WK	Billboard.	NOVEMBER 17, 1979	HOT 100.
①	3	8	**Still**..*Commodores* ... Motown 1474
②	2	13	**Dim All The Lights** ....*Donna Summer* ... Casablanca 2201
③	7	5	No More Tears (Enough Is Enough).....................................
			Barbra Streisand/Donna Summer ... Columbia 11125
④	6	7	Babe ....*Styx* ... A&M 2188
⑤	1	7	Heartache Tonight ....*Eagles* ... Asylum 46545
⑥	4	17	Rise ....*Herb Alpert* ... A&M 2151
⑦	9	11	**You Decorated My Life**.................*Kenny Rogers* ... United Artists 1315
⑧	8	7	Tusk...*Fleetwood Mac* ... Warner 49077
⑨	10	13	Please Don't Go ...........................*K.C. & The Sunshine Band* ... T.K. 1035
⑩	5	15	Pop Muzik...*M* ... Sire 49033

★ **HIGHEST DEBUT** ★ POS 63
Coward Of The County ....*Kenny Rogers*

★ **BIGGEST MOVER** ★ 63 to 43
Head Games ....*Foreigner*

TW	LW	WK	Billboard.	NOVEMBER 24, 1979	HOT 100.
①	3	6	**No More Tears (Enough Is Enough)** ....
			Barbra Streisand/Donna Summer ... Columbia 11125
②	4	8	**Babe** ....*Styx* ... A&M 2188
③	1	9	**Still**..*Commodores* ... Motown 1474
④	2	14	**Dim All The Lights** ....*Donna Summer* ... Casablanca 2201
⑤	5	8	**Heartache Tonight** ....*Eagles* ... Asylum 46545
⑥	9	14	**Please Don't Go** ...........................*K.C. & The Sunshine Band* ... T.K. 1035
⑦	7	12	**You Decorated My Life**.................*Kenny Rogers* ... United Artists 1315
⑧	14	4	**Send One Your Love** ....*Stevie Wonder* ... Tamla 54303
⑨	8	8	**Tusk**...*Fleetwood Mac* ... Warner 49077
⑩	10	16	**Pop Muzik**...*M* ... Sire 49033

★ **HIGHEST DEBUT** ★ POS 82
Forever Mine.................................*The O'Jays*

★ **BIGGEST MOVER** ★ 59 to 35
Rock With You ....*Michael Jackson*

TW	LW	WK	Billboard.	DECEMBER 1, 1979	HOT 100.
①	1	7	**No More Tears (Enough Is Enough)** ....
			Barbra Streisand/Donna Summer ... Columbia 11125
②	2	9	**Babe** ....*Styx* ... A&M 2188
③	3	10	**Still**..*Commodores* ... Motown 1474
④	6	15	**Please Don't Go** ...........................*K.C. & The Sunshine Band* ... T.K. 1035
⑤	5	9	**Heartache Tonight** ....*Eagles* ... Asylum 46545
⑥	12	7	**Escape (The Pina Colada Song)** ....*Rupert Holmes* ... Infinity 50035
⑦	8	5	**Send One Your Love** ....*Stevie Wonder* ... Tamla 54303
⑧	4	15	**Dim All The Lights** ....*Donna Summer* ... Casablanca 2201
⑨	11	8	**Ships** ....*Barry Manilow* ... Arista 0464
⑩	10	17	**Pop Muzik**...*M* ... Sire 49033

★ **HIGHEST DEBUT** ★ POS 84
Romeo's Tune ....*Steve Forbert*

★ **BIGGEST MOVER** ★ 65 to 44
Video Killed The Radio Star ....*The Buggles*

Billboard ⊙ DECEMBER 8, 1979 ⊙ HOT 100.

TW	LW	WK		
❶	2	10	**Babe** ....*Styx* ... A&M 2188	
②	1	8	**No More Tears (Enough Is Enough)** .... *Barbra Streisand/Donna Summer* ... Columbia 11125	
③	3	11	**Still** ....*Commodores* ... Motown 1474	
④	4	16	**Please Don't Go** ...............................*K.C. & The Sunshine Band* ... T.K. 1035	
⑤	6	8	**Escape (The Pina Colada Song)** ....*Rupert Holmes* ... Infinity 50035	
⑥	7	6	**Send One Your Love** ....*Stevie Wonder* ... Tamla 54303	
⑦	5	10	**Heartache Tonight** ....*Eagles* ... Asylum 46545	
⑧	11	14	**You're Only Lonely** ..................................*J.D. Souther* ... Columbia 11079	
⑨	9	9	**Ships** ....*Barry Manilow* ... Arista 0464	
❿	14	8	**Do That To Me One More Time** ....*The Captain & Tennille* ... Casablanca 2215	

★ **HIGHEST DEBUT** ★ POS 33	★ **BIGGEST MOVER** ★ 76 to 40
The Long Run ....*Eagles*	I Wanna Be Your Lover ....*Prince*

Billboard ⊙ DECEMBER 15, 1979 ⊙ HOT 100.

TW	LW	WK		
❶	1	11	**Babe** ....*Styx* ... A&M 2188	
②	3	12	**Still** ....*Commodores* ... Motown 1474	
③	4	17	**Please Don't Go** ...............................*K.C. & The Sunshine Band* ... T.K. 1035	
④	5	9	**Escape (The Pina Colada Song)** ....*Rupert Holmes* ... Infinity 50035	
⑤	6	7	**Send One Your Love** ....*Stevie Wonder* ... Tamla 54303	
⑥	2	9	**No More Tears (Enough Is Enough)** .... *Barbra Streisand/Donna Summer* ... Columbia 11125	
⑦	8	15	**You're Only Lonely** ..................................*J.D. Souther* ... Columbia 11079	
⑧	10	9	**Do That To Me One More Time** ....*The Captain & Tennille* ... Casablanca 2215	
⑨	7	11	**Heartache Tonight** ....*Eagles* ... Asylum 46545	
❿	11	10	**Take The Long Way Home** ....*Supertramp* ... A&M 2193	

★ **HIGHEST DEBUT** ★ POS 45	★ **BIGGEST MOVER** ★ 33 to 19
Sara ....*Fleetwood Mac*	The Long Run ....*Eagles*

Billboard ⊙ DECEMBER 22, 1979 ⊙ HOT 100.

TW	LW	WK		
❶	4	10	**Escape (The Pina Colada Song)** ....*Rupert Holmes* ... Infinity 50035	
❷	3	18	**Please Don't Go** ...............................*K.C. & The Sunshine Band* ... T.K. 1035	
③	1	12	**Babe** ....*Styx* ... A&M 2188	
④	5	8	**Send One Your Love** ....*Stevie Wonder* ... Tamla 54303	
⑤	2	13	**Still** ....*Commodores* ... Motown 1474	
⑥	8	10	**Do That To Me One More Time** ....*The Captain & Tennille* ... Casablanca 2215	
⑦	7	16	**You're Only Lonely** ..................................*J.D. Souther* ... Columbia 11079	
⑧	6	10	**No More Tears (Enough Is Enough)** .... *Barbra Streisand/Donna Summer* ... Columbia 11125	
⑨	11	12	**Ladies Night** ....*Kool & The Gang* ... De-Lite 801	
❿	10	11	**Take The Long Way Home** ....*Supertramp* ... A&M 2193	

★ **HIGHEST DEBUT** ★ POS 58	★ **BIGGEST MOVER** ★ 45 to 35
Crazy Little Thing Called Love ....*Queen*	Sara ....*Fleetwood Mac*

Billboard ⬤ JANUARY 5, 1980 ⬤ HOT 100

TW	LW	WK		
❶	2	20	**Please Don't Go**	*K.C. & The Sunshine Band* . . . T.K. 1035
②	1	12	Escape (The Pina Colada Song)	*Rupert Holmes* . . . Infinity 50035
❸	11	10	Rock With You	*Michael Jackson* . . . Epic 50797
❹	4	10	**Send One Your Love**	*Stevie Wonder* . . . Tamla 54303
❺	6	12	Do That To Me One More Time	*The Captain & Tennille* . . . Casablanca 2215
⑥	3	14	Babe	*Styx* . . . A&M 2188
⑦	5	15	Still	*Commodores* . . . Motown 1474
❽	22	8	Coward Of The County	*Kenny Rogers* . . . United Artists 1327
⑨	9	14	Ladies Night	*Kool & The Gang* . . . De-Lite 801
⑩	13	12	We Don't Talk Anymore	*Cliff Richard* . . . EMI America 8025

★ **HIGHEST DEBUT** ★ POS 81
I'm Alive ....*Gamma*

★ *BIGGEST MOVER* ★ 64 to 42
Fool In The Rain ....*Led Zeppelin*

Billboard ⬤ JANUARY 12, 1980 ⬤ HOT 100

TW	LW	WK		
❶	2	13	**Escape (The Pina Colada Song)**	*Rupert Holmes* . . . Infinity 50035
❷	3	11	Rock With You	*Michael Jackson* . . . Epic 50797
❸	5	13	Do That To Me One More Time	*The Captain & Tennille* . . . Casablanca 2215
④	4	11	**Send One Your Love**	*Stevie Wonder* . . . Tamla 54303
⑤	1	21	Please Don't Go	*K.C. & The Sunshine Band* . . . T.K. 1035
⑥	7	16	Still	*Commodores* . . . Motown 1474
❼	8	9	Coward Of The County	*Kenny Rogers* . . . United Artists 1327
❽	9	15	**Ladies Night**	*Kool & The Gang* . . . De-Lite 801
⑨	10	13	We Don't Talk Anymore	*Cliff Richard* . . . EMI America 8025
⑩	6	15	Babe	*Styx* . . . A&M 2188

★ **HIGHEST DEBUT** ★ POS 81
Too Late ....*Journey*

★ *BIGGEST MOVER* ★ 59 to 33
An American Dream ....*The Dirt Band*

Billboard ⬤ JANUARY 19, 1980 ⬤ HOT 100

TW	LW	WK		
❶	2	12	**Rock With You**	*Michael Jackson* . . . Epic 50797
❷	3	14	Do That To Me One More Time	*The Captain & Tennille* . . . Casablanca 2215
③	1	14	Escape (The Pina Colada Song)	*Rupert Holmes* . . . Infinity 50035
④	7	10	Coward Of The County	*Kenny Rogers* . . . United Artists 1327
⑤	4	12	Send One Your Love	*Stevie Wonder* . . . Tamla 54303
⑥	12	16	Cruisin'	*Smokey Robinson* . . . Tamla 54306
❼	9	14	**We Don't Talk Anymore**	*Cliff Richard* . . . EMI America 8025
⑧	8	16	**Ladies Night**	*Kool & The Gang* . . . De-Lite 801
⑨	5	22	Please Don't Go	*K.C. & The Sunshine Band* . . . T.K. 1035
⑩	11	14	**Cool Change**	*Little River Band* . . . Capitol 4789

★ **HIGHEST DEBUT** ★ POS 72
Him...*Rupert Holmes*

★ *BIGGEST MOVER* ★ 86 to 49
On The Radio ....*Donna Summer*

Billboard — JANUARY 26, 1980 — HOT 100

TW	LW	WK			
❶	1	13	Rock With You	Michael Jackson	Epic 50797
❷	2	15	Do That To Me One More Time	The Captain & Tennille	Casablanca 2215
❸	4	11	Coward Of The County	Kenny Rogers	United Artists 1327
④	3	15	Escape (The Pina Colada Song)	Rupert Holmes	Infinity 50035
⑤	6	17	Cruisin'	Smokey Robinson	Tamla 54306
⑥	5	13	Send One Your Love	Stevie Wonder	Tamla 54303
⑦	7	15	We Don't Talk Anymore	Cliff Richard	EMI America 8025
⑧	18	6	Crazy Little Thing Called Love	Queen	Elektra 46579
⑨	11	8	The Long Run	Eagles	Asylum 46569
⑩	15	7	Sara	Fleetwood Mac	Warner 49150

★ HIGHEST DEBUT ★ POS 44
Desire ....Andy Gibb

★ BIGGEST MOVER ★ 72 to 56
Him...Rupert Holmes

Billboard — FEBRUARY 2, 1980 — HOT 100

TW	LW	WK			
❶	1	14	Rock With You	Michael Jackson	Epic 50797
❷	2	16	Do That To Me One More Time	The Captain & Tennille	Casablanca 2215
❸	3	12	Coward Of The County	Kenny Rogers	United Artists 1327
④	5	18	Cruisin'	Smokey Robinson	Tamla 54306
⑤	8	7	Crazy Little Thing Called Love	Queen	Elektra 46579
⑥	4	16	Escape (The Pina Colada Song)	Rupert Holmes	Infinity 50035
❼	10	8	Sara	Fleetwood Mac	Warner 49150
❽	9	9	The Long Run	Eagles	Asylum 46569
⑨	16	12	Yes, I'm Ready	Teri DeSario with K.C.	Casablanca 2227
⑩	14	12	Don't Do Me Like That	Tom Petty & The Heartbreakers	Backstreet 41138

★ HIGHEST DEBUT ★ POS 68
How Do I Make You ....Linda Ronstadt

★ BIGGEST MOVER ★ 44 to 22
Desire ....Andy Gibb

Billboard — FEBRUARY 9, 1980 — HOT 100

TW	LW	WK			
❶	1	15	Rock With You	Michael Jackson	Epic 50797
②	2	17	Do That To Me One More Time	The Captain & Tennille	Casablanca 2215
❸	3	13	Coward Of The County	Kenny Rogers	United Artists 1327
④	4	19	Cruisin'	Smokey Robinson	Tamla 54306
⑤	5	8	Crazy Little Thing Called Love	Queen	Elektra 46579
⑥	9	13	Yes, I'm Ready	Teri DeSario with K.C.	Casablanca 2227
❼	7	9	Sara	Fleetwood Mac	Warner 49150
⑧	8	10	The Long Run	Eagles	Asylum 46569
⑨	17	9	Longer	Dan Fogelberg	Full Moon 50824
⑩	10	13	Don't Do Me Like That	Tom Petty & The Heartbreakers	Backstreet 41138

★ HIGHEST DEBUT ★ POS 73
Baby Talks Dirty ....The Knack

★ BIGGEST MOVER ★ 68 to 35
How Do I Make You ....Linda Ronstadt

Billboard — FEBRUARY 16, 1980 — HOT 100

TW	LW	WK	Title	Artist
1	2	18	**Do That To Me One More Time**	*The Captain & Tennille* ... Casablanca 2215
2	5	9	**Crazy Little Thing Called Love**	*Queen* ... Elektra 46579
3	3	14	**Coward Of The County**	*Kenny Rogers* ... United Artists 1327
4	4	20	**Cruisin'**	*Smokey Robinson* ... Tamla 54306
5	1	16	**Rock With You**	*Michael Jackson* ... Epic 50797
6	6	14	**Yes, I'm Ready**	*Teri DeSario with K.C.* ... Casablanca 2227
7	7	10	**Sara**	*Fleetwood Mac* ... Warner 49150
8	9	10	**Longer**	*Dan Fogelberg* ... Full Moon 50824
9	14	6	**On The Radio**	*Donna Summer* ... Casablanca 2236
10	13	4	**Desire**	*Andy Gibb* ... RSO 1019

★ **HIGHEST DEBUT** ★ POS 53
Off The Wall .... *Michael Jackson*

★ **BIGGEST MOVER** ★ 71 to 56
Come Back .... *The J. Geils Band*

Billboard — FEBRUARY 23, 1980 — HOT 100

TW	LW	WK	Title	Artist
1	2	10	**Crazy Little Thing Called Love**	*Queen* ... Elektra 46579
2	1	19	**Do That To Me One More Time**	*The Captain & Tennille* ... Casablanca 2215
3	6	15	**Yes, I'm Ready**	*Teri DeSario with K.C.* ... Casablanca 2227
4	4	21	**Cruisin'**	*Smokey Robinson* ... Tamla 54306
5	5	17	**Rock With You**	*Michael Jackson* ... Epic 50797
6	8	11	**Longer**	*Dan Fogelberg* ... Full Moon 50824
7	9	7	**On The Radio**	*Donna Summer* ... Casablanca 2236
8	10	5	**Desire**	*Andy Gibb* ... RSO 1019
9	3	15	**Coward Of The County**	*Kenny Rogers* ... United Artists 1327
10	7	11	**Sara**	*Fleetwood Mac* ... Warner 49150

★ **HIGHEST DEBUT** ★ POS 60
I Can't Tell You Why .... *Eagles*

★ **BIGGEST MOVER** ★ 53 to 37
Off The Wall .... *Michael Jackson*

Billboard — MARCH 1, 1980 — HOT 100

TW	LW	WK	Title	Artist
1	1	11	**Crazy Little Thing Called Love**	*Queen* ... Elektra 46579
2	3	16	**Yes, I'm Ready**	*Teri DeSario with K.C.* ... Casablanca 2227
3	2	20	**Do That To Me One More Time**	*The Captain & Tennille* ... Casablanca 2215
4	6	12	**Longer**	*Dan Fogelberg* ... Full Moon 50824
5	8	6	**Desire**	*Andy Gibb* ... RSO 1019
6	7	8	**On The Radio**	*Donna Summer* ... Casablanca 2236
7	4	22	**Cruisin'**	*Smokey Robinson* ... Tamla 54306
8	5	18	**Rock With You**	*Michael Jackson* ... Epic 50797
9	13	12	**Working My Way Back To You/Forgive Me, Girl**	*Spinners* ... Atlantic 3637
10	15	7	**Another Brick In The Wall**	*Pink Floyd* ... Columbia 11187

★ **HIGHEST DEBUT** ★ POS 63
Hold On To My Love...................... *Jimmy Ruffin*

★ **BIGGEST MOVER** ★ 60 to 32
I Can't Tell You Why .... *Eagles*

Billboard — MARCH 8, 1980 — HOT 100

TW	LW	WK	Title	Artist	Label
1	1	12	**Crazy Little Thing Called Love**	*Queen*	Elektra 46579
2	2	17	**Yes, I'm Ready**	*Teri DeSario with K.C.*	Casablanca 2227
3	4	13	**Longer**	*Dan Fogelberg*	Full Moon 50824
4	5	7	**Desire**	*Andy Gibb*	RSO 1019
5	6	9	**On The Radio**	*Donna Summer*	Casablanca 2236
6	10	8	**Another Brick In The Wall**	*Pink Floyd*	Columbia 11187
7	3	21	**Do That To Me One More Time**	*The Captain & Tennille*	Casablanca 2215
8	9	13	**Working My Way Back To You/Forgive Me, Girl**	*Spinners*	Atlantic 3637
9	16	8	**Him**	*Rupert Holmes*	MCA 41173
10	14	14	**The Second Time Around**	*Shalamar*	Solar 11709

★ **HIGHEST DEBUT** ★ POS 76
Do Right ....*Paul Davis*

★ **BIGGEST MOVER** ★ 61 to 28
Call Me ....*Blondie*

Billboard — MARCH 15, 1980 — HOT 100

TW	LW	WK	Title	Artist	Label
1	1	13	**Crazy Little Thing Called Love**	*Queen*	Elektra 46579
2	3	14	**Longer**	*Dan Fogelberg*	Full Moon 50824
3	6	9	**Another Brick In The Wall**	*Pink Floyd*	Columbia 11187
4	4	8	**Desire**	*Andy Gibb*	RSO 1019
5	5	10	**On The Radio**	*Donna Summer*	Casablanca 2236
6	8	14	**Working My Way Back To You/Forgive Me, Girl**	*Spinners*	Atlantic 3637
7	2	18	**Yes, I'm Ready**	*Teri DeSario with K.C.*	Casablanca 2227
8	9	9	**Him**	*Rupert Holmes*	MCA 41173
9	10	15	**The Second Time Around**	*Shalamar*	Solar 11709
10	11	9	**Too Hot**	*Kool & The Gang*	De-Lite 802

★ **HIGHEST DEBUT** ★ POS 53
You May Be Right ....*Billy Joel*

★ **BIGGEST MOVER** ★ 48 to 31
Sexy Eyes ....*Dr. Hook*

Billboard — MARCH 22, 1980 — HOT 100

TW	LW	WK	Title	Artist	Label
1	3	10	**Another Brick In The Wall**	*Pink Floyd*	Columbia 11187
2	2	15	**Longer**	*Dan Fogelberg*	Full Moon 50824
3	1	14	**Crazy Little Thing Called Love**	*Queen*	Elektra 46579
4	4	9	**Desire**	*Andy Gibb*	RSO 1019
5	6	15	**Working My Way Back To You/Forgive Me, Girl**	*Spinners*	Atlantic 3637
6	5	11	**On The Radio**	*Donna Summer*	Casablanca 2236
7	8	10	**Him**	*Rupert Holmes*	MCA 41173
8	9	16	**The Second Time Around**	*Shalamar*	Solar 11709
9	10	10	**Too Hot**	*Kool & The Gang*	De-Lite 802
10	11	8	**How Do I Make You**	*Linda Ronstadt*	Asylum 46602

★ **HIGHEST DEBUT** ★ POS 72
Let Me Be ....*Korona*

★ **BIGGEST MOVER** ★ 53 to 27
You May Be Right ....*Billy Joel*

Billboard Hot 100 — MARCH 29, 1980

TW	LW	WK	Title	Artist	Label
1	1	11	**Another Brick In The Wall**	Pink Floyd	Columbia 11187
2	5	16	**Working My Way Back To You/Forgive Me, Girl**	Spinners	Atlantic 3637
③	3	15	Crazy Little Thing Called Love	Queen	Elektra 46579
④	4	10	**Desire**	Andy Gibb	RSO 1019
⑤	11	7	Call Me	Blondie	Chrysalis 2414
⑥	7	11	Him	Rupert Holmes	MCA 41173
⑦	9	11	Too Hot	Kool & The Gang	De-Lite 802
⑧	8	17	**The Second Time Around**	Shalamar	Solar 11709
⑨	14	7	Ride Like The Wind	Christopher Cross	Warner 49184
⑩	10	9	**How Do I Make You**	Linda Ronstadt	Asylum 46602

★ **HIGHEST DEBUT** ★ POS 56
Don't Fall In Love With A Dreamer...........Kenny Rogers with Kim Carnes

★ **BIGGEST MOVER** ★ 70 to 50
Stomp! ....The Brothers Johnson

Billboard Hot 100 — APRIL 5, 1980

TW	LW	WK	Title	Artist	Label
1	1	12	**Another Brick In The Wall**	Pink Floyd	Columbia 11187
②	2	17	**Working My Way Back To You/Forgive Me, Girl**	Spinners	Atlantic 3637
3	5	8	Call Me	Blondie	Chrysalis 2414
④	3	16	Crazy Little Thing Called Love	Queen	Elektra 46579
⑤	7	12	**Too Hot**	Kool & The Gang	De-Lite 802
⑥	6	12	Him	Rupert Holmes	MCA 41173
⑦	9	8	Ride Like The Wind	Christopher Cross	Warner 49184
⑧	11	11	Special Lady	Ray, Goodman & Brown	Polydor 2033
⑨	4	11	Desire	Andy Gibb	RSO 1019
⑩	10	10	**How Do I Make You**	Linda Ronstadt	Asylum 46602

★ **HIGHEST DEBUT** ★ POS 60
Biggest Part Of Me...........................Ambrosia

★ **BIGGEST MOVER** ★ 65 to 47
Breakdown Dead Ahead ....Boz Scaggs

Billboard Hot 100 — APRIL 12, 1980

TW	LW	WK	Title	Artist	Label
1	1	13	**Another Brick In The Wall**	Pink Floyd	Columbia 11187
2	3	9	Call Me	Blondie	Chrysalis 2414
③	2	18	Working My Way Back To You/Forgive Me, Girl	Spinners	Atlantic 3637
④	7	9	Ride Like The Wind	Christopher Cross	Warner 49184
⑤	5	13	**Too Hot**	Kool & The Gang	De-Lite 802
⑥	8	12	Special Lady	Ray, Goodman & Brown	Polydor 2033
⑦	15	19	With You I'm Born Again	Billy Preston & Syreeta	Motown 1477
⑧	4	17	Crazy Little Thing Called Love	Queen	Elektra 46579
⑨	11	8	I Can't Tell You Why	Eagles	Asylum 46608
⑩	12	9	**Off The Wall**	Michael Jackson	Epic 50838

★ **HIGHEST DEBUT** ★ POS 46
Hurt So Bad...........................Linda Ronstadt

★ **BIGGEST MOVER** ★ 44 to 26
Don't Fall In Love With A Dreamer...........Kenny Rogers with Kim Carnes

Billboard — APRIL 19, 1980 — HOT 100

TW	LW	WK	Title	Artist ... Label
1	2	10	**Call Me**	*Blondie* ... Chrysalis 2414
2	1	14	**Another Brick In The Wall**	*Pink Floyd* ... Columbia 11187
3	4	10	**Ride Like The Wind**	*Christopher Cross* ... Warner 49184
4	7	20	**With You I'm Born Again**	*Billy Preston & Syreeta* ... Motown 1477
5	6	13	**Special Lady**	*Ray, Goodman & Brown* ... Polydor 2033
6	12	11	**Lost In Love**	*Air Supply* ... Arista 0479
7	11	9	**Fire Lake**	*Bob Seger* ... Capitol 4836
8	9	9	**I Can't Tell You Why**	*Eagles* ... Asylum 46608
9	3	19	**Working My Way Back To You/Forgive Me, Girl**	*Spinners* ... Atlantic 3637
10	10	10	**Off The Wall**	*Michael Jackson* ... Epic 50838

★ **HIGHEST DEBUT** ★ POS 57
She's Out Of My Life ... *Michael Jackson*

★ **BIGGEST MOVER** ★ 61 to 37
Funkytown ... *Lipps, Inc.*

Billboard — APRIL 26, 1980 — HOT 100

TW	LW	WK	Title	Artist ... Label
1	1	11	**Call Me**	*Blondie* ... Chrysalis 2414
2	3	11	**Ride Like The Wind**	*Christopher Cross* ... Warner 49184
3	2	15	**Another Brick In The Wall**	*Pink Floyd* ... Columbia 11187
4	4	21	**With You I'm Born Again**	*Billy Preston & Syreeta* ... Motown 1477
5	5	14	**Special Lady**	*Ray, Goodman & Brown* ... Polydor 2033
6	6	12	**Lost In Love**	*Air Supply* ... Arista 0479
7	7	10	**Fire Lake**	*Bob Seger* ... Capitol 4836
8	8	10	**I Can't Tell You Why**	*Eagles* ... Asylum 46608
9	12	7	**You May Be Right**	*Billy Joel* ... Columbia 11231
10	13	11	**Sexy Eyes**	*Dr. Hook* ... Capitol 4831

★ **HIGHEST DEBUT** ★ POS 73
Coming Up ... *Paul McCartney & Wings*

★ **BIGGEST MOVER** ★ 75 to 59
Steal Away ... *Robbie Dupree*

Billboard — MAY 3, 1980 — HOT 100

TW	LW	WK	Title	Artist ... Label
1	1	12	**Call Me**	*Blondie* ... Chrysalis 2414
2	2	12	**Ride Like The Wind**	*Christopher Cross* ... Warner 49184
3	6	13	**Lost In Love**	*Air Supply* ... Arista 0479
4	4	22	**With You I'm Born Again**	*Billy Preston & Syreeta* ... Motown 1477
5	3	16	**Another Brick In The Wall**	*Pink Floyd* ... Columbia 11187
6	7	11	**Fire Lake**	*Bob Seger* ... Capitol 4836
7	9	8	**You May Be Right**	*Billy Joel* ... Columbia 11231
8	8	11	**I Can't Tell You Why**	*Eagles* ... Asylum 46608
9	10	12	**Sexy Eyes**	*Dr. Hook* ... Capitol 4831
10	12	10	**Hold On To My Love**	*Jimmy Ruffin* ... RSO 1021

★ **HIGHEST DEBUT** ★ POS 54
Against The Wind ... *Bob Seger*

★ **BIGGEST MOVER** ★ 59 to 33
Steal Away ... *Robbie Dupree*

MAY 10, 1980 — Billboard HOT 100

TW	LW	WK	Title	Artist ... Label
①	1	13	Call Me	Blondie ... Chrysalis 2414
②	2	13	Ride Like The Wind	Christopher Cross ... Warner 49184
③	3	14	Lost In Love	Air Supply ... Arista 0479
④	4	23	With You I'm Born Again	Billy Preston & Syreeta ... Motown 1477
⑤	5	17	Another Brick In The Wall	Pink Floyd ... Columbia 11187
⑥	6	12	Fire Lake	Bob Seger ... Capitol 4836
⑦	7	9	You May Be Right	Billy Joel ... Columbia 11231
⑧	9	13	Sexy Eyes	Dr. Hook ... Capitol 4831
⑨	11	7	Don't Fall In Love With A Dreamer	Kenny Rogers with Kim Carnes ... United Artists 1345
⑩	10	11	Hold On To My Love	Jimmy Ruffin ... RSO 1021

★ **HIGHEST DEBUT** ★ POS 71
Tired Of Toein' The Line .... Rocky Burnette

★ **BIGGEST MOVER** ★ 54 to 26
Against The Wind .... Bob Seger

MAY 17, 1980 — Billboard HOT 100

TW	LW	WK	Title	Artist ... Label
①	1	14	Call Me	Blondie ... Chrysalis 2414
②	2	14	Ride Like The Wind	Christopher Cross ... Warner 49184
③	3	15	Lost In Love	Air Supply ... Arista 0479
④	19	8	Funkytown	Lipps, Inc. ... Casablanca 2233
⑤	4	24	With You I'm Born Again	Billy Preston & Syreeta ... Motown 1477
⑥	8	14	Sexy Eyes	Dr. Hook ... Capitol 4831
⑦	7	10	You May Be Right	Billy Joel ... Columbia 11231
⑧	9	8	Don't Fall In Love With A Dreamer	Kenny Rogers with Kim Carnes ... United Artists 1345
⑨	5	18	Another Brick In The Wall	Pink Floyd ... Columbia 11187
⑩	11	7	Biggest Part Of Me	Ambrosia ... Warner 49225

★ **HIGHEST DEBUT** ★ POS 67
Cupid/I've Loved You For A Long Time .... Spinners

★ **BIGGEST MOVER** ★ 19 to 4
Funkytown .... Lipps, Inc.

MAY 24, 1980 — Billboard HOT 100

TW	LW	WK	Title	Artist ... Label
①	1	15	Call Me	Blondie ... Chrysalis 2414
②	4	9	Funkytown	Lipps, Inc. ... Casablanca 2233
③	3	16	Lost In Love	Air Supply ... Arista 0479
④	8	9	Don't Fall In Love With A Dreamer	Kenny Rogers with Kim Carnes ... United Artists 1345
⑤	6	15	Sexy Eyes	Dr. Hook ... Capitol 4831
⑥	10	8	Biggest Part Of Me	Ambrosia ... Warner 49225
⑦	16	11	Stomp!	The Brothers Johnson ... A&M 2216
⑧	11	7	Hurt So Bad	Linda Ronstadt ... Asylum 46624
⑨	2	15	Ride Like The Wind	Christopher Cross ... Warner 49184
⑩	12	15	Cars	Gary Numan ... Atco 7211

★ **HIGHEST DEBUT** ★ POS 38
It's Still Rock And Roll To Me .... Billy Joel

★ **BIGGEST MOVER** ★ 67 to 29
Cupid/I've Loved You For A Long Time .... Spinners

TW	LW	WK	Billboard	MAY 31, 1980	HOT 100
①	2	10	**Funkytown** ....*Lipps, Inc.* ... Casablanca 2233
②	1	16	**Call Me** ....*Blondie* ... Chrysalis 2414
③	14	6	**Coming Up** ....*Paul McCartney & Wings* ... Columbia 11263
④	4	10	**Don't Fall In Love With A Dreamer** .... *Kenny Rogers with Kim Carnes* ... United Artists 1345
⑤	5	16	**Sexy Eyes** ....*Dr. Hook* ... Capitol 4831
⑥	6	9	**Biggest Part Of Me** ....*Ambrosia* ... Warner 49225
⑦	7	12	**Stomp!** ....*The Brothers Johnson* ... A&M 2216
⑧	8	8	**Hurt So Bad** ....*Linda Ronstadt* ... Asylum 46624
⑨	11	5	**Against The Wind** ....*Bob Seger* ... Capitol 4863
⑩	10	16	**Cars** ....*Gary Numan* ... Atco 7211

★ HIGHEST DEBUT ★ POS 75	★ BIGGEST MOVER ★ 77 to 56
More Love ....*Kim Carnes*	Angel Say No ....*Tommy Tutone*

TW	LW	WK	Billboard	JUNE 7, 1980	HOT 100
①	1	11	**Funkytown** ....*Lipps, Inc.* ... Casablanca 2233
②	3	7	**Coming Up** ....*Paul McCartney & Wings* ... Columbia 11263
③	6	10	**Biggest Part Of Me** ....*Ambrosia* ... Warner 49225
④	4	11	**Don't Fall In Love With A Dreamer** .... *Kenny Rogers with Kim Carnes* ... United Artists 1345
⑤	2	17	**Call Me** ....*Blondie* ... Chrysalis 2414
⑥	11	12	**The Rose** ....*Bette Midler* ... Atlantic 3656
⑦	9	6	**Against The Wind** ....*Bob Seger* ... Capitol 4863
⑧	8	9	**Hurt So Bad** ....*Linda Ronstadt* ... Asylum 46624
⑨	10	17	**Cars** ....*Gary Numan* ... Atco 7211
⑩	13	6	**Little Jeannie** ....*Elton John* ... MCA 41236

★ HIGHEST DEBUT ★ POS 80	★ BIGGEST MOVER ★ 64 to 50
The Very Last Time ....*Utopia*	Magic ....*Olivia Newton-John*

TW	LW	WK	Billboard	JUNE 14, 1980	HOT 100
①	1	12	**Funkytown** ....*Lipps, Inc.* ... Casablanca 2233
②	2	8	**Coming Up** ....*Paul McCartney & Wings* ... Columbia 11263
③	3	11	**Biggest Part Of Me** ....*Ambrosia* ... Warner 49225
④	6	13	**The Rose** ....*Bette Midler* ... Atlantic 3656
⑤	7	7	**Against The Wind** ....*Bob Seger* ... Capitol 4863
⑥	5	18	**Call Me** ....*Blondie* ... Chrysalis 2414
⑦	11	4	**It's Still Rock And Roll To Me** ....*Billy Joel* ... Columbia 11276
⑧	10	7	**Little Jeannie** ....*Elton John* ... MCA 41236
⑨	9	18	**Cars** ....*Gary Numan* ... Atco 7211
⑩	13	10	**Steal Away** ....*Robbie Dupree* ... Elektra 46621

★ HIGHEST DEBUT ★ POS 68	★ BIGGEST MOVER ★ 65 to 37
Empire Strikes Back ....*Meco*	More Love ....*Kim Carnes*

Billboard — JUNE 21, 1980 — HOT 100

TW	LW	WK	Title	Artist	Label
①	1	13	**Funkytown**	*Lipps, Inc.*	Casablanca 2233
②	2	9	Coming Up	*Paul McCartney & Wings*	Columbia 11263
③	3	12	**Biggest Part Of Me**	*Ambrosia*	Warner 49225
④	4	14	The Rose	*Bette Midler*	Atlantic 3656
⑤	5	8	**Against The Wind**	*Bob Seger*	Capitol 4863
⑥	7	5	It's Still Rock And Roll To Me	*Billy Joel*	Columbia 11276
⑦	8	8	Little Jeannie	*Elton John*	MCA 41236
⑧	10	11	Steal Away	*Robbie Dupree*	Elektra 46621
⑨	9	19	Cars	*Gary Numan*	Atco 7211
⑩	11	10	She's Out Of My Life	*Michael Jackson*	Epic 50871

★ **HIGHEST DEBUT** ★ POS 44
Love The World Away ....*Kenny Rogers*

★ **BIGGEST MOVER** ★ 58 to 45
In America ....*The Charlie Daniels Band*

Billboard — JUNE 28, 1980 — HOT 100

TW	LW	WK	Title	Artist	Label
①	2	10	**Coming Up**	*Paul McCartney & Wings*	Columbia 11263
②	1	14	Funkytown	*Lipps, Inc.*	Casablanca 2233
③	4	15	**The Rose**	*Bette Midler*	Atlantic 3656
④	6	6	It's Still Rock And Roll To Me	*Billy Joel*	Columbia 11276
⑤	5	9	**Against The Wind**	*Bob Seger*	Capitol 4863
⑥	7	9	Little Jeannie	*Elton John*	MCA 41236
⑦	8	12	Steal Away	*Robbie Dupree*	Elektra 46621
⑧	3	13	Biggest Part Of Me	*Ambrosia*	Warner 49225
⑨	11	7	Cupid/I've Loved You For A Long Time	*Spinners*	Atlantic 3664
⑩	10	11	**She's Out Of My Life**	*Michael Jackson*	Epic 50871

★ **HIGHEST DEBUT** ★ POS 67
Play The Game..............................*Queen*

★ **BIGGEST MOVER** ★ 82 to 61
Take A Little Rhythm ....*Ali Thomson*

Billboard — JULY 5, 1980 — HOT 100

TW	LW	WK	Title	Artist	Label
①	1	11	**Coming Up**	*Paul McCartney & Wings*	Columbia 11263
②	2	15	Funkytown	*Lipps, Inc.*	Casablanca 2233
③	3	16	**The Rose**	*Bette Midler*	Atlantic 3656
④	4	7	It's Still Rock And Roll To Me	*Billy Joel*	Columbia 11276
⑤	6	10	Little Jeannie	*Elton John*	MCA 41236
⑥	5	10	Against The Wind	*Bob Seger*	Capitol 4863
⑦	7	13	Steal Away	*Robbie Dupree*	Elektra 46621
⑧	9	8	Cupid/I've Loved You For A Long Time	*Spinners*	Atlantic 3664
⑨	8	14	Biggest Part Of Me	*Ambrosia*	Warner 49225
⑩	11	15	Let's Get Serious	*Jermaine Jackson*	Motown 1469

★ **HIGHEST DEBUT** ★ POS 33
Emotional Rescue..................*The Rolling Stones*

★ **BIGGEST MOVER** ★ 74 to 54
I Can't Let Go ....*Linda Ronstadt*

Billboard — JULY 12, 1980 — HOT 100

TW	LW	WK	Title	Artist	Label
1	1	12	**Coming Up**	Paul McCartney & Wings	Columbia 11263
2	4	8	It's Still Rock And Roll To Me	Billy Joel	Columbia 11276
3	3	17	**The Rose**	Bette Midler	Atlantic 3656
4	5	11	Little Jeannie	Elton John	MCA 41236
5	8	9	Cupid/I've Loved You For A Long Time	Spinners	Atlantic 3664
6	7	14	**Steal Away**	Robbie Dupree	Elektra 46621
7	2	16	Funkytown	Lipps, Inc.	Casablanca 2233
8	14	8	Magic	Olivia Newton-John	MCA 41247
9	10	16	Let's Get Serious	Jermaine Jackson	Motown 1469
10	11	10	**Let Me Love You Tonight**	Pure Prairie League	Casablanca 2266

★ HIGHEST DEBUT ★ POS 67
Lookin' For Love ....Johnny Lee

★ BIGGEST MOVER ★ 59 to 37
Old-Fashion Love ....Commodores

Billboard — JULY 19, 1980 — HOT 100

TW	LW	WK	Title	Artist	Label
1	2	9	**It's Still Rock And Roll To Me**	Billy Joel	Columbia 11276
2	1	13	Coming Up (Live at Glasgow)	Paul McCartney & Wings	Columbia 11263
3	4	12	**Little Jeannie**	Elton John	MCA 41236
4	5	10	**Cupid/I've Loved You For A Long Time**	Spinners	Atlantic 3664
5	11	13	**Shining Star**	Manhattans	Columbia 11222
6	6	15	**Steal Away**	Robbie Dupree	Elektra 46621
7	8	9	Magic	Olivia Newton-John	MCA 41247
8	3	18	The Rose	Bette Midler	Atlantic 3656
9	9	17	**Let's Get Serious**	Jermaine Jackson	Motown 1469
10	10	11	**Let Me Love You Tonight**	Pure Prairie League	Casablanca 2266

★ HIGHEST DEBUT ★ POS 74
Hot Rod Hearts ....Robbie Dupree

★ BIGGEST MOVER ★ 58 to 43
Why Not Me ....Fred Knoblock

Billboard — JULY 26, 1980 — HOT 100

TW	LW	WK	Title	Artist	Label
1	1	10	**It's Still Rock And Roll To Me**	Billy Joel	Columbia 11276
2	7	10	**Magic**	Olivia Newton-John	MCA 41247
3	3	13	**Little Jeannie**	Elton John	MCA 41236
4	4	11	**Cupid/I've Loved You For A Long Time**	Spinners	Atlantic 3664
5	5	14	**Shining Star**	Manhattans	Columbia 11222
6	2	14	Coming Up (Live at Glasgow)	Paul McCartney & Wings	Columbia 11263
7	6	16	Steal Away	Robbie Dupree	Elektra 46621
8	12	12	**Tired Of Toein' The Line**	Rocky Burnette	EMI America 8043
9	11	9	Take Your Time (Do It Right)	The S.O.S. Band	Tabu 5522
10	8	19	The Rose	Bette Midler	Atlantic 3656

★ HIGHEST DEBUT ★ POS 72
You Better Run ....Pat Benatar

★ BIGGEST MOVER ★ 48 to 33
Boulevard ....Jackson Browne

TW	LW	WK	**Billboard**		AUGUST 2, 1980		**HOT 100**

TW	LW	WK		
❶	2	11	**Magic** ....*Olivia Newton-John* . . . MCA 41247	
②	1	11	It's Still Rock And Roll To Me ....*Billy Joel* . . . Columbia 11276	
③	3	14	**Little Jeannie** ....*Elton John* . . . MCA 41236	
④	4	12	**Cupid/I've Loved You For A Long Time** ....*Spinners* . . . Atlantic 3664	
⑤	5	15	**Shining Star**................................*Manhattans* . . . Columbia 11222	
❻	9	10	Take Your Time (Do It Right) ....*The S.O.S. Band* . . . Tabu 5522	
⑦	6	15	Coming Up (Live at Glasgow) ....*Paul McCartney & Wings* . . . Columbia 11263	
⑧	8	13	**Tired Of Toein' The Line** ....*Rocky Burnette* . . . EMI America 8043	
❾	11	5	Emotional Rescue.....................*The Rolling Stones* . . . Rolling Stones 20001	
⑩	17	8	Sailing ....*Christopher Cross* . . . Warner 49507	

★ HIGHEST DEBUT ★ POS 61	★ BIGGEST MOVER ★ 53 to 36
All Over The World ....*Electric Light Orchestra*	You're The Only Woman (You & I) ....*Ambrosia*

TW	LW	WK	**Billboard**		AUGUST 9, 1980		**HOT 100**

TW	LW	WK		
❶	1	12	**Magic** ....*Olivia Newton-John* . . . MCA 41247	
②	2	12	It's Still Rock And Roll To Me ....*Billy Joel* . . . Columbia 11276	
③	3	15	**Little Jeannie** ....*Elton John* . . . MCA 41236	
❹	6	11	Take Your Time (Do It Right) ....*The S.O.S. Band* . . . Tabu 5522	
❺	10	9	Sailing ....*Christopher Cross* . . . Warner 49507	
⑥	5	16	Shining Star................................*Manhattans* . . . Columbia 11222	
❼	9	6	Emotional Rescue.....................*The Rolling Stones* . . . Rolling Stones 20001	
⑧	4	13	Cupid/I've Loved You For A Long Time................................*Spinners* . . . Atlantic 3664	
⑨	7	16	Coming Up (Live at Glasgow) ....*Paul McCartney & Wings* . . . Columbia 11263	
⑩	49	5	Upside Down ....*Diana Ross* . . . Motown 1494	

★ HIGHEST DEBUT ★ POS 46	★ BIGGEST MOVER ★ 49 to 10
Late In The Evening ....*Paul Simon*	Upside Down.................................*Diana Ross*

TW	LW	WK	**Billboard**		AUGUST 16, 1980		**HOT 100**

TW	LW	WK		
❶	1	13	**Magic**..*Olivia Newton-John* . . . MCA 41247	
❷	5	10	Sailing..*Christopher Cross* . . . Warner 49507	
❸	4	12	**Take Your Time (Do It Right)** ....*The S.O.S. Band* . . . Tabu 5522	
❹	7	7	Emotional Rescue.....................*The Rolling Stones* . . . Rolling Stones 20001	
❺	10	6	Upside Down ....*Diana Ross* . . . Motown 1494	
⑥	2	13	It's Still Rock And Roll To Me ....*Billy Joel* . . . Columbia 11276	
⑦	6	17	Shining Star................................*Manhattans* . . . Columbia 11222	
⑧	3	16	Little Jeannie ....*Elton John* . . . MCA 41236	
⑨	19	10	**Let My Love Open The Door** ....*Pete Townshend* . . . Atco 7217	
⑩	12	12	**More Love** ....*Kim Carnes* . . . EMI America 8045	

★ HIGHEST DEBUT ★ POS 67	★ BIGGEST MOVER ★ 33 to 15
Another One Bites The Dust...................*Queen*	Give Me The Night ....*George Benson*

TW	LW	WK	Billboard.	AUGUST 23, 1980	HOT 100.
❶	1	14	**Magic**..*Olivia Newton-John* . . . MCA 41247
❷	2	11	**Sailing**..*Christopher Cross* . . . Warner 49507
❸	3	13	**Take Your Time (Do It Right)** ....*The S.O.S. Band* . . . Tabu 5522
❹	4	8	**Emotional Rescue**......................*The Rolling Stones* . . . Rolling Stones 20001
❺	5	7	**Upside Down** ....*Diana Ross* . . . Motown 1494
❻	6	14	**It's Still Rock And Roll To Me** ....*Billy Joel* . . . Columbia 11276
❼	13	11	**Fame** ....*Irene Cara* . . . RSO 1034
❽	21	11	**All Out Of Love** ....*Air Supply* . . . Arista 0520
❾	9	11	**Let My Love Open The Door** ....*Pete Townshend* . . . Atco 7217
❿	10	13	**More Love** ....*Kim Carnes* . . . EMI America 8045

★ *HIGHEST DEBUT* ★ POS 69	★ *BIGGEST MOVER* ★ 63 to 43
Look What You've Done To Me........*Boz Scaggs*	**Xanadu**.................*Olivia Newton-John/Electric Light Orchestra*

TW	LW	WK	Billboard.	AUGUST 30, 1980	HOT 100.
❶	2	12	**Sailing** ....*Christopher Cross* . . . Warner 49507
❷	5	8	**Upside Down** ....*Diana Ross* . . . Motown 1494
❸	1	15	**Magic** ....*Olivia Newton-John* . . . MCA 41247
❹	4	9	**Emotional Rescue**......................*The Rolling Stones* . . . Rolling Stones 20001
❺	3	14	**Take Your Time (Do It Right)** ....*The S.O.S. Band* . . . Tabu 5522
❻	7	12	**Fame** ....*Irene Cara* . . . RSO 1034
❼	8	12	**All Out Of Love** ....*Air Supply* . . . Arista 0520
❽	11	9	**Give Me The Night**................*George Benson* . . . Warner 49505
❾	9	12	**Let My Love Open The Door** ....*Pete Townshend* . . . Atco 7217
❿	10	14	**More Love** ....*Kim Carnes* . . . EMI America 8045

★ *HIGHEST DEBUT* ★ POS 69	★ *BIGGEST MOVER* ★ 69 to 45
Midnight Rocks.................*Al Stewart*	Look What You've Done To Me........*Boz Scaggs*

TW	LW	WK	Billboard.	SEPTEMBER 6, 1980	HOT 100.
❶	2	9	**Upside Down**..*Diana Ross* . . . Motown 1494
❷	1	13	**Sailing**..*Christopher Cross* . . . Warner 49507
❸	4	10	**Emotional Rescue**................*The Rolling Stones* . . . Rolling Stones 20001
❹	7	13	**All Out Of Love** ....*Air Supply* . . . Arista 0520
❺	6	13	**Fame** ....*Irene Cara* . . . RSO 1034
❻	3	16	**Magic** ....*Olivia Newton-John* . . . MCA 41247
❼	8	10	**Give Me The Night**................................*George Benson* . . . Warner 49505
❽	5	15	**Take Your Time (Do It Right)** ....*The S.O.S. Band* . . . Tabu 5522
❾	11	5	**Late In The Evening** ....*Paul Simon* . . . Warner 49511
❿	13	9	**Lookin' For Love**................................*Johnny Lee* . . . Full Moon/Asylum 47004

★ *HIGHEST DEBUT* ★ POS 40	★ *BIGGEST MOVER* ★ 64 to 51
Real Love...........................*The Doobie Brothers*	Who'll Be The Fool Tonight ....*Larsen-Feiten Band*

TW	LW	WK	Billboard	SEPTEMBER 13, 1980	HOT 100
①	1	10	**Upside Down**..................................*Diana Ross* . . . Motown 1494
②	4	14	**All Out Of Love**..............................*Air Supply* . . . Arista 0520
③	3	11	**Emotional Rescue**.................*The Rolling Stones* . . . Rolling Stones 20001
④	5	14	**Fame**..*Irene Cara* . . . RSO 1034
⑤	2	14	**Sailing**.......................................*Christopher Cross* . . . Warner 49507
⑥	7	11	**Give Me The Night**............................*George Benson* . . . Warner 49505
⑦	9	6	**Late In The Evening**...........................*Paul Simon* . . . Warner 49511
⑧	10	10	**Lookin' For Love**................................*Johnny Lee* . . . Full Moon/Asylum 47004
⑨	23	5	**Another One Bites The Dust**..................*Queen* . . . Elektra 47031
⑩	13	13	**Drivin' My Life Away** ....*Eddie Rabbitt* . . . Elektra 46656

★ HIGHEST DEBUT ★ POS 77	★ BIGGEST MOVER ★ 49 to 33
Dreaming.....................................*Cliff Richard*	Woman In Love.........................*Barbra Streisand*

TW	LW	WK	Billboard	SEPTEMBER 20, 1980	HOT 100
①	1	11	**Upside Down**..................................*Diana Ross* . . . Motown 1494
②	2	15	**All Out Of Love**..............................*Air Supply* . . . Arista 0520
③	9	6	**Another One Bites The Dust**..................*Queen* . . . Elektra 47031
④	4	15	**Fame**..*Irene Cara* . . . RSO 1034
⑤	8	11	**Lookin' For Love** ....*Johnny Lee* . . . Full Moon/Asylum 47004
⑥	6	12	**Give Me The Night**............................*George Benson* . . . Warner 49505
⑦	7	7	**Late In The Evening** ....*Paul Simon* . . . Warner 49511
⑧	10	14	**Drivin' My Life Away** ....*Eddie Rabbitt* . . . Elektra 46656
⑨	15	13	**One In A Million You** ....*Larry Graham* . . . Warner 49221
⑩	3	12	**Emotional Rescue**.....................*The Rolling Stones* . . . Rolling Stones 20001

★ HIGHEST DEBUT ★ POS 43	★ BIGGEST MOVER ★ 77 to 52
The Wanderer ....*Donna Summer*	Dreaming...*Cliff Richard*

TW	LW	WK	Billboard	SEPTEMBER 27, 1980	HOT 100
①	1	12	**Upside Down**..................................*Diana Ross* . . . Motown 1494
②	2	16	**All Out Of Love**..............................*Air Supply* . . . Arista 0520
③	3	7	**Another One Bites The Dust**..................*Queen* . . . Elektra 47031
④	6	13	**Give Me The Night**............................*George Benson* . . . Warner 49505
⑤	5	12	**Lookin' For Love** ....*Johnny Lee* . . . Full Moon/Asylum 47004
⑥	7	8	**Late In The Evening** ....*Paul Simon* . . . Warner 49511
⑦	8	15	**Drivin' My Life Away** ....*Eddie Rabbitt* . . . Elektra 46656
⑧	4	16	**Fame**..*Irene Cara* . . . RSO 1034
⑨	9	14	**One In A Million You** ....*Larry Graham* . . . Warner 49221
⑩	11	12	**I'm Alright** ....*Kenny Loggins* . . . Columbia 11317

★ HIGHEST DEBUT ★ POS 68	★ BIGGEST MOVER ★ 67 to 46
You've Lost That Lovin' Feeling........*Daryl Hall & John Oates*	Dreamer...................................*Supertramp*

Billboard — OCTOBER 4, 1980 — HOT 100

TW	LW	WK	Title	Artist	Label
1	3	8	Another One Bites The Dust	Queen	Elektra 47031
2	2	17	All Out Of Love	Air Supply	Arista 0520
3	1	13	Upside Down	Diana Ross	Motown 1494
4	4	14	Give Me The Night	George Benson	Warner 49505
5	7	16	Drivin' My Life Away	Eddie Rabbitt	Elektra 46656
6	6	9	Late In The Evening	Paul Simon	Warner 49511
7	12	5	Woman In Love	Barbra Streisand	Columbia 11364
8	10	13	I'm Alright	Kenny Loggins	Columbia 11317
9	5	13	Lookin' For Love	Johnny Lee	Full Moon/Asylum 47004
10	11	9	Xanadu	Olivia Newton-John/Electric Light Orchestra	MCA 41285

★ HIGHEST DEBUT ★ POS 39
Lady ....Kenny Rogers

★ BIGGEST MOVER ★ 62 to 32
Master Blaster (Jammin') ....Stevie Wonder

Billboard — OCTOBER 11, 1980 — HOT 100

TW	LW	WK	Title	Artist	Label
1	1	9	Another One Bites The Dust	Queen	Elektra 47031
2	7	6	Woman In Love	Barbra Streisand	Columbia 11364
3	3	14	Upside Down	Diana Ross	Motown 1494
4	2	18	All Out Of Love	Air Supply	Arista 0520
5	5	17	Drivin' My Life Away	Eddie Rabbitt	Elektra 46656
6	6	10	Late In The Evening	Paul Simon	Warner 49511
7	8	14	I'm Alright	Kenny Loggins	Columbia 11317
8	10	10	Xanadu	Olivia Newton-John/Electric Light Orchestra	MCA 41285
9	11	6	Real Love	The Doobie Brothers	Warner 49503
10	4	15	Give Me The Night	George Benson	Warner 49505

★ HIGHEST DEBUT ★ POS 75
Never Be The Same ....Christopher Cross

★ BIGGEST MOVER ★ 39 to 20
Lady ....Kenny Rogers

Billboard — OCTOBER 18, 1980 — HOT 100

TW	LW	WK	Title	Artist	Label
1	1	10	Another One Bites The Dust	Queen	Elektra 47031
2	2	7	Woman In Love	Barbra Streisand	Columbia 11364
3	3	15	Upside Down	Diana Ross	Motown 1494
4	4	19	All Out Of Love	Air Supply	Arista 0520
5	12	13	He's So Shy	Pointer Sisters	Planet 47916
6	9	7	Real Love	The Doobie Brothers	Warner 49503
7	7	15	I'm Alright	Kenny Loggins	Columbia 11317
8	8	11	Xanadu	Olivia Newton-John/Electric Light Orchestra	MCA 41285
9	5	18	Drivin' My Life Away	Eddie Rabbitt	Elektra 46656
10	6	11	Late In The Evening	Paul Simon	Warner 49511

★ HIGHEST DEBUT ★ POS 79
Deep Inside My Heart ....Randy Meisner

★ BIGGEST MOVER ★ 75 to 55
Never Be The Same ....Christopher Cross

Billboard — OCTOBER 25, 1980 — HOT 100

TW	LW	WK	Title	Artist	Label
1	2	8	Woman In Love	Barbra Streisand	Columbia 11364
2	1	11	Another One Bites The Dust	Queen	Elektra 47031
3	5	14	He's So Shy	Pointer Sisters	Planet 47916
4	3	16	Upside Down	Diana Ross	Motown 1494
5	6	8	Real Love	The Doobie Brothers	Warner 49503
6	17	4	Lady	Kenny Rogers	Liberty 1380
7	11	6	The Wanderer	Donna Summer	Geffen 49563
8	4	20	All Out Of Love	Air Supply	Arista 0520
9	7	16	I'm Alright	Kenny Loggins	Columbia 11317
10	12	12	Never Knew Love Like This Before	Stephanie Mills	20th Century 2460

★ **HIGHEST DEBUT** ★ POS 78
One-Trick Pony ... Paul Simon

★ **BIGGEST MOVER** ★ 58 to 41
I'm Happy That Love Has Found You ... Jimmy Hall

Billboard — NOVEMBER 1, 1980 — HOT 100

TW	LW	WK	Title	Artist	Label
1	1	9	Woman In Love	Barbra Streisand	Columbia 11364
2	2	12	Another One Bites The Dust	Queen	Elektra 47031
3	3	15	He's So Shy	Pointer Sisters	Planet 47916
4	6	5	Lady	Kenny Rogers	Liberty 1380
5	5	9	Real Love	The Doobie Brothers	Warner 49503
6	7	7	The Wanderer	Donna Summer	Geffen 49563
7	4	17	Upside Down	Diana Ross	Motown 1494
8	10	13	Never Knew Love Like This Before	Stephanie Mills	20th Century 2460
9	11	9	I'm Coming Out	Diana Ross	Motown 1491
10	15	7	Master Blaster (Jammin')	Stevie Wonder	Tamla 54317

★ **HIGHEST DEBUT** ★ POS 32
Love On The Rocks ... Neil Diamond

★ **BIGGEST MOVER** ★ 86 to 63
It's My Turn ... Diana Ross

Billboard — NOVEMBER 8, 1980 — HOT 100

TW	LW	WK	Title	Artist	Label
1	1	10	Woman In Love	Barbra Streisand	Columbia 11364
2	4	6	Lady	Kenny Rogers	Liberty 1380
3	3	16	He's So Shy	Pointer Sisters	Planet 47916
4	2	13	Another One Bites The Dust	Queen	Elektra 47031
5	6	8	The Wanderer	Donna Summer	Geffen 49563
6	9	10	I'm Coming Out	Diana Ross	Motown 1491
7	8	14	Never Knew Love Like This Before	Stephanie Mills	20th Century 2460
8	10	8	Master Blaster (Jammin')	Stevie Wonder	Tamla 54317
9	5	10	Real Love	The Doobie Brothers	Warner 49503
10	7	18	Upside Down	Diana Ross	Motown 1494

★ **HIGHEST DEBUT** ★ POS 30
Hungry Heart ... Bruce Springsteen

★ **BIGGEST MOVER** ★ 68 to 43
Guilty ... Barbra Streisand & Barry Gibb

TW	LW	WK	Billboard	NOVEMBER 15, 1980	HOT 100.
1	2	7	**Lady**..*Kenny Rogers* . . . Liberty 1380
2	1	11	**Woman In Love** ....*Barbra Streisand* . . . Columbia 11364
3	5	9	**The Wanderer**.................................*Donna Summer* . . . Geffen 49563
4	4	14	**Another One Bites The Dust**..........................*Queen* . . . Elektra 47031
5	6	11	**I'm Coming Out** ....*Diana Ross* . . . Motown 1491
6	7	15	**Never Knew Love Like This Before** .... *Stephanie Mills* . . . 20th Century 2460
7	8	9	**Master Blaster (Jammin')** ....*Stevie Wonder* . . . Tamla 54317
8	3	17	**He's So Shy** ....*Pointer Sisters* . . . Planet 47916
9	14	8	**More Than I Can Say** ....*Leo Sayer* . . . Warner 49565
10	32	3	**(Just Like) Starting Over**.........................*John Lennon* . . . Geffen 49604

★ HIGHEST DEBUT ★ POS 79	★ BIGGEST MOVER ★ 32 to 10
Turn And Walk Away.........................*The Babys*	(Just Like) Starting Over ....*John Lennon*

TW	LW	WK	Billboard	NOVEMBER 22, 1980	HOT 100.
1	1	8	**Lady**..*Kenny Rogers* . . . Liberty 1380
2	2	12	**Woman In Love** ....*Barbra Streisand* . . . Columbia 11364
3	3	10	**The Wanderer**.................................*Donna Summer* . . . Geffen 49563
4	4	15	**Another One Bites The Dust**..........................*Queen* . . . Elektra 47031
5	5	12	**I'm Coming Out** ....*Diana Ross* . . . Motown 1491
6	6	16	**Never Knew Love Like This Before** .... *Stephanie Mills* . . . 20th Century 2460
7	7	10	**Master Blaster (Jammin')** ....*Stevie Wonder* . . . Tamla 54317
8	9	9	**More Than I Can Say** ....*Leo Sayer* . . . Warner 49565
9	10	4	**(Just Like) Starting Over**.........................*John Lennon* . . . Geffen 49604
10	11	11	**Dreaming** ....*Cliff Richard* . . . EMI America 8057

★ HIGHEST DEBUT ★ POS 41	★ BIGGEST MOVER ★ 81 to 58
Tell It Like It Is ....*Heart*	The Tide Is High...........................*Blondie*

TW	LW	WK	Billboard	NOVEMBER 29, 1980	HOT 100.
1	1	9	**Lady**..*Kenny Rogers* . . . Liberty 1380
2	2	13	**Woman In Love** ....*Barbra Streisand* . . . Columbia 11364
3	3	11	**The Wanderer**.................................*Donna Summer* . . . Geffen 49563
4	4	16	**Another One Bites The Dust**..........................*Queen* . . . Elektra 47031
5	5	13	**I'm Coming Out** ....*Diana Ross* . . . Motown 1491
6	8	10	**More Than I Can Say** ....*Leo Sayer* . . . Warner 49565
7	7	11	**Master Blaster (Jammin')** ....*Stevie Wonder* . . . Tamla 54317
8	9	5	**(Just Like) Starting Over**.........................*John Lennon* . . . Geffen 49604
9	11	5	**Love On The Rocks**...........................*Neil Diamond* . . . Capitol 4939
10	10	12	**Dreaming** ....*Cliff Richard* . . . EMI America 8057

★ HIGHEST DEBUT ★ POS 65	★ BIGGEST MOVER ★ 58 to 38
Hey Nineteen ....*Steely Dan*	The Tide Is High...........................*Blondie*

Billboard HOT 100 — DECEMBER 6, 1980

TW	LW	WK	Title	Artist	Label
1	1	10	**Lady**	Kenny Rogers	Liberty 1380
2	6	11	**More Than I Can Say**	Leo Sayer	Warner 49565
3	4	17	**Another One Bites The Dust**	Queen	Elektra 47031
4	2	14	**Woman In Love**	Barbra Streisand	Columbia 11364
5	7	12	**Master Blaster (Jammin')**	Stevie Wonder	Tamla 54317
6	8	6	**(Just Like) Starting Over**	John Lennon	Geffen 49604
7	9	6	**Love On The Rocks**	Neil Diamond	Capitol 4939
8	11	5	**Hungry Heart**	Bruce Springsteen	Columbia 11391
9	5	14	**I'm Coming Out**	Diana Ross	Motown 1491
10	10	13	**Dreaming**	Cliff Richard	EMI America 8057

★ **HIGHEST DEBUT** ★ POS 81
I Can't Stop The Feelin' ....Pure Prairie League

★ **BIGGEST MOVER** ★ 65 to 45
Hey Nineteen ....Steely Dan

Billboard HOT 100 — DECEMBER 13, 1980

TW	LW	WK	Title	Artist	Label
1	1	11	**Lady**	Kenny Rogers	Liberty 1380
2	2	12	**More Than I Can Say**	Leo Sayer	Warner 49565
3	3	18	**Another One Bites The Dust**	Queen	Elektra 47031
4	6	7	**(Just Like) Starting Over**	John Lennon	Geffen 49604
5	5	13	**Master Blaster (Jammin')**	Stevie Wonder	Tamla 54317
6	7	7	**Love On The Rocks**	Neil Diamond	Capitol 4939
7	8	6	**Hungry Heart**	Bruce Springsteen	Columbia 11391
8	4	15	**Woman In Love**	Barbra Streisand	Columbia 11364
9	14	7	**Guilty**	Barbra Streisand & Barry Gibb	Columbia 11390
10	11	11	**Hit Me With Your Best Shot**	Pat Benatar	Chrysalis 2464

★ **HIGHEST DEBUT** ★ POS 75
Same Old Lang Syne...................Dan Fogelberg

★ **BIGGEST MOVER** ★ 90 to 69
Giving It Up For Your Love ....Delbert McClinton

Billboard HOT 100 — DECEMBER 20, 1980

TW	LW	WK	Title	Artist	Label
1	1	12	**Lady**	Kenny Rogers	Liberty 1380
2	2	13	**More Than I Can Say**	Leo Sayer	Warner 49565
3	4	8	**(Just Like) Starting Over**	John Lennon	Geffen 49604
4	6	8	**Love On The Rocks**	Neil Diamond	Capitol 4939
5	5	14	**Master Blaster (Jammin')**	Stevie Wonder	Tamla 54317
6	7	7	**Hungry Heart**	Bruce Springsteen	Columbia 11391
7	3	19	**Another One Bites The Dust**	Queen	Elektra 47031
8	9	8	**Guilty**	Barbra Streisand & Barry Gibb	Columbia 11390
9	10	12	**Hit Me With Your Best Shot**	Pat Benatar	Chrysalis 2464
10	11	9	**Every Woman In The World**	Air Supply	Arista 0564

★ **HIGHEST DEBUT** ★ POS 64
Seven Bridges Road ....Eagles

★ **BIGGEST MOVER** ★ 69 to 38
Giving It Up For Your Love ....Delbert McClinton

Billboard 🎵 DECEMBER 27, 1980 🎵 **HOT 100**

TW	LW	WK			
1	3	9	**(Just Like) Starting Over**	*John Lennon* . . .	Geffen 49604
②	2	14	**More Than I Can Say**	*Leo Sayer* . . .	Warner 49565
3	4	9	**Love On The Rocks**	*Neil Diamond* . . .	Capitol 4939
④	1	13	**Lady**	*Kenny Rogers* . . .	Liberty 1380
5	6	8	**Hungry Heart**	*Bruce Springsteen* . . .	Columbia 11391
6	10	10	**Every Woman In The World**	*Air Supply* . . .	Arista 0564
7	8	9	**Guilty**	*Barbra Streisand & Barry Gibb* . . .	Columbia 11390
8	11	7	**The Tide Is High**	*Blondie* . . .	Chrysalis 2465
⑨	9	13	**Hit Me With Your Best Shot**	*Pat Benatar* . . .	Chrysalis 2464
10	12	6	**Tell It Like It Is**	*Heart* . . .	Epic 50950

★ **HIGHEST DEBUT** ★ POS 81	★ **BIGGEST MOVER** ★ 59 to 37
United Together ....*Aretha Franklin*	Same Old Lang Syne ....*Dan Fogelberg*

Billboard · JANUARY 10, 1981 · HOT 100

TW	LW	WK	Title	Artist / Label
1	1	11	**(Just Like) Starting Over**	*John Lennon* . . . Geffen 49604
2	3	11	**Love On The Rocks**	*Neil Diamond* . . . Capitol 4939
3	7	11	**Guilty**	*Barbra Streisand & Barry Gibb* . . . Columbia 11390
4	8	9	The Tide Is High	*Blondie* . . . Chrysalis 2465
5	5	10	**Hungry Heart**	*Bruce Springsteen* . . . Columbia 11391
6	6	12	Every Woman In The World	*Air Supply* . . . Arista 0564
7	11	8	Passion	*Rod Stewart* . . . Warner 49617
8	10	8	**Tell It Like It Is**	*Heart* . . . Epic 50950
9	4	15	Lady	*Kenny Rogers* . . . Liberty 1380
10	2	16	More Than I Can Say	*Leo Sayer* . . . Warner 49565

★ **HIGHEST DEBUT** ★ POS 86
Toccata . . . . *Sky*

★ **BIGGEST MOVER** ★ 55 to 35
Seven Bridges Road . . . . *Eagles*

Billboard · JANUARY 17, 1981 · HOT 100

TW	LW	WK	Title	Artist / Label
1	1	12	**(Just Like) Starting Over**	*John Lennon* . . . Geffen 49604
2	2	12	**Love On The Rocks**	*Neil Diamond* . . . Capitol 4939
3	3	12	**Guilty**	*Barbra Streisand & Barry Gibb* . . . Columbia 11390
4	4	10	**The Tide Is High**	*Blondie* . . . Chrysalis 2465
5	5	11	**Hungry Heart**	*Bruce Springsteen* . . . Columbia 11391
6	6	13	Every Woman In The World	*Air Supply* . . . Arista 0564
7	7	9	Passion	*Rod Stewart* . . . Warner 49617
8	8	9	**Tell It Like It Is**	*Heart* . . . Epic 50950
9	9	16	Lady	*Kenny Rogers* . . . Liberty 1380
10	11	13	**De Do Do Do, De Da Da Da**	*The Police* . . . A&M 2275

★ **HIGHEST DEBUT** ★ POS 36
Woman . . . . *John Lennon*

★ **BIGGEST MOVER** ★ 49 to 32
I Ain't Gonna Stand For It . . . . *Stevie Wonder*

Billboard · JANUARY 24, 1981 · HOT 100

TW	LW	WK	Title	Artist / Label
1	1	13	**(Just Like) Starting Over**	*John Lennon* . . . Geffen 49604
2	2	13	**Love On The Rocks**	*Neil Diamond* . . . Capitol 4939
3	4	11	**The Tide Is High**	*Blondie* . . . Chrysalis 2465
4	3	13	**Guilty**	*Barbra Streisand & Barry Gibb* . . . Columbia 11390
5	5	12	**Hungry Heart**	*Bruce Springsteen* . . . Columbia 11391
6	6	14	Every Woman In The World	*Air Supply* . . . Arista 0564
7	7	10	Passion	*Rod Stewart* . . . Warner 49617
8	12	12	**I Love A Rainy Night**	*Eddie Rabbitt* . . . Elektra 47066
9	11	14	**It's My Turn**	*Diana Ross* . . . Motown 1496
10	10	14	**De Do Do Do, De Da Da Da**	*The Police* . . . A&M 2275

★ **HIGHEST DEBUT** ★ POS 31
The Best Of Times . . . . *Styx*

★ **BIGGEST MOVER** ★ 68 to 50
Treat Me Right . . . . *Pat Benatar*

Billboard — JANUARY 31, 1981 — HOT 100.

TW	LW	WK			
❶	3	12	**The Tide Is High**	*Blondie*	Chrysalis 2465
②	1	14	(Just Like) Starting Over	*John Lennon*	Geffen 49604
❸	12	15	Celebration	*Kool & The Gang*	De-Lite 807
④	8	13	I Love A Rainy Night	*Eddie Rabbitt*	Elektra 47066
⑤	6	15	**Every Woman In The World**	*Air Supply*	Arista 0564
⑥	7	11	Passion	*Rod Stewart*	Warner 49617
⑦	2	14	Love On The Rocks	*Neil Diamond*	Capitol 4939
❽	18	10	9 To 5	*Dolly Parton*	RCA 12133
⑨	9	15	It's My Turn	*Diana Ross*	Motown 1496
⑩	11	11	**I Made It Through The Rain**	*Barry Manilow*	Arista 0566

★ *HIGHEST DEBUT* ★ POS 32	★ *BIGGEST MOVER* ★ 65 to 50
Hello Again ....*Neil Diamond*	Hearts On Fire ....*Randy Meisner*

Billboard — FEBRUARY 7, 1981 — HOT 100.

TW	LW	WK			
❶	3	16	**Celebration**	*Kool & The Gang*	De-Lite 807
②	1	13	The Tide Is High	*Blondie*	Chrysalis 2465
❸	4	14	I Love A Rainy Night	*Eddie Rabbitt*	Elektra 47066
④	8	11	9 To 5	*Dolly Parton*	RCA 12133
❺	6	12	**Passion**	*Rod Stewart*	Warner 49617
⑥	2	15	(Just Like) Starting Over	*John Lennon*	Geffen 49604
⑦	5	16	Every Woman In The World	*Air Supply*	Arista 0564
❽	17	4	Woman	*John Lennon*	Geffen 49644
⑨	9	16	**It's My Turn**	*Diana Ross*	Motown 1496
⑩	11	10	Giving It Up For Your Love	*Delbert McClinton*	Capitol 4948

★ *HIGHEST DEBUT* ★ POS 65	★ *BIGGEST MOVER* ★ 72 to 52
Fade Away ....*Bruce Springsteen*	What Kind Of Fool ....*Barbra Streisand & Barry Gibb*

Billboard — FEBRUARY 14, 1981 — HOT 100.

TW	LW	WK			
❶	1	17	**Celebration**	*Kool & The Gang*	De-Lite 807
②	4	12	9 To 5	*Dolly Parton*	RCA 12133
❸	3	15	I Love A Rainy Night	*Eddie Rabbitt*	Elektra 47066
④	2	14	The Tide Is High	*Blondie*	Chrysalis 2465
⑤	5	13	**Passion**	*Rod Stewart*	Warner 49617
⑥	8	5	Woman	*John Lennon*	Geffen 49644
⑦	6	16	(Just Like) Starting Over	*John Lennon*	Geffen 49604
❽	13	12	Keep On Loving You	*REO Speedwagon*	Epic 50953
⑨	10	11	Giving It Up For Your Love	*Delbert McClinton*	Capitol 4948
⑩	11	12	**Hey Nineteen**	*Steely Dan*	MCA 51036

★ *HIGHEST DEBUT* ★ POS 74	★ *BIGGEST MOVER* ★ 78 to 57
Morning Train (Nine To Five) ....*Sheena Easton*	Don't Stand So Close To Me ....*The Police*

Billboard — FEBRUARY 21, 1981 — HOT 100

TW	LW	WK	Title	Artist	Label
❶	2	13	9 To 5	Dolly Parton	RCA 12133
❷	3	16	I Love A Rainy Night	Eddie Rabbitt	Elektra 47066
③	1	18	Celebration	Kool & The Gang	De-Lite 807
❹	6	6	Woman	John Lennon	Geffen 49644
⑤	4	15	The Tide Is High	Blondie	Chrysalis 2465
❻	8	13	Keep On Loving You	REO Speedwagon	Epic 50953
❼	12	5	The Best Of Times	Styx	A&M 2300
❽	9	12	Giving It Up For Your Love	Delbert McClinton	Capitol 4948
❾	11	11	Same Old Lang Syne	Dan Fogelberg	Full Moon 50961
⑩	10	13	Hey Nineteen	Steely Dan	MCA 51036

★ HIGHEST DEBUT ★ POS 70
Angel Of The Morning ....Juice Newton

★ BIGGEST MOVER ★ 74 to 53
Morning Train (Nine To Five)........Sheena Easton

Billboard — FEBRUARY 28, 1981 — HOT 100

TW	LW	WK	Title	Artist	Label
❶	2	17	I Love A Rainy Night	Eddie Rabbitt	Elektra 47066
②	1	14	9 To 5	Dolly Parton	RCA 12133
❸	4	7	Woman	John Lennon	Geffen 49644
④	3	19	Celebration	Kool & The Gang	De-Lite 807
❺	6	14	Keep On Loving You	REO Speedwagon	Epic 50953
❻	7	6	The Best Of Times	Styx	A&M 2300
⑦	5	16	The Tide Is High	Blondie	Chrysalis 2465
❽	8	13	Giving It Up For Your Love	Delbert McClinton	Capitol 4948
⑨	9	12	Same Old Lang Syne	Dan Fogelberg	Full Moon 50961
⑩	12	15	The Winner Takes It All	Abba	Atlantic 3776

★ HIGHEST DEBUT ★ POS 63
I Can't Stand It ....Eric Clapton & His Band

★ BIGGEST MOVER ★ 65 to 41
Just The Two Of Us......Grover Washington, Jr./Bill Withers

Billboard — MARCH 7, 1981 — HOT 100

TW	LW	WK	Title	Artist	Label
❶	1	18	I Love A Rainy Night	Eddie Rabbitt	Elektra 47066
②	2	15	9 To 5	Dolly Parton	RCA 12133
❸	3	8	Woman	John Lennon	Geffen 49644
④	5	15	Keep On Loving You	REO Speedwagon	Epic 50953
❺	6	7	The Best Of Times	Styx	A&M 2300
❻	4	20	Celebration	Kool & The Gang	De-Lite 807
❼	11	7	Crying	Don McLean	Millennium 11799
❽	8	14	Giving It Up For Your Love	Delbert McClinton	Capitol 4948
❾	10	16	The Winner Takes It All	Abba	Atlantic 3776
⑩	14	6	Hello Again	Neil Diamond	Capitol 4960

★ HIGHEST DEBUT ★ POS 77
Sweetheart ....Franke & The Knockouts

★ BIGGEST MOVER ★ 54 to 36
Angel Of The Morning ....Juice Newton

TW	LW	WK	Billboard.	MARCH 14, 1981	HOT 100.
❶	2	16	**9 To 5**..*Dolly Parton* . . . RCA 12133
❷	4	16	**Keep On Loving You**.................................*REO Speedwagon* . . . Epic 50953
❸	3	9	**Woman**...*John Lennon* . . . Geffen 49644
❹	5	8	**The Best Of Times** ....*Styx* . . . A&M 2300
❺	1	19	**I Love A Rainy Night**.............................*Eddie Rabbitt* . . . Elektra 47066
❻	7	8	**Crying** ....*Don McLean* . . . Millennium 11799
❼	12	7	**Rapture** ....*Blondie* . . . Chrysalis 2485
❽	9	17	**The Winner Takes It All**...............................*Abba* . . . Atlantic 3776
❾	10	7	**Hello Again**....................................*Neil Diamond* . . . Capitol 4960
❿	6	21	**Celebration**....................................*Kool & The Gang* . . . De-Lite 807

★ *HIGHEST DEBUT* ★ POS 38	★ *BIGGEST MOVER* ★ 47 to 29
Her Town Too............*James Taylor & J.D. Souther*	I Can't Stand It................*Eric Clapton & His Band*

TW	LW	WK	Billboard.	MARCH 21, 1981	HOT 100.
❶	2	17	**Keep On Loving You** ....*REO Speedwagon* . . . Epic 50953
❷	3	10	**Woman** ....*John Lennon* . . . Geffen 49644
❸	4	9	**The Best Of Times**...*Styx* . . . A&M 2300
❹	1	17	**9 To 5**...*Dolly Parton* . . . RCA 12133
❺	6	9	**Crying** ....*Don McLean* . . . Millennium 11799
❻	7	8	**Rapture** ....*Blondie* . . . Chrysalis 2485
❼	9	8	**Hello Again** ....*Neil Diamond* . . . Capitol 4960
⑧	8	18	**The Winner Takes It All**...............................*Abba* . . . Atlantic 3776
⑨	5	20	**I Love A Rainy Night** ....*Eddie Rabbitt* . . . Elektra 47066
❿	12	8	**What Kind Of Fool** ......*Barbra Streisand & Barry Gibb* . . . Columbia 11430

★ *HIGHEST DEBUT* ★ POS 60	★ *BIGGEST MOVER* ★ 70 to 48
Too Much Time On My Hands....................*Styx*	Time Out Of Mind ....*Steely Dan*

TW	LW	WK	Billboard.	MARCH 28, 1981	HOT 100.
❶	6	9	**Rapture** ....*Blondie* . . . Chrysalis 2485
②	2	11	**Woman** ....*John Lennon* . . . Geffen 49644
③	3	10	**The Best Of Times**...*Styx* . . . A&M 2300
④	1	18	**Keep On Loving You**.................................*REO Speedwagon* . . . Epic 50953
⑤	5	10	**Crying** ....*Don McLean* . . . Millennium 11799
⑥	7	9	**Hello Again**....................................*Neil Diamond* . . . Capitol 4960
⑦	4	18	**9 To 5**...*Dolly Parton* . . . RCA 12133
⑧	23	7	**Just The Two Of Us** ....*Grover Washington, Jr./Bill Withers* . . . Elektra 47103
⑨	12	10	**Kiss On My List**...........................*Daryl Hall & John Oates* . . . RCA 12142
❿	10	9	**What Kind Of Fool** ......*Barbra Streisand & Barry Gibb* . . . Columbia 11430

★ *HIGHEST DEBUT* ★ POS 72	★ *BIGGEST MOVER* ★ 65 to 32
Love You Like I Never Loved Before ....*John O'Banion*	Take It On The Run................*REO Speedwagon*

TW	LW	WK	Billboard	APRIL 4, 1981	HOT 100
❶	1	10	**Rapture** ....*Blondie* ... Chrysalis 2485
②	2	12	**Woman** ....*John Lennon* ... Geffen 49644
③	3	11	**The Best Of Times**...*Styx* ... A&M 2300
❹	9	11	**Kiss On My List**...............................*Daryl Hall & John Oates* ... RCA 12142
⑤	5	11	**Crying** ....*Don McLean* ... Millennium 11799
⑥	6	10	**Hello Again**...*Neil Diamond* ... Capitol 4960
❼	8	8	**Just The Two Of Us** ....*Grover Washington, Jr./Bill Withers* ... Elektra 47103
⑧	4	19	**Keep On Loving You**...............................*REO Speedwagon* ... Epic 50953
⑨	11	9	**While You See A Chance** ....*Steve Winwood* ... Island 49656
⑩	10	10	**What Kind Of Fool** ....*Barbra Streisand & Barry Gibb* ... Columbia 11430

★ HIGHEST DEBUT ★ POS 81	★ BIGGEST MOVER ★ 59 to 32
Find Your Way Back ....*Jefferson Starship*	Living Inside Myself ....*Gino Vannelli*

TW	LW	WK	Billboard	APRIL 11, 1981	HOT 100
❶	4	12	**Kiss On My List**...........................*Daryl Hall & John Oates* ... RCA 12142
②	1	11	**Rapture** ....*Blondie* ... Chrysalis 2485
③	3	12	**The Best Of Times**...*Styx* ... A&M 2300
④	2	13	**Woman**...*John Lennon* ... Geffen 49644
❺	7	9	**Just The Two Of Us** ....*Grover Washington, Jr./Bill Withers* ... Elektra 47103
❻	11	9	**Morning Train (Nine To Five)** ....*Sheena Easton* ... EMI America 8071
⑦	5	12	**Crying**...*Don McLean* ... Millennium 11799
⑧	9	10	**While You See A Chance** ....*Steve Winwood* ... Island 49656
⑨	8	20	**Keep On Loving You**...............................*REO Speedwagon* ... Epic 50953
⑩	12	10	**Don't Stand So Close To Me** ....*The Police* ... A&M 2301

★ HIGHEST DEBUT ★ POS 71	★ BIGGEST MOVER ★ 57 to 33
Since I Don't Have You ....*Don McLean*	Bette Davis Eyes.............................*Kim Carnes*

TW	LW	WK	Billboard	APRIL 18, 1981	HOT 100
❶	1	13	**Kiss On My List**...........................*Daryl Hall & John Oates* ... RCA 12142
②	2	12	**Rapture** ....*Blondie* ... Chrysalis 2485
③	6	10	**Morning Train (Nine To Five)** ....*Sheena Easton* ... EMI America 8071
❹	5	10	**Just The Two Of Us** ....*Grover Washington, Jr./Bill Withers* ... Elektra 47103
⑤	4	14	**Woman**...*John Lennon* ... Geffen 49644
⑥	12	9	**Angel Of The Morning** ....*Juice Newton* ... Capitol 4976
❼	8	11	**While You See A Chance** ....*Steve Winwood* ... Island 49656
⑧	14	10	**Being With You**...............................*Smokey Robinson* ... Tamla 54321
⑨	3	13	**The Best Of Times** ....*Styx* ... A&M 2300
⑩	10	11	**Don't Stand So Close To Me** ....*The Police* ... A&M 2301

★ HIGHEST DEBUT ★ POS 81	★ BIGGEST MOVER ★ 66 to 51
One Day In Your Life.................*Michael Jackson*	Find Your Way Back ....*Jefferson Starship*

TW	LW	WK	Billboard		APRIL 25, 1981		HOT 100.
①	1	14	**Kiss On My List**............................		*Daryl Hall & John Oates* . . . RCA 12142		
②	3	11	**Morning Train (Nine To Five)**		*Sheena Easton* . . . EMI America 8071		
③	8	11	**Being With You**.....................................		*Smokey Robinson* . . . Tamla 54321		
④	4	11	**Just The Two Of Us**		*Grover Washington, Jr./Bill Withers* . . . Elektra 47103		
⑤	6	10	**Angel Of The Morning**		*Juice Newton* . . . Capitol 4976		
⑥	2	13	Rapture		*Blondie* . . . Chrysalis 2485		
⑦	7	12	**While You See A Chance**		*Steve Winwood* . . . Island 49656		
⑧	5	15	Woman..		*John Lennon* . . . Geffen 49644		
⑨	9	14	The Best Of Times		*Styx* . . . A&M 2300		
⑩	10	12	**Don't Stand So Close To Me**		*The Police* . . . A&M 2301		

★ HIGHEST DEBUT ★ POS 67	★ BIGGEST MOVER ★ 61 to 48
This Little Girl ....*Gary U.S. Bonds*	Stars on 45 medley..........................*Stars on 45*

TW	LW	WK	Billboard		MAY 2, 1981		HOT 100.
①	2	12	**Morning Train (Nine To Five)** ....*Sheena Easton* . . . EMI America 8071				
②	4	12	**Just The Two Of Us**........................*Grover Washington, Jr./Bill Withers* . . . Elektra 47103				
③	3	12	**Being With You**.....................................*Smokey Robinson* . . . Tamla 54321				
④	5	11	**Angel Of The Morning**.............................*Juice Newton* . . . Capitol 4976				
⑤	1	15	Kiss On My List.....................*Daryl Hall & John Oates* . . . RCA 12142				
⑥	6	14	Rapture ....*Blondie* . . . Chrysalis 2485				
⑦	18	6	Bette Davis Eyes.............................*Kim Carnes* . . . EMI America 8077				
⑧	7	13	While You See A Chance ....*Steve Winwood* . . . Island 49656				
⑨	16	7	Living Inside Myself ....*Gino Vannelli* . . . Arista 0588				
⑩	11	10	**I Can't Stand It** ....*Eric Clapton & His Band* . . . RSO 1060				

★ HIGHEST DEBUT ★ POS 61	★ BIGGEST MOVER ★ 76 to 39
The Waiting ....*Tom Petty & The Heartbreakers*	America ....*Neil Diamond*

TW	LW	WK	Billboard		MAY 9, 1981		HOT 100.
①	1	13	**Morning Train (Nine To Five)** ....*Sheena Easton* . . . EMI America 8071				
②	2	13	**Just The Two Of Us**........................*Grover Washington, Jr./Bill Withers* . . . Elektra 47103				
③	3	13	**Being With You**.....................................*Smokey Robinson* . . . Tamla 54321				
④	4	12	**Angel Of The Morning**.............................*Juice Newton* . . . Capitol 4976				
⑤	7	7	**Bette Davis Eyes** ....*Kim Carnes* . . . EMI America 8077				
⑥	5	16	Kiss On My List.....................*Daryl Hall & John Oates* . . . RCA 12142				
⑦	12	8	Take It On The Run ....*REO Speedwagon* . . . Epic 01054				
⑧	9	8	Living Inside Myself ....*Gino Vannelli* . . . Arista 0588				
⑨	18	10	Sukiyaki ....*A Taste Of Honey* . . . Capitol 4953				
⑩	10	11	**I Can't Stand It** ....*Eric Clapton & His Band* . . . RSO 1060				

★ HIGHEST DEBUT ★ POS 71	★ BIGGEST MOVER ★ 80 to 65
Nobody Wins ....*Elton John*	Is It You..*Lee Ritenour*

Billboard — MAY 16, 1981 — HOT 100

TW	LW	WK		
❶	5	8	**Bette Davis Eyes**....................................*Kim Carnes* . . . EMI America 8077	
②	2	14	**Just The Two Of Us**........................*Grover Washington, Jr./Bill Withers* . . . Elektra 47103	
❸	3	14	**Being With You**...................................*Smokey Robinson* . . . Tamla 54321	
④	4	13	**Angel Of The Morning**...........................*Juice Newton* . . . Capitol 4976	
⑤	1	14	**Morning Train (Nine To Five)** ....*Sheena Easton* . . . EMI America 8071	
⑥	7	9	**Take It On The Run**..............................*REO Speedwagon* . . . Epic 01054	
❼	8	9	**Living Inside Myself** ....*Gino Vannelli* . . . Arista 0588	
⑧	9	11	**Sukiyaki** ....*A Taste Of Honey* . . . Capitol 4953	
⑨	6	17	**Kiss On My List**...................*Daryl Hall & John Oates* . . . RCA 12142	
⑩	12	9	**Too Much Time On My Hands** ....*Styx* . . . A&M 2323	

★ **HIGHEST DEBUT** ★ POS 59
The One That You Love ....*Air Supply*

★ **BIGGEST MOVER** ★ 67 to 38
You Make My Dreams ......*Daryl Hall & John Oates*

Billboard — MAY 23, 1981 — HOT 100

TW	LW	WK		
❶	1	9	**Bette Davis Eyes**....................................*Kim Carnes* . . . EMI America 8077	
❷	3	15	**Being With You** ....*Smokey Robinson* . . . Tamla 54321	
③	2	15	**Just The Two Of Us** ....*Grover Washington, Jr./Bill Withers* . . . Elektra 47103	
④	4	14	**Angel Of The Morning**............................*Juice Newton* . . . Capitol 4976	
❺	14	7	**Stars on 45 medley** ....*Stars on 45* . . . Radio 3810	
⑥	6	10	**Take It On The Run** ....*REO Speedwagon* . . . Epic 01054	
❼	7	10	**Living Inside Myself** ....*Gino Vannelli* . . . Arista 0588	
⑧	8	12	**Sukiyaki** ....*A Taste Of Honey* . . . Capitol 4953	
❾	10	10	**Too Much Time On My Hands** ....*Styx* . . . A&M 2323	
⑩	11	9	**Watching The Wheels** ....*John Lennon* . . . Geffen 49695	

★ **HIGHEST DEBUT** ★ POS 33
All Those Years Ago ....*George Harrison*

★ **BIGGEST MOVER** ★ 59 to 38
The One That You Love ....*Air Supply*

Billboard — MAY 30, 1981 — HOT 100

TW	LW	WK		
❶	1	10	**Bette Davis Eyes**....................................*Kim Carnes* . . . EMI America 8077	
❷	2	16	**Being With You** ....*Smokey Robinson* . . . Tamla 54321	
❸	5	8	**Stars on 45 medley** ....*Stars on 45* . . . Radio 3810	
❹	8	13	**Sukiyaki** ....*A Taste Of Honey* . . . Capitol 4953	
❺	6	11	**Take It On The Run** ....*REO Speedwagon* . . . Epic 01054	
❻	7	11	**Living Inside Myself** ....*Gino Vannelli* . . . Arista 0588	
⑦	3	16	**Just The Two Of Us** ....*Grover Washington, Jr./Bill Withers* . . . Elektra 47103	
❽	11	13	**A Woman Needs Love (Just Like You Do)**........*Ray Parker Jr. & Raydio* . . . Arista 0592	
⑨	9	11	**Too Much Time On My Hands** ....*Styx* . . . A&M 2323	
⑩	10	10	**Watching The Wheels** ....*John Lennon* . . . Geffen 49695	

★ **HIGHEST DEBUT** ★ POS 76
Queen Of Hearts ....*Juice Newton*

★ **BIGGEST MOVER** ★ 86 to 62
Hearts ....*Marty Balin*

TW	LW	WK	Billboard	JUNE 6, 1981	HOT 100
①	1	11	Bette Davis Eyes	Kim Carnes ...	EMI America 8077
②	2	17	Being With You	Smokey Robinson ...	Tamla 54321
③	3	9	Stars on 45 medley	Stars on 45 ...	Radio 3810
④	4	14	Sukiyaki	A Taste Of Honey ...	Capitol 4953
⑤	5	12	Take It On The Run	REO Speedwagon ...	Epic 01054
⑥	6	12	Living Inside Myself	Gino Vannelli ...	Arista 0588
⑦	8	14	A Woman Needs Love (Just Like You Do)	Ray Parker Jr. & Raydio ...	Arista 0592
⑧	7	17	Just The Two Of Us	Grover Washington, Jr./Bill Withers ...	Elektra 47103
⑨	12	7	America	Neil Diamond ...	Capitol 4994
⑩	11	14	Sweetheart	Franke & The Knockouts ...	Millennium 11801

★ **HIGHEST DEBUT** ★ POS 66
Gemini Dream ....The Moody Blues

★ **BIGGEST MOVER** ★ 62 to 43
Hearts ....Marty Balin

TW	LW	WK	Billboard	JUNE 13, 1981	HOT 100
①	1	12	Bette Davis Eyes	Kim Carnes ...	EMI America 8077
②	3	10	Stars on 45 medley	Stars on 45 ...	Radio 3810
③	4	15	Sukiyaki	A Taste Of Honey ...	Capitol 4953
④	2	18	Being With You	Smokey Robinson ...	Tamla 54321
⑤	7	15	A Woman Needs Love (Just Like You Do)	Ray Parker Jr. & Raydio ...	Arista 0592
⑥	6	13	Living Inside Myself	Gino Vannelli ...	Arista 0588
⑦	11	4	All Those Years Ago	George Harrison ...	Dark Horse 49725
⑧	9	8	America	Neil Diamond ...	Capitol 4994
⑨	5	13	Take It On The Run	REO Speedwagon ...	Epic 01054
⑩	10	15	Sweetheart	Franke & The Knockouts ...	Millennium 11801

★ **HIGHEST DEBUT** ★ POS 33
I Don't Need You ....Kenny Rogers

★ **BIGGEST MOVER** ★ 66 to 37
Gemini Dream ....The Moody Blues

TW	LW	WK	Billboard	JUNE 20, 1981	HOT 100
①	2	11	Stars on 45 medley	Stars on 45 ...	Radio 3810
②	1	13	Bette Davis Eyes	Kim Carnes ...	EMI America 8077
③	3	16	Sukiyaki	A Taste Of Honey ...	Capitol 4953
④	5	16	A Woman Needs Love (Just Like You Do)	Ray Parker Jr. & Raydio ...	Arista 0592
⑤	7	5	All Those Years Ago	George Harrison ...	Dark Horse 49725
⑥	4	19	Being With You	Smokey Robinson ...	Tamla 54321
⑦	14	6	The One That You Love	Air Supply ...	Arista 0604
⑧	8	9	America	Neil Diamond ...	Capitol 4994
⑨	17	8	You Make My Dreams	Daryl Hall & John Oates ...	RCA 12217
⑩	20	13	Jessie's Girl	Rick Springfield ...	RCA 12201

★ **HIGHEST DEBUT** ★ POS 76
Touch Me When We're Dancing ....Carpenters

★ **BIGGEST MOVER** ★ 72 to 51
Don't Let Him Go ....REO Speedwagon

JUNE 27, 1981 — Billboard HOT 100

TW	LW	WK	Title	Artist	Label
❶	2	14	**Bette Davis Eyes**	*Kim Carnes*	EMI America 8077
②	1	12	**Stars on 45 medley**	*Stars on 45*	Radio 3810
③	3	17	**Sukiyaki**	*A Taste Of Honey*	Capitol 4953
④	4	17	**A Woman Needs Love (Just Like You Do)**	*Ray Parker Jr. & Raydio*	Arista 0592
❺	5	6	**All Those Years Ago**	*George Harrison*	Dark Horse 49725
❻	7	7	**The One That You Love**	*Air Supply*	Arista 0604
❼	9	9	**You Make My Dreams**	*Daryl Hall & John Oates*	RCA 12217
⑧	8	10	**America**	*Neil Diamond*	Capitol 4994
❾	10	14	**Jessie's Girl**	*Rick Springfield*	RCA 12201
❿	23	7	**Elvira**	*The Oak Ridge Boys*	MCA 51084

★ **HIGHEST DEBUT** ★ POS 75
(There's) No Gettin' Over Me ....*Ronnie Milsap*

★ **BIGGEST MOVER** ★ 84 to 66
Lady (You Bring Me Up) ....*Commodores*

JULY 4, 1981 — Billboard HOT 100

TW	LW	WK	Title	Artist	Label
❶	1	15	**Bette Davis Eyes**	*Kim Carnes*	EMI America 8077
❷	5	7	**All Those Years Ago**	*George Harrison*	Dark Horse 49725
❸	6	8	**The One That You Love**	*Air Supply*	Arista 0604
❹	9	15	**Jessie's Girl**	*Rick Springfield*	RCA 12201
❺	7	10	**You Make My Dreams**	*Daryl Hall & John Oates*	RCA 12217
❻	10	8	**Elvira**	*The Oak Ridge Boys*	MCA 51084
⑦	2	13	**Stars on 45 medley**	*Stars on 45*	Radio 3810
⑧	4	18	**A Woman Needs Love (Just Like You Do)**	*Ray Parker Jr. & Raydio*	Arista 0592
❾	12	9	**Theme From "Greatest American Hero" (Believe It or Not)**	*Joey Scarbury*	Elektra 47147
❿	13	4	**I Don't Need You**	*Kenny Rogers*	Liberty 1415

★ **HIGHEST DEBUT** ★ POS 51
Urgent ....*Foreigner*

★ **BIGGEST MOVER** ★ 75 to 42
(There's) No Gettin' Over Me ....*Ronnie Milsap*

JULY 11, 1981 — Billboard HOT 100

TW	LW	WK	Title	Artist	Label
❶	1	16	**Bette Davis Eyes**	*Kim Carnes*	EMI America 8077
❷	2	8	**All Those Years Ago**	*George Harrison*	Dark Horse 49725
❸	3	9	**The One That You Love**	*Air Supply*	Arista 0604
❹	4	16	**Jessie's Girl**	*Rick Springfield*	RCA 12201
❺	5	11	**You Make My Dreams**	*Daryl Hall & John Oates*	RCA 12217
❻	6	9	**Elvira**	*The Oak Ridge Boys*	MCA 51084
⑦	7	14	**Stars on 45 medley**	*Stars on 45*	Radio 3810
❽	9	10	**Theme From "Greatest American Hero" (Believe It or Not)**	*Joey Scarbury*	Elektra 47147
❾	10	5	**I Don't Need You**	*Kenny Rogers*	Liberty 1415
❿	18	7	**Slow Hand**	*Pointer Sisters*	Planet 47929

★ **HIGHEST DEBUT** ★ POS 54
Endless Love ....*Diana Ross & Lionel Richie*

★ **BIGGEST MOVER** ★ 75 to 55
Cool Love ....*Pablo Cruise*

Billboard — JULY 18, 1981 — HOT 100

TW	LW	WK	Title	Artist	Label
1	1	17	**Bette Davis Eyes**	*Kim Carnes*	EMI America 8077
2	2	9	**All Those Years Ago**	*George Harrison*	Dark Horse 49725
3	3	10	The One That You Love	*Air Supply*	Arista 0604
4	4	17	Jessie's Girl	*Rick Springfield*	RCA 12201
5	5	12	**You Make My Dreams**	*Daryl Hall & John Oates*	RCA 12217
6	6	10	Elvira	*The Oak Ridge Boys*	MCA 51084
7	8	11	Theme From "Greatest American Hero" (Believe It or Not)	*Joey Scarbury*	Elektra 47147
8	9	6	I Don't Need You	*Kenny Rogers*	Liberty 1415
9	10	8	Slow Hand	*Pointer Sisters*	Planet 47929
10	16	9	Boy From New York City	*The Manhattan Transfer*	Atlantic 3816

★ **HIGHEST DEBUT** ★ POS 64
Fire And Ice .... *Pat Benatar*

★ **BIGGEST MOVER** ★ 54 to 38
Endless Love .... *Diana Ross & Lionel Richie*

Billboard — JULY 25, 1981 — HOT 100

TW	LW	WK	Title	Artist	Label
1	3	11	**The One That You Love**	*Air Supply*	Arista 0604
2	1	18	Bette Davis Eyes	*Kim Carnes*	EMI America 8077
3	4	18	Jessie's Girl	*Rick Springfield*	RCA 12201
4	7	12	Theme From "Greatest American Hero" (Believe It or Not)	*Joey Scarbury*	Elektra 47147
5	6	11	**Elvira**	*The Oak Ridge Boys*	MCA 51084
6	8	7	I Don't Need You	*Kenny Rogers*	Liberty 1415
7	9	9	Slow Hand	*Pointer Sisters*	Planet 47929
8	5	13	You Make My Dreams	*Daryl Hall & John Oates*	RCA 12217
9	10	10	Boy From New York City	*The Manhattan Transfer*	Atlantic 3816
10	11	10	Hearts	*Marty Balin*	EMI America 8084

★ **HIGHEST DEBUT** ★ POS 57
Stop Draggin' My Heart Around ....*Stevie Nicks*
with Tom Petty & The Heartbreakers

★ **BIGGEST MOVER** ★ 64 to 44
Fire And Ice ....*Pat Benatar*

Billboard — AUGUST 1, 1981 — HOT 100

TW	LW	WK	Title	Artist	Label
1	3	19	**Jessie's Girl**	*Rick Springfield*	RCA 12201
2	1	12	The One That You Love	*Air Supply*	Arista 0604
3	4	13	Theme From "Greatest American Hero" (Believe It or Not)	*Joey Scarbury*	Elektra 47147
4	6	8	I Don't Need You	*Kenny Rogers*	Liberty 1415
5	5	12	Elvira	*The Oak Ridge Boys*	MCA 51084
6	7	10	Slow Hand	*Pointer Sisters*	Planet 47929
7	2	19	Bette Davis Eyes	*Kim Carnes*	EMI America 8077
8	9	11	Boy From New York City	*The Manhattan Transfer*	Atlantic 3816
9	10	11	Hearts	*Marty Balin*	EMI America 8084
10	14	10	Queen Of Hearts	*Juice Newton*	Capitol 4997

★ **HIGHEST DEBUT** ★ POS 71
I Could Never Miss You (More Than I
  Do) ....*Lulu*

★ **BIGGEST MOVER** ★ 56 to 30
Who's Crying Now...................................*Journey*

TW	LW	WK	Billboard®	AUGUST 8, 1981	HOT 100®
①	1	20	**Jessie's Girl**..................................*Rick Springfield* . . . RCA 12201		
②	14	5	**Endless Love** ....*Diana Ross & Lionel Richie* . . . Motown 1519		
③	3	14	**Theme From "Greatest American Hero" (Believe It or Not)**................ *Joey Scarbury* . . . Elektra 47147		
④	4	9	**I Don't Need You** ....*Kenny Rogers* . . . Liberty 1415		
⑤	5	13	**Elvira**...*The Oak Ridge Boys* . . . MCA 51084		
⑥	6	11	**Slow Hand**..*Pointer Sisters* . . . Planet 47929		
⑦	8	12	**Boy From New York City**.........*The Manhattan Transfer* . . . Atlantic 3816		
⑧	9	12	**Hearts**...*Marty Balin* . . . EMI America 8084		
⑨	10	11	**Queen Of Hearts** ....*Juice Newton* . . . Capitol 4997		
⑩	2	13	**The One That You Love** ....*Air Supply* . . . Arista 0604		

★ *HIGHEST DEBUT* ★ POS 56	★ *BIGGEST MOVER* ★ 62 to 45
The Voice...................*The Moody Blues*	The Beach Boys Medley ....*The Beach Boys*

TW	LW	WK	Billboard®	AUGUST 15, 1981	HOT 100®
①	2	6	**Endless Love**........................*Diana Ross & Lionel Richie* . . . Motown 1519		
②	3	15	**Theme From "Greatest American Hero" (Believe It or Not)**.... *Joey Scarbury* . . . Elektra 47147		
③	4	10	**I Don't Need You**......................................*Kenny Rogers* . . . Liberty 1415		
④	1	21	**Jessie's Girl**...*Rick Springfield* . . . RCA 12201		
⑤	5	14	**Elvira**...*The Oak Ridge Boys* . . . MCA 51084		
⑥	6	12	**Slow Hand** ....*Pointer Sisters* . . . Planet 47929		
⑦	7	13	**Boy From New York City**.........*The Manhattan Transfer* . . . Atlantic 3816		
⑧	8	13	**Hearts**...*Marty Balin* . . . EMI America 8084		
⑨	9	12	**Queen Of Hearts** ....*Juice Newton* . . . Capitol 4997		
⑩	11	8	**(There's) No Gettin' Over Me**.......................*Ronnie Milsap* . . . RCA 12264		

★ *HIGHEST DEBUT* ★ POS 71	★ *BIGGEST MOVER* ★ 72 to 53
Arthur's Theme (Best That You Can Do)...................*Christopher Cross*	Draw Of The Cards ....*Kim Carnes*

TW	LW	WK	Billboard®	AUGUST 22, 1981	HOT 100®
①	1	7	**Endless Love**........................*Diana Ross & Lionel Richie* . . . Motown 1519		
②	2	16	**Theme From "Greatest American Hero" (Believe It or Not)**.... *Joey Scarbury* . . . Elektra 47147		
③	3	11	**I Don't Need You** ....*Kenny Rogers* . . . Liberty 1415		
④	6	13	**Slow Hand** ....*Pointer Sisters* . . . Planet 47929		
⑤	4	22	**Jessie's Girl**...*Rick Springfield* . . . RCA 12201		
⑥	21	5	**Stop Draggin' My Heart Around** .... *Stevie Nicks with Tom Petty & The Heartbreakers* . . . Modern 7336		
⑦	7	14	**Boy From New York City**.........*The Manhattan Transfer* . . . Atlantic 3816		
⑧	9	13	**Queen Of Hearts** ....*Juice Newton* . . . Capitol 4997		
⑨	10	9	**(There's) No Gettin' Over Me**.......................*Ronnie Milsap* . . . RCA 12264		
⑩	11	10	**Lady (You Bring Me Up)**............................*Commodores* . . . Motown 1514		

★ *HIGHEST DEBUT* ★ POS 61	★ *BIGGEST MOVER* ★ 66 to 42
Start Me Up ....*The Rolling Stones*	In Your Letter.........................*REO Speedwagon*

Billboard · AUGUST 29, 1981 · HOT 100

TW	LW	WK		
1	1	8	**Endless Love**........................*Diana Ross & Lionel Richie* . . . Motown 1519	
2	4	14	**Slow Hand** ....*Pointer Sisters* . . . Planet 47929	
3	2	17	**Theme From "Greatest American Hero" (Believe It or Not)**................ *Joey Scarbury* . . . Elektra 47147	
4	6	6	**Stop Draggin' My Heart Around** .... *Stevie Nicks with Tom Petty & The Heartbreakers* . . . Modern 7336	
5	5	23	**Jessie's Girl**...*Rick Springfield* . . . RCA 2201	
6	8	14	**Queen Of Hearts** ....*Juice Newton* . . . Capitol 4997	
7	9	10	**(There's) No Gettin' Over Me**.......................*Ronnie Milsap* . . . RCA 12264	
8	15	9	**Urgent** ....*Foreigner* . . . Atlantic 3831	
9	10	11	**Lady (You Bring Me Up)**.............................*Commodores* . . . Motown 1514	
10	11	7	**Who's Crying Now** ....*Journey* . . . Columbia 02241	

★ **HIGHEST DEBUT** ★ POS 68
Private Eyes...................*Daryl Hall & John Oates*

★ **BIGGEST MOVER** ★ 61 to 35
Start Me Up ....*The Rolling Stones*

Billboard · SEPTEMBER 5, 1981 · HOT 100

TW	LW	WK		
1	1	9	**Endless Love**........................*Diana Ross & Lionel Richie* . . . Motown 1519	
2	2	15	**Slow Hand** ....*Pointer Sisters* . . . Planet 47929	
3	4	7	**Stop Draggin' My Heart Around**.. *Stevie Nicks with Tom Petty & The Heartbreakers* . . . Modern 7336	
4	8	10	**Urgent** ....*Foreigner* . . . Atlantic 3831	
5	7	11	**(There's) No Gettin' Over Me** ....*Ronnie Milsap* . . . RCA 12264	
6	6	15	**Queen Of Hearts** ....*Juice Newton* . . . Capitol 4997	
7	10	8	**Who's Crying Now** ....*Journey* . . . Columbia 02241	
8	9	12	**Lady (You Bring Me Up)** ....*Commodores* . . . Motown 1514	
9	5	24	**Jessie's Girl**...*Rick Springfield* . . . RCA 12201	
10	3	18	**Theme From "Greatest American Hero" (Believe It or Not)**.............. *Joey Scarbury* . . . Elektra 47147	

★ **HIGHEST DEBUT** ★ POS 47
Share Your Love With Me ....*Kenny Rogers*

★ **BIGGEST MOVER** ★ 65 to 43
I've Done Everything For You ......*Rick Springfield*

Billboard · SEPTEMBER 12, 1981 · HOT 100

TW	LW	WK		
1	1	10	**Endless Love**........................*Diana Ross & Lionel Richie* . . . Motown 1519	
2	2	16	**Slow Hand** ....*Pointer Sisters* . . . Planet 47929	
3	3	8	**Stop Draggin' My Heart Around**.. *Stevie Nicks with Tom Petty & The Heartbreakers* . . . Modern 7336	
4	4	11	**Urgent**...*Foreigner* . . . Atlantic 3831	
5	5	12	**(There's) No Gettin' Over Me** ....*Ronnie Milsap* . . . RCA 12264	
6	6	16	**Queen Of Hearts** ....*Juice Newton* . . . Capitol 4997	
7	7	9	**Who's Crying Now** ....*Journey* . . . Columbia 02241	
8	8	13	**Lady (You Bring Me Up)** ....*Commodores* . . . Motown 1514	
9	24	5	**Arthur's Theme (Best That You Can Do)**..................*Christopher Cross* . . . Warner 49787	
10	12	8	**Step By Step**................................*Eddie Rabbitt* . . . Elektra 47174	

★ **HIGHEST DEBUT** ★ POS 61
Tryin' To Live My Life Without You.....*Bob Seger*

★ **BIGGEST MOVER** ★ 54 to 34
Private Eyes...................*Daryl Hall & John Oates*

Billboard ⊙ SEPTEMBER 19, 1981 ⊙ HOT 100®

TW	LW	WK	Title	Artist / Label
❶	1	11	Endless Love	Diana Ross & Lionel Richie ... Motown 1519
❷	6	17	Queen Of Hearts	Juice Newton ... Capitol 4997
❸	3	9	Stop Draggin' My Heart Around	Stevie Nicks with Tom Petty & The Heartbreakers ... Modern 7336
❹	4	12	Urgent	Foreigner ... Atlantic 3831
❺	5	13	(There's) No Gettin' Over Me	Ronnie Milsap ... RCA 12264
❻	7	10	Who's Crying Now	Journey ... Columbia 02241
❼	9	6	Arthur's Theme (Best That You Can Do)	Christopher Cross ... Warner 49787
⑧	8	14	Lady (You Bring Me Up)	Commodores ... Motown 1514
⑨	10	9	Step By Step	Eddie Rabbitt ... Elektra 47174
⑩	2	17	Slow Hand	Pointer Sisters ... Planet 47929

★ HIGHEST DEBUT ★ POS 77
Atlanta Lady (Something About Your Love) ... Marty Balin

★ BIGGEST MOVER ★ 45 to 29
Hard To Say ... Dan Fogelberg

Billboard ⊙ SEPTEMBER 26, 1981 ⊙ HOT 100®

TW	LW	WK	Title	Artist / Label
❶	1	12	Endless Love	Diana Ross & Lionel Richie ... Motown 1519
②	2	18	Queen Of Hearts	Juice Newton ... Capitol 4997
❸	3	10	Stop Draggin' My Heart Around	Stevie Nicks with Tom Petty & The Heartbreakers ... Modern 7336
④	4	13	Urgent	Foreigner ... Atlantic 3831
❺	5	14	(There's) No Gettin' Over Me	Ronnie Milsap ... RCA 12264
❻	6	11	Who's Crying Now	Journey ... Columbia 02241
❼	7	7	Arthur's Theme (Best That You Can Do)	Christopher Cross ... Warner 49787
⑧	9	10	Step By Step	Eddie Rabbitt ... Elektra 47174
⑨	8	15	Lady (You Bring Me Up)	Commodores ... Motown 1514
⑩	11	6	Start Me Up	The Rolling Stones ... Rolling Stones 21003

★ HIGHEST DEBUT ★ POS 54
Here I Am (Just When I Thought I Was Over You) ... Air Supply

★ BIGGEST MOVER ★ 77 to 60
Atlanta Lady (Something About Your Love) ... Marty Balin

Billboard ⊙ OCTOBER 3, 1981 ⊙ HOT 100®

TW	LW	WK	Title	Artist / Label
❶	1	13	Endless Love	Diana Ross & Lionel Richie ... Motown 1519
❷	7	8	Arthur's Theme (Best That You Can Do)	Christopher Cross ... Warner 49787
③	3	11	Stop Draggin' My Heart Around	Stevie Nicks with Tom Petty & The Heartbreakers ... Modern 7336
❹	6	12	Who's Crying Now	Journey ... Columbia 02241
⑤	5	15	(There's) No Gettin' Over Me	Ronnie Milsap ... RCA 12264
⑥	2	19	Queen Of Hearts	Juice Newton ... Capitol 4997
❼	8	11	Step By Step	Eddie Rabbitt ... Elektra 47174
⑧	4	14	Urgent	Foreigner ... Atlantic 3831
❾	10	7	Start Me Up	The Rolling Stones ... Rolling Stones 21003
⑩	11	11	Hold On Tight	ELO ... Jet 02408

★ HIGHEST DEBUT ★ POS 66
Physical ... Olivia Newton-John

★ BIGGEST MOVER ★ 66 to 44
Every Little Thing She Does Is Magic ... The Police

Billboard · OCTOBER 10, 1981 · HOT 100

TW	LW	WK			
①	1	14	**Endless Love**...................Diana Ross & Lionel Richie ... Motown 1519
②	2	9	Arthur's Theme (Best That You Can Do)................. Christopher Cross ... Warner 49787
③	3	12	**Stop Draggin' My Heart Around**.............. Stevie Nicks with Tom Petty & The Heartbreakers ... Modern 7336
④	4	13	**Who's Crying Now**..............................Journey ... Columbia 02241
⑤	11	12	For Your Eyes Only ....Sheena Easton ... Liberty 1418
⑥	7	12	Step By Step..............................Eddie Rabbitt ... Elektra 47174
⑦	9	8	Start Me Up...............The Rolling Stones ... Rolling Stones 21003
⑧	13	7	Private Eyes.............Daryl Hall & John Oates ... RCA 12296
⑨	8	15	Urgent ....Foreigner ... Atlantic 3831
⑩	10	12	**Hold On Tight** ....ELO ... Jet 02408

★ HIGHEST DEBUT ★ POS 42	★ BIGGEST MOVER ★ 61 to 39
Waiting For A Girl Like You ....Foreigner	Oh No......................................Commodores

Billboard · OCTOBER 17, 1981 · HOT 100

TW	LW	WK			
①	2	10	**Arthur's Theme (Best That You Can Do)**.......... Christopher Cross ... Warner 49787
②	1	15	Endless Love ....Diana Ross & Lionel Richie ... Motown 1519
③	7	9	Start Me Up...................The Rolling Stones ... Rolling Stones 21003
④	5	13	**For Your Eyes Only** ....Sheena Easton ... Liberty 1418
⑤	6	13	**Step By Step** ....Eddie Rabbitt ... Elektra 47174
⑥	8	8	**Private Eyes**.............Daryl Hall & John Oates ... RCA 12296
⑦	3	13	Stop Draggin' My Heart Around .... Stevie Nicks with Tom Petty & The Heartbreakers ... Modern 7336
⑧	4	14	Who's Crying Now ....Journey ... Columbia 02241
⑨	13	8	Hard To Say ....Dan Fogelberg ... Full Moon 02488
⑩	11	9	The Night Owls ....Little River Band ... Capitol 5033

★ HIGHEST DEBUT ★ POS 56	★ BIGGEST MOVER ★ 85 to 65
Why Do Fools Fall In Love ....Diana Ross	Never Too Much ....Luther Vandross

Billboard · OCTOBER 24, 1981 · HOT 100

TW	LW	WK			
①	1	11	**Arthur's Theme (Best That You Can Do)**.......... Christopher Cross ... Warner 49787
②	2	16	Endless Love ....Diana Ross & Lionel Richie ... Motown 1519
③	3	10	Start Me Up...................The Rolling Stones ... Rolling Stones 21003
④	4	14	**For Your Eyes Only** ....Sheena Easton ... Liberty 1418
⑤	5	14	**Step By Step** ....Eddie Rabbitt ... Elektra 47174
⑥	6	9	**Private Eyes**.............Daryl Hall & John Oates ... RCA 12296
⑦	7	14	Stop Draggin' My Heart Around .... Stevie Nicks with Tom Petty & The Heartbreakers ... Modern 7336
⑧	9	9	**Hard To Say** ....Dan Fogelberg ... Full Moon 02488
⑨	10	10	The Night Owls ....Little River Band ... Capitol 5033
⑩	12	10	I've Done Everything For You ....Rick Springfield ... RCA 12166

★ HIGHEST DEBUT ★ POS 73	★ BIGGEST MOVER ★ 61 to 41
Leather And Lace......Stevie Nicks with Don Henley	Young Turks ....Rod Stewart

Billboard OCTOBER 31, 1981 — HOT 100

TW	LW	WK	Title	Artist	Label
1	1	12	Arthur's Theme (Best That You Can Do)	Christopher Cross	Warner 49787
2	3	11	Start Me Up	The Rolling Stones	Rolling Stones 21003
3	6	10	Private Eyes	Daryl Hall & John Oates	RCA 12296
4	4	15	For Your Eyes Only	Sheena Easton	Liberty 1418
5	2	17	Endless Love	Diana Ross & Lionel Richie	Motown 1519
6	11	8	Tryin' To Live My Life Without You	Bob Seger	Capitol 5042
7	8	10	Hard To Say	Dan Fogelberg	Full Moon 02488
8	9	11	The Night Owls	Little River Band	Capitol 5033
9	10	11	I've Done Everything For You	Rick Springfield	RCA 12166
10	5	15	Step By Step	Eddie Rabbitt	Elektra 47174

★ HIGHEST DEBUT ★ POS 56
Don't Stop Believin'......................Journey

★ BIGGEST MOVER ★ 73 to 50
Leather And Lace......Stevie Nicks with Don Henley

Billboard NOVEMBER 7, 1981 — HOT 100

TW	LW	WK	Title	Artist	Label
1	3	11	Private Eyes	Daryl Hall & John Oates	RCA 12296
2	2	12	Start Me Up	The Rolling Stones	Rolling Stones 21003
3	1	13	Arthur's Theme (Best That You Can Do)	Christopher Cross	Warner 49787
4	4	16	For Your Eyes Only	Sheena Easton	Liberty 1418
5	6	9	Tryin' To Live My Life Without You	Bob Seger	Capitol 5042
6	8	12	The Night Owls	Little River Band	Capitol 5033
7	7	11	Hard To Say	Dan Fogelberg	Full Moon 02488
8	9	12	I've Done Everything For You	Rick Springfield	RCA 12166
9	11	7	Here I Am (Just When I Thought I Was Over You)	Air Supply	Arista 0626
10	15	5	Waiting For A Girl Like You	Foreigner	Atlantic 3868

★ HIGHEST DEBUT ★ POS 51
Yesterday's Songs........................Neil Diamond

★ BIGGEST MOVER ★ 55 to 30
Trouble................................Lindsey Buckingham

Billboard NOVEMBER 14, 1981 — HOT 100

TW	LW	WK	Title	Artist	Label
1	1	12	Private Eyes	Daryl Hall & John Oates	RCA 12296
2	2	13	Start Me Up	The Rolling Stones	Rolling Stones 21003
3	14	7	Physical	Olivia Newton-John	MCA 51182
4	10	6	Waiting For A Girl Like You	Foreigner	Atlantic 3868
5	5	10	Tryin' To Live My Life Without You	Bob Seger	Capitol 5042
6	6	13	The Night Owls	Little River Band	Capitol 5033
7	9	8	Here I Am (Just When I Thought I Was Over You)	Air Supply	Arista 0626
8	8	13	I've Done Everything For You	Rick Springfield	RCA 12166
9	3	14	Arthur's Theme (Best That You Can Do)	Christopher Cross	Warner 49787
10	12	13	The Theme From Hill Street Blues	Mike Post featuring Larry Carlton	Elektra 47186

★ HIGHEST DEBUT ★ POS 59
I Can't Go For That (No Can Do).......Daryl Hall & John Oates

★ BIGGEST MOVER ★ 70 to 50
Centerfold................................The J. Geils Band

Billboard — NOVEMBER 21, 1981 — HOT 100

TW	LW	WK	Title	Artist / Label
1	3	8	**Physical**	Olivia Newton-John ... MCA 51182
2	1	13	Private Eyes	Daryl Hall & John Oates ... RCA 12296
3	4	7	Waiting For A Girl Like You	Foreigner ... Atlantic 3868
4	2	14	Start Me Up	The Rolling Stones ... Rolling Stones 21003
5	7	9	**Here I Am (Just When I Thought I Was Over You)**	Air Supply ... Arista 0626
6	5	11	Tryin' To Live My Life Without You	Bob Seger ... Capitol 5042
7	6	14	The Night Owls	Little River Band ... Capitol 5033
8	12	9	Every Little Thing She Does Is Magic	The Police ... A&M 2371
9	9	15	Arthur's Theme (Best That You Can Do)	Christopher Cross ... Warner 49787
10	10	14	**The Theme From Hill Street Blues**	Mike Post featuring Larry Carlton ... Elektra 47186

★ **HIGHEST DEBUT** ★ POS 76
Shake It Up ... The Cars

★ **BIGGEST MOVER** ★ 59 to 32
I Can't Go For That (No Can Do) ... Daryl Hall & John Oates

Billboard — NOVEMBER 28, 1981 — HOT 100

TW	LW	WK	Title	Artist / Label
1	1	9	**Physical**	Olivia Newton-John ... MCA 51182
2	3	8	**Waiting For A Girl Like You**	Foreigner ... Atlantic 3868
3	2	14	Private Eyes	Daryl Hall & John Oates ... RCA 12296
4	8	10	**Every Little Thing She Does Is Magic**	The Police ... A&M 2371
5	5	10	**Here I Am (Just When I Thought I Was Over You)**	Air Supply ... Arista 0626
6	11	10	**Oh No**	Commodores ... Motown 1527
7	4	15	Start Me Up	The Rolling Stones ... Rolling Stones 21003
8	6	12	Tryin' To Live My Life Without You	Bob Seger ... Capitol 5042
9	9	16	Arthur's Theme (Best That You Can Do)	Christopher Cross ... Warner 49787
10	12	7	Why Do Fools Fall In Love	Diana Ross ... RCA 12349

★ **HIGHEST DEBUT** ★ POS 78
You Could Have Been With Me ... Sheena Easton

★ **BIGGEST MOVER** ★ 76 to 58
Shake It Up ... The Cars

Billboard — DECEMBER 5, 1981 — HOT 100

TW	LW	WK	Title	Artist / Label
1	1	10	**Physical**	Olivia Newton-John ... MCA 51182
2	2	9	**Waiting For A Girl Like You**	Foreigner ... Atlantic 3868
3	4	11	**Every Little Thing She Does Is Magic**	The Police ... A&M 2371
4	6	11	**Oh No**	Commodores ... Motown 1527
5	5	11	**Here I Am (Just When I Thought I Was Over You)**	Air Supply ... Arista 0626
6	3	15	Private Eyes	Daryl Hall & John OOtes ... RCA 12296
7	11	10	Let's Groove	Earth, Wind & Fire ... ARC 02536
8	12	8	Young Turks	Rod Stewart ... Warner 49843
9	10	8	Why Do Fools Fall In Love	Diana Ross ... RCA 12349
10	7	16	Start Me Up	The Rolling Stones ... Rolling Stones 21003

★ **HIGHEST DEBUT** ★ POS 70
Waiting On A Friend ... The Rolling Stones

★ **BIGGEST MOVER** ★ 58 to 43
Shake It Up ... The Cars

TW	LW	WK	Billboard	DECEMBER 12, 1981	HOT 100.
①	1	11	**Physical** ....Olivia Newton-John ... MCA 51182		
②	2	10	**Waiting For A Girl Like You** ....Foreigner ... Atlantic 3868		
③	3	12	**Every Little Thing She Does Is Magic** ....The Police ... A&M 2371		
④	4	12	**Oh No** ....Commodores ... Motown 1527		
⑤	7	11	**Let's Groove** ....Earth, Wind & Fire ... ARC 02536		
⑥	8	9	**Young Turks** ....Rod Stewart ... Warner 49843		
⑦	5	12	**Here I Am (Just When I Thought I Was Over You)** .... Air Supply ... Arista 0626		
⑧	9	9	**Why Do Fools Fall In Love** ....Diana Ross ... RCA 12349		
⑨	14	9	**Harden My Heart** ....Quarterflash ... Geffen 49824		
⑩	11	7	**Don't Stop Believin'** ....Journey ... Columbia 02567		

★ HIGHEST DEBUT ★ POS 74	★ BIGGEST MOVER ★ 70 to 36
Sweet Dreams ....Air Supply	Waiting On A Friend ....The Rolling Stones

TW	LW	WK	Billboard	DECEMBER 19, 1981	HOT 100.
①	1	12	**Physical** ....Olivia Newton-John ... MCA 51182		
②	2	11	**Waiting For A Girl Like You** ....Foreigner ... Atlantic 3868		
③	5	12	**Let's Groove** ....Earth, Wind & Fire ... ARC 02536		
④	4	13	**Oh No** ....Commodores ... Motown 1527		
⑤	6	10	**Young Turks** ....Rod Stewart ... Warner 49843		
⑥	13	6	**I Can't Go For That (No Can Do)** ...Daryl Hall & John Oates ... RCA 12357		
⑦	8	10	**Why Do Fools Fall In Love** ....Diana Ross ... RCA 12349		
⑧	9	10	**Harden My Heart** ....Quarterflash ... Geffen 49824		
⑨	10	8	**Don't Stop Believin'** ....Journey ... Columbia 02567		
⑩	11	9	**Leather And Lace** ....Stevie Nicks with Don Henley ... Modern 7341		

★ HIGHEST DEBUT ★ POS 76	★ BIGGEST MOVER ★ 74 to 53
Somewhere Down The Road ....Barry Manilow	Sweet Dreams ....Air Supply

TW	LW	WK	Billboard	DECEMBER 26, 1981	HOT 100.
①	1	13	**Physical** ....Olivia Newton-John ... MCA 51182		
②	2	12	**Waiting For A Girl Like You** ....Foreigner ... Atlantic 3868		
③	3	13	**Let's Groove** ....Earth, Wind & Fire ... ARC 02536		
④	6	7	**I Can't Go For That (No Can Do)** ...Daryl Hall & John Oates ... RCA 12357		
⑤	5	11	**Young Turks** ....Rod Stewart ... Warner 49843		
⑥	8	11	**Harden My Heart** ....Quarterflash ... Geffen 49824		
⑦	7	11	**Why Do Fools Fall In Love** ....Diana Ross ... RCA 12349		
⑧	10	10	**Leather And Lace** ....Stevie Nicks with Don Henley ... Modern 7341		
⑨	9	9	**Don't Stop Believin'** ....Journey ... Columbia 02567		
⑩	11	10	**Trouble** ....Lindsey Buckingham ... Asylum 47223		

★ HIGHEST DEBUT ★ POS 71	★ BIGGEST MOVER ★ 67 to 54
Abacab ....Genesis	All Our Tomorrows ....Eddie Schwartz

Billboard — JANUARY 9, 1982 — HOT 100

TW	LW	WK			
❶	1	15	**Physical** ....*Olivia Newton-John* ... MCA 51182
❷	2	14	**Waiting For A Girl Like You** ....*Foreigner* ... Atlantic 3868
❸	3	15	**Let's Groove**................................*Earth, Wind & Fire* ... ARC 02536
❹	4	9	**I Can't Go For That (No Can Do)** ...*Daryl Hall & John Oates* ... RCA 12357
⑤	5	13	**Young Turks**..*Rod Stewart* ... Warner 49843
❻	6	13	**Harden My Heart**...*Quarterflash* ... Geffen 49824
❼	8	12	**Leather And Lace**.................*Stevie Nicks with Don Henley* ... Modern 7341
❽	11	10	**Centerfold** ....*The J. Geils Band* ... EMI America 8102
❾	14	12	**Turn Your Love Around** ....*George Benson* ... Warner 49846
➓	10	12	**Trouble** ....*Lindsey Buckingham* ... Asylum 47223

★ *HIGHEST DEBUT* ★ POS 76	★ *BIGGEST MOVER* ★ 63 to 49
Pac-Man Fever.........................*Buckner & Garcia*	Somewhere Down The Road.........*Barry Manilow*

Billboard — JANUARY 16, 1982 — HOT 100

TW	LW	WK			
❶	1	16	**Physical** ....*Olivia Newton-John* ... MCA 51182
❷	2	15	**Waiting For A Girl Like You** ....*Foreigner* ... Atlantic 3868
③	3	16	**Let's Groove**................................*Earth, Wind & Fire* ... ARC 02536
❹	4	10	**I Can't Go For That (No Can Do)** ...*Daryl Hall & John Oates* ... RCA 12357
❺	8	11	**Centerfold** ....*The J. Geils Band* ... EMI America 8102
❻	6	14	**Harden My Heart**...*Quarterflash* ... Geffen 49824
❼	7	13	**Leather And Lace**.................*Stevie Nicks with Don Henley* ... Modern 7341
❽	9	13	**Turn Your Love Around** ....*George Benson* ... Warner 49846
❾	10	13	**Trouble** ....*Lindsey Buckingham* ... Asylum 47223
➓	13	14	**The Sweetest Thing (I've Ever Known)** ....*Juice Newton* ... Capitol 5046

★ *HIGHEST DEBUT* ★ POS 57	★ *BIGGEST MOVER* ★ 68 to 35
Open Arms ....*Journey*	Through The Years ....*Kenny Rogers*

Billboard — JANUARY 23, 1982 — HOT 100

TW	LW	WK			
❶	1	17	**Physical** ....*Olivia Newton-John* ... MCA 51182
❷	2	16	**Waiting For A Girl Like You** ....*Foreigner* ... Atlantic 3868
❸	5	12	**Centerfold** ....*The J. Geils Band* ... EMI America 8102
❹	4	11	**I Can't Go For That (No Can Do)** ...*Daryl Hall & John Oates* ... RCA 12357
❺	6	15	**Harden My Heart**...*Quarterflash* ... Geffen 49824
❻	7	14	**Leather And Lace** ....*Stevie Nicks with Don Henley* ... Modern 7341
❼	8	14	**Turn Your Love Around** ....*George Benson* ... Warner 49846
⑧	3	17	**Let's Groove** ....*Earth, Wind & Fire* ... ARC 02536
❾	9	14	**Trouble** ....*Lindsey Buckingham* ... Asylum 47223
➓	10	15	**The Sweetest Thing (I've Ever Known)** ....*Juice Newton* ... Capitol 5046

★ *HIGHEST DEBUT* ★ POS 74	★ *BIGGEST MOVER* ★ 57 to 29
Tonight I'm Yours (Don't Hurt Me) ....*Rod Stewart*	Open Arms ....*Journey*

TW	LW	WK	Billboard	JANUARY 30, 1982	HOT 100.
①	4	12	**I Can't Go For That (No Can Do)**.................. *Daryl Hall & John Oates* ... RCA 12357
②	2	17	**Waiting For A Girl Like You** ....*Foreigner* ... Atlantic 3868
③	3	13	**Centerfold** ....*The J. Geils Band* ... EMI America 8102
④	1	18	**Physical** ....*Olivia Newton-John* ... MCA 51182
⑤	5	16	**Harden My Heart**................................*Quarterflash* ... Geffen 49824
⑥	6	15	**Leather And Lace** ....*Stevie Nicks with Don Henley* ... Modern 7341
⑦	7	15	**Turn Your Love Around** ....*George Benson* ... Warner 49846
⑧	8	18	**Let's Groove** ....*Earth, Wind & Fire* ... ARC 02536
⑨	10	16	**The Sweetest Thing (I've Ever Known)** ....*Juice Newton* ... Capitol 5046
⑩	11	14	**Hooked On Classics**.....*The Royal Philharmonic Orchestra* ... RCA 12304

★ **HIGHEST DEBUT** ★ POS 79
We Got The Beat.................................*Go-Go's*

★ **BIGGEST MOVER** ★ 82 to 62
Should I Do It.........................*The Pointer Sisters*

TW	LW	WK	Billboard	FEBRUARY 6, 1982	HOT 100.
①	3	14	**Centerfold**....................................*The J. Geils Band* ... EMI America 8102
②	1	13	**I Can't Go For That (No Can Do)** ...*Daryl Hall & John Oates* ... RCA 12357
③	2	18	**Waiting For A Girl Like You**...............................*Foreigner* ... Atlantic 3868
④	5	17	**Harden My Heart**...............................*Quarterflash* ... Geffen 49824
⑤	7	16	**Turn Your Love Around** ....*George Benson* ... Warner 49846
⑥	6	16	**Leather And Lace** ....*Stevie Nicks with Don Henley* ... Modern 7341
⑦	4	19	**Physical** ....*Olivia Newton-John* ... MCA 51182
⑧	9	17	**The Sweetest Thing (I've Ever Known)** ....*Juice Newton* ... Capitol 5046
⑨	13	12	**Shake It Up**.................................*The Cars* ... Elektra 47250
⑩	10	15	**Hooked On Classics**.....*The Royal Philharmonic Orchestra* ... RCA 12304

★ **HIGHEST DEBUT** ★ POS 63
I Love Rock 'N Roll .....*Joan Jett & The Blackhearts*

★ **BIGGEST MOVER** ★ 62 to 44
Should I Do It........................*The Pointer Sisters*

TW	LW	WK	Billboard	FEBRUARY 13, 1982	HOT 100.
①	1	15	**Centerfold**....................................*The J. Geils Band* ... EMI America 8102
②	2	14	**I Can't Go For That (No Can Do)** ...*Daryl Hall & John Oates* ... RCA 12357
③	4	18	**Harden My Heart**....................................*Quarterflash* ... Geffen 49824
④	15	5	**Open Arms** ....*Journey* ... Columbia 02687
⑤	5	17	**Turn Your Love Around** ....*George Benson* ... Warner 49846
⑥	9	13	**Shake It Up**.................................*The Cars* ... Elektra 47250
⑦	8	18	**The Sweetest Thing (I've Ever Known)** ....*Juice Newton* ... Capitol 5046
⑧	7	20	**Physical** ....*Olivia Newton-John* ... MCA 51182
⑨	3	19	**Waiting For A Girl Like You**...............................*Foreigner* ... Atlantic 3868
⑩	12	10	**Sweet Dreams**....................................*Air Supply* ... Arista 0655

★ **HIGHEST DEBUT** ★ POS 69
Make A Move On Me ....*Olivia Newton-John*

★ **BIGGEST MOVER** ★ 64 to 31
We Got The Beat................................*Go-Go's*

TW	LW	WK	Billboard	FEBRUARY 20, 1982	HOT 100
①	1	16	**Centerfold**......................................*The J. Geils Band* . . . EMI America 8102
②	2	15	I Can't Go For That (No Can Do) ...*Daryl Hall & John Oates* . . . RCA 12357
③	3	19	**Harden My Heart**................................*Quarterflash* . . . Geffen 49824
④	4	6	Open Arms ....*Journey* . . . Columbia 02687
⑤	6	14	Shake It Up ....*The Cars* . . . Elektra 47250
⑥	22	6	That Girl ....*Stevie Wonder* . . . Tamla 1602
⑦	7	19	**The Sweetest Thing (I've Ever Known)** ....*Juice Newton* . . . Capitol 5046
⑧	10	11	Sweet Dreams.....................................*Air Supply* . . . Arista 0655
⑨	8	21	Physical ....*Olivia Newton-John* . . . MCA 51182
⑩	12	13	Leader Of The Band ....*Dan Fogelberg* . . . Full Moon 02647

★ HIGHEST DEBUT ★ POS 67	★ BIGGEST MOVER ★ 39 to 18
Freeze-Frame......................*The J. Geils Band*	I Love Rock 'N Roll .....*Joan Jett & The Blackhearts*

TW	LW	WK	Billboard	FEBRUARY 27, 1982	HOT 100
①	1	17	**Centerfold**......................................*The J. Geils Band* . . . EMI America 8102
②	4	7	**Open Arms** ....*Journey* . . . Columbia 02687
③	2	16	I Can't Go For That (No Can Do) ...*Daryl Hall & John Oates* . . . RCA 12357
④	5	15	**Shake It Up** ....*The Cars* . . . Elektra 47250
⑤	6	7	That Girl ....*Stevie Wonder* . . . Tamla 1602
⑥	8	12	Sweet Dreams.....................................*Air Supply* . . . Arista 0655
⑦	3	20	Harden My Heart.................................*Quarterflash* . . . Geffen 49824
⑧	7	20	The Sweetest Thing (I've Ever Known) ....*Juice Newton* . . . Capitol 5046
⑨	18	4	I Love Rock 'N Roll............*Joan Jett & The Blackhearts* . . . Boardwalk 135
⑩	10	14	Leader Of The Band ....*Dan Fogelberg* . . . Full Moon 02647

★ HIGHEST DEBUT ★ POS 69	★ BIGGEST MOVER ★ 73 to 60
Baby Makes Her Blue Jeans Talk ....*Dr. Hook*	Edge Of Seventeen (Just Like The White Winged Dove) ....*Stevie Nicks*

TW	LW	WK	Billboard	MARCH 6, 1982	HOT 100
①	1	18	**Centerfold**......................................*The J. Geils Band* . . . EMI America 8102
②	2	8	**Open Arms** ....*Journey* . . . Columbia 02687
③	9	5	I Love Rock 'N Roll..............*Joan Jett & The Blackhearts* . . . Boardwalk 135
④	4	16	**Shake It Up** ....*The Cars* . . . Elektra 47250
⑤	5	8	That Girl ....*Stevie Wonder* . . . Tamla 1602
⑥	6	13	Sweet Dreams.....................................*Air Supply* . . . Arista 0655
⑦	3	17	I Can't Go For That (No Can Do) ...*Daryl Hall & John Oates* . . . RCA 12357
⑧	12	9	**Mirror, Mirror**..................................*Diana Ross* . . . RCA 13021
⑨	10	15	**Leader Of The Band** ....*Dan Fogelberg* . . . Full Moon 02647
⑩	11	14	**Take It Easy On Me** ....*Little River Band* . . . Capitol 5057

★ HIGHEST DEBUT ★ POS 57	★ BIGGEST MOVER ★ 56 to 34
Don't Talk To Strangers..............*Rick Springfield*	Freeze-Frame.......................*The J. Geils Band*

TW	LW	WK	Billboard	MARCH 13, 1982	HOT 100.
❶	1	19	Centerfold..................................The J. Geils Band ... EMI America 8102
❷	2	9	Open Arms ....Journey ... Columbia 02687
❸	3	6	I Love Rock 'N Roll..............Joan Jett & The Blackhearts ... Boardwalk 135
④	4	17	Shake It Up ....The Cars ... Elektra 47250
⑤	5	9	That Girl ....Stevie Wonder ... Tamla 1602
⑥	6	14	Sweet Dreams ....Air Supply ... Arista 0655
❼	11	7	We Got The Beat...Go-Go's ... I.R.S. 9903
❽	8	10	Mirror, Mirror...Diana Ross ... RCA 13021
⑨	9	16	Leader Of The Band ....Dan Fogelberg ... Full Moon 02647
⑩	10	15	Take It Easy On Me ....Little River Band ... Capitol 5057

★ HIGHEST DEBUT ★ POS 80
I'll Try Something New.............A Taste Of Honey

★ BIGGEST MOVER ★ 57 to 36
Don't Talk To Strangers.............Rick Springfield

TW	LW	WK	Billboard	MARCH 20, 1982	HOT 100.
❶	3	7	I Love Rock 'N Roll ....Joan Jett & The Blackhearts ... Boardwalk 135
❷	2	10	Open Arms ....Journey ... Columbia 02687
③	1	20	Centerfold ....The J. Geils Band ... EMI America 8102
④	5	10	That Girl ....Stevie Wonder ... Tamla 1602
⑤	6	15	Sweet Dreams ....Air Supply ... Arista 0655
⑥	7	8	We Got The Beat...Go-Go's ... I.R.S. 9903
❼	17	6	Make A Move On Me ....Olivia Newton-John ... MCA 52000
⑧	8	11	Mirror, Mirror...Diana Ross ... RCA 13021
⑨	4	18	Shake It Up...The Cars ... Elektra 47250
⑩	12	11	Pac-Man Fever.................................Buckner & Garcia ... Columbia 02673

★ HIGHEST DEBUT ★ POS 66
Did It In A Minute.............Daryl Hall & John Oates

★ BIGGEST MOVER ★ 75 to 59
I've Never Been To Me ....Charlene

TW	LW	WK	Billboard	MARCH 27, 1982	HOT 100.
❶	1	8	I Love Rock 'N Roll ....Joan Jett & The Blackhearts ... Boardwalk 135
❷	2	11	Open Arms ....Journey ... Columbia 02687
❸	6	9	We Got The Beat...Go-Go's ... I.R.S. 9903
④	4	11	That Girl ....Stevie Wonder ... Tamla 1602
⑤	5	16	Sweet Dreams ....Air Supply ... Arista 0655
⑥	7	7	Make A Move On Me ....Olivia Newton-John ... MCA 52000
⑦	3	21	Centerfold ....The J. Geils Band ... EMI America 8102
⑧	14	16	Chariots Of Fire - Titles...............................Vangelis ... Polydor 2189
⑨	10	12	Pac-Man Fever.................................Buckner & Garcia ... Columbia 02673
⑩	18	6	Freeze-Frame.................................The J. Geils Band ... EMI America 8108

★ HIGHEST DEBUT ★ POS 70
The Beatles' Movie Medley.............The Beatles

★ BIGGEST MOVER ★ 66 to 46
Did It In A Minute.............Daryl Hall & John Oates

TW	LW	WK	Billboard	APRIL 3, 1982	HOT 100
①	1	9	**I Love Rock 'N Roll** ....Joan Jett & The Blackhearts ... Boardwalk 135		
②	2	12	**Open Arms** ....Journey ... Columbia 02687		
③	3	10	**We Got The Beat**...Go-Go's ... I.R.S. 9903		
④	4	12	**That Girl**..Stevie Wonder ... Tamla 1602		
⑤	6	8	**Make A Move On Me**......................Olivia Newton-John ... MCA 52000		
⑥	8	17	**Chariots Of Fire - Titles**...............................Vangelis ... Polydor 2189		
⑦	10	7	**Freeze-Frame**...............................The J. Geils Band ... EMI America 8108		
⑧	14	5	**Don't Talk To Strangers**............................Rick Springfield ... RCA 13070		
⑨	9	13	**Pac-Man Fever**................................Buckner & Garcia ... Columbia 02673		
⑩	11	21	**Key Largo** ....Bertie Higgins ... Kat Family 02524		

★ *HIGHEST DEBUT* ★ POS 65	★ *BIGGEST MOVER* ★ 67 to 45
Run For The Roses ....*Dan Fogelberg*	Hang Fire................................*The Rolling Stones*

TW	LW	WK	Billboard	APRIL 10, 1982	HOT 100
①	1	10	**I Love Rock 'N Roll** ....Joan Jett & The Blackhearts ... Boardwalk 135		
②	3	11	**We Got The Beat** ....Go-Go's ... I.R.S. 9903		
③	6	18	**Chariots Of Fire - Titles**...............................Vangelis ... Polydor 2189		
④	7	8	**Freeze-Frame** ....The J. Geils Band ... EMI America 8108		
⑤	5	9	**Make A Move On Me**......................Olivia Newton-John ... MCA 52000		
⑥	8	6	**Don't Talk To Strangers**............................Rick Springfield ... RCA 13070		
⑦	2	13	**Open Arms** ....Journey ... Columbia 02687		
⑧	4	13	**That Girl**..Stevie Wonder ... Tamla 1602		
⑨	10	22	**Key Largo** ....Bertie Higgins ... Kat Family 02524		
⑩	12	10	**Do You Believe In Love**.............Huey Lewis & The News ... Chrysalis 2589		

★ *HIGHEST DEBUT* ★ POS 29	★ *BIGGEST MOVER* ★ 71 to 45
Ebony And Ivory ....*Paul McCartney with Stevie Wonder*	Stars on 45 III ....*Stars on 45*

TW	LW	WK	Billboard	APRIL 17, 1982	HOT 100
①	1	11	**I Love Rock 'N Roll** ....Joan Jett & The Blackhearts ... Boardwalk 135		
②	2	12	**We Got The Beat** ....Go-Go's ... I.R.S. 9903		
③	3	19	**Chariots Of Fire - Titles**...............................Vangelis ... Polydor 2189		
④	4	9	**Freeze-Frame** ....The J. Geils Band ... EMI America 8108		
⑤	5	10	**Make A Move On Me**......................Olivia Newton-John ... MCA 52000		
⑥	6	7	**Don't Talk To Strangers**............................Rick Springfield ... RCA 13070		
⑦	10	11	**Do You Believe In Love** ....Huey Lewis & The News ... Chrysalis 2589		
⑧	9	23	**Key Largo** ....Bertie Higgins ... Kat Family 02524		
⑨	7	14	**Open Arms** ....Journey ... Columbia 02687		
⑩	8	14	**That Girl**..Stevie Wonder ... Tamla 1602		

★ *HIGHEST DEBUT* ★ POS 68	★ *BIGGEST MOVER* ★ 69 to 55
Heat Of The Moment ....*Asia*	My Girl....................................*Donnie Iris*

Billboard — APRIL 24, 1982 — HOT 100

TW	LW	WK				
①	1	12	I Love Rock 'N Roll	Joan Jett & The Blackhearts	Boardwalk 135
②	2	13	We Got The Beat	Go-Go's	I.R.S. 9903
③	3	20	Chariots Of Fire - Titles	Vangelis	Polydor 2189
④	4	10	Freeze-Frame	The J. Geils Band	EMI America 8108
⑤	6	8	Don't Talk To Strangers	Rick Springfield	RCA 13070
⑥	21	3	Ebony And Ivory	Paul McCartney with Stevie Wonder	Columbia 02860
⑦	7	12	Do You Believe In Love	Huey Lewis & The News	Chrysalis 2589
⑧	8	24	Key Largo	Bertie Higgins	Kat Family 02524
⑨	13	9	'65 Love Affair	Paul Davis	Arista 0661
⑩	15	14	867-5309/Jenny	Tommy Tutone	Columbia 02646

★ **HIGHEST DEBUT** ★ POS 81
Baby, Come To Me ....Patti Austin with James Ingram

★ **BIGGEST MOVER** ★ 80 to 64
Secret Journey ....The Police

Billboard — MAY 1, 1982 — HOT 100

TW	LW	WK				
①	1	13	I Love Rock 'N Roll	Joan Jett & The Blackhearts	Boardwalk 135
②	3	21	Chariots Of Fire - Titles	Vangelis	Polydor 2189
③	6	4	Ebony And Ivory	Paul McCartney with Stevie Wonder	Columbia 02860
④	4	11	Freeze-Frame	The J. Geils Band	EMI America 8108
⑤	5	9	Don't Talk To Strangers	Rick Springfield	RCA 13070
⑥	2	14	We Got The Beat	Go-Go's	I.R.S. 9903
⑦	7	13	Do You Believe In Love	Huey Lewis & The News	Chrysalis 2589
⑧	10	15	867-5309/Jenny	Tommy Tutone	Columbia 02646
⑨	9	10	'65 Love Affair	Paul Davis	Arista 0661
⑩	20	12	I've Never Been To Me	Charlene	Motown 1611

★ **HIGHEST DEBUT** ★ POS 63
Crimson And Clover ....Joan Jett & The Blackhearts

★ **BIGGEST MOVER** ★ 55 to 20
Heat Of The Moment ....Asia

Billboard — MAY 8, 1982 — HOT 100

TW	LW	WK				
①	2	22	Chariots Of Fire - Titles	Vangelis	Polydor 2189
②	3	5	Ebony And Ivory	Paul McCartney with Stevie Wonder	Columbia 02860
③	1	14	I Love Rock 'N Roll	Joan Jett & The Blackhearts	Boardwalk 135
④	5	10	Don't Talk To Strangers	Rick Springfield	RCA 13070
⑤	4	12	Freeze-Frame	The J. Geils Band	EMI America 8108
⑥	8	16	867-5309/Jenny	Tommy Tutone	Columbia 02646
⑦	6	15	We Got The Beat	Go-Go's	I.R.S. 9903
⑧	9	11	'65 Love Affair	Paul Davis	Arista 0661
⑨	10	13	I've Never Been To Me	Charlene	Motown 1611
⑩	11	8	Did It In A Minute	Daryl Hall & John Oates	RCA 13065

★ **HIGHEST DEBUT** ★ POS 70
Love's Been A Little Bit Hard On Me ....Juice Newton

★ **BIGGEST MOVER** ★ 59 to 38
Rosanna ....Toto

Billboard — MAY 15, 1982 — HOT 100

TW	LW	WK	Title	Artist ... Label
1	2	6	**Ebony And Ivory**	*Paul McCartney with Stevie Wonder* ... Columbia 02860
2	1	23	**Chariots Of Fire - Titles**	*Vangelis* ... Polydor 2189
3	4	11	**Don't Talk To Strangers**	*Rick Springfield* ... RCA 13070
4	3	15	**I Love Rock 'N Roll**	*Joan Jett & The Blackhearts* ... Boardwalk 135
5	6	17	**867-5309/Jenny**	*Tommy Tutone* ... Columbia 02646
6	9	14	**I've Never Been To Me**	*Charlene* ... Motown 1611
7	8	12	**'65 Love Affair**	*Paul Davis* ... Arista 0661
8	5	13	**Freeze-Frame**	*The J. Geils Band* ... EMI America 8108
9	13	9	**The Other Woman**	*Ray Parker Jr.* ... Arista 0669
10	10	9	**Did It In A Minute**	*Daryl Hall & John Oates* ... RCA 13065

★ **HIGHEST DEBUT** ★ POS 70
Break It Up ... *Foreigner*

★ **BIGGEST MOVER** ★ 62 to 33
Body Language ... *Queen*

Billboard — MAY 22, 1982 — HOT 100

TW	LW	WK	Title	Artist ... Label
1	1	7	**Ebony And Ivory**	*Paul McCartney with Stevie Wonder* ... Columbia 02860
2	3	12	**Don't Talk To Strangers**	*Rick Springfield* ... RCA 13070
3	6	15	**I've Never Been To Me**	*Charlene* ... Motown 1611
4	5	18	**867-5309/Jenny**	*Tommy Tutone* ... Columbia 02646
5	9	10	**The Other Woman**	*Ray Parker Jr.* ... Arista 0669
6	7	13	**'65 Love Affair**	*Paul Davis* ... Arista 0661
7	2	24	**Chariots Of Fire - Titles**	*Vangelis* ... Polydor 2189
8	16	12	**Don't You Want Me**	*The Human League* ... A&M 2397
9	10	10	**Did It In A Minute**	*Daryl Hall & John Oates* ... RCA 13065
10	11	13	**Get Down On It**	*Kool & The Gang* ... De-Lite 818

★ **HIGHEST DEBUT** ★ POS 69
Take Me Down ... *Alabama*

★ **BIGGEST MOVER** ★ 66 to 41
Play The Game Tonight ... *Kansas*

Billboard — MAY 29, 1982 — HOT 100

TW	LW	WK	Title	Artist ... Label
1	1	8	**Ebony And Ivory**	*Paul McCartney with Stevie Wonder* ... Columbia 02860
2	2	13	**Don't Talk To Strangers**	*Rick Springfield* ... RCA 13070
3	3	16	**I've Never Been To Me**	*Charlene* ... Motown 1611
4	4	19	**867-5309/Jenny**	*Tommy Tutone* ... Columbia 02646
5	5	11	**The Other Woman**	*Ray Parker Jr.* ... Arista 0669
6	6	14	**'65 Love Affair**	*Paul Davis* ... Arista 0661
7	8	13	**Don't You Want Me**	*The Human League* ... A&M 2397
8	11	13	**Always On My Mind**	*Willie Nelson* ... Columbia 02741
9	9	11	**Did It In A Minute**	*Daryl Hall & John Oates* ... RCA 13065
10	10	14	**Get Down On It**	*Kool & The Gang* ... De-Lite 818

★ **HIGHEST DEBUT** ★ POS 52
Do I Do ... *Stevie Wonder*

★ **BIGGEST MOVER** ★ 87 to 70
Angel In Blue ... *The J. Geils Band*

Billboard — JUNE 5, 1982 — HOT 100

TW	LW	WK	Title	Artist	Label
1	1	9	Ebony And Ivory	Paul McCartney with Stevie Wonder	Columbia 02860
2	2	14	Don't Talk To Strangers	Rick Springfield	RCA 13070
3	3	17	I've Never Been To Me	Charlene	Motown 1611
4	4	20	867-5309/Jenny	Tommy Tutone	Columbia 02646
5	5	12	The Other Woman	Ray Parker Jr.	Arista 0669
6	7	14	Don't You Want Me	The Human League	A&M 2397
7	8	14	Always On My Mind	Willie Nelson	Columbia 02741
8	11	8	Heat Of The Moment	Asia	Geffen 50040
9	6	15	'65 Love Affair	Paul Davis	Arista 0661
10	16	8	Rosanna	Toto	Columbia 02811

★ HIGHEST DEBUT ★ POS 57
What Kind Of Fool Am I .... Rick Springfield

★ BIGGEST MOVER ★ 56 to 33
Take Me Down .... Alabama

Billboard — JUNE 12, 1982 — HOT 100

TW	LW	WK	Title	Artist	Label
1	1	10	Ebony And Ivory	Paul McCartney with Stevie Wonder	Columbia 02860
2	2	15	Don't Talk To Strangers	Rick Springfield	RCA 13070
3	6	15	Don't You Want Me	The Human League	A&M 2397
4	5	13	The Other Woman	Ray Parker Jr.	Arista 0669
5	7	15	Always On My Mind	Willie Nelson	Columbia 02741
6	8	9	Heat Of The Moment	Asia	Geffen 50040
7	10	9	Rosanna	Toto	Columbia 02811
8	11	7	Crimson And Clover	Joan Jett & The Blackhearts	Boardwalk 144
9	4	21	867-5309/Jenny	Tommy Tutone	Columbia 02646
10	12	11	It's Gonna Take A Miracle	Deniece Williams	ARC 02812

★ HIGHEST DEBUT ★ POS 52
Keep The Fire Burnin' .... REO Speedwagon

★ BIGGEST MOVER ★ 49 to 34
Still They Ride .... Journey

Billboard — JUNE 19, 1982 — HOT 100

TW	LW	WK	Title	Artist	Label
1	1	11	Ebony And Ivory	Paul McCartney with Stevie Wonder	Columbia 02860
2	3	16	Don't You Want Me	The Human League	A&M 2397
3	7	10	Rosanna	Toto	Columbia 02811
4	4	14	The Other Woman	Ray Parker Jr.	Arista 0669
5	5	16	Always On My Mind	Willie Nelson	Columbia 02741
6	6	10	Heat Of The Moment	Asia	Geffen 50040
7	8	8	Crimson And Clover	Joan Jett & The Blackhearts	Boardwalk 144
8	16	9	Let It Whip	Dazz Band	Motown 1609
9	17	9	Hurts So Good	John Cougar	Riva 209
10	10	12	It's Gonna Take A Miracle	Deniece Williams	ARC 02812

★ HIGHEST DEBUT ★ POS 33
Hold Me .... Fleetwood Mac

★ BIGGEST MOVER ★ 51 to 31
What Kind Of Fool Am I .... Rick Springfield

Billboard — JUNE 26, 1982 — HOT 100

TW	LW	WK	Title	Artist ... Label
1	1	12	**Ebony And Ivory**	*Paul McCartney with Stevie Wonder* ... Columbia 02860
2	2	17	Don't You Want Me	*The Human League* ... A&M 2397
3	3	11	Rosanna	*Toto* ... Columbia 02811
4	6	11	**Heat Of The Moment**	*Asia* ... Geffen 50040
5	5	17	**Always On My Mind**	*Willie Nelson* ... Columbia 02741
6	9	10	Hurts So Good	*John Cougar* ... Riva 209
7	7	9	**Crimson And Clover**	*Joan Jett & The Blackhearts* ... Boardwalk 144
8	8	10	Let It Whip	*Dazz Band* ... Motown 1609
9	12	8	Love's Been A Little Bit Hard On Me	*Juice Newton* ... Capitol 5120
10	4	15	The Other Woman	*Ray Parker Jr.* ... Arista 0669

★ **HIGHEST DEBUT** ★   POS 48
Wasted On The Way............*Crosby, Stills & Nash*

★ **BIGGEST MOVER** ★   42 to 19
Eye Of The Tiger ....*Survivor*

Billboard — JULY 3, 1982 — HOT 100

TW	LW	WK	Title	Artist ... Label
1	2	18	**Don't You Want Me**	*The Human League* ... A&M 2397
2	3	12	**Rosanna**	*Toto* ... Columbia 02811
3	1	13	Ebony And Ivory	*Paul McCartney with Stevie Wonder* ... Columbia 02860
4	4	12	**Heat Of The Moment**	*Asia* ... Geffen 50040
5	6	11	Hurts So Good	*John Cougar* ... Riva 209
6	5	18	Always On My Mind	*Willie Nelson* ... Columbia 02741
7	8	11	Let It Whip	*Dazz Band* ... Motown 1609
8	9	9	Love's Been A Little Bit Hard On Me	*Juice Newton* ... Capitol 5120
9	19	5	Eye Of The Tiger..................................	*Survivor* ... Scotti Brothers 02912
10	12	10	**Caught Up In You**	*38 Special* ... A&M 2412

★ **HIGHEST DEBUT** ★   POS 55
Love Will Turn You Around ....*Kenny Rogers*

★ **BIGGEST MOVER** ★   48 to 29
Wasted On The Way............*Crosby, Stills & Nash*

Billboard — JULY 10, 1982 — HOT 100

TW	LW	WK	Title	Artist ... Label
1	1	19	**Don't You Want Me**	*The Human League* ... A&M 2397
2	2	13	**Rosanna**	*Toto* ... Columbia 02811
3	5	12	Hurts So Good	*John Cougar* ... Riva 209
4	4	13	**Heat Of The Moment**	*Asia* ... Geffen 50040
5	9	6	Eye Of The Tiger..................................	*Survivor* ... Scotti Brothers 02912
6	7	12	Let It Whip	*Dazz Band* ... Motown 1609
7	8	10	Love's Been A Little Bit Hard On Me......................	*Juice Newton* ... Capitol 5120
8	3	14	Ebony And Ivory	*Paul McCartney with Stevie Wonder* ... Columbia 02860
9	11	26	Tainted Love	*Soft Cell* ... Sire 49855
10	10	11	**Caught Up In You**	*38 Special* ... A&M 2412

★ **HIGHEST DEBUT** ★   POS 55
Take It Away ....*Paul McCartney*

★ **BIGGEST MOVER** ★   65 to 51
Love Is In Control (Finger On The Trigger)................................*Donna Summer*

'82

TW	LW	WK	**Billboard.**		JULY 17, 1982		**HOT 100.**
❶	1	20	**Don't You Want Me**		*The Human League* . . . A&M 2397		
❷	2	14	**Rosanna**		*Toto* . . . Columbia 02811		
❸	3	13	**Hurts So Good**		*John Cougar* . . . Riva 209		
❹	5	7	**Eye Of The Tiger**		*Survivor* . . . Scotti Brothers 02912		
❺	6	13	**Let It Whip**		*Dazz Band* . . . Motown 1609		
❻	12	5	**Hold Me**		*Fleetwood Mac* . . . Warner 29966		
❼	7	11	**Love's Been A Little Bit Hard On Me**		*Juice Newton* . . . Capitol 5120		
❽	9	27	**Tainted Love**		*Soft Cell* . . . Sire 49855		
❾	11	13	**Only The Lonely**		*The Motels* . . . Capitol 5114		
❿	10	12	**Caught Up In You**		*38 Special* . . . A&M 2412		

★ **HIGHEST DEBUT** ★ POS 75
Valley Girl.........*Frank Zappa with Moon Unit Zappa*

★ **BIGGEST MOVER** ★ 55 to 31
Take It Away ....*Paul McCartney*

TW	LW	WK	**Billboard.**		JULY 24, 1982		**HOT 100.**
❶	4	8	**Eye Of The Tiger**		*Survivor* . . . Scotti Brothers 02912		
❷	2	15	**Rosanna**		*Toto* . . . Columbia 02811		
❸	3	14	**Hurts So Good**		*John Cougar* . . . Riva 209		
❹	6	6	**Hold Me**		*Fleetwood Mac* . . . Warner 29966		
❺	5	14	**Let It Whip**		*Dazz Band* . . . Motown 1609		
❻	11	9	**Abracadabra**		*The Steve Miller Band* . . . Capitol 5126		
❼	1	21	**Don't You Want Me**		*The Human League* . . . A&M 2397		
❽	8	28	**Tainted Love**		*Soft Cell* . . . Sire 49855		
❾	9	14	**Only The Lonely**		*The Motels* . . . Capitol 5114		
❿	12	7	**Keep The Fire Burnin'**		*REO Speedwagon* . . . Epic 02967		

★ **HIGHEST DEBUT** ★ POS 69
Jack & Diane.............................*John Cougar*

★ **BIGGEST MOVER** ★ 59 to 41
And I Am Telling You I'm Not Going ......*Jennifer Holliday*

TW	LW	WK	**Billboard.**		JULY 31, 1982		**HOT 100.**
❶	1	9	**Eye Of The Tiger**		*Survivor* . . . Scotti Brothers 02912		
②	2	16	**Rosanna**		*Toto* . . . Columbia 02811		
❸	3	15	**Hurts So Good**		*John Cougar* . . . Riva 209		
❹	4	7	**Hold Me**		*Fleetwood Mac* . . . Warner 29966		
❺	6	10	**Abracadabra**		*The Steve Miller Band* . . . Capitol 5126		
❻	11	9	**Hard To Say I'm Sorry**		*Chicago* . . . Full Moon 29979		
❼	7	22	**Don't You Want Me**		*The Human League* . . . A&M 2397		
❽	14	8	**Even The Nights Are Better**		*Air Supply* . . . Arista 0692		
❾	9	15	**Only The Lonely**		*The Motels* . . . Capitol 5114		
❿	10	8	**Keep The Fire Burnin'**		*REO Speedwagon* . . . Epic 02967		

★ **HIGHEST DEBUT** ★ POS 69
Do You Wanna Touch Me (Oh Yeah) ....*Joan Jett & The Blackhearts*

★ **BIGGEST MOVER** ★ 69 to 47
Jack & Diane.............................*John Cougar*

TW	LW	WK	Billboard	AUGUST 7, 1982	HOT 100
❶	1	10	**Eye Of The Tiger** ....*Survivor* . . . Scotti Brothers 02912
❷	3	16	**Hurts So Good** ....*John Cougar* . . . Riva 209
❸	5	11	**Abracadabra**.................................*The Steve Miller Band* . . . Capitol 5126
❹	4	8	**Hold Me** ....*Fleetwood Mac* . . . Warner 29966
❺	6	10	**Hard To Say I'm Sorry** ....*Chicago* . . . Full Moon 29979
⑥	2	17	Rosanna...*Toto* . . . Columbia 02811
❼	8	9	**Even The Nights Are Better** ....*Air Supply* . . . Arista 0692
❽	10	9	**Keep The Fire Burnin'** ....*REO Speedwagon* . . . Epic 02967
⑨	9	16	**Only The Lonely** ....*The Motels* . . . Capitol 5114
⑩	7	23	Don't You Want Me ....*The Human League* . . . A&M 2397

★ HIGHEST DEBUT ★ POS 69	★ BIGGEST MOVER ★ 64 to 45
I Keep Forgettin' (Every Time You're Near)......................*Michael McDonald*	Only Time Will Tell ....*Asia*

TW	LW	WK	Billboard	AUGUST 14, 1982	HOT 100
❶	1	11	**Eye Of The Tiger** ....*Survivor* . . . Scotti Brothers 02912
❷	2	17	**Hurts So Good** ....*John Cougar* . . . Riva 209
❸	3	12	**Abracadabra**.................................*The Steve Miller Band* . . . Capitol 5126
❹	4	9	**Hold Me** ....*Fleetwood Mac* . . . Warner 29966
❺	5	11	**Hard To Say I'm Sorry** ....*Chicago* . . . Full Moon 29979
❻	7	10	**Even The Nights Are Better** ....*Air Supply* . . . Arista 0692
❼	8	10	**Keep The Fire Burnin'**.....................*REO Speedwagon* . . . Epic 02967
⑧	6	18	Rosanna ....*Toto* . . . Columbia 02811
⑨	12	7	Vacation...*Go-Go's* . . . I.R.S. 9907
⑩	11	8	**Wasted On The Way** ....*Crosby, Stills & Nash* . . . Atlantic 4058

★ HIGHEST DEBUT ★ POS 72	★ BIGGEST MOVER ★ 61 to 41
Hold On..*Santana*	Somebody's Baby.....................*Jackson Browne*

TW	LW	WK	Billboard	AUGUST 21, 1982	HOT 100
❶	1	12	**Eye Of The Tiger** ....*Survivor* . . . Scotti Brothers 02912
❷	2	18	**Hurts So Good** ....*John Cougar* . . . Riva 209
❸	3	13	**Abracadabra**.................................*The Steve Miller Band* . . . Capitol 5126
❹	4	10	**Hold Me**...*Fleetwood Mac* . . . Warner 29966
❺	5	12	**Hard To Say I'm Sorry** ....*Chicago* . . . Full Moon 29979
❻	6	11	**Even The Nights Are Better** ....*Air Supply* . . . Arista 0692
❼	7	11	**Keep The Fire Burnin'**.....................*REO Speedwagon* . . . Epic 02967
❽	9	8	**Vacation**...*Go-Go's* . . . I.R.S. 9907
❾	10	9	**Wasted On The Way** ....*Crosby, Stills & Nash* . . . Atlantic 4058
⑩	12	7	**Take It Away**................................*Paul McCartney* . . . Columbia 03018

★ HIGHEST DEBUT ★ POS 69	★ BIGGEST MOVER ★ 72 to 51
You Keep Runnin' Away...................*38 Special*	Hold On...*Santana*

Billboard — AUGUST 28, 1982 — HOT 100

TW	LW	WK			
1	1	13	Eye Of The Tiger	Survivor	Scotti Brothers 02912
2	2	19	Hurts So Good	John Cougar	Riva 209
3	3	14	Abracadabra	The Steve Miller Band	Capitol 5126
4	4	11	Hold Me	Fleetwood Mac	Warner 29966
5	5	13	Hard To Say I'm Sorry	Chicago	Full Moon 29979
6	6	12	Even The Nights Are Better	Air Supply	Arista 0692
7	7	12	Keep The Fire Burnin'	REO Speedwagon	Epic 02967
8	8	9	Vacation	Go-Go's	I.R.S. 9907
9	9	10	Wasted On The Way	Crosby, Stills & Nash	Atlantic 4058
10	10	8	Take It Away	Paul McCartney	Columbia 03018

★ HIGHEST DEBUT ★ POS 67
You Don't Want Me Anymore ....Steel Breeze

★ BIGGEST MOVER ★ 74 to 53
Break It To Me Gently ....Juice Newton

Billboard — SEPTEMBER 4, 1982 — HOT 100

TW	LW	WK			
1	3	15	Abracadabra	The Steve Miller Band	Capitol 5126
2	1	14	Eye Of The Tiger	Survivor	Scotti Brothers 02912
3	5	14	Hard To Say I'm Sorry	Chicago	Full Moon 29979
4	4	12	Hold Me	Fleetwood Mac	Warner 29966
5	6	13	Even The Nights Are Better	Air Supply	Arista 0692
6	11	16	You Should Hear How She Talks About You	Melissa Manchester	Arista 0676
7	2	20	Hurts So Good	John Cougar	Riva 209
8	8	10	Vacation	Go-Go's	I.R.S. 9907
9	9	11	Wasted On The Way	Crosby, Stills & Nash	Atlantic 4058
10	10	9	Take It Away	Paul McCartney	Columbia 03018

★ HIGHEST DEBUT ★ POS 67
Heart Attack ....Olivia Newton-John

★ BIGGEST MOVER ★ 75 to 53
The One You Love ....Glenn Frey

Billboard — SEPTEMBER 11, 1982 — HOT 100

TW	LW	WK			
1	3	15	Hard To Say I'm Sorry	Chicago	Full Moon 29979
2	2	15	Eye Of The Tiger	Survivor	Scotti Brothers 02912
3	1	16	Abracadabra	The Steve Miller Band	Capitol 5126
4	11	8	Jack & Diane	John Cougar	Riva 210
5	5	14	Even The Nights Are Better	Air Supply	Arista 0692
6	6	17	You Should Hear How She Talks About You	Melissa Manchester	Arista 0676
7	4	13	Hold Me	Fleetwood Mac	Warner 29966
8	7	21	Hurts So Good	John Cougar	Riva 209
9	9	12	Wasted On The Way	Crosby, Stills & Nash	Atlantic 4058
10	10	10	Take It Away	Paul McCartney	Columbia 03018

★ HIGHEST DEBUT ★ POS 69
Heartlight ....Neil Diamond

★ BIGGEST MOVER ★ 64 to 36
Big Fun ....Kool & The Gang

Billboard ● SEPTEMBER 18, 1982 ● HOT 100.

TW	LW	WK		
❶	1	16	**Hard To Say I'm Sorry**	*Chicago* ... Full Moon 29979
②	3	17	Abracadabra	*The Steve Miller Band* ... Capitol 5126
③	2	16	Eye Of The Tiger	*Survivor* ... Scotti Brothers 02912
④	4	9	Jack & Diane	*John Cougar* ... Riva 210
❺	6	18	**You Should Hear How She Talks About You**	
				Melissa Manchester ... Arista 0676
⑥	5	15	Even The Nights Are Better	*Air Supply* ... Arista 0692
⑦	7	14	Hold Me	*Fleetwood Mac* ... Warner 29966
⑧	8	22	Hurts So Good	*John Cougar* ... Riva 209
⑨	14	12	Eye In The Sky	*The Alan Parsons Project* ... Arista 0696
⑩	10	11	**Take It Away**	*Paul McCartney* ... Columbia 03018

★ HIGHEST DEBUT ★ POS 69	★ BIGGEST MOVER ★ 63 to 49
Southern Cross .... *Crosby, Stills & Nash*	Love Come Down .... *Evelyn King*

Billboard ● SEPTEMBER 25, 1982 ● HOT 100.

TW	LW	WK		
❶	2	18	**Abracadabra**	*The Steve Miller Band* ... Capitol 5126
❷	4	10	Jack & Diane	*John Cougar* ... Riva 210
③	1	17	Hard To Say I'm Sorry	*Chicago* ... Full Moon 29979
④	3	17	Eye Of The Tiger	*Survivor* ... Scotti Brothers 02912
❺	5	19	**You Should Hear How She Talks About You**	
				Melissa Manchester ... Arista 0676
⑥	9	13	Eye In The Sky	*The Alan Parsons Project* ... Arista 0696
❼	12	12	Who Can It Be Now?	*Men At Work* ... Columbia 02888
⑧	18	9	Somebody's Baby	*Jackson Browne* ... Asylum 69982
⑨	8	23	Hurts So Good	*John Cougar* ... Riva 209
⑩	11	14	**Love Is In Control (Finger On The Trigger)**	*Donna Summer* ... Geffen 29982

★ HIGHEST DEBUT ★ POS 72	★ BIGGEST MOVER ★ 80 to 64
Pressure .... *Billy Joel*	Rock This Town .... *Stray Cats*

Billboard ● OCTOBER 2, 1982 ● HOT 100.

TW	LW	WK		
❶	2	11	**Jack & Diane**	*John Cougar* ... Riva 210
②	1	19	Abracadabra	*The Steve Miller Band* ... Capitol 5126
③	3	18	Hard To Say I'm Sorry	*Chicago* ... Full Moon 29979
④	4	18	Eye Of The Tiger	*Survivor* ... Scotti Brothers 02912
⑤	5	20	**You Should Hear How She Talks About You**	
				Melissa Manchester ... Arista 0676
⑥	6	14	Eye In The Sky	*The Alan Parsons Project* ... Arista 0696
❼	7	13	Who Can It Be Now?	*Men At Work* ... Columbia 02888
⑧	8	10	Somebody's Baby	*Jackson Browne* ... Asylum 69982
❾	15	9	I Keep Forgettin' (Every Time You're Near)	*Michael McDonald* ... Warner 29933
⑩	9	24	Hurts So Good	*John Cougar* ... Riva 209

★ HIGHEST DEBUT ★ POS 61	★ BIGGEST MOVER ★ 39 to 13
Muscles .... *Diana Ross*	Heart Attack .... *Olivia Newton-John*

Billboard — OCTOBER 9, 1982 — HOT 100

TW	LW	WK	Title	Artist	Label
1	1	12	Jack & Diane	John Cougar	Riva 210
2	2	20	Abracadabra	The Steve Miller Band	Capitol 5126
3	3	19	Hard To Say I'm Sorry	Chicago	Full Moon 29979
4	6	15	Eye In The Sky	The Alan Parsons Project	Arista 0696
5	7	14	Who Can It Be Now?	Men At Work	Columbia 02888
6	4	19	Eye Of The Tiger	Survivor	Scotti Brothers 02912
7	9	10	I Keep Forgettin' (Every Time You're Near)	Michael McDonald	Warner 29933
8	8	11	Somebody's Baby	Jackson Browne	Asylum 69982
9	11	11	You Can Do Magic	America	Capitol 5142
10	14	14	I Ran (So Far Away)	A Flock Of Seagulls	Jive 102

★ HIGHEST DEBUT ★ POS 56
I.G.Y. (What A Beautiful World)......Donald Fagen

★ BIGGEST MOVER ★ 53 to 33
New World Man ......Rush

Billboard — OCTOBER 16, 1982 — HOT 100

TW	LW	WK	Title	Artist	Label
1	1	13	Jack & Diane	John Cougar	Riva 210
2	5	15	Who Can It Be Now?	Men At Work	Columbia 02888
3	4	16	Eye In The Sky	The Alan Parsons Project	Arista 0696
4	3	20	Hard To Say I'm Sorry	Chicago	Full Moon 29979
5	2	21	Abracadabra	The Steve Miller Band	Capitol 5126
6	7	11	I Keep Forgettin' (Every Time You're Near)	Michael McDonald	Warner 29933
7	8	12	Somebody's Baby	Jackson Browne	Asylum 69982
8	9	12	You Can Do Magic	America	Capitol 5142
9	11	7	Heart Attack	Olivia Newton-John	MCA 52100
10	10	15	I Ran (So Far Away)	A Flock Of Seagulls	Jive 102

★ HIGHEST DEBUT ★ POS 65
Maneater ......Daryl Hall & John Oates

★ BIGGEST MOVER ★ 62 to 47
Get Closer......Linda Ronstadt

Billboard — OCTOBER 23, 1982 — HOT 100

TW	LW	WK	Title	Artist	Label
1	1	14	Jack & Diane	John Cougar	Riva 210
2	2	16	Who Can It Be Now?	Men At Work	Columbia 02888
3	3	17	Eye In The Sky	The Alan Parsons Project	Arista 0696
4	6	12	I Keep Forgettin' (Every Time You're Near)	Michael McDonald	Warner 29933
5	11	10	Up Where We Belong	Joe Cocker & Jennifer Warnes	Island 99996
6	9	8	Heart Attack	Olivia Newton-John	MCA 52100
7	7	13	Somebody's Baby	Jackson Browne	Asylum 69982
8	8	13	You Can Do Magic	America	Capitol 5142
9	10	16	I Ran (So Far Away)	A Flock Of Seagulls	Jive 102
10	5	22	Abracadabra	The Steve Miller Band	Capitol 5126

★ HIGHEST DEBUT ★ POS 76
Whatcha Gonna Do ......Chilliwack

★ BIGGEST MOVER ★ 50 to 36
Truly......Lionel Richie

Billboard — OCTOBER 30, 1982 — HOT 100

TW	LW	WK	Title	Artist	Label
1	2	17	**Who Can It Be Now?**	*Men At Work*	Columbia 02888
2	1	15	Jack & Diane	*John Cougar*	Riva 210
3	3	18	**Eye In The Sky**	*The Alan Parsons Project*	Arista 0696
4	4	13	**I Keep Forgettin' (Every Time You're Near)**	*Michael McDonald*	Warner 29933
5	5	11	Up Where We Belong	*Joe Cocker & Jennifer Warnes*	Island 99996
6	6	9	Heart Attack	*Olivia Newton-John*	MCA 52100
7	7	14	**Somebody's Baby**	*Jackson Browne*	Asylum 69982
8	8	14	**You Can Do Magic**	*America*	Capitol 5142
9	9	17	**I Ran (So Far Away)**	*A Flock Of Seagulls*	Jive 102
10	13	8	Heartlight	*Neil Diamond*	Columbia 03219

★ **HIGHEST DEBUT** ★ POS 31
It's Raining Again ....*Supertramp*

★ **BIGGEST MOVER** ★ 36 to 14
Truly....................................*Lionel Richie*

Billboard — NOVEMBER 6, 1982 — HOT 100

TW	LW	WK	Title	Artist	Label
1	5	12	**Up Where We Belong**	*Joe Cocker & Jennifer Warnes*	Island 99996
2	1	18	Who Can It Be Now?	*Men At Work*	Columbia 02888
3	6	10	**Heart Attack**	*Olivia Newton-John*	MCA 52100
4	4	14	**I Keep Forgettin' (Every Time You're Near)**	*Michael McDonald*	Warner 29933
5	2	16	Jack & Diane	*John Cougar*	Riva 210
6	3	19	Eye In The Sky	*The Alan Parsons Project*	Arista 0696
7	10	9	Heartlight	*Neil Diamond*	Columbia 03219
8	8	15	**You Can Do Magic**	*America*	Capitol 5142
9	13	18	Gloria	*Laura Branigan*	Atlantic 4048
10	14	5	Truly	*Lionel Richie*	Motown 1644

★ **HIGHEST DEBUT** ★ POS 45
The Girl Is Mine...................*Michael Jackson/Paul McCartney*

★ **BIGGEST MOVER** ★ 73 to 55
Dirty Laundry ....*Don Henley*

Billboard — NOVEMBER 13, 1982 — HOT 100

TW	LW	WK	Title	Artist	Label
1	1	13	**Up Where We Belong**	*Joe Cocker & Jennifer Warnes*	Island 99996
2	10	6	Truly	*Lionel Richie*	Motown 1644
3	3	11	**Heart Attack**	*Olivia Newton-John*	MCA 52100
4	9	19	**Gloria**	*Laura Branigan*	Atlantic 4048
5	7	10	**Heartlight**	*Neil Diamond*	Columbia 03219
6	2	19	Who Can It Be Now?	*Men At Work*	Columbia 02888
7	5	17	Jack & Diane	*John Cougar*	Riva 210
8	8	16	**You Can Do Magic**	*America*	Capitol 5142
9	4	15	I Keep Forgettin' (Every Time You're Near)	*Michael McDonald*	Warner 29933
10	14	7	**Muscles**	*Diana Ross*	RCA 13348

★ **HIGHEST DEBUT** ★ POS 58
You Got Lucky ....*Tom Petty & The Heartbreakers*

★ **BIGGEST MOVER** ★ 36 to 12
Maneater ....*Daryl Hall & John Oates*

Billboard — NOVEMBER 20, 1982 — HOT 100.

TW	LW	WK		
①	1	14	**Up Where We Belong** ......*Joe Cocker & Jennifer Warnes* ... Island 99996	
②	2	7	**Truly**..*Lionel Richie* ... Motown 1644	
③	3	12	**Heart Attack**..............................*Olivia Newton-John* ... MCA 52100	
④	4	20	**Gloria**..*Laura Branigan* ... Atlantic 4048	
⑤	5	11	**Heartlight**..*Neil Diamond* ... Columbia 03219	
⑥	6	20	**Who Can It Be Now?**....................*Men At Work* ... Columbia 02888	
⑦	13	12	**Mickey**...*Toni Basil* ... Chrysalis 2638	
⑧	12	6	**Maneater**........................*Daryl Hall & John Oates* ... RCA 13354	
⑨	14	14	**Steppin' Out**....................................*Joe Jackson* ... A&M 2428	
⑩	10	8	**Muscles**...*Diana Ross* ... RCA 13348	

★ *HIGHEST DEBUT* ★ POS 56	★ *BIGGEST MOVER* ★ 52 to 19
I Do...*The J. Geils Band*	Sexual Healing.............................*Marvin Gaye*

Billboard — NOVEMBER 27, 1982 — HOT 100.

TW	LW	WK		
①	2	8	**Truly** ....*Lionel Richie* ... Motown 1644	
②	4	21	**Gloria** ....*Laura Branigan* ... Atlantic 4048	
③	3	13	**Heart Attack**..............................*Olivia Newton-John* ... MCA 52100	
④	1	15	**Up Where We Belong** ....*Joe Cocker & Jennifer Warnes* ... Island 99996	
⑤	5	12	**Heartlight**..*Neil Diamond* ... Columbia 03219	
⑥	7	13	**Mickey**...*Toni Basil* ... Chrysalis 2638	
⑦	8	7	**Maneater**........................*Daryl Hall & John Oates* ... RCA 13354	
⑧	9	15	**Steppin' Out**....................................*Joe Jackson* ... A&M 2428	
⑨	14	4	**The Girl Is Mine** ....*Michael Jackson/Paul McCartney* ... Epic 03288	
⑩	10	9	**Muscles**...*Diana Ross* ... RCA 13348	

★ *HIGHEST DEBUT* ★ POS 59	★ *BIGGEST MOVER* ★ 43 to 31
Heart To Heart ....*Kenny Loggins*	Down Under.................................*Men At Work*

Billboard — DECEMBER 4, 1982 — HOT 100.

TW	LW	WK		
①	1	9	**Truly** ....*Lionel Richie* ... Motown 1644	
②	2	22	**Gloria** ....*Laura Branigan* ... Atlantic 4048	
③	6	14	**Mickey** ....*Toni Basil* ... Chrysalis 2638	
④	7	8	**Maneater**........................*Daryl Hall & John Oates* ... RCA 13354	
⑤	5	13	**Heartlight**..*Neil Diamond* ... Columbia 03219	
⑥	4	16	**Up Where We Belong** ....*Joe Cocker & Jennifer Warnes* ... Island 99996	
⑦	8	16	**Steppin' Out**....................................*Joe Jackson* ... A&M 2428	
⑧	9	5	**The Girl Is Mine** ....*Michael Jackson/Paul McCartney* ... Epic 03288	
⑨	11	6	**Dirty Laundry**....................................*Don Henley* ... Asylum 69894	
⑩	10	10	**Muscles** ....*Diana Ross* ... RCA 13348	

★ *HIGHEST DEBUT* ★ POS 70	★ *BIGGEST MOVER* ★ 72 to 51
Bad Boy...*Ray Parker Jr.*	Love In Store................................*Fleetwood Mac*

Billboard — DECEMBER 11, 1982 — HOT 100

TW	LW	WK	Title	Artist
1	3	15	**Mickey**	*Toni Basil* ... Chrysalis 2638
2	2	23	**Gloria**	*Laura Branigan* ... Atlantic 4048
3	4	9	**Maneater**	*Daryl Hall & John Oates* ... RCA 13354
4	1	10	**Truly**	*Lionel Richie* ... Motown 1644
5	8	6	**The Girl Is Mine**	*Michael Jackson/Paul McCartney* ... Epic 03288
6	7	17	**Steppin' Out**	*Joe Jackson* ... A&M 2428
7	9	7	**Dirty Laundry**	*Don Henley* ... Asylum 69894
8	12	7	**Sexual Healing**	*Marvin Gaye* ... Columbia 03302
9	11	13	**Rock This Town**	*Stray Cats* ... EMI America 8132
10	10	11	**Muscles**	*Diana Ross* ... RCA 13348

★ **HIGHEST DEBUT** ★ POS 70
Your Love Is Driving Me Crazy ......*Sammy Hagar*

★ **BIGGEST MOVER** ★ 47 to 31
Heart To Heart ....*Kenny Loggins*

Billboard — DECEMBER 18, 1982 — HOT 100

TW	LW	WK	Title	Artist
1	3	10	**Maneater**	*Daryl Hall & John Oates* ... RCA 13354
2	1	16	**Mickey**	*Toni Basil* ... Chrysalis 2638
3	2	24	**Gloria**	*Laura Branigan* ... Atlantic 4048
4	5	7	**The Girl Is Mine**	*Michael Jackson/Paul McCartney* ... Epic 03288
5	4	11	**Truly**	*Lionel Richie* ... Motown 1644
6	6	18	**Steppin' Out**	*Joe Jackson* ... A&M 2428
7	7	8	**Dirty Laundry**	*Don Henley* ... Asylum 69894
8	8	8	**Sexual Healing**	*Marvin Gaye* ... Columbia 03302
9	9	14	**Rock This Town**	*Stray Cats* ... EMI America 8132
10	10	12	**Muscles**	*Diana Ross* ... RCA 13348

★ **HIGHEST DEBUT** ★ POS 40
Shame On The Moon ....*Bob Seger & The Silver Bullet Band*

★ **BIGGEST MOVER** ★ 70 to 54
Your Love Is Driving Me Crazy ......*Sammy Hagar*

Billboard — DECEMBER 25, 1982 — HOT 100

TW	LW	WK	Title	Artist
1	1	11	**Maneater**	*Daryl Hall & John Oates* ... RCA 13354
2	2	17	**Mickey**	*Toni Basil* ... Chrysalis 2638
3	4	8	**The Girl Is Mine**	*Michael Jackson/Paul McCartney* ... Epic 03288
4	7	9	**Dirty Laundry**	*Don Henley* ... Asylum 69894
5	3	25	**Gloria**	*Laura Branigan* ... Atlantic 4048
6	6	19	**Steppin' Out**	*Joe Jackson* ... A&M 2428
7	8	9	**Sexual Healing**	*Marvin Gaye* ... Columbia 03302
8	12	8	**Down Under**	*Men At Work* ... Columbia 03303
9	9	15	**Rock This Town**	*Stray Cats* ... EMI America 8132
10	5	12	**Truly**	*Lionel Richie* ... Motown 1644

★ **HIGHEST DEBUT** ★ POS 43
Stray Cat Strut............................*Stray Cats*

★ **BIGGEST MOVER** ★ 78 to 60
The Woman In Me.....................*Donna Summer*

Billboard — JANUARY 8, 1983 — HOT 100

TW	LW	WK	Title	Artist	Label
1	1	13	**Maneater**	Daryl Hall & John Oates	RCA 13354
2	3	10	**The Girl Is Mine**	Michael Jackson/Paul McCartney	Epic 03288
3	4	11	**Dirty Laundry**	Don Henley	Asylum 69894
4	8	10	**Down Under**	Men At Work	Columbia 03303
5	7	11	**Sexual Healing**	Marvin Gaye	Columbia 03302
6	2	19	**Mickey**	Toni Basil	Chrysalis 2638
7	5	27	**Gloria**	Laura Branigan	Atlantic 4048
8	6	21	**Steppin' Out**	Joe Jackson	A&M 2428
9	9	17	**Rock This Town**	Stray Cats	EMI America 8132
10	10	14	**Truly**	Lionel Richie	Motown 1644

★ HIGHEST DEBUT ★ POS 82
Got To Be There .... Chaka Khan

★ BIGGEST MOVER ★ 43 to 31
Stray Cat Strut .... Stray Cats

Billboard — JANUARY 15, 1983 — HOT 100

TW	LW	WK	Title	Artist	Label
1	4	11	**Down Under**	Men At Work	Columbia 03303
2	2	11	**The Girl Is Mine**	Michael Jackson/Paul McCartney	Epic 03288
3	3	12	**Dirty Laundry**	Don Henley	Asylum 69894
4	1	14	**Maneater**	Daryl Hall & John Oates	RCA 13354
5	5	12	**Sexual Healing**	Marvin Gaye	Columbia 03302
6	6	20	**Mickey**	Toni Basil	Chrysalis 2638
7	12	12	**Africa**	Toto	Columbia 03335
8	13	18	**Baby, Come To Me**	Patti Austin with James Ingram	Qwest 50036
9	14	16	**Rock The Casbah**	The Clash	Epic 03245
10	11	15	**Heartbreaker**	Dionne Warwick	Arista 1015

★ HIGHEST DEBUT ★ POS 49
You Are .... Lionel Richie

★ BIGGEST MOVER ★ 52 to 31
Pass The Dutchie .... Musical Youth

Billboard — JANUARY 22, 1983 — HOT 100

TW	LW	WK	Title	Artist	Label
1	1	12	**Down Under**	Men At Work	Columbia 03303
2	2	12	**The Girl Is Mine**	Michael Jackson/Paul McCartney	Epic 03288
3	3	13	**Dirty Laundry**	Don Henley	Asylum 69894
4	5	13	**Sexual Healing**	Marvin Gaye	Columbia 03302
5	7	13	**Africa**	Toto	Columbia 03335
6	4	15	**Maneater**	Daryl Hall & John Oates	RCA 13354
7	8	19	**Baby, Come To Me**	Patti Austin with James Ingram	Qwest 50036
8	9	17	**Rock The Casbah**	The Clash	Epic 03245
9	6	21	**Mickey**	Toni Basil	Chrysalis 2638
10	10	16	**Heartbreaker**	Dionne Warwick	Arista 1015

★ HIGHEST DEBUT ★ POS 29
All Right .... Christopher Cross

★ BIGGEST MOVER ★ 73 to 53
Breaking Us In Two .... Joe Jackson

Billboard — JANUARY 29, 1983 — HOT 100

TW	LW	WK	Title	Artist	Label
❶	1	13	**Down Under**	*Men At Work*	Columbia 03303
❷	5	14	**Africa**	*Toto*	Columbia 03335
❸	4	14	**Sexual Healing**	*Marvin Gaye*	Columbia 03302
④	3	14	**Dirty Laundry**	*Don Henley*	Asylum 69894
⑤	2	13	**The Girl Is Mine**	*Michael Jackson/Paul McCartney*	Epic 03288
⑥	6	16	**Maneater**	*Daryl Hall & John Oates*	RCA 13354
❼	7	20	**Baby, Come To Me**	*Patti Austin with James Ingram*	Qwest 50036
❽	8	18	**Rock The Casbah**	*The Clash*	Epic 03245
❾	12	7	**Shame On The Moon**	*Bob Seger & The Silver Bullet Band*	Capitol 5187
❿	11	17	**You And I**	*Eddie Rabbitt with Crystal Gayle*	Elektra 69936

★ **HIGHEST DEBUT** ★ POS 36
We've Got Tonight...........*Kenny Rogers & Sheena Easton*

★ **BIGGEST MOVER** ★ 78 to 54
Fall In Love With Me ....*Earth, Wind & Fire*

Billboard — FEBRUARY 5, 1983 — HOT 100

TW	LW	WK	Title	Artist	Label
❶	2	15	**Africa**	*Toto*	Columbia 03335
②	1	14	**Down Under**	*Men At Work*	Columbia 03303
❸	3	15	**Sexual Healing**	*Marvin Gaye*	Columbia 03302
④	7	21	**Baby, Come To Me**	*Patti Austin with James Ingram*	Qwest 50036
⑤	9	8	**Shame On The Moon**	*Bob Seger & The Silver Bullet Band*	Capitol 5187
⑥	6	17	**Maneater**	*Daryl Hall & John Oates*	RCA 13354
⑦	4	15	**Dirty Laundry**	*Don Henley*	Asylum 69894
❽	8	19	**Rock The Casbah**	*The Clash*	Epic 03245
❾	10	18	**You And I**	*Eddie Rabbitt with Crystal Gayle*	Elektra 69936
❿	11	14	**You Can't Hurry Love**	*Phil Collins*	Atlantic 89933

★ **HIGHEST DEBUT** ★ POS 36
Separate Ways (Worlds Apart)..............*Journey*

★ **BIGGEST MOVER** ★ 90 to 74
It Might Be You ....*Stephen Bishop*

Billboard — FEBRUARY 12, 1983 — HOT 100

TW	LW	WK	Title	Artist	Label
❶	2	15	**Down Under**	*Men At Work*	Columbia 03303
❷	4	22	**Baby, Come To Me**	*Patti Austin with James Ingram*	Qwest 50036
③	3	16	**Sexual Healing**	*Marvin Gaye*	Columbia 03302
④	5	9	**Shame On The Moon**	*Bob Seger & The Silver Bullet Band*	Capitol 5187
⑤	1	16	**Africa**	*Toto*	Columbia 03335
⑥	6	18	**Maneater**	*Daryl Hall & John Oates*	RCA 13354
❼	9	19	**You And I**	*Eddie Rabbitt with Crystal Gayle*	Elektra 69936
⑧	8	20	**Rock The Casbah**	*The Clash*	Epic 03245
❾	12	8	**Stray Cat Strut**	*Stray Cats*	EMI America 8122
❿	10	15	**You Can't Hurry Love**	*Phil Collins*	Atlantic 89933

★ **HIGHEST DEBUT** ★ POS 40
Mr. Roboto ....*Styx*

★ **BIGGEST MOVER** ★ 61 to 49
Poison Arrow................................*ABC*

Billboard FEBRUARY 19, 1983 HOT 100.

TW	LW	WK	Title	Artist	Label
❶	2	23	**Baby, Come To Me** ....*Patti Austin with James Ingram* ...	Qwest 50036
②	1	16	**Down Under**...*Men At Work* ...	Columbia 03303
❸	4	10	**Shame On The Moon** ...*Bob Seger & The Silver Bullet Band* ...	Capitol 5187
❹	9	9	**Stray Cat Strut**...............................*Stray Cats* ...	EMI America 8122
⑤	5	17	**Africa**..*Toto* ...	Columbia 03335
❻	23	5	**Billie Jean**.................................*Michael Jackson* ...	Epic 03509
❼	7	20	**You And I**......................*Eddie Rabbitt with Crystal Gayle* ...	Elektra 69936
❽	18	12	**Do You Really Want To Hurt Me**.............*Culture Club* ...	Epic/Virgin 03368
❾	19	9	**Hungry Like The Wolf**.................................*Duran Duran* ...	Harvest 5195
⑩	10	16	**You Can't Hurry Love**..............................*Phil Collins* ...	Atlantic 89933

★ HIGHEST DEBUT ★ POS 73	★ BIGGEST MOVER ★ 23 to 6
Whirly Girl ....*Oxo*	Billie Jean ....*Michael Jackson*

Billboard FEBRUARY 26, 1983 HOT 100.

TW	LW	WK	Title	Artist	Label
❶	1	24	**Baby, Come To Me** ....*Patti Austin with James Ingram* ...	Qwest 50036
❷	3	11	**Shame On The Moon** ....*Bob Seger & The Silver Bullet Band* ... Capitol 5187	
❸	4	10	**Stray Cat Strut**.....................................*Stray Cats* ...	EMI America 8122
❹	6	6	**Billie Jean** ....*Michael Jackson* ...	Epic 03509
❺	8	13	**Do You Really Want To Hurt Me**.............*Culture Club* ...	Epic/Virgin 03368
❻	9	10	**Hungry Like The Wolf**.................................*Duran Duran* ...	Harvest 5195
❼	7	21	**You And I**......................*Eddie Rabbitt with Crystal Gayle* ...	Elektra 69936
⑧	2	17	**Down Under**...*Men At Work* ...	Columbia 03303
❾	21	5	**We've Got Tonight**............*Kenny Rogers & Sheena Easton* ...	Liberty 1492
⑩	13	12	**Pass The Dutchie** ....*Musical Youth* ...	MCA 52149

★ HIGHEST DEBUT ★ POS 54	★ BIGGEST MOVER ★ 76 to 58
Change Of Heart.....*Tom Petty & The Heartbreakers*	I Don't Care Anymore ....*Phil Collins*

Billboard MARCH 5, 1983 HOT 100.

TW	LW	WK	Title	Artist	Label
❶	4	7	**Billie Jean** ....*Michael Jackson* ...	Epic 03509
❷	2	12	**Shame On The Moon** ....*Bob Seger & The Silver Bullet Band* ... Capitol 5187	
❸	3	11	**Stray Cat Strut**.......................................*Stray Cats* ...	EMI America 8122
❹	5	14	**Do You Really Want To Hurt Me**.............*Culture Club* ...	Epic/Virgin 03368
❺	6	11	**Hungry Like The Wolf**.................................*Duran Duran* ...	Harvest 5195
❻	1	25	**Baby, Come To Me**.............*Patti Austin with James Ingram* ...	Qwest 50036
⑦	7	22	**You And I**......................*Eddie Rabbitt with Crystal Gayle* ...	Elektra 69936
❽	9	6	**We've Got Tonight**............*Kenny Rogers & Sheena Easton* ...	Liberty 1492
❾	11	13	**Back On The Chain Gang**...............................*Pretenders* ...	Sire 29840
⑩	10	13	**Pass The Dutchie** ....*Musical Youth* ...	MCA 52149

★ HIGHEST DEBUT ★ POS 73	★ BIGGEST MOVER ★ 55 to 31
Love My Way..........................*Psychedelic Furs*	Der Kommissar...........................*After The Fire*

Billboard — MARCH 12, 1983 — HOT 100

TW	LW	WK	Title / Artist
1	1	8	**Billie Jean** ....*Michael Jackson* ... Epic 03509
2	2	13	**Shame On The Moon** ....*Bob Seger & The Silver Bullet Band* ... Capitol 5187
3	3	12	**Stray Cat Strut**..*Stray Cats* ... EMI America 8122
4	4	15	**Do You Really Want To Hurt Me**.............*Culture Club* ... Epic/Virgin 03368
5	5	12	**Hungry Like The Wolf** ....*Duran Duran* ... Harvest 5195
6	9	14	**Back On The Chain Gang**.................................*Pretenders* ... Sire 29840
7	11	9	**You Are**..*Lionel Richie* ... Motown 1657
8	8	7	**We've Got Tonight**............*Kenny Rogers & Sheena Easton* ... Liberty 1492
9	6	26	**Baby, Come To Me**............*Patti Austin with James Ingram* ... Qwest 50036
10	15	6	**Separate Ways (Worlds Apart)**.................*Journey* ... Columbia 03513

★ **HIGHEST DEBUT** ★ POS 65
Welcome To Heartlight ....*Kenny Loggins*

★ **BIGGEST MOVER** ★ 65 to 44
Beat It.......................................*Michael Jackson*

Billboard — MARCH 19, 1983 — HOT 100

TW	LW	WK	Title / Artist
1	1	9	**Billie Jean** ....*Michael Jackson* ... Epic 03509
2	2	14	**Shame On The Moon** ....*Bob Seger & The Silver Bullet Band* ... Capitol 5187
3	4	16	**Do You Really Want To Hurt Me**.............*Culture Club* ... Epic/Virgin 03368
4	5	13	**Hungry Like The Wolf**...*Duran Duran* ... Harvest 5195
5	6	15	**Back On The Chain Gang**...........................*Pretenders* ... Sire 29840
6	7	10	**You Are**..*Lionel Richie* ... Motown 1657
7	8	8	**We've Got Tonight**............*Kenny Rogers & Sheena Easton* ... Liberty 1492
8	10	7	**Separate Ways (Worlds Apart)**.................*Journey* ... Columbia 03513
9	11	8	**One On One** ....*Daryl Hall & John Oates* ... RCA 13421
10	13	6	**Mr. Roboto**...*Styx* ... A&M 2525

★ **HIGHEST DEBUT** ★ POS 65
Solitaire ....*Laura Branigan*

★ **BIGGEST MOVER** ★ 74 to 50
Even Now ....*Bob Seger & The Silver Bullet Band*

Billboard — MARCH 26, 1983 — HOT 100

TW	LW	WK	Title / Artist
1	1	10	**Billie Jean** ....*Michael Jackson* ... Epic 03509
2	3	17	**Do You Really Want To Hurt Me**................................*Culture Club* ... Epic/Virgin 03368
3	4	14	**Hungry Like The Wolf** ....*Duran Duran* ... Harvest 5195
4	6	11	**You Are**..*Lionel Richie* ... Motown 1657
5	5	16	**Back On The Chain Gang**...........................*Pretenders* ... Sire 29840
6	7	9	**We've Got Tonight** ....*Kenny Rogers & Sheena Easton* ... Liberty 1492
7	10	7	**Mr. Roboto**...*Styx* ... A&M 2525
8	8	8	**Separate Ways (Worlds Apart)**.................*Journey* ... Columbia 03513
9	9	9	**One On One** ....*Daryl Hall & John Oates* ... RCA 13421
10	13	18	**Twilight Zone** ....*Golden Earring* ... 21 Records 103

★ **HIGHEST DEBUT** ★ POS 54
Let's Dance ....*David Bowie*

★ **BIGGEST MOVER** ★ 65 to 48
Solitaire ....*Laura Branigan*

TW	LW	WK	Billboard	APRIL 2, 1983	HOT 100.
❶	1	11	**Billie Jean** ....*Michael Jackson* . . . Epic 03509
❷	2	18	**Do You Really Want To Hurt Me**.................................. *Culture Club* . . . Epic/Virgin 03368
③	3	15	**Hungry Like The Wolf** ....*Duran Duran* . . . Harvest 5195
④	4	12	**You Are**..*Lionel Richie* . . . Motown 1657
⑤	5	17	**Back On The Chain Gang**................................*Pretenders* . . . Sire 29840
⑥	6	10	**We've Got Tonight**.........*Kenny Rogers & Sheena Easton* . . . Liberty 1492
❼	7	8	**Mr. Roboto**...*Styx* . . . A&M 2525
⑧	8	9	**Separate Ways (Worlds Apart)**................*Journey* . . . Columbia 03513
⑨	9	10	**One On One** ....*Daryl Hall & John Oates* . . . RCA 13421
⑩	10	19	**Twilight Zone** ....*Golden Earring* . . . 21 Records 103

★ HIGHEST DEBUT ★ POS 58	★ BIGGEST MOVER ★ 73 to 55
Rio..*Duran Duran*	Mornin' ....*Jarreau*

TW	LW	WK	Billboard	APRIL 9, 1983	HOT 100.
❶	1	12	**Billie Jean** ....*Michael Jackson* . . . Epic 03509
②	2	19	**Do You Really Want To Hurt Me**.................................. *Culture Club* . . . Epic/Virgin 03368
③	3	16	**Hungry Like The Wolf** ....*Duran Duran* . . . Harvest 5195
❹	11	12	**Come On Eileen** ....*Dexys Midnight Runners* . . . Mercury 76189
⑤	7	9	**Mr. Roboto**..*Styx* . . . A&M 2525
⑥	6	11	**We've Got Tonight** ....*Kenny Rogers & Sheena Easton* . . . Liberty 1492
❼	9	11	**One On One** ....*Daryl Hall & John Oates* . . . RCA 13421
⑧	8	10	**Separate Ways (Worlds Apart)**................*Journey* . . . Columbia 03513
⑨	12	11	**Jeopardy**.................................*Greg Kihn Band* . . . Beserkley 69847
⑩	14	7	**Beat It**....................................*Michael Jackson* . . . Epic 03759

★ HIGHEST DEBUT ★ POS 28	★ BIGGEST MOVER ★ 77 to 52
Overkill ....*Men At Work*	Flashdance...What A Feeling ....*Irene Cara*

TW	LW	WK	Billboard	APRIL 16, 1983	HOT 100.
❶	1	13	**Billie Jean** ....*Michael Jackson* . . . Epic 03509
❷	4	13	**Come On Eileen** ....*Dexys Midnight Runners* . . . Mercury 76189
❸	5	10	**Mr. Roboto** ....*Styx* . . . A&M 2525
❹	9	12	**Jeopardy**.................................*Greg Kihn Band* . . . Beserkley 69847
❺	10	8	**Beat It**....................................*Michael Jackson* . . . Epic 03759
⑥	3	17	**Hungry Like The Wolf**...........................*Duran Duran* . . . Harvest 5195
⑦	7	12	**One On One** ....*Daryl Hall & John Oates* . . . RCA 13421
⑧	8	11	**Separate Ways (Worlds Apart)**................*Journey* . . . Columbia 03513
⑨	12	10	**Der Kommissar** ....*After The Fire* . . . Epic 03559
⑩	2	20	**Do You Really Want To Hurt Me** ....*Culture Club* . . . Epic/Virgin 03368

★ HIGHEST DEBUT ★ POS 53	★ BIGGEST MOVER ★ 55 to 37
Affair Of The Heart ....*Rick Springfield*	My Love.......................................*Lionel Richie*

TW	LW	WK	Billboard.	APRIL 23, 1983	HOT 100.
❶	2	14	**Come On Eileen**......................*Dexys Midnight Runners* . . . Mercury 76189
❷	5	9	Beat It..*Michael Jackson* . . . Epic 03759
❸	3	11	**Mr. Roboto** ....*Styx* . . . A&M 2525
❹	4	13	Jeopardy............................*Greg Kihn Band* . . . Beserkley 69847
❺	1	14	Billie Jean..*Michael Jackson* . . . Epic 03509
❻	9	11	Der Kommissar ....*After The Fire* . . . Epic 03559
❼	7	13	**One On One** ....*Daryl Hall & John Oates* . . . RCA 13421
❽	8	12	**Separate Ways (Worlds Apart)**.................*Journey* . . . Columbia 03513
❾	15	5	Let's Dance ....*David Bowie* . . . EMI America 8158
❿	13	10	She Blinded Me With Science....................*Thomas Dolby* . . . Capitol 5204

★ **HIGHEST DEBUT** ★ POS 71
Looking For A Stranger ....*Pat Benatar*

★ **BIGGEST MOVER** ★ 100 to 79
I Won't Be Home Tonight ....*Tony Carey*

TW	LW	WK	Billboard.	APRIL 30, 1983	HOT 100.
❶	2	10	**Beat It** ....*Michael Jackson* . . . Epic 03759
②	1	15	Come On Eileen ....*Dexys Midnight Runners* . . . Mercury 76189
③	4	14	Jeopardy.................................*Greg Kihn Band* . . . Beserkley 69847
④	3	12	Mr. Roboto...*Styx* . . . A&M 2525
⑤	6	12	**Der Kommissar** ....*After The Fire* . . . Epic 03559
⑥	9	6	Let's Dance ....*David Bowie* . . . EMI America 8158
⑦	5	15	Billie Jean..*Michael Jackson* . . . Epic 03509
⑧	10	11	**She Blinded Me With Science**....................*Thomas Dolby* . . . Capitol 5204
⑨	15	4	Overkill..*Men At Work* . . . Columbia 03795
⑩	12	10	Little Red Corvette ....*Prince* . . . Warner 29746

★ **HIGHEST DEBUT** ★ POS 35
Don't Let It End ....*Styx*

★ **BIGGEST MOVER** ★ 80 to 60
Never Gonna Let You Go.............*Sergio Mendes*

TW	LW	WK	Billboard.	MAY 7, 1983	HOT 100.
❶	1	11	**Beat It** ....*Michael Jackson* . . . Epic 03759
②	3	15	**Jeopardy**.................................*Greg Kihn Band* . . . Beserkley 69847
③	6	7	Let's Dance ....*David Bowie* . . . EMI America 8158
④	2	16	Come On Eileen ....*Dexys Midnight Runners* . . . Mercury 76189
⑤	5	13	**Der Kommissar** ....*After The Fire* . . . Epic 03559
⑥	9	5	Overkill..*Men At Work* . . . Columbia 03795
⑦	8	12	**She Blinded Me With Science**....................*Thomas Dolby* . . . Capitol 5204
⑧	4	13	Mr. Roboto...*Styx* . . . A&M 2525
⑨	10	11	Little Red Corvette ....*Prince* . . . Warner 29746
⑩	11	9	**I Won't Hold You Back**.............................*Toto* . . . Columbia 03597

★ **HIGHEST DEBUT** ★ POS 56
I'm Still Standing ....*Elton John*

★ **BIGGEST MOVER** ★ 70 to 50
Too Shy ....*Kajagoogoo*

TW	LW	WK	Billboard		MAY 14, 1983		HOT 100.
❶	1	12	**Beat It** ....*Michael Jackson* . . . Epic 03759
❷	3	8	Let's Dance ....*David Bowie* . . . EMI America 8158
③	2	16	Jeopardy...*Greg Kihn Band* . . . Beserkley 69847
❹	6	6	Overkill ....*Men At Work* . . . Columbia 03795
❺	7	13	**She Blinded Me With Science**..............*Thomas Dolby* . . . Capitol 5204
❻	4	17	Come On Eileen ....*Dexys Midnight Runners* . . . Mercury 76189
❼	13	7	**Flashdance...What A Feeling** ....*Irene Cara* . . . Casablanca 811440
❽	9	12	Little Red Corvette ....*Prince* . . . Warner 29746
❾	11	9	Solitaire..*Laura Branigan* . . . Atlantic 89868
⑩	5	14	Der Kommissar ....*After The Fire* . . . Epic 03559

★ *HIGHEST DEBUT* ★ POS 76	★ *BIGGEST MOVER* ★ 89 to 71
Inside Love (So Personal) ....*George Benson*	The Closer You Get ....*Alabama*

TW	LW	WK	Billboard		MAY 21, 1983		HOT 100.
❶	2	9	**Let's Dance**...*David Bowie* . . . EMI America 8158
②	1	13	Beat It..*Michael Jackson* . . . Epic 03759
❸	7	8	**Flashdance...What A Feeling** ....*Irene Cara* . . . Casablanca 811440
❹	4	7	Overkill ....*Men At Work* . . . Columbia 03795
❺	5	14	**She Blinded Me With Science**..............*Thomas Dolby* . . . Capitol 5204
❻	8	13	**Little Red Corvette** ....*Prince* . . . Warner 29746
❼	9	10	Solitaire ....*Laura Branigan* . . . Atlantic 89868
❽	3	17	Jeopardy...*Greg Kihn Band* . . . Beserkley 69847
❾	12	7	My Love ....*Lionel Richie* . . . Motown 1677
⑩	17	6	Time (Clock Of The Heart).....................*Culture Club* . . . Epic/Virgin 03796

★ *HIGHEST DEBUT* ★ POS 49	★ *BIGGEST MOVER* ★ 72 to 50
The Woman In You ....*The Bee Gees*	Come Dancing ....*The Kinks*

TW	LW	WK	Billboard		MAY 28, 1983		HOT 100.
❶	3	9	**Flashdance...What A Feeling** ....*Irene Cara* . . . Casablanca 811440
❷	1	10	Let's Dance ....*David Bowie* . . . EMI America 8158
③	2	14	Beat It..*Michael Jackson* . . . Epic 03759
❹	4	8	Overkill ....*Men At Work* . . . Columbia 03795
❺	5	15	**She Blinded Me With Science**..............*Thomas Dolby* . . . Capitol 5204
❻	6	14	**Little Red Corvette** ....*Prince* . . . Warner 29746
❼	7	11	Solitaire ....*Laura Branigan* . . . Atlantic 89868
❽	10	7	Time (Clock Of The Heart).....................*Culture Club* . . . Epic/Virgin 03796
❾	9	8	My Love ....*Lionel Richie* . . . Motown 1677
⑩	13	12	**Straight From The Heart**...........................*Bryan Adams* . . . A&M 2536

★ *HIGHEST DEBUT* ★ POS 41	★ *BIGGEST MOVER* ★ 78 to 57
Wanna Be Startin' Somethin' ......*Michael Jackson*	Sweet Dreams (Are Made of This) .....*Eurythmics*

TW	LW	WK	Billboard®	JUNE 4, 1983	HOT 100®
❶	1	10	**Flashdance...What A Feeling** ....*Irene Cara* . . . Casablanca 811440		
❷	2	11	Let's Dance ....*David Bowie* . . . EMI America 8158		
❸	4	9	**Overkill** ....*Men At Work* . . . Columbia 03795		
❹	8	8	Time (Clock Of The Heart).....................*Culture Club* . . . Epic/Virgin 03796		
❺	5	16	**She Blinded Me With Science**..............*Thomas Dolby* . . . Capitol 5204		
❻	3	15	Beat It...*Michael Jackson* . . . Epic 03759		
❼	9	9	**My Love** ....*Lionel Richie* . . . Motown 1677		
❽	6	15	Little Red Corvette ....*Prince* . . . Warner 29746		
❾	7	12	Solitaire...*Laura Branigan* . . . Atlantic 89868		
❿	10	13	**Straight From The Heart**...........................*Bryan Adams* . . . A&M 2536		
★ *HIGHEST DEBUT* ★ POS 36			★ *BIGGEST MOVER* ★ 41 to 22		
Every Breath You Take ....*The Police*			Wanna Be Startin' Somethin' ......*Michael Jackson*		

TW	LW	WK	Billboard®	JUNE 11, 1983	HOT 100®
❶	1	11	**Flashdance...What A Feeling** ....*Irene Cara* . . . Casablanca 811440		
②	2	12	Let's Dance ....*David Bowie* . . . EMI America 8158		
❸	4	9	Time (Clock Of The Heart).....................*Culture Club* . . . Epic/Virgin 03796		
④	3	10	Overkill ....*Men At Work* . . . Columbia 03795		
❺	7	10	**My Love**..*Lionel Richie* . . . Motown 1677		
⑥	6	16	Beat It...*Michael Jackson* . . . Epic 03759		
⑦	5	17	She Blinded Me With Science....................*Thomas Dolby* . . . Capitol 5204		
⑧	12	14	**Always Something There To Remind Me** ....*Naked Eyes* . . . EMI America 8155		
❾	14	7	**Don't Let It End** ....*Styx* . . . A&M 2543		
❿	11	9	Affair Of The Heart ....*Rick Springfield* . . . RCA 13497		
★ *HIGHEST DEBUT* ★ POS 60			★ *BIGGEST MOVER* ★ 70 to 52		
Hot Girls In Love ....*Loverboy*			1999...*Prince*		

TW	LW	WK	Billboard®	JUNE 18, 1983	HOT 100®
❶	1	12	**Flashdance...What A Feeling** ....*Irene Cara* . . . Casablanca 811440		
❷	3	10	**Time (Clock Of The Heart)** ....*Culture Club* . . . Epic/Virgin 03796		
❸	2	13	Let's Dance ....*David Bowie* . . . EMI America 8158		
❹	11	10	Electric Avenue ....*Eddy Grant* . . . Portrait 03793		
❺	4	11	Overkill ....*Men At Work* . . . Columbia 03795		
❻	5	11	My Love ....*Lionel Richie* . . . Motown 1677		
❼	9	8	Don't Let It End ....*Styx* . . . A&M 2543		
❽	8	15	**Always Something There To Remind Me** ....*Naked Eyes* . . . EMI America 8155		
❾	10	10	**Affair Of The Heart**...............................*Rick Springfield* . . . RCA 13497		
❿	13	8	Family Man.............................*Daryl Hall & John Oates* . . . RCA 13507		
★ *HIGHEST DEBUT* ★ POS 59			★ *BIGGEST MOVER* ★ 69 to 52		
Take Me To Heart ....*Quarterflash*			Cuts Like A Knife ....*Bryan Adams*		

Billboard — HOT 100 — JUNE 25, 1983

TW	LW	WK	Title	Artist ... Label
❶	1	13	Flashdance...What A Feeling	Irene Cara ... Casablanca 811440
❷	2	11	Time (Clock Of The Heart)	Culture Club ... Epic/Virgin 03796
❸	4	11	Electric Avenue	Eddy Grant ... Portrait 03793
❹	14	4	Every Breath You Take	The Police ... A&M 2542
❺	3	14	Let's Dance	David Bowie ... EMI America 8158
❻	10	9	Family Man	Daryl Hall & John Oates ... RCA 13507
❼	7	9	Don't Let It End	Styx ... A&M 2543
❽	13	11	Never Gonna Let You Go	Sergio Mendes ... A&M 2540
❾	9	11	Affair Of The Heart	Rick Springfield ... RCA 13497
❿	15	10	Too Shy	Kajagoogoo ... EMI America 8161

★ **HIGHEST DEBUT** ★ POS 57
Rock 'N' Roll Is King ....ELO

★ **BIGGEST MOVER** ★ 59 to 43
Take Me To Heart ....Quarterflash

Billboard — HOT 100 — JULY 2, 1983

TW	LW	WK	Title	Artist ... Label
❶	1	14	Flashdance...What A Feeling	Irene Cara ... Casablanca 811440
❷	3	12	Electric Avenue	Eddy Grant ... Portrait 03793
❸	4	5	Every Breath You Take	The Police ... A&M 2542
④	2	12	Time (Clock Of The Heart)	Culture Club ... Epic/Virgin 03796
❺	8	12	Never Gonna Let You Go	Sergio Mendes ... A&M 2540
❻	7	10	Don't Let It End	Styx ... A&M 2543
❼	10	11	Too Shy	Kajagoogoo ... EMI America 8161
⑧	6	10	Family Man	Daryl Hall & John Oates ... RCA 13507
❾	15	6	Wanna Be Startin' Somethin'	Michael Jackson ... Epic 03914
❿	14	13	She's A Beauty	The Tubes ... Capitol 5217

★ **HIGHEST DEBUT** ★ POS 42
It's A Mistake ....Men At Work

★ **BIGGEST MOVER** ★ 70 to 56
War Games ....Crosby, Stills & Nash

Billboard — HOT 100 — JULY 9, 1983

TW	LW	WK	Title	Artist ... Label
❶	3	6	Every Breath You Take	The Police ... A&M 2542
❷	2	13	Electric Avenue	Eddy Grant ... Portrait 03793
③	1	15	Flashdance...What A Feeling	Irene Cara ... Casablanca 811440
❹	5	13	Never Gonna Let You Go	Sergio Mendes ... A&M 2540
❺	7	12	Too Shy	Kajagoogoo ... EMI America 8161
❻	9	7	Wanna Be Startin' Somethin'	Michael Jackson ... Epic 03914
⑦	4	13	Time (Clock Of The Heart)	Culture Club ... Epic/Virgin 03796
❽	11	10	Come Dancing	The Kinks ... Arista 1054
❾	6	11	Don't Let It End	Styx ... A&M 2543
❿	13	10	Our House	Madness ... Geffen 29668

★ **HIGHEST DEBUT** ★ POS 59
Lawyers In Love ....Jackson Browne

★ **BIGGEST MOVER** ★ 64 to 48
I'll Tumble 4 Ya ....Culture Club

Billboard — JULY 16, 1983 — HOT 100

TW	LW	WK	Title	Artist	Label
1	1	7	Every Breath You Take	The Police	A&M 2542
2	2	14	Electric Avenue	Eddy Grant	Portrait 03793
3	3	16	Flashdance...What A Feeling	Irene Cara	Casablanca 811440
4	4	14	Never Gonna Let You Go	Sergio Mendes	A&M 2540
5	6	8	Wanna Be Startin' Somethin'	Michael Jackson	Epic 03914
6	8	11	Come Dancing	The Kinks	Arista 1054
7	5	13	Too Shy	Kajagoogoo	EMI America 8161
8	10	11	Our House	Madness	Geffen 29668
9	13	7	Is There Something I Should Know	Duran Duran	Capitol 5233
10	7	14	Time (Clock Of The Heart)	Culture Club	Epic/Virgin 03796

★ **HIGHEST DEBUT** ★ POS 71
Promises, Promises ....Naked Eyes

★ **BIGGEST MOVER** ★ 59 to 40
Lawyers In Love ....Jackson Browne

Billboard — JULY 23, 1983 — HOT 100

TW	LW	WK	Title	Artist	Label
1	1	8	Every Breath You Take	The Police	A&M 2542
2	2	15	Electric Avenue	Eddy Grant	Portrait 03793
3	3	17	Flashdance...What A Feeling	Irene Cara	Casablanca 811440
4	4	15	Never Gonna Let You Go	Sergio Mendes	A&M 2540
5	5	9	Wanna Be Startin' Somethin'	Michael Jackson	Epic 03914
6	6	12	Come Dancing	The Kinks	Arista 1054
7	8	12	Our House	Madness	Geffen 29668
8	9	8	Is There Something I Should Know	Duran Duran	Capitol 5233
9	11	8	Stand Back	Stevie Nicks	Modern 99863
10	14	9	She Works Hard For The Money	Donna Summer	Mercury 812370

★ **HIGHEST DEBUT** ★ POS 48
Human Nature ....Michael Jackson

★ **BIGGEST MOVER** ★ 62 to 42
The Safety Dance ....Men Without Hats

Billboard — JULY 30, 1983 — HOT 100

TW	LW	WK	Title	Artist	Label
1	1	9	Every Breath You Take	The Police	A&M 2542
2	2	16	Electric Avenue	Eddy Grant	Portrait 03793
3	3	18	Flashdance...What A Feeling	Irene Cara	Casablanca 811440
4	4	16	Never Gonna Let You Go	Sergio Mendes	A&M 2540
5	8	9	Is There Something I Should Know	Duran Duran	Capitol 5233
6	11	12	Sweet Dreams (Are Made of This)	Eurythmics	RCA 13533
7	5	10	Wanna Be Startin' Somethin'	Michael Jackson	Epic 03914
8	10	10	She Works Hard For The Money	Donna Summer	Mercury 812370
9	9	9	Stand Back	Stevie Nicks	Modern 99863
10	7	13	Our House	Madness	Geffen 29668

★ **HIGHEST DEBUT** ★ POS 38
Tell Her About It ....Billy Joel

★ **BIGGEST MOVER** ★ 87 to 68
Lady Love Me (One More Time)..............George Benson

Billboard — AUGUST 6, 1983 — HOT 100

TW	LW	WK	Title	Artist	Label
1	1	10	Every Breath You Take	The Police	A&M 2542
2	6	13	Sweet Dreams (Are Made of This)	Eurythmics	RCA 13533
3	8	11	She Works Hard For The Money	Donna Summer	Mercury 812370
4	5	10	Is There Something I Should Know	Duran Duran	Capitol 5233
5	3	19	Flashdance...What A Feeling	Irene Cara	Casablanca 811440
6	2	17	Electric Avenue	Eddy Grant	Portrait 03793
7	11	10	Maniac	Michael Sembello	Casablanca 812516
8	4	17	Never Gonna Let You Go	Sergio Mendes	A&M 2540
9	9	10	Stand Back	Stevie Nicks	Modern 99863
10	7	11	Wanna Be Startin' Somethin'	Michael Jackson	Epic 03914

★ HIGHEST DEBUT ★ POS 51
(She's) Sexy + 17 .... Stray Cats

★ BIGGEST MOVER ★ 69 to 49
Far From Over .... Frank Stallone

Billboard — AUGUST 13, 1983 — HOT 100

TW	LW	WK	Title	Artist	Label
1	1	11	Every Breath You Take	The Police	A&M 2542
2	2	14	Sweet Dreams (Are Made of This)	Eurythmics	RCA 13533
3	3	12	She Works Hard For The Money	Donna Summer	Mercury 812370
4	7	11	Maniac	Michael Sembello	Casablanca 812516
5	4	11	Is There Something I Should Know	Duran Duran	Capitol 5233
6	9	11	Stand Back	Stevie Nicks	Modern 99863
7	5	20	Flashdance...What A Feeling	Irene Cara	Casablanca 811440
8	11	7	It's A Mistake	Men At Work	Columbia 03959
9	8	18	Never Gonna Let You Go	Sergio Mendes	A&M 2540
10	13	12	(Keep Feeling) Fascination	The Human League	A&M 2547

★ HIGHEST DEBUT ★ POS 65
Tell Her No .... Juice Newton

★ BIGGEST MOVER ★ 86 to 69
Big Log .... Robert Plant

Billboard — AUGUST 20, 1983 — HOT 100

TW	LW	WK	Title	Artist	Label
1	1	12	Every Breath You Take	The Police	A&M 2542
2	2	15	Sweet Dreams (Are Made of This)	Eurythmics	RCA 13533
3	3	13	She Works Hard For The Money	Donna Summer	Mercury 812370
4	4	12	Maniac	Michael Sembello	Casablanca 812516
5	6	12	Stand Back	Stevie Nicks	Modern 99863
6	8	8	It's A Mistake	Men At Work	Columbia 03959
7	5	12	Is There Something I Should Know	Duran Duran	Capitol 5233
8	10	13	(Keep Feeling) Fascination	The Human League	A&M 2547
9	12	9	Puttin' On The Ritz	Taco	RCA 13574
10	15	8	I'll Tumble 4 Ya	Culture Club	Epic/Virgin 03912

★ HIGHEST DEBUT ★ POS 67
Telefone (Long Distance Love Affair) ..... Sheena Easton

★ BIGGEST MOVER ★ 84 to 62
How Can I Refuse .... Heart

Billboard — AUGUST 27, 1983 — HOT 100

TW	LW	WK	Title	Artist	Label
1	1	13	**Every Breath You Take**	The Police	A&M 2542
2	2	16	**Sweet Dreams (Are Made of This)**	Eurythmics	RCA 13533
3	4	13	**Maniac**	Michael Sembello	Casablanca 812516
4	3	14	**She Works Hard For The Money**	Donna Summer	Mercury 812370
5	9	10	**Puttin' On The Ritz**	Taco	RCA 13574
6	6	9	**It's A Mistake**	Men At Work	Columbia 03959
7	5	13	**Stand Back**	Stevie Nicks	Modern 99863
8	8	14	**(Keep Feeling) Fascination**	The Human League	A&M 2547
9	10	9	**I'll Tumble 4 Ya**	Culture Club	Epic/Virgin 03912
10	12	13	**China Girl**	David Bowie	EMI America 8165

★ **HIGHEST DEBUT** ★ POS 37
King Of Pain .... The Police

★ **BIGGEST MOVER** ★ 67 to 52
Telefone (Long Distance Love Affair) ..... Sheena Easton

Billboard — SEPTEMBER 3, 1983 — HOT 100

TW	LW	WK	Title	Artist	Label
1	2	17	**Sweet Dreams (Are Made of This)**	Eurythmics	RCA 13533
2	3	14	**Maniac**	Michael Sembello	Casablanca 812516
3	1	14	**Every Breath You Take**	The Police	A&M 2542
4	5	11	**Puttin' On The Ritz**	Taco	RCA 13574
5	4	15	**She Works Hard For The Money**	Donna Summer	Mercury 812370
6	11	11	**The Safety Dance**	Men Without Hats	Backstreet 52232
7	12	6	**Tell Her About It**	Billy Joel	Columbia 04012
8	6	10	**It's A Mistake**	Men At Work	Columbia 03959
9	9	10	**I'll Tumble 4 Ya**	Culture Club	Epic/Virgin 03912
10	13	7	**Human Nature**	Michael Jackson	Epic 04026

★ **HIGHEST DEBUT** ★ POS 56
Sitting At The Wheel .... The Moody Blues

★ **BIGGEST MOVER** ★ 70 to 48
It Must Be Love .... Madness

Billboard — SEPTEMBER 10, 1983 — HOT 100

TW	LW	WK	Title	Artist	Label
1	2	15	**Maniac**	Michael Sembello	Casablanca 812516
2	1	18	**Sweet Dreams (Are Made of This)**	Eurythmics	RCA 13533
3	6	12	**The Safety Dance**	Men Without Hats	Backstreet 52232
4	4	12	**Puttin' On The Ritz**	Taco	RCA 13574
5	7	7	**Tell Her About It**	Billy Joel	Columbia 04012
6	3	15	**Every Breath You Take**	The Police	A&M 2542
7	5	16	**She Works Hard For The Money**	Donna Summer	Mercury 812370
8	15	9	**Total Eclipse Of The Heart**	Bonnie Tyler	Columbia 03906
9	10	8	**Human Nature**	Michael Jackson	Epic 04026
10	9	11	**I'll Tumble 4 Ya**	Culture Club	Epic/Virgin 03912

★ **HIGHEST DEBUT** ★ POS 61
If Anyone Falls .... Stevie Nicks

★ **BIGGEST MOVER** ★ 83 to 59
This Time .... Bryan Adams

TW	LW	WK	Billboard	SEPTEMBER 17, 1983	HOT 100.
❶	1	16	Maniac..*Michael Sembello* . . . Casablanca 812516		
❷	5	8	Tell Her About It...*Billy Joel* . . . Columbia 04012		
❸	3	13	The Safety Dance ....*Men Without Hats* . . . Backstreet 52232		
❹	8	10	Total Eclipse Of The Heart........................*Bonnie Tyler* . . . Columbia 03906		
❺	2	19	Sweet Dreams (Are Made of This)...................*Eurythmics* . . . RCA 13533		
❻	6	16	Every Breath You Take ....*The Police* . . . A&M 2542		
❼	9	9	Human Nature ....*Michael Jackson* . . . Epic 04026		
❽	4	13	Puttin' On The Ritz ....*Taco* . . . RCA 13574		
❾	15	8	Making Love Out Of Nothing At All ....*Air Supply* . . . Arista 9056		
❿	11	8	Don't Cry...*Asia* . . . Geffen 29571		

★ HIGHEST DEBUT ★ POS 62	★ BIGGEST MOVER ★ 55 to 37
All Night Long (All Night).................*Lionel Richie*	Delirious ....*Prince*

TW	LW	WK	Billboard	SEPTEMBER 24, 1983	HOT 100.
❶	2	9	Tell Her About It ....*Billy Joel* . . . Columbia 04012		
❷	4	11	Total Eclipse Of The Heart........................*Bonnie Tyler* . . . Columbia 03906		
❸	3	14	The Safety Dance ....*Men Without Hats* . . . Backstreet 52232		
❹	1	17	Maniac ....*Michael Sembello* . . . Casablanca 812516		
❺	9	9	Making Love Out Of Nothing At All ....*Air Supply* . . . Arista 9056		
❻	5	20	Sweet Dreams (Are Made of This)...................*Eurythmics* . . . RCA 13533		
❼	7	10	Human Nature ....*Michael Jackson* . . . Epic 04026		
❽	8	14	Puttin' On The Ritz ....*Taco* . . . RCA 13574		
❾	12	8	(She's) Sexy + 17 ....*Stray Cats* . . . EMI America 8168		
❿	10	9	Don't Cry...*Asia* . . . Geffen 29571		

★ HIGHEST DEBUT ★ POS 70	★ BIGGEST MOVER ★ 72 to 51
Uptown Girl...*Billy Joel*	Modern Love...................................*David Bowie*

TW	LW	WK	Billboard	OCTOBER 1, 1983	HOT 100.
❶	2	12	Total Eclipse Of The Heart.................*Bonnie Tyler* . . . Columbia 03906		
②	1	10	Tell Her About It..*Billy Joel* . . . Columbia 04012		
③	3	15	The Safety Dance ....*Men Without Hats* . . . Backstreet 52232		
④	5	10	Making Love Out Of Nothing At All ....*Air Supply* . . . Arista 9056		
⑤	9	9	(She's) Sexy + 17 ....*Stray Cats* . . . EMI America 8168		
⑥	11	6	King Of Pain...*The Police* . . . A&M 2569		
⑦	13	9	True ....*Spandau Ballet* . . . Chrysalis 42720		
⑧	4	18	Maniac ....*Michael Sembello* . . . Casablanca 812516		
⑨	17	6	Islands In The Stream ....*Kenny Rogers & Dolly Parton* . . . RCA 13615		
⑩	12	10	Far From Over.....................................*Frank Stallone* . . . RSO 815023		

★ HIGHEST DEBUT ★ POS 72	★ BIGGEST MOVER ★ 87 to 67
My Town ....*Michael Stanley Band*	Send Her My Love ....*Journey*

TW	LW	WK	Billboard. OCTOBER 8, 1983 HOT 100.
❶	1	13	**Total Eclipse Of The Heart**...............*Bonnie Tyler* . . . Columbia 03906
❷	4	11	**Making Love Out Of Nothing At All** ....*Air Supply* . . . Arista 9056
❸	6	7	**King Of Pain** ....*The Police* . . . A&M 2569
❹	7	10	**True**...................................*Spandau Ballet* . . . Chrysalis 42720
⑤	5	10	**(She's) Sexy + 17** ....*Stray Cats* . . . EMI America 8168
❻	9	8	**Islands In The Stream** ....*Kenny Rogers & Dolly Parton* . . . RCA 13615
⑦	2	11	**Tell Her About It**....................................*Billy Joel* . . . Columbia 04012
⑧	3	16	**The Safety Dance** ....*Men Without Hats* . . . Backstreet 52232
❾	17	7	**One Thing Leads To Another**...................*The Fixx* . . . MCA 52264
⑩	10	11	**Far From Over**............................*Frank Stallone* . . . RSO 815023

★ HIGHEST DEBUT ★ POS 75	★ BIGGEST MOVER ★ 51 to 32
P.Y.T. (Pretty Young Thing) ....*Michael Jackson*	Uptown Girl...*Billy Joel*

TW	LW	WK	Billboard. OCTOBER 15, 1983 HOT 100.
❶	1	14	**Total Eclipse Of The Heart**...............*Bonnie Tyler* . . . Columbia 03906
❷	2	12	**Making Love Out Of Nothing At All** ....*Air Supply* . . . Arista 9056
❸	3	8	**King Of Pain** ....*The Police* . . . A&M 2569
❹	4	11	**True** ....*Spandau Ballet* . . . Chrysalis 42720
❺	6	8	**Islands In The Stream** ....*Kenny Rogers & Dolly Parton* . . . RCA 13615
❻	9	8	**One Thing Leads To Another**...................*The Fixx* . . . MCA 52264
❼	14	5	**All Night Long (All Night)** ....*Lionel Richie* . . . Motown 1698
⑧	8	17	**The Safety Dance** ....*Men Without Hats* . . . Backstreet 52232
⑨	7	12	**Tell Her About It**....................................*Billy Joel* . . . Columbia 04012
⑩	5	11	**(She's) Sexy + 17** ....*Stray Cats* . . . EMI America 8168

★ HIGHEST DEBUT ★ POS 26	★ BIGGEST MOVER ★ 53 to 31
Say Say Say ......*Paul McCartney & Michael Jackson*	Cum On Feel The Noize ....*Quiet Riot*

TW	LW	WK	Billboard. OCTOBER 22, 1983 HOT 100.
❶	1	15	**Total Eclipse Of The Heart**...............*Bonnie Tyler* . . . Columbia 03906
❷	2	13	**Making Love Out Of Nothing At All** ....*Air Supply* . . . Arista 9056
❸	5	9	**Islands In The Stream** ....*Kenny Rogers & Dolly Parton* . . . RCA 13615
❹	4	12	**True** ....*Spandau Ballet* . . . Chrysalis 42720
❺	7	6	**All Night Long (All Night)** ....*Lionel Richie* . . . Motown 1698
❻	6	9	**One Thing Leads To Another**...................*The Fixx* . . . MCA 52264
⑦	3	9	**King Of Pain**...*The Police* . . . A&M 2569
⑧	13	8	**Delirious** ....*Prince* . . . Warner 29503
⑨	12	13	**Burning Down The House**......................*Talking Heads* . . . Sire 29565
⑩	11	10	**Telefone (Long Distance Love Affair)**...........................*Sheena Easton* . . . EMI America 8172

★ HIGHEST DEBUT ★ POS 54	★ BIGGEST MOVER ★ 55 to 32
Church Of The Poison Mind ....*Culture Club*	P.Y.T. (Pretty Young Thing) ....*Michael Jackson*

Billboard 🔴 OCTOBER 29, 1983 🔴 HOT 100

TW	LW	WK	Title	Artist
❶	3	10	Islands In The Stream........*Kenny Rogers & Dolly Parton* ... RCA 13615	
②	1	16	Total Eclipse Of The Heart.....................*Bonnie Tyler* ... Columbia 03906	
❸	5	7	All Night Long (All Night) ....*Lionel Richie* ... Motown 1698	
④	4	13	True ....*Spandau Ballet* ... Chrysalis 42720	
❺	6	10	One Thing Leads To Another.................................*The Fixx* ... MCA 52264	
⑥	2	14	Making Love Out Of Nothing At All ....*Air Supply* ... Arista 9056	
⑦	7	10	King Of Pain...*The Police* ... A&M 2569	
⑧	8	9	Delirious ....*Prince* ... Warner 29503	
⑨	10	11	Telefone (Long Distance Love Affair) ....*Sheena Easton* ... EMI America 8172	
⑩	15	6	Uptown Girl ....*Billy Joel* ... Columbia 04149	

★ **HIGHEST DEBUT** ★ POS 30
Say It Isn't So......................*Daryl Hall-John Oates*

★ **BIGGEST MOVER** ★ 73 to 51
In A Big Country...........................*Big Country*

Billboard 🔴 NOVEMBER 5, 1983 🔴 HOT 100

TW	LW	WK	Title	Artist
❶	1	11	Islands In The Stream........*Kenny Rogers & Dolly Parton* ... RCA 13615	
❷	3	8	All Night Long (All Night) ....*Lionel Richie* ... Motown 1698	
③	2	17	Total Eclipse Of The Heart.....................*Bonnie Tyler* ... Columbia 03906	
❹	5	11	One Thing Leads To Another ....*The Fixx* ... MCA 52264	
❺	10	7	Uptown Girl ....*Billy Joel* ... Columbia 04149	
⑥	11	4	Say Say Say ....*Paul McCartney & Michael Jackson* ... Columbia 04168	
⑦	6	15	Making Love Out Of Nothing At All ....*Air Supply* ... Arista 9056	
⑧	8	10	Delirious ....*Prince* ... Warner 29503	
⑨	9	12	Telefone (Long Distance Love Affair) ....*Sheena Easton* ... EMI America 8172	
⑩	4	14	True ....*Spandau Ballet* ... Chrysalis 42720	

★ **HIGHEST DEBUT** ★ POS 49
Twist Of Fate........................*Olivia Newton-John*

★ **BIGGEST MOVER** ★ 40 to 26
Church Of The Poison Mind ....*Culture Club*

Billboard 🔴 NOVEMBER 12, 1983 🔴 HOT 100

TW	LW	WK	Title	Artist
❶	2	9	All Night Long (All Night) ....*Lionel Richie* ... Motown 1698	
②	1	12	Islands In The Stream ....*Kenny Rogers & Dolly Parton* ... RCA 13615	
❸	5	8	Uptown Girl..*Billy Joel* ... Columbia 04149	
❹	6	5	Say Say Say ....*Paul McCartney & Michael Jackson* ... Columbia 04168	
⑤	3	18	Total Eclipse Of The Heart.....................*Bonnie Tyler* ... Columbia 03906	
⑥	4	12	One Thing Leads To Another.............................*The Fixx* ... MCA 52264	
❼	12	9	Cum On Feel The Noize ....*Quiet Riot* ... Pasha 04005	
⑧	8	11	Delirious ....*Prince* ... Warner 29503	
⑨	7	16	Making Love Out Of Nothing At All ....*Air Supply* ... Arista 9056	
⑩	11	11	Suddenly Last Summer ....*The Motels* ... Capitol 5271	

★ **HIGHEST DEBUT** ★ POS 48
Undercover Of The Night..............*Rolling Stones*

★ **BIGGEST MOVER** ★ 59 to 42
Union Of The Snake ....*Duran Duran*

Billboard — NOVEMBER 19, 1983 — HOT 100

TW	LW	WK	Title	Artist	Label
1	1	10	All Night Long (All Night)	Lionel Richie	Motown 1698
2	4	6	Say Say Say	Paul McCartney & Michael Jackson	Columbia 04168
3	3	9	Uptown Girl	Billy Joel	Columbia 04149
4	2	13	Islands In The Stream	Kenny Rogers & Dolly Parton	RCA 13615
5	7	10	Cum On Feel The Noize	Quiet Riot	Pasha 04005
6	5	19	Total Eclipse Of The Heart	Bonnie Tyler	Columbia 03906
7	13	9	Love Is A Battlefield	Pat Benatar	Chrysalis 42732
8	6	13	One Thing Leads To Another	The Fixx	MCA 52264
9	10	12	Suddenly Last Summer	The Motels	Capitol 5271
10	17	4	Say It Isn't So	Daryl Hall-John Oates	RCA 13654

★ HIGHEST DEBUT ★ POS 53
Read 'Em And Weep .... Barry Manilow

★ BIGGEST MOVER ★ 42 to 24
Union Of The Snake .... Duran Duran

Billboard — NOVEMBER 26, 1983 — HOT 100

TW	LW	WK	Title	Artist	Label
1	1	11	All Night Long (All Night)	Lionel Richie	Motown 1698
2	2	7	Say Say Say	Paul McCartney & Michael Jackson	Columbia 04168
3	3	10	Uptown Girl	Billy Joel	Columbia 04149
4	4	14	Islands In The Stream	Kenny Rogers & Dolly Parton	RCA 13615
5	5	11	Cum On Feel The Noize	Quiet Riot	Pasha 04005
6	7	10	Love Is A Battlefield	Pat Benatar	Chrysalis 42732
7	10	5	Say It Isn't So	Daryl Hall-John Oates	RCA 13654
8	12	12	Heart And Soul	Huey Lewis & The News	Chrysalis 42726
9	14	7	Crumblin' Down	John Cougar Mellencamp	Riva 214
10	13	8	P.Y.T. (Pretty Young Thing)	Michael Jackson	Epic 04165

★ HIGHEST DEBUT ★ POS 57
Running With The Night .... Lionel Richie

★ BIGGEST MOVER ★ 88 to 67
In The Mood .... Robert Plant

Billboard — DECEMBER 3, 1983 — HOT 100

TW	LW	WK	Title	Artist	Label
1	1	12	All Night Long (All Night)	Lionel Richie	Motown 1698
2	2	8	Say Say Say	Paul McCartney & Michael Jackson	Columbia 04168
3	3	11	Uptown Girl	Billy Joel	Columbia 04149
4	4	15	Islands In The Stream	Kenny Rogers & Dolly Parton	RCA 13615
5	7	6	Say It Isn't So	Daryl Hall-John Oates	RCA 13654
6	6	11	Love Is A Battlefield	Pat Benatar	Chrysalis 42732
7	5	12	Cum On Feel The Noize	Quiet Riot	Pasha 04005
8	8	13	Heart And Soul	Huey Lewis & The News	Chrysalis 42726
9	9	8	Crumblin' Down	John Cougar Mellencamp	Riva 214
10	11	7	Church Of The Poison Mind	Culture Club	Epic/Virgin 04144

★ HIGHEST DEBUT ★ POS 52
Karma Chameleon .... Culture Club

★ BIGGEST MOVER ★ 57 to 35
Running With The Night .... Lionel Richie

TW	LW	WK	Billboard.	DECEMBER 10, 1983	HOT 100.
①	2	9	**Say Say Say**...........*Paul McCartney & Michael Jackson* . . . Columbia 04168
②	1	13	**All Night Long (All Night)** ....*Lionel Richie* . . . Motown 1698
③	3	12	**Uptown Girl**...*Billy Joel* . . . Columbia 04149
④	5	7	**Say It Isn't So** ....*Daryl Hall-John Oates* . . . RCA 13654
⑤	6	12	**Love Is A Battlefield** ....*Pat Benatar* . . . Chrysalis 42732
⑥	4	16	**Islands In The Stream** ....*Kenny Rogers & Dolly Parton* . . . RCA 13615
⑦	11	6	**Union Of The Snake** ....*Duran Duran* . . . Capitol 5290
⑧	7	13	**Cum On Feel The Noize** ....*Quiet Riot* . . . Pasha 04005
⑨	9	9	**Crumblin' Down** ....*John Cougar Mellencamp* . . . Riva 214
⑩	10	8	**Church Of The Poison Mind**.............*Culture Club* . . . Epic/Virgin 04144

★ HIGHEST DEBUT ★ POS 45	★ BIGGEST MOVER ★ 84 to 63
Pink Houses ....*John Cougar Mellencamp*	The Curly Shuffle.................*Jump 'n The Saddle*

TW	LW	WK	Billboard.	DECEMBER 17, 1983	HOT 100.
①	1	10	**Say Say Say**...........*Paul McCartney & Michael Jackson* . . . Columbia 04168
②	4	8	**Say It Isn't So** ....*Daryl Hall-John Oates* . . . RCA 13654
③	2	14	**All Night Long (All Night)** ....*Lionel Richie* . . . Motown 1698
④	3	13	**Uptown Girl** ....*Billy Joel* . . . Columbia 04149
⑤	7	7	**Union Of The Snake** ....*Duran Duran* . . . Capitol 5290
⑥	5	13	**Love Is A Battlefield**.............................*Pat Benatar* . . . Chrysalis 42732
⑦	11	7	**Owner Of A Lonely Heart** ....*Yes* . . . Atco 99817
⑧	6	17	**Islands In The Stream** ....*Kenny Rogers & Dolly Parton* . . . RCA 13615
⑨	12	7	**Twist Of Fate** ....*Olivia Newton-John* . . . MCA 52284
⑩	10	9	**Church Of The Poison Mind** ....*Culture Club* . . . Epic/Virgin 04144

★ HIGHEST DEBUT ★ POS 50	★ BIGGEST MOVER ★ 67 to 47
Middle Of The Road ....*The Pretenders*	Think Of Laura ....*Christopher Cross*

TW	LW	WK	Billboard.	DECEMBER 24, 1983	HOT 100.
①	1	11	**Say Say Say**...........*Paul McCartney & Michael Jackson* . . . Columbia 04168
②	2	9	**Say It Isn't So** ....*Daryl Hall-John Oates* . . . RCA 13654
③	5	8	**Union Of The Snake** ....*Duran Duran* . . . Capitol 5290
④	7	8	**Owner Of A Lonely Heart** ....*Yes* . . . Atco 99817
⑤	3	15	**All Night Long (All Night)** ....*Lionel Richie* . . . Motown 1698
⑥	4	14	**Uptown Girl** ....*Billy Joel* . . . Columbia 04149
⑦	6	14	**Love Is A Battlefield** ....*Pat Benatar* . . . Chrysalis 42732
⑧	9	8	**Twist Of Fate** ....*Olivia Newton-John* . . . MCA 52284
⑨	11	7	**Undercover Of The Night** ....*Rolling Stones* . . . Rolling Stones 99813
⑩	18	15	**Break My Stride**.................................*Matthew Wilder* . . . Private I 04113

★ HIGHEST DEBUT ★ POS 49	★ BIGGEST MOVER ★ 73 to 50
So Bad.................................*Paul McCartney*	Yah Mo B There...........*James Ingram with Michael McDonald*

JANUARY 7, 1984 — Billboard HOT 100

TW	LW	WK	Title	Artist	Label
❶	1	13	**Say Say Say**	*Paul McCartney & Michael Jackson*	Columbia 04168
❷	2	11	**Say It Isn't So**	*Daryl Hall-John Oates*	RCA 13654
❸	3	10	**Union Of The Snake**	*Duran Duran*	Capitol 5290
❹	4	10	**Owner Of A Lonely Heart**	*Yes*	Atco 99817
❺	8	10	**Twist Of Fate**	*Olivia Newton-John*	MCA 52284
❻	12	14	**Talking In Your Sleep**	*The Romantics*	Nemperor 04135
❼	10	17	**Break My Stride**	*Matthew Wilder*	Private I 04113
❽	11	11	**I Guess That's Why They Call It The Blues**	*Elton John*	Geffen 29460
❾	9	9	**Undercover Of The Night**	*Rolling Stones*	Rolling Stones 99813
❿	5	17	**All Night Long (All Night)**	*Lionel Richie*	Motown 1698

★ **HIGHEST DEBUT** ★ POS 61
Wrapped Around Your Finger ....*The Police*

★ **BIGGEST MOVER** ★ 49 to 34
So Bad ....*Paul McCartney*

JANUARY 14, 1984 — Billboard HOT 100

TW	LW	WK	Title	Artist	Label
❶	1	14	**Say Say Say**	*Paul McCartney & Michael Jackson*	Columbia 04168
❷	4	11	**Owner Of A Lonely Heart**	*Yes*	Atco 99817
③	2	12	**Say It Isn't So**	*Daryl Hall-John Oates*	RCA 13654
④	3	11	**Union Of The Snake**	*Duran Duran*	Capitol 5290
❺	5	11	**Twist Of Fate**	*Olivia Newton-John*	MCA 52284
❻	6	15	**Talking In Your Sleep**	*The Romantics*	Nemperor 04135
❼	7	18	**Break My Stride**	*Matthew Wilder*	Private I 04113
❽	8	12	**I Guess That's Why They Call It The Blues**	*Elton John*	Geffen 29460
❾	13	7	**Karma Chameleon**	*Culture Club*	Epic/Virgin 04221
❿	15	8	**Running With The Night**	*Lionel Richie*	Motown 1710

★ **HIGHEST DEBUT** ★ POS 47
Jump ....*Van Halen*

★ **BIGGEST MOVER** ★ 61 to 44
Wrapped Around Your Finger ....*The Police*

JANUARY 21, 1984 — Billboard HOT 100

TW	LW	WK	Title	Artist	Label
❶	2	12	**Owner Of A Lonely Heart**	*Yes*	Atco 99817
②	1	15	**Say Say Say**	*Paul McCartney & Michael Jackson*	Columbia 04168
❸	9	8	**Karma Chameleon**	*Culture Club*	Epic/Virgin 04221
❹	6	16	**Talking In Your Sleep**	*The Romantics*	Nemperor 04135
❺	7	19	**Break My Stride**	*Matthew Wilder*	Private I 04113
❻	8	13	**I Guess That's Why They Call It The Blues**	*Elton John*	Geffen 29460
⑦	5	12	**Twist Of Fate**	*Olivia Newton-John*	MCA 52284
❽	13	12	**Joanna**	*Kool & The Gang*	De-Lite 829
❾	10	9	**Running With The Night**	*Lionel Richie*	Motown 1710
❿	3	13	**Say It Isn't So**	*Daryl Hall-John Oates*	RCA 13654

★ **HIGHEST DEBUT** ★ POS 36
Nobody Told Me ....*John Lennon*

★ **BIGGEST MOVER** ★ 89 to 70
For A Rocker ....*Jackson Browne*

Billboard — JANUARY 28, 1984 — HOT 100

TW	LW	WK	Title	Artist	Label
①	1	13	**Owner Of A Lonely Heart**	*Yes*	Atco 99817
②	3	9	Karma Chameleon	*Culture Club*	Epic/Virgin 04221
③	4	17	**Talking In Your Sleep**	*The Romantics*	Nemperor 04135
④	6	14	**I Guess That's Why They Call It The Blues**	*Elton John*	Geffen 29460
⑤	5	20	**Break My Stride**	*Matthew Wilder*	Private I 04113
⑥	8	13	**Joanna**	*Kool & The Gang*	De-Lite 829
⑦	2	16	Say Say Say	*Paul McCartney & Michael Jackson*	Columbia 04168
⑧	9	10	**Running With The Night**	*Lionel Richie*	Motown 1710
⑨	7	13	Twist Of Fate	*Olivia Newton-John*	MCA 52284
⑩	12	10	**That's All!**	*Genesis*	Atlantic 89724

★ **HIGHEST DEBUT** ★ POS 44
Got A Hold On Me ....*Christine McVie*

★ **BIGGEST MOVER** ★ 86 to 69
Runner ....*Manfred Mann's Earth Band*

Billboard — FEBRUARY 4, 1984 — HOT 100

TW	LW	WK	Title	Artist	Label
①	2	10	**Karma Chameleon**	*Culture Club*	Epic/Virgin 04221
②	1	14	Owner Of A Lonely Heart	*Yes*	Atco 99817
③	3	18	**Talking In Your Sleep**	*The Romantics*	Nemperor 04135
④	6	14	**Joanna**	*Kool & The Gang*	De-Lite 829
⑤	5	21	**Break My Stride**	*Matthew Wilder*	Private I 04113
⑥	4	15	I Guess That's Why They Call It The Blues	*Elton John*	Geffen 29460
⑦	8	11	**Running With The Night**	*Lionel Richie*	Motown 1710
⑧	10	11	That's All!	*Genesis*	Atlantic 89724
⑨	11	9	**Think Of Laura**	*Christopher Cross*	Warner 29658
⑩	12	9	Pink Houses	*John Cougar Mellencamp*	Riva 215

★ **HIGHEST DEBUT** ★ POS 59
The Language Of Love ....*Dan Fogelberg*

★ **BIGGEST MOVER** ★ 73 to 52
Somebody's Watching Me....................*Rockwell*

Billboard — FEBRUARY 11, 1984 — HOT 100

TW	LW	WK	Title	Artist	Label
①	1	11	**Karma Chameleon**	*Culture Club*	Epic/Virgin 04221
②	4	15	**Joanna**	*Kool & The Gang*	De-Lite 829
③	3	19	**Talking In Your Sleep**	*The Romantics*	Nemperor 04135
④	2	15	Owner Of A Lonely Heart	*Yes*	Atco 99817
⑤	11	5	**Jump**	*Van Halen*	Warner 29384
⑥	8	12	**That's All!**	*Genesis*	Atlantic 89724
⑦	7	12	**Running With The Night**	*Lionel Richie*	Motown 1710
⑧	10	10	**Pink Houses**	*John Cougar Mellencamp*	Riva 215
⑨	9	10	**Think Of Laura**	*Christopher Cross*	Warner 29658
⑩	6	16	I Guess That's Why They Call It The Blues	*Elton John*	Geffen 29460

★ **HIGHEST DEBUT** ★ POS 20
Thriller ....*Michael Jackson*

★ **BIGGEST MOVER** ★ 83 to 59
She Was Hot ....*Rolling Stones*

TW	LW	WK	Billboard.	FEBRUARY 18, 1984	HOT 100.
❶	1	12	**Karma Chameleon**.....................*Culture Club* ... Epic/Virgin 04221
❷	5	6	**Jump**...*Van Halen* ... Warner 29384
③	2	16	**Joanna** ....*Kool & The Gang* ... De-Lite 829
❹	12	11	**99 Luftballons**.......................................*Nena* ... Epic 04108
⑤	3	20	**Talking In Your Sleep**.................*The Romantics* ... Nemperor 04135
⑥	6	13	**That's All!** ....*Genesis* ... Atlantic 89724
❼	20	2	**Thriller** ....*Michael Jackson* ... Epic 04364
⑧	4	16	**Owner Of A Lonely Heart** ....*Yes* ... Atco 99817
⑨	15	10	**Girls Just Want To Have Fun**..............*Cyndi Lauper* ... Portrait 04120
⑩	13	15	**Let The Music Play**............................*Shannon* ... Mirage 99810

★ HIGHEST DEBUT ★ POS 43	★ BIGGEST MOVER ★ 73 to 49
Adult Education ....*Daryl Hall-John Oates*	Hold Me Now....................*Thompson Twins*

TW	LW	WK	Billboard.	FEBRUARY 25, 1984	HOT 100.
❶	2	7	**Jump**..*Van Halen* ... Warner 29384
②	1	13	**Karma Chameleon** ....*Culture Club* ... Epic/Virgin 04221
❸	4	12	**99 Luftballons**..*Nena* ... Epic 04108
❹	9	11	**Girls Just Want To Have Fun**..............*Cyndi Lauper* ... Portrait 04120
⑤	7	3	**Thriller** ....*Michael Jackson* ... Epic 04364
❻	3	17	**Joanna** ....*Kool & The Gang* ... De-Lite 829
❼	12	6	**Nobody Told Me**.......................*John Lennon* ... Polydor 817254
⑧	10	16	**Let The Music Play**............................*Shannon* ... Mirage 99810
⑨	14	8	**Wrapped Around Your Finger** ....*The Police* ... A&M 2614
⑩	13	11	**An Innocent Man** ....*Billy Joel* ... Columbia 04259

★ HIGHEST DEBUT ★ POS 63	★ BIGGEST MOVER ★ 65 to 43
They Don't Know......................*Tracey Ullman*	Radio Ga-Ga...*Queen*

TW	LW	WK	Billboard.	MARCH 3, 1984	HOT 100.
❶	1	8	**Jump**..*Van Halen* ... Warner 29384
❷	3	13	**99 Luftballons** ....*Nena* ... Epic 04108
❸	4	12	**Girls Just Want To Have Fun**..............*Cyndi Lauper* ... Portrait 04120
❹	5	4	**Thriller** ....*Michael Jackson* ... Epic 04364
❺	7	7	**Nobody Told Me**.......................*John Lennon* ... Polydor 817254
⑥	2	14	**Karma Chameleon** ....*Culture Club* ... Epic/Virgin 04221
❼	12	6	**Somebody's Watching Me**..................*Rockwell* ... Motown 1702
❽	9	9	**Wrapped Around Your Finger** ....*The Police* ... A&M 2614
⑨	8	17	**Let The Music Play**............................*Shannon* ... Mirage 99810
⑩	13	8	**I Want A New Drug**.................*Huey Lewis & The News* ... Chrysalis 42766

★ HIGHEST DEBUT ★ POS 40	★ BIGGEST MOVER ★ 75 to 50
Miss Me Blind..............................*Culture Club*	Hello ....*Lionel Richie*

TW	LW	WK	Billboard.	MARCH 10, 1984	HOT 100.
①	1	9	**Jump**..	*Van Halen* ...	Warner 29384
②	3	13	**Girls Just Want To Have Fun**..............	*Cyndi Lauper* ...	Portrait 04120
③	2	14	99 Luftballons..	*Nena* ...	Epic 04108
④	4	5	**Thriller**...	*Michael Jackson* ...	Epic 04364
⑤	7	7	Somebody's Watching Me.........................	*Rockwell* ...	Motown 1702
⑥	5	8	Nobody Told Me......................................	*John Lennon* ...	Polydor 817254
⑦	10	9	I Want A New Drug	*Huey Lewis & The News* ...	Chrysalis 42766
⑧	11	7	Here Comes The Rain Again.....................	*Eurythmics* ...	RCA 13725
⑨	16	7	Footloose...	*Kenny Loggins* ...	Columbia 04310
⑩	6	15	Karma Chameleon	*Culture Club* ...	Epic/Virgin 04221

★ HIGHEST DEBUT ★ POS 49	★ BIGGEST MOVER ★ 79 to 60
Love Somebody.........................*Rick Springfield*	To All The Girls I've Loved Before.............*Julio Iglesias & Willie Nelson*

TW	LW	WK	Billboard.	MARCH 17, 1984	HOT 100.
①	1	10	**Jump**..	*Van Halen* ...	Warner 29384
②	2	14	**Girls Just Want To Have Fun**..............	*Cyndi Lauper* ...	Portrait 04120
③	5	8	Somebody's Watching Me.........................	*Rockwell* ...	Motown 1702
④	3	15	99 Luftballons..	*Nena* ...	Epic 04108
⑤	9	8	Footloose...	*Kenny Loggins* ...	Columbia 04310
⑥	4	6	Thriller...	*Michael Jackson* ...	Epic 04364
⑦	7	10	I Want A New Drug	*Huey Lewis & The News* ...	Chrysalis 42766
⑧	8	8	Here Comes The Rain Again.....................	*Eurythmics* ...	RCA 13725
⑨	6	9	Nobody Told Me......................................	*John Lennon* ...	Polydor 817254
⑩	12	10	**New Moon On Monday**..........................	*Duran Duran* ...	Capitol 5309

★ HIGHEST DEBUT ★ POS 58	★ BIGGEST MOVER ★ 59 to 36
Head Over Heels ....*Go-Go's*	Eat It ....*"Weird Al" Yankovic*

TW	LW	WK	Billboard.	MARCH 24, 1984	HOT 100.
①	1	11	**Jump**..	*Van Halen* ...	Warner 29384
②	3	9	**Somebody's Watching Me**	*Rockwell* ...	Motown 1702
③	2	15	Girls Just Want To Have Fun....................	*Cyndi Lauper* ...	Portrait 04120
④	5	9	**Footloose**	*Kenny Loggins* ...	Columbia 04310
⑤	8	9	Here Comes The Rain Again.....................	*Eurythmics* ...	RCA 13725
⑥	7	11	**I Want A New Drug**	*Huey Lewis & The News* ...	Chrysalis 42766
⑦	4	16	99 Luftballons..	*Nena* ...	Epic 04108
⑧	12	9	**Automatic**...	*Pointer Sisters* ...	Planet 13730
⑨	13	6	**Adult Education**....................	*Daryl Hall-John Oates* ...	RCA 13714
⑩	11	9	**Got A Hold On Me**	*Christine McVie* ...	Warner 29372

★ HIGHEST DEBUT ★ POS 59	★ BIGGEST MOVER ★ 36 to 18
The Longest Time.................................*Billy Joel*	Eat It ....*"Weird Al" Yankovic*

Billboard — MARCH 31, 1984 — HOT 100

TW	LW	WK	Title	Artist	Label
1	4	10	**Footloose**	Kenny Loggins	Columbia 04310
2	2	10	**Somebody's Watching Me**	Rockwell	Motown 1702
3	1	12	Jump	Van Halen	Warner 29384
4	5	10	**Here Comes The Rain Again**	Eurythmics	RCA 13725
5	3	16	Girls Just Want To Have Fun	Cyndi Lauper	Portrait 04120
6	6	12	**I Want A New Drug**	Huey Lewis & The News	Chrysalis 42766
7	12	6	Against All Odds (Take A Look At Me Now)	Phil Collins	Atlantic 89700
8	8	10	**Automatic**	Pointer Sisters	Planet 13730
9	9	7	**Adult Education**	Daryl Hall-John Oates	RCA 13714
10	14	5	Miss Me Blind	Culture Club	Epic/Virgin 04388

★ **HIGHEST DEBUT** ★ POS 71
Give Me Tonight ....Shannon

★ **BIGGEST MOVER** ★ 71 to 49
Breakdance............................Irene Cara

Billboard — APRIL 7, 1984 — HOT 100

TW	LW	WK	Title	Artist	Label
1	1	11	**Footloose**	Kenny Loggins	Columbia 04310
2	2	11	**Somebody's Watching Me**	Rockwell	Motown 1702
3	7	7	**Against All Odds (Take A Look At Me Now)**	Phil Collins	Atlantic 89700
4	4	11	**Here Comes The Rain Again**	Eurythmics	RCA 13725
5	3	13	Jump	Van Halen	Warner 29384
6	8	11	Automatic	Pointer Sisters	Planet 13730
7	10	6	Miss Me Blind	Culture Club	Epic/Virgin 04388
8	9	8	**Adult Education**	Daryl Hall-John Oates	RCA 13714
9	5	17	Girls Just Want To Have Fun	Cyndi Lauper	Portrait 04120
10	13	7	Hello	Lionel Richie	Motown 1722

★ **HIGHEST DEBUT** ★ POS 47
Oh Sherrie ....Steve Perry

★ **BIGGEST MOVER** ★ 76 to 58
Rock You Like A Hurricane ....Scorpions

Billboard — APRIL 14, 1984 — HOT 100

TW	LW	WK	Title	Artist	Label
1	1	12	**Footloose**	Kenny Loggins	Columbia 04310
2	3	8	Against All Odds (Take A Look At Me Now)	Phil Collins	Atlantic 89700
3	2	12	Somebody's Watching Me	Rockwell	Motown 1702
4	10	8	Hello	Lionel Richie	Motown 1722
5	6	12	**Automatic**	Pointer Sisters	Planet 13730
6	7	7	Miss Me Blind	Culture Club	Epic/Virgin 04388
7	4	12	Here Comes The Rain Again	Eurythmics	RCA 13725
8	11	10	Hold Me Now	Thompson Twins	Arista 9164
9	8	9	Adult Education	Daryl Hall-John Oates	RCA 13714
10	5	14	Jump	Van Halen	Warner 29384

★ **HIGHEST DEBUT** ★ POS 44
I'll Wait ....Van Halen

★ **BIGGEST MOVER** ★ 56 to 38
Let's Hear It For The Boy ....Deniece Williams

Billboard — APRIL 21, 1984 — HOT 100

TW	LW	WK	Title	Artist
1	2	9	**Against All Odds (Take A Look At Me Now)**	*Phil Collins* ... Atlantic 89700
2	1	13	Footloose	*Kenny Loggins* ... Columbia 04310
3	4	9	Hello	*Lionel Richie* ... Motown 1722
4	8	11	Hold Me Now	*Thompson Twins* ... Arista 9164
5	6	8	**Miss Me Blind**	*Culture Club* ... Epic/Virgin 04388
6	5	13	Automatic	*Pointer Sisters* ... Planet 13730
7	3	13	Somebody's Watching Me	*Rockwell* ... Motown 1702
8	13	7	Love Somebody	*Rick Springfield* ... RCA 13738
9	7	13	Here Comes The Rain Again	*Eurythmics* ... RCA 13725
10	14	9	They Don't Know	*Tracey Ullman* ... MCA 52347

★ **HIGHEST DEBUT** ★ POS 46
The Reflex ....*Duran Duran*

★ **BIGGEST MOVER** ★ 53 to 36
Time After Time ....*Cyndi Lauper*

Billboard — APRIL 28, 1984 — HOT 100

TW	LW	WK	Title	Artist
1	1	10	**Against All Odds (Take A Look At Me Now)**	*Phil Collins* ... Atlantic 89700
2	3	10	Hello	*Lionel Richie* ... Motown 1722
3	2	14	Footloose	*Kenny Loggins* ... Columbia 04310
4	4	12	Hold Me Now	*Thompson Twins* ... Arista 9164
5	5	9	**Miss Me Blind**	*Culture Club* ... Epic/Virgin 04388
6	8	8	Love Somebody	*Rick Springfield* ... RCA 13738
7	11	8	**You Might Think**	*The Cars* ... Elektra 69744
8	10	10	They Don't Know	*Tracey Ullman* ... MCA 52347
9	6	14	Automatic	*Pointer Sisters* ... Planet 13730
10	13	9	To All The Girls I've Loved Before	*Julio Iglesias & Willie Nelson* ... Columbia 04217

★ **HIGHEST DEBUT** ★ POS 54
Love Will Show Us How ....*Christine McVie*

★ **BIGGEST MOVER** ★ 88 to 67
Dance Hall Days ....*Wang Chung*

Billboard — MAY 5, 1984 — HOT 100

TW	LW	WK	Title	Artist
1	1	11	**Against All Odds (Take A Look At Me Now)**	*Phil Collins* ... Atlantic 89700
2	2	11	Hello	*Lionel Richie* ... Motown 1722
3	4	13	**Hold Me Now**	*Thompson Twins* ... Arista 9164
4	3	15	Footloose	*Kenny Loggins* ... Columbia 04310
5	6	9	**Love Somebody**	*Rick Springfield* ... RCA 13738
6	10	10	To All The Girls I've Loved Before	*Julio Iglesias & Willie Nelson* ... Columbia 04217
7	7	9	**You Might Think**	*The Cars* ... Elektra 69744
8	8	11	**They Don't Know**	*Tracey Ullman* ... MCA 52347
9	12	5	Let's Hear It For The Boy	*Deniece Williams* ... Columbia 04417
10	5	10	Miss Me Blind	*Culture Club* ... Epic/Virgin 04388

★ **HIGHEST DEBUT** ★ POS 49
Stay The Night ....*Chicago*

★ **BIGGEST MOVER** ★ 69 to 55
Whisper To A Scream (Birds Fly) .....*Icicle Works*

Billboard — MAY 12, 1984 — HOT 100

TW	LW	WK	Title	Artist / Label
1	2	12	**Hello**	*Lionel Richie* . . . Motown 1722
2	1	12	**Against All Odds (Take A Look At Me Now)**	*Phil Collins* . . . Atlantic 89700
3	3	14	**Hold Me Now**	*Thompson Twins* . . . Arista 9164
4	9	6	**Let's Hear It For The Boy**	*Deniece Williams* . . . Columbia 04417
5	5	10	**Love Somebody**	*Rick Springfield* . . . RCA 13738
6	6	11	**To All The Girls I've Loved Before**	*Julio Iglesias & Willie Nelson* . . . Columbia 04217
7	7	10	**You Might Think**	*The Cars* . . . Elektra 69744
8	4	16	**Footloose**	*Kenny Loggins* . . . Columbia 04310
9	11	6	**Oh Sherrie**	*Steve Perry* . . . Columbia 04391
10	14	5	**Time After Time**	*Cyndi Lauper* . . . Portrait 04432

★ **HIGHEST DEBUT** ★ POS 42
It's A Miracle ....*Culture Club*

★ **BIGGEST MOVER** ★ 61 to 45
Who's That Girl? ....*Eurythmics*

Billboard — MAY 19, 1984 — HOT 100

TW	LW	WK	Title	Artist / Label
1	1	13	**Hello**	*Lionel Richie* . . . Motown 1722
2	4	7	**Let's Hear It For The Boy**	*Deniece Williams* . . . Columbia 04417
3	2	13	**Against All Odds (Take A Look At Me Now)**	*Phil Collins* . . . Atlantic 89700
4	3	15	**Hold Me Now**	*Thompson Twins* . . . Arista 9164
5	6	12	**To All The Girls I've Loved Before**	*Julio Iglesias & Willie Nelson* . . . Columbia 04217
6	10	6	**Time After Time**	*Cyndi Lauper* . . . Portrait 04432
7	5	11	**Love Somebody**	*Rick Springfield* . . . RCA 13738
8	9	7	**Oh Sherrie**	*Steve Perry* . . . Columbia 04391
9	7	11	**You Might Think**	*The Cars* . . . Elektra 69744
10	8	17	**Footloose**	*Kenny Loggins* . . . Columbia 04310

★ **HIGHEST DEBUT** ★ POS 59
Magic ....*The Cars*

★ **BIGGEST MOVER** ★ 65 to 40
Almost Paradise...Love Theme From
Footloose ....*Mike Reno & Ann Wilson*

Billboard — MAY 26, 1984 — HOT 100

TW	LW	WK	Title	Artist / Label
1	2	8	**Let's Hear It For The Boy**	*Deniece Williams* . . . Columbia 04417
2	1	14	**Hello**	*Lionel Richie* . . . Motown 1722
3	6	7	**Time After Time**	*Cyndi Lauper* . . . Portrait 04432
4	3	14	**Against All Odds (Take A Look At Me Now)**	*Phil Collins* . . . Atlantic 89700
5	8	8	**Oh Sherrie**	*Steve Perry* . . . Columbia 04391
6	5	13	**To All The Girls I've Loved Before**	*Julio Iglesias & Willie Nelson* . . . Columbia 04217
7	12	6	**The Reflex**	*Duran Duran* . . . Capitol 5345
8	16	12	**Sister Christian**	*Night Ranger* . . . MCA/Camel 52350
9	13	10	**Breakdance**	*Irene Cara* . . . Geffen 29328
10	4	16	**Hold Me Now**	*Thompson Twins* . . . Arista 9164

★ **HIGHEST DEBUT** ★ POS 36
Dancing In The Dark ....*Bruce Springsteen*

★ **BIGGEST MOVER** ★ 59 to 39
Magic ....*The Cars*

TW	LW	WK	Billboard	JUNE 2, 1984	HOT 100
①	1	9	Let's Hear It For The Boy..............Deniece Williams . . . Columbia 04417
②	3	8	Time After Time................................Cyndi Lauper . . . Portrait 04432
③	2	15	Hello...Lionel Richie . . . Motown 1722
④	5	9	Oh Sherrie ....Steve Perry . . . Columbia 04391
⑤	7	7	The Reflex.......................................Duran Duran . . . Capitol 5345
⑥	8	13	Sister Christian ....Night Ranger . . . MCA/Camel 52350
⑦	4	15	Against All Odds (Take A Look At Me Now) .... Phil Collins . . . Atlantic 89700
⑧	13	7	The Heart Of Rock & Roll ....Huey Lewis & The News . . . Chrysalis 42782
⑨	9	11	Breakdance ....Irene Cara . . . Geffen 29328
⑩	6	14	To All The Girls I've Loved Before..............Julio Iglesias & Willie Nelson . . . Columbia 04217

★ HIGHEST DEBUT ★ POS 57	★ BIGGEST MOVER ★ 81 to 58
When Doves Cry.....................Prince	Farewell My Summer Love.........Michael Jackson

TW	LW	WK	Billboard	JUNE 9, 1984	HOT 100
①	2	9	Time After Time................................Cyndi Lauper . . . Portrait 04432
②	1	10	Let's Hear It For The Boy..................Deniece Williams . . . Columbia 04417
③	4	10	Oh Sherrie..Steve Perry . . . Columbia 04391
④	5	8	The Reflex.......................................Duran Duran . . . Capitol 5345
⑤	6	14	Sister Christian ....Night Ranger . . . MCA/Camel 52350
⑥	8	8	The Heart Of Rock & Roll .... Huey Lewis & The News . . . Chrysalis 42782
⑦	3	16	Hello...Lionel Richie . . . Motown 1722
⑧	9	12	Breakdance ....Irene Cara . . . Geffen 29328
⑨	11	9	Self Control...................................Laura Branigan . . . Atlantic 89676
⑩	14	7	Jump (For My Love)........................Pointer Sisters . . . Planet 13780

★ HIGHEST DEBUT ★ POS 49	★ BIGGEST MOVER ★ 57 to 36
Sad Songs (Say So Much) ....Elton John	When Doves Cry.....................Prince

TW	LW	WK	Billboard	JUNE 16, 1984	HOT 100
①	1	10	Time After Time................................Cyndi Lauper . . . Portrait 04432
②	4	9	The Reflex.......................................Duran Duran . . . Capitol 5345
③	2	11	Let's Hear It For The Boy..................Deniece Williams . . . Columbia 04417
④	3	11	Oh Sherrie ....Steve Perry . . . Columbia 04391
⑤	5	15	Sister Christian ....Night Ranger . . . MCA/Camel 52350
⑥	6	9	The Heart Of Rock & Roll .... Huey Lewis & The News . . . Chrysalis 42782
⑦	9	10	Self Control...................................Laura Branigan . . . Atlantic 89676
⑧	10	8	Jump (For My Love)........................Pointer Sisters . . . Planet 13780
⑨	14	4	Dancing In The Dark ....Bruce Springsteen . . . Columbia 04463
⑩	11	15	Borderline ....Madonna . . . Sire 29354

★ HIGHEST DEBUT ★ POS 50	★ BIGGEST MOVER ★ 36 to 17
I'm Free (Heaven Helps The Man) ....Kenny Loggins	When Doves Cry.....................Prince

Billboard — JUNE 23, 1984 — HOT 100

TW	LW	WK	Title	Artist	Label
1	2	10	**The Reflex**	Duran Duran	Capitol 5345
2	1	11	Time After Time	Cyndi Lauper	Portrait 04432
3	3	12	Let's Hear It For The Boy	Deniece Williams	Columbia 04417
4	9	5	Dancing In The Dark	Bruce Springsteen	Columbia 04463
5	7	11	Self Control	Laura Branigan	Atlantic 89676
6	6	10	The Heart Of Rock & Roll	Huey Lewis & The News	Chrysalis 42782
7	8	9	Jump (For My Love)	Pointer Sisters	Planet 13780
8	17	4	When Doves Cry	Prince	Warner 29286
9	4	12	Oh Sherrie	Steve Perry	Columbia 04391
10	11	8	Eyes Without A Face	Billy Idol	Chrysalis 42786

★ **HIGHEST DEBUT** ★ POS 52
Panama .... Van Halen

★ **BIGGEST MOVER** ★ 68 to 46
Ghostbusters .... Ray Parker Jr.

Billboard — JUNE 30, 1984 — HOT 100

TW	LW	WK	Title	Artist	Label
1	1	11	**The Reflex**	Duran Duran	Capitol 5345
2	4	6	**Dancing In The Dark**	Bruce Springsteen	Columbia 04463
3	8	5	When Doves Cry	Prince	Warner 29286
4	5	12	Self Control	Laura Branigan	Atlantic 89676
5	7	10	Jump (For My Love)	Pointer Sisters	Planet 13780
6	6	11	The Heart Of Rock & Roll	Huey Lewis & The News	Chrysalis 42782
7	2	12	Time After Time	Cyndi Lauper	Portrait 04432
8	10	9	Eyes Without A Face	Billy Idol	Chrysalis 42786
9	3	13	Let's Hear It For The Boy	Deniece Williams	Columbia 04417
10	12	8	Almost Paradise...Love Theme From Footloose	Mike Reno & Ann Wilson	Columbia 04418

★ **HIGHEST DEBUT** ★ POS 30
State Of Shock .... Jacksons

★ **BIGGEST MOVER** ★ 72 to 49
Stuck On You .... Lionel Richie

Billboard — JULY 7, 1984 — HOT 100

TW	LW	WK	Title	Artist	Label
1	3	6	**When Doves Cry**	Prince	Warner 29286
2	2	7	**Dancing In The Dark**	Bruce Springsteen	Columbia 04463
3	5	11	**Jump (For My Love)**	Pointer Sisters	Planet 13780
4	4	13	**Self Control**	Laura Branigan	Atlantic 89676
5	1	12	**The Reflex**	Duran Duran	Capitol 5345
6	8	10	Eyes Without A Face	Billy Idol	Chrysalis 42786
7	7	13	Time After Time	Cyndi Lauper	Portrait 04432
8	10	9	Almost Paradise...Love Theme From Footloose	Mike Reno & Ann Wilson	Columbia 04418
9	6	12	The Heart Of Rock & Roll	Huey Lewis & The News	Chrysalis 42782
10	13	8	Legs	ZZ Top	Warner 29272

★ **HIGHEST DEBUT** ★ POS 51
Rock Me Tonite .... Billy Squier

★ **BIGGEST MOVER** ★ 63 to 45
Sexy Girl .... Glenn Frey

Billboard — JULY 14, 1984 — HOT 100

TW	LW	WK	Title	Artist	Label
①	1	7	When Doves Cry	Prince	Warner 29286
②	2	8	Dancing In The Dark	Bruce Springsteen	Columbia 04463
③	3	12	Jump (For My Love)	Pointer Sisters	Planet 13780
④	6	11	Eyes Without A Face	Billy Idol	Chrysalis 42786
⑤	5	13	The Reflex	Duran Duran	Capitol 5345
⑥	4	14	Self Control	Laura Branigan	Atlantic 89676
⑦	8	10	Almost Paradise...Love Theme From Footloose	Mike Reno & Ann Wilson	Columbia 04418
⑧	19	5	Ghostbusters	Ray Parker Jr.	Arista 9212
⑨	9	13	The Heart Of Rock & Roll	Huey Lewis & The News	Chrysalis 42782
⑩	10	9	Legs	ZZ Top	Warner 29272

★ **HIGHEST DEBUT** ★ POS 56
Lights Out.....................Peter Wolf

★ **BIGGEST MOVER** ★ 85 to 60
All Of You....................Julio Iglesias & Diana Ross

Billboard — JULY 21, 1984 — HOT 100

TW	LW	WK	Title	Artist	Label
①	1	8	When Doves Cry	Prince	Warner 29286
②	2	9	Dancing In The Dark	Bruce Springsteen	Columbia 04463
③	8	6	Ghostbusters	Ray Parker Jr.	Arista 9212
④	4	12	Eyes Without A Face	Billy Idol	Chrysalis 42786
⑤	3	13	Jump (For My Love)	Pointer Sisters	Planet 13780
⑥	15	4	State Of Shock	Jacksons	Epic 04503
⑦	7	11	Almost Paradise...Love Theme From Footloose	Mike Reno & Ann Wilson	Columbia 04418
⑧	10	10	Legs	ZZ Top	Warner 29272
⑨	16	7	Sad Songs (Say So Much)	Elton John	Geffen 29292
⑩	11	9	Infatuation	Rod Stewart	Warner 29256

★ **HIGHEST DEBUT** ★ POS 45
If This Is It.....................Huey Lewis & The News

★ **BIGGEST MOVER** ★ 72 to 54
When You Close Your Eyes...........Night Ranger

Billboard — JULY 28, 1984 — HOT 100

TW	LW	WK	Title	Artist	Label
①	1	9	When Doves Cry	Prince	Warner 29286
②	3	7	Ghostbusters	Ray Parker Jr.	Arista 9212
③	2	10	Dancing In The Dark	Bruce Springsteen	Columbia 04463
④	6	5	State Of Shock	Jacksons	Epic 04503
⑤	4	13	Eyes Without A Face	Billy Idol	Chrysalis 42786
⑥	10	10	Infatuation	Rod Stewart	Warner 29256
⑦	9	8	Sad Songs (Say So Much)	Elton John	Geffen 29292
⑧	8	11	Legs	ZZ Top	Warner 29272
⑨	16	11	What's Love Got To Do With It	Tina Turner	Capitol 5354
⑩	5	14	Jump (For My Love)	Pointer Sisters	Planet 13780

★ **HIGHEST DEBUT** ★ POS 68
Only When You Leave.................Spandau Ballet

★ **BIGGEST MOVER** ★ 76 to 55
Cruel Summer.....................Bananarama

TW	LW	WK	Billboard		AUGUST 4, 1984		HOT 100.
❶	1	10	**When Doves Cry**		*Prince* . . . Warner 29286		
❷	2	8	Ghostbusters		*Ray Parker Jr.* . . . Arista 9212		
❸	4	6	**State Of Shock**		*Jacksons* . . . Epic 04503		
④	3	11	Dancing In The Dark		*Bruce Springsteen* . . . Columbia 04463		
❺	9	12	**What's Love Got To Do With It**		*Tina Turner* . . . Capitol 5354		
❻	6	11	**Infatuation**		*Rod Stewart* . . . Warner 29256		
❼	7	9	Sad Songs (Say So Much)		*Elton John* . . . Geffen 29292		
❽	15	7	Stuck On You		*Lionel Richie* . . . Motown 1746		
❾	11	10	**Breakin'...There's No Stopping Us**		*Ollie & Jerry* . . . Polydor 821708		
❿	13	14	I Can Dream About You		*Dan Hartman* . . . MCA 52378		

★ *HIGHEST DEBUT* ★ POS 45
Let's Go Crazy ....*Prince & The Revolution*

★ *BIGGEST MOVER* ★ 80 to 57
We're Not Gonna Take It ....*Twisted Sister*

TW	LW	WK	Billboard		AUGUST 11, 1984		HOT 100.
❶	2	9	**Ghostbusters**		*Ray Parker Jr.* . . . Arista 9212		
②	1	11	**When Doves Cry**		*Prince* . . . Warner 29286		
❸	3	7	**State Of Shock**		*Jacksons* . . . Epic 04503		
④	5	13	**What's Love Got To Do With It**		*Tina Turner* . . . Capitol 5354		
❺	7	10	**Sad Songs (Say So Much)**		*Elton John* . . . Geffen 29292		
❻	8	8	Stuck On You		*Lionel Richie* . . . Motown 1746		
⑦	4	12	Dancing In The Dark		*Bruce Springsteen* . . . Columbia 04463		
❽	10	15	I Can Dream About You		*Dan Hartman* . . . MCA 52378		
⑨	6	12	Infatuation		*Rod Stewart* . . . Warner 29256		
❿	17	12	Sunglasses At Night		*Corey Hart* . . . EMI America 8203		

★ *HIGHEST DEBUT* ★ POS 52
Cover Me ....*Bruce Springsteen*

★ *BIGGEST MOVER* ★ 87 to 65
I'm So Excited.............................*Pointer Sisters*

TW	LW	WK	Billboard		AUGUST 18, 1984		HOT 100.
❶	1	10	**Ghostbusters**		*Ray Parker Jr.* . . . Arista 9212		
❷	4	14	**What's Love Got To Do With It**		*Tina Turner* . . . Capitol 5354		
❸	3	8	**State Of Shock**		*Jacksons* . . . Epic 04503		
④	2	12	**When Doves Cry**		*Prince* . . . Warner 29286		
❺	6	9	Stuck On You		*Lionel Richie* . . . Motown 1746		
❻	8	16	**I Can Dream About You**		*Dan Hartman* . . . MCA 52378		
❼	12	9	Missing You		*John Waite* . . . EMI America 8212		
⑧	5	11	Sad Songs (Say So Much)		*Elton John* . . . Geffen 29292		
⑨	10	13	Sunglasses At Night		*Corey Hart* . . . EMI America 8203		
❿	13	15	**If Ever You're In My Arms Again**		*Peabo Bryson* . . . Elektra 69728		

★ *HIGHEST DEBUT* ★ POS 48
Torture ....*Jacksons*

★ *BIGGEST MOVER* ★ 65 to 50
I'm So Excited.............................*Pointer Sisters*

Billboard — AUGUST 25, 1984 — HOT 100.

TW	LW	WK	Title	Artist	Label
1	1	11	Ghostbusters	Ray Parker Jr.	Arista 9212
2	2	15	What's Love Got To Do With It	Tina Turner	Capitol 5354
3	5	10	Stuck On You	Lionel Richie	Motown 1746
4	4	13	When Doves Cry	Prince	Warner 29286
5	7	10	Missing You	John Waite	EMI America 8212
6	6	17	I Can Dream About You	Dan Hartman	MCA 52378
7	3	9	State Of Shock	Jacksons	Epic 04503
8	9	14	Sunglasses At Night	Corey Hart	EMI America 8203
9	15	6	She Bop	Cyndi Lauper	Portrait 04516
10	10	16	If Ever You're In My Arms Again	Peabo Bryson	Elektra 69728

★ HIGHEST DEBUT ★ POS 49
Lucky Star....................Madonna

★ BIGGEST MOVER ★ 86 to 70
On The Dark Side........John Cafferty & The Beaver Brown Band

Billboard — SEPTEMBER 1, 1984 — HOT 100.

TW	LW	WK	Title	Artist	Label
1	2	16	What's Love Got To Do With It	Tina Turner	Capitol 5354
2	5	11	Missing You	John Waite	EMI America 8212
3	3	11	Stuck On You	Lionel Richie	Motown 1746
4	1	12	Ghostbusters	Ray Parker Jr.	Arista 9212
5	4	14	When Doves Cry	Prince	Warner 29286
6	9	7	She Bop	Cyndi Lauper	Portrait 04516
7	8	15	Sunglasses At Night	Corey Hart	EMI America 8203
8	16	5	Let's Go Crazy	Prince & The Revolution	Warner 29216
9	11	7	If This Is It	Huey Lewis & The News	Chrysalis 42803
10	10	17	If Ever You're In My Arms Again	Peabo Bryson	Elektra 69728

★ HIGHEST DEBUT ★ POS 62
Swept Away..................Diana Ross

★ BIGGEST MOVER ★ 80 to 63
You Take Me Up....................Thompson Twins

Billboard — SEPTEMBER 8, 1984 — HOT 100.

TW	LW	WK	Title	Artist	Label
1	1	17	What's Love Got To Do With It	Tina Turner	Capitol 5354
2	2	12	Missing You	John Waite	EMI America 8212
3	6	8	She Bop	Cyndi Lauper	Portrait 04516
4	4	13	Ghostbusters	Ray Parker Jr.	Arista 9212
5	3	12	Stuck On You	Lionel Richie	Motown 1746
6	8	6	Let's Go Crazy	Prince & The Revolution	Warner 29216
7	9	8	If This Is It	Huey Lewis & The News	Chrysalis 42803
8	11	11	The Warrior	Scandal Featuring Patty Smyth	Columbia 04424
9	7	16	Sunglasses At Night	Corey Hart	EMI America 8203
10	14	6	Drive	The Cars	Elektra 69706

★ HIGHEST DEBUT ★ POS 54
Who Wears These Shoes?................Elton John

★ BIGGEST MOVER ★ 50 to 36
Caribbean Queen (No More Love On The Run) ....Billy Ocean

Billboard ⚬ SEPTEMBER 15, 1984 ⚬ HOT 100

TW	LW	WK	Title	Artist	Label
❶	1	18	What's Love Got To Do With It	Tina Turner	Capitol 5354
❷	2	13	Missing You	John Waite	EMI America 8212
❸	3	9	She Bop	Cyndi Lauper	Portrait 04516
❹	6	7	Let's Go Crazy	Prince & The Revolution	Warner 29216
⑤	5	13	Stuck On You	Lionel Richie	Motown 1746
⑥	7	9	If This Is It	Huey Lewis & The News	Chrysalis 42803
❼	10	7	Drive	The Cars	Elektra 69706
❽	8	12	The Warrior	Scandal Featuring Patty Smyth	Columbia 04424
⑨	4	14	Ghostbusters	Ray Parker Jr.	Arista 9212
❿	13	14	The Glamorous Life	Sheila E.	Warner 29285

★ **HIGHEST DEBUT** ★ POS 54
Blue Jean ....David Bowie

★ **BIGGEST MOVER** ★ 80 to 59
Wake Me Up Before You Go-Go ....Wham!

Billboard ⚬ SEPTEMBER 22, 1984 ⚬ HOT 100

TW	LW	WK	Title	Artist	Label
❶	2	14	Missing You	John Waite	EMI America 8212
❷	4	8	Let's Go Crazy	Prince & The Revolution	Warner 29216
③	3	10	She Bop	Cyndi Lauper	Portrait 04516
④	1	19	What's Love Got To Do With It	Tina Turner	Capitol 5354
❺	7	8	Drive	The Cars	Elektra 69706
⑥	6	10	If This Is It	Huey Lewis & The News	Chrysalis 42803
❼	8	13	The Warrior	Scandal Featuring Patty Smyth	Columbia 04424
❽	10	15	The Glamorous Life	Sheila E.	Warner 29285
⑨	18	6	I Just Called To Say I Love You	Stevie Wonder	Motown 1745
❿	13	10	Cruel Summer	Bananarama	London 810127

★ **HIGHEST DEBUT** ★ POS 68
Left In The Dark ....Barbra Streisand

★ **BIGGEST MOVER** ★ 85 to 64
I Can't Hold Back ....Survivor

Billboard ⚬ SEPTEMBER 29, 1984 ⚬ HOT 100

TW	LW	WK	Title	Artist	Label
❶	2	9	Let's Go Crazy	Prince & The Revolution	Warner 29216
②	1	15	Missing You	John Waite	EMI America 8212
❸	5	9	Drive	The Cars	Elektra 69706
④	3	11	She Bop	Cyndi Lauper	Portrait 04516
❺	9	7	I Just Called To Say I Love You	Stevie Wonder	Motown 1745
⑥	4	20	What's Love Got To Do With It	Tina Turner	Capitol 5354
⑦	7	14	The Warrior	Scandal Featuring Patty Smyth	Columbia 04424
❽	8	16	The Glamorous Life	Sheila E.	Warner 29285
⑨	10	11	Cruel Summer	Bananarama	London 810127
❿	11	8	Cover Me	Bruce Springsteen	Columbia 04561

★ **HIGHEST DEBUT** ★ POS 48
Out Of Touch ....Daryl Hall John Oates

★ **BIGGEST MOVER** ★ 49 to 38
I Feel For You ....Chaka Khan

Billboard — OCTOBER 6, 1984 — HOT 100

TW	LW	WK	Title	Artist ... Label
❶	1	10	**Let's Go Crazy**	*Prince & The Revolution* ... Warner 29216
❷	5	8	I Just Called To Say I Love You	*Stevie Wonder* ... Motown 1745
❸	3	10	**Drive**	*The Cars* ... Elektra 69706
④	2	16	Missing You	*John Waite* ... EMI America 8212
⑤	4	12	She Bop	*Cyndi Lauper* ... Portrait 04516
❻	12	10	Hard Habit To Break	*Chicago* ... Full Moon 29214
⑦	8	17	**The Glamorous Life**	*Sheila E.* ... Warner 29285
❽	13	7	Lucky Star	*Madonna* ... Sire 29177
⑨	7	15	The Warrior	*Scandal Featuring Patty Smyth* ... Columbia 04424
❿	10	9	Cover Me	*Bruce Springsteen* ... Columbia 04561

★ **HIGHEST DEBUT** ★ POS 28
Purple Rain ....*Prince & The Revolution*

★ **BIGGEST MOVER** ★ 77 to 60
I Can't Drive 55 ....*Sammy Hagar*

Billboard — OCTOBER 13, 1984 — HOT 100

TW	LW	WK	Title	Artist ... Label
❶	2	9	**I Just Called To Say I Love You**	*Stevie Wonder* ... Motown 1745
②	1	11	Let's Go Crazy	*Prince & The Revolution* ... Warner 29216
❸	3	11	**Drive**	*The Cars* ... Elektra 69706
④	6	11	Hard Habit To Break	*Chicago* ... Full Moon 29214
⑤	8	8	Lucky Star	*Madonna* ... Sire 29177
❻	11	10	Caribbean Queen (No More Love On The Run)	*Billy Ocean* ... Jive 9199
⑦	4	17	Missing You	*John Waite* ... EMI America 8212
❽	10	10	Cover Me	*Bruce Springsteen* ... Columbia 04561
⑨	7	18	The Glamorous Life	*Sheila E.* ... Warner 29285
❿	5	13	She Bop	*Cyndi Lauper* ... Portrait 04516

★ **HIGHEST DEBUT** ★ POS 48
No More Lonely Nights ....*Paul McCartney*

★ **BIGGEST MOVER** ★ 54 to 38
Penny Lover ....*Lionel Richie*

Billboard — OCTOBER 20, 1984 — HOT 100

TW	LW	WK	Title	Artist ... Label
❶	1	10	**I Just Called To Say I Love You**	*Stevie Wonder* ... Motown 1745
❷	6	11	Caribbean Queen (No More Love On The Run)	*Billy Ocean* ... Jive 9199
❸	4	12	**Hard Habit To Break**	*Chicago* ... Full Moon 29214
④	5	9	**Lucky Star**	*Madonna* ... Sire 29177
⑤	2	12	Let's Go Crazy	*Prince & The Revolution* ... Warner 29216
⑥	3	12	Drive	*The Cars* ... Elektra 69706
⑦	8	11	**Cover Me**	*Bruce Springsteen* ... Columbia 04561
❽	12	19	On The Dark Side	*John Cafferty & The Beaver Brown Band* ... Scotti Brothers 04594
⑨	18	3	Purple Rain	*Prince & The Revolution* ... Warner 29174
❿	13	28	I'm So Excited	*Pointer Sisters* ... Planet 13857

★ **HIGHEST DEBUT** ★ POS 53
Walking On A Thin Line ....*Huey Lewis & The News*

★ **BIGGEST MOVER** ★ 62 to 46
Sea Of Love ....*The Honeydrippers*

Billboard ⦿ OCTOBER 27, 1984 ⦿ HOT 100.

TW	LW	WK			
❶	1	11	**I Just Called To Say I Love You**	*Stevie Wonder*	Motown 1745
❷	2	12	**Caribbean Queen (No More Love On The Run)**	*Billy Ocean*	Jive 9199
❸	3	13	**Hard Habit To Break**	*Chicago*	Full Moon 29214
❹	9	4	**Purple Rain**	*Prince & The Revolution*	Warner 29174
❺	4	10	**Lucky Star**	*Madonna*	Sire 29177
❻	13	8	**Wake Me Up Before You Go-Go**	*Wham!*	Columbia 04552
❼	8	20	**On The Dark Side**	*John Cafferty & The Beaver Brown Band*	Scotti Brothers 04594
❽	5	13	**Let's Go Crazy**	*Prince & The Revolution*	Warner 29216
❾	10	29	**I'm So Excited**	*Pointer Sisters*	Planet 13857
❿	14	10	**Some Guys Have All The Luck**	*Rod Stewart*	Warner 29215

★ HIGHEST DEBUT ★ POS 45	★ BIGGEST MOVER ★ 53 to 39
We Belong ....*Pat Benatar*	**Walking On A Thin Line** ....*Huey Lewis & The News*

Billboard ⦿ NOVEMBER 3, 1984 ⦿ HOT 100.

TW	LW	WK			
❶	2	13	**Caribbean Queen (No More Love On The Run)**	*Billy Ocean*	Jive 9199
②	1	12	**I Just Called To Say I Love You**	*Stevie Wonder*	Motown 1745
③	4	5	**Purple Rain**	*Prince & The Revolution*	Warner 29174
④	3	14	**Hard Habit To Break**	*Chicago*	Full Moon 29214
⑤	6	9	**Wake Me Up Before You Go-Go**	*Wham!*	Columbia 04552
⑥	5	11	**Lucky Star**	*Madonna*	Sire 29177
⑦	7	21	**On The Dark Side**	*John Cafferty & The Beaver Brown Band*	Scotti Brothers 04594
⑧	13	8	**Blue Jean**	*David Bowie*	EMI America 8231
⑨	16	8	**Better Be Good To Me**	*Tina Turner*	Capitol 5387
⑩	15	9	**I Feel For You**	*Chaka Khan*	Warner 29195

★ HIGHEST DEBUT ★ POS 38	★ BIGGEST MOVER ★ 70 to 50
The Wild Boys ....*Duran Duran*	**Stranger In Town** ....*Toto*

Billboard ⦿ NOVEMBER 10, 1984 ⦿ HOT 100.

TW	LW	WK			
❶	1	14	**Caribbean Queen (No More Love On The Run)**	*Billy Ocean*	Jive 9199
②	2	13	**I Just Called To Say I Love You**	*Stevie Wonder*	Motown 1745
③	3	6	**Purple Rain**	*Prince & The Revolution*	Warner 29174
④	5	10	**Wake Me Up Before You Go-Go**	*Wham!*	Columbia 04552
⑤	10	10	**I Feel For You**	*Chaka Khan*	Warner 29195
⑥	12	7	**Out Of Touch**	*Daryl Hall John Oates*	RCA 13916
⑦	9	9	**Better Be Good To Me**	*Tina Turner*	Capitol 5387
⑧	8	9	**Blue Jean**	*David Bowie*	EMI America 8231
⑨	4	15	**Hard Habit To Break**	*Chicago*	Full Moon 29214
⑩	11	10	**Desert Moon**	*Dennis DeYoung*	A&M 2666

★ HIGHEST DEBUT ★ POS 52	★ BIGGEST MOVER ★ 74 to 55
Born In The U.S.A. ....*Bruce Springsteen*	**Pride (In The Name Of Love)** *U2*

Billboard — NOVEMBER 17, 1984 — HOT 100

TW	LW	WK	Title	Artist ... Label
1	4	11	**Wake Me Up Before You Go-Go**	*Wham!* ... Columbia 04552
2	3	7	**Purple Rain**	*Prince & The Revolution* ... Warner 29174
3	1	15	**Caribbean Queen (No More Love On The Run)**	*Billy Ocean* ... Jive 9199
4	5	11	**I Feel For You**	*Chaka Khan* ... Warner 29195
5	2	14	**I Just Called To Say I Love You**	*Stevie Wonder* ... Motown 1745
6	6	8	**Out Of Touch**	*Daryl Hall John Oates* ... RCA 13916
7	7	10	**Better Be Good To Me**	*Tina Turner* ... Capitol 5387
8	11	13	**Strut**	*Sheena Easton* ... EMI America 8227
9	12	7	**All Through The Night**	*Cyndi Lauper* ... Portrait 04639
10	13	7	**Penny Lover**	*Lionel Richie* ... Motown 1762

★ HIGHEST DEBUT ★ POS 48	★ BIGGEST MOVER ★ 82 to 66
Like A Virgin ....*Madonna*	Call To The Heart ....*Giuffria*

Billboard — NOVEMBER 24, 1984 — HOT 100

TW	LW	WK	Title	Artist ... Label
1	1	12	**Wake Me Up Before You Go-Go**	*Wham!* ... Columbia 04552
2	2	8	**Purple Rain**	*Prince & The Revolution* ... Warner 29174
3	4	12	**I Feel For You**	*Chaka Khan* ... Warner 29195
4	6	9	**Out Of Touch**	*Daryl Hall John Oates* ... RCA 13916
5	7	11	**Better Be Good To Me**	*Tina Turner* ... Capitol 5387
6	3	16	**Caribbean Queen (No More Love On The Run)**	*Billy Ocean* ... Jive 9199
7	8	14	**Strut**	*Sheena Easton* ... EMI America 8227
8	9	8	**All Through The Night**	*Cyndi Lauper* ... Portrait 04639
9	10	8	**Penny Lover**	*Lionel Richie* ... Motown 1762
10	5	15	**I Just Called To Say I Love You**	*Stevie Wonder* ... Motown 1745

★ HIGHEST DEBUT ★ POS 63	★ BIGGEST MOVER ★ 81 to 62
Easy Lover ....*Philip Bailey with Phil Collins*	Bruce ....*Rick Springfield*

Billboard — DECEMBER 1, 1984 — HOT 100

TW	LW	WK	Title	Artist ... Label
1	1	13	**Wake Me Up Before You Go-Go**	*Wham!* ... Columbia 04552
2	4	10	**Out Of Touch**	*Daryl Hall John Oates* ... RCA 13916
3	3	13	**I Feel For You**	*Chaka Khan* ... Warner 29195
4	2	9	**Purple Rain**	*Prince & The Revolution* ... Warner 29174
5	5	12	**Better Be Good To Me**	*Tina Turner* ... Capitol 5387
6	8	9	**All Through The Night**	*Cyndi Lauper* ... Portrait 04639
7	12	5	**The Wild Boys**	*Duran Duran* ... Capitol 5417
8	9	9	**Penny Lover**	*Lionel Richie* ... Motown 1762
9	7	15	**Strut**	*Sheena Easton* ... EMI America 8227
10	11	8	**No More Lonely Nights**	*Paul McCartney* ... Columbia 04581

★ HIGHEST DEBUT ★ POS 56	★ BIGGEST MOVER ★ 83 to 59
Loverboy ....*Billy Ocean*	Foolish Heart ....*Steve Perry*

Billboard · DECEMBER 8, 1984 · HOT 100

TW	LW	WK	Title	Artist	Label
1	2	11	**Out Of Touch**	Daryl Hall John Oates	RCA 13916
2	1	14	Wake Me Up Before You Go-Go	Wham!	Columbia 04552
3	3	14	**I Feel For You**	Chaka Khan	Warner 29195
4	7	6	The Wild Boys	Duran Duran	Capitol 5417
5	6	10	**All Through The Night**	Cyndi Lauper	Portrait 04639
6	10	9	**No More Lonely Nights**	Paul McCartney	Columbia 04581
7	11	9	Sea Of Love	The Honeydrippers	Es Paranza 99701
8	8	10	**Penny Lover**	Lionel Richie	Motown 1762
9	13	12	Cool It Now	New Edition	MCA 52455
10	14	7	We Belong	Pat Benatar	Chrysalis 42826

★ **HIGHEST DEBUT** ★ POS 45
I Want To Know What Love Is............Foreigner

★ **BIGGEST MOVER** ★ 56 to 40
Loverboy ....Billy Ocean

Billboard · DECEMBER 15, 1984 · HOT 100

TW	LW	WK	Title	Artist	Label
1	1	12	**Out Of Touch**	Daryl Hall John Oates	RCA 13916
2	4	7	**The Wild Boys**	Duran Duran	Capitol 5417
3	11	5	Like A Virgin	Madonna	Sire 29210
4	3	15	I Feel For You	Chaka Khan	Warner 29195
5	7	10	Sea Of Love	The Honeydrippers	Es Paranza 99701
6	6	10	**No More Lonely Nights**	Paul McCartney	Columbia 04581
7	9	13	Cool It Now	New Edition	MCA 52455
8	2	15	Wake Me Up Before You Go-Go	Wham!	Columbia 04552
9	10	8	We Belong	Pat Benatar	Chrysalis 42826
10	5	11	All Through The Night	Cyndi Lauper	Portrait 04639

★ **HIGHEST DEBUT** ★ POS 42
I Would Die 4 U ....Prince & The Revolution

★ **BIGGEST MOVER** ★ 81 to 64
The Heat Is On.................................Glenn Frey

Billboard · DECEMBER 22, 1984 · HOT 100

TW	LW	WK	Title	Artist	Label
1	3	6	**Like A Virgin**	Madonna	Sire 29210
2	2	8	**The Wild Boys**	Duran Duran	Capitol 5417
3	1	13	Out Of Touch	Daryl Hall John Oates	RCA 13916
4	5	11	Sea Of Love	The Honeydrippers	Es Paranza 99701
5	7	14	Cool It Now	New Edition	MCA 52455
6	9	9	We Belong	Pat Benatar	Chrysalis 42826
7	4	16	I Feel For You	Chaka Khan	Warner 29195
8	6	11	No More Lonely Nights	Paul McCartney	Columbia 04581
9	14	10	All I Need	Jack Wagner	Qwest 29238
10	12	10	Valotte	Julian Lennon	Atlantic 89609

★ **HIGHEST DEBUT** ★ POS 37
Careless Whisper............Wham! featuring George Michael

★ **BIGGEST MOVER** ★ 90 to 74
Treat Her Like A Lady................The Temptations

Billboard — JANUARY 5, 1985 — HOT 100

TW	LW	WK	Title	Artist
1	1	8	**Like A Virgin**	*Madonna* . . . Sire 29210
2	2	10	**The Wild Boys**	*Duran Duran* . . . Capitol 5417
3	4	13	**Sea Of Love**	*The Honeydrippers* . . . Es Paranza 99701
4	5	16	**Cool It Now**	*New Edition* . . . MCA 52455
5	6	11	**We Belong**	*Pat Benatar* . . . Chrysalis 42826
6	9	12	**All I Need**	*Jack Wagner* . . . Qwest 29238
7	3	15	**Out Of Touch**	*Daryl Hall John Oates* . . . RCA 13916
8	12	10	**Run To You**	*Bryan Adams* . . . A&M 2686
9	15	8	**You're The Inspiration**	*Chicago* . . . Full Moon 29126
10	10	12	**Valotte**	*Julian Lennon* . . . Atlantic 89609

★ **HIGHEST DEBUT** ★ POS 76
Knocking At Your Back Door ....*Deep Purple*

★ **BIGGEST MOVER** ★ 65 to 20
Do They Know It's Christmas? ....*Band Aid*

Billboard — JANUARY 12, 1985 — HOT 100

TW	LW	WK	Title	Artist
1	1	9	**Like A Virgin**	*Madonna* . . . Sire 29210
2	6	13	**All I Need**	*Jack Wagner* . . . Qwest 29238
3	2	11	**The Wild Boys**	*Duran Duran* . . . Capitol 5417
4	3	14	**Sea Of Love**	*The Honeydrippers* . . . Es Paranza 99701
5	5	12	**We Belong**	*Pat Benatar* . . . Chrysalis 42826
6	9	9	**You're The Inspiration**	*Chicago* . . . Full Moon 29126
7	8	11	**Run To You**	*Bryan Adams* . . . A&M 2686
8	4	17	**Cool It Now**	*New Edition* . . . MCA 52455
9	10	13	**Valotte**	*Julian Lennon* . . . Atlantic 89609
10	11	10	**Born In The U.S.A.**	*Bruce Springsteen* . . . Columbia 04680

★ **HIGHEST DEBUT** ★ POS 90
Gotta Get You Home Tonight ....*Eugene Wilde*

★ **BIGGEST MOVER** ★ 76 to 64
Knocking At Your Back Door ....*Deep Purple*

Billboard — JANUARY 19, 1985 — HOT 100

TW	LW	WK	Title	Artist
1	1	10	**Like A Virgin**	*Madonna* . . . Sire 29210
2	2	14	**All I Need**	*Jack Wagner* . . . Qwest 29238
3	6	10	**You're The Inspiration**	*Chicago* . . . Full Moon 29126
4	11	7	**I Want To Know What Love Is**	*Foreigner* . . . Atlantic 89596
5	13	9	**Easy Lover**	*Philip Bailey with Phil Collins* . . . Columbia 04679
6	7	12	**Run To You**	*Bryan Adams* . . . A&M 2686
7	3	12	**The Wild Boys**	*Duran Duran* . . . Capitol 5417
8	5	13	**We Belong**	*Pat Benatar* . . . Chrysalis 42826
9	10	11	**Born In The U.S.A.**	*Bruce Springsteen* . . . Columbia 04680
10	20	5	**Careless Whisper**	*Wham! featuring George Michael* . . . Columbia 04691

★ **HIGHEST DEBUT** ★ POS 43
California Girls ....*David Lee Roth*

★ **BIGGEST MOVER** ★ 68 to 48
Rockin' At Midnight ....*The Honeydrippers*

TW	LW	WK	Billboard.	JANUARY 26, 1985	HOT 100.
❶	1	11	**Like A Virgin**...*Madonna* . . . Sire 29210
❷	4	8	**I Want To Know What Love Is** ....*Foreigner* . . . Atlantic 89596
❸	3	11	**You're The Inspiration**..............................*Chicago* . . . Full Moon 29126
❹	5	10	**Easy Lover**.........................*Philip Bailey with Phil Collins* . . . Columbia 04679
❺	10	6	**Careless Whisper**.........*Wham! featuring George Michael* . . . Columbia 04691
❻	2	15	**All I Need** ....*Jack Wagner* . . . Qwest 29238
❼	6	13	**Run To You** ....*Bryan Adams* . . . A&M 2686
❽	12	12	**The Boys Of Summer**...................................*Don Henley* . . . Geffen 29141
❾	16	9	**Loverboy** ....*Billy Ocean* . . . Jive 9284
❿	14	7	**I Would Die 4 U** ....*Prince & The Revolution* . . . Warner 29121

★ **HIGHEST DEBUT** ★ POS 43
Only The Young................................*Journey*

★ **BIGGEST MOVER** ★ 70 to 45
Relax..........................*Frankie Goes To Hollywood*

TW	LW	WK	Billboard.	FEBRUARY 2, 1985	HOT 100.
❶	2	9	**I Want To Know What Love Is** ....*Foreigner* . . . Atlantic 89596
❷	4	11	**Easy Lover** ....*Philip Bailey with Phil Collins* . . . Columbia 04679
❸	5	7	**Careless Whisper**.........*Wham! featuring George Michael* . . . Columbia 04691
④	3	12	**You're The Inspiration** ....*Chicago* . . . Full Moon 29126
❺	9	10	**Loverboy** ....*Billy Ocean* . . . Jive 9284
❻	8	13	**The Boys Of Summer**...................................*Don Henley* . . . Geffen 29141
⑦	1	12	**Like A Virgin**...*Madonna* . . . Sire 29210
❽	10	8	**I Would Die 4 U**.......................*Prince & The Revolution* . . . Warner 29121
❾	12	8	**Method Of Modern Love** ....*Daryl Hall John Oates* . . . RCA 13970
❿	13	11	**Neutron Dance** ....*Pointer Sisters* . . . Planet 13951

★ **HIGHEST DEBUT** ★ POS 53
Save A Prayer...................................*Duran Duran*

★ **BIGGEST MOVER** ★ 29 to 13
The Heat Is On................................*Glenn Frey*

TW	LW	WK	Billboard.	FEBRUARY 9, 1985	HOT 100.
❶	1	10	**I Want To Know What Love Is** ....*Foreigner* . . . Atlantic 89596
❷	2	12	**Easy Lover** ....*Philip Bailey with Phil Collins* . . . Columbia 04679
❸	3	8	**Careless Whisper**.........*Wham! featuring George Michael* . . . Columbia 04691
❹	5	11	**Loverboy** ....*Billy Ocean* . . . Jive 9284
❺	6	14	**The Boys Of Summer** ....*Don Henley* . . . Geffen 29141
❻	4	13	**You're The Inspiration** ....*Chicago* . . . Full Moon 29126
❼	9	9	**Method Of Modern Love** ....*Daryl Hall John Oates* . . . RCA 13970
❽	10	12	**Neutron Dance** ....*Pointer Sisters* . . . Planet 13951
⑨	7	13	**Like A Virgin**...*Madonna* . . . Sire 29210
❿	8	9	**I Would Die 4 U** ....*Prince & The Revolution* . . . Warner 29121

★ **HIGHEST DEBUT** ★ POS 43
Material Girl................................*Madonna*

★ **BIGGEST MOVER** ★ 59 to 47
Somebody ....*Bryan Adams*

Billboard FEBRUARY 16, 1985 HOT 100.

TW	LW	WK	Title	Artist	Label
1	3	9	**Careless Whisper** .....*Wham! featuring George Michael* . . . Columbia 04691		
2	1	11	I Want To Know What Love Is ....*Foreigner* . . . Atlantic 89596		
3	2	13	Easy Lover.........................*Philip Bailey with Phil Collins* . . . Columbia 04679		
4	4	12	Loverboy ....*Billy Ocean* . . . Jive 9284		
5	7	10	**Method Of Modern Love**...............*Daryl Hall John Oates* . . . RCA 13970		
6	8	13	**Neutron Dance**..*Pointer Sisters* . . . Planet 13951		
7	16	5	Can't Fight This Feeling ....*REO Speedwagon* . . . Epic 04713		
8	11	11	The Heat Is On...*Glenn Frey* . . . MCA 52512		
9	5	15	The Boys Of Summer..................................*Don Henley* . . . Geffen 29141		
10	13	5	California Girls ....*David Lee Roth* . . . Warner 29102		

★ **HIGHEST DEBUT** ★ POS 54
I'm On Fire ....*Bruce Springsteen*

★ **BIGGEST MOVER** ★ 90 to 69
When The Rain Begins To Fall ....*Jermaine Jackson/Pia Zadora*

Billboard FEBRUARY 23, 1985 HOT 100.

TW	LW	WK	Title	Artist	Label
1	1	10	**Careless Whisper** .....*Wham! featuring George Michael* . . . Columbia 04691		
2	4	13	**Loverboy** ....*Billy Ocean* . . . Jive 9284		
3	3	14	Easy Lover.........................*Philip Bailey with Phil Collins* . . . Columbia 04679		
4	7	6	Can't Fight This Feeling ....*REO Speedwagon* . . . Epic 04713		
5	2	12	I Want To Know What Love Is ....*Foreigner* . . . Atlantic 89596		
6	6	14	**Neutron Dance**..*Pointer Sisters* . . . Planet 13951		
7	8	12	The Heat Is On...*Glenn Frey* . . . MCA 52512		
8	10	6	California Girls ....*David Lee Roth* . . . Warner 29102		
9	5	11	Method Of Modern Love ....*Daryl Hall John Oates* . . . RCA 13970		
10	11	10	Sugar Walls...*Sheena Easton* . . . EMI America 8253		

★ **HIGHEST DEBUT** ★ POS 60
Along Comes A Woman......................*Chicago*

★ **BIGGEST MOVER** ★ 65 to 50
Rhythm Of The Night ....*DeBarge*

Billboard MARCH 2, 1985 HOT 100.

TW	LW	WK	Title	Artist	Label
1	1	11	**Careless Whisper** .....*Wham! featuring George Michael* . . . Columbia 04691		
2	4	7	Can't Fight This Feeling ....*REO Speedwagon* . . . Epic 04713		
3	8	7	California Girls ....*David Lee Roth* . . . Warner 29102		
4	7	13	The Heat Is On...*Glenn Frey* . . . MCA 52512		
5	2	14	Loverboy ....*Billy Ocean* . . . Jive 9284		
6	6	15	Neutron Dance..*Pointer Sisters* . . . Planet 13951		
7	5	13	I Want To Know What Love Is ....*Foreigner* . . . Atlantic 89596		
8	3	15	Easy Lover.........................*Philip Bailey with Phil Collins* . . . Columbia 04679		
9	10	11	Sugar Walls ....*Sheena Easton* . . . EMI America 8253		
10	11	11	The Old Man Down The Road ....*John Fogerty* . . . Warner 29100		

★ **HIGHEST DEBUT** ★ POS 55
Crazy For You....................................*Madonna*

★ **BIGGEST MOVER** ★ 95 to 68
We Close Our Eyes ....*Go West*

TW	LW	WK	Billboard.	MARCH 9, 1985	HOT 100.
①	2	8	**Can't Fight This Feeling** ....*REO Speedwagon* . . . Epic 04713
②	1	12	**Careless Whisper**.........*Wham! featuring George Michael* . . . Columbia 04691
③	4	14	**The Heat Is On**....................................*Glenn Frey* . . . MCA 52512
④	3	8	**California Girls**..............................*David Lee Roth* . . . Warner 29102
⑤	18	5	**Material Girl**...*Madonna* . . . Sire 29083
⑥	15	7	**Too Late For Goodbyes**...........................*Julian Lennon* . . . Atlantic 89589
⑦	6	16	**Neutron Dance** ....*Pointer Sisters* . . . Planet 13951
⑧	7	14	**I Want To Know What Love Is** ....*Foreigner* . . . Atlantic 89596
⑨	9	12	**Sugar Walls** ....*Sheena Easton* . . . EMI America 8253
⑩	13	16	**Misled**.................................*Kool & The Gang* . . . De-Lite 880431

★ *HIGHEST DEBUT* ★ POS 64	★ *BIGGEST MOVER* ★ 75 to 56
Forever Man.............................*Eric Clapton*	The Bird...*The Time*

TW	LW	WK	Billboard.	MARCH 16, 1985	HOT 100.
①	1	9	**Can't Fight This Feeling** ....*REO Speedwagon* . . . Epic 04713
②	3	15	**The Heat Is On**....................................*Glenn Frey* . . . MCA 52512
③	5	6	**Material Girl**...*Madonna* . . . Sire 29083
④	4	9	**California Girls** ....*David Lee Roth* . . . Warner 29102
⑤	14	6	**One More Night** ....*Phil Collins* . . . Atlantic 89588
⑥	6	8	**Too Late For Goodbyes**...........................*Julian Lennon* . . . Atlantic 89589
⑦	2	13	**Careless Whisper**.........*Wham! featuring George Michael* . . . Columbia 04691
⑧	12	14	**Lovergirl** ....*Teena Marie* . . . Epic 04619
⑨	15	9	**Private Dancer** ....*Tina Turner* . . . Capitol 5433
⑩	17	16	**Relax**....................................*Frankie Goes To Hollywood* . . . Island 99805

★ *HIGHEST DEBUT* ★ POS 47	★ *BIGGEST MOVER* ★ 62 to 49
That Was Yesterday ....*Foreigner*	Don't You (Forget About Me) ....*Simple Minds*

TW	LW	WK	Billboard.	MARCH 23, 1985	HOT 100.
①	1	10	**Can't Fight This Feeling** ....*REO Speedwagon* . . . Epic 04713
②	3	7	**Material Girl**...*Madonna* . . . Sire 29083
③	5	7	**One More Night** ....*Phil Collins* . . . Atlantic 89588
④	2	16	**The Heat Is On**....................................*Glenn Frey* . . . MCA 52512
⑤	6	9	**Too Late For Goodbyes** ....*Julian Lennon* . . . Atlantic 89589
⑥	8	15	**Lovergirl** ....*Teena Marie* . . . Epic 04619
⑦	9	10	**Private Dancer**....................................*Tina Turner* . . . Capitol 5433
⑧	14	9	**High On You** ....*Survivor* . . . Scotti Brothers 04685
⑨	11	9	**Only The Young**....................................*Journey* . . . Geffen 29090
⑩	10	17	**Relax**....................................*Frankie Goes To Hollywood* . . . Island 99805

★ *HIGHEST DEBUT* ★ POS 21	★ *BIGGEST MOVER* ★ 57 to 43
We Are The World......................*USA for Africa*	Some Like It Hot ....*The Power Station*

TW	LW	WK	Billboard	MARCH 30, 1985	HOT 100
①	3	8	One More Night	Phil Collins	Atlantic 89588
②	2	8	Material Girl	Madonna	Sire 29083
③	1	11	Can't Fight This Feeling	REO Speedwagon	Epic 04713
④	6	16	Lovergirl	Teena Marie	Epic 04619
⑤	21	2	We Are The World	USA for Africa	Columbia 04839
⑥	5	10	Too Late For Goodbyes	Julian Lennon	Atlantic 89589
⑦	7	11	Private Dancer	Tina Turner	Capitol 5433
⑧	8	10	High On You	Survivor	Scotti Brothers 04685
⑨	20	5	Crazy For You	Madonna	Geffen 29051
⑩	15	10	Nightshift	Commodores	Motown 1773

★ HIGHEST DEBUT ★ POS 65	★ BIGGEST MOVER ★ 21 to 5
One Lonely Night......REO Speedwagon	We Are The World......USA for Africa

TW	LW	WK	Billboard	APRIL 6, 1985	HOT 100
①	1	9	One More Night	Phil Collins	Atlantic 89588
②	5	3	We Are The World	USA for Africa	Columbia 04839
③	2	9	Material Girl	Madonna	Sire 29083
④	9	6	Crazy For You	Madonna	Geffen 29051
⑤	4	17	Lovergirl	Teena Marie	Epic 04619
⑥	3	12	Can't Fight This Feeling	REO Speedwagon	Epic 04713
⑦	10	11	Nightshift	Commodores	Motown 1773
⑧	14	8	I'm On Fire	Bruce Springsteen	Columbia 04772
⑨	18	8	Rhythm Of The Night	DeBarge	Gordy 1770
⑩	6	11	Too Late For Goodbyes	Julian Lennon	Atlantic 89589

★ HIGHEST DEBUT ★ POS 60	★ BIGGEST MOVER ★ 69 to 52
Celebrate Youth......Rick Springfield	Axel F......Harold Faltermeyer

TW	LW	WK	Billboard	APRIL 13, 1985	HOT 100
①	2	4	We Are The World	USA for Africa	Columbia 04839
②	1	10	One More Night	Phil Collins	Atlantic 89588
③	4	7	Crazy For You	Madonna	Geffen 29051
④	7	12	Nightshift	Commodores	Motown 1773
⑤	3	10	Material Girl	Madonna	Sire 29083
⑥	8	9	I'm On Fire	Bruce Springsteen	Columbia 04772
⑦	9	9	Rhythm Of The Night	DeBarge	Gordy 1770
⑧	5	18	Lovergirl	Teena Marie	Epic 04619
⑨	14	12	Obsession	Animotion	Mercury 880266
⑩	13	20	Missing You	Diana Ross	RCA 13966

★ HIGHEST DEBUT ★ POS 81	★ BIGGEST MOVER ★ 84 to 66
Voices Carry......'til Tuesday	Welcome To The Pleasuredome.....Frankie Goes To Hollywood

TW	LW	WK	Billboard.	APRIL 20, 1985	HOT 100.
①	1	5	**We Are The World**..............................USA for Africa . . . Columbia 04839		
②	3	8	**Crazy For You** ....Madonna . . . Geffen 29051		
③	4	13	**Nightshift** ....Commodores . . . Motown 1773		
④	2	11	One More Night ....Phil Collins . . . Atlantic 89588		
⑤	7	10	Rhythm Of The Night..............................DeBarge . . . Gordy 1770		
⑥	6	10	**I'm On Fire**..Bruce Springsteen . . . Columbia 04772		
⑦	9	13	Obsession...Animotion . . . Mercury 880266		
⑧	11	9	Don't You (Forget About Me) ....Simple Minds . . . A&M 2703		
⑨	12	9	One Night In Bangkok ....Murray Head . . . RCA 13988		
⑩	10	21	**Missing You** ....Diana Ross . . . RCA 13966		

★ **HIGHEST DEBUT** ★ POS 52
Heaven ....Bryan Adams

★ **BIGGEST MOVER** ★ 61 to 49
Smuggler's Blues ....Glenn Frey

TW	LW	WK	Billboard.	APRIL 27, 1985	HOT 100.
①	1	6	**We Are The World**..............................USA for Africa . . . Columbia 04839		
②	2	9	**Crazy For You** ....Madonna . . . Geffen 29051		
③	5	11	**Rhythm Of The Night** ....DeBarge . . . Gordy 1770		
④	3	14	Nightshift..Commodores . . . Motown 1773		
⑤	8	10	Don't You (Forget About Me) ....Simple Minds . . . A&M 2703		
⑥	9	10	One Night In Bangkok ....Murray Head . . . RCA 13988		
⑦	7	14	Obsession...Animotion . . . Mercury 880266		
⑧	12	7	Some Like It Hot ....The Power Station . . . Capitol 5444		
⑨	6	11	I'm On Fire ....Bruce Springsteen . . . Columbia 04772		
⑩	11	10	All She Wants To Do Is Dance ....Don Henley . . . Geffen 29065		

★ **HIGHEST DEBUT** ★ POS 48
Angel..............................Madonna

★ **BIGGEST MOVER** ★ 52 to 35
Heaven ....Bryan Adams

TW	LW	WK	Billboard.	MAY 4, 1985	HOT 100.
①	1	7	**We Are The World**..............................USA for Africa . . . Columbia 04839		
②	2	10	**Crazy For You** ....Madonna . . . Geffen 29051		
③	3	12	**Rhythm Of The Night** ....DeBarge . . . Gordy 1770		
④	5	11	Don't You (Forget About Me) ....Simple Minds . . . A&M 2703		
⑤	6	11	One Night In Bangkok ....Murray Head . . . RCA 13988		
⑥	7	15	**Obsession**...Animotion . . . Mercury 880266		
⑦	8	8	Some Like It Hot ....The Power Station . . . Capitol 5444		
⑧	4	15	Nightshift..Commodores . . . Motown 1773		
⑨	10	11	**All She Wants To Do Is Dance**................Don Henley . . . Geffen 29065		
⑩	12	10	Smooth Operator....................................Sade . . . Portrait 04807		

★ **HIGHEST DEBUT** ★ POS 77
Dangerous ....Natalie Cole

★ **BIGGEST MOVER** ★ 62 to 46
Would I Lie To You? ....Eurythmics

TW	LW	WK	Billboard	MAY 11, 1985	HOT 100
①	2	11	**Crazy For You**	*Madonna*	Geffen 29051
②	1	8	We Are The World	*USA for Africa*	Columbia 04839
③	4	12	Don't You (Forget About Me)	*Simple Minds*	A&M 2703
④	3	13	Rhythm Of The Night	*DeBarge*	Gordy 1770
⑤	5	12	One Night In Bangkok	*Murray Head*	RCA 13988
⑥	7	9	**Some Like It Hot**	*The Power Station*	Capitol 5444
⑦	10	11	Smooth Operator	*Sade*	Portrait 04807
⑧	11	8	Everything She Wants	*Wham!*	Columbia 04840
⑨	6	16	Obsession	*Animotion*	Mercury 880266
⑩	14	9	Everybody Wants To Rule The World	*Tears For Fears*	Mercury 880659

★ **HIGHEST DEBUT** ★ POS 39
Sussudio ....*Phil Collins*

★ **BIGGEST MOVER** ★ 82 to 66
Wake Up (Next To You).......*Graham Parker & The Shot*

TW	LW	WK	Billboard	MAY 18, 1985	HOT 100
①	3	13	**Don't You (Forget About Me)**	*Simple Minds*	A&M 2703
②	1	12	Crazy For You	*Madonna*	Geffen 29051
③	5	13	**One Night In Bangkok**	*Murray Head*	RCA 13988
④	8	9	Everything She Wants	*Wham!*	Columbia 04840
⑤	7	12	**Smooth Operator**	*Sade*	Portrait 04807
⑥	6	10	**Some Like It Hot**	*The Power Station*	Capitol 5444
⑦	4	14	Rhythm Of The Night	*DeBarge*	Gordy 1770
⑧	2	9	We Are The World	*USA for Africa*	Columbia 04839
⑨	10	10	Everybody Wants To Rule The World	*Tears For Fears*	Mercury 880659
⑩	12	8	Axel F	*Harold Faltermeyer*	MCA 52536

★ **HIGHEST DEBUT** ★ POS 37
Raspberry Beret ....*Prince & The Revolution*

★ **BIGGEST MOVER** ★ 70 to 53
Everytime You Go Away ....*Paul Young*

TW	LW	WK	Billboard	MAY 25, 1985	HOT 100
①	4	10	**Everything She Wants**	*Wham!*	Columbia 04840
②	1	14	Don't You (Forget About Me)	*Simple Minds*	A&M 2703
③	9	11	Everybody Wants To Rule The World	*Tears For Fears*	Mercury 880659
④	10	9	Axel F	*Harold Faltermeyer*	MCA 52536
⑤	5	13	**Smooth Operator**	*Sade*	Portrait 04807
⑥	2	13	Crazy For You	*Madonna*	Geffen 29051
⑦	3	14	One Night In Bangkok	*Murray Head*	RCA 13988
⑧	11	10	Suddenly	*Billy Ocean*	Jive 9323
⑨	6	11	Some Like It Hot	*The Power Station*	Capitol 5444
⑩	15	10	Things Can Only Get Better	*Howard Jones*	Elektra 69651

★ **HIGHEST DEBUT** ★ POS 51
Getcha Back ....*The Beach Boys*

★ **BIGGEST MOVER** ★ 80 to 62
Little By Little ....*Robert Plant*

Billboard — JUNE 1, 1985 — HOT 100

TW	LW	WK	Title	Artist
❶	1	11	**Everything She Wants**	*Wham!* ... Columbia 04840
❷	3	12	Everybody Wants To Rule The World	*Tears For Fears* ... Mercury 880659
❸	4	10	**Axel F**	*Harold Faltermeyer* ... MCA 52536
④	2	15	Don't You (Forget About Me)	*Simple Minds* ... A&M 2703
❺	8	11	**Suddenly**	*Billy Ocean* ... Jive 9323
⑥	5	14	Smooth Operator	*Sade* ... Portrait 04807
❼	12	7	Heaven	*Bryan Adams* ... A&M 2729
❽	10	11	Things Can Only Get Better	*Howard Jones* ... Elektra 69651
❾	13	13	In My House	*Mary Jane Girls* ... Gordy 1741
❿	11	11	Fresh	*Kool & The Gang* ... De-Lite 880623

★ HIGHEST DEBUT ★ POS 48
Glory Days ... *Bruce Springsteen*

★ BIGGEST MOVER ★ 75 to 52
Cannonball ... *Supertramp*

Billboard — JUNE 8, 1985 — HOT 100

TW	LW	WK	Title	Artist
❶	2	13	**Everybody Wants To Rule The World**	*Tears For Fears* ... Mercury 880659
②	1	12	Everything She Wants	*Wham!* ... Columbia 04840
③	3	11	**Axel F**	*Harold Faltermeyer* ... MCA 52536
④	5	12	**Suddenly**	*Billy Ocean* ... Jive 9323
❺	7	8	Heaven	*Bryan Adams* ... A&M 2729
❻	8	12	Things Can Only Get Better	*Howard Jones* ... Elektra 69651
❼	9	14	**In My House**	*Mary Jane Girls* ... Gordy 1741
⑧	4	16	Don't You (Forget About Me)	*Simple Minds* ... A&M 2703
❾	10	12	**Fresh**	*Kool & The Gang* ... De-Lite 880623
❿	11	12	Walking On Sunshine	*Katrina & The Waves* ... Capitol 5466

★ HIGHEST DEBUT ★ POS 44
If You Love Somebody Set Them Free ... *Sting*

★ BIGGEST MOVER ★ 75 to 54
Who's Holding Donna Now ... *DeBarge*

Billboard — JUNE 15, 1985 — HOT 100

TW	LW	WK	Title	Artist
❶	1	14	**Everybody Wants To Rule The World**	*Tears For Fears* ... Mercury 880659
❷	5	9	Heaven	*Bryan Adams* ... A&M 2729
③	3	12	**Axel F**	*Harold Faltermeyer* ... MCA 52536
④	4	13	**Suddenly**	*Billy Ocean* ... Jive 9323
❺	6	13	**Things Can Only Get Better**	*Howard Jones* ... Elektra 69651
❻	12	6	Sussudio	*Phil Collins* ... Atlantic 89560
❼	7	15	**In My House**	*Mary Jane Girls* ... Gordy 1741
⑧	2	13	Everything She Wants	*Wham!* ... Columbia 04840
❾	11	8	Angel	*Madonna* ... Sire 29008
❿	10	13	Walking On Sunshine	*Katrina & The Waves* ... Capitol 5466

★ HIGHEST DEBUT ★ POS 66
Shout ... *Tears For Fears*

★ BIGGEST MOVER ★ 68 to 45
Never Surrender ... *Corey Hart*

Billboard — JUNE 22, 1985 — HOT 100

TW	LW	WK	Title	Artist
❶	2	10	**Heaven**	*Bryan Adams* . . . A&M 2729
❷	6	7	**Sussudio**	*Phil Collins* . . . Atlantic 89560
③	1	15	**Everybody Wants To Rule The World**	*Tears For Fears* . . . Mercury 880659
❹	11	6	**Raspberry Beret**	*Prince & The Revolution* . . . Paisley Park 28972
❺	12	6	**A View To A Kill**	*Duran Duran* . . . Capitol 5475
❻	9	9	**Angel**	*Madonna* . . . Sire 29008
⑦	7	16	**In My House**	*Mary Jane Girls* . . . Gordy 1741
⑧	5	14	**Things Can Only Get Better**	*Howard Jones* . . . Elektra 69651
❾	10	14	**Walking On Sunshine**	*Katrina & The Waves* . . . Capitol 5466
❿	13	10	**The Search Is Over**	*Survivor* . . . Scotti Brothers 04871

★ HIGHEST DEBUT ★ POS 54
Freeway Of Love .... *Aretha Franklin*

★ BIGGEST MOVER ★ 63 to 41
You Spin Me Round (Like A Record) ..... *Dead Or Alive*

Billboard — JUNE 29, 1985 — HOT 100

TW	LW	WK	Title	Artist
❶	1	11	**Heaven**	*Bryan Adams* . . . A&M 2729
❷	2	8	**Sussudio**	*Phil Collins* . . . Atlantic 89560
❸	5	7	**A View To A Kill**	*Duran Duran* . . . Capitol 5475
❹	4	7	**Raspberry Beret**	*Prince & The Revolution* . . . Paisley Park 28972
❺	6	10	**Angel**	*Madonna* . . . Sire 29008
❻	10	11	**The Search Is Over**	*Survivor* . . . Scotti Brothers 04871
⑦	3	16	**Everybody Wants To Rule The World**	*Tears For Fears* . . . Mercury 880659
❽	14	10	**Would I Lie To You?**	*Eurythmics* . . . RCA 14078
❾	8	15	**Things Can Only Get Better**	*Howard Jones* . . . Elektra 69651
❿	7	17	**In My House**	*Mary Jane Girls* . . . Gordy 1741

★ HIGHEST DEBUT ★ POS 46
The Power Of Love .... *Huey Lewis & The News*

★ BIGGEST MOVER ★ 90 to 74
St. Elmo's Fire (Man In Motion) .... *John Parr*

Billboard — JULY 6, 1985 — HOT 100

TW	LW	WK	Title	Artist
❶	2	9	**Sussudio**	*Phil Collins* . . . Atlantic 89560
❷	3	8	**A View To A Kill**	*Duran Duran* . . . Capitol 5475
❸	4	8	**Raspberry Beret**	*Prince & The Revolution* . . . Paisley Park 28972
④	1	12	**Heaven**	*Bryan Adams* . . . A&M 2729
❺	6	12	**The Search Is Over**	*Survivor* . . . Scotti Brothers 04871
❻	8	11	**Would I Lie To You?**	*Eurythmics* . . . RCA 14078
❼	13	9	**You Give Good Love**	*Whitney Houston* . . . Arista 9274
❽	14	9	**Everytime You Go Away**	*Paul Young* . . . Columbia 04867
❾	12	13	**Voices Carry**	*'til Tuesday* . . . Epic 04795
❿	5	11	**Angel**	*Madonna* . . . Sire 29008

★ HIGHEST DEBUT ★ POS 52
We Don't Need Another Hero (Thunderdome) .... *Tina Turner*

★ BIGGEST MOVER ★ 74 to 53
St. Elmo's Fire (Man In Motion) .... *John Parr*

Billboard — JULY 13, 1985 — HOT 100

TW	LW	WK	Title	Artist	Label
1	2	9	A View To A Kill	Duran Duran	Capitol 5475
2	1	10	Sussudio	Phil Collins	Atlantic 89560
3	3	9	Raspberry Beret	Prince & The Revolution	Paisley Park 28972
4	5	13	The Search Is Over	Survivor	Scotti Brothers 04871
5	6	12	Would I Lie To You?	Eurythmics	RCA 14078
6	8	10	Everytime You Go Away	Paul Young	Columbia 04867
7	7	10	You Give Good Love	Whitney Houston	Arista 9274
8	9	14	Voices Carry	'til Tuesday	Epic 04795
9	11	7	Glory Days	Bruce Springsteen	Columbia 04924
10	12	9	The Goonies 'R' Good Enough	Cyndi Lauper	Portrait 04918

★ **HIGHEST DEBUT** ★ POS 50
You're Only Human (Second Wind).......Billy Joel

★ **BIGGEST MOVER** ★ 86 to 71
Lay It Down ....Ratt

Billboard — JULY 20, 1985 — HOT 100

TW	LW	WK	Title	Artist	Label
1	1	10	A View To A Kill	Duran Duran	Capitol 5475
2	3	10	Raspberry Beret	Prince & The Revolution	Paisley Park 28972
3	6	11	Everytime You Go Away	Paul Young	Columbia 04867
4	7	11	You Give Good Love	Whitney Houston	Arista 9274
5	2	11	Sussudio	Phil Collins	Atlantic 89560
6	4	14	The Search Is Over	Survivor	Scotti Brothers 04871
7	11	7	If You Love Somebody Set Them Free	Sting	A&M 2738
8	9	8	Glory Days	Bruce Springsteen	Columbia 04924
9	14	6	Shout	Tears For Fears	Mercury 880294
10	5	13	Would I Lie To You?	Eurythmics	RCA 14078

★ **HIGHEST DEBUT** ★ POS 46
Don't Lose My Number ....Phil Collins

★ **BIGGEST MOVER** ★ 78 to 58
Live Every Moment ....REO Speedwagon

Billboard — JULY 27, 1985 — HOT 100

TW	LW	WK	Title	Artist	Label
1	3	12	Everytime You Go Away	Paul Young	Columbia 04867
2	9	7	Shout	Tears For Fears	Mercury 880294
3	4	12	You Give Good Love	Whitney Houston	Arista 9274
4	1	11	A View To A Kill	Duran Duran	Capitol 5475
5	7	8	If You Love Somebody Set Them Free	Sting	A&M 2738
6	8	9	Glory Days	Bruce Springsteen	Columbia 04924
7	2	11	Raspberry Beret	Prince & The Revolution	Paisley Park 28972
8	12	10	Sentimental Street	Night Ranger	MCA/Camel 52591
9	13	8	Never Surrender	Corey Hart	EMI America 8268
10	14	8	Get It On	The Power Station	Capitol 5479

★ **HIGHEST DEBUT** ★ POS 43
Freedom ....Wham!

★ **BIGGEST MOVER** ★ 84 to 65
Only For Love ....Limahl

Billboard — AUGUST 3, 1985 — HOT 100

TW	LW	WK	Title	Artist	Label
1	2	8	**Shout**	Tears For Fears	Mercury 880294
2	1	13	Everytime You Go Away	Paul Young	Columbia 04867
3	5	9	**If You Love Somebody Set Them Free**	Sting	A&M 2738
4	3	13	You Give Good Love	Whitney Houston	Arista 9274
5	6	10	Glory Days	Bruce Springsteen	Columbia 04924
6	9	9	Never Surrender	Corey Hart	EMI America 8268
7	16	6	The Power Of Love	Huey Lewis & The News	Chrysalis 42876
8	8	11	**Sentimental Street**	Night Ranger	MCA/Camel 52591
9	10	9	**Get It On**	The Power Station	Capitol 5479
10	14	10	Who's Holding Donna Now	DeBarge	Gordy 1793

★ **HIGHEST DEBUT** ★ POS 64
There Must Be An Angel (Playing With My Heart) .... Eurythmics

★ **BIGGEST MOVER** ★ 83 to 52
Do You Want Crying .... Katrina & The Waves

Billboard — AUGUST 10, 1985 — HOT 100

TW	LW	WK	Title	Artist	Label
1	1	9	**Shout**	Tears For Fears	Mercury 880294
2	2	14	Everytime You Go Away	Paul Young	Columbia 04867
3	3	10	**If You Love Somebody Set Them Free**	Sting	A&M 2738
4	6	10	Never Surrender	Corey Hart	EMI America 8268
5	7	7	The Power Of Love	Huey Lewis & The News	Chrysalis 42876
6	10	11	**Who's Holding Donna Now**	DeBarge	Gordy 1793
7	5	11	Glory Days	Bruce Springsteen	Columbia 04924
8	12	8	Freeway Of Love	Aretha Franklin	Arista 9354
9	9	10	**Get It On**	The Power Station	Capitol 5479
10	4	14	You Give Good Love	Whitney Houston	Arista 9274

★ **HIGHEST DEBUT** ★ POS 62
Every Step Of The Way .... John Waite

★ **BIGGEST MOVER** ★ 85 to 61
Oh Sheila .... Ready For The World

Billboard — AUGUST 17, 1985 — HOT 100

TW	LW	WK	Title	Artist	Label
1	1	10	**Shout**	Tears For Fears	Mercury 880294
2	5	8	The Power Of Love	Huey Lewis & The News	Chrysalis 42876
3	4	11	**Never Surrender**	Corey Hart	EMI America 8268
4	3	11	If You Love Somebody Set Them Free	Sting	A&M 2738
5	8	9	**Freeway Of Love**	Aretha Franklin	Arista 9354
6	2	15	Everytime You Go Away	Paul Young	Columbia 04867
7	11	9	St. Elmo's Fire (Man In Motion)	John Parr	Atlantic 89541
8	6	12	Who's Holding Donna Now	DeBarge	Gordy 1793
9	12	8	Summer Of '69	Bryan Adams	A&M 2739
10	14	7	We Don't Need Another Hero (Thunderdome)	Tina Turner	Capitol 5491

★ **HIGHEST DEBUT** ★ POS 36
Dress You Up .... Madonna

★ **BIGGEST MOVER** ★ 52 to 39
Cry .... Godley & Creme

Billboard — AUGUST 24, 1985 — HOT 100

TW	LW	WK		
1	2	9	**The Power Of Love** ....*Huey Lewis & The News* . . . Chrysalis 42876	
(2)	1	11	Shout...*Tears For Fears* . . . Mercury 880294	
(3)	3	12	**Never Surrender**..................................*Corey Hart* . . . EMI America 8268	
(4)	7	10	St. Elmo's Fire (Man In Motion)......................*John Parr* . . . Atlantic 89541	
(5)	5	10	Freeway Of Love ....*Aretha Franklin* . . . Arista 9354	
(6)	10	8	We Don't Need Another Hero (Thunderdome) ....*Tina Turner* . . . Capitol 5491	
7	9	9	Summer Of '69...............................*Bryan Adams* . . . A&M 2739	
(8)	4	12	If You Love Somebody Set Them Free....................*Sting* . . . A&M 2738	
(9)	6	16	Everytime You Go Away ....*Paul Young* . . . Columbia 04867	
(10)	12	13	**What About Love?** ....*Heart* . . . Capitol 5481	

★ **HIGHEST DEBUT** ★ POS 40
Lonely Ol' Night..............*John Cougar Mellencamp*

★ **BIGGEST MOVER** ★ 50 to 33
Oh Sheila............................*Ready For The World*

Billboard — AUGUST 31, 1985 — HOT 100

TW	LW	WK		
1	1	10	**The Power Of Love** ....*Huey Lewis & The News* . . . Chrysalis 42876	
2	4	11	St. Elmo's Fire (Man In Motion)......................*John Parr* . . . Atlantic 89541	
3	5	11	**Freeway Of Love**...................................*Aretha Franklin* . . . Arista 9354	
4	6	9	We Don't Need Another Hero (Thunderdome) ....*Tina Turner* . . . Capitol 5491	
5	7	10	**Summer Of '69**.................................*Bryan Adams* . . . A&M 2739	
(6)	2	12	Shout...*Tears For Fears* . . . Mercury 880294	
(7)	3	13	Never Surrender ....*Corey Hart* . . . EMI America 8268	
(8)	12	9	Cherish ....*Kool & The Gang* . . . De-Lite 880869	
(9)	14	8	**You're Only Human (Second Wind)**........*Billy Joel* . . . Columbia 05417	
(10)	17	8	Money For Nothing ....*Dire Straits* . . . Warner 28950	

★ **HIGHEST DEBUT** ★ POS 47
Dancing In The Street.....*Mick Jagger/David Bowie*

★ **BIGGEST MOVER** ★ 92 to 69
Love Theme From St. Elmo's Fire ....*David Foster*

Billboard — SEPTEMBER 7, 1985 — HOT 100

TW	LW	WK		
1	2	12	**St. Elmo's Fire (Man In Motion)** ....*John Parr* . . . Atlantic 89541	
(2)	1	11	The Power Of Love...................*Huey Lewis & The News* . . . Chrysalis 42876	
(3)	4	10	We Don't Need Another Hero (Thunderdome) ....*Tina Turner* . . . Capitol 5491	
(4)	3	12	Freeway Of Love ....*Aretha Franklin* . . . Arista 9354	
(5)	5	11	**Summer Of '69**.................................*Bryan Adams* . . . A&M 2739	
(6)	10	9	Money For Nothing ....*Dire Straits* . . . Warner 28950	
7	8	10	Cherish ....*Kool & The Gang* . . . De-Lite 880869	
(8)	11	8	Don't Lose My Number..........................*Phil Collins* . . . Atlantic 89536	
(9)	9	9	**You're Only Human (Second Wind)**........*Billy Joel* . . . Columbia 05417	
(10)	13	7	Pop Life................................*Prince & The Revolution* . . . Paisley Park 28998	

★ **HIGHEST DEBUT** ★ POS 43
Part-Time Lover ....*Stevie Wonder*

★ **BIGGEST MOVER** ★ 47 to 33
Dancing In The Street.....*Mick Jagger/David Bowie*

Billboard · SEPTEMBER 14, 1985 · HOT 100.

TW	LW	WK	Title / Artist / Label
1	1	13	St. Elmo's Fire (Man In Motion) ....*John Parr* ... Atlantic 89541
2	3	11	We Don't Need Another Hero (Thunderdome) ....*Tina Turner* ... Capitol 5491
3	6	10	Money For Nothing ....*Dire Straits* ... Warner 28950
4	7	11	Cherish ....*Kool & The Gang* ... De-Lite 880869
5	2	12	The Power Of Love ....*Huey Lewis & The News* ... Chrysalis 42876
6	8	9	Don't Lose My Number ....*Phil Collins* ... Atlantic 89536
7	4	13	Freeway Of Love ....*Aretha Franklin* ... Arista 9354
8	12	8	Freedom...*Wham!* ... Columbia 05409
9	10	8	Pop Life...........................*Prince & The Revolution* ... Paisley Park 28998
10	11	11	Invincible...*Pat Benatar* ... Chrysalis 42877

★ HIGHEST DEBUT ★ POS 49	★ BIGGEST MOVER ★ 73 to 51
Head Over Heels.....................*Tears For Fears*	We Built This City ....*Starship*

Billboard · SEPTEMBER 21, 1985 · HOT 100.

TW	LW	WK	Title / Artist / Label
1	3	11	Money For Nothing ....*Dire Straits* ... Warner 28950
2	4	12	Cherish..*Kool & The Gang* ... De-Lite 880869
3	1	14	St. Elmo's Fire (Man In Motion).....................*John Parr* ... Atlantic 89541
4	2	12	We Don't Need Another Hero (Thunderdome) ....*Tina Turner* ... Capitol 5491
5	6	10	Don't Lose My Number ....*Phil Collins* ... Atlantic 89536
6	8	9	Freedom...*Wham!* ... Columbia 05409
7	9	9	Pop Life ....*Prince & The Revolution* ... Paisley Park 28998
8	5	13	The Power Of Love ....*Huey Lewis & The News* ... Chrysalis 42876
9	15	8	Oh Sheila...............................*Ready For The World* ... MCA 52636
10	14	6	Dress You Up ....*Madonna* ... Sire 28919

★ HIGHEST DEBUT ★ POS 56	★ BIGGEST MOVER ★ 69 to 51
Lay Your Hands On Me ....*Thompson Twins*	Boy In The Box ....*Corey Hart*

Billboard · SEPTEMBER 28, 1985 · HOT 100.

TW	LW	WK	Title / Artist / Label
1	1	12	Money For Nothing ....*Dire Straits* ... Warner 28950
2	2	13	Cherish..*Kool & The Gang* ... De-Lite 880869
3	6	10	Freedom...*Wham!* ... Columbia 05409
4	5	11	Don't Lose My Number ....*Phil Collins* ... Atlantic 89536
5	9	9	Oh Sheila................................*Ready For The World* ... MCA 52636
6	10	7	Dress You Up ....*Madonna* ... Sire 28919
7	13	12	Take On Me ....*a-ha* ... Warner 29011
8	3	15	St. Elmo's Fire (Man In Motion).....................*John Parr* ... Atlantic 89541
9	14	7	Saving All My Love For You.....................*Whitney Houston* ... Arista 9381
10	15	6	Lonely Ol' Night ....*John Cougar Mellencamp* ... Riva 880984

★ HIGHEST DEBUT ★ POS 51	★ BIGGEST MOVER ★ 84 to 66
Who's Zoomin' Who...................*Aretha Franklin*	Broken Wings ....*Mr. Mister*

Billboard OCTOBER 5, 1985 HOT 100

TW	LW	WK	Title	Artist	Label
1	1	13	**Money For Nothing**	*Dire Straits*	Warner 28950
2	2	14	**Cherish**	*Kool & The Gang*	De-Lite 880869
3	5	10	Oh Sheila	*Ready For The World*	MCA 52636
4	7	13	Take On Me	*a-ha*	Warner 29011
5	6	8	**Dress You Up**	*Madonna*	Sire 28919
6	9	8	Saving All My Love For You	*Whitney Houston*	Arista 9381
7	3	11	Freedom	*Wham!*	Columbia 05409
8	10	7	Lonely Ol' Night	*John Cougar Mellencamp*	Riva 880984
9	11	6	Dancing In The Street	*Mick Jagger/David Bowie*	EMI America 8288
10	15	5	Part-Time Lover	*Stevie Wonder*	Tamla 1808

★ **HIGHEST DEBUT** ★ POS 45
Separate Lives ....*Phil Collins & Marilyn Martin*

★ **BIGGEST MOVER** ★ 81 to 64
Like To Get To Know You Well......*Howard Jones*

Billboard OCTOBER 12, 1985 HOT 100

TW	LW	WK	Title	Artist	Label
1	3	11	**Oh Sheila**	*Ready For The World*	MCA 52636
2	1	14	Money For Nothing	*Dire Straits*	Warner 28950
3	4	14	Take On Me	*a-ha*	Warner 29011
4	6	9	Saving All My Love For You	*Whitney Houston*	Arista 9381
5	10	6	Part-Time Lover	*Stevie Wonder*	Tamla 1808
6	8	8	**Lonely Ol' Night**	*John Cougar Mellencamp*	Riva 880984
7	9	7	**Dancing In The Street**	*Mick Jagger/David Bowie*	... EMI America 8288
8	2	15	Cherish	*Kool & The Gang*	De-Lite 880869
9	13	6	Miami Vice Theme	*Jan Hammer*	MCA 52666
10	5	9	Dress You Up	*Madonna*	Sire 28919

★ **HIGHEST DEBUT** ★ POS 84
To Live And Die In L.A. ....*Wang Chung*

★ **BIGGEST MOVER** ★ 72 to 52
Girls Are More Fun ....*Ray Parker Jr.*

Billboard OCTOBER 19, 1985 HOT 100

TW	LW	WK	Title	Artist	Label
1	3	15	**Take On Me**	*a-ha*	Warner 29011
2	4	10	Saving All My Love For You	*Whitney Houston*	Arista 9381
3	5	7	Part-Time Lover	*Stevie Wonder*	Tamla 1808
4	1	12	Oh Sheila	*Ready For The World*	MCA 52636
5	9	7	Miami Vice Theme	*Jan Hammer*	MCA 52666
6	6	9	**Lonely Ol' Night**	*John Cougar Mellencamp*	Riva 880984
7	2	15	Money For Nothing	*Dire Straits*	Warner 28950
8	7	8	Dancing In The Street	*Mick Jagger/David Bowie*	EMI America 8288
9	11	9	Fortress Around Your Heart	*Sting*	A&M 2767
10	13	6	Head Over Heels	*Tears For Fears*	Mercury 880899

★ **HIGHEST DEBUT** ★ POS 49
Sleeping Bag ....*ZZ Top*

★ **BIGGEST MOVER** ★ 84 to 71
To Live And Die In L.A. ....*Wang Chung*

TW	LW	WK	Billboard.	OCTOBER 26, 1985	HOT 100.
❶	2	11	**Saving All My Love For You**	*Whitney Houston* . . .	Arista 9381
❷	3	8	Part-Time Lover	*Stevie Wonder* . . .	Tamla 1808
③	1	16	Take On Me	*a-ha* . . .	Warner 29011
❹	5	8	Miami Vice Theme	*Jan Hammer* . . .	MCA 52666
❺	10	7	Head Over Heels	*Tears For Fears* . . .	Mercury 880899
⑥	4	13	Oh Sheila..	*Ready For The World* . . .	MCA 52636
⑦	6	10	Lonely Ol' Night	*John Cougar Mellencamp* . . .	Riva 880984
⑧	9	10	**Fortress Around Your Heart**	*Sting* . . .	A&M 2767
⑨	11	8	**I'm Goin' Down**	*Bruce Springsteen* . . .	Columbia 05603
❿	15	7	You Belong To The City	*Glenn Frey* . . .	MCA 52651

★ *HIGHEST DEBUT* ★ POS 46	★ *BIGGEST MOVER* ★ 62 to 45
Election Day ....*Arcadia*	Sisters Are Doin' It For Themselves ....*Eurythmics & Aretha Franklin*

TW	LW	WK	Billboard.	NOVEMBER 2, 1985	HOT 100.
❶	2	9	**Part-Time Lover**	*Stevie Wonder* . . .	Tamla 1808
❷	4	9	**Miami Vice Theme**..	*Jan Hammer* . . .	MCA 52666
③	1	12	Saving All My Love For You....................	*Whitney Houston* . . .	Arista 9381
❹	5	8	Head Over Heels	*Tears For Fears* . . .	Mercury 880899
⑤	3	17	Take On Me	*a-ha* . . .	Warner 29011
❻	10	8	You Belong To The City	*Glenn Frey* . . .	MCA 52651
❼	13	9	We Built This City	*Starship* . . .	Grunt 14170
⑧	8	11	**Fortress Around Your Heart**	*Sting* . . .	A&M 2767
⑨	11	11	**Lovin' Every Minute Of It**.....................	*Loverboy* . . .	Columbia 05569
❿	16	11	Be Near Me	*ABC* . . .	Mercury 880626

★ *HIGHEST DEBUT* ★ POS 51	★ *BIGGEST MOVER* ★ 80 to 58
Small Town ....*John Cougar Mellencamp*	You're A Friend Of Mine........*Clarence Clemons & Jackson Browne*

TW	LW	WK	Billboard.	NOVEMBER 9, 1985	HOT 100.
❶	2	10	**Miami Vice Theme**	*Jan Hammer* . . .	MCA 52666
②	1	10	Part-Time Lover	*Stevie Wonder* . . .	Tamla 1808
❸	4	9	**Head Over Heels**...............................	*Tears For Fears* . . .	Mercury 880899
❹	6	9	You Belong To The City	*Glenn Frey* . . .	MCA 52651
❺	7	10	We Built This City	*Starship* . . .	Grunt 14170
⑥	3	13	Saving All My Love For You....................	*Whitney Houston* . . .	Arista 9381
❼	15	6	**Separate Lives**....................*Phil Collins & Marilyn Martin* . . .	Atlantic 89498
⑧	5	18	Take On Me	*a-ha* . . .	Warner 29011
❾	10	12	**Be Near Me**	*ABC* . . .	Mercury 880626
❿	18	8	Lay Your Hands On Me..........................	*Thompson Twins* . . .	Arista 9396

★ *HIGHEST DEBUT* ★ POS 40	★ *BIGGEST MOVER* ★ 61 to 45
Say You, Say Me...........................*Lionel Richie*	Walk Of Life ....*Dire Straits*

Billboard — NOVEMBER 16, 1985 — HOT 100

TW	LW	WK	Title	Artist	Label
1	5	11	**We Built This City**	Starship	Grunt 14170
2	4	10	**You Belong To The City**	Glenn Frey	MCA 52651
3	1	11	Miami Vice Theme	Jan Hammer	MCA 52666
4	3	10	Head Over Heels	Tears For Fears	Mercury 880899
5	2	11	Part-Time Lover	Stevie Wonder	Tamla 1808
6	7	7	Separate Lives	Phil Collins & Marilyn Martin	Atlantic 89498
7	11	9	Broken Wings	Mr. Mister	RCA 14136
8	12	10	Never	Heart	Capitol 5512
9	9	13	**Be Near Me**	ABC	Mercury 880626
10	10	9	Lay Your Hands On Me	Thompson Twins	Arista 9396

★ **HIGHEST DEBUT** ★ POS 66
Talk To Me ....Stevie Nicks

★ **BIGGEST MOVER** ★ 71 to 53
Sun City ....Artists United Against Apartheid

Billboard — NOVEMBER 23, 1985 — HOT 100

TW	LW	WK	Title	Artist	Label
1	1	12	**We Built This City**	Starship	Grunt 14170
2	2	11	**You Belong To The City**	Glenn Frey	MCA 52651
3	6	8	Separate Lives	Phil Collins & Marilyn Martin	Atlantic 89498
4	7	10	Broken Wings	Mr. Mister	RCA 14136
5	8	11	Never	Heart	Capitol 5512
6	10	10	**Lay Your Hands On Me**	Thompson Twins	Arista 9396
7	4	11	Head Over Heels	Tears For Fears	Mercury 880899
8	3	12	Miami Vice Theme	Jan Hammer	MCA 52666
9	11	9	Who's Zoomin' Who	Aretha Franklin	Arista 9410
10	5	12	Part-Time Lover	Stevie Wonder	Tamla 1808

★ **HIGHEST DEBUT** ★ POS 53
It's Only Love.................Bryan Adams/Tina Turner

★ **BIGGEST MOVER** ★ 66 to 47
Talk To Me ....Stevie Nicks

Billboard — NOVEMBER 30, 1985 — HOT 100

TW	LW	WK	Title	Artist	Label
1	3	9	**Separate Lives**	Phil Collins & Marilyn Martin	Atlantic 89498
2	1	13	We Built This City	Starship	Grunt 14170
3	4	11	Broken Wings	Mr. Mister	RCA 14136
4	2	12	You Belong To The City	Glenn Frey	MCA 52651
5	5	12	Never	Heart	Capitol 5512
6	6	11	**Lay Your Hands On Me**	Thompson Twins	Arista 9396
7	9	10	**Who's Zoomin' Who**	Aretha Franklin	Arista 9410
8	13	6	Election Day	Arcadia	Capitol 5501
9	17	9	Party All The Time	Eddie Murphy	Columbia 05609
10	14	7	Sleeping Bag	ZZ Top	Warner 28884

★ **HIGHEST DEBUT** ★ POS 55
I'm Your Man.......................................Wham!

★ **BIGGEST MOVER** ★ 72 to 56
Sex As A Weapon ....Pat Benatar

Billboard — DECEMBER 7, 1985 — HOT 100

TW	LW	WK	Title	Artist	Label
1	3	12	**Broken Wings**	Mr. Mister	RCA 14136
2	1	10	Separate Lives	Phil Collins & Marilyn Martin	Atlantic 89498
3	2	14	We Built This City	Starship	Grunt 14170
4	5	13	**Never**	Heart	Capitol 5512
5	12	5	Say You, Say Me	Lionel Richie	Motown 1819
6	4	13	You Belong To The City	Glenn Frey	MCA 52651
7	8	7	Election Day	Arcadia	Capitol 5501
8	7	11	Who's Zoomin' Who	Aretha Franklin	Arista 9410
9	9	10	Party All The Time	Eddie Murphy	Columbia 05609
10	10	8	Sleeping Bag	ZZ Top	Warner 28884

★ **HIGHEST DEBUT** ★ POS 55
My Hometown .... Bruce Springsteen

★ **BIGGEST MOVER** ★ 74 to 54
Everything In My Heart .... Corey Hart

Billboard — DECEMBER 14, 1985 — HOT 100

TW	LW	WK	Title	Artist	Label
1	1	13	**Broken Wings**	Mr. Mister	RCA 14136
2	2	11	Separate Lives	Phil Collins & Marilyn Martin	Atlantic 89498
3	5	6	Say You, Say Me	Lionel Richie	Motown 1819
4	9	11	Party All The Time	Eddie Murphy	Columbia 05609
5	4	14	Never	Heart	Capitol 5512
6	7	8	**Election Day**	Arcadia	Capitol 5501
7	11	9	Alive & Kicking	Simple Minds	A&M 2783
8	10	9	**Sleeping Bag**	ZZ Top	Warner 28884
9	13	14	I Miss You	Klymaxx	Constellation 52606
10	3	15	We Built This City	Starship	Grunt 14170

★ **HIGHEST DEBUT** ★ POS 85
Day By Day .... Hooters

★ **BIGGEST MOVER** ★ 91 to 64
Living In America .... James Brown

Billboard — DECEMBER 21, 1985 — HOT 100

TW	LW	WK	Title	Artist	Label
1	3	7	**Say You, Say Me**	Lionel Richie	Motown 1819
2	1	14	Broken Wings	Mr. Mister	RCA 14136
3	4	12	Party All The Time	Eddie Murphy	Columbia 05609
4	7	10	Alive & Kicking	Simple Minds	A&M 2783
5	2	12	Separate Lives	Phil Collins & Marilyn Martin	Atlantic 89498
6	6	9	**Election Day**	Arcadia	Capitol 5501
7	9	15	I Miss You	Klymaxx	Constellation 52606
8	14	7	That's What Friends Are For	Dionne & Friends	Arista 9422
9	12	8	Small Town	John Cougar Mellencamp	Riva 884202
10	8	10	Sleeping Bag	ZZ Top	Warner 28884

★ **HIGHEST DEBUT** ★ POS 61
Kyrie .... Mr. Mister

★ **BIGGEST MOVER** ★ 96 to 76
He'll Never Love You (Like I Do) .... Freddie Jackson

TW	LW	WK	Billboard. ⊙ DECEMBER 28, 1985 ⊙	HOT 100.
❶	1	8	**Say You, Say Me** ....*Lionel Richie* . . . Motown 1819	
❷	3	13	**Party All The Time**...........................*Eddie Murphy* . . . Columbia 05609	
❸	4	11	**Alive & Kicking**...............................*Simple Minds* . . . A&M 2783	
❹	8	8	**That's What Friends Are For** ....*Dionne & Friends* . . . Arista 9422	
❺	7	16	**I Miss You** ....*Klymaxx* . . . Constellation 52606	
❻	9	9	**Small Town** ....*John Cougar Mellencamp* . . . Riva 884202	
⑦	2	15	**Broken Wings**.......................................*Mr. Mister* . . . RCA 14136	
⑧	5	13	**Separate Lives**....................*Phil Collins & Marilyn Martin* . . . Atlantic 89498	
⑨	12	9	**Tonight She Comes** ....*The Cars* . . . Elektra 69589	
⑩	6	10	**Election Day** ....*Arcadia* . . . Capitol 5501	

★ HIGHEST DEBUT ★ POS 65	★ BIGGEST MOVER ★ 32 to 16
Sara ....*Starship*	My Hometown ....*Bruce Springsteen*

502

Billboard — JANUARY 11, 1986 — HOT 100

TW	LW	WK	Title	Artist ... Label
1	1	10	**Say You, Say Me**	*Lionel Richie* ... Motown 1819
2	2	15	**Party All The Time**	*Eddie Murphy* ... Columbia 05609
3	4	10	**That's What Friends Are For**	*Dionne & Friends* ... Arista 9422
4	3	13	**Alive & Kicking**	*Simple Minds* ... A&M 2783
5	5	18	**I Miss You**	*Klymaxx* ... Constellation 52606
6	6	11	**Small Town**	*John Cougar Mellencamp* ... Riva 884202
7	9	11	**Tonight She Comes**	*The Cars* ... Elektra 69589
8	11	9	**Talk To Me**	*Stevie Nicks* ... Modern 99582
9	7	17	**Broken Wings**	*Mr. Mister* ... RCA 14136
10	13	11	**Walk Of Life**	*Dire Straits* ... Warner 28878

★ **HIGHEST DEBUT** ★ POS 87
Your Personal Touch .....*Evelyn "Champagne" King*

★ **BIGGEST MOVER** ★ 80 to 66
Secret Lovers ....*Atlantic Starr*

Billboard — JANUARY 18, 1986 — HOT 100

TW	LW	WK	Title	Artist ... Label
1	3	11	**That's What Friends Are For**	*Dionne & Friends* ... Arista 9422
2	1	11	**Say You, Say Me**	*Lionel Richie* ... Motown 1819
3	2	16	**Party All The Time**	*Eddie Murphy* ... Columbia 05609
4	4	14	**Alive & Kicking**	*Simple Minds* ... A&M 2783
5	5	19	**I Miss You**	*Klymaxx* ... Constellation 52606
6	6	12	**Small Town**	*John Cougar Mellencamp* ... Riva 884202
7	8	10	**Talk To Me**	*Stevie Nicks* ... Modern 99582
8	12	12	**Burning Heart**	*Survivor* ... Scotti Brothers 05663
9	10	12	**Walk Of Life**	*Dire Straits* ... Warner 28878
10	7	12	**Tonight She Comes**	*The Cars* ... Elektra 69589

★ **HIGHEST DEBUT** ★ POS 52
King For A Day ....*Thompson Twins*

★ **BIGGEST MOVER** ★ 66 to 45
Secret Lovers ....*Atlantic Starr*

Billboard — JANUARY 25, 1986 — HOT 100

TW	LW	WK	Title	Artist ... Label
1	1	12	**That's What Friends Are For**	*Dionne & Friends* ... Arista 9422
2	2	12	**Say You, Say Me**	*Lionel Richie* ... Motown 1819
3	8	13	**Burning Heart**	*Survivor* ... Scotti Brothers 05663
4	7	11	**Talk To Me**	*Stevie Nicks* ... Modern 99582
5	12	9	**I'm Your Man**	*Wham!* ... Columbia 05721
6	11	8	**My Hometown**	*Bruce Springsteen* ... Columbia 05728
7	9	13	**Walk Of Life**	*Dire Straits* ... Warner 28878
8	5	20	**I Miss You**	*Klymaxx* ... Constellation 52606
9	3	17	**Party All The Time**	*Eddie Murphy* ... Columbia 05609
10	13	10	**Spies Like Us**	*Paul McCartney* ... Capitol 5537

★ **HIGHEST DEBUT** ★ POS 64
Sanctify Yourself ....*Simple Minds*

★ **BIGGEST MOVER** ★ 87 to 61
This Could Be The Night ....*Loverboy*

Billboard — FEBRUARY 1, 1986 — HOT 100

TW	LW	WK			
❶	1	13	That's What Friends Are For	Dionne & Friends	Arista 9422
❷	3	14	Burning Heart	Survivor	Scotti Brothers 05663
❸	5	10	I'm Your Man	Wham!	Columbia 05721
④	4	12	Talk To Me	Stevie Nicks	Modern 99582
⑤	2	13	Say You, Say Me	Lionel Richie	Motown 1819
⑥	6	9	My Hometown	Bruce Springsteen	Columbia 05728
❼	11	10	When The Going Gets Tough, The Tough Get Going	Billy Ocean	Jive 9432
❽	10	11	Spies Like Us	Paul McCartney	Capitol 5537
⑨	7	14	Walk Of Life	Dire Straits	Warner 28878
❿	13	11	Go Home	Stevie Wonder	Tamla 1817

★ **HIGHEST DEBUT** ★ POS 54
R.O.C.K. In The U.S.A. .....*John Cougar Mellencamp*

★ **BIGGEST MOVER** ★ 84 to 56
Superbowl Shuffle.......*The Chicago Bears Shufflin' Crew*

Billboard — FEBRUARY 8, 1986 — HOT 100

TW	LW	WK			
❶	1	14	That's What Friends Are For	Dionne & Friends	Arista 9422
❷	2	15	Burning Heart	Survivor	Scotti Brothers 05663
❸	3	11	I'm Your Man	Wham!	Columbia 05721
❹	7	11	When The Going Gets Tough, The Tough Get Going	Billy Ocean	Jive 9432
❺	11	10	How Will I Know	Whitney Houston	Arista 9434
❻	13	8	Kyrie	Mr. Mister	RCA 14258
⑦	8	12	Spies Like Us	Paul McCartney	Capitol 5537
⑧	4	13	Talk To Me	Stevie Nicks	Modern 99582
⑨	15	10	Living In America	James Brown	Scotti Brothers 05682
❿	12	17	Conga	Miami Sound Machine	Epic 05457

★ **HIGHEST DEBUT** ★ POS 79
Rock Me Amadeus...................................*Falco*

★ **BIGGEST MOVER** ★ 91 to 69
Calling America.................*Electric Light Orchestra*

Billboard — FEBRUARY 15, 1986 — HOT 100

TW	LW	WK			
❶	5	11	How Will I Know	Whitney Houston	Arista 9434
❷	4	12	When The Going Gets Tough, The Tough Get Going	Billy Ocean	Jive 9432
③	2	16	Burning Heart	Survivor	Scotti Brothers 05663
④	6	9	Kyrie	Mr. Mister	RCA 14258
⑤	1	15	That's What Friends Are For	Dionne & Friends	Arista 9422
⑥	3	12	I'm Your Man	Wham!	Columbia 05721
⑦	9	11	Living In America	James Brown	Scotti Brothers 05682
⑧	12	13	The Sweetest Taboo	Sade	Portrait 05713
⑨	15	8	Sara	Starship	Grunt 14253
❿	10	18	Conga	Miami Sound Machine	Epic 05457

★ **HIGHEST DEBUT** ★ POS 73
Le Bel Age ....*Pat Benatar*

★ **BIGGEST MOVER** ★ 79 to 56
Rock Me Amadeus...................................*Falco*

Billboard — FEBRUARY 22, 1986 — HOT 100

TW	LW	WK			
①	1	12	How Will I Know	Whitney Houston	Arista 9434
②	4	10	Kyrie	Mr. Mister	RCA 14258
③	2	13	When The Going Gets Tough, The Tough Get Going	Billy Ocean	Jive 9432
④	9	9	Sara	Starship	Grunt 14253
⑤	7	12	Living In America	James Brown	Scotti Brothers 05682
⑥	8	14	The Sweetest Taboo	Sade	Portrait 05713
⑦	11	13	Life In A Northern Town	The Dream Academy	Warner 28841
⑧	12	14	Silent Running (On Dangerous Ground)	Mike + The Mechanics	Atlantic 89488
⑨	3	17	Burning Heart	Survivor	Scotti Brothers 05663
⑩	5	16	That's What Friends Are For	Dionne & Friends	Arista 9422

★ HIGHEST DEBUT ★ POS 52	★ BIGGEST MOVER ★ 56 to 40
Kiss .... Prince & The Revolution	Rock Me Amadeus .... Falco

Billboard — MARCH 1, 1986 — HOT 100

TW	LW	WK			
①	2	11	Kyrie	Mr. Mister	RCA 14258
②	1	13	How Will I Know	Whitney Houston	Arista 9434
③	4	10	Sara	Starship	Grunt 14253
④	5	13	Living In America	James Brown	Scotti Brothers 05682
⑤	6	15	The Sweetest Taboo	Sade	Portrait 05713
⑥	3	14	When The Going Gets Tough, The Tough Get Going	Billy Ocean	Jive 9432
⑦	7	14	Life In A Northern Town	The Dream Academy	Warner 28841
⑧	8	15	Silent Running (On Dangerous Ground)	Mike + The Mechanics	Atlantic 89488
⑨	11	10	Secret Lovers	Atlantic Starr	A&M 2788
⑩	14	7	These Dreams	Heart	Capitol 5541

★ HIGHEST DEBUT ★ POS 66	★ BIGGEST MOVER ★ 95 to 75
So Far Away .... Dire Straits	What Have You Done For Me Lately .... Janet Jackson

Billboard — MARCH 8, 1986 — HOT 100

TW	LW	WK			
①	1	12	Kyrie	Mr. Mister	RCA 14258
②	3	11	Sara	Starship	Grunt 14253
③	2	14	How Will I Know	Whitney Houston	Arista 9434
④	10	8	These Dreams	Heart	Capitol 5541
⑤	9	11	Secret Lovers	Atlantic Starr	A&M 2788
⑥	8	16	Silent Running (On Dangerous Ground)	Mike + The Mechanics	Atlantic 89488
⑦	5	16	The Sweetest Taboo	Sade	Portrait 05713
⑧	4	14	Living In America	James Brown	Scotti Brothers 05682
⑨	7	15	Life In A Northern Town	The Dream Academy	Warner 28841
⑩	12	8	King For A Day	Thompson Twins	Arista 9450

★ HIGHEST DEBUT ★ POS 73	★ BIGGEST MOVER ★ 71 to 50
I Do What I Do .... John Taylor	West End Girls .... Pet Shop Boys

MARCH 15, 1986 — Billboard HOT 100

TW	LW	WK	Title	Artist	Label
1	2	12	**Sara**	*Starship*	Grunt 14253
2	4	9	**These Dreams**	*Heart*	Capitol 5541
3	1	13	Kyrie	*Mr. Mister*	RCA 14258
4	5	12	Secret Lovers	*Atlantic Starr*	A&M 2788
5	3	15	How Will I Know	*Whitney Houston*	Arista 9434
6	11	7	R.O.C.K. In The U.S.A.	*John Cougar Mellencamp*	Riva 884455
7	14	6	Rock Me Amadeus	*Falco*	A&M 2821
8	6	17	Silent Running (On Dangerous Ground)	*Mike + The Mechanics*	Atlantic 89488
9	10	9	King For A Day	*Thompson Twins*	Arista 9450
10	13	9	Nikita	*Elton John*	Geffen 28800

★ **HIGHEST DEBUT** ★ POS 47
Harlem Shuffle .... *Rolling Stones*

★ **BIGGEST MOVER** ★ 76 to 55
Bad Boy .... *Miami Sound Machine*

MARCH 22, 1986 — Billboard HOT 100

TW	LW	WK	Title	Artist	Label
1	2	10	**These Dreams**	*Heart*	Capitol 5541
2	1	13	Sara	*Starship*	Grunt 14253
3	4	13	**Secret Lovers**	*Atlantic Starr*	A&M 2788
4	7	7	Rock Me Amadeus	*Falco*	A&M 2821
5	6	8	R.O.C.K. In The U.S.A.	*John Cougar Mellencamp*	Riva 884455
6	3	14	Kyrie	*Mr. Mister*	RCA 14258
7	10	10	Nikita	*Elton John*	Geffen 28800
8	9	10	King For A Day	*Thompson Twins*	Arista 9450
9	11	10	What You Need	*INXS*	Atlantic 89460
10	15	5	Kiss	*Prince & The Revolution*	Paisley Park 28751

★ **HIGHEST DEBUT** ★ POS 72
Stick Around .... *Julian Lennon*

★ **BIGGEST MOVER** ★ 73 to 47
Take Me Home .... *Phil Collins*

MARCH 29, 1986 — Billboard HOT 100

TW	LW	WK	Title	Artist	Label
1	4	8	**Rock Me Amadeus**	*Falco*	A&M 2821
2	1	11	These Dreams	*Heart*	Capitol 5541
3	3	14	**Secret Lovers**	*Atlantic Starr*	A&M 2788
4	5	9	R.O.C.K. In The U.S.A.	*John Cougar Mellencamp*	Riva 884455
5	10	6	Kiss	*Prince & The Revolution*	Paisley Park 28751
6	9	11	What You Need	*INXS*	Atlantic 89460
7	7	11	**Nikita**	*Elton John*	Geffen 28800
8	2	14	Sara	*Starship*	Grunt 14253
9	13	14	Let's Go All The Way	*Sly Fox*	Capitol 5552
10	11	11	**This Could Be The Night**	*Loverboy*	Columbia 05765

★ **HIGHEST DEBUT** ★ POS 54
Greatest Love Of All .... *Whitney Houston*

★ **BIGGEST MOVER** ★ 43 to 24
Why Can't This Be Love .... *Van Halen*

Billboard 🔵 APRIL 5, 1986 🔵 HOT 100.

TW	LW	WK		
①	1	9	**Rock Me Amadeus** ....*Falco* ... A&M 2821
②	4	10	**R.O.C.K. In The U.S.A.**..............*John Cougar Mellencamp* ... Riva 884455
③	5	7	**Kiss** ....*Prince & The Revolution* ... Paisley Park 28751
④	3	15	**Secret Lovers** ....*Atlantic Starr* ... A&M 2788
⑤	2	12	**These Dreams** ....*Heart* ... Capitol 5541
⑥	6	12	**What You Need**..*INXS* ... Atlantic 89460
⑦	11	11	**Manic Monday** ....*Bangles* ... Columbia 05757
⑧	9	15	**Let's Go All The Way** ....*Sly Fox* ... Capitol 5552
⑨	13	9	**Addicted To Love** ....*Robert Palmer* ... Island 99570
⑩	7	12	**Nikita**...*Elton John* ... Geffen 28800

★ **HIGHEST DEBUT** ★ POS 68	★ **BIGGEST MOVER** ★ 78 to 60
Move Away.............................*Culture Club*	On My Own ....*Patti LaBelle & Michael McDonald*

Billboard 🔵 APRIL 12, 1986 🔵 HOT 100.

TW	LW	WK		
①	1	10	**Rock Me Amadeus** ....*Falco* ... A&M 2821
②	3	8	**Kiss** ....*Prince & The Revolution* ... Paisley Park 28751
③	7	12	**Manic Monday** ....*Bangles* ... Columbia 05757
④	2	11	**R.O.C.K. In The U.S.A.** ....*John Cougar Mellencamp* ... Riva 884455
⑤	6	13	**What You Need**..*INXS* ... Atlantic 89460
⑥	9	10	**Addicted To Love** ....*Robert Palmer* ... Island 99570
⑦	8	16	**Let's Go All The Way**.......................................*Sly Fox* ... Capitol 5552
⑧	12	7	**West End Girls**................................*Pet Shop Boys* ... EMI America 8307
⑨	14	5	**Harlem Shuffle** ....*Rolling Stones* ... Rolling Stones 05802
⑩	11	11	**Tender Love** ....*Force M.D.'s* ... Warner 28818

★ **HIGHEST DEBUT** ★ POS 49	★ **BIGGEST MOVER** ★ 71 to 53
Live To Tell ....*Madonna*	Tomorrow Doesn't Matter Tonight ....*Starship*

Billboard 🔵 APRIL 19, 1986 🔵 HOT 100.

TW	LW	WK		
①	2	9	**Kiss** ....*Prince & The Revolution* ... Paisley Park 28751
②	3	13	**Manic Monday** ....*Bangles* ... Columbia 05757
③	6	11	**Addicted To Love** ....*Robert Palmer* ... Island 99570
④	1	11	**Rock Me Amadeus**..*Falco* ... A&M 2821
⑤	8	8	**West End Girls**................................*Pet Shop Boys* ... EMI America 8307
⑥	5	14	**What You Need**..*INXS* ... Atlantic 89460
⑦	7	17	**Let's Go All The Way**.......................................*Sly Fox* ... Capitol 5552
⑧	9	6	**Harlem Shuffle** ....*Rolling Stones* ... Rolling Stones 05802
⑨	12	6	**Why Can't This Be Love** ....*Van Halen* ... Warner 28740
⑩	10	12	**Tender Love** ....*Force M.D.'s* ... Warner 28818

★ **HIGHEST DEBUT** ★ POS 61	★ **BIGGEST MOVER** ★ 84 to 67
There'll Be Sad Songs (To Make You Cry) ....*Billy Ocean*	I Wanna Be A Cowboy ....*Boys Don't Cry*

Billboard — HOT 100 — APRIL 26, 1986

TW	LW	WK	Title	Artist	Label
1	1	10	**Kiss**	*Prince & The Revolution*	Paisley Park 28751
2	3	12	**Addicted To Love**	*Robert Palmer*	Island 99570
3	5	9	**West End Girls**	*Pet Shop Boys*	EMI America 8307
4	2	14	**Manic Monday**	*Bangles*	Columbia 05757
5	9	7	**Why Can't This Be Love**	*Van Halen*	Warner 28740
6	8	7	**Harlem Shuffle**	*Rolling Stones*	Rolling Stones 05802
7	4	12	**Rock Me Amadeus**	*Falco*	A&M 2821
8	12	10	**What Have You Done For Me Lately**	*Janet Jackson*	A&M 2812
9	13	11	**Your Love**	*The Outfield*	Columbia 05796
10	14	7	**Take Me Home**	*Phil Collins*	Atlantic 89472

★ **HIGHEST DEBUT** ★ POS 57
A Different Corner......................*George Michael*

★ **BIGGEST MOVER** ★ 91 to 67
The Love Parade.................*The Dream Academy*

Billboard — HOT 100 — MAY 3, 1986

TW	LW	WK	Title	Artist	Label
1	2	13	**Addicted To Love**	*Robert Palmer*	Island 99570
2	3	10	**West End Girls**	*Pet Shop Boys*	EMI America 8307
3	1	11	**Kiss**	*Prince & The Revolution*	Paisley Park 28751
4	5	8	**Why Can't This Be Love**	*Van Halen*	Warner 28740
5	6	8	**Harlem Shuffle**	*Rolling Stones*	Rolling Stones 05802
6	8	11	**What Have You Done For Me Lately**	*Janet Jackson*	A&M 2812
7	12	6	**Greatest Love Of All**	*Whitney Houston*	Arista 9466
8	9	12	**Your Love**	*The Outfield*	Columbia 05796
9	10	8	**Take Me Home**	*Phil Collins*	Atlantic 89472
10	4	15	**Manic Monday**	*Bangles*	Columbia 05757

★ **HIGHEST DEBUT** ★ POS 75
Like No Other Night..........................*38 Special*

★ **BIGGEST MOVER** ★ 75 to 59
Who's Johnny......................................*El DeBarge*

Billboard — HOT 100 — MAY 10, 1986

TW	LW	WK	Title	Artist	Label
1	2	11	**West End Girls**	*Pet Shop Boys*	EMI America 8307
2	1	14	**Addicted To Love**	*Robert Palmer*	Island 99570
3	7	7	**Greatest Love Of All**	*Whitney Houston*	Arista 9466
4	4	9	**Why Can't This Be Love**	*Van Halen*	Warner 28740
5	6	12	**What Have You Done For Me Lately**	*Janet Jackson*	A&M 2812
6	8	13	**Your Love**	*The Outfield*	Columbia 05796
7	9	9	**Take Me Home**	*Phil Collins*	Atlantic 89472
8	11	10	**Bad Boy**	*Miami Sound Machine*	Epic 05805
9	5	9	**Harlem Shuffle**	*Rolling Stones*	Rolling Stones 05802
10	12	10	**If You Leave**	*Orchestral Manoeuvres In The Dark*	A&M 2811

★ **HIGHEST DEBUT** ★ POS 74
When The Heart Rules The Mind................*GTR*

★ **BIGGEST MOVER** ★ 75 to 56
Like No Other Night...........................*38 Special*

Billboard — MAY 17, 1986 — HOT 100

TW	LW	WK		
1	3	8	Greatest Love Of All	Whitney Houston ... Arista 9466
2	1	12	West End Girls	Pet Shop Boys ... EMI America 8307
3	4	10	Why Can't This Be Love	Van Halen ... Warner 28740
4	5	13	What Have You Done For Me Lately	Janet Jackson ... A&M 2812
5	11	6	Live To Tell	Madonna ... Sire 28717
6	6	14	Your Love	The Outfield ... Columbia 05796
7	7	10	Take Me Home	Phil Collins ... Atlantic 89472
8	8	11	Bad Boy	Miami Sound Machine ... Epic 05805
9	10	11	If You Leave	Orchestral Manoeuvres In The Dark ... A&M 2811
10	2	15	Addicted To Love	Robert Palmer ... Island 99570

★ HIGHEST DEBUT ★ POS 71
One Hit (To The Body) .... The Rolling Stones

★ BIGGEST MOVER ★ 85 to 60
Danger Zone .... Kenny Loggins

Billboard — MAY 24, 1986 — HOT 100

TW	LW	WK		
1	1	9	Greatest Love Of All	Whitney Houston ... Arista 9466
2	5	7	Live To Tell	Madonna ... Sire 28717
3	11	10	On My Own	Patti LaBelle & Michael McDonald ... MCA 52770
4	2	13	West End Girls	Pet Shop Boys ... EMI America 8307
5	9	12	If You Leave	Orchestral Manoeuvres In The Dark ... A&M 2811
6	4	14	What Have You Done For Me Lately	Janet Jackson ... A&M 2812
7	7	11	Take Me Home	Phil Collins ... Atlantic 89472
8	8	12	Bad Boy	Miami Sound Machine ... Epic 05805
9	12	12	I Can't Wait	Nu Shooz ... Atlantic 89446
10	14	10	All I Need Is A Miracle	Mike + The Mechanics ... Atlantic 89450

★ HIGHEST DEBUT ★ POS 55
Dreams .... Van Halen

★ BIGGEST MOVER ★ 76 to 51
Sledgehammer .... Peter Gabriel

Billboard — MAY 31, 1986 — HOT 100

TW	LW	WK		
1	1	10	Greatest Love Of All	Whitney Houston ... Arista 9466
2	2	8	Live To Tell	Madonna ... Sire 28717
3	3	11	On My Own	Patti LaBelle & Michael McDonald ... MCA 52770
4	5	13	If You Leave	Orchestral Manoeuvres In The Dark ... A&M 2811
5	9	13	I Can't Wait	Nu Shooz ... Atlantic 89446
6	10	11	All I Need Is A Miracle	Mike + The Mechanics ... Atlantic 89450
7	12	16	Something About You	Level 42 ... Polydor 883362
8	14	10	Is It Love	Mr. Mister ... RCA 14313
9	13	8	Be Good To Yourself	Journey ... Columbia 05869
10	6	15	What Have You Done For Me Lately	Janet Jackson ... A&M 2812

★ HIGHEST DEBUT ★ POS 45
Invisible Touch .... Genesis

★ BIGGEST MOVER ★ 56 to 38
Like A Rock ...... Bob Seger & The Silver Bullet Band

Billboard — JUNE 7, 1986 — HOT 100

TW	LW	WK	Title	Artist	Label
1	2	9	**Live To Tell**	*Madonna*	Sire 28717
2	3	12	On My Own	*Patti LaBelle & Michael McDonald*	MCA 52770
3	1	11	Greatest Love Of All	*Whitney Houston*	Arista 9466
4	5	14	I Can't Wait	*Nu Shooz*	Atlantic 89446
5	6	12	**All I Need Is A Miracle**	*Mike + The Mechanics*	Atlantic 89450
6	4	14	If You Leave	*Orchestral Manoeuvres In The Dark*	A&M 2811
7	7	17	**Something About You**	*Level 42*	Polydor 883362
8	11	9	**Crush On You**	*The Jets*	MCA 52774
9	13	8	There'll Be Sad Songs (To Make You Cry)	*Billy Ocean*	Jive 9465
10	15	7	A Different Corner	*George Michael*	Columbia 05888

★ **HIGHEST DEBUT** ★ POS 54
Modern Woman ....*Billy Joel*

★ **BIGGEST MOVER** ★ 65 to 51
Opportunities (Let's Make Lots Of Money) ....*Pet Shop Boys*

Billboard — JUNE 14, 1986 — HOT 100

TW	LW	WK	Title	Artist	Label
1	2	13	**On My Own**	*Patti LaBelle & Michael McDonald*	MCA 52770
2	1	10	Live To Tell	*Madonna*	Sire 28717
3	4	15	**I Can't Wait**	*Nu Shooz*	Atlantic 89446
4	9	9	There'll Be Sad Songs (To Make You Cry)	*Billy Ocean*	Jive 9465
5	8	10	Crush On You	*The Jets*	MCA 52774
6	3	12	Greatest Love Of All	*Whitney Houston*	Arista 9466
7	10	8	**A Different Corner**	*George Michael*	Columbia 05888
8	14	10	No One Is To Blame	*Howard Jones*	Elektra 69549
9	5	13	All I Need Is A Miracle	*Mike + The Mechanics*	Atlantic 89450
10	7	18	Something About You	*Level 42*	Polydor 883362

★ **HIGHEST DEBUT** ★ POS 76
Sweet Freedom ....*Michael McDonald*

★ **BIGGEST MOVER** ★ 62 to 49
Glory Of Love ....*Peter Cetera*

Billboard — JUNE 21, 1986 — HOT 100

TW	LW	WK	Title	Artist	Label
1	1	14	**On My Own**	*Patti LaBelle & Michael McDonald*	MCA 52770
2	4	10	There'll Be Sad Songs (To Make You Cry)	*Billy Ocean*	Jive 9465
3	5	11	**Crush On You**	*The Jets*	MCA 52774
4	2	11	Live To Tell	*Madonna*	Sire 28717
5	3	16	I Can't Wait	*Nu Shooz*	Atlantic 89446
6	8	11	No One Is To Blame	*Howard Jones*	Elektra 69549
7	7	9	**A Different Corner**	*George Michael*	Columbia 05888
8	11	12	Holding Back The Years	*Simply Red*	Elektra 69564
9	14	9	Who's Johnny	*El DeBarge*	Gordy 1842
10	12	10	**Nothin' At All**	*Heart*	Capitol 5572

★ **HIGHEST DEBUT** ★ POS 63
Suzanne ....*Journey*

★ **BIGGEST MOVER** ★ 68 to 51
Hyperactive ....*Robert Palmer*

Billboard 🔴 JUNE 28, 1986 🔴 HOT 100.

TW	LW	WK				
❶	1	15	**On My Own**	*Patti LaBelle & Michael McDonald*	MCA 52770
❷	2	11	**There'll Be Sad Songs (To Make You Cry)**	*Billy Ocean*	Jive 9465
③	3	12	**Crush On You**	*The Jets*	MCA 52774
④	8	13	**Holding Back The Years**	*Simply Red*	Elektra 69564
⑤	6	12	**No One Is To Blame**	*Howard Jones*	Elektra 69549
⑥	9	10	**Who's Johnny**	*El DeBarge*	Gordy 1842
❼	7	10	**A Different Corner**	*George Michael*	Columbia 05888
⑧	17	5	**Invisible Touch**	*Genesis*	Atlantic 89407
⑨	14	7	**Nasty**	*Janet Jackson*	A&M 2830
❿	15	8	**Sledgehammer**	*Peter Gabriel*	Geffen 28718

★ *HIGHEST DEBUT* ★ POS 42	★ *BIGGEST MOVER* ★ 96 to 77
Papa Don't Preach.....................*Madonna*	Take My Breath Away ....*Berlin*

Billboard 🔴 JULY 5, 1986 🔴 HOT 100.

TW	LW	WK				
❶	2	12	**There'll Be Sad Songs (To Make You Cry)**	*Billy Ocean*	Jive 9465
❷	4	14	**Holding Back The Years**	*Simply Red*	Elektra 69564
❸	6	11	**Who's Johnny**	*El DeBarge*	Gordy 1842
④	5	13	**No One Is To Blame**	*Howard Jones*	Elektra 69549
⑤	9	8	**Nasty**	*Janet Jackson*	A&M 2830
⑥	8	6	**Invisible Touch**	*Genesis*	Atlantic 89407
⑦	3	13	**Crush On You**	*The Jets*	MCA 52774
⑧	1	16	**On My Own**	*Patti LaBelle & Michael McDonald*	MCA 52770
⑨	10	9	**Sledgehammer**	*Peter Gabriel*	Geffen 28718
❿	14	9	**Danger Zone**	*Kenny Loggins*	Columbia 05893

★ *HIGHEST DEBUT* ★ POS 47	★ *BIGGEST MOVER* ★ 89 to 57
The Edge Of Heaven ....*Wham!*	Venus ....*Bananarama*

Billboard 🔴 JULY 12, 1986 🔴 HOT 100.

TW	LW	WK				
❶	2	15	**Holding Back The Years**	*Simply Red*	Elektra 69564
❷	6	7	**Invisible Touch**	*Genesis*	Atlantic 89407
③	1	13	**There'll Be Sad Songs (To Make You Cry)**	*Billy Ocean*	Jive 9465
④	5	9	**Nasty**	*Janet Jackson*	A&M 2830
⑤	3	12	**Who's Johnny**	*El DeBarge*	Gordy 1842
⑥	9	10	**Sledgehammer**	*Peter Gabriel*	Geffen 28718
❼	10	10	**Danger Zone**	*Kenny Loggins*	Columbia 05893
⑧	4	14	**No One Is To Blame**	*Howard Jones*	Elektra 69549
⑨	12	13	**Your Wildest Dreams**	*The Moody Blues*	Polydor 883906
❿	11	13	**Tuff Enuff**	*The Fabulous Thunderbirds*	CBS Associated 05838

★ *HIGHEST DEBUT* ★ POS 74	★ *BIGGEST MOVER* ★ 85 to 64
Walk Like A Man ....*Mary Jane Girls*	Man Size Love ....*Klymaxx*

Billboard — JULY 19, 1986 — HOT 100

TW	LW	WK	Title	Artist ... Label
1	2	8	Invisible Touch	Genesis ... Atlantic 89407
2	6	11	Sledgehammer	Peter Gabriel ... Geffen 28718
3	4	10	Nasty	Janet Jackson ... A&M 2830
4	7	11	Danger Zone	Kenny Loggins ... Columbia 05893
5	1	16	Holding Back The Years	Simply Red ... Elektra 69564
6	5	13	Who's Johnny	El DeBarge ... Gordy 1842
7	11	7	Glory Of Love	Peter Cetera ... Full Moon 28662
8	3	14	There'll Be Sad Songs (To Make You Cry)	Billy Ocean ... Jive 9465
9	9	14	Your Wildest Dreams	The Moody Blues ... Polydor 883906
10	17	8	Love Touch	Rod Stewart ... Warner 28668

★ HIGHEST DEBUT ★ POS 40
Dancing On The Ceiling ....Lionel Richie

★ BIGGEST MOVER ★ 86 to 59
Don't Forget Me (When I'm Gone) .....Glass Tiger

Billboard — JULY 26, 1986 — HOT 100

TW	LW	WK	Title	Artist ... Label
1	2	12	Sledgehammer	Peter Gabriel ... Geffen 28718
2	4	12	Danger Zone	Kenny Loggins ... Columbia 05893
3	1	9	Invisible Touch	Genesis ... Atlantic 89407
4	3	11	Nasty	Janet Jackson ... A&M 2830
5	7	8	Glory Of Love	Peter Cetera ... Full Moon 28662
6	12	5	Papa Don't Preach	Madonna ... Sire 28660
7	10	9	Love Touch	Rod Stewart ... Warner 28668
8	11	11	Mad About You	Belinda Carlisle ... I.R.S. 52815
9	5	17	Holding Back The Years	Simply Red ... Elektra 69564
10	15	8	Modern Woman	Billy Joel ... Epic 06118

★ HIGHEST DEBUT ★ POS 65
Love Zone ....Billy Ocean

★ BIGGEST MOVER ★ 89 to 66
Somebody Like You ....38 Special

Billboard — AUGUST 2, 1986 — HOT 100

TW	LW	WK	Title	Artist ... Label
1	5	9	Glory Of Love	Peter Cetera ... Full Moon 28662
2	1	13	Sledgehammer	Peter Gabriel ... Geffen 28718
3	2	13	Danger Zone	Kenny Loggins ... Columbia 05893
4	6	6	Papa Don't Preach	Madonna ... Sire 28660
5	3	10	Invisible Touch	Genesis ... Atlantic 89407
6	8	12	Mad About You	Belinda Carlisle ... I.R.S. 52815
7	7	10	Love Touch	Rod Stewart ... Warner 28668
8	4	12	Nasty	Janet Jackson ... A&M 2830
9	12	12	We Don't Have To Take Our Clothes Off	Jermaine Stewart ... Arista 9424
10	11	10	Opportunities (Let's Make Lots Of Money)	Pet Shop Boys ... EMI America 8330

★ HIGHEST DEBUT ★ POS 42
Stuck With You ....Huey Lewis & The News

★ BIGGEST MOVER ★ 73 to 55
Walk This Way ....Run-D.M.C.

Billboard — AUGUST 9, 1986 — HOT 100

TW	LW	WK	Title	Artist ... Label
1	1	10	Glory Of Love	Peter Cetera ... Full Moon 28662
2	4	7	Papa Don't Preach	Madonna ... Sire 28660
3	6	13	Mad About You	Belinda Carlisle ... I.R.S. 52815
4	2	14	Sledgehammer	Peter Gabriel ... Geffen 28718
5	9	13	We Don't Have To Take Our Clothes Off	Jermaine Stewart ... Arista 9424
6	7	11	Love Touch	Rod Stewart ... Warner 28668
7	3	14	Danger Zone	Kenny Loggins ... Columbia 05893
8	12	9	Higher Love	Steve Winwood ... Island 28710
9	15	7	Venus	Bananarama ... London 886056
10	13	9	Rumors	Timex Social Club ... Jay 7001

★ HIGHEST DEBUT ★ POS 60
When I Think Of You ... Janet Jackson

★ BIGGEST MOVER ★ 72 to 56
Heaven In Your Eyes ... Loverboy

Billboard — AUGUST 16, 1986 — HOT 100

TW	LW	WK	Title	Artist ... Label
1	2	8	Papa Don't Preach	Madonna ... Sire 28660
2	1	11	Glory Of Love	Peter Cetera ... Full Moon 28662
3	3	14	Mad About You	Belinda Carlisle ... I.R.S. 52815
4	8	10	Higher Love	Steve Winwood ... Island 28710
5	5	14	We Don't Have To Take Our Clothes Off	Jermaine Stewart ... Arista 9424
6	9	8	Venus	Bananarama ... London 886056
7	13	5	Dancing On The Ceiling	Lionel Richie ... Motown 1843
8	10	10	Rumors	Timex Social Club ... Jay 7001
9	18	9	Take My Breath Away	Berlin ... Columbia 05903
10	12	7	The Edge Of Heaven	Wham! ... Columbia 06182

★ HIGHEST DEBUT ★ POS 54
Throwing It All Away ... Genesis

★ BIGGEST MOVER ★ 89 to 65
Twist And Shout ... The Beatles

Billboard — AUGUST 23, 1986 — HOT 100

TW	LW	WK	Title	Artist ... Label
1	1	9	Papa Don't Preach	Madonna ... Sire 28660
2	4	11	Higher Love	Steve Winwood ... Island 28710
3	6	9	Venus	Bananarama ... London 886056
4	3	15	Mad About You	Belinda Carlisle ... I.R.S. 52815
5	2	12	Glory Of Love	Peter Cetera ... Full Moon 28662
6	7	6	Dancing On The Ceiling	Lionel Richie ... Motown 1843
7	9	10	Take My Breath Away	Berlin ... Columbia 05903
8	5	15	We Don't Have To Take Our Clothes Off	Jermaine Stewart ... Arista 9424
9	8	11	Rumors	Timex Social Club ... Jay 7001
10	10	8	The Edge Of Heaven	Wham! ... Columbia 06182

★ HIGHEST DEBUT ★ POS 67
Heartbeat ... Don Johnson

★ BIGGEST MOVER ★ 74 to 57
Sweet Love ... Anita Baker

Billboard — AUGUST 30, 1986 — HOT 100

TW	LW	WK	Title	Artist	Label
1	2	12	Higher Love	Steve Winwood	Island 28710
2	3	10	Venus	Bananarama	London 886056
3	1	10	Papa Don't Preach	Madonna	Sire 28660
4	7	11	Take My Breath Away	Berlin	Columbia 05903
5	6	7	Dancing On The Ceiling	Lionel Richie	Motown 1843
6	12	9	Friends And Lovers	Gloria Loring & Carl Anderson	USA Carrere 06122
7	11	12	Sweet Freedom	Michael McDonald	MCA 52857
8	9	12	Rumors	Timex Social Club	Jay 7001
9	15	5	Stuck With You	Huey Lewis & The News	Chrysalis 43019
10	4	16	Mad About You	Belinda Carlisle	I.R.S. 52815

★ HIGHEST DEBUT ★ POS 49
Typical Male .... Tina Turner

★ BIGGEST MOVER ★ 67 to 46
Heartbeat .... Don Johnson

Billboard — SEPTEMBER 6, 1986 — HOT 100

TW	LW	WK	Title	Artist	Label
1	2	11	Venus	Bananarama	London 886056
2	4	12	Take My Breath Away	Berlin	Columbia 05903
3	1	13	Higher Love	Steve Winwood	Island 28710
4	5	8	Dancing On The Ceiling	Lionel Richie	Motown 1843
5	6	10	Friends And Lovers	Gloria Loring & Carl Anderson	USA Carrere 06122
6	9	6	Stuck With You	Huey Lewis & The News	Chrysalis 43019
7	7	13	Sweet Freedom	Michael McDonald	MCA 52857
8	13	13	Words Get In The Way	Miami Sound Machine	Epic 06120
9	3	11	Papa Don't Preach	Madonna	Sire 28660
10	15	7	Walk This Way	Run-D.M.C.	Profile 5112

★ HIGHEST DEBUT ★ POS 81
25 Or 6 To 4 .... Chicago

★ BIGGEST MOVER ★ 63 to 44
True Colors .... Cyndi Lauper

Billboard — SEPTEMBER 13, 1986 — HOT 100

TW	LW	WK	Title	Artist	Label
1	2	13	Take My Breath Away	Berlin	Columbia 05903
2	4	9	Dancing On The Ceiling	Lionel Richie	Motown 1843
3	6	7	Stuck With You	Huey Lewis & The News	Chrysalis 43019
4	5	11	Friends And Lovers	Gloria Loring & Carl Anderson	USA Carrere 06122
5	1	12	Venus	Bananarama	London 886056
6	3	14	Higher Love	Steve Winwood	Island 28710
7	7	14	Sweet Freedom	Michael McDonald	MCA 52857
8	8	14	Words Get In The Way	Miami Sound Machine	Epic 06120
9	10	8	Walk This Way	Run-D.M.C.	Profile 5112
10	11	13	Baby Love	Regina	Atlantic 89417

★ HIGHEST DEBUT ★ POS 71
Human .... Human League

★ BIGGEST MOVER ★ 61 to 46
Girl Can't Help It .... Journey

Billboard — SEPTEMBER 20, 1986 — HOT 100

TW	LW	WK	Title	Artist	Label
1	3	8	Stuck With You	Huey Lewis & The News	Chrysalis 43019
2	2	10	Dancing On The Ceiling	Lionel Richie	Motown 1843
3	4	12	Friends And Lovers	Gloria Loring & Carl Anderson	USA Carrere 06122
4	1	14	Take My Breath Away	Berlin	Columbia 05903
5	8	15	Words Get In The Way	Miami Sound Machine	Epic 06120
6	9	9	Walk This Way	Run-D.M.C.	Profile 5112
7	5	13	Venus	Bananarama	London 886056
8	11	11	Don't Forget Me (When I'm Gone)	Glass Tiger	Manhattan 50037
9	12	8	Dreamtime	Daryl Hall	RCA 14387
10	10	14	Baby Love	Regina	Atlantic 89417

★ HIGHEST DEBUT ★ POS 66
I Am By Your Side .... Corey Hart

★ BIGGEST MOVER ★ 94 to 72
The Rain .... Oran "Juice" Jones

Billboard — SEPTEMBER 27, 1986 — HOT 100

TW	LW	WK	Title	Artist	Label
1	1	9	Stuck With You	Huey Lewis & The News	Chrysalis 43019
2	3	13	Friends And Lovers	Gloria Loring & Carl Anderson	USA Carrere 06122
3	2	11	Dancing On The Ceiling	Lionel Richie	Motown 1843
4	6	10	Walk This Way	Run-D.M.C.	Profile 5112
5	8	12	Don't Forget Me (When I'm Gone)	Glass Tiger	Manhattan 50037
6	9	9	Dreamtime	Daryl Hall	RCA 14387
7	14	8	When I Think Of You	Janet Jackson	A&M 2855
8	15	12	Two Of Hearts	Stacey Q	Atlantic 89381
9	4	15	Take My Breath Away	Berlin	Columbia 05903
10	11	10	Love Zone	Billy Ocean	Jive 9510

★ HIGHEST DEBUT ★ POS 51
Amanda .... Boston

★ BIGGEST MOVER ★ 72 to 49
The Rain .... Oran "Juice" Jones

Billboard — OCTOBER 4, 1986 — HOT 100

TW	LW	WK	Title	Artist	Label
1	1	10	Stuck With You	Huey Lewis & The News	Chrysalis 43019
2	2	14	Friends And Lovers	Gloria Loring & Carl Anderson	USA Carrere 06122
3	7	9	When I Think Of You	Janet Jackson	A&M 2855
4	5	13	Don't Forget Me (When I'm Gone)	Glass Tiger	Manhattan 50037
5	6	10	Dreamtime	Daryl Hall	RCA 14387
6	8	13	Two Of Hearts	Stacey Q	Atlantic 89381
7	12	8	Throwing It All Away	Genesis	Atlantic 89372
8	4	11	Walk This Way	Run-D.M.C.	Profile 5112
9	13	6	Typical Male	Tina Turner	Capitol 5615
10	3	12	Dancing On The Ceiling	Lionel Richie	Motown 1843

★ HIGHEST DEBUT ★ POS 40
True Blue .... Madonna

★ BIGGEST MOVER ★ 74 to 59
Jody .... Jermaine Stewart

TW	LW	WK	Billboard®	OCTOBER 11, 1986	HOT 100®
❶	3	10	When I Think Of You	Janet Jackson	A&M 2855
❷	4	14	Don't Forget Me (When I'm Gone)	Glass Tiger	Manhattan 50037
❸	6	14	Two Of Hearts	Stacey Q	Atlantic 89381
❹	7	9	Throwing It All Away	Genesis	Atlantic 89372
❺	9	7	Typical Male	Tina Turner	Capitol 5615
❻	1	11	Stuck With You	Huey Lewis & The News	Chrysalis 43019
❼	12	8	Heartbeat	Don Johnson	Epic 06285
❽	2	15	Friends And Lovers	Gloria Loring & Carl Anderson	USA Carrere 06122
❾	14	7	True Colors	Cyndi Lauper	Portrait 06247
❿	5	11	Dreamtime	Daryl Hall	RCA 14387

★ **HIGHEST DEBUT** ★ POS 75
Where Did Your Heart Go? .... Wham!

★ **BIGGEST MOVER** ★ 82 to 57
Everybody Have Fun Tonight .... Wang Chung

TW	LW	WK	Billboard®	OCTOBER 18, 1986	HOT 100®
❶	1	11	When I Think Of You	Janet Jackson	A&M 2855
❷	5	8	Typical Male	Tina Turner	Capitol 5615
❸	9	8	True Colors	Cyndi Lauper	Portrait 06247
④	4	10	Throwing It All Away	Genesis	Atlantic 89372
⑤	7	9	Heartbeat	Don Johnson	Epic 06285
⑥	3	15	Two Of Hearts	Stacey Q	Atlantic 89381
⑦	2	15	Don't Forget Me (When I'm Gone)	Glass Tiger	Manhattan 50037
⑧	13	10	I Didn't Mean To Turn You On	Robert Palmer	Island 99537
⑨	11	13	All Cried Out	Lisa Lisa & Cult Jam with Full Force	Columbia 05844
⑩	15	11	A Matter Of Trust	Billy Joel	Columbia 06108

★ **HIGHEST DEBUT** ★ POS 42
Hip To Be Square .... Huey Lewis & The News

★ **BIGGEST MOVER** ★ 93 to 68
C'est La Vie .... Robbie Nevil

TW	LW	WK	Billboard®	OCTOBER 25, 1986	HOT 100®
❶	3	9	True Colors	Cyndi Lauper	Portrait 06247
❷	2	9	Typical Male	Tina Turner	Capitol 5615
③	1	12	When I Think Of You	Janet Jackson	A&M 2855
④	8	11	I Didn't Mean To Turn You On	Robert Palmer	Island 99537
⑤	5	10	Heartbeat	Don Johnson	Epic 06285
⑥	15	5	Amanda	Boston	MCA 52756
⑦	4	11	Throwing It All Away	Genesis	Atlantic 89372
⑧	9	14	All Cried Out	Lisa Lisa & Cult Jam with Full Force	Columbia 05844
⑨	14	7	Human	Human League	A&M 2861
⑩	11	11	Sweet Love	Anita Baker	Elektra 69557

★ **HIGHEST DEBUT** ★ POS 74
Is This Love .... Survivor

★ **BIGGEST MOVER** ★ 69 to 52
You Know I Love You...Don't You? .... Howard Jones

TW	LW	WK	Billboard.	NOVEMBER 1, 1986	HOT 100.
①	1	10	True Colors	Cyndi Lauper	Portrait 06247
②	2	10	Typical Male	Tina Turner	Capitol 5615
③	4	12	I Didn't Mean To Turn You On	Robert Palmer	Island 99537
④	6	6	Amanda	Boston	MCA 52756
⑤	9	8	Human	Human League	A&M 2861
⑥	13	5	True Blue	Madonna	Sire 28591
⑦	3	13	When I Think Of You	Janet Jackson	A&M 2855
⑧	10	12	Sweet Love	Anita Baker	Elektra 69557
⑨	15	12	Take Me Home Tonight	Eddie Money	Columbia 06231
⑩	8	15	All Cried Out	Lisa Lisa & Cult Jam with Full Force	Columbia 05844

★ HIGHEST DEBUT ★ POS 56	★ BIGGEST MOVER ★ 74 to 55
Notorious ....Duran Duran	Is This Love ....Survivor

TW	LW	WK	Billboard.	NOVEMBER 8, 1986	HOT 100.
①	4	7	Amanda	Boston	MCA 52756
②	3	13	I Didn't Mean To Turn You On	Robert Palmer	Island 99537
③	1	11	True Colors	Cyndi Lauper	Portrait 06247
④	5	9	Human	Human League	A&M 2861
⑤	6	6	True Blue	Madonna	Sire 28591
⑥	9	13	Take Me Home Tonight	Eddie Money	Columbia 06231
⑦	11	10	You Give Love A Bad Name	Bon Jovi	Mercury 884953
⑧	2	11	Typical Male	Tina Turner	Capitol 5615
⑨	12	9	Word Up	Cameo	Atlanta Artists 884933
⑩	13	9	The Rain	Oran "Juice" Jones	Def Jam 06209

★ HIGHEST DEBUT ★ POS 81	★ BIGGEST MOVER ★ 97 to 78
Talk To Me ....Chico DeBarge	Coming Around Again ....Carly Simon

TW	LW	WK	Billboard.	NOVEMBER 15, 1986	HOT 100.
①	1	8	Amanda	Boston	MCA 52756
②	4	10	Human	Human League	A&M 2861
③	5	7	True Blue	Madonna	Sire 28591
④	6	14	Take Me Home Tonight	Eddie Money	Columbia 06231
⑤	7	11	You Give Love A Bad Name	Bon Jovi	Mercury 884953
⑥	2	14	I Didn't Mean To Turn You On	Robert Palmer	Island 99537
⑦	9	10	Word Up	Cameo	Atlanta Artists 884933
⑧	12	9	The Next Time I Fall	Peter Cetera with Amy Grant	Full Moon 28597
⑨	10	10	The Rain	Oran "Juice" Jones	Def Jam 06209
⑩	3	12	True Colors	Cyndi Lauper	Portrait 06247

★ HIGHEST DEBUT ★ POS 78	★ BIGGEST MOVER ★ 55 to 38
This Is The Time ....Billy Joel	Love Is Forever ....Billy Ocean

TW	LW	WK	Billboard.	NOVEMBER 22, 1986	HOT 100.
❶	2	11	**Human**...*Human League* ... A&M 2861
②	1	9	Amanda...*Boston* ... MCA 52756
③	3	8	**True Blue**..*Madonna* ... Sire 28591
❹	5	12	**You Give Love A Bad Name**.........................*Bon Jovi* ... Mercury 884953
⑤	4	15	Take Me Home Tonight ....*Eddie Money* ... Columbia 06231
❻	7	11	**Word Up**..*Cameo* ... Atlanta Artists 884933
❼	8	10	The Next Time I Fall ....*Peter Cetera with Amy Grant* ... Full Moon 28597
❽	11	6	Hip To Be Square ....*Huey Lewis & The News* ... Chrysalis 43065
❾	14	10	The Way It Is ....*Bruce Hornsby & The Range* ... RCA 5023
❿	13	8	Love Will Conquer All ....*Lionel Richie* ... Motown 1866

★ HIGHEST DEBUT ★ POS 45	★ BIGGEST MOVER ★ 77 to 61
War.............*Bruce Springsteen & The E Street Band*	Tasty Love...*Freddie Jackson*

TW	LW	WK	Billboard.	NOVEMBER 29, 1986	HOT 100.
❶	4	13	**You Give Love A Bad Name**....................*Bon Jovi* ... Mercury 884953
②	1	12	Human ....*Human League* ... A&M 2861
③	3	9	**True Blue**..*Madonna* ... Sire 28591
❹	7	11	**The Next Time I Fall** ....*Peter Cetera with Amy Grant* ... Full Moon 28597
❺	8	7	Hip To Be Square ....*Huey Lewis & The News* ... Chrysalis 43065
⑥	6	12	**Word Up**..*Cameo* ... Atlanta Artists 884933
⑦	2	10	Amanda...*Boston* ... MCA 52756
❽	9	11	The Way It Is ....*Bruce Hornsby & The Range* ... RCA 5023
❾	10	9	**Love Will Conquer All** ....*Lionel Richie* ... Motown 1866
❿	16	10	Walk Like An Egyptian ....*Bangles* ... Columbia 06257

★ HIGHEST DEBUT ★ POS 67	★ BIGGEST MOVER ★ 69 to 50
Change Of Heart ....*Cyndi Lauper*	At This Moment ....*Billy Vera & The Beaters*

TW	LW	WK	Billboard.	DECEMBER 6, 1986	HOT 100.
❶	4	12	**The Next Time I Fall** .....*Peter Cetera with Amy Grant* ... Full Moon 28597
②	1	14	You Give Love A Bad Name...........................*Bon Jovi* ... Mercury 884953
❸	5	8	**Hip To Be Square**.................*Huey Lewis & The News* ... Chrysalis 43065
❹	8	12	The Way It Is ....*Bruce Hornsby & The Range* ... RCA 5023
❺	10	11	Walk Like An Egyptian ....*Bangles* ... Columbia 06257
⑥	6	13	**Word Up**..*Cameo* ... Atlanta Artists 884933
❼	11	10	Everybody Have Fun Tonight ....*Wang Chung* ... Geffen 28562
❽	2	13	Human ....*Human League* ... A&M 2861
❾	9	10	**Love Will Conquer All** ....*Lionel Richie* ... Motown 1866
❿	12	10	To Be A Lover..*Billy Idol* ... Chrysalis 43024

★ HIGHEST DEBUT ★ POS 51	★ BIGGEST MOVER ★ 79 to 60
Open Your Heart ....*Madonna*	Keep Your Hands To Yourself...............*Georgia Satellites*

Billboard 🔴 DECEMBER 13, 1986 🔴 HOT 100.

TW	LW	WK	Title	Artist / Label
1	4	13	**The Way It Is**	*Bruce Hornsby & The Range* . . . RCA 5023
2	5	12	Walk Like An Egyptian	*Bangles* . . . Columbia 06257
3	3	9	**Hip To Be Square**	*Huey Lewis & The News* . . . Chrysalis 43065
4	1	13	The Next Time I Fall	*Peter Cetera with Amy Grant* . . . Full Moon 28597
5	7	11	Everybody Have Fun Tonight	*Wang Chung* . . . Geffen 28562
6	2	15	You Give Love A Bad Name	*Bon Jovi* . . . Mercury 884953
7	10	11	To Be A Lover	*Billy Idol* . . . Chrysalis 43024
8	11	7	Notorious	*Duran Duran* . . . Capitol 5648
9	15	9	Shake You Down	*Gregory Abbott* . . . Columbia 06191
10	13	25	Stand By Me	*Ben E. King* . . . Atlantic 89361

★ HIGHEST DEBUT ★ POS 79	★ BIGGEST MOVER ★ 94 to 73
Can't Help Falling In Love .... *Corey Hart*	Jimmy Lee .... *Aretha Franklin*

Billboard 🔴 DECEMBER 20, 1986 🔴 HOT 100.

TW	LW	WK	Title	Artist / Label
1	2	13	**Walk Like An Egyptian**	*Bangles* . . . Columbia 06257
2	1	14	The Way It Is	*Bruce Hornsby & The Range* . . . RCA 5023
3	5	12	Everybody Have Fun Tonight	*Wang Chung* . . . Geffen 28562
4	8	8	Notorious	*Duran Duran* . . . Capitol 5648
5	9	10	Shake You Down	*Gregory Abbott* . . . Columbia 06191
6	7	12	**To Be A Lover**	*Billy Idol* . . . Chrysalis 43024
7	3	10	Hip To Be Square	*Huey Lewis & The News* . . . Chrysalis 43065
8	14	11	C'est La Vie	*Robbie Nevil* . . . Manhattan 50047
9	10	26	**Stand By Me**	*Ben E. King* . . . Atlantic 89361
10	4	14	The Next Time I Fall	*Peter Cetera with Amy Grant* . . . Full Moon 28597

★ HIGHEST DEBUT ★ POS 73	★ BIGGEST MOVER ★ 83 to 56
I Wanna Go Back .... *Eddie Money*	Livin' On A Prayer .... *Bon Jovi*

Billboard 🔴 DECEMBER 27, 1986 🔴 HOT 100.

TW	LW	WK	Title	Artist / Label
1	1	14	**Walk Like An Egyptian**	*Bangles* . . . Columbia 06257
2	3	13	**Everybody Have Fun Tonight**	*Wang Chung* . . . Geffen 28562
3	4	9	Notorious	*Duran Duran* . . . Capitol 5648
4	5	11	Shake You Down	*Gregory Abbott* . . . Columbia 06191
5	2	15	The Way It Is	*Bruce Hornsby & The Range* . . . RCA 5023
6	8	12	C'est La Vie	*Robbie Nevil* . . . Manhattan 50047
7	13	9	Control	*Janet Jackson* . . . A&M 2877
8	11	6	War	*Bruce Springsteen & The E Street Band* . . . Columbia 06432
9	9	27	**Stand By Me**	*Ben E. King* . . . Atlantic 89361
10	12	12	**Don't Get Me Wrong**	*The Pretenders* . . . Sire 28630

★ HIGHEST DEBUT ★ POS 77	★ BIGGEST MOVER ★ 86 to 68
Without Your Love .... *Toto*	(You Gotta) Fight For Your Right (To Party!) .... *Beastie Boys*

Billboard — JANUARY 10, 1987 — HOT 100

TW	LW	WK	Title	Artist	Label
①	1	16	**Walk Like An Egyptian**	Bangles	Columbia 06257
②	3	11	**Notorious**	Duran Duran	Capitol 5648
❸	4	13	Shake You Down	Gregory Abbott	Columbia 06191
④	2	15	Everybody Have Fun Tonight	Wang Chung	Geffen 28562
⑤	6	14	C'est La Vie	Robbie Nevil	Manhattan 50047
⑥	7	11	Control	Janet Jackson	A&M 2877
⑦	5	17	The Way It Is	Bruce Hornsby & The Range	RCA 5023
⑧	8	8	War	Bruce Springsteen & The E Street Band	Columbia 06432
⑨	15	13	At This Moment	Billy Vera & The Beaters	Rhino 74403
⑩	12	12	Is This Love	Survivor	Scotti Brothers 06381

★ HIGHEST DEBUT ★ POS 90	★ BIGGEST MOVER ★ 48 to 39
Coming Up Close ....'Til Tuesday	Livin' On A Prayer..............................Bon Jovi

Billboard — JANUARY 17, 1987 — HOT 100

TW	LW	WK	Title	Artist	Label
❶	3	14	**Shake You Down**	Gregory Abbott	Columbia 06191
❷	5	15	**C'est La Vie**	Robbie Nevil	Manhattan 50047
③	2	12	Notorious	Duran Duran	Capitol 5648
④	1	17	Walk Like An Egyptian	Bangles	Columbia 06257
❺	9	14	At This Moment	Billy Vera & The Beaters	Rhino 74403
❻	6	12	Control	Janet Jackson	A&M 2877
❼	15	7	Open Your Heart	Madonna	Sire 28508
⑧	11	12	Land Of Confusion	Genesis	Atlantic 89336
⑨	10	13	**Is This Love**	Survivor	Scotti Brothers 06381
⑩	4	16	Everybody Have Fun Tonight	Wang Chung	Geffen 28562

★ HIGHEST DEBUT ★ POS 40	★ BIGGEST MOVER ★ 39 to 22
Jacob's Ladder...............Huey Lewis & The News	Livin' On A Prayer..............................Bon Jovi

Billboard — JANUARY 24, 1987 — HOT 100

TW	LW	WK	Title	Artist	Label
❶	5	15	**At This Moment**	Billy Vera & The Beaters	Rhino 74403
②	2	16	**C'est La Vie**	Robbie Nevil	Manhattan 50047
③	1	15	Shake You Down	Gregory Abbott	Columbia 06191
④	7	8	Open Your Heart	Madonna	Sire 28508
⑤	6	13	**Control**	Janet Jackson	A&M 2877
⑥	8	13	Land Of Confusion	Genesis	Atlantic 89336
❼	12	13	**Someday**	Glass Tiger	Manhattan 50048
⑧	13	9	Change Of Heart	Cyndi Lauper	Portrait 06431
⑨	9	14	**Is This Love**	Survivor	Scotti Brothers 06381
⑩	11	13	**Victory**	Kool & The Gang	Mercury 888074

★ HIGHEST DEBUT ★ POS 72	★ BIGGEST MOVER ★ 69 to 51
Don't Need A Gun ....Billy Idol	Mandolin Rain............Bruce Hornsby & The Range

TW	LW	WK	Billboard	JANUARY 31, 1987	HOT 100.
①	1	16	**At This Moment**	.........................*Billy Vera & The Beaters* . . .	Rhino 74403
②	4	9	**Open Your Heart**	....*Madonna* . . .	Sire 28508
③	2	17	C'est La Vie	....*Robbie Nevil* . . .	Manhattan 50047
④	6	14	**Land Of Confusion**	....*Genesis* . . .	Atlantic 89336
⑤	8	10	Change Of Heart	...............................*Cyndi Lauper* . . .	Portrait 06431
⑥	5	14	Control	.................................*Janet Jackson* . . .	A&M 2877
⑦	7	14	**Someday**	.....................................*Glass Tiger* . . .	Manhattan 50048
⑧	3	16	Shake You Down	..........................*Gregory Abbott* . . .	Columbia 06191
⑨	15	8	Livin' On A Prayer	.................................*Bon Jovi* . . .	Mercury 888184
⑩	12	14	Touch Me (I Want Your Body)	.................*Samantha Fox* . . .	Jive 1006

★ *HIGHEST DEBUT* ★ POS 64	★ *BIGGEST MOVER* ★ 74 to 53
Nothing's Gonna Stop Us Now.............*Starship*	Let's Go!...*Wang Chung*

TW	LW	WK	Billboard	FEBRUARY 7, 1987	HOT 100.
❶	2	10	**Open Your Heart**	....*Madonna* . . .	Sire 28508
②	1	17	At This Moment	.........................*Billy Vera & The Beaters* . . .	Rhino 74403
❸	9	9	Livin' On A Prayer	....*Bon Jovi* . . .	Mercury 888184
④	5	11	Change Of Heart	.............................*Cyndi Lauper* . . .	Portrait 06431
❺	10	15	Touch Me (I Want Your Body)	.................*Samantha Fox* . . .	Jive 1006
⑥	4	15	Land Of Confusion	...............................*Genesis* . . .	Atlantic 89336
❼	11	12	Keep Your Hands To Yourself	.............*Georgia Satellites* . . .	Elektra 69502
⑧	7	15	Someday	...........................*Glass Tiger* . . .	Manhattan 50048
⑨	13	13	Will You Still Love Me?	........................*Chicago* . . .	Full Moon 28512
⑩	12	10	We're Ready	.....................................*Boston* . . .	MCA 52985

★ *HIGHEST DEBUT* ★ POS 74	★ *BIGGEST MOVER* ★ 80 to 59
What You Get Is What You See ....*Tina Turner*	Fire.............*Bruce Springsteen & The E Street Band*

TW	LW	WK	Billboard	FEBRUARY 14, 1987	HOT 100.
❶	3	10	**Livin' On A Prayer**	....*Bon Jovi* . . .	Mercury 888184
②	1	11	Open Your Heart	....*Madonna* . . .	Sire 28508
③	4	12	**Change Of Heart**	.............................*Cyndi Lauper* . . .	Portrait 06431
④	5	16	**Touch Me (I Want Your Body)**	..................*Samantha Fox* . . .	Jive 1006
❺	7	13	Keep Your Hands To Yourself	.............*Georgia Satellites* . . .	Elektra 69502
❻	9	14	Will You Still Love Me?	........................*Chicago* . . .	Full Moon 28512
⑦	2	18	At This Moment	.........................*Billy Vera & The Beaters* . . .	Rhino 74403
❽	15	5	Jacob's Ladder	.......................*Huey Lewis & The News* . . .	Chrysalis 43097
⑨	10	11	**We're Ready**	.....................................*Boston* . . .	MCA 52985
⑩	12	11	Ballerina Girl	....*Lionel Richie* . . .	Motown 1873

★ *HIGHEST DEBUT* ★ POS 45	★ *BIGGEST MOVER* ★ 95 to 72
Tonight, Tonight, Tonight ....*Genesis*	The Finer Things.......................*Steve Winwood*

Billboard — FEBRUARY 21, 1987 — HOT 100

TW	LW	WK	Title	Artist	Label
1	1	11	Livin' On A Prayer	Bon Jovi	Mercury 888184
2	5	14	Keep Your Hands To Yourself	Georgia Satellites	Elektra 69502
3	6	15	Will You Still Love Me?	Chicago	Full Moon 28512
4	8	6	Jacob's Ladder	Huey Lewis & The News	Chrysalis 43097
5	4	17	Touch Me (I Want Your Body)	Samantha Fox	Jive 1006
6	11	15	You Got It All	The Jets	MCA 52968
7	10	12	Ballerina Girl	Lionel Richie	Motown 1873
8	2	12	Open Your Heart	Madonna	Sire 28508
9	12	13	Love You Down	Ready For The World	MCA 52947
10	3	13	Change Of Heart	Cyndi Lauper	Portrait 06431

★ **HIGHEST DEBUT** ★ POS 59
I Knew You Were Waiting (For Me) ....Aretha Franklin & George Michael

★ **BIGGEST MOVER** ★ 95 to 71
Walking Down Your Street....................Bangles

Billboard — FEBRUARY 28, 1987 — HOT 100

TW	LW	WK	Title	Artist	Label
1	1	12	Livin' On A Prayer	Bon Jovi	Mercury 888184
2	4	7	Jacob's Ladder	Huey Lewis & The News	Chrysalis 43097
3	2	15	Keep Your Hands To Yourself	Georgia Satellites	Elektra 69502
4	3	16	Will You Still Love Me?	Chicago	Full Moon 28512
5	6	16	You Got It All	The Jets	MCA 52968
6	11	11	Somewhere Out There	Linda Ronstadt & James Ingram	MCA 52973
7	12	7	Respect Yourself	Bruce Willis	Motown 1876
8	14	11	(You Gotta) Fight For Your Right (To Party!)	Beastie Boys	Def Jam 06595
9	13	14	Big Time	Peter Gabriel	Geffen 28503
10	7	13	Ballerina Girl	Lionel Richie	Motown 1873

★ **HIGHEST DEBUT** ★ POS 71
Come As You Are ....Peter Wolf

★ **BIGGEST MOVER** ★ 37 to 22
Lean On Me ....Club Nouveau

Billboard — MARCH 7, 1987 — HOT 100

TW	LW	WK	Title	Artist	Label
1	1	13	Livin' On A Prayer	Bon Jovi	Mercury 888184
2	2	8	Jacob's Ladder	Huey Lewis & The News	Chrysalis 43097
3	5	17	You Got It All	The Jets	MCA 52968
4	6	12	Somewhere Out There	Linda Ronstadt & James Ingram	MCA 52973
5	7	8	Respect Yourself	Bruce Willis	Motown 1876
6	3	16	Keep Your Hands To Yourself	Georgia Satellites	Elektra 69502
7	8	12	(You Gotta) Fight For Your Right (To Party!)	Beastie Boys	Def Jam 06595
8	9	15	Big Time	Peter Gabriel	Geffen 28503
9	12	8	Mandolin Rain	Bruce Hornsby & The Range	RCA 5087
10	15	8	Let's Wait Awhile	Janet Jackson	A&M 2906

★ **HIGHEST DEBUT** ★ POS 59
Sign 'O' The Times................................Prince

★ **BIGGEST MOVER** ★ 78 to 60
Light Of Day ....The Barbusters (Joan Jett & The Blackhearts)

TW	LW	WK	Billboard.	MARCH 14, 1987	HOT 100.
❶	2	9	**Jacob's Ladder**......................*Huey Lewis & The News* . . . Chrysalis 43097
❷	4	13	**Somewhere Out There**......................*Linda Ronstadt & James Ingram* . . . MCA 52973
❸	10	9	Let's Wait Awhile.......................................*Janet Jackson* . . . A&M 2906
④	1	14	Livin' On A Prayer ....*Bon Jovi* . . . Mercury 888184
❺	12	5	Lean On Me.......................................*Club Nouveau* . . . Warner 28430
❻	9	9	Mandolin Rain.......................*Bruce Hornsby & The Range* . . . RCA 5087
⑦	5	9	Respect Yourself.......................................*Bruce Willis* . . . Motown 1876
⑧	8	16	**Big Time**.......................................*Peter Gabriel* . . . Geffen 28503
❾	3	18	You Got It All ....*The Jets* . . . MCA 52968
❿	13	7	Nothing's Gonna Stop Us Now ....*Starship* . . . Grunt 5109

★ HIGHEST DEBUT ★ POS 63	★ BIGGEST MOVER ★ 80 to 51
What's Going On ....*Cyndi Lauper*	(I Just) Died In Your Arms..............*Cutting Crew*

TW	LW	WK	Billboard.	MARCH 21, 1987	HOT 100.
❶	5	6	**Lean On Me**.......................................*Club Nouveau* . . . Warner 28430
❷	3	10	**Let's Wait Awhile**.......................................*Janet Jackson* . . . A&M 2906
❸	10	8	Nothing's Gonna Stop Us Now ....*Starship* . . . Grunt 5109
❹	6	10	**Mandolin Rain**.......................*Bruce Hornsby & The Range* . . . RCA 5087
⑤	2	14	Somewhere Out There........*Linda Ronstadt & James Ingram* . . . MCA 52973
❻	12	6	Tonight, Tonight, Tonight.......................................*Genesis* . . . Atlantic 89290
⑦	1	10	Jacob's Ladder......................*Huey Lewis & The News* . . . Chrysalis 43097
⑧	7	10	Respect Yourself.......................................*Bruce Willis* . . . Motown 1876
❾	13	9	Come Go With Me.......................................*Expose* . . . Arista 9555
❿	8	17	Big Time ....*Peter Gabriel* . . . Geffen 28503

★ HIGHEST DEBUT ★ POS 49	★ BIGGEST MOVER ★ 63 to 39
La Isla Bonita ....*Madonna*	What's Going On ....*Cyndi Lauper*

TW	LW	WK	Billboard.	MARCH 28, 1987	HOT 100.
❶	1	7	**Lean On Me**.......................................*Club Nouveau* . . . Warner 28430
❷	3	9	Nothing's Gonna Stop Us Now ....*Starship* . . . Grunt 5109
③	2	11	Let's Wait Awhile.......................................*Janet Jackson* . . . A&M 2906
❹	6	7	Tonight, Tonight, Tonight.......................................*Genesis* . . . Atlantic 89290
⑤	4	11	Mandolin Rain.......................*Bruce Hornsby & The Range* . . . RCA 5087
❻	5	15	Somewhere Out There........*Linda Ronstadt & James Ingram* . . . MCA 52973
❼	9	10	Come Go With Me.......................................*Expose* . . . Arista 9555
⑧	11	10	**The Final Countdown** ....*Europe* . . . Epic 06416
❾	14	11	Don't Dream It's Over ....*Crowded House* . . . Capitol 5614
❿	17	6	I Knew You Were Waiting (For Me)......*Aretha Franklin & George Michael* . . . Arista 9559

★ HIGHEST DEBUT ★ POS 52	★ BIGGEST MOVER ★ 64 to 44
Big Love ....*Fleetwood Mac*	With Or Without You *U2*

Billboard — APRIL 4, 1987 — HOT 100

TW	LW	WK	Title	Artist	Label
❶	2	10	Nothing's Gonna Stop Us Now	Starship	Grunt 5109
②	1	8	Lean On Me	Club Nouveau	Warner 28430
③	4	8	Tonight, Tonight, Tonight	Genesis	Atlantic 89290
④	3	12	Let's Wait Awhile	Janet Jackson	A&M 2906
❺	7	11	Come Go With Me	Expose	Arista 9555
❻	10	7	I Knew You Were Waiting (For Me)	Aretha Franklin & George Michael	Arista 9559
❼	9	12	Don't Dream It's Over	Crowded House	Capitol 5614
⑧	8	11	The Final Countdown	Europe	Epic 06416
⑨	5	12	Mandolin Rain	Bruce Hornsby & The Range	RCA 5087
⑩	11	11	Let's Go!	Wang Chung	Geffen 28531

★ **HIGHEST DEBUT** ★ POS 54
I Know What I Like ....Huey Lewis & The News

★ **BIGGEST MOVER** ★ 96 to 70
You Keep Me Hangin' On...................Kim Wilde

Billboard — APRIL 11, 1987 — HOT 100

TW	LW	WK	Title	Artist	Label
①	1	11	Nothing's Gonna Stop Us Now	Starship	Grunt 5109
②	2	9	Lean On Me	Club Nouveau	Warner 28430
❸	6	8	I Knew You Were Waiting (For Me)	Aretha Franklin & George Michael	Arista 9559
④	3	9	Tonight, Tonight, Tonight	Genesis	Atlantic 89290
❺	7	13	Don't Dream It's Over	Crowded House	Capitol 5614
⑥	5	12	Come Go With Me	Expose	Arista 9555
❼	12	6	Sign 'O' The Times	Prince	Paisley Park 28399
❽	11	11	Midnight Blue	Lou Gramm	Atlantic 89304
⑨	10	12	Let's Go!	Wang Chung	Geffen 28531
⑩	14	10	The Finer Things	Steve Winwood	Island 28498

★ **HIGHEST DEBUT** ★ POS 62
Wanted Dead Or Alive ....Bon Jovi

★ **BIGGEST MOVER** ★ 70 to 51
You Keep Me Hangin' On...................Kim Wilde

Billboard — APRIL 18, 1987 — HOT 100

TW	LW	WK	Title	Artist	Label
❶	3	9	I Knew You Were Waiting (For Me)	Aretha Franklin & George Michael	Arista 9559
②	1	12	Nothing's Gonna Stop Us Now	Starship	Grunt 5109
❸	5	14	Don't Dream It's Over	Crowded House	Capitol 5614
④	7	7	Sign 'O' The Times	Prince	Paisley Park 28399
❺	8	12	Midnight Blue	Lou Gramm	Atlantic 89304
⑥	12	7	Looking For A New Love	Jody Watley	MCA 52956
⑦	2	10	Lean On Me	Club Nouveau	Warner 28430
❽	10	11	The Finer Things	Steve Winwood	Island 28498
⑨	6	13	Come Go With Me	Expose	Arista 9555
⑩	17	7	(I Just) Died In Your Arms	Cutting Crew	Virgin 99481

★ **HIGHEST DEBUT** ★ POS 88
Wild Horses ....Gino Vannelli

★ **BIGGEST MOVER** ★ 84 to 58
Diamonds ....Herb Alpert

TW	LW	WK	Billboard. APRIL 25, 1987 HOT 100.
①	1	10	**I Knew You Were Waiting (For Me)**... *Aretha Franklin & George Michael* . . . Arista 9559
②	3	15	**Don't Dream It's Over** ....*Crowded House* . . . Capitol 5614
③	4	8	**Sign 'O' The Times**...............................*Prince* . . . Paisley Park 28399
④	6	8	Looking For A New Love.........................*Jody Watley* . . . MCA 52956
⑤	10	8	(I Just) Died In Your Arms.....................*Cutting Crew* . . . Virgin 99481
⑥	2	13	Nothing's Gonna Stop Us Now....................*Starship* . . . Grunt 5109
⑦	12	6	La Isla Bonita ....*Madonna* . . . Sire 28425
⑧	8	12	**The Finer Things**...............................*Steve Winwood* . . . Island 28498
⑨	5	13	Midnight Blue..*Lou Gramm* . . . Atlantic 89304
⑩	13	6	With Or Without You ....*U2* . . . Island 99469

★ HIGHEST DEBUT ★ POS 51	★ BIGGEST MOVER ★ 84 to 69
In Too Deep.................................*Genesis*	Don't Disturb This Groove...............*The System*

TW	LW	WK	Billboard. MAY 2, 1987 HOT 100.
❶	5	9	**(I Just) Died In Your Arms** ....*Cutting Crew* . . . Virgin 99481
❷	4	9	**Looking For A New Love** ....*Jody Watley* . . . MCA 52956
③	2	16	Don't Dream It's Over ....*Crowded House* . . . Capitol 5614
❹	7	7	**La Isla Bonita** ....*Madonna* . . . Sire 28425
⑤	3	9	Sign 'O' The Times.............................*Prince* . . . Paisley Park 28399
❻	10	7	With Or Without You ....*U2* . . . Island 99469
⑦	1	11	I Knew You Were Waiting (For Me)......*Aretha Franklin & George Michael* . . . Arista 9559
⑧	8	13	**The Finer Things**.................................*Steve Winwood* . . . Island 28498
⑨	6	14	Nothing's Gonna Stop Us Now............................*Starship* . . . Grunt 5109
⑩	12	13	**Stone Love**.......................................*Kool & The Gang* . . . Mercury 888292

★ HIGHEST DEBUT ★ POS 77	★ BIGGEST MOVER ★ 94 to 70
Soul City ....*Partland Brothers*	Sweet Sixteen..*Billy Idol*

TW	LW	WK	Billboard. MAY 9, 1987 HOT 100.
❶	1	10	**(I Just) Died In Your Arms** ....*Cutting Crew* . . . Virgin 99481
❷	2	10	**Looking For A New Love** ....*Jody Watley* . . . MCA 52956
❸	6	8	With Or Without You ....*U2* . . . Island 99469
④	4	8	**La Isla Bonita** ....*Madonna* . . . Sire 28425
⑤	3	17	Don't Dream It's Over ....*Crowded House* . . . Capitol 5614
⑥	5	10	Sign 'O' The Times.............................*Prince* . . . Paisley Park 28399
❼	13	7	Heat Of The Night.............................*Bryan Adams* . . . A&M 2921
⑧	16	13	The Lady In Red..............................*Chris DeBurgh* . . . A&M 2848
⑨	18	7	Big Love..*Fleetwood Mac* . . . Warner 28398
⑩	7	12	I Knew You Were Waiting (For Me)......*Aretha Franklin & George Michael* . . . Arista 9559

★ HIGHEST DEBUT ★ POS 68	★ BIGGEST MOVER ★ 88 to 61
Point Of No Return ....*Expose*	Something So Strong ....*Crowded House*

Billboard — MAY 16, 1987 — HOT 100

TW	LW	WK	Title	Artist	Label
①	3	9	With Or Without You	U2	Island 99469
②	2	11	Looking For A New Love	Jody Watley	MCA 52956
③	1	11	(I Just) Died In Your Arms	Cutting Crew	Virgin 99481
④	4	9	La Isla Bonita	Madonna	Sire 28425
⑤	8	14	The Lady In Red	Chris DeBurgh	A&M 2848
⑥	7	8	Heat Of The Night	Bryan Adams	A&M 2921
⑦	9	8	Big Love	Fleetwood Mac	Warner 28398
⑧	14	8	You Keep Me Hangin' On	Kim Wilde	MCA 53024
⑨	11	10	Talk Dirty To Me	Poison	Capitol 5686
⑩	17	8	Always	Atlantic Starr	Warner 28455

★ **HIGHEST DEBUT** ★ POS 38
I Wanna Dance With Somebody (Who Loves Me)......................Whitney Houston

★ **BIGGEST MOVER** ★ 88 to 71
Variety Tonight.......................REO Speedwagon

Billboard — MAY 23, 1987 — HOT 100

TW	LW	WK	Title	Artist	Label
①	1	10	With Or Without You	U2	Island 99469
②	2	12	Looking For A New Love	Jody Watley	MCA 52956
③	5	15	The Lady In Red	Chris DeBurgh	A&M 2848
④	8	9	You Keep Me Hangin' On	Kim Wilde	MCA 53024
⑤	3	12	(I Just) Died In Your Arms	Cutting Crew	Virgin 99481
⑥	6	9	Heat Of The Night	Bryan Adams	A&M 2921
⑦	7	9	Big Love	Fleetwood Mac	Warner 28398
⑧	10	9	Always	Atlantic Starr	Warner 28455
⑨	4	10	La Isla Bonita	Madonna	Sire 28425
⑩	9	11	Talk Dirty To Me	Poison	Capitol 5686

★ **HIGHEST DEBUT** ★ POS 52
Shakedown................................Bob Seger

★ **BIGGEST MOVER** ★ 83 to 59
Funky Town ....Pseudo Echo

Billboard — MAY 30, 1987 — HOT 100

TW	LW	WK	Title	Artist	Label
①	1	11	With Or Without You	U2	Island 99469
②	4	10	You Keep Me Hangin' On	Kim Wilde	MCA 53024
③	3	16	The Lady In Red	Chris DeBurgh	A&M 2848
④	8	10	Always	Atlantic Starr	Warner 28455
⑤	7	10	Big Love	Fleetwood Mac	Warner 28398
⑥	15	8	Head To Toe	Lisa Lisa & Cult Jam	Columbia 07008
⑦	11	12	Right On Track	Breakfast Club	MCA 52954
⑧	6	10	Heat Of The Night	Bryan Adams	A&M 2921
⑨	12	9	I Know What I Like	Huey Lewis & The News	Chrysalis 43108
⑩	14	8	Wanted Dead Or Alive	Bon Jovi	Mercury 888467

★ **HIGHEST DEBUT** ★ POS 66
Rhythm Is Gonna Get You..........Gloria Estefan & Miami Sound Machine

★ **BIGGEST MOVER** ★ 78 to 60
The Pleasure Principle ....Janet Jackson

TW	LW	WK	Billboard	JUNE 6, 1987	HOT 100
❶	2	11	**You Keep Me Hangin' On**......................*Kim Wilde* ... MCA 53024
❷	4	11	Always......................................*Atlantic Starr* ... Warner 28455
❸	6	9	Head To Toe ....*Lisa Lisa & Cult Jam* ... Columbia 07008
④	3	17	The Lady In Red............................*Chris DeBurgh* ... A&M 2848
⑤	1	12	With Or Without You ....*U2* ... Island 99469
❻	11	7	In Too Deep..................................*Genesis* ... Atlantic 89316
❼	10	9	**Wanted Dead Or Alive**......................*Bon Jovi* ... Mercury 888467
⑧	5	11	Big Love............................*Fleetwood Mac* ... Warner 28398
❾	14	9	Diamonds....................................*Herb Alpert* ... A&M 2929
❿	18	4	I Wanna Dance With Somebody (Who Loves Me) ...... *Whitney Houston* ... Arista 9598

★ **HIGHEST DEBUT** ★ POS 51
I Want Your Sex ....*George Michael*

★ **BIGGEST MOVER** ★ 85 to 62
Back In The High Life Again........*Steve Winwood*

TW	LW	WK	Billboard	JUNE 13, 1987	HOT 100
❶	2	12	**Always**......................................*Atlantic Starr* ... Warner 28455
②	1	12	You Keep Me Hangin' On..........................*Kim Wilde* ... MCA 53024
❸	3	10	**Head To Toe** ....*Lisa Lisa & Cult Jam* ... Columbia 07008
④	6	8	In Too Deep..................................*Genesis* ... Atlantic 89316
❺	10	5	I Wanna Dance With Somebody (Who Loves Me) ...... *Whitney Houston* ... Arista 9598
⑥	4	18	The Lady In Red............................*Chris DeBurgh* ... A&M 2848
❼	7	10	**Wanted Dead Or Alive**......................*Bon Jovi* ... Mercury 888467
⑧	9	10	Diamonds....................................*Herb Alpert* ... A&M 2929
⑨	5	13	With Or Without You ....*U2* ... Island 99469
❿	13	12	Just To See Her ....*Smokey Robinson* ... Motown 1877

★ **HIGHEST DEBUT** ★ POS 51
I Still Haven't Found What I'm Looking
For *U2*

★ **BIGGEST MOVER** ★ 84 to 63
Rock Steady ....*Whispers*

TW	LW	WK	Billboard	JUNE 20, 1987	HOT 100
❶	3	11	**Head To Toe** ....*Lisa Lisa & Cult Jam* ... Columbia 07008
②	1	13	Always......................................*Atlantic Starr* ... Warner 28455
❸	5	6	I Wanna Dance With Somebody (Who Loves Me) ...... *Whitney Houston* ... Arista 9598
④	4	9	In Too Deep..................................*Genesis* ... Atlantic 89316
⑤	8	11	**Diamonds** ....*Herb Alpert* ... A&M 2929
⑥	12	6	Alone..*Heart* ... Capitol 44002
⑦	7	11	**Wanted Dead Or Alive**......................*Bon Jovi* ... Mercury 888467
⑧	2	13	You Keep Me Hangin' On..........................*Kim Wilde* ... MCA 53024
⑨	13	12	Songbird......................................*Kenny G* ... Arista 9588
❿	10	13	Just To See Her ....*Smokey Robinson* ... Motown 1877

★ **HIGHEST DEBUT** ★ POS 52
Seven Wonders........................*Fleetwood Mac*

★ **BIGGEST MOVER** ★ 71 to 51
Hearts On Fire ....*Bryan Adams*

Billboard — JUNE 27, 1987 — HOT 100

TW	LW	WK	Title / Artist
1	3	7	**I Wanna Dance With Somebody (Who Loves Me)** .... *Whitney Houston* . . . Arista 9598
2	1	12	**Head To Toe** .... *Lisa Lisa & Cult Jam* . . . Columbia 07008
3	4	10	**In Too Deep** .... *Genesis* . . . Atlantic 89316
4	6	7	**Alone** .... *Heart* . . . Capitol 44002
5	2	14	**Always** .... *Atlantic Starr* . . . Warner 28455
6	9	13	**Songbird** .... *Kenny G* . . . Arista 9588
7	12	6	**Shakedown** .... *Bob Seger* . . . MCA 53094
8	5	12	**Diamonds** .... *Herb Alpert* . . . A&M 2929
9	10	14	**Just To See Her** .... *Smokey Robinson* . . . Motown 1877
10	7	12	**Wanted Dead Or Alive** .... *Bon Jovi* . . . Mercury 888467

★ HIGHEST DEBUT ★ POS 67	★ BIGGEST MOVER ★ 95 to 73
It's Not Over ('Til It's Over) .... *Starship*	Good Times .... *INXS & Jimmy Barnes*

Billboard — JULY 4, 1987 — HOT 100

TW	LW	WK	Title / Artist
1	1	8	**I Wanna Dance With Somebody (Who Loves Me)** .... *Whitney Houston* . . . Arista 9598
2	4	8	**Alone** .... *Heart* . . . Capitol 44002
3	7	7	**Shakedown** .... *Bob Seger* . . . MCA 53094
4	2	13	**Head To Toe** .... *Lisa Lisa & Cult Jam* . . . Columbia 07008
5	6	14	**Songbird** .... *Kenny G* . . . Arista 9588
6	3	11	**In Too Deep** .... *Genesis* . . . Atlantic 89316
7	11	13	**Don't Disturb This Groove** .... *The System* . . . Atlantic 89320
8	9	15	**Just To See Her** .... *Smokey Robinson* . . . Motown 1877
9	14	9	**Point Of No Return** .... *Expose* . . . Arista 9579
10	16	8	**Funky Town** .... *Pseudo Echo* . . . RCA 5217

★ HIGHEST DEBUT ★ POS 80	★ BIGGEST MOVER ★ 84 to 60
Here I Go Again .... *Whitesnake*	La Bamba .... *Los Lobos*

Billboard — JULY 11, 1987 — HOT 100

TW	LW	WK	Title / Artist
1	2	9	**Alone** .... *Heart* . . . Capitol 44002
2	1	9	**I Wanna Dance With Somebody (Who Loves Me)** ...... *Whitney Houston* . . . Arista 9598
3	3	8	**Shakedown** .... *Bob Seger* . . . MCA 53094
4	5	15	**Songbird** .... *Kenny G* . . . Arista 9588
5	7	14	**Don't Disturb This Groove** .... *The System* . . . Atlantic 89320
6	9	10	**Point Of No Return** .... *Expose* . . . Arista 9579
7	10	9	**Funky Town** .... *Pseudo Echo* . . . RCA 5217
8	11	11	**Something So Strong** .... *Crowded House* . . . Capitol 5695
9	4	14	**Head To Toe** .... *Lisa Lisa & Cult Jam* . . . Columbia 07008
10	17	5	**I Still Haven't Found What I'm Looking For** .... *U2* . . . Island 99430

★ HIGHEST DEBUT ★ POS 43	★ BIGGEST MOVER ★ 78 to 60
Who's That Girl .... *Madonna*	Dreamin' .... *Will To Power*

Billboard — JULY 18, 1987 — HOT 100

TW	LW	WK	Title	Artist	Label
①	1	10	**Alone**	Heart	Capitol 44002
❷	3	9	**Shakedown**	Bob Seger	MCA 53094
③	2	10	**I Wanna Dance With Somebody (Who Loves Me)**	Whitney Houston	Arista 9598
④	5	15	**Don't Disturb This Groove**	The System	Atlantic 89320
⑤	6	11	**Point Of No Return**	Expose	Arista 9579
⑥	7	10	**Funky Town**	Pseudo Echo	RCA 5217
❼	10	6	**I Still Haven't Found What I'm Looking For**	U2	Island 99430
⑧	8	12	**Something So Strong**	Crowded House	Capitol 5695
❾	11	7	**I Want Your Sex**	George Michael	Columbia 07164
⑩	12	8	**Rhythm Is Gonna Get You**	Gloria Estefan & Miami Sound Machine	Epic 07059

★ **HIGHEST DEBUT** ★ POS 63
Doing It All For My Baby..........Huey Lewis & The News

★ **BIGGEST MOVER** ★ 66 to 49
Love Power........Dionne Warwick & Jeffrey Osborne

Billboard — JULY 25, 1987 — HOT 100

TW	LW	WK	Title	Artist	Label
①	1	11	**Alone**	Heart	Capitol 44002
❷	2	10	**Shakedown**	Bob Seger	MCA 53094
❸	7	7	**I Still Haven't Found What I'm Looking For**	U2	Island 99430
④	3	11	**I Wanna Dance With Somebody (Who Loves Me)**	Whitney Houston	Arista 9598
❺	9	8	**I Want Your Sex**	George Michael	Columbia 07164
❻	10	9	**Rhythm Is Gonna Get You**	Gloria Estefan & Miami Sound Machine	Epic 07059
⑦	8	13	**Something So Strong**	Crowded House	Capitol 5695
❽	12	13	**Heart And Soul**	T'Pau	Virgin 99466
⑨	4	16	**Don't Disturb This Groove**	The System	Atlantic 89320
⑩	5	12	**Point Of No Return**	Expose	Arista 9579

★ **HIGHEST DEBUT** ★ POS 77
Touch Of Grey..........Grateful Dead

★ **BIGGEST MOVER** ★ 63 to 45
Doing It All For My Baby..........Huey Lewis & The News

Billboard — AUGUST 1, 1987 — HOT 100

TW	LW	WK	Title	Artist	Label
❶	2	11	**Shakedown**	Bob Seger	MCA 53094
❷	3	8	**I Still Haven't Found What I'm Looking For**	U2	Island 99430
③	1	12	**Alone**	Heart	Capitol 44002
④	5	9	**I Want Your Sex**	George Michael	Columbia 07164
❺	6	10	**Rhythm Is Gonna Get You**	Gloria Estefan & Miami Sound Machine	Epic 07059
❻	8	14	**Heart And Soul**	T'Pau	Virgin 99466
❼	14	9	**Cross My Broken Heart**	The Jets	MCA 53123
❽	15	9	**Luka**	Suzanne Vega	A&M 2937
⑨	4	12	**I Wanna Dance With Somebody (Who Loves Me)**	Whitney Houston	Arista 9598
⑩	16	10	**Wot's It To Ya**	Robbie Nevil	Manhattan 50075

★ **HIGHEST DEBUT** ★ POS 50
Didn't We Almost Have It All......Whitney Houston

★ **BIGGEST MOVER** ★ 87 to 66
Jump Start ....Natalie Cole

TW	LW	WK	Billboard	AUGUST 8, 1987	HOT 100.
①	2	9	**I Still Haven't Found What I'm Looking For** ......*U2* ... Island 99430		
②	4	10	**I Want Your Sex** ....*George Michael* ... Columbia 07164		
③	1	12	Shakedown ....*Bob Seger* ... MCA 53094		
④	6	15	**Heart And Soul** ....*T'Pau* ... Virgin 99466		
⑤	8	10	Luka..*Suzanne Vega* ... A&M 2937		
⑥	5	11	Rhythm Is Gonna Get You .... *Gloria Estefan & Miami Sound Machine* ... Epic 07059		
⑦	11	5	**Who's That Girl** ....*Madonna* ... Sire 28341		
⑧	7	10	**Cross My Broken Heart**.......................................*The Jets* ... MCA 53123		
⑨	3	13	Alone...*Heart* ... Capitol 44002		
⑩	10	11	**Wot's It To Ya**...*Robbie Nevil* ... Manhattan 50075		

★ **HIGHEST DEBUT** ★ POS 37	★ **BIGGEST MOVER** ★ 93 to 76
I Just Can't Stop Loving You ......*Michael Jackson with Siedah Garrett*	Misfit ....*Curiosity Killed The Cat*

TW	LW	WK	Billboard	AUGUST 15, 1987	HOT 100.
①	1	10	**I Still Haven't Found What I'm Looking For** ......*U2* ... Island 99430		
②	7	6	**Who's That Girl** ....*Madonna* ... Sire 28341		
③	2	11	I Want Your Sex...................................*George Michael* ... Columbia 07164		
④	5	11	Luka..*Suzanne Vega* ... A&M 2937		
⑤	11	8	La Bamba ....*Los Lobos* ... Slash 28336		
⑥	4	16	Heart And Soul...*T'Pau* ... Virgin 99466		
⑦	12	10	Don't Mean Nothing................................*Richard Marx* ... Manhattan 50079		
⑧	8	11	Cross My Broken Heart.......................................*The Jets* ... MCA 53123		
⑨	13	15	Only In My Dreams ....*Debbie Gibson* ... Atlantic 89322		
⑩	6	12	Rhythm Is Gonna Get You .... *Gloria Estefan & Miami Sound Machine* ... Epic 07059		

★ **HIGHEST DEBUT** ★ POS 62	★ **BIGGEST MOVER** ★ 37 to 16
Paper In Fire ....*John Cougar Mellencamp*	I Just Can't Stop Loving You ......*Michael Jackson with Siedah Garrett*

TW	LW	WK	Billboard	AUGUST 22, 1987	HOT 100.
①	2	7	**Who's That Girl** ....*Madonna* ... Sire 28341		
②	5	9	**La Bamba** ....*Los Lobos* ... Slash 28336		
③	4	12	**Luka** ....*Suzanne Vega* ... A&M 2937		
④	7	11	**Don't Mean Nothing**................................*Richard Marx* ... Manhattan 50079		
⑤	3	12	I Want Your Sex...................................*George Michael* ... Columbia 07164		
⑥	1	11	I Still Haven't Found What I'm Looking For ....*U2* ... Island 99430		
⑦	9	16	**Only In My Dreams** ....*Debbie Gibson* ... Atlantic 89322		
⑧	11	12	**Rock Steady** ....*Whispers* ... Solar 70006		
⑨	6	17	Heart And Soul...*T'Pau* ... Virgin 99466		
⑩	16	3	**I Just Can't Stop Loving You** .... *Michael Jackson with Siedah Garrett* ... Epic 07253		

★ **HIGHEST DEBUT** ★ POS 73	★ **BIGGEST MOVER** ★ 90 to 63
Something Real (Inside Me/Inside You) ....*Mr. Mister*	Casanova..*Levert*

Billboard — AUGUST 29, 1987 — HOT 100

TW	LW	WK	Title	Artist	Label
1	2	10	**La Bamba**	*Los Lobos*	Slash 28336
2	1	8	Who's That Girl	*Madonna*	Sire 28341
3	4	12	**Don't Mean Nothing**	*Richard Marx*	Manhattan 50079
4	3	13	Luka	*Suzanne Vega*	A&M 2937
5	7	17	Only In My Dreams	*Debbie Gibson*	Atlantic 89322
6	10	4	I Just Can't Stop Loving You	*Michael Jackson with Siedah Garrett*	Epic 07253
7	8	13	**Rock Steady**	*Whispers*	Solar 70006
8	16	5	Didn't We Almost Have It All	*Whitney Houston*	Arista 9616
9	11	10	**It's Not Over ('Til It's Over)**	*Starship*	RCA/Grunt 5225
10	12	13	Can't We Try	*Dan Hill with Vonda Sheppard*	Columbia 07050

★ **HIGHEST DEBUT** ★ POS 65
You Are The Girl ....*The Cars*

★ **BIGGEST MOVER** ★ 75 to 54
Victim Of Love ....*Bryan Adams*

Billboard — SEPTEMBER 5, 1987 — HOT 100

TW	LW	WK	Title	Artist	Label
1	1	11	**La Bamba**	*Los Lobos*	Slash 28336
2	6	5	I Just Can't Stop Loving You	*Michael Jackson with Siedah Garrett*	Epic 07253
3	2	9	Who's That Girl	*Madonna*	Sire 28341
4	5	18	**Only In My Dreams**	*Debbie Gibson*	Atlantic 89322
5	8	6	**Didn't We Almost Have It All**	*Whitney Houston*	Arista 9616
6	3	13	**Don't Mean Nothing**	*Richard Marx*	Manhattan 50079
7	10	14	Can't We Try	*Dan Hill with Vonda Sheppard*	Columbia 07050
8	15	10	Here I Go Again	*Whitesnake*	Geffen 28339
9	7	14	Rock Steady	*Whispers*	Solar 70006
10	14	8	Doing It All For My Baby	*Huey Lewis & The News*	Chrysalis 43143

★ **HIGHEST DEBUT** ★ POS 70
It's A Sin ....*Pet Shop Boys*

★ **BIGGEST MOVER** ★ 84 to 63
I Think We're Alone Now ....*Tiffany*

Billboard — SEPTEMBER 12, 1987 — HOT 100

TW	LW	WK	Title	Artist	Label
1	1	12	**La Bamba**	*Los Lobos*	Slash 28336
2	2	6	I Just Can't Stop Loving You	*Michael Jackson with Siedah Garrett*	Epic 07253
3	5	7	**Didn't We Almost Have It All**	*Whitney Houston*	Arista 9616
4	8	11	**Here I Go Again**	*Whitesnake*	Geffen 28339
5	4	19	Only In My Dreams	*Debbie Gibson*	Atlantic 89322
6	7	15	**Can't We Try**	*Dan Hill with Vonda Sheppard*	Columbia 07050
7	10	9	Doing It All For My Baby	*Huey Lewis & The News*	Chrysalis 43143
8	11	11	When Smokey Sings	*ABC*	Mercury 888604
9	3	10	Who's That Girl	*Madonna*	Sire 28341
10	17	9	I Heard A Rumour	*Bananarama*	London 886165

★ **HIGHEST DEBUT** ★ POS 41
Causing A Commotion ....*Madonna*

★ **BIGGEST MOVER** ★ 72 to 51
Mony Mony "Live" ....*Billy Idol*

TW	LW	WK	Billboard	SEPTEMBER 19, 1987	HOT 100
1	2	7	**I Just Can't Stop Loving You** ..... *Michael Jackson with Siedah Garrett* ... Epic 07253		
2	3	8	**Didn't We Almost Have It All** .... *Whitney Houston* ... Arista 9616		
3	1	13	La Bamba .... *Los Lobos* ... Slash 28336		
4	4	12	Here I Go Again .... *Whitesnake* ... Geffen 28339		
5	8	12	**When Smokey Sings** .... *ABC* ... Mercury 888604		
6	7	10	**Doing It All For My Baby** ..... *Huey Lewis & The News* ... Chrysalis 43143		
7	6	16	**Can't We Try** .... *Dan Hill with Vonda Sheppard* ... Columbia 07050		
8	10	10	I Heard A Rumour .... *Bananarama* ... London 886165		
9	16	8	Lost In Emotion .... *Lisa Lisa & Cult Jam* ... Columbia 07267		
10	11	9	Touch Of Grey .... *Grateful Dead* ... Arista 9606		

★ *HIGHEST DEBUT* ★ POS 40	★ *BIGGEST MOVER* ★ 91 to 72
Bad .... *Michael Jackson*	Sugar Free .... *Wa Wa Nee*

TW	LW	WK	Billboard	SEPTEMBER 26, 1987	HOT 100
1	2	9	**Didn't We Almost Have It All** .... *Whitney Houston* ... Arista 9616		
2	4	13	**Here I Go Again** .... *Whitesnake* ... Geffen 28339		
3	1	8	I Just Can't Stop Loving You .... *Michael Jackson with Siedah Garrett* ... Epic 07253		
4	8	11	**I Heard A Rumour** .... *Bananarama* ... London 886165		
5	9	9	Lost In Emotion .... *Lisa Lisa & Cult Jam* ... Columbia 07267		
6	5	13	When Smokey Sings .... *ABC* ... Mercury 888604		
7	11	9	Carrie .... *Europe* ... Epic 07282		
8	3	14	La Bamba .... *Los Lobos* ... Slash 28336		
9	10	10	**Touch Of Grey** .... *Grateful Dead* ... Arista 9606		
10	15	9	U Got The Look .... *Prince* ... Paisley Park 28289		

★ *HIGHEST DEBUT* ★ POS 64	★ *BIGGEST MOVER* ★ 91 to 70
Should've Known Better .... *Richard Marx*	Boys Night Out .... *Timothy B. Schmit*

TW	LW	WK	Billboard	OCTOBER 3, 1987	HOT 100
(1)	1	10	**Didn't We Almost Have It All** .... *Whitney Houston* ... Arista 9616		
(2)	2	14	Here I Go Again .... *Whitesnake* ... Geffen 28339		
(3)	5	10	Lost In Emotion .... *Lisa Lisa & Cult Jam* ... Columbia 07267		
(4)	4	12	**I Heard A Rumour** .... *Bananarama* ... London 886165		
(5)	7	10	Carrie .... *Europe* ... Epic 07282		
(6)	10	10	U Got The Look .... *Prince* ... Paisley Park 28289		
(7)	13	8	**Who Will You Run To** .... *Heart* ... Capitol 44040		
(8)	6	14	When Smokey Sings .... *ABC* ... Mercury 888604		
(9)	14	8	**Paper In Fire** .... *John Cougar Mellencamp* ... Mercury 888763		
(10)	16	12	One Heartbeat .... *Smokey Robinson* ... Motown 1897		

★ *HIGHEST DEBUT* ★ POS 40	★ *BIGGEST MOVER* ★ 73 to 54
Brilliant Disguise .... *Bruce Springsteen*	(I've Had) The Time Of My Life .... *Bill Medley &* *Jennifer Warnes*

Billboard — OCTOBER 10, 1987 — HOT 100

TW	LW	WK	Title	Artist	Label
1	2	15	Here I Go Again	Whitesnake	Geffen 28339
2	3	11	Lost In Emotion	Lisa Lisa & Cult Jam	Columbia 07267
3	5	11	Carrie	Europe	Epic 07282
4	4	13	I Heard A Rumour	Bananarama	London 886165
5	6	11	U Got The Look	Prince	Paisley Park 28289
6	1	11	Didn't We Almost Have It All	Whitney Houston	Arista 9616
7	7	9	Who Will You Run To	Heart	Capitol 44040
8	16	4	Bad	Michael Jackson	Epic 07418
9	9	9	Paper In Fire	John Cougar Mellencamp	Mercury 888763
10	11	9	Casanova	Levert	Atlantic 89217

★ **HIGHEST DEBUT** ★ POS 59
We'll Be Together..Sting

★ **BIGGEST MOVER** ★ 54 to 35
(I've Had) The Time Of My Life........Bill Medley & Jennifer Warnes

Billboard — OCTOBER 17, 1987 — HOT 100

TW	LW	WK	Title	Artist	Label
1	2	12	Lost In Emotion	Lisa Lisa & Cult Jam	Columbia 07267
2	5	12	U Got The Look	Prince	Paisley Park 28289
3	3	12	Carrie	Europe	Epic 07282
4	8	5	Bad	Michael Jackson	Epic 07418
5	11	6	Causing A Commotion	Madonna	Sire 28224
6	1	16	Here I Go Again	Whitesnake	Geffen 28339
7	7	10	Who Will You Run To	Heart	Capitol 44040
8	10	10	Casanova	Levert	Atlantic 89217
9	9	10	Paper In Fire	John Cougar Mellencamp	Mercury 888763
10	4	14	I Heard A Rumour	Bananarama	London 886165

★ **HIGHEST DEBUT** ★ POS 66
Skeletons..Stevie Wonder

★ **BIGGEST MOVER** ★ 70 to 51
Shake Your Love ....Debbie Gibson

Billboard — OCTOBER 24, 1987 — HOT 100

TW	LW	WK	Title	Artist	Label
1	4	6	Bad	Michael Jackson	Epic 07418
2	5	7	Causing A Commotion	Madonna	Sire 28224
3	2	13	U Got The Look	Prince	Paisley Park 28289
4	1	13	Lost In Emotion	Lisa Lisa & Cult Jam	Columbia 07267
5	11	9	I Think We're Alone Now	Tiffany	MCA 53167
6	8	11	Casanova	Levert	Atlantic 89217
7	14	8	Mony Mony "Live"	Billy Idol	Chrysalis 43161
8	12	11	Let Me Be The One	Expose	Arista 9617
9	13	9	Little Lies	Fleetwood Mac	Warner 28291
10	3	13	Carrie	Europe	Epic 07282

★ **HIGHEST DEBUT** ★ POS 53
Is This Love ....Whitesnake

★ **BIGGEST MOVER** ★ 56 to 40
Don't You Want Me ....Jody Watley

Billboard — OCTOBER 31, 1987 — HOT 100

TW	LW	WK	Title	Artist
①	1	7	**Bad**	*Michael Jackson* ... Epic 07418
②	2	8	**Causing A Commotion**	*Madonna* ... Sire 28224
③	5	10	I Think We're Alone Now	*Tiffany* ... MCA 53167
④	7	9	Mony Mony "Live"	*Billy Idol* ... Chrysalis 43161
⑤	6	12	**Casanova**	*Levert* ... Atlantic 89217
⑥	9	10	Little Lies	*Fleetwood Mac* ... Warner 28291
⑦	8	12	**Let Me Be The One**	*Expose* ... Arista 9617
⑧	3	14	**U Got The Look**	*Prince* ... Paisley Park 28289
⑨	13	12	Breakout	*Swing Out Sister* ... Mercury 888016
⑩	16	5	Brilliant Disguise	*Bruce Springsteen* ... Columbia 07595

★ HIGHEST DEBUT ★ POS 47	★ BIGGEST MOVER ★ 97 to 74
So Emotional .... *Whitney Houston*	Power Of Love .... *Laura Branigan*

Billboard — NOVEMBER 7, 1987 — HOT 100

TW	LW	WK	Title	Artist
①	3	11	**I Think We're Alone Now**	*Tiffany* ... MCA 53167
②	2	9	**Causing A Commotion**	*Madonna* ... Sire 28224
③	4	10	Mony Mony "Live"	*Billy Idol* ... Chrysalis 43161
④	6	11	**Little Lies**	*Fleetwood Mac* ... Warner 28291
⑤	1	8	Bad	*Michael Jackson* ... Epic 07418
⑥	12	7	(I've Had) The Time Of My Life	*Bill Medley & Jennifer Warnes* ... RCA 5224
⑦	9	13	Breakout	*Swing Out Sister* ... Mercury 888016
⑧	10	6	Brilliant Disguise	*Bruce Springsteen* ... Columbia 07595
⑨	7	13	Let Me Be The One	*Expose* ... Arista 9617
⑩	11	10	It's A Sin	*Pet Shop Boys* ... EMI America 43027

★ HIGHEST DEBUT ★ POS 68	★ BIGGEST MOVER ★ 71 to 54
Candle In The Wind .... *Elton John*	Need You Tonight .... *INXS*

Billboard — NOVEMBER 14, 1987 — HOT 100

TW	LW	WK	Title	Artist
①	1	12	**I Think We're Alone Now**	*Tiffany* ... MCA 53167
②	3	11	Mony Mony "Live"	*Billy Idol* ... Chrysalis 43161
③	6	8	(I've Had) The Time Of My Life	*Bill Medley & Jennifer Warnes* ... RCA 5224
④	4	12	**Little Lies**	*Fleetwood Mac* ... Warner 28291
⑤	11	8	Heaven Is A Place On Earth	*Belinda Carlisle* ... MCA 53181
⑥	7	14	**Breakout**	*Swing Out Sister* ... Mercury 888016
⑦	8	7	**Brilliant Disguise**	*Bruce Springsteen* ... Columbia 07595
⑧	2	10	Causing A Commotion	*Madonna* ... Sire 28224
⑨	10	11	**It's A Sin**	*Pet Shop Boys* ... EMI America 43027
⑩	14	8	Should've Known Better	*Richard Marx* ... Manhattan 50083

★ HIGHEST DEBUT ★ POS 72	★ BIGGEST MOVER ★ 90 to 66
Don't Shed A Tear .... *Paul Carrack*	I Live For Your Love .... *Natalie Cole*

Billboard — NOVEMBER 21, 1987 — HOT 100

TW	LW	WK	Title	Artist	Label
1	2	12	Mony Mony "Live"	Billy Idol	Chrysalis 43161
2	3	9	(I've Had) The Time Of My Life	Bill Medley & Jennifer Warnes	RCA 5224
3	5	9	Heaven Is A Place On Earth	Belinda Carlisle	MCA 53181
4	1	13	I Think We're Alone Now	Tiffany	MCA 53167
5	7	8	Brilliant Disguise	Bruce Springsteen	Columbia 07595
6	6	15	Breakout	Swing Out Sister	Mercury 888016
7	10	9	Should've Known Better	Richard Marx	Manhattan 50083
8	4	13	Little Lies	Fleetwood Mac	Warner 28291
9	12	12	I've Been In Love Before	Cutting Crew	Virgin 99425
10	19	5	Faith	George Michael	Columbia 07623

★ HIGHEST DEBUT ★ POS 44
The Way You Make Me Feel ......Michael Jackson

★ BIGGEST MOVER ★ 81 to 56
I Could Never Take The Place Of Your Man ......Prince

Billboard — NOVEMBER 28, 1987 — HOT 100

TW	LW	WK	Title	Artist	Label
1	2	10	(I've Had) The Time Of My Life	Bill Medley & Jennifer Warnes	RCA 5224
2	3	10	Heaven Is A Place On Earth	Belinda Carlisle	MCA 53181
3	1	13	Mony Mony "Live"	Billy Idol	Chrysalis 43161
4	7	10	Should've Known Better	Richard Marx	Manhattan 50083
5	10	6	Faith	George Michael	Columbia 07623
6	5	9	Brilliant Disguise	Bruce Springsteen	Columbia 07595
7	4	14	I Think We're Alone Now	Tiffany	MCA 53167
8	11	8	We'll Be Together	Sting	A&M 2983
9	9	13	I've Been In Love Before	Cutting Crew	Virgin 99425
10	14	9	Shake Your Love	Debbie Gibson	Atlantic 89187

★ HIGHEST DEBUT ★ POS 57
Seasons Change ......Expose

★ BIGGEST MOVER ★ 94 to 76
You And Me Tonight ......Deja

Billboard — DECEMBER 5, 1987 — HOT 100

TW	LW	WK	Title	Artist	Label
1	2	11	Heaven Is A Place On Earth	Belinda Carlisle	MCA 53181
2	1	11	(I've Had) The Time Of My Life	Bill Medley & Jennifer Warnes	RCA 5224
3	5	7	Faith	George Michael	Columbia 07623
4	4	11	Should've Known Better	Richard Marx	Manhattan 50083
5	11	7	Is This Love	Whitesnake	Geffen 28233
6	10	10	Shake Your Love	Debbie Gibson	Atlantic 89187
7	8	9	We'll Be Together	Sting	A&M 2983
8	16	6	So Emotional	Whitney Houston	Arista 9642
9	12	12	The One I Love	R.E.M.	I.R.S. 53171
10	14	10	Don't You Want Me	Jody Watley	MCA 53162

★ HIGHEST DEBUT ★ POS 57
Tunnel Of Love ......Bruce Springsteen

★ BIGGEST MOVER ★ 86 to 52
Could've Been ......Tiffany

Billboard DECEMBER 12, 1987 HOT 100

TW	LW	WK	Title	Artist ... Label
1	3	8	**Faith**	*George Michael* ... Columbia 07623
2	1	12	Heaven Is A Place On Earth	*Belinda Carlisle* ... MCA 53181
3	4	12	**Should've Known Better**	*Richard Marx* ... Manhattan 50083
4	2	12	(I've Had) The Time Of My Life................	*Bill Medley & Jennifer Warnes* ... RCA 5224
5	5	8	**Is This Love**	*Whitesnake* ... Geffen 28233
6	6	11	Shake Your Love	*Debbie Gibson* ... Atlantic 89187
7	8	7	So Emotional..	*Whitney Houston* ... Arista 9642
8	7	10	We'll Be Together..	*Sting* ... A&M 2983
9	10	11	Don't You Want Me	*Jody Watley* ... MCA 53162
10	11	8	Got My Mind Set On You	*George Harrison* ... Dark Horse 28178

★ **HIGHEST DEBUT** ★ POS 60
What Have I Done To Deserve This? ....*Pet Shop Boys & Dusty Springfield*

★ **BIGGEST MOVER** ★ 83 to 66
Pump Up The Volume ....*M/A/R/R/S*

Billboard DECEMBER 19, 1987 HOT 100

TW	LW	WK	Title	Artist ... Label
1	1	9	**Faith**	*George Michael* ... Columbia 07623
2	5	9	**Is This Love**	*Whitesnake* ... Geffen 28233
3	7	8	So Emotional..	*Whitney Houston* ... Arista 9642
4	6	12	**Shake Your Love**	*Debbie Gibson* ... Atlantic 89187
5	10	9	Got My Mind Set On You	*George Harrison* ... Dark Horse 28178
6	9	12	**Don't You Want Me**	*Jody Watley* ... MCA 53162
7	2	13	Heaven Is A Place On Earth	*Belinda Carlisle* ... MCA 53181
8	11	13	**Catch Me (I'm Falling)**................	*Pretty Poison* ... Virgin 99416
9	13	15	**Valerie**	*Steve Winwood* ... Island 28231
10	8	11	We'll Be Together..	*Sting* ... A&M 2983

★ **HIGHEST DEBUT** ★ POS 71
Never Gonna Give You Up.................*Rick Astley*

★ **BIGGEST MOVER** ★ 81 to 65
Hot In The City.......................................*Billy Idol*

Billboard DECEMBER 26, 1987 HOT 100

TW	LW	WK	Title	Artist ... Label
1	1	10	**Faith**	*George Michael* ... Columbia 07623
2	3	9	**So Emotional**..................................	*Whitney Houston* ... Arista 9642
3	2	10	Is This Love	*Whitesnake* ... Geffen 28233
4	5	10	**Got My Mind Set On You**	*George Harrison* ... Dark Horse 28178
5	4	13	Shake Your Love	*Debbie Gibson* ... Atlantic 89187
6	6	13	**Don't You Want Me**	*Jody Watley* ... MCA 53162
7	11	6	The Way You Make Me Feel.....................	*Michael Jackson* ... Epic 07645
8	8	14	**Catch Me (I'm Falling)**............................	*Pretty Poison* ... Virgin 99416
9	13	10	Cherry Bomb ....*John Cougar Mellencamp* ... Mercury 888934
10	16	10	Need You Tonight	*INXS* ... Atlantic 89188

★ **HIGHEST DEBUT** ★ POS 80
Live My Life ....*Boy George*

★ **BIGGEST MOVER** ★ 84 to 55
She's Like The Wind ....*Patrick Swayze featuring Wendy Fraser*

Billboard — JANUARY 9, 1988 — HOT 100

TW	LW	WK			
❶	2	11	**So Emotional**	Whitney Houston	Arista 9642
❷	4	12	Got My Mind Set On You	George Harrison	Dark Horse 28178
③	1	12	Faith	George Michael	Columbia 07623
④	3	12	Is This Love	Whitesnake	Geffen 28233
⑤	7	8	The Way You Make Me Feel	Michael Jackson	Epic 07645
⑥	10	12	Need You Tonight	INXS	Atlantic 89188
⑦	5	15	Shake Your Love	Debbie Gibson	Atlantic 89187
⑧	9	12	**Cherry Bomb**	John Cougar Mellencamp	Mercury 888934
⑨	12	14	Tell It To My Heart	Taylor Dayne	Arista 9612
⑩	6	15	Don't You Want Me	Jody Watley	MCA 53162

★ HIGHEST DEBUT ★ POS 82	★ BIGGEST MOVER ★ 96 to 83
Love Overboard .... Gladys Knight & The Pips	Never Let Me Down Again .... Depeche Mode

Billboard — JANUARY 16, 1988 — HOT 100

TW	LW	WK			
❶	2	13	**Got My Mind Set On You**	George Harrison	Dark Horse 28178
②	1	12	So Emotional	Whitney Houston	Arista 9642
❸	5	9	The Way You Make Me Feel	Michael Jackson	Epic 07645
④	6	13	Need You Tonight	INXS	Atlantic 89188
⑤	14	8	Could've Been	Tiffany	MCA 53231
⑥	12	10	Hazy Shade Of Winter	Bangles	Def Jam 07630
⑦	11	11	Candle In The Wind	Elton John	MCA 53196
⑧	9	15	Tell It To My Heart	Taylor Dayne	Arista 9612
⑨	3	13	Faith	George Michael	Columbia 07623
⑩	4	13	Is This Love	Whitesnake	Geffen 28233

★ HIGHEST DEBUT ★ POS 49	★ BIGGEST MOVER ★ 82 to 65
Father Figure .... George Michael	Love Overboard .... Gladys Knight & The Pips

Billboard — JANUARY 23, 1988 — HOT 100

TW	LW	WK			
❶	3	10	**The Way You Make Me Feel**	Michael Jackson	Epic 07645
❷	4	14	Need You Tonight	INXS	Atlantic 89188
❸	5	9	Could've Been	Tiffany	MCA 53231
④	1	14	Got My Mind Set On You	George Harrison	Dark Horse 28178
⑤	6	11	Hazy Shade Of Winter	Bangles	Def Jam 07630
⑥	7	12	**Candle In The Wind**	Elton John	MCA 53196
⑦	8	16	**Tell It To My Heart**	Taylor Dayne	Arista 9612
⑧	11	9	Seasons Change	Expose	Arista 9640
⑨	2	13	So Emotional	Whitney Houston	Arista 9642
⑩	15	11	I Want To Be Your Man	Roger	Reprise 28229

★ HIGHEST DEBUT ★ POS 53	★ BIGGEST MOVER ★ 64 to 49
Endless Summer Nights .... Richard Marx	Be Still My Beating Heart .... Sting

Billboard — JANUARY 30, 1988 — HOT 100

TW	LW	WK	Title	Artist	Label
1	2	15	**Need You Tonight**	INXS	Atlantic 89188
2	3	10	Could've Been	Tiffany	MCA 53231
3	5	12	Hazy Shade Of Winter	Bangles	Def Jam 07630
4	1	11	The Way You Make Me Feel	Michael Jackson	Epic 07645
5	8	10	Seasons Change	Expose	Arista 9640
6	10	12	I Want To Be Your Man	Roger	Reprise 28229
7	4	15	Got My Mind Set On You	George Harrison	Dark Horse 28178
8	11	13	Hungry Eyes	Eric Carmen	RCA 5315
9	6	13	Candle In The Wind	Elton John	MCA 53196
10	7	17	Tell It To My Heart	Taylor Dayne	Arista 9612

★ **HIGHEST DEBUT** ★ POS 57
Out Of The Blue ....Debbie Gibson

★ **BIGGEST MOVER** ★ 64 to 48
I Want Her......................................Keith Sweat

Billboard — FEBRUARY 6, 1988 — HOT 100

TW	LW	WK	Title	Artist	Label
1	2	11	**Could've Been**	Tiffany	MCA 53231
2	3	13	**Hazy Shade Of Winter**	Bangles	Def Jam 07630
3	1	16	**Need You Tonight**	INXS	Atlantic 89188
4	5	11	**Seasons Change**	Expose	Arista 9640
5	6	13	**I Want To Be Your Man**	Roger	Reprise 28229
6	8	14	**Hungry Eyes**	Eric Carmen	RCA 5315
7	12	9	**What Have I Done To Deserve This?** Pet Shop Boys & Dusty Springfield		EMI-Manhattan 50107
8	13	10	**Say You Will**	Foreigner	Atlantic 89169
9	14	10	**Tunnel Of Love**	Bruce Springsteen	Columbia 07663
10	11	13	**I Could Never Take The Place Of Your Man**	Prince	Paisley Park 28288

★ **HIGHEST DEBUT** ★ POS 48
Man In The Mirror....................Michael Jackson

★ **BIGGEST MOVER** ★ 81 to 58
Angel..Aerosmith

Billboard — FEBRUARY 13, 1988 — HOT 100

TW	LW	WK	Title	Artist	Label
1	1	12	**Could've Been**	Tiffany	MCA 53231
2	4	12	Seasons Change	Expose	Arista 9640
3	5	14	**I Want To Be Your Man**	Roger	Reprise 28229
4	6	15	**Hungry Eyes**	Eric Carmen	RCA 5315
5	7	10	What Have I Done To Deserve This? Pet Shop Boys & Dusty Springfield		EMI-Manhattan 50107
6	3	17	Need You Tonight	INXS	Atlantic 89188
7	2	14	Hazy Shade Of Winter	Bangles	Def Jam 07630
8	8	11	Say You Will	Foreigner	Atlantic 89169
9	11	14	**Don't Shed A Tear**	Paul Carrack	Chrysalis 43164
10	15	9	She's Like The Wind	Patrick Swayze featuring Wendy Fraser	RCA 5363

★ **HIGHEST DEBUT** ★ POS 49
Get Outta My Dreams, Get Into My Car.......Billy Ocean

★ **BIGGEST MOVER** ★ 72 to 52
Rock Of Life ....Rick Springfield

Billboard — FEBRUARY 20, 1988 — HOT 100

TW	LW	WK	Title	Artist
1	2	13	**Seasons Change**	*Expose* . . . Arista 9640
2	5	11	**What Have I Done To Deserve This?**	*Pet Shop Boys & Dusty Springfield* . . . EMI-Manhattan 50107
3	1	13	**Could've Been**	*Tiffany* . . . MCA 53231
4	12	6	**Father Figure**	*George Michael* . . . Columbia 07682
5	4	16	**Hungry Eyes**	*Eric Carmen* . . . RCA 5315
6	8	12	**Say You Will**	*Foreigner* . . . Atlantic 89169
7	10	10	**She's Like The Wind**	*Patrick Swayze featuring Wendy Fraser* . . . RCA 5363
8	11	10	**Never Gonna Give You Up**	*Rick Astley* . . . RCA 5347
9	9	15	**Don't Shed A Tear**	*Paul Carrack* . . . Chrysalis 43164
10	3	15	**I Want To Be Your Man**	*Roger* . . . Reprise 28229

★ **HIGHEST DEBUT** ★ POS 67
What A Wonderful World .... *Louis Armstrong*

★ **BIGGEST MOVER** ★ 88 to 68
Electric Blue .... *Icehouse*

Billboard — FEBRUARY 27, 1988 — HOT 100

TW	LW	WK	Title	Artist
1	4	7	**Father Figure**	*George Michael* . . . Columbia 07682
2	2	12	**What Have I Done To Deserve This?**	*Pet Shop Boys & Dusty Springfield* . . . EMI-Manhattan 50107
3	7	11	**She's Like The Wind**	*Patrick Swayze featuring Wendy Fraser* . . . RCA 5363
4	8	11	**Never Gonna Give You Up**	*Rick Astley* . . . RCA 5347
5	5	17	**Hungry Eyes**	*Eric Carmen* . . . RCA 5315
6	1	14	**Seasons Change**	*Expose* . . . Arista 9640
7	6	13	**Say You Will**	*Foreigner* . . . Atlantic 89169
8	12	7	**I Get Weak**	*Belinda Carlisle* . . . MCA 53242
9	9	16	**Don't Shed A Tear**	*Paul Carrack* . . . Chrysalis 43164
10	11	15	**Can't Stay Away From You**	*Gloria Estefan & Miami Sound Machine* . . . Epic 07641

★ **HIGHEST DEBUT** ★ POS 47
Where Do Broken Hearts Go ...... *Whitney Houston*

★ **BIGGEST MOVER** ★ 84 to 65
Pamela .... *Toto*

Billboard — MARCH 5, 1988 — HOT 100

TW	LW	WK	Title	Artist
1	1	8	**Father Figure**	*George Michael* . . . Columbia 07682
2	4	12	**Never Gonna Give You Up**	*Rick Astley* . . . RCA 5347
3	3	12	**She's Like The Wind**	*Patrick Swayze featuring Wendy Fraser* . . . RCA 5363
4	8	8	**I Get Weak**	*Belinda Carlisle* . . . MCA 53242
5	2	13	**What Have I Done To Deserve This?**	*Pet Shop Boys & Dusty Springfield* . . . EMI-Manhattan 50107
6	10	16	**Can't Stay Away From You**	*Gloria Estefan & Miami Sound Machine* . . . Epic 07641
7	12	8	**Just Like Paradise**	*David Lee Roth* . . . Warner 28119
8	15	7	**Endless Summer Nights**	*Richard Marx* . . . EMI-Manhattan 50113
9	17	5	**Man In The Mirror**	*Michael Jackson* . . . Epic 07668
10	14	16	**I Found Someone**	*Cher* . . . Geffen 28191

★ **HIGHEST DEBUT** ★ POS 67
Pink Cadillac .... *Natalie Cole*

★ **BIGGEST MOVER** ★ 73 to 52
Going Back To Cali .... *L.L. Cool J*

Billboard — MARCH 12, 1988 — HOT 100

TW	LW	WK	Title	Artist
1	2	13	**Never Gonna Give You Up**	*Rick Astley* . . . RCA 5347
2	1	9	Father Figure	*George Michael* . . . Columbia 07682
3	3	13	**She's Like The Wind**	*Patrick Swayze featuring Wendy Fraser* . . . RCA 5363
4	4	9	I Get Weak	*Belinda Carlisle* . . . MCA 53242
5	8	8	Endless Summer Nights	*Richard Marx* . . . EMI-Manhattan 50113
6	7	9	**Just Like Paradise**	*David Lee Roth* . . . Warner 28119
7	9	6	Man In The Mirror	*Michael Jackson* . . . Epic 07668
8	12	7	Out Of The Blue	*Debbie Gibson* . . . Atlantic 89129
9	16	9	I Want Her	*Keith Sweat* . . . Vintertainment 69431
10	6	17	Can't Stay Away From You	*Gloria Estefan & Miami Sound Machine* . . . Epic 07641

★ **HIGHEST DEBUT** ★ POS 63
Anything For You......*Gloria Estefan & Miami Sound Machine*

★ **BIGGEST MOVER** ★ 67 to 49
Pink Cadillac ....*Natalie Cole*

Billboard — MARCH 19, 1988 — HOT 100

TW	LW	WK	Title	Artist
1	1	14	**Never Gonna Give You Up**	*Rick Astley* . . . RCA 5347
2	4	10	**I Get Weak**	*Belinda Carlisle* . . . MCA 53242
3	2	10	**Father Figure**	*George Michael* . . . Columbia 07682
4	7	7	**Man In The Mirror**	*Michael Jackson* . . . Epic 07668
5	5	9	Endless Summer Nights	*Richard Marx* . . . EMI-Manhattan 50113
6	3	14	She's Like The Wind	*Patrick Swayze featuring Wendy Fraser* . . . RCA 5363
7	8	8	Out Of The Blue	*Debbie Gibson* . . . Atlantic 89129
8	6	10	Just Like Paradise	*David Lee Roth* . . . Warner 28119
9	9	10	I Want Her	*Keith Sweat* . . . Vintertainment 69431
10	12	6	Get Outta My Dreams, Get Into My Car	*Billy Ocean* . . . Jive 9678

★ **HIGHEST DEBUT** ★ POS 63
Shattered Dreams...............*Johnny Hates Jazz*

★ **BIGGEST MOVER** ★ 86 to 71
Strange But True...........................*Times Two*

Billboard — MARCH 26, 1988 — HOT 100

TW	LW	WK	Title	Artist
1	4	8	**Man In The Mirror**	*Michael Jackson* . . . Epic 07668
2	5	10	**Endless Summer Nights**	*Richard Marx* . . . EMI-Manhattan 50113
3	1	15	Never Gonna Give You Up	*Rick Astley* . . . RCA 5347
4	7	9	Out Of The Blue	*Debbie Gibson* . . . Atlantic 89129
5	10	7	Get Outta My Dreams, Get Into My Car	*Billy Ocean* . . . Jive 9678
6	2	11	I Get Weak	*Belinda Carlisle* . . . MCA 53242
7	9	11	I Want Her	*Keith Sweat* . . . Vintertainment 69431
8	3	11	Father Figure	*George Michael* . . . Columbia 07682
9	12	10	Rocket 2 U	*The Jets* . . . MCA 53254
10	11	10	**Hysteria**	*Def Leppard* . . . Mercury 870004

★ **HIGHEST DEBUT** ★ POS 61
Always On My Mind....................*Pet Shop Boys*

★ **BIGGEST MOVER** ★ 86 to 69
One Good Reason.......................*Paul Carrack*

Billboard — APRIL 2, 1988 — HOT 100

TW	LW	WK	Title	Artist	Label
1	1	9	Man In The Mirror	Michael Jackson	Epic 07668
2	2	11	Endless Summer Nights	Richard Marx	EMI-Manhattan 50113
3	5	8	Get Outta My Dreams, Get Into My Car	Billy Ocean	Jive 9678
4	4	10	Out Of The Blue	Debbie Gibson	Atlantic 89129
5	7	12	I Want Her	Keith Sweat	Vintertainment 69431
6	9	11	Rocket 2 U	The Jets	MCA 53254
7	12	8	Devil Inside	INXS	Atlantic 89144
8	3	16	Never Gonna Give You Up	Rick Astley	RCA 5347
9	13	10	Girlfriend	Pebbles	MCA 53185
10	16	6	Where Do Broken Hearts Go	Whitney Houston	Arista 9674

★ **HIGHEST DEBUT** ★ POS 79
Nightime ....Pretty Poison

★ **BIGGEST MOVER** ★ 61 to 44
Always On My Mind ....Pet Shop Boys

Billboard — APRIL 9, 1988 — HOT 100

TW	LW	WK	Title	Artist	Label
1	3	9	Get Outta My Dreams, Get Into My Car	Billy Ocean	Jive 9678
2	1	10	Man In The Mirror	Michael Jackson	Epic 07668
3	4	11	Out Of The Blue	Debbie Gibson	Atlantic 89129
4	7	9	Devil Inside	INXS	Atlantic 89144
5	10	7	Where Do Broken Hearts Go	Whitney Houston	Arista 9674
6	6	12	Rocket 2 U	The Jets	MCA 53254
7	2	12	Endless Summer Nights	Richard Marx	EMI-Manhattan 50113
8	9	11	Girlfriend	Pebbles	MCA 53185
9	5	13	I Want Her	Keith Sweat	Vintertainment 69431
10	12	13	Wishing Well	Terence Trent D'Arby	Columbia 07675

★ **HIGHEST DEBUT** ★ POS 67
I'm Still Searching.......................Glass Tiger

★ **BIGGEST MOVER** ★ 79 to 57
Nightime ....Pretty Poison

Billboard — APRIL 16, 1988 — HOT 100

TW	LW	WK	Title	Artist	Label
1	1	10	Get Outta My Dreams, Get Into My Car	Billy Ocean	Jive 9678
2	4	10	Devil Inside	INXS	Atlantic 89144
3	5	8	Where Do Broken Hearts Go	Whitney Houston	Arista 9674
4	2	11	Man In The Mirror	Michael Jackson	Epic 07668
5	10	14	Wishing Well	Terence Trent D'Arby	Columbia 07675
6	8	12	Girlfriend	Pebbles	MCA 53185
7	6	13	Rocket 2 U	The Jets	MCA 53254
8	12	12	Angel	Aerosmith	Geffen 28249
9	11	8	I Saw Him Standing There	Tiffany	MCA 53285
10	13	12	Some Kind Of Lover	Jody Watley	MCA 53235

★ **HIGHEST DEBUT** ★ POS 40
One More Try...........................George Michael

★ **BIGGEST MOVER** ★ 84 to 64
We All Sleep Alone ....Cher

Billboard — APRIL 23, 1988 — HOT 100

TW	LW	WK	Title	Artist	Label
1	3	9	Where Do Broken Hearts Go	Whitney Houston	Arista 9674
2	2	11	Devil Inside	INXS	Atlantic 89144
3	1	11	Get Outta My Dreams, Get Into My Car	Billy Ocean	Jive 9678
4	5	15	Wishing Well	Terence Trent D'Arby	Columbia 07675
5	6	13	Girlfriend	Pebbles	MCA 53185
6	8	13	Angel	Aerosmith	Geffen 28249
7	9	9	I Saw Him Standing There	Tiffany	MCA 53285
8	15	7	Anything For You	Gloria Estefan & Miami Sound Machine	Epic 07759
9	12	8	Pink Cadillac	Natalie Cole	EMI-Manhattan 50117
10	13	10	Prove Your Love	Taylor Dayne	Arista 9676

★ HIGHEST DEBUT ★ POS 57
Foolish Beat....................Debbie Gibson

★ BIGGEST MOVER ★ 79 to 55
Make It Real........................The Jets

Billboard — APRIL 30, 1988 — HOT 100

TW	LW	WK	Title	Artist	Label
1	1	10	Where Do Broken Hearts Go	Whitney Houston	Arista 9674
2	4	16	Wishing Well	Terence Trent D'Arby	Columbia 07675
3	6	14	Angel	Aerosmith	Geffen 28249
4	2	12	Devil Inside	INXS	Atlantic 89144
5	8	8	Anything For You	Gloria Estefan & Miami Sound Machine	Epic 07759
6	3	12	Get Outta My Dreams, Get Into My Car	Billy Ocean	Jive 9678
7	9	9	Pink Cadillac	Natalie Cole	EMI-Manhattan 50117
8	10	11	Prove Your Love	Taylor Dayne	Arista 9676
9	7	10	I Saw Him Standing There	Tiffany	MCA 53285
10	5	14	Girlfriend	Pebbles	MCA 53185

★ HIGHEST DEBUT ★ POS 58
The Valley Road ....Bruce Hornsby & The Range

★ BIGGEST MOVER ★ 82 to 63
Nothin' But A Good Time........................Poison

Billboard — MAY 7, 1988 — HOT 100

TW	LW	WK	Title	Artist	Label
1	2	17	Wishing Well	Terence Trent D'Arby	Columbia 07675
2	5	9	Anything For You	Gloria Estefan & Miami Sound Machine	Epic 07759
3	3	15	Angel	Aerosmith	Geffen 28249
4	1	11	Where Do Broken Hearts Go	Whitney Houston	Arista 9674
5	7	10	Pink Cadillac	Natalie Cole	EMI-Manhattan 50117
6	11	7	Always On My Mind	Pet Shop Boys	EMI-Manhattan 50123
7	8	12	Prove Your Love	Taylor Dayne	Arista 9676
8	15	8	Shattered Dreams	Johnny Hates Jazz	Virgin 99383
9	12	13	Electric Blue	Icehouse	Chrysalis 43201
10	13	11	Naughty Girls (Need Love Too)	Samantha Fox	Jive 1089

★ HIGHEST DEBUT ★ POS 53
Dirty Diana....................Michael Jackson

★ BIGGEST MOVER ★ 75 to 59
Pour Some Sugar On Me ....Def Leppard

Billboard — HOT 100 — MAY 14, 1988

TW	LW	WK	Title	Artist / Label
1	2	10	**Anything For You**	Gloria Estefan & Miami Sound Machine ... Epic 07759
2	8	9	**Shattered Dreams**	Johnny Hates Jazz ... Virgin 99383
3	1	18	Wishing Well	Terence Trent D'Arby ... Columbia 07675
4	14	5	One More Try	George Michael ... Columbia 07773
5	5	11	**Pink Cadillac**	Natalie Cole ... EMI-Manhattan 50117
6	6	8	Always On My Mind	Pet Shop Boys ... EMI-Manhattan 50123
7	3	16	Angel	Aerosmith ... Geffen 28249
8	10	12	Naughty Girls (Need Love Too)	Samantha Fox ... Jive 1089
9	9	14	Electric Blue	Icehouse ... Chrysalis 43201
10	11	9	I Don't Want To Live Without You	Foreigner ... Atlantic 89101

★ **HIGHEST DEBUT** ★ POS 63
New Sensation ...... INXS

★ **BIGGEST MOVER** ★ 90 to 69
Rush Hour ...... Jane Wiedlin

Billboard — HOT 100 — MAY 21, 1988

TW	LW	WK	Title	Artist / Label
1	1	11	**Anything For You**	Gloria Estefan & Miami Sound Machine ... Epic 07759
2	4	6	One More Try	George Michael ... Columbia 07773
3	2	10	Shattered Dreams	Johnny Hates Jazz ... Virgin 99383
4	6	9	**Always On My Mind**	Pet Shop Boys ... EMI-Manhattan 50123
5	8	13	**Naughty Girls (Need Love Too)**	Samantha Fox ... Jive 1089
6	10	10	I Don't Want To Live Without You	Foreigner ... Atlantic 89101
7	9	15	**Electric Blue**	Icehouse ... Chrysalis 43201
8	12	13	**Wait**	White Lion ... Atlantic 89126
9	16	6	Everything Your Heart Desires	Daryl Hall John Oates ... Arista 9684
10	13	13	**Two Occasions**	The Deele ... Solar 70015

★ **HIGHEST DEBUT** ★ POS 66
Black And Blue ...... Van Halen

★ **BIGGEST MOVER** ★ 95 to 70
Paradise ...... Sade

Billboard — HOT 100 — MAY 28, 1988

TW	LW	WK	Title	Artist / Label
1	2	7	**One More Try**	George Michael ... Columbia 07773
2	3	11	**Shattered Dreams**	Johnny Hates Jazz ... Virgin 99383
3	1	12	Anything For You	Gloria Estefan & Miami Sound Machine ... Epic 07759
4	5	14	Naughty Girls (Need Love Too)	Samantha Fox ... Jive 1089
5	6	11	**I Don't Want To Live Without You**	Foreigner ... Atlantic 89101
6	4	10	Always On My Mind	Pet Shop Boys ... EMI-Manhattan 50123
7	9	7	Everything Your Heart Desires	Daryl Hall John Oates ... Arista 9684
8	14	7	Together Forever	Rick Astley ... RCA 8319
9	8	14	Wait	White Lion ... Atlantic 89126
10	11	15	Piano In The Dark	Brenda Russell ... A&M 3003

★ **HIGHEST DEBUT** ★ POS 72
Sign Your Name ...... Terence Trent D'Arby

★ **BIGGEST MOVER** ★ 78 to 54
Make Me Lose Control ...... Eric Carmen

TW	LW	WK	Billboard		JUNE 4, 1988		HOT 100.
❶	1	8	**One More Try** ....*George Michael* . . . Columbia 07773
②	2	12	**Shattered Dreams** ....*Johnny Hates Jazz* . . . Virgin 99383
③	4	15	**Naughty Girls (Need Love Too)** ....*Samantha Fox* . . . Jive 1089
❹	7	8	**Everything Your Heart Desires** ....*Daryl Hall John Oates* . . . Arista 9684
❺	8	8	**Together Forever**....................................*Rick Astley* . . . RCA 8319
⑥	10	16	**Piano In The Dark**...................................*Brenda Russell* . . . A&M 3003
❼	15	7	**Foolish Beat** ....*Debbie Gibson* . . . Atlantic 89109
⑧	5	12	**I Don't Want To Live Without You**...................*Foreigner* . . . Atlantic 89101
⑨	13	8	**Make It Real**...*The Jets* . . . MCA 53311
⑩	3	13	**Anything For You**.......*Gloria Estefan & Miami Sound Machine* . . . Epic 07759

★ *HIGHEST DEBUT* ★ POS 71	★ *BIGGEST MOVER* ★ 98 to 79
I Don't Wanna Live Without Your Love ....*Chicago*	Little Walter..............................*Tony! Toni! Tone!*

TW	LW	WK	Billboard		JUNE 11, 1988		HOT 100.
①	1	9	**One More Try** ....*George Michael* . . . Columbia 07773
❷	5	9	**Together Forever**....................................*Rick Astley* . . . RCA 8319
❸	4	9	**Everything Your Heart Desires**......................*Daryl Hall John Oates* . . . Arista 9684
④	2	13	**Shattered Dreams**...................*Johnny Hates Jazz* . . . Virgin 99383
⑤	3	16	**Naughty Girls (Need Love Too)** ....*Samantha Fox* . . . Jive 1089
⑥	7	8	**Foolish Beat** ....*Debbie Gibson* . . . Atlantic 89109
❼	9	9	**Make It Real**...*The Jets* . . . MCA 53311
⑧	12	6	**Dirty Diana** ....*Michael Jackson* . . . Epic 07739
⑨	11	9	**Circle In The Sand** ....*Belinda Carlisle* . . . MCA 53308
⑩	14	7	**The Valley Road**........................*Bruce Hornsby & The Range* . . . RCA 7645

★ *HIGHEST DEBUT* ★ POS 53	★ *BIGGEST MOVER* ★ 98 to 78
Roll With It..................................*Steve Winwood*	I Know You're Out There Somewhere ....*The Moody Blues*

TW	LW	WK	Billboard		JUNE 18, 1988		HOT 100.
❶	2	10	**Together Forever**...*Rick Astley* . . . RCA 8319
②	1	10	**One More Try** ....*George Michael* . . . Columbia 07773
❸	6	9	**Foolish Beat** ....*Debbie Gibson* . . . Atlantic 89109
❹	8	7	**Dirty Diana** ....*Michael Jackson* . . . Epic 07739
⑤	7	10	**Make It Real**...*The Jets* . . . MCA 53311
⑥	3	10	**Everything Your Heart Desires** ....*Daryl Hall John Oates* . . . Arista 9684
⑦	9	10	**Circle In The Sand**.............................*Belinda Carlisle* . . . MCA 53308
⑧	10	8	**The Valley Road**........................*Bruce Hornsby & The Range* . . . RCA 7645
⑨	13	11	**The Flame** ....*Cheap Trick* . . . Epic 07745
⑩	12	8	**Alphabet St.** ....*Prince* . . . Paisley Park 27900

★ *HIGHEST DEBUT* ★ POS 60	★ *BIGGEST MOVER* ★ 53 to 33
I Don't Wanna Go On With You Like That ....*Elton John*	Roll With It................................*Steve Winwood*

Billboard — JUNE 25, 1988 — HOT 100

TW	LW	WK	Title	Artist	Label
1	3	10	**Foolish Beat**	*Debbie Gibson*	Atlantic 89109
2	4	8	Dirty Diana	*Michael Jackson*	Epic 07739
③	1	11	Together Forever	*Rick Astley*	RCA 8319
4	5	11	**Make It Real**	*The Jets*	MCA 53311
5	9	12	The Flame	*Cheap Trick*	Epic 07745
6	8	9	The Valley Road	*Bruce Hornsby & The Range*	RCA 7645
⑦	2	11	One More Try	*George Michael*	Columbia 07773
8	10	9	**Alphabet St.**	*Prince*	Paisley Park 27900
9	11	8	Mercedes Boy	*Pebbles*	MCA 53279
⑩	18	10	Pour Some Sugar On Me	*Def Leppard*	Mercury 870298

★ **HIGHEST DEBUT** ★ POS 76
Sweet Child O' Mine .... *Guns N' Roses*

★ **BIGGEST MOVER** ★ 79 to 55
The Twist .... *The Fat Boys with Chubby Checker*

Billboard — JULY 2, 1988 — HOT 100

TW	LW	WK	Title	Artist	Label
1	2	9	**Dirty Diana**	*Michael Jackson*	Epic 07739
②	1	11	Foolish Beat	*Debbie Gibson*	Atlantic 89109
3	5	13	The Flame	*Cheap Trick*	Epic 07745
④	4	12	**Make It Real**	*The Jets*	MCA 53311
⑤	6	10	**The Valley Road**	*Bruce Hornsby & The Range*	RCA 7645
6	9	9	Mercedes Boy	*Pebbles*	MCA 53279
7	10	11	Pour Some Sugar On Me	*Def Leppard*	Mercury 870298
8	11	11	Nothin' But A Good Time	*Poison*	Capitol 44145
9	16	8	New Sensation	*INXS*	Atlantic 89080
⑩	3	12	Together Forever	*Rick Astley*	RCA 8319

★ **HIGHEST DEBUT** ★ POS 52
Love Will Save The Day .... *Whitney Houston*

★ **BIGGEST MOVER** ★ 80 to 64
Here With Me .... *REO Speedwagon*

Billboard — JULY 9, 1988 — HOT 100

TW	LW	WK	Title	Artist	Label
1	3	14	**The Flame**	*Cheap Trick*	Epic 07745
2	6	10	Mercedes Boy	*Pebbles*	MCA 53279
3	7	12	Pour Some Sugar On Me	*Def Leppard*	Mercury 870298
4	9	9	New Sensation	*INXS*	Atlantic 89080
⑤	1	10	Dirty Diana	*Michael Jackson*	Epic 07739
6	8	12	**Nothin' But A Good Time**	*Poison*	Capitol 44145
7	2	12	Foolish Beat	*Debbie Gibson*	Atlantic 89109
8	15	8	Hold On To The Nights	*Richard Marx*	EMI-Manhattan 50106
9	5	11	The Valley Road	*Bruce Hornsby & The Range*	RCA 7645
⑩	11	14	Nite And Day	*Al B. Sure!*	Warner 28192

★ **HIGHEST DEBUT** ★ POS 42
Monkey .... *George Michael*

★ **BIGGEST MOVER** ★ 69 to 50
When It's Love .... *Van Halen*

THE SONG TITLES

This section lists, alphabetically, all Top 10 titles listed in the chart section of this book. The artist's name is listed next to each title along with the date each record first hit its peak position in the Top 10. The highest debuts and biggest movers are not included in this section, unless they went on to make the Top 10.

A song with more than one charted version is listed once, with the artist's names listed below it in chronological order. Songs that have the same title, but are different tunes, are listed separately in chronological order.

A

4/25/70 **ABC** *Jackson 5*
9/04/82 **Abracadabra** *Steve Miller Band*
Abraham, Martin And John
12/14/68 *Dion*
8/14/71 *Tom Clay (medley)*
5/03/86 **Addicted To Love** *Robert Palmer*
4/07/84 **Adult Education**
  Daryl Hall-John Oates
6/18/83 **Affair Of The Heart**
  Rick Springfield
2/05/83 **Africa** *Toto*
9/15/79 **After The Love Has Gone**
  Earth, Wind & Fire
1/22/77 **After The Lovin'**
  Engelbert Humperdinck
7/10/76 **Afternoon Delight**
  Starland Vocal Band
4/21/84 **Against All Odds (Take A Look At Me Now)** *Phil Collins*
6/14/80 **Against The Wind** *Bob Seger*
8/04/62 **Ahab, The Arab** *Ray Stevens*
9/19/70 **Ain't No Mountain High Enough**
  Diana Ross
9/18/71 **Ain't No Sunshine** *Bill Withers*
10/11/75 **Ain't No Way To Treat A Lady**
  Helen Reddy
4/07/73 **Ain't No Woman (Like The One I've Got)** *Four Tops*
5/25/68 **Ain't Nothing Like The Real Thing**
  Marvin Gaye & Tammi Terrell
11/20/65 **Ain't That Peculiar** *Marvin Gaye*
8/03/74 **Air That I Breathe** *Hollies*
7/07/62 **Al Di La'** *Emilio Pericoli*
12/28/85 **Alive & Kicking** *Simple Minds*
11/10/62 **All Alone Am I** *Brenda Lee*
2/02/59 **All American Boy** *Bill Parsons*
3/06/76 **All By Myself** *Eric Carmen*
10/25/86 **All Cried Out** *Lisa Lisa & Cult Jam*
2/06/65 **All Day And All Of The Night**
  Kinks
12/25/71 **All I Ever Need Is You**
  Sonny & Cher
11/10/73 **All I Know** *Garfunkel*
6/17/67 **All I Need** *Temptations*
1/12/85 **All I Need** *Jack Wagner*
6/07/86 **All I Need Is A Miracle**
  Mike + The Mechanics
11/12/83 **All Night Long (All Night)**
  Lionel Richie
9/13/80 **All Out Of Love** *Air Supply*
10/17/70 **All Right Now** *Free*
5/04/85 **All She Wants To Do Is Dance**
  Don Henley
7/04/81 **All Those Years Ago**
  George Harrison
12/08/84 **All Through The Night**
  Cyndi Lauper
8/19/67 **All You Need Is Love** *Beatles*
9/29/62 **Alley Cat** *Bent Fabric*
7/11/60 **Alley-Oop** *Hollywood Argyles*

7/14/84 **Almost Paradise...Love Theme From Footloose**
  Mike Reno & Ann Wilson
7/11/87 **Alone** *Heart*
7/29/72 **Alone Again (Naturally)**
  Gilbert O'Sullivan
11/28/60 **Alone At Last** *Jackie Wilson*
6/22/59 **Along Came Jones** *Coasters*
7/16/66 **Along Comes Mary** *Association*
6/25/88 **Alphabet St.** *Prince*
3/31/73 **Also Sprach Zarathustra (2001)**
  Deodato
3/16/59 **Alvin's Harmonica** *Chipmunks*
6/13/87 **Always** *Atlantic Starr*
Always On My Mind
6/12/82 *Willie Nelson*
5/21/88 *Pet Shop Boys*
6/11/83 **Always Something There To Remind Me** *Naked Eyes*
11/08/86 **Amanda** *Boston*
1/09/65 **Amen** *Impressions*
6/13/81 **America** *Neil Diamond*
1/15/72 **American Pie** *Don McLean*
5/09/70 **American Woman** *Guess Who*
2/09/74 **Americans** *Byron MacGregor*
12/28/59 **Among My Souvenirs**
  Connie Francis
2/27/71 **Amos Moses** *Jerry Reed*
11/29/69 **And When I Die**
  Blood, Sweat & Tears
6/29/85 **Angel** *Madonna*
4/30/88 **Angel** *Aerosmith*
1/23/61 **Angel Baby** *Rosie & The Originals*
7/16/77 **Angel In Your Arms** *Hot*
Angel Of The Morning
6/29/68 *Merrilee Rush*
5/02/81 *Juice Newton*
10/20/73 **Angie** *Rolling Stones*
12/28/74 **Angie Baby** *Helen Reddy*
7/27/74 **Annie's Song** *John Denver*
3/22/80 **Another Brick In The Wall**
  Pink Floyd
4/17/71 **Another Day** *Paul McCartney*
10/04/80 **Another One Bites The Dust**
  Queen
Another Saturday Night
5/25/63 *Sam Cooke*
10/12/74 *Cat Stevens*
Another Somebody Done Somebody Wrong Song..*see:*
  (Hey Won't You Play)
2/15/64 **Anyone Who Had A Heart**
  Dionne Warwick
5/14/88 **Anything For You**
  Gloria Estefan & Miami Sound Machine
4/03/61 **Apache** *Jorgen Ingmann*
Apartment..*see: Theme From*
9/23/67 **Apples, Peaches, Pumpkin Pie**
  Jay & The Techniques
4/12/69 **Aquarius/Let The Sunshine In**
  5th Dimension
11/28/60 **Are You Lonesome To-night?**
  Elvis Presley

9/01/58 **Are You Really Mine**	6/27/70 **Ball Of Confusion** *Temptations*
Jimmie Rodgers	4/13/68 **Ballad Of Bonnie And Clyde**
2/14/70 **Arizona** *Mark Lindsay*	*Georgie Fame*
10/17/81 **Arthur's Theme (Best That You**	7/12/69 **Ballad Of John And Yoko** *Beatles*
Can Do) *Christopher Cross*	3/05/66 **Ballad Of The Green Berets**
9/04/61 **As If I Didn't Know** *Adam Wade*	*SSgt Barry Sadler*
1/29/66 **As Tears Go By** *Rolling Stones*	2/21/87 **Ballerina Girl** *Lionel Richie*
4/17/61 **Asia Minor** *Kokomo*	10/18/75 **Ballroom Blitz** *Sweet*
9/13/75 **At Seventeen** *Janis Ian*	7/25/70 **Band Of Gold** *Freda Payne*
1/24/87 **At This Moment**	6/08/74 **Band On The Run**
Billy Vera & The Beaters	*Paul McCartney & Wings*
5/24/69 **Atlantis** *Donovan*	**Bang A Gong (Get It On)**
4/14/84 **Automatic** *Pointer Sisters*	3/04/72 *T. Rex*
6/01/85 **Axel F** *Harold Faltermeyer*	8/03/85 *Power Station*
	4/23/66 **Bang Bang (My Baby Shot Me**
B	**Down)** *Cher*
	1/29/66 **Barbara Ann** *Beach Boys*
12/08/79 **Babe** *Styx*	6/18/66 **Barefootin'** *Robert Parker*
3/01/69 **Baby, Baby Don't Cry** *Miracles*	6/01/59 **Battle Of New Orleans**
1/14/78 **Baby Come Back** *Player*	*Johnny Horton*
2/19/83 **Baby, Come To Me**	5/31/86 **Be Good To Yourself** *Journey*
Patti Austin with James Ingram	10/12/63 **Be My Baby** *Ronettes*
9/23/72 **Baby Don't Get Hooked On Me**	12/07/59 **Be My Guest** *Fats Domino*
Mac Davis	11/09/85 **Be Near Me** *ABC*
10/09/65 **Baby Don't Go** *Sonny & Cher*	6/29/74 **Be Thankful For What You Got**
9/09/67 **Baby I Love You** *Aretha Franklin*	*William DeVaughn*
7/26/69 **Baby, I Love You** *Andy Kim*	12/21/63 **Be True To Your School**
3/11/67 **Baby I Need Your Lovin'**	*Beach Boys*
Johnny Rivers	10/05/74 **Beach Baby** *First Class*
11/27/71 **Baby I'm-A Want You** *Bread*	11/11/78 **Beast Of Burden** *Rolling Stones*
Baby It's You	2/25/67 **Beat Goes On** *Sonny & Cher*
2/03/62 *Shirelles*	4/30/83 **Beat It** *Michael Jackson*
11/01/69 *Smith*	5/25/68 **Beautiful Morning** *Rascals*
10/31/64 **Baby Love** *Supremes*	10/01/66 **Beauty Is Only Skin Deep**
9/13/86 **Baby Love** *Regina*	*Temptations*
3/13/61 **Baby Sittin' Boogie** *Buzz Clifford*	9/12/64 **Because** *Dave Clark Five*
9/14/59 **Baby Talk** *Jan & Dean*	7/04/60 **Because They're Young**
12/03/77 **Baby, What A Big Surprise**	*Duane Eddy*
Chicago	12/01/58 **Beep Beep** *Playmates*
4/13/63 **Baby Workout** *Jackie Wilson*	5/31/75 **Before The Next Teardrop Falls**
3/21/60 **Baby (You've Got What It**	*Freddy Fender*
Takes)	8/14/71 **Beginnings** *Chicago*
Dinah Washington & Brook Benton	5/23/81 **Being With You** *Smokey Robinson*
11/09/74 **Back Home Again** *John Denver*	**Believe It Or Not**..see: Theme From
Back In Love Again..see: (Every	*"Greatest American Hero"*
Time I Turn Around)	10/14/72 **Ben** *Michael Jackson*
6/12/65 **Back In My Arms Again**	1/27/68 **Bend Me, Shape Me**
Supremes	*American Breed*
5/13/72 **Back Off Boogaloo** *Ringo Starr*	4/13/74 **Bennie And The Jets** *Elton John*
3/19/83 **Back On The Chain Gang**	4/08/67 **Bernadette** *Four Tops*
Pretenders	3/01/75 **Best Of My Love** *Eagles*
10/07/72 **Back Stabbers** *O'Jays*	8/20/77 **Best Of My Love** *Emotions*
12/13/69 **Backfield In Motion** *Mel & Tim*	3/21/81 **Best Of Times** *Styx*
10/24/87 **Bad** *Michael Jackson*	**Best That You Can Do**..see:
7/21/73 **Bad, Bad Leroy Brown** *Jim Croce*	*Arthur's Theme*
10/11/75 **Bad Blood** *Neil Sedaka*	4/27/74 **Best Thing That Ever Happened**
5/10/86 **Bad Boy** *Miami Sound Machine*	**To Me** *Gladys Knight & The Pips*
7/14/79 **Bad Girls** *Donna Summer*	5/06/72 **Betcha By Golly, Wow** *Stylistics*
6/28/69 **Bad Moon Rising**	12/04/76 **Beth** *Kiss*
Creedence Clearwater Revival	5/16/81 **Bette Davis Eyes** *Kim Carnes*
6/07/75 **Bad Time** *Grand Funk*	11/24/84 **Better Be Good To Me**
6/27/64 **Bad To Me** *Billy J. Kramer*	*Tina Turner*
6/24/78 **Baker Street** *Gerry Rafferty*	2/29/60 **Beyond The Sea** *Bobby Darin*

11/06/61	**Big Bad John** *Jimmy Dean*	
11/17/62	**Big Girls Don't Cry** *4 Seasons*	
8/10/59	**Big Hunk O' Love** *Elvis Presley*	
12/28/59	**Big Hurt** *Miss Toni Fisher*	
5/30/87	**Big Love** *Fleetwood Mac*	
3/07/87	**Big Time** *Peter Gabriel*	
6/07/80	**Biggest Part Of Me** *Ambrosia*	
3/05/83	**Billie Jean** *Michael Jackson*	
6/15/74	**Billy, Don't Be A Hero**	
	Bo Donaldson & The Heywoods	

11/06/61 **Big Bad John** *Jimmy Dean*
11/17/62 **Big Girls Don't Cry** *4 Seasons*
8/10/59 **Big Hunk O' Love** *Elvis Presley*
12/28/59 **Big Hurt** *Miss Toni Fisher*
5/30/87 **Big Love** *Fleetwood Mac*
3/07/87 **Big Time** *Peter Gabriel*
6/07/80 **Biggest Part Of Me** *Ambrosia*
3/05/83 **Billie Jean** *Michael Jackson*
6/15/74 **Billy, Don't Be A Hero**
　　　　Bo Donaldson & The Heywoods
8/25/58 **Bird Dog** *Everly Brothers*
3/20/65 **Birds And The Bees** *Jewel Akens*
11/02/74 **Bitch Is Back** *Elton John*
5/02/64 **Bits And Pieces** *Dave Clark Five*
9/16/72 **Black & White** *Three Dog Night*
10/01/66 **Black Is Black** *Los Bravos*
1/09/71 **Black Magic Woman** *Santana*
3/15/75 **Black Water** *Doobie Brothers*
3/02/63 **Blame It On The Bossa Nova**
　　　　Eydie Gorme
2/19/77 **Blinded By The Light**
　　　　Manfred Mann's Earth Band
　　　　Blowin' In The Wind
8/17/63 　*Peter, Paul & Mary*
9/03/66 　*Stevie Wonder*
11/07/60 **Blue Angel** *Roy Orbison*
12/17/77 **Blue Bayou** *Linda Ronstadt*
11/03/84 **Blue Jean** *David Bowie*
4/03/61 **Blue Moon** *Marcels*
7/06/63 **Blue On Blue** *Bobby Vinton*
9/21/63 **Blue Velvet** *Bobby Vinton*
7/06/59 **Bobby Sox To Stockings**
　　　　Frankie Avalon
12/01/62 **Bobby's Girl** *Marcie Blane*
4/24/76 **Bohemian Rhapsody** *Queen*
7/10/61 **Boll Weevil Song** *Brook Benton*
12/23/67 **Boogaloo Down Broadway**
　　　　Fantastic Johnny C
3/09/74 **Boogie Down** *Eddie Kendricks*
5/15/76 **Boogie Fever** *Sylvers*
11/12/77 **Boogie Nights** *Heatwave*
2/01/75 **Boogie On Reggae Woman**
　　　　Stevie Wonder
9/09/78 **Boogie Oogie Oogie**
　　　　A Taste Of Honey
7/14/79 **Boogie Wonderland**
　　　　Earth, Wind & Fire with The Emotions
7/21/73 **Boogie Woogie Bugle Boy**
　　　　Bette Midler
6/16/84 **Borderline** *Madonna*
12/17/66 **Born Free** *Roger Williams*
1/19/85 **Born In The U.S.A.**
　　　　Bruce Springsteen
8/24/68 **Born To Be Wild** *Steppenwolf*
9/15/58 **Born Too Late** *Poni-Tails*
11/16/63 **Bossa Nova Baby** *Elvis Presley*
12/21/68 **Both Sides Now** *Judy Collins*
3/02/68 **Bottle Of Wine** *Fireballs*
5/17/69 **Boxer, The** *Simon & Garfunkel*
　　　　Boy From New York City
2/27/65 　*Ad Libs*
8/08/81 　*Manhattan Transfer*
8/23/69 **Boy Named Sue** *Johnny Cash*

7/13/59 **Boy Without A Girl** *Frankie Avalon*
2/09/85 **Boys Of Summer** *Don Henley*
12/25/71 **Brand New Key** *Melanie*
6/12/71 **Brand New Me** *Aretha Franklin*
8/26/72 **Brandy (You're A Fine Girl)**
　　　　Looking Glass
9/19/64 **Bread And Butter** *Newbeats*
3/03/62 **Break It To Me Gently**
　　　　Brenda Lee
1/21/84 **Break My Stride** *Matthew Wilder*
4/07/73 **Break Up To Make Up** *Stylistics*
6/09/84 **Breakdance** *Irene Cara*
5/29/61 **Breakin' In A Brand New Broken**
　　　　Heart *Connie Francis*
8/04/84 **Breakin'...There's No Stopping**
　　　　Us *Ollie & Jerry*
　　　　Breaking Up Is Hard To Do
8/11/62 　*Neil Sedaka*
2/21/76 　*Neil Sedaka*
11/14/87 **Breakout** *Swing Out Sister*
11/05/77 **Brick House** *Commodores*
　　　　Bridge Over Troubled Water
2/28/70 　*Simon & Garfunkel*
6/05/71 　*Aretha Franklin*
11/21/87 **Brilliant Disguise**
　　　　Bruce Springsteen
10/23/61 **Bristol Stomp** *Dovells*
9/07/59 **Broken-Hearted Melody**
　　　　Sarah Vaughan
12/07/85 **Broken Wings** *Mr. Mister*
8/25/73 **Brother Louie** *Stories*
9/30/67 **Brown Eyed Girl** *Van Morrison*
5/29/71 **Brown Sugar** *Rolling Stones*
2/22/69 **Build Me Up Buttercup**
　　　　Foundations
6/13/60 **Burning Bridges** *Jack Scott*
10/22/83 **Burning Down The House**
　　　　Talking Heads
2/01/86 **Burning Heart** *Survivor*
10/28/72 **Burning Love** *Elvis Presley*
9/17/66 **Bus Stop** *Hollies*
10/19/63 **Busted** *Ray Charles*
4/24/61 **But I Do** *Clarence Henry*

C

　　　　C.C. Rider..*see: See See Rider*
1/17/87 **C'est La Vie** *Robbie Nevil*
2/13/61 **Calcutta** *Lawrence Welk*
2/13/61 **Calendar Girl** *Neil Sedaka*
3/12/66 **California Dreamin'**
　　　　Mamas & The Papas
　　　　California Girls
8/28/65 　*Beach Boys*
3/02/85 　*David Lee Roth*
2/29/64 **California Sun** *Rivieras*
4/19/80 **Call Me** *Blondie*
4/14/73 **Call Me (Come Back Home)**
　　　　Al Green
8/10/74 **Call On Me** *Chicago*
10/11/75 **Calypso** *John Denver*
2/22/69 **Can I Change My Mind**
　　　　Tyrone Davis

4/04/64 **Can't Buy Me Love** *Beatles*	**Cherish**
3/09/85 **Can't Fight This Feeling**	9/24/66 *Association*
REO Speedwagon	12/25/71 *David Cassidy*
11/02/74 **Can't Get Enough** *Bad Company*	9/21/85 **Cherish** *Kool & The Gang*
9/21/74 **Can't Get Enough Of Your Love,**	1/09/88 **Cherry Bomb**
Babe *Barry White*	*John Cougar Mellencamp*
3/15/75 **Can't Get It Out Of My Head**	10/15/66 **Cherry, Cherry** *Neil Diamond*
Electric Light Orchestra	5/03/75 **Chevy Van** *Sammy Johns*
4/13/63 **Can't Get Used To Losing You**	5/08/71 **Chick-A-Boom** *Daddy Dewdrop*
Andy Williams	8/27/83 **China Girl** *David Bowie*
2/03/62 **Can't Help Falling In Love**	3/03/62 **Chip Chip** *Gene McDaniels*
Elvis Presley	12/22/58 **Chipmunk Song** *Chipmunks*
4/22/78 **Can't Smile Without You**	7/07/79 **Chuck E.'s In Love**
Barry Manilow	*Rickie Lee Jones*
3/05/88 **Can't Stay Away From You**	11/07/64 **Chug-A-Lug** *Roger Miller*
Gloria Estefan & Miami Sound Machine	12/03/83 **Church Of The Poison Mind**
Can't Take My Eyes Off You	*Culture Club*
7/22/67 *Frankie Valli*	6/23/62 **Cindy's Birthday** *Johnny Crawford*
2/10/68 *Lettermen (medley)*	6/18/88 **Circle In The Sand**
9/12/87 **Can't We Try**	*Belinda Carlisle*
Dan Hill with Vonda Sheppard	4/28/73 **Cisco Kid** *War*
3/27/65 **Can't You Hear My Heartbeat**	12/30/72 **Clair** *Gilbert O'Sullivan*
Herman's Hermits	10/05/74 **Clap For The Wolfman**
7/18/64 **Can't You See That She's Mine**	*Guess Who*
Dave Clark Five	4/24/65 **Clapping Song** *Shirley Ellis*
10/03/70 **Candida** *Dawn*	8/03/68 **Classical Gas** *Mason Williams*
1/23/88 **Candle In The Wind** *Elton John*	1/29/72 **Clean Up Woman** *Betty Wright*
8/24/63 **Candy Girl** *4 Seasons*	**Close To You**..*see: (They Long To*
6/10/72 **Candy Man** *Sammy Davis, Jr.*	*Be)*
1/29/77 **Car Wash** *Rose Royce*	5/06/67 **Close Your Eyes** *Peaches & Herb*
7/31/65 **Cara, Mia** *Jay & The Americans*	5/13/78 **Closer I Get To You**
11/09/74 **Carefree Highway**	*Roberta Flack with Donny Hathaway*
Gordon Lightfoot	1/04/69 **Cloud Nine** *Temptations*
2/16/85 **Careless Whisper** *Wham!*	**C'mon**..*see: Come On*
11/03/84 **Caribbean Queen (No More Love**	8/26/72 **Coconut** *Nilsson*
On The Run) *Billy Ocean*	10/22/77 **Cold As Ice** *Foreigner*
10/10/87 **Carrie** *Europe*	8/26/67 **Cold Sweat** *James Brown*
8/12/67 **Carrie-Anne** *Hollies*	7/19/69 **Color Him Father** *Winstons*
6/07/80 **Cars** *Gary Numan*	8/14/71 **Colour My World** *Chicago*
10/31/87 **Casanova** *Levert*	11/21/64 **Come A Little Bit Closer**
5/08/65 **Cast Your Fate To The Wind**	*Jay & The Americans*
Sounds Orchestral	4/18/70 **Come And Get It** *Badfinger*
12/21/74 **Cat's In The Cradle** *Harry Chapin*	4/13/74 **Come And Get Your Love**
12/19/87 **Catch Me (I'm Falling)**	*Redbone*
Pretty Poison	9/09/67 **Come Back When You Grow Up**
9/25/65 **Catch Us If You Can**	*Bobby Vee*
Dave Clark Five	7/16/83 **Come Dancing** *Kinks*
5/23/60 **Cathy's Clown** *Everly Brothers*	4/04/87 **Come Go With Me** *Expose*
7/03/82 **Caught Up In You** *38 Special*	**Come On**..*also see: Cum On*
10/24/87 **Causing A Commotion** *Madonna*	8/29/64 **C'mon And Swim** *Bobby Freeman*
5/30/70 **Cecilia** *Simon & Garfunkel*	7/08/67 **Come On Down To My Boat**
2/07/81 **Celebration** *Kool & The Gang*	*Every Mothers' Son*
2/06/82 **Centerfold** *J. Geils Band*	4/23/83 **Come On Eileen**
11/17/62 **Cha-Cha-Cha** *Bobby Rydell*	*Dexys Midnight Runners*
10/03/60 **Chain Gang** *Sam Cooke*	7/15/67 **C'mon Marianne** *4 Seasons*
1/20/68 **Chain Of Fools** *Aretha Franklin*	1/28/78 **Come Sail Away** *Styx*
2/14/87 **Change Of Heart** *Cyndi Lauper*	12/19/64 **Come See About Me** *Supremes*
11/03/58 **Chantilly Lace** *Big Bopper*	4/13/59 **Come Softly To Me** *Fleetwoods*
6/06/64 **Chapel Of Love** *Dixie Cups*	11/29/69 **Come Together** *Beatles*
5/08/82 **Chariots Of Fire - Titles** *Vangelis*	6/28/80 **Coming Up (Live at Glasgow)**
3/09/59 **Charlie Brown** *Coasters*	*Paul McCartney & Wings*
	2/08/86 **Conga** *Miami Sound Machine*
	1/24/87 **Control** *Janet Jackson*

11/18/72	**Convention '72** *Delegates*			
1/10/76	**Convoy** *C.W. McCall*			
1/19/80	**Cool Change** *Little River Band*			
1/05/85	**Cool It Now** *New Edition*			
7/02/66	**Cool Jerk** *Capitols*			

11/18/72 **Convention '72** *Delegates*
1/10/76 **Convoy** *C.W. McCall*
1/19/80 **Cool Change** *Little River Band*
1/05/85 **Cool It Now** *New Edition*
7/02/66 **Cool Jerk** *Capitols*
8/12/78 **Copacabana (At The Copa)**
    Barry Manilow
1/09/61 **Corinna, Corinna** *Ray Peterson*
3/03/73 **Could It Be I'm Falling In Love**
    Spinners
9/20/75 **Could It Be Magic** *Barry Manilow*
2/06/88 **Could've Been** *Tiffany*
5/21/77 **Couldn't Get It Right**
    Climax Blues Band
5/08/65 **Count Me In**
    Gary Lewis & The Playboys
5/13/78 **Count On Me** *Jefferson Starship*
10/20/84 **Cover Me** *Bruce Springsteen*
3/17/73 **Cover Of "Rolling Stone"**
    Dr. Hook & The Medicine Show
1/26/80 **Coward Of The County**
    Kenny Rogers
5/18/68 **Cowboys To Girls** *Intruders*
4/29/72 **Cowboys Work Is Never Done**
    Sonny & Cher
10/10/70 **Cracklin' Rosie** *Neil Diamond*
5/02/60 **Cradle Of Love** *Johnny Preston*
11/27/61 **Crazy** *Patsy Cline*
5/11/85 **Crazy For You** *Madonna*
2/23/80 **Crazy Little Thing Called Love**
    Queen
6/03/67 **Creeque Alley**
    Mamas & The Papas
    Crimson And Clover
2/01/69   *Tommy James & The Shondells*
6/19/82   *Joan Jett*
2/03/73 **Crocodile Rock** *Elton John*
    Crooked Little Man..*see: Don't Let*
    The Rain Come Down
8/01/87 **Cross My Broken Heart** *Jets*
9/29/84 **Cruel Summer** *Bananarama*
2/02/80 **Cruisin'** *Smokey Robinson*
11/26/83 **Crumblin' Down**
    John Cougar Mellencamp
6/21/86 **Crush On You** *Jets*
10/12/63 **Cry Baby**
    Garnet Mimms & The Enchanters
4/27/68 **Cry Like A Baby** *Box Tops*
    Crying
10/09/61   *Roy Orbison*
3/21/81   *Don McLean*
6/12/65 **Crying In The Chapel**
    Elvis Presley
3/03/62 **Crying In The Rain**
    Everly Brothers
2/19/66 **Crying Time** *Ray Charles*
7/26/69 **Crystal Blue Persuasion**
    Tommy James & The Shondells
11/19/83 **Cum On Feel The Noize**
    Quiet Riot
7/19/80 **Cupid/I've Loved You For A Long**
    Time *Spinners*
6/21/75 **Cut The Cake** *AWB*

D

    Da Doo Ron Ron
6/08/63   *Crystals*
7/16/77   *Shaun Cassidy*
2/10/79 **Da Ya Think I'm Sexy?**
    Rod Stewart
8/05/72 **Daddy Don't You Walk So Fast**
    Wayne Newton
    Daddy's Home
5/29/61   *Shep & The Limelites*
3/17/73   *Jermaine Jackson*
12/19/64 **Dance, Dance, Dance**
    Beach Boys
2/23/78 **Dance, Dance, Dance (Yowsah,**
    Yowsah, Yowsah) *Chic*
7/10/61 **Dance On Little Girl** *Paul Anka*
4/20/68 **Dance To The Music**
    Sly & The Family Stone
10/18/75 **Dance With Me** *Orleans*
7/08/78 **Dance With Me** *Peter Brown*
6/30/84 **Dancing In The Dark**
    Bruce Springsteen
    Dancing In The Street
10/17/64   *Martha & The Vandellas*
10/12/85   *Mick Jagger/David Bowie*
5/18/74 **Dancing Machine** *Jackson 5*
9/13/86 **Dancing On The Ceiling**
    Lionel Richie
4/09/77 **Dancing Queen** *Abba*
11/05/66 **Dandy** *Herman's Hermits*
8/01/64 **Dang Me** *Roger Miller*
7/26/86 **Danger Zone** *Kenny Loggins*
6/02/73 **Daniel** *Elton John*
12/07/59 **Danny Boy** *Conway Twitty*
4/14/73 **Danny's Song** *Anne Murray*
3/23/74 **Dark Lady** *Cher*
2/22/64 **Dawn (Go Away)** *4 Seasons*
2/05/72 **Day After Day** *Badfinger*
5/06/72 **Day Dreaming** *Aretha Franklin*
1/22/66 **Day Tripper** *Beatles*
4/09/66 **Daydream** *Lovin' Spoonful*
12/02/67 **Daydream Believer** *Monkees*
1/29/77 **Dazz** *Brick*
1/17/81 **De Do Do Do, De Da Da Da**
    Police
5/09/64 **Dead Man's Curve** *Jan & Dean*
2/24/62 **Dear Lady Twist**
    Gary (U.S.) Bonds
3/13/76 **December, 1963 (Oh, What a**
    Night) *Four Seasons*
11/02/59 **Deck Of Cards** *Wink Martindale*
    Dedicated To The One I Love
3/27/61   *Shirelles*
3/25/67   *Mamas & The Papas*
11/16/63 **Deep Purple**
    Nino Tempo & April Stevens
10/22/83 **Delirious** *Prince*
9/15/73 **Delta Dawn** *Helen Reddy*
8/24/63 **Denise** *Randy & The Rainbows*
4/30/83 **Der Kommissar** *After The Fire*
11/10/84 **Desert Moon** *Dennis DeYoung*
12/04/71 **Desiderata** *Les Crane*

3/08/80	**Desire** *Andy Gibb*
	Devil In Disguise..*see: (You're The)*
4/16/88	**Devil Inside** *INXS*
10/17/60	**Devil Or Angel** *Bobby Vee*
9/15/79	**Devil Went Down To Georgia**
	Charlie Daniels Band
11/26/66	**Devil With A Blue Dress On &**
	Good Golly Miss Molly
	Mitch Ryder/Detroit Wheels
9/25/76	**Devil Woman** *Cliff Richard*
9/22/58	**Devoted To You** *Everly Brothers*
7/28/73	**Diamond Girl** *Seals & Crofts*
6/20/87	**Diamonds** *Herb Alpert*
6/20/64	**Diane** *Bachelors*
5/22/82	**Did It In A Minute**
	Daryl Hall & John Oates
6/11/66	**Did You Ever Have To Make Up**
	Your Mind? *Lovin' Spoonful*
3/21/70	**Didn't I (Blow Your Mind This**
	Time) *Delfonics*
9/26/87	**Didn't We Almost Have It All**
	Whitney Houston
	Died In Your Arms..*see: (I Just)*
6/14/86	**Different Corner** *George Michael*
11/10/79	**Dim All The Lights**
	Donna Summer
7/02/88	**Dirty Diana** *Michael Jackson*
1/08/83	**Dirty Laundry** *Don Henley*
10/16/76	**Disco Duck**
	Rick Dees & His Cast Of Idiots
4/03/76	**Disco Lady** *Johnnie Taylor*
3/15/69	**Dizzy** *Tommy Roe*
2/10/73	**Do It Again** *Steely Dan*
11/16/74	**Do It ('Til You're Satisfied)**
	B.T. Express
2/16/80	**Do That To Me One More Time**
	Captain & Tennille
4/13/63	**Do The Bird** *Dee Dee Sharp*
10/17/64	**Do Wah Diddy Diddy**
	Manfred Mann
	Do You..*also see: Da Ya*
4/17/82	**Do You Believe In Love**
	Huey Lewis & The News
10/16/65	**Do You Believe In Magic**
	Lovin' Spoonful
11/13/76	**Do You Feel Like We Do**
	Peter Frampton
5/18/68	**Do You Know The Way To San**
	Jose *Dionne Warwick*
10/09/71	**Do You Know What I Mean**
	Lee Michaels
	Do You Know Where You're
	Going To..*see: Theme From*
	Mahogany
10/20/62	**Do You Love Me** *Contours*
3/26/83	**Do You Really Want To Hurt Me**
	Culture Club
8/06/77	**Do You Wanna Make Love**
	Peter McCann
5/09/64	**Do You Want To Know A Secret**
	Beatles
	Dock Of The Bay..*see: (Sittin' On)*
	Doctor..*also see: Dr.*

5/06/72	**Doctor My Eyes** *Jackson Browne*
1/02/71	**Does Anybody Really Know What**
	Time It Is? *Chicago*
9/25/61	**Does Your Chewing Gum Lose**
	It's Flavor (On The Bedpost
	Over Night) *Lonnie Donegan*
3/27/71	**Doesn't Somebody Want To Be**
	Wanted *Partridge Family*
9/19/87	**Doing It All For My Baby**
	Huey Lewis & The News
12/07/63	**Dominique** *Singing Nun*
1/02/71	**Domino** *Van Morrison*
8/28/61	**Don't Bet Money Honey**
	Linda Scott
3/31/62	**Don't Break The Heart That**
	Loves You *Connie Francis*
9/08/79	**Don't Bring Me Down**
	Electric Light Orchestra
3/29/75	**Don't Call Us, We'll Call You**
	Sugarloaf/Jerry Corbetta
9/17/83	**Don't Cry** *Asia*
1/31/70	**Don't Cry Daddy** *Elvis Presley*
3/31/79	**Don't Cry Out Loud**
	Melissa Manchester
7/18/87	**Don't Disturb This Groove**
	System
2/02/80	**Don't Do Me Like That** *Tom Petty*
4/25/87	**Don't Dream It's Over**
	Crowded House
2/17/73	**Don't Expect Me To Be Your**
	Friend *Lobo*
5/24/80	**Don't Fall In Love With A**
	Dreamer
	Kenny Rogers with Kim Carnes
10/11/86	**Don't Forget Me (When I'm**
	Gone) *Glass Tiger*
12/27/86	**Don't Get Me Wrong** *Pretenders*
4/16/77	**Don't Give Up On Us** *David Soul*
8/07/76	**Don't Go Breaking My Heart**
	Elton John & Kiki Dee
12/08/62	**Don't Hang Up** *Orlons*
11/26/77	**Don't It Make My Brown Eyes**
	Blue *Crystal Gayle*
8/14/65	**Don't Just Stand There**
	Patty Duke
4/23/77	**Don't Leave Me This Way**
	Thelma Houston
7/02/83	**Don't Let It End** *Styx*
5/02/64	**Don't Let The Rain Come Down**
	(Crooked Little Man)
	Serendipity Singers
7/04/64	**Don't Let The Sun Catch You**
	Crying *Gerry & The Pacemakers*
7/27/74	**Don't Let The Sun Go Down On**
	Me *Elton John*
10/07/78	**Don't Look Back** *Boston*
9/28/85	**Don't Lose My Number**
	Phil Collins
8/29/87	**Don't Mean Nothing** *Richard Marx*
2/26/66	**Don't Mess With Bill** *Marvelettes*
7/17/71	**Don't Pull Your Love**
	Hamilton, Joe Frank & Reynolds

4/27/63	**Don't Say Nothin' Bad (About My Baby)** *Cookies*
2/13/88	**Don't Shed A Tear** *Paul Carrack*
7/08/67	**Don't Sleep In The Subway** *Petula Clark*
4/11/81	**Don't Stand So Close To Me** *Police*
9/24/77	**Don't Stop** *Fleetwood Mac*
12/19/81	**Don't Stop Believin'** *Journey*
10/13/79	**Don't Stop 'Til You Get Enough** *Michael Jackson*
5/22/82	**Don't Talk To Strangers** *Rick Springfield*
10/26/63	**Don't Think Twice, It's All Right** *Peter, Paul & Mary*
3/20/61	**Don't Worry** *Marty Robbins*
5/13/67	**Don't You Care** *Buckinghams*
5/18/85	**Don't You (Forget About Me)** *Simple Minds*
11/30/59	**Don't You Know** *Della Reese*
7/03/82	**Don't You Want Me** *Human League*
12/19/87	**Don't You Want Me** *Jody Watley*
2/23/59	**Donna** *Ritchie Valens*
10/26/63	**Donna The Prima Donna** *Dion DiMucci*
11/14/64	**Door Is Still Open To My Heart** *Dean Martin*
11/18/78	**Double Vision** *Foreigner*
11/30/63	**(Down At) Papa Joe's** *Dixiebelles*
3/04/72	**Down By The Lazy River** *Osmonds*
8/28/65	**Down In The Boondocks** *Billy Joe Royal*
12/20/69	**Down On The Corner** *Creedence Clearwater Revival*
1/15/83	**Down Under** *Men At Work*
1/23/65	**Downtown** *Petula Clark*
	Dr. Kildare ..see: *Theme From*
	Dr. Zhivago ..see: *Somewhere, My Love*
1/18/64	**Drag City** *Jan & Dean*
8/14/71	**Draggin' The Line** *Tommy James*
3/31/62	**Dream Baby** *Roy Orbison*
6/08/59	**Dream Lover** *Bobby Darin*
4/10/76	**Dream On** *Aerosmith*
3/27/76	**Dream Weaver** *Gary Wright*
11/22/80	**Dreaming** *Cliff Richard*
6/18/77	**Dreams** *Fleetwood Mac*
10/04/86	**Dreamtime** *Daryl Hall*
10/05/85	**Dress You Up** *Madonna*
5/12/73	**Drift Away** *Dobie Gray*
12/28/63	**Drip Drop** *Dion DiMucci*
9/29/84	**Drive** *Cars*
10/04/80	**Drivin' My Life Away** *Eddie Rabbitt*
2/24/73	**Dueling Banjos** *Eric Weissberg & Steve Mandell*
2/17/62	**Duke Of Earl** *Gene Chandler*
7/31/61	**Dum Dum** *Brenda Lee*
4/15/78	**Dust In The Wind** *Kansas*
8/02/75	**Dynomite** *Bazuka*

E

10/12/74	**Earache My Eye Featuring Alice Bowie** *Cheech & Chong*
7/06/63	**Easier Said Than Done** *Essex*
8/27/77	**Easy** *Commodores*
4/11/70	**Easy Come, Easy Go** *Bobby Sherman*
2/02/85	**Easy Lover** *Philip Bailey/Phil Collins*
9/27/69	**Easy To Be Hard** *Three Dog Night*
1/08/66	**Ebb Tide** *Righteous Brothers*
5/15/82	**Ebony And Ivory** *Paul McCartney with Stevie Wonder*
3/20/61	**Ebony Eyes** *Everly Brothers*
8/16/86	**Edge Of Heaven** *Wham!*
3/13/65	**Eight Days A Week** *Beatles*
5/22/82	**867-5309/Jenny** *Tommy Tutone*
6/15/63	**18 Yellow Roses** *Bobby Darin*
1/04/60	**El Paso** *Marty Robbins*
12/14/85	**Election Day** *Arcadia*
7/02/83	**Electric Avenue** *Eddy Grant*
5/21/88	**Electric Blue** *Icehouse*
11/02/68	**Elenore** *Turtles*
11/29/69	**Eli's Coming** *Three Dog Night*
3/12/66	**Elusive Butterfly** *Bob Lind*
7/25/81	**Elvira** *Oak Ridge Boys*
4/26/75	**Emma** *Hot Chocolate*
3/18/78	**Emotion** *Samantha Sang*
9/06/80	**Emotional Rescue** *Rolling Stones*
2/13/61	**Emotions** *Brenda Lee*
10/13/58	**End, The** *Earl Grant*
3/23/63	**End Of The World** *Skeeter Davis*
8/15/81	**Endless Love** *Diana Ross & Lionel Richie*
3/26/88	**Endless Summer Nights** *Richard Marx*
6/12/65	**Engine Engine #9** *Roger Miller*
12/18/65	**England Swings** *Roger Miller*
2/19/77	**Enjoy Yourself** *Jacksons*
	Enough Is Enough ..see: *No More Tears*
5/18/74	**Entertainer, The** *Marvin Hamlisch*
3/23/74	**Eres Tu (Touch The Wind)** *Mocedades*
12/22/79	**Escape (The Pina Colada Song)** *Rupert Holmes*
9/25/65	**Eve Of Destruction** *Barry McGuire*
9/04/82	**Even The Nights Are Better** *Air Supply*
	Evergreen ..see: *Love Theme From "A Star Is Born"*
11/23/74	**Everlasting Love** *Carl Carlton*
9/23/78	**Everlasting Love** *Andy Gibb*
7/10/61	**Every Beat Of My Heart** *Pips*
7/09/83	**Every Breath You Take** *Police*
12/05/81	**Every Little Thing She Does Is Magic** *Police*
2/10/79	**Every 1's A Winner** *Hot Chocolate*
12/24/77	**(Every Time I Turn Around) Back In Love Again** *L.T.D.*

1/31/81	**Every Woman In The World** *Air Supply*
12/07/63	**Everybody** *Tommy Roe*
12/27/86	**Everybody Have Fun Tonight** *Wang Chung*
2/14/70	**Everybody Is A Star** *Sly & The Family Stone*
11/06/65	**Everybody Loves A Clown** *Gary Lewis & The Playboys*
5/26/62	**Everybody Loves Me But You** *Brenda Lee*
8/15/64	**Everybody Loves Somebody** *Dean Martin*
10/14/72	**Everybody Plays The Fool** *Main Ingredient*
6/08/85	**Everybody Wants To Rule The World** *Tears For Fears*
6/27/60	**Everybody's Somebody's Fool** *Connie Francis*
10/11/69	**Everybody's Talkin'** *Nilsson*
2/15/69	**Everyday People** *Sly & The Family Stone*
3/04/72	**Everything I Own** *Bread*
5/30/70	**Everything Is Beautiful** *Ray Stevens*
5/25/85	**Everything She Wants** *Wham!*
3/02/68	**Everything That Touches You** *Association*
6/11/88	**Everything Your Heart Desires** *Daryl Hall John Oates*
7/27/85	**Everytime You Go Away** *Paul Young*
3/21/70	**Evil Ways** *Santana*
2/14/76	**Evil Woman** *Electric Light Orchestra*
1/23/61	**Exodus** *Ferrante & Teicher*
3/29/75	**Express** *B.T. Express*
11/04/67	**Expressway To Your Heart** *Soul Survivors*
10/16/82	**Eye In The Sky** *Alan Parsons Project*
7/24/82	**Eye Of The Tiger** *Survivor*
7/14/84	**Eyes Without A Face** *Billy Idol*

F

12/12/87	**Faith** *George Michael*
8/23/75	**Fallin' In Love** *Hamilton, Joe Frank & Reynolds*
9/20/75	**Fame** *David Bowie*
9/13/80	**Fame** *Irene Cara*
12/04/71	**Family Affair** *Sly & The Family Stone*
6/25/83	**Family Man** *Daryl Hall & John Oates*
10/01/83	**Far From Over** *Frank Stallone*
	Fascination..*see: (Keep Feeling)*
2/27/88	**Father Figure** *George Michael*
8/10/74	**Feel Like Makin' Love** *Roberta Flack*
9/20/75	**Feel Like Makin' Love** *Bad Company*

8/18/73	**Feelin' Stronger Every Day** *Chicago*
10/25/75	**Feelings** *Morris Albert*
6/18/77	**Feels Like The First Time** *Foreigner*
6/10/78	**Feels So Good** *Chuck Mangione*
3/20/65	**Ferry Across The Mersey** *Gerry & The Pacemakers*
	Fever
8/25/58	*Peggy Lee*
12/25/65	*McCoys*
10/09/76	**Fifth Of Beethoven** *Walter Murphy & The Big Apple Band*
2/07/76	**50 Ways To Leave Your Lover** *Paul Simon*
	Fight..*see: Main Event*
	Fight For Your Right..*see: (You Gotta)*
9/27/75	**Fight The Power** *Isley Brothers*
3/28/87	**Final Countdown** *Europe*
4/18/87	**Finer Things** *Steve Winwood*
8/15/60	**Finger Poppin' Time** *Hank Ballard*
8/10/63	**Fingertips - Pt 2** *Little Stevie Wonder*
10/19/68	**Fire** *Crazy World Of Arthur Brown*
2/08/75	**Fire** *Ohio Players*
2/24/79	**Fire** *Pointer Sisters*
10/31/70	**Fire And Rain** *James Taylor*
5/03/80	**Fire Lake** *Bob Seger*
4/15/72	**First Time Ever I Saw Your Face** *Roberta Flack*
11/16/63	**500 Miles Away From Home** *Bobby Bare*
1/15/66	**Five O'Clock World** *Vogues*
7/09/88	**Flame, The** *Cheap Trick*
5/28/83	**Flashdance...What A Feeling** *Irene Cara*
9/17/77	**Float On** *Floaters*
1/08/66	**Flowers On The Wall** *Statler Brothers*
11/13/61	**Fly, The** *Chubby Checker*
3/12/77	**Fly Like An Eagle** *Steve Miller*
11/29/75	**Fly, Robin, Fly** *Silver Convention*
11/13/61	**Fool #1** *Brenda Lee*
9/28/68	**Fool On The Hill** *Sergio Mendes & Brasil '66*
	Fool Such As I..*see: (Now And Then There's)*
6/05/76	**Fool To Cry** *Rolling Stones*
5/22/76	**Fooled Around And Fell In Love** *Elvin Bishop*
6/25/88	**Foolish Beat** *Debbie Gibson*
5/25/63	**Foolish Little Girl** *Shirelles*
3/31/84	**Footloose** *Kenny Loggins* *(also see: Almost Paradise)*
4/04/60	**Footsteps** *Steve Lawrence*
3/13/71	**For All We Know** *Carpenters*
12/28/68	**For Once In My Life** *Stevie Wonder*
6/15/74	**For The Love Of Money** *O'Jays*
3/25/67	**For What It's Worth** *Buffalo Springfield*
2/15/64	**For You** *Rick Nelson*

6/13/70	**For You Blue** *Beatles*
10/17/81	**For Your Eyes Only**
	Sheena Easton
7/03/65	**For Your Love** *Yardbirds*
3/28/60	**Forever** *Little Dippers*
1/18/64	**Forget Him** *Bobby Rydell*
3/29/80	**Forgive Me, Girl (medley)**
	Spinners
10/26/85	**Fortress Around Your Heart**
	Sting
12/20/69	**Fortunate Son**
	Creedence Clearwater Revival
7/27/59	**Forty Miles Of Bad Road**
	Duane Eddy & The Rebels
1/17/76	**Fox On The Run** *Sweet*
5/26/73	**Frankenstein** *Edgar Winter Group*
7/06/59	**Frankie** *Connie Francis*
11/04/72	**Freddie's Dead (Theme From**
	"Superfly") *Curtis Mayfield*
12/07/74	**Free Wheelin'**
	Bachman-Turner Overdrive
9/28/85	**Freedom** *Wham!*
8/31/85	**Freeway Of Love** *Aretha Franklin*
4/10/82	**Freeze-Frame** *J. Geils Band*
6/08/85	**Fresh** *Kool & The Gang*
9/27/86	**Friends And Lovers**
	Gloria Loring & Carl Anderson
2/16/63	**From A Jack To A King**
	Ned Miller
3/21/64	**Fun, Fun, Fun** *Beach Boys*
9/30/67	**Funky Broadway** *Wilson Pickett*
	Funkytown
5/31/80	*Lipps, Inc.*
7/18/87	*Pseudo Echo*
1/06/73	**Funny Face** *Donna Fargo*
5/19/62	**Funny Way Of Laughin'** *Burl Ives*

G

9/26/64	**G.T.O.** *Ronny & The Daytonas*
4/12/69	**Galveston** *Glen Campbell*
4/24/65	**Game Of Love**
	Wayne Fontana & The Mindbenders
11/04/72	**Garden Party** *Rick Nelson*
3/27/61	**Gee Whiz (Look At His Eyes)**
	Carla Thomas
11/14/60	**Georgia On My Mind** *Ray Charles*
2/04/67	**Georgy Girl** *Seekers*
5/24/69	**Get Back** *Beatles*
7/24/76	**Get Closer** *Seals & Crofts*
2/08/75	**Get Dancin'**
	Disco Tex & The Sex-O-Lettes
8/18/73	**Get Down** *Gilbert O'Sullivan*
6/21/75	**Get Down, Get Down (Get On The**
	Floor) *Joe Simon*
5/22/82	**Get Down On It** *Kool & The Gang*
8/30/75	**Get Down Tonight**
	K.C. & The Sunshine Band
	Get It On..*see: Bang A Gong*
11/11/78	**Get Off** *Foxy*
11/06/65	**Get Off Of My Cloud**
	Rolling Stones

4/09/88	**Get Outta My Dreams, Get Into**
	My Car *Billy Ocean*
6/13/70	**Get Ready** *Rare Earth*
9/06/69	**Get Together** *Youngbloods*
6/12/76	**Get Up And Boogie (That's**
	Right) *Silver Convention*
8/11/84	**Ghostbusters** *Ray Parker Jr.*
7/18/70	**Gimme Dat Ding** *Pipkins*
10/14/67	**Gimme Little Sign** *Brenton Wood*
2/25/67	**Gimme Some Lovin'**
	Spencer Davis Group
11/17/62	**Gina** *Johnny Mathis*
9/01/58	**Ginger Bread** *Frankie Avalon*
7/18/64	**Girl From Ipanema**
	Stan Getz/Astrud Gilberto
1/08/83	**Girl Is Mine**
	Michael Jackson/Paul McCartney
8/12/67	**Girl Like You** *Young Rascals*
10/05/68	**Girl Watcher** *O'Kaysions*
5/27/67	**Girl, You'll Be A Woman Soon**
	Neil Diamond
4/23/88	**Girlfriend** *Pebbles*
3/10/84	**Girls Just Want To Have Fun**
	Cyndi Lauper
5/31/69	**Gitarzan** *Ray Stevens*
	Give Me..*also see: Gimme*
3/21/70	**Give Me Just A Little More**
	Time *Chairmen Of The Board*
6/30/73	**Give Me Love (Give Me Peace On**
	Earth) *George Harrison*
9/27/80	**Give Me The Night**
	George Benson
2/21/81	**Giving It Up For Your Love**
	Delbert McClinton
4/25/64	**Glad All Over** *Dave Clark Five*
10/06/84	**Glamorous Life** *Sheila E.*
5/07/66	**Gloria** *Shadows Of Knight*
11/27/82	**Gloria** *Laura Branigan*
8/03/85	**Glory Days** *Bruce Springsteen*
8/02/86	**Glory Of Love** *Peter Cetera*
10/07/72	**Go All The Way** *Raspberries*
	Go Away Little Girl
1/12/63	*Steve Lawrence*
9/11/71	*Donny Osmond*
2/01/86	**Go Home** *Stevie Wonder*
2/01/60	**Go, Jimmy, Go** *Jimmy Clanton*
4/17/65	**Go Now!** *Moody Blues*
3/12/77	**Go Your Own Way** *Fleetwood Mac*
	Goin' Out Of My Head
12/26/64	*Little Anthony & The Imperials*
2/10/68	*Lettermen (medley)*
8/04/79	**Gold** *John Stewart*
4/03/76	**Golden Years** *David Bowie*
3/27/65	**Goldfinger** *Shirley Bassey*
7/02/77	**Gonna Fly Now (Theme From**
	"Rocky") *Bill Conti*
	Good Golly Miss Molly..*see: Devil*
	With The Blue Dress
4/30/66	**Good Lovin'** *Young Rascals*
4/21/62	**Good Luck Charm** *Elvis Presley*
7/12/69	**Good Morning Starshine** *Oliver*
6/01/68	**Good, The Bad And The Ugly**
	Hugo Montenegro

1/14/67	**Good Thing**
	Paul Revere & The Raiders
11/04/72	**Good Time Charlie's Got The**
	Blues *Danny O'Keefe*
8/18/79	**Good Times** *Chic*
5/23/60	**Good Timin'** *Jimmy Jones*
12/10/66	**Good Vibrations** *Beach Boys*
2/16/59	**Goodbye Baby** *Jack Scott*
12/04/61	**Goodbye Cruel World**
	James Darren
8/26/72	**Goodbye To Love** *Carpenters*
12/08/73	**Goodbye Yellow Brick Road**
	Elton John
5/19/79	**Goodnight Tonight** *Wings*
7/13/85	**Goonies 'R' Good Enough**
	Cyndi Lauper
3/24/84	**Got A Hold On Me** *Christine McVie*
1/16/88	**Got My Mind Set On You**
	George Harrison
12/11/71	**Got To Be There** *Michael Jackson*
	Got To Get You Into My Life
7/24/76	*Beatles*
9/16/78	*Earth, Wind & Fire*
6/25/77	**Got To Give It Up** *Marvin Gaye*
1/12/59	**Gotta Travel On** *Billy Grammer*
7/14/62	**Gravy (For My Mashed**
	Potatoes) *Dee Dee Sharp*
	Grazing In The Grass
7/20/68	*Hugh Masekela*
6/07/69	*Friends Of Distinction*
8/26/78	**Grease** *Frankie Valli*
	Greatest American Hero ..*see:*
	Theme From
5/17/86	**Greatest Love Of All**
	Whitney Houston
	Green Berets ..*see: Ballad Of*
10/17/70	**Green-Eyed Lady** *Sugarloaf*
6/18/66	**Green Grass**
	Gary Lewis & The Playboys
9/29/62	**Green Onions**
	Booker T. & The MG's
9/27/69	**Green River**
	Creedence Clearwater Revival
2/03/68	**Green Tambourine** *Lemon Pipers*
4/18/60	**Greenfields** *Brothers Four*
7/15/78	**Groove Line** *Heatwave*
1/30/71	**Groove Me** *King Floyd*
5/20/67	**Groovin'** *Young Rascals*
5/28/66	**Groovy Kind Of Love**
	Mindbenders
9/17/66	**Guantanamera** *Sandpipers*
1/10/81	**Guilty**
	Barbra Streisand & Barry Gibb
4/27/59	**Guitar Boogie Shuffle** *Virtues*
9/15/73	**Gypsy Man** *War*
12/05/70	**Gypsy Woman** *Brian Hyland*
11/06/71	**Gypsys, Tramps & Thieves** *Cher*

H

5/10/69	**Hair** *Cowsills*
10/06/73	**Half-Breed** *Cher*

	Handy Man
2/29/60	*Jimmy Jones*
9/10/77	*James Taylor*
2/08/69	**Hang 'Em High**
	Booker T. & The MG's
10/05/74	**Hang On In There Baby**
	Johnny Bristol
10/02/65	**Hang On Sloopy** *McCoys*
7/16/66	**Hanky Panky**
	Tommy James & The Shondells
5/13/67	**Happening, The** *Supremes*
1/06/62	**Happy Birthday, Sweet Sixteen**
	Neil Sedaka
6/05/76	**Happy Days** *Pratt & McClain*
6/13/60	**Happy-Go-Lucky-Me** *Paul Evans*
5/11/59	**Happy Organ** *Dave 'Baby' Cortez*
3/25/67	**Happy Together** *Turtles*
3/28/60	**Harbor Lights** *Platters*
8/01/64	**Hard Day's Night** *Beatles*
10/20/84	**Hard Habit To Break** *Chicago*
10/31/81	**Hard To Say** *Dan Fogelberg*
9/11/82	**Hard To Say I'm Sorry** *Chicago*
2/13/82	**Harden My Heart** *Quarterflash*
5/03/86	**Harlem Shuffle** *Rolling Stones*
9/21/68	**Harper Valley P.T.A.**
	JeannieeC. Riley
7/31/61	**Hats Off To Larry** *Del Shannon*
11/14/64	**Have I The Right?** *Honeycombs*
3/13/71	**Have You Ever Seen The Rain**
	Creedence Clearwater Revival
3/08/75	**Have You Never Been Mellow**
	Olivia Newton-John
12/11/71	**Have You Seen Her** *Chi-Lites*
10/29/66	**Have You Seen Your Mother,**
	Baby, Standing In The
	Shadow? *Rolling Stones*
5/10/69	**Hawaii Five-O** *Ventures*
2/06/88	**Hazy Shade Of Winter** *Bangles*
3/21/70	**He Ain't Heavy, He's My**
	Brother *Hollies*
5/03/75	**He Don't Love You (Like I Love**
	You) *Tony Orlando & Dawn*
12/05/60	**He Will Break Your Heart**
	Jerry Butler
	He'll Have To Go (Stay)
3/07/60	*Jim Reeves*
5/30/60	*Jeanne Black*
11/03/62	**He's A Rebel** *Crystals*
3/30/63	**He's So Fine** *Chiffons*
10/25/80	**He's So Shy** *Pointer Sisters*
5/12/79	**He's The Greatest Dancer**
	Sister Sledge
11/09/85	**Head Over Heels** *Tears For Fears*
6/20/87	**Head To Toe** *Lisa Lisa & Cult Jam*
11/26/83	**Heart And Soul**
	Huey Lewis & The News
8/08/87	**Heart And Soul** *T'Pau*
11/06/82	**Heart Attack** *Olivia Newton-John*
9/25/65	**Heart Full Of Soul** *Yardbirds*
4/28/79	**Heart Of Glass** *Blondie*
3/18/72	**Heart Of Gold** *Neil Young*
6/09/84	**Heart Of Rock & Roll**
	Huey Lewis & The News

11/10/79	**Heartache Tonight** *Eagles*	2/21/70	**Hey There Lonely Girl**
11/27/61	**Heartaches** *Marcels*		*Eddie Holman*
12/14/59	**Heartaches By The Number**	4/26/75	**(Hey Won't You Play) Another**
	Guy Mitchell		**Somebody Done Somebody**
10/18/86	**Heartbeat** *Don Johnson*		**Wrong Song** *B.J. Thomas*
11/17/73	**Heartbeat – It's A Lovebeat**	2/03/73	**Hi, Hi, Hi** *Wings*
	DeFranco Family	3/23/85	**High On You** *Survivor*
1/15/83	**Heartbreaker** *Dionne Warwick*	10/13/73	**Higher Ground** *Stevie Wonder*
11/13/82	**Heartlight** *Neil Diamond*	8/30/86	**Higher Love** *Steve Winwood*
8/08/81	**Hearts** *Marty Balin*		**Hill Street Blues**..see: *Theme From*
3/16/85	**Heat Is On** *Glenn Frey*	3/29/80	**Him** *Rupert Holmes*
6/26/82	**Heat Of The Moment** *Asia*	6/10/67	**Him Or Me – What's It Gonna**
5/16/87	**Heat Of The Night** *Bryan Adams*		**Be?** *Paul Revere & The Raiders*
	Heat Wave	12/06/86	**Hip To Be Square**
9/21/63	*Martha & The Vandellas*		*Huey Lewis & The News*
11/15/75	*Linda Ronstadt*		**His Latest Flame**..see: *(Marie's the*
6/22/85	**Heaven** *Bryan Adams*		*Name)*
11/28/70	**Heaven Help Us All**	12/20/80	**Hit Me With Your Best Shot**
	Stevie Wonder		*Pat Benatar*
12/05/87	**Heaven Is A Place On Earth**	10/09/61	**Hit The Road Jack** *Ray Charles*
	Belinda Carlisle	6/27/70	**Hitchin' A Ride** *Vanity Fare*
3/17/79	**Heaven Knows**	6/02/73	**Hocus Pocus** *Focus*
	Donna Summer with Brooklyn Dreams	7/24/82	**Hold Me** *Fleetwood Mac*
11/26/77	**Heaven On The 7th Floor**	5/05/84	**Hold Me Now** *Thompson Twins*
	Paul Nicholas	8/28/65	**Hold Me, Thrill Me, Kiss Me**
1/12/74	**Helen Wheels**		*Mel Carter*
	Paul McCartney & Wings	11/09/68	**Hold Me Tight** *Johnny Nash*
5/12/84	**Hello** *Lionel Richie*	10/03/81	**Hold On Tight** *ELO*
3/28/81	**Hello Again** *Neil Diamond*	5/03/80	**Hold On To My Love** *Jimmy Ruffin*
5/09/64	**Hello, Dolly!** *Louis Armstrong*	7/09/88	**Hold On To The Nights**
12/30/67	**Hello Goodbye** *Beatles*		*Richard Marx*
8/03/68	**Hello, I Love You** *Doors*	1/13/79	**Hold The Line** *Toto*
12/22/73	**Hello It's Me** *Todd Rundgren*	1/30/65	**Hold What You've Got** *Joe Tex*
5/22/61	**Hello Mary Lou** *Ricky Nelson*	8/26/72	**Hold Your Head Up** *Argent*
8/24/63	**Hello Mudduh, Hello Fadduh!**	7/12/86	**Holding Back The Years**
	Allan Sherman		*Simply Red*
6/22/63	**Hello Stranger** *Barbara Lewis*	12/27/69	**Holly Holy** *Neil Diamond*
9/04/65	**Help!** *Beatles*	7/06/74	**Hollywood Swinging**
6/08/74	**Help Me** *Joni Mitchell*		*Kool & The Gang*
3/27/71	**Help Me Make It Through The**	3/26/66	**Homeward Bound**
	Night *Sammi Smith*		*Simon & Garfunkel*
5/29/65	**Help Me, Rhonda** *Beach Boys*	4/13/68	**Honey** *Bobby Goldsboro*
3/17/62	**Her Royal Majesty** *James Darren*	9/23/72	**Honky Cat** *Elton John*
7/06/68	**Here Comes The Judge**	8/23/69	**Honky Tonk Women**
	Shorty Long		*Rolling Stones*
3/31/84	**Here Comes The Rain Again**		**Hooked On A Feeling**
	Eurythmics	1/11/69	*B.J. Thomas*
9/08/73	**Here I Am (Come And Take Me)**	4/06/74	*Blue Swede*
	Al Green	1/30/82	**Hooked On Classics**
11/21/81	**Here I Am (Just When I Thought I**		*Royal Philharmonic Orchestra*
	Was Over You) *Air Supply*	11/05/66	**Hooray For Hazel** *Tommy Roe*
10/10/87	**Here I Go Again** *Whitesnake*	9/23/78	**Hopelessly Devoted To You**
1/14/78	**Here You Come Again**		*Olivia Newton-John*
	Dolly Parton	6/29/68	**Horse, The** *Cliff Nobles & Co.*
3/10/62	**Hey! Baby** *Bruce Channel*	3/25/72	**Horse With No Name** *America*
1/14/78	**Hey Deanie** *Shaun Cassidy*	9/09/78	**Hot Blooded** *Foreigner*
	Hey, Girl	10/28/78	**Hot Child In The City** *Nick Gilder*
9/07/63	*Freddie Scott*	10/18/69	**Hot Fun In The Summertime**
1/15/72	*Donny Osmond*		*Sly & The Family Stone*
9/28/68	**Hey Jude** *Beatles*	1/29/77	**Hot Line** *Sylvers*
2/08/64	**Hey Little Cobra** *Rip Chords*	6/03/72	**Hot Rod Lincoln**
2/14/81	**Hey Nineteen** *Steely Dan*		*Commander Cody*
2/09/63	**Hey Paula** *Paul & Paula*	6/02/79	**Hot Stuff** *Donna Summer*

5/07/77	**Hotel California**	*Eagles*
1/19/63	**Hotel Happiness**	*Brook Benton*
12/28/59	**Hound Dog Man**	*Fabian*
	House Of The Rising Sun	
9/05/64	*Animals*	
4/04/70	*Frijid Pink*	
9/07/68	**House That Jack Built**	
	Aretha Franklin	
10/21/67	**How Can I Be Sure**	
	Young Rascals	
8/07/71	**How Can You Mend A Broken**	
	Heart	*Bee Gees*
12/24/77	**How Deep Is Your Love**	
	Bee Gees	
3/22/80	**How Do I Make You**	
	Linda Ronstadt	
9/05/64	**How Do You Do It?**	
	Gerry & The Pacemakers	
7/22/72	**How Do You Do?**	
	Mouth & MacNeal	
5/14/66	**How Does That Grab You,**	
	Darlin'?	*Nancy Sinatra*
5/31/75	**How Long**	*Ace*
11/18/78	**How Much I Feel**	*Ambrosia*
	How Sweet It Is (To Be Loved By	
	You)	
1/30/65	*Marvin Gaye*	
8/30/75	*James Taylor*	
2/15/86	**How Will I Know**	*Whitney Houston*
11/22/86	**Human**	*Human League*
9/17/83	**Human Nature**	*Michael Jackson*
5/08/61	**Hundred Pounds Of Clay**	
	Gene McDaniels	
7/30/66	**Hungry**	*Paul Revere & The Raiders*
2/13/88	**Hungry Eyes**	*Eric Carmen*
12/27/80	**Hungry Heart**	*Bruce Springsteen*
3/26/83	**Hungry Like The Wolf**	
	Duran Duran	
8/03/68	**Hurdy Gurdy Man**	*Donovan*
9/11/61	**Hurt**	*Timi Yuro*
	Hurt So Bad	
3/13/65	*Little Anthony & The Imperials*	
5/24/80	*Linda Ronstadt*	
2/26/72	**Hurting Each Other**	*Carpenters*
8/07/82	**Hurts So Good**	*John Cougar*
9/21/68	**Hush**	*Deep Purple*
6/26/65	**Hush, Hush, Sweet Charlotte**	
	Patti Page	
7/26/75	**Hustle, The**	*Van McCoy*
3/26/88	**Hysteria**	*Def Leppard*

I

6/11/66	**I Am A Rock**	*Simon & Garfunkel*
5/08/71	**I Am...I Said**	*Neil Diamond*
12/09/72	**I Am Woman**	*Helen Reddy*
	I Can Dance..see: Long Tall	
	Glasses	
8/18/84	**I Can Dream About You**	
	Dan Hartman	
11/23/74	**I Can Help**	*Billy Swan*
12/11/65	**I Can Never Go Home Anymore**	
	Shangri-Las	

11/04/72	**I Can See Clearly Now**	
	Johnny Nash	
11/25/67	**I Can See For Miles**	*Who*
10/18/69	**I Can't Get Next To You**	
	Temptations	
7/10/65	**(I Can't Get No) Satisfaction**	
	Rolling Stones	
1/30/82	**I Can't Go For That (No Can Do)**	
	Daryl Hall & John Oates	
6/19/65	**I Can't Help Myself**	*Four Tops*
5/02/81	**I Can't Stand It**	*Eric Clapton*
11/02/63	**I Can't Stay Mad At You**	
	Skeeter Davis	
8/24/68	**I Can't Stop Dancing**	
	Archie Bell & The Drells	
6/02/62	**I Can't Stop Loving You**	
	Ray Charles	
4/19/80	**I Can't Tell You Why**	*Eagles*
6/14/86	**I Can't Wait**	*Nu Shooz*
2/06/88	**I Could Never Take The Place Of**	
	Your Man	*Prince*
8/20/66	**I Couldn't Live Without Your**	
	Love	*Petula Clark*
2/23/59	**I Cried A Tear**	*LaVern Baker*
	I Didn't Get To Sleep At All..see:	
	(Last Night)	
11/08/86	**I Didn't Mean To Turn You On**	
	Robert Palmer	
9/23/67	**I Dig Rock And Roll Music**	
	Peter, Paul & Mary	
5/24/75	**I Don't Like To Sleep Alone**	
	Paul Anka	
8/15/81	**I Don't Need You**	*Kenny Rogers*
5/28/88	**I Don't Want To Live Without**	
	You	*Foreigner*
12/26/64	**I Feel Fine**	*Beatles*
11/24/84	**I Feel For You**	*Chaka Khan*
11/12/77	**I Feel Love**	*Donna Summer*
6/05/61	**I Feel So Bad**	*Elvis Presley*
6/19/71	**I Feel The Earth Move**	
	Carole King	
3/12/66	**I Fought The Law**	
	Bobby Fuller Four	
3/05/88	**I Found Someone**	*Cher*
8/01/70	**I Found That Girl**	*Jackson 5*
7/04/64	**I Get Around**	*Beach Boys*
3/19/88	**I Get Weak**	*Belinda Carlisle*
3/18/78	**I Go Crazy**	*Paul Davis*
2/20/65	**I Go To Pieces**	*Peter & Gordon*
11/10/58	**I Got A Feeling**	*Ricky Nelson*
11/17/73	**I Got A Name**	*Jim Croce*
5/27/67	**I Got Rhythm**	*Happenings*
11/24/58	**I Got Stung**	*Elvis Presley*
4/27/68	**I Got The Feelin'**	*James Brown*
8/14/65	**I Got You Babe**	*Sonny & Cher*
12/18/65	**I Got You (I Feel Good)**	
	James Brown	
5/06/72	**I Gotcha**	*Joe Tex*
1/28/84	**I Guess That's Why They Call It**	
	The Blues	*Elton John*
11/20/65	**I Hear A Symphony**	*Supremes*
2/13/71	**I Hear You Knocking**	
	Dave Edmunds	

9/26/87	**I Heard A Rumour** *Bananarama*	7/30/66	**I Saw Her Again**
	I Heard It Through The		*Mamas & The Papas*
	Grapevine	4/23/88	**I Saw Him Standing There**
12/16/67	*Gladys Knight & The Pips*		*Tiffany*
12/14/68	*Marvin Gaye*		**I Say A Little Prayer**
10/05/74	**I Honestly Love You**	12/09/67	*Dionne Warwick*
	Olivia Newton-John	10/05/68	*Aretha Franklin*
10/13/84	**I Just Called To Say I Love You**	12/16/67	**I Second That Emotion** *Miracles*
	Stevie Wonder	9/14/74	**I Shot The Sheriff** *Eric Clapton*
8/22/70	**I Just Can't Help Believing**	2/08/69	**I Started A Joke** *Bee Gees*
	B.J. Thomas	8/08/87	**I Still Haven't Found What I'm**
9/19/87	**I Just Can't Stop Loving You**		**Looking For** *U2*
	Michael Jackson with Siedah Garrett	3/23/68	**I Thank You** *Sam & Dave*
5/02/87	**(I Just) Died In Your Arms**	11/21/70	**I Think I Love You**
	Cutting Crew		*Partridge Family*
12/09/78	**I Just Wanna Stop** *Gino Vannelli*		**I Think We're Alone Now**
7/30/77	**I Just Want To Be Your**	4/22/67	*Tommy James & The Shondells*
	Everything *Andy Gibb*	11/07/87	*Tiffany*
9/11/71	**I Just Want To Celebrate**	12/04/61	**I Understand (Just How You**
	Rare Earth		**Feel)** *G-Clefs*
10/23/82	**I Keep Forgettin' (Every Time**	6/27/87	**I Wanna Dance With Somebody**
	You're Near) *Michael McDonald*		**(Who Loves Me)**
4/18/87	**I Knew You Were Waiting (For**		*Whitney Houston*
	Me)	5/07/77	**I Wanna Get Next To You**
	Aretha Franklin & George Michael		*Rose Royce*
1/15/72	**I Knew You When** *Donny Osmond*	8/08/64	**I Wanna Love Him So Bad**
5/01/65	**I Know A Place** *Petula Clark*		*Jelly Beans*
	(I Know) I'm Losing You	3/24/84	**I Want A New Drug**
12/31/66	*Temptations*		*Huey Lewis & The News*
10/03/70	*Rare Earth*	4/02/88	**I Want Her** *Keith Sweat*
5/30/87	**I Know What I Like**	10/24/60	**I Want To Be Wanted** *Brenda Lee*
	Huey Lewis & The News	2/13/88	**I Want To Be Your Man** *Roger*
1/27/62	**I Know (You Don't Love Me No**	2/01/64	**I Want To Hold Your Hand**
	More) *Barbara George*		*Beatles*
3/12/77	**I Like Dreamin'** *Kenny Nolan*	2/02/85	**I Want To Know What Love Is**
	I Like It Like That		*Foreigner*
7/31/61	*Chris Kenner*	9/14/59	**I Want To Walk You Home**
8/07/65	*Dave Clark Five*		*Fats Domino*
2/28/81	**I Love A Rainy Night**	1/31/70	**I Want You Back** *Jackson 5*
	Eddie Rabbitt	7/21/79	**I Want You To Want Me**
	I Love How You Love Me		*Cheap Trick*
10/30/61	*Paris Sisters*	5/05/79	**I Want Your Love** *Chic*
12/14/68	*Bobby Vinton*	8/08/87	**I Want Your Sex** *George Michael*
1/24/76	**I Love Music** *O'Jays*	2217/79	**I Was Made For Dancin'**
3/20/82	**I Love Rock 'N Roll** *Joan Jett*		*Leif Garrett*
12/23/78	**I Love The Nightlife (Disco**	7/29/67	**I Was Made To Love Her**
	'Round) *Alicia Bridges*		*Stevie Wonder*
4/11/60	**I Love The Way You Love**	12/11/65	**I Will** *Dean Martin*
	Marv Johnson	4/27/63	**I Will Follow Him**
6/01/63	**I Love You Because** *Al Martino*		*Little Peggy March*
3/21/64	**I Love You More And More Every**	3/10/79	**I Will Survive** *Gloria Gaynor*
	Day *Al Martino*	1/22/77	**I Wish** *Stevie Wonder*
1/31/81	**I Made It Through The Rain**	2/17/68	**I Wish It Would Rain** *Temptations*
	Barry Manilow	5/07/83	**I Won't Hold You Back** *Toto*
12/28/85	**I Miss You** *Klymaxx*	2/24/68	**I Wonder What She's Doing**
7/01/72	**I Need You** *America*		**Tonite**
4/20/59	**I Need Your Love Tonight**		*Tommy Boyce & Bobby Hart*
	Elvis Presley	2/02/85	**I Would Die 4 U**
4/15/67	**I Never Loved A Man (The Way I**		*Prince & The Revolution*
	Love You) *Aretha Franklin*	1/17/76	**I Write The Songs** *Barry Manilow*
10/23/82	**I Ran (So Far Away)**	1/15/72	**I'd Like To Teach The World To**
	A Flock Of Seagulls		**Sing** *New Seekers*
10/13/62	**I Remember You** *Frank Ifield*	11/18/72	**I'd Love You To Want Me** *Lobo*

9/25/76	**I'd Really Love To See You Tonight**	2/01/86	**I'm Your Man** *Wham!*
	England Dan & John Ford Coley	11/26/66	**I'm Your Puppet**
11/18/72	**I'll Be Around** *Spinners*		*James & Bobby Purify*
5/15/65	**I'll Be Doggone** *Marvin Gaye*	11/21/87	**I've Been In Love Before**
7/10/76	**I'll Be Good To You**		*Cutting Crew*
	Brothers Johnson	5/11/74	**(I've Been) Searchin' So Long**
10/17/70	**I'll Be There** *Jackson 5*		*Chicago*
4/27/74	**I'll Have To Say I Love You In A Song** *Jim Croce*	11/07/81	**I've Done Everything For You**
			Rick Springfield
6/12/71	**I'll Meet You Halfway**	11/13/71	**I've Found Someone Of My Own**
	Partridge Family		*Free Movement*
9/13/69	**I'll Never Fall In Love Again**	4/30/77	**I've Got Love On My Mind**
	Tom Jones		*Natalie Cole*
2/07/70	**I'll Never Fall In Love Again**	1/19/74	**I've Got To Use My Imagination**
	Dionne Warwick		*Gladys Knight & The Pips*
5/15/65	**I'll Never Find Another You**	10/15/66	**I've Got You Under My Skin**
	Seekers		*4 Seasons*
10/20/79	**I'll Never Love This Way Again**	9/28/68	**I've Gotta Get A Message To You** *Bee Gees*
	Dionne Warwick		
6/03/72	**I'll Take You There**	3/09/59	**I've Had It** *Bell Notes*
	Staple Singers	11/28/87	**(I've Had) The Time Of My Life**
8/27/83	**I'll Tumble 4 Ya** *Culture Club*		*Bill Medley & Jennifer Warnes*
12/31/66	**I'm A Believer** *Monkees*		**I've Loved You For A Long Time**..see: Cupid
5/06/67	**I'm A Man** *Spencer Davis Group*		
10/11/80	**I'm Alright** *Kenny Loggins*	5/22/82	**I've Never Been To Me** *Charlene*
11/15/80	**I'm Coming Out** *Diana Ross*	5/01/61	**I've Told Every Little Star**
10/26/85	**I'm Goin' Down** *Bruce Springsteen*		*Linda Scott*
12/12/64	**I'm Gonna Be Strong** *Gene Pitney*	5/15/71	**If** *Bread*
9/14/59	**I'm Gonna Get Married**	8/18/84	**If Ever You're In My Arms Again** *Peabo Bryson*
	Lloyd Price		
6/23/73	**I'm Gonna Love You Just A Little More Baby** *Barry White*	5/13/78	**If I Can't Have You**
			Yvonne Elliman
1/11/69	**I'm Gonna Make You Love Me**	1/20/68	**If I Could Build My Whole World Around You**
	Supremes & Temptations		*Marvin Gaye & Tammi Terrell*
10/25/69	**I'm Gonna Make You Mine**	11/25/72	**If I Could Reach You**
	Lou Christie		*5th Dimension*
8/07/65	**I'm Henry VIII, I Am**		**If I Had A Hammer**
	Herman's Hermits	10/13/62	*Peter, Paul & Mary*
7/30/77	**I'm In You** *Peter Frampton*	9/07/63	*Trini Lopez*
	I'm Leaving It Up To You	11/05/66	**If I Were A Carpenter**
11/23/63	*Dale & Grace*		*Bobby Darin*
9/14/74	*Donny & Marie Osmond*	2/13/71	**If I Were Your Woman**
2/22/69	**I'm Livin' In Shame**		*Gladys Knight & The Pips*
	Diana Ross & The Supremes	8/05/72	**(If Loving You Is Wrong) I Don't Want To Be Right** *Luther Ingram*
7/26/75	**I'm Not In Love** *10cc*		
6/21/75	**I'm Not Lisa** *Jessi Colter*	9/15/84	**If This Is It**
4/13/85	**I'm On Fire** *Bruce Springsteen*		*Huey Lewis & The News*
12/10/66	**I'm Ready For Love**	2/20/71	**If You Could Read My Mind**
	Martha & The Vandellas		*Gordon Lightfoot*
10/27/84	**I'm So Excited** *Pointer Sisters*	12/09/72	**If You Don't Know Me By Now**
4/09/66	**I'm So Lonesome I Could Cry**		*Harold Melvin & The Bluenotes*
	B.J. Thomas	5/31/86	**If You Leave**
7/18/60	**I'm Sorry** *Brenda Lee*		*Orchestral Manoeuvres In The Dark*
9/27/75	**I'm Sorry** *John Denver*	10/23/76	**If You Leave Me Now** *Chicago*
9/02/72	**I'm Still In Love With You**	8/29/70	**(If You Let Me Make Love To You Then) Why Can't I Touch You?** *Ronnie Dyson*
	Al Green		
12/09/72	**I'm Stone In Love With You**	6/29/74	**If You Love Me (Let Me Know)**
	Stylistics		*Olivia Newton-John*
4/10/65	**I'm Telling You Now**	8/03/85	**If You Love Somebody Set Them Free** *Sting*
	Freddie & The Dreamers		
6/11/77	**I'm Your Boogie Man**		
	KC & The Sunshine Band		

564

10/16/71	**If You Really Love Me** *Stevie Wonder*
5/18/63	**If You Wanna Be Happy** *Jimmy Soul*
12/22/73	**If You're Ready (Come Go With Me)** *Staple Singers*
8/01/60	**Image Of A Girl** *Safaris*
6/03/78	**Imaginary Lover** *Atlanta Rhythm Section*
11/13/71	**Imagine** *John Lennon Plastic Ono Band*
12/09/67	**In And Out Of Love** *Diana Ross & The Supremes*
10/09/65	**"In" Crowd** *Ramsey Lewis Trio*
3/30/63	**In Dreams** *Roy Orbison*
6/08/85	**In My House** *Mary Jane Girls*
8/29/60	**In My Little Corner Of The World** *Anita Bryant*
6/14/69	**In The Ghetto** *Elvis Presley*
12/14/59	**In The Mood** *Ernie Field's Orch.*
5/19/79	**In The Navy** *Village People*
4/22/72	**In The Rain** *Dramatics*
9/12/70	**In The Summertime** *Mungo Jerry*
7/12/69	**In The Year 2525** *Zager & Evans*
6/27/87	**In Too Deep** *Genesis*
11/25/67	**Incense And Peppermints** *Strawberry Alarm Clock*
3/22/69	**Indian Giver** *1910 Fruitgum o.*
7/13/68	**Indian Lake** *Cowsills*
7/24/67	**Indian Reservation** *Raiders*
11/07/70	**Indiana Wants Me** *R. Dean Taylor*
7/28/84	**Infatuation** *Rod Stewart*
11/06/71	**Inner City Blues (Make Me Wanna Holler)** *Marvin Gaye*
2/25/84	**Innocent Man** *Billy Joel*
3/28/70	**Instant Karma (We All Shine On)** *John Ono Lennon*
9/14/85	**Invincible** *Pat Benatar*
7/19/86	**Invisible Touch** *Genesis*
5/31/86	**Is It Love** *Mr. Mister*
8/06/83	**Is There Something I Should Know** *Duran Duran*
1/17/87	**Is This Love** *Survivor*
12/19/87	**Is This Love** *Whitesnake*
12/26/70	**Isn't It A Pity** *George Harrison*
11/01/75	**Island Girl** *Elton John*
10/29/83	**Islands In The Stream** *Kenny Rogers & Dolly Parton*
6/28/69	**Israelites** *Desmond Dekker & The Aces*
9/18/65	**It Ain't Me Babe** *Turtles*
6/05/71	**It Don't Come Easy** *Ringo Starr*
11/14/70	**It Don't Matter To Me** *Bread*
10/03/64	**It Hurts To Be In Love** *Gene Pitney*
6/16/62	**It Keeps Right On A-Hurtin'** *Johnny Tillotson*
11/04/67	**It Must Be Him** *Vikki Carr*
12/16/72	**It Never Rains In Southern California** *Albert Hammond*
10/25/75	**It Only Takes A Minute** *Tavares*
6/24/78	**It's A Heartache** *Bonnie Tyler*

6/04/66	**It's A Man's Man's Man's World** *James Brown*
8/20/83	**It's A Mistake** *Men At Work*
11/14/87	**It's A Sin** *Pet Shop Boys*
9/29/58	**It's All In The Game** *Tommy Edwards*
11/09/63	**It's All Right** *Impressions*
11/12/77	**It's Ecstasy When You Lay Down Next To Me** *Barry White*
6/12/82	**It's Gonna Take A Miracle** *Deniece Williams*
1/23/71	**It's Impossible** *Perry Como*
	It's In His Kiss ..*see: Shoop Shoop Song*
4/06/59	**It's Just A Matter Of Time** *Brook Benton*
4/06/59	**It's Late** *Ricky Nelson*
6/01/63	**It's My Party** *Lesley Gore*
1/24/81	**It's My Turn** *Diana Ross*
8/29/87	**It's Not Over ('Til It's Over)** *Starship*
5/29/65	**It's Not Unusual** *Tom Jones*
8/15/60	**It's Now Or Never** *Elvis Presley*
	It's Only Make Believe
11/10/58	*Conway Twitty*
10/31/70	*Glen Campbell*
5/23/64	**It's Over** *Roy Orbison*
12/10/77	**It's So Easy** *Linda Ronstadt*
7/19/80	**It's Still Rock And Roll To Me** *Billy Joel*
8/28/65	**It's The Same Old Song** *Four Tops*
12/28/59	**It's Time To Cry** *Paul Anka*
6/19/71	**It's Too Late** *Carole King*
2/02/63	**It's Up To You** *Rick Nelson*
5/03/69	**It's Your Thing** *Isley Brothers*
8/08/60	**Itsy Bitsy Teenie Weenie Yellow Polkadot Bikini** *Brian Hyland*

J

10/02/82	**Jack & Diane** *John Cougar*
4/15/78	**Jack And Jill** *Raydio*
5/17/75	**Jackie Blue** *Ozark Mountain Daredevils*
3/14/87	**Jacob's Ladder** *Huey Lewis & The News*
1/17/70	**Jam Up Jelly Tight** *Tommy Roe*
2/29/64	**Java** *Al Hirt*
11/09/74	**Jazzman** *Carole King*
10/04/69	**Jean** *Oliver*
	Jenny ..*see: 867-5309*
1/29/66	**Jenny Take A Ride!** *Mitch Ryder/Detroit Wheels*
5/07/83	**Jeopardy** *Greg Kihn*
1/16/65	**Jerk, The** *Larks*
8/01/81	**Jessie's Girl** *Rick Springfield*
3/30/74	**Jet** *Paul McCartney & Wings*
7/09/77	**Jet Airliner** *Steve Miller Band*
4/15/67	**Jimmy Mack** *Martha & The Vandellas*
2/07/70	**Jingle Jangle** *Archies*
8/09/75	**Jive Talkin'** *Bee Gees*

2/11/84	**Joanna** *Kool & The Gang*
4/07/62	**Johnny Angel** *Shelley Fabares*
7/21/62	**Johnny Get Angry**
	Joanie Sommers
1/12/74	**Joker, The** *Steve Miller Band*
3/06/65	**Jolly Green Giant** *Kingsmen*
2/26/72	**Joy** *Apollo 100*
4/17/71	**Joy To The World**
	Three Dog Night
1/20/68	**Judy In Disguise (With Glasses)**
	John Fred & His Playboy Band
8/17/63	**Judy's Turn To Cry** *Lesley Gore*
9/19/70	**Julie, Do Ya Love Me**
	Bobby Sherman
2/25/84	**Jump** *Van Halen*
7/07/84	**Jump (For My Love)**
	Pointer Sisters
7/06/68	**Jumpin' Jack Flash**
	Rolling Stones
3/09/74	**Jungle Boogie** *Kool & The Gang*
3/25/72	**Jungle Fever** *Chakachas*
1/11/75	**Junior's Farm**
	Paul McCartney & Wings
3/20/76	**Junk Food Junkie** *Larry Groce*
8/25/58	**Just A Dream** *Jimmy Clanton*
6/05/65	**Just A Little** *Beau Brummels*
10/16/65	**Just A Little Bit Better**
	Herman's Hermits
8/17/59	**Just A Little Too Much**
	Ricky Nelson
8/27/77	**Just A Song Before I Go**
	Crosby, Stills & Nash
10/26/59	**Just Ask Your Heart**
	Frankie Avalon
5/04/74	**Just Don't Want To Be Lonely**
	Main Ingredient
3/16/68	**Just Dropped In (To See What Condition My Condition Was In)** *First Edition*
3/12/88	**Just Like Paradise**
	David Lee Roth
5/30/64	**(Just Like) Romeo & Juliet**
	Reflections
12/27/80	**(Just Like) Starting Over**
	John Lennon
4/03/71	**Just My Imagination (Running Away With Me)** *Temptations*
5/15/65	**Just Once In My Life**
	Righteous Brothers
7/27/63	**Just One Look** *Doris Troy*
5/02/81	**Just The Two Of Us**
	Grover Washington, Jr./Bill Withers
2/18/78	**Just The Way You Are** *Billy Joel*
11/27/76	**Just To Be Close To You**
	Commodores
7/04/87	**Just To See Her**
	Smokey Robinson
6/16/79	**Just When I Needed You Most**
	Randy Vanwarmer
12/08/73	**Just You 'N' Me** *Chicago*

K

5/18/59	**Kansas City** *Wilbert Harrison*
2/04/84	**Karma Chameleon** *Culture Club*
8/20/83	**(Keep Feeling) Fascination**
	Human League
10/01/77	**Keep It Comin' Love**
	KC & The Sunshine Band
10/30/65	**Keep On Dancing** *Gentrys*
3/21/81	**Keep On Loving You**
	REO Speedwagon
7/18/64	**Keep On Pushing** *Impressions*
8/24/74	**Keep On Smilin'** *Wet Willie*
11/10/73	**Keep On Truckin'** *Eddie Kendricks*
1/30/65	**Keep Searchin'** *Del Shannon*
8/14/82	**Keep The Fire Burnin'**
	REO Speedwagon
2/21/87	**Keep Your Hands To Yourself**
	Georgia Satellites
1/13/73	**Keeper Of The Castle** *Four Tops*
4/17/82	**Key Largo** *Bertie Higgins*
5/14/66	**Kicks** *Paul Revere & The Raiders*
9/19/60	**Kiddio** *Brook Benton*
2/24/73	**Killing Me Softly With His Song**
	Roberta Flack
2/18/67	**Kind Of A Drag** *Buckinghams*
3/22/86	**King For A Day** *Thompson Twins*
10/08/83	**King Of Pain** *Police*
3/20/65	**King Of The Road** *Roger Miller*
4/19/86	**Kiss** *Prince & The Revolution*
7/24/76	**Kiss And Say Goodbye**
	Manhattans
4/11/81	**Kiss On My List**
	Daryl Hall & John Oates
9/30/78	**Kiss You All Over** *Exile*
4/21/79	**Knock On Wood** *Amii Stewart*
1/23/71	**Knock Three Times** *Dawn*
7/07/73	**Kodachrome** *Paul Simon*
5/11/59	**Kookie, Kookie (Lend Me Your Comb)**
	Edward Byrnes & Connie Stevens
12/07/74	**Kung Fu Fighting** *Carl Douglas*
3/01/86	**Kyrie** *Mr. Mister*

L

8/29/87	**La Bamba** *Los Lobos*
5/02/87	**La Isla Bonita** *Madonna*
1/10/70	**La La La (If I Had You)**
	Bobby Sherman
4/06/68	**La - La - Means I Love You**
	Delfonics
1/12/80	**Ladies Night** *Kool & The Gang*
3/08/75	**Lady** *Styx*
4/07/79	**Lady** *Little River Band*
11/15/80	**Lady** *Kenny Rogers*
12/10/66	**Lady Godiva** *Peter & Gordon*
5/23/87	**Lady In Red** *Chris DeBurgh*
4/20/68	**Lady Madonna** *Beatles*
3/29/75	**Lady Marmalade** *LaBelle*
7/20/68	**Lady Willpower**
	Gary Puckett & The Union Gap

6/13/64	**Little Children** *Billy J. Kramer*
8/18/62	**Little Diane** *Dion*
7/09/66	**Little Girl** *Syndicate Of Sound*
10/26/68	**Little Green Apples** *O.C. Smith*
10/31/64	**Little Honda** *Hondells*
7/19/80	**Little Jeannie** *Elton John*
11/07/87	**Little Lies** *Fleetwood Mac*
2/17/79	**Little More Love**
	Olivia Newton-John
8/01/64	**Little Old Lady (From**
	Pasadena) *Jan & Dean*
10/14/67	**Little Ole Man**
	(Uptight-Everything's Alright)
	Bill Cosby
5/21/83	**Little Red Corvette** *Prince*
10/02/61	**Little Sister** *Elvis Presley*
8/25/58	**Little Star** *Elegants*
5/05/73	**Little Willy** *Sweet*
10/04/69	**Little Woman** *Bobby Sherman*
8/11/73	**Live And Let Die** *Wings*
6/07/86	**Live To Tell** *Madonna*
2/14/87	**Livin' On A Prayer** *Bon Jovi*
1/12/74	**Living For The City**
	Stevie Wonder
3/01/86	**Living In America** *James Brown*
5/30/81	**Living Inside Myself** *Gino Vannelli*
	Loco-Motion
8/25/62	*Little Eva*
5/04/74	*Grand Funk*
6/16/79	**Logical Song** *Supertramp*
10/24/74	**Lola** *Kinks*
2/08/60	**Lonely Blue Boy** *Conway Twitty*
7/13/59	**Lonely Boy** *Paul Anka*
6/11/77	**Lonely Boy** *Andrew Gold*
12/08/62	**Lonely Bull** *Tijuana Brass*
1/30/71	**Lonely Days** *Bee Gees*
3/27/76	**Lonely Night (Angel Face)**
	Captain & Tennille
10/12/85	**Lonely Ol' Night**
	John Cougar Mellencamp
3/08/75	**Lonely People** *America*
11/09/59	**Lonely Street** *Andy Williams*
2/09/59	**Lonely Teardrops** *Jackie Wilson*
9/29/79	**Lonesome Loser** *Little River Band*
12/01/58	**Lonesome Town** *Ricky Nelson*
6/13/70	**Long And Winding Road** *Beatles*
10/03/70	**Long As I Can See The Light**
	Creedence Clearwater Revival
9/02/72	**Long Cool Woman (In A Black**
	Dress) *Hollies*
2/02/80	**Long Run** *Eagles*
5/03/75	**Long Tall Glasses (I Can**
	Dance) *Leo Sayer*
6/30/73	**Long Train Runnin'**
	Doobie Brothers
3/15/80	**Longer** *Dan Fogelberg*
11/23/74	**Longfellow Serenade**
	Neil Diamond
7/06/68	**Look Of Love**
	Sergio Mendes & Brasil '66
5/27/72	**Look What You Done For Me**
	Al Green

4/27/74	**Lookin' For A Love**
	Bobby Womack
9/20/80	**Lookin' For Love** *Johnny Lee*
10/03/70	**Lookin' Out My Back Door**
	Creedence Clearwater Revival
5/02/87	**Looking For A New Love**
	Jody Watley
7/23/77	**Looks Like We Made It**
	Barry Manilow
2/09/63	**Loop De Loop** *Johnny Thunder*
4/13/74	**Lord's Prayer** *Sister Janet Mead*
5/25/63	**Losing You** *Brenda Lee*
10/17/87	**Lost In Emotion**
	Lisa Lisa & Cult Jam
5/03/80	**Lost In Love** *Air Supply*
2/19/77	**Lost Without Your Love** *Bread*
2/17/79	**Lotta Love** *Nicolette Larson*
12/14/63	**Louie Louie** *Kingsmen*
12/22/62	**Love Came To Me** *Dion*
5/31/69	**Love (Can Make You Happy)**
	Mercy
11/30/68	**Love Child**
	Diana Ross & The Supremes
3/28/70	**Love Grows (Where My**
	Rosemary Goes)
	Edison Lighthouse
5/29/76	**Love Hangover** *Diana Ross*
3/13/76	**Love Hurts** *Nazareth*
12/08/73	**Love I Lost**
	Harold Melvin & The Bluenotes
12/10/83	**Love Is A Battlefield** *Pat Benatar*
11/15/75	**Love Is A Rose** *Linda Ronstadt*
7/31/76	**Love Is Alive** *Gary Wright*
5/18/68	**Love Is All Around** *Troggs*
2/10/68	**Love Is Blue** *Paul MMuriat*
3/11/67	**Love Is Here And Now You're**
	Gone *Supremes*
9/25/82	**Love Is In Control (Finger On The**
	Trigger) *Donna Summer*
10/14/78	**Love Is In The Air**
	John Paul Young
5/28/66	**Love Is Like An Itching In My**
	Heart *Supremes*
6/24/78	**Love Is Like Oxygen** *Sweet*
5/26/79	**Love Is The Answer**
	England Dan & John Ford Coley
3/04/78	**(Love Is) Thicker Than Water**
	Andy Gibb
4/14/62	**Love Letters** *Ketty Lester*
3/06/76	**Love Machine** *Miracles*
5/30/64	**Love Me Do** *Beatles*
10/19/74	**Love Me For A Reason** *Osmonds*
6/13/64	**Love Me With All Your Heart**
	Ray Charles Singers
5/30/70	**Love On A Two-Way Street**
	Moments
1/10/81	**Love On The Rocks** *Neil Diamond*
5/02/70	**Love Or Let Me Be Lonely**
	Friends Of Distinction
1/16/65	**Love Potion Number Nine**
	Searchers
1/31/76	**Love Rollercoaster** *Ohio Players*
11/20/76	**Love So Right** *Bee Gees*

5/05/84	**Love Somebody** *Rick Springfield*	
	Love Story ..see: (Where Do I Begin)	
3/05/77	**Love Theme From "A Star Is Born" (Evergreen)**	
	Barbra Streisand	
6/28/69	**Love Theme From Romeo & Juliet** *Henry Mancini*	
2/07/76	**Love To Love You Baby**	
	Donna Summer	
8/09/86	**Love Touch** *Rod Stewart*	
3/24/73	**Love Train** *O'Jays*	
11/29/86	**Love Will Conquer All**	
	Lionel Richie	
8/26/78	**Love Will Find A Way**	
	Pablo Cruise	
6/21/75	**Love Will Keep Us Together**	
	Captain & Tennille	
6/21/75	**Love Won't Let Me Wait**	
	Major Harris	
2/21/87	**Love You Down**	
	Ready For The World	
6/09/79	**Love You Inside Out** *Bee Gees*	
6/27/70	**Love You Save** *Jackson 5*	
6/13/60	**Love You So** *Ron Holden*	
9/27/86	**Love Zone** *Billy Ocean*	
7/10/82	**Love's Been A Little Bit Hard On Me** *Juice Newton*	
2/09/74	**Love's Theme**	
	Love Unlimited Orchestra	
4/21/62	**Lover Please** *Clyde McPhatter*	
10/30/65	**Lover's Concerto** *Toys*	
1/19/59	**Lover's Question** *Clyde McPhatter*	
2/23/85	**Loverboy** *Billy Ocean*	
3/30/85	**Lovergirl** *Teena Marie*	
6/09/62	**Lovers Who Wander** *Dion*	
10/06/73	**Loves Me Like A Rock**	
	Paul Simon	
11/02/85	**Lovin' Every Minute Of It**	
	Loverboy	
4/05/75	**Lovin' You** *Minnie Riperton*	
11/29/75	**Low Rider** *War*	
10/09/76	**Lowdown** *Boz Scaggs*	
6/18/77	**Lucille** *Kenny Rogers*	
10/20/84	**Lucky Star** *Madonna*	
1/04/75	**Lucy In The Sky With Diamonds**	
	Elton John	
8/22/87	**Luka** *Suzanne Vega*	
11/08/75	**Lyin' Eyes** *Eagles*	

M

3/14/70	**Ma Belle Amie** *Tee Set*	
	MacArthur Park	
6/22/68	*Richard Harris*	
11/11/78	*Donna Summer*	
10/05/59	**Mack The Knife** *Bobby Darin*	
8/09/86	**Mad About You** *Belinda Carlisle*	
10/02/71	**Maggie May** *Rod Stewart*	
7/12/75	**Magic** *Pilot*	
8/02/80	**Magic** *Olivia Newton-John*	
11/30/68	**Magic Carpet Ride** *Steppenwolf*	
11/06/76	**Magic Man** *Heart*	
8/26/78	**Magnet And Steel** *Walter Egan*	

	Mahogany ..see: Theme From	
8/11/79	**Main Event/Fight**	
	Barbra Streisand	
4/03/82	**Make A Move On Me**	
	Olivia Newton-John	
6/25/88	**Make It Real** *Jets*	
8/22/70	**Make It With You** *Bread*	
6/06/70	**Make Me Smile** *Chicago*	
12/25/65	**Make The World Go Away**	
	Eddy Arnold	
7/21/79	**Makin' It** *David Naughton*	
10/08/83	**Making Love Out Of Nothing At All** *Air Supply*	
4/11/60	**Mama** *Connie Francis*	
8/25/79	**Mama Can't Buy You Love**	
	Elton John	
6/27/70	**Mama Liked The Roses**	
	Elvis Presley	
5/29/61	**Mama Said** *Shirelles*	
7/11/70	**Mama Told Me (Not To Come)**	
	Three Dog Night	
2/27/71	**Mama's Pearl** *Jackson 5*	
	Man In Motion ..see: St. Elmo's Fire	
3/26/88	**Man In The Mirror**	
	Michael Jackson	
6/16/62	**(Man Who Shot) Liberty Valance** *Gene Pitney*	
3/21/87	**Mandolin Rain** *Bruce Hornsby*	
1/18/75	**Mandy** *Barry Manilow*	
12/18/82	**Maneater** *Daryl Hall & John Oates*	
2/09/59	**Manhattan Spiritual** *Reg Owen*	
9/10/83	**Maniac** *Michael Sembello*	
4/19/86	**Manic Monday** *Bangles*	
12/26/60	**Many Tears Ago** *Connie Francis*	
7/23/77	**Margaritaville** *Jimmy Buffett*	
11/16/63	**Maria Elena** *Los Indios Tabajaras*	
9/18/61	**(Marie's the Name) His Latest Flame** *Elvis Presley*	
5/05/62	**Mashed Potato Time**	
	Dee Dee Sharp	
12/06/80	**Master Blaster (Jammin')**	
	Stevie Wonder	
4/28/73	**Masterpiece** *Temptations*	
3/23/85	**Material Girl** *Madonna*	
10/18/86	**Matter Of Trust** *Billy Joel*	
4/02/77	**Maybe I'm Amazed** *Wings*	
3/20/71	**Me And Bobby McGee**	
	Janis Joplin	
12/16/72	**Me And Mrs. Jones** *Billy Paul*	
5/15/71	**Me And You And A Dog Named Boo** *Lobo*	
11/02/63	**Mean Woman Blues** *Roy Orbison*	
12/10/66	**Mellow Yellow** *Donovan*	
	Memphis	
7/20/63	*Lonnie Mack*	
7/11/64	*Johnny Rivers*	
2/05/66	**Men In My Little Girl's Life**	
	Mike Douglas	
7/09/88	**Mercedes Boy** *Pebbles*	
8/12/67	**Mercy, Mercy, Mercy**	
	Buckinghams	
5/14/66	**Message To Michael**	
	Dionne Warwick	

2/16/85	**Method Of Modern Love** *Daryl Hall John Oates*
10/02/61	**Mexico** *Bob Moore*
11/09/85	**Miami Vice Theme** *Jan Hammer*
9/04/61	**Michael** *Highwaymen*
12/11/82	**Mickey** *Toni Basil*
9/21/63	**Mickey's Monkey** *Miracles*
6/01/74	**Midnight At The Oasis** *Maria Muldaur*
8/09/75	**Midnight Blue** *Melissa Manchester*
4/18/87	**Midnight Blue** *Lou Gramm*
11/02/68	**Midnight Confessions** *Grass Roots*
1/17/70	**Midnight Cowboy** *Ferrante & Teicher*
3/17/62	**Midnight In Moscow** *Kenny Ball*
1/04/64	**Midnight Mary** *Joey Powers*
10/27/73	**Midnight Train To Georgia** *Gladys Knight & The Pips*
4/13/68	**Mighty Quinn (Quinn The** **Eskimo)** *Manfred Mann*
9/26/60	**Million To One** *Jimmy Charles*
10/18/75	**Miracles** *Jefferson Starship*
6/17/67	**Mirage** *Tommy James & The Shondells*
3/06/82	**Mirror, Mirror** *Diana Ross*
3/09/85	**Misled** *Kool & The Gang*
4/21/84	**Miss Me Blind** *Culture Club*
8/05/78	**Miss You** *Rolling Stones*
9/22/84	**Missing You** *John Waite*
4/13/85	**Missing You** *Diana Ross*
9/05/60	**Mission Bell** *Donnie Brooks*
	Mister..see: Mr.
6/12/76	**Misty Blue** *Dorthy Moore*
	Mockingbird
9/07/63	*Inez & Charlie Foxx*
3/23/74	*Carly Simon & James Taylor*
7/26/86	**Modern Woman** *Billy Joel*
5/07/66	**Monday, Monday** *Mamas & The Papas*
9/21/85	**Money For Nothing** *Dire Straits*
4/03/76	**Money Honey** *Bay City Rollers*
9/07/63	**Monkey Time** *Major Lance*
	Monster Mash
10/20/62	*Bobby "Boris" Pickett*
8/11/73	*Bobby "Boris" Pickett*
11/28/70	**Montego Bay** *Bobby Bloom*
	Mony Mony
6/15/68	*Tommy James & The Shondells*
11/21/87	*Billy Idol*
6/19/61	**Moody River** *Pat Boone*
7/31/76	**Moonlight Feels Right** *Starbuck*
8/24/63	**More** *Kai Winding*
8/16/80	**More Love** *Kim Carnes*
7/17/76	**More, More, More** *Andrea True Connection*
12/25/76	**More Than A Feeling** *Boston*
12/06/80	**More Than I Can Say** *Leo Sayer*
8/04/73	**Morning After** *Maureen McGovern*
5/27/72	**Morning Has Broken** *Cat Stevens*
1/25/75	**Morning Side Of The Mountain** *Donny & Marie Osmond*

5/02/81	**Morning Train (Nine To Five)** *Sheena Easton*
12/15/73	**Most Beautiful Girl** *Charlie Rich*
4/01/72	**Mother And Child Reunion** *Paul Simon*
5/22/61	**Mother-In-Law** *Ernie K-Doe*
8/13/66	**Mothers Little Helper** *Rolling Stones*
12/05/64	**Mountain Of Love** *Johnny Rivers*
9/25/61	**Mountain's High** *Dick & DeeDee*
8/14/71	**Mr. Big Stuff** *Jean Knight*
11/16/59	**Mr. Blue** *Fleetwoods*
2/20/71	**Mr. Bojangles** *Nitty Gritty Dirt Band*
10/10/60	**Mr. Custer** *Larry Verne*
10/11/75	**Mr. Jaws** *Dickie Goodman*
12/12/64	**Mr. Lonely** *Bobby Vinton*
4/16/83	**Mr. Roboto** *Styx*
6/26/65	**Mr. Tambourine Man** *Byrds*
5/01/65	**Mrs. Brown You've Got A Lovely** **Daughter** *Herman's Hermits*
6/01/68	**Mrs. Robinson** *Simon & Garfunkel*
7/11/60	**Mule Skinner Blues** *Fendermen*
11/13/82	**Muscles** *Diana Ross*
5/05/79	**Music Box Dancer** *Frank Mills*
11/20/76	**Muskrat Love** *Captain & Tennille*
1/22/66	**Must To Avoid** *Herman's Hermits*
7/04/64	**My Boy Lollipop** *Millie Small*
8/31/63	**My Boyfriend's Back** *Angels*
7/26/69	**My Cherie Amour** *Stevie Wonder*
3/25/67	**My Cup Runneth Over** *Ed Ames*
1/26/63	**My Dad** *Paul Petersen*
10/21/72	**My Ding-A-Ling** *Chuck Berry*
2/06/61	**My Empty Arms** *Jackie Wilson*
3/22/75	**My Eyes Adored You** *Frankie Valli*
3/06/65	**My Girl** *Temptations*
5/16/64	**My Guy** *Mary Wells*
1/19/59	**My Happiness** *Connie Francis*
7/30/77	**My Heart Belongs To Me** *Barbra Streisand*
3/28/64	**My Heart Belongs To Only You** *Bobby Vinton*
9/26/60	**My Heart Has A Mind Of Its** **Own** *Connie Francis*
8/03/59	**My Heart Is An Open Book** *Carl Dobkins, Jr.*
7/04/60	**My Home Town** *Paul Anka*
1/25/86	**My Hometown** *Bruce Springsteen*
1/06/79	**My Life** *Billy Joel*
12/13/75	**My Little Town** *Simon & Garfunkel*
2/05/66	**My Love** *Petula Clark*
6/02/73	**My Love** *Paul McCartney & Wings*
6/11/83	**My Love** *Lionel Richie*
9/29/73	**My Maria** *B.W. Stevenson*
11/16/74	**My Melody Of Love** *Bobby Vinton*
8/25/79	**My Sharona** *Knack*
10/12/68	**My Special Angel** *Vogues*
12/26/70	**My Sweet Lord** *George Harrison*
8/18/58	**My True Love** *Jack Scott*
9/11/61	**My True Story** *Jive Five*
3/29/69	**My Whole World Ended (The** **Moment You Left Me)** *David Ruffin*

8/26/67	**Ode To Billie Joe** *Bobbie Gentry*	
4/12/80	**Off The Wall** *Michael Jackson*	
2/17/73	**Oh, Babe, What Would You Say?** *Hurricane Smith*	
12/07/59	**Oh! Carol** *Neil Sedaka*	
5/27/72	**Oh Girl** *Chi-Lites*	
5/31/69	**Oh Happy Day**	
	Edwin Hawkins' Singers	
4/27/74	**Oh My My** *Ringo Starr*	
12/05/81	**Oh No** *Commodores*	
9/26/64	**Oh, Pretty Woman** *Roy Orbison*	
10/12/85	**Oh Sheila** *Ready For The World*	
6/09/84	**Oh Sherrie** *Steve Perry*	
6/01/74	**Oh Very Young** *Cat Stevens*	
9/27/69	**Oh, What A Night** *Dells*	
	(also see: December, 1963)	
4/17/71	**Oh Woman Oh Why**	
	Paul McCartney	
6/07/75	**Old Days** *Chicago*	
12/18/71	**Old Fashioned Love Song**	
	Three Dog Night	
5/02/60	**Old Lamplighter** *Browns*	
3/02/85	**Old Man Down The Road**	
	John Fogerty	
5/26/62	**Old Rivers** *Walter Brennan*	
7/13/74	**On And On**	
	Gladys Knight & The Pips	
	On Broadway	
4/27/63	*Drifters*	
6/10/78	*George Benson*	
6/14/86	**On My Own**	
	Patti LaBelle & Michael McDonald	
10/27/84	**On The Dark Side**	
	John Cafferty/Beaver Brown Band	
3/08/80	**On The Radio** *Donna Summer*	
4/17/61	**On The Rebound** *Floyd Cramer*	
4/12/75	**Once You Get Started**	
	Rufus Featuring Chaka Khan	
6/28/69	**One** *Three Dog Night*	
2/13/71	**One Bad Apple** *Osmonds*	
7/13/63	**One Fine Day** *Chiffons*	
10/03/87	**One Heartbeat** *Smokey Robinson*	
12/05/87	**One I Love** *R.E.M.*	
9/20/80	**One In A Million You**	
	Larry Graham	
12/26/70	**One Less Bell To Answer**	
	5th Dimension	
1/25/75	**One Man Woman/One Woman Man** *Paul Anka/Odia Coates*	
5/01/61	**One Mint Julep** *Ray Charles*	
3/30/85	**One More Night** *Phil Collins*	
5/28/88	**One More Try** *George Michael*	
12/15/58	**One Night** *Elvis Presley*	
5/18/85	**One Night In Bangkok**	
	Murray Head	
8/02/75	**One Of These Nights** *Eagles*	
4/09/83	**One On One**	
	Daryl Hall & John Oates	
7/25/81	**One That You Love** *Air Supply*	
11/05/83	**One Thing Leads To Another** *Fixx*	
4/10/71	**One Toke Over The Line**	
	Brewer & Shipley	

9/18/61	**One Track Mind** *Bobby Lewis*	
11/20/65	**1-2-3** *Len Barry*	
9/14/68	**1, 2, 3 Red Light**	
	1910 Fruitgum Co.	
6/09/62	**One Who Really Loves You**	
	Mary Wells	
9/05/87	**Only In My Dreams**	
	Debbie Gibson	
11/03/62	**Only Love Can Break A Heart**	
	Gene Pitney	
4/17/76	**Only Sixteen** *Dr. Hook*	
7/25/60	**Only The Lonely** *Roy Orbison*	
7/17/82	**Only The Lonely** *Motels*	
4/19/69	**Only The Strong Survive**	
	Jerry Butler	
3/23/85	**Only The Young** *Journey*	
5/24/75	**Only Yesterday** *Carpenters*	
	Only You	
6/01/59	*Franck Pourcel*	
1/11/75	*Ringo Starr*	
1/20/79	**Ooh Baby Baby** *Linda Ronstadt*	
7/18/70	**O-o-h Child** *Five Stairsteps*	
2/27/82	**Open Arms** *Journey*	
12/02/67	**Open Letter To My Teenage Son** *Victor Lundberg*	
2/07/87	**Open Your Heart** *Madonna*	
8/02/86	**Opportunities (Let's Make Lots Of Money)** *Pet Shop Boys*	
6/12/82	**Other Woman** *Ray Parker Jr.*	
3/23/63	**Our Day Will Come**	
	Ruby & The Romantics	
7/23/83	**Our House** *Madness*	
4/15/78	**Our Love** *Natalie Cole*	
12/16/78	**(Our Love) Don't Throw It All Away** *Andy Gibb*	
3/30/63	**Our Winter Love** *Bill Pursell*	
2/01/64	**Out Of Limits** *Marketts*	
4/09/88	**Out Of The Blue** *Debbie Gibson*	
12/08/84	**Out Of Touch**	
	Daryl Hall John Oates	
7/08/72	**Outa-Space** *Billy Preston*	
12/25/65	**Over And Over** *Dave Clark Five*	
10/26/68	**Over You**	
	Gary Puckett & The Union Gap	
6/04/83	**Overkill** *Men At Work*	
1/21/84	**Owner Of A Lonely Heart** *Yes*	

P

6/06/64	**P.S. I Love You** *Beatles*	
5/26/62	**P.T. 109** *Jimmy Dean*	
11/26/83	**P.Y.T. (Pretty Young Thing)**	
	Michael Jackson	
3/27/82	**Pac-Man Fever** *Buckner & Garcia*	
6/11/66	**Paint It, Black** *Rolling Stones*	
6/23/62	**Palisades Park** *Freddy Cannon*	
8/16/86	**Papa Don't Preach** *Madonna*	
	Papa Joe's..*see: Down At*	
12/02/72	**Papa Was A Rollin' Stone**	
	Temptations	
9/04/65	**Papa's Got A Brand New Bag**	
	James Brown	

10/03/87	**Paper In Fire**	3/14/64	**Please Please Me** *Beatles*
	John Cougar Mellencamp	11/14/60	**Poetry In Motion** *Johnny Tillotson*
	Paper Roses	4/12/75	**Poetry Man** *Phoebe Snow*
6/13/60	*Anita Bryant*	7/18/87	**Point Of No Return** *Expose*
11/03/73	*Marie Osmond*	10/12/59	**Poison Ivy** *Coasters*
6/25/66	**Paperback Writer** *Beatles*	8/23/69	**Polk Salad Annie** *Tony Joe White*
11/02/85	**Part-Time Lover** *Stevie Wonder*	2/27/61	**Pony Time** *Chubby Checker*
12/28/85	**Party All The Time** *Eddie Murphy*	8/04/58	**Poor Little Fool** *Ricky Nelson*
9/01/62	**Party Lights** *Claudine Clark*	11/12/66	**Poor Side Of Town** *Johnny Rivers*
2/26/83	**Pass The Dutchie** *Musical Youth*	9/21/85	**Pop Life** *Prince & The Revolution*
2/07/81	**Passion** *Rod Stewart*	11/03/79	**Pop Muzik** *M*
10/06/62	**Patches** *Dickey Lee*	10/21/72	**Popcorn** *Hot Butter*
9/19/70	**Patches** *Clarence Carter*	11/10/62	**Popeye The Hitchhiker**
11/06/71	**Peace Train** *Cat Stevens*		*Chubby Checker*
3/18/67	**Penny Lane** *Beatles*	1/11/64	**Popsicles And Icicles** *Murmaids*
12/01/84	**Penny Lover** *Lionel Richie*	5/08/61	**Portrait Of My Love**
6/27/64	**People** *Barbra Streisand*		*Steve Lawrence*
8/17/68	**People Got To Be Free** *Rascals*	11/06/65	**Positively 4th Street** *Bob Dylan*
1/12/63	**Pepino The Italian Mouse**	7/09/88	**Pour Some Sugar On Me**
	Lou Monte		*Def Leppard*
1/27/62	**Peppermint Twist**	8/24/85	**Power Of Love**
	Joey Dee & The Starliters		*Huey Lewis & The News*
3/17/62	**Percolator (Twist)**	2/26/72	**Precious And Few** *Climax*
	Billy Joe & The Checkmates	1/04/60	**Pretty Blue Eyes** *Steve Lawrence*
6/15/59	**Personality** *Lloyd Price*	8/07/61	**Pretty Little Angel Eyes**
3/02/59	**Peter Gunn** *Ray Anthony*		*Curtis Lee*
3/02/59	**Petite Fleur**	7/20/63	**Pride And Joy** *Marvin Gaye*
	Chris Barber's Jazz Band	10/26/59	**Primrose Lane** *Jerry Wallace*
4/12/75	**Philadelphia Freedom**	3/23/85	**Private Dancer** *Tina Turner*
	Elton John Band	11/07/81	**Private Eyes**
11/24/73	**Photograph** *Ringo Starr*		*Daryl Hall & John Oates*
11/21/81	**Physical** *Olivia Newton-John*	12/15/58	**Problems** *Everly Brothers*
6/04/88	**Piano In The Dark** *Brenda Russell*	1/20/79	**Promises** *Eric Clapton*
2/22/75	**Pick Up The Pieces** *AWB*		**Proud Mary**
7/23/66	**Pied Piper** *Crispian St. Peters*	3/08/69	*Creedence Clearwater Revival*
6/09/73	**Pillow Talk** *Sylvia*	3/27/71	*Ike & Tina Turner*
	Pina Colada Song ..*see: Escape*	5/07/88	**Prove Your Love** *Taylor Dayne*
5/07/88	**Pink Cadillac** *Natalie Cole*	2/28/70	**Psychedelic Shack** *Temptations*
2/11/84	**Pink Houses**	10/15/66	**Psychotic Reaction** *Count Five*
	John Cougar Mellencamp	5/11/63	**Puff The Magic Dragon**
4/13/59	**Pink Shoe Laces** *Dodie Stevens*		*Peter, Paul & Mary*
5/04/63	**Pipeline** *Chantay's*		**Puppy Love**
12/24/66	**Place In The Sun** *Stevie Wonder*	4/04/60	*Paul Anka*
9/18/76	**Play That Funky Music**	4/01/72	*Donny Osmond*
	Wild Cherry	11/17/84	**Purple Rain**
6/23/62	**Playboy** *Marvelettes*		*Prince & The Revolution*
6/16/73	**Playground In My Mind**	8/30/69	**Put A Little Love In Your Heart**
	Clint Holmes		*Jackie DeShannon*
8/19/67	**Pleasant Valley Sunday**	5/01/71	**Put Your Hand In The Hand**
	Monkees		*Ocean*
8/10/74	**Please Come To Boston**	3/02/74	**Put Your Hands Together** *O'Jays*
	Dave Loggins	10/05/59	**Put Your Head On My Shoulder**
1/05/80	**Please Don't Go**		*Paul Anka*
	K.C. & The Sunshine Band	9/03/83	**Puttin' On The Ritz** *Taco*
8/01/60	**Please Help Me, I'm Falling**		
	Hank Locklin		
11/18/67	**Please Love Me Forever**		**Q**
	Bobby Vinton		
8/09/75	**Please Mr. Please**	6/26/61	**Quarter To Three** *U.S. Bonds*
	Olivia Newton-John	9/19/81	**Queen Of Hearts** *Juice Newton*
	Please Mr. Postman	11/17/58	**Queen Of The Hop** *Bobby Darin*
12/11/61	*Marvelettes*	1/04/64	**Quicksand** *Martha & The Vandellas*
1/25/75	*Carpenters*	6/01/59	**Quiet Village** *Martin Denny*

573

R

4/05/86 **R.O.C.K. In The U.S.A.**
   John Cougar Mellencamp
7/18/64 **Rag Doll** *4 Seasons*
11/15/86 **Rain, The** *Oran "Juice" Jones*
11/19/66 **Rain On The Roof** *Lovin' Spoonful*
12/02/67 **Rain, The Park & Other Things**
   Cowsills
6/26/61 **Raindrops** *Dee Clark*
1/03/70 **Raindrops Keep Fallin' On My**
   Head *B.J. Thomas*
5/21/66 **Rainy Day Women #12 & 35**
   Bob Dylan
6/19/71 **Rainy Days And Mondays**
   Carpenters
3/07/70 **Rainy Night In Georgia**
   Brook Benton
10/13/73 **Ramblin Man**
   Allman Brothers Band
9/22/62 **Ramblin' Rose** *Nat King Cole*
3/21/70 **Rapper, The** *Jaggerz*
3/28/81 **Rapture** *Blondie*
7/20/85 **Raspberry Beret**
   Prince & The Revolution
10/15/66 **Reach Out I'll Be There**
   Four Tops
6/22/68 **Reach Out Of The Darkness**
   Friend And Lover
10/25/80 **Real Love** *Doobie Brothers*
10/02/71 **Reason To Believe** *Rod Stewart*
9/07/59 **Red River Rock**
   Johnny & The Hurricanes
4/03/65 **Red Roses For A Blue Lady**
   Vic Dana
7/09/66 **Red Rubber Ball** *Cyrkle*
9/09/67 **Reflections**
   Diana Ross & The Supremes
5/09/70 **Reflections Of My Life**
   Marmalade
6/23/84 **Reflex, The** *Duran Duran*
3/16/85 **Relax** *Frankie Goes To Hollywood*
   Release Me (And Let Me Love
   Again)
12/22/62 *"Little Esther" Phillips*
5/27/67 *Engelbert Humperdinck*
9/26/64 **Remember (Walkin' In The**
   Sand) *Shangri-Las*
10/28/78 **Reminiscing** *Little River Band*
11/20/65 **Rescue Me** *Fontella Bass*
6/03/67 **Respect** *Aretha Franklin*
3/07/87 **Respect Yourself** *Bruce Willis*
11/17/62 **Return To Sender** *Elvis Presley*
5/05/79 **Reunited** *Peaches & Herb*
5/18/63 **Reverend Mr. Black** *Kingston Trio*
9/06/75 **Rhinestone Cowboy**
   Glen Campbell
8/01/87 **Rhythm Is Gonna Get You**
   Gloria Estefan & Miami Sound Machine
4/27/85 **Rhythm Of The Night** *DeBarge*
3/09/63 **Rhythm Of The Rain** *Cascades*
3/26/77 **Rich Girl** *Daryl Hall & John Oates*
12/08/62 **Ride!** *Dee Dee Sharp*

7/11/70 **Ride Captain Ride** *Blues Image*
4/26/80 **Ride Like The Wind**
   Christopher Cross
5/01/76 **Right Back Where We Started**
   From *Maxine Nightingale*
5/30/87 **Right On Track** *Breakfast Club*
6/30/73 **Right Place Wrong Time**
   Dr. John
5/07/77 **Right Time Of The Night**
   Jennifer Warnes
8/03/74 **Rikki Don't Lose That Number**
   Steely Dan
6/30/79 **Ring My Bell** *Anita Ward*
12/05/64 **Ringo** *Lorne Greene*
9/15/62 **Rinky Dink** *Baby Cortez*
10/20/79 **Rise** *Herb Alpert*
   Rock..*also see: R.O.C.K.*
9/09/72 **Rock And Roll (Part 2)**
   Gary Glitter
7/20/74 **Rock And Roll Heaven**
   Righteous Brothers
8/14/76 **Rock And Roll Music** *Beach Boys*
4/19/69 **Rock Me** *Steppenwolf*
3/29/86 **Rock Me Amadeus** *Falco*
9/28/74 **Rock Me Gently** *Andy Kim*
3/09/74 **Rock On** *David Essex*
11/27/71 **Rock Steady** *Aretha Franklin*
8/29/87 **Rock Steady** *Whispers*
7/06/74 **Rock The Boat** *Hues Corporation*
1/22/83 **Rock The Casbah** *Clash*
12/11/82 **Rock This Town** *Stray Cats*
1/19/80 **Rock With You** *Michael Jackson*
7/13/74 **Rock Your Baby** *George McCrae*
7/15/72 **Rocket Man** *Elton John*
4/02/88 **Rocket 2 U** *Jets*
8/09/75 **Rockford Files** *Mike Post*
8/02/75 **Rockin' Chair** *Gwen McCrae*
6/27/60 **Rockin' Good Way**
   Dinah Washington & Brook Benton
11/06/76 **Rock'n Me** *Steve Miller*
1/20/73 **Rockin' Pneumonia - Boogie**
   Woogie Flu *Johnny Rivers*
   Rockin' Robin
10/13/58 *Bobby Day*
4/22/72 *Michael Jackson*
10/11/75 **Rocky** *Austin Roberts*
3/03/73 **Rocky Mountain High**
   John Denver
   Romeo & Juliet..*see: (Just Like)*
   and Love Theme From
5/16/64 **Ronnie** *4 Seasons*
7/03/82 **Rosanna** *Toto*
6/28/80 **Rose, The** *Bette Midler*
2/13/71 **Rose Garden** *Lynn Anderson*
7/14/62 **Roses Are Red** *Bobby Vinton*
1/09/61 **Rubber Ball** *Bobby Vee*
12/04/76 **Rubberband Man** *Spinners*
1/31/70 **Rubberneckin'** *Elvis Presley*
2/23/63 **Ruby Baby** *Dion*
8/02/69 **Ruby, Don't Take Your Love To**
   Town
   Kenny Rogers & The First Edition
3/04/67 **Ruby Tuesday** *Rolling Stones*

8/16/86	**Rumors** *Timex Social Club*
3/29/69	**Run Away Child, Running Wild**
	Temptations
10/04/75	**Run Joey Run** *David Geddes*
6/06/70	**Run Through The Jungle**
	Creedence Clearwater Revival
12/25/61	**Run To Him** *Bobby Vee*
1/19/85	**Run To You** *Bryan Adams*
10/23/61	**Runaround Sue** *Dion*
4/24/61	**Runaway** *Del Shannon*
1/18/60	**Running Bear** *Johnny Preston*
6/05/61	**Running Scared** *Roy Orbison*
2/04/84	**Running With The Night**
	Lionel Richie

S

	S.W.A.T...*see: Theme From*
10/06/79	**Sad Eyes** *Robert John*
10/23/61	**Sad Movies (Make Me Cry)**
	Sue Thompson
8/11/84	**Sad Songs (Say So Much)**
	Elton John
9/10/83	**Safety Dance** *Men Without Hats*
10/13/79	**Sail On** *Commodores*
8/30/80	**Sailing** *Christopher Cross*
12/19/60	**Sailor (Your Home Is The Sea)**
	Lolita
	Saint..*see: St.*
1/11/75	**Sally G** *Paul McCartney & Wings*
9/28/63	**Sally, Go 'Round The Roses**
	Jaynetts
2/21/81	**Same Old Lang Syne**
	Dan Fogelberg
7/17/61	**San Antonio Rose** *Floyd Cramer*
9/16/67	**San Franciscan Nights**
	Eric Burdon & The Animals
7/01/67	**San Francisco (Be Sure To Wear**
	Flowers In Your Hair)
	Scott McKenzie
2/02/80	**Sara** *Fleetwood Mac*
3/15/86	**Sara** *Starship*
6/26/76	**Sara Smile**
	Daryl Hall & John Oates
	Satisfaction..*see: (I Can't Get No)*
9/23/72	**Saturday In The Park** *Chicago*
1/03/76	**Saturday Night** *Bay City Rollers*
9/26/64	**Save It For Me** *4 Seasons*
10/17/60	**Save The Last Dance For Me**
	Drifters
8/21/65	**Save Your Heart For Me**
	Gary Lewis & The Playboys
10/26/85	**Saving All My Love For You**
	Whitney Houston
9/15/73	**Say, Has Anybody Seen My**
	Sweet Gypsy Rose
	Tony Orlando & Dawn
12/17/83	**Say It Isn't So**
	Daryl Hall-John Oates
10/19/68	**Say It Loud - I'm Black And I'm**
	Proud *James Brown*
12/10/83	**Say Say Say**
	Paul McCartney & Michael Jackson

12/21/85	**Say You, Say Me** *Lionel Richie*
2/20/88	**Say You Will** *Foreigner*
9/04/61	**School Is Out** *Gary (U.S.) Bonds*
7/29/72	**School's Out** *Alice Cooper*
1/08/72	**Scorpio** *Dennis Coffey*
	Sea Of Love
8/24/59	*Phil Phillips*
1/05/85	*Honeydrippers*
7/28/62	**Sealed With A Kiss** *Brian Hyland*
7/13/85	**Search Is Over** *Survivor*
	Searchin' So Long..*see: (I've Been)*
2/20/88	**Seasons Change** *Expose*
3/02/74	**Seasons In The Sun** *Terry Jacks*
6/09/62	**Second Hand Love**
	Connie Francis
3/22/80	**Second Time Around** *Shalamar*
4/23/66	**Secret Agent Man** *Johnny Rivers*
3/22/86	**Secret Lovers** *Atlantic Starr*
10/22/66	**See See Rider**
	Eric Burdon & The Animals
3/14/64	**See The Funny Little Clown**
	Bobby Goldsboro
8/27/66	**See You In September**
	Happenings
6/30/84	**Self Control** *Laura Branigan*
12/22/79	**Send One Your Love**
	Stevie Wonder
1/07/78	**Sentimental Lady** *Bob Welch*
7/27/85	**Sentimental Street** *Night Ranger*
11/30/85	**Separate Lives**
	Phil Collins & Marilyn Martin
3/19/83	**Separate Ways (Worlds Apart)**
	Journey
2/10/79	**September** *Earth, Wind & Fire*
11/09/59	**Seven Little Girls Sitting In The**
	Back Seat *Paul Evans*
7/03/65	**Seventh Son** *Johnny Rivers*
1/29/83	**Sexual Healing** *Marvin Gaye*
	Sexy + 17..*see: (She's)*
5/24/80	**Sexy Eyes** *Dr. Hook*
12/21/74	**Sha-La-La (Make Me Happy)**
	Al Green
6/17/78	**Shadow Dancing** *Andy Gibb*
	Shaft..*see: Theme From*
2/27/65	**Shake** *Sam Cooke*
2/27/82	**Shake It Up** *Cars*
9/11/76	**(Shake, Shake, Shake) Shake**
	Your Booty
	KC & The Sunshine Band
1/17/87	**Shake You Down** *Gregory Abbott*
5/19/79	**Shake Your Body (Down To The**
	Ground) *Jacksons*
3/17/79	**Shake Your Groove Thing**
	Peaches & Herb
12/19/87	**Shake Your Love** *Debbie Gibson*
8/01/87	**Shakedown** *Bob Seger*
7/28/73	**Shambala** *Three Dog Night*
9/09/78	**Shame** *Evelyn "Champagne" King*
2/26/83	**Shame On The Moon** *Bob Seger*
6/05/76	**Shannon** *Henry Gross*
12/05/70	**Share The Land** *Guess Who*
1/06/79	**Sharing The Night Together**
	Dr. Hook

5/14/88	**Shattered Dreams**
	Johnny Hates Jazz
7/07/79	**She Believes In Me** *Kenny Rogers*
5/14/83	**She Blinded Me With Science**
	Thomas Dolby
9/08/84	**She Bop** *Cyndi Lauper*
5/19/62	**She Cried** *Jay & The Americans*
3/21/64	**She Loves You** *Beatles*
8/06/83	**She Works Hard For The Money**
	Donna Summer
6/17/67	**She'd Rather Be With Me** *Turtles*
7/02/83	**She's A Beauty** *Tubes*
12/07/63	**She's A Fool** *Lesley Gore*
3/20/71	**She's A Lady** *Tom Jones*
12/26/64	**She's A Woman** *Beatles*
10/30/76	**She's Gone**
	Daryl Hall & John Oates
1/08/66	**She's Just My Style**
	Gary Lewis & The Playboys
2/27/88	**She's Like The Wind**
	Patrick Swayze featuring Wendy Fraser
12/12/64	**She's Not There** *Zombies*
9/08/62	**She's Not You** *Elvis Presley*
6/21/80	**She's Out Of My Life**
	Michael Jackson
10/01/83	**(She's) Sexy + 17** *Stray Cats*
9/01/62	**Sheila** *Tommy Roe*
9/15/62	**Sherry** *4 Seasons*
7/21/79	**Shine A Little Love**
	Electric Light Orchestra
5/24/75	**Shining Star** *Earth, Wind & Fire*
7/19/80	**Shining Star** *Manhattans*
12/01/79	**Ships** *Barry Manilow*
5/25/68	**Shoo-Be-Doo-Be-Doo-Da-Day**
	Stevie Wonder
4/11/64	**Shoop Shoop Song (It's In His Kiss)** *Betty Everett*
	Shop Around
2/20/61	*Miracles*
7/10/76	*Captain & Tennille*
1/28/78	**Short People** *Randy Newman*
4/03/65	**Shotgun** *Jr. Walker & The All Stars*
12/12/87	**Should've Known Better**
	Richard Marx
8/03/85	**Shout** *Tears For Fears*
5/05/62	**Shout** *Joey Dee & The Starliters*
5/19/62	**Shout! Shout! (Knock Yourself Out)** *Ernie Maresca*
1/19/74	**Show And Tell** *Al Wilson*
5/08/76	**Show Me The Way**
	Peter Frampton
5/25/74	**Show Must Go On**
	Three Dog Night
8/10/74	**Sideshow** *Blue Magic*
4/25/87	**Sign 'O' The Times** *Prince*
8/08/70	**Signed, Sealed, Delivered I'm Yours** *Stevie Wonder*
8/28/71	**Signs** *Five Man Electrical Band*
3/08/86	**Silent Running (On Dangerous Ground)** *Mike + The Mechanics*
5/15/65	**Silhouettes** *Herman's Hermits*
5/22/76	**Silly Love Songs** *Wings*
3/09/68	**Simon Says** *1910 Fruitgum Co.*

12/28/63	**Since I Fell For You** *Lenny Welch*
	Since You've Been Gone..*see:*
	(Sweet Sweet Baby)
4/21/73	**Sing** *Carpenters*
2/07/76	**Sing A Song** *Earth, Wind & Fire*
4/25/60	**Sink The Bismarck**
	Johnny Horton
5/21/77	**Sir Duke** *Stevie Wonder*
6/09/84	**Sister Christian** *Night Ranger*
6/14/75	**Sister Golden Hair** *America*
3/16/68	**(Sittin' On) The Dock Of The Bay** *Otis Redding*
5/02/60	**Sixteen Reasons** *Connie Stevens*
5/22/82	**'65 Love Affair** *Paul Davis*
12/30/67	**Skinny Legs And All** *Joe Tex*
12/06/75	**Sky High** *Jigsaw*
7/26/86	**Sledgehammer** *Peter Gabriel*
9/21/59	**Sleep Walk** *Santo & Johnny*
12/14/85	**Sleeping Bag** *ZZ Top*
10/05/68	**Slip Away** *Clarence Carter*
1/28/78	**Slip Slidin' Away** *Paul Simon*
5/07/66	**Sloop John B** *Beach Boys*
	Slow Dancin'..*see: Swayin' To The Music*
8/29/81	**Slow Hand** *Pointer Sisters*
4/14/62	**Slow Twistin'** *Chubby Checker*
12/28/85	**Small Town**
	John Cougar Mellencamp
11/22/69	**Smile A Little Smile For Me**
	Flying Machine
9/04/71	**Smiling Faces Sometimes**
	Undisputed Truth
9/17/77	**Smoke From A Distant Fire**
	Sanford/Townsend Band
1/19/59	**Smoke Gets In Your Eyes**
	Platters
7/28/73	**Smoke On The Water**
	Deep Purple
1/19/74	**Smokin' In The Boy's Room**
	Brownsville Station
5/18/85	**Smooth Operator** *Sade*
7/07/62	**Snap Your Fingers**
	Joe Henderson
4/05/75	**Snookeroo** *Ringo Starr*
12/31/66	**Snoopy Vs. The Red Baron**
	Royal Guardsmen
9/26/70	**Snowbird** *Anne Murray*
1/09/88	**So Emotional** *Whitney Houston*
4/30/77	**So In To You**
	Atlanta Rhythm Section
11/23/59	**So Many Ways** *Brook Benton*
8/03/63	**So Much In Love** *Tymes*
10/10/60	**So Sad (To Watch Good Love Go Bad)** *Everly Brothers*
3/25/67	**Sock It To Me-Baby!**
	Mitch Ryder/Detroit Wheels
5/05/62	**Soldier Boy** *Shirelles*
5/21/83	**Solitaire** *Laura Branigan*
10/27/84	**Some Guys Have All The Luck**
	Rod Stewart
4/16/88	**Some Kind Of Lover** *Jody Watley*
2/22/75	**Some Kind Of Wonderful**
	Grand Funk

5/11/85	**Some Like It Hot** *Power Station*
6/17/67	**Somebody To Love**
	Jefferson Airplane
10/16/82	**Somebody's Baby**
	Jackson Browne
11/14/70	**Somebody's Been Sleeping**
	100 Proof Aged In Soul
3/24/84	**Somebody's Watching Me**
	Rockwell
1/24/87	**Someday** *Glass Tiger*
12/27/69	**Someday We'll Be Together**
	Diana Ross & The Supremes
8/16/75	**Someone Saved My Life**
	Tonight *Elton John*
4/15/67	**Somethin' Stupid**
	Nancy & Frank Sinatra
11/15/69	**Something** *Beatles*
5/31/86	**Something About You** *Level 42*
7/25/87	**Something So Strong**
	Crowded House
3/04/78	**Sometimes When We Touch**
	Dan Hill
2/17/79	**Somewhere In The Night**
	Barry Manilow
8/13/66	**Somewhere, My Love**
	Ray Conniff & The Singers
3/14/87	**Somewhere Out There**
	Linda Ronstadt & James Ingram
1/18/69	**Son-Of-A Preacher Man**
	Dusty Springfield
7/01/72	**Song Sung Blue** *Neil Diamond*
7/11/87	**Songbird** *Kenny G*
7/31/71	**Sooner Or Later** *Grass Roots*
5/11/59	**Sorry (I Ran All The Way Home)**
	Impalas
12/25/76	**Sorry Seems To Be The Hardest**
	Word *Elton John*
11/04/67	**Soul Man** *Sam & Dave*
1/18/69	**Soulful Strut** *Young-Holt Unlimited*
1/01/66	**Sounds Of Silence**
	Simon & Garfunkel
4/13/63	**South Street** *Orlons*
4/30/77	**Southern Nights** *Glen Campbell*
11/24/73	**Space Race** *Billy Preston*
	Spanish Harlem
3/13/61	*Ben E. King*
9/11/71	*Aretha Franklin*
4/19/80	**Special Lady**
	Ray, Goodman & Brown
7/28/62	**Speedy Gonzales** *Pat Boone*
3/02/74	**Spiders & Snakes** *Jim Stafford*
2/08/86	**Spies Like Us** *Paul McCartney*
8/22/70	**Spill The Wine** *Eric Burdon & War*
7/05/69	**Spinning Wheel**
	Blood, Sweat & Tears
4/18/70	**Spirit In The Sky**
	Norman Greenbaum
8/04/58	**Splish Splash** *Bobby Darin*
2/10/68	**Spooky** *Classics IV*
9/07/85	**St. Elmo's Fire (Man In Motion)**
	John Parr
2/09/59	**Stagger Lee** *Lloyd Price*
5/09/60	**Stairway To Heaven** *Neil Sedaka*

8/20/83	**Stand Back** *Stevie Nicks*
	Stand By Me
6/12/61	*Ben E. King*
12/20/86	*Ben E. King*
1/08/77	**Stand Tall** *Burton Cummings*
1/21/67	**Standing In The Shadows Of**
	Love *Four Tops*
	Star Is Born ..see: *Love Theme*
	From
	Star Wars Theme
9/17/77	*John Williams/*
	London Symphony Orchestra
10/01/77	*Meco*
6/20/81	**Stars on 45 medley** *Stars on 45*
10/31/81	**Start Me Up** *Rolling Stones*
	Starting Over ..see: *(Just Like)*
8/04/84	**State Of Shock** *Jacksons*
11/21/60	**Stay** *Maurice Williams*
5/01/71	**Stay Awhile** *Bells*
8/24/68	**Stay In My Corner** *Dells*
2/04/78	**Stayin' Alive** *Bee Gees*
7/12/80	**Steal Away** *Robbie Dupree*
10/17/81	**Step By Step** *Eddie Rabbitt*
12/11/82	**Steppin' Out** *Joe Jackson*
10/26/74	**Steppin' Out (Gonna Boogie**
	Tonight) *Tony Orlando & Dawn*
6/08/63	**Still** *Bill Anderson*
11/17/79	**Still** *Commodores*
10/23/76	**Still The One** *Orleans*
7/22/78	**Still The Same** *Bob Seger*
5/24/80	**Stomp!** *Brothers Johnson*
5/02/87	**Stone Love** *Kool & The Gang*
12/19/70	**Stoned Love** *Supremes*
7/27/68	**Stoned Soul Picnic** *5th Dimension*
1/23/71	**Stoney End** *Barbra Streisand*
10/26/74	**Stop And Smell The Roses**
	Mac Davis
3/07/64	**Stop And Think It Over**
	Dale & Grace
9/05/81	**Stop Draggin' My Heart Around**
	Stevie Nicks with Tom Petty
3/27/65	**Stop! In The Name Of Love**
	Supremes
12/10/66	**Stop Stop Stop** *Hollies*
12/28/68	**Stormy** *Classics IV*
5/28/83	**Straight From The Heart**
	Bryan Adams
5/26/62	**Stranger On The Shore**
	Mr. Acker Bilk
7/02/66	**Strangers In The Night**
	Frank Sinatra
4/01/67	**Strawberry Fields Forever**
	Beatles
9/24/77	**Strawberry Letter 23**
	Brothers Johnson
2/26/83	**Stray Cat Strut** *Stray Cats*
5/18/74	**Streak, The** *Ray Stevens*
7/07/62	**Stripper, The** *David Rose*
11/24/84	**Strut** *Sheena Easton*
5/12/73	**Stuck In The Middle With You**
	Stealers Wheel
4/25/60	**Stuck On You** *Elvis Presley*
8/25/84	**Stuck On You** *Lionel Richie*

9/20/86	**Stuck With You**
	Huey Lewis & The News
5/12/79	**Stumblin' In**
	Suzi Quatro & Chris Norman
6/08/85	**Suddenly** *Billy Ocean*
11/19/83	**Suddenly Last Summer** *Motels*
1/22/72	**Sugar Daddy** *Jackson 5*
10/12/63	**Sugar Shack**
	Jimmy Gilmer & The Fireballs
9/20/69	**Sugar, Sugar** *Archies*
12/31/66	**Sugar Town** *Nancy Sinatra*
3/02/85	**Sugar Walls** *Sheena Easton*
	Sukiyaki
6/15/63	*Kyu Sakamoto*
6/13/81	*A Taste Of Honey*
4/07/79	**Sultans Of Swing** *Dire Straits*
9/25/76	**Summer** *War*
11/25/72	**Summer Breeze** *Seals & Crofts*
8/13/66	**Summer In The City**
	Lovin' Spoonful
9/30/78	**Summer Nights**
	John Travolta & Olivia Newton-John
8/31/85	**Summer Of '69** *Bryan Adams*
	Summer Place..*see: Theme From A*
10/17/64	**Summer Song**
	Chad Stuart & Jeremy Clyde
8/27/66	**Summertime** *Billy Stewart*
9/29/58	**Summertime Blues**
	Eddie Cochran
6/24/67	**Sunday Will Never Be The**
	Same *Spanky & Our Gang*
6/29/74	**Sundown** *Gordon Lightfoot*
9/01/84	**Sunglasses At Night** *Corey Hart*
8/20/66	**Sunny** *Bobby Hebb*
1/15/72	**Sunshine** *Jonathan Edwards*
8/31/68	**Sunshine Of Your Love** *Cream*
3/30/74	**Sunshine On My Shoulders**
	John Denver
9/03/66	**Sunshine Superman** *Donovan*
1/13/73	**Superfly** *Curtis Mayfield*
	(also see: Freddie's Dead)
4/26/75	**Supernatural Thing** *Ben E. King*
10/16/71	**Superstar** *Carpenters*
1/27/73	**Superstition** *Stevie Wonder*
4/09/66	**Sure Gonna Miss Her**
	Gary Lewis & The Playboys
7/20/63	**Surf City** *Jan & Dean*
9/14/63	**Surfer Girl** *Beach Boys*
1/25/64	**Surfin' Bird** *Trashmen*
5/25/63	**Surfin' U.S.A.** *Beach Boys*
3/20/61	**Surrender** *Elvis Presley*
10/13/58	**Susie Darlin'** *Robin Luke*
4/11/64	**Suspicion** *Terry Stafford*
11/01/69	**Suspicious Minds** *Elvis Presley*
7/06/85	**Sussudio** *Phil Collins*
10/22/77	**Swayin' To The Music (Slow**
	Dancin') *Johnny Rivers*
7/26/75	**Swearin' To God** *Frankie Valli*
6/05/71	**Sweet And Innocent**
	Donny Osmond
8/16/69	**Sweet Caroline** *Neil Diamond*
5/03/69	**Sweet Cherry Wine**
	Tommy James & The Shondells

10/23/71	**Sweet City Woman** *Stampeders*
3/20/82	**Sweet Dreams** *Air Supply*
9/03/83	**Sweet Dreams (Are Made of**
	This) *Eurythmics*
8/30/86	**Sweet Freedom**
	Michael McDonald
8/21/71	**Sweet Hitch-Hiker**
	Creedence Clearwater Revival
10/26/74	**Sweet Home Alabama**
	Lynyrd Skynyrd
4/24/76	**Sweet Love** *Commodores*
11/01/86	**Sweet Love** *Anita Baker*
2/27/71	**Sweet Mary** *Wadsworth Mansion*
4/18/60	**Sweet Nothin's** *Brenda Lee*
7/30/66	**Sweet Pea** *Tommy Roe*
3/04/72	**Sweet Seasons** *Carole King*
5/13/67	**Sweet Soul Music** *Arthur Conley*
3/30/68	**(Sweet Sweet Baby) Since**
	You've Been Gone
	Aretha Franklin
6/25/66	**Sweet Talkin' Guy** *Chiffons*
4/03/76	**Sweet Thing**
	Rufus Featuring Chaka Khan
8/03/59	**Sweeter Than You** *Ricky Nelson*
3/01/86	**Sweetest Taboo** *Sade*
2/13/82	**Sweetest Thing (I've Ever**
	Known) *Juice Newton*
6/06/81	**Sweetheart**
	Franke & The Knockouts
6/20/60	**Swingin' School** *Bobby Rydell*
6/03/72	**Sylvia's Mother**
	Dr. Hook & The Medicine Show

T

4/20/74	**TSOP (The Sound Of**
	Philadelphia)
	MFSB featuring The Three Degrees
7/17/82	**Tainted Love** *Soft Cell*
7/08/78	**Take A Chance On Me** *Abba*
11/22/69	**Take A Letter Maria**
	R.B. Greaves
	Take A Look At Me Now..*see:*
	Against All Odds
5/01/61	**Take Good Care Of Her**
	Adam Wade
9/18/61	**Take Good Care Of My Baby**
	Bobby Vee
8/21/82	**Take It Away** *Paul McCartney*
3/06/82	**Take It Easy On Me**
	Little River Band
5/30/81	**Take It On The Run**
	REO Speedwagon
3/13/76	**Take It To The Limit** *Eagles*
5/12/79	**Take Me Home** *Cher*
5/10/86	**Take Me Home** *Phil Collins*
8/28/71	**Take Me Home, Country Roads**
	John Denver
11/15/86	**Take Me Home Tonight**
	Eddie Money
9/13/86	**Take My Breath Away** *Berlin*
10/19/85	**Take On Me** *a-ha*

12/15/79	**Take The Long Way Home**	1/18/86	**That's What Friends Are For**
	Supertramp		*Dionne & Friends*
5/25/63	**Take These Chains From My**	2/22/60	**Theme From "A Summer Place"**
	Heart *Ray Charles*		*Percy Faith*
8/16/80	**Take Your Time (Do It Right)**	8/04/62	**Theme From Dr. Kildare (Three**
	S.O.S. Band		**Stars Will Shine Tonight)**
1/04/64	**Talk Back Trembling Lips**		*Richard Chamberlain*
	Johnny Tillotson		**Theme From Exorcist** *..see:*
5/16/87	**Talk Dirty To Me** *Poison*		*Tubular Bells*
1/25/86	**Talk To Me** *Stevie Nicks*	8/15/81	**Theme From "Greatest American**
1/28/84	**Talking In Your Sleep** *Romantics*		**Hero" (Believe It or Not)**
2/23/59	**Tall Paul** *Annette*		*Joey Scarbury*
6/29/59	**Tallahassee Lassie**	11/14/81	**Theme From Hill Street Blues**
	Freddy Cannon		*Mike Post featuring Larry Carlton*
11/27/65	**Taste Of Honey** *Herb Alpert*		**Theme From Love Story** *..see:*
11/03/58	**Tea For Two Cha Cha**		*(Where Do I Begin)*
	Tommy Dorsey	1/24/76	**Theme From Mahogany (Do You**
12/12/70	**Tears Of A Clown** *Miracles*		**Know Where You're Going To)**
10/13/58	**Tears On My Pillow**		*Diana Ross*
	Little Anthony & The Imperials		**Theme From "Rocky"** *..see: Gonna*
9/22/62	**Teen Age Idol** *Rick Nelson*		*Fly Now*
2/08/60	**Teen Angel** *Mark Dinning*	2/28/76	**Theme From S.W.A.T.**
10/19/59	**Teen Beat** *Sandy Nelson*		*Rhythm Heritage*
5/18/59	**Teenager In Love**	11/20/71	**Theme From Shaft** *Isaac Hayes*
	Dion & The Belmonts		**Theme From "Superfly"** *..see:*
10/29/83	**Telefone (Long Distance Love**		*Freddie's Dead*
	Affair) *Sheena Easton*	9/05/60	**Theme From The Apartment**
9/24/77	**Telephone Line**		*Ferrante & Teicher*
	Electric Light Orchestra	2/24/68	**(Theme From) Valley Of The**
9/24/83	**Tell Her About It** *Billy Joel*		**Dolls** *Dionne Warwick*
2/27/65	**Tell Her No** *Zombies*	10/26/74	**Then Came You**
1/19/63	**Tell Him** *Exciters*		*Dionne Warwicke & Spinners*
4/27/59	**Tell Him No** *Travis & Bob*	9/14/63	**Then He Kissed Me** *Crystals*
	Tell It Like It Is	3/11/67	**Then You Can Tell Me Goodbye**
1/28/67	*Aaron Neville*		*Casinos*
1/10/81	*Heart*	8/17/59	**There Goes My Baby** *Drifters*
1/23/88	**Tell It To My Heart** *Taylor Dayne*	1/04/64	**There! I've Said It Again**
1/21/67	**Tell It To The Rain** *4 Seasons*		*Bobby Vinton*
8/01/60	**Tell Laura I Love Her**	7/05/86	**There'll Be Sad Songs (To Make**
	Ray Peterson		**You Cry)** *Billy Ocean*
8/24/74	**Tell Me Something Good** *Rufus*	3/25/67	**There's A Kind Of Hush**
12/22/62	**Telstar** *Tornadoes*		*Herman's Hermits*
4/12/86	**Tender Love** *Force M.D.'s*	2/27/61	**There's A Moon Out Tonight**
6/07/75	**Thank God I'm A Country Boy**		*Capris*
	John Denver	9/05/81	**(There's) No Gettin' Over Me**
2/14/70	**Thank You (Falettinme Be Mice**		*Ronnie Milsap*
	Elf Agin) *Sly & The Family Stone*	2/26/66	**These Boots Are Made For**
3/20/82	**That Girl** *Stevie Wonder*		**Walkin'** *Nancy Sinatra*
10/06/73	**That Lady** *Isley Brothers*	3/22/86	**These Dreams** *Heart*
2/11/84	**That's All!** *Genesis*	5/31/69	**These Eyes** *Guess Who*
7/04/60	**That's All You Gotta Do**	4/28/84	**They Don't Know** *Tracey Ullman*
	Brenda Lee	10/25/75	**They Just Can't Stop It the**
12/24/66	**That's Life** *Frank Sinatra*		**(Games People Play)** *Spinners*
6/23/62	**That's Old Fashioned**	7/25/70	**(They Long To Be) Close To**
	Everly Brothers		**You** *Carpenters*
10/22/77	**That's Rock 'N' Roll**	8/13/66	**They're Coming To Take Me**
	Shaun Cassidy		**Away, Ha-Haaa!** *Napoleon XIV*
11/22/75	**That's The Way (I Like It)**		**Thicker Than Water** *..see: (Love Is)*
	KC & The Sunshine Band	8/25/62	**Things** *Bobby Darin*
7/10/71	**That's The Way I've Always**	6/15/85	**Things Can Only Get Better**
	Heard It Should Be *Carly Simon*		*Howard Jones*
10/18/69	**That's The Way Love Is**	4/16/77	**Things We Do For Love** *10cc*
	Marvin Gaye	6/15/68	**Think** *Aretha Franklin*

Date	Song	Artist
2/04/84	**Think Of Laura**	*Christopher Cross*
3/29/86	**This Could Be The Night**	
	Loverboy	
2/20/65	**This Diamond Ring**	
	Gary Lewis & The Playboys	
10/11/69	**This Girl Is A Woman Now**	
	Gary Puckett & The Union Gap	
	This Guy's (Girl's) In Love With You	
6/22/68	*Herb Alpert*	
3/08/69	*Dionne Warwick*	
4/15/67	**This Is My Song**	*Petula Clark*
3/08/69	**This Magic Moment**	
	Jay & The Americans	
8/28/76	**This Masquerade**	*George Benson*
10/23/61	**This Time**	*Troy Shondell*
6/03/78	**This Time I'm In It For Love**	
	Player	
11/22/75	**This Will Be**	*Natalie Cole*
6/29/63	**Those Lazy-Hazy-Crazy Days Of Summer**	*Nat King Cole*
6/26/61	**Those Oldies But Goodies**	
	Little Caesar & The Romans	
11/02/68	**Those Were The Days**	
	Mary Hopkin	
12/12/60	**Thousand Stars**	
	Kathy Young with The Innocents	
8/24/59	**Three Bells**	*Browns*
	Three Stars Will Shine Tonight..see: Theme From Dr. Kildare	
8/12/78	**Three Times A Lady**	
	Commodores	
3/03/84	**Thriller**	*Michael Jackson*
10/11/86	**Throwing It All Away**	*Genesis*
4/01/78	**Thunder Island**	*Jay Ferguson*
5/22/65	**Ticket To Ride**	*Beatles*
1/31/81	**Tide Is High**	*Blondie*
4/21/73	**Tie A Yellow Ribbon Round The Ole Oak Tree**	
	Dawn featuring Tony Orlando	
7/13/63	**Tie Me Kangaroo Down, Sport**	
	Rolf Harris	
7/20/59	**Tiger**	*Fabian*
5/18/68	**Tighten Up**	
	Archie Bell & The Drells	
8/08/70	**Tighter, Tighter**	*Alive & Kicking*
9/21/59	**('Til) I Kissed You**	*Everly Brothers*
6/09/84	**Time After Time**	*Cyndi Lauper*
6/18/83	**Time (Clock Of The Heart)**	
	Culture Club	
12/29/73	**Time In A Bottle**	*Jim Croce*
12/05/64	**Time Is On My Side**	
	Rolling Stones	
5/03/69	**Time Is Tight**	
	Booker T. & The MG's	
	Time Of My Life..see: (I've Had)	
3/29/69	**Time Of The Season**	*Zombies*
12/09/78	**Time Passages**	*Al Stewart*
4/16/66	**Time Won't Let Me**	*Outsiders*
2/07/76	**Times Of Your Life**	*Paul Anka*
11/09/74	**Tin Man**	*America*

Date	Song	Artist
7/26/80	**Tired Of Toein' The Line**	
	Rocky Burnette	
4/24/65	**Tired Of Waiting For You**	*Kinks*
5/19/84	**To All The Girls I've Loved Before**	
	Julio Iglesias & Willie Nelson	
12/20/86	**To Be A Lover**	*Billy Idol*
12/01/58	**To Know Him, Is To Love Him**	
	Teddy Bears	
10/21/67	**To Sir With Love**	*Lulu*
8/07/61	**Together**	*Connie Francis*
6/18/88	**Together Forever**	*Rick Astley*
11/17/58	**Tom Dooley**	*Kingston Trio*
12/11/61	**Tonight**	*Ferrante & Teicher*
1/11/86	**Tonight She Comes**	*Cars*
4/04/87	**Tonight, Tonight, Tonight**	
	Genesis	
11/13/76	**Tonight's The Night (Gonna Be Alright)**	*Rod Stewart*
6/28/69	**Too Busy Thinking About My Baby**	*Marvin Gaye*
4/05/80	**Too Hot**	*Kool & The Gang*
3/23/85	**Too Late For Goodbyes**	
	Julian Lennon	
7/15/72	**Too Late To Turn Back Now**	
	Cornelius Brothers & Sister Rose	
1/06/79	**Too Much Heaven**	*Bee Gees*
5/23/81	**Too Much Time On My Hands**	
	Styx	
6/03/78	**Too Much, Too Little, Too Late**	
	Johnny Mathis/Deniece Williams	
7/09/83	**Too Shy**	*Kajagoogoo*
12/01/73	**Top Of The World**	*Carpenters*
10/20/58	**Topsy II**	*Cozy Cole*
2/05/77	**Torn Between Two Lovers**	
	Mary MacGregor	
7/10/61	**Tossin' And Turnin'**	*Bobby Lewis*
10/01/83	**Total Eclipse Of The Heart**	
	Bonnie Tyler	
2/15/69	**Touch Me**	*Doors*
2/14/87	**Touch Me (I Want Your Body)**	
	Samantha Fox	
8/18/73	**Touch Me In The Morning**	
	Diana Ross	
9/26/87	**Touch Of Grey**	*Grateful Dead*
11/13/61	**Tower Of Strength**	
	Gene McDaniels	
3/29/69	**Traces**	*Classics IV*
7/08/67	**Tracks Of My Tears**	
	Johnny Rivers	
10/25/69	**Tracy**	*Cuff Links*
	Tragedy	
3/23/59	*Thomas Wayne*	
5/29/61	*Fleetwoods*	
3/24/79	**Tragedy**	*Bee Gees*
3/07/70	**Travelin' Band**	
	Creedence Clearwater Revival	
5/29/61	**Travelin' Man**	*Ricky Nelson*
7/03/71	**Treat Her Like A Lady**	
	Cornelius Brothers & Sister Rose	
10/16/65	**Treat Her Right**	*Roy Head*
6/24/72	**Troglodyte (Cave Man)**	
	Jimmy Castor Bunch	

1/16/82	**Trouble**	*Lindsey Buckingham*
2/03/73	**Trouble Man**	*Marvin Gaye*
10/08/83	**True**	*Spandau Ballet*
11/15/86	**True Blue**	*Madonna*
10/25/86	**True Colors**	*Cyndi Lauper*
11/27/82	**Truly**	*Lionel Richie*

5/22/76 **Tryin' To Get The Feeling Again**
    Barry Manilow

11/07/81 **Tryin' To Live My Life Without**
    You *Bob Seger*

4/30/77 **Tryin' To Love Two** *William Bell*

5/11/74 **Tubular Bells** *Mike Oldfield*

7/12/86 **Tuff Enuff** *Fabulous Thunderbirds*

5/27/72 **Tumbling Dice** *Rolling Stones*

2/06/88 **Tunnel Of Love** *Bruce Springsteen*

8/17/68 **Turn Around, Look At Me**
    Vogues

5/23/70 **Turn Back The Hands Of Time**
    Tyrone Davis

5/11/59 **Turn Me Loose** *Fabian*

8/14/76 **Turn The Beat Around**
    Vicki Sue Robinson

12/04/65 **Turn! Turn! Turn!** *Byrds*

2/06/82 **Turn Your Love Around**
    George Benson

11/03/79 **Tusk** *Fleetwood Mac*

4/28/73 **Twelfth Of Never** *Donny Osmond*

4/26/69 **Twenty-Five Miles** *Edwin Starr*

9/12/70 **25 Or 6 To 4** *Chicago*

3/26/83 **Twilight Zone** *Golden Earring*

Twist, The
9/19/60		*Chubby Checker*
1/13/62		*Chubby Checker*

4/04/64 **Twist And Shout** *Beatles*

1/07/84 **Twist Of Fate** *Olivia Newton-John*

5/12/62 **Twist, Twist Senora**
    Gary "U.S." Bonds

3/24/62 **Twistin' The Night Away**
    Sam Cooke

6/01/63 **Two Faces Have I** *Lou Christie*

1/19/63 **Two Lovers** *Mary Wells*

5/21/88 **Two Occasions** *Deele*

10/11/86 **Two Of Hearts** *Stacey Q*

2001..*see: Also Sprach Zarathustra*

10/18/86 **Typical Male** *Tina Turner*

U

10/17/87 **U Got The Look** *Prince*

2/08/64 **Um, Um, Um, Um, Um, Um**
    Major Lance

1/13/62 **Unchain My Heart** *Ray Charles*

8/28/65 **Unchained Melody**
    Righteous Brothers

9/04/71 **Uncle Albert/Admiral Halsey**
    Paul & Linda McCartney

8/22/64 **Under The Boardwalk** *Drifters*

7/09/77 **Undercover Angel** *Alan O'Day*

12/24/83 **Undercover Of The Night**
    Rolling Stones

8/11/73 **Uneasy Rider** *Charlie Daniels*

5/25/68 **Unicorn** *Irish Rovers*

12/24/83 **Union Of The Snake** *Duran Duran*

2/23/74 **Until You Come Back To Me**
    (That's What I'm Gonna Do)
    Aretha Franklin

6/06/70 **Up Around The Bend**
    Creedence Clearwater Revival

2/09/63 **Up On The Roof** *Drifters*

4/18/70 **Up The Ladder To The Roof**
    Supremes

7/08/67 **Up-Up And Away** *5th Dimension*

11/06/82 **Up Where We Belong**
    Joe Cocker & Jennifer Warnes

9/06/80 **Upside Down** *Diana Ross*

2/12/66 **Uptight (Everything's Alright)**
    Stevie Wonder
    (also see: Little Ole Man)

11/12/83 **Uptown Girl** *Billy Joel*

9/05/81 **Urgent** *Foreigner*

10/14/72 **Use Me** *Bill Withers*

7/08/78 **Use Ta Be My Girl** *O'Jays*

V

9/01/62 **Vacation** *Connie Francis*

8/21/82 **Vacation** *Go-Go's*

12/19/87 **Valerie** *Steve Winwood*

3/30/68 **Valleri** *Monkees*

Valley Of The Dolls..*see: Theme*
    From

7/02/88 **Valley Road** *Bruce Hornsby*

1/12/85 **Valotte** *Julian Lennon*

5/23/70 **Vehicle** *Ides Of March*

12/09/72 **Ventura Highway** *America*

3/09/59 **Venus** *Frankie Avalon*

Venus
2/07/70		*Shocking Blue*
9/06/86		*Bananarama*

10/06/62 **Venus In Blue Jeans**
    Jimmy Clanton

1/24/87 **Victory** *Kool & The Gang*

7/13/85 **View To A Kill** *Duran Duran*

1/25/60 **Village Of St. Bernadette**
    Andy Williams

7/13/85 **Voices Carry** *'Til Tuesday*

Volare
8/18/58		*Domenico Modugno*
9/05/60		*Bobby Rydell*

W

7/21/62 **Wah Watusi** *Orlons*

5/21/88 **Wait** *White Lion*

11/28/81 **Waiting For A Girl Like You**
    Foreigner

11/17/84 **Wake Me Up Before You Go-Go**
    Wham!

1/24/76 **Walk Away From Love**
    David Ruffin

10/29/66 **Walk Away Renee** *Left Banke*

Walk--Don't Run
8/29/60		*Ventures*
8/22/64		*Ventures ('64)*

3/02/63 **Walk Like A Man** *4 Seasons*

12/20/86 **Walk Like An Egyptian** *Bangles*

1/25/86 **Walk Of Life** *Dire Straits*

12/11/61	**Walk On By** *Leroy Van Dyke*	12/05/87	**We'll Be Together** *Sting*
6/13/64	**Walk On By** *Dionne Warwick*	4/15/78	**We'll Never Have To Say**

12/11/61 **Walk On By** *Leroy Van Dyke*
6/13/64 **Walk On By** *Dionne Warwick*
3/27/61 **Walk Right Back** *Everly Brothers*
1/26/63 **Walk Right In** *Rooftop Singers*
         Walk This Way
1/29/77   *Aerosmith*
9/27/86   *Run-D.M.C.*
5/10/75 **Walking In Rhythm** *Blackbyrds*
6/22/85 **Walking On Sunshine**
         Katrina & The Waves
12/07/63 **Walking The Dog** *Rufus Thomas*
8/15/60 **Walking To New Orleans**
         Fats Domino
2/24/62 **Wanderer, The** *Dion*
11/15/80 **Wanderer, The** *Donna Summer*
7/16/83 **Wanna Be Startin' Somethin'**
         Michael Jackson
6/12/71 **Want Ads** *Honey Cone*
6/06/87 **Wanted Dead Or Alive** *Bon Jovi*
         War
8/29/70   *Edwin Starr*
12/27/86   *Bruce Springsteen*
9/22/84 **Warrior**
         Scandal Featuring Patty Smyth
11/23/63 **Washington Square**
         Village Stompers
9/27/75 **Wasted Days And Wasted**
         Nights *Freddy Fender*
8/21/82 **Wasted On The Way**
         Crosby, Stills & Nash
5/23/81 **Watching The Wheels**
         John Lennon
7/13/59 **Waterloo** *Stonewall Jackson*
8/24/74 **Waterloo** *Abba*
4/27/63 **Watermelon Man**
         Mongo Santamaria
1/11/60 **Way Down Yonder In New**
         Orleans *Freddie Cannon*
11/29/75 **Way I Want To Touch You**
         Captain & Tennille
12/13/86 **Way It Is** *Bruce Hornsby*
3/25/72 **Way Of Love** *Cher*
2/02/74 **Way We Were** *Barbra Streisand*
1/23/88 **Way You Make Me Feel**
         Michael Jackson
2/11/67 **(We Ain't Got) Nothin' Yet**
         Blues Magoos
         We All Shine On..see: Instant
         Karma
6/16/79 **We Are Family** *Sister Sledge*
2/04/78 **We Are The Champions** *Queen*
4/13/85 **We Are The World** *USA for Africa*
1/05/85 **We Belong** *Pat Benatar*
11/16/85 **We Built This City** *Starship*
1/08/66 **We Can Work It Out** *Beatles*
8/09/86 **We Don't Have To Take Our**
         Clothes Off *Jermaine Stewart*
9/14/85 **We Don't Need Another Hero**
         (Thunderdome) *Tina Turner*
1/19/80 **We Don't Talk Anymore**
         Cliff Richard
12/07/59 **We Got Love** *Bobby Rydell*
4/10/82 **We Got The Beat** *Go-Go's*

12/05/87 **We'll Be Together** *Sting*
4/15/78 **We'll Never Have To Say**
         Goodbye Again
         England Dan & John Ford Coley
10/17/64 **We'll Sing In The Sunshine**
         Gale Garnett
11/26/77 **We're All Alone** *Rita Coolidge*
9/29/73 **We're An American Band**
         Grand Funk
2/14/87 **We're Ready** *Boston*
3/26/83 **We've Got Tonight**
         Kenny Rogers & Sheena Easton
10/31/70 **We've Only Just Begun**
         Carpenters
1/02/65 **Wedding, The** *Julie Rogers*
11/08/69 **Wedding Bell Blues**
         5th Dimension
2/26/77 **Weekend In New England**
         Barry Manilow
5/08/76 **Welcome Back** *John Sebastian*
5/10/86 **West End Girls** *Pet Shop Boys*
9/15/58 **Western Movies** *Olympics*
4/22/67 **Western Union** *Five Americans*
8/10/59 **What A Diff'rence A Day Makes**
         Dinah Washington
         What A Feeling..see: Flashdance
4/14/79 **What A Fool Believes**
         Doobie Brothers
8/24/85 **What About Love?** *Heart*
4/19/75 **What Am I Gonna Do With You**
         Barry White
10/29/66 **What Becomes Of The**
         Brokenhearted *Jimmy Ruffin*
8/09/69 **What Does It Take (To Win Your**
         Love) *Jr. Walker & The All Stars*
2/20/88 **What Have I Done To Deserve**
         This?
         Pet Shop Boys & Dusty Springfield
5/17/86 **What Have You Done For Me**
         Lately *Janet Jackson*
2/22/60 **What In The World's Come Over**
         You *Jack Scott*
3/27/71 **What Is Life** *George Harrison*
3/21/81 **What Kind Of Fool**
         Barbra Streisand & Barry Gibb
2/22/64 **What Kind Of Fool (Do You Think**
         I Am) *Tams*
         What The World Needs Now Is
         Love
7/24/65   *Jackie DeShannon*
8/14/71   *Tom Clay (medley)*
3/09/63 **What Will Mary Say**
         Johnny Mathis
4/12/86 **What You Need** *INXS*
3/24/79 **What You Won't Do For Love**
         Bobby Caldwell
8/17/59 **What'd I Say** *Ray Charles*
         What's..also see: Wot's
4/10/71 **What's Going On** *Marvin Gaye*
9/01/84 **What's Love Got To Do With It**
         Tina Turner
7/31/65 **What's New Pussycat?**
         Tom Jones

Date	Song	Artist
3/17/62	**What's Your Name**	*Don & Juan*
8/20/77	**Whatcha Gonna Do?**	*Pablo Cruise*
9/25/71	**Whatcha See Is Whatcha Get**	
	Dramatics	
11/16/74	**Whatever Gets You Thru The Night**	
	John Lennon/Plastic Ono Band	
3/06/61	**Wheels**	*String-A-Longs*
8/04/58	**When**	*Kalin Twins*
5/28/66	**When A Man Loves A Woman**	
	Percy Sledge	
7/07/84	**When Doves Cry**	*Prince*
1/27/62	**When I Fall In Love**	*Lettermen*
10/17/64	**When I Grow Up (To Be A Man)**	
	Beach Boys	
5/14/77	**When I Need You**	*Leo Sayer*
10/11/86	**When I Think Of You**	
	Janet Jackson	
9/19/87	**When Smokey Sings**	*ABC*
1/13/62	**When The Boy In Your Arms (Is The Boy In Your Heart)**	
	Connie Francis	
2/15/86	**When The Going Gets Tough, The Tough Get Going**	
	Billy Ocean	
9/18/61	**When We Get Married**	
	Dreamlovers	
	When Will I Be Loved	
7/18/60		*Everly Brothers*
6/21/75		*Linda Ronstadt*
12/14/74	**When Will I See You Again**	
	Three Degrees	
6/26/71	**When You're Hot, You're Hot**	
	Jerry Reed	
8/11/79	**When You're In Love With A Beautiful Woman**	*Dr. Hook*
10/28/78	**Whenever I Call You "Friend"**	
	Kenny Loggins	
8/22/64	**Where Did Our Love Go**	
	Supremes	
4/23/88	**Where Do Broken Hearts Go**	
	Whitney Houston	
4/03/71	**(Where Do I Begin) Love Story**	
	Andy Williams	
8/12/72	**Where Is The Love**	
	Roberta Flack & Donny Hathaway	
2/08/60	**Where Or When**	
	Dion & The Belmonts	
3/20/61	**Where The Boys Are**	
	Connie Francis	
6/06/70	**Which Way You Goin' Billy?**	
	Poppy Family	
4/18/81	**While You See A Chance**	
	Steve Winwood	
5/16/64	**White On White**	*Danny Williams*
7/29/67	**White Rabbit**	*Jefferson Airplane*
11/09/68	**White Room**	*Cream*
4/25/60	**White Silver Sands**	
	Bill Black's Combo	
7/29/67	**Whiter Shade Of Pale**	
	Procol Harum	
10/30/82	**Who Can It Be Now?**	
	Men At Work	
11/15/75	**Who Loves You**	*Four Seasons*
9/25/61	**Who Put The Bomp (In The Bomp, Bomp, Bomp)**	
	Barry Mann	
10/03/87	**Who Will You Run To**	*Heart*
3/07/70	**Who'll Stop The Rain**	
	Creedence Clearwater Revival	
10/03/81	**Who's Crying Now**	*Journey*
8/10/85	**Who's Holding Donna Now**	
	DeBarge	
7/05/86	**Who's Johnny**	*El DeBarge*
12/07/68	**Who's Making Love**	
	Johnnie Taylor	
8/22/87	**Who's That Girl**	*Madonna*
11/30/85	**Who's Zoomin' Who**	
	Aretha Franklin	
1/31/70	**Whole Lotta Love**	*Led Zeppelin*
1/12/59	**Whole Lotta Loving**	*Fats Domino*
12/28/59	**Why**	*Frankie Avalon*
5/17/86	**Why Can't This Be Love**	
	Van Halen	
8/23/75	**Why Can't We Be Friends?**	*War*
2/10/73	**Why Can't We Live Together**	
	Timmy Thomas	
12/19/81	**Why Do Fools Fall In Love**	
	Diana Ross	
1/11/69	**Wichita Lineman**	*Glen Campbell*
12/15/84	**Wild Boys**	*Duran Duran*
3/28/60	**Wild One**	*Bobby Rydell*
7/30/66	**Wild Thing**	*Troggs*
3/09/63	**Wild Weekend**	*Rebels*
6/21/75	**Wildfire**	*Michael Murphey*
5/26/73	**Wildflower**	*Skylark*
8/24/74	**Wildwood Weed**	*Jim Stafford*
7/07/73	**Will It Go Round In Circles**	
	Billy Preston	
1/30/61	**Will You Love Me Tomorrow**	
	Shirelles	
2/21/87	**Will You Still Love Me?**	*Chicago*
8/04/58	**Willie And The Hand Jive**	
	Johnny Otis Show	
12/03/66	**Winchester Cathedral**	
	New Vaudeville Band	
7/01/67	**Windy**	*Association*
3/14/81	**Winner Takes It All**	*Abba*
8/10/63	**Wipe Out**	*Surfaris*
8/01/64	**Wishin' And Hopin'**	
	Dusty Springfield	
5/07/88	**Wishing Well**	*Terence Trent D'Arby*
11/18/72	**Witchy Woman**	*Eagles*
5/20/78	**With A Little Luck**	*Wings*
5/16/87	**With Or Without You**	*U2*
4/19/80	**With You I'm Born Again**	
	Billy Preston & Syreeta	
1/31/70	**Without Love (There Is Nothing)**	
	Tom Jones	
9/18/61	**Without You**	*Johnny Tillotson*
2/19/72	**Without You**	*Nilsson*
7/21/62	**Wolverton Mountain**	*Claude King*
3/21/81	**Woman**	*John Lennon*
10/25/80	**Woman In Love**	*Barbra Streisand*
6/20/81	**Woman Needs Love (Just Like You Do)**	*Ray Parker Jr. & Raydio*

1/13/68	**Woman, Woman** *Union Gap*	
6/27/70	**Wonder Of You** *Elvis Presley*	
9/28/63	**Wonderful! Wonderful!** *Tymes*	
7/10/65	**Wonderful World**	
	Herman's Hermits	
1/09/61	**Wonderland By Night**	
	Bert Kaempfert	
8/28/61	**Wooden Heart** *Joe Dowell*	
6/05/65	**Wooly Bully**	
	Sam The Sham & The Pharoahs	
11/22/86	**Word Up** * *Cameo*	
9/20/86	**Words Get In The Way**	
	Miami Sound Machine	
1/21/67	**Words Of Love**	
	Mamas & The Papas	
9/03/66	**Working In The Coal Mine**	
	Lee Dorsey	
	Working My Way Back To You	
3/05/66	*4 Seasons*	
3/29/80	*Spinners (medley)*	
2/10/73	**World Is A Ghetto** *War*	
6/27/64	**World Without Love**	
	Peter & Gordon	
2/01/69	**Worst That Could Happen**	
	Brooklyn Bridge	
8/01/87	**Wot's It To Ya** *Robbie Nevil*	
7/13/85	**Would I Lie To You?** *Eurythmics*	
9/17/66	**Wouldn't It Be Nice** *Beach Boys*	
3/03/84	**Wrapped Around Your Finger**	
	Police	
11/20/76	**Wreck Of The Edmund**	
	Fitzgerald *Gordon Lightfoot*	
7/03/61	**Writing On The Wall** *Adam Wade*	

X

10/11/80	**Xanadu** *Olivia Newton-John/*	
	Electric Light Orchestra	

Y

2/03/79	**Y.M.C.A.** *Village People*	
10/30/61	**Ya Ya** *Lee Dorsey*	
3/05/77	**Year Of The Cat** *Al Stewart*	
7/24/61	**Yellow Bird** *Arthur Lyman Group*	
9/17/66	**Yellow Submarine** *Beatles*	
	Yes, I'm Ready	
7/31/65	*Barbara Mason*	
3/01/80	*Teri DeSario with K.C.*	
12/13/69	**Yester-Me, Yester-You,**	
	Yesterday *Stevie Wonder*	
10/09/65	**Yesterday** *Beatles*	
7/28/73	**Yesterday Once More** *Carpenters*	
10/16/71	**Yo-Yo** *Osmonds*	
9/19/60	**Yogi** *Ivy Three*	
	You...*also see: U*	
11/09/74	**You Ain't Seen Nothing Yet**	
	Bachman-Turner Overdrive	
2/12/83	**You And I**	
	Eddie Rabbitt with Crystal Gayle	
8/13/77	**You And Me** *Alice Cooper*	
9/07/74	**You And Me Against The World**	
	Helen Reddy	
3/26/83	**You Are** *Lionel Richie*	

1/22/72	**You Are Everything** *Stylistics*	
12/29/62	**You Are My Sunshine**	
	Ray Charles	
3/29/75	**You Are So Beautiful** *Joe Cocker*	
5/19/73	**You Are The Sunshine Of My**	
	Life *Stevie Wonder*	
12/11/76	**You Are The Woman** *Firefall*	
9/22/62	**You Beat Me To The Punch**	
	Mary Wells	
9/22/62	**You Belong To Me** *Duprees*	
6/24/78	**You Belong To Me** *Carly Simon*	
11/16/85	**You Belong To The City**	
	Glenn Frey	
12/23/67	**You Better Sit Down Kids** *Cher*	
5/08/61	**You Can Depend On Me**	
	Brenda Lee	
10/16/82	**You Can Do Magic** *America*	
8/18/79	**You Can't Change That** *Raydio*	
	You Can't Hurry Love	
9/10/66	*Supremes*	
2/05/83	*Phil Collins*	
6/15/63	**You Can't Sit Down** *Dovells*	
11/17/79	**You Decorated My Life**	
	Kenny Rogers	
1/22/66	**You Didn't Have To Be So Nice**	
	Lovin' Spoonful	
12/02/78	**You Don't Bring Me Flowers**	
	Barbra Streisand & Neil Diamond	
12/21/63	**You Don't Have To Be A Baby To**	
	Cry *Caravelles*	
1/08/77	**You Don't Have To Be A Star (To**	
	Be In My Show)	
	Marilyn McCoo & Billy Davis, Jr.	
7/16/66	**You Don't Have To Say You Love**	
	Me *Dusty Springfield*	
9/08/62	**You Don't Know Me** *Ray Charles*	
9/04/61	**You Don't Know What You've**	
	Got (Until You Lose It)	
	Ral Donner	
9/02/72	**You Don't Mess Around With**	
	Jim *Jim Croce*	
2/01/64	**You Don't Own Me** *Lesley Gore*	
7/27/85	**You Give Good Love**	
	Whitney Houston	
11/29/86	**You Give Love A Bad Name**	
	Bon Jovi	
3/07/87	**You Got It All** *Jets*	
	You Got What It Takes	
2/08/60	*Marv Johnson*	
5/13/67	*Dave Clark Five*	
3/07/87	**(You Gotta) Fight For Your Right**	
	(To Party!) *Beastie Boys*	
11/02/74	**You Haven't Done Nothin**	
	Stevie Wonder	
	You Keep Me Hangin' On	
11/19/66	*Supremes*	
8/31/68	*Vanilla Fudge*	
6/06/87	*Kim Wilde*	
10/15/77	**You Light Up My Life**	
	Debby Boone	
8/13/77	**You Made Me Believe In Magic**	
	Bay City Rollers	

12/17/77	**You Make Loving Fun** *Fleetwood Mac*
6/15/74	**You Make Me Feel Brand New** *Stylistics*
1/15/77	**You Make Me Feel Like Dancing** *Leo Sayer*
7/04/81	**You Make My Dreams** *Daryl Hall & John Oates*
5/03/80	**You May Be Right** *Billy Joel*
4/28/84	**You Might Think** *Cars*
10/16/61	**You Must Have Been A Beautiful Baby** *Bobby Darin*
11/04/78	**You Needed Me** *Anne Murray*
11/18/78	**You Never Done It Like That** *Captain & Tennille*
12/23/72	**You Ought To Be With Me** *Al Green*
11/28/64	**You Really Got Me** *Kinks*
2/07/76	**You Sexy Thing** *Hot Chocolate*
9/04/76	**You Should Be Dancing** *Bee Gees*
9/18/82	**You Should Hear How She Talks About You** *Melissa Manchester*
3/01/69	**You Showed Me** *Turtles*
6/23/79	**You Take My Breath Away** *Rex Smith*
11/14/60	**You Talk Too Much** *Joe Jones*
7/17/65	**You Turn Me On** *Ian Whitcomb*
9/25/65	**You Were On My Mind** *We Five*
7/13/74	**You Won't See Me** *Anne Murray*
8/11/62	**You'll Lose A Good Thing** *Barbara Lynn*
9/04/76	**You'll Never Find Another Love Like Mine** *Lou Rawls*
9/14/68	**You're All I Need To Get By** *Marvin Gaye & Tammi Terrell*
8/24/74	**(You're) Having My Baby** *Paul Anka*
1/14/78	**You're In My Heart (The Final Acclaim)** *Rod Stewart*
9/16/67	**You're My Everything** *Temptations*
4/09/66	**(You're My) Soul And Inspiration** *Righteous Brothers*
2/15/75	**You're No Good** *Linda Ronstadt*
8/31/85	**You're Only Human (Second Wind)** *Billy Joel*
12/15/79	**You're Only Lonely** *J.D. Souther*
	You're Sixteen
12/26/60	*Johnny Burnette*
1/26/74	*Ringo Starr*
1/06/73	**You're So Vain** *Carly Simon*
8/10/63	**(You're the) Devil In Disguise** *Elvis Presley*
1/04/75	**You're The First, The Last, My Everything** *Barry White*
1/19/85	**You're The Inspiration** *Chicago*
11/13/65	**You're The One** *Vogues*
6/10/78	**You're The One That I Want** *John Travolta & Olivia Newton-John*
3/16/63	**You're The Reason I'm Living** *Bobby Darin*
7/31/71	**You've Got A Friend** *James Taylor*
11/27/65	**You've Got To Hide Your Love Away** *Silkie*
10/09/65	**You've Got Your Troubles** *Fortunes*
2/06/65	**You've Lost That Lovin' Feelin'** *Righteous Brothers*
4/12/69	**You've Made Me So Very Happy** *Blood, Sweat & Tears*
2/09/63	**You've Really Got A Hold On Me** *Miracles*
	Young And The Restless *..see:* *Nadia's Theme*
4/06/68	**Young Girl** *Union Gap*
4/20/63	**Young Lovers** *Paul & Paula*
12/19/81	**Young Turks** *Rod Stewart*
4/21/62	**Young World** *Rick Nelson*
5/10/86	**Your Love** *Outfield*
	(Your Love Keeps Lifting Me) Higher And Higher
10/07/67	*Jackie Wilson*
9/10/77	*Rita Coolidge*
1/27/73	**Your Mama Don't Dance** *Kenny Loggins & Jim Messina*
11/04/67	**Your Precious Love** *Marvin Gaye & Tammi Terrell*
1/23/71	**Your Song** *Elton John*
7/12/86	**Your Wildest Dreams** *Moody Blues*
6/15/68	**Yummy Yummy Yummy** *Ohio Express*

Z

1/12/63	**Zip-A-Dee Doo-Dah** *Bob B. Soxx & The Blue Jeans*

THE HIGHEST DEBUTS AND BIGGEST MOVERS

This section highlights the highest-debuting and biggest-moving singles in **Hot 100** history. The highest debuts and fastest movers are arranged according to:

Top 3 by Year
Top 5 by Decade
All-Time Top 10

In the highest debuts segment, the debut position is listed to the left of the title. The date of debut appears next to the artist name. In the case of highest debut ties, the single with the earlier date is listed first.

For the biggest movers section, the total positions climbed appears at the left, followed by the previous and the current weeks' chart positions. Listed to the right of the artist name is the chart date of its biggest move. In the event of biggest mover ties, the record positioned at a higher ranking appears first.

HIGHEST DEBUTS — BY YEAR

1958
30 One Night ... *Elvis Presley* – 11/10/58
39 (All Of A Sudden) My Heart Sings ... *Paul Anka* – 12/22/58
40 It's All In The Game ... *Tommy Edwards* – 8/25/58

1959
33 I Need Your Love Tonight ... *Elvis Presley* – 3/30/59
39 My Wish Came True ... *Elvis Presley* – 7/13/59
43 A Big Hunk O' Love ... *Elvis Presley* – 7/6/59

1960
35 Are You Lonesome To-night? ... *Elvis Presley* – 11/14/60
37 He'll Have To Stay ... *Jeanne Black* – 5/2/60
40 Angel Baby ... *Rosie & The Originals* – 12/12/60

1961
24 Surrender ... *Elvis Presley* – 2/20/61
42 Runaround Sue ... *Dion* – 9/25/61
43 I'm Learning About Love ... *Brenda Lee* – 1/30/61
43 I Feel So Bad ... *Elvis Presley* – 5/15/61

1962
50 All Alone Am I ... *Brenda Lee* – 9/29/62
51 Good Luck Charm ... *Elvis Presley* – 3/17/62
55 Dear Ivan ... *Jimmy Dean* – 1/6/62

1963
40 Walk Like A Man ... *The 4 Seasons* – 1/26/63
45 Hello Mudduh, Hello Fadduh! ... *Allan Sherman* – 8/3/63
50 There! I've Said It Again ... *Bobby Vinton* – 11/30/63

1964
21 A Hard Day's Night ... *The Beatles* – 7/18/64
22 I Feel Fine ... *The Beatles* – 12/5/64
27 Can't Buy Me Love ... *The Beatles* – 3/28/64

1965
12 Mrs. Brown You've Got A Lovely Daughter ... *Herman's Hermits* – 4/17/65
36 We Can Work It Out ... *The Beatles* – 12/18/65
39 I Hear A Symphony ... *The Supremes* – 10/30/65

1966
25 Nowhere Man ... *The Beatles* – 3/5/66
28 Paperback Writer ... *The Beatles* – 6/11/66
30 Snoopy Vs. The Red Baron ... *The Royal Guardsmen* – 12/17/66

1967
32 A Little Bit Me, A Little Bit You ... *The Monkees* – 3/25/67
33 Daydream Believer ... *The Monkees* – 11/18/67
45 Hello Goodbye ... *The Beatles* – 12/2/67

1968
10 Hey Jude ... *The Beatles* – 9/14/68
23 Lady Madonna ... *The Beatles* – 3/23/68
24 Valleri ... *The Monkees* – 3/9/68

1969
10 Get Back ... *The Beatles* – 5/10/69
20 Something ... *The Beatles* – 10/18/69
23 Come Together ... *The Beatles* – 10/18/69

1970
6 Let It Be ... *The Beatles* – 3/21/70
35 The Long And Winding Road ... *The Beatles* – 5/23/70
40 I'll Be There ... *The Jackson 5* – 9/19/70

1971
20 Imagine ... *John Lennon/ Plastic Ono Band* – 10/23/71
40 Brown Sugar ... *The Rolling Stones* – 5/1/71
41 Battle Hymn Of Lt. Calley ... *C Company featuring Terry Nelson* – 4/24/71

1972
44 Look What You Done For Me ... *Al Green* – 4/1/72
50 Tumbling Dice ... *The Rolling Stones* – 4/29/72
55 Sweet Surrender ... *Bread* – 11/11/72

1973
54 Killing Me Softly With His Song ... *Roberta Flack* – 1/27/73
58 I'm Just A Singer (In A Rock And Roll Band) ... *The Moody Blues* – 2/3/73
59 Give Me Love (Give Me Peace On Earth) ... *George Harrison* – 5/19/73

1974

45 Skin Tight ... *Ohio Players* – 9/7/74
48 Lucy In The Sky With Diamonds ... *Elton John* – 11/30/74
51 Then Came You ... *Dionne Warwicke & Spinners* – 7/27/74
51 Can't Get Enough Of Your Love, Babe ... *Barry White* – 8/3/74

1975

44 The Last Game Of The Season (The Blind Man In The Bleachers) ...
    David Geddes – 11/15/75
47 Fox On The Run ... *Sweet* – 11/15/75
48 I Write The Songs ... *Barry Manilow* – 11/15/75

1976

40 I Wish ... *Stevie Wonder* – 12/4/76
45 Somebody To Love ... *Queen* – 11/27/76
47 Lost Without Your Love ... *Bread* – 11/27/76

1977

50 Got To Give It Up (Pt. I) ... *Marvin Gaye* – 4/16/77
52 My Heart Belongs To Me ... *Barbra Streisand* – 5/21/77
56 Bite Your Lip (Get up and dance!) ... *Elton John* – 2/12/77

1978

35 Too Much Heaven ... *The Bee Gees* – 11/18/78
40 Da Ya Think I'm Sexy ... *Rod Stewart* – 12/23/78
48 You Don't Bring Me Flowers ... *Barbra Streisand & Neil Diamond* – 10/28/78

1979

29 Tragedy ... *The Bee Gees* – 2/10/79
33 The Long Run ... *Eagles* – 12/8/79
37 Love You Inside Out ... *The Bee Gees* – 4/21/79

1980

30 Hungry Heart ... *Bruce Springsteen* – 11/8/80
32 Love On The Rocks ... *Neil Diamond* – 11/1/80
33 Emotional Rescue ... *The Rolling Stones* – 7/5/80

1981

31 The Best Of Times ... *Styx* – 1/24/81
32 Hello Again ... *Neil Diamond* – 1/31/81
33 All Those Years Ago ... *George Harrison* – 5/23/81
33 I Don't Need You ... *Kenny Rogers* – 6/13/81

1982

29 Ebony And Ivory ... *Paul McCartney with Stevie Wonder* – 4/10/82
31 It's Raining Again ... *Supertramp* – 10/30/82
33 Hold Me ... *Fleetwood Mac* – 6/19/82

1983

26 Say Say Say ... *Paul McCartney & Michael Jackson* – 10/15/83
28 Overkill ... *Men At Work* – 4/9/83
29 All Right ... *Christopher Cross* – 1/22/83

1984

20 Thriller ... *Michael Jackson* – 2/11/84
28 Purple Rain ... *Prince & The Revolution* – 10/6/84
30 State Of Shock ... *The Jacksons* – 6/30/84

1985

21 We Are The World ... *USA for Africa* – 3/23/85
36 Dress You Up ... *Madonna* – 8/17/85
37 Raspberry Beret ... *Prince* – 5/18/85

1986

40 Dancing On The Ceiling ... *Lionel Richie* – 7/19/86
40 True Blue ... *Madonna* – 10/4/86
42 Papa Don't Preach ... *Madonna* – 6/28/86
42 Stuck With You ... *Huey Lewis & The News* – 8/2/86
42 Hip To Be Square ... *Huey Lewis & The News* – 10/18/86

1987

37 I Just Can't Stop Loving You ... *Michael Jackson* – 8/8/87
38 I Wanna Dance With Somebody (Who Loves Me) ... *Whitney Houston* – 5/16/87
40 Jacob's Ladder ... *Huey Lewis & The News* – 1/17/87
40 Bad ... *Michael Jackson* – 9/19/87
40 Brilliant Disguise ... *Bruce Springsteen* – 10/3/87

1988

40 One More Try ... *George Michael* – 4/16/88
42 Monkey ... *George Michael* – 7/9/88
46 Everything Your Heart Desires ... *Daryl Hall John Oates* – 4/16/88

BIGGEST MOVERS — BY YEAR

1958
68: 86-18 **Lonesome Town** ... *Ricky Nelson* – 10/27/58
67: 93-26 **Are You Really Mine** ... *Jimmie Rodgers* – 8/11/58
59: 88-29 **The Little Drummer Boy** ... *The Harry Simeone Chorale* – 12/29/58

1959
57: 93-36 **The Battle Of New Orleans** ... *Johnny Horton* – 5/4/59
57: 100-43 **Wont'cha Come Home** ... *Lloyd Price* – 11/16/59
56: 84-28 **Teen Beat** ... *Sandy Nelson* – 9/14/59

1960
67: 84-17 **Stuck On You** ... *Elvis Presley* – 4/11/60
59: 74-15 **Cathy's Clown** ... *The Everly Brothers* – 5/2/60
53: 96-43 **The Theme From "A Summer Place"** ... *Percy Faith* – 1/18/60

1961
51: 75-24 **This Time** ... *Troy Shondell* – 9/25/61
51: 79-28 **Dance The Mess Around** ... *Chubby Checker* – 5/1/61
51: 85-34 **Flaming Star** ... *Elvis Presley* – 4/24/61

1962
49: 66-17 **Big Girls Don't Cry** ... *The 4 Seasons* – 10/27/62
48: 68-20 **Return To Sender** ... *Elvis Presley* – 10/27/62
44: 93-49 **Duke Of Earl** ... *Gene Chandler* – 1/20/62

1963
48: 68-20 **Surf City** ... *Jan & Dean* – 6/22/63
46: 65-19 **Sugar Shack** ... *Jimmy Gilmer & The Fireballs* – 9/28/63
46: 87-41 **He's So Fine** ... *The Chiffons* – 3/2/63

1964
51: 75-24 **Dawn (Go Away)** ...*The Four Seasons* – 2/8/64
50: 60-10 **The House Of The Rising Sun** ... *The Animals* – 8/15/64
48: 55-7 **Twist And Shout** ... *The Beatles* – 3/21/64
48: 69-21 **She Loves You** ... *The Beatles* – 2/1/64

1965
54: 68-14 **I Got You (I Feel Good)** ... *James Brown* – 11/20/65
50: 64-14 **Get Off Of My Cloud** ... *The Rolling Stones* – 10/16/65
44: 94-50 **I Know A Place** ... *Petula Clark* – 3/27/65

1966
45: 79-34 **Monday, Monday** ... *The Mamas & The Papas* – 4/16/66
45: 90-45 **(You're My) Soul And Inspiration** ... *The Righteous Brothers* – 3/12/66
44: 52-8 **Yellow Submarine** ... *The Beatles* – 8/27/66

1967
52: 80-28 **A Whiter Shade Of Pale** ... *Procol Harum* – 7/1/67
50: 71-21 **Ode To Billie Joe** ... *Bobbie Gentry* – 8/12/67
49: 85-36 **Penny Lane** ... *The Beatles* – 3/4/67
49: 98-49 **Sunday Will Never Be The Same** ... *Spanky & Our Gang* – 5/27/67

1968
74: 81-7 **Harper Valley P.T.A.** ... *Jeannie C. Riley* – 8/31/68
57: 78-21 **Ain't No Way** ... *Aretha Franklin* – 4/13/68
55: 77-22 **Hello, I Love You** ... *The Doors* – 7/13/68

1969
56: 96-40 **Eleanor Rigby** ... *Aretha Franklin* – 11/15/69
52: 89-37 **Aquarius/Let The Sunshine In** ... *The 5th Dimension* – 3/15/69
52: 92-40 **This Girl's In Love With You** ... *Dionne Warwick* – 2/8/69

1970
59: 72-13 **My Sweet Lord** ... *George Harrison* – 12/5/70
57: 95-38 **Psychedelic Shack** ... *The Temptations* – 1/24/70
56: 96-40 **Kentucky Rain** ... *Elvis Presley* – 2/21/70

1971
50: 89-39 **Got To Be There** ... *Michael Jackson* – 11/6/71
48: 87-39 **For All We Know** ... *Carpenters* – 2/13/71
47: 87-40 **Cherish** ... *David Cassidy* – 11/13/71

1972
58: 100-42 **Hi, Hi, Hi** ... *Wings* – 12/23/72
46: 88-42 **Back Off Boogaloo** ... *Ringo Starr* – 4/8/72
45: 80-35 **Oh Girl** ... *The Chi-Lites* – 4/15/72

1973
44: 86-42 **The Morning After** ... *Maureen McGovern* – 7/7/73
40: 74-34 **Saturday Night's Alright For Fighting** ... *Elton John* – 8/11/73
36: 76-40 **I Got A Name** ... *Jim Croce* – 10/13/73

1974

45: 79-34 It's Only Rock 'N Roll (But I Like It) ... *The Rolling Stones* – 8/17/74
42: 93-51 You Haven't Done Nothin ... *Stevie Wonder* – 8/10/74
38: 86-48 Promised Land ... *Elvis Presley* – 11/2/74

1975

53: 82-29 Convoy ... *C.W. McCall* – 12/13/75
47: 80-33 The Way I Want To Touch You ... *Captain & Tennille* – 10/4/75
43: 85-42 Express ... *B.T. Express* – 2/1/75

1976

48: 83-35 I.O.U. ... *Jimmy Dean* – 5/22/76
39: 59-20 Welcome Back ... *John Sebastian* – 4/10/76
32: 60-28 If You Leave Me Now ... *Chicago* – 8/21/76

1977

49: 89-40 The King Is Gone ... *Ronnie McDowell* – 9/17/77
35: 72-37 Lido Shuffle ... *Boz Scaggs* – 3/19/77
35: 89-54 The Greatest Love Of All ... *George Benson* – 8/13/77

1978

44: 76-32 Night Fever ... *The Bee Gees* – 2/11/78
41: 79-38 Flash Light ... *Parliament* – 2/25/78
40: 57-17 With A Little Luck ... *Wings* – 4/8/78
40: 78-38 Hollywood Nights ... *Bob Seger & The Silver Bullet Band* – 8/19/78

1979

50: 79-29 Hot Stuff ... *Donna Summer* – 4/28/79
40: 66-26 Reunited ... *Peaches & Herb* – 3/31/79
37: 52-15 Heartache Tonight ... *Eagles* – 10/13/79
37: 77-40 Heaven Knows ... *Donna Summer with Brooklyn Dreams* – 1/20/79

1980

39: 49-10 Upside Down ... *Diana Ross* – 8/9/80
38: 67-29 Cupid/I've Loved You For A Long Time ... *Spinners* – 5/24/80
37: 86-49 On The Radio ... *Donna Summer* – 1/19/80

1981

37: 76-39 America ... *Neil Diamond* – 5/2/81
34: 70-36 Waiting On A Friend ... *The Rolling Stones* – 12/12/81
33: 65-32 Take It On The Run ... *Reo Speedwagon* – 3/21/81
33: 75-42 (There's) No Gettin' Over Me ... *Ronnie Milsap* – 7/4/81
33: 82-49 Take It Easy On Me ... *Little River Band* – 12/12/81

1982

35: 55-20 Heat Of The Moment ... *Asia* – 5/1/82
33: 52-19 Sexual Healing ... *Marvin Gaye* – 11/20/82
33: 64-31 We Got The Beat ... *Go-Go's* – 2/13/82
33: 68-35 Through The Years ... *Kenny Rogers* – 1/16/82

1983

25: 77-52 Flashdance...What A Feeling ... *Irene Cara* – 4/9/83
24: 55-31 Der Kommissar ... *After The Fire* – 3/5/83
24: 74-50 Even Now ... *Bob Seger* – 3/19/83
24: 78-54 Fall In Love With Me ... *Earth, Wind & Fire* – 1/29/83
24: 83-59 This Time ... *Bryan Adams* – 9/10/83

1984

25: 65-40 Almost Paradise...Love Theme From Footloose ...
Mike Reno & Ann Wilson – 5/19/84
25: 75-50 Hello ... *Lionel Richie* – 3/3/84
25: 85-60 All Of You ... *Julio Iglesias & Diana Ross* – 7/14/84

1985

45: 65-20 Do They Know It's Christmas? ... *Band Aid* – 1/5/85
31: 83-52 Do You Want Crying ... *Katrina & The Waves* – 8/3/85
28: 84-56 Spanish Eddie ... *Laura Branigan* – 8/3/85

1986

32: 89-57 Venus ... *Bananarama* – 7/5/86
28: 84-56 Superbowl Shuffle ... *The Chicago Bears Shufflin' Crew* – 2/1/86
27: 83-56 Livin' On A Prayer ... *Bon Jovi* – 12/20/86
27: 86-59 Don't Forget Me (When I'm Gone) ... *Glass Tiger* – 7/19/86

1987

34: 86-52 Could've Been ... *Tiffany* – 12/5/87
29: 80-51 (I Just) Died In Your Arms ... *Cutting Crew* – 3/14/87
29: 84-55 She's Like The Wind ... *Patrick Swayze with Wendy Fraser* – 12/26/87

1988

25: 95-70 Paradise ... *Sade* – 5/21/88
24: 78-54 Make Me Lose Control ... *Eric Carmen* – 5/28/88
24: 79-55 Make It Real ... *The Jets* – 4/23/88
24: 79-55 The Twist ... *The Fat Boys* – 6/25/88

HIGHEST DEBUTS — BY DECADE

FIFTIES

30 One Night ... *Elvis Presley* – 11/10/58
33 I Need Your Love Tonight ... *Elvis Presley* – 3/30/59
39 (All Of A Sudden) My Heart Sings ... *Paul Anka* – 12/22/58
39 My Wish Came True ... *Elvis Presley* – 7/13/59
40 It's All In The Game ... *Tommy Edwards* – 8/25/58

SIXTIES

10 Hey Jude ... *The Beatles* – 9/14/68
10 Get Back ... *The Beatles* – 5/10/69
12 Mrs. Brown You've Got A Lovely Daughter ... *Herman's Hermits* – 4/17/65
20 Something ... *The Beatles* – 10/18/69
21 A Hard Day's Night ... *The Beatles* – 7/18/64

SEVENTIES

6 Let It Be ... *The Beatles* – 3/21/70
20 Imagine ... *John Lennon/Plastic Ono Band* – 10/23/71
29 Tragedy ... *The Bee Gees* – 2/10/79
33 The Long Run ... *Eagles* – 12/8/79
35 The Long And Winding Road ... *The Beatles* – 5/23/70
35 Too Much Heaven ... *The Bee Gees* – 11/18/78

EIGHTIES

20 Thriller ... *Michael Jackson* – 2/11/84
21 We Are The World ... *USA for Africa* – 3/23/85
26 Say Say Say ... *Paul McCartney & Michael Jackson* – 10/15/83
28 Overkill ... *Men At Work* – 4/9/83
28 Purple Rain ... *Prince & The Revolution* – 10/6/84

BIGGEST MOVERS — BY DECADE

FIFTIES

68: 86-18 **Lonesome Town** ... *Ricky Nelson* – 10/27/58
67: 93-26 **Are You Really Mine** ... *Jimmie Rodgers* – 8/11/58
59: 88-29 **The Little Drummer Boy** ... *The Harry Simeone Chorale* – 12/29/58
58: 92-34 **Bird Dog** ... *The Everly Brothers* – 8/11/58
57: 93-36 **The Battle Of New Orleans** ... *Johnny Horton* – 5/4/59
57: 100-43 **Wont'cha Come Home** ... *Lloyd Price* – 11/16/59

SIXTIES

74: 81-7 **Harper Valley P.T.A.** ... *Jeannie C. Riley* – 8/31/68
67: 84-17 **Stuck On You** ... *Elvis Presley* – 4/11/60
59: 74-15 **Cathy's Clown** ... *The Everly Brothers* – 5/2/60
57: 78-21 **Ain't No Way** ... *Aretha Franklin* – 4/13/68
56: 96-40 **Eleanor Rigby** ... *Aretha Franklin* – 11/15/69

SEVENTIES

59: 72-13 **My Sweet Lord** ... *George Harrison* – 12/5/70
58: 100-42 **Hi, Hi, Hi** ... *Wings* – 12/23/72
57: 95-38 **Psychedelic Shack** ... *The Temptations* – 1/24/70
56: 96-40 **Kentucky Rain** ... *Elvis Presley* – 2/21/70
53: 82-29 **Convoy** ... *C.W. McCall* – 12/13/75

EIGHTIES

45: 65-20 **Do They Know It's Christmas?** ... *Band Aid* – 1/5/85
39: 49-10 **Upside Down** ... *Diana Ross* – 8/9/80
38: 67-29 **Cupid/I've Loved You For A Long Time** ... *Spinners* – 5/24/80
37: 76-39 **America** ... *Neil Diamond* – 5/2/81
37: 86-49 **On The Radio** ... *Donna Summer* – 1/19/80

ALL-TIME *HOT 100* HIGHEST DEBUTS

 6 Let It Be ... *The Beatles* – 3/21/70
10 Hey Jude ... *The Beatles* – 9/14/68
10 Get Back ... *The Beatles* – 5/10/69
12 Mrs. Brown You've Got A Lovely Daughter ... *Herman's Hermits* – 4/17/65
20 Something ... *The Beatles* – 10/18/69
20 Imagine ... *John Lennon/Plastic Ono Band* – 10/23/71
20 Thriller ... *Michael Jackson* – 2/11/84
21 A Hard Day's Night ... *The Beatles* – 7/18/64
21 We Are The World ... *USA for Africa* – 3/23/85
22 I Feel Fine ... *The Beatles* – 12/5/64

ALL-TIME *HOT 100* BIGGEST MOVERS

74: 81-7   Harper Valley P.T.A. ... *Jeannie C. Riley* – 8/31/68
68: 86-18 Lonesome Town ... *Ricky Nelson* – 10/27/58
67: 84-17 Stuck On You ... *Elvis Presley* – 4/11/60
67: 93-26 Are You Really Mine ... *Jimmie Rodgers* – 8/11/58
59: 72-13 My Sweet Lord ... *George Harrison* – 12/5/70
59: 74-15 Cathy's Clown ... *The Everly Brothers* – 5/2/60
59: 88-29 The Little Drummer Boy ... *The Harry Simeone Chorale* – 12/29/58
58: 92-34 Bird Dog ... *The Everly Brothers* – 8/11/58
58: 100-42 Hi, Hi, Hi ... *Wings* – 12/23/72
57: 78-21 Ain't No Way ... *Aretha Franklin* – 4/13/68
57: 93-36 The Battle Of New Orleans ... *Johnny Horton* – 5/4/59
57: 95-38 Psychedelic Shack ... *The Temptations* – 1/24/70
57: 100-43 Wont'cha Come Home ... *Lloyd Price* – 11/16/59

Up And Coming on next page

UP AND COMING!

TOP R&B SINGLES 1942-1988

We've gone back further than ever before! Our research has been expanded to not only include every single to hit *Billboard's* **Hot R&B (Black/Soul) Singles** charts, but also their **Best Selling, Disc Jockey,** and **Juke Box** R&B charts. The book will include well over a thousand artist biographies.

TOP COUNTRY SINGLES 1944-1988

Here's the revision you've been waiting for — featuring thousands of artist biographies, title trivia and greatly expanded research. This book will begin with the first **Most Played Juke Box Folk Records** chart in 1944 and will list every single to ever hit *Billboard's* **Best Selling, Disc Jockey, Juke Box,** and **Hot Country Singles** country charts.

BILLBOARD'S TOP VIDEOCASSETTES 1979-1988

Our first venture into the film industry. The over 1400 hottest videocassette movies to hit *Billboard's* **Top Videocassettes Rentals and Sales** charts over the past 10 years, researched and compiled in a concise, easy-to-use volume. Includes a brief description of each film's plot or content.

THE RECORD RESEARCH COLLECTION

BOOK TITLE	Quantity	Price	Total
1. Top Pop Singles 1955-1986 (Hardcover)	_____	$60.00	_____
2. Top Pop Singles 1955-1986 (Softcover)	_____	$50.00	_____
3. Pop Singles Annual 1955-1986 (Hardcover)	_____	$60.00	_____
4. Pop Singles Annual 1955-1986 (Softcover)	_____	$50.00	_____
5. Top 10 Charts 1958-1988 (Hardcover)	_____	$60.00	_____
6. Top 10 Charts 1958-1988 (Softcover)	_____	$50.00	_____
7. Pop Memories 1890-1954 (Hardcover)	_____	$60.00	_____
8. Pop Memories 1890-1954 (Softcover)	_____	$50.00	_____
9. Top Pop Albums 1955-1985	_____	$50.00	_____
10. Top 3000+ 1955-1987	_____	$30.00	_____
11. Music & Video Yearbook 1987	_____	$30.00	_____
12. Music Yearbook 1986	_____	$30.00	_____
13. Music Yearbook 1985	_____	$30.00	_____
14. Music Yearbook 1984	_____	$30.00	_____
15. Music Yearbook 1983	_____	$30.00	_____
16. Bubbling Under The Hot 100 1959-1981	_____	$30.00	_____

All books are softcover except items 1, 3, 5 & 7.

Shipping & Handling (see below).. _____

Total Payment $ _____

Shipping & Handling

Please include a check or money order for full amount plus **$4.00** for postage and handling. All *Canadian* and *foreign* orders add $4.00 per order. Canadian and foreign orders are shipped via surface mail. Call or write for air mail shipping rates.

For more information on the complete line of *Record Research* books, please write for a free catalog.

Payment Method ☐ Check ☐ Money Order
☐ MasterCard ☐ VISA

MasterCard or VISA # _____ _____ _____ _____

Expiration Date ____ / ____
Mo. Yr.

Signature _____

To Charge Your Order By Phone, Call 414-251-5408
(office hours: 8AM-5PM CST)

Name _____

Address _____

City _____

State _____ Zip _____

Record Research Inc.
P.O. Box 200
Menomonee Falls, Wisconsin 53051